Moores Rowland's Orange Tax Guide

Moores Rowland's Orange Tax Guide 1990-91

Covering
Inheritance Tax
National Insurance Contributions
Stamp Duty (including Stamp Duty Reserve Tax)
Value Added Tax

LONDON · BUTTERWORTHS · 1990

England	Butterworth & Co (Publishers) Ltd, 88 Kingsway, LONDON WC2B 6AB and 4 Hill Street, EDINBURGH EH2 3LJ
Australia	Butterworths Pty Ltd, SYDNEY, MELBOURNE, BRISBANE, ADELAIDE, PERTH, CANBERRA and HOBART
Canada	Butterworth & Co (Canada) Ltd, TORONTO Butterworth & Co (Western Canada) Ltd, VANCOUVER
New Zealand	Butterworths of New Zealand Ltd, WELLINGTON and AUCKLAND
Singapore	Butterworth & Co (Asia) Pte Ltd, SINGAPORE
USA	Butterworth Legal Publishers, SEATTLE, Washington; BOSTON, Massachusetts; and AUSTIN, Texas D and S Publishers, CLEARWATER, Florida

ISBN 0 406 36504 0

ISSN 0951–8223

Printed in Great Britain by The Bath Press, Avon

Preface

This annual, prepared by practitioners for practitioners, is of practical help to anyone involved in the day-to-day application of inheritance tax, national insurance contributions, stamp duties or value added tax. It is essentially a brief explanation in plain words of all the detailed tax legislation which is printed in *Butterworths Orange Tax Handbook*.

Every section, paragraph and regulation is explained, with references to case law, extra-statutory concessions, statements of practice, press releases and other useful information. Where appropriate the notes contain helpful tax planning suggestions and highlight practical danger areas which might otherwise be overlooked. For readers who require a more detailed treatment, references are made to the relevant paragraphs in Foster's Capital Taxes Encyclopaedia, Sergeant and Sims on Stamp Duties or De Voil on Value Added Tax, as the case may be. We must emphasise that no commentary can replace study of the precise wording of the legislation.

The appendices contain a unique easy-to-find collection of press releases, extra-statutory concessions, statements of practice, certain booklets and other useful information.

A similar treatment for income tax, corporation tax and capital gains tax is contained in the twin publication *Moores Rowland's Yellow Tax Guide*.

We gratefully acknowledge the help received in the preparation of this edition from Michael Walter and Charles Barcroft.

The law is stated as at July 1990 and includes the relevant parts of the Social Security Act 1990 and of the Finance Act 1990. This edition covers the legislation applicable in the year 1990–91 only, so readers should keep the earlier editions of the guide for dealing with past years.

We welcome any suggestions for improving the book to serve tax practitioners. Please write to the Editor, Moores Rowland's Orange Tax Guide, at the address shown below.

Clifford's Inn   MOORES ROWLAND
Fetter Lane
London EC4A 1AS
July 1990

Abbreviations

BTR	British Tax Review
CCAB	Consultative Committee of Accountancy Bodies
CGTA 1979	Capital Gains Tax Act 1979
COR	Contracted-out rate
CTT	Capital Transfer Tax (now Inheritance Tax)
DSS	Department of Social Security
EB	Earnings bracket
FA	Finance Act
FSA 1986	Financial Services Act 1986
ICAEW	Institute of Chartered Accountants in England and Wales
IHT	Inheritance Tax
IHTA 1984	Inheritance Tax Act 1984 (formerly Capital Transfer Tax Act 1984)
LEL	Lower earnings limit
PCTA 1968	Provisional Collection of Taxes Act 1968
RR	Reduced rate
s.	Section
SA 1891	Stamp Act 1891
Sch.	Schedule
SFO	Superannuation Funds Office
SI	Statutory Instrument
SP	Statement of Practice
SR	Standard rate
SSA	Social Security Act
SSPA	Social Security Pensions Act
STC	Simon's Tax Cases
STI	Simon's Tax Intelligence
TA 1988	Income and Corporation Taxes Act 1988
TC	Tax Cases (HMSO)
TMA 1970	Taxes Management Act 1970
UEL	Upper earnings limit
VATA 1983	Value Added Tax Act 1983

Contents

Contents

Part I Inheritance Tax

Contents

All references, in this style **B2.07**, in this Part are to Foster's Capital Taxes Encyclopaedia.

Note: Capital transfer tax is renamed inheritance tax by FA 1986, s. 100 with effect from 25 July 1986.

Finance Act 1978
1978 Chapter 42

PART V MISCELLANEOUS AND SUPPLEMENTARY

77. Disclosure of information to tax authorities in other member States. (L1.10; L2.31)
The Revenue are authorised to disclose information relating to the affairs of taxpayers to the tax authorities of other EC member States.

Inheritance Tax Act 1984

1984 Chapter 51

PART I GENERAL

MAIN CHARGES AND DEFINITIONS

1. Charge on transfers.

Inheritance tax is charged on the value transferred by a chargeable transfer.

2. Chargeable transfers and exempt transfers. (B1.01–03; C1.01)

Any transfer of value by an individual made after 26 March 1974 is a chargeable transfer unless it is an exempt transfer or a potentially exempt transfer made after 17 March 1986 (see IHTA 1984, s. 3A). A notional transfer can result from a mere failure to exercise a right if as a result of that failure a person's estate is diminished and another's increased or if settled property is increased where there is no interest in possession. Such circumstances could arise for example, in deliberately failing to subscribe for a favourable rights issue of shares in a private company where other members so subscribe, thus increasing their proportional holding.

As to winnings by football pool syndicates see SP/E14, 16 September 1977.

References to chargeable transfers are normally taken to include occasions when exit charges apply.

3. Transfers of value. (C1.01)

The basic proposition is that the tax is calculated on the value transferred which is usually the reduction in total value of the transferor's estate as a result of a transfer—other than of excluded property (see IHTA 1984, ss. 6, 82) or which is exempt (see IHTA 1984, ss. 18–42) or is a potentially exempt transfer made after 17 March 1986 (see IHTA 1984, s. 3A)—and not on the value of the asset actually transferred, which may or may not give the same result. For example, if 2 per cent. of the share capital in a private company is given away by a shareholder then owning 51 per cent. he is left with a 49 per cent. holding. The net value of the transfer is the difference between the value of a 51 per cent. holding which would control the company and a 49 per cent. holding which would not, and usually this would be very much in excess of the value of a 2 per cent. holding in isolation. The value of the 2 per cent. holding on its own is still relevant so far as capital gains tax and stamp duty are concerned. If the transferor bears the inheritance tax the value transferred is the gross equivalent of the net transfer, *i.e.* such a sum as after the tax thereon is equivalent to the net transfer. A gift by cheque is made when cleared through the donee's bank account, *Re Owen, Owen* v. *I.R. Comrs.* [1949] 1 All ER 901; as to a gift of shares see *Re Rose, Rose and Others* v. *I.R. Comrs.* [1952] 1 All ER 1217 where the gift was complete when the donor had done all necessary to divest himself of the shares, even though the donee was not then registered as the member. Oral agreements did not make valid dispositions in *Grey and Another* v. *I.R. Comrs.* [1960] AC 1 (a stamp duty case) and in *Oughtred* v. *I.R. Comrs.* [1959] 3 All ER 623 where agreements in writing were required.

3A. Potentially exempt transfers. (Division C4)

The concept of the potentially exempt transfer is introduced by IHTA 1984, s. 3A in respect of transfers occurring on, or after, 18 March 1986. A potentially exempt transfer means a transfer by an individual (which apart from this section would be chargeable to inheritance tax) by way of gift to (*a*) another individual, or (*b*) an accumulation and maintenance trust (see IHTA 1984, s. 71) or (*c*) a disabled persons trust (see IHTA 1984, s. 89). It should be noted that generally only actual transfers (see sub-s. (6)) and not deemed transfers can qualify as potentially exempt transfers and the recipients must be as specified. However, after 16 March 1987, gifts by an individual into a life interest settlement for another individual, or terminations of life interest settlements may qualify as potentially exempt transfers on the normal inheritance tax premise that a life tenant is deemed to be the owner of the underlying assets (see IHTA 1984, s. 49). Close company transfers under IHTA 1984, s. 98 cannot qualify as potentially exempt transfers. In value terms a potentially exempt transfer will only qualify to the extent that the value transferred is attributable to the donor's property becoming comprised in the estate of the donee individual by virtue of the transfer (this can prevent the payment of school fees by a grandparent direct to the school from being a potentially exempt transfer), although this should extend to the diminution in value of the transferor's estate—see SP/E13, 15 April 1976, and I.C.A.E.W. TR 631, 22 August 1986, para. 2. However, where no property changes hands the potentially exempt transfer is limited to the gain to the donee's estate.

Provided that a donor individual survives for a minimum period of seven years from the date of making the gift, a potentially exempt transfer becomes wholly exempt. However, if the donor dies within the seven-year period it becomes a chargeable transfer and the tax liability is computed in accordance with IHTA 1984, s. 7 at the current table death rates and subject to the appropriate taper relief provided for in that section. Note that until a potentially exempt transfer becomes chargeable it is regarded as exempt for all purposes so that it would not be aggregated with a subsequent chargeable transfer (for example, a transfer to a discretionary trust) for the purposes of establishing the rate of tax appropriate to the chargeable transfer. However, the position is totally changed on the potentially exempt transfer becoming chargeable and this will affect the rate of tax on subsequent transfers. Note that the annual exemption (IHTA 1984, s. 19) is utilised first against chargeable transfers and then against potentially exempt transfers on becoming chargeable. See also IHTA 1984, ss. 113A, 113B, 124A and 124B where the potentially exempt transfer comprises respectively relevant business property and agricultural property, ss. 30–35 (conditional exemption), s. 199 (liability for tax), s. 216 (delivery of accounts), s. 227 (payment by instalments), FA 1986, s. 102 (gifts with reservation) and CGTA 1979, s. 126 (capital gains tax—relief for gifts of business assets, after 13 March 1989. See also IHTA 1984, s. 165).

4. Transfers on death. (D1.01)

Inheritance tax is charged on death at the full scale in accordance with IHTA 1984, s. 7, as if the whole of the deceased's estate had been disposed of immediately prior to death, but assets such as life policies maturing on death would be included on the basis of the proceeds receivable under IHTA 1984, s. 171. For deaths after 17 March 1986 the deceased's estate is deemed to include gifts made by the deceased after that date in which a benefit has been retained see—FA 1986, s. 102.

The deceased is deemed to have an absolute interest in settled property of which he was life tenant (IHTA 1984, s. 49), unless the property reverts to the settler or his spouse and was not acquired for value by the settlor or his spouse or following the transfer of a reversionary interest in settlement after 9 March 1981.

Inheritance tax applies to deaths on or after 13 March 1975, but the estate duty rules were substantially changed in respect of deaths on or after 13 November 1974. Prior to that date estate duty applied to deaths and under those rules if a surviving spouse had been left a life interest in an estate there would have been no further estate duty payable on her subsequent death (surviving spouse exemption). In such circumstances inheritance tax or capital transfer tax would be payable on the subsequent death of the surviving spouse, and would be exempt on the first death under IHTA 1984, s. 18. It is therefore provided that where estate duty had been paid on the first death no inheritance tax or capital transfer tax is payable on the death of the surviving spouse. In such circumstances it is advisable if possible to invest in appreciating assets.

Inheritance tax on death is payable in respect of deaths after 12 March 1975, but if estate duty had remained in existence transfers prior to that date would have been subject to estate duty under the seven year gift *inter vivos* provisions. If, as a result of a death liable to inheritance tax or capital transfer tax, estate duty would have been payable on gifts *inter vivos* the amount which would have been liable to estate duty, *i.e.* after relief for industrial hereditaments, agricultural property or taper relief etc. is charged to inheritance tax or capital transfer tax as a transfer on death. The provisions relating to pre 1968 life insurance policies which formed an estate on their own for estate duty are retained for inheritance tax and capital transfer tax.

For the purposes of the section the trustees of a settlement will be regarded as non-resident in the U.K. unless the majority of them (or of each class, if more than one) are U.K. resident and the general administration of the settlement is ordinarily carried on in the U.K.

5. Meaning of estate. (B3.01)

Estate includes all assets beneficially owned by a transferor, other than excluded property, on death or for deaths after 8 March 1982, non-residents' bank accounts (see IHTA 1984, s. 96), and including property over which the transferor had a general power of appointment as to which see *Estate and Gift Duty Comrs.* v. *Fiji Resorts Ltd P.C.* 1982, [1982] STC 871. A person having a beneficial interest in possession in settled property is deemed to be the beneficial owner of the appropriate part of the trust capital. From 18 March 1986 FA 1986, s. 102 extends the definition of estate to include gifts made by the deceased on or after that date in which a benefit has been retained. Excluded property does not form part of the estate, but note that a reversionary interest is not necessarily excluded property (IHTA 1984, s. 48 (1), (3)).

See also Extra-statutory concessions F2 and F13 (1988) for further exclusions.

Where it is necessary to ascertain the value of a transferor's estate, liabilities incurred for consideration in money's worth or imposed by law may be deducted. However see FA 1986, s. 103 where a deduction is precluded if the creditor has received gifts from the deceased or where the deceased derived no benefit from the debt where incurred after 17 March 1986. If it is necessary to calculate the transferor's tax, but not any other taxes resulting from the transfer *e.g.* capital gains tax. Apart from the liability for the inheritance tax itself any liability to be discharged later is taken at its discount value.

A charge on any property shall be taken as far as possible as reducing the value of that property.

A liability to a non-U.K. resident is deducted as far as possible in the first instance from property outside the U.K., unless it is to be discharged in the U.K. or is charged on property in the U.K.

Reasonable expense for mourning is deductible as is development gains and development land tax in certain circumstances (Extra-statutory concessions F1 and F14 (1985)).

6. Excluded property. (J3.11; 21, 22)

This section is subject to the provisions of IHTA 1984, ss. 48 (3), 267 and contains further definitions of excluded property. See also IHTA 1984, s. 82.

Property situated outside the U.K. (or deemed to be so situated under the gift provisions of any double death duty agreement) if held beneficially by an individual not domiciled in the U.K., nor deemed to be domiciled by IHTA 1984, s. 267, is excluded property. It is irrelevant how he acquired his beneficial entitlement.

Unlike capital gains tax (see CGTA 1979, s. 18 (4)) the inheritance tax legislation contains no situs rules for determining whether property is located in the U.K. or overseas and consequently the common law situs rules will apply:

(i) *Registered securities* are situated where they are registered which is generally the place where the share register is kept and where the shares can be dealt with, *See R* v. *Williams and Another* [1942] AC 541; where dealings may take place in two or more countries the situs is the country in which the registered owner would ordinarily deal, *Treasurer for Ontario* v. *Aberdein* [1947] AC 24 and *Standard Chartered Bank Ltd.* v. *I.R. Comrs.* [1978] STC 272.

(ii) *Bearer securities* are situated in the country in which the title documents are kept, *Winans and Another* v. *A.-G.* (No. 2) [1910] AC 27. However, where Eurobonds are held through the Euroclear system the CTO appear to have regard to the location of the broker.

(iii) *Renounceable letters of allotment* of shares in U.K. companies were held to have a U.K. situs irrespective of the location of the documents, in a CGT case, *Young and Another* v. *Phillips* [1984] STC 520.

(iv) *Debts* A simple contract debt is generally situated in the country where the debtor resides. Where there is more than one country regard will be had to the contract terms to localise the debt, *New York Life Insurance Co. Ltd* v. *Public Trustee* [1924] 2 Ch. 101. A speciality debt (that is debts based on a document under seal) including mortgages under seal is located where the document is situate at the time of the disposition by the creditor, *Royal Trust Co.* v. *A.-G. for Alberta* [1930] AC 144.

(v) *Freehold and leasehold land* is located where the property is situated.

(vi) *Movable property* is located where physically situated. However, see Extra-statutory concession F7 (1988) where foreign works of art temporarily in the U.K. are not charged to tax. Ships are generally situated where registered unless within U.K. territorial or national waters, see *The Trustees Executors and Agency Co. Ltd and Others* v. *I.R. Comrs.* [1973] STC 96.

Gilt-edged securities issued as free of taxation if in the beneficial ownership of a non-ordinarily resident, non-U.K. domiciled person are excluded property and therefore free of inheritance tax if in the beneficial ownership of such a person or if held in trust and such a person has a qualifying interest in possession therein, see IHTA 1984, s. 59. Such issues ceased between 18 March 1977 and 1985. The securities maturing in 1987 or later covered by this exemption are as follows:

3½ per cent. War Loan 1952 or after, Savings Certificates issued before 1 September 1922, and also the 7th and 8th and the £1 issues.

Rate	Stock	Year	Rate	Stock	Year
9%	Conversion Stock	2000	8¾%	Treasury Stock	1997
9¾%	Conversion Stock	2003	9%	Treasury Stock	1994
11%	Exchequer Stock	1990	9%	Treasury Stock	1992–96
13¼%	Exchequer Stock	1996	9%	Treasury Stock	2008
5¾%	Funding Stock	1987–91	9½%	Treasury Stock	1999
6%	Funding Stock	1993	10%	Treasury Stock	1993
6½%	Funding Stock	1985–87	10%	Treasury Stock	1994
2%	Index Linked Treasury Stock	1992	10%	Treasury Convertible Stock	1991
2½%	Index Linked Treasury Stock	2024	10½%	Treasury Convertible Stock	1992
5½%	Treasury Stock	2008–12	12½%	Treasury Stock	1993
6¾%	Treasury Stock	1995–98	12¾%	Treasury Stock	1992
7¾%	Treasury Stock	1985–88	12¾%	Treasury Stock	1995
7¾%	Treasury Stock	2012–15	13%	Treasury Stock	1990
8%	Treasury Stock	1992	13¼%	Treasury Stock	1997
8%	Treasury Stock	2002–6	13¾%	Treasury Stock	1993
8¼%	Treasury Stock	1987–90	14½%	Treasury Stock	1994
8½%	Treasury Stock	2000	15¼%	Treasury Stock	1996
8½%	Treasury Stock	2007	15½%	Treasury Stock	1998

It would appear that a non-domiciled non-ordinary resident person deemed to be domiciled under IHTA 1984, s. 267 could make transfers free of inheritance tax by acquiring such exempt gilts and transferring them *in specie* to the proposed beneficiary. In appropriate circumstances trustees might wish to switch investments to hold such securities if the person having a qualified interest in possession qualifies for the exemption *i.e.* actually a non-domiciled, non-ordinarily resident person.

There are anti-avoidance provisions to minimise exploitation of the relief where after 19 April 1978 property has been resettled in particular circumstances. It is provided that on a re-settlement it is necessary for both settlements to comply with the requirements of exclusion (see above) and IHTA 1984, s. 48.

If a person domiciled in the Channel Islands or Isle of Man is beneficially entitled to savings of the type mentioned, they are treated as excluded property and therefore exempt from inheritance tax.

The pay and chattels of a member of visiting forces resident in the U.K. (who is not a British citizen, British Dependent Territories citizen or British Overseas citizen) is excluded property.

RATES

7. Rates. (B1.42)
The rates are set out in Schedule 1 to this Act.

From 18 March 1986 it is necessary to aggregate a transfer on death or during life only with transfers made within the previous seven-year period (from 27 July 1981 to 17 March 1986 a ten year period applied). However, note that when computing tax on a transfer after 17 March 1986 transfers made within the previous seven years will be aggregated even if made pre-18 March 1986.

From 18 March 1984 there is one table of death rates (previously for capital transfer tax there were two tables, one for lifetime transfers and the other for transfers on death) and chargeable lifetime transfers are charged at one half of the death scale. However, where the donor dies the tax situation of all gifts made within the previous seven years will be reviewed and the tax charge on each gift computed separately at the death rates at the time of the donor's death but subject to a taper relief on the tax where the gift was made more than three years before the death.

Note that potentially exempt transfers within seven years of death become chargeable transfers, see IHTA 1984, s. 3A. When computing the tax, the value of each gift is the amount of the original transfer (not the current value of property representing it) and each gift is essentially regarded as a "mini-estate" on its own (entirely separate from the estate on death) and is aggregated as the top slice with gifts made in the seven years prior to it (even though some of the earlier gifts may have been made more than seven years before death). The resultant tax is tapered where the death occurs more than three years before the gift as follows:

Tax payable
Gift within 4 years of death—80% of normal rates
Gift within 5 years of death—60% of normal rates
Gift within 6 years of death—40% of normal rates
Gift within 7 years of death—20% of normal rates

The tapered rates do not apply to chargeable transfers made before 18 March 1986 even where the transferor dies after that date.

The tax charge on a previously chargeable gift (for example a gift to a discretionary trust) is computed in the same way except (*a*) where the tax exceeds the tax charge on the original transfer only the excess is payable and (*b*) where the tax charge is less than the original charge no repayment is given.

Note that in computing inheritance tax on the estate at death the full value of all gifts made within the seven years of death are aggregated with the estate the latter being regarded as the top slice when applying the table rates.

See also IHTA 1984, s. 264 for transfers reported late.

8. Indexation of rate bands. (D4.02)
Unless Parliament determines otherwise the inheritance tax rate band is index linked. The increase applied each year (assuming that there is one) is measured by reference to the increase in the general index of retail prices (RPI) during the year to the December ending in the preceding tax year. For example the 1990–91 band was increased by reference to the movement in the RPI between December 1988 and December 1989. The figure is rounded up to a multiple of £1,000.

The Treasury, before each 6 April, publish a statutory instrument specifying the revised rate table which is a similar procedure to that adopted for the indexation of income tax thresholds and allowances under TA 1988, s. 1.

9. Transitional provisions on reduction of tax. (B1.41)
IHTA 1984, Sch. 2 is introduced with provisions that apply on any change in rates of tax.

DISPOSITIONS THAT ARE NOT TRANSFERS OF VALUE

10. Dispositions not intended to confer gratuitous benefit. (C1.01, 21)
A disposition is not a transfer of value provided it can be shown that there was no gratuitous intent in favour of anyone, not necessarily the transferee, and that either it was a transaction at arm's length between unconnected persons or a disposition that might be expected to be made in an arm's length transaction between unconnected persons. Gratuitous intent was established in *Macpherson* v. *I.R. Comrs.* [1987] STC 73. See also the estate duty cases of *A.-G.* v. *Boden and Another* [1912] 1 KB 539 and *A.-G.* v. *Ralli* (1936) 15 ATC 523 where the transactions were held to be commercial for full consideration. If the disposition is a sale of shares or debentures in an unquoted company it is also necessary to show that the price was freely negotiated at the time of sale, or was at such a price.
For partnership assurance policies, see Extra-statutory concession F 10 (1988).

11. Dispositions for maintenance of family. (C1.22–23)
Transfers during life are exempt if made by one party to a marriage in favour of the other or of a child of either party which is for the maintenance of the other party, or for the maintenance, education or training of a child under 18 or undergoing full-time education, or after that age until such education ceases.
Relief is also available for such transfers to a child not in the care of a parent with a restriction that relief is only available after age 18 if the child has for substantial periods been in the care of the transferor. Relief is available for an illegitimate child or for an adopted child. Transfers for the reasonable maintenance of dependent relatives are also exempt.
If the transfer is a disposal of an interest in possession in settled property the interest is not deemed to have ceased under IHTA 1984, s. 51.
Marriage and other terms are defined. A lump sum payment such as for an education policy or school fees in advance may come within these provisions. Divorce settlements will not generally give rise to chargeable transfers.
See also Extra-statutory concession F 12 (1988).

12. Dispositions allowable for income tax or conferring retirement benefits. (C1.25, 26)
An allowable expense for income tax or corporation tax is not a chargeable transfer. In addition, it should be noted that a contribution to an approved occupational, retirement annuity or personal pension scheme is not a transfer. Other pension provisions not greater than allowable under an approved scheme to non-connected former employees or their dependants are also exempt. Rent free or reduced rent occupation is to be regarded as a pension equivalent to rent forgone. This section applies to all inheritance tax dispositions other than on death and partial relief is given where a payment partially qualifies.
The fact that a disposition is a payment not allowable in computing profits or gains for income tax purposes because, for example, it is an entertaining expense or a payment for a capital asset does not necessarily mean that it would be treated as a transfer of value, but it appears technically necessary to satisfy the provisions of IHTA 1984, s. 10 to show it is not a transfer of value. It might also be necessary to consider IHTA 1984, s. 94 (close companies).

13. Dispositions by close companies for benefit of employees. (C1.27)
A transfer after 6 April 1976 to trusts for the benefit of employees within IHTA 1984, s. 86 by a close company is not a chargeable transfer for inheritance tax provided that the employees benefiting include all or most of the company's employees. A transfer by an individual of shares so that after the transfer the trustees of the employees' trust hold more than half the ordinary shares in the company and have voting control, is an exempt transfer. (IHTA 1984, s. 28 amendment with effect from 11 April 1978 as previously the transferee had to divest himself of all his shares). There are restrictions on the trust making dispositions to existing or former participators (within ten years prior to the disposition) with the exception that persons entitled to, or entitled to acquire less than 5 per cent. of the issued share capital of any class, or who would be entitled to less than 5 per cent. of the company's assets on a winding up are ignored. Capital gains tax relief for such a transfer is given under CGTA 1979, s. 149.
It should be noted that it is no longer necessary for the transferor to dispose of all his shares to the trust as the section provides that no person connected with the transferor must be able to benefit from the trusts.
See SP/E11.

14. Waiver of remuneration. (C1.28)
The waiver or repayment of remuneration is not a transfer of value for inheritance tax where apart from the waiver or repayment a Schedule E tax liability would arise. The payer's accounts must be

adjusted accordingly so that the amount waived or repaid is brought into charge for tax. It is suggested that in order to be effective the waiver should be under seal.

15. Waiver of dividends. (C1.29)
A waiver of a dividend within twelve months before the due date of payment is not a transfer of value for inheritance tax purposes and it is suggested that in order to be effective the waiver document should be made under seal.

16. Grant of tenancies of agricultural property. (C2.22)
The grant of a tenancy of agricultural property in the U.K., Channel Islands or the Isle of Man for full consideration in money or money's worth is not regarded as a transfer of value. The Revenue have previously argued that because of the substantial difference in value between tenanted and untenanted agricultural land the mere grant of a tenancy even for full value could be a chargeable transfer for inheritance tax purposes. The section applies to tenancies granted at any time, whether before or after the passing of FA 1981, and to this extent is retrospective in effect.

17. Changes in distribution of deceased's estate, etc. (D5.01–05, 31, 42–44, 61)
A deed of family arrangement or any instrument made in writing within two years of death can override the will or intestacy as at the date of death for inheritance tax purposes provided (*a*) that written notice of the instrument of variation or disclaimer is given to the Revenue within six months of its execution (or such longer period as the Board may allow), and (*b*) that the other conditions contained in IHTA 1984 s. 142 are complied with. Only one variation can be made within these provisions: *Russell* v. *I.R. Comrs.* [1988] STC 195. As to precatory bequests within two years of death see IHTA 1984, s. 143. The effect under both IHTA 1984, ss. 142 and 143 is that the deceased is deemed to have bequeathed his estate originally in the manner in which it is ultimately divided.

In Scotland, subject to any renunciation of the legitim, the inheritance tax on the death is chargeable as if the dispositions to the spouse did not include any part which would encroach upon the legitim.

PART II EXEMPT TRANSFERS

CHAPTER I GENERAL

18. Transfers between spouses. (B2.01; C3.11)
Transfers between spouses are exempt to an unlimited extent if both are domiciled or non-domiciled in the U.K., or if only the transferee is domiciled here. If, however, the transferee spouse is not domiciled in the U.K. and the transferor spouse is domiciled in the U.K., the exemption is limited to £55,000 which is an addition to the nil rate band under IHTA 1984, s. 37. However after 17 March 1986 excess gifts above the £55,000 threshold may qualify as potentially exempt transfers under IHTA 1984, s. 3A. Note that the gifts with reservation provisions contained in FA 1986, s. 102 and effective after 17 March 1986 do not apply to exempt spouse transfers.

Note that this section provides that if a condition has to be satisfied for the spouse to take an interest in the property, it must be so satisfied within 12 months of the transfer. The usual condition would be that the spouse survives the testator for a specified period of no more than twelve months. This should be compared with the six months *commorientes* period allowed by IHTA 1984, s. 92.

There are exceptions to certain of the exemptions. The exceptions are:

(*a*) if the disposition takes effect (in possession) after any period or a prior interest terminating but subject to the proviso that this does not apply if the period relates only to surviving the other spouse for a stated period. Thus exemption may unwittingly be lost by granting prior powers of maintenance, or occupation of property, for example to a housekeeper, the residue ultimately passing to the spouse or a charity. Such provisions in wills should be incorporated after a detailed consideration of the consequences.

(*b*) if the disposition is subject to a condition not satisfied within 12 months. Having regard to the reference to satisfying and to the defeasible provision mentioned below for IHTA 1984, ss. 23–25, it is unclear if this refers only to conditions precedent *e.g.* a contingent gift which does not vest until the condition is satisfied, and not to conditions subsequent such as a defeasible interest where there is immediate vesting but subsequently on breach of a condition the property is taken away.

(*c*) if after 15 April 1976 a reversionary interest in settled property has been acquired by the donee spouse for money or money's worth, para. 1 does not apply in relation to the property when it falls into possession on the termination of the immediate prior interest.

(*d*) if after 9 March 1981 property is given in consideration for the transfer of a reversionary interest in settled property where the latter, by virtue of IHTA 1984, s. 55 does not form part of the acquirers estate. There is an exemption for reversionary interests acquired before 10 March 1981 and for an interest under a settlement created before 16 April 1976.

See also IHTA 1984, s. 268 for the "associated operations" provisions and the Revenue view as to the application of *Furniss* v. *Dawson* [1984] STC 153.

19. Annual exemption. (C3.01, 02)

Each individual is entitled to exempt lifetime transfers of up to £3,000 (without grossing up) in each tax year. To the extent that a transferor's chargeable transfers are less than £3,000 in any tax year the shortfall may be carried forward for one year only, and added to the annual exemption available in the next year to the extent that transfers in that year exceed £3,000. Note that the annual exemption for each tax year has to be utilised against transfers in that year before any unused balance of the annual allowance brought forward from the previous year may be used. From 18 March 1986 the annual exemption is applied first against non-potentially exempt transfers and then against potentially exempt transfers which become chargeable and which are deemed to have been made later in the year than any other transfer. Consequently it would be possible for a carried forward exemption applied against a chargeable transfer to be withdrawn in favour of a potentially exempt transfer becoming chargeable in the previous year.

The Revenue do not generally require a return where cash gifts are made within the annual exemptions, and for gifts after 31 March 1981, there has been a further relaxation in the account provisions. See IHTA 1984, s. 216 and Inland Revenue Press Release, dated 9 October 1981.

See *Ray and Redman's Inheritance Tax Planning*, (1989, Butterworths) for the planning possibilities from this and other exemptions.

This exemption does not apply to deemed dispositions such as by settlements or on death except on the termination of an interest in possession from 6 April 1981, see IHTA 1984, s. 7. There is an exception for close company apportionments under IHTA 1984, s. 94. See also IHTA 1984, s. 57.

As to capital gains tax holdover on chargeable disposals after 13 March 1989 where covered by the annual exemption see CGTA 1979, s. 147A.

20. Small gifts. (C3.03)

Lifetime gifts not exceeding £250 per recipient (without grossing up) made by individuals (but not by trusts) in each tax year are exempt. The gifts with reservation provisions contained in FA 1986, s. 102 do not apply to gifts exempt under this section.

This exemption does not apply to deemed dispositions.

21. Normal expenditure out of income. (C3.01, 04)

A lifetime transfer of value is exempt from inheritance tax if it was made as part of the normal expenditure of the transferor and taking one year with another is made out of his income, provided he was on average left with sufficient income to maintain his usual standard of living. What is "normal" may be a difficult matter to resolve particularly when the expenditure first commences, but a transfer will usually be considered normal if it is made three times with the intention of continuing to make similar transfers. If there is a contract or it can be shown there is an intention to make continuing payments, for example, under a life assurance policy it is thought it would probably be treated as normal expenditure from the first such payment. Whether the income is net after tax paid (or payable) is unclear and in particular whether an individual can claim (provided it can be shown) that he meets his taxes wholly or partially out of capital resources is open to doubt. However, if a married woman is in receipt of income in her own right, but her husband pays the tax thereon and she does not contribute to the household living expenses, it could be argued that the whole of her gross income was available to make normal expenditure transfers. The case is similar if one can identify the whole or part of the income going into a separate bank or other account from which the "normal expenditure" payments are made. For the Revenue view see Inland Revenue letter, 9 June 1976.

What is a person's usual standard of living may also be a matter of some argument and especially, if the standard changes, *e.g.* on an individual's retirement or move to a different area where the social life is much more limited.

An insurance premium on a policy on the transferor's life is not treated as part of normal expenditure if the insurance policy and a purchased annuity are linked unless it can be shown they were not associated operations within IHTA 1984, s. 268. It would therefore be necessary to show that both the insurance policy and the annuity were taken out on the insurance company's normal terms for the life assured. It may be prudent to take them out with different companies.

It is also provided that the capital element of a purchased life annuity (as defined in TA 1988, s. 656) purchased after 12 November 1974 is not to be included as income for the normal expenditure rules which is an adverse change from the estate duty practice but it demonstrates that the term "income" is not confined to "income" in the taxation sense.

An important use of the normal expenditure rules in practice, is to enable an individual to provide for the future payment of inheritance tax through, for example, joint whole life last survivor insurance policies written on the lives of himself and his spouse in favour of his children or grandchildren where he gifts the annual premiums (or amounts thereof).

The exemption does not apply to deemed disposals. See also FA 1986, s. 102 (gifts with reservation) after 17 March 1986.

22. Gifts in consideration of marriage. (C3.01, 05)
There is an additional exemption of up to £5,000 (calculated without grossing up) by a parent of the bride or groom in respect of an outright lifetime gift or gift in trust to either or both of them. If the transferor is a grandparent or remoter ancestor or is the bride giving to the groom or vice versa, the limit is £2,500. For other persons the limit of the exempt transfer is £1,000. From 18 March 1986 such gifts may qualify as potentially exempt transfers under IHTA 1984, s. 3A.

The gifts must be in consideration of the particular marriage which has been arranged and should therefore be made prior to the marriage taking place, or under an enforceable agreement made prior to the marriage.

If the gift is under a marriage settlement the beneficiaries must be within the classes defined by IHTA 1984, s. 21.

From 6 April 1981 this exemption is extended to the termination of an interest in possession as a result of which trust property is transferred to the parties to the marriage absolutely or resettled in trust for them. The beneficiary becoming absolutely entitled is the deemed transferor within the normal marriage exemption limits. In order to qualify for the relief the transferor must give six months' notice to the trustees (from the date of the transfer) informing them of the extent of any marriage exemption available.

The exemption only applies to actual disposals and not deemed disposals. See also IHTA 1984, s. 57. Note that the "gifts with reservation" provisions contained in FA 1986, s. 102 do not apply to gifts exempt under this section.

23. Gifts to charities. (B2.02; C3.12)
Subject to the anti-avoidance provisions in IHTA 1984, s. 23, gifts to charities are exempt from inheritance tax without limit whether made during lifetime or on death.

Note that the "gifts with reservation" provisions contained in FA 1986, s. 102 do not apply to gifts exempt under this section which already contains extensive anti-avoidance provisions summarised below.

The exceptions (*b*), (*c*) and (*d*) to the exemptions in s. 18 above also apply here and further provisions also apply and the relief is not available if:
(i) the disposition is defeasible
(ii) what is given is an interest in other property and the donor still retains any interest therein
(iii) the disposition is for a limited period
(iv) the disposition is of an interest in settled property and the property remains comprised in the settlement
(v) in relation to land (or a building) the donor has created an interest or reserved an interest and that interest entitles him (or his spouse or a connected person) to occupation or possession of the land or building (or part) rent free or below an arm's length rent. It appears that if someone other than the donor had created or reserved the interest this provision would be inapplicable
(vi) property not within (v) above is subject to an interest created or reserved by the donor, unless he received full consideration in money or money's worth for the creation, or the interest does not substantially affect the donee's enjoyment of the gift.
It appears that the creation or reservation in (v) and (vi) above could have happened many years ago.
(vii) the property (or part) may become applicable other than for charitable purposes unless it becomes property of a body specified in ss. 24, 25 or 26 or s. 24A where the property is land for transfers after 13 March 1989.
The position 12 months after the disposition is considered in deciding if (ii), (v) or (vi) apply. Thus if originally the donor had retained part of an interest in other property but within the 12 months also gifts that part, the exception would not apply. Furthermore for (i) if the defeasance period does not exceed 12 months and at the expiration the gift has not been defeated, it is regarded as indefeasible originally.

The restrictions on exemptions for gifts to charities, political parties, for national purposes or for public benefit are modified so that the exemption does not apply if the property was comprised in a trust and the exempt body, including the trustees of an approved maintenance fund under IHTA 1984, Sch. 4, para. 1, for events after 8 March 1982, had acquired an interest in the trust for money or money's worth—this applies for acquisitions after 11 April 1978—IHTA 1984, s. 53.

It should be noted that a gift is regarded as made if it becomes the property of, or is held on trust for, the recipient and "donor" is construed accordingly. Thus a sale of property at under-value is "a gift" for this purpose.

24. Gifts to political parties. (B2.03; C3.13; D2.05)
Transfers in favour of qualifying political parties (defined by reference to general election voting criteria) are exempt. Transfers before 15 March 1988 were exempt, but the exemption for those made during the year before death was limited to £100,000. See IHTA 1984, s. 23 for the conditions of such a transfer. Note that the "gifts with reservation" provisions contained in FA 1986, s. 102 do not apply to gifts exempt under this section.
As to capital gains tax for disposals after 13 March 1989 see CGTA 1979, s. 147A.

24A. Gifts to housing associations. (B2.03A)
A gift of land after 13 March 1989 in favour of a registered housing association is exempt from inheritance tax to the extent that the value transferred is attributable to land in the U.K. The extensive anti-avoidance provisions contained in IHTA 1984, s. 23 applicable to gifts to charities (and various other gifts) also apply to gifts under this section. In addition the gifted property will be related property of the donor under the IHTA 1984, s. 161 (2). As to the equivalent capital gains tax exemption, see CGTA 1979, s. 146A.

25. Gifts for national purposes, etc. (B2.04; C3.14)
Transfers to the national institutions listed and referred to are exempt without limit. Distributions etc. from discretionary trusts are exempt under IHTA 1984, s. 96. See Department of Education and Science Press Release, March 1977 and Appendix 5 (Capital taxation and the national heritage). For CGT exemption see CGTA 1979, s. 147 (2).
See also IHTA 1984, s. 23 for conditions for such a transfer and note that condition (ii) does not apply if what is given is the benefit of an agreement restricting the use of land, *e.g.* a restrictive covenant. Note that the "gifts with reservation" provisions contained in FA 1986, s. 102 do not apply to gifts exempt under this section.

26. Gifts for public benefit. (B2.05; C3.15)
Transfers for the public benefit to a non-profit-making organisation may, if the Treasury so direct, be treated as exempt transfers. Distributions etc. from discretionary trusts are exempt under IHTA 1984, s. 76. For CGT exemption see CGTA 1979, ss. 147 (1), 147A.
See s. 23 above for the conditions for such a transfer. Note that the "gifts with reservation" provisions contained in FA 1986, s. 102 do not apply to gifts exempt under this section.

26A. Potentially exempt transfer of property subsequently held for national purposes, etc. (Division C4)
A potentially exempt transfer that becomes chargeable to tax after 17 March 1986 on the death of the donor within seven years of the gift comprising property that either has or could be designated by the Treasury under IHTA 1984, s. 31 as being of historic, scenic or scientific interest, etc. will in certain circumstances be regarded as an exempt transfer. The circumstances are a disposal of such property during the period beginning with the date of original transfer and ending with the date of the transferors death by way of (*a*) sale by private treaty or gift to a national institution as listed in IHTA 1984, Sch. 3, or (*b*) a disposal in satisfaction of tax under IHTA 1984, s. 230.

27. Maintenance funds for historic buildings, etc. (B2.06; G5.41–43)
A transfer of value is an exempt transfer if made to a fund approved by the Treasury under IHTA 1984, Sch. 4 either at the time of transfer or subsequently.
The anti-avoidance provisions contained in s. 23 above are applied. In broad terms this means that the transfer should be an outright unconditional transfer of the whole of the donor's interest in the property and must not be subject to any prior interest before receipt by a maintenance fund. See IHTA 1984, s. 57A where property accrues to a fund on termination of an interest in possession after 16 March 1987. Note that the "gifts with reservation" provisions contained in FA 1986, s. 102 do not apply to gifts exempt under this section. As to capital gains tax for disposals after 13 March 1989 see CGTA 1979, s. 147A.

28. Employee trusts. (B2.07)
The rules relating to an exempt transfer into an employee trust for inheritance tax purposes are modified where the property is held in trust as prescribed by IHTA 1984, s. 86 (1) for the benefit of all or most of the employees of the company. It is also necessary for the trustees to hold more than half the ordinary shares of the company and have voting control on all questions affecting the company as a whole ignoring limited class rights. There must be no conditions under which the trustees may be relieved of their powers without consent. The beneficiaries must not include a participator in the company or a participator in any close company which had transferred funds to the trust, or who has been such a participator or a person connected with a participator during the

previous ten years. Participators who are not beneficially entitled to 5 per cent. or more of the shares of any class are excluded. The rules apply to transfers of value made after 10 April 1978. Note that the "gifts with reservation" provisions contained in FA 1986, s. 102 do not apply to gifts exempt under this section.

29. Loans—modifications of exemptions. (B2.02; G3.12–13)
For the purpose of the exemptions under the above sections where there is a transfer of value involving a loan transaction (whether of money or other property), it is specifically provided that the notional cost to the lender is deemed to be a normal one out of income so that it is only necessary to show that after allowing for all transfers of value part of his normal expenditure the transferor was left sufficient income to maintain his usual standard of living, in order to qualify for the exemption under section 21 above.

29A. Abatement of exemption where claim settled out of beneficiary's own resources. (D5.34)
This section applies in relation to deaths occurring after 26 July 1989 where a beneficiary (the exempt beneficiary) receives an exempt transfer from a deceased's estate and settles a claim against the estate out of his own resources. The exempt transfers referred to are to a spouse, to charities, political parties, for national purposes or public benefit and to maintenance funds and to employee trusts.

The original exempt transfer is reduced to the extent that the beneficiary uses funds to settle the claim, calculated by reference to the diminution in his estate as a result of the transfer. Where the beneficiary's disposition itself results in a transfer of value, any resultant tax liability and business or agricultural property reliefs available to the beneficiary are ignored. As a further complexity the grossing up provisions of IHTA 1984, s. 38 (attribution of value to specific gifts) will apply because the beneficiary's disposition is deemed to be a specific gift not bearing its own tax.

CHAPTER II CONDITIONAL EXEMPTION

30. Conditionally exempt transfers. (G5.11; K1.22)
Lifetime transfers of historic houses, works of art etc. may be conditionally exempt from inheritance tax provided that the transferor or his spouse had between them been beneficially entitled to the property throughout the six years ended with the transfer, or the asset was acquired on death when the asset was conditionally exempt or left out of account under the relevant estate duty rules. Whether or not a transfer will qualify as a potentially exempt transfer made after 17 March 1986 will be decided without reference to this section—probably on the grounds that under IHTA 1984, s. 3A (1) (*b*) a transfer already exempt cannot qualify as being potentially exempt. It will be noted that a claim for conditional exemption will not be allowed until after the transferor's death and that conditional exemption will not be available to the extent that property comprised in a potentially exempt transfer has been sold by the transferee before the transferor's death. This section applies to transfers after 6 April 1976. See also FA 1985, Sch. 26.

IHTA 1984, ss. 30–35 inclusive provide the detailed rules applicable to such assets.

Capital gains tax relief on such transfers is given by CGTA 1979, ss. 147, 147A.

The relief also applies on death without the necessity of having owned the asset for six years or having inherited it.

31. Designation and undertakings. (G5.12)
The objects which the Treasury has power to designate as qualifying works of art etc. are defined and include pictures, books, works of art, scientific collections, land or buildings, amenity land and historical objects. Land essential for the protection of the character and amenities of a building of outstanding historic or architectural interest no longer has to adjoin the building for exemption to apply. The Treasury may require separate undertakings where different people are entitled to different properties. The owner has to give an undertaking that the property will be kept permanently in the U.K. and that reasonable steps will be taken for its preservation and for securing reasonable access to the public. See H.C. Written Ans., 9 February 1987, Appendix 5, Capital taxation and the national heritage, and Appendix 6, Capital taxation and works of art. Where a claim for designation is made in respect of a transfer of value occurring after 17 March 1986 which qualified as a potentially exempt transfer under IHTA 1984, s. 3A but which becomes chargeable (because of the donors death within seven years of the gift) a decision as to whether the property is suitable for designation will be based on the circumstances existing following the transferor's death.

32. Chargeable events. (G5.11; K1.22)
A conditionally exempt transfer becomes liable to inheritance tax on the happening of a chargeable event at the rates in force at that time unless the transfer qualified as a potentially exempt transfer made after 17 March 1986 (see IHTA 1984, s. 3A) when tax will be chargeable only if the transferor

dies within seven years of making the gift. This can happen when an undertaking has not been observed in a material respect or on death, sale, gift or other disposal, unless the disposal is a sale to an approved institution or the asset is transferred to the Board in satisfaction of inheritance tax. However, a death or gift is not a chargeable event if the transfer is itself a conditionally exempt transfer with the legatee or donee giving the appropriate undertakings to the Treasury. See H.C. Written Ans., 25 June 1980, Vol. 987, col. 202.

32A. Associated properties. (G5.11; K1.22)

As various people may be required to give undertakings, this section provides conditional exemption for associated properties, that is an historic building, its amenity land and objects historically associated with it. The death of the owner or the disposal of any of the associated properties is a chargeable event for inheritance tax, unless the personal representatives or trustees dispose of the property by private treaty to a museum or similar body, or the property is transferred in specie in settlement of tax or the disposal qualifies as a potentially exempt transfer made after 17 March 1986 (see IHTA 1984, s. 3A). If there is a part disposal, the exemption does not extend to the remainder unless the appropriate undertaking is given over the remaining property. If the disposal occurs on death and the appropriate undertaking is given, the transfer may again be conditionally exempt. If there is a partial disposal which is not itself exempt, it is regarded as a disposal of the whole property unless the appropriate undertaking is given for the remainder and it still qualifies under the heritage property rules.

33. Amount of charge under section 32. (E5.51; G5.11, 31, 32; K1.22)

Inheritance tax will be payable on a chargeable event on a transfer of value equal to the value of the property at the time of the chargeable event and at one half the table rate from 18 March 1986 under IHTA 1984, s. 7, if what is termed the relevant person is alive, and if he is dead at the appropriate table rate as if it were the highest part of his estate. As a transitional measure following the introduction of inheritance tax from 18 March 1986 when calculating tax on a chargeable event on, or after that date by reference to a death occurring before that date it is to be assumed that the amendments to IHTA 1984, s. 7 (rates) made by FA 1986 were in force at the time of the earlier death—thus securing the benefit of the shorter seven year cumulation period and higher tax threshold. Note that under sub-s. (2A) the death of the relevant person after a lifetime chargeable event will not result in a recomputation of the tax rate on that earlier event—this should exclude the possibility of potentially exempt transfers made after 17 March 1986 but prior to the chargeable event entering into the tax calculation at that time, should they become chargeable on the donors death within seven years. See IHTA 1984, s. 3A. A sale at an arm's length value not intended to confer any gratuitous benefit is deemed to take place at the sale price. See *Tyser* v. *A.-G.* [1938] Ch 426 where in a similarly worded estate duty provision "proceeds of sale" was interpreted as meaning the net proceeds of sale after deducting the expenses of sale. See IHTA 1984, s. 78 where in certain circumstances for discretionary trusts the rates of tax under sub-s. (1) (*b*) (i) and (1) (*b*) (ii) of this section are modified.

For the purposes of computing the inheritance tax payable on a chargeable event (other than one within IHTA 1984, s. 79) it is necessary to identify the "relevant person" who will be deemed to have made the transfer. However, this section is concerned only with chargeable events following transactions which have either been conditionally exempt transfers, or have occurred on "conditionally exempt occasions", *i.e.,* generally transfers by trustees which are not chargeable under IHTA 1984, ss. 58–85 because of IHTA 1984, s. 78. Where the "last transaction" (see below) was a conditionally exempt transfer the relevant person is the original transferor. However, where the last transaction was a "conditionally exempt occasion", the relevant person is the settlor (or if there is more than one, such person as the Board may select).

Where there have been two or more transactions the "last transaction" will be the latest transaction within the period of thirty years prior to the chargeable event. Where there has been more than one transaction within the thirty year period the Board may select the "last transaction". Inheritance tax on the chargeable event is calculated as though the relevant person had made an additional chargeable transfer. If the relevant person is alive the amount is added to his cumulative gifts total and computed at one half the table rate, whereas if he has died it is added to the amount of his estate.

34. Reinstatement of transferor's cumulative total. (G5.15)

It is provided that a chargeable event is treated as part of the cumulative total of the person who made the last conditionally exempt transfer before the chargeable event. Note he may not have been designated the relevant person for IHTA 1984, s. 38 above. If he is alive this affects subsequent chargeable transfers by him. If he is dead the amount on which the tax becomes payable on the chargeable event is added to the value of his estate at his death. It is also provided that if the property has been comprised in a settlement made less than thirty years before the chargeable event a settlor who has made a conditionally exempt transfer of the property can be placed in the position of a person who made the last conditionally exempt transfer before the chargeable event.

35. Conditional exemption on death before 7 April 1976. (G5.21)
Schedule 5 is introduced. IHTA 1984, Sch. 5 relating to conditional exemption for works of art etc. on death does not apply in respect of any death after 6 April 1976. The provisions relating to sales only apply to arm's length sales where there was no intention to confer gratuitous benefits. There are provisions for events originally dealt with under FA 1975, ss. 31–34 (or FA 1930, s. 40 (2)) to be taken into account as appropriate for the new conditionally exempt transfer sections.

CHAPTER III ALLOCATION OF EXEMPTIONS

36. Preliminary. (D2.11)
The purpose of the supplementary provisions is to ascertain the tax payable on a transfer of value to which IHTA 1984, ss. 18, 23–27 and 30 apply, which is only partly exempt. Such a situation would usually arise on death where, for example, a share of the residue has been left to a surviving spouse, but the remainder of the residue has been left to a chargeable beneficiary.

Usually there will not be any significant difference in the total tax payable whether the legacies are left free of, or subject to, inheritance tax.

37. Abatement of gifts. (D2.12)
If gifts have to abate owing to an insufficiency of assets without regard to inheritance tax chargeable, all the calculations proceed as if they were gifts of a lesser sum.

If, as a result of the provisions of IHTA 1984, s. 38 attributing value to specific gifts, these in aggregate exceed the value transferred then the specific gifts have to be regarded as reduced to the value transferred. The individual specific gifts do not necessarily abate proportionately. It is necessary to consider under any rule of law or term of the disposition what could happen on a distribution of assets. If a foreign law applies to distribution of assets the order to be considered is under that law.

38. Attribution of value to specific gifts. (D2.13)
In the first instance it is necessary to ascertain the specific bequest where the inheritance tax falls on residue, *i.e.* specific gifts of personalty not given subject to bearing their own tax, or specific gifts of realty specifically made free of tax. The gift of realty will bear its own tax unless the will otherwise directs under IHTA 1984, s. 211. See IHTA 984, s. 39A for establishing the exempt part of an estate for transfers on or after 18 March 1986. Note that any liability not allowed as a deduction from the estate under IHTA 1984, s. 5 (5) or under FA 1986, s. 103 is treated as a specific gift.

Other than exempt gifts, those free of tax gifts have to be added together as if they were an estate on their own, and grossed at the appropriate death scale under IHTA 1984, s. 7. If all other bequests are exempt, for example if the residue is left to the widow, this grossing calculation will give the tax payable out of residue and the balance will pass to the surviving spouse.

If, however, apart from exempt gifts the estate includes specific gifts which do bear their own tax for example, realty and personalty expressly given subject to bearing their own tax, or a share of the residue in a chargeable estate, it is necessary to continue the calculations.

The gross equivalent of the free of tax gifts is deducted from the total estate and the balance divided between the chargeable gifts, *i.e.* chargeable share of residue and specific gifts subject to tax, and the exempt gifts, either an exempt share of residue or exempt specific gifts.

The gross equivalent of the free of tax gifts as calculated, is added to the specific gifts subject to tax, and the non-exempt share of residue to arrive at a new total of gross chargeable gifts.

A notional amount of tax is chargeable on this amount and an assumed notional rate of tax is arrived at by showing as a percentage the notional amount of tax divided by the notional total of chargeable gifts arrived at above.

This notional estate rate is applied to the net free of tax specific gifts to re-gross them once more at this notional estate rate.

The newly re-grossed free of tax gifts are added to any specific gifts bearing their own tax and deducted from the total estate to arrive at the exempt and chargeable shares of residue.

Figures should now be available for specific gifts subject to tax, the gross equivalent of the specific gifts free of tax, and the chargeable share of residue. Inheritance tax is calculated on these figures at the appropriate estate rate applicable to the aggregate of them.

This somewhat complex calculation can best be illustrated by examples.

EXAMPLE—Attribution of value to specific gifts
Peter Singer died on 7 August 1989, leaving an estate of £400,000. His will provided for pecuniary legacies free of IHT to his son Robert of £100,000 and to his nephew James of £30,000. The residue

was left equally to his daughter, Susan and his widow Ann. The legacy to Ann is exempt from tax under IHTA 1984, s. 18. There were no lifetime transfers except to utilise the inheritance tax annual exemptions.

(I) The free of IHT legacies total £130,000 and assuming these were the only transfers they would be equivalent to gross legacies of £138,000 on which tax at the death rate would be £8,000.

(II) On this basis the residue would be £400,000 − £138,000 = £262,000. Only one half of this, £131,000, would be chargeable (Susan's share) so the chargeable notional gross transfers total £138,000 + £131,000 = £269,000 on first grossing.

(III) Inheritance tax at the death scale on £269,000 is £60,400 giving an estate rate for regrossing of 22·45 per cent. *i.e.* (60,400/269,000) × 100. At this rate free of IHT legacies gross to (100,000/77·55) × 100 = £167,634.

(IV) The residue now becomes (£400,000 − £167,634) = £232,366 of which Ann's one half share of £116,183 is exempt leaving £283,817 liable to tax (*i.e.* £116,183 + £167,634) on which the IHT is £66,327 leaving a final estate rate of 23·37 per cent.

	£	£
Gross estate		400,000
Legacies—Robert	100,000	
Andrew	30,000	
	130,000	
Inheritance tax on notional figure of £167,634 at 23·37 per cent.		
(final estate rate)	39,176	
		169,176
Residue left		£230,824
Susan's legacy (¹/₂ of residue)		115,412
Inheritance tax on notional figure of £116,183 at 23·37 per cent.		27,152
		£88,260
Ann's legacy (¹/₂) (exempt)		£115,412

SUMMARY—	
Robert (son)	100,000
James (nephew)	30,000
Susan (daughter)	88,260
Ann (widow)	115,412
Inheritance tax £39,176 + £27,152	66,328
	£400,000

In the example had the residue of the estate comprised business or agricultural property reference would first be made to IHTA 1984, s. 39A to establish the exempt element of the estate before proceeding with the grossing calculations in respect of transfers after 17 March 1986.

39. Attribution of value to residuary gifts. (D2.14)
Residue is the amount left after deducting from the estate specific gifts and any inheritance tax payable out of them. See also IHTA 1984, s. 39A.

39A. Operation of sections 38 and 39 in cases of business or agricultural relief. (D2.16A)
This section prevents the exploitation of the rules under IHTA 1984, ss. 38, 39 whereby in a partially exempt estate all available business and agricultural reliefs (see IHTA 1984, ss. 104, 116) could accrue against the chargeable part of the estates even though part of the business or agricultural property passed to an exempt beneficiary. In a partly exempt estate comprising business or agricultural and other property, instead of specific gifts (for example a pecuniary legacy) of business or agricultural property being attributed gross against the transfer of value on death it will be reduced to the "appropriate fraction" of its value.

Specific gifts of business or agricultural property must first be reduced by the attributable business or agricultural property relief. The effect where for example a pecuniary legacy is left to an exempt spouse may be to reduce the exempt proportion of the estate consequently increasing the chargeable proportion, other business and agricultural reliefs being shared rateably between the exempt and chargeable parts of the estate. The numerator and denominator of the "appropriate fraction" are calculated as follows:

Numerator =   Total value transferred (after deducting business/agricultural relief) *less* specific gifts of business/agricultural property (after deducting reliefs).
Denominator =   Total value transferred (before deducting business/agricultural property reliefs) *less* specific gifts of business/agricultural property (before deducting reliefs).

Where an estate includes no business or agricultural property other than covered by specific bequests the numerator and denominator will be the same and there will be no reduction.

Where the grossing up provisions prescribed by IHTA 1984, s. 38 apply (for example where in a partially exempt estate there are chargeable bequests above the IHT nil rate band) the value of specific gifts is first calculated in accordance with this section before applying s. 38 provisions. For cases where pecuniary legacies are charged on business or agricultural property, see s. 39A (6).

EXAMPLE

	Estate (gross)	Estate (after reliefs)
	£	£
Partnership share (50% business relief)	200,000	100,000
Tenanted farmland (30% agricultural relief)	400,000	280,000
Vacate farmland (50% agricultural relief)	500,000	250,000
Other estate	100,000	100,000
	£1,200,000	
Transfer of value		£730,000

Terms of will
Legacy to widow £400,000
Tenanted farmland to daughter—Susie
Residue to sons—Peter, Robert and James
All bequests bearing their own tax

Attribution of gifts
  (i) Attribute value to specific gifts qualifying for business or agricultural property reliefs after deducting reliefs:
      To Susie—tenanted farmland   £280,000

 (ii) Attribute value to specific gifts of other property as reduced by the "appropriate fraction":
      To widow—pecuniary legacy   £400,000
      Appropriate fraction:

$$\frac{£730,000 - £280,000}{£1,200,000 - £400,000} = \frac{£450,000}{£800,000} \times £400,000 \qquad\qquad 225,000$$

(iii) Balance attributable to residue   225,000

                                                                                               £730,000

      Thus—Exempt portion of estate to widow   £225,000
           —Chargeable   505,000

                                                                                               £730,000

40. Gifts made separately out of different funds. (D2.14)
It is necessary to make separate multiple calculations where gifts are made out of separate funds, *e.g.* free estate and where a limited interest in settled property for a fixed number of years is partly

gifted as a specific legacy and partly falls into residue (partially exempt). It is unclear whether it is necessary to calculate two assumed rates as if each fund was a separate estate and then the revised two funds aggregated to get to the total estate for the true inheritance tax payable.

41. Burden of tax. (D2.15)
Inheritance tax is payable either by the donee or out of a chargeable proportion of residue and not out of exempt specific gifts or exempt shares of residue and this over-rides any terms of a disposition to the contrary.

42. Supplementary. (D2.11–15)
Provision is made for claims under the Scottish law of legitim to be treated as specific gifts bearing their own inheritance tax.
   Various terms are defined.

PART III SETTLED PROPERTY

CHAPTER I PRELIMINARY

43. Settlement and related expressions. (E1.11, 15, 16)
Settlement means any disposition whereby property is:
   (a) held in trust for persons in succession or for any persons subject to a contingency, or
   (b) held by trustees on trust to accumulate income or under discretionary powers, or
   (c) charged with the payment of any annuity or periodic payment otherwise than for full consideration.
   A lease for life or for a period related to a death is to be treated as a settlement unless granted for full consideration. Reciprocal partnership assurances may not be settlements (Extra-statutory concession F10 (1985)).

44. Settlor. (E1.21)
Settlor in relation to a settlement includes any person by whom the settlement was made directly or indirectly.

45. Trustee. (E1.22)
Trustee means, where there would otherwise be no trustee, the persons in whose name the property is vested.

46. Interest in possession: Scotland. (E1.44)
The making of a trust is a normal chargeable transfer by the settlor and taxed accordingly. See IHTA 1984, ss. 51 to 53 for further situations treated as settlements in Scotland. As to the timing of a distribution in a Scottish case, see *Stenhouse's Trustees* v. *Lord Advocate,* CS 1983, [1984] STC 195.

47. Reversionary interest. (Division E6)
A reversionary interest means a future interest under a settlement, whether vested or contingent.
   In Scotland an interest in the fee of property subject to a proper liferent is also a reversionary interest.

48. Excluded property. (E1.91, 101, 111)
A reversionary interest (defined in IHTA 1984, s. 47) is excluded property except in the circumstances specified below. Thus a reversionary interest acquired at any time by the person entitled to it, or a person previously so entitled, for a consideration in money or money's worth is not excluded property nor is a reversionary interest to which either the settlor, or his spouse is, or has been beneficially entitled. If Adam so acquired it (even pre March 1974) and on his death now, it is left to Benjamin, apparently Benjamin cannot claim that it is excluded property.
   Excluded property is not relevant property by virtue of IHTA 1984, s. 58(1) and is not therefore subject to the discretionary trust charging provisions contained in IHTA 1984, ss. 58–85. However, it should be noted that reversionary interests are not treated as excluded property for the purposes of IHTA 1984, s. 65 permitting, for example, re-investment in overseas property without crystallising a capital transfer tax charge.
   The reason why a reversionary interest acquired for value is not excluded property is in order to avoid a life tenant, who is deemed to be entitled to the entire trust fund, reducing his estate by paying for the reversionary interest, as he would then have an absolute interest in the trust fund, which he is already deemed to have, and his estate would have been reduced by the cash paid for the reversionary interest.
   See *Von Ernst & Cie S.A. and Others* v. *I.R. Comrs* [1980] STC 111 as to the material time for determining whether exempt securities constitute excluded property.

Property situated outside the U.K. comprised in a settlement wherever made is excluded property (although a reversionary interest in it is usually not) provided that the settlor was domiciled outside the U.K. at the time the property was transferred to the settlement (Inland Revenue letter, 3 December 1975). For events after 8 March 1982 excluded property is not relevant property by virtue of IHTA 1984, s. 58, and as such is not subject to the discretionary trust charging provisions contained in IHTA 1984, ss. 58–85. Domicile has its normal meaning in respect of settlements made before 10 December 1974, and thereafter its meaning as extended by IHTA 1984, s. 267.

A reversionary interest in property comprised in a settlement but situated outside the U.K.—

(1) is excluded property if the person beneficially entitled to it is domiciled outside the U.K. no matter how he acquired the interest.

(2) is also excluded property, whoever is beneficially entitled, unless it has been acquired for consideration or the settlor or his spouse is or has been entitled or it is a reversionary interest in a lease for life.

See also IHTA 1984, s. 82.

Where no qualifying interest in possession subsists in gilt-edged stocks specified (see IHTA 1984, s. 6) they also will be regarded as excluded property, provided that it can be shown that all current or prospective beneficiaries of the trust are neither domiciled nor ordinarily resident in the U.K. For this purpose domicile has its normal meaning not that extended by IHTA 1984, s. 267 but see *Von Ernst & Cie S.A. and others* v. *I.R. Comrs.* [1980] STC 111 and *Minden Trust (Cayman) Ltd.* v. *I.R. Comrs.* [1985] STC 758 where the scheme involved became ineffective after 19 April 1978 by amendments to sub-sections (4) and (5). A scheme to exploit this relief failed in *I.R. Comrs.* v. *Brandenburg* [1982] STC 555 and in *Montague Trust Co. (Jersey) Ltd.* [1989] STC 307.

CHAPTER II INTERESTS IN POSSESSION AND REVERSIONARY INTERESTS

49. Treatment of interests in possession. (E2.01)

A beneficiary with a beneficial interest in possession in settled property is treated as beneficially entitled to the same proportion of the property as his limited share in the income therefrom bears to the total income. See also IHTA 1984, ss. 50, 59.

This does not apply for the purposes of determining the extent of a chargeable transfer where the interest arises as a result of a disposition for money or money's worth and from 18 March 1986 and prior to 17 March 1987 if a transfer of value resulted from such disposition it could not qualify as a potentially exempt transfer under IHTA 1984, s. 3A. Termination of interests in possession or gifts to interest in possession settlements may qualify as potentially exempt transfers; see IHTA 1984, s. 3A (2).

50. Interests in part, etc. (B3.12; E2.02)

The interest of a person not entitled to any income, but entitled to the use and enjoyment of settled property, is a fractional share as computed by reference to the annual value of his interest compared with the total annual value of all interests in the property. If such a person also has a small interest in income it is unclear how his share is to be determined.

Where a person is entitled to an annuity or other specified amount of income it would be possible to vary the capital value of his share by changing the investment policy into say, high-yielding assets instead of low-yielding assets. For the purpose of computing inheritance tax there are therefore limits within which the yield on the trust fund supporting the annuity must be deemed to fall. The yield must not exceed that available on $2^{1}/_{2}$ per cent. Consols and must not be below the gross dividend yield of the F.T. Actuaries All Shares Index (S.I. 1975 No. 610). For transfers of value on or after 15 August 1980 the higher yield must not exceed that shown in the *FT-Actuaries Shares Indices* for British Government Stocks ("Irredeemables") and which replaces that on $2^{1}/_{2}$ per cent. Consols—the yield from the All-Share-Index is retained for the lower yield (S.I. 1980 No. 1000) and see Inland Revenue Press Release, 25 July 1980. The capital value of the appropriate share of the property is first calculated in the normal way. A second calculation is then made using the overriding limits, Inland Revenue Press Releases, 8 May 1975, 25 July 1980. See Extra-statutory concession F11 (1985) where an annuity is charged on property.

The calculations are made by reference to the specific amount.

See SP/E6, 5 November 1975 on power to augment income and SP/D16, 12 February 1976, and *Pearson and Others* v. *I.R. Comrs.* [1980] STC 318 on definition of interest in possession.

See also IHTA 1984, s. 59—essentially an interest in possession means a present right to present enjoyment and there is a distinction between the exercise of a power to terminate an interest in possession, and a power which will prevent such an interest arising in the first place.

EXAMPLE—Overriding limits

Albert is entitled to £1,000 and property income is £5,000 pa; he has a 1/5th interest in the supporting capital of say £50,000 = £10,000. Bertha is entitled to all the income after Albert's annuity; Bertha has a 4/5th interest in the supporting capital *i.e.* £40,000. By increasing the income to £12,000 pa. Albert's share would be only 1/12th. The second calculation presumes the yield not to be higher than that available on irredeemables—say £50,000 @ 15% = £7,500 so the final share on Albert's death is

$$\frac{1000}{7500} \times £50,000 = £6,667.$$

By decreasing the income to £2,000, Bertha's share would be $^1/_2$ only *i.e.* £25,000. The second calculation presumes the yield not to be lower than the gross dividend yield of the F.T. Actuaries All Shares Index—say £50,000 @ $4^1/_2$% = £2,250.

So the final share on Bertha's death is 5/9ths × £50,000 = £27,777.

Because the life tenant is deemed to have an interest in the whole of the capital and not merely an actuarial valuation of his life interest a reversionary interest is usually excluded property under IHTA 1984, s. 48; as otherwise the same trust assets would be deemed to be the property of the life tenant and the remainderman.

51. Disposal of interest in possession. (E2.12)
The disposal by a person of a beneficial interest in possession or a part thereof, *Pearson & Others* v. *I.R. Comrs.* [1980] STC 318 (SP/D16, 12 February 1976) is not a transfer of value but is treated as a cessation of his interest. See also *I.R. Comrs.* v. *Brandenburg* [1982] STC 555.

However if the IHTA 1984, s. 11 conditions are satisfied the interest is not treated as coming to an end.

52. Charge on termination of interest in possession. (E2.14)
On the *inter vivos* cessation of a beneficial interest in possession inheritance tax shall be charged as if he had made a transfer of value of an amount equal to the whole value of the capital of the settlement, or his proportionate interest therein. See *I.R. Comrs.* v. *Brandenburg* [1982] STC 555. On his death IHTA 1984, s. 4 applies to make a similar charge.

There are transitional arrangements for the cesser of interest before 10 December 1974 in a settlement made before 27 March 1974, see IHTA 1984, Sch. 6. Part disposals and interests in part of the trust fund are apportioned. There are provisions to prevent the artificial depreciation of values. See Extra-statutory concession F11 (1985) where an annuity is charged on property.

As to power to allow a beneficiary to occupy a house see Inland Revenue Press Releases, 6 August 1975 and 15 August 1979.

The termination of an interest in possession after 17 March 1986 and before 17 March 1987 could not qualify as a potentially exempt transfer within IHTA 1984, s. 3A. See IHTA 1984, s. 57A in connection with approved maintenance funds for historic buildings for terminations after 16 March 1987.

53. Exceptions from charge under section 52. (E2.21–31)
Inheritance tax is not charged to the extent to which a beneficiary becomes beneficially entitled to the property or a proportion of it as against the trustees, except to the extent stated in IHTA 1984, s. 52. Except on death, capital gains tax would be payable on appropriate assets in such circumstances, under CGTA 1979, s. 54 (1), unless roll-over under FA 1982, s. 82 applies on disposals after 5 April 1982 and before 14 March 1989.

On a disposal of an interest in possession for value the capital transfer tax chargeable is calculated as if the value of the property was reduced by the consideration received, ignoring as consideration the value of a reversionary interest or other property comprised in the settlement. Inheritance tax is not chargeable on the beneficiary's cesser of interest if the settled property then reverts to the settlor unless he (or his spouse after 11 April 1978) had acquired a reversionary interest in the property for money or money's worth. If the settlor's spouse (or widow within two years of the settlor's death) becomes beneficially entitled to the settled property on an interest coming to an end then, provided that she is domiciled in the U.K. and neither the settlor nor the spouse had acquired a reversionary interest for money or money's worth, there will be no inheritance tax charged on the interest coming to an end.

In respect of transfers on or after 10 March 1981 the capital transfer tax avoidance device was stopped whereby an interest in property was created for a short period and the reversionary interest transferred as excluded property into settlement followed by a tax free termination of the interest, the interest meanwhile having been acquired for its market value which was nearly equivalent to the full capital value as the interest in possession was for a very short period, say, three months.

There is an exemption for reversionary interests acquired before 10 March 1981 or in respect of an interest under a settlement created before 16 April 1976.

There are a number of anti-avoidance modifications. For the purpose of the provisions, indirect or circuitous consideration in establishing whether a person has acquired an interest under settlement for money for money's worth is caught.

The provisions apply to acquisitions of interest in settlements after 11 April 1978, and after 13 June 1978 to the extent that they relate to persons becoming entitled to interests in possession in trusts acquired for money's worth after that date.

54. Exceptions from charge on death. (D1.01, 12, 44; E2.11–15, 17–19; M1.01)
The deceased is deemed to have an absolute interest in settled property of which he was life tenant (IHTA 1984, s. 49 (1)), unless the property reverts to the settlor or his spouse and was not acquired for value by the settlor or his spouse or following the transfer of a reversionary interest into settlement after 9 March 1981.

Where it is not known which spouse survived the other they shall be assumed to have died at the same instant.

54A. Special rate of charge where settled property affected by potentially exempt transfer. (C4.13)
This is an anti-avoidance provision to prevent the reduction of the tax charge on transfers to discretionary trusts through the use of short-term interests in possession. It applies where after 16 March 1987 a settlor (*a*) makes a potentially exempt transfer to an interest in possession trust and (*b*) during the lifetime of the settlor and within seven years of the potentially exempt transfer the interest in possession ("the relevant interest") terminates either wholly or in part ("the relevant transfer"), either during the lifetime, or on the death of the life tenant and (*c*) the whole or part of the property supporting the life interest (referred to as "the special rate property") falls into a discretionary trust, *i.e.*, where there is no interest in possession (other than a qualifying accumulation and maintenance trust; see IHTA 1984, s. 71).

The tax charge is either the normal charge under IHTA 1984, s. 52 on the termination of the interest in possession based on the life tenant's situation, or if greater, tax calculated as the aggregate of (*a*) and (*b*) below.

(*a*) Tax at half the table rate on a notional transfer by the settlor at the date of the relevant transfer and of an amount equal to the part of the relevant transfer falling into the discretionary settlement *i.e.*, "the special rate property" and assuming previous cumulative chargeable transfers equal to the settlors actual chargeable transfers during the seven year period prior to the date of the potentially exempt transfer that gave rise to the settlement. Note that other potentially exempt transfers made by the settlor in that period are ignored.

(*b*) Tax based on the life tenant's situation attributable to the part (if any) of the relevant transfer that does not comprise special rate property—where all the property so devolves the tax under this head will be nil.

See also IHTA 1984, s. 54B for further provisions supplementary to this section.

54B. Provisions supplementary to section 54A. (C4.13)
The deaths of the settlor or life tenant after a chargeable transfer to which IHTA 1984, s. 54A applies is not to affect the tax charged under s. 54A unless the death would result in a higher charge, and then only in relation to either the settlor, or the life tenant depending upon which calculation under s. 54A (4) and (5) gives rise to the higher charge.

When calculating the settlor's cumulative gifts for the purposes of IHTA 1984, s. 54A (4) it is necessary to include previous transfers chargeable under s. 54A for the same settlor occurring within the seven years.

55. Reversionary interest acquired by beneficiary. (E6.21)
IHTA 1984, s. 5 (1) notwithstanding, a reversionary interest is not part of a person's estate where he acquires that interest expectant on an interest, whether in possession or not and IHTA 1984, s. 10 (1) does not apply to a disposition by which a reversionary interest is so acquired. Where such a disposition constituted a transfer of value before 17 March 1987 it could not qualify as a potentially exempt transfer under IHTA 1984, s. 3A.

56. Exclusion of certain exemptions. (B2.01; C3.11, 13–15; E3.23)
This section contains exceptions to certain of the exemptions contained in IHTA 1984, ss. 18, 23, 27.

See also IHTA 1984, s. 24.

57. Application of certain exemptions. (G5.42)
The "gifts in consideration of marriage" exemption and the "annual" exemption are extended to the termination of an interest in possession as a result of which trust property is transferred to the parties to the marriage absolutely or resettled in trust for them. The beneficiary becoming absolutely entitled is the deemed transferor within the normal marriage exemption limits in IHTA 1984, s. 21. In order to qualify for the relief the transferor must give six months' notice to the trustees (from the date of the transfer) informing them of the extent of any marriage exemption available.

See Inland Revenue Press Release, 9 October 1981 as to relaxation of accounting requirements for termination of interests after 5 April 1981.

A transfer of value is an exempt transfer if made to a fund approved by the Treasury under IHTA 1984, s. 27 and Sch. 4 either at the time of transfer or subsequently.

57A. Relief where property enters maintenance fund. (G5.44)
The purpose of these provisions is to exempt settled property from inheritance tax on the death on or after 17 March 1987 of a person who has an interest in possession in the property, *e.g.* a life

tenant, if the terms on which the property is held are altered after the death so that it passes into an approved maintenance fund for historic buildings etc. (see IHTA 1984, Sch. 4) within two years of the death, or three years if court proceedings are necessary. The provisions will not apply if the disposition is conditional or defeasible, or if the property passing to the maintenance fund is itself settled property or has been acquired for a consideration in money or money's worth.

As to capital gains tax for disposals after 13 March 1989, see CGTA 1979, s. 147A.

CHAPTER III SETTLEMENTS WITHOUT INTERESTS IN POSSESSION

INTERPRETATION

58. Relevant property. (E4.02)
The inheritance tax charges apply to relevant property and this is defined as meaning settled property in which no qualifying interest in possession subsists but excluding trusts of the following types:
  (a) charitable trusts
  (b) accumulation and maintenance trusts
  (c) maintenance funds for historic buildings
  (d) pension schemes
  (e) employee and newspaper trusts, etc.
  (f) protective trusts under Trustee Act 1925, s. 33 (1) (ii) held pre-12 April 1978
  (g) trusts for the disabled settled pre- 10 March 1981
  (h) trade or professional compensation funds
  (i) trusts comprising excluded property
In the case of pension schemes ((d) above) exemption does not extend to benefits which, having become payable, are re-settled
See IHTA 1984, s. 48 (1).

59. Qualifying interest in possession. (E1.41)
An interest in possession is defined as meaning an interest in possession to which an individual or a company is beneficially entitled, although in the case of the company its business must consist wholly or mainly of the acquisition of interests in settled property and such acquisitions must have been made for full consideration in money or money's worth from an individual who was beneficially entitled to it. Where a company acquired the interest before 14 March 1975 the condition as to the company's business will be deemed to be satisfied currently if it would have qualified at the date of acquisition, or the company is authorised to carry on long-term insurance business. Unfortunately there is still no full statutory definition of an interest in possession so that the law established in *Pearson* v. *I.R. Comrs.* [1980] STC 318, *i.e.,* "a current right to current enjoyment" still applies. See also *Moore and Osborne* v. *I.R. Comrs., Re Trafford's Settlement Trusts* [1984] STC 236, *Miller and another* v. *I.R. Comrs.* [1987] STC 108 and estate duty cases *Gartside* v. *I.R. Comrs.* [1968] AC 553, *A.-G.* v. *Power and Another* [1906] 2 IR 272 for further commentary on interests in possession, and for the effect of Trustee Act 1925, s. 31 see *Swales and Others* v. *I.R. Comrs.* [1984] STC 413 and *Re Delamere's Settlement Trusts, Kenny and Others* v. *Cunningham-Reid and Others* [1984] 1 All ER 584. See also IHTA 1984, ss. 48–53.

60. Commencement of settlement. (E4.03)
It is made clear that references in the legislation to the commencement of the settlement are references to the time when property is first comprised in it.

61. Ten-year anniversary. (E4.03)
The term "ten-year anniversary" is defined. Ten-year anniversary in relation to a settlement means each ten-year anniversary of the date of commencement of the settlement falling after 31 March 1983. Where the first ten-year anniversary would fall within the year ended 31 March 1984 and during that year there is a payment or transfer of assets out of the trust fund which could not have been made except as the result of some court proceedings, and which would have been chargeable to tax (ignoring the election available to pre- 27 March 1974 settlements under IHTA 1984, s. 68, the first ten-year anniversary is postponed until 1 April 1984, but this does not affect the date of subsequent ten-year anniversaries.

62. Related settlements. (E4.04)
Settlements made on the same day by the same settlor are related unless one or both of them are charitable (otherwise than for a limited period).

63. Minor interpretative provisions. (E4.45)
Various terms are defined, a payment includes a transfer of assets other than money and quarter means a period of three months.

PRINCIPAL CHARGE TO TAX

64. Charge at ten-year anniversary. (E4.11)

This section provides for an inheritance tax charge on all relevant property held on the ten-year anniversary. There is relief where property has not been relevant property for the entire ten-year period, for example, property held under an interest in possession for part of the time, or additions to the fund, and the rate of tax is reduced by 1/40th for each quarter which had expired in the ten-year period prior to the property becoming relevant property. Income which has been neither distributed nor accumulated is not to be treated as a trust asset for the purposes of the charge, and accumulated income is to be treated as becoming a trust asset on the date of the accumulation: see Inland Revenue Press Release and SP 8/86; 10 November 1986.

For the calculation of the tax see IHTA 1984, ss. 66, 67.

65. Charge at other times. (E4.12, 13, 21–31)

This section provides for a charge to inheritance tax where property ceases to be relevant property or where there is a depreciatory transaction by the trustees. The amount liable to tax is computed on the reduction in the value of the trust property as a result of the disposition (as reduced by business or agricultural property relief where appropriate) which brings discretionary trusts into line with individuals where the "consequential loss" formula has always applied.

The likely situations where a charge will occur will be on an actual distribution of trust property, or on the trustees granting an interest in possession in trust property (*i.e.,* in relevant property). Where tax on the charge is not borne by the recipient (*i.e.,* it is paid out of other relevant property in the trust) then the diminution in value as a result of the disposition is grossed up to arrive at the exit value for tax purposes. The rate of tax is prescribed under IHTA 1984, ss. 68, 69.

There is no charge where property ceases to be relevant property during the quarter following a ten-year anniversary and this may provide tax-planning opportunities for trustees.

There is no tax charge on the payment of reasonable management expenses of the relevant property nor on payments treated as income of any person for U.K. tax purposes whether or not that income is liable to tax because the person is non-U.K. resident. Where the trustees have made a depreciatory disposition (including a disposition by associated operations—see IHTA 1984, s. 16 for definition of disposition), there is no charge where there is no intention to confer gratuitous benefit, or where IHTA 1984 (grant of tenancies of agricultural property) would prevent the disposition from being a transfer of value. However, a deliberate omission by the trustees to exercise a right will constitute a disposition.

There is no tax charge on settled property becoming excluded property under s. 48 (where the settlor was domiciled outside the U.K. at the time the settlement was made), for example, on reinvestment from U.K. assets into overseas property. It should be noted that the conversion into excluded property does not cover excluded property under IHTA 1984, s. 99, *i.e.,* reversionary interests.

RATES OF PRINCIPAL CHARGE

66. Rate of ten-yearly charge. (E4.43, 44)

The rate of charge to tax on a ten-year anniversary is 3/10ths of the effective rate. The effective rate is arrived at by calculating the tax at one half the table rate from 18 March 1986 (previously at the lifetime table rate) on a notional transfer and expressing it as a percentage thereof. The effective rate is then applied to the relevant property in the settlement at the date of charge to establish the tax payable. There is relief where property has not been relevant property for the entire ten-year period, for example, property held under an interest in possession for part of the time, or additions to the fund, and the rate of tax attributable to it is reduced by 1/40th for each quarter which had expired in the ten-year period prior to the property becoming relevant property.

The notional transfer is the aggregate of (*a*)–(*c*) assuming prior cumulative transfers of (*d*)–(*g*) where relevant:

(*a*) The value of the relevant property in the trust at the ten-year date.

(*b*) The value of any trust property (whether on creation or from subsequent additions) which has never been relevant property whilst comprised in the settlement, *e.g.*, property in which there is an interest in possession.

(*c*) The value of property in any related settlement (see IHTA 1984, s. 62) immediately after its creation.

(*d*) Any chargeable transfers made by the settlor in the seven years (ten years for transfers before 18 March 1986) prior to creation of the trust excluding the initial transfer to the trust itself or any other transfers made on that day.

   Items (*b*), (*c*) and (*d*) do not apply to trusts created before 27 March 1974.

(*e*) In respect of the first ten-year anniversary only of pre-27 March 1974 settlements the amount of any distribution payments (calculated under the old rules) during the period 27 March 1974 to 8 March 1982.

(*f*) The gross amounts charged under IHTA 1984, s. 65 (property ceasing to be relevant property) after 8 March 1982 and within the ten years before the anniversary concerned.

(*g*) Any further amounts or adjustments to be included by virtue of IHTA 1984, s. 67 (added property, etc.).

Settlors should avoid making additions after 8 March 1982 to pre-27 March 1974 trusts as the notional transfer will be increased by the seven-year cumulative transfers (ten years for transfers before 18 March 1986) prior to the addition as referred to above. The section will be triggered by a very small addition provided that it is a chargeable transfer and if the settlor's other transfers within the seven-year period have been material the effective rate of capital transfer tax may be substantially increased.

The amount of the notional transfer in computing the effective rate of tax on a ten-yearly charge under IHTA 1984, s. 64 is modified for pre-27 March 1974 settlements.

67. Added property, etc. (E4.45)

This section covers the position where after 8 March 1982 a settlor makes a chargeable transfer as a result of which the value of the property of a pre-existing trust is increased. It is immaterial whether the amount of the property is increased, the section applying where there has been an increase in value. There is a relieving provision where the transferor has no primary intention to increase the value, there has been no increase in the amount, and the increase in value does not exceed 5 per cent. of its value immediately prior to the transfer.

Where the section applies the figure to be included under IHTA 1984, s. 66 (5) (*a*) (settlor's transfers during the seven years (ten years for transfers before 18 March 1986) prior to the creation of the settlement—item (*d*) in the commentary above) will be substituted by the settlor's cumulative chargeable transfers during the seven years prior to the later addition if that gives a larger figure. If there is more than one later addition then transfers within the seven years prior to each addition are reviewed and the greatest figure taken.

There are relieving provisions to cover double-charging where trust assets have both ceased, and become relevant property in the ten years prior to an anniversary when they would be charged again where after 8 March 1982 a settlor has added property to a pre-27 March 1974 settlement. The effect is to enhance the notional transfer under IHTA 1984, s. 66 by the amount of the settlor's other cumulative transfers during the seven-year period immediately prior to the addition. If there has been more than one later addition then transfers within the seven years prior to each addition are reviewed and the greatest figure taken.

68. Rate before first ten-year anniversary. (E4.41–44)

The rate of tax charged on property ceasing to be relevant property before the first ten-year anniversary under IHTA 1984, s. 65 (charges between subsequent ten-year anniversaries are dealt with under s. 69 below) is at the appropriate fraction of the effective rate of tax computed at one half the table rate under IHTA 1984, s. 7 (2) from 18 March 1986 (previously at the lifetime table rate) rates on a notional transfer (made on the occasion of charge) comprising the aggregate of the following:

(*a*) The value of the property comprised in the settlement immediately after its creation together with the value on creation of the property in any related settlement (a settlement created by the same settlor on the same day, see IHTA 1984, s. 66. It is immaterial whether on creation part of the property is held under an interest in possession as it is still included in this calculation.

(*b*) The value of any addition to the settlement (as at the date of such addition) since its creation and prior to the occasion of charge (whether or not still retained) but assuming prior cumulative chargeable transfers equal to the total chargeable transfers made by the settlor in the seven years (ten years for transfers before 18 March 1986) prior to the creation of the settlement, and ignoring any transfers made on that day.

The appropriate fraction is 3/10ths × q/40 where q is the number of complete quarters which have expired between the date of creation of the settlement and the day immediately prior to the occasion of charge. There is further relief where any property comprised in the exit value has not been relevant property during any complete quarter in the period referred to above and any such quarter will not count in arriving at q in the fraction. However, where property becomes relevant property in the quarter in which it is subject to the exit charge then that quarter counts as 1. Where the relief applies it will be necessary to compute the appropriate fraction separately for the particular property concerned. It should be noted that these reliefs have no application to trusts created before 27 March 1974 where the appropriate fraction will be 3/10ths or 1/5th (if transitional relief applies, see below).

The rules are modified for pre-27 March 1974 settlements, in particular as to the calculation of the notional transfer. For distributions before 1 April 1983 the appropriate fraction is 1/5th and this applies until 31 March 1984 where in specified situations court proceedings are necessary. In other cases the appropriate fraction is 3/10ths. See *Rowland's Tax Guide 1983–84* commentary on FA 1982, s. 101 and Sch. 15, paras. 1 to 9. The notional transfer is computed assuming prior cumulative chargeable transfers of the following amounts:

(*a*) The cumulative total of amounts on which tax has already been charged under IHTA 1984, s. 65 (*i.e.,* previous exit charges), and (*b*) The amount of any distribution payments under the old rules during the period 27 March 1974 to 8 March 1982 inclusive and within the ten-year period prior to the charge in question. The tax is calculated in the usual way on the notional transfer subject to the possible application of the transitional rate.

See IHTA 1984, s. 264 (transfers reported late). Note that a potentially exempt transfer (see IHTA 1984, s. 3A) on becoming chargeable could increase the tax rate on subsequent exit charges. See also IHTA 1984, s. 226 (payment) and s. 233 (interest).

69. Rate between ten-year anniversaries. (E4.46)

The exit charge under IHTA 1984, s. 65 on property ceasing to be relevant property after the first or a subsequent ten-year anniversary is calculated at the appropriate fraction (see below) of the rate applicable to the immediately preceding ten-year anniversary. Where the exit charge event occurs after 17 March 1986 and the last ten year anniversary occurred before that date FA 1986, Sch. 19, para. 43 provides that the last periodic charge may be computed as though the revised charging rules contained in FA 1966 were then in force—the most important of these is the reduction in the settlors cumulative transfer period from ten to seven years. However, where there have been any additions to the trust property since the last ten-year anniversary (whether or not such property was or has become relevant property) or, property which was comprised in the settlement at the time of the preceding ten-year anniversary but was not then relevant property (for example, property held under an interest in possession trust at that time) has subsequently become relevant property, it is necessary to recompute a notional rate as if such property had been included at the ten-year anniversary. The property is included at its value on becoming comprised in the settlement where either it became relevant property at that time, or has never become relevant property—in any other case it is valued at the date that it becomes relevant property.

The appropriate fraction is $q/40$ where q is the number of complete quarters which have expired on the day prior to the date of charge since the previous ten-year anniversary.

There is similar relief to that under IHTA 1984, s. 68 (3) where any property comprised in the exit value had not been relevant property during any complete quarter in the period referred to above and such quarters will not count in arriving at q in the fraction. However, where property becomes relevant property in the quarter in which it is subject to the exit charge then that quarter will count as 1. Where relief applies it will be necessary to compute the appropriate fraction separately for the particular property concerned.

These rules apply (with the exception of the reliefs referred to above) to pre-27 March 1974 trusts as well as to those created subsequently. Where tax rates have decreased since the previous ten-year anniversary the rates at that time are notionally recomputed using the new table when computing the exit charge. See IHTA 1984, Sch. 2, para. 3.

SPECIAL CASES—CHARGES TO TAX

70. Property leaving temporary charitable trusts. (E5.02)

Property held for charitable purposes is not relevant property (see IHTA 1984, s. 58) and accordingly whilst so held is not subject to exit or ten-year anniversary charges. However, where property is held for charitable purposes for a limited period only there will be a charge to tax at rates prescribed in this section on the trust's termination, or on property being applied other than for charitable purposes. The charge is on the diminution in the value of the trust property as a result of the disposition and this is grossed up where the tax is paid out of trust funds. Depreciatorytransactions by the trustees (unless without gratuitous intent, or where grant of tenancies of agricultural property, would prevent the disposition from being a transfer of value) and omissions to exercise rights (unless not deliberate) are chargeable events. The rate of tax depends on the period during which the property subject to the disposition has been held by the charitable trust (the relevant period) and is the aggregate of the following percentages:

0·25 per cent. for each of the first 40 complete successive quarters in the relevant period,

0·20 per cent. for each of the next 40,

0·15 per cent. for each of the next 40,

0·10 per cent. for each of the next 40,

0·05 per cent. for each of the next 40.

The maximum aggregate percentage is 20 per cent. and the charge would not be levied for periods before 13 March 1975. There is a transitional provision where the property chargeable under this section was relevant property before 10 December 1981, for example, where held on a general discretionary trust, and became held for charitable purposes before 9 March 1982. In such a case when computing the percentage rate under sub-s. (6) the relevant period is deemed to have begun on the date (not being earlier than 13 March 1975) on which the property last became relevant property, for example, on an interest in possession settlement terminating, subsequently being held on the discretionary trust.

There is no charge under the section for property applied in the payment of reasonable management expenses of the trust property, nor where any payment is treated as income in the hands of the recipient, or would be so treated if the person were a U.K. resident.

See also IHTA 1984, s. 68 above regarding elections.

71. Accumulation and maintenance trusts. (E5.11–29)
Property held under accumulation and maintenance trusts satisfying the detailed conditions in the section is not relevant property by virtue of IHTA 1984, s. 58, and as such is not subject to exit and ten-yearly charges under the discretionary trust rules. Whilst the conditions are satisfied there is no inheritance tax charge on a qualifying beneficiary becoming entitled to trust property (or an interest in possession in trust property) on, or before attaining a specified age (see below); or on the death of a qualifying beneficiary before obtaining the specified age. The conditions to enjoy these advantages, all of which need to be satisfied are as follows:

(*a*) One or more beneficiaries will become entitled to the settled property, or an interest in possession in it by age twenty-five at the latest. This is an absolute requirement and a trustee's power to revoke a trust will result in loss of qualification, see *Lord Inglewood* v. *I.R. Comrs.* [1983] STC 133. However an appointment by Trustees subject to, and with the possibility of becoming void on the grounds of illegality did not infringe this condition in *Maitland's Trustees* v. *Lord Advocate* [1982] SLT 483. See also Extra-statutory concession F8 (1988).

(*b*) There is no interest in possession in the settled property and income not applied for the maintenance, education or benefit of a beneficiary is to be accumulated.

(*c*) Not more than twenty-five years must have elapsed since commencement of the settlement or at such later time as the conditions in (*a*) and (*b*) above become satisfied. Alternatively, all the beneficiaries must be, or were grandchildren of a common grandparent, or children, widows or widowers of such grandchildren who died before the time when, had they survived, they would have become entitled to the settled property or an interest in possession in it. There are transitional provisions for pre- 15 April 1976 settlements which satisfied the basic (*a*) and (*b*) conditions above on that day.

It is necessary that there is, or has been, at least one living beneficiary. For the purposes of the provisions a person's children includes illegitimate children, step-children and adopted children. A person includes an unborn person.

There will be an inheritance tax charge where settled property ceases to satisfy the qualification requirements, or where the trustees make a depreciatory disposition (including an omission to act) unless not deliberate and without gratuitous intent. See *Egerton and another* v. *I.R. Comrs.* [1983] STC 531 where a charge arose on creation of protective trusts.

The amount and the tapering charge is calculated in the same manner as for property leaving temporary charitable trusts, see IHTA 1984, s. 70. It is to be noted that the charge under s. 70 is independent of any previous history of transfers by the settlor or by the trustees but is related solely to the amount of time during which the property has been comprised in the settlement and the diminution in the value of the fund at the date of the occasion to charge. Any tax charge on creation of the settlement is calculated in the normal way. However from 18 March 1986 transfers by individuals on or after that date to accumulation and maintenance trusts should qualify as potentially exempt transfers within IHTA 1984, s. 3A. The creation of an accumulation and maintenance settlement by discretionary trustees will be an occasion of charge under IHTA 1984, s. 65 on property ceasing to be relevant property.

See also SP/E1, 11 June 1975; SP/E2, 9 September 1975 and Inland Revenue Press Releases, 24 September 1975, 8 October 1975 and 19 January 1976. *Note:* these all refer to the original provisions contained in FA 1975, Sch. 5, para. 15 but as the current provisions are essentially similar they should be of application.

See also *Hart* v. *Briscoe and others; Hoare Trustees* v. *Gardner* [1978] STC 89 for possible capital gains tax problems. As to age of majority under pre- 1970 settlements, see Inland Revenue letter, dated 1 June 1977.

See *Egerton* v. *I.R. Comrs.* [1983] STC 531 on previous legislation.

72. Property leaving employee trusts and newspaper trusts. (E5.37, 38)
Property held on the terms of employee trusts as defined in IHTA 1984, s. 86 is not relevant property provided that there is no interest in possession subsisting. Accordingly the property is not subject to exit and ten-yearly charges. However, there will be an inheritance tax charge calculated in the same way as for property leaving temporary charitable settlements under IHTA 1984, s. 70 in the following situations:

(*a*) Where property ceases to be held on the terms of the trust, otherwise than by virtue of a payment out of the trust fund (but subject to (*b*) below).

(*b*) Where a payment is made out of the trust fund for the benefit of a person (or to any person connected with him) who either (i) has provided directly or indirectly property for the settlement (additions not exceeding £1,000 in any one year are ignored), or (ii) where the trust is for employees of a close company the person in question is a participator who owns, or is entitled to acquire not less than 5 per cent. of the company's share capital of any class or who would be entitled to not less than 5 per cent. of the assets in a winding-up, or (iii) where the person has acquired his interest in the property for a consideration in money or money's worth.

(*c*) Where the trustees make any depreciatory disposition (including an omission to act) unless not deliberate and without any gratuitous intent.

73. Pre-1978 protective trusts. (E5.34)

A protective trust is defined as one where property is held on trusts to the like effect as under the Trustee Act 1925, s. 33 (1), for example, one in favour of a spendthrift beneficiary, and which was triggered before 12 April 1978, for example, by the beneficiary's bankruptcy. In such a case the property became held upon a discretionary trust for specified beneficiaries and IHTA 1984, s. 58 provides that such property is not relevant property and accordingly not subject to exit and ten-yearly charges; *Thomas & Thomas* v. *I.R. Comrs.* [1981] STC 382. For protective trusts triggered after 11 April 1978 the property becomes held on a deemed interest in possession trust in favour of the principal beneficiary and as such is not relevant property.

74. Pre-1981 trusts for disabled persons. (E5.35, 36)

A somewhat similar situation to IHTA 1984, s. 73 applies for trusts for the benefit of mentally or physically disabled persons where the property was settled before 10 March 1981 and is held on discretionary trusts. Such property is not relevant property, see IHTA 1984, s. 58. For settlements after 9 March 1981 the beneficiary is deemed to have an interest in possession so that the discretionary trust rules will not apply.

However, there will be a tax charge where in the case of a protective or disabled person's trust the funds are applied other than for the benefit of the beneficiary, or where the trustees make a depreciatory transaction (including an omission to act) unless not deliberate and without gratuitous intent. The amount of the charge and the rate of tax are calculated in the same way as for property leaving a temporary charitable trust under IHTA 1984, s. 70. The trusts for the benefit of the disabled are as defined in IHTA 1984, s. 74.

SPECIAL CASES—RELIEFS

75. Property becoming subject to employee trusts. (E4.21–31)

There is no charge under IHTA 1984, s. 65 where shares or securities of a company cease to be relevant property on becoming comprised in an employee trust as defined in IHTA 1984, s. 86 (1), provided that the following conditions are satisfied:

(*a*) The beneficiaries of the trust must include all or most of the company's employees or office holders.

(*b*) That the conditions contained in IHTA 1984, s. 28 are satisfied, namely, that the trustees must hold more than half of the ordinary shares of the company (ignoring shares held in any other trusts) and must have voting control on all questions affecting the company as a whole (ignoring limited class rights on winding-up, etc.) and there must be no provisions whereby the trustees may be relieved of their powers without consent. The conditions must be satisfied at the time in question or within one year thereafter.

(*c*) The beneficiaries must not include a participator in the company or a participator in any close company which had transferred funds to the trust, or who has been such a participator or a person connected with a participator during the previous ten years. Participators who are not beneficially entitled to 5 per cent. or more of the shares of any class are excluded.

76. Property becoming held for charitable purposes, etc. (E4.21–31)

There is no tax charge where after 8 March 1982 property ceases to be relevant property, or ceases to be property of time-limited charities (IHTA 1984, s. 70), accumulation and maintenance trusts (IHTA 1984, s. 71), employee and newspaper trusts (IHTA 1984, s. 72), protective trusts for disabled persons (IHTA 1984, ss. 73, 74), or maintenance funds for historic buildings (IHTA 1984, Sch. 4) on becoming the property of:

(*a*) Charities (unlimited as to time).

(*b*) Political parties, under IHTA 1984, s. 24.

(*c*) National bodies, *e.g.*, National Gallery, National Trust, etc., see IHTA 1984, s. 25.

(*d*) Non-profit making bodies approved by the Treasury where the property is of outstanding scenic, historic or scientific interest, see IHTA 1984, s. 26.

There are provisions to prevent exploitation of the relief in particular by devaluing the transferor fund, for example, by losing control of a company on selling a minority shareholding to a charity. It is necessary to compute the amount of the transfer in the normal way (ignoring business and agricultural property relief) and assuming no grossing up. If this amount exceeds the value of the property received by the charity (less any consideration paid) inheritance tax is charged on the excess.

Relief is not available unless a transfer is irrevocable (ability to revoke within the first twelve months provided not in fact revoked will not effect relief) and the property must be applied only for the purposes of the bodies (*a*)–(*d*) above.

See also IHTA 1984, s. 23.

WORKS OF ART, HISTORIC BUILDINGS, ETC.

77. Maintenance funds for historic buildings, etc.
Schedule 4 is introduced.

78. Conditionally exempt occasions. (E5.51; G5.31, 32)
There is no tax exit charge on property ceasing to be relevant property, for example, on a distribution, provided that the work of art has been comprised in the settlement throughout the six-year period ending with the transfer and provided also that an appropriate claim is made to the Treasury for designation under IHTA 1984, s. 31 and the necessary undertakings given. Where such a transaction is or was free of tax it is referred to as a "conditionally exempt occasion", and the transfer as a "conditionally exempt transfer".

Under IHTA 1984, s. 34 where there is a chargeable event, for example, on the conditions for approval of the work of art being breached, this normally affects the cumulative gifts total of the person who made the last conditionally exempt transfer before the chargeable event. However, the application of s. 34 is specifically excluded where a chargeable event follows a conditionally exempt occasion.

Where the settlor is the relevant person and the settlement was created on his death then the full table rate prescribed by IHTA 1984, s. 7 (1) applies and in other cases one half table rate: (from 18 March 1986). Where the last transaction regarding property before a chargeable event was a conditionally exempt occasion, and the relevant person died before 13 March 1975, the amount is added to his estate liable to estate duty in order to compute the tax due; in other cases if the conditionally exempt occasion occurred before the settlement's first ten-year anniversary (see IHTA 1984, s. 64) the tax will be at 30 per cent. of what would otherwise be payable, and if after the first and before the second ten-year anniversary at 60 per cent. of such tax. The method of computation referred to above depending upon whether the relevant person is alive or dead will apply. In all cases tax rates current at the time of the chargeable event are used. As to capital gains tax on disposals after 13 March 1989, see CGTA 1979, s. 147A.

79. Exemption from ten-yearly charge. (E5.03; G5.31)
Works of art held in a discretionary trust are free of the ten-yearly charge under IHTA 1984, s. 64 where on or before becoming comprised in the settlement the property has been the subject of a conditionally exempt transfer (see IHTA 1984, s. 78), or alternatively the subject of a gift where the donor has elected under CGTA 1979, s. 147 (4) for the gain to be rolled over to the donee. In such cases there will be no ten-yearly anniversary falling before either an actual sale of the property, or on the Treasury's undertakings being breached.

Exemption from the ten-yearly charge will also apply to other property (not having previously been the subject of a prior conditional exempt transfer, or claim under CGTA 1979, s. 147 (4) before becoming comprised in the settlement) provided that on the trustees' claim, the Treasury designates the property as a work of art under IHTA 1984, s. 31 and the necessary undertakings are given. However, there will be a tax charge on a subsequent breach of the undertakings or on a sale, or other chargeable event referred to in IHTA 1984, s. 32 unless there is a conditionally exempt occasion (see IHTA 1984, s. 78) before the occurrence of the breach etc. and after the property became comprised in the settlement. The method of calculating tax is very similar to that used for property leaving temporary charitable trusts etc. under IHTA 1984, s. 70 and is independent of the settlor's or the trustees' history of chargeable transfers. The tax is computed by applying a percentage to the value of the property at the time of the event. The percentage depends upon the "relevant period" and this starts at the latest of the following dates:
  (*a*) the commencement of the settlement,
  (*b*) the date of the last ten-year anniversary prior to the property becoming comprised in the settlement, or
  (*c*) 13 March 1975.
and ends on the day prior to the chargeable event. Having measured the length of the relevant period the rate of tax is the aggregate of the following percentages:
  0·25 per cent. for each of the first 40 complete successive quarters (*i.e.*, a period of three months) in the relevant period.
  0·20 per cent. for each of the next 40,
  0·15 per cent. for each of the next 40,
  0·10 per cent. for each of the next 40, and
  0·05 per cent. for each of the next 40.
There is an anti-avoidance provision to cover the position where the trustees have purchased works of art and made the appropriate claim to the Treasury under IHTA 1984, s. 31 so that such property will be exempt from subsequent ten-yearly charges. However, in computing the rate of tax on the first ten-yearly charge after the acquisition (under IHTA 1984, s. 66) it is necessary to include the consideration paid by the trustees for the works of art as part of the notional transfer in

calculating the tax rate applicable to the other property in the settlement. The persons liable for the tax are the trustees and any person for whose benefit the property (including attributable income) has been applied on or after the event.

MISCELLANEOUS

80. Initial interest of settlor or spouse. (E4.51)
Where after 26 March 1974 a settlor (including the spouse or widow or widower) has an interest in possession in settled property immediately on creation of the settlement but that interest is later terminated without any of the persons referred to above having an interest in possession, the settlor, or spouse, etc., is deemed to have made a separate settlement at the date of the termination. However, this does not affect the dates of the ten-year anniversaries which are still geared to the date of creation of the original settlement, see IHTA 1984, s. 61 (2).

81. Property moving between settlements. (E4.52, 53)
Where property held by one settlement becomes held by another settlement without any beneficiary becoming beneficially entitled to the property (an interest in possession is not sufficient for this purpose) it will be treated as having remained in the first settlement. This applies where the property ceased to be held after 9 December 1981. Property ceasing to be held after 26 March 1974 and before 10 December 1981 will only be regarded as remaining in the first settlement where there was a direct transfer between settlements by the same disposition.

82. Excluded property. (E1.101)
The definition of excluded property for the purposes of IHTA 1984, ss. 80 and 81, is made more stringent particularly in connection with the holding of exempt government securities (treated as excluded property under IHTA 1984, s. 48). Under IHTA 1984, s. 65 there is no exit charge on re-investment by trustees into exempt stocks provided that the settlor was not domiciled in the U.K. on creation of the settlement and the other requirements of IHTA 1984, s. 48 are met (primarily that all known beneficiaries are not domiciled, or resident or ordinarily resident in the U.K.). However, where property moves between settlements under IHTA 1984, s. 81, it is specifically provided that the settlor of the second settlement must have been not domiciled in the U.K. on its creation and there is a similar requirement under IHTA 1984, s. 80 (initial interest of settlor or spouse) as to the settlor of the first settlement referred to therein. This appears to be aimed at avoidance possibilities as between U.K. domiciled and non-domiciled spouses. For IHTA 1984, s. 65 purposes the extended definition of domicile in IHTA 1984, s. 267 does not apply in relation to property settled before 10 December 1974.
   See also IHTA 1984, ss. 6, 48.

83. Property becoming settled on a death. (E1.51)
Property which becomes settled on the death of any person under a will or an intestacy is deemed to have become comprised in the settlement on the testator's death.

84. Income applied for charitable purposes. (E4.02; E5.02, 32)
Where a trust provides for part of the income to be applied for charitable purposes a corresponding part of the settled property will be regarded as held for charitable purposes.

85. Credit for annual charges under Finance Act 1975. (E3.31, 32)
The annual capital transfer tax charge for non-resident trustees under FA 1975, Sch. 5, para. 12 was terminated with effect from 1 January 1982. Any capital transfer tax previously charged but not already allowed as a credit will be deducted from tax payable under the subsequent provisions.

CHAPTER IV MISCELLANEOUS

86. Trusts for benefit of employees. (B2.07; C1.27; E5.37, 38)
Trusts (after 8 March 1982 approved profit-sharing schemes specifically qualify as employee trusts) which do not permit the funds to be applied other than for the benefit of employees (which covers all or most of the employees), and their families, relations or dependants or charities are entitled to favourable inheritance tax treatment.
   See IHTA 1984, s. 13 for setting up such a trust.
   An interest in possession of less than 5 per cent. of the trust property is ignored, and whilst the conditions are met (for events after 8 March 1982), such property is not relevant property (see IHTA 1984, s. 58) and accordingly is not subject to the discretionary trust charging provisions.

87. Newspaper trusts. (E5.40)
From 7 April 1976 by IHTA 1984, s. 87 trusts whose main or principal assets are shares in a newspaper publishing or holding company subject to meeting conditions specified are brought within the provisions as applying to employee trusts.

See IHTA 1984, s. 75 for discretionary trust property becoming subject to employee and newspaper trusts and IHTA 1984, s. 72 for the charge on property leaving such trusts—after 8 March 1982.

88. Protective trusts. (E5.34)
A protective trust is defined as one where property is held on trusts to the like effect as under the Trustee Act, 1925, s. 33 (1). This is one in favour of a beneficiary possibly a spendthrift or wealthy young adult which determines on certain events such as bankruptcy or attempted alienation or mortgage of the interest in the trust. On such an event occurring after 11 April 1978 the property becomes held on a deemed interest in possession trust in favour of the principal beneficiary, and is not therefore relevant property under IHTA 1984, s. 58. Prior to 11 April 1978 on such an event the property became held on specified discretionary trusts basically in favour of the principal benefici-ary, a spouse, issue or next of kin (*see Thomas* v. *I.R. Comrs.* [1981] STC 382 and *Cholmondeley and another* v. *I.R. Comrs.* [1986] STC 384). See SP/E7, 3 March 1976.

A transfer to create a protective trust is a chargeable transfer unless the settlor is the principal beneficiary.

It is specified that IHTA 1984, s. 52 does not apply if on the principal beneficiary's interest ceasing the property is then held under the protective trusts.

See IHTA 1984, s. 73 for trusts triggered before 12 April 1978.

89. Trusts for disabled persons. (E5.35, 36)
The relief applies where after 9 March 1981 (previously more limited provisions applied) property is transferred into a trust where there is no interest in possession (for example, a discretionary trust), and the terms of the trust provide that at least one half of that property is applied for the benefit of a disabled beneficiary during his lifetime. The beneficiary is deemed to have an interest in possession in the trust property and consequently such property is not relevant property under IHTA 1984, s. 58 and exit and ten-yearly charges etc. under the rules for taxing discretionary trusts will not apply. A disabled person is defined.

See IHTA 1984, s. 73 for trusts settled before 10 March 1981.

From 18 March 1986 transfers by individuals to disabled persons trusts on or after that date should qualify as potentially exempt transfers under IHTA 1984, s. 3A.

90. Trustees' annuities, etc. (E2.21–31)
If under the terms of a settlement a trustee is left an annuity as remuneration for his services to the extent it is reasonable, he is not deemed to have an interest in the trust fund and there is no inheritance tax charge on his death or on his interest in possession coming to an end.

91. Administration period. (E1.51)
If a person would have become entitled to an interest in possession in any part of residue on the completion of the administration period, for inheritance tax purposes, the same consequences follow as if he had obtained such an interest in the ascertained residue and the unadministered estate, from the earliest date income would have been attributable to that interest if the residue had been ascertained immediately after the death. A disposal of his interest by a beneficiary but not a disclaimer would therefore incur a charge to tax even though legally he never had an interest in possession of the property bequeathed. (See *Commissioner of Stamp Duties (Queensland)* v. *Livingstone* [1964] 3 All ER 692). This is subject to the provisions relating to variations and disclaimers and discretionary will trusts, under IHTA 1984, ss. 17, 142 and 144.

Practical difficulties can arise in valuing the relevant property of an estate in administration for any tax charge under these provisions having regard to the definitions contained in this section.

92. Survivorship clauses. (E1.61)
These provisions allow a *commorientes* period of up to six months, and if the beneficiary fails to survive this period the beneficiaries then acquiring the property are deemed to have become entitled to the property as if from the commencement of the period. These provisions nullify the "General Franco" scheme to distribute free of tax from a discretionary trust.

93. Disclaimers. (E2.21–31)
A person entitled to an interest in settled property who disclaims that interest other than for consideration will be treated as if he had not become entitled to that interest. As to disclaimers of other property, see IHTA 1984, s. 142.

PART IV CLOSE COMPANIES

TRANSFERS BY CLOSE COMPANIES

94. Charge on participators. (F1.22–29)
A transfer of value by a close company gives rise to a charge to tax as if each person to whom an amount is apportioned had made a net transfer equal to the amount apportioned, less the amount

by which his estate is increased as a result of the company transfer, ignoring for this purpose all rights and interests in the company. Such transfers tot up on the person's cumulative lifetime gifts total.

Apportionment is among the participators according to their respective rights, except that there is no apportionment to a person taxable thereon *e.g.* as a distribution or in respect of non-U.K. property to an individual not domiciled in the U.K. See *I.R. Comrs.* v. *Brandenburg* [1982] STC 555.

A transfer of value by a close company might alternatively give rise to a charge as a distribution under TA 1988, s. 209 (4) (TA 1970, s. 233 (3)) and could be apportioned among the shareholders for CGT purposes under CGTA 1979, s. 75 in which case inheritance tax would not be charged.

For definitions see s. 101.

95. Participator in two companies. (F1.26)
Where the apportionment is to another company this is sub-apportioned to the ultimate participators but the increase in the estate of the transferee company as a result of the transfer is also apportioned to offset against the sub-apportionment to them.

96. Preference shares disregarded. (F1.24)
Apportionment would not normally be made to preference shareholders if the effect would be relatively small.

97. Transfers within group, etc. (F1.24)
The surrendering of group losses or ACT is not a transfer of value under this section. If a transfer within a group within TA 1970, s. 273 free of chargeable gains has only a slight effect on minority interests these rights and interests are left out of account for calculating the apportionment to the participators. As to intra group transfers see SP/E15, March 1975.

ALTERATIONS OF CAPITAL, ETC.

98. Effect of alterations of capital, etc. (F1.11)
Any alteration to a close company's unquoted share or loan capital or any alteration in the rights attaching to the unquoted shares or debentures is treated as a disposition at that time by the participators. However such a disposition cannot qualify as a potentially exempt transfer under IHTA 1984, s. 3A. References to a person's rights and interests in a company include rights and interests in the assets of the company available for distribution among the participators in the event of a winding-up or in any other circumstances.

SETTLED PROPERTY

99. Transfers where participators are trustees. (F1.27)
Under the normal close company rules of IHTA 1984, ss. 94–97 a transfer of value by a close company is deemed to be a transfer by the participators to whom it is apportioned. If these participators are trustees, the deemed transfer takes the form of a deemed coming to an end of part of the limited interest where there is a qualifying interest in possession thus producing an inheritance tax charge under IHTA 1984, ss. 51–53, or if the trust fund is a discretionary trust there is a deemed disposition by the trustees of the amount apportioned chargeable (on events after 8 March 1982) under IHTA 1984, s. 65. The off-set against the amount so apportioned is by reference to the increase in value in the settled property exclusive of the value of rights or interests in the close company itself.

100. Alterations of capital, etc. where participators are trustees. (F1.12)
An alteration of unquoted share capital in a close company, gives rise to a capital distribution on termination of an interest in possession (not grossed up) where the shares are held by trustees.

101. Companies' interests in settled property. (F1.31)
Where a close company has an interest in possession in settled property the participators are deemed to have the interest in possession in the settled property in place of the company in proportion to their respective shareholdings (see *I.R. Comrs.* v. *Brandenburg* [1982] STC 555). For events after 8 March 1982 where the participators are themselves trustees holding under an interest in possession trust it is the beneficiary with the interest in possession who is deemed to be entitled to the company's interest in possession in place of the trustees.

See SP/E5, 11 June 1975.

Qualifying interest in possession is as defined in IHTA 1984, s. 59.

GENERAL

102. Interpretation. (F1.02)
The definition of a close company includes a non-resident company but otherwise is that in TA 1988, ss. 414, 415 (TA 1970, ss. 282, 283). A participator has the meaning in TA 1988, s. 417

(TA 1970, s. 303 (1)) but excludes a person from being a participator only because he is a loan creditor.

PART V MISCELLANEOUS RELIEFS

CHAPTER I BUSINESS PROPERTY

103. Preliminary. (G1.01)
The purpose of this Schedule is to allow for a reduction in the value transferred by a transfer of value in respect of business assets and also to reduce the value of chargeable transactions made or deemed to be made by trustees in respect of trust holdings of business assets. This paragraph defines transfer of value for the purposes of the business property relief, and is therefore given before deduction of exemptions under IHTA 1984, Part II. "Business" includes only a business carried on for gain and is extended to mean businesses carried on in the exercise of a profession or vocation.

104. The relief. (G1.02)
The relief is by way of a reduction (IHTA 1984, s. 105) in the principal value of the relevant business property transferred after 6 April 1976. This reduction takes place before any grossing up. Because the relief for business property is granted before the inheritance tax is calculated the relief in terms of tax is considerably greater than the nominal percentage if the donor bears the tax on the grossed-up equivalent of the business property transferred.

EXAMPLE—Relief for business property
ABC & Co. owned its freehold office block worth £50,000. On 8 August 1986 the four partners A, B, C, and D, gave the property jointly to interest in possession trusts for their sons. It is considered that the office block of itself is not an interest in a business, but the asset is used wholly for the purpose of the partnership business.

Unfortunately, as settled property gifts made before 17 March 1987 they did not qualify as potentially exempt transfers under IHTA 1984, s. 3A. Had the gifts been made direct to the sons they would have qualified and become totally exempt from tax on the respective fathers surviving the seven year inter vivos period.

	Transfer	Business Relief 30%	Transfer of value	Less annual exemption (see note)	Chargeable
Transaction A	12,500	3,750	8,750	2,870	5,880
B	12,500	3,750	8,750	5,000	3,750
C	12,500	3,750	8,750	1,470	7,280
D	12,500	3,750	8,750	2,100	6,650
	£50,000	£15,000	£35,000	£11,440	£23,560

Note: Maximum exemption less already used.

1985–86	3,000
1986–87	3,000
	6,000

105. Relevant business property. (G1.02, 11, 12, 22, 32, 42, 52)
This section defines relevant business property as property consisting of a business (for example, a sole proprietor business) or interest in a business (for example an interest as a partner) or shares in, or securities in, a company which gave the transferor control of the company immediately before the transfer in which case the relief is 50 per cent. For further comment on control, see IHTA 1984, s. 227.

For transfers and events occurring after 16 March 1987 the 50 per cent. relief applies to substantial minority shareholdings in unquoted companies where the transferor (including related property) has voting powers over more than 25 per cent. of total votes capable of being cast. It should be noted that after 16 March 1987 companies whose shares are dealt in on the Unlisted Securities Market (U.S.M.) are regarded as being "quoted" and therefore eligible for business relief (at 50 per cent.) only where a controlling interest is held. Note also that the higher 50 per cent.

rate will not be available where a claim for related property has been made under IHTA 1984 s. 176 and the 25 per cent. holding is exceeded only by the inclusion of related property. Note also the provisions of IHTA 1984, s. 109A.

The relief is 30 per cent. for unquoted minority shareholdings (not qualifying for the 50 per cent. rate and subject to exclusions referred to below) and for any land or building, plant or machinery which immediately prior to the transfer were used wholly or mainly for the purposes of the business carried on by a company controlled by the transferor or by a partnership in which he was then a partner. The 30 per cent. relief applies provided firstly that the transferor's interest in the business or (as the case may be if a company carries on the business) in the shares or securities of the company are themselves relevant business property, and secondly, if further conditions are satisfied as to their use for business purposes stipulated in s. 112 below.

After 9 March 1981 business relief at 30 per cent. applies to transfers or distributions of trust land or buildings, machinery or plant used wholly or mainly for the purpose of a business carried on by a beneficiary with an interest in possession in the settlement. However the case of *Fetherstonhaugh and others* v. *I.R. Comrs.* [1984] STC 261 would indicate that a life tenant carrying on a sole proprietor business would be entitled to business relief at 50 per cent. and this is confirmed by Law Society correspondence with the Revenue 21 April 1986, when the whole or part of the business is transferred. Land or share dealing or investment holding businesses are specifically excluded from relief except for stock jobbers ("marketmaker" from the date of the Stock Exchange reforms of October 1986—"marketmaker" is defined and the Revenue are given power to modify by statutory instrument the categories of excluded businesses), discount houses or holding companies of mainly qualifying companies.

The relief does not apply where the company is in liquidation unless for the purpose of reconstruction or amalgamation, nor if a contract of sale has been entered into unless either the property is a business or interest therein and is being sold to a company to carry on the business and the consideration is wholly or mainly shares or securities of that company, or the property is shares or securities of a company, and the sale is for the purpose of a reconstruction or amalgamation.

Woodlands qualify for 50 per cent. relief on death. For Lloyd's underwriters see Lloyd's circular to Names, 29 September 1977. Business relief may be available for furnished holiday accommodation where the services provided by the owner go well beyond that of being a landlord—see ICAEW Taxation anomalies 1984 and prior years (TR 581), para. 23: *Simon's Tax Intelligence* 1985, p. 316. Business relief was available following deeds of variation giving amounts payable from the sale of business assets: *Russell and another* v. *I.R. Comrs.* [1988] STC 195.

106. Minimum period of ownership. (G1.13, 24, 52)
To qualify as relevant business property, property has to be owned by the transferor for a period of at least two years immediately preceding the transfer. But see s. 107 below.

107. Replacements. (G1.14, 25, 52)
The assets transferred must be owned throughout the two years immediately preceding the transfer, although there are provisions for property replacing other property. There is a limitation on the value to which the relief can apply for replaced assets except if the replaced assets are held by virtue of
    (i)   a partnership formation or change or
    (ii) by a company controlled by the former owner of a business which was acquired by the company.

108. Successions. (G1.15, 25, 52)
A legatee is deemed to have owned the assets from the date of death unless the legacy was from his spouse in which case the spouse's period of ownership is also deemed to be his.

109. Successive transfers. (G1.16, 27, 52)
Even though the conditions of IHTA 1984, s. 109 cannot be satisfied, relief will still be given if an earlier transfer of value was eligible for relief under this Chapter (ss. 103 to 114) (or would have been if the rules then existed) and the property (or part) of the earlier transfer became the property of the person (or spouse) who is the subsequent transferor provided that the subsequent transfer is relevant business property (or is prevented from being such only by IHTA 1984, s. 109), and either the earlier or later transfer was made on the death of the transferor.

109A. Additional requirement in case of minority shareholdings. (G1.41, 42)
For transfers after 16 March 1987 to obtain the 50 per cent. reduction for minority shareholdings in unquoted companies it is necessary for the transferor to have retained voting power in excess of 25 per cent. throughout the two year period prior to the transfer, or throughout the shorter periods of ownership under IHTA 1984, s. 108 (Successions) and s. 109 (Successive transfers).

110. Value of business. (G1.01)
The value of the business on which the relief is available is the net value *i.e.* the value of assets, including goodwill, used in the business less any liabilities incurred for business purposes. See *Finch and others* v. *I. R. Comrs.* [1983] STC 157.

111. Value of certain shares and securities. (G1.32)
If a group of companies only partly qualifies the non qualifying companies in the group are omitted for the purpose of calculating the relief.

112. Exclusion of value of excepted assets. (G1.19, 31, 54)
Excepted assets are excluded in calculating the value for relief purposes of the relevant business property. Thus they reduce the value of qualifying shares and securities or of a business or interest therein.

To obtain relief the asset must have been used throughout the entire two years wholly or mainly for the purposes of the business or at the time of the transfer be required for future use for those purposes. There are special provisions concerning groups of companies.

Items must have been used throughout the two years preceding the transfer, or, subject to certain qualifications, for a replaced asset, if the replaced and original assets were so used for two out of the preceding five years.

It seems there may be considerable areas of doubt as to whether an asset is used wholly or mainly for business purposes, *e.g.* large bank balances where part may be in excess of business needs, or part of a building sublet.

It seems that if the asset qualifies as being mainly used for business purposes, this would allow the entire value of the asset to qualify even if there is some non-business user, but if the asset is mainly for non-business use, there may be no relief available.

113. Contracts for sale. (G1.28, 29, 53)
Business relief may be lost where "buy and sell agreements" have been entered for example, by partners agreeing to purchase an outgoing partner's interest. See SP 12/80, 23 December 1980.

113A. Transfers within seven years before death of transferor. (G1.91)
These provisions apply to restrict the availability of business relief where a transferor dies within seven years of making on, or after 18 March 1986 either (*a*) a potentially exempt transfer of relevant business property which becomes chargeable, or (*b*) a previously chargeable transfer of relevant business property the tax on which falls to be recomputed in accordance with IHTA 1984, s. 7.

Business relief will only be available where the transferee has retained ownership of the original property throughout from the date of transfer to the date of death and that the property would qualify as relevant business property at the latter date apart from the minimum two year ownership requirement contained in IHTA 1984, s. 106. If the transferee predeceases the transferor the qualification conditions must be met at the date of transferee's death. Where the original property consisted of shares or securities business relief is preserved for transfers after 16 March 1987 if the original transfers were made either from (*a*) a controlling quoted holding and therefore eligible for 50 per cent. relief, or (*b*) a controlling unquoted holding (and have remained unquoted during the donee's ownership). Where only part of the transfer of value is attributable to the original property then only that part qualifies for business relief.

113B. Application of s. 113A to replacement property. (G1.91)
Where the transferee has disposed of all or part of the property before the transferor's death, the availability of business relief is retained provided that he applies all the proceeds in the acquisition of replacement business property within 12 months of the disposal and both transactions are on arm's length terms and the replacement property is owned by the transferee at the date of the transferor's death.

114. Avoidance of double relief. (G1.02, 74)
Assets eligible for agricultural relief under IHTA 1984, s. 115 etc. do not also qualify for business relief but agricultural assets such as stock and plant not qualifying for relief under the agricultural relief provisions do qualify for the business property relief.

Where woodlands are the subject of a chargeable transfer so as to crystallise a transfer both on the gift and on a disposal in relation to the previous death under IHTA 1984, s. 129 the business relief is calculated on the value as reduced by the tax chargeable in relation to the previous death.

CHAPTER II AGRICULTURAL PROPERTY

115. Preliminary. (G3.01–04)
A transfer of value for agricultural property relief purposes includes an amount chargeable under the discretionary trust provisions contained in IHTA 1984, s. 58–85.

Agricultural land is defined as agricultural land and pasture in the U.K., the Channel Islands or the Isle of Man including:
> (*a*) woodlands; buildings used in the intensive rearing of livestock [effectively enacting Extrastatutory concession J3 (1988)—provided that their occupation is ancillary to the occupation of

the agricultural land or pasture;

(*b*) cottages, farm buildings and farm-houses together with the land occupied with them of a character appropriate to the property.

The relief is on the basis of the agricultural value of such property which is taken to be the value if the property were subject to a perpetual covenant prohibiting its use otherwise than as agricultural property.

116. The relief. (G3.01–04)

Provided that the ownership and occupation rules are satisfied (see IHTA 1984, ss. 117 to 124 below) the value transferred which is attributable to agricultural property is reduced by 50 per cent. if:

(*a*) the transferor had vacant possession in the property immediately prior to its transfer, or the right to obtain it within the next 12 months; or

(*b*) the transferor had owned his interest in the land prior to 10 March 1981 and would have been entitled to the 50 per cent. relief under the old rules (see FA 1975, Sch. 8) had he disposed of the land on 9 March 1981, for example land occupied by a member of the transferor's family (see FA 1975, Sch. 8, para. 3 (4)). Where the old relief would have been restricted by the overriding limits of £250,000 or 1,000 acres (see FA 1975, Sch. 8, para. 5), the new relief is similarly restricted, although the 30 per cent. relief (20 per cent. prior to 15 March 1983) will apply to the remainder of the land. In such situations it is also necessary to take account of any other transfers of land (whether on, or after (under the new rules) or before 10 March 1981) to see whether the limits have been reached, which is an unfortunate complication. However the limits will not apply to transfers after 9 March 1981 if the property is held with vacant possession or if the tenancy was created after that date. Finally the 50 per cent. relief is not available if prior to the transfer of value (but after 9 March 1981) the transferor's interest gave any right to, or to obtain, vacant possession, or if the transferor has failed to take up such a right by any omission to act.

In other cases, that is tenanted land to which the 50 per cent. relief does not apply, the relief is 30 per cent. (20 per cent. prior to 15 March 1983).

Provided that the aggregate interests of all joint tenants or tenants in common (or their Scottish counterparts) give vacant possession then each joint tenant or tenant in common is deemed to have vacant possession.

The recasting of agricultural relief brings it in line with business relief in that the deduction is given before deducting annual exemptions. Also, it is not necessary to be a working farmer, as the requirement to carry on a trade has been repealed.

117. Minimum period of occupation or ownership. (G3.01–04, 21)

The transferor must have occupied the property for the purposes of agriculture for two years before the transfer, or owned it for a period of seven years during which it was occupied by the transferor or another person for the purposes of agriculture. In both cases the minimum periods end with the date of the transfer.

118. Replacements. (G3.13, 22)

Relief on replacement property transferred is allowed where the total period of occupation consists of at least two years within the five years ending with the transfer or in the case of tenanted property where the original and replacement property were held for seven years in the ten years ending with the transfer. Partnership changes are ignored. In other cases the relief cannot exceed that which would have been due had the land not been replaced.

119. Occupation by company or partnership. (G3.12)

Occupation by a company controlled by the transferor is treated as occupation by the transferor for the purposes of establishing the period of occupancy (IHTA 1984, s. 117) and the period of occupancy of replacement property (IHTA 1984, s. 118). Land occupied by a Scottish partnership, although a separate legal entity, is deemed to be occupied by the partners.

120. Successions. (G3.14, 23)

A legatee is deemed to have owned and occupied (provided that he does subsequently occupy the property) the property from the date of death except in the case of a spouse in which case the ownership and occupation of both spouses can be aggregated.

Where the transferor became entitled to his interest in the agricultural property on the death of his spouse after 9 March 1981 the conditions under IHTA 1984, s. 116 are deemed to have been satisfied by the transferor if previously satisfied by the spouse. Thus where a deceased spouse could have obtained agricultural property relief on a transfer prior to 10 March 1981, for example under FA 1975, Sch. 8, para. 3 (4) (land occupied by a member of the transferor's family) relief under the new rules will be extended to a transfer by the surviving spouse.

121. Successive transfers. (G3.15, 24)

The minimum occupancy and ownership conditions contained in IHTA 1984, s. 117 above are not applied where:

(*a*) the transferor or his spouse obtained his interest in the agricultural property, either by gift or by inheritance, and on the earlier occasion agricultural property relief under this Schedule was available (or would have been available if then in force); and

(*b*) at the time of the later transfer the property was occupied for agricultural purposes by the transferor or by the personal representative of the original transferor; and

(*c*) the later transfer would have qualified for agricultural property relief were it not for the minimum occupancy and ownership conditions; and

(*d*) either the earlier or the later transfer was on a death.

Illustration
Farmer John dies on 28 February leaving his 2,000 acre farm to his nephew Jim who commenced to farm on 1 December following release by John's personal representatives. Jim died on 26 December.

Agricultural property relief will be available on Jim's death, notwithstanding Jim's short period of occupancy of the property.

There are provisions dealing with replacement property or where part only of the property qualified for relief under the earlier transfer.

122. Agricultural property of companies. (G3.31)
If shares in a company are transferred, agricultural relief is available to the extent that the value is attributable to the agricultural value of agricultural property which forms part of the company's assets and can be attributed to the value of the shares provided that the transferor had control of the company. For this purpose related property cannot be included to give control if an election has been made to value them as unrelated property under IHTA 1984, s. 176.

In the case of a company references to the transferor's interest in agricultural property are construed as references to the company's interest. The requisite period of occupancy is dealt with in IHTA 1984, s. 123.

123. Provisions supplementary to s. 122. (G3.31–37)
To qualify for the relief the company has to have owned and occupied the property for two years prior to the transfer or held tenanted land for seven years before the transfer and the shares must have been held by the transferor throughout the same two or seven-year periods respectively.

There are provisions allowing replacement of agricultural property within the company and where the shares in the company replace other eligible agricultural property; provided that the minimum period is two years out of five in the case of owner-occupied property and seven out of ten for tenanted property.

The company is treated as having occupied agricultural property at any time when it was occupied by a person who subsequently controls the company, which means that the relief is available if, for example, a farming business is incorporated.

124. Contracts for sale. (G3.41–42)
Relief is not available where there is a binding contract for sale of the property or shares in a company, otherwise than on a transfer of a business to a company wholly or mainly in consideration of shares in the company where the transferor secures control of the company, or for the purposes of a reconstruction or amalgamation of the company.

124A. Transfers within seven years before death of transferor. (G3.81)
This section applies to restrict the availability of agricultural relief in the computation of additional tax (see IHTA 1984, s. 7) following a transferor's death within seven years of making on, or after, 18 March 1986, either (*a*) a potentially exempt transfer of agricultural property, or (*b*) a previously chargeable transfer of agricultural property.

Agricultural relief will not be available unless property comprised in the gift is owned by the transferee throughout the period from the date of transfer to the date of death ("the relevant period") and that throughout the relevant period the property is agricultural property occupied either by the transferee or another for the purposes of agriculture. Where the original agricultural property comprised shares in a farming company (see IHTA 1984, s. 122) the company must have owned the agricultural land throughout the relevant period. Where the transferee predeceases the transferor the conditions must be satisfied at the transferee's death. For transfers after 16 March 1987 the donee's period of ownership of the original property is aggregated with the period of ownership of the shares into which it has been transferred. Where only a part of the transfer can be attributed to the original property, agricultural relief is only available in respect of that part.

124B. Application of s. 124A to replacement property
Where the transferee has disposed of all or part of the property before the transferor's death, the availability of agricultural relief is retained provided that he applies all the proceeds in the acquisition of replacement agricultural property within 12 months of the disposal and both transactions are on arm's length terms and the replacement property is owned by the transferee at the time of the transferors death.

CHAPTER III WOODLANDS

125. The relief. (G4.01–03)
Relief for woodlands is available if claimed by notice in writing within two years of death or such longer time as the Board may allow and if certain conditions are met. Relief is only available if the deceased held the land beneficially for the five years preceding his death or acquired it otherwise than for money or money's worth. The land must be situated in the U.K. which excludes the Channel Islands and the Isle of Man, unlike for agricultural property. The relief only applies on death. It does not apply where the woodlands are included as agricultural property under Ch. II above. The value of the trees or underwood is left out of account at death, but inheritance tax will probably become chargeable at a later date under IHTA 1984, s. 126.

126. Charge to tax on disposal of trees or underwood. (G4.04, 05)
Inheritance tax is payable on a disposal in relation to the last death on which the trees or underwood passed. A person entitled to the sale proceeds (or who would be so entitled if the disposal was a sale) is liable to the tax. An inter-spouse disposal is ignored. Inheritance tax is only charged on the first disposal following the death, at the death rates in force at the time of the disposal, and it is not charged again in relation to the same death on a subsequent disposal of the same trees or underwood.

127. Amount subject to charge. (G4.04, 05)
Inheritance tax is calculated on the net sale proceeds on a sale for full consideration in money or money's worth and on the net value at the date of disposal in other cases. The amount of tax is calculated as if the chargeable amount were added to the estate of the latest person on whose death the property passed, and the amount payable is the additional tax so calculated.

It should be noted that the amount left out of account on a death is the value of the trees and underwood at that time, but the amount subsequently charged on a disposal is calculated by adding in the value at the date of the disposal at which time the value may be considerably in excess of the value at death.

Provided that at the date of death the trees or underwood would have qualified as relevant business property for business relief under IHTA 1984, Pt. V, Ch. I, a 50 per cent. deduction is allowed from the disposal proceeds when computing the tax liability. This applies to disposals after 26 October 1977, even if the death occurred prior to that time.

EXAMPLE—Disposal of trees or underwood: basis and rate of tax
Mitchel died on 30 September 1989 and left the following estate, there having been no lifetime transfers within the seven years before death and ignoring business relief).

		£
Sundry assets		150,000
Value of trees and underwood		60,000
		£210,000
Inheritance tax payable at death: On £150,000		£12,800
On 1 January 1998 the trees and underwood were sold for:		120,000
after allowing for selling and replanting expenses		
Other assets at death		150,000
		£270,000
Inheritance tax payable		
First	£118,000	nil
Next	152,000 @ 40%	60,800
	£270,000	60,800
Less: Paid on death		12,800
Payable on sale of timber		£48,000
If no claim were made, inheritance tax on death would have been:		
First	£118,000	nil
Next	92,000 @ 40%	36,800
	£210,000	£36,800

However the additional £24,000 which would have been payable on the death would have been expended nine years earlier and at a time when the cash may not have been available even taking into account the instalments payments option, IHTA 1984, s. 229.

128. Rate of charge. (G4.05)
The charge under IHTA 1984, s. 126 in respect of a sum determined under IHTA 1984, s. 127 above is computed at the rate in force at the date of death, the amount being so charged being the highest part of the estate.

129. Credit for tax charged. (G4.08)
If the later disposal is itself a chargeable transfer the value of the trees or underwood for the later transfer is regarded as diminished by the tax chargeable under IHTA 1984, s. 126. See also IHTA 1984, s. 114 (2) for avoidance of double relief.

130. Interpretation. (D4.05)
Net values are after selling expenses and expenses of replanting within three years or such longer time as the Board may allow.

CHAPTER IV TRANSFERS WITHIN [SEVEN] YEARS BEFORE DEATH

131. The relief. (D4.03)
Where a transfer falls in the seven year gift *inter vivos* period before a death and the value of property at the date of death or at the date of sale, if it has been sold, is less than the value at the date of the transfer, the tax or additional tax payable by the donee is calculated as if the value transferred were the lower amount. This will apply to potentially exempt transfers on becoming chargeable (see IHTA 1984, s. 3A) and to other previously chargeable transfers where additional tax may be payable—see IHTA 1984, s. 7. This section does not apply to tangible movable property which is a wasting asset and the sale will only qualify if it is an arm's length sale to a non-connected party. The appropriate claim has to be made within the normal six year time limit.

132. Wasting assets. (D4.03)
IHTA 1984, s. 131 does not apply to tangible moveable property which is a wasting asset.

133. Shares—capital receipts. (D4.04)
If a capital payment is received prior to the relevant date in respect of shares, for example a sale of rights, it has to be added to the sale proceeds or value on death.

134. Payments of calls. (D4.04)
Conversely any payment of calls etc., made before the relevant time would be deducted from the valuation of the sale proceeds or value at death.

135. Reorganisation of share capital, etc. (D4.04)
Provision is made for following through a reorganisation of share capital within the capital gains tax definitions of CGTA 1979, ss. 77–86.

136. Transactions of close companies. (D4.05)
There are provisions for increasing the value of shares in a close company which has made a transfer of value or altered the rights attaching to its shares since the chargeable transfer and before the relevant time.

137. Interests in land. (D4.06)
Provision is made for changes in the value of interests in land to take account of changes during the gift *inter vivos* period such as compensation for the grant of an easement etc.

138. Leases. (D4.07)
Provision is made for the depreciation of leases where the interest in land is a lease with less than 50 years to run. An appropriate fraction addition is made to the sale proceeds or value at death. The appropriate fraction is $P(1)-P(2)/P(1)$ where $P(1)$ is the appropriate percentage from the curved line depreciation table for a premium on leases (contained in CGTA 1979, Sch. 3) at the date of the gift *inter vivos* and $P(2)$ is the percentage at the date of sale or death.

139. Other property. (D4.09)
A general provision is introduced where the property is neither shares nor an interest in land to take account of changes in the property between the relevant dates.

Provision is also made for increasing the value at the date of death or sale by the excess of any benefits received over a reasonable return on the asset.

140. Interpretation. (H2.01)
Various terms are defined in connection with the calculation of a reduction in value of a transfer of value within three years prior to the death and also the reduction of value in respect of a spouse transfer which has fallen in value between the date of the transfer and the date of the Revenue claim under IHTA 1984, s. 203 (1).

CHAPTER V MISCELLANEOUS

SUCCESSIVE CHARGES

141. Two or more transfers within five years. (E2.41, 42)
Quick succession relief is available where the value of a person's estate has been increased by a chargeable transfer within five years prior to: (*a*) his death; or (*b*) a lifetime transfer of settled property in which the transferor had an interest in possession, and where the first transfer was made by reference to the value of the same settled property either on the making of the settlement or on a subsequent transfer.

The relief is calculated as a percentage reduction in tax payable on the first transfer (to the extent that the transferor's estate is increased by the first transfer) and is allowed as a deduction against tax due on the later transfer. It amounts to 100 per cent. where the transfers occur within one year, 80 per cent. within the second year, 60 per cent. within the third year, 40 per cent. within the fourth year and 20 per cent. within the fifth year.

Relief is given only on the first subsequent transfer except to the extent that the tax or the appropriate percentage of it remains unrelieved, when it may be allowed against subsequent transfers of the same property within the original five-year period.

An increase in the estate by the acquisition of a reversionary interest on or before the later transfer which was excluded property is ignored.

See also FA 1986, s. 104 in respect of certain events occurring after 17 March 1986.

CHANGES IN DISTRIBUTION OF DECEASED'S ESTATE, ETC.

142. Alteration of dispositions taking effect on death. (D5.44)
It is possible under this section and IHTA 1984, ss. 143 and 144 effectively to reorganise and redirect dispositions contained in a person's will or under the law of intestacy provided that this is done within two years of the death.

Variations or disclaimers must be made in writing within two years of the death and must relate to a disposition made (*a*) by the deceased's will, or (*b*) under the law of intestacy or otherwise. A variation or disclaimer must not be made for consideration in money or money's worth, unless the consideration is itself a qualifying variation or disclaimer relating to another of the deceased's dispositions. Variations or disclaimers extend only to property comprised in the deceased's estate, including excluded property but not to property in which the deceased had a life interest or which is deemed to be included by virtue of FA 1986, s. 102 (gifts with reservation). Written notice must be given to the Revenue within six months of the date of variation or disclaimer, or during such longer period as the Board may allow. Rectification of errors in a deed of variation was allowed in *Lake* v. *Lake and others* [1989] STC 865.

The effect of the variation or disclaimer for inheritance tax purposes is as if the original benefit had never been conferred, and the property concerned falls into the residue of the estate. It is not possible to make a valid disclaimer where a benefit has been derived since the death from the property concerned; this might for example make it difficult if not impossible for a surviving spouse to disclaim an inheritance in the matrimonial home. See also IHTA 1984, ss. 17, 146, 146A. The Revenue failed to prove a composite transaction in *Hastings and another* v. *I.R. Comrs.* and *Countess Fitzwilliam and others* v. *I.R. Comrs.* [1990] STC 65.

143. Compliance with testator's request. (D5.45)
Where property is left to a legatee with an informal request to transfer the property to other persons and this is in fact done within two years of the death, the transferee is deemed for inheritance tax purposes to have inherited directly from the deceased.

144. Distribution etc. from property settled by will. (D5.11)
Where a testator settles a discretionary will trust and before there is any interest in possession in the property the trustees make a capital distribution or some other event occurs within two years of the death there will be no inheritance tax liability as a result of such transaction (which would otherwise arise under IHTA 1984, Part III, Chapter III) and tax is payable as if the distribution or event had been provided for in the will. As far as inheritance tax is concerned this is a very flexible and useful

means of bequeathing an estate or part of it where it is not clear at the time of making the will of the most beneficial manner or making the proposed distribution. As to CGT see CGTA 1979, s. 49 (6)–(9). As to income tax see Inland Revenue Press Release, 11 April 1989.

145. Redemption of surviving spouse's life interest. (D5.32, 33)
If the surviving spouse makes an election under Administration of Estates Act 1925, s. 47A he will be treated as having been entitled to a sum equal to the capital sum mentioned in that section and not the life interest.

146. Inheritance (Provision for Family and Dependants) Act 1975. (D5.32, 33)
If property passes in accordance with an order under the Inheritance (Provision for Family and Dependants) Act 1975, s. 2 it is treated for inheritance tax purposes as if it were a disposition made on death. Any inheritance tax already paid may be reclaimed together with interest from the date of claim.

If there was a disposition by the deceased prior to death which was comprised in a chargeable transfer and under s. 10 of the above-mentioned Act, the recipient has to provide money or other property by reason thereof the amount provided is treated as if left by the deceased at death, and adjustments and repayments of inheritance tax made accordingly. This section applies in relation to deaths after 6 April 1976.

Action taken in compliance with orders under the Act will not constitute chargeable occasions under IHTA 1984, s. 52 (lifetime termination of an interest in possession) or under the discretionary trust charging provisions, for events after 8 March 1982, contained in IHTA 1984, ss. 58–85.

147. Scotland: legitim. (D5.63, 64)
This section applies in respect of deaths after 12 November 1974 where the will or testamentary document is governed by the law of Scotland, and the deceased left a surviving spouse and a person under the age of 18 able to claim legitim *i.e.* the legal rights of the survivors to a portion of the estate which over-rides any provision of the will. The section applies only if the disposition to the spouse would encroach upon the legitim share.

MUTUAL AND VOIDABLE TRANSFERS

148. Mutual transfers: exemption for donee's gift. (C2.51, 52)
These provisions are repealed in respect of donee transfers after 17 March 1986.

149. Mutual transfers: relief for donor's gift. (C2.53)
These provisions are repealed in respect of donee transfers after 17 March 1986.

150. Voidable transfers. (C2.55)
A claim can be made if a chargeable transfer made at any time after 26 March 1974 is or becomes voidable or otherwise defeasible because of an enactment or rule of law. Any inheritance tax paid is repaid and the transfer is treated as if it had never been made. This means that all subsequent transfers are recalculated and any tax refunded as necessary. Repayment is to carry interest from the date of claim which would have to be made within the normal six year time limit.

PENSION SCHEMES, ETC.

151. Treatment of pension rights, etc. (D1.19; E5.31)
The right to a pension or annuity from an approved superannuation fund which terminates and is not within IHTA 1984, s. 151 (2) (*b*), is ignored when ascertaining the value of assets passing on death. Superannuation fund property is not (after 8 March 1982) relevant property under IHTA 1984, s. 58, and accordingly is not subject to the discretionary trust charging provisions contained in IHTA 1984, ss. 58–85. As to death benefits, see SP10/86.

152. Cash options. (E5.31)
If a pension is payable to a surviving spouse or dependants under a self-employed retirement annuity contract or approved personal pension scheme and at his option under the terms of the

contract a capital sum might have been payable to the estate instead of the pension, the deceased is not treated as beneficially entitled to the capital sum which might have been obtained (see also TA 1988, s. 621.

153. Overseas pensions. (D1.21; J3.25)

Certain pensions payable by the U.K. Government in respect of overseas service are exempt from inheritance tax.

154. Death on active service, etc. (D2.02)

Death on active service, as defined, means that inheritance tax is not payable in respect of the death. It should be noted that the Defence Council or Secretary of State must certify for the exemption to be obtained. Also the death may take place many years after the individual has ceased to be a person who at the relevant time satisfied the conditions. Members of the Royal Ulster Constabulary are included by Extra-statutory concession F 5 (1985). *Barty King and another* v. *Minister of Defence* [1979] STC 218. Hansard, 26 November 1979, as are those killed on active service in the Falklands dispute. See Inland Revenue Press Release, 23 June 1982.

155. Visiting forces, etc. (J3.28)

The stipulated property of a member of visiting forces resident in the U.K. (who is not a citizen of the U.K. and Colonies) is excluded property if the individual also comes within the terms of this paragraph.

156. Apsley House and Chevening Estate. (G6.01, 02)

The inheritance tax provisions will not apply in respect of the rights conferred by s. 3 of the Wellington Museum Act 1947 or property held on the trusts of the trust instrument set out in the schedule to the Chevening Estate Act 1959.

157. Non-residents' bank accounts. (E2.29)

For deaths occurring after 8 March 1982 foreign currency accounts (*i.e.*, non-sterling accounts with the Bank of England, the Post Office, a recognised bank or licensed institution) situated in the U.K. will be left out of account for inheritance tax purposes where the deceased at the time of his death was not domiciled, resident or ordinarily resident in the U.K. The exemption also extends to such an account held by trustees where the deceased was beneficially entitled to an interest in possession provided that the settlor was not U.K. domiciled when he made the settlement and provided that the trustees were not domiciled, resident or ordinarily resident immediately prior to the beneficiary's death.

Residence and ordinary residence are determined as for income tax purposes and the trustees will not be regarded as being U.K. resident unless the general administration of the settlement is ordinarily carried on in the U.K. and a majority of the trustees are U.K. resident and ordinarily resident.

158. Double taxation conventions. (J5.03)

Power is given to enter into double taxation agreements with overseas countries covering inheritance tax (including when required provisions for the exchange of information between the U.K. and other territories to combat fiscal evasion), and any existing arrangements relating to estate duty are extended to cover inheritance tax. Double taxation agreements exist with France, India, Irish Republic, Italy, Netherlands, Pakistan, South Africa, Sweden, Switzerland and United States of America.

159. Unilateral relief. (J5.01, 02)

Overseas taxes similar to inheritance tax or chargeable by reference to a gift *inter vivos* or on death are relieved as a credit against U.K. inheritance tax. If the property is situated in the overseas territory and not in the U.K. the credit is equal to the full overseas tax charged. Where, however, the property is situated neither in the U.K. nor the overseas territory, or is situated both in the U.K. and the overseas territory, and in each case is subject to inheritance tax or the equivalent in both countries, the credit is calculated in accordance with the formula (IHT (A)/IHT(A) + Overseas tax (B)) × smaller of IHT or the overseas tax (C).

If the property is situated as above and is subject to tax imposed in more than one overseas territory, the formula is modified. The overseas tax (B) in the above formula is the aggregate of the taxes in each of the overseas countries, but C in the formula is the aggregate of all except the largest of the U.K. inheritance tax and each of the overseas equivalent taxes.

Double taxation relief is given at the higher of any treaty relief under IHTA 1984, s. 158 or unilateral relief under this section. The calculation of the unilateral relief is in fact the same as that given in the agreements with the United States of America, South Africa, India and Pakistan.

PART VI VALUATION

CHAPTER I GENERAL

160. Market value. (H2.01)
Property is to be valued at open market value with no reduction for flooding the market by disposing of the whole of the property at one time. This basis which is now statutory was approved in the estate duty case *Duke of Buccleuch and another* v. *I.R. Comrs.* [1967] 1 AC 506. For valuations of unquoted shares and securities see IHTA 1984, s. 168. Determinations on appeal of land valuations are dealt with by the Lands Tribunal; see IHTA 1984, s. 222 (4). As to the valuation of a jointly owned house see *Wight and another* v. *I.R. Comrs., Lands Tribunal* (1982) 264 EG 935. As to the valuation of tenanted agricultural land see *Willett and another* v. *I.R. Comrs., Lands Tribunal* (1982) 264 EG 257.

The market value of quoted securities in practice is as for capital gains tax, namely the lower of one quarter of the difference between the lower and higher closing prices added to the lower price ($^1/_4$ up) or mid-way between the highest and lowest prices at which the bargains were marked. There are exceptions where the quoted price is not a proper measure of the market value, but in view of *Crabtree* v. *Hinchcliffe* (1971) 47 TC 419 it would be necessary to find as a fact that special circumstances affecting the share price had been unjustifiably withheld from the stock exchange.

Unit trusts are valued at the lower (manager's buying) quoted price.

EXAMPLE—Valuation: quoted shares.
AB Ltd. was quoted at 44/46 on Friday 5 February and at 41/43 (ex div) on Monday 8 February. Bargains were made at 45, $44^1/_2$, $45^1/_2$, $44^3/_4$ on the Friday and at $41^1/_4$, 42, $42^1/_2$, $42^1/_4$ on the Monday.

The cash dividend declared was $2^1/_2$p per share (ignoring tax credit).

Mr. X died with 1,000 shares on Saturday 6 February.

Values—

Friday   —$^1/_4$ up.

$46-44=2\times{}^1/_4={}^1/_2+44=$ $44^1/_2$

Friday   —bargains marked $\dfrac{44^1/_2+45^1/_2}{2}=$ 45

Monday —$^1/_4$ up.

$43-41=2\times{}^1/_4={}^1/_2+41=41^1/_2+2^1/_2=$ 44

Monday —bargains marked $\dfrac{41^1/_4+42^1/_2}{2}=41^7/_8+2^1/_2=$ $44^3/_8$

Value

$44\times1,000=$ £440

161. Related property. (H2.41–43)
The concept of related property is extremely important for inheritance tax and the most common practical application will be in relation to shares in unquoted companies but it does apply to other property and it is unclear if and how it could affect different interests in land. The concept appreciates that the aggregate value of fragmented assets can be proportionately much less than the value of the whole as a unit and therefore provides that for valuation calculation purposes relevant assets of the transferor must be aggregated with those of his spouse, and with any property which has been held by a charity or similar exempt body at any time within five years of the transfer where the property was originally transferred to the charity after 15 April 1976 by the transferor or his spouse.

Having ascertained the total value of the related property as if held by one notional person it is then necessary to apportion this among the parties concerned. This is done basically in proportion to the usual non-related values of the assets of each party which were aggregated under the related properties provisions, unless the assets concerned are shares or debentures etc. identifiable as of the same class (as defined) in which case the apportionment is made on the basis of the number of shares or nominal value of the debenture stock etc.

EXAMPLE—Valuation of related property
Mr. Shavrov held 30 per cent. of the shares in Historia Ltd., his wife held 21 per cent. of the shares and his 1978 charitable settlement held 20 per cent. of the shares. Any disposal by Mr. or Mrs. Shavrov would therefore take place on the basis of a proportion of a 71 per cent. shareholding. A disposal by the trust however would be on the basis of a 20 per cent. shareholding, because the trust property is related to the shareholdings of Mr. & Mrs. Shavrov but not the other way around. If Mr. Shavrov gave away 25 per cent. of the shares the reduction in his estate would be the difference between $^{30}/_{71}$sts of a 71 per cent. holding before the transfer, and $^{5}/_{46}$ths of a 46 per cent. holding after the transfer. A 71 per cent. shareholding would control the company and would usually be calculated on an earnings basis, whereas a 46 per cent. shareholding although a substantial minority holding would not control the company and would therefore normally be calculated on a yield basis. It appears that if he first gave 5 per cent. to Mrs. Shavrov the diminution of his estate would be confined to $^{25}/_{71}$sts of a 71 per cent. holding as he would now be left with no shares, which may be lower than mentioned above as $^{5}/_{46}$ths may have only a negligible value.

It should be noted that although the related shareholding provisions to an extent aggregate various holdings, the effect is not the same as if the shares were held by one person. For example, a 51 per cent. shareholder with no related property disposing of two per cent. of the shares would be assessed to IHT on the difference between a 51 per cent. shareholding and a 49 per cent. shareholding. If, however, a shareholder held two per cent. of the share capital and his spouse held 49 per cent. they would be valued as related property as a 51 per cent. shareholding. However, if the two per cent. shareholder disposed of his entire interest his estate would be reduced by the difference between $^{2}/_{51}$sts of a 51 per cent. shareholding and nil, all his shares having been disposed of, which would normally be very much less than the loss of control on reducing from a 51 per cent. to a 49 per cent. shareholding. In each case the disposal of the remaining 49 per cent. would give rise to a similar charge. The Revenue might invoke the associated operations provisions of IHTA 1984, s. 268 if an attempt was made to utilise the inter-spouse exemption to ensure that the controlling hump could be disposed of at a cost of tax on $^{2}/_{51}$sts of the 51 per cent. value, but this may depend on what happens to the shares then held by the spouse.

It should be noted that the transfer in favour of a charity or other exempt body is merely a delaying anti-avoidance provision and if for example, a two per cent. shareholding was given to a charity, which would be exempt, and if the charity then sold the shares to say a merchant bank in a non-associated operation, after five years the property held by the charity would cease to be related to that owned by the transferor, and if he were then left with 49 per cent. of the shares *prima facie* one may consider that a disposal at the reduced value could then take place. However it is unclear if and how the Revenue might seek to invoke IHTA 1984, s. 268 (associated operations) on the later disposal and might require justifiable reasons for the original 2 per cent. transactions and why control was "dissipated" in that way. The related property provisions effectively replace the artificial assets value basis in FA 1940, ss. 46 and 55 which applied for estate duty and which have no place under inheritance tax.

162. Liabilities. (H2.27)
Where it is necessary to ascertain the value of a transferor's estate, liabilities incurred for consideration in money or money's worth or imposed by law may be deducted. If it is necessary to calculate the transferor's estate immediately after a transfer the liabilities to be deducted include the inheritance tax (if any, for example if a potentially exempt transfer is made after 17 March 1986—see IHTA 1984, s. 3A), but not any other taxes resulting from the transfer *e.g.* CGT. Apart from the liability for the inheritance tax itself any liability to be discharged later is taken at its discount value. See also IHTA 1984, s. 165.

A charge on any property shall be taken as far as possible as reducing the value of that property.

A liability to a non U.K. resident is deducted as far as possible in the first instance from property outside the U.K., unless it is to be discharged in the U.K. or is charged on property in the U.K.

See also IHTA 1984, s. 5 and FA 1986, s. 103 in respect of deaths after 17 March 1986 where further restrictions as to deductibility may be imposed.

163. Restriction on freedom to dispose. (H2.31)
If property suffers from a contractual restriction on its subsequent disposal, for the purposes of the first relevant event after the contract, the restrictive effect on the valuation of the property is taken into account only to the extent that money or money's worth was given for it. This does not apply if the contract giving rise to the restriction with or without associated operations was itself a chargeable transfer. In such a case an allowance is to be made (*i.e.* allowing a liability deduction) for so much of the earlier value transferred without grossing as is attributable to the contractual exclusion or restriction. If the contract was made before 27 March 1974 the restriction is taken into account only where the first relevant event (as defined) is a transfer on death.

The question of whether a contract was made is important. It is also to be noted that it is the freedom of disposal which is in point, for example if a person gifts an easement over his land in favour of an adjoining owner. The donee can still freely dispose of the land but an acquirer takes it subject to the easement or any other relevant rights etc. attaching to the land.

164. Transferor's expenses. (C2.24, 25)
Expenses of a transfer other than inheritance tax are to be ignored if borne by the transferor and treated as reducing the value of the transfer if borne by the transferee.

165. Tax on capital gains. (C2.24, 25)
If any CGT is payable by a donee the value of a chargeable transfer is reduced by the tax so payable. This rule also applies to chargeable transfers by trustees where any CGT on the trustees' gain is borne by a beneficiary becoming absolutely entitled to the property. For disposals after 13 March 1989 it may be beneficial for a CGT holdover election to be made under the provisions of CGTA 1979, s. 126 (gifts of business assets) or under CGTA 1979, s. 147A (gifts on which inheritance tax is chargeable) although under CGTA 1979, s. 147A a holdover election is not available on a gift constituting a potentially exempt transfer. Previously the more generous holdover provisions contained in FA 1980, s. 79 applied. Any inheritance tax paid on the original gift is allowed as a deduction in the donee's CGT computation.

166. Creditors' rights. (H3.72)
The value of a right to receive a loan etc. or what is due under an obligation is to be based on the assumption that it is a good debt, or that the obligation will be met except to the extent that it can be proved that recovery is impossible or not reasonably practicable and this situation arose without any act or omission of the creditor. If, however, the debt is due or obligation is to be met at some specified date in the future and not on demand then it would be appropriately discounted. (See IHTA 1984, s. 162).

167. Life policies, etc. (H3.75)
Life policies and annuities due are valued on the basis of the higher of the market value or the total premiums paid less returned through partial surrender. The market value cannot be less than the surrender value, but could be greater if for example there had been an unexpected deterioration in the life assured's health.

These provisions do not apply on death where the insurance proceeds are chargeable under IHTA 1984, s. 171 or to term assurance policies where the indemnity period is in excess of three years and the premiums are paid at normal intervals. Nor do they apply where the policy does not cease to be part of the estate of the transferor nor to certain mutual transfers IHTA 1984, ss. 148, 149 before 18 March 1986.

See also FA 1986, s. 102 and Sch. 20, para. 7 in respect of gifts with reservation made after 17 March 1986.

Where the policy is unit linked and the payment of each premium secures the allocation of a specified number of such units, then if the value of the units allocated to the policy on the payment of the premiums is less than the aggregate value of those units at the time of the allocation, the total of premiums paid is reduced by any such difference.

A premium paid on a trust policy is usually a transfer of the net premium, see Inland Revenue Press Release, 17 January 1979.

These provisions in general apply to transfers by trustees of discretionary trusts for events after 8 March 1982.

168. Unquoted shares and securities. (H3.11)
Unquoted shares or unquoted securities are valued on the basis of the price reasonably expected on a sale in the open market on the assumption that there is available to any prospective purchaser all the information which a prudent prospective purchaser might reasonably require for a purchase from a willing vendor by private treaty at arm's length. This is similar to the CGT provisions in CGTA 1979, s. 152 (3) and to this extent is contrary to the decision in *re Lynall* (deceased) (1971) 47 TC 375. The information deemed to be available in each case will depend on the circumstances. For example, if a 20 per cent. shareholding is being valued it is probable that the information that could reasonably be required is far less than for the acquisition of a 60 per cent. controlling interest. If, however, the price to be paid for the 20 per cent. interest was substantial, additional information would reasonably be required compared with an investment of a much more modest amount. It is not to be envisaged that the prospective purchaser could reasonably ask the willing vendor to commit a breach of trust or disclose confidential information which the board, on request, would not be expected to authorise him to divulge. When considering the valuation of shares in unquoted companies it is important to bear in mind the nature of a share. Following the case of *Borlands Trustee* v. *Steel Bros. & Co. Ltd.* (1901) 1 CA 279 it was held that a share is no more than a collection of rights between the shareholders *inter se* and between the shareholders and the company itself.

Many companies contain in their articles a restriction on the transfer of shares and this restriction has to be taken into account in the valuation. It is however necessary to assume that the hypothetical purchaser will in fact be registered as the new shareholder and it is not necessary to show that as a matter of fact the directors would not approve a transfer other than for example to a family member. The effect of a restriction on transfer is probably depreciatory in that it must be assumed that the shares acquired would be subject to the restrictions for any future transfer. On the other hand it could be argued that the existence of the restrictions makes it possible for the hypothetical purchaser to acquire further shares at less than their true value on any other party making a disposal, and as such the restrictions could tend to increase the value of the shares. The effect of a restriction on transfer has been considered in such cases as *Salvesen's Trustees* v. *R. Commissioners* (1930) SLT 387 and *I.R Comrs.* v. *Crossman* [1926] 1 All ER 762.

It is important to consider the factors involved in valuing shares. The importance of particular factors in any given set of circumstances will depend very much on the facts of the case and the percentage shareholding being considered. Clearly the purchaser of the whole of the share capital is much less interested in the ability of the directors, who are in any event likely to retire, than the purchaser of 10 per cent. of the shares who would himself be unable to influence the board to any marked degree and is therefore very dependent upon the managerial ability within the company.

Other factors which should be considered as having a greater or lesser bearing on the valuation would be the state of the industry in which the company trades and its significance within that industry. The general economic and political climate at the time of the valuation must also be considered. The profit record and trends are important points to consider but a minority share-holder is likely to be even more interested in the dividend record and cover which in turn determine the yield of his investment. It is important to consider the general commercial standing of the company such as its dependence on a small number of suppliers or customers. It is also necessary to consider whether the company is properly capitalised and whether the gearing between loan capital and equity capital is reasonable. The short and long term cash requirements of the business should be considered in the light of the resources available. The asset backing of the shares is important for both minority and majority shareholders, albeit for different reasons. The majority shareholder on the other hand looks to the asset backing to give security to his investment and therefore reduce the yield required compared with a more speculative investment without such backing.

The asset backing could take the form of the company's premises the value of which would be affected by whether they were freehold or leasehold and the physical age and condition of the property, development plans and potential, and in the case of leasehold premises the length of lease and likelihood of renewal. With regard to other fixed assets such as plant and machinery the age, condition and replacement policy are all of considerable relevance to a potential of shares and the underlying value of any investments or non-trading assets held by the company would have considerable significance.

Any abnormal income or expenditure should be reviewed and it may be necessary to make a deduction for contingent liabilities. If, for example, a majority shareholding was being valued on the basis of the company's realisable assets on a proposed liquidation it would be necessary to provide for the corporation tax liability on any chargeable gain on property or balancing charges which would result from the liquidation following the decision in *Winter (Executor of Sutherland)* v. *I.R. Comrs.* [1961] 3 All ER 855. If, however, the assets are being considered only on the basis of supporting the possible sale of the business as a going concern or as backing for an earnings or yield basis valuation, it would merely be necessary to include a discounted figure for contingent liabilities including corporation tax on unrealised gains the degree of discount reflecting the probability materialising within the foreseeable future.

Other special factors can be extremely important in the question of share valuation such as relationship between the remaining shareholders, because of a non-family purchaser of say, 10 per cent. of the shares would be unlikely to have much influence in the company where the remaining 90 per cent. of the shares were all held within a closely knit family. Other possibilities would include a possible sale of shares, to, say, a venture capital company or even potential flotation on the stock exchange.

It has been stressed that the value of shares depends on the rights attaching to those shares. In the simplest of cases there is but one class of shares with equal rights to dividends, votes and any surplus on winding up. It is, however, possible to have many classes of shares and it is common to have, for example, preference shares where the right to dividend is limited and the voting rights and entitlement to a surplus on winding up are severely limited. It is by no means uncommon to find companies where there are various classes of ordinary, preference and deferred shares with different rights as to voting, entitlement to dividend and surplus on winding up. In each case it is necessary to look at the rights attaching to the shares in order to arrive at a valuation. A fundamental entitlement would be to the voting powers at a company meeting and the number of such voting shares held would normally determine the relative value attached to them.

90 per cent. +
The holder of 90 per cent. or more of the shares could not only sell his shares but could give the

purchaser compulsory purchase powers under the Companies Act 1985, s. 428 to enable him to buy the remaining shares outstanding, whether the other shareholders wished to sell or not.

75 per cent. +
The holder of 75 per cent. or more of the shares can pass a special resolution which would enable him to place the company into liquidation, or to sell the business as a going concern. Because of such ability the lowest value which would apply to such a shareholding would be on the basis of the realisable value on a liquidation, including all contingent liabilities such as additional taxation and redundancy payments and subject to a further discount to enable the person actually doing the liquidation to make a reasonable profit. Such a discount might be in the order of, say 25 to 33 per cent. (*re Courthorpe* (1928) 7 ATC 538).

50 per cent. +
A holder of more than 50 per cent. of the voting share capital has day to day control over the company in that he can appoint himself or his nominees as the directors in charge of his business. He also has control over the remuneration policy and can probably pay a large proportion of the profits to himself as a director. He also has control over the dividend policy and may decide to pay small or large dividends or even decide to pay no dividend at all, but to roll up the profits within the company. The holder of more than 50 per cent. of the shares therefore will value his shares on the basis of the potential earnings of the company. It is normal to measure the potential earnings on the basis of, say, the last three years' available accounts, but any profit trend may be taken into consideration as can any special factors such as non-recurring items or excessive directors remuneration, which in reality may be a profit distribution.

50 per cent. exactly
Once the shareholding drops to 50 per cent. there is no longer any control but at exactly 50 per cent. no other party has control either. In the circumstances it depends very much on how the other shares are held. Clearly if the remaining 50 per cent. are held by a single individual the possibilities of deadlock are reasonably high, whereas if the remaining shares are held by 30 different individuals the possibility of securing an ally or at least an abstainer and thereby achieve effective control might be very considerable. If effective control is available the shares would still be valued on an earnings basis, even if the holding were marginally less than 50 per cent.

If effective control is not available the value of the shares is going to be based on what is known as the yield basis which would depend on the dividends paid on the shares. On such a basis the assets and earnings are only of importance in so far as they indicate the probability of the dividend being maintained or increased and therefore the likely future yield on the shares. It very often happens however that an unquoted company does not pay a dividend and in such a case the valuation has to proceed on the basis of a notional dividend. It is then necessary to decide the dividend which a reasonable board of directors would in the circumstances pay on the shares in view of the company's trading results; this might well be a dividend of, say, one-sixth of the available profit after corporation tax and the valuation would be based on such a notional dividend. It would, however, be further discounted for the fact that it is merely a notional dividend and the company has no dividend history.

25 per cent. +
A shareholding in excess of 25 per cent. is sufficient to block a special resolution and as such is marginally more valuable than a shareholding of 25 per cent. or less. Depending on the manner in which the shares are held it may be that a shareholding in excess of say, 33 per cent. may begin to give powers equivalent to control. On the other hand a shareholding as high as 49 per cent. may be totally without influence, if the remaining shares are held by a single party.

25 per cent. −
A shareholding of 25 per cent. or below is also valued on a yield basis, but a slightly higher yield would be required in view of the vulnerability of not being able to block a special resolution and therefore to prevent a liquidation or sale of the business. A holding of 10 per cent. or less is subject to compulsory purchase under the Companies Act 1985, ss. 429–430 and the required yield would therefore be marginally higher than that required for a larger shareholding.

Price earnings ratio
The valuation of the earnings basis is often computed on the basis of what is know as the price earnings ratio. The price earnings ratio is basically the number of years purchase of the after tax profits of the company, or expressed in a different way—

$$\text{share capital} \times \frac{\text{price per share}}{\text{maintainable profit after tax}}$$

Yield
The dividend yield is usually expressed as a percentage and the gross equivalent yield (*i.e.* on the

dividend declared plus tax credit) that is required for a minority interest in a private company would usually be within the region of 25 or 30 per cent. per annum for a trading company and 10 to 15 per cent. for a property investment company. These percentages are merely broad guide-lines. It will be appreciated that the earnings divided by the dividend gives the number of times the dividend is covered by the profits and valuations on the basis of yield and earnings are to that extent related to each other.

In ascertaining the yield required by a prospective purchaser it is often suggested that reference should be made to comparable quoted companies but there are major objections to such a procedure. In the first instance the prices at which quoted shares change hands are subject to very much wider fluctuations than those applicable to unquoted shares, because shares in a quoted company are in a volatile market of easily marketable assets, whereas a purchaser of shares in a private company tends to hold on to them for a considerable period. In the period from 1983 to 1987 the ordinary share index on the stock exchange varied from 383 to 1238. In 1987 alone it varied between 785 and 1238.

The other problem with any comparison with a quoted company is the improbability of finding a comparable quoted company. If the unquoted company being valued is generally comparable in size, structure, history and expectations to a quoted public company such comparisons may well be meaningful. It is not however realistic to value the shares in Joe Bloggs Engineering Ltd., with ten employees, by reference to the share price of a public company merely because both companies are engaged in engineering. The basis of valuation of shares by reference to an addition for non-marketability of, say, 35 per cent. to the value of a quoted company is unlikely to give a realistic value, at least in the case of ordinary shares (*McNamee* v. *Revenue Commissioners* [1954] I.R. 214).

If preference shares and debentures are being valued however, a comparison with quoted public companies is likely to be very much more meaningful, as it would probably be reasonable to assume that both companies would meet their dividend liabilities and a purchaser of preference shares would be influenced by the yield available on similar shares in respect of an investment on the stock market. It has been held in the case of *AG of Ceylon* v. *Mackie* [1952] 2 All ER 775 that if a transferor or deceased person holds preference and ordinary shares or various classes of shares, such that the combined value is greater than the value of each class in isolation, it is necessary to value the holdings together.

There is also a tendency with property and investment companies to value the shares by applying some suitable method of discount to the underlying value of the assets. If, however, a minority interest is being considered it is most unlikely that this basis will produce a reasonable valuation and even for a holding of between say, 50 and 75 per cent. the basis is probably unrealistic when considering the rights of the shareholders. It might, however be argued, if the break-up value is considerably in excess of the earnings basis valuation, that a shareholder with a controlling interest could probably be able to obtain sufficient support to place the company into liquidation, which might make a discounted assets basis appropriate in the circumstances. However, each case must be considered on its merits to establish whether such an argument is realistic.

In practice, the valuation of shares in unquoted companies has to be agreed by the Shares Valuation Division of the Inland Revenue. If a valuation has to be agreed it is highly desirable to ascertain all the relevant facts relating to the shares to be valued and on that basis arriving at what is considered to be a fair and reasonable valuation such as could be recommended to both the prospective purchaser and hypothetical vendor. If the valuation could be recommended to both parties with conviction it is likely that this value would ultimately be accepted by the Shares Valuation Division. It is desirable to formulate a detailed and supportable valuation which may be submitted to the Shares Valuation Division in the first instance, rather than arrive at a figure which is incapable of rational support and then haggle with the Shares Valuation Division to try and reach an acceptable valuation. Appeals on the question of share valuation for unquoted companies may be made to the Special Commissioners, whose decision on a matter of fact is final, *McBrearty* v. *I.R. Comrs.* [1975] STC 614.

169. Farm cottages. (H3.65)
In valuing agricultural property, if this includes cottages which are occupied by persons employed solely for agricultural purposes in connection with the agricultural property, any increased value attributable to the cottages on the basis they are suitable for residential purposes for other persons is ignored. The identity of the legal occupier may be relevant unless the Revenue would concede that physical occupation is required by the context.

170. Leases for life, etc. (H2.51)
The value of a lessor's interest where the lease of property is treated as a settlement is to be calculated by applying a fraction to the value of the property at the date of valuation. The denominator is effectively the full premium foregone or otherwise calculated notional capital value at the time the lease was granted and the numerator is the value of the consideration actually obtained at that time.

CHAPTER II ESTATE ON DEATH

171. Changes occuring on death. (D1.03)
Value on death includes changes in the value of the estate which have occurred by reason of the death, for example, a life policy maturing, apart from the termination on the death of any interest or the passing of any interest by survivorship, which are therefore valued at the full value. IHTA 1984, s. 176 deals with related property sales within three years of death, IHTA 1984, ss. 178–189 deal with the sale of qualifying investments (shares etc.) within twelve months of death and IHTA 1984, ss. 190–198 deal with sales of land sold within three years of death.

172. Funeral expenses. (D1.11)
Reasonable funeral expenses are allowable deductions. These now include the cost of a tombstone: SP7/87.

173. Expenses incurred abroad. (D1.12)
An allowance of a maximum of 5 per cent. of the value of the property may be made for the expenses of administering or realising such property situated outside the U.K.

174. Income tax and unpaid inheritance tax. (D1.14)
Any previous undischarged tax liability at death is only an allowable deduction on the estate if paid out of the estate and not by another party, *e.g.* the donee.
   Similar rules apply to tax due in respect of deep discount securities and offshore funds.

175. Liability to make future payments, etc. (C2.31)
A liability for future payments or transfer of assets reduces the value of the property passing on death but is to be computed by reducing the payments or assets by what would be the chargeable portion.

176. Related property, etc.—sales. (D3.21)
A claim may be made where related property is sold by a qualifying sale (see sub-s. (3) for conditions) within three years of death by the legatee or personal representative at arm's length for a then freely negotiated price to an unconnected purchaser. A claim may also be made if the property was valued in connection with other property (not by virtue of IHTA 1984, s. 161) and is similarly so sold and the other property has not been vested in the vendors since the death. For example, if the deceased in his own name left a 75 per cent. holding in an unquoted company and leaves it in three equal parts each legatee would have had his 25 per cent. valued in connection with the other 50 per cent. as ⅓rd of a 75 per cent. interest. Where this paragraph applies the probate value of the qualifying sale is revised to what it would have been if it had not been valued as related property or in conjunction with other property. The paragraph only applies if the proceeds are less than the original probate value, taking into account all relevant changes of circumstances. The relief applies in respect of deaths after 6 April 1976, but does not apply where the property is shares or securities in a close company where between the death and sale their value has been reduced by more than 5 per cent. as a result of an alteration in the company's share or loan capital or rights attaching to them. Close company and alteration for that purpose are defined by reference to IHTA 1984, s. 102.
   It should be noted that it is not the sale proceeds that are substituted for the related property value. The value at the date of death of the property *i.e.* the subject of each qualifying sale is recalculated to the value at death considered in isolation and that is the value to be substituted for probate purposes for that item of property.

177. Scottish agricultural leases. (G3.64)
Under Scottish law when a lease comes to an end there is a statutory right whereby it will continue on the same terms except in relation to its duration. If the lease is for a period of less than one year, there is a renewal for a similar period, and if the lease is for one year or more, there is a renewal for a further year and from year to year thereafter. This is termed a continuance of the lease by tacit relocation. On the death of a tenant holding either by tacit relocation, or under the unexpired portion of a lease there are rights of succession in the tenancy in favour of a limited class of persons. This is unlike the situation in England and Wales and the intention of this section is to bring the inheritance tax position in Scotland, as far as possible, into line with the former. Accordingly in respect of a death after 14 November 1976 of a tenant having at the time of his death an interest in the unexpired portion of a fixed-term lease of Scottish agricultural property, any value attributable to the prospect of renewal of the lease by tacit relocation is to be excluded from the estate provided (*a*) he had been a tenant of the property for a continuous period of at least two years immediately preceding his death, or (*b*) he had become the tenant of the property by succession.
   Where a deceased person's estate includes value attributable to his interest as a tenant in agricultural property in Scotland and the interest is held by virtue of tacit relocation (*i.e.*, under a lease the term of which has expired) the value of the interest will be excluded for inheritance tax purposes provided:

(*a*) he had been the tenant of the property for a continuous period of two years prior to his death, or he had become the tenant by succession; and

(*b*) the interest is acquired on his death by a new tenant.

It is made clear that the value of tenant's improvements in respect of which the tenant may have a right of compensation is to be included in the estate.

CHAPTER III SALE OF SHARES ETC. FROM DECEASED'S ESTATE

178. Preliminary. (D3.01–09)

The purpose of IHTA 1984, ss. 179–188 inclusive is to enable quoted investments (which after 16 March 1987 includes shares dealt in on the U.S.M.) sold within a year of death to be revalued for probate purposes at the lower sale proceeds instead of the value at the date of death. The relief is very similar to that which applied for estate duty under FA 1973, s. 45.

This section defines various phrases and provides that a claim, if made, relates to all the securities disposed of within the period. The term "qualifying investments" is of particular importance and note that only an "appropriate person" can claim, being one who is liable for and pays the tax attributable to those qualifying investments at death which are the subject of his claim.

Personal representatives and trustees shall be treated as a separate and continuing body of persons distinct from the persons actually involved.

If the market value is substituted for the sale proceeds on a sale at under value no allowance is made for notional expenses. Incidental expenses for the purchase, sale or ascertaining the best consideration which could have been obtained on a sale are not to be taken into account.

179. The relief. (D3.02)

The relief is calculated as being the excess of the probate value of the investment sold within 12 months of the death over for those particular investments the greater of (*a*) the actual sale proceeds, or (*b*) the best consideration which could reasonably have been obtained at sale date.

For inheritance tax purposes the investments are treated as being reduced by this loss on sale compared with the original probate value, and are therefore effectively revalued for probate purposes as the sale proceeds.

A claim made under these provisions has to specify the capacity in which a claimant is acting for example, as personal representative, trustee or legatee.

180. Effect of purchases. (D3.03)

To prevent people selling investments and reacquiring them very shortly afterwards it is provided that if any qualifying investments are reacquired in the same capacity for example as personal representatives, within a period ending two months after the last sale for which a claim is made which could be as much as fourteen months after the death, the relief has to be reduced by the proportion which the purchased price bears to the sale price. For example, if investments were valued on death at £20,000 but sold within twelve months for £15,000, the relief under s. 179 would be £5,000. If, however, during that period and within two months after the last sale further qualifying investments had been acquired at a cost of £8,000 the relief would be reduced by $(8,000/15,000) \times 5,000 = £2,667$. The relief will therefore be lost entirely if the cost of the investments purchased equals or exceeds the sale proceeds. A similar adjustment for purchases is made for claims on property sales under IHTA 1984, s. 192.

If, however, the claim is being made by a person not in a capacity as a personal representative or trustee, but for example, by a legatee of a "subject to tax" bequest, no account is taken of investments made by him, unless they consist of a reacquisition of the same investments as those disposed of and for which the claim is being made.

181. Capital receipts. (D3.05)

If any capital sum which does not constitute income for the purposes of income tax is received by the appropriate person in respect of investments sold such amount must be deemed to be added to the sale proceeds for s. 179 calculations for a sale within the 12 months. This appears to be without future time limit. A disposal of rights in a provisional allotment of shares or debentures is regarded as equivalent to such a capital sum received. Thus a sale ex capital rights would be within these provisions.

182. Payment of calls. (D3.05)

If a call is made in respect of qualifying investments sold within the 12 months period the amount paid on the call for purposes of s. 179 calculations has to be added to the unaltered probate value. This is the converse of the s. 181 situation above.

The amount paid on the call is deducted in arriving at the final "sale values" (probate value and acquisition cost at death for capital gains tax—see IHTA 1984, s. 187.

183. Changes in holdings. (D3.07)

If an investment is exchanged for another as a result of a CGT free reorganisation within CGTA 1979, ss. 77–88 the investments acquired as a result of the exchange are deemed to have been held at death. Any amount payable on the exchange is added to the probate value and any amount paid on the additional contributions to the new holding on the exchange is deducted from the eventual probate value under IHTA 1984, s. 187 for capital gains tax which restores the original probate value.

If part of the investments are sold the formula to apply is set out in IHTA 1984, s. 183.

184. Exchanges. (D3.03)
If investments are exchanged for other assets and their market value at that date is greater than the probate value, they are deemed to have been sold at the market value. If they are exchanged at a market value less than the probate value on the wording of the legislation, it seems doubtful that they could be treated as having been sold in order to obtain relief under IHTA 1984, s. 179 (2).

If the exchange is within IHTA 1984, s. 183 this section does not apply.

185. Acquisition of like investments. (D3.08)
If a holding of investments is sold only part of which would be eligible for relief under IHTA 1984, s. 179 (2) because further qualifying investments of that description have been acquired since the death in the same capacity, the disposal is deemed to take place *pro rata* between the investments acquired post death and those held (or deemed to be held) at death.

If in the example given for IHTA 1984, s. 186, subsequent to the death the legatee had acquired another 20,000 shares of the same class, the following provisions would apply:

In this section it appears $^2/_5$ of the 12,000 shares sold would be attributed to *post death* acquisitions viz. 4,800 shares. Then the balance of 7,200 shares sold would be apportioned under IHTA 1984, s. 186 in the ratio of $^2/_3$ eligible for relief = 4,800 shares and $^1/_3$ not eligible = 2,400 shares. The IHTA 1984, s. 186 relief would be £1,200 and the revised probate value £18,800.

186. Value of part of a fund. (D3.07)
This section applies when part only of a holding of qualifying investments is comprised in a person's estate, for example, if prior to the death a legatee already held 10,000 shares of the same description as the 20,000 left to him at death and valued at £20,000. In such circumstances it is assumed that the entire 30,000 were held at date of death (see also how this affects IHTA 1984, s. 185). However, because of this assumption if a claim is made under IHTA 1984, s. 179 for relief, what would otherwise be the loss on sale is scaled down by reference to a fraction (the taxable fraction).

The numerator of the fraction is the value of those qualifying investments actually comprised in the estate at death. The denominator is the value of the entire holding at that date. Thus if the legatee already held 10,000 of the same shares and 20,000 were comprised in the estate the value of which at death was £20,000:

Then 12,000 shares are sold for £9,000 (probate value £12,000)
Therefore $(20/30) \times £9,000 = £6,000$ sale proceeds compared with probate value
$(20/30) \times £12,000 = £8,000$ giving loss on sale £2,000
Therefore the revised probate value would be £20,000 less £2,000 = £18,000.

187. Attribution of values to specific investments. (D3.09)
When the total relief under IHTA 1984, s. 179 has been arrived at it is apportioned among the various specific investments held at death in order to arrive at the revised probate value which is also the CGT acquisition base of personal representatives (or legatees). In most cases the value will be the sale value of the specific investment, but if the relief is reduced because of additional purchases the relevant proportion *i.e.* the proportion by which the loss is reduced under IHTA 1984, s. 180 is added to the sale value, if that is below the original probate value, or deducted from the sale value if that is in excess of the original probate value. Relevant proportion is defined in IHTA 1984, s. 178. Calls and additional contributions on an exchange under IHTA 1984, s. 182 and s. 183 are deducted from the appropriate investments.

Sale price is defined by IHTA 1984, s. 179.

188. Limitation of loss on sale. (D3.02)
If there is, as a result of calls or cash contributions under IHTA 1984, ss. 182 or 183, any loss on sale, it is restricted to the revised probate value so producing a nil value at death.

189. Date of sale or purchase. (D3.02).
For a purchase or sale the relevant dates are the contract date or (if the purchase or sale is from anyone exercising an option) the date granted, not when it was exercised. The position is not clear if

a person allows an option to lapse in consideration of being granted a new option, the latter grant being outside the period.

Note that there is no time limit during which the option must have been granted unlike for land under IHTA 1984, s. 198 (2).

CHAPTER IV SALE OF LAND FROM DECEASED'S ESTATE

190. Preliminary. (D3.13)
The purpose of IHTA 1984, ss. 190–198 is to enable the probate value of land to be revised to the sale proceeds if it is sold by the personal representative or trustees of a will settlement, or by a legatee who can qualify as an "appropriate person" as defined.

No incidental expenses can be taken into account for a purchase or sale (or deemed sale).

Various terms are defined.

191. The relief. (D3.12)
A claim may be made where the sale value of the land differs from the probate value by at least 5 per cent. of the probate value or £1,000 whichever is the less. The sale has to be an arm's length sale, within three years of death, to a non-connected person as defined by this section.

Note that this is a more restricted definition of connected person compared with that under IHTA 1984, s. 270. If, however, the sale is to such a person the relief is not available even if the sale is at the full market value.

The revised value applies also for capital gains tax: CGTA 1979, s. 153. If the sale value is *higher,* but no inheritance tax is payable, a claim would eliminate capital gains tax on the gain. The Revenue refuse such claims on the grounds that there is no appropriate person liable for inheritance tax.

192. Effect of purchases. (D3.17)
If land is acquired within four months of the last sale for which a claim is made, which could be up to 40 months after death, there will be no claim if the aggregate purchase prices of the land exceeds the sale proceeds of land for which a claim is made. If, however, the sale proceeds exceed the purchase prices there has to be added to the sale price where a claim has been made, an appropriate fraction. This is to be calculated as the difference between the probate value and the sale proceeds *i.e.*

$$\frac{\text{Aggregate purchase prices}}{\text{Aggregate sale prices}} \times \text{loss on sale (as adjusted IHTA 1984, ss. 193–196)}$$

This adjustment for purchases may be compared with that relating to the purchase of investments under IHTA 1984, s. 180.

It seems that if a spouse makes the new acquisitions this is in order even if after the period ends she transfers the land to her spouse. This may also apply for qualifying investments reacquired.

193. Changes between death and sale. (D3.13)
The sale value is the actual net sale proceeds but if due to changed circumstances or conditions (see IHTA 1984, s. 193 (2)) between to the date of death and the date of sale, it is necessary to increase the sale price to reflect such changes if appropriate. The addition thereto is the excess of what the probate value of the land would have been if the changed circumstances had prevailed at the date of death over the original value at death. Provision is made for a reduction if the original probate value exceeds the revised value. Certain compensation payments received between date of death and sale have to be addedto the sale price.

194. Leases. (D3.14)
Where the interest in land is a lease with less than 50 years to run an appropriate fraction addition is made to the sale proceeds. The appropriate fraction is $[P (1) - P (2)]P (1)$ where $P (1)$ is the appropriate percentage (from the curved line depreciation tables for premiums on leases contained in CGTA 1979, Sch. 3) at the date of death, and $P (2)$ is the percentage at the date of sale. By this means account is taken of the expected depreciation of a short lease between the date of death and the date of sale.

195. Valuation by reference to other interests. (D3.15)
The later sale price of the interest in the land would usually be unaffected by any other interests in that land or other land. However, on the death, for inheritance tax such other interests may have been taken into account and increased what would otherwise have been the probate value of the interest in the land. In such circumstances the excess of the probate value over what the lower value would have been if the other interests had not been taken into account, has to be added to the sale proceeds for determining the relief claim.

196. Sales to beneficiaries etc. and exchanges. (D3.16)
Unlike for investments under IHTA 1984, ss. 178–188, a claim may but need not be made for each interest in land disposed of. If there has been a disposal or exchange of any land even to a connected

person under IHTA 1984, s. 191 at *more* than the probate value the claim is reduced by this excess and if there is more than one claim the excess is apportioned rateably. Therefore for interests in land on which a loss would arise, the disposal should take place within the three years and any other interests in land which were held at the death, should be disposed of *after* that time so as to eliminate the off-set position.

197. Compulsory acquisition more than three years after death. (D3.18)
If an interest in land is acquired under a compulsory purchase order in respect of which notice to treat has been served before death or within three years afterwards, a claim may be made for relief under IHTA 1984, s. 191 as if there had been a sale within the three year period.

198. Date of sale or purchase. (D3.19)
The appropriate disposal or acquisition dates for this relief is the contract date, not the date of completion. If, however, the purchase or sale takes place as a result of an option granted not more than six months earlier the date the option was granted is substituted for the contract date or the date the option was exercised.
   Note the restrictive period of the option which contrasts with IHTA 1984, s. 189 where there is no time limit on the option for securities. Subject to s. 198 (4) the date of sale to an authority possessing compulsory purchase powers follows the CGT rules. But see IHTA 1984, s. 197 above.

PART VII LIABILITY

GENERAL RULES

199. Dispositions by transferor. (K1.11, 17)
The liability to pay tax on a chargeable lifetime disposition falls on the transferor with secondary liabilities falling on the donee or persons in whom the property concerned becomes vested, or where the property becomes comprised in a trust, the beneficiaries benefiting under that settlement from the property. However, the order of priority is modified for inheritance tax in respect of the tax, or additional tax due on chargeable transfers made after 17 March 1986 and within seven years of the transferor's death. The liability will comprise tax on potentially exempt transfers becoming chargeable and any additional tax on previous chargeable transfers. In this case the transferor's personal representative is included among the persons liable for the additional tax although because of the application of IHTA 1984, s. 204 (7) and (8) the personal representative's liability is secondary to the other persons mentioned above so that in most cases the donee remains primarily liable but subject to the overall limitations provided in IHTA 1984, s. 204.
   Under the capital transfer tax regime as for inheritance tax a chargeable lifetime transfer will be calculated in a similar manner. The value transferred will be found after deducting available business or agricultural property reliefs and any unused annual exemption (see IHTA 1984, s. 19). The resulting amount will be the value transferred on the basis that the transferee bears the tax. If he does not and, for example, an asset is transferred in specie to the donee, the amount will be grossed-up to arrive at the value transferred on which tax is calculated. It would not seem that it will be necessary to gross-up potentially exempt transfers (see IHTA 1984, s. 3A) because no tax is chargeable at the time, and should the transfer become chargeable on the donor's death within seven years, the primary liability for tax will fall upon the donee.
   There are various anti-avoidance provisions enabling the Revenue to recover inheritance tax from third parties receiving property or intermeddling in an estate, see *I.R. Comrs.* v. *Stype Investments (Jersey) Ltd. Re Clore dec'd* [1982] STC 625 and *I.R. Comrs.* v. *Stannard* [1984] STC 245, and to prevent a transferor disposing of assets to his spouse without retaining sufficient assets to meet the tax liabilities in respect of other transfers. See IHTA 1984, s. 203 for some relaxation of the spouse's liability if the transfer to the spouse preceded the chargeable transfer.

200. Transfer on death. (K1.12, 25)
The deceased's personal representatives are primarily liable for the inheritance tax or capital transfer tax (before 25 July 1986) payable on death so far as the assets were not comprised in a settlement or if so comprised was land in the U.K. vesting in those representatives. From 18 March 1986 the personal representatives retain a secondary liability to pay tax on potentially exempt transfers and the additional tax on previous chargeable transfers as a result of the donees' death within seven years (see IHTA 1984, ss. 7, 199). They are similarly liable for the tax arising on gifts with reservation (see FA 1986, s. 102) but in this case only if the tax remains unpaid by the donee for more than 12 months and subject to the limitation as to the assets in the personal representatives' hands.
   In the case of settled property the primary liability is on the trustees, although tax may be recovered from the beneficiary by agreement or in the circumstances specified. The Revenue do not regard a settlor as retaining an interest in a settlement (for income tax purposes) where the trustees have power to, or do, pay the inheritance tax on a gift into settlement: SP1/82.
   See also notes to IHTA 1984, s. 199 above.

201. Settled property. (K1.13)

In the case of settled property the primary liability is on the trustees, although inheritance tax may be recovered from the beneficiary by agreement or in the circumstances specified. The Revenue do not regard a settlor as retaining an interest in a settlement (for income tax purposes) where the trustees have power to, or do, pay the inheritance tax on a gift into settlement: SP1/82.

A live settlor with non-resident trustees may be liable for the inheritance tax but see the limitation of the liability under sub-s. (2) for chargeable transfers which are not potentially exempt transfers—note also that the settlor of a potentially exempt transfer retains a liability for the tax on his death within seven years. There is transitional relief for settlements made before 17 March 1987 provided that the trustees were U.K. resident from inception but have not been U.K. resident since 16 March 1987. Under IHTA 1984, s. 7 from 18 March 1986 the full table rates of tax apply not only to transfers on death but also to transfers within a seven years gift *inter vivos* period. The additional tax recoverable from the transferee is computed in accordance with IHTA 1984, s. 7 but subject to possible relief under IHTA 1984, s. 131.

The Revenue's claim against the settlor for tax where the trustees are non-resident cannot apply if the settlement was made before 11 December 1974, and the trustees were then U.K. residents when the settlement was made but have not been resident in the U.K. at any time during the period from 10 December 1974 to the date of any chargeable transfer. (See also IHTA 1984, s. 2 (3)). References to chargeable transfers include references to occasions of charge on discretionary trusts under IHTA 1984, Pt. III, Ch. III.

202. Close companies. (K1.14)

The inheritance tax resulting from the transfer is payable by the company in the first instance then by persons to whom the apportionment or transfer is made, limited for each person to the tax on the value apportioned to him or the increase in his estate as a result of the transfer. A person to whom not more than 5 per cent. of the value transferred is apportioned is not liable for any of the tax.

See also IHTA 1984, ss. 94 and 99.

203. Liability of spouse. (K1.15)

Inheritance tax on a chargeable transfer may be recovered from a wife in respect of a transfer to her by her husband (or vice versa) up to the market value of the transfer when it was made. If the chargeable transfer was made after the spouse transfer and that spouse transfer was not of tangible moveable property, the limit is now amended to that value or if lower and the spouse still holds the property, the market value of the assets transferred to the wife at the time of the chargeable transfer giving rise to the Revenue's claim against the wife. If in the meantime the wife has sold the assets transferred to her (as defined) by a qualifying sale, the Revenue's claim is limited to the value at the date of the qualifying sale.

The provisions of IHTA 1984, ss. 133–140 which relate to the reduction in value of gifts *inter vivos* in the seven years from 18 March 1986 prior to death are also applied for calculating the reduction in value of the spouse transfer under this section. There are various anti-avoidance provisions to prevent a transferor disposing of assets to his spouse without retaining sufficient assets to meet the tax liability in respect of other transfers. There is some relaxation of the spouse's liability if the transfer to the spouse preceded the chargeable transfer.

204. Limitation of liability. (K1.16)

The liability for inheritance tax of persons acting in a representative capacity for example, as trustee or personal representative, is limited to the value of the assets which they have or should have control over. The liability of a beneficiary under IHTA 1984, s. 200 (1), (3) or s. 201 (1) to whom income is applied is limited to the net income after tax. Those primarily liable to inheritance tax are the transferor or the trustees of a settlement. From 18 March 1986 the donee has the primary liability to pay the tax on potentially exempt transfers and the additional tax on previous chargeable transfers where the donor has died within seven years of making such gifts. The donor's personal representatives retain a secondary liability as "last resort"—see IHTA 1984, s. 199. If anybody else has to pay the tax for example, a donee, he is liable to the tax as if the transfer had been tax inclusive instead of tax exclusive, *i.e.* without grossing up.

205. More than one person liable. (K1.11, 17)

Where two or more persons are liable for the same tax each shall be liable for the whole of it.

SPECIAL CASES

207. Conditional exemption, etc. (G5.11; K1.22)

A conditionally exempt transfer becomes liable to inheritance tax on the happening of a chargeable event at the rates in force at that time. This can happen when an undertaking has not been observed in a material respect or on death, sale, gift or other disposal, unless the disposal is a sale to an approved institution or the asset is transferred to the Board in satisfaction of tax, see IHTA 1984, ss. 32 and 32A. However, a death or gift is not a chargeable event if the transfer is itself a conditionally exempt transfer with the legatee or donee giving the appropriate undertakings to the Treasury. See H.C. Written Ans., 25 June 1980, Vol. 987, col. 202.

The persons liable for the tax are the trustees and any person for whose benefit the property (including attributable income) has been applied on or after the event.

See IHTA 1984, Pt. III, Ch. III (ss. 58 to 85).

If the undertaking made to the Treasury under IHTA 1984, Sch. 5, para. 5 is broken, or if the asset is sold or otherwise disposed of inheritance tax will be chargeable. On a breach of the undertaking the person liable for the tax is the person who, on a sale, would be entitled to the proceeds or income therefrom. On an actual disposal the person by or for whose benefit it took place is liable. Inheritance tax will be charged in respect of the last death on which the transfer took place provided this was before 7 April 1976, unless the disposal is a sale to an approved museum etc. or a gift where the donee gives the undertaking.

208. Woodlands. (G4.04; K1.23)
The person liable under IHTA 1984, s. 126 is the person entitled to the proceeds if a sale took place.

209. Succession in Scotland. (K1.24)
The persons liable for tax are those who claim legitim under IHTA 1984, s. 147.

210. Pension rights, etc. (K1.25)
The trustees of the scheme are not liable but if the transfer is made on death of a person entitled to an interest the persons liable include his personal representatives.

BURDEN OF TAX, ETC.

211. Burden of tax on death. (L6.03)
Where property situated in the U.K. is transferred on death after 26 July 1983 the inheritance tax paid by the personal representatives attributable to the U.K. property which vests in them (and was not immediately prior to the death comprised in a settlement) is to be treated as a general testamentary and administration expense of the estate and payable out of residue—this is however subject to any contrary provision in the will. Provision is made for the personal representatives to recover any taxpaid by them which is not a testamentary expense and is attributable to other property. This gives statutory effect to the Scottish case of *Re Dougal and Another* [1981] STC 514, subject to any direction to the contrary in the will. If the personal representatives have or could have paid inheritance tax by instalments which is borne by a devisee he in turn may pay by instalments in the same manner and with the same interest arrangements. There are specific powers to enable transferees, beneficiaries etc. who are compelled to pay the tax to enable them to sell or mortgage their interests in order to do so.

212. Powers to raise tax. (K2.05; L4.06)
Provision is made for the personal representatives to recover any inheritance tax paid by them which is not a testamentary expense and is attributable to other property. This gives statutory effect to the Scottish case of *Re Dougal and Another* [1981] STC 514, subject to any direction to the contrary in the will. There are specific powers to enable transferees, beneficiaries etc. who are compelled to pay the tax to enable them to sell or mortgage their interests in order to do so.

213. Refund by instalments. (K2.07; L4.07)
Where tax paid or payable by instalments is recoverable from another person that other person shall be permitted to refund by instalments including interest unless the parties otherwise agree.

214. Certificates of tax paid. (K2.08; L4.08)
Where a person has paid tax for which he is not liable the Board may issue a certificate of payment.

PART VIII ADMINISTRATION AND COLLECTION

MANAGEMENT

215. General. (L4.09)
Inheritance tax is under the care and management of the Board of Inland Revenue, Capital Taxes Office (CTO). Transfers on death and settlement matters are dealt with from Minford House,

Rockley Road, West Kensington, London W14 0DS, 01–603 4622. *Inter vivos* transfers are dealt with by the CTO at Lynwood Road, Thames Ditton, Surrey KT7 0EB, 01–398 4242 and in Edinburgh and Belfast for Scotland and Northern Ireland respectively.

ACCOUNTS AND INFORMATION

216. Delivery of accounts. (L2.01, 11, 12, 31)
Returns are to be made in a number of specified situations and in particular by the personal representatives of a deceased person and every person who as transferor or trustee of a settlement is or could be liable for tax in respect of any transfer after 26 March 1974. Foreign trustees are within the scope of the legislation, *Re Clore (deceased) (No. 3), I.R. Comrs.* v. *Stype Trustees (Jersey) Ltd. and others* [1985] STC 394, however in that case a former trustee was held liable to make a return only of information in his possession—he could not be required to solicit further information from others. The personal representatives must make a return of all property which formed part of the deceased's estate immediately before his death. Provisional returns may be made. Personal representatives must make a return within 12 months of the end of the month in which the death occurs, or if later within three months of the first acting. If there are no personal representatives the beneficiaries or trustees must submit an account. Other persons must make a return within twelve months or if later three months after becoming liable for tax.

From 18 March 1986 donees of potentially exempt transfers which become chargeable (see IHTA 1984, s. 3A) and of gifts with reservation (see FA 1986, s. 102) must also deliver an account within 12 months of the end of the month in which the transferor's death occurs. Similarly, the duty to make a return in respect of a potentially exempt transfer arising from the termination of an interest in possession in settled property after 16 March 1987 which becomes chargeable is extended to persons entitled to interests in possession in the property or for whose benefit the property is applied after the transfer, and the settlor. A return must also be made within three months of the end of the month in which an exempt or relieved transfer ceases to be exempt or held-over. See IHTA 1984, s. 226 for payment of inheritance tax.

See IHTA 1984, s. 256 as to power to make regulations.

To simplify the administration of small estates and to dispense with the need to deliver an account regulations were introduced in 1981 (S.I. 1981 Nos. 880, 881). From 1 July 1990, for deaths after 31 March 1990, the "excepted estates" level is £115,000 (see Inland Revenue Press Release 5 June 1990 and S.I. 1990 Nos. 1110, 1111 and 1112). It was £100,000 for deaths after 31 March 1989 (see Inland Revenue Press Release 30 June 1989).

For some relaxation in the provisions for submitting accounts of gifts (other than potentially exempt transfers from 18 March 1986), see S.I. 1981 No. 1440 and Inland Revenue Press Release 24 July 1984.

217. Defective accounts. (L2.14)
Corrective accounts must be rendered to the Revenue within six months of obtaining any additional information.

218. Non-resident trustees. (L2.21)
Any professional other than a barrister who has been concerned with the making after 26 March 1974 of a settlement where the settlor was domiciled in the U.K. and the trustees of the settlement are not resident in the U.K., must within three months make a return to the Board stating the names and addresses of the settlor and the trustees of the settlement, unless the settlement is made by will or a return has been lodged by some other person. It would seem that this may extend to cases where resident trustees are appointed but it is known that it is intended subsequently to appoint non-resident trustees. The trustees of a settlement will not be regarded as resident in the U.K. unless the majority of them (or of each class, if more than one) are U.K. residents and the general administration of the trust is ordinarily carried on in the U.K.

219. Power to require information. (L2.31)
The Board may serve a notice in writing requiring any person to furnish them with such information as they may require in respect of inheritance tax. A barrister or solicitor can claim privilege, except to the extent that he must disclose the name and address of his client or, in the case of a non-resident client, his U.K. associates. For notices served after 25 July 1990 the prior consent of a Special Commissioner is required.

220. Inspection of property. (L2.32, 33)
The Revenue have power to authorise any person to inspect a property for valuation purposes.

DETERMINATIONS AND APPEALS

221. Notices of determination. (L3.01–04, 11)
The Board of Inland Revenue may in respect of any transfer or suspected transfer give a notice of determination specifying:

(*a*) the date of the transfers

(*b*) the value transferred and the value of any property to which the value transferred is wholly or partly attributable

(*c*) the transferor,

(*d*) the tax chargeable (if any) and the persons who are liable for the whole or part of it,

(*e*) the amount of any payment made in excess of the tax for which a person is liable and the date from which and the rate at which tax or any repayment of inheritance tax overpaid carries interest, and

(*f*) any other matters that appear relevant.

A determination by the Board will be final against the person on whom the notice is served unless it is appealed against. Such a determination for inheritance tax is the equivalent of an assessment for other taxation purposes.

222. Appeals against determinations. (L3.11–15, 35)

An appeal may be made within 30 days to the Special Commissioners, except where the only point in dispute is a matter of law. Leave may then be given for the appeal to go straight to the High Court, except in the case of a valuation of land which is to be dealt with by the Lands Tribunal.

223. Appeals out of time. (L3.12)

The Board or the Special Commissioners have power to extend the time for lodging an appeal.

224. Procedure before Special Commissioners. (L3.31)

The appellant may be represented by a barrister, solicitor or accountant, or, with leave, by any other person, and the Special Commissioners may give notice to any party to the proceedings other than the Board requiring the production of documents, books and accounts etc. and giving access to the Revenue. Special Commissioners have power to summon any person to appear as a witness, and may examine him on oath.

225. Statement of case for opinion of High Court. (L3.51)

A case stated may be requested within 30 days of the Special Commissioners' determination by means of a written request accompanied by a fee of £25.

PAYMENT

226. Payment: general rules. (L4.01–05)

Inheritance tax is due on a chargeable transfer within six months after the end of the month in which the chargeable transfer is made, except that if the transfer is made after 5 April and before 1 October in any year the tax is due on 30 April in the following year. It follows from this that tax may be due for payment before the return has to be submitted, see IHTA 1984, s. 216 and that a transfer on 6 April gives the longest credit before tax is payable.

See Extra-statutory concession F6 (1985) for relief on foreign assets.

Personal representatives must pay all the inheritance tax for which they are liable on delivery of their account. This perpetuates the problem of having to pay the duty on the Revenue affidavit or its equivalent before being able to obtain probate. From 18 March 1986 the additional tax due by the donee of a gift *inter vivos* as a result of death within seven years is due six months after the month in which the death occurs—this includes tax due on potentially exempt transfers on becoming chargeable and by trustees of discretionary trusts where in the early years of a settlement a potentially exempt transfer by the settlor on becoming chargeable will affect the subsequent tax rate on exit charges. Tax on a non-chargeable or relieved transfer becoming chargeable or ceasing to be held over shall be due six months after theend of the month in which the transfer ceases to be non chargeable. There is an overriding limit preventing a personal representative being liable to pay tax in excess of the assets in his hands.

227. Payment by instalments—land, shares and businesses. (L5.01, 11–14)

It is possible to pay the tax by instalments in respect of transfers in certain cases of:

(*a*) land, or

(*b*) shares or securities which gave the deceased control of the company. The anomalous definition of control was amended to exclude control by a majority of the votes on any particular question affecting the company as a whole in respect of transfers made after 19 April 1978. Class rights giving voting powers in certain cases for example, on liquidation or on matters affecting shares of that class, are ignored. Corresponding changes were made for the purposes of agricultural property relief, business property relief and excluded property held by people domiciled in the Channel Islands or the Isle of Man which use the same definition of control.

(*c*) shares or securities of an unquoted company if the Board are satisfied that otherwise undue hardship would result, or

(*d*) for shares or securities of an unquoted company where not less than 20 per cent. of the tax chargeable on the chargeable transfer is attributable to the shares or securities, or is otherwise payable by instalments, or (*e*) so much of the value transferred relating to unquoted shares as exceeds £20,000 (£5,000 pre 15 March 1983) where the shares represent not less than 10 per cent. of the nominal value of the issued share capital, or 10 per cent. of the nominal value of the ordinary shares if it is ordinary shares as defined which are being transferred.

An election has to be made for payment by ten equal yearly instalments (prior to 15 March 1983 such payments may have been either eight equal yearly or sixteen equal half-yearly instalments), the first instalment being due six months after the end of the month in which the death occurred. Payments by instalments are available only on death or on life-time transfers where the tax is to be borne by the donee, or, otherwise than on death in respect of certain events in relation to a settlement, such as where the property continues to be comprised in the settlement on the termination of an interest in possession. From 18 March 1986 many lifetime gifts qualify as potentially exempt transfers (see IHTA 1984, s. 3A) and consequently no tax is payable at the time the gift is made. However on becoming chargeable, where the donor dies within seven years of that time the instalment basis of payment of the tax is only available to the extent that the donee retains the qualifying property at the date of the transferor's death. For transfers occurring after 16 March 1987 similar relief is extended to the additional tax payable on an original chargeable transfer on the donor's death within seven years. In both cases relief is also available where the business or agricultural property replacement provisions contained in IHTA 1984 ss. 113B, 124B are satisfied. However in the case of unquoted shares and unquoted securities relief will only be available if they remain unquoted throughout *i.e.* from the date of the chargeable transfer until the death of the transferor (or earlier death of the donee).

For transfers made on death if the property is subsequently sold all outstanding instalments become payable forthwith. For a life time transfer where tax is borne by the donee the outstanding instalments become payable on sale or a chargeable transfer made otherwise than on death. Where instalment payments apply subject to the property remaining comprised in a settlement any outstanding instalments become payable forthwith if it ceases to be so comprised.

Where a transfer is other than on death the transfer date is used and the 20 per cent. rule for unquoted shares is dropped, although in that case the question as to whether undue hardship would result if payment by instalments were not allowed is to be determined on the assumption that the shares etc. transferred were retained by the person liable to pay the tax. A person is treated as having control of a company if he has voting control on all questions affecting the company as a whole. For this purpose related shares *i.e.* shares owned by a spouse or shares transferred to a charity, or certain other exempt bodies within five years under the related properties provisions are aggregated with the transferor's shares.

Where shares are comprised in a settlement the voting powers of the trustees shall be deemed to be given to the person beneficially entitled in possession to the shares or securities (except where no individual is so entitled).

Provision is also made for payment by instalments in respect of transfers of the net value of a business or an interest in a business on death, or where the transferee bears the tax or the transfer is in respect of certain events in relation to a settlement, where the property continues to be held in the settlement. See Lloyd's circular to Names, 29 September 1977.

228. Shares, etc. within s. 227. (L5.01, 11–14)
Terms are defined, see IHTA 1984, s. 227 for further information.

229. Payment by instalments—woodlands. (L5.21)
Payment by instalments may also be claimed in respect of a transfer of commercial woodlands.

230. Acceptance of property in satisfaction of tax. (L5.41)
The Board may accept, if they think fit, and on application of the person liable to pay the inheritance tax, certain assets *in specie* in whole or partial satisfaction of the tax due. The acceptable assets are land, certain buildings and their contents, works of art and other items of national, scientific or historic interest. See Department of Education and Science Press Release, March 1977 and Chancellor of the Duchy of Lancaster, House of Commons, Written Answer, 7 August 1980, col. 274. See also the National Heritage Act 1980, s. 9. By S.I. 1986 No. 600, made 26 March 1986, the functions exercised by the Chancellor of the Duchy of Lancaster are transferred to the Lord President of the Council.

See IR67 Capital taxation and the national heritage (December 1986), Appendix 5, and SP6/87. See IHTA 1984, s. 233 for interest provisions where property is accepted after 16 March 1987.

231. Powers to transfer property in satisfaction of tax. (L5.41)
Property transferred *in specie* in payment of inheritance tax is not itself a chargeable transfer. A person who has power to sell the property in order to pay the tax can agree to transfer it *in specie* to the Board so as to satisfy the tax.

232. Administration actions. (L4.15)
A court shall, out of the property under its control or in its possession provide for the unpaid tax due and interest attributable thereto when proceedings are undertaken to determine the correct administration of any property.

INTEREST

233. Interest on unpaid tax. (L4.05; L5.42)

Overdue tax is charged at a single rate from 16 December 1986 in respect of both chargeable transfers during lifetime and on death: see Inland Revenue Press Release, 19 November 1986. Recent rates are: 11 per cent. from 6 July 1989 (S.I. 1989 No. 1002), 9 per cent. from 6 October 1988 (S.I. 1988 No. 1623), 8 per cent. from 6 August 1988 (S.I. 1988 No. 1280), 6 per cent. from 6 June 1987 (S.I. 1987 No. 887), 8 per cent. from 16 December 1986 and 9 per cent. (death) or 11 per cent. (other cases) from 30 April 1985. From 18 March 1986 the death rate (the single rate from 16 December 1986) also applies to the tax on potentially exempt transfers which become chargeable, or to other additional tax payable as a result of the transferor's, or settlor's death within seven years of such dispositions. There is no relief for income tax in respect of the interest paid, but overpayments are repaid together with interest at the same rate.

The Treasury have made regulations, the Taxes (Interest Rate) Regulations 1989, S.I. 1989 No. 1297, which set out formulae to fix the rate of interest according to average base rates. When the rate changes, the Board must by order specify the new rate and when it takes effect; this is not made by statutory instrument.

Where after 16 March 1987 property is accepted in lieu of tax under IHTA 1984, s. 230 the agreement with the Board may provide for the property to be valued at the date of the offer and not at the date of acceptance in which case interest ceases to run from the offer date—see Inland Revenue Press Release, 8 April 1987. See also F(No. 2)A 1987, s. 97.

234. Interest on instalments. (L5.31)

Interest is due on instalments from the date each instalment becomes due not from the date of the principal transaction for shares and securities, businesses, woodlands and property qualifying for agricultural property relief. This does not apply in the case of shares of an investment company or one dealing in land or securities unless it is a holding company (as defined) or a jobber ("marketmaker" as defined in sub-s. (4) from 27 October 1986. From this date the Revenue are empowered to modify by statutory instrument the categories of favoured business) or discount house or where any of the tax is attributable to qualifying agricultural property. In other cases interest runs from the normal date of payment of tax irrespective of the fact that payment may be postponed under the instalment provisions. As interest is charged at relatively penal rates under IHTA 1984, s. 233 the advantage of payment by instalments in such cases is substantially lost.

235. Interest on overpaid tax. (L4.05; L5.42)

Repayments of overpaid tax carry interest from the date of payment at the rates prescribed under IHTA 1984, s. 233. Interest so received is not subject to income tax.

236. Special cases. (L5.32)

IHTA 1984, s. 233 also applies to tax payable in respect of *inter vivos* gifts.

INLAND REVENUE CHARGE FOR UNPAID TAX

237. Imposition of charge. (L6.01–03)

The general rule is that property transferred is subject to an automatic Revenue charge which takes effect subject to any encumbrance already on the property. The Revenue charge does not apply to personalty or movable property passing on death. Personalty includes leaseholds and individual shares in land held on a trust for sale.

If property subject to a Revenue charge is disposed of to a purchaser (as defined) it must be considered at the time of the disposal.

(1) For land in England and Wales.
Unless the charge is registered as a land charge, or a notice is filed for registered land, the charge ceases to apply but the sale proceeds are subject to the charge.

(2) Similar provisions apply to land in Northern Ireland.

(3) For personal property situated in the U.K. (or any property situated outside) not already within (1) and (2) above, if the purchaser had no notice of the charge it will not apply but attaches to the sale proceeds etc.

(4) The charge ceases to apply if a certificate of discharge has been given for the property and the purchaser had no notice that the certificate could be invalid. Again the charge transfers to the sale proceeds.

From 18 March 1986 the charge applies to potentially exempt transfers which become chargeable provided that the property is retained by the donee at the date of the transferor's death. The property is freed from the charge if it has been sold (but not if disposed of in any other way) but the charge is re-imposed on the sale proceeds (or property representing them) to the extent of the original transfer of value.

The rules as to notice may be construed as actual, constructive or implied notice.
See also IHTA 1984, s. 256.

238. Effect of purchases. (L6.03)
If the Revenue charge remains on a disposal to a *bona fide* purchaser for value without notice it will
then lapse six years from the later of the date on which the tax became due, or the date on which a
full and proper account was delivered to the Revenue. For the purposes of this paragraph the time
of the disposition means in the case of registered land the time of registration of the disposition and
for other property, the completion date.

CERTIFICATES OF DISCHARGE

239. Certificates of discharge. (L4.13, 14)
If the Board are satisfied as to payment of inheritance tax, they may, on application give a
certificate of discharge and must give one if the chargeable transfer was made on death or where the
transferor has died. Application is made to the Board after the expiration of two years from the
transfer, or earlier at the Revenue's discretion. However a minimum two year period is prescribed
in respect of tax on potentially exempt transfers becoming chargeable from 18 March 1986. A
certificate is subject to all material facts being disclosed.
See also IHTA 1984, s. 256.

ADJUSTMENTS

240. Underpayments. (L4.10)
Where too little tax has been paid the underpayment will be recoverable together with interest
within the usual six-year time limit. In the case of fraud, wilful default or neglect the six-year period
runs from the date when the defect comes to the notice of the Board. For the procedure in relation
to transfers reported late, see IHTA 1984, s. 264.

241. Overpayments. (L4.11)
Overpayments of tax and interest must be claimed within six years of the date of the final payment.

RECOVERY OF TAX

242. Recovery of tax. (L4.09)
The Board is prevented from taking legal action for the recovery of inheritance tax until the amount
due has been agreed or determined, or if under appeal up to the amount of tax not in dispute.

243. Scotland: recovery of tax in sheriff court. (L3.21)
In Scotland tax and interest thereon may, subject to court limits, be recovered in the sheriff court.

244. Right to address court. (L3.21)
An officer of the Board may address the court.

PENALTIES

245. Failure to provide information. (L7.02)
There are penalties which may be levied of up to £50 for failure to deliver an account or make a
return or comply with a notice, together with a further penalty, after it is declared by a Court or the
Special Commissioners, of £10 a day if the default continues.

246. Failure to appear before Special Commissioners, etc. (L7.02)
There is a penalty of up to £50 for failing to appear before the Special Commissioners if summoned,
or for refusing to be sworn or answer lawful questions.

247. Provision of incorrect information. (L7.03)
In the case of fraud the maximum penalty for a person liable to inheritance tax is £50 plus twice the
tax lost and in the case of negligence is £50 plus an amount equal to the tax lost. In each case the tax
lost is also payable together with interest.
   There is a penalty for persons liable to inheritance tax of up to £500 for fraudulently assisting in
the production of any information known to be incorrect, and £250 for negligently doing so.
   It should be noted that the negligence and fraud penalties apply on the production of incorrect
information. The policy of inactivity would appear only to attract the penalties for failing to make a
return under IHTA 1984, s. 245 above. Interest would also be chargeable under IHTA 1984, ss. 264
and 233.

248. Failure to remedy errors. (L7.03)
An error which arose without there having been fraud or negligence, that is not corrected without
unreasonable delay is treated as being negligence.

249. Recovery of penalties. (L7.05)
Provision is made for the recovery of penalties before the Special Commissioners or the High Court or in Scotland the Court of Session. Proceedings are commenced by the Special Commissioners (or Lord Advocate) subject to appeal to the High Court (or Court of Session).

250. Time limit for recovery. (L7.05)
Proceedings for the recovery of penalties must be made within three years of the date the amount of the inheritance tax properly payable was notified by the Board to the persons liable. Personal representatives are also covered.

251. Summary award. (L7.04)
Special Commissioners may award specified penalties summarily for failure to comply with a notice or for failing to appear before them.

252. Effect of award by Special Commissioners. (L7.05)
A penalty awarded by the Special Commissioners may be recoverable as a Crown debt.

253. Mitigation of penalties. (L7.07)
The Board have power to mitigate penalties, or stay or compound proceedings for their recovery.

MISCELLANEOUS

254. Evidence. (L7.06)
A notice under IHTA 1984, s. 221 which has become final shall be treated as sufficient evidence of the matters determined therein.

255. Determination of questions on previous view of law. (L4.12)
Agreements reached in accordance with the prevailing practice will not be changed if subsequent court action proves that practice to have been wrong.

256. Regulations about accounts, etc. (L2.12, 13, 21, 31)
The Board is given powers to make regulations by statutory instrument on various administrative matters connected with inheritance tax, and the section has extended the obligation to submit accounts to beneficiaries and trustees where there are no personal representatives. See IHTA 1984 s. 216.

257. Form, etc. of accounts. (L2.01)
The Revenue have powers to prescribe the appropriate forms and to compel verification of books and records, including on oath.

258. Service of documents. (L2.01)
A notice is duly served if delivered to a person or if it is left at, or sent by post to, a usual or last known place of residence, or if posted to such residence or to the place of business or employment.

259. Inspection of records. (L2.33)
The Stamp Act provisions dealing with inspection of records do apply to inheritance tax.

260. Inland Revenue Regulation Act 1890. (L2.01; L7.07)
The Inland Revenue Regulation Act 1890 dealing with proceedings for fines, powers of mitigation etc. does not apply to inheritance tax as they are dealt with above.

261. Scotland: inventories. (L2.01)
The appropriate powers are taken to apply to Scotland the provisions of Part VIII (IHTA 1984, ss. 215–261).

PART IX MISCELLANEOUS AND SUPPLEMENTARY

MISCELLANEOUS

262. Tax chargeable in certain cases of future payments, etc. (C2.31)
Where there is a transfer of value under which assets are transferred or payments are made over a period exceeding one year inheritance tax is charged as if there were a deemed disposal on each such occasion and the amount of the transfer has to be recalculated each time.

EXAMPLE—Future payments: tax chargeable in certain cases
On 31 August 1986 Christopher Angus agrees to sell shares in the family company to a discretionary trust for £30,000 in six annual tranches of £5,000 each (discounted present value of future

payments say £20,000) the market value of an outright sale is £90,000 and the value transferred is therefore £70,000. When the third instalment is paid the value of the shares had increased to £120,000. The formula to be applied to this later instalment (ignoring business relief) is as follows—

Value of asset transferred at date of transfer × original value transferred (gift element)

total value at time of original gift

$$(£120,000/6) \times (£70,000/90,000) = £15,555$$

Which is the gift element of the third instalment that has to be grossed up in order to calculate the inheritance tax if payable by Christopher although this would not be necessary if the trustees pay the tax.

263. Annuity purchased in conjunction with life policy. (C1.15)
A back to back arrangement with an annuity and a life policy where the beneficiary under the life policy is a person other than the annuitant, gives rise to a transfer of value at the time the benefit of the policy becomes vested. The charge is on the lower of the aggregate of the cost of the annuity and the premiums paid or other consideration given under the life policy, on or before the transfer, or the maximum benefit capable of being conferred at any time under the life policy but calculated as if that was the date of transfer under the life policy. This section applies to policies issued or varied after 27 March 1974. Refer to IHTA 1984, s. 21 in respect of purchased annuities for normal expenditure out of income rules.

This section would not apply where the annuity and life policy are taken out on normal terms so that it can be shown that they are not associated operations. See SP/E4, 5 February 1975.

264. Transfers reported late. (C2.42)
If a chargeable transfer is not reported until a later transfer has already taken place and the inheritance tax has been paid on the later transfer, the earlier transfer shall be treated for IHTA 1984, s. 7 purposes (except as respects whether full or half table rate applies) as having been made on the date on which it was discovered, but tax is charged at the rates applicable at the date of the actual transfer, or if the later transfer was on death, immediately before that date. If the later transfer was at a nil rate, tax is deemed to have been paid when the transfer was notified under IHTA 1984, s. 216. For transfers reported from 27 July 1981 the tax due on the earlier transfer (provided made within 10 years of the later transfer) is the sum of (i) the tax which would have been payable on the transfer if it had been reported on time, and (ii) the additional tax which would have been payable on the later transfer if the earlier transfer had been duly included. Where no tax is payable on the later transfer the tax payable is treated as nil. Note that after 17 March 1986 the maximum cumulation period is seven years (see IHTA 1984, s. 7) so that unreported gifts will not affect the tax on subsequent gifts made more than seven years later. Where more than one transfer is reported late the additional tax due on the later transfer is apportioned between them on a *pro rata* basis. However, where the tax on one of the earlier transfers has already been settled with the Revenue the additional tax will be charged on the other (or others).

If a transfer is an event after 8 March 1982 to which IHTA 1984, s. 68 applies (an event for a pre-27 March 1974 discretionary trust before its first ten-year anniversary) the provisions of this section will apply as if it were a transfer of value in the normal way and any payments, distributions etc. from the trust will be treated as made by the same person.

See IHTA 1984, s. 256 as to power to make regulations under this section.

This is a policy of convenience so far as the Revenue is concerned, as the tax chargeable will be the same provided that the transfer is added to the seven year cumulative transfers at any stage. So far as the donee of the earlier transfer is concerned however, he is substantially prejudiced by these provisions to the benefit of later donees. It therefore behoves a donee to ensure that the Revenue are duly informed of the transfers as they are made.

For a period of six months from the date of discovery of the earlier transfer, interest on the inheritance tax underpaid is calculated on the basis of the amount of tax which would have been payable, had the transfer been charged to inheritance tax in the correct order. It would seem that after the six months if any part of the higher tax is unpaid, interest is chargeable on that higher amount.

It would seem that such an omission to notify a transfer, could give rise to penalties under IHTA 1984, s. 245 but not under s. 247.

265. Chargeable transfers affecting more than one property. (C2.28)
Where value transferred relates to more than one property the tax chargeable is rateably apportioned.

266. More than one chargeable transfer on one day. (C2.30)
The tax chargeable on composite transfers is allocated rateably to the property concerned. If there is more than one transfer on the same day tax is calculated as if the transfers had been made in the order which produces the lowest charge to inheritance tax.

Inheritance tax is calculated on all the transfers on a particular day and apportioned rateably according to the value of the assets transferred.

267. Persons treated as domiciled in United Kingdom. (J2.06)
A person not domiciled in the U.K. at the time of the transfer shall be treated as if he were domiciled in the U.K. if:

(*a*) he was domiciled under general law in the U.K. on or after 10 December 1974 and within the three years immediately preceding the transfer, or

(*b*) he was resident in the U.K. on or after 10 December 1974 and in at least seventeen out of the previous twenty years.

For the purpose of this section residence is to be determined in accordance with the usual income tax rules except that any house available for use in the U.K. is ignored. See TA 1988, ss. 334–336 and notes thereto in *Moores Rowland's Yellow Tax Guide.* See also *Re Clore (deceased) (No. 2), Official Solicitor* v. *Clore and Others* [1984] STC 609 where the deceased failed to lose his English domicile.

It should be noted that the deemed domiciled provisions do not apply to certain excluded property. See IHTA 1984, ss. 6, 48.

As to the Domicile and Matrimonial Proceedings Act 1973, see [1979] *British Tax Review,* 31 December.

INTERPRETATION

268. Associated operations. (C1.11; C2.27)
Associated operations are widely defined as any two or more operations where the same property is affected, or where one operation affects a further operation. Operation includes an omission. The operations can be effected by the same or different persons not necessarily at the same time. A lease granted for full consideration is not to be associated with any operation effected more than three years after the grant of the lease, and no operation effected after 27 March 1974 shall be associated with an operation effected before that date. A transfer of value made by associated operations at different times is treated as made at the date of the last operation.

These provisions relating to associated operations are extremely widely drawn and could be applied to almost any series of transactions. The provisions should therefore be viewed with considerable caution in any proposed planning for inheritance tax. The provisions are likely to have considerable application and may well apply to attempts to avoid transfers of value by means of a sale and a transfer of cash (whether before or after the sale) to enable the purchaser to pay for the property.

In the House of Commons Debates on 10 March 1975 the Chief Secretary to the Treasury stated that a transfer of money from one spouse to another to enable the spouse to make a gift to a son or daughter for example, on marriage, would not be taxed as an associated operation. Such an arrangement technically may be within the definition under IHTA 1984, s. 268, but at present it appears that the Revenue intend to save the associated operations provisions only for blatant cases of tax avoidance. For the Revenue view as to the application of *Furniss* v. *Dawson* [1984] STC 153 see also ICAEW Guidance Note 25 September 1985, TR 588 para. 11, *Simon's Tax Intelligence,* p. 571. Associated operations were established in *Macpherson* v. *I.R. Comrs.* [1988] STC 362.

However it appears that an arrangement whereby an asset is sold, albeit for market value, the consideration remaining outstanding and subsequently reduced by annual waivers within the annual inheritance tax exemptions, may be viewed by the Revenue as associated operations. If the Revenue contention were found to be correct then a transfer of value might occur at the time of the final loan waiver of an amount equal to the value of the asset at that time including any appreciation in value from the date of the actual sale. See *Law Society's Gazette,* 1 March 1978.

269. Control of company. (G1.21–23)
A person is treated as having control of a company if he has voting control on all questions affecting the company as a whole. For this purpose related shares *i.e.* shares owned by a spouse or shares transferred to a charity, or certain other exempt bodies within five years under the related properties provisions of IHTA 1984, s. 161 are aggregated with the transferor's shares.

Where shares are comprised in a settlement the voting powers of the trustees shall be deemed to be given to the person beneficially entitled in possession to the shares or securities (except where no individual is so entitled).

270. Connected persons. (C1.21)
Various terms are defined. For inheritance tax purposes connected persons include uncle, aunt, nephew and niece in addition to the capital gains tax definition of connected persons under CGTA 1979, s. 63.

271. Property of corporations sole. (B3.16)
Property to which a person is beneficially entitled does not include property to which he is entitled as a corporation sole.

272. General interpretation
Various terms are defined. Note that "quoted shares" includes shares quoted on a recognised stock exchange, or dealt in on the U.S.M.—however the "Over the Counter" and "Third Market" are not included.

SUPPLEMENTARY

273. Transition from estate duty
Schedule 6 is introduced.

274. Commencement
The Act comes into force on 1 January 1985 subject to supplementary rules in Schedule 7.

275. Continuity and construction of references to old and new law
Continuity is not affected by the introduction of this Act.

276. Consequential amendments
Schedule 8 is introduced.

277. Repeals

278. Short title
The Act was cited as the Capital Transfer Tax Act 1984 until 25 July 1986 and then as the Inheritance Tax Act 1984 (see FA 1986, s. 100).

SCHEDULES

SCHEDULE 1 TABLE OF RATES OF TAX (Section 7) **(B1.42)**

The rates of tax applicable on death, or on gifts *inter-vivos* within seven years of death, are nil on the first £128,000 and 40 per cent. on the excess from 6 April 1990 (£118,000 and 40 per cent. on the excess, from 6 April 1989). From 15 March 1988 to 5 April 1989 the rates were nil on the first £110,000 and 40 per cent. on the excess.
    See IHTA 1984, Sch. 2 for the transitional provisions on reduction of tax.
    If a person dies within seven years of making a transfer, additional tax is payable if it would be due by reference to the death scale at the date of death. See IHTA 1984, ss. 3A, 7.
    It is necessary to aggregate a transfer on death or during life with transfers made within the previous seven-year period.
    For indexation of rate bands, see IHTA 1984, s. 8.

SCHEDULE 2 PROVISIONS APPLYING ON REDUCTION OF TAX (Section 9)

Interpretation
1.—(B1.42) References in the Schedule are to events occurring before, on or after a reduction in inheritance tax by the substitution of new rates.

Death within seven years of potentially exempt transfer
1A.—Tax payable on potentially exempt transfers made and becoming chargeable from 18 March 1986 will be computed in accordance with the table rates in force at the date of the transferor's death.

Death within seven years of chargeable transfer
2.—(C2.45) If a person dies within seven years of making a chargeable transfer (other than a potentially exempt transfer) additional tax is only payable if it would be due by reference to the death scale in force at the date of death. These provisions also apply on the introduction of Inheritance tax where the death occurs on, after 18 March 1986 and the chargeable transfer was prior to that date—see FA 1986, Sch. 19, para. 44.

Settlement without interest in possession
3.—(E4.46) Where there is an exit charge on property ceasing to be relevant property between ten-year anniversaries, the rate of tax prescribed under IHTA 1984, s. 69 is that applying (or

deemed to have applied) at the previous ten-year anniversary. However, where there has been a reduction in tax rates, the rate at the last ten-year anniversary will be notionally re-computed at the currently reduced table rate in IHTA 1984, Sch. 1 and that rate applied to the exit charge.

Disposal of trees etc. following exemption on death
4.—(G4.04) If the value of trees is left out of an estate on death for inheritance tax purposes and is subsequently sold, tax is calculated in accordance with the death scale applicable to a death at the time of sale. This applies following the introduction of Inheritance tax even where the death occured before 18 March 1986. See FA 1986, Sch. 19, para. 45.

Conditionally exempt transfers
5.—(G5.11; K1.22) If a conditionally exempt transfer on for example, a work of art, ceases to be exempt, tax is calculated in accordance with the appropriate table rate in force at the time the asset ceases to qualify for exemption.

Maintenance funds for historic buildings
6.—(E5.41) Where there is a chargeable transfer from a maintenance fund (after 8 March 1982) under IHTA 1984, Sch. 4, para 8, and the tax rate is computed under para. 14 of that Schedule (in relation to a settlor's death before a reduction in rates) it is to be assumed that the death rates current on the occasion of charge were in force at the time of the death.

SCHEDULE 3 GIFTS FOR NATIONAL PURPOSES, ETC. (Sections 25, 32, 230 etc.) (B2.04, 05; C3.13, 15)

Transfers to the national institutions listed and referred to are exempt without limit. Distributions etc. from discretionary trusts are exempt under IHTA 1984, s. 76. See Department of Education and Science Press Release, March 1977 and Appendix 15 (Capital taxation and the national heritage). For CGT exemption see CGTA 1979, s. 147 (2).

SCHEDULE 4 MAINTENANCE FUNDS FOR HISTORIC BUILDINGS, ETC. (Sections 27, 58, 77 etc.)

PART I TREASURY DIRECTIONS (G5.42, 43)

Giving of directions
1.—The Treasury may give a direction in respect of a property provided that the conditions in para. 2 are met.

Conditions
2.—The Treasury will approve a fund provided that the trustees are approved by the Treasury and must include one trustee being a trust corporation, solicitor or accountant and the trustees must be resident in the U.K., *i.e.,* the general administration being carried on, and a majority of the trustees being resident, in the U.K.
     Various terms are defined, "accountant" meaning a member of an incorporated society of accountants, "trust corporation" as defined for the purposes of the Law of Property Act 1925, or for the purposes of Art. 9 of the Administration of Estates (Northern Ireland) Order 1979.
     Paragraph 3 sets out the requirements in connection with this paragraph.
3.—The requirements to be met in para. 2 above are:
     (*a*) That within the period of six years of becoming an approved trust its funds must not be capable of being used for any purpose other than for the maintenance, repair or preservation of the historic buildings etc., (for the definition of qualifying property see below, or for the maintenance, repair, preservation or improvement of the trust's own property).
     (*b*) That should any of the property cease to be held on the trusts within the six year period, or prior to the settlor's death or former life tenant's death after 16 March 1987—see para. 15A below (within that time), it can pass only to a national body (museums etc.) or a qualifying charity existing for the preservation of maintaining historic buildings, etc.
     (*c*) That any income arising from trust property at any time and not applied for the maintenance, repair etc. of the building must be applied for the benefit of national bodies or qualifying charities as (*c*) above.
After the six-year period, income remains subject to the same restrictions, although capital is not, albeit the latter is subject to the consequences contained in Sch. 4, para. 8 on property leaving the maintenance fund.
     Under the old rules (see FA 1980, s. 89 (4) (*d*)) and under the new provisions property may be

transferred between approved maintenance funds within the prescribed time scales without crystallising a tax charge. In such cases the six-year period during which the property of the fund is restricted will run from the date of approval of the transferor fund.

Qualifying property is defined to include land which in the opinion of the Treasury is of outstanding scenic or historic or scientific interest; buildings of outstanding historic or architectural interest and ancillary land and objects historically associated with such buildings. See IHTA 1984, s. 31. Property will qualify only where the requisite undertaking has been given to the Treasury (as to the preservation of the property, facilities for public access, etc.) and provided that such undertaking has not been breached.

4.—Where property is comprised in a settlement exempt under the old provisions it will be deemed to be approved under para. 3 above.

Withdrawal
5.—The Treasury may withdraw approval of a fund if they consider that its property or its administration cease to warrant its continuance.

Information
6.—The Treasury have power to request the trustees to provide them with such accounts and other information as they may require relating to the fund and also have power to approve funds in advance of transfers of property to them.

Enforcement of trusts
7.—The Treasury have the right and powers of a beneficiary as respects the appointment, removal and retirement of trustees where a direction has been issued under para. 1 above.

PART II PROPERTY LEAVING MAINTENANCE FUNDS (E5.41; G5.45)

Charge to tax
8.—Property held in an approved maintenance fund for historic buildings etc., is not relevant property and as such is not subject to exit and ten-yearly charges under the normal discretionary trust rules. However, where property ceases to be so held, or is applied other than for the prescribed purposes of the fund either directly or by a depreciatory transaction, or where there is an omission to exercise a right (unless without gratuitous intent) there is a tax charge under this paragraph. Dispositions which would be exempt under IHTA 1984, s. 16 (grant of tenancies of agricultural property) are excluded. The tax charge is calculated on the diminution in the value of the trust property as a result of the disposition and this is grossed up where the tax is paid out of the trust funds. The rate of tax is as prescribed in paras. 11–15 below. There are avoidance provisions where an interest under the settlement has been acquired by a charity for a consideration in money or money's worth.

See also IHTA 1984, Sch. 2, para. 6.

Exceptions from charge
9.—Where property leaves an approved maintenance fund the charge may be avoided if the property is resettled within 30 days on another approved maintenance fund by an exempt transfer under IHTA 1984, s. 27. The 30-day period is increased to two years where the occasion of charge is the death of the settlor. There are similar anti-avoidance provisions and rules as to calculation of any excess which may be chargeable as under paras. 16–18 below. As to capital gains tax for disposals after 13 March 1989, see CGTA 1979, s. 147A.

10.—Whilst the revertor to settlor provisions have generally been abolished they still apply to approved maintenance funds and there will be no charge under para. 8 on property leaving such a fund and reverting to the settlor or his spouse, or where the settlor has died and the property reverts to the widow or widower within a two year period from the death. There are similar anti-avoidance provisions and calculation of a tax charge on any excess transfer as under paras. 16–18 below.

Rates of charge
11.—Paragraphs 11–15 contain a number of relatively complex calculations as to the rate of tax applicable on property leaving an approved maintenance fund. The rate prescribed in this paragraph will apply to most situations where the property in the maintenance fund has been derived from a previous discretionary trust, or where discretionary trust property has been distributed to an individual who has made an exempt transfer under IHTA 1984, s. 27 to a maintenance fund. Paragraph 12 applies in other cases and provides for further rates (computed in accordance with paras. 13 and 14) the higher of which will be applied.

The rate of tax under this paragraph depends upon the relevant period which is defined as commencing at the latest of (*a*) the date of the last ten-year anniversary of the settlement in which the property was comprised before it last ceased to be relevant property (in most cases on transfer to the maintenance fund, or to an individual who makes the transfer), (*b*) the date the property became (or last became) relevant property before ceasing to be as such and (*c*) 13 March 1975. The relevant period ends on the day prior to the event giving rise to the charge.

The rate of tax is the aggregate of the following percentages:

0·25 per cent. for each of the first 40 complete successive quarters in the relevant period,

0·20 per cent. for each of the next 40,

0·15 per cent. for each of the next 40,

0·10 per cent. for each of the next 40,

0·05 per cent. for each of the next 40.

The aggregate percentage (the maximum being 30 per cent.) is applied to the amount of the transfer calculated under para. 8.

12.—This paragraph applies where tax is chargeable under para. 8 and where the tax rate under para. 11 does not apply. The rate of tax under this paragraph is the greater of the first rate (as calculated under para. 13) and the second rate (as calculated under para. 14).

13.—The first rate is the aggregate of the same percentages as defined in para. 11 above although the relevant period is redefined and commences with the date that the property became held by an approved maintenance fund(s) and ends on the day prior to the occasion of charge. No period prior to a previous occasion of charge under para. 8 in respect of the same property is included in the relevant period.

14.—This paragraph sets out the calculation of the second rate as referred to in para. 12 above. If the settlor is alive the second rate is the effective rate which would be charged on a notional lifetime transfer by the settlor on the date (and on the amount under para. 8) of the occasion of charge.

The subsequent death of the settlor is not to affect the rate of tax on any earlier lifetime charge—this should exclude the possibility of any previous potentially exempt transfers made by the settlor after 17 March 1986 (see IHTA 1984, s. 3A) from entering into the calculations should they become chargeable on his death within seven years. As a transitional measure following the introduction of inheritance tax rules from 18 March 1986, when calculating tax on a chargeable event on or after that date by reference to a pre-18 March 1986 death, it is to be assumed that the amendments to IHTA 1984, s. 7 (rates) made by FA 1986 were then in force—thus securing the benefit of the shorter seven year cumulation period and higher tax threshold.

If the settlor is dead, the second rate is the effective rate arrived at by including the amount under para. 8 as the top slice of his estate, see IHTA 1984, Sch. 2, para. 6 where there has been a reduction in rates of inheritance tax. However, if the settlor died before 13 March 1975 the second rate is found by including the amount as the top slice of the estate subject to estate duty and recomputing the tax at the death rates at the date of the occasion of charge.

There are detailed provisions to cover the position where the property has been comprised in more than one settlement and enabling the Board to select the settlor for the purposes of this paragraph. The effective rate is defined as the fraction found by expressing the tax chargeable as a percentage of the amount on which it is charged.

15.—Where property became comprised in a maintenance fund under the old rules it will be deemed to have been so held under the new rules in para. 8 above for the purposes of paras. 11–14 above.

Maintenance fund following interest in possession

15A.—(G5.42–45) The rules for charges where property leaves an approved maintenance fund for non-qualifying purposes are modified in respect of deaths or charges after 16 March 1987 so that the charge on property formerly held on an interest in possession trust may, if the Board so determine, be based on the cumulative chargeable gifts of the former life tenant.

PART III PROPERTY BECOMING COMPRISED IN MAINTENANCE FUNDS

16–18.—(E4.26; E5.41; G5.42) There is no exit charge under IHTA 1984, s. 65 where property on ceasing to be relevant property after 8 March 1982 becomes comprised in a maintenance fund for historic buildings, etc. approved under this schedule. The relief is not available where an interest under the settlement has previously been acquired by the trustees for a consideration in money or money's worth or if they became entitled to the interest as a result of transactions (either directly or indirectly) including a disposition for such consideration, *i.e.*, the associated operations provisions contained in s. 268 may be appropriate in view of the definition of disposition. There will, however, be a charge where the value of the transfer computed on the consequential loss basis (without grossing up) but ignoring business and agricultural property relief exceeds the value of the property received by the maintenance fund (less any consideration given by them).

Where an individual becomes entitled to trust property (which thus ceases to be relevant property) the exit charge under IHTA 1984, s. 65 does not apply provided that the individual resettles the property within thirty days on an approved maintenance trust by an exempt transfer under this Schedule. The limit is extended to two years where the person became entitled to the property on death. Similar rules apply to individuals as for the trustees where the individual has acquired an interest in the property for a consideration in money or money's worth, or where an excess transfer is chargeable to tax as discussed above. As to capital gains tax for disposals after 13 March 1989, see CGTA 1979, s. 147A.

SCHEDULE 5 CONDITIONAL EXEMPTION: DEATHS BEFORE 7 APRIL 1976 (Section 35)

Charge on failure of condition of exemption—objects
1.—(G5.22) If the undertaking made to the Treasury under para. 5 below is broken, or if the asset is sold or otherwise disposed of tax will be chargeable. On a breach of the undertaking the person liable for the tax is the person who, on a sale, would be entitled to the proceeds or income therefrom. On an actual disposal the person by or for whose benefit it took place is liable. Tax will be charged in respect of the last death on which the transfer took place provided this was before 7 April 1976, unless the disposal is a sale to an approved museum etc. or a gift where the donee gives the undertaking.
2.—(G5.22) If the chargeable event in relation to the work of art exempt from capital transfer tax under para. 5 below occurred within three years of the death prior to 7 April 1976 the whole computation on death was recomputed and tax was payable as if the exemption had never applied. If the disposal or breach of the Treasury undertaking takes place more than three years after the death the recomputation is made by bringing in the market value at that date or the sale proceeds of an arm's length sale and not the value at the date of death. There are anti-avoidance provisions to prevent assets being disposed of piecemeal.

Charge on failure of condition of exemption—buildings etc.
3.—(G5.23) Relief was available in respect of deaths prior to 7 April 1976 in respect of historic houses, which was broadly similar to the relief available for works of art under para. 5. It was necessary to make the appropriate claim to the Treasury and for them to designate land as being of outstanding scenic or historic or scientific interest, and buildings, together with their surrounding land, and any object historically associated with them to be of outstanding historical or architectural interest.
    If such an asset is subsequently sold, or the Treasury undertaking breached, similar consequences follow as for works of art under paras. 1 and 2.
4.—(G5.23; L5.41) The tax chargeable under para. 3 is charged at death rates on the value of the property at the time the tax becomes chargeable, as if it had been sold at that date.

Further undertaking on disposal
5.—(G5.21–23) In respect of deaths on or before 6 April 1976 it was possible to make a claim to the Treasury to designate various works of art etc. as being of national, scientific, historic or artistic interest; and provided an undertaking was given that the object would be kept permanently in the U.K., that reasonable steps would be taken for its preservation and reasonable facilities granted to the public for its examination, its value could be left out of the estate for capital transfer tax purposes, subject to para. 1 above.

Requirements of sale
6.—(G5.21–23) The provisions apply to arm's length sales where there was no intention to confer gratuitous benefits.

SCHEDULE 6 TRANSITION FROM ESTATE DUTY (Section 273)

General
1.—(M1.01) Transfers of assets liable to estate duty under that legislation will not also be liable to inheritance tax, thus the tax on lifetime transfer between 26 March 1974 and 13 March 1975 is cancelled where the death takes place before 13 March 1975. The value of woodlands was left out of account for estate duty under FA 1909–10, s. 61 (5) until sale. Where the sale had not occurred by 26 March 1974 the estate duty exemption is regarded as ending immediately after the first transfer of value, other than an exempt inter-spouse transfer made after 13 March 1975.
    References to estate duty include references to inheritance tax on death.

Surviving spouse or former spouse
2.—(M1.04) Inheritance tax only applies to deaths on or after 13 March 1975, but the estate duty rules were substantially changed in respect of deaths on or after 13 November 1974. Prior to that date estate duty applied to deaths and under those rules if a surviving spouse had been left a life interest in an estate there would have been no further estate duty payable on her subsequent death

(surviving spouse exemption). In such circumstances inheritance tax or capital transfer tax would be payable on the subsequent death of the surviving spouse, and would be exempt on the first death under FA 1975, Sch. 6, para. 1. It is therefore provided that where estate duty had been paid on the first death no inheritance tax or capital transfer tax is payable on the death of the surviving spouse. In such circumstances it is advisable if possible to invest in appreciating assets.

Sales and mortgages of reversionary interests
3.—(M1.06) Where a purchaser or mortgagee of a reversionary interest in settled property acquired his interest or loan for full consideration in money or money's worth on the security of such a reversionary interest prior to 27 March 1974, inheritance tax payable by the purchaser or mortgagee when the interest falls into possession, will not exceed the estate duty which would have been payable by him had FA 1975 not been enacted (*i.e.* under estate duty rules as prevailed previously). There are restrictions on this relief if the purchaser or mortgagee of the reversionary interest was a close company in which the vendor was a participator.

Objects of national etc. interest left out of account on death
4.—(M1.06) The provisions of Schedule 5 relating to conditional exemption for works of art etc. on death do not apply in respect of any death after 6 April 1976. The provisions relating to sales only apply to arm's length sales where there was no intention to confer gratuitous benefits. There are provisions for events originally dealt with under Sch. 5 (or FA 1930, s. 40 (2)) to be taken into account as appropriate for the new conditionally exempt transfer sections.

SCHEDULE 7 COMMENCEMENT: SUPPLEMENTARY RULES (Section 274)

The Act generally came into force on 1 January 1985.

SCHEDULE 8 CONSEQUENTIAL AMENDMENTS (Section 276)

Finance Act 1986
1986 Chapter 41

PART V INHERITANCE TAX

100. Capital transfer tax to be known as inheritance tax. (A1.18)

Capital transfer tax became known as inheritance tax from 25 July 1986. The Capital Transfer Tax Act 1984 may also be referred to as the Inheritance Tax Act 1984. The change in title is automatically applied to documents such as wills drafted with reference to capital transfer tax and incidentally allowed the Revenue to continue to use CTT forms until IHT forms became available.

101. Lifetime transfers potentially exempt etc. (C4.02, 03; D4.11)

FA 1986, Sch. 19 is introduced to provide for potentially exempt transfers and make other alterations to introduce inheritance tax.

For CGT purposes, following a claim for hold-over relief on a gift, in determining the amount of the chargeable gain accruing to the transferee the deduction of CTT continues to apply where the gift becomes a chargeable transfer for inheritance tax.

102. Gifts with reservation. (Division B5)

Property given subject to a reservation is treated as property to which the donor was still beneficially entitled immediately before his death, if the reservation is still in existence at that time, and is thus liable to inheritance tax as part of his estate. This includes cases where a settlor is a potential beneficiary under a discretionary trust: *A-G* v. *Heywood* (1887) 19 QB 326, *A-G* v. *Farrell* (1931) 1 KB 81, *Gartside* v. *I.R. Comrs.* (1968) AC 553. If the reservation ceases before the donor's death, he is treated as having made a potentially exempt transfer, *i.e.* a gift that is exempt from inheritance tax provided that he survives the seven-year gift *inter vivos* period at the time the reservation ceases. FA 1986, Sch. 20 introduces rules (similar to the estate duty rules) to cover cases where the property changes hands after the gift or where the donee pre-deceases the donor. Note the reference to "gift" as opposed to "transfer of value"—see Revenue comments in I.C.A.E.W. Memorandum TR631, 21 August 1986, Section B, para. 13.

A gift is regarded as a gift with reservation if the property is not enjoyed to the entire exclusion, or virtually to the entire exclusion of the donee. Gifts made under the terms of regular premium insurance policies made before 18 March 1986 and not altered thereafter will be excluded from the definition of gifts with reservation. Discretionary death benefits payable under approved occupational pension schemes, personal pension schemes and retirement annuity contracts do not constitute reserved benefits—SP10/86.

The reservation rules do not apply to inter spouse transfers, small gifts, gifts in consideration of marriage, gifts to charities, gifts to political parties, gifts, after 13 March 1989 to housing associations, gifts for national purposes, gifts for public benefit, maintenance funds for historic buildings or employee trusts. They can, however apply to gifts otherwise exempt under the "annual exemption" or "normal expenditure" out of income provisions.

A distinction must be made between a reservation of a benefit and the extraction of an interest followed by the gift of the remainder subject to that interest. For example, if a donor grants a lease or property to himself and his spouse and gives away the freehold reversion there is no reservation of benefit. If, however, he gives away the freehold subject to a condition of lease back he has reserved a benefit, see *Nichols* v. *I.R. Comrs.* (1975) STC 278. See also *Chick* v. *Stamp Duties Commissioner* (1958) AC 425, *Munro* v. *Stamp Duties Commissioner* (1934) AC 61, *A-G* v. *Seacombe* (1911) 2 KB 688, *Stamp Duties Commissioner* v. *Permanent Trustee Co of New South Wales Ltd.* (1956) AC 512, *A-G* v. *Earl Grey* (1900) AC 124, *A-G* v. *Worrall* (1895) 1 QB 99, *Oakes* v. *Stamp Duties Commissioner* (1954) AC 57, *Stamp Duties Commissioner* v. *Perpetual Trustee Co. Ltd.* (1943) AC 425.

See *Law Society's Gazette*, 10 December 1986 for letter of 29 October 1986 from Capital Taxes Office.

103. Treatment of certain debts and incumbrances. (D1.23, 24; D4.22)

Debts or incumbrances created on or after 18 March 1986 are subject to abatement if the loan is received from a person to whom the deceased had transferred property. This consists not only of property derived from the deceased and lent back, but other consideration lent by the donee from property derived from the deceased other than property already included in the consideration, unless it can be shown that the gift was not made to enable or facilitate the loan-back.

The repayment of a loan, which is non-deductible under these provisions, is itself treated as a transfer of value which is a potentially exempt transfer.

A liability in respect of a life insurance policy made after 30 June 1986 can be deducted only if the policy proceeds form part of the estate.

104. Regulations for avoiding double charges etc. (D4.31–34)
It will be appreciated that a gift with a reservation can also be a chargeable transfer and regulations introduced by statutory instrument have been made to avoid such double charges whilst preserving the higher amount of tax (S.I. 1987 No. 1130). The regulations provide for the reduction of the value transferred by one transfer by the amount of the other transfer, or by way of credit for the tax payable on one transfer against the tax payable on the other and apply to transfers and other events occurring after 17 March 1986; see Inland Revenue Press Release, 2 July 1987 and Appendix 8.

106. Changes in financial institutions: business property. (G1.12, 23)
Business property relief is not available to investment holders or dealers apart from stock jobbers. With the abolition of stock jobbers in the Big Bang, business property relief will instead be available to market makers. The Revenue have power to add to the category of "market maker" by statutory instrument.

107. Changes in financial institutions: interest. (L5.31)
As for business property relief, interest on inheritance tax payable by instalments makes a specific exemption for stock jobbers and after the Big Bang instead refers to market makers with power for the Revenue to add to the definition of "market maker" by statutory instrument.

SCHEDULE 19 INHERITANCE TAX (Section 101)

PART II TRANSITIONAL PROVISIONS

40.—A death or chargeable event occuring on or after 18 March 1986 does not affect the tax chargeable on a transfer of value before that date. This does not however enable the mutual transfer provisions to be claimed where the donee's transfer occurs on or after that date.
41.—Where tax is chargeable on a conditionally exempt transfer ceasing to be exempt on a chargeable event occurring on or after 18 March 1986 the rate of tax to be used is the current rate as if it had been in force at the time of death.
42.—Similarly where on a chargeable event on or after 18 March 1986 tax becomes payable in respect of a maintenance fund for historic buildings by reference to a death which occurred before that date tax will be calculated at the current rates as if they had been in force at the time of death.
43.—Where a discretionary trust is subject to an exit charge on an occasion falling on or after 18 March 1986 and the most recent ten year anniversary fell before that date the current rate at one-half the new table rate is applicable.
44.—The provisions of IHTA 1984, Sch. 2, para. 2 relating to the reduction in rate of tax following a gift inter vivos are amended to apply the new single table rates.
45.—The reduction in tax provisions of FA 1984, Sch. 2, para. 4 in respect of a disposal of trees on or after 18 March 1986 are amended to reflect the substitution of a single table.
46.—A transfer of value made on or after 1 July 1986 which brings to an end the estate duty deferment on timber is not a potentially exempt transfer.

SCHEDULE 20 GIFTS WITH RESERVATION (Section 102)

Interpretation and application
1.—The material date is defined as the date of the donor's death, where the reservation of interest was retained until death, and in other cases the date on which it ceases to be subject to a reservation. Other terms are defined by reference to FA 1986, s. 102 and IHTA 1984. The gifts with reservation provisions only apply to disposals on or after 18 March 1986.

Substitutions and accretions
2.—(B5.21–24) The gift with reservation provisions may be traced through a disposal by the donee in exchange for other property unless it becomes settled property or is a disposal of a sum of money in sterling or any other currency. If the donee gives away property subject to a reservation he is deemed still to hold it so that if the reservation ceases it may cease to be treated as a gift with a reservation by the original donor from the date the reservation ceases. Bonus shares or rights issues on shares given to a donee are treated as included in the property of the gift subject to reservation.
3.—(B5.21–24) Any consideration given for shares, securities, options etc. by the donee will be allowed as a reduction in the value of the gift subject to the reservation unless the consideration consists of property received by the donor and forming part of his estate on death. Capitalisation of reserves on a bonus issue does not count as additional consideration for this purpose.

Donee predeceasing the material date
4.—(B5.21–24) The donee who dies before the material date is deemed not to have died and acts of

his personal representatives are treated as his acts and bequests or assets passing on intestacy are treated as gifts made at the date of the donee's death.

Settled gifts

5.—(B5.21–24) Where there is a gift into settlement the property comprised in the settlement shall be treated as the property comprised in the gift and if the settlement comes to an end before the material date any property other than property taken absolutely and benefically by the donor, and any consideration given by him for property so taken, shall be treated as comprised in the gift. If the donee subsequently settles the gifted property, subject to the donor's reservation, the donor is treated as if he were the settlor for these purposes. Where property comprised in the settlement at the material date is directly or indirectly derived from a loan made by the donor to the trustees of the settlement it shall be treated as property originally comprised in the gift. Accumulations of income are not treated as property derived from the gift.

Exclusion of benefit

6.—(B5.14, 16) Occupation of land or possession of chattels by the donor is not regarded as a reservation of benefit where the asset is rented for full consideration in money or money's worth. An interest in land occupied by the donor as a result of an unforeseen change in circumstances which results in the donor being unable to maintain himself through old age or infirmity or otherwise, and represents a reasonable provision by the donee for the care and maintenance of the donor who is a relative, will not be treated as a reservation of a benefit. A reservation of benefit by virtue of an associated operation is included as a reservation of benefit.

7.—Where there is an insurance scheme consisting of a policy of insurance on the life of the donor or his spouse, or on their joint lives, and the benefits which accrue to the donee are measured by reference to benefits accruing to the donor or his spouse under that or another policy, it shall be treated as a gift with reservation.

Agricultural property and business property

8.—(G1.13, G3.11, 21) Where the asset disposed of by way of gift is relevant business property, agricultural property or shares representing agricultural property of companies and the property is subject to reservation, business or agricultural relief will be given on the death of the donor or on the property ceasing to be subject to a reservation, as if the property comprised in the gift was a transfer of value by the donee. For this purpose ownership by the donor prior to the disposal with reservation will be treated as ownership by the donee and occupation by the donor prior to or after the disposal will be treated as occupation by the donee. However, for transfers after 16 March 1987 for the purpose of deciding whether shares qualify for the 50 per cent. relief as a controlling shareholding or as an unquoted holding with more than 25 per cent. of the votes, the donor is deemed to own the shares at the date of cesser of the reservation, or at the donor's death as appropriate—this is helpful and means that the donor's own shares and related property may be taken into account. Otherwise it is the circumstances of the donee that govern the availability of relief. In the case of agricultural property of companies the shares must be held by the donee as if it was the agricultural value of agricultural property of the donor.

   If the donee dies before the transfer references to the donee include his personal representatives or beneficiaries.

Finance Act 1987
1987 Chapter 16

PART IV INHERITANCE TAX

60. Acceptance in lieu: waiver of interest. (L5.41)

If the Board agree to accept property, such as works of art, in satisfaction of any inheritance tax, on terms that the value to be attributed to the property is to be determined at the date of offer rather than the date of acceptance of the property, interest is only charged up to the date of offer in respect of an acceptance after 16 March 1987.

Finance (No. 2) Act 1987
1987 Chapter 51

PART II INHERITANCE TAX

97. Acceptance in lieu: capital transfer tax and estate duty. (L5.41)

This is a provision parallel to FA 1987, s. 60 and extends similar treatment to certain capital transfer tax and estate duty liabilities which the Board agree may be settled by the transfer of property such as works of art in lieu of the tax. If the terms on which the Board so agree provide that the value to be attributed to the property is to be determined at a date prior to that of the formal acceptance (and probably usually at the offer date) interest and outstanding tax is only charged up to the earlier date. The section applies to acceptances occurring after 16 March 1987 and will become of diminishing importance with the passage of time.

Finance Act 1989
1989 Chapter 26

PART III MISCELLANEOUS AND GENERAL

INTEREST ETC.

178. Setting of rates of interest. (L4.05)

From an appointed day (18 August 1989, see S.I. 1989 No. 1298) rates of interest on unpaid tax under IHTA 1984, ss. 233, 235 together with their dates of application are determined by Treasury regulations, the Taxes (Interest Rate) Regulations 1989, S.I. 1989 No. 1297, which set out formulae to fix the rate of interest according to average base rates. When the rate changes, the Board must by order specify the new rate and when it takes effect.

MISCELLANEOUS

182. Disclosure of information. (L1.08, 10; L2.31)

It is a criminal offence for officials or former officials of the Revenue to reveal any information relating to the tax affairs of any indentifiable person. The measure also covers staff working for the Special Commissioners, the Parliamentary Commissioner for Administration, the Comptroller and Auditor General and their officers, all of whom may have access to private tax information from time to time as part of their functions.

Disclosure is permitted with the prior consent of the taxpayer, when specifically allowed by statute, when the courts order a disclosure to be made or when made for the purposes of a prosecution for a tax offence.

Any person found guilty may be liable to imprisonment for up to two years, or a fine, or both. The decision to prosecute for an alleged breach of confidentiality may be made by the Board of Inland Revenue or the Director of Public Prosecutions.

This section replaces the Official Secrets Act 1911, s. 2 with effect from 1 March 1990.

Finance Act 1990
1990 Chapter 29

PART III MISCELLANEOUS AND GENERAL

MISCELLANEOUS

124. Inheritance tax: restriction on power to require information. (L2.31)
IHTA 1984, s. 219 is modified to provide that the exercise by the Revenue of its IHT information powers requires the prior approval of a Special Commissioner. The amendment applies to any notice given after 25 July 1990.

125. Information for tax authorities in other member States. (L1.10; L2.31)
FA 1978, s. 77 is extended so that the Revenue have authority to pass on to the revenue authorities of other EC member States not only information that they have obtained for U.K. tax purposes, but also to seek information specially requested for the purposes of tax liability in another member State.

126. Pools payments for football ground improvements. (E4.03)
The pools promoters have agreed with the Football League and the Scottish Football League that amounts equal to the reduction in the pool betting duty from 42.5% to 40% will be paid to the trustees of the Football Trust 1990. The trustees have resolved to spend the money on capital works to improve the safety and comfort of spectators at football grounds in accordance with the recommendations in Lord Justice Taylor's report on the Hillsborough disaster published on 18 January 1990 (Cm 962).

Inheritance tax charges cannot arise on payments which are either distributed to the football clubs or held in the Trust.

Index

Inheritance Tax

R

RATES OF IHT
indexation, IHTA 1984, s. 8
special, potentially exempt transfers, IHTA 1984, s. 54A
Table of, IHTA 1984, Sch. 1
RELEVANT BUSINESS PROPERTY
meaning, IHTA 1984, s. 105
relief, unquoted companies, substantial minority shareholdings in, IHTA 1984, s. 105
RELATED PROPERTY
valuation, IHTA 1984, s. 161
—relief for sales after death, IHTA 1984, s. 176
RELIEFS
agricultural property. *See* AGRICULTURAL RELIEF
business property. *See* BUSINESS RELIEF
woodlands. *See* WOODLANDS
RESIDUARY GIFTS
attribution of value, IHTA 1984, s. 39
RETURNS
on behalf of settlor, IHTA 1984, s. 218
personal representatives, by, IHTA 1984, s. 216
REVERSIONARY INTEREST
excluded property, IHTA 1984, ss. 48, 267
mortgage or sale of, IHTA 1984, Sch. 6, para. 3
settled property, IHTA 1984, ss. 54–56

S

SCOTTISH AGRICULTURAL LEASES
fixed terms, IHTA 1984, s. 177
tacit relocation, IHTA 1984, s. 177
SECURITIES
payment of tax by instalments, IHTA 1984, s. 227
Unlisted Securities Market, in, IHTA 1984, s. 272
unquoted, valuation of, IHTA 1984, s. 168
valuation of, IHTA 1984, ss. 119, 160, 178
SERVICE OF DOCUMENTS
generally, IHTA 1984, s. 256
SETTLED PROPERTY. *See also* TRUSTEE
close companies, IHTA 1984, s. 99
deemed absolute interest in, IHTA 1984, s. 49
definitions, IHTA 1984, s. 43
disposal of interest is for maintenance of family, IHTA 1984, s. 11
excluded property, IHTA 1984, ss. 48, 267
generally, IHTA 1984, Part III, Chapter I
liability for IHT
—beneficiary and trustees, IHTA 1984, ss. 199–205

SETTLED PROPERTY—*cont.*
—settlor, IHTA 1984, s. 201
maintenance fund entering relief for, IHTA 1984, s. 57A
potentially exempt transfer, IHTA 1984, ss. 54A, 54B
reversionary interest, mortgage or sale of, IHTA 1984, Sch. 6, para. 3
reverter to settlor exemption, limitation, IHTA 1984, ss. 51–53
settlor, liability for IHT, IHTA 1984, s. 201
shares payment of IHT by instalments, IHTA 1984, s. 227
successive charges, relief for, IHTA 1984, s. 141
SETTLEMENTS WITHOUT INTEREST IN POSSESSION
accumulation and maintenance trusts, IHTA 1984, ss. 58, 71
added property, IHTA 1984, ss. 66, 67
annual charges, IHTA 1984, s. 85
charge to tax,
—before first ten-year anniversary, IHTA 1984, s. 68
—between ten-year anniversaries, IHTA 1984, s. 69
—rate of ten-yearly charge, IHTA 1984, s. 66
charitable purposes,
—exempt bodies, property held for, by, IHTA 1984, s. 76
—income applied for, IHTA 1984, s. 84
charitable trusts, property leaving, IHTA 1984, s. 70
commencement of settlement, IHTA 1984, s. 60
death, property becoming settled on, IHTA 1984, s. 83
definitions,
—qualifying interest in possession, IHTA 1984, s. 59
—relevant property, IHTA 1984, s. 58
disabled persons, trusts for, IHTA 1984, s. 118
employee trusts,
—property becoming subject to, IHTA 1984, s. 115
—property leaving, IHTA 1984, s. 72
excluded property, IHTA 1984, s. 82
exempt bodies, charitable purposes, property held for, by, IHTA 1984, s. 76
historic buildings, maintenance funds, IHTA 1984, ss. 77–79
interpretation, IHTA 1984, s. 63
maintenance funds, historic buildings, IHTA 1984, ss. 77–79
newspaper trusts, property leaving, IHTA 1984, s. 72
potentially exempt transfers, IHTA 1984, ss. 54A, 54B
property moving, between, IHTA 1984, s. 81

Appendices

APPENDIX 1. PRESS RELEASES—INLAND REVENUE AND OTHERS

10 March 1975. Hansard
CTT—associated operations

The Chief Secretary to the Treasury (Mr. Joel Barnett)

I want to explain the reason for the clause [now IHTA 1984, s. 268]. As I said in Committee, it is reasonable for a husband to share capital with his wife when she has no means of her own. If she chooses to make gifts out of the money she has received from her husband, there will be no question of using the associated operation provisions to treat them as gifts made by the husband and taxable as such.

In a blatant case, where a transfer by a husband to a wife was made on condition that the wife should at once use the money to make gifts to others, a charge on a gift by the husband might arise under the clause. The hon. Gentleman fairly recognised that.

I want to give an example of certain circumstances that could mean the clause having to be invoked. There are complex situations involving transactions between husband and wife and others where, for example, a controlling shareholder with a 60 per cent. holding in a company wished to transfer his holding to his son. If he gave half to his son, having first transferred half to his wife, and later his wife transferred her half share to the son, the effect would be to pass a controlling shareholding from father to son. The Revenue would then use the associated operations provisions to ensure that the value of a controlling holding was taxed.

There are ordinary, perfectly innocent transfers between husband and wife. For example, where a husband has the money and the wife has no money—or the other way round, which happens from time to time—and the one with the money gives something to the other to enable the spouse to make a gift to a son or a daughter on marriage, that transaction would not be caught by the clause. It would be a reasonable thing to do. I have made that clear in Committee upstairs, and I make it clear again now.

H.C. Deb., 10 March 1975, Vol. 888, col. 56.

8 May 1975. Inland Revenue
CTT—Income Yield Attributable to Settled Property (FA 1975, Sch. 5, para. 3, now IHTA 1984, s. 50)

1. The Capital Transfer Tax (Settled Property Income Yield) Order 1975 S.I. 1975 No. 610 comes into operation on 8 May 1975. Its broad effect is to prescribe maximum and minimum rates of income yield where an interest in possession in settled property comes to an end and part of the property is attributable to an annuity.

2. Under FA 1975, Sch. 5, para. 3 a person who is beneficially entitled to the income of settled property is treated for capital transfer tax purposes as beneficially entitled to the property. Where the income to which a person is entitled is a specified amount (*e.g.* an annuity), or the whole less a specified amount, the part of the property to be attributed to his interest is calculated by reference to the income yield of the property. Under Sch. 5, para. 3 (4), the Treasury have power to prescribe higher and lower rates which operate as limits beyond which variations in the actual income yield of the property are disregarded. The higher rate applies when the interest in the annuity comes to an end, the lower rate applies when the interest in the remainder of the property comes to an end. This Order prescribes the higher and lower rates by reference to the Financial Times Actuaries Share Indices. The higher rate is the current yield from $2\frac{1}{2}$ per cent. Consols, the lower rate is the current gross dividend yield from the Financial Times Actuaries All Share Index. If no yield has been calculated for the date on which the property falls to be valued then the relevant indices for the latest earlier date are used. Details of these yields may be obtained between 9 a.m. and 5 p.m. on any working day from the [Capital Taxes Office], Minford House, Rockley Road, London W14 (01-603 4622); 16 Picardy Place, Edinburgh EH1 3NB (031-556 8511); or Law Courts Building, Chichester Street, Belfast BT1 3NV (0232-35111).

3. The Order does not apply where the interest in possession came to an end before 8 May 1975.

6 August 1975. Inland Revenue (see also SP10/79)
Power to allow beneficiary to occupy house

"Commonly such a power is ancillary to a primary trust created by the will and we should not regard its presence as affecting any interest in possession existing under that trust. If there is no such interest it could perhaps be argued that the exercise of the power might create one, but in the ordinary case we should not take this view unless the trustees were empowered to, and did, grant a lease for life within the terms of FA 1975, Sch. 5. para. 1 (3) [now IHTA 1984, s. 43 (3)].

"If the exercise of the power reduces the value of the settled property, as it would if the trustees could and did grant a lease for a fixed term at less than a rack rent, we should in practice seek the alternative charge given by para. 6 (3) [repealed 1982] or 4 (9) [now IHTA 1984, s. 52 (3), (4)] of the Schedule."

24 September 1975. Inland Revenue
FA 1975—CTT—settled property (FA 1975, Sch. 5, para. 15 [repealed 1982])

1. This Press Notice deals with points on the application of the provisions of FA 1975, Sch. 5 which have been raised with the Board of Inland Revenue. The Board feel that their views on the interpretation of the provisions of FA 1975 as regards these points may be of general interest.
2. Transitional relief for capital distribution from pre-March 1974 settlements on conversion to an accumulation and maintenance settlement satisfying the conditions of FA 1975, Sch. 5, para. 15 (1).

Where a charge arises under FA 1975, Sch. 5, para. 15 (3), (*i.e.* where a discretionary settlement is converted into an accumulation and maintenance trust satisfying the conditions of para. 15 (1)). Sch. 5, para. 14 (5) *(b)* provides that the transitional relief for capital distributions from pre-March 1974 settlements does not apply unless each of the "beneficiaries" is domiciled and resident in the United Kingdom. The condition is regarded as satisfied if all the existing "beneficiaries" under the trust as modified are so domiciled and resident. For this purpose possible unborn beneficiaries will be disregarded.
3. Accumulation and maintenance settlements; effect of the Trustee Act 1925 s. 31 (1) (ii) on application of conditions of FA 1975, Sch. 5, para. 15 (1).

The entitlement of a beneficiary to the income of settled property in accordance with the Trustee Act 1925, s. 31 (1) (ii) on his attaining his majority is regarded as giving him an interest in possession on attaining a specified age not exceeding 25 for the purpose of FA 1975, Sch. 5, para. 15 (1), irrespective of the time at which his interest is expressly limited to vest.
See IHTA 1984, s. 71.

8 October 1975. Inland Revenue letter
Accumulation and maintenance settlements: powers of appointment

The inclusion of issue as possible objects of a special power of appointment would exclude a settlement from the benefit of FA 1975, Sch. 5, para. 15 [repealed 1982] if the power would allow the trustees to prevent any interest in possession in the settled property from commencing before the beneficiary concerned attained the age specified. It would depend on the precise words of the settlement and the facts to which they had to be applied whether a particular settlement satisfied the conditions of para. 15 (1). In many cases the rules against perpetuity and accumulations would operate to prevent an effective appointment outside those conditions. Perhaps I should add that the application of para. 15 is not a matter for a once-for-all decision. It is a question that needs to be kept in mind at all times when there is settled property in which no interest in possession subsists.

I am afraid that I do not understand why Mr. . . should think inequality between the beneficiaries fatal to the application of para. 15. There is nothing in that paragraph requiring the "beneficiaries" to be identified or their interests to be quantified, much less equal. (Letter from the Inland Revenue quoted in *Law Society's Gazette*, October 1975.)
See IHTA 1984, s. 71.

6 January 1976. Inland Revenue
Payments to employees under accident insurance schemes—CTT/IHT liability (FA 1975, s. 20 (4) [now IHTA 1984, s. 10])

The Board of Inland Revenue understand that there is uncertainty about the capital transfer tax position of payments by an employer to an employee or his dependants following a claim by the employer under the terms of an accident insurance policy effected by the employer under the terms of which the benefits are payable to him absolutely.

The Board wish to make it clear that FA 1975, s. 20 (4) provides that there will not be a "transfer of value" where the employer and employee are at arm's length and not connected with each other and where there is no intention to confer a gratuitous benefit. Where the employer and employee are connected there will be no liability if the payment was such as might reasonably be expected between non-connected persons.

In many cases the payment will be covered by the exemption in FA 1975, Sch. 6, para. 9 as being allowable as a deduction in computing the taxable profits of a trade, profession or vocation, so that no question of a capital transfer tax liability can arise. If a payment not covered by FA 1975, Sch. 6, para. 9 [repealed] is allowable for income tax or corporation tax purposes, *e.g.* under the TA 1970, ss. 72, 304 provisions, the Board will accept that this of itself establishes that the requirements of s. 20 (4) are met.

19 January 1976. Inland Revenue
CTT: accumulation and maintenance settlements (FA 1975, Sch. 5, para. 15 [repealed 1982])

This notice deals with some points of detail on the application of FA 1975, Sch. 5, para. 15 which have been raised with the Board of Inland Revenue. The Board feel that their views on these points may be of general interest. Apart from the first two points the questions were expressed as specific examples of situations which might arise under a settlement. These questions, with the answers, are set out at para. 3.

See IHTA 1984, s. 71.

1. Powers of Appointment and Revocation limited to the Class of Beneficiaries
Where there is a trust for accumulation and maintenance of a class of persons who become entitled to the property (or to an interest in possession in it) at a specified age not exceeding 25 it would not be disqualified under para. 15 (1) *(a)* by the existence of a power to vary or determine the respective shares of members of the class (even to the extent of excluding some members altogether) provided the power is exercisable only in favour of a person under 25 who is a member of the class.

2. Transitional Relief under FA 1975, Sch. 5, para. 14
The transitional relief provided by FA 1975, Sch. 5, para. 14 applies to any capital distribution treated as made under para. 15 (3), provided that the conditions in para. 14 (5) are met.
3. The examples set out below are based on a settlement for the children of X contingently on attaining 25, the trustees being required to accumulate the income so far as it is not applied for the maintenance of X's children.

A. The Settlement was made on X's marriage and he has as yet no children.

FA 1975, Sch. 5, para. 15 will not apply until a child is born and that event will give rise to a charge for tax under sub-para. (3), subject, if it occurs before 1 April 1980, to relief under para. 14 of that Schedule.

B. The trustees have power to apply income for the benefit of X's unmarried sister.

Para. 15 does not apply because the condition of sub-para. (1) *(b)* is not met.

C. The trustees have power to apply capital for the benefit of X's unmarried sister.

Para. 15 does not apply because the condition of sub-para. (1) *(a)* is not met.

D. X has power to appoint the capital not only among his children but also among his remoter issue.

E. The trustees have an overriding power of appointment in favour of other persons.

Para. 15 does not apply (unless the power can be exercised only in favour of persons who would thereby acquire interests in possession on or before attaining 25). A release of the disqualifying power would give rise to a charge for tax under para. 15 (3). Its exercise would give rise to a charge under para. 6 (2). Either charge is subject to relief under para. 14.

F. The settled property has been revocably appointed to one of the children contingently on his attaining 25 and the appointment is now made irrevocable.

If the power to revoke prevents para. 15 from applying (as it would, for example, if the property thereby became subject to a power of appointment as at D or E) tax will be chargeable under sub-para. (3) when the appointment is made irrevocable. This is subject to relief under para. 14.

G. The trust to accumulate income is expressed to be during the life of the settlor.

As the settlor may live beyond the 25th birthday of any of his children, the trust does not satisfy the condition in sub-para. (1) *(a)* and the paragraph does not apply.

4 February 1976. Inland Revenue letter
Reversionary interests

"A reversionary interest is excluded property if
    (a) Wherever it is situated it has not been acquired for consideration and it is not expectant on the determination of a lease for life *etc.* granted otherwise than for full consideration, or
    (b) if the interest itself is situated outside the U.K. and is either

(i) in the actual beneficial ownership of someone domiciled outside the U.K. or

(ii) itself settled property comprised in a settlement made by someone who was domiciled outside the U.K. when he made the settlement."

Letter from the Inland Revenue, *Law Society's Gazette,* 4 February 1976.

3 March 1976. Inland Revenue letter
Reversionary interests, created on purchase

"In your letter of 15 October you asked about the protection from capital transfer tax of *bona fide* purchasers of reversionary interests.

You were concerned in particular with the situation in which a settlement is created by the sale of a reversionary interest in property wholly owned by the vendor. In that situation, FA 1894, s. 3 would normally have excluded any claim for estate duty on the death of the vendor to the extent that the purchase price represented full consideration for the interest purchased.

I confirm that where such an interest was purchased by the reversioner *before* 27 March 1974, FA 1975, Sch. 5, para. 23 (1) [now IHTA 1984, Sch. 6, para. 3] will protect the purchaser from any capital transfer tax in excess of the estate duty which he would have had to pay had that Act not been passed. Thus, if the purchaser had paid the full actuarial value of the interest concerned he would not have to pay any tax on the death of the vendor. The interest itself when purchased is not 'excluded property' for capital transfer tax and must be taken into account in the estate of the purchaser." Letter from the Inland Revenue, *Law Society's Gazette,* 3 March 1976.

7 May 1976. Inland Revenue
CTT: pension schemes (FA 1975, Sch. 5, para. 16 [now IHTA 1984, ss. 151, 210])

1. This note has been prepared at the request of The National Association of Pension Funds primarily to enable the administrators of pension schemes to answer enquiries about the capital transfer tax liability of benefits payable under such schemes.
2. No liability to capital transfer tax arises in respect of benefits payable on a person's death under a normal pension scheme except in the circumstances explained below.
3. Such benefits are liable to capital transfer tax if:
   (a) they form part of his freely disposable property passing under his will or intestacy. (This applies only if his executors or administrators have a legally enforceable claim to the benefits: if they were payable to them only at the discretion of the trustees of the pension fund or some similar persons they are not liable to capital transfer tax.), or
   (b) he had the power, immediately before his death, to nominate or appoint the benefits to anyone he pleased.
In these cases the benefits should be included in the personal representatives' account (schedule of the deceased's assets) which has to be completed when applying for a grant of probate or letters of administration. The capital transfer tax (if any) which is assessed on the personal representatives' account has to be paid before the grant can be obtained.
4. On some events other than the death of a member information should be given to the appropriate Estate Duty Office. These are:
   (a) the payment of contributions to a scheme which has not been approved for income tax purposes;
   (b) the making of an irrevocable nomination or the disposal of a benefit by a member in his lifetime (otherwise than in favour of his spouse) which reduces the value of his estate (*e.g.* the surrender of part of his pension or his lump sum benefit in exchange for a pension for the life of another).
If capital transfer tax proves to be payable the Estate Duty Office will communicate with the persons liable to pay the tax.

9 June 1976. Inland Revenue letter
Normal expenditure out of income (IHTA 1984, s. 21)

"The statute does not lay down a precise definition of income for the purposes of this exemption. We would therefore take the view that the word has to be interpreted in accordance with normal accountancy rules. This implies taking income net of tax; as regards taking into account the tax on a wife's income, I think it implies adopting a factual test—*i.e.* looking to see what tax is actually borne by the spouse concerned. Of course this is an area in which it is difficult to lay down an inflexible rule, and the circumstances of individual cases will doubtless be diverse." Letter from Inland Revenue, *Law Society's Gazette*, 9 June 1976.

March 1977. Department of Education and Science
The tax position of gifts to the arts and sales of artistic objects

CTT and CGT
4. Many bodies in the arts field are registered as charities. Gifts of money or objects to charities are exempt from CTT without limit if they are made more than one year before the donor's death. Gifts made to charities on death or within one year before death are exempt up to a cumulative total of £100,000 per donor. The tax is not charged either on gifts or bequests to certain national institutions concerned with the preservation of the national heritage (or similar bodies approved by the Treasury), for example the National Gallery or the British Museum. [IHTA 1984, Sch. 3] sets out the relevant national heritage bodies. Gifts to charities and to these national heritage bodies are not charged with CGT.
5. Gifts to non-profit-making bodies of works of art and other objects which in the opinion of the Treasury are of national, historic, artistic or scientific interest may be conditionally exempt from CTT and CGT if the Treasury so direct. The conditions are that the property is given to a body approved by the Treasury as appropriate for its preservation, and that suitable undertakings are given regarding the use or disposal of the property, its preservation, and reasonable access to the public.

Acceptance of works of art and other objects in lieu of CTT
6. Objects or collections of objects may be accepted in lieu of CTT if the Treasury are satisfied that they are of pre-eminent national, scientific, historic or artistic interest. This also applies to objects which are not pre-eminent if they have been kept in a building which is itself accepted in lieu of tax or is owned by the Crown or by one of the bodies covered by [IHTA 1984, Sch. 3], provided that in the opinion of the Treasury the objects should remain associated with the building.

Artistic objects in private hands: CTT
7. An object of national, scientific, historic or artistic interest (referred to in the following paragraphs as an "object") may be conditionally exempted from CTT on the owner's death, even though it continues to be held in private ownership. It may also be similarly exempted from CTT on a lifetime gift if the donor, or his spouse, has owned it for at least 6 years before the gift or if he inherited it on a death on which it was conditionally exempt from estate duty or from CTT. Objects held on trust can qualify for exemption on broadly similar lines.
8. The objects covered include pictures, prints, books, manuscripts, works of art, and scientific collections. The qualifying test for exemption is whether the object would be good enough to be displayed in a public collection, whether national, local authority or university. The exemption is subject to the giving of certain undertakings as set out in the legislation (*e.g.* reasonable access for the public). It is withdrawn if there is a breach of the undertakings or if the object is sold, other than by private treaty to one of the bodies covered by [IHTA 1984, Sch. 3]. Exemption is not withdrawn if the object is accepted in lieu of all or part of a CTT liability.
9. If an exemption is withdrawn as a result of an open market sale or a breach of the undertakings, CTT is then charged, generally on the sale proceeds or the current market value of the object. The precise way in which the tax is calculated, under the rules in [IHTA 1984, s. 35, Sch. 5], will depend on whether the last exempt transfer of the object took place before 7 April 1976.

The special purchase scheme for artistic objects
11. The combined liability to CTT and CGT on an open market sale of an exempt object can be very substantial. The owner may decide instead to take advantage of the special purchase scheme and give a public collection of his choice the opportunity to acquire the object by private treaty. The first step is to reach agreement on a valuation accepted by both parties as a fair assessment of the market price. It is for the owner to propose the valuation, which is then considered by the body's expert advisers. Once the valuation has been agreed the next step is to calculate the special private treaty sale price.
12. To enable the special sale price to be calculated the agreed valuation is split into two components—
  (i) The potential liability to CTT and CGT on what is mutually agreed would be the sale proceeds of the object on the open market;
  (ii) The net proceeds which would accrue to the owner from an open market sale (*i.e.* the gross valuation minus (i))
If the approved body paid the owner an amount equivalent to (ii), the owner would be no better or worse off than under an open market sale. To encourage sales to these approved bodies, however,

the special sale price is calculated as (ii) plus 25 per cent. of (i). By taking advantage of the special purchase scheme the owner is thus increasing his net proceeds from the sale by 25 per cent. of the tax due on an open market sale.

1 March 1978. Inland Revenue letter
Associated operations

"You wrote on 7 November to say that you had received enquiries about the applications of FA 1975, s. 44 [now IHTA 1984, s. 268] (associated operations) to what I may perhaps loosely describe as schemes designed to maximise the advantage of the capital transfer tax £2,000 annual exemption. I am sorry I have not been able to reply earlier.

Your first example concerned the case where A sold an asset to B but left the price outstanding on loan, part of which was written-off each year. We will obviously need to consider any actual case of this kind in the light of the full facts but on the facts as given in the example it seems clear that the sale of the asset and the writing-off of the loans are associated with each other as a single arrangement and, *prima facie*, we would consider s. 44 relevant, whether or not interest was payable on the loan. If section 44 does apply it may well follow that under s. 44 (3) we would have to look at the value of the asset at the date of the release of the last part of the debt.

Your second example involved a gift of shares on terms that the son would pay the CTT by instalments, the father subsequently making further gifts of cash to the son. In this case we agree that s. 44 does not apply; the mere fact that the father made later gifts within the annual exemption to enable the son to pay the tax would not therefore require the value transferred by the original gift to be reviewed."

11 April 1978. Inland Revenue
CTT: deeds of family arrangement etc. (FA 1975, s. 47 [now IHTA 1984, s. 142])

This press release outlines the changes the Government proposes to include in the Finance Bill relating to deeds of family arrangement. The changes take effect as from today. The press release also explains how the Capital Taxes Office will deal with deeds of family arrangement and other similar instruments that have already been entered into.
1. FA 1975, s. 47 provides that if within two years of a death the dispositions under the deceased person's will or under the rules of intestacy are varied by a "deed of family arrangement or similar instrument" the variation is not treated as a transfer of value by any of the beneficiaries. The tax chargeable on the death is moreover adjusted as if the variation were incorporated in the dispositions under the will or intestacy. The Section also provides that when a legacy or any other interest in a deceased person's estate is disclaimed gratuitously within two years of the death, the beneficiary is not treated as having made a gift.
2. Hitherto the Inland Revenue have taken the view that the provision dealing with deeds of family arrangement or similar instruments does not apply where the beneficiary seeks to redirect property which he has already accepted or from which he has already received some benefit. They have also taken the view that the provision does not apply where property is redirected and the recipient is neither a member of the family nor a beneficiary under the will. These and other matters arising from the interpretation of the provision have given rise to considerable practical difficulty. It is accordingly proposed to redefine in the Finance Bill the provisions dealing both with deeds of family arrangement and with disclaimers of legacies and other interests in a deceased person's estate.
3. Under the new rules the tax treatment described in paragraph 1 will apply to any written instrument made within two years of death and varying, or disclaiming a benefit under, a disposition of property (other than settled property), forming part of the deceased person's estate. The rule dealing with "variations" will not be limited to variation in favour of members of the family or beneficiaries under the will. It will also apply notwithstanding that a beneficiary who is giving up an interest had,before the date of the instrument, taken possession of the property or taken a benefit from it. The provision will not however apply where the variation or disclaimer is made for a consideration which does not itself consist of a variation or disclaimer affecting non-settled property forming part of the deceased's estate. The new rules apply to instruments made on or after 11 April 1978; they do not apply to income tax, capital gains tax or stamp duty.
4. Instruments entered into before 11 April will continue to be governed by the existing legislation. However, the Inland Revenue will no longer regard an instrument as outside the scope of that legislation solely on the grounds that it introduced a beneficiary who would not have benefited under the deceased person's will or the rules of intestacy and who was not a member of the family, or that a beneficiary has redirected a gift from which he had already accepted some advantage for himself. This new practice will be applied subject to the statutory provisions which restrict the reopening of settled cases and in particular FA 1975, Sch. 4, para. 26 [now IHTA 1984, s. 255] (Determination of questions on previous view of the law).

4 October 1978. C.C.A.B. TR. 309
Inland Revenue answer to accountants' complaints on accounts examination procedures (TA 1970, s. 115)

Introduction
1. In March 1977 the accountancy bodies held a meeting with the Inland Revenue to consider the selective examination of business accounts by Inspectors of Taxes introduced in 1977. The opportunity was also taken to clarify a number of other operational matters which had been causing difficulty. The outcome of these discussions was published in two practice notes issued by the accountancy bodies in 1977, one of which, TR 246 "Examination of Business Accounts by Inspectors of Taxes", published 18 October 1977, the other, TR 249, published 2 September 1977. See also Inland Revenue letters 15 October and 16 November 1976.
2. It was considered to be to the mutual advantage of both the Revenue and the C.C.A.B. to hold a further meeting to review the selective system which had now been working almost eighteen months. As well as discussing the examination of business accounts the opportunity was taken to discuss a number of other matters.
3. These are the agreed notes of the meeting held on 1 June 1978 and, for this purpose, includes notes relating to some matters which were on the agenda but covered separately by correspondence.

Valuation of unquoted shares by valuation division
23. The C.C.A.B. pointed out a common difficulty where separate negotiations took place for valuations for stamp duty, capital gains tax and capital transfer tax. It was suggested that all valuations required should be agreed at the same time.
24. The value for stamp duty purposes was usually required very quickly after the transaction and if the other values were negotiated at the same time (often on a different basis) then there could be inconvenient delay in the stamp duty valuation. The Revenue promised to refer the points to its Technical Division to see if the processes could be streamlined but it was stressed that nobody wanted a solution which would cause delays in the stamp duty valuations. They have since written as follows:
"The Technical Division can offer no other solution to that given at our meetings, *i.e.* the parties request the Capital Taxes Office or Tax District soon after the transaction to start the valuation procedure. It is insisted that the facts to determine the value for CTT and CGT purposes are not usually available at the stamp duty valuation stage and without them Shares Valuation Division can make no progress.
Technical Division suggest that if the history of specific cases were instanced they could then identify where the material delays arose and perhaps see if there is anything basically wrong with the system."

17 January 1979. Inland Revenue
Life assurance premiums: measure of value for purpose of CTT (FA 1975, Sch. 10, para. 11 [now IHTA 1984, s. 167])

Where a person pays a life assurance premium for the benefit of someone else (for example where the policy is held in trust for another person) this may constitute a transfer of value for the purposes of capital transfer tax. From 6 April 1979 there will be a right in many cases for the payer to make a deduction from the premium in accordance with the system of relief introduced by FA 1976, s. 34. The Board of Inland Revenue take the view that where the payment of a premium on a life assurance policy is a transfer of value for the purposes of capital transfer tax, the amount of the transfer is:
(a) the net amount of the premium after any deduction made under the authority of FA 1976, Sch. 4, para. 5;
(b) the gross premium where the premium is paid without deduction.

31 December 1979. BTR 398
Domicile: effect of Domicile and Matrimonial Proceedings Act 1973 (IHTA 1984, s. 267)

In the course of an action for a declaration as to the validity of a marriage it was contended that the effect of the Domicile and Matrimonial Proceedings Act 1973 was that a married woman could avoid taking a dependent domicile if she did not want it but that she could still take it if she wished. Sir George Baker P. held that the effect of the Act was that dependent domicile had been abolished. If for example an English girl married an American she would not acquire an American domicile unless and until she went to America. "Of course, a marriage as normally understood would be strong evidence that a woman had acquired the same domicile as her husband, for example, when a foreign woman comes here and marries an Englishman and they settle down as a married couple, have children and so on; but it is only one factor in her choice." *Puttick* v. *Attorney-General*, 8 May 1979, [1979] 3 WLR 542; [1979] 3 All ER 463.

25 July 1980. Inland Revenue
CTT: settled property income yields

1. An Order (S.I. 1980 No. 1000) has today been laid before the House of Commons to replace an earlier Statutory Instrument (S.I. 1975 No. 610) relating to capital transfer tax and settled property. This notice explains the effect of the new Order, which comes into effect on 15 August 1980, and invites application from taxpayers who feel that they may have been prejudiced by the Inland Revenue's treatment of cases since 16 May 1977, when the earlier Order became inoperative in part.

The purpose of the order
2. Under FA 1975, Sch. 5, para. 3 [now IHTA 1984, s. 49 (1)] a person who has a beneficial entitlement to the income of settled property is treated for capital transfer tax purposes as being beneficially entitled to the property itself. Thus someone who has a life interest in property is treated as owning that property absolutely, so that on his death there is a charge to tax on the value of the property. But if a person's entitlement to income from settled property is expressed as a specified amount (*i.e.* typically if he has an annuity), special rules are needed to determine the proportion of the value of the settled property which is to be attributed to the annuitant or, conversely, to the person who has the right to receive the balance of the income after the annuity has been paid.
3. The rule for cases of this kind is contained in Sch. 5, para. 3 (3) [now IHTA 1984, s. 50 (2)] which provides that the value of the annuitant's share or of the balance is to be found by reference to the income yield of the property in the settlement. Thus if, at the date when the interest has to be valued, settled property worth £5,000 is producing an income yield of 10 per cent. per annum, and an annuity of £100 is payable, the annuitant will be treated as owning one-fifth of the settled property (*i.e.* £1,000) since he is entitled to one-fifth of the income; a person entitled to the balance will be treated as owning the remaining four-fifths.
4. The legislation recognises that taxpayers could take undue advantage of the rule by switching to high or low yielding investments shortly before the termination of one or other of the interests in the settled property. Sch. 5, para. 3 (4) [now s. 50 (3)] therefore provides that the Treasury may prescribe upper and lower limits to the income yield that can be used for the calculation of the value of either portion. This was done in 1975 by an Order (S.I. 1975 No. 610) which prescribed rates appearing in the FT-Actuaries Shares Indices compiled by the Financial Times, the Institute of Actuaries and the Faculty of Actuaries, and published in the Financial Times. The yield from 2½ per cent. Consols was designated as the higher rate, and the gross dividend yield of the All-Share Index as the lower rate.
5. The constituents of the FT-Actuaries Share Indices were changed on 16 May 1977; since then they have not contained a separate entry for the yield of 2½ per cent. Consols. The yield continued, however, to be published elsewhere and the Capital Taxes Office has since that date used the 2½ per cent. Consols yield derived from other sources as the higher rate limit. But following legal advice that there is no authority for this practice, it has been decided to provide a new higher rate by the making of a new Order.

The new Order
6. The new Order retains the yield from the All-Shares Index as the measure of the lower rate but provides that the higher designated rate is to be that shown in the FT-Actuaries Share Indices for British Government Stocks ("Irredeemables"), a category which subsumes the former 2½ per cent. Consols listing and responding to market conditions in very much the same way. It applies to transfers of value taking place on or after 15 August 1980.

Revision of liability
7. Where liability to tax in respect of events which occurred on or after 16 May 1977 and before the making of the new Order has been settled on the basis of the yield from 2½ per cent. Consols, the liability should now be adjusted on the basis of the actual yield which the settled property was producing at the time. FA 1975, Sch. 4, para. 2 [now IHTA 1984, s. 216] (which prohibits the reopening of settled liabilities) is not considered to preclude such adjustments. The Capital Taxes Office will initiate the adjustments in any cases which it is able to identify. It may however not be possible to identify all relevant cases: taxpayers who consider that they may have been prejudiced by the use of the yield of 2½ per cent. Consols are therefore invited to apply to the appropriate Office to have their liabilities adjusted. The addresses are:

England and Wales: Minford House, Rockley Road, London W14 ODE
Scotland: 16 Picardy Place, Edinburgh EH1 3NB
Northern Ireland: Law Courts Buildings, Chichester Street, Belfast BT1 3NU

7 August 1980. Hansard
Objects in lieu of tax

The Rt. Hon. Norman St. John-Stevas, M.P., Chancellor of the Duchy of Lancaster and Minister for the Arts announced today that the present system of obtaining expert advice on the pre-eminence of objects offered in satisfaction of tax should be revised. The Chancellor of the Duchy has also issued new detailed guidelines on the interpretation of pre-eminence.

Replying to a Written Parliamentary Question from Mr. Andrew Faulds, M.P. (Warley, East), who asked whether the Chancellor of the Duchy would make a statement on the interpretation of pre-eminence of works of art and museum objects accepted in satisfaction of capital transfer tax, he said:

"Following consultations with the national museums and galleries and the relevant advisory bodies, I have decided that the present system of obtaining expert advice on the pre-eminence of objects offered in satisfaction of tax should be revised and detailed guidelines issued on the interpretation of pre-eminence. I shall continue to rely on the directors of the national museums and galleries as my principal source of advice but shall expect them usually to consult widely, particularly where an object has local significance or could be of especial interest within a local context, before formulating their advice. In cases of doubt they will be expected to consult the Standing Commission on Museums and Galleries or the Royal Commission on Historical Manuscripts who will then, if necessary, convene an informal panel of independent advisers which may include a representative of the relevant Historic Buildings Council. The new procedure will be kept under review."

(H.C. Written Ans. 7 Aug. 1980, col. 274).

Guidelines on the interpretation of pre-eminence in respect of objects offered in satisfaction of tax
The following guidelines are intended as a framework of reference for the expert advisers (who are chosen from the directors of the relevant national museums and galleries), to help them in formulating their advice on whether an item is pre-eminent.

(*i*) Does the object have an especially close association with our history and national life?

This category includes foreign as well as British works, for example, gifts that foreign sovereigns or governments have made, and objects that have been acquired abroad in circumstances closely associated with our history. It includes objects closely associated with some part of the United Kingdom, or with the development of its institutions and industries. Some objects which fall under this category will be of such national importance that they deserve to enter a national museum or gallery. Others may well be of a lesser degree of national importance, though they will be nonetheless significant in a local context. This category will also include works which derive their significance from a local connection, and which may therefore qualify as pre-eminent only in a local or university museum.

(*ii*) Is the object of especial artistic or art-historical interest?

This category, like (*iii*) below, includes objects deserving of entering a national museum or gallery as well as other objects which may not be pre-eminent in a national museum or gallery in London, Edinburgh or Cardiff, but will be pre-eminent in museums or galleries elsewhere which do not already possess items of a similar genre or a similar quality.

(*iii*) Is the object of especial importance for the study of some particular form of art, learning or history?

This category includes a wide variety of objects, not restricted to works of art, which are of especial importance for the study of, say, a particular scientific development. The category also includes objects forming part of a historical unity, series or collection either in one place or in the country as a whole. Without a particular object or group of objects both a unity and a series may be impaired.

(*iv*) Does the object have an especially close association with a particular historic setting?

This category will include primarily works of art, manuscripts, furniture or other items which have an especially close association with an important historic building. They will fall to be considered pre-eminent by virtue of the specific contribution they make to the understanding of an outstanding historic building. Thus, the category may include paintings or furniture specially commissioned for a particular house or a group of paintings having an association with a particular location.

9 March 1981. Hansard
Association for Business Sponsorship of the Arts

Capital transfer tax
10. Gifts made in sponsorship of the arts may qualify for certain exemptions from the charge to capital transfer tax on gratuitous transfers of property by individuals and close companies.
11. There is a general exemption for the first £2,000 of gifts by an individual in any one tax year and, in addition, gifts by an individual to any one person in one tax year are exempt up to a value of

£250. Outright gifts to charity are exempt from capital transfer tax, whatever their value, if they are made more than one year before the death of the donor; if the gift takes place on or within one year of the donor's death they are exempt up to a cumulative total of £200,000 for each donor. (Prior to 26 March 1980 the limit was £100,000).

12. There is an unlimited exemption for gifts or bequests to certain national institutions concerned with the preservation of the national heritage (for example, the British Museum or the National Trust) or to certain bodies specified in FA 1975, Sch. 6, para. 12 [now IHTA 1984, Sch. 3] such as universities and local authorities. There is also an exemption under Sch. 6, para. 13 [now IHTA 1984, s. 26] (matched by a corresponding exemption from capital gains tax) for gifts or bequests of certain national heritage property (outstanding land and historic buildings, works of art etc. of national, scientific, historic or artistic interest, and property given as a source of income for the upkeep of such items) to non-profit-making bodies approved by the Treasury. Under FA 1976, s. 84 [repealed 1982] exemption may be claimed for transfers of property to, or capital distributions from, a special trust fund approved by the Treasury and devoted to the maintenance and preservation of buildings outstanding for their historic or architectural interest, together with their historically associated contents and amenity land; such a fund would also be exempt from the periodic charge to tax on discretionary trusts. FA 1976, s. 55 [now CGTA 1979, s. 148] "rolls over" for CGT purposes any accrued gain arising on the disposal of assets to such a trust fund.

13. Transfers by close companies may give rise to capital transfer tax. The liability is calculated by apportioning the value transferred among the participators of the company making the transfer, and the £2,000 annual exemption applies to the value allocated to each individual participator. So far as the company's transfer of value relates to property given to charity or to the national institutions or bodies mentioned above, then the exemptions for gifts to those bodies extend to the amounts apportioned to the individual participators. Capital transfer tax does not apply to gifts by incorporated bodies other than close companies.

14. Capital transfer tax is not charged on dispositions which are allowed for income tax or corporation tax purposes.

26 November 1981. Inland Revenue letter
Trusts: CTT and income tax

"It is the Inland Revenue's view that the provisions of TA 1988, ss. 673 and 683 (TA 1970, ss. 447 and 457) apply to all settlements under the terms of which the trustees are directed or empowered to meet the settlor's personal capital gains tax or capital transfer tax liabilities from the settled funds.

"In the case of a settlement whose terms were silent on the matter of payment of such liabilities the Inland Revenue would not normally seek to apply the provisions of TA 1988, ss. 673 and 683 (TA 1970, ss. 447 and 457), where the trustees did in fact pay any capital transfer tax due. I would however draw your attention to the amendments to TA 1970, s. 451 contained in FA 1981, s. 42 (7) (now TA 1988, s. 677), under which such a payment might be assessable upon the settlor as being a capital sum applied by the trustees for the settlor's benefit."

23 June 1982. Inland Revenue
CTT: killed in war exemption: Falkland Islands

In reply to the Parliamentary Question:
   "To ask Mr Chancellor of the Exchequer, what will be the CTT position of those killed in the Falklands dispute."
the Financial Secretary yesterday gave the following reply:
   "I can confirm that the estates of those killed on active service on the Falklands dispute will be exempt from capital transfer tax."

Note
It is for the Ministry of Defence to issue certificates in qualifying cases.
   See FA 1975, Sch. 7, para. 1 [now IHTA 1984, s. 154].

30 July 1982. Inland Revenue
CTT: works of art: form 700A

1. Form 700A, on which conditional exemption from capital transfer tax and capital gains tax may be claimed in respect of works of art and other objects, has been revised in the light of the Government's response to the third (interim) report of the Education, Science and Arts Committee (ESAC).

2. The exemption applies to any pictures, prints, books, manuscripts, works of art, scientific collections or other things not yielding income which appear to the Treasury to be of national,

scientific, historic or artistic interest. It is conditional on the new owner undertaking to preserve the object and to take steps to secure reasonable access to the public to view the object.
3. The Government's reply to the ESAC report set out new arrangements through which the public access undertakings could be satisfied, and these are set out in the revised form.
4. Copies of the revised Form 700A are available from the Capital Taxes Office, Minford House, Rockley Road, London W14 0DF (telephone 01-603 4622).

Notes
1. To obtain conditional exemption from capital transfer tax and capital gains tax an owner of a work of art or other object must undertake to take reasonable steps to secure reasonable public access to the object. In the application form for the exemption—Form 700A—the owner is asked to state how he intends to arrange access by the public to view his object and the notes on p. 4 of the form—which are intended for guidance—list three ways in which the undertaking may be fulfilled.
2. For the future an owner who does not live in a house which is or will be open to the public will be able to choose between:
  (*a*) lending his objects for display in a house which is regularly open to the public; or
  (*b*) lending his objects to public collections on a long term basis; or
  (*c*) asking the Capital Taxes Office to arrange for details of the objects (and how to contact the owner or his agent) to put on a register maintained by the National Art Library of the Victoria and Albert Museum. Copies of this register are held also at the National Library of Scotland, the National Museum of Wales and the Public Record Office of Northern Ireland. The register will be made available to museums and galleries and to members of the public. Owners will if requested be required to lend objects for special exhibitions for up to six months in any two year period and to make arrangements for members of the public to view the objects.
3. The revised form makes it clear that the register need not identify the owner or the address at which the object is held.

30 July 1982. Inland Revenue
CTT: Scotland: inventory forms

Cap Form A-3 and Cap Form B-3 have hitherto been the forms of Inland Revenue Inventory prescribed for use in Scotland, B-3 where confirmation was to be obtained under the Small Estates Acts, and the twelve-page A-3 for use in all other cases.
  In the interests of simplicity and economy a six-page form, Cap Form B-4, has been introduced for use where the estate is an excepted estate as defined in the Capital Transfer Tax (Delivery of Accounts) (Scotland) Regulations 1981 (S.I. 1981, No 881) to the effect that:
  (*a*) the value of the estate is attributable wholly to property passing under the deceased's will or intestacy or under a nomination of an asset taking effect on death or by survivorship;
  (*b*) the total gross value of that property did not exceed £25,000;
  (*c*) of that property not more than 10 per cent. of the total gross value or £1,000, whichever figure is the higher, represented value attributable to property then situated outside the U.K.
  (*d*) the deceased died on or after 1 April 1981 domiciled in the U.K. and without having made any chargeable transfer during his lifetime.
  A–3 and B–3, which will remain available for use in appropriate cases, have been redesigned to take account of recent changes in the law.
  Revised instructions for completing inventory forms are now available; the instruction booklet is designated Cap Form A–5 (1982). The new prints of the Inventory forms are designated Cap Form A–3 (1981), Cap Form B–3 (1981) and Cap Form B–4 (1981); they may be obtained from the Registrar, Capital Taxes Office, Inland Revenue, 16 Picardy Place, Edinburgh EH1 3NB or at Sheriff Clerk's Offices and authorised Stamp and Post Offices in Scotland.

24 November 1982. The Law Society's Gazette
CTT and specific devises

The following correspondence appeared in the Law Society's Gazette 24 November, p. 1518:
Over the past few months, the Non-Contentious Business Committee and the Revenue Law Committee have given lengthy consideration to the implication of the decision in *Re Dougal* [1981] STC 514. A full note about the decision appeared in [1981] *Gazette*, 4 November, 1213.
  Briefly, the case decided that, in the absence of any provision to the contrary in the will of a deceased person, all capital transfer tax, whether in respect of real or personal property, is a testamentary expense; previously it had been thought both by the Inland Revenue and by the profession that capital transfer tax attributable to real property was payable out of that property.
  The decision in *Re Dougal* was based on the construction of the provisions of FA 1975 which had introduced capital transfer tax. Previously, the law had been clear that, in the absence of a direction

to the contrary, estate duty in respect of real property had been payable out of that property, and it is understood that it was the Government's intention that the same provisions should apply for capital transfer tax purposes. However, the case of *Re Dougal* found otherwise.

Re Dougal was a decision of the Court of Session in Scotland. Scottish decisions are, of course, not binding in England and Wales but would be of persuasive authority if the matter were to be litigated in the High Court. If such litigation does take place then the High Court judgment will be declaratory of the law either way. If the High Court follows the Court of Session, and decides that in England and Wales the capital transfer tax in respect of real property is a testamentary expense, then questions will arise as to the administration of estates since 1975 which were concluded on the previous view of the law. If the High Court does not follow *Re Dougal*, then the uncertainty will continue until there has been a decision of the House of Lords which is the only court that can speak with authority for both England and Wales and Scotland.

In April 1982, the Inland Revenue wrote seeking the views of The Society as to whether any change or clarification of the law would be desirable following the decision in *Re Dougal*. The letter mentioned three possibilities for reform: first, that all tax payable on a deceased's estate should be treated as a testamentary expense whether in respect of real or personal property; secondly, that bequests, whether real or personal should bear their own tax, and finally, that real property should bear its own tax but that tax on personal property should fall on the residue. Whatever change was contemplated there would be the question of the date on which it would take effect and here the possibilities would be either the introduction of capital transfer tax (1975) or deaths after the *Dougal* case (1981) or deaths after the introduction of any new legislation.

The Revenue Law Committee took the view that a clause should be inserted in the Finance Bill 1982; as a matter of urgency, confirming the law as both sides had believed it to be before the case of *Re Dougal*, such provision to be retrospective to 1975 (the introduction of capital transfer tax). Such provision would then regularise the administration of the estates which had taken place since that date on the previous view of the law. As far as the future was concerned, however, the Revenue Law Committee were of the view that legislation should be introduced to confirm the decision in *Re Dougal*.

The Non-Contentious Business Committee, however, were concerned at the principle of retrospective legislation, especially as this could create difficulties for solicitors who had prepared estate accounts on the basis of *Re Dougal* after the decision in June 1981. The Non-Contentious Business Committee, however, agreed with the Revenue Law Committee that for the future, legislation should be enacted as soon as possible to provide that all capital transfer tax should be payable out of residue; the differentiation between real and personal property was archaic and should be abandoned.

Representations were therefore then made to the Inland Revenue that a clause should be included in the 1982 Finance Bill providing that the tax payable on the whole of the deceased's free property in the U.K. was a testamentary expense, the tax being payable by the executors and effectively borne by the residuary legatees; although such a statutory provision would in fact confirm the decision in *Re Dougal*, nevertheless, the legislation should provide that it should apply to all deaths taking place after the Finance Act came into force.

In the event, however, no such clause was included in the Finance Bill 1982. In the absence, therefore, of immediate amending legislation, the Non-Contentious Business Committee considered how best the profession could be assisted in view of the continuing uncertainty and resolved to ask the Inland Revenue if they would be prepared to publish a statement of their views for the assistance of the profession.

The Inland Revenue wrote fully in reply to that request and subsequently further representations were made to the Inland Revenue that legislation should be included in the Finance Bill 1983. The correspondence is published below for the information of the profession:

Mrs. A. N. Brice
Senior Assistant Secretary
The Law Society

Dear Mrs. Brice

Incidence of capital transfer tax on death

You asked if I would write to you about our current practice outside Scotland in relation to the incidence of capital transfer tax on death.

In a press release of 8 June 1978 we set out our understanding, based on the advice of Scottish counsel, of the incidence of capital transfer tax under Scots law where heritable properties or other legacies had been specifically bequeathed and the will contained no directions as to who should ultimately bear the burden of the tax. This was to the effect that the tax attributable to heritable property was a debt to be paid out of that property which the executors were entitled to recover from the person or persons in whom it had vested beneficially while the capital transfer tax attributable to a specific bequest of moveable property was a testamentary expense the burden of which fell to be borne by the residuary estate.

On 5 June 1981, however, the Court of Session decided in *Re Dougal* [1981] S.T.C. 514; *sub nom Cowie's Trs, Petitioners* 1982 S.L.T. 326, that FA 1975 had made a radical change in the law and that for capital transfer tax no distinction fell to be made between one kind of property and another; hence a specific legacy of heritable property, like a specific legacy of moveables, should not bear any proportion of capital transfer tax when the will was silent.

Elsewhere in the U.K. the position has been that where the will is silent as to the incidence of tax, the tax on a specific bequest of real property in the U.K. is borne by the legatees and of free personal property by the residuary estate. Following *Re Dougal* doubts have been expressed about the correctness of this practice.

We have been advised that there are no relevant differences between Scots law and the law in the rest of the U.K. and therefore that there is nothing to prevent the decision in *Re Dougal* from applying in England, Wales and Northern Ireland.

We consider, however, that in the absence of any judgment on the point by a non-Scottish court, the incidence of tax on specific devises of free real property where the will contains no direction is primarily a matter for decision between the specific and residuary beneficiaries. Outside Scotland we shall normally therefore be prepared for the time being to follow the course adopted in the administration of the particular estate. Where, however, the beneficiaries cannot reach agreement between themselves, or where it is necessary to consider any proceedings before a court, so that we have to take a stance, then as presently advised we shall follow the decision in *Re Dougal*.

We appreciate that personal representatives and others may remain in some uncertainty how they should properly act in the absence of express directions in the will. At the request of Ministers therefore we have been consulting those directly concerned with the administration of estates about the possibility of legislation to clarify the position and about the form any such legislation might take. No decision has however been reached on whether it will be possible to deal with this issue in the 1983 Finance Bill even if it is agreed that in principle legislation is desirable.

Yours sincerely,
L. J. H. Beighton
Inland Revenue
12 October 1982

L. J. H. Beighton Esq.,
Inland Revenue
Somerset House,
London WC2R 1LB.

Dear Mr. Beighton,

Further to my letter to you of 20 October, I am now able to reply a little more fully to your (longer) letter of 12 October which has been considered both by the Non-Contentious Business Committee and by the Revenue Law Committee.

First, the Committees have asked me to thank you for the statement of your views which will be of great interest to the profession. The Committees would like to publish a note in The Law Society's *Gazette* which will refer to your views and I attach a copy of a draft of such note for your information. I would be glad if you could please confirm that you would have no objection to the publication of your letter in this context. This is a matter which has given rise to a large number of representations from members of the profession, and to correspondence in the columns of The Law Society's *Gazette*, which indicates the degree of importance as well as of concern that is felt by the profession as a whole about the matter. Secondly, the Committees are grateful to Ministers for requesting consultation about the possibility of legislation to clarify the position and the form such legislation should take. The Committees agree with the conclusion that the position should be clarified by legislation rather than litigation for two main reasons. First, final certainty could only be reached by litigation if the case were decided by the House of Lords, which is the only court that can speak for the whole of the U.K.; the expense of such litigation, and the time involved before certainty is achieved, are both cogent arguments in favour of legislation, sooner rather than later.

The second reason why legislation is preferable is that any decision of the court would be declaratory of the law as from 1975; although FA 1975, Sch. 4, para. 26 will assist for capital transfer tax purposes, it would still be open to beneficiaries to question the procedure adopted by the personal representatives; again, although the Trustee Act 1925, s. 61 would be of help, it could be necessary for an application to be made to the court in each case.

Having concluded that legislation is desirable, the Committees have considered how best this can be formulated and here they feel that due regard must be paid to the fact that, because of the uncertainty which has existed since the decision in *Re Dougal*, it has been open to personal representatives to adopt either of the two courses outlined in your letter; a simple re-statement of the law as both sides believed it to be prior to the decision would, therefore, penalise those personal representatives who have, since the decision, regarded CTT on realty as a testamentary expense.

The Committees therefore suggest that the proposed amending legislation should borrow from the principles set out in FA 1976, s. 46 which followed the decision in *Sime Darby London Ltd.* v. *Sime Darby Holdings Ltd.* [1975] STC 562 and, in particular, from s. 46 (5), as to validate transactions concluded on either view of the law.

At the same time as the legislation suggested in this letter is enacted to regularise past transactions, the opportunity should also be taken of clarifying the position for the future and enacting the first possibility of reform outlined in your letter of 7 April. You will recall that that suggestion was that, in the absence of express provision to the contrary in a will, the tax payable on the whole of a deceased's free property (both real and personal) in the U.K. should be treated as a testamentary expense, leaving the tax attributable to free foreign property to be borne by the person entitled to it and that attributable to settled property (wherever situate) to be borne by the settled funds; such legislative provision should take effect in respect of all deaths occurring after the date upon which the Finance Bill receives the Royal Assent.

In view of the fact that the legislation suggested in this letter will affect the administration of estates, the Committees have asked me to write similarly to the Lord Chancellor's Department, so that they will be kept informed of the Committee's views.

Whilst appreciating what you say in the final sentence of your letter, the Committees nevertheless take the view that it is essential that these matters should be clarified by legislation and, in view of the fact that the present difficulties have arisen out of the wording of the capital transfer tax legislation in 1975, they take the view that it would be appropriate for the amending legislation to be included in the Finance Bill 1983.

If the Committees can be of any assistance during the preparation of the new legislation, please let me know; I know that they would welcome an opportunity of commenting on any draft that might be prepared.

Yours sincerely,
(Mrs.) A. N. Brice,
Senior Assistant Secretary
9 November 1982

Meanwhile, however, solicitors may wish to bear in mind the provisions of FA 1975, Sch. 4, para. 26 [now IHTA 1984, s. 255] which provides that where any payment of capital transfer tax has been made and accepted in satisfaction of any liability on a view of the law which was then generally believed or adopted in practice, any question of whether too little or too much has been paid or what was the right amount of tax payable shall be determined on the same view, notwithstanding that it appears from subsequent legal decision or otherwise that the view was, or may have been, wrong.

Solicitors advising personal representatives may also wish to bear in mind the provisions of the Trustee Act 1925, s. 61 which gives the court the power to relieve any trustee (including a personal representative) from liability if he has acted honestly and reasonably.

9 June 1983. C.C.A.B. TR 508
Notes on taxation anomalies and practical difficulties

In December 1982 a submission entitled Memorandum of Taxation Anomalies and Practical Difficulties 1982 (TR 488) was made to the Chairman of the Board of Inland Revenue on behalf of the Councils of the constituent members of the Consultative Committee of Accountancy Bodies.

On 11 January 1983 a meeting was held at Somerset House between representatives of the accountancy bodies and the Inland Revenue to discuss the above memorandum.

A note of that meeting is attached. The paragraph numbers are those used in the memorandum.

CAPITAL TRANSFER TAX

Agricultural property relief (FA 1981, Sch. 14 para 9 (1) [now IHTA 1984, s. 122 (1)])

77–79. The Revenue said that, though agricultural relief was not available, business relief was available. The amount of relief was the same under both schemes.

Discretionary trusts (FA 1982 ss. 101 to 127 [now IHTA 1984 ss. 58 to 85])
80. The Revenue said that the Policy Division would be happy to meet the C.C.A.B. for the further discussions requested.

Rate of ten-yearly charge (FA 1982, s. 109 [now IHTA 1984, s. 66])
81–82. The Revenue said that the C.C.A.B.'s first proposals would significantly complicate the

present law, and the fragmentation resulting from the second proposal would effectively eliminate the ten year charge.

29 September 1983. Inland Revenue
CAP Form 202—Inland Revenue Account where a Deceased's Estate is below the CTT threshold

This capital transfer tax account has been revised and its scope extended. The new four page form may be used where the total net value of the estate, after deducting any exemptions and reliefs claimed, does not exceed the threshold above which capital transfer tax is payable at the date of death and both

(*a*) the deceased died on or after 27 March 1981 domiciled in the U.K.; and
(*b*) the estate comprises only property which has passed under the deceased's will or intestacy or by nomination or beneficially by survivorship; and all that property was situate in the U.K.

In all other estates form 200 (U.K. domicile) or 201 (overseas domicile) should be used, *unless* the estate is an excepted estate under the CTT (Delivery of Account) Regulations in which case no account need be completed, although exceptionally one may be required later.

See also Press Release 7 October 1983.

7 October 1983. Inland Revenue
CAP Form 202—Inland Revenue Account

Further to the Press Release of 29 September, the Revenue point out that this form, like its predecessor, applies to England and Wales only and that copies of the form are available from the Capital Taxes Office, Minford House, Rockley Road, London W14 0DF and Head Post Offices in England and Wales.

A similar form for Northern Ireland is being prepared and should soon be available from the Capital Taxes Office, Law Courts Building, Chichester Street, Belfast BT1 3NU and Head Post Offices in Northern Ireland.

In Scotland, the CAP Form B-4 is the nearest equivalent to the Form 202. Regulations which introduced the B-4 (see *Simon's Tax Intelligence* 1982, p. 351), have recently been amended so that for deaths on or after 1 April 1983, £40,000 replaces £25,000 at (*b*) and £2,000 replaces £1,000 at (*c*). It is intended that a revised form for use in Scotland will be available in the new year from the Capital Taxes Office, 16 Picardy Place, Edinburgh EH1 3NB or at Sheriff Clerks' Offices and authorised Stamp and Post Offices in Scotland. In the meantime, the present form, amended where appropriate, may be used.

2 November 1983. Hansard
Bloodstock industry (taxation)

Mr. Latham asked the Chancellor of the Exchequer on what authority the capital taxes office indicated that horse owners and breeders will not be permitted 50 per cent. agricultural relief on capital transfer tax and also, in certain circumstances, not be permitted 50 per cent. business relief; and if he will instruct the office to reverse this decision.

Mr. Moore: Under the provisions of the capital transfer tax, agricultural relief is given for agricultural property occupied for agricultural purposes. Business relief is given if the business is carried on for gain. Whether any particular property qualifies under these provisions is a matter of the proper interpretation of the law in relation to the fact of the particular case. If the taxpayer does not accept the view of the Inland Revenue he may appeal.

HC, 2 November 1983, Vol. 47, col. 380.

3 May 1984. Inland Revenue
Estate duty: calculation of duty payable on a chargeable event affecting heritage objects previously granted conditional exemption

Under the estate duty provisions, an object which in the opinion of the Treasury was of national, scientific, historic or artistic interest could be exempt from duty if undertakings were given to preserve it and keep it in the U.K. If an object which had been exempted from duty was subsequently sold (unless the purchaser was a national institution or similar body), or if the undertaking was broken, duty became chargeable, generally either on the sale proceeds or on the value of the object at the date of the charge. These "clawback" charges may still apply now in relation to objects which have previously been exempted from estate duty.

Estate duty applied not only to property passing on death but also to property given away by the deceased within a certain period before his death. In these latter cases the duty chargeable could be reduced by a taper relief (FA 1960, s. 64). The exemption described in the preceding paragraph could also apply to an object which came within the charge to duty because it was the subject of an inter vivos gift. The Board have been advised that in these circumstances taper relief under s. 64 is not available to reduce the amount liable to the clawback charge, and that the amount chargeable to duty is the full value or sale proceeds. The Board understand that the Capital Taxes Office have in the past applied taper relief to reduce the amount liable to the clawback charge. Assessments made on that basis before the date of this notice will not be reopened.

Note
Estate duty applied broadly to the value of all property passing on death. In addition, property given away by the deceased with a certain period before his death (latterly 7 years) was treated as passing on death. Depending on the period between the gift and the death a "taper relief" applied to reduce the value chargeable to duty by varying percentages.

The exemption from duty available—as now from capital transfer tax which superseded estate duty in 1975—for objects of national, scientific, historic or artistic interest could also apply to objects which became liable to duty because they were the subject of a lifetime gift. This notice explains how estate duty charges are to be calculated in future when objects of this kind are sold.

24 July 1984. Inland Revenue
CTT: delivery of Accounts of lifetime transfers

This Press Release acts as a reminder that accounts of transfers within the capital transfer tax nil rate band often need not be made.
1. Under Regulations introduced in December 1981 arrangements were made to relieve taxpayers and their agents of the need to deliver accounts of certain gifts, including terminations of interests in possession in settled property, which are wholly covered by the annual or marriage gifts exemption. Despite that, a substantial number of gifts and terminations covered by the Order are still being notified to the Capital Taxes Offices—either in correspondence or by delivery of an account. This Press Release is therefore by way of a reminder of the existence of the Order, the purpose of which is to simplify the administration of capital transfer tax in circumstances where liability to the tax is unlikely to arise.

Gifts
2. The Order provides that no account need be sent to the Inland Revenue of what is called an "excepted transfer". This term covers a gift made by an individual where—
(a) the amount of the gift and of any other chargeable transfers previously made by the individual in the same income tax year does not exceed £10,000; and
(b) the amount of the gift and of any other chargeable transfers made by the individual in the previous ten years (or since the introduction of the tax on 26 March 1974 when shorter) does not exceed £40,000.

Note
Strictly the amount on which tax is charged is measured not by the value of the gift but by the reduction in the value of the transferor's estate. The word "gift" should be understood in this sense.
3. However, taxpayers should keep their own records of such gifts so that an account can be lodged if required at a later date. In addition if an individual who has not reported a gift in the belief that it was covered by these regulations later finds that it was not, he must deliver an account of it within six months of the time he discovers the omission.
4. Where there has been no account for an excepted transfer and an earlier transfer is discovered, an account of the excepted transfer will be treated as having been delivered on the last day on which it would otherwise have been done, i.e. twelve months after the end of the month in which it was made. This provision facilitates the proper operation of the rules in FA 1976, s. 114 (6) [now IHTA 1984, s. 264 (8)] governing transfers reported late.

Terminations of interests in possession in settled property
5. Under FA 1981, s. 94 [now IHTA 1984, s. 57] an individual may allocate to the trustees of settled property in which he has an interest in possession the whole or part of the annual exemption and of any exemption for marriage gifts to which he may be entitled: the trustees can then apply these exemptions against the termination of that interest (details of this procedure were set out in the Revenue's press notice of 3 April 1981). If the value transferred by the termination is not greater than any exemption thus set against it—an "excepted termination" in the words of the Order—no account need be sent to the Inland Revenue.
6. The Inland Revenue may require the trustee to account to them for any excepted termination but, unless they do so within six months of its date (and except in cases of fraud or failure to disclose material facts), the trustees will then be automatically discharged from the claim to tax (if any) in respect of that termination.

Effective date
7. The Order came into effect on 1 December 1981 in respect of gifts made on or after 1 April 1981 and in respect of terminations of interests on or after 6 April when, s. 94 came into effect.

19 September 1984. I.C.A.E.W.
I.C.A.E.W. Memorandum (TR 557): CTT: "Buy and Sell" agreements

Introduction
1. This guidance note reproduces correspondence between the Inland Revenue and the accountancy bodies regarding the availability of business relief under FA 1976, Sch. 10, para. 3 (4) [now IHTA 1984, s. 113], where, on the death before retirement of a member of a partnership, the deceased's interest is to, or may, pass to the surviving partners.
2. In October 1980 the Inland Revenue issued a Statement of Practice (SP 12/80) entitled "Capital transfer tax—business relief from capital transfer tax: 'buy and sell' agreements".
3. In its issue of 6 May 1981 the *Law Society's Gazette* published a table which summarises the position in various circumstances. It is emphasized that although the Revenue have agreed that this table outlines the general position regard must be had to the construction of the particular agreement and the correct conclusion on the availability of business relief can only be drawn after careful scrutiny of the agreement in each individual case.

Extracts from correspondence
4. Extracts from the correspondence referred to in paragraph 1 are set out in paragraphs 5 to 8 below.

5. Letter dated 10 May 1982 from the accountancy bodies to the Inland Revenue.

The Inland Revenue Statement of Practice SP 12/80 dated 13 October 1980 sets out the views of the Board as to the effect of FA 1976, Sch. 10, para. 3 (4) [now IHTA 1984, s. 113] on agreements between partners or shareholder directors whereby, in the event of death before retirement, the deceased's personal representatives must sell, and the survivors must buy, the deceased's interest in the business.

Paragraph 3 (4) [s. 113] denies relief where business property is the subject of a binding contract of sale which has been entered into at the time of transfer, and the Statement of Practice states that agreements of the type referred to above, commonly known as "buy and sell" agreements, fall within this definition.

It has generally been assumed that paragraph 3 (4) [s. 113] was intended to deny relief where the transferor had decided to cease trading, had entered into a binding contract for the sale of his business, and had subsequently died or given away his interest before completion of the sale. In the words of *Dymond's Capital Taxes*, "There is no point in giving business relief where the property is, in effect, cash realised on the sale of a business" [(para. 24.733)].

However, the Statement of Practice extends the application of paragraph 3 (4) [s. 113] to situations where the sale is to take place only in the event of death before retirement. By inference it is assumed that business relief will also be denied in such circumstances to lifetime transfers, even though there was no intention to cease trading and the sale on death might be expected to be many years away. We consider this practice to be contrary to the intention of the legislation and to give rise to many anomalies because business relief will depend upon the form of words used ratherthan the substance. The following are examples of various forms of partnership provisions and the apparent effect on the availability of business relief.

Partnership provision	*Apparent effect*
(a) On the death in service or retirement of a partner the surviving partners shall purchase his share in the partnership for £X.	If a partner gives away part of his partnership share in his lifetime, or dies in service, business relief will presumably not be available.
(b) On the death in service or retirement of a partner the surviving partners have an option to buy and the retiring partner (or his personal representatives) have an option to sell his share in the partnership.	If a partner gives away part of his partnership share in his lifetime, or dies in service, 50% business relief will be available as an option is not a binding contract for sale.
(c) There is no provision for the purchase of a partner's share. By his will a partner directs that if he dies in service his partnership interest is to be sold.	If he gives away part of his partnership share in his lifetime or dies in service, 50% business relief will be available as there is no binding contract for sale.
(d) On the death in service or retirement of a partner his share is to accrue to the surviving partners who shall pay an annuity to the partner or his widow as appropriate.	If a partner gives away part of his partnership share in his lifetime, or dies in service, is this to be constituted as a binding contract for sale?

We are aware that an article appeared on this subject in the *Law Society's Gazette* of 6 May 1981 ... but it is not clear whether this interpretation has the approval of the Revenue.

6. Reply from the Inland Revenue dated 5 July 1982.

The purpose of paragraph 3 (4) [s. 113] was to limit business relief to transfers of business property. To that end paragraph 3 (4) [s. 113] denies relief when—because of a binding contract for sale—what the transferor passes to the transferee is in effect an entitlement to the sale consideration rather than the right to a continuing business interest. While in principle therefore relief is not available on a transfer of business property which is bound by a contract for sale, the decision in any case involving the transfer of an interest in a partnership will depend on the terms of the partnership agreement. It was this situation which our Statement of Practice SP 12/80 was designed to illuminate (its purpose was not to—nor, of course, could it—extend the scope of paragraph 3 (4) [s. 113]).

In your examples (b) and (c) business relief will be available, but taking example (a) against this background it is clear that business relief will not be available on a partner's death in service or retirement. But if the contract for sale is not operative in his lifetime so that he can give his interest away—and it continues as a business interest in the hands of the recipient—then business relief will be available. Similarly in example (d) business relief will be available on a lifetime transfer of a partner's interest if the accrual clause and annuity provision does not then come into operation; but if it does, spouse exemption may be due to the extent of the value of the annuity. On death in service there would again be no business relief, but exemption would be due on the widow's annuity. In the case of example (d) the capital gains tax Statement of Practice of 17 January 1975 may also be in point. Any chargeable gains accruing to a retired partner would be computed by comparing the consideration received (including the capitalised value of the annuity) with the capital gains tax "cost", or the market value at the date of death for the personal representatives of a deceased partner.

While I accept that this is not a straightforward area, the effect does not seem to me to be contrary to the intention of the legislation, nor would there appear to be anomalies. The substance of the agreement is different in the different examples so it is not surprising that the tax consequences are also different.

Finally, for the sake of completeness, the article in the *Law Society's Gazette* for 6 May 1981 correctly states the general position since it is only in the final case that a binding contract for sale exists before the death of the partner.

7. Letter dated 19 January 1983 from the accountancy bodies to the Inland Revenue.

We think it would be helpful to publish our substantive correspondence, but before doing so it would be useful to clarify one point, which relates to FA 1976, Sch. 10, para. 3 (4) [now IHTA 1984, s. 113], and the view expressed in SP 12/80. This Statement of Practice states that a "buy and sell" agreement is outlined therein, is a binding contract for sale within paragraph 3 (4) [s. 113] so that it is not relevant business property and therefore business relief will not be due.

The argument against this view is that tax is charged on the death of any person "as if, *immediately before his death*, he had made a transfer of value and the value transferred by it had been equal to the value of his estate immediately before his death, but subject to the following provisions of this section". (FA 1975, s. 22 (1) [now IHTA 1984, s. 4 (1)].) The deemed transfer of value is, by definition, treated as made at a time when the deceased was alive. Paragraph 3 (4), [s. 113] provides:

"Where any property would be relevant business property in relation to a transfer of value but a binding contract for its sale has been entered into *at the time of the transfer*, it is not relevant business property in relation to the transfer . . .".

At the time of the deemed transfer value, the terms of the "buy and sell" agreement will not have been operative. In the case of a partnership, the agreement is conditional upon the death of a partner.

We suggest that the view in SP 12/80 ignores the effect of section 22 (1) [now s. 4 (1)], and treats the transfer as taking place on, or immediately after, the death of the partner. On a strict construction (and if the Revenue are to withhold the relief, a strict construction is called for) it is submitted that the Revenue view is incorrect.

It should be added, for the avoidance of doubt, that FA 1975, Sch. 10, para. 9 [now IHTA 1984, s. 171 (1)] is not applicable in these circumstances. That paragraph [subsection] is relevant only for the purposes of determining changes in the value of a person's estate occurring by reason of his death. This has no bearing on the question of the availability of relief in respect of the value of property comprised in a person's estate.

8. Reply from the Inland Revenue dated 8 February 1983.

Thank you for your letter of 19 January. It brings into focus the cause of our differing views on the application of paragraph 3 (4) [s. 113].

It is common ground that paragraph 3 (4) [s. 113] excludes from the CTT business relief property which is subject to a binding contract for sale at "the time of the transfer". You argue that FA 1975, s. 22 (1) [IHTA 1984, s. 4 (1)] is authority for the view that for the purposes of the tax the time of a transfer on death is immediately before the death. A buy and sell agreement in a partnership deed which comes into operation only at the moment of death cannot be taken to fetter a partner's interest immediately before his death. Hence on this view it could not amount to a binding contract for sale at the time of the transfer and the partner's interest would qualify for business relief.

We consider however that this approach overlooks the complementary effect of FA 1975, s. 51 (2) [now IHTA 1984, s. 3 (4)]. Section 22 (1) [s. 4 (1)] provides that an event—namely death— shall be an occasion of charge and requires a valuation to be made by reference to a hypothetical transfer before death. Section 51 (2) [s. 3 (4)] effectively provides that the "event", *i.e.* the death, is itself a transfer of value. It follows therefore that when a binding contract for sale exists at the date of death, *i.e.* at the time of the statutory transfer of value within section 51 (2) [s. 3 (4)], paragraph 3 (4) [s. 113] operates to exclude business relief.

I do not consider this to be an unreasonably strict interpretation of the legislation. It is consistent with the scheme of the tax to charge on death the value of the property which is transferred and a partner whose interest is bound by a buy and sell agreement which becomes effective at the moment of his death can only transfer his interest subject to that agreement. It is equally consistent with the scheme of business relief to deny relief in circumstances in which the deceased partner's estate receives, and is taxed on, a sum of money.

I have not commented on your penultimate paragraph since, as you will see, our construction does not rely on Sch. 10, para. 9 [s. 171 (1)].

22 May 1985. Law Society's Gazette
Deeds of variation (IHTA 1984, s. 142)

The Revenue have taken further advice on the interpretation of IHTA 1984, s. 142 and have indicated that the following conditions must be satisfied by an instrument if it is to be brought within that provision—
1. the instrument in writing must be made by the persons or any of the persons who benefit or would benefit under the dispositions of the property comprised in the deceased's estate immediately before his death;
2. the instrument must be made within two years after the death;
3. the instrument must clearly indicate the dispositions that are the subject of it, and vary their destination as laid down by the deceased's will, or under the law relating to intestate estates, or otherwise;
4. a notice of election must be given within six months of the date of the instrument, unless the Board see fit to accept a late election; and
5. the notice of election must refer to the appropriate statutory provisions.

It is likely that the application of these principles will mean that most cases in which there were thought to be technical objections to instruments of variation will now be accepted. It will not be contended that the instrument of variation, to be eligible, has in terms to purport to vary the will or intestacy provisions themselves: it is sufficient if the instrument of variation identifies the disposition to be varied and varies its destination. It is emphasised, however, that the Revenue will continue to require that the provisions of IHTA 1984, s. 142 as interpreted above, are satisfied.

There have been some cases in which a number of instruments of variation have been executed in relation to the same will or intestacy. The Revenue emphasise that these cases must be considered on their precise facts, but in broad terms their views will be as follows—
(*a*) an election which is validly made is irrevocable;
(*b*) an instrument will not fall within IHTA 1984, s. 142 if it *further* redirects any item or any part of an item that has *already* been redirected under an earlier instrument; and
(*c*) to avoid any uncertainty, variations covering a number of items should ideally be made in one instrument.

25 July 1985. Inland Revenue
Capital Taxes Office

The movement of work relating to CTT matters in England and Wales, from the office at Hinchley Wood to the main Capital Taxes Office at Minford House, Rockley Road, London W14 0DF (telephone: 071-603 4622) is now entering a new phase.

The examination of estates prima facie below the capital transfer tax threshold is being moved in stages to Minford House over the coming months. Practitioners may therefore receive letters in such cases from either building. They should reply to the address from which the letter originated, though arrangements will be made to ensure replies are redirected to the appropriate building if necessary. Practitioners and members of the public should now also direct general enquiries concerning non-taxpaying cases to the Minford House enquiries section (071-603 4622 ext 214 and 241).

Some work on individual cases prior to a grant of representation is also being moved in stages to Minford House, but certain internal Revenue work such as indexing remains at Hinchley Wood.

This does not affect the information and enquiries normally sent to CTOs in Edinburgh or Belfast, which should continue to be directed there.

25 September 1985. ICAEW
TR 588: Furniss v. Dawson

Guidance note TR588 was issued in September 1985 by the Institute of Chartered Accountants in England and Wales, comprising—

Text of a letter dated 8 July 1985 to the Inland Revenue following a meeting between representatives of the Institute of Chartered Accountants in England and Wales, The Law Society and the Inland Revenue.
Text of a reply dated 20 September 1985 from the Board of Inland Revenue.

The Revenue reply is reproduced in full below, following the corresponding paragraphs from the Institute's letter.

From the text of a letter dated 8 July 1985 from the Institute of Chartered Accountants in England and Wales—

Furniss v. Dawson

We are grateful to you and your colleagues for meeting representatives of the Institute and The Law Society on 10 June 1985.

Introduction
1. The meeting can conveniently be divided into two parts: the need for short-term guidance and the longer-term aspects. As explained at the meeting, although both we and The Law Society are concerned with both aspects it was felt appropriate for us to concern ourselves primarily with the former and for the The Law Society to cover the latter aspect. We identified certain areas which are of immediate concern, although as stated at the meeting this is by no means intended to be exhaustive.
2. We agreed to write further on certain aspects of the matters to which we referred and, for the sake of completeness, all of the areas which we mentioned are set out in paragraphs 4–21 below. We have also referred to the need for clarification as to the instructions given to inspectors.
3. As we mentioned at our meeting the areas which we have identified below arise from no more than a quick review of topics which have been raised following the *Furniss v Dawson* decision ([1984] STC 153, HL). The fact that they have been raised is indicative of their importance but, as stated at the meeting, the list is not exhaustive and further areas might need to be covered in due course. ....

Note
The rest of this letter (paras 4–29) is reproduced below, before the corresponding paragraphs of the Revenue's reply.

From the text of a reply dated 20 September 1985 from the Board of Inland Revenue

I am writing in reply to your letter of 8 July.

As you know, the Board very much welcomed the recent opportunity to discuss with the Institute of Chartered Accountants and The Law Society the implications of the judgments handed down by the House of Lords in the cases of *Ramsay, Burmah* and *Dawson*.

Clearly, the interpretation of the *Ramsay* and *Dawson* judgments is a matter for the courts. It will be for the courts, not for officials, to determine the law. However, you have explained that, meanwhile, there are a number of points on which practitioners and businesses would find it helpful to have a note of how the Revenue understands the position, and in this letter I try to respond accordingly.

We start with much common ground between us. Perhaps the shortest and simplest explanation of the "new approach" was given by Lord Wilberforce, when he said that "legislation cannot be required . . . to enable the courts to arrive at a conclusion which corresponds with the parties' own intentions". I think many of us accept that this "new approach" brings interpretation of the law in this area closer to the reality, or if you like the substance, of the transactions with which it has to deal. We are also conscious that it has also brought with it a measure of uncertainty: partly because by its nature it requires us all to take a rather broader view of the legal implications of a transaction or series of transactions; but partly also because the approach is "new" and (as the House of Lords themselves have emphasised) will no doubt be refined further, as the courts come to consider more cases.

I do not want to get this out of proportion. It is commonplace that the courts in North America and a number of European countries have been following somewhat similar approaches for many years. And even in this country a number of fundamental questions for tax purposes—for example, the existence of a "partnership", of "employment", of "income" itself—have always been left undefined in the taxing statutes: there is such a wide and complex variety of facts and real-life relationships that, accepting some inevitable uncertainty at the margin, the tax code does not attempt to capture them in a mechanical formula but leaves them to be determined in the last resort by the courts, having regard to the actual facts of the particular case. Having said that, we are all agreed that the line of reasoning in *Ramsay* and subsequent cases represents a new and important development. When we discussed these issues with the Institute and the Society, we in the Revenue confirmed our readiness to co-operate with you in reducing uncertainties of this kind and (where possible) removing them. Taxpayers should not be burdened by unnecessary uncertainty in judging the likely tax consequences of their actions; and I might add that uncertainty of this kind can also make more difficult the work of those who are responsible for administering the Taxes Acts.

On your side, the Institute recognised that, whilst we could try to help with guidance and clarification of the Revenue's attitude in the normal or more straightforward case, we are not in a position to give categorical assurances. In particular, we might well take one view of a transaction standing on its own; we might take another view—and I think this follows necessarily from the approach described by Lord Wilberforce—where a similar transaction was one step in a series of transactions apparently designed to avoid tax. You have therefore said that the Institute appreciates that any response which we are able to give must be subject to the caveat that, even where it is agreed that the Revenue would not as a rule seek to invoke the *Ramsay* and *Dawson* principle, there may well be individual cases where, because of the circumstances, the Revenue would nevertheless feel it was obliged to follow the *Ramsay* and *Dawson* approach. In particular, we may need to look at all the facts of the case in order to establish the nature and legal implications of the transaction. What follows is to be read in that spirit.

I thought that it would be helpful to spell out all this, even at the cost of some length. And it is against this background that I now try to give you as positive and helpful a response as we can, at this stage, to the 10 specific questions which the Institute has raised with us. . . .

Capital transfer tax
11. (*a*) The CTT regime contains anti-avoidance legislation of a wide-ranging nature relating to associated operations, basically IHTA 1984, s. 268, under which gifts are to include other associated transactions affecting the same property. The doctrine arising from *Furniss v Dawson* makes for additional uncertainty and it would be helpful to have an assurance that where, as in this case, specific anti-avoidance legislation exists, an attempt will not be made to extend it.

(*b*) We understand that, in response to our enquiry at the meeting, you agreed that the Revenue would not seek to disturb existing practice under which taxpayers arrange their affairs so as to take advantage of the exemption for inter-spouse transfers.

(*c*) We sought confirmation that the *Furniss v Dawson* principle would not apply to inheritance trusts.

Revenue response: You suggest it would be helpful to have an assurance that where *specific anti-avoidance legislation* like IHTA 1984, s. 286 exists no attempt will be made to extend it by using a *Ramsay* approach. You will recall that the question of the relationship between the emerging principle in *Ramsay* and anti-avoidance provisions was considered in the *Ramsay* case. Lord Wilberforce said—

"I have a full respect for the principles which have been stated but I do not consider that they should exclude the approach for which the Crown contends. That does not introduce a new principle: it would be to apply to new and sophisticated legal devices the undoubted power and duty of the courts to determine their nature in law and to relate them to existing legislation. While the techniques of tax avoidance progress and are technically improved, the courts are not obliged to stand still. Such immobility must result either in loss of tax, to the prejudice of other taxpayers, or to Parliamentary congestion or (most likely) to both."

It is our understanding, therefore, that the *Ramsay* approach is applicable in the context of specific anti-avoidance legislation and outside it, depending upon the facts of the case.

I can confirm that we would not seek to disturb existing practices in relation to *inter-spouse transfers*. It should, however, be borne in mind that the circumstances of such transfers always need to be carefully examined to ensure, among other things, that the transaction has substance as well as form. (For example, an understanding between the spouses on the ultimate destination of the assets would be important in this connection.) In general the terms of the Press Release of 8 April 1975 (see *Simon's Tax Intelligence* 1975, p. 180) remain valid as a description of the practice in this area.

The wide-ranging nature of the term "*inheritance trusts*" makes it difficult to give the confirmation you seek. The term can be used rather loosely in the context of insurance schemes and, while some of these may be regarded as not open to challenge, others are; and cases will be going to the Special Commissioners in due course.

21 April 1986. Law Society's Gazette
Assets used for life tenant's business: business property relief

Under the code in IHTA 1984, ss. 103 to 114, business property relief is given at either 30 per cent. or 50 per cent. by adjusting the valuation of "relevant business property" as defined in s. 105. In *Featherstonehaugh* v. *Commissioners of Inland Revenue* [1984] STC 261, it was decided that relief at what is now the 50 per cent. rate was available for land on which a sole trader was life tenant and on which he had carried on a farming business prior to the transfer on his death.

The Inland Revenue's understanding of this decision is that, where there is a transfer of value of a life tenant's business or interest in a business (including assets of which he was life tenant which were used in that business), the case falls within s. 105 (1) (*a*) and the 50 per cent. relief is available. Where, by contrast, the transfer of value is only of any land, building, machinery or plant, used wholly or mainly for the purposes of a business carried on by the life tenant and in which he had an interest in possession under a settlement, the relief is only available at the rate of 30 per cent. if the transfer takes place in circumstances in which the business itself is not being disposed of.

Thus, if land in a settlement has been used for the purpose of the life tenant's business, the 50 per cent. relief is only available if the transfer of value is one of his business as a whole (or an interest in it), including the property in which he has a life interest.

10 June 1986. Hansard
Gifts with reservation

See Inland Revenue letter, 18 May 1987.

9 July 1986. Inland Revenue
IHT: death benefits under superannuation arrangements

See SP10/86, Appendix 2.

21 August 1986. I.C.A.E.W.
TR631: Finance Bill 1986 Section B: inheritance tax

Notes of meeting with the Revenue on 4 June 1986.

Clause 80 and Schedule 18 (now s. 101 and Sch. 19): lifetime transfers potentially exempt etc.

Paragraph 1 (IHTA 1984, s. 3A)
1. The Institute regretted the extra complexity and uncertainty flowing from the new regime; and contrasted the treatment of trusts and absolute gifts. The Revenue commented that Ministers had taken a firm decision to restrict the favourable potentially exempt transfer treatment to outright gifts between individuals.
2. The Revenue said that the value regarded as a potentially exempt transfer would generally be the same as the amount that would otherwise have been a chargeable transfer. For example, where one individual made an outright gift to another of shares out of a controlling shareholding, the amount of the potentially exempt transfer would be the loss to the donor's estate rather than the value of the shares in isolation. In response to a point not in the representations, the Revenue agreed that there could in theory be some rare and contrived situations (*e.g.*, waiver of rights) where the quantum of the chargeable transfer could be greater than the potentially exempt transfer exemption. These would be considered if they ever arose.
3. The potentially exempt transfer treatment of gifts into accumulation and maintenance settlements recognised the fact that it was often not possible or practicable to make outright gifts to minors. Arguably, the age 25 ceiling for these trusts was too generous for special regime designed for those under legal disability. The Institute argued that there were some over the age of 25 who might be thought unable to manage large sums of capital, and asked for their views about the relatively harsh treatment of trusts for the over-25s to be passed to Ministers.
4. Where a settlor of an accumulation and maintenance trust wanted to get potentially exempt treatment for the payment of premiums on a life policy, written upon trust for beneficiaries, he could provide the trust with the funds from which the trustees could pay the premiums.
5. The Institute felt that the CTT regime of contemporary accounts of transfers had led to disciplined record-keeping. Under the new regime, there could be large contingent liabilities, and

large items to enter settlor's cumulation, for up to seven years. Investigation of transfers after the donor's death would be difficult both for Revenue and taxpayer, especially where matters like share valuations were involved. The Revenue felt that the taxpayers who were used to the record-keeping disciplines of the CTT era might find it no great burden to keep records appropriate to the return to estate duty-style queries after the death.

Paragraph 3 (2) (IHTA 1984, s. 8)
6. The Institute accepted that in a provision determining what tax rate scale would apply, it was sufficient to look at the date rather than the moment of death.

Paragraph 13 (now 20) (IHTA 1984, s. 98)
7. It was agreed that a close company's transfer of value apportioned under IHTA 1984, s. 94 was treated as if each participator had made a separate transfer of an appropriate amount, and was thus not a potentially exempt transfer because of new s. 3A (6) introduced by paragraph 1 of this Schedule.

Paragraph 14 (now 21) (IHTA 1984, ss. 113A, 113B)
8. The shift to inheritance tax meant that the date of death joined the date of gift as being relevant to relief on qualifying property. Where, say, a business was gifted and the donor died within seven years, then as a general matter of policy the relief attributable to qualifying property should be available only if appropriate qualifying property were held at the time the tax charge arose. Report Stage amendments allowed for the replacement of one qualifying property with similar qualifying property
9. Since business and agricultural relief were only relevant to chargeable transfers, the new legislation could appropriately refer to potentially exempt transfers proving to be chargeable transfers rather than referring to transfers of value. Problems of identification of shares where the donee acquired and disposed of shares of the same type existed already.

Paragraph 15 (now 22) (IHTA 1984, ss. 124A, 124B)
10. Report Stage amendments covered conversion in the period between gift and death of agricultural land into shares in a company holding the land.

Paragraph 22 (now 29) (IHTA 1984, s. 216)
11. The Revenue thought it unlikely that donees would be unaware of the fate of a donor, but agreed to consider how to publicise the accounting duties placed on donees by this year's legislation. Arguably, the problems were no worse than under estate duty. Possible changes to the enforcement or penalty regime resulting from the Keith Committee recommendations would be the subject of consultation.

Paragraph 24 (now 31) (IHTA 1984, s. 217)
12. Under CTT, if a person in life settled property on discretionary trusts, the entitlement to the instalment option ended when the property passed out of the trust to a beneficiary. The inheritance tax position would be no worse.

Clause 81 and Schedule 19 (now s. 97 and Schedule 20)—gifts with reservation
13. It was true that the new legislation greatly increased the importance of the concept of a gift. This was because the gifts with reservation rules focussed on the disposition of property, while CTT focussed on transfers of value. "Gift" was not defined, but was left to its natural meaning of disposition of property with an element of bounty. While some estate duty case law on gifts with reservation was uncertain, this corpus of law would nevertheless be of assistance.
14. The Revenue noted that the regulation-making powers had been extended to cover other cases not yet identified. The Institute would be invited to comment of the coverage of the proposed regulations. However, it might be that some areas of apparent double charge were on closer inspection separate occasions of charge. The Revenue would consider whether relief was appropriate where, for example, the removal of property from a discretionary trust where it had been subject to a reservation for the settlor gave rise both to a discretionary trust proportionate charge and to a later gift with remuneration charge on the settlor's death.
15. The Revenue did not see there need to be reservation of benefit merely because a donor was a trustee of his settlement, as he could not benefit from his trust without specific provisions to this effect. IHTA 1984, s. 90 would take some if not all trustees' remuneration out of any gift with reservation charge.
16. There was no intention for the gifts with reservations provisions to alter the present treatment of pension and retirement annuity schemes.

Schedule 19 (now Schedule 20), paragraph 6 (2)
17. The point of paragraph 6 (2) had been dealt with at Committee.

Clause 82 (now s. 103)—Treatment of certain debts and encumbrances
18. In practice, the Revenue treated guarantee debts as incurred for full consideration (*e.g.*, the

granting of credit by the creditor to the principal debtor). Such a debt would be allowed as a deduction from the death estate, subject to the general rule in IHTA 1984, s. 162 (1), for all debts with a right to reimbursement—the deduction is limited to what cannot reasonably be expected to be reimbursed. Bona fide commercial debts did not need a specific exemption. They would come within [FA 1986, s. 103 (1)] if the creditor had had property derived from the deceased. If they did, there was no reason to allow a deduction for them simply because a full rate of interest was charged, but the escape route in [s. 103 (2) (*b*)] could help.

19. The Revenue did not feel it was right in principle that the escape under the "purpose" test in [s. 103 (2) (*b*)] should be extended to the case where the consideration for the loan was property derived from the deceased. In practice under estate duty, the loan was in genuine cases made out of property which neither was nor represented property derived from the deceased; hence no problem.

Effective date for new tax tables
20. Amendents had been made to provide an explicit rather than implicit table of tax rates. This would indeed be effective from 18 March 1986.

10 November 1986. Inland Revenue
IHT/CTT treatment of income of discretionary trusts

1. Following legal advice the Revenue today announced a change in the way that income of discretionary trusts is treated in determining the liability to IHT/CTT.
2. The change in practice means that:
   (*a*) income which has neither been distributed to beneficiaries of the trust nor been accumulated—*i.e.* added to the trust—will be excluded from the tax charge on discretionary trusts; and
   (*b*) accumulated income will be treated as an asset of the trust separate from the original property from which it derives, in calculating the rate of charge on that income.
3. Statement of Practice (SP 8/86), see Appendix 2, contains details of the change.

Note
1. A discretionary trust is one under which no particular individual has the right to receive the income arising from the trust assets—for example, where the income can be distributed at the trustees' discretion—or where the trustees can or must accumulate the income.
2. All the assets held in a discretionary trust immediately before each 10-year anniversary of the trust are taxed at 10-yearly intervals.
3. Property leaving the discretionary regime is liable to a proportionate charge—a time-based fraction of the 10-yearly charge.
4. The rate of tax is reduced for any property that has not been in the discretionary trust regime throughout the period for which the charge applies.
5. Up to now, income from trust property which has been neither distributed to beneficiaries nor accumulated has been treated as a chargeable asset. Undistributed income (whether or not accumulated) has been regarded as being in the trust for as long as the property from which it derives.
6. For all the new cases—as well as existing cases where the tax liability is yet to be settled— undistributed and unaccumulated income will not be brought into the tax charge. The rate of tax on accumulated income will be reduced according to the date on which the property from which that income derives was put into the trust.

19 November 1986. Inland Revenue
IHT: interest on unpaid and overpaid tax

In response to a Parliamentary Question the Financial Secretary to the Treasury, the Rt. Hon. Norman Lamont M.P., has announced that for the future there will be only one rate of interest on IHT (previously CTT) paid late or overpaid.

The new single rate replaces the separate rates which previously applied depending on whether the transfer took place in lifetime or on death. This will provide a worthwhile simplification for all concerned.

The new single rate will be kept broadly in line with other rates, but it is not likely to change as often as the rates for other taxes. Very frequent changes in the IHT rates of interest would cause extra work in the administration of the tax which is often paid by instalments over up to 10 years.
See IHTA 1984, s. 233 and IR Press Release 23 September 1988.

10 December 1986. Law Society's Gazette
IHT—gifts with reservation (FA 1986, s. 102).

The following exchange of correspondence between Vic Washtell of Touche Ross on 29 August 1986 and the Controller of the Capital Taxes Office on 29 October 1986 was published in *The Law Society's Gazette* on 10 December 1986.

Could you please let us know whether the Inland Revenue intends to issue a statement of practice regarding the Revenue's view on various types of gift which they would treat as gifts with reservation under the new inheritance tax legislation, If not, could you please let us know whether or not the Revenue would regard gifts in the following situations as gifts with reservation.

As you will doubtless appreciate, any question about the existence and/or extent of any future liability to tax can be determined only in accordance with the particular facts on the basis of the law as it is understood to be. However, in order to be as helpful to you as I can at this stage, I would offer the following comments on the situations outlined in your letter.

1. *A transfers assets into a discretionary settlement. The class of beneficiaries includes A's wife at the trustees' discretion on a regular basis.*

The mere fact that the donor's spouse is a member of the class of potential beneficiaries would not suffice to bring the gift within the provisions of FA 1986 s. 102, *[gifts with reservation]*. I should, however, draw your attention to Sch. 20 para. 6 (1) (c) and 7 *[associated operations and certain life assurance arrangements]*.

2. *B transfers assets into a discretionary settlement under which he is not included in the class of beneficiaries (including B) to the class of beneficiaries in future.*

As you probably know the inclusion of the settlor among the class of beneficiaries subject to powers contained in his trust is considered to be sufficient to constitute his gift as a gift with reservation. Where there is a possibility of the settlor becoming included in the class of beneficiaries by exercise of a power in the settlement, it is considered likely that this would again constitute a gift with reservation.

3. *C buys a house and puts it into the name of himself and his wife as tenants in common. On the death of the wife her share of the house passes to the son absolutely. C remains in occupation of the property. On the death of C is the whole or only C's half of the property treated as part of his estate for inheritance tax purposes?*

Having regard to FA 1986, s. 102 (5) (a), *[exempt transfers between spouses]* it is not considered that the original gift to C's wife would constitute a gift with reservation. However, the death of C might give rise to a claim for tax on other grounds but this would fall for consideration in the light of the precise facts as they were shown to be at that time.

4. *D owns freehold property and grants a lease to himself and his wife for twenty years at a peppercorn. D then gifts the reversionary interest in the property to his son.*

If the true construction of the transactions here is that the gift to the son is of the reversionary interest only in the property then the gift would not constitute a gift with reservation.

5. *E gifts all of his shares in his family company into an accumulation and maintenance settlement for his children under which E is a trustee.*

The mere fact that E is a trustee of an accumulation and maintenance settlement for his children would not of itself involve a reservation to him.

6. *F owns a home and some adjacent land. F gifts the land but retains the house.*

If the situation is such that the subject matter of the gift is the land only, I do not see that this constitutes a gift with reservation.

7. *G, a non-domiciliary, gifts excluded property into a discretionary settlement under which he is in the class of beneficiaries. G dies domiciled in the U.K. Are the "excluded property" assets in the settlement treated as part of G's estate?*

Here it seems to me that the settled property would be "property subject to a reservation" in relation to the settlor. Accordingly it would fall within FA 1986, s. 102 (3) to be treated as property to which he was beneficially entitled immediately before his death. The effect would be to lock the property into the settlor's estate within the meaning of CTTA/IHTA 1984, s. 5 (1), which is subject to the exception for "excluded property". It would follow that in the case of settled property, relief for foreign assets could continue to be available under *ibid.*, s. 48 (3) provided that the settlor was domiciled outside the U.K. at the time the settlement was made.

8. *Kindly confirm that Statement of Practice E10 will apply for inheritance tax purposes* [vendor retaining a lease for life].

As you will know SP/E10 applies in the context of the FA 1975, Sch. 5 now para. 1 (3), CTTA/IHTA 1984, *[lease for life treated as a settlement]*. In the context of gifts with reservation, I might perhaps draw your attention to FA 1986, Sch. 20 para. 6 (1) (a) *[occupation, enjoyment or possession by the donor to be disregarded if for full consideration]*.

The Controller's letter concludes:

I would emphasise that each case must be looked at in the light of its own particular facts. Too much should not be read, therefore, into general comments on the bare situations outlined in your letter which may not, in the event, be found to apply to the facts of an individual case.

In a separate development, the Revenue has confirmed to the Association of British Insurers that the following do **not** constitute gifts with reservation:

(*a*) A whole life policy effected by the life assured in trusts for X should X survive the life assured, but otherwise for the life assured.

(*b*) An endowment effected by the life assured in trust for X if living at the death of the life assured before the maturity date but otherwise for the life assured.

Also, the Revenue has confirmed that if a gift with reservation is made into a pre-Budget day trust, this will **not** 'taint' the whole trust fund so as to make the funds settled before Budget day liable to inheritance tax.

9 February 1986. Hansard
CTT: heritage property

Mr. David Clark asked the Chancellor of the Exchequer what machinery he has established about publicising landscape schemes offset against capital transfer tax under FA 1976.

Mr. Norman Lamont: Publicity about public access to heritage property which has been conditionally exempted from capital tax is incorporated in the terms of the management agreement which is negotiated to give effect to the undertakings about preservation and public access that are required as a precondition of exemption. Requirements will differ from case to case but, outstanding chattels apart (for which different arrangements apply), these will normally comprise some or all of the following:

(*a*) Owner to inform the British Tourist Authority (the Scottish Tourist Board and the Highlands and Islands Development Board in Scotland) of the opening arrangements and subsequent changes.

(*b*) Owner to advertise the opening arrangements in one or more suitable publications with national circulation.

(*c*) Owner to display a notice outside the property giving details of the opening arrangements.

(*d*) Owner to agree that the advisory body or bodies (or its/or their agents), which confirmed the property's eligible quality and with whom the terms of the detailed management agreement will have been negotiated, can divulge the access arrangements to anyone who enquires about them.

(*e*) Owner to agree to such other publicity as the advisory body, or bodies, consider to be appropriate. This could include displaying a notice in some public place in the locality (*e.g.* the local post office, local library, local tourist office or town hall) or in a local preservation society's newsletter.

The managment agreement would also normally provide scope for additional measures to be agreed, if appropriate, between the owner and the advisory body or bodies at a later stage.

See IHTA 1984, s. 27 and Sch. 4.

8 April 1987. Inland Revenue
Acceptance of property in lieu of IHT, CTT and estate duty

See SP6/87, Appendix 2.

18 May 1987. Inland Revenue letter
IHT: gifts with reservation

I am now able to write to you about the points concerning the provisions on gifts with reservation.

It does not seem realistic to think in terms of precise and comprehensive guidance on how the gifts with reservation provisions will be interpreted and applied since so much will turn on the particular facts of individual cases. However, as the provisions are similar to those adopted for estate duty, the relevant estate duty case law and practice provide a helpful guide to the interpretation and application of the IHT legislation. That said, may I turn to your specific concerns.

Gifts of land
1. Consistent with the assurance given last year by the Minister of State in Standing Committee G (Hansard, 10 June 1986, col. 425) the estate duty practice on the treatment of gifts involving a share in a house where the gifted property is occupied by all the joint owners including the donor will apply. The donor's retention of a share in the property will not by itself amount to a reservation. If, and for so long as, all the joint owners remain in occupation, the donor's occupation will not be

treated as a reservation provided the gift is itself unconditional and there is no collateral benefit to the donor. The payment by the donee of the donor's share of the running costs, for example, might be such a benefit. An arrangement will not necessarily be jeopardised merely because it involves a gift of an unequal share in a house.

2. In other cases the donor's occupation or enjoyment of the gifted land will only be disregarded if the occupation is for full consideration in money or money's worth as provided in FA 1986, Sch. 20, para. 6 (1) (*a*) (or if it is by way of a reasonable "care and maintenance" provision within para. 6 (1) (*b*)). Whether an arrangement is for full consideration will of course depend on the precise facts. But among the attributes of an acceptable arrangement would be the existence of a bargain negotiated at arm's length by parties who were independently advised and which followed the normal commercial criteria in force at the time it was negotiated.

3. You raised the possibility that a donor might give his house subject to a prior lease created in his own favour. Consistent with the principles established in the case of *Munro* v. *Commissioners of Stamp Duties (New South Wales)* [1934] AC 61, we would not normally expect the donor's retention of the lease to constitute a reservation, assuming that the creation of the lease and the subsequent gift of the property subject to that lease are independent transactions. The application or otherwise of the decision in *Re Nichols* [1975] 1 WLR 534 concerning a (donee) landlord's covenants would be a matter for determination in the light of all the facts at the time of the donor's death.

Gifts involving family businesses or farms
4. A gift involving a family business or farm will not necessarily amount to a gift with reservation merely because the donor remains in the business, perhaps as a director or a partner. For example, where the gift is of shares of a company, the continuation of reasonable commercial arrangements in the form of remuneration for the donor's ongoing services to the company entered into before the gift will not of itself amount to a reservation provided the remuneration is in no way linked to or beneficially affected by the gift. Similar considerations will apply in the case where the gift is into trust which empowered a trustee, who may be the donor, to retain director's fees etc. for his own benefit.

5. The "Munro" principle will also be relevant in determining the tax treatment of gifts affecting family farms where the donor and the donee continue to farm the land in pursuance of arrangements entered into prior to and independently of the gift. In cases where this principle does not apply, the test of "full consideration" for the purposes of para. 6 (1) (*a*) will need to be satisfied with regard to the donor's occupation of the land. In applying that test we shall take account of all the circumstances surrounding the arrangement including the sharing of profits and losses, the donor's and the donee's interests in the land, and their respective commitment and expertise.

Gifts of chattels
6. You referred to potential difficulties in determining what amounts to "full consideration" for the donor's continued enjoyment of gifted chattels, particularly pictures and paintings, for the purposes of Sch. 20, para. 6. These may not be insuperable, as appears from the recent case of *I.R. Comrs.* v. *Macpherson* [[1987] STC 73], and in any event it would be difficult to overturn an arm's length, commercial arrangement entered into by parties who were independently advised.

Settlor's retention of reversion
7. In the case where a gift is made into trust, the retention by the settlor (donor) of a reversionary interest under the trust is not considered to constitute a reservation, whether the retained interest arises under the express terms of the trust or it arises by operation of general law e.g. a resulting trust.

2 July 1987. Inland Revenue
IHT: reduction in requirements for delivery of accounts on death

1. In order to simplify the administration of small estates, regulations were introduced in 1981 to dispense with the need in smaller straightforward estates to deliver an account for the purposes of capital transfer tax—now inheritance tax. These regulations (the "excepted estates" regulations) were amended in 1983 so that, provided the criteria were met, there was no requirement to deliver an account where the gross value of the deceased's estate did not exceed £40,000.

2. Regulations were laid on 1 July 1987 that will increase the "excepted estates" limit to £70,000 in England and Wales, Scotland and Northern Ireland.

Details of the new regulations
3. Under these new regulations, with effect from 1 August 1987, an account need not be delivered for inheritance tax purposes of the estate, called an "excepted estate", of any person who died on or after 1 April 1987 where:

(i) the total gross value of the estate for tax purposes does not exceed £70,000 (formerly £40,000);

(ii) the estate comprises only property which has passed under the deceased's will or intestacy, or by nomination, or beneficially by survivorship;

(iii) not more than £10,000 (formerly £2,000) consists of property situated outside the U.K.; and

(iv) the deceased died domiciled in the U.K. and had made no lifetime gifts chargeable to either inheritance tax or CTT.

4. Estates where the deceased had an interest in settled property are not "excepted estates".

5. Where the value of an estate is attributable in part to property passing by survivorship in joint tenancy, it is the value of the deceased's beneficial interest in that property which is taken into account for the purpose of the £70,000 limit.

6. Three orders have been laid:

—The Inheritance Tax (Delivery of Accounts) Regulations 1987—S.I. 1987 No. 1127 applies to England and Wales.

—The Inheritance Tax (Delivery of Accounts) (Scotland) Regulations 1987—S.I. 1987 No. 1128 applies to Scotland.

—The Inheritance Tax (Delivery of Accounts) (Northern Ireland) Regulations 1987—S.I. 1987 No. 1129 applies to Northern Ireland.

All have the same effective date.

7. Each order amends the Principal Regulations made for capital transfer tax in 1981 (S.I. 1981 No. 880, S.I. 1981 No. 881 and S.I. 1981 No. 1441 respectively) which were first amended in 1983 (S.I. 1983 No. 1039, S.I. 1983 No. 1040 and S.I. 1983 No. 1911 respectively). Copies of the new and the earlier regulations are obtainable from HM Stationery Office. Until the new regulations come into force the previous regulations will continue to operate.

8. These regulations do not affect the present requirements on lifetime transfers (S.I. 1981 No. 1440) that were introduced in 1981.

Potentially exempt transfers and gifts with reservation

9. A "potentially exempt transfer" is a transfer of value made by an individual on or after 18 March 1986 which constitutes a gift to another individual or a gift into an accumulation and maintenance trust or a trust for the disabled. Where the deceased had made a lifetime transfer of value that was a potentially exempt transfer and the potentially exempt transfer becomes chargeable to inheritance tax on the death of the donor within 7 years, the estate cannot qualify as an "excepted estate".

10. Special rules apply on the death of a donor who has given away property on or after 18 March 1986 subject to a reservation. A gift is one with reservation if:

—the donee does not assume bona fide possession and enjoyment of the property, or

—the property is not enjoyed to the entire exclusion, or virtually the entire exclusion, of the donor and of any benefit to him by contract or otherwise.

If the reservation subsists at the death or if the property has ceased to be subject to a reservation within seven years before the donor's death, the estate of the donor is not an "excepted estate" under the new regulations.

Grants of representation

11. Where the definition of an "excepted estate" is wholly met there is no need for an account of the estate to be presented for inheritance tax purposes. This is so whether the grant of representation is the first made in respect of the deceased or whether the grant is limited in duration in respect of property or to any special purpose.

12. The Lord Chancellor's Department is amending with effect from 1 August 1987 its Non-Contentious Probate Fees Order to introduce a fixed fee of £150 for all estates within the range £40,001 to £70,000. This will assist personal representatives, making it unnecessary for them to calculate the precise value of an estate.

13. No changes are being made in Scotland in the rules governing applications for confirmation to an estate. The inventory must therefore continue to be completed and presented to the Sheriff Clerk in the normal way.

Accounts

14. As at present, the Board will retain the right to call for an account within the "prescribed period" of 35 days of the grant of probate (60 days of the issue of confirmation in Scotland). In England and Wales and Northern Ireland the 35 days do not begin to run until the first grant is made which is not a grant limited in duration, in respect of property or to any special purpose. To ensure these arrangements work properly, the Board exercise this power in a small number of cases by issuing a form for completion by personal representatives requiring details of the estate.

15. As at present, a person who obtains a grant of representation or confirmation without delivery of an account and later discovers that the estate is not an "excepted estate", must deliver a form of account to the Board within six months of his discovery.

Discharges

16. If the Board do not issue a written notice in the "prescribed period" the personal representatives will be automatically discharged from any claims for tax in respect of the property comprised in the estate, and any charge on that property will be extinguished at the end of the "prescribed period". If, however, a notice is issued by the Board, personal representatives are not automatically discharged, and if they want a certificate of discharge they must apply for it in the normal way. Automatic discharge does not have any effect in cases of fraud or failure to disclose material facts. Nor does it affect the tax position when it is later discovered that there is further property in the estate and as a result the estate is no longer an "excepted estate".

Transfers reported late

17. In cases where no account of an excepted estate has been delivered and an earlier chargeable lifetime transfer which had not been reported is later disclosed, an account of the estate will continue to be treated as having been delivered on the last day of the prescribed period in relation to the estate. This provision modifies IHTA 1984, s. 264 (8) which provides that where tax is payable at a nil rate the date of payment shall be treated as the date on which the transfer was notified in an account. The provision ensures the proper operation of the rules governing transfers reported late by fixing a nominal date of delivery.

Other estates and lifetime transfers

18. The rules governing delivery of accounts in estates falling outside the conditions laid down in the regulations and for lifetime transfers are not affected by these regulations, and the provisions of IHTA 1984, s. 216 continue to apply without modification in these cases.

Estates where no grant of representation or confirmation is obtained

19. IHTA 1984, s. 216 (2) provides that where no grant of representation or confirmation in the U.K. is obtained within 12 months of the end of the month in which the death took place, the beneficiaries and others in whom property forming part of the estate rests after the death are required to deliver an account of the property. If the estate is an "excepted estate" that requirement is dispensed with by these Regulations.

Notes

1. FA 1987, which was passed before the Election, increased the starting point for inheritance tax from £71,000 to £90,000. In order to reduce the administrative costs of smaller estates, an increase is being made from £40,000 to £70,000 in the level below which accounts of estates do not need to be supplied to the Capital Taxes Office. Such estates are called "excepted estates".

2. The new limit comes into force from 1 August 1987 and applies to the estate of anyone who died on or after 1 April 1987. In order to be an excepted estate, the estate must have total gross value of no more than £70,000, contain no settled property, nor more than £10,000 in property situated outside the U.K.; and the deceased must have made no transfers within seven years of death nor any gifts where a benefit has been reserved.

3. The regulations apply throughout the U.K.

2 July 1987. Inland Revenue
IHT: Double Charges Relief Regulations

The Board of Inland Revenue have made regulations (S.I. 1987 No. 1130) which provide for relief in certain circumstances where the same property falls to be charged and cumulated twice as a result of the transferor's death. The Regulations apply to transfers and other events occurring on or after 18 March 1986.

The Regulations (The Inheritance Tax (Double Charges Relief) Regulations 1987) are reproduced in Appendix 8.

Notes

1 Inheritance tax was introduced in 1986, and applies to transfers and other events occurring on or after 18 March 1986.

2 The structure of the tax means that in certain circumstances the same property can be charged twice and entered twice into the cumulation of chargeable transfers as a result of a transferor's death. For example, a gift with reservation to a discretionary trust may be taxable when made and if the reservation continues until the donor's death, the gifted property is also chargeable on the death.

3 The legislation (FA 1986 s 104) empowered the Board to make regulations for the avoidance of double charges and double cumulation in these and certain other circumstances.
4 In such cases, the Regulations preserve the higher amount of tax, but also eliminate double charge and double cumulation arising as a result of the transferor's death.

17 March 1988. Hansard
IHT and family companies

Viscount Mackintosh of Halifax asked whether, given their stated aim of creating a climate where family companies can flourish, it is their intention that clearance under FA 1982 s. 53 (2) will in all cases be refused on the death of a controlling shareholder where sufficient dividends can be voted by the executors to enable the inheritance tax liability to be met by instalments on the basis that hardship would not arise as the executors control the company and thus control the flow of dividends.
Lord Brabazon of Tara: I understand that there have been very few cases of the kind in question. However, where the company has surplus funds sufficient to discharge the inheritance tax liability, the Revenue take the view that there would be no hardship since the liability could be met by dividend payments from the company.
  HL Written Answer, Vol. 494, col. 1349

29 April 1988. Hansard
Political parties: IHT exemption

Mr Gordon Brown asked which of the political parties are currently treated by the Revenue as qualifying political parties for the purposes of IHTA 1984, s. 24.
Mr Norman Lamont: The political parties which currently qualify are: Conservative; Labour; Labour and Co-operative; Social and Liberal Democratic; Social Democratic; Scottish Nationalist; Plaid Cymru; Ulster Unionist; Democratic Unionist; Social Democratic and Labour.
  HC Written Answer, Vol. 132, col. 329
  The Liberal Party and the Social Democratic Party, before and after the establishment of the Social and Liberal Democratic Party, also currently qualify: *HC Written Answer, 25 July 1988, Vol. 138, col. 106.*

August 1988. I.C.A.E.W.
Memorandum TR 713: taxation representations (miscellaneous matters): 1987 and prior years

The Institute has issued a memorandum containing a summary of unsettled points submitted to the Revenue and the Revenue's responses. Section 1 of the memoradum summarises uncleared points for years going back to 1975. Section 2, reproduced below [as regards IHT], sets out the Institute's detailed submission to the Revenue for 1987.

SECTION 2
TAXATION REPRESENTATIONS: 1987

INHERITANCE TAX

(All references are to IHTA 1984)

Potentially exempt transfers (s. 3A (2))
29. Where a potentially exempt transfer is made to an individual, property must become comprised in the donee's estate or the donee's estate must be increased. This prevents the payment of school fees by a grandparent from being a potentially exempt transfer. If the payment were to the son who spends it on his children's education that is a potentially exempt transfer. In our submission of May 1987 we pointed out that it would be much simpler if every transfer by way of gift were a potentially exempt transfer save those to companies and to discretionary trusts.
  Revenue response: This requirement is not peculiar to potentially exempt transfers. A broadly similar one has applied to the exemption for transfers between spouses since the introduction of capital transfer tax. Your proposed change could facilitate the manipulation of the relief for tax avoidance purposes. The present rules do not militate against the payment of school fees by grandparents since, as you recognise, such payment qualifies as a potentially exempt transfer if made through a parent.

Transfers between spouses (s. 18)
31. The limit for the exemption where the spouse is non-domiciled is £55,000. This is the amount of the nil rate band introduced in March 1982 and does not now seem to be relevant.

Revenue response: Transfers where the transferor but not the transferee spouse is domiciled in the U.K. are rarely met in practice. Moreover few other countries allow unlimited exemption for transfers between spouses even where both are domiciled within the jurisdiction.

Annual exemption (s. 19 (1))
32. The annual exemption of £3,000 was last increased in April 1981. We consider it should be increased substantially.

Small gifts (s. 20 (1))
33. The small gift exemption of £250 was last increased in April 1980. Similarly, we consider that it should be increased substantially.

Revenue response: The abolition of the lifetime charge on most gifts decreased the importance of the exemptions significantly and for most people and most gifts they will prove to be irrelevant. The representations will be borne in mind.

Normal expenditure out of income (s. 21)
34. The normal income expenditure can apply only "if it is shown that" clauses (*a*), (*b*) and (*c*) of subsection 1 apply. This indicates that the taxpayer has to explain such gifts to the CTO. The investment income surcharge has been abolished and income tax rate bands widened so that normal income gifts are now most important. We consider that it should not be necessary to have to show the CTO that the normal income gift was within the section.

Revenue response: As eligibility for this relief depends on satisfying conditions which are personal to each individual, it is fair and reasonable to ask for evidence of entitlement to the relief.

Gifts in consideration of marriage (s. 22)
35. The exemption for marriage gifts are at the same figures as they were in 1974. We consider that they should be substantially increased.

Revenue response: See 32 and 33 above.

Annual exemption (s. 19 (3A))
36. When potentially exempt transfer becomes chargeable due to premature death the annual exemption is set against it unless already set against earlier transfers. In cases where, in the next year, s. 19 (2) has been invoked and the allowance has been used in that year, the allowance is attributed to the potentially exempt transfer in the earlier year and the later year's tax has to be recalculated. This leads to difficulties. We suggest that the potentially exempt transfer which has become chargeable should not have annual exemption in such a case.

Revenue response: We agree that the interaction of ss. 19 (1) and 3A (1) (*b*) may need to be adjusted, if it leads to difficulties which prove troublesome in practice. The matter will be kept under review.

Related settlements (s. 62)
37. We consider an interest in possession settlement or a disabled trust should not be a related settlement. In this way the tax consequences of an interest in possession settlement, etc. would be no different from the consequences of outright ownership. Related settlements do exist and in the main they are to be found in the trusts set up by wills.

Revenue response: Section 62 applies only for the purposes of the charges under Chapter III of Part III on discretionary trusts. Amending the provision, as you suggest, would facilitate the avoidance or mitigation of the charge on these trusts through fragmentation.

Charge at ten year anniversary (s. 64)
38. Discretionary settlements are often the vehicle for holding a family's principal asset such as shares in a family company or a firm. If such an asset is sold within a year or two of a ten year anniversary it is possible that gains tax will reduce the capital to a figure lower than that assessed to the ten year charge. Some allowance should be given where this happens. Trusts invested in quoted shares are not so seriously affected as there will generally be some turnover of investments year by year.

Revenue response: There is already such an allowance. Capital gains tax liability arising after the date of a ten-year anniversary will reduce the amount of the trust capital taxable at the next ten-year anniversary, irrespective of the nature of the trust assets . Considerations of parity of tax treatment apart, the proposal for giving a retrospective deduction for CGT liability on particular types of assets would lead to the same CGT liability being allowed twice. It would also delay the finalisation of the inheritance tax liability for up to two years after the ten-yearly charge.

Rate of ten-yearly charge (s. 66 (2))
39. Where property was not comprised in a discretionary settlement for the whole of the ten years the rate is shaded. Therefore it is necessary to identify the assets in existence at the ten year anniversary which derive from property which either become relevant property or become com-

prised in the settlement during the ten year period. It would be helpful if practice notes were available as this seems a subject not suited to further legislation.

Revenue response: Given the diversity of arrangements it does not seem realistic to think in terms of precise and all-embracing practice notes. Although the CTO are not aware of any real problems in this area, nevertheless they will be happy to consider with you any reasonable approach proposed in individual cases.

Property moving between settlements (s. 81)

40. For the purposes of the ten year charges, etc. where property ceases to be comprised in one settlement and becomes comprised in another it is treated as remaining in the first settlement. Where it becomes comprised in an interest in possession settlement it should be treated as having left the original settlement. It this is not the case the consequences of property being subject to an interest in possession are not the same as if it were owned by an individual.

Revenue response: The provision recognises the fact that a person entitled to an interest in possession in settled property cannot actually make a fresh settlement of that property, and is necessary to prevent the avoidance or mitigation of the charge on discretionary trusts through fragmentation.

Transfers within seven years before death of transferor (s. 113A)

41. When testing a transfer for business property relief, where a potentially exempt transfer has been caught by the premature death of the donor, s. 113A (3) requires the transferee to have held the property since the transfer. Where the potentially exempt transfer was settled, perhaps on accumulation and maintenance trusts, beneficiaries may have become entitled to the settled capital or an interest in possession therein. Therefore the business property relief is lost. This seems wrong. An accumulation and maintenance trust is the conventional way of providing management for an infant's capital and is always treated as part of the inheritance tax regime for individuals not as a discretionary settlement.

Revenue response: The present rule, which applies equally to transfers between individuals and to all trusts, is that the relief is lost if the transferee disposes of the property (other than on death) in the transferor's lifetime without acquiring qualifying replacement property. It is necessary therefore to compare the identity of the transferee at both dates. Prior to the appointment of property by the trustees, the beneficial interests under an accumulation and maintenance trusts are no different from those under other discretionary trusts. So, for this purpose, the same rules apply to them. The case where a trustee of an accumulation and maintenance trust could be obliged to transfer relievable property to a beneficiary within seven years of its settlement because vesting may not be postponed beyond age 25, is only likely to arise in practice if the beneficiary has attained the age of majority before the qualifying property is put into trust.

Application of s. 113A to replacement property (s. 113B)

42. When the original relevant business property is replaced, s. 113B (1) (*b*) requires the whole of the consideration to be applied to the replacement property. We are most concerned that this will cause the relief to be lost in many cases. The retailer who moves can hardly be expected to eschew all businesses which are a little less in value than that which he is selling.

43. Furthermore, the section extends business property relief to cases where relevant business property has been sold and replaced. It does not give relief where the replacement is agricultural property.

Revenue response: The present replacement property rules were not intended to be comprehensive but reflected judgment about the more probable situations which are likely to arise, if at all. The matter will be kept under review for evidence of practical needs that changes are warranted.

Transfers within seven years before death of transferor (s. 124A)

44. This repeats for agricultural property relief the anomaly in respect of s. 113A (3) referred to above.

Revenue response: See 41 above.

Application of s. 134A to replacement property

45. This repeats for agricultural property relief the anomaly in respect of s. 113B referred to above where one cannot transfer from agricultural to business property.

Revenue response: See 42 and 43 above.

Distribution etc. from property settled by will (s. 144)

46. Where a will settles property on discretionary terms and within two years of death the discretion is exercised so that capital vests in individuals, etc. that is not an occasion of charge and the tax is recalculated as if the distribution has been made by the will. However, a discretion can only be exercised by trustees and therefore the executors must obtain probate, paying tax on the basis that the will will not alter, they assent the estate to themselves and then exercise their discretion. In many cases the result will be a repayment of tax as they will favour the surviving spouse. It should be possible for the likely exercise of the discretion to be taken into account when probate is extracted, so saving payment and repayment of tax.

Revenue response: The general rule that tax must be paid on an estate before probate is granted has proved to be a valuable safeguard of the interests of the Exchequer, the personal representative and the beneficiaries. The tax payable is normally calculated by reference to the existing circumstances, any any attempt at that stage to anticipate future possible events would undermine the efficacy of the present arrangements.

Delivery of accounts (s. 216 (1) (bb))
47. Where the premature death of the donor causes a potentially exempt transfer to become chargeable the donee is required to report his gifts. Where large sums are involved, business-trained people will also be involved and compliance may be expected. We still believe that, where the gifts are small and might easily be exempt (*e.g.* under £1,000), it is unlikely that it will occur to the donee that he has any such responsibility.

Revenue response: The legal personal representatives are obliged to make the fullest possible enquiries about lifetime transfers by the deceased before submitting the Revenue account. This should usually reveal the extent of the deceased's gift-making. Moreover most modest gifts will be covered by the small gift and annual exemptions.

Appeals against determinations (s. 222)
48. The appeal where there is disagreement over the value of unquoted shares, is to the Special Commissioners. Their decisions are unreported. Were they available to the profession it would improve the quality of the valuations made by them and shorten many negotiations. The obvious benefit to SVD and to the profession makes it desirable for these decisions to be reported.

Revenue response: As you know, decisions of the Special Commissioners are not reported, irrespective of the nature of the appeal, and it would be difficult to justify a change in this practice for a particular kind of decision only. However, as responsibility for the Special Commissioners was transferred from the Revenue to the Lord Chancellor's Department a copy of your recommendation has been forwarded to them.

15 June 1989. Inland Revenue
IHT: interest on unpaid and overpaid tax

The rate of interest charged on inheritance tax paid late and paid in respect of inheritance tax overpaid is to be increased from 9 per cent. to 11 per cent. with effect from 6 July 1989. This is in line with other interest rates which have risen recently.
1. Orders have been laid altering the rate of interest charged on tax paid late. The Orders provide for a new rate of 11 per cent. p.a. applying to IHT, CTT and estate duty.
2. The Orders also provide for the rate of interest paid by the Revenue on repayments of IHT, CTT and estate duty to be increased to 11 per cent. p.a.
3. The change applies from 6 July 1989 whether or not on that date interest has already started to run.
4. The Orders will be published as S.I. 1989 No. 998, S.I. 1989 No. 999 and S.I. 1989 No. 1002.

Note
The Orders are entitled The IHT and CTT (Interest on Unpaid Tax) Order 1989, The Estate Duty (Interest on Unpaid Duty) Order 1989 and the Estate Duty (Northern Ireland) (Interest on Unpaid Duty) Order 1989.

30 June 1989. Inland Revenue
IHT: "excepted estates": limit increased

[*See Inland Revenue Press Release, 5 June 1990.*]

DETAILS

1. Where the value of an estate is attributable in part to property passing by survivorship in joint tenancy, it is the value of the deceased's beneficial interest in that property which is taken into account for the purpose of the [£115,000] limit.

Potentially exempt transfers and gifts with reservation

2. A "potentially exempt transfer" is a transfer of value made by an individual on or after:

(*a*) *18 March 1986* which constitutes a gift to another individual or a gift into an accumulation and maintenance trust, or trust for the disabled,

(*b*) *17 March 1987* relating to certain gifts involving interest in possession trusts.

Where the deceased had made a lifetime transfer of value that was a potentially exempt transfer, and the potentially exempt transfer becomes chargeable to inheritance tax on the death of the donor within seven years, the estate cannot qualify as an "excepted estate".

3. Special rules apply on the death of a donor who has given away property on or after 18 March 1986 subject to a reservation. A gift is one with reservation if:

(*a*) the donee does not assume *bona fide* possession and enjoyment of the property, or

(*b*) the property is not enjoyed to the entire exclusion, or virtually to the entire exclusion, of the donor and of any benefit to him by contract or otherwise.

If the reservation subsists at the death or if the property has ceased to be subject to a reservation within seven years before the donor's death, the estate of the donor is not an "excepted estate" under the new regulations.

Grants of representation

4. Where the definition of an "excepted estate" is satisfied as a whole there is no need for an account of the estate to be presented for inheritance tax purposes. This is so whether the grant of representation is the first made in respect of the deceased or whether the grant is limited in duration in respect of property or to any special purpose.

5. The Lord Chancellor's Department is amending with effect from 1 August 1989 its Non-Contentious Probate Fees Order to introduce a fixed fee of £215 for all estates within the range £70,001 to £100,000. This will assist personal representatives, making it unnecessary for them to calculate the precise value of an estate.

6. No changes are being made in Scotland in the rules governing applications for confirmation to an estate. The inventory must therefore continue to be completed and presented to the Sheriff Clerk in the normal way.

Accounts

7. As at present, the Board will retain the right to call for an account within the "prescribed period" of 35 days of the grant of probate (60 days of the issue of confirmation in Scotland). In England and Wales and Northern Ireland the 35 days do not begin to run until the first grant is made which is not a grant limited in duration, in respect of property or to any special purpose. To ensure these arrangements work properly, the Board exercise this power in a small number of cases by issuing (other than in Scotland) a form for completion by personal representatives requiring deatils of the estate.

8. As at present, a person who obtains a grant of representation or confirmation without delivery of an account and later discovers that the estate is not an "excepted estate", must deliver a form of account to the Board within six months of the discovery.

Discharges

9. If the Board do not issue a written notice in the "prescribed period" the personal representatives will be automatically discharged from any claims for tax in respect of the property comprised in the estate, and any charge on that property will be extinguished at the end of the "prescribed period". If, however a notice is issued by the Board, personal representatives are not automatically discharged, and if they want a certificate of discharge they must apply for it in the normal way. Automatic discharge does not have any effect in cases of fraud or failure to disclose material facts. Nor does it affect the tax position when it is later discovered that there is a further property in the estate and as a result the estate is no longer an "excepted estate".

Transfers reported late

10. In cases where no account of an excepted estate has been delivered and an earlier *chargeable* lifetime transfer which had not been reported is later disclosed, an account of the estate will (as before) be treated as having been delivered on the last day of the prescribed period in relation to the estate. This modifies the general rule that where tax is payable at a nil rate the date of payment shall be treated as the date on which the transfer was notified in an account. The provision ensures the proper operation of the rules governing transfers reported late by fixing a nominal date of delivery.

Other estates and lifetime transfers
11. The rules governing delivery of accounts in estates falling outside the conditions laid down in the regulations and for lifetime transfers are not affected by these regulations, and the provisions of IHTA 1984, s. 216 continue to apply without modification in these cases.

Estates where no grant of representation or confirmation is obtained
12. IHTA 1984, s. 216 (2) provides that where no grant of representation or confirmation in the U.K. is obtained within 12 months of the end of the month in which the death took place, the beneficiaries and others in whom property forming part of the estate vests after the death are required to deliver an account of the property. If the estate is an "excepted estate" that requirement is dispensed with by these Regulations.

1 August 1989. Inland Revenue
Setting Revenue rates of interest

1. The Treasury has, with ministerial approval, laid regulations giving details of how interest rates used by the Revenue are calculated.
2. The regulations set out the formulae by which Revenue interest rates are calculated. These formulae have been in use for some years though not previously published. The formulae are based on the average of base lending rate of certain clearing banks rounded to the nearest whole number, and are:
   Main Taxes Acts provisions:
      ...
   Official rate for Schedule E benefits:
      ...
   IHT and earlier capital taxes:
      (Base rate plus 2 per cent. reduced by basic rate tax) minus 1 per cent.
The current rate of interest for each of these taxes using the present average base lending rate of 14 per cent. are ... and 11 per cent. respectively.
3. The regulations are made under FA 1989, s. 178 which introduces a new procedure for setting Revenue interest rates. Under this procedure, the formulae used for setting the interest rates are to be published by the Treasury in regulations and the rates then set automatically in accordance with the formulae. The regulations take effect from 18 August 1989.

Notes
1. The Treasury has laid regulations setting out the formulae to be used for setting the rates of interest used by the Revenue. These formulae have been in use for some years, though not previously published. The rates are based on an average of the base lending rates of the following high street banks—Barclays, Lloyds, Midland, National Westminster, Bank of Scotland, Royal Bank of Scotland—rounded to the nearest whole number with halves rounded downwards. Revenue rates will then change when this average changes, with the new rate coming into effect from the beginning of the next tax month. Changes will be announced in Revenue press releases.
2.–4. ...
5. The interest rate on capital taxes is (base rate plus 2 per cent. reduced by basic rate tax) minus 1 per cent. This rate applies to unpaid tax and repayments of IHT, CTT and estate duty. The formula is based on a broad average of the net of tax cost of borrowing taking into account that these taxing provisions may run on for a great many years.

25 January 1990. Tax Journal
IHT tax payments

On 30 November 1989 the Senior Registrar of the Family Division made a Practice Direction with regard to IHT. It reads:

"For many years it has been common practice for solicitors to send Inland Revenue accounts to probate registries with cheques for the payment of IHT. The cheques are forwarded to the Inland Revenue Finance Division (Cashier), where the accounts are receipted and then returned to the registries. With effect from 2 January 1990 this practice will cease and accounts from solicitors must be sent to the Inland Revenue, Finance Division (Cashier), Barrington Road, Worthing, West Sussex BN12 4XH in order that they may be properly receipted prior to presentation to the probate registries."

9 May 1990. The Law Society
IHT: changes in Revenue practice

In a recent letter to the Law Society (published in the *Law Society's Gazette*, 9 May 1990) the Revenue notified two changes of inheritance tax practice as follows.

Partly exempt transfers
IHTA 1984, s. 40 directs that "where gifts taking effect on a transfer of value take effect separately out of different funds"—for example where on a death there are gifts out of the free estate and out of settlements—then each fund is to be considered separately for the purpose of the allocation of exemptions under Ch III, including the grossing-up of the gifts. The rate of tax used by the Capital Taxes Office to gross-up separate gifts out of different funds has until now been the rate applicable to the total value of *all* property chargeable on the testator's death. The Board now accepts that the rate of tax to be used for grossing-up should be found by looking at each fund separately and in isolation.

Coming to an end of an interest in possession in settled property
When an interest in possession in settled property comes to an end during the lifetime of the person entitled to it, IHTA 1984, s. 52 (1) states that the value for inheritance tax purposes is ". . . equal to the value of the property in which his interest subsisted". Until now this value has been deterimined as a rateable proportion of the aggregate value of that settled property and other property of a similar kind in the person's estate. The Board now take the view that, in these circumstances, settled property in which the interest subsisted should be valued *in isolation* without reference to any similar property.

These statements of the Board's position are made without prejudice to the application in an appropriate case of the *Ramsay* principle or the provisions of IHTA 1984 relating to associated operations. The changes of view will be applied to all new cases and to existing cases where the tax liability has not been settled.

5 June 1990. Inland Revenue
IHT: "excepted estates"—limit increased

Regulations have been laid to increase the limit for "excepted estates" from £100,000 to £115,000. This increase will further simplify the administration of some 10,000 smaller estates for IHT purposes.

This means that executors or administrators of straightforward estates with a value of £115,000 or less will not have to deliver an account to the Revenue. The new limit will apply from 1 July 1990, to the estate of any person who died on or after 1 April 1990. (The limit was last increased from £70,000 to £100,000 with effect from 1 August 1989.)

DETAILS

Estates qualifying
1. Estates will qualify as "excepted estates" only where *all* the following conditions apply:
    (*a*) the total gross value of the estate for tax purposes does not exceed £115,000;
    (*b*) the estate comprises only property which has passed under the deceased's will or intestacy, or by nomination, or beneficially by survivorship. (Where the value of an estate is attributable in part to property passing by survivorship in joint tenancy, it is the value of the deceased's beneficial interest in that property that is taken into account for the purposes of the £115,000 limit);
    (*c*) not more than £15,000 consists of property situated outside the U.K.;
    (*d*) the deceased died domiciled in the United Kingdom and had not made lifetime gifts chargeable to either IHT or CTT.

Estates not qualifying
2. Estates where the deceased
(*a*) had made a chargeable potentially exempt transfer
(*b*) had made a gift with a reservation that subsists at the time of the death or within seven years of the death
(*c*) enjoyed an interest in settled property
are not "excepted estates".

Grants of representation
3. Where the definition of an "excepted estate" is satisfied as a whole there is no need for an account of the estate to be presented for inheritance tax purposes. This is so whether the grant of representation is the first made in respect of the deceased or whether the grant is limited in duration in respect of property or to any special purpose.
4. The Lord Chancellor's Department will not be making any changes to its Non-Contentious Probate Fees Order as a result of the increase in the "excepted estates" limit.

Scotland
5. No changes are being made in Scotland in the rules governing applications for confirmation to an estate. The inventory must therefore continue to be completed and presented to the Sheriff Clerk in the normal way.

Notes
1. Three orders have been laid:
(*a*) The IHT (Delivery of Accounts) Regulations 1990 (S.I. 1990 No. 1110) applies to England and Wales
(*b*) The IHT (Delivery of Accounts) (Scotland) Regulations 1990 (S.I. 1990 No. 1111) applies to Scotland
(*c*) The IHT (Delivery of Accounts) (Northern Ireland) Regulations 1990 (SI 1990 No. 1112) applies to Northern Ireland.
All have the same effective date.
2. Each order amends the Principal Regulations made for capital transfer tax in 1981 (S.I. 1981 No. 880, S.I. 1981 No. 881 and S.I. 1981 No. 441 respectively).
These were amended in—
—1983 (S.I. 1983/1039, S.I. 1983/1040 and S.I. 1983/1911)
—1987 (S.I. 1987/1127, S.I. 1987/1128 and S.I. 1987/1129)
—1989 (S.I. 1989/1078, S.I. 1989/1079 and S.I. 1989/1080
Copies of the new and the earlier regulations are obtainable from HMSO. Until the new regulations come into force the previous regulations will continue to operate.
3. These regulations do not affect the present requirements on lifetime transfers (S.I. 1981 No. 1440) that were introduced in 1981.
4. The Press Release issued on 30 June 1989 [see above] contains a more detailed explanation of the rules for "expected estates". These rules continue unchanged.

APPENDIX 2. INLAND REVENUE STATEMENTS OF PRACTICE

Following a review of their methods of publishing information on administrative practice with a view to making it available to the public in a uniform, accessible and more readily identifiable way, the Revenue introduced a new series of Statements of Practice on 18 July 1978.

Before 18 July 1978 information on administrative practice was disseminated in a variety of ways including Statements in Parliament. Written Parliamentary Answers (often reproduced in Revenue Press Releases), letters to professional bodies and to journals, etc.

An index of statements issued before 18 July 1978 which remain valid was published in a Revenue Press Release on 18 June 1979 and revised by further Press Releases dated 29 October 1980, 23 March 1982 and 14 July 1987. The index with full texts is reproduced below.

STATEMENTS ISSUED BEFORE 18 JULY 1978 WHICH REMAIN VALID

Contents

Accumulation and maintenance settlements: **([IHTA 1984, s. 71] formerly FA 1975, Sch. 5, para. 15)**
E1. Powers of appointment *(11 June 1975)*

"It must be appreciated that in any particular case the exemption will depend on the precise terms
of the trust and power concerned, and on the facts to which they apply. In general, however, the
official view is that the conditions do not restrict the application of [IHTA 1984, s. 71] (formerly FA
Sch. 5, para. 15) to settlements where the interests of individual beneficiaries are defined and
indefeasible.

The requirement of [IHTA 1984, s. 71] (formerly FA 1975 Sch. 5, para. 15 (1) *(a)*) is that 'one or
more persons will, on or before attaining a specified age not exceeding twenty five, become entitled
to, or to an interest in possession in, the settled property or part of it.' It is considered that settled
property would meet this condition if at the relevant time it can be seen that it must vest for an
interest in possession in some member of an existing class of potential beneficiaries on or before his
attaining 25. The existence of a special power of appointment would not of itself exclude para. 15 if
neither the exercise nor the release of the power could break the condition. To achieve this effect
might, however, require careful drafting."
See Law Society's Gazette 11 June 1975; British Tax Review 1975, p. 436.

E2. Powers of advancement *(September 1975)*

With regard to the effect of the application of the Trustee Act 1925, s. 32 (as interpreted in
Pilkington v. *I.R. Comrs.* [1964] AC 612) to a settlement otherwise within [IHTA 1984, s. 71]
(formerly FA 1975, Sch. 5, para. 15 (1)) the view of the Revenue is that the existence of a common
form power of advancement does not prevent a settlement from satisfying the terms of [IHTA
1984, s. 71] (formerly FA 1975, Sch. 5, para. 15).
See British Tax Review 1975, p. 437.

E2a. Examples

The examples set out below are based on a settlement for the children of X contingently on
attaining 25, the trustees being required to accumulate the income so far as it is not applied for the
maintenance of X's children.

A. The Settlement was made on X's marriage
and he has as yet no children.

> [IHTA 1984, s. 71] (formerly FA 1975, Sch. 5,
> para. 15) will not apply until a child is born and
> that event will give rise to a charge for tax under
> sub-para. (3), subject, if it occurs before 1 April
> 1980, to relief under para. 14 of that Schedule.

B. The trustees have power to apply income
for the benefit of X's unmarried sister.

> [IHTA 1984, s. 71] (formerly FA 1975, Sch. 5
> para. 15) does not apply because the condition
> of sub-para (1) *(b)* is not met.

C. The trustees have power to apply capital for
the benefit of X's unmarried sister.

> [IHTA 1984, s. 71] (formerly FA 1975, Sch. 5
> para 15) does not apply because the condition
> of sub-para (1) *(a)* is not met.

D. X has power to appoint the capital not only
among his children but also among his remoter
issue.

E. The trustees have an overriding power of
appointment in favour of other persons.

> [IHTA 1984, s. 71] (formerly FA 1975, Sch. 5
> para. 15) does not apply (unless the power can
> be exercised only in favour of persons who
> would thereby acquire interests in possession
> on or before attaining 25). A release of the
> disqualifying power would give rise to a charge
> for tax under para. 15 (3). Its exercise would
> give rise to a charge under para. 6 (2). Either
> charge is subject to relief under para. 14.

F. The settled property has been revocably
appointed to one of the children contingently
on his attaining 25 and the appointment is now
made irrevocable.

> If the power to revoke prevents [IHTA 1984, s.
> 71] (formerly FA 1975, Sch. 5 para. 15) from
> applying, (as it would, for example, if the prop-
> erty thereby became subject to a power of
> appointment as at D or E) tax will be charge-
> able under sub-para. (3) when the appointment
> is made irrevocable. This is subject to relief
> under para. 14.

Superannuation, life insurance and accident schemes
E3. Superannuation schemes *(September 1975)*

"It is not intended to charge [IHT] on payments made by the trustees of a superannuation scheme within [IHTA 1984, s. 151] (formerly FA 1975, Sch. 5, para. 16) in direct exercise of a discretion to pay a lump sum death benefit to any one or more of a member's dependants. It is not considered that pending the exercise of the discretion the benefit should normally be regarded as property comprised in a settlement so as to bring it within the scope of the former FA 1975, Sch. 5. The protection of [IHTA 1984, s. 151] (formerly FA 1975 Sch. 5, para. 16) would not of course extend further if the trustees themselves then settled the property so paid."
See British Tax Review 1975, p. 439.

E4. Associated operations *(5 February 1975)*

The present practice—as for estate duty, the intention is to follow that on the introduction of CTT [now IHT]—is to regard policies and annuities as not being affected by the associated operations rule if, first, the policy was issued on full medical evidence of the assured's health, and secondly, it would have been issued on the same terms if the annuity had not been bought.
See Hansard Standing Committee A, 5 February 1975, Vol. 2, col. 872.

Interest in possession
E5. Close companies *(11 June 1975)*

"The Revenue confirms that the general intention of [IHTA 1984, s. 101] (formerly FA 1975, Sch. 5, para. 24 (5)) is to treat the participators as beneficial owners for all the purposes of that section. On this footing the Revenue would in practice regard the conditions of [IHTA 1984, ss. 52 (2) and 53 (2)] (formerly FA 1975 Sch. 5 paras. 4 (3) and 4 (4)) as satisfied where it is the company that in fact becomes entitled to the property or disposes of the interest."
See Law Society's Gazette, 11 June 1975.

E6. Power to augment income *(5 November 1975)*

The effect for [IHT] of the exercise by the trustees of a will of a power to augment the income of a beneficiary out of capital is outlined below.

In the normal case, where the beneficiary concerned is life tenant of the settled property this will have no immediate consequences for [IHT]. The life tenant already has an interest in possession and under the provisions of [IHTA 1984, s. 49] (formerly FA 1975, Sch. 5, para. 3 (1), is treated as beneficially entitled to the property. The enlargement of that interest to an absolute interest does not change this position ([IHTA 1984, s. 53 (2)]) (formerly FA 1975 Sch. 5, para. 4 (3)) and it is not affected by the relationship of the beneficiary to the testator.

In the exceptional case, where the beneficiary is not the life tenant, or in which there is no subsisting interest in possession, the exercise of the power would give rise to a charge for tax under [IHTA 1984, s. 53 (2)] (formerly FA 1975 Sch. 5, para. 4 (2)). But if the life tenant is the surviving spouse of a testator who died before 13 November 1974, exemption might be available under [IHTA 1984, Sch. 6, para. 2] (formerly FA 1975 Sch. 5 para. 4 (7)) of that Schedule.

The exercise of the power would be regarded as distributing the settled property rather than as reducing its value, so that [IHTA 1984, s. 52 (3)] (formerly FA 1975 Sch. 5 paras. 4 (9) and 6 (3)) of the Schedule would not be in point.
See Law Society's Gazette, 5 November 1975.

E7. Protective trusts *(3 March 1976)*

"I have been asked to reply to your letter about the relief from [IHT] for property held on protective trusts.

In our view trusts "to the like effect" as those set out in the Trustee Act 1925, s. 33 (1) are trusts which are not materially different in their tax consequences. We should not wish to distinguish a trust by reason of a minor variation or additional administrative powers or duties. But in the first situation which you mention the extension of the list of potential beneficiaries to brothers and sisters of the principal beneficiary could be a means of giving relief to a trust primarily intended to benefit them. Such a trust would be regarded as outside the scope of [IHTA 1984, ss. 88 (2) and 89 (1)] (formerly FA 1975, Sch. 5, para. 18).

On the other hand it is clear from the existence of [IHTA 1984, s. 88 (2) *(b)*] (formerly FA 1975, Sch. 5 para. 18 (2) *(b)*) that the insertion of a power to apply capital for the benefit of this primary beneficiary was contemplated as a possible feature of a settlement entitled to relief."

"You wrote to us again about the special exemptions from capital transfer tax provided for protective trusts.

I appreciate that so long as the principal beneficiary has no spouse or issue the statutory trusts extend to the next of kin for the time being who might well be brothers and sisters. But this is not at all the same thing as including them in the primary class of beneficiaries *ab initio* on an equal footing with the spouse and issue. In that event the brothers and sisters could receive the income of settled property to the entire exclusion of the principal beneficiary his spouse and issue. I confirm that trusts which could produce this result would not be regarded as 'to the like effect' as those specified in Trustee Act 1925, s. 33 (1)."

See Law Society's Gazette, 31 March 1976.

E8. Age of majority *(1 June 1977)*

The Family Law Reform Act 1969, Sch. 3, para. 5 provides that section 1 of that Act, which reduces the age of majority to 18 and amends various statutory provisions including the Trustee Act 1925, s. 31 is not to affect the latter section 'in its application to an interest under an instrument made before the commencement date.'

For the purposes of the Family Law Reform Act, Sch. 3, para. 5 (1) (*a*) an interest appointed after the commencement date of s. 1 of that Act under a special power of appointment created by an instrument made before that date is not an 'interest under an instrument made before the commencement date.'

See Law Society's Gazette, 1 June, 1977.

Settled property: Miscellaneous
E9. Excluded property *(3 December 1975)*

"You wrote to me on 14 October about [IHTA 1984, s. 48 (3) and 267 (3)] (formerly FA 1975, Sch. 5, para. 2) and asked whether any account would be taken of the deemed domicile provisions.

I gather that your main doubt concerns the wording of [IHTA 1984, s. 267 (3)] (formerly FA 1975, Sch. 5 para. 2 (2)), and in particular the time at which property is regarded as having become comprised in a settlement. We think that in the context of [IHTA 1984, s. 48 (3)] (formerly FA 1975 Sch. 5 para. 2 (1)) property becomes comprised in a settlement when it, or other property which it represents is introduced by the settlor. Thus in your example the foreign investments are re-investments of settled property already comprised in the settlement before 10 December 1974, and would accordingly be excluded property."

See Law Society's Gazette, 3 December 1975.

E10. Leases for life *(7 December 1977)*

"You wrote to me on 10 June about [IHTA 1984, s. 43 (3)] (formerly FA 1975, Sch. 5, para. 1 (3)).

You were concerned that a vendor of property who wished to retain a lease for his life might be barred from the relief afforded by the exception for leases granted for full consideration if the creation of the the lease was by way of a reservation out of the interest conveyed rather than by a separate grant of the leasehold interest. I can confirm that we would not seek to exclude relief solely on these grounds. Whether or not full consideration is given is a matter which depends upon the facts of the individual case, but for this purpose we would take into account a reduction in the price obtained by the vendor because of the reservation of the leasehold interest."

See Law Society's Gazette, 7 December 1977.

E11. Employee trusts *(1 December 1976)*

The Revenue interprets [IHTA 1984, s. 13 (1)] (formerly FA 1976, s. 90 (1)), and in particular para. (*b*) quite as restrictively as you suggest. We regard the section as requiring where the trust is to benefit employees of a subsidiary of the company making the provision those eligible to benefit must include all or most of the employees and officers of the subsidiary and the employees and officers of the holding company taken as a single class. So it would be possible to exclude all of the officers and employees of the holding company without losing the exemption if they comprised only a minority of the combined class. But the exemption would not be available for a contribution to a fund for the sole benefit of the employees of a small subsidiary. This is because it would otherwise have been easy to create such a situation artificially in order to benefit a favoured group of a company's officeholders or employees.

This construction should not normally give rise to the difficulty which you envisage. It is true that there are some close companies in which the participators outnumber the other employees. But even here the exemption is not irretrievably lost. The requirement to exclude participators and those connected with them from benefit is modified by [IHTA 1984, s. 13 (3), (4)] (formerly s. 90 (4)). This limits the meaning of "a participator" for this purpose to those having a substantial stake in the assets being transferred and makes an exception in favour of income benefits. So even where most of the employees are also major participators or their relatives an exempt transfer could be made if the trust provided only for income benefits and the eventual disposal of the capital away from the participators and their families.

I should perhaps add that these restrictions do not affect the exemptions offered by [IHTA 1984, s. 86] (formerly FA 1975, Sch. 5, para. 17), from tax charges during the continuance of a trust for employees which meets the conditions of that paragraph and I am sure that you will recognise the need to ensure that the major shareholders in a close company cannot make an exempt transfer of capital to a trust which can at a later date distribute it to members of their families who may well be employed by the company.

See Law Society's Gazette, 1 December 1976.

Non-settled property
E12. Orders in matrimonial proceedings *(20 August 1975)*

Transfers of money or property pursuant to an order of the court in consequence of a decree of divorce or nullity of marriage will in general be regarded as exempt from [IHT] as transactions at arm's length which are not intended to confer any gratuitous benefit.

If, exceptionally, such a benefit is intended it is the duty of the transferor to deliver a capital transfer tax account to the Controller, Capital Taxes Office, Minford House, Rockley Road, London W14 0DS.

See Practice Note, 20 August 1975.

E13. Charities *(15 April 1976)*

1. [IHTA 1984, ss. 25 and 26] (formerly FA 1975, Sch. 6, paras. 10 and 11) exempt from capital transfer tax certain gifts to charities and political parties to the extent that the value transferred is attributable to property given to a charity etc. [IHTA 1984, ss. 25 and 26] (formerly FA 1975, Sch. 6, paras. 12 and 13) exempt in similar terms gifts for national purposes and for the public benefit.
2. Where the value transferred (*i.e.* the loss to transferor's estate as a result of the disposition) exceeds the value of the gift in the hands of a charity, etc., the Board of Inland Revenue have hitherto taken the view that the transfer is exempt only to the extent of the value of the property in the hands of the transferee. The Board wish it to be known that they are now advised that the exemption extends to the whole value transferred.

See Inland Revenue Press Release, 15 April 1976.

E14. Pools etc. syndicates *(16 September 1977)*

It has recently been suggested that [IHT] may be payable on winnings by football pools syndicates. The Board of Inland Revenue wish to make it clear that this is not so. Where winnings are shared out among the members of the syndicate in accordance with the terms of an agreement drawn up before the win, no liability to capital transfer tax is incurred.

Where for example football pool winnings are paid out, in accordance with a pre-existing enforceable arrangement, among the members of the syndicate in proportion to the share of the stake money each has provided, each member of the syndicate receives what already belongs to him or her. There is therefore no "gift" or "chargeable transfer" by the person who, on behalf of the members, receives the winnings from the pools promoter.

Members of a pool syndicate may think it wise to record in a written, signed and dated statement, the existence and terms of the agreement between them. But the Inland Revenue cannot advise on the wording or legal effect of such a statement, nor do they wish copies of such statements to be sent to them for approval or registration.

Where following a pools win the terms of an agreement are varied or part of the winnings are distributed to persons who are not members of the syndicate, [IHT] liability may be incurred. The same principles apply to premium bonds syndicates and other similar arrangements.

See Inland Revenue Press Release, 16 September 1977.

E15. Close companies—group transfers *(March 1975)*

Whether or not a disposition is a transfer of value for the purposes of the [IHT] has to be determined by reference to [IHTA 1984, ss. 65 (3) and 237] (formerly s. 20, and s. 20 (4)) which provide that a disposition is not a transfer of value if it was not intended to confer any gratuitous benefit on any person, subject to the other provisions of that subsection. In the Board's view, the effect is that a dividend paid by a subsidiary company to its parent is not a transfer of value and so [IHTA 1984, s. 257] (formerly FA 1975 s. 39) does not start to operate in relation to such dividends.

Nor does the Board feel that they can justifiably treat a transfer of assets between a wholly-owned subsidiary and its parent or between two wholly-owned subsidiaries as a transfer of value.

See 1975 British Tax Review, p. 139.

IHT and Scots law
E16. Missives of sale *(8 June 1978)*

Where a person sells heritable property situated in Scotland, the sale is effected by way of missives of sale followed, usually sometime later, by the delivery of a disposition of the property. The question has arisen as to whether the purchaser or the seller is entitled to any [IHT] reliefs which may be attributable to heritable property if a transfer of value, *e.g.* on the occasion of a death, occurs during the period between completion of the missives of sale and delivery of the disposition of the property. Hitherto, it has been the practice both for estate duty and CTT [now IHT] to give reliefs attributable to heritable property to the purchaser's estate.

In a recent non-tax case (*Gibson* v. *Hunter Home Designs Ltd. (in liquidation)* 1976 SLT 94) the Court of Session ruled that, between the date of completion of the missives and the date of delivery of the disposition of the property, the seller is not divested of any part of his right of property, in the subjects of sale. The Board of Inland Revenue have accordingly been advised that any CTT [now IHT] or estate duty reliefs which are attributable to heritable property fall to be given to the seller. Where, for example, the seller of agricultural property dies between completion of the missives and delivery of the disposition of the property, any [IHT] agricultural or business reliefs due will be given to his estate. If the purchaser dies between these two dates these reliefs will not be available. This view of the law will be applied to existing cases, subject to the statutory provisions which restrict the re-opening of settled cases, in particular for IHT [IHTA 1984, s. 255] (formerly FA 1975, Sch. 4, para. 26) (determination of questions on previous view of the law) and for estate duty FA 1951, s. 35 (restriction on re-opening cases on the ground of legal mistake).

See Inland Revenue Press Release, 8 June 1978.

E17. Incidence of tax

Withdrawn by Inland Revenue Press Release, 29 June 1984.

E18. Partial disclaimers of residue *(8 June 1978)*

Doubts have arisen as to whether under Scots law the provisions of [IHTA 1984, s. 142] (formerly FA 1975, s. 47) (deeds of family arrangement, etc.) which deal with disclaimers apply to partial disclaimers of residue. Hitherto the Revenue have taken the view that a residuary legatee could not disclaim part of his interest in the residuary estate. The Revenue have, however, been advised that under Scots law in certain circumstances a residuary legatee can make a partial disclaimer. Where, therefore, as a matter of general law such a partial disclaimer is possible, the Inland Revenue now accept that the provisions of [IHTA 1984, s. 142] (formerly FA 1975, s. 47) which deal with disclaimers apply. This view of the law will also be applied to existing cases subject to the statutory provisions which restrict the re-opening of settled cases.

See Inland Revenue Press Release, 8 June 1978.

STATEMENTS ISSUED AFTER 17 JULY 1978

SP10/79 *(15 August 1979)*
Power for trustees to allow a beneficiary to occupy dwelling-house

Many wills and settlements contain a clause empowering the trustees to permit a beneficiary to occupy a dwelling-house which forms part of the trust property on such terms as they think fit. The Revenue do not regard the existence of such a power as excluding any interest in possession in the property.

Where there is no interest in possession in the property in question, the Revenue do not regard the exercise of the power as creating one if the effect is merely to allow non-exclusive occupation or to create a contractual tenancy for full consideration. The Revenue also take the view that no interest in possession arises on the creation of a lease for a term or a periodic tenancy for less than full consideration, though this will normally give rise to a charge for tax under [IHTA 1984, s. 65]. On the other hand (1) (*b*) (formerly FA 1975, Sch. 5, para. 6 (3)), if the power is drawn in terms wide enough to cover the creation of an exclusive or joint right of residence, albeit revocable, for a definite or indefinite period, and is exercised with the intention of providing a particular beneficiary with a permanent home, the Revenue will normally regard the exercise of the power as creating an interest in possession. And if the trustees in exercise of their powers grant a lease for life for less than full consideration, this will also be regarded as creating an interest in possession in view of [IHTA 1984, ss. 43(3), 50(6)] (formerly FA 1975, Sch. 5, paras. 1 (3) and 3 (6)).

A similar view will be taken where the power is exercised over property in which another beneficiary had an interest in possession up to the time of the exercise.

See also Inland Revenue Press Release, 6 August 1975.

SP1/80 *(16 January 1980)*
Legal entitlement and administrative practices

The following is the text of a Written Answer given by the Minister of State, Treasury, Mr. Peter Rees, Q.C., M.P., today:

"Where an assessment has been made, and this shows a repayment due to the taxpayer, repayment is invariably made of the full amount.

For [IHT], assessments which lead to repayments of sums overpaid are not initiated automatically by the Capital Taxes Office if the amount involved is £10 or less.

The aim of these tolerances is to minimise work which is highly cost-ineffective; they cannot operate to deny a repayment to a taxpayer who has claimed his full entitlement."

SP12/80 *(13 October 1980)*
Business relief from [IHT]: "buy and sell" agreements

The Revenue understands that it is sometimes the practice for partners or shareholder directors of companies to enter into an agreement (known as a "Buy & Sell" Agreement) whereby, in the event of the death before retirement of one of them, the deceased's personal representatives are obliged to sell and the survivors are obliged to purchase the deceased's business interest of shares, funds for the purchase being frequently provided by means of appropriate life assurance policies.

In the Revenue's view such an agreement, requiring as it does a sale and purchase and not merely conferring an option to sell or buy, is a binding contract for sale within [IHTA 1984, s. 113] (formerly FA 1976, Sch. 10, para. 3 (4)). As a result the [IHT] business relief will not be due on the business interest or shares. ([IHTA 1984, s. 113]) (formerly FA 1975, Sch. 10, para. 3 (4)) provides that where any property would be relevant business property for the purpose of business relief in relation to atransfer of value but a binding contract for its sale has been entered into at the time of the transfer, it is not relevant business property in relation to that transfer).

See I.C.A.E.W. TR 557, 18 September 1984.

SP18/80 *(23 December 1980)*
Securities dealt in on the Stock Exchange Unlisted Securities Market: status and valuation for tax purposes

The Stock Exchange introduced an organised market in unlisted securities—the Unlisted Securities Market—on 10 November 1980.

In the view of the Revenue securities dealt in on the Unlisted Securities Market will not fall to be treated as "listed" or "quoted" for the purposes of those sections of the Taxes Acts which use these terms in relation to securities. The securities will, however, satisfy the tests of being "authorised to be dealt in" and "dealt in (regularly or from time to time)" on a recognised stock exchange.

Where it is necessary for tax purposes to agree the open market value of such securities on a given date, initial evidence of their value will be suggested by the details of the bargains done at or near the relevant date. However other factors may also be relevant and the Shares Valuation Division of the Capital Taxes Office will consider whether a value offered on the basis of those bargains can be accepted as an adequate reflection of the open market value.

SP1/82 *(6 April 1982)*
The interaction of income tax and [IHT] on assets put into settlements

1. For many years the tax code has contained legislation to prevent a person avoiding higher rate income tax by making a settlement, while still retaining some rights to enjoy the income or capital of the settlement. This legislation, which is embodied in TA 1970, Part XVI, provides in general terms that the income of a settlement shall, for income tax purposes, be treated as that of the settlor in all circumstances where the settlor might benefit directly or indirectly from the settlement.
2. If the trustees have power to pay or do in fact pay capital transfer tax due on assets which the settlor puts into the settlement the Inland Revenue have taken the view that the settlor has thereby an interest in the income or property of the settlement, and that the income of the settlement should be treated as his for tax purposes under TA 1970, Part XVI.
3. The [IHT] legislation [IHTA 1984, ss. 199–201] (formerly FA 1975, s. 25 (2) and (3)) however provides that both the settlor and the trustees are liable for any capital transfer tax payable when a settlor puts assets into a settlement. The Board of Inland Revenue have therefore decided that they will no longer, in these circumstances, treat the income of the settlement as that of the settlor for income tax purposes solely because the trustees have power to pay or do in fact pay [IHT] on assets put into settlements.
4. This change of practice applies to settlement income for 1981–82, *et seq.*

SP8/86 *(10 November 1986)*
IHT: treatment of income of discretionary trusts

1. This statement modified the Revenue's existing practice concerning the IHT treatment of income of discretionary trusts.
2. The view had been taken that undistributed and unaccumulated income in the trustees' hands is a taxable trust asset. For the purpose of determining the rate of charge, income (whether or not accumulated) was regarded as having been comprised in the trust for as long as the original trust from which the income or accumulation had derived.
3. However, in view of the opinions expressed in some cases recently, the Inland Revenue have sought fresh legal advice on this interpretation of the legislation.

Change of practice
4. In the light of that advice the Board of Inland Revenue now take the view—

(*a*) that *undistributed and unaccumulated income* should not be treated as a taxable trust asset, and

(*b*) that, for the purpose of determining the rate of charge on *accumulated income*, the income should be treated as becoming a taxable asset of the trust on the date when the accumulation is made.

Application of revised practice
5. This change in practice will be applied to all new cases and to existing cases where the tax liability has not been settled.

SP10/86 *(9 July 1986)*
IHT: death benefits under superannuation arrangements

The Board of Inland Revenue have confirmed that their existing practice of not charging capital transfer tax on death benefits that are payable from tax-approved occupational pension and retirement annuity schemes under discretionary trusts, will also apply to inheritance tax.

The practice will extend to tax under the gifts with reservation rules as well as to tax under the ordinary inheritance tax rules.

Notes
1. A gift with reservation is one where the donor retains some benefit from the property he has given away. A contribution to a pension scheme might be a gift with reservation if it was meant to provide (as alternative benefits) either a pension for the contributor or death benefits payable to a third party. A declaration of trust relating to death benefits would be a gift with reservation if the contributor was one of the possible beneficiaries.
2. Many occupational pension schemes and self-employed retirement annuity schemes provide for death benefits to be paid through a discretionary trust, to be distributed to selected beneficiaries within two years of the death. The death benefit is not charged to capital transfer tax if the scheme itself has tax approval.
3. Some pensions experts have suggested that the inheritance tax rules about gifts with reservation might override this exemption. This is not so. The inheritance tax proposals effectively restore the former estate duty practice in relation to gifts with reservation. If the death benefit would have been exempt under CTT, it will also be exempt under IHT—even if it arose from a gift with reservation.
4. The schemes to which the practice applies are occupational pension schemes, retirement annuity contracts and retirement annuity trust schemes that have been approved by the Revenue for tax purposes, and the equivalent statutory schemes.

SP6/87 *(8 April 1987)*
Acceptance of property in lieu of IHT, CTT and estate duty

In his Budget, the Chancellor proposed that people who offer heritage property in lieu of inheritance tax on other property will be given the option of having the offset against tax calculated by reference to the value of the property at the date of the offer instead of its value at the date of acceptance. When this option is chosen, interest on the tax will cease to accrue from the date of the offer.

Clause 151 of the Finance Bill [now FA 1987, s. 60], published today, contains provisions that will allow the Revenue to accept property on these terms. Amendments will be proposed to extend the provisions so that they also cover acceptances in satisfaction of capital transfer tax, estate duty, and interest on tax or duty.

How the arrangements will work
1. The Revenue may, with the agreement of the departmental ministers with responsibility for the environment and the arts, accept heritage property in whole or part satisfaction of an inheritance tax, capital transfer tax or estate duty debt. Property can be accepted in satisfaction of interest accrued on the tax as well as the tax itself. Full details of the arrangements are given in Chapter 11 of the Revenue booklet "Capital Taxation and the National Heritage" (IR 67), see Appendix 5.
2. No capital tax is payable on property that is accepted in lieu of tax. The amount of tax satisfied is determined by agreeing a special price at which the departmental ministers reimburse the Revenue. This price is found by establishing an agreed value for the item and deducting a proportion of the tax given up on the item itself, using an agreement known as the "douceur".
3. Until now, the special price has been calculated from the value of the item at the time the Revenue accepted it. Interest was payable on the outstanding tax up to that date.
4. In future, if the provisions in the current Finance Bill are enacted, the persons liable for the tax which is to be satisfied by an acceptance in lieu will be able to choose between the exisiting

arrangements and new arrangements under which the special price will be calculated from the value of the item on the date they offer it. When they choose the new "offer date" arrangements, interest on the tax satisfied by the item will cease to accrue on that date.

5. The terms on which property is accepted are a matter for negotiation. Since most offers are made initially on the basis of the current value of the item, the Revenue propose to consider them on the new "offer date" basis unless the offerer notifies them that he wishes to adopt the present "acceptance date" basis of valuation. The offerer's option will normally remain open until the item is formally accepted. But this will be the subject of review if more than two years elapse from the date of the offer without the terms being settled. The Revenue may then give six months' notice that they will no longer be prepared to accept the item of the "offer date" basis.

6. If the Finance Bill provisions are enacted, the "offer date" basis will be available for formal acceptances on or after 17 March 1987 (Budget Day). This will include acceptances of items under consideration before them. The Revenue will consider provisional acceptances on the "offer date" basis pending Royal Assent if the offerer wishes them to do so. Acceptances given before 17 March cannot be reopened.

See IHTA 1984, ss. 230, 234.

SP7/87 *(15 July 1987)*
IHT: deduction for reasonable funeral expenses

The term "funeral expenses" in IHTA 1984, s. 172 has previously been construed as excluding the cost of a tombstone. However, the Board of Inland Revenue now take the view that the term allows a deduction from the value of a deceased's estate for the cost of a tombstone or gravestone.

APPENDIX 3. EXTRA-STATUTORY CONCESSIONS

(Note judicial comments in *I.R. Comrs.* v. *Frere* [1965] AC 402, at 409, *I.R. Comrs.* v. *Bates* [1968] AC 483, at 516, *Vestey* v. *I.R. Comrs.* (*No. 2*) [1978] STC 567).

LIST OF CONCESSIONS

CONCESSIONS IN BOOKLET IR1 (1988)

Concessions relating to IHT (and CTT)

No.

F1   Mourning
F2   Roman Catholic religious communities
F3   *Inter vivos gifts to charities.* (See concession J1)
F4   *Agricultural property.* (See concession J2)
F5   Deaths of members of the Royal Ulster Constabulary
F6   Foreign assets
F7   Foreign owned works of art
F8   Accumulation and maintenance settlements
F9   *Relief for successive charges.* (See concession J3)
F10 Partnership assurance policies
F11 Property chargeable on the ceasing of an annuity
F12 Disposition for maintenance of dependent relative
F13 Subsequent devolutions of property under the wills of persons dying before 12 March 1952 whose estates were wholly exempted from estate duty under FA 1894, s. 8 (1)
F14 *Inter vivos gifts: deduction for development gains tax and development land tax.* (See concession J4)

Concessions relating to CTT only

No.

J1   Inter vivos gifts to charities
J2   Agricultural property
J3   Relief for successive charges
J4   Inter vivos gifts: deduction for development gains tax and development land tax

F
INHERITANCE TAX (AND CAPITAL TRANSFER TAX)

F1. Mourning
A reasonable amount for mourning for the family and servants is allowed as a funeral expense.

F2. Roman Catholic religious communities
The property of Roman Catholic religious communities whose purposes are charitable is treated as trust property, held for a charitable purpose even where there is no enforceable trust, with the result that IHT is not claimed on the death of one of the nominal owners of the property.

F3. *(Superseded by Concession J1).*

F4. *(Superseded by Concession J2).*

F5. Deaths of members of the Royal Ulster Constabulary
The relief from IHT under IHTA 1984, s. 154 granted in certain circumstances to the estates of members of the armed forces, is applied to the estates of members of the Royal Ulster Constabulary who die from injuries caused in Northern Ireland by terrorist activity.

F6. Foreign assets
Where, because of restrictions imposed by the foreign government, executors cannot immediately transfer to this country sufficient of the deceased's foreign assets for the payment of the IHT attributable to them, they are given the option of deferring payment until the transfer can be effected. If the amount in sterling that the executors finally succeed in bringing to this country is less than this tax, the balance is waived.

F7. Foreign owned works of art
Where a work of art normally kept overseas becomes liable to IHT on the owner's death solely because it is physically situated in the U.K. at the relevant date, the liability will—by concession—be waived if the work was brought into the U.K. solely for public exhibition, cleaning or restoration. If the work of art is held by a discretionary trust (or is otherwise comprised in settled property in which there is no interest in possession), the charge to tax arising under IHTA 1984, s. 64 will, similarly, be waived.

F8. Accumulation and maintenance settlements
The requirement of FA 1975, Sch. 5 para. 15 (1) (*a*) [repealed] or IHTA 1984, s. 71 (1) (*a*) is regarded as being satisfied even if no age is specified in the trust instrument, provided that it is clear that a beneficiary will in fact become entitled to the settled property (or to an interest in possession in it) by the age of 25.

F9. *(Superseded by Concession J3).*

F10. Partnership assurance policies
A partnership assurance scheme under which each partner effects a policy on his own life in trust for the other partners is not regarded as a settlement for IHT purposes if the following conditions are fulfilled:
  —The premiums paid on the policy fall within IHTA 1984, s. 10 (exemption for dispositions not intended to confer a gratuitous benefit on any person).
  —The policy was effected prior to 15 September 1976 and has not been varied on or after that date (but the exercise of a power of appointment under a "discretionary" trust policy would not be regarded as a variation for this purpose).
  —The trusts of the policy are governed by English law or by Scots law, provided that in the latter case the policy does not directly or indirectly involve a partnership itself as a separate persona.

F11. Property chargeable on the ceasing of an annuity
Where an IHT charge arises when an annuitant under a settlement either dies or disposes of his interest and
  —the annuity is charged wholly or in part on real or leasehold property, and
  —the Board is satisfied that a capital valuation of the property at the relevant date restricted to its existing use, reflects an anticipated increase in rents obtainable for that use after that date appropriate relief will be given in calculating the proportion of the property on which tax is chargeable.

F12. Disposition for maintenance of dependent relative
A disposition by a child in favour of his unmarried mother (so far as it represents a reasonable provision for her care or maintenance) qualifies for exemption under IHTA 1984, s. 11 (3) if the mother is incapacitated by old age or infirmity from maintaining herself. By concession such a disposition is also treated as exempt if the mother (although not so incapacitated) is genuinely financially dependent on the child making the disposition.

F13. Subsequent devolutions of property under the wills of persons dying before 12 March 1952 whose estates were wholly exempted from estate duty under FA 1894, s. 8 (1).
Where a person died before 12 March 1952 and his estate was wholly exempted from estate duty as the property of a common seaman, marine or soldier who dies in the service of the Crown and under his will he left a limited interest to someone who dies on or after 12 March 1975, IHT is not charged on any property exempted on the original death which passes under the terms of the will on the termination of the limited interest.

F14. *(Superseded by Concession J4).*

J
CAPITAL TRANSFER TAX ONLY

J1. Inter vivos gifts to charities
Where, at the donor's death, there is no existing fund which has been and continues to be directly benefited by the gift, the claim to tax is not pursued against the charitable institution.

J2. Agricultural property
For the purposes of the CTT relief for agricultural property, buildings used in connection with the intensive rearing of livestock or fish on a commercial basis for the production of food for human consumption are treated as "agricultural property".

J3. Relief for successive charges
Where there is a chargeable transfer of settled property in which there is an interest in possession, and the transferor became entitled to his interest not more than 4 years earlier on a death on which estate duty was payable in respect of the settled property, FA 1975, Sch. 5, para. 5 (2) [repealed] provides for a reduction in the taxable value of the settled property on the second occasion. If however the transferor acquired his interest on an occasion on which neither estate duty nor CTT was payable but, on or after the making of the settlement, and within 4 years of the chargeable transfer, there had been a death on which estate duty was payable in respect of the settled property, relief under this paragraph will be given by reference to the latter death.

J4. Inter vivos gifts: deductions for development gains tax and development land tax
 Lapsed 19 March 1985.

APPENDIX 4. INTESTACY RULES

The following information has been compiled from "The Solicitors' and Barristers' Directory and Diary" and is reproduced by kind permission of Waterlow Publishers Ltd.

Administration of Estates Act 1925 as amended for deaths after 1 June 1987

Surviving relative(s)	Person(s) entitled to the estate	Person(s) entitled to grant of letters of Administration
1. Spouse[1] only	Surviving Spouse[1] absolutely	Surviving Spouse[1]
2. Spouse[1] and Issue[2]	(a) Surviving Spouse[1] takes (i) Personal chattels (ii) £75,000[3] (iii) Life interest in half residuary estate (b) Issue[2] take residuary estate at age 18[6] subject to life interest in half of surviving spouse in equal shares per stirpes	Surviving Spouse[1] and one other person[4]
3. Spouse[1] and Parent(s)	(a) Surviving Spouse[1] takes (i) Personal chattels (ii) £125,000[3] (iii) Half residuary estate absolutely (b) Parent(s) take half residuary estate (in equal shares)	Surviving Spouse[1]
4. Spouse[1] and Brother(s) and/or Sister(s) of the whole blood and/or issue of such who predeceased the intestate	(a) Surviving Spouse[1] takes (i) Personal chattels (ii) £125,000[3] (iii) Half residuary estate absolutely (b) Brother(s) and Sister(s) and/or issue takes half residuary estate at age 18[6] in equal shares per stirpes	Surviving Spouse (and one other person)[4]
5. Issue	Issue at age 18[6] in equal shares per stirpes	Issue
6. Parent(s)	Parent(s) in equal shares	Parent
7. Brother(s) and/or Sister(s) of the whole blood and/or issue of such who predeceased the intestate	Brother(s) and Sister(s) and/or issue at age 18[6] in equal shares per stirpes	Brother or Sister or issue etc (and one other person)[4]
8. Brother(s) and/or Sister(s) of the half blood and/or issue of such who predeceased the intestate	Half Brother(s) and Sister(s) and/or issue at age 18[6] in equal shares per stirpes	Half Brother or Sister or issue etc (and one other person)[4]
9. Grandparent(s)	Grandparent(s) in equal shares	Grandparent
10. Uncle(s) and/or Aunt(s) of the whole blood and/or issue of such who predeceased the intestate	Uncle(s) and Aunt(s) and/or issue at age 18[6] in equal shares per stirpes	Uncle or Aunt or issue etc (and one other person)[4]
11. Uncle(s) and/or Aunt(s) of the half blood and/or issue of such who predeceased intestate	Such Uncle(s) and Aunt(s) and/or issue at age 18[6] in equal shares per stirpes	Such Uncle, Aunt or issue etc (and one other person)[4]
12. No relative as mentioned above	The Crown as bona vacantia	The Crown

Notes

1. Where a decree of judicial separation is in force and the separation is continuing at the date of death the estate of the intestate devolves as if his or her surviving spouse were dead.

2. "Issue" includes issue through all degrees.

(*a*) *Illegitimate children* took no interest before 1926; between 1926 and 1970 on the death of his or her mother, provided no legitimate issue survived her, an illegitimate child took such interest as if he or she had been born legitimate; after 1970, an illegitimate child has the same right of inheritance of his or her parent's estate as a legitimate child.

(*b*) *Adopted children*: from 1949 on the death of the adopter his or her estate devolves as if the adopted person had been born in wedlock and was not the child of any person other than his or her adopters. An adopted person is deemed to become the brother or sister of the whole blood of the other lawful or adopted children of the adopters; of the half blood, in other cases.

(*c*) *Legitimated children* take as if legitimate save as to real or personal property devolving with a dignity or title of honour.

3. The sum payable to the surviving spouse must be paid out of capital. Interest at the rate of 6 per cent. a year being the current rate with effect from 1 October 1983 up to the date of payment should if possible be paid out of income. For deaths in earlier years the relevant lump sums were as follows:

Date of Death	Issue surviving	No Issue surviving
	£	£
1.1.26 to 31.12.52	1,000	1,000*
1.1.53 to 31.12.66	5,000	20,000
1.1.67 to 30.6.72	8,750	30,000
1.7.72 to 14.3.77	15,000	40,000
15.3.77 to 30.4.81	25,000	55,000
1.5.81 to 31.5.87	40,000	85,000

* Up to 1952 where no issue survived, in place of the larger capital sum the surviving spouse took a life interest in the whole estate, subject to which the residue was held on the statutory trusts for the other relatives in classes 6 to 11 above. If no such relatives survived the surviving spouse took the whole estate absolutely.

4. If there is a minority or life interest arising under the distribution of the estate of the intestate there must be at least two (but not more than four) administrators.

5. The surviving spouse may elect under the Administration of Estates Act 1925, s. 47A, to have his or her life interest redeemed for a capital sum.

6. (i) Age 21 if the death was before 1 January 1970.

(ii) In the event that a minor beneficiary under the distribution aforesaid dies before attaining the age of 18 and without leaving issue capable of taking his share by substitution, the distribution of the estate is completed as if such deceased beneficiary had predeceased the intestate.

(iii) The Trustee Act 1925, ss. 31 and 32, will apply to any fund in which under the foregoing rules there subsist minority or life interests.

APPENDIX 5. CAPITAL TAXATION AND THE NATIONAL HERITAGE

December 1986. Inland Revenue (IR 67)
February 1988. Inland Revenue (IR 67 Finance Acts 1987 Supplement)

This booklet outlines the scope of the legislation on capital taxation at 1 December 1986 and its effect on the national heritage, and gives guidance on the approach which is adopted in administering its provisions. It replaces the memorandum published by the Treasury in 1983. The booklet itself has no binding force. If further information is required please refer to the Capital Taxes Office (Designated Property Section).

This material is Crown copyright, reproduced with the permission of the Controller of Her Majesty's Stationery Office.

CONTENTS

Chapter 1 INTRODUCTION

Preservation of the heritage—general policy

1.1 Buildings of historic or architectural interest, land of historic, scenic or scientific interest, and objects and collections of national, artistic, historic or scientific interest form an integral and major part of the cultural life of this country. It has been the policy of successive Governments that this national heritage should be conserved and protected for the benefit of the community. They have taken the view that so far as possible property of this kind should remain in private hands and that its owners should be encouraged to retain and care for it and display it to the public; and that where this is no longer possible the owners should dispose of it to those bodies in this country which have been set up specifically to hold such property in trust for the community.

1.2 Over the past 90 years a succession of fiscal and other measures have been introduced to help preserve the heritage. The latter include:

(*a*) The allocation of substantial financial resources to maintain and enhance the collections in our national museums and galleries and to preserve historic buildings and monuments owned by, or in the guardianship of, the Secretaries of State.

(*b*) Grant aid to owners towards the repair of historic buildings. (Information about these is available from the Historic Buildings and Monuments Commission for England or the Historic Buildings Councils for Scotland, Wales and Northern Ireland.)

(*c*) Establishment with Exchequer grant aid of the Countryside Commissions and the Nature Conservancy Council who advise on conservation and whose duties include administering grants for the acquisition and management of outstanding scenic and scientific land.

(*d*) Annual grants to the National Heritage Memorial Fund which was set up on 1 April 1980 to assist in the acquisition, preservation and maintenance of outstanding land, buildings and objects. The Fund's trustees have wide discretion to make grants and loans to public and private bodies concerned with preserving the heritage in its widest sense.

(*e*) Introduction of successive legislative measures including the Wildlife and Countryside Act 1981 (and corresponding provisions in Northern Ireland and Scotland) which, among other things, empowers local planning authorities to make management agreements, with payments, for conservation of the natural beauty and amenity of the countryside and, in National Parks, to give grants and loans for that purpose.

Purpose of booklet
1.3 This booklet describes the current *fiscal* provisions relating to heritage property. It sets out the capital tax reliefs available, the arrangements for dealing with claims for these reliefs, the arrangements for private treaty sales to national collections and certain other bodies, and the procedures for offering property in satisfaction of inheritance tax, capital transfer tax or estate duty. It also describes the income tax arrangements relating to maintenance funds (Chapter 8 and Appendix 5) and contains some pointers on the application of stamp duty (Chapters **8.4, 8.6, 9.2, 9.3** and **11.1** and Appendix 5) and VAT (Chapters **10.9** and **11.1**).
1.4 A number of Government Departments and other bodies are referred to in this booklet. They and their addresses are listed in Appendix 8.

Developments since last edition
1.5 This booklet replaces the memorandum published by the Treasury in July 1983 and reflects legislative and other changes made up to 1 December 1986.
1.6 The booklet's production by the Inland Revenue reflects the fact that, as a result of FA 1985, s. 95, the Department took over the former responsibilities of the Treasury for capital tax reliefs for heritage property with effect from 25 July 1985. These functions include:
   (*a*) Assessing, in conjunction with the advisory agencies, the suitability of property for relief.
   (*b*) Obtaining appropriate undertakings about maintenance and preservation of, and public access to, the heritage property and then formally designating qualifying property.
   (*c*) Monitoring whether the undertakings are subsequently observed.
   (*d*) Approving the terms of maintenance funds set up to support qualifying heritage property and monitoring the activities of those funds.
   (*e*) Related second-order responsibilities such as approving public institutions as recipients of exempt heritage property and approving the temporary export of qualifying works of art.
1.7 Of the other changes which have been made since July 1983, the most significant relate to CTT. Two specific heritage measures were included in FA 1985 and apply with effect from 19 March 1985. They are as follows:
   (*a*) Alterations have been made to the conditions for exemption of land essential for the protection of the character and amenities of a building of outstanding historical or architectural interest. Details of the revised conditions are given in Chapter 6.
   (*b*) Owners are required to agree with the Inland Revenue the detailed steps necessary to give effect to the general undertakings—see Chapters **4.4, 5.7** and **6.6**.
1.8 The more general changes have included the following:
   (*a*) The CTT legislation was consolidated in CTTA 1984 which came into force on 1 January 1985. It applies to transfers of value and other events occurring on or after that date. The consolidated Act re-enacts all the earlier provisions.
   (*b*) CTT was replaced by IHT with effect from 18 March 1986. The new tax is charged under an amended version of the CTTA, referred to in this booklet by its new alternative title IHTA 1984.

Other relevant official publications
1.9 In the case of works of art, other leaflets have been produced by the Office of Arts and Libraries which summarise and illustrate the benefits of the tax reliefs and provide guidance on the administrative procedures involved in particular cirumstances. These are:
   (*a*) Works of Art: A basic Guide to Capital Taxation and the National Heritage.
   (*b*) Private Treaty Sales of Works of Art.
   (*c*) Works of Art: Guidelines on in situ offers in lieu of capital taxation.
   See Appendix 6.
1.10 For land of outstanding scenic interest, the Countryside Commission has published a general leaflet on capital tax reliefs and what is involved in obtaining them, and a guide to preparing simple management plans as a format for the conditions of exemption:

(*a*) Capital Tax Relief for Outstanding Scenic Land CCP 204.

(*b*) Heritage Landscapes Management Plans CCP 205.

These can be obtained free of charge from Countryside Commission Publications Despatch Department, 19/23 Albert Road, Manchester M19 2EQ.

Chapter 2 THE CAPITAL TAXES BRIEFLY DESCRIBED

2.1 There are four capital taxes from which reliefs are available in respect of national heritage property: capital transfer tax (CTT), inheritance tax (IHT), estate duty (ED) and capital gains tax (CGT).

2.2 *Capital transfer tax* was introduced in FA 1975. It applies to lifetime transfers of value made after 26 March 1974 and before 18 March 1986 and to all deaths occurring after 12 March 1975 and before 18 March 1986. Lifetime transfers are cumulated for 10 years and are charged at half of the rate applicable to transfers made on, or within three years of, death. For transfers between 6 April 1985 and 17 March 1986, the threshold below which tax is not charged is £67,000. CTT is not charged on the first £3,000 of the lifetime transfers which a person makes in any one tax year. Transfers between spouses domiciled in the U.K. are also exempt.

2.3* *Inheritance tax*, was introduced in FA 1986. It applies to transfers made, deaths and certain other events occurring on or after 18 March 1986. Like its predecessor, it is a tax on gratuitous transfers by individuals. The *major difference* between the two is the treatment of *lifetime transfers*. Outright transfers between individuals, termed "potentially exempt transfers", are exempt from IHT if the transferor lives on for seven years. Gifts made within seven years of death are charged at death rates but the charge is tapered where the gift occurs more than three years before death. Special charging rules apply where gifts are made but the donor reserves or enjoys a benefit. The charge on *death* is retained and most of the CTT exemptions and reliefs (*e.g.* inter-spouse transfers) have been continued. Subject to some minor adjustments, IHT adopts the existing CTT regime for the taxation of *trust related transfers*, which remain subject to the full range of charges at the time they are made (the rates of charge are still half those of the death scale). The *cumulation period* for all chargeable transfers (trust and other) has been reduced from 10 to seven years. At the time of publication, the threshold below which tax is not chargeable is £71,000.*

*See 1987 Supplement, p. 213 below.

2.4 *Estate duty*, which applies to property passing on a death *before 13 March 1975*, may be relevant on the *sale* now of heritage objects which have previously been exempted from estate duty. The statutory provisions are described in Appendix 3.

2.5 *Capital gains tax* is chargeable at 30 per cent. on gains arising since 6 April 1965 (or a later acquisition date) on the disposal of assets. In broad terms the amount of a chargeable gain is the difference between the cost of an asset and the proceeds received on its sale less an adjustment ("indexation allowance") which broadly takes account of the inflationary element of the gain accruing since March 1982. An individual (or married couple living together) is entitled to an annual personal exemption, which for 1986–87 is £6,300* but whose value has in recent years been adjusted annually in line with increases in retail prices. Only net gains (*i.e.* total gains less losses) above this figure are charged to CGT. Chargeable gains arising on gifts of assets by individuals and on distributions of assets by trustees may be held over until a subsequent disposal of the asset. There is no charge to the tax on unrealised gains on assets held by an individual at his death. The gains accruing on the disposal of an individual chattel is exempt if the consideration received for it does not exceed £3,000.

Chapter 3 CAPITAL TAXES: SUMMARY OF HERITAGE RELIEFS AVAILABLE

3.1 This chapter gives a brief description of the reliefs which are available to owners of national heritage property. The various categories of property which may qualify for the reliefs and the conditions which have to be met are dealt with in greater detail in subsequent chapters. The procedures for making a claim are set out in Appendix 1.

3.2 In this and succeeding Chapters the CTT and IHT heritage provisions are described together because they are broadly similar. A number of essentially technical changes have been made to the CTT heritage provisions to ensure that they mesh in with the new IHT general structure. These are detailed in the appropriate parts of the remainder of this booklet and are summarised in Appendix 6.

Capital transfer tax and inheritance tax

Conditional exemption (see Chapters 4–6)

3.3 A chargeable transfer of qualifying national heritage property is conditionally exempt from CTT or IHT (as the case may be) when formally designated following receipt of undertakings given by an appropriate person—usually the new owner—to preserve the property and allow reasonable public access to it, and, in the case of works of art and other objects, not to send it out of the U.K. Where an exemption claim is made in respect of property gifted in lifetime on or after 18 March 1986 which becomes chargeable to IHT because of the donor's death within seven years of the gift and undertakings are already in force (in respect of an associated maintenance fund or a CGT exemption claim), those undertakings are normally accepted for the purposes of the IHT conditional exemption claim and do *not* need to be duplicated (IHTA 1984, s. 31 (4G)—as introduced by FA 1986, Sch. 19, para. 8 (2)). In practice, there will normally be no need for duplication either where there is an undertaking in force given under IHTA 1984, s. 31 (4A). As is explained below, a breach of the undertakings or a sale of the property will normally lead to a loss of the exemption, and that is why it is called "conditional". The form of the undertakings which are required varies according to the type of property transferred and is discussed in **Chapters 4–6**. When a claim has been allowed the heritage property concerned is formally 'designated'.

3.4 Conditional exemption from CTT can be claimed:

(a) for a transfer made on death; and

(b) for a lifetime if the transferor (or his spouse or the two between them) has been beneficially entitled to the property for at least the preceding six years; or if the transferor has inherited the property on a death when it was conditionally exempted from CTT or ED. (IHTA 1984, s. 30).

3.5* Conditional exemption from IHT can be claimed:

*See 1987 Supplement, p. 213 below.

(a) for a transfer made on death;

(b) for a lifetime transfer to someone other than an individual, for example a transfer into trust (other than an accumulation and maintenance settlement or a trust for disabled persons) or to a company;

(c) for a lifetime transfer to an individual where the donor reserves or enjoys a benefit which subsists until, or which is given up within seven years of, his or her death; and

(d) for an outright lifetime transfer to an individual where the donor dies within the following seven years.

In the cases described in subparagraphs (b) and (d) (and in those described in subparagraph (c) where the benefit is given up within seven years of death), the conditions mentioned in para. 3.4 (b) have to be met. In the cases described in subparagraphs (c) and (d), conditional exemption cannot be claimed *unless or until the transfer becomes chargeable as a result of the donor's death* (IHTA 1984, s. 30 (3B)—as introduced by FA 1986, Sch. 19, para. 7). *Title to exemption in such circumstances is determined by reference to the circumstances existing at the time of the claim* (IHTA 1984, s. 31 (1A)—as introduced by FA 1986, Sch. 19 para. 8 (1)).

3.6* *Special rules apply* where, between the respective dates of a lifetime gift "caught" on death (because the gift was made within the preceding seven years) and the death itself, there have been certain intermediate events:

(a) If the property has meanwhile been given, or sold by private treaty, to one of the national bodies listed in IHTA 1984, Sch. 3 (see **3.9** (iii)) or if it has been accepted in satisfaction of tax (see **3.9** (iv)), the charge on death is exempted outright without the need for undertakings to be given (IHTA 1984, s. 26A—as introduced by FA 1986, Sch. 19 para. 6).

(b) If the property has meanwhile been sold in other circumstances, a conditional exemption claim is precluded in respect of the charge arising on the donor's subsequent death (IHTA 1984, s. 30 (3C)—as introduced by FA 1986, Sch. 19 para. 7). (In contrast, if in the interim the property has been the subject of a further gift, a claim for exemption in respect of the first gift can be made if the existing owner is prepared to give the necessary undertakings.)

Disposal of conditionally exempt property (see Chapter 7)

3.7 Once the property has been designated for conditional exemption, both the property itself and the undertakings given in respect of it will be monitored to check whether the property has been sold and whether the undertakings are being honoured. A breach of the undertakings or a sale of the property will normally lead to a loss of the exemption.

3.8 The consequences can be illustrated by taking the example of a man who inherited a picture of national heritage quality from his mother and gave undertakings of the kind described in **3.3** so that no CTT or IHT was paid on the picture as part of his mother's estate.

3.9 If he now wants to part with his picture there are several options open to him. Some will not involve him in paying any CTT or IHT. Others will.

(a) *No CTT or IHT to pay*

(i) He can give the picture away with the recipient renewing the undertakings mentioned in paragraph **3.3** above. In this case the conditional exemption runs on (IHTA 1984, s. 32 (5)).

(ii) He can give the picture to one of the bodies listed in IHTA 1984, Sch. 3 (see Appendix 10). Gifts and bequests to these bodies are exempt from CTT and IHT altogether so that if he does this the conditional exemption becomes absolute (IHTA 1984, s. 32 (4) (a) Chapter 9).

(iii) He can sell the picture *by private treaty* to one of the Sch. 3 bodies, when again the conditional exemption becomes absolute (IHTA 1984, s. 32 (4) (*a*)). In these circumstances the value of the tax exemption is shared between the vendor and the purchasing body under an administrative arrangement known as the "douceur". The vendor and the purchaser will negotiate the market value of the picture (the Government does not intervene in this process in any way) and then deduct the tax which would have been payable if it had been sold for that amount in the open market. The vendor will receive the net sum together with a proportion of the notional tax and the purchasing body will get the benefit of the balance of the notional tax by paying less than the estimated market price. On a sale, by private treaty, of land and buildings the vendor may in general receive 10 per cent. of the value of the tax exemption; on a sale of objects by private treaty, he may in general receive 25 per cent. of that value, but in both cases the precise amount will be determined in negotiation between the vendor and the purchaser. Further details of this arrangement are given in Chapter 10 and illustrative examples are shown in Appendices 11 and 12.

(iv) If he has CTT or IHT to pay on some other transfer or if he has an outstanding ED liability, he can offer the picture to the Government in whole or part satisfaction of his liability. If the Government agree to take it this is known as *acceptance in lieu*. The amount which he can pay by this means will be worked out in a similar way as described in paragraph **3.9** (*a*) (iii) above—in other words it will be arrived at just as if he had made a private treaty sale to the Government—*except* that when property is accepted in lieu the "douceur" is fixed at 25 per cent. for objects and 10 per cent. for land and there is no flexibility in these percentages. The valuation used is that agreed at the date of acceptance, not the date of the offer, of the property (Chapter 11).*

*See 1987 Supplement, p. 213 below.

(*b*) *CTT or IHT to pay*

If instead of any of these options, the owner of the picture either

(i) sells it on the open market, or
(ii) gives or bequeaths it to somebody who does *not* renew the undertakings, or
(iii) breaks the undertakings himself

he will lose the conditional exemption and will have to pay CTT or IHT in place of the tax which was not charged on the picture when he acquired it (IHTA 1984, s. 32 (2)). This will be calculated on the sale proceeds, or the open market value of the picture at the time the conditional exemption was lost, as appropriate (IHTA 1984, s. 33 (1) (*a*) and (3)). In case (ii) there could also be tax to pay on the gift or bequest of the picture but in such cases, there are rules to ensure that in effect only the higher of the two charges is payable (IHTA 1984, s. 33 (7), (8), the latter being introduced by FA 1986, Sch. 19, para. 11 (4).

Property held in trust

3.10 In general the arrangements described in the preceding subparagraphs apply also to transfers of heritage property held in trust (see Appendix 2).

Help with maintenance etc. of property (see Chapter 8 and Appendix 5)

3.11 The owner of an outstanding building, land essential for the protection of the character and amenities of it, or objects historically associated with it, or land of outstanding scenic, historic or scientific interest may want to set up a trust fund—a "Maintenance Fund"—to provide for the maintenance, repair or preservation of the property and for the provision of reasonable public access to it. Exemption can be claimed from the CTT or IHT normally payable on the setting up of a trust fund for this purpose (IHTA 1984, s. 27 and Sch. 4). The assets of such a fund are exempt from the ten-yearly CTT and IHT charges on discretionary trusts (IHTA 1984, s. 58 (1) (*c*)) and distributions out for qualifying heritage purposes are exempt from the proportionate CTT or IHT charge which normally falls on discretionary trust distributions (IHTA 1984, Sch. 4 para. 8 (2)). (These funds may also be favourably treated for income tax purposes—see **8.4** (*c*)).

Capital gains tax

3.12 Provided that the conditions for conditional exemption are satisfied, relief from CGT will be available in all the situations described at paragraph **3.9** (*a*) (i)–(iii) above. Property cannot be accepted in lieu of CGT—paragraph **3.9** (*a*) (iv)—but no CGT is charged if property is accepted in lieu of CTT or IHT (although the notional CGT charge is taken into account in the douceur calculation (see Chapter 11).

3.13 The relief from CGT takes two forms:

(*a*) *Outright exemption* is available:

(i) for gifts or bequests to a Sch. 3 body listed in Appendix 10 if the property has been the subject of a conditionally exempt transfer for CTT, IHT or CGT and the appropriate undertakings—described in Chapters 4–6 are in force (CGTA 1979, s. 147 (2) (*a*));

(ii) for gifts of heritage property (as defined in IHTA 1984, s. 26 (2)), or property given as a source of income for the upkeep of thereof, made for public benefit to a body not established or conducted for profit (CGTA, s. 147 (1))—see **9.4**;

(iii) for private treaty sales to a Sch. 3 body (see para. **3.9** (*a*) (iii)—if the property has been the subject of a conditionally exempt transfer for CTT, IHT or CGT and the appropriate undertakings—described in Chapters 4–6—are in force (CGTA 1979, s. 147 (2) (*a*)). If such undertakings have not been given, exemption may be allowed by concession provided that the "douceur" arrangement, as described in para. **3.9** (*a*) (iii) and **10.4**, has been used; and

(iv) for property accepted in lieu of CTT or IHT—see **3.12**.

(*b*) *Deferment of charge* is available:

(i) for gifts to charity—see **3.14**—or to a Sch. 3 body where outright exemption is not available because the property is not the subject of current heritage undertakings. The transfer is treated as not giving rise to any gain and any charge to tax is deferred by carrying forward the gain until there is a subsequent disposal of the property (CGTA 1979, 146);

(ii) for gifts of property for which *conditional exemption* is claimed (CGTA 1979 s. 147 (3) and (4)) (any gain will be charged only if the asset is transferred again without once more qualifying for relief, or if the coinditions of the undertakings are breached—CGTA 1979, s. 147 (5) and (6));

(iii) for gifts of property for which *holdover relief* is claimed. This is available when property is given by one individual to another, or transferred into or out of settlement. In the cases of gifts between individuals and of transfers from a serttlement to an individual, relief has to be claimed by both of them, but in the case of gifts by an individual into trust, including a maintenance fund, or transfers between settlements, by the transferor only. In that event the charge is deferred until there is a subsequent chargeable disposal by the asset's new owner. If that disposal is itself a transfer qualifying for the relief, the charge will be deferred again. (FA 1980, s. 79 as amended by FA 1981, s. 78 and FA 1982, s. 82).

CHARITIES

3.14. This booklet is not about charities. But an owner may wish to consider the possibility of putting his property into a charitable trust. The general law of charities would apply to such a trust and it would benefit from a wide range of tax exemptions. This is a possibility on which owners may wish to take legal advice. (See also Chapter 9.)

Chapter 4 CONDITIONAL EXEMPTION FROM CAPITAL TAXES: WORKS OF ART AND OTHER OBJECTS OF MUSEUM QUALITY

Eligible objects

4.1 The objects eligible for conditional exemption are *"any pictures, prints, books, manuscripts, works of art, scientific collections or other things not yielding income which appear to the Commissioners of Inland Revenue to be of national, scientific, historic or artistic interest"* (IHTA 1984, s. 31 (1) (*a*). In practice, the Capital Taxes Office seeks advice from expert advisers in the national museums or galleries on whether an object or collection is of a sufficiently high quality to be displayed in a public collection, whether national, local authority or university. An inspection of the property is normally required and the inspection process may take some time especially if the exemption claim covers a number of different items requiring different advice from different experts.

Collections

4.2 Conditional exemption is designed primarily for individual objects; however scientific and other specialised collections or homogeneous groups of objects can also be considered if most of the individual items are of a standard which would entitle them to exemption. If a collection of the appropriate standard is transferred during the owner's lifetime each object must satisfy the rule in paragraph **3.4** (*b*) that it must have been held for six years or been acquired on a death.

4.3 When considering the transfer of a collection the owner may well find that—because the objects forming part of the collection have been acquired at different times—some objects will not immediately be eligible for conditional exemption because he has owned them for less than six years. In these circumstances, he can transfer the qualifying part of the collection straightaway, and can *lend* the non-qualifying part to a body or person who is prepared to observe the conditions of exemption that apply to the whole collection. Once the six year period in relation to the non-qualifying part of the collection has elapsed, that part can then be transferred.

Conditions for exemption

4.4 In order that conditional exemption may be given, undertakings are required from the owner that:
  (i) the object will be kept permanently in the U.K. and will not leave it temporarily except for an approved purpose and period (*e.g.* temporary public exhibition abroad). Any application to send an object abroad temporarily should be made to the appropriate Capital Taxes Office (see Appendix 8) in the first instance before applying for an export licence (the latter may be required from the Department of Trade and Industry, in the case of objects more than 50 years old);
  (ii) agreed steps will be taken to preserve the object; and
  (iii) agreed steps will be taken to secure reasonable public access to it (IHTA 1984, s. 31 (2)).
  As from 19 March 1985, owners are statutorily required to agree with the Revenue the detailed steps necessary to fulfil the general undertakings (FA 1985, Sch. 26 para. 2 (3)). For eligible objects, claimants are required to complete the form 700A which is available from Capital Taxes Offices (addresses are given in Appendix 8). Where the underatkings have been given, their performance will be closely monitored.

Reasonable public access

4.5 Successive Governments have taken the view that where conditional exemption from tax has been given—and, therefore, tax revenue has been forgone—the public should have reasonable access to the object concerned. Conditional exemption cannot be granted unless reasonable access is ensured. The person making a claim should say how he intends to fulfil the undertaking to provide such access. The ways in which the public access condition can be satisfied are as follows.
4.6 *Where the object is or will be on display in a privately-owned house or room open to the public;* The owner may arrange to display the object in a privately-owned house or room which is or will be open to the public. If the owner himself has a house or room which is suitable for opening to the public and in which the object can be reasonably exhibited, he may be required to display it there. The frequency of opening will be a matter for negotiation in the light of the circumstances of each case, and appropriate publicity for the opening of the house will be required.
4.7 *Where the object is not or will not be on display in a privately-owned house or room open to the public, the owner may either:*
  (*a*) arrange to lend the object (anonymously if desired) for the purpose of display on a long-term loan to a public collection, whether national, local authority or university, or to a museum, gallery or historic house run by a charitable trust and open to the public,
  or
  (*b*) agree to allow viewing by appointment to the public *and* also—unless this cannot be done without physical risk to the object—to lend it (anonymously if desired) on request to a public collection (as defined above) for special exhibitions which are properly organised and meet adequate security standards. The duration of such a loan need not exceed six months in any two year period, or such longer loan and period as would be reasonable in appropriate cases, except that the duration need not exceed 25 per cent. of the period. Exhibitions organised by the national museums, galleries and libraries would qualify for this purpose; and so normally would exhibitions by the Arts Council of Great Britain, by the Royal Academy of Arts, by the National Trusts and by those local authority and university collections whose security arrangements have received the approval of the National Security Adviser to the Museums and Galleries Commission.
4.8 The availability of an object for viewing by appointment will be publicised by means of an entry on the Register of conditionally exempt property held by the National Art Library in the Victoria and Albert Museum. Copies of this Register are held by the National Library of Scotland, the National Museum of Wales and the Public Record Office for Northern Ireland. The Register will contain a detailed description of the object, the broad geographical location (*e.g.* county or metropolitan area) in which it may be viewed, and the name and address of the person to whom application to view it should be made. *There is no need for the entry to identify the owner or the address at which the object is held; owners who are concerned about the security of their objects may arrange for the Register entry to invite enquirers to apply in the first instance to an agent.* However the owner himself must bear the expense of any arrangement he makes to preserve his anonymity. When it is confirmed that conditional exemption for the object can be given, the Capital Taxes Office will provide forms on which the information which is to be included on the Register will need to be entered. Public collections will be advised of the arrangements for consulting the Register of conditionally exempt objects; the public will also be able to consult the Register. The details of any such arrangements can be discussed with the Capital Taxes Office before a decision to apply for exemption is made.
4.9 The arrangements for displaying the object in a house or room open to the public, and for viewing the object by appointment, which are described in paragraphs **4.5** to **4.8**, may include provision for a reasonable entry charge.

4.10 The Capital Taxes Office should be consulted if it is proposed to alter any agreed arrangement for public access. If formal agreement to any change is not obtained the exemption may be lost.
4.11 If documents which are conditionally exempted contain information which for personal or other reasons ought to be treated as confidential the law permits these documents—subject to the approval of the Revenue—to be excluded from the public access requirements (IHTA 1984, s. 31 (3)).
4.12 Loans to public collections may be covered by the Government Indemnity Scheme to relieve the borrower of the need to take out commercial insurance. For further information, the borrower should consult the Museums and Galleries Commission.

Foreign owned works of art
4.13 Where a work of art normally kept overseas becomes liable to CTT or IHT on the owner's death solely because it is physically situated in the U.K. at the time, the liability will—by concession—be waived if the work was brought into the U.K. solely for public exhibition, cleaning or restoration. If the work of art is held by the trustees of a discretionary trust, the ten-yearly charge to tax will similarly be waived.

Chapter 5 CONDITIONAL EXEMPTION FROM CAPITAL TAXES: OUTSTANDING LAND

Eligible land: general

5.1 Conditional exemption may be given for land which in the opinion of the Revenue is of *outstanding scenic, historic or scientific interest* (IHTA 1984, s. 31 (1) (*b*)). These three categories cover botanical, horticultural, silvicultural, arboricultural, agricultural, archaeological, physiographic and ecological features interest, and include man-made landscapes. Buildings erected on outstanding land may qualify on their own merits as outstanding buildings—see Chapter 6. However where they do not the exemption for the land will nonetheless extend to the buildings which stand on it, provided that they contribute to the scenic, historic or scientific interest of the land.
5.2 Before a decision is taken on whether the land is or is not of outstanding interest the Capital Taxes Office will seek the views of the relevant advisory bodies, which are listed in Appendix 9. The appropriate territorial advisory bodies mentioned at 1. to 3. in that Appendix will be consulted about every claim; and those at 4 and 5. in appropriate cases when silvicultural, arboricultural, botanical or horticultural considerations are involved. Where land meets the requirements for exemption on more than one count, (for example, both scenic and scientific grounds) appropriate undertakings will be required to protect all the qualifying interests, regardless of the basis on which the claim was made. In such cases the advisory bodies will liaise with one another. To minimise the delay and duplication of effort, a lead agency is nominated by the Capital Taxes Office to act as the conduit for a composite recommendation. (Similar administrative arrangements apply where the exemption claim also includes a building of outstanding historic or architectural interest.)

(i) Scenic land

5.3 An area of land will be judged to be outstanding for its scenic interest only if it has qualities well in excess of scenic land of its general type. A starting point for consideration will be if the land is in one of the National Parks in England or Wales, in a designated Area of Outstanding Natural Beauty in England, Wales or Northern Ireland or in a National Scenic Area in Scotland. Nevertheless within these identifiable areas there may be land which will not meet the high standards applicable to conditional exemption. Conversely there may be some land outside such areas which will qualify. Buildings on the land, and trees and underwood, may share in the exemption if they contribute to the scenic interest.
5.4 The Countryside Commissions and [the Department for the Environment for Northern Ireland (Conservation Service)] will advise in what respects the land is of outstanding interest. Relevant factors might include diversity of land form and feature, relative relief, vegetation cover including trees and woods, presence of water, land use and man-made features, or the contribution which the land makes to its wider setting, all assessed by national and not regional or local standards.

(ii) Scientific land

5.5 Land may be of outstanding scientific interest because of its flora (natural or cultivated), fauna, geological or physiographical features. Subject to the appropriate conditions being met (see **5.7—5.10**) and the scientific quality of the land being confirmed at the time of the exemption claim, land qualifies for conditional exemption if it is within a Site of Special Scientific Interest notified by the Nature Conservancy Council under the Wildlife and Countryside Act 1981, s. 28 in Great Britain, or in a National Nature Reserve or an Area of special scientific interest declared by the Department of the Environment for Northern Ireland. Some land outside these identified areas might qualify for designation and for exemption if it is of the requisite standard. Buildings on the land, and trees and underwood, may share in the exemption if they contribute to the scientific interest.

(iii) Historic land

5.6 In order to qualify as being of outstanding historic interest land must have a very special historic significance in national or international terms. For example it might be judged to be outstanding because of its association with a particularly important historic event. Earthworks archaeological sites, or archaeological landscapes which have been scheduled as ancient monuments will clearly be eligible for consideration for conditional exemption, but each case will need to be considered on its merits. Buildings on the land and trees and underwood, may share in the exemption if they contribute to the historic interest.

Conditions for exemption

5.7 Before conditional exemption is given for qualifying land, undertakings are required that agreed steps will be taken for the maintenance of the land, for the preservation of its character and for securing reasonable public access to it (IHTA 1984, s. 31 (4)). As from 19 March 1985, owners are statutorily required to agree with the Inland Revenue the detailed steps necessary to fulfil these general undertakings (FA 1985, Sch. 26, para. 2 (3)). In practice, a schedule of detailed management conditions is appended to the general undertakings. The content of the undertakings will reflect the advice from the relevant advisory agencies, which will aim to preserve the scenic, or historic qualities justifying the conditional exemption. Owners will be required to:
(*a*) manage the land with regard to conserving its natural and historic features including trees and woods, flora and fauna, hedges, walls and specified man-made relics or structures;
(*b*) agree not to carry out any proposals for change or development which would adversely affect the scenic, scientific or historic interest unless specified bodies have given written consent;
(*c*) afford reasonable public access for walking and riding on existing rights of way and permissive paths, supplemented where necessary by new access of either type. For some land of outstanding scientific interest, it may be appropriate to limit public access. For buildings exempted for their contribution to the interest of the land rather than on their own merits, access to the interiors will not usually be appropriate.
A simple management plan on these lines, specific to the estate and agreed with the appropriate advisory body or bodies, will often be an appropriate practical approach. An advisory publication on such plans is mentioned in **1.10**.
5.8 The relevant advisory agencies (see Appendix 9) will be prepared to advise ownes on appropriate management practices, including the desirability or otherwise of proposed changes which might have a significant effect on the eligibility of the land.

Woodlands

5.9 Land qualifying as of outstanding scenic, historic or scientific interest, or as essential to protect an outstanding building (**6.2**), often includes woodlands which are an integral part or primary part of the interest justifying conditional exemption. In such cases, undertakings will be sought, requiring the management, thinning, felling and replanting of the woodlands to take account of the need to conserve the qualities for which the exemption has been granted. A woodland management plan, aimed at preserving the woodland's character and agreed with the advisory bodies, will often be the appropriate form of such undertakings. (If the woodland is already being managed under one of the Foresty Commission's grant-aid schemes, the plan of operations agreed between the Commission and the woodland owner under the scheme may be used, varied, where appropriate, on the advice of the other advisory bodies making recommendations on the conditional exemption claim). In these circumstances the incidental sale of timber would not breach the undertakings.
5.10 Ancient semi-natural woodlands which are, or could be, properly included on the Nature Conservancy Council's Inventory of Ancient Woodland will be eligible for consideration for exemption on scientific as well as scenic or historic grounds, but each case will need to be considered on its merits. Other woodlands on ancient woodland sites, including plantations, would normally be expected to qualify on scientific grounds, but may be accepted if they satisfy the criteria relating to land of outstanding scenic or historic interest.
5.11 There is separate CTT and IHT relief for woodlands which may be claimed instead of conditional exemption (IHTA 1984, ss. 125–130). Under this relief the owner may elect to have the value of the trees standing on death left out of account in calculating the CTT or IHT liability and for the tax to be deferred until the trees are sold or otherwise disposed of. In such cases the tax is assessed on the value of the trees at the time of disposal (less 50 per cent. business relief where the woodland is run as a business). This deferment relief is described in detail in Leaflet 12 "*Taxation of Woodlands*", available from the Forestry Commission (address given in Appendix 8).

Chapter 6 CONDITIONAL EXEMPTION FROM CAPITAL TAXES: BUILDINGS OF OUT-STANDING HISTORIC OR ARCHITECTURAL INTEREST, ESSENTIAL AMENITY LAND AND HISTORICALLY ASSOCIATED OBJECTS

Eligible buildings

6.1 Conditional exemption may be given for buildings of *outstanding historic or architectural interest* (IHTA 1984, s. 31 (1) (*c*)). If a grant has been given under the Historic Buildings and Ancient Monuments Act 1953, s. 3A (as introduced by the National Heritage Act 1983) for a particular building that will be a prima facie indication that it will be accepted as outstanding for CTT and IHT purposes. If a building or ancient monument scheduled under the National Heritage Act 1983 has been listed under the Town and Country Planning Acts the grading will give an indication of its merits; but any building or ancient monument is eligible for consideration. Before a decision is taken on whether or not a building is eligiblethe Capital Taxes Office will consult the Historic Buildings and Monuments Commission for England or the appropriate department in England, Scotland, Wales or Northern Ireland, which will in turn consult the relevant Historic Buildings Council. [The Department of the Environment for Northern Ireland (Conservation Service) has replaced the Ulster Countryside Committee and the Historic Buildings Council for Northern Ireland.]

Essential amenity land

6.2 Land essential for the protection of the character and amenities of an outstanding building is also eligible for exemption (IHTA 1984, s. 31 (1) (*d*)). The factors to be taken into account here include the need to protect the views from an outstanding building (*e.g.* to landscaped park land); and the views of and approaches to it; and the need to prevent undesirable development close to it. Trees and underwood on the land may share in the exemption if they contribute to the qualifying interest. Advice will be sought on exemption claims for such land in the same way as for the outstanding building itself.

6.3 *The qualifying conditions for exemption were altered for chargeable transfers and other events occurring on or after 19 March 1985.* Prior to that date the land had to *adjoin* (*i.e.* actually abut;) an outstanding building in order to qualify for relief. *This restriction no longer applies* and the land now has to satisfy one test only—that is essential for the protection of the character and amenities of the outstanding building. (FA 1985, s. 94 and Sch. 26, para. 2).

Buildings on essential amenity land

6.4 Buildings on essential amenity land qualify for exemption in their own right if they meet the standards set out in **6.1**. When they are not eligible for exemption in their own right, the exemption granted to such essential amenity land will nonetheless extend to buildings on it provided that they make some positive contribution and are essential for the protection of the character and amenities of the outstanding building.

Historically associated objects

6.5 Objects historically associated with an outstanding building are also eligible for conditional exemption (IHTA 1984, s. 31 (1) (*e*)). The fact that the object belongs to the same historical period as the building is not in itself sufficient for exemption to be granted. To qualify for exemption the object must have a close association with a particular building and make a significant contribution, whether individually or as part of a collection or a scheme of decoration, to the appreciation of that building or its history. The object need not necessarily be of U.K. origin, nor would it be expected that every item should be contemporary with the building as changes will have taken place which reflect the individual taste of different owners. In the case of claims for such objects advice will be sought in the same way as for the outstanding building itself.

Conditions for exemption

(*a*) *General*

6.6 In order that conditional exemption may be given, undertakings are required that agreed steps will be taken:
    (*a*) for the maintenance, repair and preservation of the property;
    (*b*) for securing reasonable public access to it; and
    (*c*) additionally, in the case of historically associated objects, for ensuring their continued association with the building (IHTA 1984, s. 31 (4)).
As from 19 March 1985, owners are statutorily required to agree with the Revenue the detailed steps necessary to fulfil the general undertakings (FA 1985, Sch. 26 para. 2 (3)). In practice, a

schedule of detailed management conditions is appended to the general undertakings. The final decision on the nature of the undertakings will take account of the advice from the relevant advisory agency (see **6.1**).

(b) Essential amenity land

6.7 In the case of essential amenity land, a further condition relating to undertakings was introduced in respect of chargeable transfers and other events occurring on or after 19 March 1985. Exemption is dependent not only on undertakings (as outlined in the preceding paragraph) being given for the land itself but also on corresponding "supportive undertakings" being given in respect of:

(i) the outstanding building whose character and amenities the land protects;

(ii) any other qualifying essential amenity land which lies between the outstanding building and the area of land for which exemption is sought; and

(iii) any other qualifying essential amenity land which, in the Revenue's opinion, is "physically closely connected" with either that claimed area of land or the outstanding building.

So, for example, in a case where A owns the outstanding building and B and C own concentric rings of qualifying land around it, a claim for exemption by C will be dependent on "supportive undertakings" being given by both A and B. (IHTA 1984, s. 31 (4A) to (4F)—as introduced by FA 1985, s. 94, and Sch. 26 para. 2 (4).

6.8 The requirement for "supportive undertakings" to be given for (*a*) the outstanding building and (*b*) any intervening land between that building and the area of land for which exemption is sought is *mandatory*. Whether the similar undertakings will also be required for "physically closely connected" land will be determined by the Revenue, in the light of the circumstances of the particular case and of advice from the advisory agencies.

6.9 The intention behind the scheme of undertakings is to establish and preserve security and continuty of amenity of a sensible heritage entity with the outstanding building as the focal point. In many cases the setting of the building is crucial to its full appreciation; often it was specifically designed to provide striking views of the building or to complement its style with appropriate surrounding landscape. Whether by specific design or by the simple process of sympathetic integration over the years, a building and its surrounding landscape often form an entity in heritage terms of which the whole is greater than the competent parts. The object of including "physically closely connected" land (which is not specifically defined) within the scope of undertakings is to further this general aim. It introduces flexibility (dependent upon the circumstances of indivdual cases) permitting the Revenue to bring some related land within the entity, where that related land is considered to have a real contribution to make the establishment of, and public access to, a viable heritage entity. Regard will be paid to its relationship to the land for which the exemption claim is made and to the outstanding building. This does not mean that "supportive undertakings" will be required as a general rule for the total area of potentially qualifying amenity land. But it ensures that such understandings are not limited to the intervening land alone. This could be inappropriate, for example, in a case where the land claimed gave only a restricted view of, and access to, the back or side of an outstanding building.

6.10 The revised rules enable exemption claims to be made for parts of an entity where the latter is in divided ownership, but they also apply where the entity is in single ownership.

6.11 Where "supportive undertakings" are required for property which has already been conditionally exempted, exemption is dependent on those original undertakings being renewed—if in the example quoted in **6.7** the owner of the building A had claimed, and been granted, exemption prior to C's claim, the latter could succeed only if A was prepared to agree to the wider area becoming subject to inter-dependent undertakings.

6.12 Where the entity is in divided ownership, separate undertakings are required in respect of each component part and the responsibility for obtaining the "supportive undertakings" rests with the person seeking conditional exemption for the relevant amenity land. Exemption is not denied to an owner of part of an entity merely because some or all of the remainder of that entity is owned by an institution, such as the National Trust, or by a non-profit making body approved under IHTA 1984, s. 26 or by a charity or a company. But relief would depend on appropriate "supportive undertakings" being given by the particular body.

6.13 "Supportive undertakings" are *not* required, in relation to a conditional exemption claim for essential amenity land, in respect of objects historically associated with an outstanding building. Nor does the regime for "supportive undertakings" apply where a conditional exemption claim is made for an outstanding building or for historically associated chattels alone.

Reasonable public access

6.14 The degree of public access considered reasonable will vary from property to property depending on factors such as features of interest, size, location, contents and other individual circumstances. There is, therefore, no hard and fast rule. As a general guide, access to the interior of a smaller building on at least one day a week during the spring and summer months plus the

Spring and Summer Bank holidays, or their equivalent in Scotland and Northern Ireland, would normally be sought (*i.e.* as a working rule, 28 days per annum, although this might be slighly lower in Scotland, Wales and Northern Ireland). This would be subject to review in the case of buildings of specialised interest or buildings whose structure, contents or decoration would suffer from the normal level of access. For larger buildings liable to attract, and capable of handling, larger numbers of visitors greater access would usually be required. Depending on the circumstances, this might range from 60 to 156 days. Access to amenity land will depend on the nature of the land, its use and all the circumstances. Owners will be expected to give appropriate publicity to whatever degree of access is agreed. An agreed level of public access can be altered to reflect changed circumstances.

6.15 It should be noted that opening an historic house to the public for the first time, or extending the annual period of such opening, may constitute a change of use requiring the consent of the local planning authority.

6.16 The arrangements for public access may include provision for a reasonable entry charge.

Chapter 7 DISPOSAL OF HERITAGE PROPERTY: CAPITAL TAX CONSEQUENCES

Capital transfer tax and inheritance tax

(a) General principles

CONDITIONAL EXEMPTION PRESERVED

7.1 Conditional exemption from CTT or IHT is not lost on a disposal of heritage property if:
  (*a*) ownership passes on *death* and the transfer is itself conditionally exempt (*i.e.* the under-takings previously given are renewed by the new owner);
  (*b*) the disposal is a *lifetime* transfer and the undertakings previously given are renewed (for CTT purposes, the transfer would thereby itself be conditionally exempt—unless the six-year ownership rule precluded this);
  (*c*) the disposal is a bequest or a gift which is exempt from CTT or IHT under some other provision—*e.g.* the exemptions for transfers between spouses or for transfers to charities or to bodies within IHTA 1984, s. 26 (see Chapter 9)—provided that the undertakings previously given are renewed by the recipient;
  (*d*) the property is bequeathed, given or sold by private treaty to a body listed in IHTA 1984, Sch. 3 (see [Chapter 9,] Chapter 10 and Appendix 9); or
  (*e*) the property is offered and accepted in lieu of of CTT, IHT or ED (see Chapter 11). (IHTA 1984, s. 32 (4) and (5)).

CONDITIONAL EXEMPTION LOST

7.2 Exemption is lost, or CTT or IHT becomes payable, if:
  (*a*) the undertakings given at the time the exemption was granted are breached in any material respect (IHTA 1984, s. 32 (2)); but the Revenue will usually give the person concerned due notice and an opportunity to remedy matters before taking steps to withdraw the exemption;
  (*b*) the property is disposed of in any way other than those listed in **7.1** (IHTA 1984, s. 32 (1) and (3)).

(b) Special rules for "associated properties"

7.3 The general principles outlined in the preceding paragraphs apply also where there are "associated properties" comprising an outstanding building and, to the extent that any exist in a particular case, an area or areas of essential amenity land and an object or objects historically associated with that building. But there are special rules which apply to such property (IHTA 1984, s. 32A—as introduced, with effect from 19 March 1985, by FA 1985, Sch. 26 para. 4). Their object is to establish and preserve security and continuity of amenity of the heritage entity and in consequence the basic rule is that any event which breaks up the entity—a disposal of the whole, or a part, of an associated property (as defined), a failure to renew undertakings, either on death or during lifetime, or the breach of an undertaking—gives rise to a tax charge on *the whole of each associated property which has been conditionally exempted from CTT or IHT unless a specific exception applies* (see **7.5** to **7.7**).

7.4 Although this charge is limited to the properties which have been conditionally exempted, it can be triggered by an event in relation to a part of the entity which has itself not been so exempted but in respect of which "supportive undertakings" have been given (**6.7**). But a charge is *not* triggered by an event affecting an associated property if no undertakings exist in respect of it. The position can be illustrated by the following example where A owns the outstanding building, B and C own concentric rings of qualifyng land around it and claim for exemption by B has previously been accepted—because "supporting undertakings" were given by A. If A breaches his undertakings, a charge will fall on B (his property alone has been conditionally exempted). But no charge will arise on B if C sells his land (because C's land is not part of the entity protected by undertakings). Furthermore, the disposal of historically associated objects will not be a chargeable event with respect to a conditionally exempted building or its amenity land unless the objects themselves are the subject of current undertakings given to secure conditional exemption for them on an earlier transfer. So if, in the above example, C owns the historically associated contents, conditional exemption has been claimed by both A and B and C dies leaving the contents to his son D, no charge will arise at that juncture on A and B. But if C had previously claimed exemption for the contents and D was not prepared to renew the undertaking in respect of them, C's death would trigger a charge on A and B. (IHTA 1984, s. 32A (3) and (4)).

7.5 A disposal of conditionally exempted associated property to a Sch. 3 body or by way of acceptance in lieu of tax makes the conditional exemption of that property absolute (**7.1**). Where only part of the conditionally exempted associated property or properties is so disposed of, that event will give rise to a charge on *the remainder*, unless the appropriate undertakings are renewed by the recipient body in respect of the property which it takes under the disposal. Similarly, undertakings would have to be renewed to prevent a charge on conditionally exempted property which remains in private hands where the disposal is of associated property which itself has not been conditionally exempted but is the subject of "supportive undertakings". (IHTA 1984, s. 32A (6)). The thought here is that, notwithstanding its special heritage status, the acquiring body has become a part-owner of a continuing heritage entity. If the body subsequently disposes of its part, the event remains a potential trigger for a charge on the remainder.

7.6 The sale of an associated property, or part of an associated property, will not affect any part of the rest of the heritage entity if the purchaser continues the vendor's undertakings. There will however be a charge in respect of the property sold if that property has been conditionally exempted. (IHTA 1984, s. 32A (9)).

7.7 There is also a limitation of the charge if the heritage entity is not materially affected by a chargeable event (IHTA 1984, s. 32A (10)). It applies when the whole or part of an associated property which has either been conditionally exempted or the subject of "supportive undertakings" is disposed of or when an undertaking given in respect of such property is breached. If the Revenue consider that the disposal or breach does not materially affect the heritage entity as a whole, the charge applies *only* to the property or part concerned, and *only* if that property has been conditionally exempted. (In that case, the provisions in IHTA 1984, s. 32A (5) to (9) do *not* come into play). In applying this rule to individual cases the Revenue will consider all the relevant factors in the light of the advice of appropriate advisory bodies. A relevant factor to which weight will be given will be whether what remains of the entity after the chargeable event might qualify for exemption as a viable heritage unit looked at on its own merits. In the case of a sale of conditionally exempted historically associated objects, it is of relatively less concern to the continuing viability of an entity if a few objects happen to be so disposed of. So, as a sale of one or two items is unlikely to be considered to have materially affected the entity.

Quantum of charge

7.8 The way in which CTT or IHT on these chargeable events is calculated is explained in Appendix 2.

Effect on a maintenance fund

7.9 Where heritage property which is conditionally exempted from CTT or IHT is supported by a maintenance fund as described in Chapter 8, the loss of conditional exemption could also lead to a CTT or IHT charge on the assets of the fund (see Appendix 5).

Capital gains tax

7.10 Any charge to CGT which was deferred when an asset was acquired will be activated if and when the asset is sold, together with a charge on any gain arising since its acquisition, unless the sale was by private treaty to a Sch. 3 body (see Chapter 10 and Appendix 10). The tax which is payable by the vendor is calculated as illustrated in Appendix 14.

Loss or damage to heritage property

7.11 The ensuing paragraphs summarise the capital tax consequences of the loss of, or damage to, conditionally exempt heritage property. The position is outlined in more detail in Appendix 7.

Capital transfer tax and inheritance tax consequences

7.12 The theft or loss of, or damage to, any property does not in general constitute a chargeable event for CTT or IHT. But if the property has been the subject of a conditionally exempt transfer, so that the present owner is obliged by his undertaking to the Revenue to take reasonable steps for its preservation, any theft, loss or damage may imply that there has been a breach of that undertaking. If it were evident that there has been such a clear breach a charge would arise, whether or not insurance monies were available. Where there has been no such breach, the destruction of the focal point of a heritage entity (the house) would *not* trigger at that stage a charge on any reamining conditionally exempted supporting property (for example, amenity land) providing the undertakings in force in respect of it continued to be observed. But a charge would arise in the normal way at some later stage—if the undertakings were breached or when the property next changes hands. Where the propety destroyed has been supported by a maintenance fund, the special tax privileges of the fund are likely to be withdrawn, with consequent tax charges.

Capital gains tax consequences

7.13 For CGT the position is that the loss of an asset, *e.g.* by theft, fire or vandalism, irrespective of whether or not it has previously been the subject of a conditionally exempt transfer, is normally treated as a disposal. But if such a disposal gives rise to a gain, because for example the owner receives an amount of compensation for the loss which exceeds the acquisition cost of the real asset, any CGT liability can generally be deferred until a later disposal. The owner of the asset may claim deferment provided that within a year of receiving the insurance or other compensation proceeds (or such longer period as the Inspector of Taxes considers reasonable) he uses these proceeds to acquire a comparable replacement. In constrast, there would be no immediate charge to CGT on any remaining conditionally exempted supporting property, providing the undertakings in force in respect of it continued to be observed. But tax would become payable if and when there was a chargeable event for CTT or IHT purposes.

7.14 Similarly deferment of CGT may be claimed when compensation is received for damage to an asset if the compensation proceeds are wholly applied to restoring it.

Chapter 8 MAINTENANCE FUNDS*

Introduction

8.1 This Chapter and Appendix 5 deal with the special tax arrangements which apply to trust funds—"maintenance funds"—set up to maintain and preserve qualifying heritage property. Paragraph **8.3** below explains what kinds of heritage property qualify for this purpose.

*See 1987 Supplement, p. 213 below.

8.2 The principle behind these specially favourable arrangements is that it is generally considered desirable for outstanding land and buildings—together with any eligible adjoining land and objects historically associated with the buildings—to remain in private ownership (rather than to be taken over by the State) and for the owners to be encouraged to set aside capital both to keep their property in a good state of repair and to make provision for a reasonable measure of public access to it.

What sort of property can be supported by a maintenance fund?

8.3 A maintenance fund may qualify for the special arrangements if it is set up for the benefit of:
   (*a*) a building which is outstanding by reason of its architectural or historic interest;
   (*b*) objects historically associated with such a building;
   (*c*) land which adjoins such a building and which is essential for the protection of the character and amenities of that building (which may include its garden); and/or
   (*d*) land of outstanding scenic, scientific or historic interest (which can include gardens which are outstanding by reason of their horticultural, arboricultural or historic interest).
If undertakings are not already in force in relation to the heritage property to be supported by the fund, that property has to meet the appropriate test for designation described in Chapters 5 and 6 and the appropriate undertakings have to be given (IHTA 1984, Sch. 4, para. 3 (3)).

Summary of the special tax arrangements

8.4 If a maintenance fund satisfies the necessary conditions, which are described in detail in **8.5** then:
   (*a*) no CTT or IHT has to be paid at the time when property is put into the fund (IHTA 1984, s. 27), and the charge to CGT may be deferred (see **3.13**(*b*));

(*b*) the trustees of the fund will not be liable to the CTT and IHT ten-yearly charge on discretionary trusts in respect of the assets in the fund (IHTA 1984, s. 58 (1) (*c*));

(*c*) the trustees will be able to elect for any tax year that the income of the fund is not to be treated for income tax purposes as the income of the person who set the fund up, but is to bear income tax only at the basic rate and the additional rate (currently 16 per cent.)* which applies to the trustees of certain trusts (FA 1977, s. 38). Further, if they so elect, no sum applied out of the fund for heritage purposes will be treated as the income of any person by virtue of that person's occupation of the heritage property in question.

Even if the trustees do not make the election for any tax year, no sum applied out of the fund in that year for heritage purposes will be treated as the income of any person by virtue of that person's occupation of the heritage property in question, provided the income of the funds is treated for tax purposes as the income of the person who set up the fund; and

(*d*) when capital is taken out of the fund for a purpose connected with the heritage (including resettlement in a new maintenance fund), there will be no charge to CTT or IHT (as there normally would be when property is distributed from a discretionary trust); in addition, where assets are distributed in specie to another trust (including a maintenance fund) or to an individual, the charge to CGT may be deferred (FA 1980, s. 79 as amended by FA 1981, s. 78 and FA 1982, s. 82) and the liability to stamp duty will be restricted to a single charge of fixed conveyance duty of 50p; but

(*e*) when capital taken out of the fund for a purpose unconnected with the heritage (*e.g.* for personal benefit), there may be CTT or IHT charges, depending on who receives the capital withdrawn (see **8.6**). In addition, there will be a charge to income tax at 30 per cent. on so much of the income of the fund as has borne income tax only at the basic rate and the additional rate and has not, up to that time, been used for a heritage purpose (FA 1980, s. 52). The normal CGT consequences follow (*i.e.* the charge may be deferred in certain circumstances—see sub-paragraph (*d*) above) and stamp duty could be chargeable in certain circumstances.

The conditions to be satisfied for the arrangements to apply

8.5 These arrangements will apply to any transfer to a maintenance fund only if the Revenue give a direction in relation to the property transferred. In order that a direction may be given:

(*a*) The Revenue must be satisfied that the property to be included in the fund is of an appropriate character and amount, having regard to other sources of upkeep available to the owner. Assets which provide little or no income would seem prima facie unsuitable, particularly if their own maintenance might make excessive demands on the resources of the fund. The property transferred should not be excessive in relation to the likely qualifying expenditure (see **8.5** (*c*)). It is possible for a small, initial fund (of a few hundred pounds) to be accepted in practice, providing there is adequate evidence of intention to settle funds at a later stage.

(*b*) The trustees of the fund must be approved by the Revenue and must include either a trust corporation, a solicitor, and accountant, or a member of such other professional body as the Revenue may allow. The trustees, or a majority of them, must also be resident in the U.K. and the general administration of the fund must ordinarily be carried on here.

(*c*) The trusts on which the property is held must provide that during the first six years from the time when the property is put into the fund or from the time when any property is added to the fund both that property itself, *i.e.* the capital of the fund, and the income from it, may be used only for:

    (i) the maintenance, repair or preservation of the heritage property for which the fund has been set up;

    (ii) making provision for public access to it;

    (iii) the maintenance, repair, preservation or reasonable improvement of the property which has itself been put into the fund; and

    (iv) defraying the expenses of the trustees (see paragraphs **8.7** to **8.15**).

Any income which is not applied in this way, and not accumulated, must go to one of the bodies listed in IHTA 1984, Sch. 3 (see Appendix 10) or to a charity which is wholly or mainly concerned with the maintenance, repair or preservation of heritage property (a heritage charity). The trusts may allow the capital of the fund to devolve at any time on any such body or charity.

(*d*) The trusts must also provide that for the whole life of the fund (not just the first six years) the income and any accumulated income (but not necessarily the capital—see **8.6**) from the property may be used by the trustees only for the purposes specified in **8.5** (*c*) (IHTA 1984, Sch. 4, paras. 2, 3).

(*e*) Finally, the tax reliefs mentioned in **8.4** (*a*) will not apply to a transfer made into the fund by an individual if the transfer does not take immediate effect, or if it depends on conditions which are not satisfied within 12 months, or if it is defeasible (*e.g.* if it can be revoked), or if the donor transfers less that his full interest in the property, or if what is being transferred is an interest in possession in settled property and the settlement has not come to an end. And they will not apply in a case where the transfer into an existing maintenance fund results in the trustees of the fund acquiring a reversionary interest by purchase, or where property is transferred into the fund in exchange for a reversionary interest which does not form part of the estate of the person acquiring that interest (IHTA 1984, s. 27 (2)).

Tax position when capital is taken out of a maintenance fund after six years or earlier death of the settlor

8.6 Subject to the terms of the trust deed, capital may be withdrawn from a maintenance fund for any purpose whatsoever after it has been in the fund for a period of six years, or—in the case of funds set up in lifetime—on the death of the settlor of the fund if that occurs before that six year period expires. Where the capital is not applied for heritage purposes, such a withdrawal will normally give rise to income tax and CTT or IHT charges (IHTA 1984, Sch. 4 para. 8). Generally speaking no CTT or IHT charge is levied if the recipient is the settlor, his spouse or his widow (IHTA 1984, Sch. 4, para. 10).* There may also be CGT charges, but these may, as a general rule, be deferred (see **8.4** (*e*)). The circumstances in which these tax charges may arise, and the way in which the tax is calculated, are explained in more detail in Appendix 5. But it should be noted here that there will normally be no CTT or IHT or immediate CGT charge, and the charge to stamp duty will be restricted to one payment of 50p, if property is distributed out of a maintenance fund to an individual beneficiary who within 30 days—or two years if the distribution occurs on a death—resettles it on the trusts of a new maintenance fund in respect of which the Revenue give a direction; nor will there be an income tax charge if *all* of the property comes out of the first fund and goes into the second (FA 1980, s. 52 (6)). No new six year restriction described in **8.5** (*c*) will apply to the new fund in relation to such resettled property. But if property comes out of the first fund following the death of the settlor before the six year period has elapsed, the unexpired portion of that period will apply to the second fund.*

*See 1987 Supplement, p. 213 below.

How may the income and capital of the fund be used?

8.7 References are made in paragraphs **8.5** (*c*) and (*d*) to the income and capital of a fund being used for purposes connected with the heritage. The following examples of what this means in practice are given for general guidance but the position will depend on the precise circumstances of individual cases.

(i) Maintenance etc of the heritage property

8.8 Structural repairs to the heritage property will normally qualify, but structural alterations will do so only in so far as they are necessary to preserve the existing property and are not going further—*e.g.* the provision of a new roof for a house would generally qualify. Expenditure on the acquisition of new heritage property will not qualify.

8.9 Running repairs and maintenance costs will normally qualify. These might include:
(*a*) in the case of a *building*, preservation of the stonework and fabric, internal redecoration and general maintenance. Heating costs will qualify to the extent that they can be shown to be necessary either to maintain or preserve the building or its qualifying contents or as a consequence of public access;
(*b*) in the case of *land*, conservation measures such as bracken control, scrub clearance where appropriate, woodland management with regard to age and species effect, provision for the replacement of mature trees (for example, in parkland—by successor planting of appropriate species), fencing, maintenance of hedges, hedgebanks and walls, and upkeep of ditches and drainage;
(*c*) in the case of *gardens*, the cost of seeds, plants, materials, implements and the repair and heating costs of greenhouses and gardeners' wages; and
(*d*) in the case of historically associated *objects*, cleaning and restoration of pictures, repairs to tapestries, curtains, carpets, clocks, furniture and suchlike.

(ii) Public access to the heritage property

8.10 This covers capital or income expenditure on the provision and upkeep of *e.g.* car parks and public lavatories, the wages of guides and attendants and special fire precautions. Lighting, heating and security costs and the upkeep of roads and drives will qualify to the extent that they are made necessary by public access.

(iii) Maintenance etc of the property in the fund

8.11 Generally, all expenses for prudent manangement will qualify. Thus in a case where the property in the fund is an agricultural estate, this will allow the trustees to make both capital and revenue expenditure on repairs and maintenance of the property in the fund.

(iv) Improvement of the property in the fund

8.12 This covers improvements made in order to generate a higher income for the fund, *e.g.* the purchase of additional farm land, as well as those which are conducive to the good management of the trust assets, *e.g.* the renovation of farm workers' cottages or the construction of a new silo. The improvements must however be "reasonable having regard to the purposes of the trust" and should therefore be undertaken only after proper provision has been made for the maintenance etc. requirements of the heritage property.

(v)　Expenses of the trustees

8.13 This covers the administrative costs incurred by the fund—for example payments of professional fees rates and taxes in respect of the property and income of the fund.

(vi)　Particular items

8.14 *Insurance.* In the case of an outstanding house, the insurance of the building itself, and of any historically associated contents, will qualify, as will the cost of public liability insurance in relation to access by the public.
8.15 The trustees may also (see **8.5** (*c*)) pay income to a national heritage body or heritage charity.

Loss or damage to heritage property

8.16 If the heritage property supported by a maintenance fund is destroyed, this is likely to lead to the withdrawal of the direction, with consequent tax charges (see Appendix 7 para. 6).

Inland Revenue powers in relation to maintenance funds

8.17 After a maintenance fund has been set up and a Revenue direction issued in respect of property transferred into it, then:
(*a*) The Revenue may take any necessary steps to enforce the trusts of the fund and will have the same powers in connection with the appointment, removal etc. of the trustees as any beneficiary under the trusts (IHTA 1984, Sch. 4, para. 7).
(*b*) The Revenue may—by notice in writing—withdraw the direction if the facts concerning the fund or its administration cease to warrant the application of the special tax arrangements described in this Chapter (IHTA 1984, Sch. 4, para. 5). This might happen where, for example, the trustees' powers of accumulation or investment were exercised in a manner inconsistent with the purposes of the fund. But the Revenue will usually give the trustees an opportunity to remedy matters before taking steps to withdraw the direction. In the event of a direction being withdrawn there would be a charge to CTT or IHT and income tax (see Appendix 5 paras. 4(*f*), 8.
(*c*) The trustees are required to furnish the Revenue with such accounts and other information in relation to the property as the Revenue may reasonably require (IHTA 1984, Sch. 4 para. 6). The Revenue will expect to receive an annual audited statement of accounts, including a balance sheet and a statement of income and expenditure, together with an annual report on the activities of the fund describing its operations during the year. Adequate records of any accumulations of income should be maintained because, in the event of charges on the fund (see **8.4** (*e*)), it would be necessary to establish how its income had been taxed, what income had been accumulated and how the accumulations had been applied.

Chapter 9 GIFTS TO CHARITIES, FOR NATIONAL PURPOSES OR FOR THE PUBLIC BENEFIT

9.1 As explained in the introduction to this booklet, the policy of successive Governments has been to encourage heritage property to remain in private hands so far as possible and for its owners to care for it and to allow the public to see it. Chapters 3 to 8 have described the tax reliefs which have been designed with this aim in view. But the owners of heritage property may nevertheless wish, or feel obliged to, dispose of the property, in which case the Government policy is to encourage them to do so to a body whose aim is to look after the heritage. The remaining Chapter describes the tax reliefs which are then available. This Chapter describes the treatment of gifts to such bodies; Chapter 10 describes the advantages of selling assets to such a body by private treaty rather than on the market; while Chapter 11 deals with handling assets to the State in lieu of CTT. The exemptions from CTT and IHT described in this Chapter are, subject to certain exceptions, specified in IHTA 1984, s. 23 (2)–(6), 25 (2), 26 (7). These exceptions are similar to, but more extensive than, those mentioned in **8.5** (*e*).

(a)　Charities

9.2 Gifts or bequests—of any property—to charities, including those concerned with the national heritage, are exempt from CTT or IHT without limit (IHTA 1984, s. 23). Gifts or bequests to charities are not chargeable to CGT (CGTA 1979, ss. 146, 49) or stamp duty.

(b)　National purposes

9.3 As a general rule, gifts and other transfers made below value otherwise than by way of a bargain at arm's length are treated for CGT purposes as made for a consideration equal to market value. It follows that CGT may be payable in these circumstances as well as CTT or IHT. Gifts and bequests of any property to the bodies listed in Appendix 10 to this booklet are entirely exempt from CTT, IHT and CGT (IHTA 1984, s. 25 and CGTA 1979, ss. 146, 147 (2) (*a*) and 49). There is also relief from CGT on sales made to these bodies below market value. Where exemption is not sought by means of the special rules relating to private treaty sales (see Chapter 10), full relief will be due for any element of gift. If, however, the actual sale price exceeds the vendor's acquisition cost, that excess is chargeable to CGT (CGTA 1979, ss. 146 (1) and (2)). All transfers to the Trustees of the National Heritage Memorial Fund and to those bodies that are charities are free of stamp duty.

(c) Public benefit

9.4 Gifts of certain types of property to an appropriate non-profit making body may be exempted—subject to a Revenue direction—from CTT, IHT, and CGT (IHTA 1984, s. 26, CGTA 1979, s. 147 (1)). This exemption applies to:
  (i) land of outstanding scenic or historic or scientific interest;
  (ii) buildings of outstanding historic or architectural or aesthetic interest, together with land used as the grounds of the building *e.g.* its garden or park, and chattels associated with the building; and
  (iii) a picture, print, book, manuscript, work of art or scientific collection which is considered of national, historic, scientific or artistic interest.
  The criteria for determining whether property should be exempted are similar to those set out in relation to tax exemption for transfers between individuals (see Chapters 4 to 6), but see also **9.5** with respect to supporting property.
9.5 To ensure reasonable provision for the upkeep of the heritage property an endowment may be transferred to the recipient body along with the property. An endowment given in this way as a source of income is exempt from CTT or IHT provided that the income it will produce is not excessive in relation to the estimated cost (allowing a reasonable margin) of the upkeep of the heritage property. Only the income from the endowment may be used. If a source of capital is required it is possible to set up a maintenance fund (see Chapter 8) instead of or in addition to an endowment fund.
9.6 A direction that the gift is exempt from CTT will be made only if the body receiving the gift is suitable to assume responsibility for the preservation of the property. This means that:
  (i) one of its aims must be the preservation of the property for the public benefit;
  (ii) it must have the financial capacity to maintain the property (see also **9.5**);
  (iii) undertakings will be required in respect of public access, restriction of use and disposal of the property, and its preservation; and
  (iv) the donor cannot reserve any interest in the property for himself.
Accordingly, draft Memoranda, Articles of Association, Trust Deeds (or other similar documents) relating to the body concerned and full details of its assets, expected income and forecast expenditure should be submitted when an application for the exemption is made. Applications should be made to the appropriate Capital Taxes Office (see Appendix 8).

Chapter 10 PUBLIC PURCHASE: PRIVATE TREATY SALES

10.1 Private treaty sales to the museums or other bodies listed in Appendix 10 frequently offer substantial financial advantages to owners. If conditionally exempt property is sold on the open market any CTT, IHT or ED exemption is lost and the vendor may also be liable to CGT on the sale proceeds. The tax charges can be substantial and the final net amount retained by the seller significantly less than the proceeds of sale. However, sale by private treaty to a body listed in Appendix 10 does not lead to the withdrawal of the conditional exemption or to a charge to CTT or IHT (IHTA 1984, ss. 32(4)(*a*), 32A (5) (*a*)). Nor is there any liability to CGT (see **3.13** (*a*)). Because the vendor receives the proceeds without any liability to tax it is not unreasonable that the acquiring institution should offer, and the vendor be prepared to accept, a lower price than would prevail if the proceeds were taxable. In this way the vendor and the acquiring institution share the value of the tax exemption. An administrative arrangement, designed to reflect this and to enable both parties to negotiate on a firm basis has been in existence for many years. This arrangement, which follows the principles recommended by the Waverley Committee (Report of the Committee on the Export of Works of Art etc, September 1952), brings what is known as the "douceur" into the calculation. Under it a tax free private treaty sale for a given value will always be financially more advantageous to the owner than a sale for that amount on the open market involving a charge to tax, and it will also benefit the public by enhancing a public collection.
10.2 There may be further benefits. If a contradictory exempt item is sold on the open market the sale proceeds are added to the cumulative total of transfers made by the last person who made a conditionally exempt transfer to the item or, in certain circumstances, the cumulative total of the settlor of a settlement which included the item (see Appendix 2). However, if the property is sold

by private treaty to a public collection or body, there will be no increase in either cumulative total. This in turnwill be likely to reduce the CTT liability of the person concerned in relation to his subsequent transfers and where subsequently a chargeable event arises with respect to which he is the relevant transferor, the tax paid thereon can be affected similarly.

10.3 The method of fixing the special price in private treaty sales is set out below.

(a) Objects

10.4 If someone is contemplating selling an item by private treaty he or she can consult the Museums and Galleries Commission for advice on the public institutions most likely to be interested in acquiring it. Thereafter, the parties negotiate—with the aid of their own advisers if necessary—an agreed value. The Government does not intervene in this process in any way. The potential liability to CGT and CTT or IHT is then calculated on this agreed value (costs of sale, such as professional fees, are not taken into account in the notional tax calculation). The special purchase price is then arrived at in accordance with the "douceur" arrangement mentioned in paragraph **10.1** above. As a general guideline, the special price would normally be the net value of the object (the market price less the notional tax liability) *plus* 25 per cent. of the value of the tax exemption. However, there will be occasions on which a figure above or below 25 per cent. would be appropriate. For example, a higher figure may be necessary to provide an adequate inducement in respect of low value objects and a lower figure may well be reasonable for very high value items.

10.5 Any institution considering a purchase will always need to know how the negotiations will be affected by the tax position of the vendor. The Capital Taxes Office should be asked to disclose the potential liability to the purchaser and confirm the exemption.

10.6 When the market value has been agreed by the parties and the taxe(s) applicable to that value deducted therefrom, the difference plus the vendor's share of the tax exemption (the "douceur") is the special price the purchaser has to pay.

10.7 An illustrative example is given at Appendix 11.

10.8 Under these arrangements gains accruing on private treaty sales are exempt from CGT and as a result other CGT reliefs are not normally available. Thus, for example, loss relief or rollover relief for the replacement of business assets is not applicable and is not taken into account in working out the special sale price. However in certain circumstances some reliefs (such as the chattels exemption and the private residence relief) may still be available and the Capital Taxes Office should be consulted about this.

10.9 Private treaty sales to the bodies listed in Appendix 10 are relieved from VAT (VATA 1983, Sch. 6 Gp. 11). Information about this is given in VAT leaflet No. 701/12/84 which is available from the local VAT office of HM Customs and Excise.

10.10 As indicated in **1.9** the office of Arts and Libraries have published a leaflet on private treaty sale arrangements for objects of national heritage quality.

(b) Land and buildings

10.11 Private treaty sales of outstanding land and historic buildings can be made to any of the bodies listed in Appendix 10 of this booklet. The views of the District Valuer are sought by the Capital Taxes Office on the market valuation proposed by the owner or executor. Once the market valuation has been agreed the approach will be similar to that for objects, except that, because neither buildings nor land can normally be exported, 10 per cent. rather than 25 per cent. of the value of the tax exemptionwill normally be used in the calculation of the special price.

10.12 Paragraphs **10.5–10.9** apply equally to private treaty sales of land and buildings.

10.13 An illustrative example is given in Appendix 12.

Chapter 11 ACCEPTANCE OF PROPERTY IN LIEU OF TAX

11.1 The Board of Inland Revenue may, with the agreement of the departmental Ministers with responsibility for the environment and the arts, accept property in whole or part satisfaction of a CTT or IHT debt (IHTA 1984, ss. 230, 231). There are similar provisions for the acceptance of property in whole or part satisfaction of an ED debt. Property may also be accepted in satisfaction of interest accrued on CTT, IHT or ED as well as in lieu of the tax itself. Where property is accepted in lieu of CTT, IHT neither CGT, stamp duty nor VAT is charged (VATA 1983, Sch. 6 Gp. 11). Details of the VAT relief are given in VAT leaflet No. 701/12/84 which is available from the local VAT office of HM Customs and Excise.

11.2 Acceptance of heritage property in lieu of tax has similar financial advantages for the vendor as a private treaty sale. It may be more convenient or attractive, particularly in the case of objects which have an especially close association with an important historic building, since in some instances the departmental Ministers may allow them to remain where they are after they have been accepted.

11.3 The types of property which may be accepted in satisfaction of tax are as follows:
  (*a*) Land (which includes buildings and any other structures and land covered by water).

(*b*) Any objects which are or have been in any building if:
  (i) the building is being or has been accepted in lieu of tax;
  (ii) the building or any interest in it belongs to the Crown or a Government department;
  (iii) the building is under the guardship of the Secretary of State for the Environment, Scotland or Wales or of the Department of the Environment for Northen Ireland; or
  (iv) the building belongs to a body listed in IHTA 1984, Sch. 3 (see Appendix 10);
and it appears to the Ministers desirable for the objects to remain associated with the building.
(*c*) Any object or collection or group of objects which the Ministers are satisfied is pre-eminent for its national, scientific, historic or artistic interest. "National interest" includes interest within any part of the U.K., and in determining whether an object or collection or group of objects is pre-eminent, regard shall be had to any significant asociation it has with a particular place.
11.4 The standard of objects within **11.3** (*c*) which can be accepted in lieu of tax is very much higher than applicable for conditional exemption (see **4.1**). Any object which is accepted in lieu of tax is automatically treated as qualifying for exemption. The position for land and buildings would generally—but not always (see **11.7** and **11.10**)—be the same.

Procedure

11.5 Advice on the acceptance in lieu procedure should be sought from the Capital Taxes Office, to whom any offer of property in satisfaction of tax should be made. An offer of property should be accompanied by full details of the property, including an indication of its current market value, as well as details of the name, address and telephone number of whoever should be contacted to arrange an inspection. Normally a colour photograph (print or transparency) of any object offered in lieu will also be required. It sometimes happens that when items which may themselves qualify for conditional exemption are offered in lieu of CTT and IHT the processing of the claim for exemption and the offer itself are telescoped. It is not necessary to await formal designation before putting the item forward as a candidate for acceptance in lieu of tax. Indeed, in such cases the necessary consideration of an exemption claim and offer can be subsumed into one exercise.
11.6 When an offer of property in lieu of tax is received, the Capital Taxes Office consults the Museums and Galleries Commission in respect of offers of chattels and the Department of Environment (or its national counterparts) in respect of offers of land buildings. They in turn obtain advice from experts on the quality and valuation of the property and advise Ministers on whether the offer should be accepted. The procedures for seeking expert advice, and the criteria applied, are set out below.

Land

11.7 Land qualifying for acceptance in lieu of tax will normally be of outstanding scenic, scientific or historic interest. Other land may however be accepted, for example land with a high amenity value, such as a nature park, or land which has a close link with an historic building. The "douceur" arrangement however only applies on the acceptance of land and buildings of outstanding interest.
11.8 Advice on the quality of the land, the suitability of potential recipients and any undertakings on management and on the provisions of public access to be required from a recipient will be sought from the bodies listed in Appendix 8 in the manner described in **5.2**. Advice on the valuation of the land will be obtained from the District Valuer.
11.9 Land will normally be accepted only if a suitable recipient for it can be found, for example, the National Trusts, national park authorities, local authorities or charitable organisations such as the local nature conservation trusts. The recipient will be required to give an undertaking not to dispose of the property without the consent of the Ministers (or in Northern Ireland the department concerned). The acceptance in lieu procedure will not be followed if the potential recipient of a piece of land is wholly or nearly entirely financed direct by Central Government (for example a Government department itself or a body such as the Nature Conservancy Council). In such a case the owner or executors of the estate would be invited to negotiate a private treaty sale direct with the body concerned.

Buildings

11.10 Buildings of architectural or historic interest may be accepted. They would generally have to be capable of being used for the public benefit. Advice on buildings offered in satisfaction of tax will be taken from the department concerned who would in turn consult the Historic Buildings and Monuments Commission for England or the relevant Historic Buildings Council elsewhere. Acceptance of buildings normally depends, like acceptance of land, upon an appropriate recipient being found who is prepared to look after the property on the same conditions as apply to the acceptance of land.

Objects associated with a building

11.11 If it is considered desirable that objects of any description which are or to have been kept in a building should remain associated with that building, they may be accepted with the building. Such objects may also be accepted where the associated building is already in some form of public ownership (see **11.3** (*b*)) or is owned by one of the bodies listed in IHTA 1984, Sch. 3 (reproduced in Appendix 10). Advice on whether such objects should be accepted and on their valuation is obtained by the MGC who consult the appropriate expert advisers in the national museums and galleries. The "douceur" arrangment, as described in **3.9** (*a*) (iv) and **11.14,** would apply only to such of the objects which fall within the ambit of IHTA 1984, s. 31 (1) (*a*) or (*c*).

Pre-eminent objects

11.12 Objects—pictures, prints, books, manuscripts, works of art, scientific objects etc—may be accepted in satisfaction of tax if it is considered that they will constitute a pre-eminent addition to a national, local authority or university collection or that they are pre-eminent in association with a particular building. The following guidelines are intended as a framework of reference for the expert advisers (who are chosen from the directors of the relevant national museums and galleries), to help them in formulating their advice on whether an item is pre-eminent (an object may fall into more than one category: for example it may have an especially close association with a particular historic setting and also may be pre-eminent, irrespective of this association, under one or more of the other categories). The MGC is responsible for obtaining this advice and is expected to consult widely particularly where the object has local significance. In appropriate cases it may in turn consult the Royal Commission on Historical Manuscripts or, when offers are made on condition that an object remains in situ (see **11.17**), the Historic Buildings and Monuments Commission for England or the relevant Historic Buildings Council elsewhere, as appropriate. If need be, the MGC may convene an informal panel of independent advisers.

(a) Does the object have an especially close association with our history and national life?

This category includes foreign as well as British works, for example, gifts from foreign sovereigns or governments and objects that have been acquired abroad in circumstances closely associated with our history. It includes objects closely associated with some part of the U.K., or with the development of its institutions and industries. Some objects which fall under this category will be of such national importance that they deserve to enter a national museum or gallery. Others may well be of a lesser degree of national importance, though they will be nonetheless significant in a local context. This category will also include works which derive their significance from a local connection, and may therefore qualify as a pre-eminent addition to a local authority or university museum.

(b) Is the object of especial artistic or art-historical interest?

This category, like (*c*) below, includes objects deserving of entering a national museum or gallery as well as other objects which may not be pre-eminent in a national museum or gallery in London, Edinburgh or Cardiff, but will be pre-eminent in local authority or university museums or galleries elsewhere which do not already possess items of a similar genre or a similar quality.

(c) Is the object of especial importance for the study of some particular form of art, learning or history?

This category includes a wide variety of objects, not restricted to works of art, which are of especial importance for the study of, say, a particular scientific development. The category also includes objects forming part of an historical unity, series or collection either in one place or in the country as a whole. Without a particular object or group of objects both a unity and a series may be impaired.

(d) Does the object have an especially close association with a particular historic setting?

This category will include primarily works of art, manuscripts, furniture or other items which have an especially close association with an important historic building. They will fall to be considered pre-eminent by virtue of the specific contribution they make to the understanding of an outstanding historic building. Thus, the category may include paintings or furniture specially commissioned for a particular house or a group of paintings having an association with a particular location.

Acceptance

11.13* Once the necessary advice has been obtained and recommendations put forward, it is for the Ministers (or in Northern Ireland the department concerned) to decide whether the property offered qualifies for acceptance in lieu of tax and to approve its valuation. In England the decision will be taken by the Minister for the Arts and the Secretary of State for the Environment. In Scotland and Wales the decision will be for the appropriate Secretary of State. In Northern Ireland the decision will be for the Department of Education for Northern Ireland or the Department of the Environment for Northen Ireland. Following the decision, the Capital Taxes Office will be authorised to negotiate acceptance up to a certain figure or instructed to reject the offer.

*See 1987 Supplement, p. 213 below.

11.14* Once agreement has been reached on the market valuation of the property offered at the date of acceptance, the Capital Taxes Office will calculate the amount of tax satisfied by the acceptance of the property. The calulation is normally carried out in a similar way as the calculation of the special price paid in a private treaty sale (see Chapter 10), taking advantage of the "douceur" arrangement (where applicable), except that fixed proportitons of the value of the tax exemption will always be usedto arrive at the special price: 25 per cent. in the case of objects and 10 per cent. in the case of outstanding land and buildings. Illustrative examples are given in Appendices 11 and 12. The acceptance of the property does not give rise to any loss of conditional exemption in respect of any previously exempt transfers of that property nor does it give rise to any CGT charge.

*See 1987 Supplement, p. 213 below.

Allocation

11.15 As stated in paragraphs **11.9** and **11.10**, land and buildings will normally be accepted only if an appropriate recipient can be found in advance. Objects accepted because of their association with a building which has also been accepted or which is already in some form or public ownership (see **11.3** (*b*)) will normally be allocated to the owner of the building. Allocation of these objects is the responsibility of the Secretary of State for the Environment in England the appropriate terretorial Secretary of State in Scotland or Wales or the appropriate department in Northern Ireland.

11.16 The allocation of objects accepted because they are pre-eminent (see **11.12**) will be decided by the Minister for the Arts or by the appropriate territorial Secretary of State or Northern Ireland department. The Minister (or in Northern Ireland the department) concerned will consult the Museums and Galleries Commission or the Royal Commission on Historical Manuscripts for advice on the appropriate recipient. Applications are invited from interested institutions or bodies through advertisements in the Museums' Bulletin (published by the Museums Association, 34 Bloomsbury Way, London WC1A2SF) or, in the case of books and manuscripts, the *Times Literary Supplement*. An object may be allocated to any institution or body within the National Heritage Act 1980, s. 3 (6) (*a*), (*b*), or (*c*), to the National Art Collections Fund or the Friends of the National Libraries or to any person who is willing to accept it.

Conditional offers

11.17 Objects may be offered on condition that they pass to a particular institution or body or, in the case of objects having a significant association with a particular setting, that they remain in that setting (in situ). Expert advice on the pre-eminence of the objects will be sought as described in **11.12**. The Museums and Galleries Commission (or the Royal Commission on Historical Manuscripts in appropriate cases) will be asked to advise on the approriateness of the recipient or the location specified in the offer. In the case of an object accepted on condition that it passes to a private institution or body or remains in situ, formal ownership will normally be vested in an appropriate public body which is prepared to lend the object so that the conditions of the offer are complied with. In all cases the recipient will be required to give undertakings concerning the care, conservation and inalienablity of the objects and their accessibility to the public.

11.18 As indicated in **1.9**, the Office of Arts and Libraries have published a leaflet containing general advice on the main issues likely to arise in in situ cases.

APPENDIX 1. MAKING A CLAIM FOR CONDITIONAL EXEMPTION OR DESIGNATION

1. Claims should be addressed to the Capital Taxes Office in London, Edinburgh or Belfast, as appropriate. But it should be noted that in practice all claims for heritage exemption are dealt with by the London office.

2. The prospective ten-yearly charge on certain heritage property in discretionary trust apart (see Appendix 2, para. 20), claims for designation or exemption can be considered formally only when a charge to CTT or IHT has arisen or where there is evidence (such as a draft conveyance) that a transfer will occur as soon as exemptibility is confirmed. However, some of the advisory bodies, like the Countryside Commission, the Countryside Commission for Scotland, the Historic Buildings and Monuments Commission for England, the Scottish Development Department (Historic Buildings and Monuments Directorate), the Historic Buildings Council for Scotland and the Nature Conservancy Council are prepared to offer informal advice on the prospects of securing exemption, *at their discretion and in so far as this is possible within limited staff resources*. The Historic Buildings and Monument Commission for England is unable to make site inspections for the purpose of reaching an informal view, and the advice which it can give on this basis is limited to

offering a view, on the basis of photographs and a brief description, of whether a building is of outstanding architectural or historic interest. *It must be emphasized that any opinion offered in this way is preliminary and informal in nature and does not in any way commit the Revenue*, with whom the statutory responsibility for designation rests.

3. When making a claim the following information should be provided. It is important for the claim to be complete and in the correct form, otherwise it might lead to delay.

(*a*) *Works of art and other objects*
   (i) Full details of the property (photographs may occasionally be required).
   (ii) The address or addresses at which the object or objects may be inspected.
   (iii) Details of any previous exemptions.
   (iv) The measures proposed for providing for reasonable public access.

(*b*) *Outstanding land*
   (i) Particulars and description of the landscape, identifying those features considered to be of outstanding merit on account of the scenic, scientific or historic interest.
   (ii) Details of the transfer in respect of which the claim has arisen and the statutory provision under which the claim is made.
   (iii) Name, address and telephone number of the person with whom the advisory body may arrange a visit.
   (iv) six copies of a map of 1:10,000 (or 1:25,000 for very large estates) on an ordnance survey base, clearly marked with:
     (*a*) land claimed;
     (*b*) so far is practicable, all buildings which, though not eligible in their own right, are considered to make some positive contribution to the qualifying interest of the land on which they are situated (please also provide a supporting schedule indicating their location (by Grid reference, farm or village name, or by cross reference to symbols on the map supplied), approximate age and construction materials);
     (*c*) all public rights of way, differentiating between footpaths and bridleways;
     (*d*) any scheduled ancient monuments (quoting the relevant County Site and Monuments Record reference number, if possible) and listed buildings (with grades);
     (*e*) any Sites of Special Scientific Interest or in Northern Ireland any Areas of Special Scientifc Interest;
     (*f*) any nature reserve;
     (*g*) any woodlands on the Nature Conservancy Council's Inventory of Ancient Woodland (describe their age and species and indicate whether subject to any Forestry Commission scheme);
     (*h*) any other contiguous land in the same ownership; and
     (*i*) any land subject to tenancy or other burden.
   (v) Details of the measures proposed for providing reasonable public access.

(*c*) *Buildings of outstanding historic or architectural interest and supporting property*
   (i) Particulars and description of the property, including any essential amenity land and any historically associated objects for which exemption is also being claimed. In particular:
     (*a*) Up-to-date photographs of the main building to show the principal elevations of the exterior and interiors of the principal rooms. Black and white or coloured photographs are acceptable but not transparencies. (Good photographs are important in advancing a claim; submission of uniformative photographs can lead to delay in processing a claim).
     (*b*) Photographs of the exteriors of all other buildings included in the claim with their identification marked on the backs.
     (*c*) Photographs which show clearly the relationship between any essential amenity land for which exemption is being claimed and including the principal views to and from the main building concerned.
   (ii) Six copies of an appropriate scale Ordnance Survey base map with the information as listed in sub-paragraph (*b*)(iv) above.
   (iii) Details of the measures proposed for reasonable public access to the outstanding building and land (if any).
   (iv) Where the claim is for essential amenity land and "supportive undertakings" are required in respect of other property—the outstanding building (and possibly other essential amenity land)—appropriate details, as outlined in sub-paragraphs (i) to (iii) above, of that other property.
   (v) In cases where historically associated objects are detailed in catalogues, please indicate clearly for which items exemption is being sought.

APPENDIX 2. CONDITIONAL EXEMPTION: CTT AND IHT CHARGES ON LOSS OF EXEMPTION

1. This Appendix supplements Chapters 3–7 by explaining how tax is charged when conditional exemption from CTT or IHT ceases to apply and a tax charge arises. The special rules relating to property held in trust are also explained in this Appendix.

Property owned by individuals

Amount on which tax is charged

2. If the conditionally exempted property is sold, tax is charged on the proceeds provided that the sale was on arm's length terms and was not intended to confer a gratuitous benefit on any person (IHTA 1984, s. 33 (3)). Otherwise tax is charged on the market value at that time of the conditional exemption ceases to apply IHTA 1984, s. 33 (1)(a).

3. In the case of an outstanding building the sale proceeds or value attributable to clearly identifiable additions or improvements made to the building since the last exemption will not in practice be charged to CTT or IHT when a chargeable event occurs.

CTT and IHT business and agricultural reliefs

4. When conditional exemption ceases to apply and tax is charged the CTT and IHT business and agricultural reliefs do *not* apply.

The "relevant person"

5. The tax on a chargeable event is calculated by reference to the circumstances of a person who has previously made a conditionally exempt transfer of the property; he is described as the "relevant person" (IHTA 1984, s. 33 (5)). If there has been only one conditionally exempt transfer of the property under the FA 1976 or IHTA 1984 rules, or there has been only one within the 30 years before the chargeable event, the relevant person is the person who made the transfer. If there have been two or more such transfers within the 30 year period, the Inland Revenue will select one of those transfers, and the relevant person will be the person who made the transfer. In practice the Inland Revenue will select whichever transfer results in the largest amount of tax being payable. Conditionally exempt transfers which took place before a previous chargeable event are not taken into account.

The rate of tax

(a) CTT—chargeable events before 18 March 1986

6. The rate of tax charged was the rate which would have applied at the time of the chargeable event the relevant person had made a gift of the amount of the sale proceeds or the market value (*i.e.* it took into account all chargeable transfers made by him within the ten years before the chargeable event). If the relevant person was then dead, the rate is that arrived at by treating the amount of the sale proceeds etc. as the top slice of his death estate (IHTA 1984, s. 33 (1) (*b*)). The rate was taken from the lifetime scale except where the transfer by the relevant person was made on his death, when the death scale was used (IHTA 1984, ss. 33 (2)). The *scale* of rates applicable was that operating at the time of the chargeable event.

(b) IHT—chargeable events on and after 18 March 1986

7. In principle, similar rules apply for IHT (*i.e.* half of the death rate tax is charged if the relevant conditionally exempt transfer was made in life and full rate if it was made on death)—IHTA 1984, s. 33 (1) and (2), as amended by FA 1986, Sch. 19, para. 11 (1) and (2). But there are certain differences and special cases:
  (*a*) Where the chargeable event occurs on or after 18 March 1986, the cumulation period is *seven* (not ten) years, irrespective of whether:
     (i) the relevant conditionally exempt transfer occurred in lifetime or on death; or
     (ii) the relevant conditionally exempt transfer occurred before or after 18 March 1986, *or*
     (iii) the relevant person died before or after 18 March 1986.
     Where the transferor is still alive at the time of the chargeable event or where he died on or after 18 March 1986, the above applies by dint of the general IHT rules. Where, however, he died *before* 18 March 1986, a special rule ensures this result (FA 1986, Sch. 19, para. 41).
  (*b*) Where the relevant person is still alive at the time of the chargeable event, any earlier potentially exempt transfers made by him are left out of account for cumulation purposes. The charge is *not* revised if the potentially exempt transfers later prove to be chargeable because the relevant person dies within seven years of making them (IHTA 1984, s. 33 (2A)—as introduced by FA 1986, Sch. 19, para. 11 (2)).
  (*c*) Tax is charged at half death rates where the relevant conditional exemption was granted in respect of an earlier lifetime transfer which became chargeable on death under the gift with reservation rules (IHTA 1984, s. 33 (2)—as amended by FA 1986, Sch. 19, para. 11 (2)).

Liability for the tax

8. Who is liable for the tax depends on the circumstances in which it becomes payable. If it becomes payable because an undertaking has been broken or the owner has died and his heirs have not given a fresh undertaking, the liability falls on the person who would have been entitled to

receive the proceeds of the sale if the property had then been sold. Normally, therefore, the owner who has broken his undertaking will be liable to pay the tax. If the chargeable event is a disposal (*e.g.* a sale or gift) the person liable is the person by whom or for whose benefit the property is disposed of (IHTA 1984, s. 207 (2)).

Effect on cumulation

9. When a chargeable event occurs, the amount of tax is normally added to the cumulative total of chargeable transfers made by the person who made the *last* conditionally exempt transfer of the property; consequently—and subject to the relevant cumulation rule (10 years for CTT, seven years for IHT)—the event may affect the rate of tax payable on any future transfers which he makes (IHTA 1984, s. 34 (1)). This happens whether or not he is the relevant person whose circumstances determine the rate of tax payable on the chargeable event itself. If the person who made the last conditionally exempt transfer is dead, the sale proceeds etc are treated as part of his estate for the purpose of calculating the rate of tax on any later chargeable event for which he is treated as the relevant person. A special rule applies, however, where the person who made the last conditionally exempt transfer is not himself selected as the relevant person and at the date of the chargeable event, or within the previous five years, the property has been comprised in a settlement made within 30 years before that date (IHTA 1984, s. 34 (3)). If in these circumstances the settlor had made a conditionally exempt transfer of the property within the 30 year period, the sale proceeds etc are added to his cumulative total (instead of to the total of the person who made the last conditionally exempt transfer).

10. A detailed example of the working of these rules is given in Appendix 13.

Double charges

11. When a conditionally exempt transfer is followed by a transfer which is not itself conditionally exempt (because for example the new owner does not renew the undertaking), the second transfer will be chargeable to CTT or IHT in the normal way. But, it will also be a chargeable event and result in a charge to tax by reference to the person who made the last conditionally exempt transfer. Thus if A made a conditionally exempt transfer to B before 18 March 1986 and B later makes a transfer to a trust and the trustees do not claim exemption there could be two charges to tax:

(*a*) on the transfer from B to the trust, under the normal IHT rules applying to a transfer of property which is not conditionally exempt; and

(*b*) on the withdrawl of the conditional exemption given on the transfer from A to B—by adding the value of the property to A's cumulative total.

12. IHTA 1984, s. 33 (7) (*a*) limits this double charge. The transfer from B to the trust is taxed in the normal way, but the tax paid on that transfer will reduce the amount of tax payable upon the withdrawal of the conditional exemption on the transfer from A to B.

13. If B's transfer to the trust takes place before B has owned the heritage property for six years and C renews the undertaking, the transfer will be a chargeable transfer but not a chargeable event. In these circumstances the tax paid on B's transfer will be credited against the tax payable on the next transfer of the property which constitutes a chargeable event (IHTA 1984, s. 33 (7) (*b*)).

14. A further rule has been incorparated to meet particular circumstances which can arise on or after 18 March 1986—where, after a conditionally exempt transfer, there is a potentially exempt transfer, the undertakings are not renewed and the potentially exempt transfer later proves to be a chargeable transfer. If, in the example at **11**, there is a potentially exempt transfer from B to C, who is not prepared to renew undertakings, that transfer will be a chargeable event in relation to the earlier transfer from A to B. The tax chargeable will be credited against the tax due if the potentially exempt transfer from B to C later proves to be a chargeable transfer (IHTA 1984, s. 33 (8)—as introduced by FA 1986, Sch. 19, para. 11 (4)).

Property held in trust: interests in possession

15.* When a person has an interest in possession (for example, a life interest) in settled property, he is in general treated for the purposes of CTT and IHT as if he were beneficially entitled to the property. Thus he is treated as making a transfer of the property when he dies or when his interest comes to an end in his lifetime. If the settled property is accepted as eligible heritage property, conditional exemption may extend to it under the rules explained above, on the same lines as for transfers of property held outright.

*See 1987 Supplement, p. 213 below.

Property held in trust: no interest in possession

16. There is in general a charge to CTT or IHT when settled property held on trusts in which there is no interest in possession (*i.e.* broadly, property held on discretionary trusts) ceases to be held on such trusts (for example when a distribution is made to a beneficiary or when an interest in possession in the trust is created). If the property in question is accepted as eligible national

heritage property, conditional exemption from this charge to tax may extend to it in certain circumstances. The occasion of the charge from which conditional exemption is given is described in the legislation as a "conditionally exempt occasion".

Conditionally exempt occasions

17. In general the rules explained above for conditionally exempt transfers apply to conditionally exempt occasions. Conditional exemption may arise if the heritage property concerned has been in the trust thoughout the six years preceding the occasion of charge, if the requisite undertakings are given and if the property is designated by the Treasury (IHTA 1984, s. 78 (1)). And if, for example, there has been both a conditionally exempt transfer and a conditionally exempt occasion in respect of the property within 30 years of a chargeable event, the Inland Revenue can select either one of those transactions to work out the rate of tax (IHTA 1984, s. 78 (3)).

18. In addition to the chargeable events described in Chapter 7, any event which gives rise to a charge to tax in the circumstances described at para. 16 (*e.g.* a distribution out of a discretionary trust) will also be a chargeable event unless that event is itself a conditionally exempt occasion. The relevant person by reference to whose circumstances tax is calculated in relation to a conditionally exempt occasion is always the settlor of the settlement; where more that one person is the settlor the Inland Revenue may select any one of them (IHTA 1984, s. 78 (2)). If the settlement was made under a will the tax charge will be calculated by reference to the death scale of rates; otherwise it will be calculated at half the death scale rate (FA 1986, Sch. 19, para. 19). The scales used will be those in force at the time of the chargeable event. The full rates of tax may in certain circumstances be reduced to thirty or sixty per cent. of those rates when the tax is being calculated by reference to a conditionally exempt occasion (IHTA 1984, s. 78 (4)). These reductions normally depend on the number of ten-yearly charges from which the heritage property in question was exempt (see para. 19). The cumulation provisions described in para. 9 do not apply to conditionally exempt occasions.

Ten-yearly charge to tax

19. Discretionary trust property is normally liable to a ten-yearly charge to tax on each tenth anniversary of the date of creation of the trust. Property which qualifies as national heritage property may be exempted from this charge as well. If the property was conditionally exempt from CTT, IHT or ED on or before the occasion when it entered the trust, it will also be exempt from any ten-yearly charge to tax which falls due before a chargeable event occurs (IHTA 1984, s. 79 (1)). A similar exemption from the ten-yearly charge applies if the corresponding relief from CGT under CGTA 1979, s. 147 was given on or before the occasion on which the property entered the trust (IHTA 1984, s. 79 (2)), *i.e.* at a time when CTT had not been imposed but after 1965.

20. If heritage property does not qualify for exemption automatically in either of the ways described in the preceding paragraph (for example because it has been purchased by the trustees of the settlement), it may still be exempt from the ten-yearly charge if it has been designated by the Revenue and the requisite undertakings have been given *before the date of the ten-yearly charge* (IHTA 1984, s. 79 (3)). It is important to make a claim well in advance so that the formalities can be completed in time. If property is exempted under s. 79 (3) and the undertakings given in respect of it are later broken, the subsection also provides for a charge to CTT or IHT on the breach. This charge is at a tapered flat rate calculated by reference to the length of time which has elapsed since 13 March 1975 or, if it is later, the date the settlement commenced, or the date of its last ten-year anniversary before the property became comprised in the settlement (IHTA 1984, s. 79 (6) and (7)). The maximum rate which can be charged is thirty per cent. and there will be no charge of this kind at all once there has been a conditionally exempt occasion in respect of the property in question (IHTA, 1984, s. 79 (4)). The persons liable for the tax includes trustees of the settlement (IHTA 1984, s. 207 (3)).

Distributions before 9 March 1982

21. Before 9 March 1982, an event which now counts as a conditionally exempt occasion (*i.e.* a distribution from a discretionary trust) was known as a conditionally exempt distribution. The rules explained above which relate to the tax charged on a chargeable event by reference to conditionally exempt occasions apply equally to chargeable events on which the tax would have been calculated by reference to a conditionally exempt distribution (IHTA 1984, s. 78 (2) (*c*)).

APPENDIX 3. ESTATE DUTY CHARGES (AND SPECIAL RULES)

1. ED applies only to property passing on a death which occurred before 13 March 1975. However, a charge to duty may still arise on objects which passed on a death (or passed inter vivos within the

statutory gift period) and which had been exempted from duty under the provisions of FA 1896, s. 20 or FA 1930, s. 40.

2. If objects exempted from ED are sold, the statutory provisions relevant at the date of death to which the exemption relates may still be effective, so as to give rise to a charge to duty. However, ED will not be charged if the exempted objects:

(i) are sold by private treaty to a qualifying national institution; or

(ii) before they are sold, have again been transferred on a death and have been conditionally exempted on that occasion under FA 1976, s. 76 or IHTA 1984, s. 30.

Special rules

3. Special rules may apply when property which has previously been exempted from ED on a death is sold after 6 April 1976. The way in which this property is taxed depends on what has happened since the original exemption was granted. If before the sale:

(a) there has been a conditionally exempt transfer on a death after 6 April 1976—CTT or IHT only is charged (IHTA 1984, Sch. 6, para. 4 (2) (b));

(b) there has been a conditionally exempt lifetime transfer after 6 April 1976—the Revenue may elect to charge either CTT or IHT (as appropriate) under the post 1976 rules or ED under the earlier rules (IHTA 1984, Sch. 6, para. 4 (2) (a);

(c) there has been a transfer after 6 April 1976—either in lifetime or on a death—of property which was exempted from ED under FA 1930, s. 40 and in respect of which conditional exemption has not been claimed—ED *will be payable i.e.*, the CTT or IHT charge does *not* wash the potential ED liability (FA 1930, s. 40 and (IHTA 1984, Sch. 6, para. 4 (4)). *But* any CTT or IHT paid on the transfer will be allowed as credit against the ED payable on the sale (IHTA 1984, Sch. 6, para. 4 (3)).

APPENDIX 4. CONDITIONAL EXEMPTION–TRANSFERS ON DEATHS BETWEEN 13 MARCH 1975 AND 6 APRIL 1976

1. The conditional exemption regime outlined in the main body of this booklet relates to chargeable transfers and events occurring on or after 7 April 1976. The rules for transfers in the period between 13 March 1975 and 6 April 1976 were different in certain respects. These differences are explained below.

2. Transfers of qualifying heritage property made on or before 6 April 1976 may be conditionally exempted from tax only if they were transfers on death (FA 1975, ss. 31–34). The same types of property can qualify for exemptions as under the current rules. The undertakings required are also the same, except that in the case of works of art and other objects of national etc interest the undertaking should provide for reasonable access for inspection of the state of preservation of the object and for purposes of research (instead of—as under the current rules—reasonable public access).

3. The chargeable events on which tax becomes payable are broadly the same as under the current rules (although the latter may apply in certain circumstances—IHTA 1984, s. 35 (2); where the Revenue have a choice of bases, in practice they will select whichever results in the largest amount of tax being payable). Tax is charged by reference to the last death on which the property was exempted from tax. The scales which will apply are those appropriate at the date of death, not those in force at the date of the chargeable event. If the chargeable event occurred within three years after the death, the property is added back to the deceased's estate and tax is charged on theestate as if conditional exemption had not been given. If the chargeable event occurred more than three years after the death, tax is charged on the sale proceeds or value of the property at the time of the chargeable event. The rate of tax at which the sale proceeds etc are then chargeable is the average rate (not the "top slice" rate as under IHTA 1984) found by adding them to the rest of the estate (including any conditionally exempt property for which there has been a chargeable event within three years after the death); but the tax charged on the rest of the estate is not increased. Credit may be given for tax on an ordinary chargeable transfer in the same way as under the current rules. In the case of sales after 6 April 1976, the sale proceeds are taken as the measure of the value only if the sale was on arm's length terms and was not intended to confer any gratuitous benefit on any person.

4. If tax becomes chargeable at different times on two or more exempt objects which formed a set at the time of death, tax is charged as if all the chargeable events had occurred at the time of the first. This rule does not, however, apply if the chargeable events are disposals to persons who are neither acting in concert nor connected with each other (IHTA 1984, Sch. 5, para. 2 (3) and (4)).

5. The rules which provide for a charge on a conditionally exempted entity of outstanding building, qualifying amenity land and historically associated objects when there is a chargeable event in respect of any part of it differ in certain detailed respects. But the basic principle is the same—a chargeable event in respect of any part triggers a charge on the whole, subject to the "materially affected" rule explained in **7.7**. (IHTA 1984, Sch. 5, paras. 3 and 4).

APPENDIX 5. MAINTENANCE FUNDS: TAX CHARGES

Introduction

1. This Appendix amplifies Chapter 8 by explaining in what circumstances there may be charges to CTT or IHT and income tax on the assets of a maintenance fund, and how these charges are calculated. It also explains the special provisions relating to one-estate elections and to CGT and stamp duty.

Capital transfer tax and inheritance tax

Exemptions available

2. If the Revenue give a direction in respect of property put (or to be put) into a maintenance fund, certain CTT and IHT exemptions follow:

   (a) Any transfer of value arising when the property is put into the fund is normally exempt from CTT or IHT (IHTA 1984, s. 2 (1)). (This includes property in which, immediately before the transfer, there was an interest in possession but in such cases either the property must pass directly to the fund during the life tenant's lifetime or arrangements must be made during his lifetime for the property to pass directly to the fund on his death).*

   (b) Where property in a discretionary settlement becomes held on the trusts of a maintenance fund while remaining comprised in the original settlement—*e.g.* by an appointment of property within the settlement—there will normally be no CTT or IHT charge (IHTA 1984, Sch. 4, para. 16).

   (c) A distribution of property from an existing discretionary trust to an individual will normally be exempt from CTT or IHT, on both the distribution and the subsequent transfer into settlement, if the individual settles the property—within 30 days (or, in some circumstances, within two years)—in a maintenance fund (IHTA 1984, Sch. 4, para. 17). Similarly a CTT or IHT charge will not normally arise when an existing maintenance fund distributes capital to an individual who transfers it to a new maintenance fund (IHTA 1984, Sch. 4, para. 9—and see paragraph 4 (b)).

   (d) While the direction is effective, the assets of the fund are not subject to the ten-yearly or other charges on discretionary trusts (IHTA 1984, s. 58 (1) (c)).

3.* As explained in **8.5**, for a period of six years after any property has been put into a maintenance fund, or until the death of the settlor of the fund (*i.e.* the person who put it into the fund in the first place) within that period, the property and any income from it may be applied only for the purposes of the maintenance etc of the heritage property, or of the maintenance or reasonable improvement of the assets of the fund, or of the payment of the trustees' expenses; or they may be paid to a body listed in IHTA 1984, Sch. 3 or to a heritage charity. Such applications do not involve any charges to CTT or IHT (IHTA 1984, s. 76 (1) and Sch. 4, para. 8 (2)).

Tax treatment of property when it ceases to be held on the trusts of a maintenance fund

4.* After the period of six years, of after the death of the settlor within that period, capital may be taken out of the fund for any purpose whatsoever. But when this happens there may be a charge to CTT or IHT depending mainly on the identity of the recipient. The detailed rules are as follows:

(a) Capital paid out for an approved heritage purpose, as summarised in paragraph 3 above

No CTT or IHT charge, except in the case where the payment is made to a heritage charity or other heritage body which had previously directly or indirectly purchased an interest under the settlement in question (IHTA 1984, Sch. 4, para. 8 (2) and (5)).

(b) Capital paid out to an individual who within 30 days of the payment (or, if the payment occurs on the death of the settlor, within two years of the death) puts it into a new maintenance fund to which a Revenue direction applies

No CTT or IHT charge unless

   (i) the individual had directly or indirectly purchased the property in question; or

   (ii) the benefit to the new fund is less than the loss to the old fund (IHTA 1984, Sch. 4, para. 9).

(c)   *Capital paid out to the settlor or to his spouse; or to the settlor's widow or widower within two years of the settlor's death*

There is generally no tax charge unless

   (i) the recipient is not domiciled in the U.K.; or

   (ii) the recipient has purchased (directly or indirectly) an interest under the settlement; or

   (iii) before entering the maintenance fund, the property was held in another settlement (either a discretionary trust or another maintenance fund) and there was no full charge to tax when the property left that settlement; or

   (iv) the benefit to the recipient is less than the loss to the maintenance fund (IHTA 1984, Sch. 4, para. 10).

(d) Capital paid out to non-heritage charities or other exempt bodies

There will generally be no charge to CTT or IHT when capital is paid out to charities or to the bodies listed in Appendix 10 or (as explained in **9.3**) for public benefit (IHTA 1984, s. 76). There are however *exceptions*; for example, there may be a tax charge if the recipient charity etc had purchased an interest under the maintenance fund settlement.

(e) Capital paid out to anybody else

This is charged to CTT or IHT at the appropriate rate (explained at paragraph 5 below). The amount liable to tax is the amount by which the value of the property in the maintenance fund is reduced as a result of the event giving rise to the change. This amount is grossed up at the appropriate rate if the tax is paid out of the assets remaining in the fund.

*See 1987 Supplement, p. 213 below.

(f) Withdrawal of the Revenue direction at any time (i.e. whether before or after the six year period has expired)

If the direction given by the Revenue in respect of property comprised in a maintenance fund is withdrawn, tax is charged on that property at the date when the direction ceases to apply (IHTA 1984, Sch. 4, para. 8 (1), (2)).

(g) Disposition by trustees

CTT or IHT is charged when the trustees of a maintenance fund do some act or deliberately fail to exercise a right which reduces the value of the property comprised in the fund. There will be no charge however where the property was applied for an approved heritage purpose (see paragraph 3 above); or if the disposition was broadly of a commercial nature; or if it was the grant of an agricultural tenancy for full value (IHTA 1984, Sch. 4, para. 8 (2), (3)).

(h) Loss of conditional exemption of property supported by a maintenance fund

If a maintenance fund is set up for the support of conditionally exempt heritage property tax may be charged on the assets of the maintenance fund when the conditional exemption is lost (see Chapter 7). When the heritage property is not subject to conditional exemption there may similarly be a CTT of IHT charge on the maintenance fund on the happening of an event which, if the heritage property were conditionally exempt, would result in that exemption being lost. (IHTA 1984, Sch. 4, paras. 3 (1), (2), (3)).

CTT and IHT: rate of tax

5. Where tax is chargeable on one of the occasions described above the rate of tax charged depends on the way in which the property on which the charge falls had previously entered the maintenance fund regime.

(a) Property transferred—tax-free or subject to only a reduced tax charge—from an existing discretionary trust, whether directly or via an individual within the period mentioned at 2 (b) above

Tax is charged at a flat rate which tapers over time and which is calculated by reference to the period—counted in complete quarters (periods of three months)—which has elapsed since the property entered the discretionary trust or was last charged to tax whilst in the trust. No period falling before 13 March 1975 is counted. The rate of tax is 0.25 per cent. for each of the first successive forty quarters; 0.2 per cent. for each of the next forty, and so on until the maximum rate of 30 per cent. is reached after 50 years (IHTA 1984, Sch. 4, para. 11).

(b) Property transferred into the maintenance fund from any other source—e.g. by way of transfer from outright ownership

The rate of tax is the higher of:

  (i) a tapered rate similar to that at paragraph 5 (a) above but calculated by reference to the period which has elapsed since the date on which the property entered the maintenance fund (IHTA 1984, Sch. 4, para. 13), and

 (ii)* a rate determined on a special basis by reference *normally* to the tax position of the settlor (*i.e.* the person who put the property into the maintenance fund in the first place) at the time the charge arises. If the settlor is then alive, this rate is the effective rate which would have applied—at lifetime rates or half the death rate scale for events on or after 18 March 1986—to a chargeable transfer made by him at that time of an amount equal to the amount on which the charge falls. If the settlor is dead when the charge arises, the effective rate is calculated as though the amount on which taxis chargeable had been added to the value transferred on his death and had formed the highest part of the value; the lifetime scale of rates is applied or half the death rate scale for events on or after 18 March 1986, unless the settlement was made on death. In establishing this rate, any previous distributions from the fund (or any similar fund) which were made within the ten (seven for events on or after 18 March 1986) years preceding the current charge are usually taken into account (IHTA 1984, Sch. 4, para. 14 as amended by FA 1986, Sch. 19, paras. 38, 42). The IHT rules described in Appendix 2 para. 7 would apply where relevant.

*See 1987 Supplement, p. 213 below.

CTT business and agricultural reliefs

6. Property paid out of maintenance funds will qualify for the CTT of IHT business relief if the trustees are themselves running a business. The CTT or IHT agricultural relief can also apply but the woodlands relief (IHTA 1984, Pt. V, Ch. III) will not apply.

Liability for CTT and IHT

7. The persons liable for the tax include the trustees of the maintenance fund (IHTA 1984, s. 201 (1)).

Income tax

8. Whenever property is taken out of a maintenance fund for any purpose other than a "heritage purpose" as summarised in paragraph 3 above where a Revenue direction is withdrawn (see para. 4 (*f*) above), there is a charge to income tax at 30 per cent. on so much of the income of the fund up to that date as has not been applied for heritage purposes. Tax is not however chargeable in respect of income which is treated as that of the settlor. In greater detail, this means that the charge will be on so much of the income of the fund, (including accumulated income), grossed up to the pre-tax figure, as has not up to that time already been applied for heritage purposes or been subject to this charge, or been charged to income tax as income of the settlor. But there is no income tax charge when property is distributed to an individual who within 30 days (or, when appropriate, two years) resettles it on a new maintenance fund in respect of which the Revenue give a direction, if the whole of the property in the first fund is resettled on the second fund; partial distributions do not qualify for this exemption (FA 1980, s. 52 [TA 1988, s. 694]).

Capital gains tax and stamp duty

9. Property transferred into trust, including into a maintenance fund, by an individual or by the trustees of a settlement can be made the subject of an election by the transferor to defer the tax on any capital gain arising at that time. A similar deferment can apply when property is transferred to another trust or is distributed to an individual. In the latter case, the election must be made by both transferor and transferee. Deferment can therefore be claimed, for example, when property is distributed to an individual who resettles it within 30 days (or, when appropriate, two years) on another maintenance fund. Moreoever, in a "30 day or two year resettlement" case, there will be only one charge to stamp duty of 50p even though the property is moved from settlement to the other by two steps (FA 1980, s. 98 (1)).

One-estate elections

10. The rules governing the taxation of income property under Schedule A contain special provisions which may affect some owners of heritage property forming part of an estate. In brief the position is that when the old Schedule A tax on owner-occupiers was abolished in 1963 certain owners of land managed as one estate were given the opportunity of making "one-estate elections" in order to preserve benefits enjoyed under the old Schedule A code. Provided that such an election was made, successive owners of the estate also had the right to make a similar election.
11. The effect of a one-estate election is that, subject to certain conditions, maintenance and repairs expenditure incurred by the owner on owner-occupied property comprised in the estate (for example a mansion house) can be set against the rental income derived from other estate properties.
12. Where part of an estate to which a one-estate election relates is transferred into a maintenance fund the part transferred continues to be treated for Schedule A purposes as forming part of the estate. Where therefore an election is in force immediately prior to the setting up of such a maintenance fund the transfer of rent producing estate properties to the fund will not disturb the existing taxation arrangements described in paragraph 10 above (FA 1980, s. 53 (1) [TA 1988, s. 27 (1)]).
13. Where part of an estate ceased to be compromised in an maintenance fund an existing election will continue to be effective if the property is resettled on another maintenance fund within 30 days or, when appropriate, two years (FA 1980, s. 53 (4) [TA 1988, s. 27 (4)]).

APPENDIX 6. SUMMARY OF CHANGES INCORPORATED IN FINANCE ACT 1986 ADAPTING THE CAPITAL TRANSFER TAX HERITAGE RULES FOR INHERITANCE TAX PURPOSES

1. The essentially technical changes which have been made to the CTT heritage regime to adapt it to the new IHT structure are detailed in the appropriate parts of this booklet. But, for ease of reference, they are summarised in this Appendix.

(a) Exemption claim in respect of lifetime gifts

(i) General

2.* Conditional exemption cannot be claimed in respect of a lifetime gift to an individual (or to an accumulation and maintenance settlement or a trust for disabled persons) of qualifying heritage property *unless or until the transfer becomes chargeable as a result of the donor's death* (IHTA 1984, s. 30 (3B)—as introduced by FA 1986, Sch. 19, para. 7). Title to conditional exemption is to be determined by reference to circumstances existing after the death of the transferor—*that is, at the time of the claim* (IHTA 1984, s. 31 (1A)—as introduced by FA 1986, Sch. 19, para. 8 (1)).

*See 1987 Supplement, p. 213 below.

(ii) Special cases

3.* Special rules apply where between the respective dates of the lifetime gift and the donor's subsequent death there have been certain intermediate events.
 (*aa*) if the property has meanwhile been given, or sold by private treaty, to one of the national bodies listed in the IHTA 1984, Sch. 3 or if it had been accepted in satisfaction of tax, the charge on death is exempted outright without the need for undertakings to be given (IHTA 1984, s. 26A—as introduced by FA 1986, Sch. 19, para. 6).
 (*bb*) If the property has meanwhile been sold in other circumstances, a conditional exemption claim is precluded in respect of the charge arising on the donor's subsequent death (IHTA) 1974, s. 30 (3C)—as introduced by FA 1986, Sch. 19, para. 7).

(iii) Undertakings—administrative arrangements

4. Where a suitable undertaking has already been given for the property in question (in respect of an associated maintenance fund or a CGT exemption claim) and this is still in force, that undertaking is normally accepted for the purposes of the conditional exemption claim and does not need to be duplicated (IHTA 1984, s. 31 (4G)—as introduced by FA 1986, Sch. 19, para. 8 (2)). In practice, there will normally be no need for duplication either where there is in force an undertaking given under IHTA 1984, s. 31 (4A).

(b) Charges when conditional exemption ends

(i) Incidence of charge

5. The existing provisions (IHTA 1984, ss. 32 and 32A) have been amended to make it clear that when a conditionally exempt transfer was initially a potentially exempt transfer, a chargeable event (that is, an event which ends conditional exemption) can only occur after the death that attracts conditional exemption (FA 1986, Sch. 19, paras. 9 and 10).

(ii) Rates of charge

6. CTT had two rate tables, one for transfers on death and another which, as from 13 March 1984, specified half the death rates for lifetime transfers. IHT achieves a similar effect using a single rate table. The provisions that apply where the charge is calculated by reference to a conditionally exempt transfer made by an individual (IHTA 1984, s. 33 (1) and (2)) have been adapted to preserve their existing effect of charging half the death tax rate if the relevant conditionally exempt transfer was made in life and the full rate if it was made on death (IHTA 1984, s. 33 (1) and (2)—as amended by FA 1986, Sch. 19, para. 11 (1) and (2)). Where the relevant conditionally exempt transfer which became chargeable on death under the gift with reservation rules, tax is chargeable at *half*, not full, death rates (IHTA 1984, s. 33 (2)—as amended by FA 1986, Sch. 19, para. 11 (2)).
7. Corresponding consequential changes have been made to the rules that apply where the charge is calculated by reference to a conditionally exempt transfer from a discretionary trust (IHTA 1984, s. 78) and where a tax charge is levied on a maintenance fund (IHTA 1984, Sch. 4, para. 14)—introduced by FA 1986, Sch. 19, paras. 19 and 38 (1) and (4) respectively.

(iii) Cumulation rules

8. Under the general IHT rules, when a donor's cumulation is calculated while he is alive (for example, for calculating the tax charge in respect of a gift into trust) transfers made to individuals after 17 March 1986 in the preceding seven years are left out of account. If his subsequent death makes any of those potentially exempt transfers chargeable, previous cumulation calculations are revised to bring them into account. *The latter rule does not apply to the charges when conditional exemption ends.* Once such a charge has been calculated with the donor's potentially exempt transfers left out of account, it will *not* be revised because the potentially exempt transfers later prove to be chargeable. Likewise, the tax is not increased to full death rates if the donor dies within seven years after the chargeable event (IHTA 1984, s. 33 (2A)—as introduced by FA 1986, Sch. 19, para. 11 (2)). Corresponding exceptions to the general rules have been incorporated in the provisions relating to charges on maintenance funds (IHTA 1984, Sch. 4, para. 14 (1A)—as introduced by FA 1986, Sch. 19, para. 38 (2)).
9. When a chargeable event occurs on or after 18 March 1986, *the charge is calculated as if the IHT rules, with seven year cumulation, had been in force when the donor died* (FA 1986, Sch. 19, para. 41). Corresponding rules apply to charges on maintenance funds (FA 1986, Sch. 19, para. 42).

10.* Where a charge on a maintenance fund is calculated by reference to the tax position of the settlor, certain previous distributions from the fund (or any similar fund) are usually taken into account (see 5 (*b*) (ii) and Appendix 5). The relevant period has been reduced from the preceding ten, to the preceding seven years (FA 1986, Sch. 19, para. 38 (3)).

*See 1987 Supplement, p. 213 below.

(iv) Double charges

11. The CTT charging rules included a credit rule that prevents a double charge in certain circumstances where there is liability on a chargeable event and a mainstream chargeable transfer charge in respect of the same property. The mainstream tax is set against the chargeable event tax (IHTA 1984, s. 33 (7)). The rule has been extended for use when after a conditionally exempt transfer a subsequent potentially exempt transfer is a chargeable event (because undertakings are not renewed) and then later the potentially exempt transfer itself becomes chargeable (because of the death of the transferor within seven years of the potentially exempt transfer). The credit rule is reversed and the chargeable event tax is set against the mainstream tax (IHTA 1984, s. 33 (8)—as introduced by FA 1986, Sch. 19, para. 11 (4)). The corresponding credit rules in cases where conditional exemption was given under the 1975 CTT legislation (relating to deaths before 7 April 1976) or under ED have been similarly extended (FA 1986, Sch. 19, paras. 12 and 39 respectively).

APPENDIX 7. CAPITAL TAX CONSEQUENCES OF LOSS OR DESTRUCTION OF CONDITONALLY EXEMPTED HERITAGE PROPERTY

1. This note outlines the capital tax consequences of the loss or destruction of conditionally exempted heritage property.

Property actually the subject of the particular event

2. For property (chattel, building or land) actually the subject of the particular event, the position is as follows. In general, the loss etc. would *not* constitute a chargeable occasion for *CTT or IHT*, whether or not insurance monies are received. A charge would however be levied if it were evident that the loss etc. had occurred because there had been a clear breach of an undertaking. It therefore does not matter for immediate purposes whether the restored building is itself of heritage quality. In a case where a building was completely destroyed, as subsequent sale (otherwise than one by private treaty to one of the bodies listed in Appendix 10) of the land on which the building had stood would be a chargeable event.

3. The rules for *CGT* are different. The loss etc. of an asset is normally treated as a disposal, giving rise to a chargeable gain if any compensation received exceeds the acquisition cost (CGTA 1979, s. 20). But the charge can be deferred if the compensation proceeds are used, within a year of receipt or such longer period as is considered reasonable), to aquire a replacement (CGTA 1979, s. 21). "Replacement" is interpreted flexibly, by reference to whether the new asset is of a similar functional type to the old. Deferment of charge would therefore be permitted, for example if jewellery is replaced by jewellery and art objects by art objects. Where a building is totally lost or destroyed and compensation monies are applied in constructing or otherwise acquiring a replacement elsewhere, s. 21 is applied concessionally by treating the building as separate assets from the land on which they each stand. Applying the functional test, a heritage property could be replaced by a modern construction which would not be suitable for designation but this fact would have no immediate relevance for CGT purposes.

Satellite exemptions

4. Turning to the implications for *satellite exemptions*, the position of supporting property is as follows. If a building is totally destroyed by fire, most, if not all, of the historically associated objects are likely to have gone up in flames with it, leaving essential amenity land as the ancilliary property potentially affected. But what follows applies to both land and such objects. For *CTT and IHT* purposes, where the destruction of the house involves no breach of an undertaking, neither its loss nor the receipt of insurance monies is a "disposal" which triggers a charge on remaining supporting property. No charge would therefore arise in respect of the latter at that stage, *providing* the undertakings originally given in respect of it continue to be observed. A charge would however arise in the normal way at some later stage—as and when an undertaking is breached, or the property is sold or otherwise next changes hands. That event may also be a chargeable transfer of the property. Conditional exemption could be claimed in respect of that transfer only if the property qualifies for exemption in its own right. Where exemption could not be claimed, the credit rules would serve to limit the double charge which would otherwise arise at that stage to the higher of the two charges.

5. The *CGT* position is basically the same. No immediate charge would arise on the supporting amenity land because of the destruction of the building (CGTA 1979, s. 147 (7) does not apply

because the only disposal is deemed disposal which is precluded by the last sentence of sub-section (6)). But tax would become payable as and when the CTT or IHT charge on loss of conditional exemption was triggered.

Maintenance funds

6. Finally, *maintenance funds*. It is not possible to be quite so forthcoming in this context because much will depend on the precise facts of each particular case. The fundamental assumption would have to be that the destruction of the building which a fund services is likely to lead to the withdrawal of the Treasury or Inland Revenue direction with consequent tax charges. In a situation where a "rump" of the heritage property survived, the Revenue would consider the matter in a constructive and sympathetic way, in so far as the facts and circumstances permitted.

7. If the insurance monies were used to acquire another qualifying building and it was desired to endow that property, like its predecessor, with a maintenance fund, a new trust would need to be established. Resettlement of some or all of the original trust funds on new maintenance trusts would not give rise to a tax charge if the provisions of IHTA 1984, Sch. 4, para. 9 were met.

APPENDIX 8. ADDRESSES OF GOVERNMENT DEPARTMENTS AND OTHER BODIES

United Kingdom

1 Inland Revenue
   Policy Division
   Room F7, West Wing
   Somerset House
   London WC2R 1LB

2 Department of Trade and Industry
   Export Licensing Branch
   Millbank Tower
   London SW1 4QU

3 National Heritage Memorial Fund
   Church House
   Great Smith Street
   London SW1 3BL

4 Museums and Galleries Commission
   7 St James's Square
   London SW1Y 4JU

5 Royal Commission on Historical
     Manuscripts
   Quality House
   Quality Court
   Chancery Lane
   London WC2A 1HP

Great Britain

6 Forestry Commission
   231 Corstorphine Road
   Edinburgh EH12 7AT

England and Wales

7 Capital Taxes Office
   Minford House
   Rockley Road
   London W14 0DF

8 Countryside Commission
   John Dower House
   Crescent Place
   Cheltenham
   Gloucestershire GL50 3RA

9 Nature Conservancy Council
   Northminster House
   Peterborough PE1 1UA

10 Royal Botanic Gardens
    Kew
    Richmond
    Surrey TW9 3AB

England

11 Office of Arts and Libraries
    Great George Street
    London SW1P 3AL

12 Department of the Environment
    Room N19/16
    2 Marsham Street
    London SW1 3EB

13 Department of the Environment
    Tollgate House
    Houlton Street
    Bristol BS2 9DJ
    (scenic and scientific land)

14 Historic Buildings and Monuments
      Commission for England
    Fortress House
    23 Savile Row
    London W1X 2HB

Scotland

15 Capital Taxes Office
    16 Picardy Place
    Edinburgh EH1 3NB

16 Scottish Education Department
    New St Andrew's House
    St James Centre
    Edinburgh EH1 3SY

17 Scottish Development Department
    Historic Buildings and Monuments
    Directorate
    20 Brandon Street
    Edinburgh EH3 5RA

18 Historic Buildings Council for Scotland
    20 Brandon Street
    Edinburgh EH3 5RA

19 Countryside Commission for Scotland
   Battleby
   Redgorton
   Perth PH1 3EW

20 Nature Conservancy Council
   HQ for Scotland
   12 Hope Terrace
   Edinburgh EH9 2AS

21 Royal Botanic Garden
   Inverleith Road
   Edinburgh EH3 5LR

Wales
22 Welsh Office
   Crown Building
   Cathays Park
   Cardiff CF1 3NQ
   (Economic and Rural Policy Division 3 for
   outstanding scenic and scientific land and
   Education Division for works of art etc)

23 Cadw Welsh Historic Monuments
   Brunel House
   2 Fitzalan House
   Cardiff CF2 1UY
   (For outstanding historic land and out-
   standing buildings and amenity land)

Northern Ireland
24 Capital Taxes Office
   Law Courts Buildings
   Chichester Street
   Belfast BT1 3NU

25 Department of Education for
   Northern Ireland
   Rathgael House
   Balloo Road
   Bangor
   County Down BT19 2PR

[Addresses 26 to 30 have been superseded by:

Historic Monuments and Buildings
   Branch Conservation Service,
Department of the Environment for
   Northern Ireland,
Calvert House,
23 Castle Place,
Belfast BT1 1FY

Countryside and Wildlife Branch
   Conservation Service,
Department of the Environment for
   Northern Ireland,
Calvert House,
23 Castle Place,
Belfast BT1 1FY]

31 Department of Agriculture for
   Northern Ireland
   Dundonald House
   Upper Newtownards Road
   Belfast BT4 3SB

APPENDIX 9. OUTSTANDING LAND: ADVISORY BODIES

Category	England	Scotland	Wales	N. Ireland
1. Scientific interest	Nature Conservancy Council	Nature Conservancy Council HQ for Scotland	As for England	Committee for Nature Conservation*
2. Scenic interest	Countryside Commission	Countryside Commission for Scotland	As for England	[Department of the Environment for Northern Ireland (Conservation Service)]
3. Historic interest (and historic buildings (with supporting amenity land) and ancient monuments)	Historic Buildings and Monuments Commission for England	Scottish Development Department, Historic Buildings and Monuments Directorate	Cadw/Welsh Historic Monuments	[Department of the Environment for Northern Ireland (Conservation Service)]
4. Arboricultural Silvicultural	Forestry Commission	As for England	As for England	Department of Agriculture for Northern Ireland
5. Horticultural Botanical	Royal Botanic Gardens Kew	Royal Botanic Gardens Edinburgh	As for England	Department of Agriculture for Northern Ireland

*Through the Department of the Environment for Northern Ireland.

APPENDIX 10. BODIES LISTED IN IHTA 1984, Sch. 3

The National Gallery.
The British Museum.
The National Museums of Scotland (the National Heritage (Scotland) Act 1985 provided for the establishment of this organisation which represented the amalgamation of the Royal Scottish Museum and the National Museum of Antiquities of Scotland.
The National Museum of Wales.
The Ulster Museum.
Any other similar national institution which exists wholly or mainly for the purpose of preserving for the public benefit a collection of scientific, historic or artistic interest and which is approved for the purposes of this Schedule by the Revenue.
Any museum or art gallery in the U.K. which exists wholly or mainly for that purpose and is maintained by a local authority or university in the U.K.
Any library the main function of which is to serve the need of teaching and research at a university in the U.K.
The Historic Buildings and Monuments Commission for England.
The National Trust for Places of Historic Interest or Natural Beauty.
The National Trust for Scotland for Places of Historic Interest or Natural Beauty.
The National Art Collections Fund.
The Trustees of the National Heritage Memorial Fund.
The Friends of the National Libraries.
The Historic Churches Preservation Trust.
The Nature Conservancy Council.
Any local authority (including National Park Authorities).
Any Government department (including the National Debt Commissioners).
Any university or university college in the U.K.

APPENDIX 11. PUBLIC PURCHASE ILLUSTRATIVE EXAMPLE

Works of art
Calculation of the price, with "douceur" (usually 25 per cent, but subject to negotiation), at which a previously conditionally exempted object can be sold to a public body by private treaty.

	£	£
Agreed current market value (say)		100,000
Tax applicable thereto:		
CGT @ 30% on gain element, assumed to be £40,000	12,000	
ED, CTT or IHT exemption granted on a previous conditionally exempt transfer, now recoverable @ say 60% on £88,000	52,800	
(*i.e.* market value less CGT)		
Total tax		64,800
Net after full tax		35,200
Add back 25% of tax (the "douceur")		16,200
Price payable by purchaser, all retained by vendor		£ 51,400

The Revenue writes off the total tax of £64,800 (£12,000+£52,800).
  The vendor has £16,200 more than if he had sold the object for £100,000 in the open market and paid the tax. The public body acquires the object for £48,600 less than its open market value.

APPENDIX 12. PUBLIC PURCHASE ILLUSTRATIVE EXAMPLE

Land and buildings
Calculation of the price, with "douceur" (usually 10 per cent. but subject to negotiation), at which previously conditionally exempted land can be sold to a public body by private treaty.

	£	£
Agreed current market value (say)		100,000
Tax applicable thereto:		
CGT @ 30% on gain element, assumed to be £50,000	15,000	
ED, CTT or IHT exemption granted on a previous conditionally exempt transfer, now recoverable @ say 60% on £85,000	51,000	
(*i.e.* market value less CGT)		
Total tax		66,000

Net after full tax	34,000
Add back 10% of tax (the "douceur")	6,600
Price payable by a purchaser, all retained by vendor	£ 40,600

The Revenue writes off the total tax of £60,000 (£15,000+£51,000).

The vendor has £6,600 more than if he had sold the land for £100,000 in the open market and paid the tax. The public body acquires the land for £59,400 less than its open market value.

APPENDIX 13. CALCULATION OF CAPITAL TRANSFER TAX OR INHERITANCE TAX CHARGE ON A CHARGEABLE EVENT

The following example illustrates the rules explained in paragraphs 5–8 of Appendix 2.

The facts

June 1969—A buys a Rembrandt.

May 1976—A dies, bequeathing the Rembrandt to B. The Treasury (prior to the transfer of responsibilities to the Inland Revenue on 25 July 1985) designate the painting. B gives the necessary undertakings, and conditional exemption is given on A's death. A's estate, apart from the Rembrandt, is £180,000 and he had previously made chargeable lifetime transfers of £40,000.

June 1979—B gives the Rembrandt to his son C. Although B has not owned the Rembrandt for 6 years, his transfer to C is eligible for conditional exemption because he inherited the painting on A's death, on which it was conditionally exempted. On B's transfer to C the painting is again designated by the Treasury, the necessary undertakings are given and the transfer is conditionally exempted.

June 1986—C sells the Rembrandt to D for £1m.

This sale is a chargeable event and tax is payable by C on the £1m sale proceeds.

Application of statutory rules

Either A or B may be selected as the relevant person for the purpose of calculating the tax:

(a) If A was selected as the relevant person, the tax would be calculated as follows:

	£
A's total of chargeable transfers	220,000
(£40,000+£180,000)	
Sale proceeds	1,000,000
	1,200,000
Tax on £1,220,000 at date of sale death rates	652,300
Less: Tax on £220,000 at date of sale death rates	59,000
Tax on chargeable event	£593,300

(b) If B was selected as the relevant person, the tax would be calculated as follows:

	£
B's cumulative total of chargeable transfers up to June 1986 (say)	100,000
Sale proceeds	1,000,000
	1,100,000
Tax on £1,100,000 at half of date of sale death rates	290,150
Less: Tax on £100,000 at half of date of sale death rates	4,475
Tax on chargeable event	£285,675

A would be selected as the relevant person in this case, as the tax on the chargeable event will then be higher than if B had been selected. But as B made the last conditionally exempt transfer of the Rembrandt, the £1m sale proceeds will be included in B's cumulative total of chargeable transfers for the purpose of calculating the tax on his future transfers in the following ten years.

APPENDIX 14. CALCULATION OF CAPITAL GAINS TAX CHARGE ON A CHARGE-ABLE EVENT

Facts as in Appendix 13; additional information as follows:

	£
Rembrandt purchased in June 1969 for	100,000
Market values: at the date of A's death	250,000
at the date B gave the picture to his son	500,000
at 31 March 1982 (assuming a claim is made under FA 1985, s. 68 (5) for the indexation adjustment to be computed by reference to this figure instead of cost)	600,000

CGT position:
1. No charge to CGT arises on A's death; the gain accrued up to the date of death (£250,000−£100,000 = £150,000) is completely exempt and B is treated as acquiring the Rembrandt for £250,000.
2. B's gain of £250,000 on the gift to C is not charged (conditionally exempt transfer) and C is treated as having acquired the Rembrandt for £250,000 (*i.e.* B's acquisition cost under 1).
3. CGT is chargeable on the sale by C; his chargeable gain before indexation is £750,000 (£1m−£250,000). The chargeable (indexed) gain is as follows:

	£
Unindexed gain	750,000
Indexation allowance (£600,000×0.231*)	138,000
Chargeable gain	£611,400

$$*\text{Indexation factor} = \frac{RD-RI}{RI} \text{ where}$$

RD = retail price index for June 1986 (385.8).
RI = retail price index for March 1982 (313.4).

IR 67 FINANCE ACTS 1987 SUPPLEMENT

This supplement modifies the outline of the fiscal legislation relating to property of national heritage quality contained in the booklet *IR 67 Capital Taxation and the National Heritage*, December 1986 (see above) to take account of FA 1987 and F(No. 2)A 1987. It also corrects some minor errors in the booklet and up-dates some of the factual information.

Like the booklet itself, the supplement has *no binding force* and does not affect a taxpayer's right of appeal on points concerning his own tax liability. The main heritage changes described in this supplement are:
(*a*) Extension of the *maintenance fund* rules to enable interest in possession trust property to be transferred free of IHT into a maintenance fund within a specified period following the life tenant's death.
(*b*) Adjustment of the rules about payment of *interest on outstanding tax in* acceptance in lieu cases.

The chapter, paragraph and page numbers referred to within the supplement are those in the booklet IR 67.

CHAPTER 2 THE CAPITAL TAXES BRIEFLY DESCRIBED

Paragraph 2.3: Inheritance tax
1. For transfers made, deaths and certain other events occurring on or after 17 March 1987:
(*a*) The tax threshold was raised to £90,000.
(*b*) Potentially exempt transfer treatment has been extended to lifetime transfers by individuals into and out of interest in possession trusts (e.g. where an individual has a life interest) (F(No. 2)A 1987, s. 96). Transfers to certain discretionary trusts and transfers involving companies remain liable to an immediate charge at half the full rates of tax.

2. The new booklet on IHT, entitled "Inheritance Tax" (IHT 1), was published in February 1987 and is available free of charge from the Capital Taxes Offices.

Paragraph 2.5: Capital gains tax
3. For 1987–88, the annual personal exemption is £6,600 [1988–89 and 1989–90, £5,000].

CHAPTER 3 SUMMARY OF CAPITAL TAX HERITAGE RELIEFS AVAILABLE

Paragraph 3.5: Conditional exemption
4. As with potentially exempt transfers generally, conditional exemption cannot be claimed for a transfer involving an interest in possession trust which is a potentially exempt transfer under the extended treatment mentioned in para. 1 above unless or until it becomes chargeable in consequence of the donor's death.

Paragraph 3.6: Intermediate events between a potentially exempt transfer and death
5. The "special rules" apply also to potentially exempt transfers under the extended treatment.

Paragraph 3.9 (a) (iv): Disposal of conditionally exempt property
6. The statement in the *final* sentence requires modification where the acceptance in lieu of IHT, CTT or ED occurs on or after 17 March 1987 (see para. 10 below).

CHAPTER 8 MAINTENANCE FUNDS

General
7. FA 1987, Sch. 9, para. 1 inserts a new s. 57A into IHTA 1984. It extends the circumstances in which property may be transferred into a maintenance fund free of IHT. For deaths on or after 17 March 1987 and subject to certain conditions, exemption is now available from the charge to tax on settled property arising on the death of a life tenant if, within a specified period after that death (generally two years, but three if the arrangements can be made only by means of a Court Order), the property is put into a maintenance fund.

Paragraph 8.4 (c): Summary of the special tax arrangements
8. For 1987–88, the additional rate is 18 per cent. [1988–89 and 1989–90, 10 per cent.]

Paragraph 8.6: Tax position when capital is taken out of maintenance fund
9. For events occurring on or after 17 March 1987, the terms of the first three sentences of this paragraph are qualified as follows. Where the property entered the maintenance fund from an interest in possession trust, capital may similarly be withdrawn if the life tenant dies before the six-year period expires. If the recipient is the life tenant's spouse or widow or widower, tax-free distribution is available only in specific circumstances. Tax-free distribution is available if the property reverts to the beneficial ownership of the former life tenant. The terms of the last sentence also apply where the life tenant dies within the six year period. (See paras. 14 and 15 below for details.)

CHAPTER 11 ACCEPTANCE OF PROPERTY IN LIEU OF TAX

Paragraphs 11.13 and 11.14: Acceptance
10. Legislation was introduced in 1987 varying the terms on which offers in lieu of IHT, CTT or ED can be made. Offerors have been given a choice that has not been available before. They are able to agree either an acceptance price based on the value of the item *at the date of offer*, and pay no interest on the tax from that date (the new option); or an acceptance price based on the value of the item when it is formally accepted, with interest running until then (the former rule). This option applies to formal acceptances on or after 17 March 1987, including acceptances of items under consideration before then. (FA 1987, s. 60 and F(No. 2)A 1987, s. 97.)
11. The Revenue will assume future offers to be made on the new "offer date" basis unless the offeror gives notice to the contrary. The offeror's option will normally remain open until the item is formally accepted but this will be subject to review if more than two years elapse from the date of the offer without the terms being settled. The Revenue may then give six months notice that they will no longer be prepared to accept the item on the offer date basis (Revenue Statement of Practice SP 6/87 issued on 8 April 1987; see Appendix 2).

APPENDIX 2. TAX CHARGES ON LOSS OF EXEMPTION

Paragraph 15: Property in interest in possession
12. As with potentially exempt transfers generally, conditional exemption cannot be claimed for a transfer involving an interest in possession trust which is a potentially exempt transfer under the extended treatment mentioned in para. 1 above unless or until it becomes chargeable in consequence of the donor's death.

APPENDIX 5. MAINTENANCE FUNDS TAX CHARGES

Paragraph 2 (a): Capital tax exemptions available
13. As indicated in para. 7 above, the exemption facility referred to in parenthesis has been *extended* for deaths on or after 17 March 1987.

Paragraphs 3 and 4: Minimum period of retention of capital in fund
14. FA 1987, Sch. 9, para. 2 enables the reference to "settlor" in the rule which removes the six-year time limit in the event of the settlor's death within that period to be read as a reference to the former "life tenant" where the property entered the maintenance fund from an interest in possession trust. This has effect for directions given on or after 17 March 1987 (FA 1987, Sch. 9, para. 5).

Paragraph 4 (c): Tax treatment of property which ceases to be held on maintenance fund trusts
15. The general rule explained in subparagraph (c)—which is set out in IHTA 1984, Sch. 4, para. 10 has been adapted, in respect of charges arising on or after 17 March 1987, where the property entered the maintenance fund from an interest in possession trust (IHTA 1984, Sch. 4, para. 15A, as introduced by FA 1987, Sch. 9, para. 3). Paragraph 10 is disapplied if the life tenant was dead when the property entered the maintenance fund. If he was alive then, tax-free distribution from the maintenance fund is permitted to:
   (*a*) the life tenant; or
   (*b*) the life tenant's spouse; or
   (*c*) the life tenant's widow or widower, if the distribution occurs within two years after the life tenant's death.
   In the case of (*b*) and (*c*), however, tax-free distribution is available only where, under the terms of the interest in possession trust, the property would have gone to the spouse, widow or widower on the termination of the interest in possession but for the creation of the maintenance fund.

Paragraph 5 (b): Rate of charge
16. The general rule explained in subparagraph (ii) has been adapted, in respect of charges arising on or after 17 March 1987, where the property entered the maintenance fund from an interest in possession trust (IHTA 1984, Sch. 4, paras. 15A (6)–(10) as introduced by FA 1987, Sch. 9, para. 3). In such cases, it is the *life tenant* who will be regarded for the purposes of this alternative recapture charge as having made the transfer *i.e.* the "life tenant" is treated as the "settlor".
17. These revised charging rules apply *both* to:
   (*a*) the new exemption facility introduced in FA 1987 (see para. 7 above); and
   (*b*) former interest in possession property that enters a maintenance fund with the benefit of the pre-1987 exemption facility (*i.e.* where the arrangements were, or are, made while the life tenant was, or is, alive), *providing the charge arises on or after 17 March 1987.*

APPENDIX 6. SUMMARY OF CHANGES ADAPTING HERITAGE RULES FOR IHT PURPOSES

Paragraphs 2 and 3: Exemption claim for lifetime gifts
18. Potentially exempt transfer treatment has been extended, on or after 17 March 1987, to certain transfers involving interest in possession trusts (see paras. 1, 4 and 12 above).

Paragraph 10: Maintenance fund cumulation rules
19. For charges arising on or after 17 March 1987 where the property entered the maintenance fund from an interest in possession trust, see paras. 16 and 17 above.

APPENDIX 6. CAPITAL TAXATION AND WORKS OF ART

The Office of Arts and Libraries has produced leaflets which summarise and illustrate the benefits of the tax reliefs and provide guidance on the administrative procedures involved in particular circumstances. These are:
(1) Works of Art: A basic Guide to Capital Taxation and the National Heritage, 1982
(2) Works of Art: Guidelines on in situ offers in lieu of capital taxation, April 1984
(3) Works of Art: Private Treaty Sales, November 1986

(1) WORKS OF ART: A BASIC GUIDE TO CAPITAL TAXATION AND THE NATIONAL HERITAGE

Do you own a work of art, such as a painting—or a manuscript or other heritage object—that may be of national, artistic, historic or scientific interest? Possibly you have just acquired it, by gift of inheritance. You may wish to keep it or, perhaps, to dispose of it, whether now or by your Will. In either case, you may well be wondering about the tax implications. If you are in this position, or if you are advising someone else who is, this booklet is intended to give you basic guidance.

If you inherit, or bequeath, a work of art on which an IHT liability could arise you may have assumed that the only option is for the tax to be paid. Similarly you may have been under the impression that if you sell your work of art you would be liable for capital taxation whatever the circumstances of sale. This booklet explains that there are several reliefs from capital taxation available: and that there are ways of disposing of your work of art which can both preserve it for the national heritage *and* provide financial advantages for you.

This booklet is only a brief guide to the tax reliefs available. If you wish to follow up any of the possibilities set out here, you will find more detailed information in a booklet published by the Revenue which covers the reliefs available on heritage property of all kinds, not just works of art (see Appendix 5).

If you acquire a work of art by inheritance or gift

1. If you acquire a work of art by inheritance or by gift, capital transfer tax will normally be payable. But you can keep the item and no pay tax on it so long as it meets certain specified criteria in terms of its quality and interest, and provided that you honour certain undertakings. This provision is known as conditional exemption; see para. 2–5 below.

Conditional exemption
2. Conditional exemption from capital transfer tax may be granted for "any pictures, prints, books, manuscripts, works of art, scientific collections or other things not yielding income which appear to the Treasury to be of national, scientific, historic or artistic interest", FA 1976, s. 77 (1) (a) [IHTA 1984, s. 31 (1)]. The yardstick applied is whether the item is of sufficient quality to be displayed in a public collection, either national or local (for example, one administered by a local authority or university). When they receive a claim for conditional exemption, the Capital Taxes office of the Inland Revenue take advice from expert advisers in the national museums and galleries as to whether the object meets this standard.
3. The grant of conditional exemption for works of art is subject to the following undertakings:
   (a) that you will keep the object permanently in the U.K. unless the Treasury agree to its leaving the country temporarily for a purpose such as temporary exhibition abroad;
   (b) that you will take reasonable steps to preserve the object; and
   (c) that you will take reasonable steps to secure reasonable public access to it.
The conditional exemption from capital transfer tax will continue so long as you fulfil these undertakings. If you decide to give the picture away, or if the object passes to you heirs, the conditional exemption will continue provided the new owner renews the undertakings. By this means a liability to capital transfer tax can be deferred indefinitely.
4. You should consider applying for conditional exemption as soon as possible after the death or transfer, if you are concerned to avoid delays in settling the estate. Professional advice on the operation of the tax rules may prove helpful to you in deciding whether or not to claim exemption at this state. Please also remember that if your application for conditional exemption is unsuccessful the full tax liability will remain. Obtaining conditional exemption leaves the options of a private treaty sale(para. 8–12) or an offer in lieu of tax (para. 13–20) open to you at a later stage.
5. Application for conditional exemption should be made on Form 700A (revised 1982) which may be obtained from: Inland Revenue, Capital Taxes Office, Minford House, Rockley Road, London W14 0DF.

You will be asked on that form to indicate how you intend to fulfil the undertaking to provide reasonable public access. Details of the options open to you are set out in Annex A.

If you decide to part with your work of art

6. You may be thinking of parting with a work of art on which conditional exemption has been granted. When you come to sell you will have to bear in mind that if you sell at auction or to a private individual you will lose the conditional exemption. This means that capital transfer tax will be payable and possibly capital gains tax as well. If you are the owner of an object exempted after 1 September 1982 and you want to sell it on the open market, you are also requested to give public collections three months' notice of this intention by writing to: The Museums and Galleries Commission, 2 Carlton Gardens, London SW1Y 5AA.

Should you sell your work of art without giving this notice there could well be problems at a later stage if an export licence is sought: the Government have powers to withhold an export licence indefinitely, and have advised the Reviewing Committee on the export of Works of Art that an indefinite stop on export should be recommended if the Museums and Galleries Commission have not been given three months' notice of an intention to sell an object conditionally exempted after 1 September 1982 for which an export licence is sought and which meets one or more of the Waverley criteria (which are used to judge whether an object is of national importance). Those criteria are as follows:

(*a*) Is the object so closely connected with our history and national life that its departure would be a misfortune?

(*b*) Is it of outstanding aesthetic importance?

(*c*) Is it of outstanding significance for the study of some particular branch of art, learning or history?

7. There are however several options which will not involve any liability to capital transfer tax:

(*a*) you can give or bequeath the object to someone who renews the undertakings for conditional exemption described in para. 3;

(*b*) you can give or bequeath the object to a public collection such as a national or local museum, gallery or library, to a university, or to certain heritage trusts and charities. The list of these bodies, set out in FA 1975, Sch. 12 [IHTA 1984, Sch. 3], is at Annex B. They are commonly known as "paragraph 12" [Sch. 3] bodies, and gifts and bequests to them are entirely exempt from capital transfer tax and capital gains tax;

(*c*) you can sell the object by private treaty Sale (see para. 8–12 below) to one of the public bodies listed in Annex B; or

(*d*) if you have to pay capital transfer tax on some other property you can offer the object to the Government for acceptance in lieu (see paras. 13–20 below). The standards for acceptance in lieu are higher than for conditional exemption; they are indicated in para. 18.

Private treaty sale

8. If you decide to sell your work of art to one of the public bodies listed in Annex B the conditional exemption from capital transfer tax and capital gains tax will not be lost. Even if your work of art has not been formally exempted from capital transfer tax, a sale of this character will nevertheless not normally attract capital gains tax.

9. The price paid by a museum or other public body in a private treaty sale will be based on the agreed valuation of the picture or object in the open market or at auction. However, the amount which the buyer will offer to pay you takes into account the tax exemption and divides the benefit of the exemption between you both. The final sum you receive will therefore be more than the net sum you could have expected in the open market (*i.e.*, the gross value less any tax) because you will share in the amount of tax saved: the addition is sometimes known as "the douceur" and the arrangement is an administrative not a statutory one.

10. Such a tax-free private treaty sale will:

(*a*) always be more financially advantageous to you, for a given value, than a sale on the open market which will entail payment of capital taxes; and

(*b*) help the public museum or gallery concerned to acquire more national heritage items than if they had to pay the full market price,

The Government have advised museums and galleries that they should in general offer the seller an amount equal to 25 per cent. of the benefit of the tax exemption, subject to negotiations above or below this figure where flexibility is appropriate. So if you want to work out roughly where you might stand, it would be reasonable for you to add, to the net price you would be left with after paying tax on an open market sale, a sum amounting to about one-quarter of that tax.

11. Your first step should be to approach a public collection of your choice and propose a figure for the market value of your work of art, preferably after taking expert advice. If the museum is interested, their staff will then seek to reach an agreement with you on this valuation. In order to agree the private treaty price with you, they will need to know how the negotiations are affected by your tax position. Institutions cannot enter into serious negotiations unless vendors are prepared to allow their tax position to be confirmed by the Capital Taxes Office; it follows that you should be ready to agree to these enquiries being made by the museum or gallery concerned.

12. By way of illustration, the following figures show how a private treaty sale price might be arrived at, on the basis of a 25 per cent. addition:

	Open market sale	Private treaty sale
Current market value *less* Capital Transfer tax at say 60 per cent.	£100,000 (say) 60,000	£100,000 (agreed estimate) 60,000
Received by seller, after CTT: *add back* 25 per cent. on total tax liability of £60,000	40,000	40,000 15,000
Received by seller	£ 40,000	£ 55,000

This is a simplified example, dependent on assumptions regarding liability to tax. In this case you would receive £15,000 more than if you had sold your work of art on the open market at the same price as the agreed estimate and paid tax to the revenue. The example does not show capital gains tax, the burden of which has been reduced by a new measure which takes account of inflation occurring after March 1982 in the calculation of gains.

Acceptance in lieu
13. If capital transfer tax has to be paid on any assets, it may be possible to offer a work or art to the Government in satisfaction of that liability. This is known as acceptance in lieu and, as with private treaty sales, a work of art accepted in lieu is exempted from capital taxation. It does not matter if this work of art or heritage object has not been formally exempted from capital transfer tax in connection with the death or transfer concerned; if it qualifies for acceptance in lieu it is automatically treated as also having qualified for exemption. Accordingly, any work of art or heritage object which is accepted in lieu benefits from exemption by virtue of that fact. The standard of objects which can be so accepted is, however, very much higher than that applicable for conditional exemption (see para. 18).

14. An object which is accepted by the Government in this way will be vested in a public body, because the Government are acting on behalf of the public in such a transaction. The benefit of the tax exemption is taken into account by adding 25 per cent. if the value of that exemption to the estimated value of the object after payment of notional tax. The amount thus calculated is offset against the tax liability of the estate on other property.

15. Since the illustration given in para. 12 has been calculated on the basis of a 25 per cent. addition, the figures would equally apply to acceptance in lieu, dependent on similar assumptions regarding liability to tax. So £55,000 would be set against the tax liability on the rest of the estate, and you would be £15,000 better off than if you had sold on the open market.

16. Another possible advantage to you with with the acceptance in lieu procedure, in addition to the tax benefit, is that the offer may be conditional. You may include in your offer a condition that the item should pass to a particular institution or body or that it should be allowed to remain where it is (in situ). The Government attach considerable importance to the desirability of items remaining in an appropriate setting, for example if they have an espcially close association with an historic building, provided that reasonable public access can be afforded and that the security and conservation arrangements are satisfactory.

17. If you wish to offer a work of art in lieu of tax you should send details to the Capital Taxes Office, whose address is given in para. 5. Your letter should include an indication of the current market valuation of the item, as well as details of a contract with whom arrangements for an inspection can be made. The Capital Taxes Office will then consult as appropriate the Departments in England, Scotland, Wales or Northern Ireland with policy responsibility for heritage issues. Decisions about the acceptance of works of art in lieu of taxation are taken by the Government Ministers concerned. Before deciding they obtain the views of expert advisers in the appropriate national museum or gallery. The expert advisers are expected to consult widely, particularly where the object has local significance, and in cases of doubt will in turn refer to the Museums and Galleries Commission or the Royal Commission on Historical manuscripts. If need be either body may convene an informal panel of independent advisers, which might include a representative of the appropriate Historic Buildings Council.

18. The standard of objects which may be accepted in lieu of tax is considerably higher than that applied in the case of claims for conditional exemption. To qualify for acceptance in lieu of tax, works of art have to satisfy a test of "pre-eminence" either in the context of a national, local authority, or university collection, or through association with a particular building. In advising on whether an item should be regarded as pre-eminent, the expert advisers refer to a set of guidelines. These are given in Annex C and they may help you to assess whether a particular work of art or other object is likely to meet the criterion of pre-eminence that is necessary for acceptance in lieu. The Government also take advice on the acceptability of any conditions attached to an acceptance in lieu offer, such as an in situ provision.

19. If the Government agree to accept the work of art in lieu of tax, the Capital Taxes Office proceed with the arrangements for acceptance. But in cases where an offer that is conditional on the work of art passing to a particular institution or body has been accepted, no further decisions are necessary concerning the allocation of the work. In cases where a work of art is offered subject to conditions about its being displayed in a particular place it will in general first be vested in a public collection, for on-lending to those responsible for the specified location. Where the item is not subject to a condition of either type, the decision about allocation will generally be taken after the acceptance arrangements are complete.

20. If the Government decline an offer, it is still open to you to offer the work of art to a museum or gallery by means of a private treaty sale, with the benefit described in para. 9.

Conclusions

21. In short, when an estate includes items of national heritage standard there are three ways in which these can qualify for tax exemption:
    (*a*) if the person to whom they pass gives the undertakings necessary for conditional exemption;
    (*b*) if they are sold by private treaty to an appropriate public body, and
    (*c*) if they are accepted in lieu of capital transfer tax.
Decisions whether or not to claim exemption may not be easy, or the settlement of the estate may be complicated; and in some cases there may be an unavoidable delay before matters are settled. No interest is charged in respect of conditionally exempt items, however late the exemption is granted: the value of such items, including those accepted in lieu of tax, is removed from the estate for the computation of interest charges. If you decide not to claim exemptions, or if your claim is rejected, tax will be payable. Other considerations in respect of conditional exemption from the owner's point of view are set out in para. 4 above.

22. Essentially, if you inherit or are given a work of art, you should ask yourself:
    Have I applied for conditional exemption from capital transfer tax?
    If you want to sell your work of art, you should ask yourself:
    Have I considered the advantage of selling it to a public body by private treaty?
    If you have a capital transfer tax liability on other property, you should ask youself:
    Have I considered the advantages of offering my work of art to the Government in lieu of that
    tax liability?

23. Taxation is a complex subject and this booklet is not intended to provide an authoritative interpretation of the various statutory and regulatory provisions that may affect you. Its aim is to draw your attention to certain taxation possibilities that exist in order to encourage the preservation of our national heritage, and which may well be of financial advantage to the private owner.

ANNEX A

Conditional exemption: How to satisfy the statutory requirement for reasonable public access

When you apply for conditional exemption from capital transfer tax on Form 700A (revised 1982) you will be asked to indicate how you intend to fulfil the undertaking to provide reasonable public access to your work of art. The options that are now open to you depend on whether or not the item can be displayed in a house which is, or will be, open to the public.

House open to the public. The condition can be met if the object is exhibited in a room which is open to the public for a reasonable number of days each year (the agreed frequency of opening depending on the circumstances of each case). The Capital Taxes Office will ask for evidence of appropriate publicity for the opening of the house or room in question, and assurances that the object will be on display.

Other cases. If the option above is not practicable you can either:
    (*a*) arrange for the object to be lent to a public collection for display on a long-term basis (or continue such an arrangement if it already exists). This could be a national, local authority or university collection, or a gallery or historic house run by a charitable trust and open to the public; or
    (*b*) ask the Capital Taxes Office to arrange for details of the object and its broad geographical location to be entered in a list of conditionally exempt items maintained at the Victoria and Albert museum, copies of which are held at the National Library of Scotland, the National Museum of Wales and the Public Record Office in Northern Ireland. This list, including information on arrangements for reasonable public access to the items, is available on request to anyone with an interest in works of art; but the entry need not identify the owner, or the precise location of the

object, and the object need not necessarily be viewed in your own home. This arrangement will be subject to an additional undertaking that, as a condition of the exemption, the object will be made available, on request, for loan to a public collection (as indicated in (a) above) for not more than one special exhibition of up to six months' duration every two years averaged over longer periods if appropriate. Public collections are advised that loans of such exempted objects can be requested for this purpose.

Before you apply to the Capital Taxes Office for conditional exemption, you should consider which method of public access you intend to offer, and make this clear in your appliction. You will have to satisfy the Capital Taxes Office that the arrangements proposed for access, which is a statutory requirement, are suitable and will be put into effect after the exemption has been confirmed. You may subsequently be asked to confirm that the undertakings you have given have been carried out.

ANNEX B

Bodies listed in FA 1975, Sch. 6, para. 12, as amended by FA 1980, s. 118 (5) [IHTA 1984, Sch. 3]

The National Gallery. The British Museum. The Royal Scottish Museum.
The National Museum of Wales. The Ulster Museum.
Any other similar national institution which exists wholly or mainly for the purpose of preserving for the public benefit a collection of scientific, historic or artistic interest and which is approved for the purposes of this paragraph by the Treasury.
Any museum or art gallery in the United Kingdom which exists wholly or mainly for that purpose and is maintained by a local authority or university in the United Kingdom.
Any library, the main function of which is to serve the needs of teaching and research at a university in the United Kingdom.
The National Trust for Places of Historic Interest or Natural Beauty.
The National Trust for Scotland for Places of Historic Interest or Natural Beauty.
The National Art Collections Fund.
The Trustees of the National Heritage Memorial Fund.
The Friends of the National Libraries.
The Historic Churches Preservation Trust.
The Nature Conservancy Council.
Any local authority (including National Park Authorities).
Any Government Department (including the National Debt Commissioners).
Any University or University College in the United Kingdom.

ANNEX C

Guidelines on the interpretation of pre-eminence in respect of objects offered in satisfaction of tax

The following guidelines are intended as a framework of reference for the Expert Advisers (who are chosen from the directors of the relevant national museums and galleries), to help them in formulating their advice on whether an item is pre-eminent. An object may fall into more than one category: for example it may have an especially close association with a particular historic setting and also be pre-eminent, irrespective of this association under one or more of the other categories.

(a) Does the object have an especially close associaton with our history and national life?

This category includes foreign as well as British works, for example, gifts that foreign sovereigns or governments have made, and objects that have been acquired abroad in circumstances closely associated with our history. It includes objects closely associated with some part of the U.K., or with the development of its institutions and industries. Some objects which fall under this category will be of such national importance that they deserve to enter a national museum or gallery. Others may well be of a lesser degree of national importance, though they will be nonetheless significant in a local context. This category will also include works which derive their significance from a local connection, and which may therefore qualify as pre-eminent only in a local or university museum.

(b) Is the object of especial artistic or art-historical interest?

This category, like (c) below, includes objects deserving of entering a national museum or gallery as well as other objects which may not be pre-eminent in a national museum or gallery in London, Edinburgh or Cardiff, but will be pre-eminent in museums or galleries elsewhere which do not already possess items of a similar genre or a similar quality.

(c) Is the object of especial importance for the study of some particular form of art, learning or history?

This category includes a wide variety of objects, not restricted to works of art, which are of especial importance for the study of, say, particular scientific development. The category also includes objects forming part of a historical unity, series or collection either in one place or in the country as a whole. Without a particular object or group of objects both a unity and a series may be impaired.

(*d*) Does the object have an especially close association with a particular historic setting?

This category will include primarily works of art, manuscripts, furniture or other items which have an especially close association with an important historic building. They will fall to be considered pre-eminent by virtue of the specific contribution they make to the understanding of an outstanding historic building. Thus, the category may include paintings or furniture specially commissioned for a particular house or a group of paintings having an association with a particular location.

(2) WORKS OF ART: GUIDELINES ON IN SITU OFFERS IN LIEU OF CAPITAL TAXATION

Background

The acceptance of a work of art of national heritage quality in lieu of capital transfer tax liabilities involves a transfer of ownership to the Government, which then arranges for ownership to be transferred to a national or local collection. Further details of the arrangements for acceptance of works of art in lieu of tax are given in the pamphlet *Works of Art: a Basic Guide to Capital Taxation and the National Heritage,* issued by the Office of Arts and Libraries, and the Revenue Booklet *Capital Taxation and the National Heritage* [reproduced in Appendix 5].

Offers of property in lieu of tax may be made on condition that the work in question remains "in situ". This note sets out guidance for private owners and public collections who may be considering such offers. In these cases agreement will have to be reached on the sharing of certain responsibilities of which details are given below.

The guidelines are intended only as general advice on the main issues likely to arise, and should not be taken as a definitive statement of policy.

Criteria

When a work of art is offered subject to a condition that it should remain "in situ" the Government has to consider and decide:
(1) whether the object should be regarded as pre-eminent;
(2) whether the proposed valuation is acceptable;
(3) whether the "in situ" condition is appropriate; and
(4) whether the financial provision available for acceptance of property in lieu of tax is sufficient to enable the offer to be accepted.
The Government also has to arrange for a suitable public institution to assume ownership of the object.

Procedure

Although the formal offer is made to the Capital Taxes Office, it is the Ministers responsible for the heritage who decide whether it should be accepted. These are the Secretary of State for the Environment and the Minister for the Arts for offers in England and the appropriate Secretary of State in the case of Wales or Scotland. In reaching a view they consult the Government's Expert Advisers on whether or not the object is pre-eminent and on its valuation; the Historic Buildings Council on the association of the object with a particular location; and the Museums and Galleries Commission (or the Royal Commission on Historical Manuscripts in appropriate cases) on the "in situ" condition itself and on a suitable public institution to assume ownership of the item.

The steps will generally take some months, following which a provisional decision on acceptability will be conveyed to the owner and any discussions about the special price can begin with the Capital Taxes Office. In addition satisfactory arrangements also have to be reached with the public institution which will eventually assume responsibility for the work of art. Owners will therefore be notified of the institution likely to be involved, and the two parties should then discuss arrangements on the issues indicated in these guidelines, involving the Office of Arts and Libraries as appropriate.

Before the "in situ" offer can be finally accepted the Government departments concerned need to establish that agreement has been reached on all the major issues in order to satisfy Ministers that appropriate undertakings will come into force once the "in situ" acceptance is effected. An agreement between the public and private collections will also need to make it clear that non-observance of the various undertakings on access and safe-keeping would lead to withdrawal of the item from its "in situ" location. Appropriate undertakings will be recorded in the Ministerial direction by which the object is transferred to a public institution.

Interest on unpaid tax

In general, interest is charged on unpaid capital transfer tax from the due date until the date of payment. If an object is accepted in lieu no tax is chargeable in respect of that object, but until the object is formally accepted interest will continue to accrue on any unpaid tax attributable to other property.

Agreements between the parties concerned

These agreements are necessary to safeguard the long-term future of an object which is to become public property, even though it will continue to be exhibited in its original location. The main points on which such agreements have to be reached between the parties are as follows:

(i) *Public access*
Although private houses are not generally open to the public for the same hours as public collections, the normal rule for "in situ" purposes would be that the opening hours of the private house must be sufficient for the purposes of public access once the object has been accepted. The Government's minimum requirement for the public access would be about 30 days a year; access by appointment only would not normally be considered sufficient.

(ii) *Environmental control*
Responsibility for environmental control will normally rest with those in charge of the private collection. Problems of environmental control will need discussion, and a pragmatic approach may need to be adopted on acceptable standards. If, for example, a picture has been hung in a house for a long period and remained in good condition, it would be unreasonable to expect new and more stringent environmental controls to be suddenly applied. On the other hand, there may be cases where additional environmental safeguards are judged necessary, and these would then have to be agreed between the parties as a pre-condition of the "in situ" acceptance.

(iii) *Conservation*
Responsibility for conservation will normally rest primarily with the public collection, but this may require consultation with, and co-operation from, those in charge of the private collection where the object is to remain. The public institution when accepting an object "in situ" will in effect also be accepting an open-ended commitment for its conservation. If required an Expert Adviser may be asked by the Government to produce a conservation report on the object, in order to give some indication of the possible future conservation needs.

(iv) *Security*
There are particular difficulties about a public collection supervising the security of an object in a physically separate private collection. The public collection, on the advice of the National Museums Security Adviser, may reasonably require certain security improvements. In general the private house will be expected to take the responsibility for security, and for the cost of any increased standards required at the time of acceptance or subsequently. However, it should also be borne in mind thatthe security measures that would apply to a public institution would not necessarily be appropriate to a house in which people live.

(v) *Insurance*
When the ownership of the work of art is transferred to the public collection, responsibility for insurance will also pass to the public institution. In some cases the institution may without difficulty be able to include insurance provision within its normal risk cover. However, the Government will be willing to consider an indemnity against damage (but not against total loss or destruction, or against loss of value following damage) under the provisions of the National Heritage Act 1980 which would cover the item while it remains "in situ".

In appropriate cases the public institution responsible for the item will be able to remove it from the premises for short periods from time to time, for study or exhibition purposes elsewhere, or for conservation work. The private collection would be consulted beforehand. In the case of removal for display on the institution's premises the indemnity cover would lapse until the item is returned to the "in situ" location.

(3) WORKS OF ART: PRIVATE TREATY SALES

Introduction
1. Private treaty sales of works of art to most public collections are exempt from capital taxation.
2. This is an important and attractive exemption for both buyer and seller and applies to pictures, furniture, manuscripts and a wide range of other heritage items which satisfy the criteria of 'museum quality' on which conditional exemption is based. For an agreed valuation, a private treaty sale will normally be financially more advantageous to the owner of art than an open market

sale on which tax is paid. The purchasing institution, usually a national or local museum, gallery or library, will also benefit from the arrangement. A full list of qualifying bodies is contained in Note A.

3. Some of the information in these guidelines has already appeared in the leaflet *Works of Art: a basic guide to Capital Taxation and the National Heritage* issued by the Office of Arts and Libraries (see above), and in the Revenue Booklet *Capital Taxation and the National Heritage* (see Appendix 5). It is repeated here for ease of reference. Sources of advice and further information are listed in Note B.

Advantages of a private treaty sale
4. If you are the owner of a heritage work which you now wish to sell, you may think that you will get your best return by an open market sale. But a private treaty sale to a qualifying public collection offers a more certain return, taking into account the tax liability to which you may be subject.
5. If a work of art is sold in the open market the vendor may be liable to CGT and to IHT (formerly CTT). However these tax charges are *not* incurred where an owner sells by private treaty to a qualifying body. A further attraction is that the value of tax exemption is shared between the vendor and the acquiring institution by what is known as the *'douceur'* arrangement (see paragraph 7).
6. Not only will such a private treaty sale normally be of greater benefit to the owner than an open market sale that entails payment of capital taxes, but a private treaty sale will also enable the seller (with the help of acquiring institution) to ensure that a part of our national heritage is retained in this country.

The 'douceur' arrangement
7. The douceur arrangement is administrative not statutory. It provides for the tax exemption to be shared between the vendor and the acquiring institution. The *special price* for the transaction, which takes account of the tax exemption, is arrived at by adding to the notional after-tax value of the heritage object a percentage (normally 25 per cent.) of the notional tax liability. This addition to the net value is known as the 'douceur'.
8. The rate of douceur is flexible, although prospective purchasing institutions will normally think in terms of 25 per cent. A higher figure may be appropriate to provide an adequate inducement in respect of low value objects or where the tax liability is relatively small. A lower figure may be appropriate in respect of an item of high value: this could still be attractive to the owner, and could bring it within the financial compass of a public purchaser.
9. The table below shows how a private treaty sale price would be calculated on the basis of a 25 per cent. douceur. In this case, the seller would receive £16,200 more than if he had sold his work of art on the open market at the same price as the agreed estimate and paid tax to the Revenue.
Calculation of the special price for a private treaty sale: douceur at 25 per cent. subject to negotiation.

	£	£
Agreed current market value, say		100,000
Tax applicable: CGT at 30 per cent. on gain element, assumed to be £40,000	12,000	
Inheritance tax (or CTT or Estate Duty) payable, say 60 per cent. on £88,000		
(market value less CGT)	52,800	
Total tax		£64,800
Net receipts after full tax		35,200
Add back 25 per cent. of tax (the douceur)		16,200
Tax exempt price paid		£51,400

The sum of £51,400 is known as the *special price*. It is what the vendor receives from the public collection; any dealer's commission must also be met from it.
The vendor has £16,200 more than if he had sold the object for £100,000 in the open market and paid the tax.
The public collection pays £51,400 which is £48,600 less than its open market value.
At the same time *the Revenue* writes off £64,800, the total tax that it would otherwise have received.
10. Costs of sale, such as professional fees, are *not* taken into account in the notional tax calculation and therefore have to be met from the sale proceeds. But by opting for a private treaty sale the vendor does *not* incur a seller's premium.

Steps to be taken by owner
11. If you are interested in a private treaty sale the steps to be taken are listed below.
  (*a*) First, approach the museum or gallery of your choice (or any other body covered by Note A) and ask them whether they are interested in acquiring your work of art.
    Once you have identified a prospective buyer, propose a current open market value for your

work of art and on this basis negotiate a valuation acceptance to both parties. It may be in your interest to seek professional help on valuation and to identify and negotiate with potential purchasers; the Museums and Galleries Commission can also advise on suitable purchasing institutions.

(*b*) Next, negotiate the special price to be paid for the object under the 'douceur' arrangement. *In considering the special price, the potential purchaser will always need to know how the calculations will be affected by the vendor's tax position.* The Capital Taxes Offices should therefore be authorised to disclose information relevant to the sale—on a strictly confidential basis—to the purchasing institution.

(*c*) When agreement has been reached on the special price, the Capital Taxes Office will be asked—usually by the acquiring institution—to check the douceur calculation.

(*d*) As soon as the Capital Taxes Office have agreed the figures, the sale can be completed.

12. If a prospective vendor does not give his consent for the Capital Taxes Office to be consulted about his tax position, the institution should seriously consider withdrawing from the negotiations. Failure to do so could result in a much higher price being paid for the object than is reasonable in a tax exempt transaction. This would be an unacceptable use of public money.

Advice to acquiring institutions

13. When approached by a vendor, the prospective purchasing institution should always seek to arrive by negotiation at a fair market price for the work of art. *The institution should never start from a figure conditioned by its own resources. If what would be a fair market price appears to be beyond its own means the institution should explore the possibility of supplementary funding from other sources.*

14. In order to satisfy itself that the rate of douceur it is offering is realistic and that it is acquiring the object for a fair price, the institution should consult the Capital Taxes Office, with the vendor's consent, during negotiations of the special price and before the transaction is concluded.

Conclusion

15. Private treaty sales of heritage items offer appreciable advantages to both parties.

16. Works of art of pre-eminent quality may also be offered to the government in settlement of capital tax liabilities. The scope for acceptances in lieu of tax in this way has recently been improved; revised guidance on acceptance in lieu is in preparation and will be issued shortly.

Note A. Bodies which are eligible to negotiate a private treaty sale

The National Gallery. The British Museum. The National Museums of Scotland. The National Museum of Wales. The Ulster Museum.

Any other similar national institution which exists wholly or mainly for the purpose of preserving for the public benefit a collection of scientific, historic or artistic interest and which is approved for the purpose of this paragraph by the Commissioners of the Inland Revenue.

Any museum or art gallery in the U.K. which exists wholly or mainly for that purpose and is maintained by a local authority or university in the U.K.

Any library, the main function of which is to serve the needs of teaching and research at a university in the U.K.

The National Trust for Places of Historic Interest or Natural Beauty
The National Trust for Scotland for Places of Historic Interest or Natural Beauty
The National Art Collections Fund
The Trustees of the National Heritage Memorial Fund
The Trustees of the National Libraries
The Historic Churches Preservation Trust
The Nature Conservancy Council
Any local authority (including National Park Authorities)
Any Government Department (including the National Debt Commissioners)
Any University or Univerity College in the United Kingdom
The Historic Buildings and Monuments Commission

Note B. Sources of advice and further information

Office of Arts and Libraries	general policy questions
Great George Street	
London SW1P 3AL	
01-233 8011	
Museums and Galleries Commission	procedural questions and liaison with
7 St James's Square	museums and galleries
London SW1Y 4JU	
01-839 8341	

Capital Taxes Office tax questions, douceur
Minford House
Rockley Road
London W14 0DF
01-603 4622

Related publications

Works of Art: A basic guide to Capital Taxation and the National Heritage OAL, 1982
Works of Art in Situ: Guidelines on in situ offers in lieu of capital taxation OAL, April 1984.
Capital Taxation and the National Heritage Inland Revenue.

APPENDIX 7. EXPECTATION OF LIFE TABLES

Tables of Complete Expectations of Life taken from the A 1967–70 Tables for Male Assured Lives and the FA 1975–78 Mortality Tables for Female Assured Lives, both published by the Institute of Actuaries and the Faculty of Actuaries.

Age	Males	Females	Age	Males	Females	Age	Males	Females
0	73.804	80.34	35	40.063	46.06	70	11.119	15.08
1	72.858	79.37	36	39.097	45.10	71	10.551	14.36
2	71.907	78.40	37	38.133	44.13	72	10.003	13.66
3	70.952	77.43	38	37.172	43.17	73	9.474	12.96
4	69.993	76.46	39	36.214	42.20	74	8.964	12.29
5	69.030	75.48	40	35.260	41.25	75	8.474	11.63
6	68.064	74.50	41	34.310	40.29	76	8.004	10.98
7	67.094	73.52	42	33.365	39.34	77	7.553	10.35
8	66.122	72.54	43	32.425	38.39	78	7.121	9.74
9	65.148	71.56	44	31.491	37.44	79	6.708	9.15
10	64.173	70.58	45	30.564	36.50	80	6.315	8.58
11	63.196	69.60	46	29.643	35.56	81	5.940	8.02
12	62.220	68.61	47	28.730	34.62	82	5.583	7.49
13	61.242	67.63	48	27.826	33.69	83	5.244	6.97
14	60.267	66.64	49	26.929	32.76	84	4.923	6.47
15	59.295	65.66	50	26.042	31.84	85	4.618	6.00
16	58.331	64.68	51	25.165	30.93	86	4.331	5.54
17	57.378	63.69	52	24.298	30.02	87	4.059	5.11
18	56.438	62.71	53	23.443	29.12	88	3.803	4.69
19	55.494	61.72	54	22.599	28.22	89	3.562	4.30
20	54.545	60.74	55	21.767	27.33	90	3.336	3.93
21	53.593	59.76	56	20.948	26.45	91	3.123	3.58
22	52.638	58.77	57	20.142	25.57	92	2.924	3.26
23	51.680	57.79	58	19.351	24.70	93	2.737	2.95
24	50.719	56.81	59	18.573	23.84	94	2.563	2.67
25	49.755	55.83	60	17.811	22.99	95	2.400	2.40
26	48.789	54.84	61	17.065	22.15	96	2.247	2.16
27	47.822	53.86	62	16.334	21.32	97	2.105	1.94
28	46.853	52.89	63	15.620	20.50	98	1.973	1.74
29	45.883	51.91	64	14.923	19.69	99	1.850	1.55
30	44.912	50.93	65	14.243	18.89	100	1.736	1.39
31	43.941	49.95	66	13.582	18.11	101	1.629	1.24
32	42.970	48.98	67	12.938	17.33	102	1.530	1.10
33	42.000	48.01	68	12.313	16.57	103	1.439	0.98
34	41.031	47.03	69	11.707	15.82	104	1.354	0.88

Index
Inheritance Tax Appendices
References in this Index are to page numbers

Part II National Insurance Contributions

Contents Page

Social Security Act 1975
1975 Chapter 14

PART I CONTRIBUTIONS

PRELIMINARY

1. Outline of contributory system
Benefits are funded by means of contributions payable to the Secretary of State. The four classes of contributions are:

(1) Class 1 contributions, earnings-related and in two forms—primary contributions from employees, and secondary contributions from employers.

(2) Class 2 contributions, payable by the self-employed at a flat rate (see s. 7).

(3) Class 3 contributions, purely voluntary and paid to provide or make up entitlement to benefits (see s. 8).

(4) Class 4 contributions, payable by the self-employed on profits.

To be liable to Class 1 or 2 contributions a person must be resident, present or ordinarily resident in Great Britain (See the Contributions Regulations 1979, S.I. 1979 No. 591, regs. 119–123). Great Britain comprises England, Wales and Scotland; Northern Ireland has its own arrangements.

2. Categories of earners
Earners are of two kinds, employed and self-employed. A person with two activities can fall into both categories. In essence, an employee has a contract of service, but a self-employed person has a contract or contracts for services.

Employed earners: The usual description of an employed earner is any person who is gainfully employed in Great Britain either under a contract of service, or in an office with emoluments chargeable to income tax under Schedule E.

A contract of service may be oral and not written. A company director holds an office although he will often also be under a contract of service.

Office holders are not employees unless they receive emoluments chargeable under Schedule E. TA 1988, s. 131 (1) defines emoluments to include all salaries, fees, wages, perquisites and profits whatsoever.

A few examples of the tests used to decide whether or not a contract of service exists are set out below.

Control. If one party has sufficient control, or right of control, even where it is seldom exercised, this may be sufficient to suggest a contract of service is in existence. Control is inferred if a person is told where, when and how to carry out his alloted tasks.

This question will always be considered (*Market Investigations Ltd.* v. *Minister of Social Security* [1969] 3 All ER 732).

The control test used to be the principal one in questions of this sort but, although remaining an important factor, it no longer carries as much weight (*Argent* v. *Minister of Social Security* [1968] 3 All ER 208).

Obligation. If there is a moral or contractual obligation for the employer to provide work and the individual to take up the work offered this may suggest a contract of service exists.

Integration. If the services provided are an integral part of the employer's business this may also suggest that a contract of service exists between the employer and the individual (*Stevenson, Jordan and Harrison Ltd.* v. *McDonald and Evans* (1952) RPC 10).

Economic reality. Where the individual providing the service is "in business on his own account", this may suggest that he is not party to a contract of service (*Market Investigations Ltd* v. *Minister of Social Security* [1969] 3 All ER 732).

Some of the aspects considered in this case were:

(*a*) does the individual risk his own capital?

(*b*) does the individual benefit from his business acumen?

(*c*) does the individual provide his own equipment?

(*d*) does the individual hire his own helpers or indeed would the company accept a substitute?

The leaflet IR 56/N.I. 39 explains this subject in further detail but the only definite point to come out of this leaflet is the instruction to contact the local DSS/Revenue office in cases of doubt.

A self-employed earner is any person who is gainfully employed in Great Britain otherwise than in "employed earner's employment". However, a person with two activities can be both an employed earner and a self-employed earner. Because categorisation as a self-employed earner will result in a liability for contributions being determined under Class 2 contribution rules, much depends on the meaning of the words "gainfully employed". Basically it is sufficient either for a motive of gain to be present, or for a gain or profit to be realised.

3. "Earnings"

Earnings include remuneration or profit derived from any trade, business, profession, office or vocation. They include consideration in the form of money for certain restrictive undertakings taxable under TA 1988, s. 313. Regulations have been made to detail the earnings to be included for contribution purposes and those that may be excluded as follows:

There are three types of income which do not come under the definition of earnings because they are not derived from employment.

The first is rent paid to a director or an employee. Where he owns the premises and rents them out to the company the payment is not considered to be earnings for contribution purposes. However, this may cause loss of CGT reliefs.

The second form of payment is a dividend. By paying a director a dividend instead of salary Class 1 contributions are avoided. However, there are a number of potential problems involving advance corporation tax, lack of relevant earnings for pension contributions, share valuation etc.

The third type of payment is interest. Where a director has a substantial credit balance to his capital or current account the company may choose to pay interest on this balance rather than salary which attracts Class 1 contributions. However, in the majority of cases the possible payments will not be great enough to allow substantial contribution savings.

Earnings for Class 1 purposes:

Earnings for contribution purposes are gross earnings. This means any deductions and reliefs admissible for income tax purposes must be ignored. Examples are superannuation contributions, personal allowances and any expenses allowable under TA 1988, s. 198.

Under Extra-statutory concession A37 (1988), para. 1, directors' fees paid to partnerships may be included in the Schedule D assessment instead of Schedule E, so contributions will be payable under Class 4 instead of Class 1.

As to payments to be excluded from earnings see the Social Security (Contributions) Regulations 1979 (S.I. 1979 No. 591, reg. 19).

Earnings for Class 2 purposes:

Class 2 contributions are not earnings related, so the definition of earnings is of no relevance.

Earnings for Class 4 purposes:

As Class 4 contributions are chargeable on an income tax assessment under Schedule D the same definition is used, namely all annual profits or gains derived from the carrying on or exercise of one or more trades, professions or vocations. The basis of assessment set out in TA 1988, ss. 60 to 63 also apply.

THE FOUR CLASSES OF CONTRIBUTIONS

4. Class 1 contributions (incidence)

There are limits set each tax year which determine when liability to primary and secondary Class 1 contributions arise in respect of earnings as an employed earner. The lower earnings limit triggers liability to Class 1 contributions. When this limit is reached contributions are due on all earnings, not just the excess over the limit. The upper earnings limit places a ceiling on the amount of primary (employee's) contributions payable but not on secondary (employer's) contributions; since 6 October 1975 secondary contributions have been due on all earnings irrespective of the amount as long as they exceed the lower earnings limit. The lower earnings limit is the level used to establish entitlement to basic contribution benefits.

The limits for 1990–91 are:

	Weekly	Monthly	Annual
Lower	£46	£200	£2,392
Upper	£350	£1,517	£18,200

Where the earnings period (see Social Security Contribution Regulations 1979, S.I. 1979 No. 591, reg. 3) is other than a week, *e.g.*, a month, the upper and lower earnings limits to be used are prescribed in the Social Security Contributions Regulations 1979, S.I. 1979 No. 591, reg. 8.

A person under the age of 16 years is not liable to pay contributions on any earnings as an employed earner, and the employer is not liable to secondary contributions.

One of the most fundamental principles of the contribution scheme is that where earnings are paid to a person in respect of any one of his employments, Class 1 contributions, both primary and secondary, are to be paid irrespective of earnings from any other employments. However, the Contribution Regulations include aggregation rules which have been introduced to avoid a person taking advantage of this principle. In contrast to Class 1, all self-employed earnings are treated for Class 2 purposes as one "single employment".

The secondary contributor in most cases will be the employed earner's employer. However, a number of regulations prescribe, in certain circumstances, others to be the secondary contributor (see the Contribution Regulations 1979, S.I. 1979 No. 591 and the Categorisation of Earners Regulations 1978, S.I. 1978 No. 1689). Where a person, employed by his or her spouse is treated as being an employed earner, the spouse is the secondary contributor.

Until 5 October 1985 both primary and secondary contributions, were charged at the same rate on all earnings if they exceeded the lower earnings limit. From 6 October 1985 to 4 October 1989 differing percentage rates were applied to both primary and secondary contributions where earnings fell into different earnings brackets. From 5 October 1989 this is true for secondary contributions only, and primary contributions are charged at a lower rate on the lower earnings level. The earnings brackets and rates for 1990–91 are:

	Weekly earnings	*Rate of primary contributions*
Below LEL*	£ 0.00 to £ 45.99	No contributions due
LEL to UEL†	£46.00 to £350.00	2% on first £46.00 9% on balance
Above UEL	Over £350.00	No further contributions due
	Weekly earnings	*Rate of secondary contributions*
	£ 0.00 to £ 45.99	Nil
Bracket 1	£ 46.00 to £ 79.99	5%
Bracket 2	£ 80.00 to £124.99	7%
Bracket 3	£125.00 to £174.99	9%
Bracket 4	£175 .00 and over	10.45%

Secondary contributions rates apply to all earnings, not only those within the earnings bracket.
*Lower earnings limit.
†Upper earnings limit.

In some cases these rates do not apply as follows:
(*a*) contracted-out employees (see SSPA 1975, s. 27);
(*b*) serving members of armed forces (S.I. 1979 No. 591, reg. 115);
(*c*) mariners (S.I. 1979 No. 591, reg. 89);
(*d*) reduced rate elections (S.I. 1979 No. 591, reg. 100).
See also the table of rates and limits in Appendix 1.

7. Class 2 contributions
A self-employed earner under the age of 16 years is not liable to pay contributions. The first week a self-employed earner becomes liable to the flat-rate contributions is the week in which his 16th birthday actually falls. The weekly flat rate for 1990–91 is £4·55. The Secretary of State has the power to impose a higher flat rate on a person who is re-categorised from an employed earner to a self-employed earner. However, to date this power has never been used.

On application to the DSS, a person may be excepted from Class 2 contributions if his earnings are below a certain level, £2,600 for 1990–91. Application for exception from Class 2 contributions is made on form CF10. Further provisions are contained in S.I. 1979 No. 591, reg. 24.

7A. Late paid Class 2 contributions
Where a Class 2 contribution is paid late it is usually payable at the rate current when it fell due as long as it is paid within the same tax year or the following tax year, or in the next tax year following if the person has undertaken (see S.I. 1979 No. 591, reg. 42 B (3)) to make the payment in that year. If there is no undertaking, the rate taken is the highest Class 2 contribution rate that applied at any time between the week in respect of which the contribution is due and the date of payment.

There is no parallel provision for late paid Class 1 contributions and they are therefore payable at the rate current at the due date.

8. Class 3 contributions
The rate is a fixed sum; for 1990–91 it is £4·45 a week. The year in which pensionable age is attained is disregarded for retirement pension purposes and as a consequence it is necessary to prohibit any person who has reached the age of 65 years from making Class 3 contributions in that year.

Late paid Class 3 contributions may be paid within the next two years following the year in which it becomes due at the rate which would have applied at the due date. Where however the delayed payment is actually made after this period the rate payable will be the higher of the rate at the time it was due and the rate at the time it was actually paid.

9. Class 4 contributions recoverable under Tax Acts
Class 4 contributions differ from the other classes in that they are based on the profits for income tax purposes from a trade, profession or vocation and are collected by means of an income tax assessment under Schedule D, Case I or II. Contributions are calculated on the profits or gains above a prescribed lower annual limit up to maximum upper annual limit. This calculation differs from the Class 1 calculation. For Class 1 purposes the lower earnings limit acts as a trigger, but all earnings are liable. The Class 4 limit is more of a threshold and the contributions are calculated as a percentage of the excess over this threshold. Profits are subject to certain adjustments, such as deductions of capital allowances, before the contributions are calculated. The 1990–91 annual limits are:

Lower £5,450
Upper £18,200
Prescribed rate   6.3%

TMA 1970 applies to contributions in the same way as income tax, with prescribed modifications. For appeal procedures see TMA 1970, ss. 31, 49 and 56. The Income Tax Acts also apply to the collection and recovery of Class 4 contributions.

Although in effect Class 4 contributions are payable by self-employed earners, it is not a requirement that they are so categorised. It is simply a case of the necessary assessment being raised. It is generally understood that the income tax case law which establishes the definition of "profits or gains" will be followed by the DSS.

The income tax rules usually apply so that a husband is liable in respect of his wife's profits or gains.

The penalty provisions under TMA 1970, Pt. X ss. 93–107 (penalties etc) and interest under TMA 1970, s. 88 apply to Class 4 contributions. However, the interest provisions of TMA 1970, s. 86 do not apply.

Certain persons qualify for exception from Class 4 liability:

   (*a*) any person under the age of 16 years at the beginning of the tax year, provided that they apply for exception;
   (*b*) any person not resident in the U.K. for tax purposes;
   (*c*) any person who is over pensionable age at the beginning of the tax year.

For other examples of exceptions see the Social Security (Contributions) Regulations 1979, No. 591, in particular where a person's income has suffered Class 1 deductions but forms part of his "profits or gains".

As to deferment of Class 2 and 4 contributions, see s. 11.

10. Class 4 contributions recoverable under regulations

Regulations may be made to impose liability to "special" Class 4 contributions. These are payable by a person who is treated as self-employed by regulation, but whose earnings are liable to income tax under Schedule E (Class 1 earnings) and the earnings exceed the lower annual limit for Class 4 purposes. "Special" contributions are payable at the same rate as ordinary contributions, currently 6.3 per cent.

It is the responsibility of the Secretary of State, and not the Revenue, to recover "Special" Class 4 contributions.

11. General power to regulate liability for contributions

Where a person has in any tax year earnings from two or more employments the Secretary of State may authorise deferment of contributions for one or more of the employments. This applies only where the earner has reason to believe his earnings, on which the collection of contributions will continue, will equal or be in excess of the maximum Class 1 limit. A similar arrangement may be made where the person is both an employed and self-employed earner. An application for deferment should be made to the DSS on a form CF379 (Class 1) or CF359 (Class 4) (available from the local DSS office) before the beginning of the tax year to which it relates. The DSS will issue a certificate showing the class(es) of contributions deferred and the period covered by the notice.

PART III DETERMINATION OF CLAIMS AND QUESTIONS

ADJUDICATION BY SECRETARY OF STATE

93. Principal questions for Secretary of State

There is no appeal procedure such as that contained in TMA 1970. This is mainly because there is no formal assessment, except of Class 4 contributions which in the main are covered by TMA 1970.

The DSS attempt to settle all disputes through correspondence and meetings but this is not always successful. The only way to resolve such problems is to put the point at issue in the form of a question to the Secretary of State for his determination. In practice the matter is delegated by the Secretary of State to his Solicitors' Office, whose findings are then reviewed by Social Security ministers. The main areas covered by the Secretary of State's jurisdiction are whether an earner is employed or self-employed and benefit contribution conditions. However, he is able to determine any question on contribution matters.

Any question of contributions must be determined by the Secretary of State before it can be considered in the courts. The Secretary of State may appoint someone to hold an inquiry into any question before determining it.

The DSS issues the forms used in this procedure. The question must be put on a form CF90; this sets out standard questions to which the applicant is requested to reply, and enables the DSS to put the question in the correct form for the Solicitors' Office to consider. Further statements may be made on a form CF91.

Form CF100 explains the procedure if a person is unable to attend an enquiry and also gives details of allowable expenses.

94. Appeal on question of law
If any question of law arises in connection with a determination by the Secretary of State, he may refer the question to the High Court. He must give written notice of his intention to the person raising the question and to any other person whom he feels is concerned with the matter. Any person who disagrees with a determination on a point of law may appeal to the High Court if the question has not already been referred to the High Court. A person must appeal and request a stated case within 28 days of receiving the written determination. This limit may be extended if there is a good reason for the delay. The DSS issues a guidance note on form CF263.

96. Review of decisions under ss. 93, 95
The Secretary of State may re-open a determination if he feels the decision was made in ignorance of a material fact or because there was a mistake in the presentation of such facts. This can only be done where the appeal time limit has expired and there is no pending appeal.

ADJUDICATION GENERALLY

114. Regulations as to determination of questions
Provision is made for regulations to cover unusual situations such as questions arising out of pre-1975 legislation and matters which do not involve appeals.

115. Procedure
The procedure to be followed at any enquiry arranged by the Secretary of State is set out in the Social Security (Adjudication) Regulations 1986, S.I. 1986 No. 2218.

117. Finality of decisions
Unless the person applying to the Secretary of State for a determination appeals against the decision it is final. However, a finding of fact or other determination in one case is not conclusive in any other case.

119. Effect of adjudication on payment and recovery
Regulations deal with liability for contributions pending a determination including any appeal or review and also with the date any decision takes effect.

PART IV GENERAL PROVISIONS AS TO OPERATION AND ADMINISTRATION OF THIS ACT

REVIEW AND RE-RATING OF CONTRIBUTIONS

120. Annual review of contributions
A report on the National Insurance Fund is made every year. It is required whenever the Secretary of State considers changing the Class 2 and 3 contribution rates or the Class 4 annual lower and upper earnings limits. The report reviews the level of earnings during the year and compares this with the previous year.

121. Orders under s. 120 (supplementary)
Whenever draft orders to change the contribution rates and limits are laid before Parliament, a copy of a Government Actuary's report on the effects that these changes will have on the National Insurance Fund must accompany the draft orders. Any order takes effect in the tax year following that in which the draft has been approved by both Houses of Parliament.

122. Additional power to alter contributions
The Secretary of State may by order change the maximum rates for Class 1 primary and secondary contributions but only by a maximum of 0.25 per cent. He may also alter the Class 2 weekly flat rate contribution and the rate of Class 3 contribution. The Class 4 rate, currently 6.3 per cent. may be increased but only up to a maximum of 8.25 per cent. Greater increases require an Act of Parliament.

123. Orders under s. 122 (supplementary)
Orders must be laid in draft and require affirmative resolutions of both the House of Lords and House of Commons. Other provisions are similar to those in s. 121 above.

123A. Further power to alter certain contributions
The Secretary of State may by order change the upper weekly earnings limits for Class 1 contributions as shown in the table in s. 4. He may also change any of the rates relating to the individual "brackets" other than the maximum which is covered in s. 122 above.

SPECIAL CLASSES OF EARNERS

127. Crown employment
Civil servants and similar employees are treated as ordinary employees for contribution purposes. However, a number of Crown employees are given different treatment, *i.e.*, members of the armed

forces, diplomatic and consular staff and civil or public servants employed in a foreign country which has a reciprocal agreement with the U.K. for National Insurance purposes.

128. Her Majesty's forces
A serving member of the armed forces is to be treated as an employed earner even if he is serving overseas. There are reduced rates of Class 1 contributions as shown in the Contributions Regulations 1979, S.I. 1979 No. 591, reg. 115. These regulations also define establishments and organisations within the armed forces and earnings for contributions purposes.

129. Mariners, airmen, etc.
A mariner due to the nature of his trade may not always be present or resident in Great Britain, which is necessary for liability to National Insurance contributions to arise. However, by reason of the regulations made under this section a mariner, airman, etc., is to be treated as an employed earner. A person who is neither domiciled nor has a place of residence in Great Britain is excepted from this section. Regulations have also been made to define the secondary contributor. Share fishermen are slightly different as they are considered self-employed earners, but pay a higher rate Class 2 contribution because they qualify for unemployment benefit.

130. Married women and widows
There are specific regulations covering the liabilities of married women and widows to National Insurance contributions.

131. Persons outside Great Britain
Persons who have been abroad at any time are covered by specific regulations.

132. Employment at sea (continental shelf operations)
The main individuals caught by this legislation are oil-rig workers, divers etc. Work in the "continental shelf", as defined by the Continental Shelf Act 1964, is not strictly in Great Britain. However, SI 1979, No. 591, reg. 85 designates anyone who is engaged in this area as liable to contributions, subject to presence and residence rules.

SOCIAL SECURITY SYSTEMS OUTSIDE GREAT BRITAIN

142. Co-ordination with Northern Ireland
Northern Ireland have their own Social Security Act 1975 and it is co-ordinated to ensure the system is similar to the one in operation in Great Britain. This means there is no need for a reciprocal agreement between the two countries. The Secretary of State has made arrangements with the head of the Northern Ireland Department to secure this end. For example, a mariner employed on a British ship who is resident or domiciled in Northern Ireland is to be regarded as resident and domiciled in Great Britain.

143. Reciprocity with other countries
Orders may be made to modify the legislation if it is necessary in respect of any agreement between Great Britain and another country.

ENFORCEMENT

146. Offences and penalties
Failure to pay contributions within the prescribed time limits renders a person liable on summary conviction to a fine at level 3. This does not apply to Class 4 contributions recoverable by the Revenue. Under the Criminal Justice Act 1982, s. 37, as amended by S.I. 1984 No. 367, art. 2 (4), Sch. 4 with effect from 1 May 1984, a level 3 fine is £400. Each time an employer fails to pay a contribution in respect of any one of his employees an offence has been committed. The same applies to a self-employed earner each time he fails to pay a Class 2 stamp. In practice the DSS prosecute for only one of the latest offences for which they have concrete evidence and then having obtained a conviction they will arrange to collect the total debt.

148. Questions arising in proceedings
Where, during proceedings a question arises relating to any contribution matter, the proceedings will be adjourned until the Secretary of State has considered the question and given his determination. Once the appeal period has expired the proceedings may continue.

UNPAID CONTRIBUTIONS

149. Evidence of non-payment
Where contributions are collected under an employer's PAYE scheme, the collector of taxes can provide the evidence to be used in proceedings. A contribution card without a stamp on a week where a contribution was due is sufficient evidence to justify proceedings for non-payment.

150. Recovery on prosecution
Where a person is convicted under s. 146 (1) and the contribution remains unpaid he continues to be liable to pay the contribution (see s. 152).

151. Proof of previous offences
Where a person has been convicted of an offence of non-payment he may, subject to available evidence, also be convicted of failures during the two-year period ending on the date the original offence was committed. If the DSS intend taking this course of action they must advise the person charged with a summons. A person who fails to pay may ultimately be sent to prison for a period of up to 90 days.

152. Provisions supplementary to ss. 150, 151
Any sum which is due from a person convicted of non-payment is recoverable as a penalty, but this penalty cannot be mitigated. This sum is then treated as contributions of the class originally payable.

PART V GENERAL

166. Orders and regulations (general provisions)
There are wide-ranging powers to make regulations or orders and these are exercised by statutory instrument. It is sometimes necessary for the Secretary of State to act in conjunction with the Treasury when orders which revise the rates and limits of contributions are proposed.

167. Parliamentary control of orders and regulations
Regulations and orders on certain topics within the contribution system must be laid in draft before Parliament and approved by each House before they are made. All regulations made by the Secretary of State, and all orders (with certain exceptions) made by him are effective unless nullified (the negative procedure).

168. Interpretation
Various definitions are given in a glossary at Sch. 20.

169. Citation, extent and commencement
This Act is known as the Social Security Act 1975 and came into force on 6 April 1975.

SCHEDULES

SCHEDULE 1 SUPPLEMENTARY PROVISIONS RELATING TO CONTRIBUTIONS OF CLASSES 1, 2 AND 3 (Section 1 (4))

Class 1 contributions where earner employed in more than one employment

1.—Earnings paid to an earner in respect of more than one employed earner's employment in a given period are usually aggregated if:
    (*a*) they are paid by the same employer, or
    (*b*) the employers carry on business in association with each other, or
    (*c*) the regulations have specifically designated one employer to be secondary contributor in respect of all employments, or
    (*d*) where the employer operates as an agency.
    There are also specific rules where one of the employments to be aggregated is a contracted-out employment.

Earnings not paid at normal intervals

2.—Regulations have been made which govern the "earnings period" where payment is made at irregular intervals (see S.I. 1979 No. 591, reg. 3).

Method of paying Class 1 contributions

3.—An employer is liable to secondary contributions on earnings paid to an employed earner and in the first instance any primary contributions liability arising on those earnings. He is however entitled to recover the primary contributions from the employee. He is not entitled to recover any secondary contributions from an employed earner's earnings, even where the employee and employer have agreed that this should be the case. This is an offence which carries a maximum fine of £400 on conviction.

General provisions as to Class 1 contributions

4.—Regulations provide for the methods of calculating Class 1 contributions and ensuring there is no avoidance or reduction in payment.

Power to combine collection of contributions with tax

5.—Class 1 contributions are collected in the same way as tax through the PAYE scheme. The collector of taxes collects both primary and secondary contributions and then pays an amount over to the DSS in respect of the contributions collected.

Provision is also made for regulations to require interest to be paid on late paid Class 1 contributions. The interest would run from not later than 14 days after the end of the tax year at a rate prescribed by statutory instrument. Interest would also be repayable on overpaid contributions but only for periods more than one year after the end of the relevant tax year. This mirrors Inland Revenue proposals to introduce interest on late paid PAYE; it is not expected to come into force until 1993.

Special penalties in the case of certain returns

5A.—Regulations may impose penalties for late or incorrect NIC returns. The main return affected is the Employer's Annual Return form P35. Similar legislation was introduced by FA 1989 for PAYE returns.

The P35 is a joint PAYE and NIC return. Tax penalties for the first 12 months of lateness are not doubled up for NIC purposes. Additional penalties, based on unpaid contributions, for lateness of more than 12 months is however added to the tax penalty. Similarly a NIC penalty may be levied in addition to a tax penalty for an incorrect return. The penalty is based on the omitted contributions.

The inspector will be able to make a determination of the penalty, which would then be treated like a tax assessment. The employer may appeal against the determination to the General Commissioners.

General regulation-making powers

6.—There are modified PAYE regulations covering this point in S.I. 1979 No. 591, Sch. 1. The earnings on which contributions become liable are recorded on the same deduction working sheet used for PAYE records, form P11 (new).

Where an employer deducts primary contributions from an employee and then fails to pay them on time, the DSS accept that they were paid on time if they are satisfied the failure or delay to pay them was neither consented to nor connived at by the employee. If a person pays the wrong contribution, the DSS does not automatically give the contributor a refund. However, the DSS may allocate the payment to the correct class of contributions. Class 2 contributions may be repaid, if they could have been excepted from liability; see also SSA 1975, s. 7. Class 2 or 3 contributions may be made by purchasing stamps and affixing them to a card, by direct debit to a bank account or by a deduction from certain pensions or allowances. In practice the DSS also accepts cheques.
7.—Regulations may provide, for contribution purposes, whether a person is treated as having attained a certain age at the beginning or end of a week.

Deduction of contributions from pension, etc.

8.—Any person receiving a pension or allowance from the DSS may allow the DSS to deduct any Class 2 or 3 (flat rate) contributions payable by him from the pension or allowance due to him.

Sickness payments counting as remuneration

9.—Where a sickness payment is made through an occupational sick pay arrangement it is treated as earnings from which Class 1 primary contributions are deductible. The employer is the secondary contributor unless arrangements have been made for someone other than the employer to be the secondary contributor.

SCHEDULE 2 LEVY OF CLASS 4 CONTRIBUTIONS WITH INCOME TAX (Section 9 (4))

Interpretation

1.— Three terms used in this Schedule are defined.

Method of computing profits or gains

2.—Class 4 contributions are payable on profits assessable to income tax under Schedule D, Case I or II, (see TA 1988, ss. 60 to 63), subject to the deduction of capital allowances from the trade, profession or vocation and the addition of balancing charges.

Reliefs

3.—In computing profits or gains on which Class 4 contributions are payable, losses may be deducted under TA 1988, ss. 380, 381, 383, 385, 388 and 389. The fact that a loss may have arisen before 6 April 1975, when Class 4 contributions were introduced, does not affect it being used for Class 4 purposes. Losses under TA 1988, ss. 380, 381 and 382 must stem from activities which, if profitable would be liable to Class 4 contributions.

No deduction is given for personal reliefs, retirement annuity premiums, interest paid, or annual payments.

Tax relief is available under TA 1988, s. 617 (5) on 50 per cent. of Class 4 contributions payable in a year of assessment and is not deductible in calculating the profits or gains on which Class 4 contributions are payable.

Husband and wife

4.—Where a wife has self-employed earnings her Class 4 contributions are calculated separately from her husband's. Once the calculation has been made the contributions are assessed in the husband's name. If an election for either separate taxation of wife's earnings or separate assessment is in force the contributions are recoverable from the wife. This regulation is nullified with effect from 6 April 1990 because of the introduction of independent taxation.

Partnerships

5.—Where the trade etc. is carried on in partnership the Class 4 liability is apportioned in the same way as the income tax liability. Each partner's share of profits is then added to any other self-employed income for the purposes of calculating the Class 4 contribution liability.

Trustees, etc.

6.—Exception from Class 4 contribution liability will be granted to a trustee who is chargeable to income tax by virtue of TA 1988, s. 59 and any person (trustee, guardian etc.) who is chargeable under TMA 1970, s. 72.

Other provisions

7.—As well as the penalty contained in TMA 1970 applying to Class 4 contributions (by virtue of s. 9 (3)) the interest provisions in TMA 1970, s. 88 (on recovery of lost tax) also apply. Interest is also chargeable under TMA 1970, s. 86 (on tax overdue) from a date to be appointed under SSA 1990, s. 18(2).

8.—Where an assessment has become final and conclusive for income tax purposes it shall be so treated for Class 4 contribution purposes.

9.—The appeal provisions relating to Schedule D Class I or II assessment, in TMA 1970, also apply to Class 4 contributions.

SCHEDULE 13 PROVISION WHICH MAY BE MADE BY PROCEDURE REGULATIONS (Section 115)

This Schedule explains in further detail the provisions which may be made by regulation as mentioned in s. 115. It covers such topics as evidence, hearings and documents.

SCHEDULE 17 CONSTITUTION, ETC., OF JOINT AUTHORITY FOR GREAT BRITIAN AND NORTHERN IRELAND (Section 142 (2))

The constitution of the Joint Authority which oversees the co-ordination between the Great Britain and Northern Ireland social security systems is laid down.

SCHEDULE 20 GLOSSARY OF EXPRESSIONS (Section 168 (1))

Various words and terms used in this Act are defined.

Social Security Pensions Act 1975
1975 Chapter 60

PART I CONTRIBUTIONS

1. Earnings limits
The limits are set each year by reference to the amount of Category A retirement pension at the start of the year for which the earnings limits are being set. The weekly lower earnings limit must be equal or not more than 99p less than the basic pension. Before 25 July 1986 the figure was 49p. The change has the effect of rounding up the contributions to the nearest £1 instead of 50p. The weekly upper earnings limit may either be equal to seven times the basic pension (£46·90 from 6 April 1990) *or* be equal to an amount between $6^{1}/_{2}$ and $7^{1}/_{2}$ times the basic pension.

3. Married women and widows
A married woman or a widow who is an employed earner may no longer elect to pay Class 1 contributions at a reduced rate. If she is self-employed she may no longer elect to be exempt from Class 2 liability. However elections already made when these rights were withdrawn are still effective in prescribed circumstances (S.I. 1979 No. 591, reg. 101). It is beneficial for a married women or widow on low earnings to revoke her reduced rate Class 1 contributions election. She then has the advantage of the 2 per cent. band on the lower earnings limit (reduced rate liability is charged on all earnings up to the upper earnings limit at 3.85 per cent.); once revoked it is not possible to reinstate the election. This section also enables the DSS to prescribe a reduced rate of Class 2 contributions though, up to now, this has not been done.

4. Persons over pensionable age
Any person over pensionable age with earnings from employment is excepted from paying Class 1 contributions. However the employer has to pay contributions on those earnings and should continue to deduct primary contributions until the employee produces a form CF384 "certificate of age exception", or other evidence, for example a birth certificate. Exception from paying Class 2 and Class 4 contributions is also granted to self-employed earners over 65 (men) or 60 (women).

5. Voluntary contributions
A person may only pay Class 3 contributions if the level of Class 1 or 2 contributions paid in any year is insufficient to produce an earnings factor which would qualify the person for full contributory benefits. A qualifying earnings factor is defined as 52 times the weekly lower earnings limit for that year.

PART III CONTRACTING-OUT

PRELIMINARY

26. Contracting-out of full contributions and benefits
Where an employer has an occupational pension scheme the rates of Class 1 contributions may be reduced because the employer's pension scheme is responsible for providing a guaranteed minimum pension instead of the state. This is known as contracting-out.

CONTRACTED-OUT RATES OF CONTRIBUTIONS AND BENEFITS

27. Contracted-out rates of Class 1 contributions
A person who is contracted out of the state scheme is still entitled to a basic pension and is therefore required to make Class 1 contributions at a reduced rate. The reduction only applies to the rate applicable to the lower and upper earnings limits, and applies to both primary and secondary contributions. The reason for this is the earnings between those limits are connected with the entitlement to the additional component of the retirement pension which a contracted-out employee gives up:

(*a*) in the case of a primary Class 1 contribution, the normal percentage less 2 per cent.;

(*b*) in the case of a secondary Class 1 contribution, the normal percentage less 3·8 per cent.

Where an employee leaves a contracted-out employment and receives earnings in the period of six weeks from the date of cessation, contributions may be deducted at the contracted-out rate.

28. Review and alteration of contracted-out rates of Class 1 contributions

The Secretary of State reviews the rates every five years and makes a report on the current position to both Houses of Parliament. He must also lay draft orders if he feels the rates require alteration.

ARRANGEMENTS FOR CONTRACTING-OUT

30. Contracted-out employment

A contracting-out certificate is issued by the Occupational Pensions Board and there must be a current contracting-out certificate in force if the reduced rates are to apply. The employed earner must be under pensionable age, the scheme must be contracted out in relation to his employment and his service must qualify him for a guaranteed minimum pension. Further subsections have been introduced by SSA 1986, s. 6 and Sch. 2 para. 4 which essentially provide for regulations to be made setting out the details covering money purchase schemes.

31. Contracting-out certificates

A certificate issued by the Occupational Pension Board specifies the rules covering the scheme. Regulations provide for an employer and the Occupational Pension Board to change or cancel the certificate.

SUPPLEMENTARY

51A. Refusal and cancellation of contracting-out certificates

There are specific time limits for the re-issue of a contracting-out certificate where it has been cancelled or surrendered. In some circumstances a certificate may be refused.

PART V GENERAL

60. Determination of questions

Any question arising on the matter of contracted-out employments must be referred by the Secretary of State to the Occupational Pensions Board for determination by that Board. SSA 1975, ss. 93 (1) and 98 (1) do not apply.

62. Other provisions about regulations and orders

Orders made by the Occupational Pensions Board need not be made by statutory instrument.

Regulations made by the Secretary of State may provide for the Occupational Pensions Board to exercise discretionary powers.

66. Interpretation

A number of terms used in this Act are defined.

67. Commencement

This Act came into force on a day appointed by the Secretary of State and different days could be appointed for different provisions.

68. Short title, citation and extent

This Act may be cited as the Social Security Pensions Act 1975 and together with SSA 1975 may be cited as the Social Security Acts 1975.

Social Security (Miscellaneous Provisions) Act 1977
1977 Chapter 5

CONTRIBUTIONS

1. Amendments relating to contributions
A number of provisions of SSA 1975 are amended including the rates of primary and secondary Class 1 contributions.

2. Amendment of regulation for crediting contributions
The amended regulations on contribution credits will not affect any benefit claimed before 18 March 1977.

OTHER MISCELLANEOUS PROVISIONS

18. Certain sums to be earnings for social security purposes
Payments made to an employed earner under various Employment Protection Acts are deemed to be earnings for contribution purposes.

GENERAL

24. Supplemental
A number of terms and phrases are defined or extended in meaning.

25. Citation, commencement and extent
This Act may be cited as the Social Security (Miscellaneous Provisions) Act 1977. This Act together with the 1975 Acts may be cited as the Social Security Acts 1975 to 1977.

Employment Protection (Consolidation) Act 1978
1978 Chapter 44

PART I PARTICULARS OF TERMS OF EMPLOYMENT

WRITTEN PARTICULARS OF TERMS OF EMPLOYMENT

1. Written particulars of terms of employment

An employee is entitled to a written statement which amongst other things must have a note stating whether or not a contracting-out certificate is in force for the respective employment, and this should be issued to him not later than 13 weeks after his employment has commenced.

ENFORCEMENT OF RIGHTS UNDER PART I

11. References to industrial tribunals

If the requirements of s. 1 are not fulfilled, an employee may refer the question to an industrial tribunal.

Social Security Act 1980
1980 Chapter 30

AMENDMENTS OF CERTAIN ENACTMENTS RELATING TO SOCIAL SECURITY

4. Miscellaneous amendments
This extends the meaning of the Social Security (Miscellaneous Provisions) Act 1977 to include the Social Security Pensions Act 1975.

ADVISORY COMMITTEES

9. The Social Security Advisory Committee
This committee was formed by combining the National Insurance Advisory Committee and the Supplementary Benefits Commission. Its functions are to review proposed regulations and advise both the Secretary of State and the Northern Ireland Department. This requires the Secretary of State and the Northern Ireland Department to furnish the Committee with all the information it requires.

The address of the Social Security Advisory Committee is: New Court, Carey Street, London WC2A 2LS.

10. Consultation with Committee on proposals for regulations
The Secretary of State is required to refer any proposed regulations to the Committee unless it is a matter of such urgency as to make any referral inexpedient. The Committee will consider the proposed regulations and make a report to either the Secretary of State or the Northern Ireland Department which may contain any recommendations the Committee thinks fit. When the draft regulations are laid before Parliament they must be accompanied by the Committee's report and a report by the Secretary of State explaining the extent to which the Committee's recommendations have been implemented, or not, as the case may be.

MISCELLANEOUS

18. Computation of age in Scotland
In Scotland, and for the purposes of the Social Security Acts 1975 to 1986, a person becomes a year older at the start of the anniversary of his date of birth.

GENERAL

21. Supplemental
This Act may be cited as the Social Security Act 1980 and together with the Social Security Acts 1975 to 1979 may be known as the Social Security Acts 1975 to 1980.

SCHEDULES

SCHEDULE 3 SOCIAL SECURITY ADVISORY COMMITTEE (Sections 9 and 10)

PART I CONSTITUTION ETC. OF COMMITTEE

1.—The Committee consists of a chairman appointed by the Secretary of State and between 10 and 13 other members.
2.—The term of office is between three and five years although the Secretary of State may, before the expiration of the term, extend it up to a further five years.
3.—Of the members, one is appointed after consultation with employers' organisations, one after consultation with workers' organisations, one after consultation with the head of the DSS for Northern Ireland and there must be at least one person with experience of work among the chronically sick and disabled.
4.—Any member may be removed by the Secretary of State on the grounds of incapacity or misbehaviour.
5.—The Committee may have a secretary and other officers as determined by the Minister of the Civil Service.
6.—The Minister also determines the expenses to be paid by the Secretary of State to the Committee.
7.—The expenses may include salary and expenses for travelling etc.
8.—The Secretary of State may provide for a pension for Committee members.

9.—The Committee may act even when there is a vacancy among its members.
10.—The Committee decides on its own procedure, including its quorum.

PART II REGULATIONS NOT REQUIRING PRIOR SUBMISSION TO COMMITTEE

Certain kinds of regulations need not be submitted to the Committee before they are made:

Social Security

12.—Regulations made simply in consequence of an order under SSA 1975, ss. 120, 122 or 123A (review of contributions) or SSA 1986, s. 63.

Social Security Pensions

13.—Regulations which simply follow on as a consequence of other regulations.

Statutory sick pay

15A.—Regulations under SSHBA 1982, s. 9.

Miscellaneous

19.—Regulations relating to tribunal procedures.
20.—Regulations for the purpose of consolidation.
21.—Regulations making provision for Northern Ireland that are similar to those made for Great Britain.

Social Security and Housing Benefits Act 1982

1982 Chapter 24

PART I STATUTORY SICK PAY

1. Employer's liability

Where an employee is unable to work due to some form of incapacity he is entitled to receive statutory sick pay if he qualifies under ss. 2 to 4 of this Act (not covered by this work).

RATE OF PAYMENT ETC.

9. Recovery by employers of amounts paid by way of statutory sick pay

An employer who has paid statutory sick pay to an employed earner is entitled, in the majority of cases, to recover it by deducting the relevant amount from the primary or secondary Class 1 contributions due to be paid by him.

MISCELLANEOUS

23. Statutory sick pay to count as remuneration for principal Act

Any sums paid to an employed earner under the statutory sick pay provisions are treated as earnings for Class 1 contribution purposes.

26. Interpretation of Part I and supplementary provisions

Various terms are defined.

27. Crown employment

The statutory sick pay provisions apply to civil servants but not to members of Her Majesty's forces when acting as such.

PART III MISCELLANEOUS

44. Application of social security legislation in relation to territorial waters

This section extends the meaning of Great Britain, U.K. and Northern Ireland to include their territorial waters.

45. Regulations

The normal provisions for making regulations, except commencement orders under s. 48 (3), apply in this Act.

47. Interpretation

Terms are defined.

48. Short title etc.

This Act may be cited as the Social Security and Housing Benefits Act 1982 and Pts. I and III of this Act, together with the Social Security Acts 1975 to 1981, may be known collectively as the Social Security Acts 1975 to 1982.

Social Security Act 1985
1985 Chapter 53

PART IV MISCELLANEOUS AND SUPPLEMENTARY

SUPPLEMENTARY

27. Other regulations
The need for the Secretary of State to refer prescribed regulations to the Social Security Advisory Committee is removed.

29. Minor and consequential amendments and repeals
Sch. 5 makes minor amendments to, and Sch. 6 repeals of, legislation.

30. Northern Ireland
Certain orders made under the Northern Ireland Act 1974, Sch. 1 are only subject to annulment by either House of Parliament.

31. Extent
Certain sections of the Act apply to Northern Ireland and the Isle of Man.

32. Commencement
Specified sections come into force on the day the Act is passed. Other sections come into force on different days or on a day specified by the Secretary of State.

33. Citation
This Act may be cited as the Social Security Act 1985 and together with the Social Security Acts 1975 to 1984 as the Social Security Acts 1975 to 1985.

Bankruptcy (Scotland) Act 1985

1985 Chapter 66

12. When sequestration is awarded

A court will award sequestration of a person's estate unless it can be shown that the petition cannnot be competently awarded. The debtor will be required to attend court but if he does not the petition may still be awarded. There are a number of reasons for not awarding sequestration.

DISTRIBUTION OF DEBTOR'S ESTATE

51. Order of priority in distribution

The order of priority of a debtor's debts are listed with further definition given in Sch. 3, Pt. I.
   Certain national insurance contributions are treated as preferred debts.

MISCELLANEOUS AND SUPPLEMENTARY

73. Interpretation

Various terms and phrases used in this Act are defined.

77. Crown application

A creditor may not apply for sequestration against the Crown as a debtor.

78. Short title, commencement and extent

This Act only relates to Scotland and came into effect on 30 October 1985.

SCHEDULES

SCHEDULE 3 PREFERRED DEBTS (Section 51)

PART I LIST OF PREFERRED DEBTS

Social Security contributions

3.—Class 1 and 2 contributions falling due in the 12 months before the "relevant date" and Class 4 contributions (restricted to one year's assessment) are all treated as preferred debts for the purposes of priority in distributing a debtor's estate.

PART II INTERPRETATION OF PART I

Meaning of "the relevant date"

7.—The relevant date is the date of sequestration or, if the debtor has died, his death.

Insolvency Act 1986
1986 Chapter 45

THE FIRST GROUP OF PARTS
COMPANY INSOLVENCY; COMPANIES WINDING UP

PART IV WINDING UP OF COMPANIES REGISTERED UNDER THE COMPANIES ACTS

CHAPTER VIII PROVISIONS OF GENERAL APPLICATION IN WINDING UP

PREFERENTIAL DEBTS

175. Preferential debts (general provision)
When a company is being wound up preferential debts are paid in priority to all other debts. Where there is insufficient funds to meet these debts in full they will be paid in equal proportions. Section 386 further defines the categories of preferential debts.

THE SECOND GROUP OF PARTS
INSOLVENCY OF INDIVIDUALS; BANKRUPTCY

PART XI BANKRUPTCY

CHAPTER IV ADMINISTRATION BY TRUSTEE

DISTRIBUTION OF BANKRUPT'S ESTATE

328. Priority of debts
The order of priority of meeting debts out of a bankrupt's estate is set out. Preferential debts, as defined by s. 386, are given priority over other debts and will be met in full. Where there are insufficient funds they will be paid in equal proportions.

THE THIRD GROUP OF PARTS
MISCELLANEOUS MATTERS BEARING ON BOTH COMPANY AND INDIVIDUAL INSOLVENCY; GENERAL INTERPRETATION; FINAL PROVISIONS

PART XII PREFERENTIAL DEBTS IN COMPANY AND INDIVIDUAL INSOLVENCY

386. Categories of preferential debts
Schedule 6 to this Act lists the preferential debts. They include the following:
tax deducted under PAYE due to the Revenue
VAT
car tax
betting and gaming duties
social security and pension scheme contributions
remuneration etc. of employees

387. "The relevant date"
The relevant date is used to determine the existence and amount of a preferential debt. The relevant date depends on a number of factors, such as whether the debtor is a company or an individual, whether voluntary liquidation, winding up or receivership is taking place, etc.

PART XVII MISCELLANEOUS AND GENERAL

434. Crown application
The Crown is only affected by this Act in relation to priorities of debts.

PART XIX FINAL PROVISIONS

440. Extent (Scotland)
The First Group of Parts (ss. 1 to 251) extend to Scotland except where stated. The Second Group of Parts (ss. 252 to 385) do not extend to Scotland.

441. Extent (Northern Ireland)
Nothing in this Act extends to Northern Ireland except any provisions relating to companies incorporated outside Great Britain.

442. Extent (other territorites)
The provisions of this Act may extend to the Channel Islands or other colony by specific order. As a result the provisions in the 1985 Act specifically dealing with such territories will continue.

443. Commencement
This Act came into force on 29 December 1986.

444. Citation
This Act may be cited as the Insolvency Act 1986.

SCHEDULES

SCHEDULE 6 THE CATEGORIES OF PREFERENTIAL DEBTS (Section 386)

Category 3: Social security contributions

6.—All Class 1 and Class 2 contributions due on the relevant date and which become due in the 12 months immediately before the relevant date are preferential debts.

7.—Class 4 contributions which have been raised on assessment and are now due or are assessed up to 5 April next before the relevant date but not exceeding, in the whole, any one year's assessment.

Social Security Act 1986

1986 Chapter 50

PART VI COMMON PROVISIONS

ADMINISTRATION

52. Adjudication
A number of provisions in SSA 1975 have been amended in accordance with Sch. 5, Pt. I.

54. Breach of regulations
The penalties for contravening or failing to comply with regulations made under any Act are revised.

56. Legal proceedings
Proceedings taken before a magistrates' court in accordance with any of the benefit Acts (as defined in s. 84) cannot be conducted on behalf of the Secretary of State by a barrister or solicitor.

57. Offences by bodies corporate
Where any offence under any of the benefit Acts (as defined in s. 84) is committed by a body corporate, but it is proved the offence was committed with the consent or connivance of any director, manager or secretary, he as well as the body corporate is guilty of the offence and is liable to be proceeded against accordingly.

59. Disclosure of information
The restrictions imposed on the Revenue regarding the passing of information do not prevent the Secretary of State or the Department of Social Security for Northern Ireland from obtaining information relating to the assessment or collection of income tax if it is relevant to benefit claims.

SUBORDINATE LEGISLATION

61. Consultations on subordinate legislation
The Secretary of State is required to consult certain committees or other bodies with regard to the preparation of proposed regulations. In certain circumstances these requirements may be waived.

PART VII MISCELLANEOUS, GENERAL AND SUPPLEMENTARY

MISCELLANEOUS

74. National insurance contributions
Various changes have been made to the Secretary of State's powers to vary the rates of contribution.

NORTHERN IRELAND

81. Orders in Council making corresponding provision for Northern Ireland
An order under the Northern Ireland Act 1974, Sch. 1, para. 1 (1) (b) which is only for the purposes of corresponding to this Act does not require affirmative resolutions of both Houses of Parliament but is subject to annulment by resolution of either House.

82. Amendments of enactments relating to social security in Northern Ireland
Certain amendments have been made to enactments relating to social security in Northern Ireland and are specified in Sch. 9.

SUPPLEMENTARY

83. Orders and regulations (general provisions)
The legislation covering extent of powers (SSA 1975, s. 166) also applies to this Act in relation to the making of orders and regulations.

84. General interpretation
Various terms and phrases are defined.

87. Extent
Only the sections (and Schedules) given in this section extend to Northern Ireland.

88. Commencement
Different days may be appointed for the commencement of the various sections in this Act.

89. Transitional
The Lord Chancellor alone, or the Lord Chancellor and the Secretary of State jointly, may make such transitional and consequential regulations as they consider necessary.

90. Citation
This Act may be cited as the Social Security Act 1986 and together with the Social Security Acts 1975 to 1985 may be cited as the Social Security Acts 1975 to 1986.

SCHEDULES

SCHEDULE 5 ADJUDICATION (Section 52)

PART II QUESTIONS FOR DETERMINATION BY THE SECRETARY OF STATE

Certain questions concerning SMP, *e.g.*, whether an employer is liable to make such payments, will be determined by the Secretary of State.

SCHEDULE 9 NORTHERN IRELAND (Section 82)

PART II TRANSFER OF FUNCTIONS RELATING TO COMMISSIONERS

2.—Certain phrases used in relation to Northern Ireland are defined.
3.—Certain functions of the DSS are transferred to the Lord Chancellor.
6.—The matters to which this paragraph applies are not "transferred matters" for the purposes of the Northern Ireland Constitution Act 1973.
7.—The normal annulment procedures apply to regulations made by the Lord Chancellor.
8.—If any enactments or instruments relating to this Part of this Schedule were made before this Schedule came into operation they will nevertheless be effective.

Income and Corporation Taxes Act 1988
1988 Chapter 1

PART XIII MISCELLANEOUS SPECIAL PROVISIONS

CHAPTER IV SUB-CONTRACTORS IN THE CONSTRUCTION INDUSTRY

559. Deductions on account of tax etc. from payments to certain sub-contractors
Where the contractor deducts tax at basic rate from payments to a sub-contractor and the deductions are more than enough to cover his income tax liability, the excess may be treated as payment of Class 4 contributions.

PART XIV PENSION SCHEMES, SOCIAL SECURITY BENEFITS, LIFE ANNUITIES, ETC.

MISCELLANEOUS

649. Minimum contributions under Social Security Act 1986
The contributions payable by the Secretary of State into an employee's personal pension scheme *i.e.,* the rebate of 2 per cent. for the first two years, (SSA 1986 Part I), is to be grossed up to account for income tax at the basic rate in force in the year of assessment for which the contributions are paid. The employee's "rebate" is to be treated as his income and will be treated as contributions paid in that year. The Inland Revenue and DSS will provide each other with sufficient information as they will need to operate this new system.

PART XIX SUPPLEMENTAL

COMMENCEMENT, SAVINGS, REPEALS, ETC.

843. Commencement
This Act applies from 1988–89.

844. Savings, transitional provisions, consequential amendments and repeals
Schedule 29 is introduced.

845. Short title
This Act may be cited as the Income and Corporation Taxes Act 1988.

SCHEDULE 29 CONSEQUENTIAL AMENDMENTS (Section 844)

The Social Security Acts

14.—Class 4 contributions are payable on enterprise allowance payments, although these are taxable under Schedule D Case VI and not Schedule D Cases I or II.

Social Security Act 1989
1989 Chapter 24

1. Amendments relating to primary class 1 contributions
From 5 October 1989 the initial primary percentage is 2 per cent. and the main primary percentage is 9 per cent. Consequential amendments are made.

2. Repayment of contributions where earnings become repayable
Regulations may provide that if earnings are repayable, contributions will be refunded.

With effect from 31 March 1990 if statutory maternity pay is repayable contributions are refunded (Social Security (Refunds) (Repayments of Contractual Maternity Pay) Regulations 1990 S.I. No. 536.

3. Abolition of Treasury supplement to contributions
The Treasury are to pay no supplement after 31 March 1989.

INFORMATION AND ADJUDICATION

21. Miscellaneous amendments relating to adjudication
Schedule 3 is introduced.

GENERAL AND SUPPLEMENTARY PROVISIONS

26. Pre-consolidation amendments
Schedule 7 is introduced. Amendments contained in Schedule 7 do not prejudice future revoking or amending orders.

31. Minor and consequential amendments, repeals and transitional provisions
Schedule 9 (repeals) is introduced and the Secretary of State's regulatory powers are extended.

33. Short title, commencement and extent
This Act may be cited as the Social Security Act 1989 and together with the Social Security Acts 1975 to 1988 may be cited as the Social Security Acts 1975 to 1989.

SCHEDULES

SCHEDULE 3 ADJUDICATION (Section 21)

Questions arising for determination by the Secretary of State

1.—Persons able to apply to the Secretary of State for determination of questions may be restricted. The Secretary of State is also enabled to make provision with respect to the formulation of questions which may arise.
3.—Certain listed authorities may refer questions of special difficulty to one or more experts, or have the assistance of one or more assessors.
4.—The procedure to be followed by an adjudication officer may be the subject of procedure regulations under SSA 1975, s. 115.

Miscellaneous

16.—Regulations made under SSA 1975 by the Lord Chancellor are subject to annulment by a resolution of either House of Parliament.

SCHEDULE 7 PRE-CONSOLIDATION AMENDMENTS (Section 26)

A number of genereal tidying-up amendments are made to prepare for the impending consolidation of the Social Security Act 1973 and subsequent Acts.

SCHEDULE 9 REPEALS (Section 31 (2))

The legislation repealed by SSA 1989 is listed.

Social Security Act 1990
1990 Chapter 27

17. Interest and penalties in respect of certain contributions
Regulations may be introduced to charge interest on late paid Class 1 contributions. Interest would run from a day not later than 14 days after the end of the tax year. Interest may be paid on Class 1 contributions repaid. The earliest date that this interest may accrue from is 12 months after the end of the relevant tax year.

Class 4 contributions attract interest under TMA 1970, s. 86 (and repayment supplement) from a date to be appointed by the Secretary of State. Formerly interest has been chargeable only under TMA 1970, s. 88.

Interest remains payable even if based on contributions which are the subject of a question to the Secretary of State.

21. Minor and consequential amendments and repeals
Sch. 6 (amendments) and Sch. 7 (repeals) are introduced.

SCHEDULE 5 SPECIAL PENALTIES IN THE CASE OF CERTAIN RETURNS (Section 17 (7))

Regulations may be introduced charging penalties under TMA 1970, s. 98A for late or incorrect contributions' returns. This will mainly apply to Employer's Annual Returns of PAYE and NIC, forms P35.

The tax penalty for the first 12 months' default is not chargeable again for NICs. Where lateness exceeds 12 months a mitigable penalty up to the NIC unpaid by the due date (14 days after the end of tax year the return relates to) is chargeable. In addition a mitigable penalty not exceeding the NIC lost due to negligent errors in the return is payable.

SCHEDULE 6 MINOR AND CONSEQUENTIAL AMENDMENTS (Section 21 (1))

Orders increasing contributions
1.—Certain amendments are made to the procedures that govern the effect of subsequent orders upon the original order.

Contributions of registered dock workers
2.—Notwithstanding the repeal of the Employment Protection (Consolidation) Act 1978, s. 145 on 3 July 1989 reduced rates of contributions will still apply to registered dock workers earnings paid or treated as paid before 6 April 1988.

Parliamentary control of regulations and orders
8.—Minor amendments are made to the conditions under which statutory instruments may be made or annulled.

Return of Class 2 contributions paid by low-earners
9.—Regulations may provide for the repayment of Class 2 contributions which could have been excepted from liability.

Tax years
11.—The definition of tax year is expanded.

SCHEDULE 7 REPEALS (Section 21 (2))

The legislation repealed by SSA 1990 is listed.

STATUTORY INSTRUMENTS

S.I. 1975 No. 556

The Social Security (Credits) Regulations 1975

Citation and commencement
1. These regulations had effect from 6 April 1975.

Interpretation
2. Various terms used in these regulations are defined.

General provisions relating to the crediting of contributions and earnings
3. Where the benefits mentioned in SSA 1975, Sch. 3 have two qualifying conditions, a credit to which a person is entitled will only count towards the second condition and it will be restricted to the amount actually required for a person to qualify for the respective benefits. Where a person is entitled to Class 1 credits for a year, they will be sufficient to complete that person's contributions record for that year. If the credit is for a week, it is calculated by taking a payment of earnings equal in amount to the lower earnings limit for that week and multiplying it by the rate set by the highest earnings bracket for primary Class 1 contributions.

For example, 1990–91:

Weekly lower earnings limit = £46
Rate of highest primary contributions = 9 %
Credit is therefore £4.14

Where a credit is due for a week which straddles two tax years, the credit will be given for the tax year in which the contribution week began.

Starting credits for the purposes of a retirement pension, a widowed mother's allowance and a widow's pension
4. For the purpose of entitlement to retirement pension, widowed mother's allowance or widow's pension, a person may be credited with the necessary Class 3 contributions to make up his other record for the year in which he reached the age of 16 and the two following years. If a person was not insured by the pre-1975 legislation, he may be allowed credits from 6 April 1974 as long as he is over 16 years of age and was in Great Britain on 6 April 1975. This is the only time such credits are given for a period before 6 April 1975.

Credits for approved training
7. Where a person was undergoing a course of training in any week, he may qualify for Class 1 credits if the course:
   (*a*) was full time; and
   (*b*) it formed part of his duties of employment; and
   (*c*) has Secretary of State approval; and
   (*d*) was not at the outset intended to be for a period exceeding 12 months or, where the person is disabled, such longer period as is reasonable in the circumstances.
   A qualifying person is defined as one who is 18 before the beginning of the tax year in which the week in question began and has paid or been credited with sufficient Class 1 or 2 contributions in one of the last three years ending in the year the course began. The level of contributions required under this provision is calculated by multiplying the lower earnings limit for the year in question by 50.

For example: 1990–91 50 × £46 = £2,300

See leaflet NI125 for further information.

Credits for invalid care allowance
7A. For any week in which a person received invalid care allowance, he may qualify for a Class 1 credit.

Credits on termination of full-time education, training or apprenticeship
8. For the purpose of entitlement to unemployment benefit or sickness benefit in the year the course finishes, a person may be credited with the necessary Class 1 contributions. This does not include persons over 21 or married women who have elected to pay reduced contributions.
   See leaflet NI125 for further information.

Credits for unemployment or incapacity for work
9. For the purpose of entitlement to any contributory benefits, a person may be allowed a Class 1 credit where he is unemployed or incapacitated. Where this involves unemployment benefit, sickness benefit or maternity allowance, the person must in the relevant year:

(1) have an earnings factor based on 13 times the weekly lower earnings limit for that year. Only Class 1 contributions actually paid will be considered for unemployment benefit and only Class 1 or 2 contributions actually paid will be considered for sickness benefit or maternity allowance; or

(2) have been for any week in that year entitled to either:
(*a*) invalidity pension;
(*b*) invalid care allowance;
(*c*) injury benefit (now abolished);
(*d*) unemployment supplement;

(3) have already satisfied the conditions, and claimed unemployment benefit, sickness benefit or maternity allowance;

(4) have been entitled to a credit under reg. 7 above;

(5) have been entitled to a credit under those provisions, but had exhausted his right to unemployment benefit or sickness benefit; this does not apply from 30 September 1989 for periods of unemployment starting on or after 1 October 1988.

The employment of a person on any day in that week may be disregarded if he was available to be employed full-time and the employment did not, together with all the other disregarded employments, engage him for more than eight hours in that week and it was not his usual main occupation or it was charitable work. If the earnings from one day's employment in any week are less than the weekly lower earnings limit, then they also may be disregarded. A week of incapacity is defined as one where each day (except Sunday, or if there is an objection, any other acceptable religious day) was:

(1) a day which was accepted for the purposes of sickness benefit or would have been accepted had a timeous claim been made; or

(2) a day on which the a person was entitled to maternity allowance or would have been entitled had a timeous claim been made; or

(3) a day which formed part of a period for which injury benefit was being paid, or would have been paid had a timeous claim been made;

(4) a day for the purpose of statutory sick pay (SSHBA 1982, s. 1).

Credits for persons approaching pensionable age
9A. A person is entitled to earnings credits for the purposes of entitlement to any benefits in any year in which he becomes 60 years old and the following four years as long as he is not absent from Great Britain for more than 182 days in any one year. This credit will only be made for a week in which a qualifying person is not liable to pay Class 2 contributions or in a week in which he is not entitled to any other credit.

Credits for jury service
9B. A person is entitled to earnings credits for the purposes of entitlement to benefits for any week during which he performs jury service if his earnings for that week are below the lower earnings limit, if he so claims by the end of the benefit year following the tax year during which he served.

Credits for maternity pay period
9C. A woman is entitled to earnings credit for the purposes of entitlement to benefits for any week during which she received statutory maternity pay, if she so claims by the end of the benefit year following the tax year during which she received that pay.

S.I. 1977 No. 622

The Social Security (Contributions) (Employment Protection) Regulations 1977

Citation, interpretation and commencement
1. These regulations came into effect on 6 April 1977.

Certain sums to be earnings
2. Where any of the payments described in Social Security (Miscellaneous Provisions) Act 1977, s. 18 (2) (*a*) or (*b*) are paid to an employed earner, they are deemed to be earnings for contribution purposes.

Modification of sections 42 and 44 of the Employment Protection Act 1975
3. Two minor modifications to these sections are made.

S.I. 1978 No. 1689

The Social Security (Categorisation of Earners) Regulations 1978

Citation, commencement and interpretation
1. These regulations came into effect on 27 December 1978. A number of terms used in these regulations are defined.

Treatment of earners in one category of earners as falling within another category and disregard of employments
2. Certain types of professions or vocations, notwithstanding they are not treated as Schedule E employments for income tax purposes, are to be treated as employed earner's employment for contribution purposes. Those affected are listed in column (A) of Sch. 1 to these regulations.

Employments treated as continuing
3. Schedule 2 to these regulations sets out when an employment is to be treated as continuing for the purposes of all contributions other than Class 4 contributions which are recovered by the Inland Revenue.

Special provisions with respect to persons declared by the High Court to be persons falling within a particular category of earners
4. Where a question of categorisation is settled in the High Court, the decision, as with all other decisions, is retrospective from the date the question first arose. However, on a point of categor-isation, the Secretary of State may prevent retrospective adjustments if he feels it is in the interests of a contributor or claimant to do so.

Persons to be treated as secondary contributors
5. In relation to employments described in Column (A) to Sch. 3 of these regulations, the secondary contributor, as described in SSA 1975, s. 4, is shown in column (B).

Revocation and general savings
6. The regulations specified in column (1) of Sch. 4 to these regulations have been revoked.

SCHEDULE 1 (Regulation 2)

PART I

The following persons are to be treated as employees and not as self-employed:
1.—Office cleaners, except those working in a private dwelling house.
2.—Agency workers if they render a personal service and are subject to supervision, direction or control and there is a continuing financial arrangement between the employed earner and the agency. There are parallel provisions for income tax in TA 1988, s. 134.

The exceptions to this rule are:
(a) any person who renders the service from his own or other premises not under the control or management of the person to whom he is supplied;
(b) actors, singers, musicians, and other entertainers; fashion, photographic and artists' mo-dels;
(c) where the agency supplied permanent staff to trades or professions and the only link is the initial introduction.
See leaflet NI192 for further information.
3.— Any person employed by his or her spouse for the purposes of the spouse's employment, whether it is self-employment or employed earner's employment.
4.—A lecturer, teacher or instructor is deemed to be an employed earner if he:
(a) gives instruction in the presence of the students, excluding the Open University; and
(b) receives earnings from the person providing the education (this therefore precludes the payment of fees directly by the individual students to the earner).
This does not apply to:
(i) an agency worker;
(ii) a part-timer, someone who has agreed, before giving the instruction, to limit the days worked to three or less in any three consecutive months; or
(iii) a person who gives public lectures.
In the majority of cases there is no dispute, but where the work is done on a part-time basis there could be a problem. Where the above provisions do not apply, the normal categorisation tests must be applied to determine whether the lecturer is self-employed. The most important case in this subject is *Argent* v. *Minister of Social Security* [1968] 3 All ER 208. The applicant was paid at an

hourly rate, was free to undertake other engagements and was not under the strict control of the person providing the education. He was therefore held to be a self-employed earner.
5.—All ministers of religion are deemed to be employed earners even where they are not under a contract of service or in an office with emoluments chargeable to tax under Schedule E. The only exception is a person whose renumeration from this employment does not consist wholly or mainly of stipend or salary.
See Press Release, 22 August 1977.

PART II

6.—Anyone who is employed as an examiner will be treated as self-employed for national insurance purposes irrespective of whether or not he is under a contract of service or in a "Schedule E office" provided that the person employing him is responsible for the administration of an examination leading to any certificate, diploma, degree or professional qualification. The duties may be as an examiner, moderator, invigilator or to set the questions for any such examinations. The only other provision is that the contract is for the work to be done within 12 months.

PART III

The following may be disregarded for contribution purposes:
7.—Where a person is employed in a dwelling-house in which both he and the employer live, the employment is not for the purposes of a trade or business carried on there by the employer, and the employer is the employee's father, mother, grandfather, stepfather, stepmother, son, daughter, grandson, grand-daughter, stepson, step-daughter, brother, sister, half-brother or half-sister.
8.—Where a person is employed by his spouse except for the purposes of the spouse's employment.
9.—Employment as a self-employed earner, including any employment described in these regulations, is to be disregarded where the person is not ordinarily employed in such employment. The meaning of ordinarily has never been defined in the courts in this context but it has for the purpose of residence. In the case of *Lysaght* v. *I.R. Comrs.* (1928) 13 TC 511 it was held to mean habitually, regularly, normally, or with a settled purpose. Basically, if a person is in regular self-employed earner's employment for 50 per cent. of his time he should be regarded as ordinarily self-employed. DHSS leaflet NI192 explains that nurses and midwives will only be regarded as not ordinarily self-employed where their work is at irregular intervals, *e.g.*, less than once a fortnight. In a case of this nature, the earnings may be disregarded for contribution purposes.
10.—Employment for the purpose of any election or referendum authorised by an Act of Parliament.
11.—Employment as a member of visiting armed forces as defined by the Visiting Forces Act 1952 and a civilian employed by such forces except any civilian who is ordinarily resident in the U.K.
12.—Employment as a member of any international headquarters or defence organisation as designated under the International Headquarters and Defence Organistations Act 1964, s. 1. The exceptions to this are serving members of the U.K. armed forces, and any officer of the Brigade of Gurkhas holding Her Majesty's commission who is not a Queen's Gurkha Officer.

SCHEDULE 2 CIRCUMSTANCES IN WHICH EMPLOYMENT IS TREATED AS CONTINUING (Regulation 3)

Self-employment is deemed to cease only when the earner is no longer ordinarily employed in such employment.

SCHEDULE 3 EMPLOYMENTS IN RESPECT OF WHICH PERSONS ARE TREATED AS SECONDARY CLASS 1 CONTRIBUTORS (Regulation 5)

Where a person is deemed to be an employee (and not self-employed), the following rules determine who is deemed to be the "employer" or secondary contributor.
1.—For an office cleaner, other than in premises used as a private dwelling-house, the secondary contributor is:
  (*a*) in the case of a person supplied by an agency, the agency;
  (*b*) in any other case (except where a company is in voluntary liquidation but is carrying on business under a liquidator) the person to whom the cleaner is contracted to do the work.
2.—For agency workers, the agency is normally the secondary contributor. If the agency is not resident, present, or with a place of business, in Great Britain, the person to whom the employee is supplied is treated as the secondary contributor.

3.—In a case of a person employed by his spouse, the spouse is the secondary contributor.

4.—Where a company is in voluntary liquidation but is carrying on business under a liquidator, the liquidator is treated as the secondary contributor.

5.—In the case of a barrister's clerk employed in chambers, the head of chambers is treated as the secondary contributor.

6.—In the case of a lecturer, teacher or instructor not supplied by an agency, the person providing the education is treated as the secondary contributor.

7.—In the case of a minister of the Church of England with no contract of service, the Church Commissioners for England is the secondary contributor.

8.—In the case of employment as a minister of religion other than (*a*) as a Church of England Minister, (*b*) under a contract of service or (*c*) mainly remunerated by a salary or stipend, the secondary contributor is:

　(*a*) where the remuneration is paid from a fund, the administrators of that fund;

　(*b*) where the remuneration is paid from more than one fund, the administrator of the fund that pays the most ministers, otherwise the administrator of the fund which first pays remuneration to the minister in any tax year.

S.I. 1979 No. 591

The Social Security (Contributions) Regulations 1979

PART I GENERAL

Citation, commencement and interpretation
1. These regulations came into force on 6 July 1979. Various terms used in these regulations are defined.

PART II ASSESSMENT OF EARNINGS-RELATED CONTRIBUTIONS

Earnings periods
2. Regulations 3 to 15 below explain earnings periods in some detail.

Earnings period for earnings normally paid or treated as paid at regular intervals
3. An earnings period is a period to which earnings paid to an employed earner are deemed to relate, irrespective of the period in which the earnings were actually earned. For an employee paid at regular intervals the earnings period is defined as follows:

　(*a*) Where an earner has only one regular pay pattern, the interval of his normal pay will be his earnings period.

　(*b*) Where an employee has two or more concurrent regular pay patterns the earnings period is the shortest of these pay intervals. For example, someone who receives a monthly salary, quarterly commission and an annual bonus has an earnings period of a month.

　(*c*) An earnings period cannot be less than one week and so where the regular pay interval is less than seven days the earnings period is defined as a week.

　(*d*) Where there is more than one regular pay interval and one is more than seven days and the other or others are less than seven days, the earnings period is a week, as long as the subsequent intervals follow on from one to the other. The first earnings period in any tax year begins on the first day of that tax year, *i.e.*, 6 April.

It is possible to avoid primary Class 1 contributions where the provisions at (*b*) above are relevant. Generally, where the greater amount of earnings are paid at the longer or longest pay intervals, this could be used to the employee's advantage. To counter this, the Secretary of State may order the longer or longest pay interval to be the deemed earnings period. Where these counter measures are enforced during a tax year, the earnings period is defined as the number of weeks from the week the change takes effect to the end of that tax year. Thereafter it will be the earnings period notified by the Secretary of State. These measures were introduced on 6 April 1983 when it was apparent that the "triple pay system", as explained at (*b*) above, was being used to avoid Class 1 contributions.

Where there is a period between the end of the last pay interval and the end of the tax year, this period, irrespective of its length, will form an earnings period. Where a payment is made after the employment has ended and it is an additional part of a payment made whilst in employment, the earnings period will be the week in which the payment is made.

Earnings period for earnings normally paid otherwise than at regular intervals and not treated as paid at regular intervals
4. Where earnings are paid at irregular intervals and do not follow any set pattern, the earnings

period is to be the length of the period for which the earnings are paid or a week, whichever is the longer. This is relevant to persons who work on projects at an hourly rate, for example employees in the film industry and casual employees. Where it is difficult to define the period to which the earnings relate, the earnings period is deemed to start on the day after the previous employment ended. Where there was no previous employment, the earnings period must be at least a week and this also applies where the payment is made before the beginning or after the end of the relevant employment.

Earnings period for sums deemed to be earnings by virtue of regulations made under section 18 of the Social Security (Miscellaneous Provisions) Act 1977
5. In the case of maternity pay and payments under the employment protection legislation, the earnings period is the longer of a week or the period to which the payment relates.

Earnings period for earnings to be aggregated where the earnings periods for those earnings otherwise would be of different lengths
5A. This regulation is relevant where there are two or more employments which fall to be aggregated. Where there is a mixture of contracted-out and non-contracted-out employments, the designated earnings period is taken to be the one relating to the contracted-out employment. Where there is more than one contracted-out employment, the earnings period is the shorter or shortest earnings period. If the aggregated employments are all contracted-out or all non-contracted out, the designated earnings period is the shorter or shortest of the earnings periods of the relevant employments.

As to the aggregation rules see SSA 1975, Sch. 1.

Treatment of earnings paid otherwise than at regular intervals
6. Where a payment which is normally made at regular intervals is made on some other date, it is deemed to be made on the date it would normally have been paid. Payments made at irregular intervals but for regular periods are deemed to be made on the last day of each regular period. This is not the case, however, where the payments fall into the wrong tax year.

Earnings periods for directors
6A. Since 6 April 1983 a director, in all cases, has an earnings period of a year. If he is appointed a director during the year, the earnings period is the number of weeks from appointment to the end of the tax year. If he ceases to be a director during the tax year, the earnings period remains a year. Where two or more employments which fall to be aggregated include at least one directorship, the common earnings period is deemed to be the longer or longest earnings period of the relevant employments. If a payment relating to the period in which he was a director is made to an ex-director in a tax year following the year in which he resigned, the director rules apply to that tax year. For example, if a director resigns during the year ended 5 April 1990 but is paid a bonus on 6 September 1990, his earnings period for 1990–91 will be a year.

Special rules apply to the 1989–90 annual earnings period, because of the introduction of the 2 per cent. primary contributions band on 5 October 1989. The benefit of the band is effectively spread over the whole of the tax year by introducing composite rates: Social Security (Contributions) (Transitional and Consequential Provisions) Regulations 1989 (S.I. 1989 No. 1677).

Earnings period for statutory maternity pay and statutory sick pay paid by the Secretary of State
6B. A week is defined as a period of seven days beginning with midnight between Saturday and Sunday, or such other period as may be prescribed in particular cases.

For the purposes of calculating Class 1 contributions a payment of SMP should not be aggregated with any other earnings and the earnings period is a week.

The earnings period for SSP is the longer of the period to which it relates or a week.

Lower and upper earnings limits
7. The lower and upper earnings limits for the year beginning 6 April 1990 are £46 and £350 respectively. These figures are always given in terms of a week.

Equivalent amounts
8. Where the earnings period is other than a week, the upper and lower limits are replaced by respective equivalents:
(*a*) Where the earnings period is a multiple of a week, the weekly limit is to be multiplied by that multiple. For example, for an earnings period of four weeks the equivalent of the 1990–91 figures in reg. 7 are £184 and £1,400 respectively.
(*b*) Where the earnings period is one month, the weekly period is multiplied by $4^{1}/_{3}$ rounded up to the next whole pound. For example for 1990–91, the respective figures are £200 and £1,517.
(*c*) Where the earnings period is a multiple of a month, the figure in (*b*) is multiplied by that multiple.

(*d*) In any other case, the weekly amount is to be divided by seven and multiplied by the number of days in the earnings period calculated to the nearest penny.

Equivalent earnings brackets for earners paid otherwise than weekly
8A. Where the earnings period is other than a week, the lower weekly secondary brackets as defined by SAA 1975, s. 4 (6E) are replaced by equivalent amounts calculated in the same manner as in reg. 8 (2) (*a*) to (*d*).

The higher weekly amount is set at one penny less than the equivalant lower amount of the next succeeding bracket. For example, in 1990–91 the lower weekly amount in bracket 2 is £80. If the earnings period is four-weekly the equivalent figure is £320 and the equivalent higher limit for bracket 1 is one penny less, £319.99.

Calculation of earnings-related contributions
9. Class 1 contributions may be calculated in two ways. The first is to calculate the primary and secondary contributions by using the standard non-contracted-out rate and round each figure to the nearest penny. This method is not commonly used.

The other method is to use the tables provided by the DSS. The two main volumes are CF391 for non-contracted-out employees and CF392 for contracted-out employees.

The tables produced are as follows:
Table A—Non-contracted-out standard rate contributions
Table B—Non-contracted-out reduced rate contributions
Table C—Contracted-out and non-contracted-out employer only contributions
Table D—Contracted-out standard rate contributions
Table E—Contracted-out reduced rate contributions
The "Table letter" referred to in the PAYE and DSS guidelines relates to A to E above and designates the rate to be used in calculating the employee's and employer's contributions.

Unless the Secretary of State agrees to the contrary, all contributions in the tax year must be calculated by using one or other of these methods. All the necessary tables, instruction cards and leaflets are supplied by the Revenue in respect of PAYE schemes and are also available from local DSS offices.

General provisions as to aggregation
10. For the purposes of earnings aggregation the reference in SSA 1975, Sch. 1, para. 1 to "a week" should be read as "earnings period".

Aggregation of earnings paid in respect of separate employed earner's employments under the same employer
11. Where earnings from two or more employments are to be aggregated but this creates practical problems because the earnings are paid from separate points, the aggregation rules may be disregarded and the contributions calculated on the earnings paid from each pay point.

Aggregation of earnings paid in respect of different employed earner's employments by different persons and apportionment of contribution liability
12. When an employed earner has more than one employment and is paid:
(*a*) by different secondary contributors (normally employer) who carry on business in association with each other; or
(*b*) by different employers, one of whom is deemed to be a secondary contributor in accordance with the Social Security (Categorisation of Earners) Regulations 1978 (S.I. 1978 No. 1689), Sch. 3; or
(*c*) by different employers where some other person is deemed to be a secondary contributor in accordance with S.I. 1978 No. 1689, Sch. 3,
the earnings shall be aggregated for Class 1 contributions purposes unless, in a case within (*a*), it is impracticable to do so.

Where the earnings are aggregated, the secondary contributors apportion their liability to secondary Class 1 contributions as they agree or in proportion to the earnings that they pay.

Aggregation of earnings paid after pensionable age
12A. A payment within reg. 20 is not to be aggregated.

Apportionment of single payment of earnings in respect of different employed earner's employments by different secondary contributors
13. When earnings are to be aggregated, the secondary contribution liability is dealt with as follows:
(*a*) where the different empoyers carry on business in association, the employer actually making the payment will be liable to the secondary contribution;
(*b*) where the employers do not carry on the business in association, the liability is to be apportioned between the employers in proportion to their payments.

Change of earnings period
14. Where the length of an employed earner's regular pay interval is changed, for example from weekly to monthly, and the new earnings period is longer than the old, this regulation ensures that contributions are not collected from the same earnings already paid in the old earnings period. The DSS instructions, given in leaflet NI269, are to calculate the contributions due in the new earnings period and deduct any paid in the old period. This does not operate where the interval does not alter but simply the actual pay day is changed.

Holiday payments
15. Where an employed earner is paid holiday pay, except where it is part of his entitlement on termination of his employment, the holiday pay shall be treated as pay in the weeks it would normally have been paid, or the earnings period may be defined as the length period to which the holiday pay relates.
See DSS leaflet NI269, paras. 66–72 which explains these methods, and certain other aspects of holiday pay.

Joint employment of husband and wife
16. Where a husband and wife are jointly employed are paid a joint income, the earnings are to be apportioned between them for contribution purposes as they are for income tax purposes, or on any basis approved by the Secretary of State.

Annual maximum
17. The annual maximum is the highest level of Class 1 or 2 contributions payable by an earner. The limit is based on $53 \times$ the primary Class 1 contributions at the standard rate.
The annual maximum for 1990–91 is £1,498.84 as shown below:

53 weeks × £46 at 2%	=	48.76
53 weeks × (£350 − £46) at 9%	=	1,450.08
		£1,498.84

Maximum standard rate means an amount equal to the weekly upper earnings limit.
Where contributions in one or all the employments are paid at a rate below the standard rate, the contributions are treated as having been paid at the standard rate. For example, contracted-out contributions at a rate of 7 per cent. (9 per cent. less 2 per cent.) are "grossed up" to the standard equivalent. Thus, if the annual contributions at the contracted-out rate of 7 per cent. are £809.94, the equivalent for annual maximum purposes is $9/7 \times £809.94 = £1,041.35$.
The rates of 5 per cent. and 7 per cent. effective from 6 October 1985 until 4 October 1989 and the 2 per cent. rate effective from 5 October 1989 are in fact standard rates and no "grossing up" is required to contributions calculated at those rates.

Payments to directors to be treated as earnings
17A. A payment made in advance or on account of earnings which would be chargeable to contributions may be regarded as earnings for contribution purposes.

Manner of making sickness payments treated as remuneration
17B. A payment of sickness pay is to be treated as remuneration derived from the person who is the secondary contributor for the employment (normally the employer). There is an exception where another person makes the sickness payment, has agreed to be secondary contributor and the necessary arrangements have been made regarding intermediate employers (see Sch. 1, para. 3 (3) (*a*)).

Calculation of earnings
18. Class 1 contributions are calculated on gross earnings from the employment or employments concerned. This means no deductions are allowed such as personal allowances for income tax. The most frequent error is the deduction of superannuation contributions where an employer has a contributory pension scheme and operates a "net pay arrangement". Special care should be taken to ensure that the gross pay before deduction of superannuation contribution is used for calculating Class 1 contributions.
See Inland Revenue booklet P7 (1989), *Employer's Guide to PAYE*, para. F82.
Lump sum payments on cessation of employment (*e.g.*, ex-gratia or compensation for loss of office) are earnings for contribution purposes if they are paid under the terms of the employee's contract. The provision which charges certain termination payments to income tax (TA 1988, s. 148) does not apply to NIC.
Where arrears of pay, (for example a backdated pay rise) arise they are treated as earnings in the week they are paid, not the weeks to which they relate.
See DSS leaflet NI269, para. 83.

Payments to be disregarded

19. A number of types of payment may be disregarded for the purposes of calculating earnings-related contribution liability. This regulation has always been important but, since the abolition of the upper limit for employer's contributions on 6 October 1985, a number of devices have been used to reduce the employer's contribution burden. The types of payment are explained below as well as the more recent contribution-saving devices.

(*a*) Where a payment on account has already been included in earnings for contribution purposes it is disregarded at the time of payment.

(*b*) Where holiday pay is paid by an employer from a central fund to which a number of employers contribute but over which they have neither management nor control, the payment is disregarded for contribution purposes. It should be noted that the payments are however taxable under PAYE.

(*c*) Where an employee receives a gratuity, offering or tip this is regarded for contribution purposes only if as the sum was previously paid to the employer and allocated by the employer to the employee. Payments made to employees through a tronc system are disregarded for contribution purposes unless the employer allocates and distributes the tips or gratuities among the employees. However, although the tronc payments are exempt for contribution purposes, they are taxable under PAYE irrespective of who actually distributes the payments. Where the employer initially collects the "tip" in the form of a service charge it must be included as earnings for contribution purposes when paid to the employee.

See DSS manual NI 269, paras. 129–132 for further information and Press Release 7 August 1980.

(*d*) Any payment in kind, other than outlined in reg. 19C below (securities etc), or by way of provision of board or lodging is disregarded for contribution purposes. This is an important principle when remuneration packages for senior employees are being designed. Although the majority of payments in kind do not avoid income tax they may be useful in delaying the employee's tax payment where PAYE does not apply.

From the Class 1 contribution viewpoint payments in kind can offer substantial savings where goods or services are provided instead of cash. It should be noted that cash payments in lieu of payments in kind are not exempt from Class 1 contributions.

One important principle is that the employer must provide the benefit and not simply settle the employee's liability. Another consideration is that the goods or services must not be capable of being converted into cash by mere surrender. The benefit is exempt if the employee has to sell it to convert it into cash.

Where the cost of the goods or services provided by the employer includes an element of VAT, that element is disregarded.

(*e*) Revoked.

(*f*) Revoked.

(*g*) Any payment made by way of a pension is disregarded for contribution purposes.

(*h*) Any payment to a minister of religion which does not form part of his salary or stipend is disregarded. This may include baptism, marriage or funeral fees.

See Press Release, 22 August 1977.

(*i*) Certain travelling allowances to disabled persons are disregarded.

(*j*) A payment by way of, or derived from, shares appropriated under a profit sharing scheme to which TA 1988, ss. 186, 187, Schs. 9, 10 applies is disregarded.

(*k*) An employer's contributions to approved personal pension arrangements made by his employee.

See Press Release, 8 December 1978.

Where an employee receives a sickness payment from a fund into which he contributed, the part of the payment attributable to his contributions is not treated as earnings.

Payments in respect of redundancy or in lieu of notice are also disregarded.

Where an employee is entitled to receive sickness benefit, invalidity benefit or maternity allowance but has obtained approval from the DSS not to claim the benefit but to receive his normal pay, the sum relating to the amount of the benefit due to the employee is disregarded.

Any specific and distinct payment of, or contribution towards, expenses actually incurred by an employed earner in carrying out his employment is disregarded. Where an employer pays a round sum or flat rate allowance to his employee this is liable to Class 1 contributions. This can be important where an employer pays an additional round sum to an employee working abroad. If the allowance is calculated by reference to "specific and distinct" expenses relating to that individual's additional costs of living abroad, *e.g.*, rent, school fees, travel or removal expenses, he may be able to pay them under this regulation without attracting Class 1 contributions liability.

Certain payments by trustees to be disregarded

19A. Certain payments when made by trustees before 6 April 1990 may be disregarded for the purposes of calculating earnings-related contributions. The principal conditions for the exclusion of such payments are:

(*a*) the trust was created before 6 April 1985, or

(*b*) if it was created after that date, it took effect immediately on termination of a trust created before that date, provided that the person now receiving payment was a beneficiary under the former trust or would have been a beneficiary had he held, at the time of the former trust, the employment in respect of which the trust is made.

Payments to directors which are to be disregarded
19B. Certain payments made to directors may be disregarded for the purposes of calculating earnings-related contributions. The conditions for the exclusion are set out. They are broadly in line with the equivalent income tax exception in TA 1988, s. 203 (PAYE).

Payments in kind not to be disregarded
19C. From 12 May 1988, certain payments which confer a beneficial interest in a security or derivative instrument may no longer be disregarded for the purposes of calculating earnings-related contributions. "Security" and "derivative instrument" are defined. These include:
(*a*) securities such as debenture stock, bonds, loan stock (including convertible loan stock), and certificates of deposit, whether any of these are issued by a government, local or public authority, company or individual (*i.e.* all debt instruments); and
(*b*) derivative instruments such as warrants, options and futures relating to debt instruments. Among the derivative instruments covered are unauthorised unit trusts holding debt instruments or their derivatives but *not* authorised untit trusts.
Where a payment in kind is not disregarded by virtue of this regulation, the amount of earnings is to be calculated or estimated by the price the security or instrument might reasonably be expected to fetch if sold in the open market on the day on which it is conferred.

Liability for Class 1 contributions in respect of earnings normally paid after pensionable age
20. Where an employee receives a payment before he reaches pensionable age but the payment would normally fall to be paid in the following tax year, the payment may be excepted for the purposes of calculating primary Class 1 contributions.

Liability for Class 1 contributions of persons over pensionable age
20A. Where an employee who has attained pensionable age receives a payment which relates to a period before he reached that age it is not to be excepted for Class 1 contributions liability.

Abnormal pay practices
21. This regulation is part of the anti-avoidance legislation provided for by SSA 1975, Sch. 1, para. 4 (*c*). It has restricted powers of retrospection, limiting any decision by the Secretary of State to contributions on payments made up to one tax year before the beginning of the tax year in which the decision is made. This regulation relates to an "abnormal pay practice". It applies where an employer or employee change the way in which earnings are paid to avoid the payment of contributions. If the Secretary of State has reason to believe there is or was an abnormal pay practice he may act on it as if a question had been raised for his determination.

Practices avoiding or reducing liability
22. This is another anti-avoidance regulation which may be used when the Secretary of State is satisfied that liability to contributions is being avoided or reduced by means of irregular or unequal payments. It is far easier for the Secretary of State to implement this power, rather than reg. 21, because it does not require the determination of a question. It simply requires the Secretary of State to be satisfied that there is the possibility of avoidance and it is not necessary for the avoidance to be wilful on part of the contributor. The counter measure will simply take the form of the DSS notifying the contributor of a change in the earnings period which will stop the avoidance. Any action of this nature is not retrospective.

PART III EXCEPTION FROM LIABILITY FOR CLASS 2 CONTRIBUTIONS, AND PROVISIONS RELATING TO CLASS 3 CONTRIBUTIONS, APPROPRIATION, REALLOCATION AND REFUND OF CONTRIBUTIONS (OTHER THAN CLASS 4 CONTRIBUTIONS)

Exception from liability for Class 2 contributions
23. A self-employed earner is excepted from Class 2 contributions liability if in any contribution week he is:
(*a*) in receipt of sickness benefit or invalidity benefit in respect of one whole week; or
(*b*) incapable of work which normally means he qualifies for sickness benefit or statutory sick pay; or
(*c*) in receipt of maternity allowance; or
(*d*) undergoing imprisonment or detention in legal custody; or
(*e*) in any part of the week in question in receipt of unemployment supplement or invalid care allowance.

A contribution week consists of seven days starting at midnight between Saturday and Sunday but does not include Sunday, or some other day where Sunday is a normal working day.

Applications for, and duration and cancellation of, certificates of exception
24. A self-employed earner may apply for exception from Class 2 contributions liability on the grounds that his income is below the small earnings limit (see SSA 1975, s. 7 (5)). The application must be made to the DSS on the prescribed form (Form CF 10) and should be accompanied by accounts and tax assessments in respect of the claim.

In the case of a new self-employed earner it is sufficient for him to claim without the necessary evidence because this would not normally be available until the time limit had expired. In this case the claimant may simply sign a statement to the effect that his earnings will be within the small earnings exception limit.

The DSS will issue a statement showing the effective date of exception; the statement expires at the end of the tax year concerned. The holder of an exemption certificate is required to produce it whenever requested, and may have it cancelled at any time.

See DSS leaflet NI 27A which contains a form CF 10 and gives further information.

Earnings for the purposes of certificates of exception
25. When any self-employed earner applies for exception the DSS may consider two periods of earnings:
(*a*) the earnings in the preceding year if they are below the small earnings exception limit and there is no reason to expect a change in the current year; or
(*b*) the earnings in the current year if they are expected to be below the specified limit.

Certificates of exception—exception from liability for, and entitlement to pay, Class 2 contributions
26. A self-employed earner may pay Class 2 contributions even where he holds an exception certificate.

Class 3 contributions
27. A person may only pay Class 3 contributions if it is for the purpose of satisfying any of the conditions of entitlement to contributory state benefits. The due date of a Class 3 contribution is the end of the tax year in which it is paid. Although the regulations relating to collection of late paid contributions apply they cannot strictly be imposed because Class 3 contributions are voluntary.

Precluded Class 3 contributions
28. No person is entitled to pay Class 3 contributions:
(*a*) if he qualifies for a credit in any event; or
(*b*) in any tax year if the aggregate of his earnings factors derived from contributions paid or credited is less than 25 times the lower earnings limit and either the contributor is time-barred from making further contributions or he has already paid Class 3 contributions but has applied for their return (see reg. 34); or
(*c*) in any tax year if the aggregate of his earnings factors derived from contributions paid or credited is more than 25 times the lower earnings limit but less than the qualifying earnings factor and as in (*b*) either a time-bar on repayment applies; or
(*d*) if it causes the aggregate of his earnings factors derived from contributions paid or credited to exceed the qualifying earnings factor by an amount which is half or more than half that year's weekly lower earnings limit; or
(*e*) in the year in which he attains pensionable age or any subsequent year; or
(*f*) in the years in which he attains the age of 17 or 18 if in an earlier year he has satisfied the first contribution condition for retirement pension or widow's pension or widowed mother's allowance (see S.I. 1975, No. 556, reg. 4).

The provisions in (*a*), (*b*) and (*c*) above may be disregarded if the payment of Class 3 contributions enables a person to satisfy (i) the first contribution condition for retirement pension, widow's pension or widowed mother's allowance or (ii) the only contribution condition for widow's payment or (iii) for certain apprentices, etc. the second contribution condition for unemployment benefit or sickness benefit. In cases (i) and (ii) he must not have satisfied the conditions at the beginning of the year.

"Credited" means credited for the purposes of retirement or widow's pension or widowed mother's allowance only. For the definition of "qualifying earnings factor" see SSPA 1975, s. 5 (3).

Class 3 contributions not paid within prescribed periods
29. If there is any failure to pay Class 3 contributions which a person is entitled to pay but it can be shown this failure was due to ignorance and error rather than a failure to exercise due care and diligence, the contribution may be paid within such further period as the Secretary of State may direct.

Appropriation of Class 3 contributions
30. Any Class 3 contributions paid in any one year may be appropriated to the earnings factor of

another year if such contributions are payable in respect of that other year. This can be done either by the contributor applying to the DSS or automatically by the Secretary of State with the consent of the contributor.

Disposal of contributions not properly paid
31. If Class 1, 2 or 3 contributions have been paid but were of the wrong class (*e.g.*, Class 2 were paid but Class 1 were due to be paid), or at the wrong rate or of the wrong amount they may be treated as paid on account of the correct contributions due.

Return of contributions
32. Subject to reg. 31 above and reg. 35 below, where Class 1, 2 or 3 contributions have been paid in error or exceed the annual maximum, the Secretary of State may grant a repayment if a request is made in writing. Where the claim for repayment relates to an error this must have been made at the time of payment and relate to some present or past matter.

The order of priority in which contributions exceeding the annual maximum are repaid is:
(*a*) primary Class 1 contributions at the reduced rate,
(*b*) Class 2 contributions,
(*c*) primary Class 1 contributions at the standard rate,
(*d*) any amount of primary Class 1 contributions at the percentages applying to contracted-out rates.

Where the employee has chosen a personal pension scheme to which the Secretary of State pays minimum contributions, in the order of priority of repayment, (*c*) and (*d*) are reversed.

Unlike the Revenue who are supposed to check every individual's end of year details to ensure no overpayment has arisen, the DSS place the onus entirely on the contributor to claim a refund.

Where a secondary contributor has not yet deducted the primary Class 1 contributions for the employee's earnings he may keep any refund of primary Class 1 contributions. If they have been deducted they should be returned to the employee unless he gives his consent in writing that the employer may receive the contributions refund.

An application for refund must be made in the form and manner prescribed by the Secretary of State. A claim for repayment of Class 1 contributions is made on Form CF28F and should be accompanied by a certificate of pay and tax on Form P60. A claim for repayment of other classes of contributions should be made on Form CF28E. The claim must be lodged within six years of the end of the year in which the contribution was paid, or such longer time as the Secretary of State may allow.

Return of Class 1 contributions paid at the non-contracted-out rate instead of at the contracted-out rate
33. The Secretary of State will also grant a repayment of contributions where the employer pays a sum on account at the non-contracted-out rate but the employment becomes contracted-out. The repayment will be the difference between the non-contracted-out rates paid and the amounts actually due. Any primary contributions will be repaid to the contributor unless he gives his permission for the employer to receive them. The time limit for making a claim in these circumstances is six years from the end of the year in which the contracted-out certificate was issued.

Return of precluded Class 3 contributions
34. Any Class 3 contributions paid by a contributor who was not entitled to pay them (see reg. 28) may be refunded as long as the application is made in the correct manner.

Calculation of return of contributions
35. If overpaid contributions are to be set against the correct liability in accordance with reg. 31, the DSS will advise the contributor of this fact in the repayment calculation. The Secretary of State must make deductions from the refund in respect of any contributory benefits paid in relation to the contributions made in error and minimum contributions and payments made by the Secretary of State under SSA 1986, ss. 1, 7.

Crediting of Class 3 contributions
36. Where a contributor's earnings factor has been derived from any or all of the contribution Classes 1, 2 or 3 and the factor falls short of a figure which is 52 times that year's lower earnings limit for Class 1 contributions by an amount which is equal to or less than half that year's lower earnings limit, he shall be credited with a Class 3 contribution for that year.

Reallocation of contributions for benefit purposes
37. Where earnings are paid at regular intervals, contributions are deducted when the earnings are paid and consequently the contributions are related to the tax year in which they are deducted. Contributions cannot therefore be treated as having been paid in any other tax year. If, however, the earnings are paid at irregular intervals but treated as regular payments by virtue of reg. 6, and the period to which the earnings relate straddles two tax years, the earner may apply to the

Secretary of State to have the contributions which were deducted in one tax year to be related to the other year for the purposes of entitlement to state benefits.

PART IV LATE PAID AND UNPAID CONTRIBUTIONS

Treatment for purpose of contributory benefit of late paid contributions under the Act
38. Any Class 2 or Class 3 contributions paid after the due date but within the next six years are deemed paid on the due date for the purposes of benefit entitlement. Class 3 contributions can be paid even later by a contributor who was undergoing a period of full-time education, apprenticeship, training, imprisonment or detention in legal custody.

Late-paid contributions can satisfy the second condition for entitlement to unemployment benefit, sickness benefit or maternity allowance.

Treatment for purpose of contributory benefit of contributions paid by virtue of regulation 27 (4)
38A. Where a person has paid Class 3 contributions late in respect of a year during any part of which a temporary allowance under the Job Release Act 1977 was payable, any contribution can be backdated to the year which it was paid.

Treatment for the purpose of any contributory benefit of late paid or unpaid primary Class 1 contributions where there was no consent, connivance or negligence by the primary contributor
39. Where Class 1 contributions are paid late by the secondary contributor but the Secretary of State is satisfied this delay was not with the consent or connivance of the primary contributor they shall be treated for contribution purposes as having been paid on the date the earnings were paid.

Voluntary Class 2 contributions not paid within permitted period
40. Where a person is entitled, but not liable, to pay Class 2 contributions but fails to pay them on the due date and this is, in the Secretary of State's opinion, not due to any lack of due care and diligence on the part of the contributor, he may be allowed a further period in which to make the payment.

Treatment for the purpose of any contributory benefit of contributions under the Act paid late through ignorance or error
41. If Class 1, 2 or 3 contributions are paid after their due date and this is due to ignorance or error on the part of the contributor, the Secretary of State may allow them to be treated as paid on any earlier date which he considers appropriate in the circumstances.

Treatment for the purpose of any contributory benefit of contributions paid under an arrangement
42. Where Class 1 or 2 contributions have been paid late under a prior arrangement with the Secretary of State they may be treated as paid on the due date for the purposes of entitlement to benefits.

Payment of contributions after death of contributor
43. If a person dies, any contributions which, immediately before his death he was entitled but not liable to pay, may be paid notwithstanding his death subject to any existing time limit.

Class 2 and Class 3 contributions paid after 5 April 1985 in respect of a period before 6 April 1983
43A. Any late paid Class 2 and 3 contributions payable in respect of a week falling in a year before 6 April 1983 is payable at the rate which was relevant on its due date.

Class 2 contributions paid late in accordance with a payment undertaking
43B. The Secretary of State may accept instalments in the settlement of Class 2 arrears and this is known as an "undertaking". The contributions are payable at the rate relevant when the contributor entered into the undertaking.

Class 2 and Class 3 contributions paid within a month from notification of amount of arrears
43C. Where the Secretary of State notifies the contributor during the last month of a tax year of arrears of Class 2 or 3 contributions due for that year they may be paid at the rate set for that year as long as they are paid within one calendar month of the date of the notification.

Class 2 and Class 3 contributions paid late through ignorance or error
43D. Where the Secretary of State accepts that due to ignorance or error a contributor has failed to pay Class 2 or Class 3 contributions other than Class 2 voluntary contributions, they may be paid at the rate applicable in the year to which they relate.

PART V COLLECTION OF CONTRIBUTIONS (OTHER THAN CLASS 4 CONTRIBUTIONS) AND RELATED MATTERS

Application for allocation of national insurance number
44. Any person who is resident or present in Great Britain, is over the age of 16 years and is an

employee or self-employed person or who wishes to pay voluntary contributions must, unless he already has a national insurance number, apply to the DSS for one on Form CF8 which is available from any local DSS Office. The DSS normally issue a number to a person within the year leading up to his 16th birthday.

A national insurance number is always in the same form, two letters, six numbers and another letter, *e.g.*, XY123456A.

Notification of national insurance numbers to secondary contributors
45. Every employee must supply his number to his employer or other person liable for secondary earnings-related contributions.

Collection and recovery of earnings-related contributions
46. The employer, or other person deemed to be the employer, is liable for earnings-related contributions in the same way as income tax under the PAYE scheme (Sch. 1 sets out the applicable parts of the Income Tax (Employments) Regulations 1973 (SI 1973 No. 334) made under TA 1970, s. 204 [now TA 1988, s. 203]).

Direct collection and recovery of earnings-related contributions
47. The Secretary of State may provide for the recovery of Class 1 contributions in any other manner he feels necessary, irrespective of the PAYE provisions in the previous regulations.

Special provisions relating to primary Class 1 contributions
48. The Secretary of State may arrange with the employee that he pays the primary Class 1 contributions liability directly. The DSS will notify the employee in writing of the arrangement and the period to which it relates. A notice is also issued to the employers advising him not to deduct Class 1 contributions from the employee's earnings. However, this does not alter the employer's liability to secondary contributions and he should continue to pay them in the normal way. The notice is sent to the employer on Form RD950 and to the employee on Form RD951.

Exception in relation to earnings to which regulation 48 applies
49. Where an employee has more than one employed earner's employment and at least one falls within reg. 48 and at least one does not, he may apply to the DSS to have payment of Class 1 contributions deferred. The application is made on Form CF379 to the Class 4 Group at DSS Headquarters in Newcastle upon Tyne. The employee cannot choose to which employment or employments the deferment should relate; the DSS alone decide. The application should be made before or as soon as possible after the beginning of the tax year to which it relates. In practice the DSS will consider any application which reaches them before 14 February in the relevant tax year. Deferment will only be granted where the employee will pay contributions, in an employment to which the deferment is not to apply, equal to at least 52 weekly or 12 monthly Class 1 contributions at the upper earnings limit. DSS leaflet NP28 gives further information.

Special provisions relating to culpable primary contributors and to secondary contributors or, as the case may be, employers exempted by treaty etc., from enforcement of the Act or from liability under it.
50. Where an employer fails to pay the employee's primary contributions, but this is due to an act or default on the part of the employee and not any negligence on the part of the employer, then the employee will be liable to the contributions. This is also the case where there is no secondary contributor resident or present in the U.K.; but the employer, although not liable to the secondary contributions, may pay them if he so wishes.

Provisions as to application for, and custody of, contribution cards etc.
51. Every person who is liable to pay Class 2 contributions, or is entitled to pay and so wishes, must apply for a contribution card (CF1). In practice this means making an application to the DSS on Form CF11. The applicant is responsible for the custody of the card, which must not be defaced, destroyed or tampered with in any way. The card must be produced for inspection on request at any reasonable time. When the card is retained by an inspector he must give a receipt for it.

Issue and currency of contribution cards
52. When the period covered by a contribution card (usually one tax year) expires it must be returned to the local DSS Office within six days (or such longer period as the Secretary of State allows). A new card, if appropriate, will be issued free of charge.

Disposal of contribution cards
53. A card must be returned to the local DSS Office as soon as the contributor is no longer liable or entitled to make contributions.

Method of, and time for, payment of Class 2 and Class 3 contributions etc.
54. Every Class 2 or Class 3 contribution must be paid on or before the last day of the contribution

week to which it relates. Payment is made by affixing of a stamp to the card or by direct debit to a bank account.

Deduction of contributions from pensions etc.—prescribed enactments and instruments under which payable
55. Liability to Class 2 or Class 3 contributions may also be discharged by consenting to a deduction to be made from any disablement pension or a pension or allowance payable under the Supplementary Benefits Act 1976, Sch. 1, para. 23 (5) and (6).

Contribution cards not to be assigned, defaced, etc.
56. A contribution card must not be sold, transferred, defaced or destroyed. Any person who removes a stamp which has been affixed to a card is considered to have defaced that card.

PART VI CONTRIBUTION STAMPS

Adaptation of Enactments
57. The Stamp Duties Act 1891 and Post Office Act 1953, as adapted in Sch. 2, apply to the issue of stamps for the purposes of these provisions.

PART VII CLASS 4 CONTRIBUTIONS

Exception from Class 4 liability of persons over pensionable age and persons not resident in the United Kingdom
58. Any person who is over pensionable age at the beginning of the year of assessment or not resident in the U.K. in the year of assessment is excepted from Class 4 contributions liability.

Exception of divers and diving supervisors from liability for Class 4 contributions
59. Any person who is employed as a diver or diving supervisor (see FA 1978, s. 29) is excepted from liability to Class 4 contributions on so much of his profits as relate to that employment.
   See Press Release, 8 December 1978.

Exception of persons under the age of 16 from liability for Class 4 contributions
60. Any person who is under 16 years old at the beginning of the year of assessment may apply for exception from Class 4 liability before the beginning of the year of assessment; the Secretary of State may accept an application after that date but before the contributions for that year become due and payable. The application should be made on Form RD901. Where the application is accepted the Secretary of State will issue a certificate of exception to the Revenue and they will not collect any contributions from the earner. This age exception should be claimed in all relevant cases because Class 4 contributions do not count towards a claimant's entitlement to contributory state benefits.

Exception from Class 4 liability by reference to Class 1 contributions paid on earnings chargeable to income tax under Schedule D
61. There are a number of trades, professions and vocations where the earner is liable to Class 1 (employed) contributions although taxed as self-employed under Schedule D Case I or II. Common examples are found within the film industry. In such cases the earner may apply for exception from Class 4 liability. A person may have difficulty in making a timeous claim for exception from liability due to the different periods involved: the current income tax year for Class 1 on earnings and a future tax year for Class 4 on Schedule D profits. Consequently, it is simpler to make a claim for deferment of Class 4 contributions or claim a repayment.

Deferment of Class 4 liability where such liability is in doubt
62. Where there is any doubt as to the extent, if any, of the contribution liability in any year, the Secretary of State may defer payment until a later date.

Application for deferment of Class 4 liability
63. An application for deferment of liability must be made before the beginning of the year of assessment or before such later date as the Secretary of State and Revenue may allow. In practice, where the Revenue issue a number of Schedule D notices of assessment at one time, the DSS may consider issuing a certificate of deferment for all years. This avoids the earner paying the Class 4 contributions and then claiming a refund.

General conditions for application for, and issue of, certificates of exception and deferment
64. An application for deferment should be made to the DSS Class 4 Group in Newcastle upon

Tyne on Form CF359 which is available from any local DSS Office. The application must include all the information the Secretary of State requires and if he subsequently discovers any of the information was erroneous he may revoke the certificate and order that the Class 4 contributions which were due for that year be paid as normal.

Revocation of certificates of exception and deferment
65. Where the Secretary of State has revoked a certificate of exception or deferment it is he and not the Revenue who is responsible for the calculation and collection of the Class 4 contribution liability.

Calculation of liability for, and recovery of, Class 4 contributions after issue of certificate of deferment
66. The Secretary of State may ask the Revenue for details of an earner's profits or gains for Class 4 contributions liability purposes of confirmation that they exceed the upper limit to enable him to calculate the Class 4 liability. The Revenue will not divulge this information unless profits or gains have become final and conclusive; or it has been agreed between the Revenue and the earner, or it is clearly the case that the profits or gains will exceed the upper limit. Once the liability has been calculated the Secretary of State will issue a notice of liability to the earner who must pay the liability within 28 days of receipt of the notice unless he appeals to, or raises a question with, the Secretary of State in relation to those contributions. If the relevant assessment is subsequently amended by the Revenue and this affects the liability, the Revenue will notify the Secretary of State who will notify the earner accordingly.

Annual maximum of Class 4 contribution due under section 9 (1) of the Act
67. Any person's liability to a mixture of Class 1 and 2 contributions is limited as described in reg. 17. This, however, does not allow for liability to Class 4 contributions. The limit for Class 4 contributions in cases where a person is also liable to Class 1 or Class 2 contributions or both in any year is the sum when added to the Class 1 or Class 2 contributions payable in the year, which equals the sum of the maximum Class 4 contributions and 53 times the Class 2 contributions payable for that year. For 1985–86 only the Class 2 figure was taken as £218.

For 1990–91 this figure is:

Class 4 £18,200 − £5,450 = £12,750 at 6.3%	=	£803.25
Class 2 £4.55 × 53 weeks		241.15
		£1,044.40

Where late paid Class 2 contributions are payable at a different rate it is that rate which should be used in this calculation. As long as maximum contributions are due under Class 1 and 2 there cannot be a further Class 4 liability.

Disposal of Class 4 contributions under section 9 (1) of the Act which are not due
68. Where Class 4 contributions have been paid in error for any reason, and the Revenue will not refund them, the Secretary of State may treat them as a payment on account of other contributions due from the contributor.

Repayment of Class 4 contributions under section 9 (1) of the Act which are not due
69. Where overpaid Class 4 contributions, as described in reg. 68, are not used towards other contributions they may be refunded. The contributor must claim in the prescribed form within six years from the end of the year of assessment *for* which the payment was made, or within a period of two years from the end of the year *in* which the payment was made. Amounts of £0.50 or less are not repaid.

Disapplication of section 47 of the Finance (No. 2) Act 1975 [TA 1988, s. 824] to repayments of Class 4 contributions paid under section 9 (1) of the Act
70. Repayment supplement does not apply to any repayment of Class 4 contributions. Under SSA 1990, this regulation may be reversed when interest under TMA 1970, s. 86 on late paid Class 4 contributions is imposed.

Class 4 liability of earners treated as self-employed earners who, but for such treatment, would be employed earners
71. A person is liable to special Class 4 contributions if he:
(a) is deemed by regulation to be self-employed; and
(b) has earnings which would otherwise be earnings liable to Class 1 contributions; and
(c) those earnings are chargeable to income tax under Schedule E; and
(d) those earnings exceed the Class 4 lower annual limit in SSA 1975, s. 10 (1) (c).

Notification of insurance number and recording of category letter on deductions working sheet
72. An earner within reg. 71 must notify his national insurance number to his employer (or the

person paying the earnings). That person will record this, and his category letter, on the earner's deductions working sheet.

Calculation of earnings for the purposes of special Class 4 contributions
73. The earnings are to be calculated as if they were employed earner's earnings. Annual earnings are rounded down to the nearest £1.

Notification and payment of special Class 4 contributions due
74. The Secretary of State will normally issue to the earner a notice of liability to special Class 4 contributions. Unless the liability is under appeal it must be paid within 28 days from the receipt of the notice.

Recovery of deferred Class 4 and special Class 4 contributions after appeal, claim or further assessment under the Income Tax Acts or after the raising of a Secretary of State's question
75. Once a claim, appeal or question in relation to deferred or special Class 4 contributions has been settled the Secretary of State will issue a notice of liability based on the outcome of the proceedings and this must be paid within 28 days of receipt of the notice.

Annual maximum of special Class 4 contributions
76. Where in any year a person is liable to both ordinary and special Class 4 contributions, the special contributions are not to exceed the difference between the ordinary Class 4 contributions payable and the maximum Class 4 contributions due in any year. This in effect limits the total special and ordinary contributions to the Class 4 annual maximum.

Disposal of special Class 4 contributions paid in excess or error
77. The Secretary of State may treat any overpayment of special Class 4 contributions as made on account of other contributions due.

Return of special Class 4 contributions paid in excess or error
78. Where any overpaid special Class 4 contributions cannot be used towards other contributions they may be refunded. The contributor must claim in the prescribed form within six years from the end of the year of assessment for which they were paid or within such longer period as the Secretary of State may allow. Amounts of 50p or less are not repaid.

Husband and wife
79. Up to 5 April 1990 a husband was liable for Class 4 contributions on his wife's profits or gains. Independent taxation means that they are separately assessed and the wife is responsible for her own Class 4 contributions.

Service of notice by post
80. Any notice the Secretary of State must give under these regulations may be sent by post.

PART VIII SPECIAL CLASSES OF EARNERS

CASE A—AIRMEN

Interpretation
81. An airman is defined as any person, except one serving in the armed forces, employed under a U.K. contract for service on an aircraft with a view to performing the duties of the contract while the aircraft is in flight. The employment may be as a pilot, commander, navigator or any other member of a crew or in any other capacity on board any aircraft for the purposes of the aircraft, crew, passengers, cargo or mails carried aboard. Thus it includes an air hostess, steward, civilian guard or policeman on duty.

Modification of employed earner's employment
82. Where an airman employed as such is either domiciled or has a place of residence in Great Britain, and his employer:
    (*a*) in the case of a British aircraft has a place of business in Great Britain, or
    (*b*) in any other case has his principal place of business in Great Britain, he is deemed to satisfy the conditions for Class 1 contributions (SSA 1975, s. 4) and earners (SSA 1975, s. 2). This is subject to reciprocal agreements with other countries under SSA 1975, s. 143.

Application of the Act and regulations
83. Where, as a consequence of an airman being out of Great Britain by reason of his employment, he is unable to meet a specified time limit or other requirement of the contributions legislation, he is given further time provided he complies as soon as is reasonably practicable.

Special transitional provision
84. Certain provisions of the National Insurance (Airmen) Regulations 1948 may continue to apply for the purposes of facilitating the winding up of the system of insurance contained in the former principal Act.

CASE B—CONTINENTAL SHELF

Application to employment in connection with continental shelf of Pt. I of the Act and so much of Pt. IV thereof as relates to contributions
85. Any person who carries out his duties of employment in areas covered by the Continental Shelf Act 1964 is treated as complying with the residence and presence rules in SSA 1975, s. 132. Where a person is working outside Great Britain but on the continental shelf he is deemed to comply with any time limits or other requirements of the legislation provided he puts right any failure as soon as is reasonably practicable on his return, even if the time limit has expired.

CASE C—MARINERS

Interpretation
86. Various terms used in regs. 86 to 99 in connection with mariners are defined.
   See leaflet NI25 for more information on this subject.

Conditions of domicile or residence
87. The usual residence or presence requirements of regs. 119 to 123 do not apply to mariners. In order for them to be liable to contributions they must be either domiciled or resident in Great Britain. A secondary contributor (employer) will only be liable if he is resident or has a place of business in Great Britain.

Modification of employed earner's employment
88. A person who is employed as a mariner under the following conditions will be treated as an employed earner irrespective of whether or not he fulfils the usual conditions for employed earners (SSA 1975, s. 2) as follows:
   (*a*) If he is employed:
      (i) on board a British ship (defined in reg. 86); or
      (ii) on board a non-British ship and the contract was entered into in the U.K. with a view to carrying out the duties, in whole or part, while the ship or vessel is on her voyage; and the person paying his earnings or, where the mariner is the ship's master or a crew member, either the person paying his earnings or the ship's owner or managing owner, has a place of business in Great Britain; or
   (*b*) if he is employed as a master, member of the crew or as a radio officer on board any ship, he may still be treated as an employed earner even where the conditions in (*a*) above do not apply.

Modification of section 4 (6E) . . . of the Act
89. From 6 April 1988, the Class 1 contribution rate for mariners is the standard rate as shown in Appendix 1. However, there is a reduction of secondary contributions where the employment is on a foreign-going ship (defined in reg. 86). This reduction is currently 0.5 per cent.

Earnings period for mariners and apportionment of earnings
90. The normal earnings period rules apply where a mariner is paid at regular intervals. In the case of mariners, however, it is more common for them to be paid at the end of a voyage. In these circumstances the earnings period is calculated by reference to the voyage period (see the definition in reg. 86).

Calculation of earnings-related contributions for mariners
91. The calculation of a mariner's contribution can become rather complicated and the DSS have produced special tables to ease this task (CF395, CF396 and CF397). The exact percentages method (see reg. 9) may be used as an alternative.

Prescribed secondary contributors
93. If the employer is not resident and does not have a place of business in Great Britain he cannot be treated as a secondary contributor. If, however, the person who actually pays the mariner is either resident or has such a place of business then he is treated as the secondary contributor.

Payments to be disregarded
94. Certain payments are disregarded in calculating a mariner's earnings for contribution purposes:

(*a*) an interim payment of earnings by way of an advance;

(*b*) a payment of his earnings allotted by him to someone else;

(*c*) a special payment while sick abroad (as defined by the National Maritime Board).

It should be noted payments under (*a*) and (*b*) are only disregarded until they actually become liable to contributions, for example when earnings fall due.

Application of the Act and regulations

96. Where a mariner is unable to comply with the requirements of the contributions legislation because he is absent from Great Britain carrying out the duties of his employment he is treated as complying with the requirements provided he fulfils them as soon as is reasonably practicable.

Modification in relation to share fishermen of Part I of the Act and so much of Part IV thereof as relates to contributions

98. A share fisherman comes within the same residence and domicile requirements as a mariner as far as contribution liability is concerned (see reg. 87). He is treated as self-employed and his rate of Class 2 contribution is increased to enable him to acquire sufficient contributions to entitle him to unemployment benefit. The prescribed rate for 1990–91 is £6.15 per week. A share fisherman is excepted from his Class 2 liability while he is unemployed.

See leaflet NI 47 for further information.

CASE D—MARRIED WOMEN AND WIDOWS

Interpretation

99. Various terms used in regs. 99 and 112 are defined.

Elections by married women and widows

100. Until 11 May 1977 certain married women and widows could elect to pay a reduced rate Class 1 contribution, if an employee, or have no liability to Class 2 contributions, if self-employed. Many of these elections are still in force.

Duration of effect of election

101. Subject to reg. 103, an election made under reg. 100 will continue in force until the first of the events shown below occur:

(*a*) the date the woman's marriage ends, except because of her husband's death; or

(*b*) the end of the tax year in which she ceases to qualify for widow's benefits, unless she remarries again during the year, is then widowed again before the end of the year and again qualifies for widow's benefits; or

(*c*) the end of any two consecutive tax years which began on or after 6 April 1978 in which she had no Class 1 earnings or self-employed income; or

(*d*) the end of the week in which she revokes her election or the end of the week prescribed by her in her revocation notice as long as it is before the end of that tax year; or

(*e*) where in any tax year after 5 April 1982 an erroneous payment on account of Class 1 contributions at the contracted-out rate are made on behalf of the woman who wishes to pay contributions at the standard rate from the next 6 April, the election will end on 5 April; or

(*f*) where in any tax year after 5 April 1982 an erroneous payment is made and she wishes to pay standard rate contributions from that date.

Continuation of elections under the former regulation 91

102. Any election having the same effect as that described in reg. 100, made under the Social Security (Contributions) Regulations 1975, (S.I. 1975 No. 492) reg. 91 still has effect.

Continuation of elections on widowhood

103. Further rules apply where a widow remarries and is then widowed again as referred to in reg. 101 (*c*) to (*f*).

Reduced rate

104. The reduced Class 1 contribution is 3.85 per cent. When an election is in force the initial primary 2 per cent. rate is not available.

Class 3 contributions

105. Any woman who has an election in force cannot pay Class 3 contributions.

Certificates of election

106. When a woman makes an election the Secretary of State issues a certificate of election (Form CF383) to the woman claimant. She is required to hand this to her employer or employers to enable them to deduct Class 1 contributions at the reduced rate.

347 Part II: National Insurance Contributions

Special transitional provisions consequent upon passing of Pensions Act
107. Detailed rules define those women who are able to make an election.

Deemed election of married women and widows excepted from contribution liability under former principal Act
108. Any election similar to that described in reg. 100 made under pre-1975 regulations (see reg. 102) may continue in force by treating the earliest election as having been made under the 1975 Regulations, reg. 91 (see reg. 102).

Special transitional provisions regarding deemed elections
109. Where an earlier election is deemed to have been made under the 1975 Regulations, reg. 91 there are further rules covering revocation.

Application of regulations 99 to 107 to elections and revocation of elections deemed made under regulations 108 and 109
110. Regs. 99 to 107, unless inconsistent with regs. 108 and 109, apply to the earlier elections under the 1975 Regulations, reg. 91.

Savings
111. For the purpose of facilitating the introduction of the scheme of social security contributions, certain provisions of the 1973 Regulations are saved.

Modifications of the Act
112. Where SSA 1975 affects married women and widows it is subject to regs. 99 to 111 above.

CASE E—MEMBERS OF THE FORCES

Establishments and organisations of which Her Majesty's forces are taken to consist
113. Her Majesty's Forces are taken to include all organisations and establishments shown in Sch. 3, Pt. I but not those in Sch. 3, Pt. II.

Treatment of serving members of the forces as present in Great Britain
114. Any serving member of the forces is treated as present in Great Britain even when serving abroad.

Reduction of rate of Class 1 contributions
115. In recognition of the fact that the state benefits payable to serving members of the armed forces are restricted, the Class 1 contributions payable by those individuals are reduced by a certain percentage. From 6 April 1990 the primary contributions are reduced by 0.7 per cent., so the maximum rate is reduced from 9.0 per cent. to 8.30 per cent. and the secondary contributions are reduced by 0.7 per cent., so the maximum rate is reduced from 10.45 per cent. to 9.75 per cent. The contributions may be calculated in accordance with the exact percentage method (reg. 9 (1)) but the DSS do provide contribution tables (CF394).

Treatment of contributions paid after due date
116. For the purpose of any entitlement to state benefits, contributions paid by a member of the armed forces after the due date are treated as paid on that date.

Special provisions concerning earnings-related contributions
117. A number of payments made to a member of the armed forces may be excluded for the purposes of contribution liability:
   (*a*) a payment of Emergency Service grant; or
   (*b*) a payment in respect of a period of voluntary service as described in TA 1988, s. 316; or
   (*c*) a bounty in recognition of liability for immediate call-up in times of emergency.
   The earnings period for a serving member of the forces is defined as follows:
   (*a*) in the case of a person serving in the regular forces, the appropriate accounting period under the Naval Pay Regulations, or the Army Pay Warrant, Queen's Regulations for the Army or those for the Royal Air Force; or
   (*b*) in the case of a person undergoing training in any of the establishments specified in Sch. 3, Pt. I, paras. 2 to 9, a month.

Application of the Act and regulations
118. If a serving member of the armed forces is unable to comply with any time limit specified in these regulations because he is serving abroad or at sea, he shall be treated as having complied if he carries out the requirement as soon as is reasonably practicable.

CASE F—RESIDENCE AND PERSONS ABROAD

Conditions as to residence or presence in Great Britain
119. To be liable to Class 1 or 2 contributions a person must be resident, present or ordinarily

resident in Great Britain. Great Britain comprises England, Wales and Scotland; Northern Ireland has its own arrangements.

An employed earner is liable to Class 1 earnings-related contributions if he is resident or ordinarily resident or present in Great Britain at the time of employment. The terms residence and ordinary residence are not defined in the legislation but it is normally accepted that the definitions for income tax purposes provide accurate guidelines. It is possible for an employed earner to be neither resident nor present in Great Britain but to be treated as ordinarily resident for contribution purposes. The DSS suggest in leaflet NI38 that where a person is absent from Great Britain for up to five years he may be treated as ordinarily resident as long as he intends to return to Great Britain. A number of tax cases involve the question of residence (see *Cooper* v. *Cadwellader* (1904) 5 TC 101; *Lysaght* v. *I.R. Comrs.* (1928) 13 TC 511; *Inchiquin* (*Lord*) v. *I.R. Comrs.* (1948) 31 TC 125; *Goodman* v. *J. Eban Ltd.* [1954] 1 All ER 763; *Reed* v. *Clark* [1985] STC 323).

There are special rules for directors of British companies who are neither resident nor ordinarily resident. If a director comes to Great Britain simply to attend board meetings and each visit is for two nights or less and there are no more than 10 visits in any tax year, the visits will be disregarded and he will be regarded as not present in Great Britain. If any visits lasts more than two weeks or there are more than 10 visits (of any duration), the director will be regarded as present and his fees will be liable to contributions.

See leaflet NI35, para. 42.

The employer who would be the secondary contributor normally, will be liable to the secondary Class 1 contributions if he is either resident, present or has a place of business in Great Britain. A place of business is defined by the DSS as a place where the employer or his agent can as of right conduct his business. A business registered under any of the Companies Acts requirement is said to have a place of business in Great Britain.

See leaflet NI132.

Where the secondary contributor (the employer) is neither resident nor present he may make the secondary contributions on a voluntary basis. If this is done he will also be required to deduct and remit the primary Class 1 contributions. If the secondary contributor is not liable and does not make voluntary contributions, the primary contributions will be recovered from the employee by using the direct collection method. An employed earner may be either resident or present in, but not ordinarily resident in, Great Britain and be employed mainly outside the U.K. by an employer whose place of business is outside the U.K. (irrespective of the fact that he also has a place of business in the U.K.). Such an employee is not liable to Class 1 primary contributions until he has been resident for more than 52 continuous weeks, beginning with the week following his last arrival in Great Britain.

A student (or, in some cases, an apprentice) not ordinarily resident in Great Britain but temporarily employed in Great Britain is not liable to Class 1 contributions until he has been resident in Great Britain for a continuous period of 52 weeks.

A self-employed earner is entitled, but not liable, to make Class 2 contributions in any week in which he is present in Great Britain. He is, however, liable to Class 2 contributions for a week in which he is ordinarily resident in Great Britain or has been resident in Great Britain for at least 26 of the last 52 contribution weeks.

Payment of contributions for periods abroad
120. A person employed outside Great Britain in employed earner's employment is liable to primary Class 1 contributions on his earnings if the employer has a place of business in Great Britain, the earner is ordinarily resident in Great Britain and immediately before the commencement of employment the earner was resident in Great Britain. The employer is liable to the secondary contributions on those earnings. Where the employment is carried out overseas the liability to both primary and secondary contributions exists only during the first 52 weeks of the overseas employment. Where a person continues working overseas after the end of the first 52-week period, he may make Class 3 voluntary contributions for any year in which he would have been entitled to make them, subject to reg. 122.

See leaflet NI132 which explains this subject in more detail.

Class 2 and Class 3 contributions for periods abroad
121. A person who is self-employed outside Great Britain is entitled to pay Class 2 contributions if he was either self-employed or an employed earner immediately before he went abroad, subject to reg. 122. The entitlement has been extended from 6 April 1989 to persons gainfully employed outside Great Britain to cover temporary periods in this country.

A person is entitled to make Class 3 contributions while he is abroad, subject to reg. 122. To qualify he must either have been resident in Great Britain for at least three years before the period to which these contributions relate or have paid minimum contributions for three years.

Entitlement or liability is subject to the reciprocal agreements between the U.K. and the other country, if one is in existence.

Conditions of payment of Class 2 or Class 3 contributions for periods abroad
122. The Class 3 contributions referred to in reg. 120 (2) (*b*) and the Class 2 or Class 3 contributions

referred to in reg. 121 must be paid within the time limits specified in reg. 27. They are subject to the qualification that the person would have been able to make these contributions if he had been present in Great Britain.

Persons outside Great Britain on the appointed day
123. There are further considerations to take into account where the person was employed abroad before 6 April 1975 (the appointed day).

CASE G—VOLUNTEER DEVELOPMENT WORKERS

Interpretation
123A. A person employed outside Great Britain as a "volunteer development worker" is entitled to pay Class 2 contributions under the provisions of reg. 123C if that person is ordinarily resident in Great Britain.
　See Press Release, 14 March 1986.

Certain volunteer development workers to be self-employed earners
123B. Where the earnings from employment as a volunteer development worker are not liable to Class 1 contributions the earner is deemed to be a self-employed earner notwithstanding that it is not employment in Great Britain.

Option to pay Class 2 contributions
123C. A person deemed to be self-employed by virtue of reg. 123B is excepted from Class 2 liability but may pay voluntarily at the rate prescribed in reg. 123D.

Special provisions as to residence, rate, annual maximum and method of payment
123D. The residence and presence conditions in Case F above (residence and persons abroad, regs. 119 to 122) do not apply to a volunteer development worker. The weekly Class 2 contributions payable is fixed for 1990–91 at 7 per cent. of the lower earnings limit. The amount payable is therefore 7 per cent. of £46.00 which equals £3.22. A volunteer development worker does not require a contribution card or Class 2 stamps to make contributions.

Late paid contributions
123E. If a volunteer development workers pays the contributions later than the due date the normal rules (SSA 1975, s. 7A) do not apply. The rate payable will be the highest rate in the period beginning with the date the contribution was due and ending on the date it was paid.

Modifications of the Act and these regulations
123F. SSA 1975 is modified in the case of volunteer development workers.

PART X MISCELLANEOUS PROVISIONS

Treatment of contribution week falling into 2 income tax years
131. Where a contribution week for Class 2 purposes is split between two tax years, the week is treated as falling wholly within the year in which it began.

Breach of regulations
132. There is no penalty for failing to comply with the requirements of the regulations relating to married women and widows (Case D—regs. 99 to 112).
　Otherwise, if any person contravenes or fails to comply with the requirements of these regulations where no specific penalty is provided for, a maximum penalty of £200 may be levied on summary conviciton. Where the offence continues after summary conviction there is a further penalty of £20 for each continuing day.

133. Revoked.

Northern Ireland
135. These regulations do not apply to Northern Ireland except Case E (regs. 113 to 117) in relation to the armed forces.

Revocation and general savings
136. A number of regulations have been revoked and are listed in Sch. 5.

SCHEDULE 1 CONTAINING THE PROVISIONS OF THE INCOME TAX (EMPLOYMENTS) REGULATIONS 1973 AS THEY APPLY TO EARNINGS-RELATED CONTRIBUTIONS UNDER THE SOCIAL SECURITY ACT 1975 (Regulation 46).

PART I GENERAL

Interpretation
2.—Various terms and words used in these regulations are defined.

Intermediate employers
3.—Where an employee works under the general control and management of a person who is not his immediate employer that person (the principal employer) is deemed to be his employer for national insurance and PAYE purposes. Where the emoluments are paid by the principal employer, the immediate employer must provide him with the necessary information which will enable him to comply with these regulations. If, however, the immediate employer actually pays the employee's emoluments the principal employer must notify him of the Class 1 deduction to be made and the principal employer may deduct this sum on making to the immediate employer the payment out of which the emoluments will be paid. In either case it is the principal employer who is liable to the Class 1 contributions. This regulation is parallel to S.I. 1973 No. 334, Reg. 3 and together they extend the definition of an employer for national insurance and PAYE purposes.
   There is a similar provision in relation to sickness payments.

Employers' earnings-related contributions
3A.—Where under these regulations a person is required to pay another person's primary and secondary Class 1 contribution liability, the person making the contribution is doing so as an agent of the other.

Inspectors and Collectors
4A.—This allows for continuity in the inspection and collection of contributions under these regulations and allows proceedings to be transferred between officers. The parallel tax provision is in TMA 1970, s. 1.

Service by post
5.—Any notice or other document may be sent by post.

Offences and penalties in relation to statutory sick pay
5A.—The penalty provisions in SSHBA 1982, s. 9 (8) and (9) apply to statutory sick pay, instead of the penalty provisions in TMA 1970, s. 98 (2). However the SSHBA 1982 provisions were repealed by SSA 1986, s. 86 (2), Sch. 11. The latest penalty provisions are in SSA 1986, s. 54.

PARTS II AND III DEDUCTION OF EARNINGS-RELATED CONTRIBUTIONS

Deduction of earnings-related contributions
6.—Every employer who pays emoluments to an employee must prepare a deductions working sheet. Although the employer is liable to both primary and secondary contributions he is permitted to deduct the primary amount from the employee's emoluments, but only in accordance with these regulations.

Calculation of deduction
13.—The employer may deduct from the employee's emoluments only the amount of primary Class 1 contributions due on those emoluments, except where payments from two or more employments fall to be aggregated. In cases of aggregation the deduction may be apportioned between the separate payments. Where, in good faith, an employer fails to deduct primary contributions from an employee's emoluments and subsequently the DSS instructs the employer to

make such deductions, the employer is able to recover the liability for the current year from the employee by deduction from future emoluments paid in that year. The employer is not permitted to recover any liability for earlier years.

The employer must record on the deductions working sheet certain details relating to the individual employee and the amounts deducted from emoluments in relation to statutory sick pay and Class 1 contributions. These records must be retained for a minimum period of three years after the end of the tax year to which they relate.

Certificate of contributions paid
25.—The employer must enter certain details on the employee's end of year certificate (P60), including the amount of pay, tax deducted and employee's national insurance contributions deducted.

PART IV PAYMENT AND RECOVERY OF EARNINGS-RELATED CONTRIBUTIONS, ETC.

Payment of earnings-related contributions by employer
26.—Where the inspector of taxes has instructed an employer to operate PAYE and remit the tax within 14 days after the end of each month the employer is also to remit the relevant earnings-related contributions. The exception to this is where the inspector has authorised the employer to deduct the tax from a fixed wage or salary by reference to the fixed sum; in these instances the payment of contributions may be made to the collector quarterly. Any overpayments made in good faith may be set against any future liability.

Employer failing to pay earnings-related contributions
27.—The collector may take action to collect contributions where the employer has not made payments on time. Before 6 April 1990 the collector calculated the amount of Class 1 contributions due on information provided by the employer. Since that date the employer must make a return of the actual contributions payable.

Specified amount of earnings-related contributions payable by the employer
27A. The collector may estimate an employer's liability and take legal proceedings to recover that sum. This route is used in preference to reg. 27. The collector is able to take similar action to recover PAYE and also deductions made from sub-contractors.

Recovery of earnings-related contributions
28.—The collector may take proceedings to recover unpaid contributions in the county court under the provisions of TMA 1970, s. 66. The unpaid duties recoverable under that section are limited to £750. In the case of national insurance contributions the limit of £750 is exclusive of any tax to be recovered by the same action.

Return by employer at end of year
30.—The employer is required to make an end of year return to the collector; in practice this is normally on Form P35. A return can however be in any form approved by the Secretary of State and agreed with the Commissioners of the Inland Revenue (who prescribe Form P35). There are a number of requirements relating to the completion of this return which should be made within 44 days after the end of the tax year.

Special return by employer at end of voyage period
30A.—The employer of a mariner is required to make a return not later than 14 days after the end of a voyage period. The return is made on Form RD386.

Inspection of employer's records
32.—The DSS may inspect all wages records to ensure that the correct deductions have been made and remitted to the collector of taxes. If the employer has not made returns or, if submitted, they are found to be incorrect, the DSS may take the appropriate action to recover the outstanding or additional contributions.

Death of employer
33.—If an employer dies, his duties under these regulations should be carried out by his personal representative or, if he pays emoluments for someone else, his successor.

Succession to a business, etc.
34.—If any person takes over as an employer he must do everything under these regulations which his predecessor was liable to do. He is liable to pay contributions which were deductible before the change, unless the contributions are no longer deductible.

PART VII ASSESSMENT AND DIRECT COLLECTION

Provisions for direct payment
50.—Where an employer does not satisfy the residence and presence rules he is not liable to secondary Class 1 contributions nor is he required to deduct the primary contributions from his employee's emoluments (reg. 119 (1) (*b*)). In such circumstances, the employee is required to pay his primary contributions direct to the collector. This arrangement is known as "direct collection" and is similar to the arrangements for income tax deductions where there is no employer liable to operate PAYE.

51.—The employee is required to complete a deductions working sheet in the same manner as his employer would have done had he been resident and present in Great Britain.

SCHEDULE 2 (Regulation 57)

PART I STAMP DUTIES MANAGEMENT ACT 1891

PART II POST OFFICE ACT 1953.

These provisions, as adapted, apply to stamps used in paying Class 2 contributions.

SCHEDULE 3 (Regulation 113)

PART I

Prescribed establishments and organisations for purposes of section 128 (3) of the Act

PART II

Establishments and organisations of which Her Majesty's Forces shall not consist.

S.I. 1979 No. 676

The Social Security (Earnings Factor) Regulations 1979

Citation, commencement and interpretation
1. Various terms used in these regulations are defined.

Ascertainment of earnings factors
2. Schedule 1 contains the formula to be used in calculating a person's earnings factor.

Evidence of official records
3. Any documents signed by a duly authorised officer of the DSS is acceptable evidence of the amount of contributions which have been paid or treated as paid.

Contributions to be treated as having been paid or as not repaid
4. Where the payment of contributions has been deferred under Reg. 49 of the Contributions Regulations (S.I. 1979 No. 591), they are treated as having been paid for the purposes of calculating a person's earnings factor. If any person receives a refund of contributions in accordance with Reg. 32 of those regulations the sum repaid is treated as having not been repaid.

Revocations
5. The regulations specified in Sch. 2 have been revoked.

SCHEDULE 1 RULES FOR THE ASCERTAINMENT OF EARNINGS FACTORS (Regulation 2)

PART I CLASS 1 CONTRIBUTIONS

The detailed rules and computations used in calculating a person's earnings factors are shown in Regs. 1 to 7.

PART II CLASS 2 AND CLASS 3 CONTRIBUTIONS

8.—The earnings factor derived from the payment of Class 2 or Class 3 contributions paid or credited is calculated by taking the Class 1 lower earnings limit for that year and multiplying it by the number of contributions made in the year.

9.—The factor derived from the calculation in para. 8 should be rounded to the nearest pound; rounded down if less than 50 pence, up if 50 pence or more.

S.I. 1982 No. 1033

The Contracting-out (Recovery of Class 1 Contributions) Regulations 1982

Citation and commencement
1. These regulations came into operation on 29 August 1982.

Prevention of recovery by employers of Class 1 contributions
2. Where an employer deducts Class 1 contributions at the contracted-out rate and subsequently discovers he should have applied the standard rate because his contracting-out certificate had been cancelled, he is unable to recover the difference from the employee. This rule applies whether or not the terms of the contract provide for the contrary.

S.I. 1983 No. 376

The Statutory Sick Pay (Compensation of Employers) and Miscellaneous Provisions Regulations 1983

Citation, commencement and interpretation
1. Various terms used in these regulations are defined.

Deductions from contributions payments
2. An employer who has made a payment of statutory sick pay may deduct the amount paid from his contributions liability before this sum is remitted to the collector of taxes, subject to a few exceptions. In practice if statutory sick pay exceeds contributions due, the excess may be set against PAYE due.

Payments to employers by or on behalf of the Secretary of State
3. The Secretary of State will repay the amount of statutory sick pay paid by an employer to an employee when he applies in writing for the refund, where the amount of the payment exceeds the contributions deducted or where the employer is not liable to pay any primary or secondary contributions.

Date when certain contributions are to be treated as paid
4. The date on which the contributions are treated as having been paid by the employer is specified.

S.I. 1985 No. 1411

The Statutory Sick Pay (Additional Compensation of Employers and Consequential Amendments) Regulations 1985

Citation, commencement and interpretation
1. These regulations may be cited as the Statutory Sick Pay (Additional Compensation of Employers and Consequential Amendments) Regulations 1985 and came into operation on 6 October 1985. Various terms used in these regulations are defined.

Right of employers to a prescribed amount
2. Where an employer pays statutory sick pay on or after 6 April 1985 and is entitled to recover this under the Statutory Sick Pay Compensation Regulations 1983, Reg. 2, he is entitled to recover an amount said to represent the secondary Class 1 contributions paid in respect of statutory sick pay as specified in Reg. 3 below.

Determination of amount
3. The employer may from 6 April 1990 recover an amount based on 7 per cent. of the statutory sick payment, from Class 1 contributions payable to the collector (Statutory Maternity Pay (Compensation of Employers) and Statutory Sick Pay (Additional Compensation of Employers) Amendment Regulation 1990 S.I. 1990 No. 218).

Deduction from contributions payments
4. There are certain rules covering the circumstances in which an employer may deduct the sum mentioned in Regs. 2 and 3.

Payments to employers by or on behalf of the Secretary of State
5. The Secretary of State must be satisfied that a number of conditions have been met before the payment will be made.

S.I. 1986 No. 2218

The Social Security (Adjudication) Regulations 1986

PART I GENERAL

Citation, commencement and interpretation
1. These regulations came into operation on 6 April 1987. Various terms and phrases are defined.

PART II COMMON PROVISIONS

Procedure in connection with determinations; and right to representation
2. A person who has the right to be heard at an inquiry may be accompanied and represented by another person.

Manner of making applications, . . .; and time limits
3. Schedule 2 describes which applications are to be made in writing; defines the appropriate officer and specifies the time limits within which certain applications must be made.
    Where an application made to the Secretary of State for the determination of a question gives insufficient information he may request further information.

Withdrawal of applications . . .
6. An application for a decision of the Secretary of State may be withdrawn at any time.

Correction of accidental errors in decisions
10. Any accidental error made in a decision may be corrected by the person who gave the decision or by an authority of like status.
    A correction made to a decision will form part of that decision.

Setting aside of decisions on certain grounds
11. A decision may be set aside by the adjudicating authority or an authority of similar status on the grounds that;
    (*a*) a person involved in the proceedings did not receive a relevant document, or
    (*b*) a party to the proceedings was not present, or
    (*c*) the interests of justice so require.

Provisions common to regulations 10 and 11
12. There is no right of appeal against a correction made under reg. 10 or a determination given under reg. 11.
    It should be noted "adjudicating authority" includes the Secretary of State.

PART III ADJUDICATING AUTHORITIES

SECTION A—THE SECRETARY OF STATE

Construction of Section A
13. In this Section "a person interested" is a person whose interest in the application or decision relates to that person's own liability under the Acts or his actual or potential rights under them. The definition concerning SSP or SMP is also defined in relation to specified legislation.

Application for decision of the Secretary of State on principal questions
14. An application form (CF90) is provided by the DSS for making applications to the Secretary of State for his determination of a question. The interested persons are notified and the Secretary of State may obtain any particulars he considers necessary.

Procedure for inquiries
15. Any person appointed by the Secretary of State to hold an inquiry may summon people to attend, to give evidence under oath and administer oaths.

The Secretary of State's decision and statement of grounds
16. Any question of law may be referred to the High Court under SSA 1975, s. 94.

Review or reference
17. A question may be reviewed by the Secretary of State on application in accordance with SSA 1975, s. 96.

PART V TRANSITIONAL PROVISIONS, SAVINGS AND REVOCATIONS

Transitional provisions
73. These provisions apply to National Insurance Acts 1965 to 1974 as they correspondingly apply to SSA 1975.

SCHEDULE 1 PROVISIONS CONFERRING POWERS EXERCISED IN MAKING THESE REGULATIONS

The powers exercised in making these regulations are specified.

SCHEDULE 2 TIME LIMITS FOR MAKING APPLICATIONS, APPEALS OR REFERENCES (Regulation 3)

7.—If any person requires the Secretary of State to review his decision, the request must be made to the DSS or DOE office from which the original decision was issued.

The request must be made within three months from the date when the Secretary of State gave the applicant notice in writing of his decision.

S.I. 1987 No. 91

The Statutory Maternity Pay (Compensation of Employers) Regulations 1987

Citation, commencement and interpretation
1. These regulations came into force on 6 April 1987. Various terms and phrases are defined.

Right of employers to prescribed amount
2. Any employer, having paid SMP, will be able to deduct a sum or receive a refund as described in reg. 3 in the circumstances stated in reg. 4 or 5 below.

Determination of the amount an employer shall be entitled to under regulation 2
3. The employer may from 6 April 1990 deduct 7 per cent. of the payment, from Class 1 contributions payable by him to the collector, being the secondary contributions due on the statutory maternity or sick payment made (The Statutory Maternity Pay (Compensation of Employers) and Statutory Sick Pay (Additional Compensation of Employers) Amendment Regulation 1990 S.I. 1990 No. 218).

Deductions from contribution payments
4. The employer may recover the amount of SMP and the 7 per cent. (see reg. 3) by deducting the total amount from contributions due except where:
  (*a*) the contributions relate to earnings paid before the beginning of the income tax month in which the statutory maternity payment was made;
  (*b*) the contributions are paid more than six years after the end of the year in which the payment was made;
  (*c*) the amounts to be recovered have already been repaid by the Secretary of State under reg. 5; or

(*d*) the employer has requested a refund under reg. 5 and this has not been refused.

Payments to employers by the Secretary of State
5. Where the amount to be deducted by the employer exceeds the contributions due to be paid, the Secretary of State may in certain circumstances make a refund.

Date when certain contributions are to be treated as paid
6. For the purposes of SSA 1986, Sch. 4, para. 5 (amount to be treated as paid and received towards discharging employer's liability to Class 1 contributions) the date on which the contributions are deemed to have been paid is:
　　(*a*) where, after deducting the relevant amounts, a payment of contributions was still to be made, the date on which the remainder was paid; and
　　(*b*) in cases where the deduction extinguished the contribution payments, the fourteenth day after the end of the income tax month during which the earnings were paid *i.e.*, the normal due date for remittance of tax and contributions deducted under the PAYE system.

S.I. 1988 No. 1409

The Social Security (Employment Training: Payments) Order 1988

Citation, commencement and interpretation
1. This order came into force on 4 September 1988. Various terms are defined.

Treatment of payments for purposes of the Social Security Act 1975
2. Payments of training premiums made to persons undergoing Employment Training (as defined in the Employment and Training Act 1973, s. 2) do not attract liability to Class 1 or 2 contributions.

S.I. 1989 No. 1238

The Social Security Act 1989 (Commencement No. 1) Order 1989

The order provides for dates when certain provisions of SSA 1989 come into force; in particular, s. 1 comes into force on 5 October 1989.

S.I. 1989 No. 1627

The Social Security (Credits) Amendment Regulations 1989

These regulations which came into force on 1 October 1989 amend S.I. 1975 No. 556. Reg. 8 is amended so that credit is awarded in respect of a tax year only if the person was undergoing full-time education, training or apprenticeship for at least part of the tax year. Conditions where credit is given for unemployment or incapacity for work, in reg. 9, are also amended

S.I. 1989 No. 1677

The Social Security (Contributions) (Transitional and Consequential Provisions) Regulations 1989

Citation, commencement and interpretation
1. These regulations came into force on 5 October 1989.

Transitional provisions for assessment of primary Class 1 contributions
2. Special rules for 1989–90 only are introduced for directors and other employees with an annual earnings period where that period straddles 5 October 1989. Composite rates are utilised to take into account the change on that date from primary earnings brackets to an initial and standard rate for primary contributions.

Amendment of principal Regulations
3. Amendments consequential to SSA 1989, s. 1 are made.

S.I. 1990 No. 218

The Statutory Maternity Pay (Compensation of Employers) and Statutory Sick Pay (Additional Compensation of Employers) Amendment Regulations 1990.

The rate of compensation available to employers on secondary contributions payable by them is reduced from $7\frac{1}{2}$ per cent. to 7 per cent. from 6 April 1990.

S.I. 1990 No. 321

The Social Security (Contributions) (Re-rating) Order 1990

These regulations came into force on 6 April 1990 and uprate secondary Class 1 earnings brackets, and Class 2, 3 and 4 rates and limits.

S.I. 1990 No. 536

The Social Security (Refunds) (Repayment of Contractual Maternity Pay) Regulations 1990

From 31 March 1990 where statutory maternity pay is repayable by the employee to the employer, because she fails to return to work after her pregnancy, the associated contributions may be refunded to the employer.

S.I. 1990 No. 604

The Social Security (Contributions) Amendment Regulations 1990

These regulations came into force on 6 April 1990 and increase the weekly LEL to £46 and the weekly UEL to £350.

Additionally, the primary Class 1 reduction for serving members of the forces is increased to 0.7 per cent. and Class 2 contributions payable by volunteer development workers is decreased to 7 per cent. of the annual LEL.

S.I. 1990 No. 605

The Social Security (Contributions) Amendment (No. 2) Regulations 1990

In the Social Security (Contributions) Regulations 1979 (S.I. 1979 No. 591) Sch. 1, a new reg. 27 requires an employer to notify the collector of the *amount* of earnings-related contributions which the employer is liable to pay to the collector for a specified period (and not just information).

Reg. 30 is amended to (*a*) extend the date for submission of the employer's end of year return from 19 April to 19 May in each year; and (*b*) provide that a single return is made in respect of all employees and that the statement, declaration and certificate accompanying the return are part of it.

Reg. 51 is amended to extend the date for submission of an employee's end of year return under the alternative direct collection procedure from 19 April to 19 May.

S.I. 1990 No. 606

The Social Security (Contributions) (Re-rating) Consequential Amendment Regulations 1990

The special rate of Class 2 contributions payable by share fishermen is increased from £5.80 to £6.15.

Index
National Insurance Contributions

Index
National Insurance Contributions

A

ADJUDICATION
appeals, S.I. 1986, No. 2218, r. 12
assessors, SSA 1989, Sch. 3, para. 3
contributions pending, determining, SSA 1975, s. 119
decisions,
—accidental errors in, S.I. 1986, No. 2218, r. 10
—application for, S.I. 1986, No. 2218, rr. 3, 6
—finality of, SSA 1975, s. 117
—setting aside, S.I. 1986, No. 2218, r. 11
experts, questions referred to, SSA 1989, Sch. 3, para. 3
inquiry,
—procedure, SSA 1975, s. 115, Sch. 13; S.I. 1986, No. 2218, r. 15
person interested, meaning, S.I. 1986, No. 2218, r. 13
procedure, SSA 1989, Sch. 3, para. 4
regulations as to, SSA 1975, s. 114
representation, right to, S.I. 1986, No. 2218, r. 2
Secretary of State, by,
—appeals, SSA 1975, ss. 93, 94
—question of law, appeal on, SSA 1975, s. 94, S.I. 1986, No. 2218, r. 16
—questions for, SSA 1975, s. 93, S.I. 1986, No. 2218, r. 14
—re-opening, SSA 1975, s. 96
—restriction of applications, SSA 1989, Sch. 3, para. 1
—review of, SSA 1975, s. 96, S.I. 1984, No. 451, r. 15, S.I. 1986, No. 2218, r. 17
statutory maternity pay, questions concerning, SSA 1986, Sch. 5
time limits, S.I. 1986, No. 2218, r. 3, Sch. 2
AGE
Scotland, computation in, SSA 1980, s. 18
AIRMEN
contributions, liability for, SSA 1975, s. 129; S.I. 1979, No. 591, rr. 82–84
meaning, S.I. 1979, No. 591, r. 81

APPRENTICESHIP
starting credits on termination of, S.I. 1975, No. 556, r. 8
APPROVED TRAINING
starting credits for, S.I. 1975, No. 556, r. 7

B

BANKRUPTCY
debts, order of priority, B(S)A 1985, s. 51, Sch. 3; IA 1986, ss. 328, 386, 387, Sch. 6
estate, sequestration of, B(S)A 1985, s. 12
BODY CORPORATE
offences by, SSA 1986, s. 57

C

CONTRIBUTIONS
abnormal pay practices, effect of, S.I. 1979, No. 591, r. 21
agent, payment as, S.I. 1979, No. 591, Sch. 1, para. 3A
airmen, liability of, SSA 1975, s. 129; S.I. 1979, No. 591, rr. 82–84
annual review, SSA 1975, s. 120
armed forces, members of, SSA 1975, s. 128
breach of regulations, S.I. 1979, No. 591, r. 132
card,
—application for, S.I. 1979, No. 591, r. 51
—currency of, S.I. 1979, No. 591, r. 52
—defacement, etc., S.I. 1979, No. 591, r. 56
—disposal of, S.I. 1979, No. 591, r. 53
—issue of, S.I. 1979, No. 591, r. 52
Class 1,
—amendments to provisions, SS(MP)A 1977, s. 1
—annual maximum, S.I. 1979, No. 591, r. 17
—assessment of, S.I. 1979, No. 591, rr. 2–22. See also EARNINGS

Appendices

Abbreviations

COR   Contracted-out rate
EB   Earnings bracket
LEL   Lower earnings limit
RR   Reduced rate
SR   Standard rate
UEL   Upper earnings limit

APPENDIX 1. RATES AND LIMITS

	1981–82	1982–83	1983–84	1984–85	1985–86 (to 5.10.85)	Reference
Class 1						
Standard rate						
Primary	7.75%	8.75%	9.00%	9.00%	9.00%	SSA 1975, s. 4
Secondary*	10.20%	10.20%	10.45%	10.45%	10.45%	
Contracted-out rate						
Primary to LEL	7.75%	8.75%	9.00%	9.00%	9.00%	SSPA 1975,
Primary above LEL	5.25%	6.25%	6.85%	6.85%	6.85%	s. 27
Secondary to LEL*	10.20%	10.20%	10.45%	10.45%	10.45%	
Secondary above LEL*	5.70%	5.70%	6.35%	6.35%	6.35%	
Reduced rate						
Primary	2.75%	3.20%	3.85%	3.85%	3.85%	S.I. 1979 No. 591,
Secondary*	10.20%	10.20%	10.45%	10.45%	10.45%	reg. 104
Lower earnings limit	£	£	£	£	£	
Weekly	27.00	29.50	32.50	34.00	35.50	SSA 1975, s. 4
Monthly	117.00	127.83	140.85	147.33	153.83	
Annual	1,404.00	1,533.96	1,689.96	1,767.96	1,845.96	
Upper earnings limit						
Weekly	200.00	220.00	235.00	250.00	265.00	SSA 1975, s. 4
Monthly	866.67	953.33	1,018.33	1,083.33	1,148.33	S.I. 1979
Annual	10,400.04	11,439.96	12,219.96	12,999.96	13,779.96	No. 591, reg. 8
NI Surcharge*						
Local authorities	3.50%	3.50%	2.50%	2.50%	—	FA 1982, s. 143
Others	3.50%	3.5%/ 2.0%	1.5%/ 1.0%	1.00%/ —	—	NISA 1976, s. 1
Class 2	£	£	£	£	£	
Normal rate						
Male	3.40	3.75	4.40	4.60	4.75	SSA 1975, s. 7
Female	3.40	3.75	4.40	4.60	4.75	
Reduced rate	—	—	—	—	—	
						S.I. 1975,
Share fisherman's rate	5.15	5.85	7.00	7.20	7.55	No. 591, reg. 98
Exception limit	1,475	1,600	1,775	1,850	1,925†	SSA 1975, s. 7
De-categorisation limit	800	800	800	800	800†	—
Class 3	3.30	3.65	4.30	4.50	4.65	SSA 1975, s. 8
Class 4						
Normal rate	5.75%	6.00%	6.30%	6.30%	6.30%	SSA 1975, s. 9
	£	£	£	£	£	
Lower annual limit	3,150	3,450	3,800	3,950	4,150	SSA 1975, s. 9
Upper annual limit	10,000	11,000	12,000	13,000	13,780	S.I. 1979, No. 591 reg. 67
Annual maximum	821.50	1,020.25	1,120.95	1,192.50	1,264.05†	S.I. 1979 No. 591, reg. 17
Class 4						
Limiting amount						
Male	574.07	651.75	749.80	813.95	824.69†	—
Female	574.07	651.75	749.80	813.95	824.69†	—

* Until its abolition in 1984 to 1985, the National Insurance Surcharge was payable as an addition to secondary class 1 contributions.

† Full year.

1985–86 (From 6 October 1985)*

Class 1

Earnings			Primary				Secondary				Reference
Weekly	Monthly	Yearly	EB	SR%[1]	RR%[1]	COR%[2]	EB	SR%[1]	RR%[1]	COR%[2]	
£0 – £35.49	£0 – £153.82	£0 – £1,845.95	–	0.00	0.00	0.00	–	0.00	0.00	0.00	SSA 1975, s. 4
£35.50 (LEL) – £54.99	£153.83 (LEL) – £238.32	£1,845.96 (LEL) – £2,859.95	1	5.00	3.85	2.85	1	5.00	5.00	0.90	
£55.00 – £89.99	£238.33 – £389.99	£2,859.96 – £4,679.99	2	7.00	3.85	4.85	2	7.00	7.00	2.90	
£90.00 – £129.99	£390.00 – £563.32	£4,680.00 – £6,759.95	3	9.00	3.85	6.85	3	9.00	9.00	4.90	
£130.00 – £259.00 (UEL)	£563.33 – £1,148.33 (UEL)	£6,759.96 – £13,779.96 (UEL)	3	9.00	3.85	6.85	4	10.45	10.45	6.35	
£265.01 or more	£13,779.95 or more	£13,779.97 or more	–	Ignore earnings above UEL			4	10.45	10.45	10.45³	

	Yearly	Reference
Class 2		
Normal weekly rate	£3.50	SSA 1975, s. 7 / S.I. 1979 No. 591, reg. 98
Share fisherman's special rate	£6.30	
Small earnings exception limit	£1,925	SSA 1975, s. 7
De-categorisation limit	£800	—
Class 3	£3.40	SSA 1975, s. 8
Class 4		
Lower annual limit	£4,150	SSA 1975, s. 9
Upper annual limit	£13,780	SSA 1975, s. 9
Rate	6.3%	SSA 1975, s. 9
Limiting amount	£824.69	S.I. 1979 No. 591, reg. 67
Annual maximum	£1,264.05	S.I. 1979 No. 591, reg. 17

[1] Rate applies to all earnings by reference to which the rate band has been selected.

[2] Rate applies only to that part of earnings which exceeds the LEL; the relevant standard rate applies to that part of earnings equal to the LEL.

[3] Rate applies only to that part of earnings which exceeds the UEL; the relevant standard rate (presently, the same rate) applies to a part of earnings which equals the LEL, and the 6.35% rate applies to earnings which exceed the LEL but do not exceed the UEL.

* For a summary of rates and limits for the first half of 1985–86 and the previous years, see table. supra.

1986–87

Class 1

Earnings			Primary				Secondary				Reference
Weekly	Monthly	Yearly	EB	SR%[1]	RR%[1]	COR%[2]	EB	SR%[1]	RR%[1]	COR%[2]	
£0 – £37.99	£0 – £164.66	£0 – £1,976.03	–	0.00	0.00	0.00	–	0.00	0.00	0.00	
£38.00 (LEL) – £59.99	£164.67 (LEL) – £259.99	£1,976.04 (LEL) – £3,779.99	1	5.00	3.85	2.85	1	5.00	5.00	0.90	
£60.00 – £94.99	£260.00 – £411.66	£3,120.00 – £4,940.03	2	7.00	3.85	4.85	2	7.00	7.00	2.90	SSA 1975, s. 4
£95.00 – £139.99	£411.67 – £606.66	£4,940.04 – £7,280.03	3	9.00	3.85	6.85	3	9.00	9.00	4.90	
£140.00 – £285.00 (UEL)	£606.67 – £1,235.00 (UEL)	£7,280.04 – £14,820.00 (UEL)	3	9.00	3.85	6.85	4	10.45	10.45	6.35	
£285.01 or more	£1,235.01 or more	£14,820.01 or more	–	Ignore earnings above UEL			4	10.45	10.45	10.45[3]	

Class 2

	Yearly										Reference
Normal weekly rate	£3.75										SSA 1975, s. 7 S.I. 1979 No. 591, reg. 98
Share fisherman's special rate	£6.55										
Small earnings exception limit	£2,075										SSA 1975, s. 7
De-categorisation limit	£800										—

Class 3

	£3.65										SSA 1975, s. 8

Class 4

Lower annual limit	£4,450										SSA 1975, s. 9
Upper annual limit	£14,820										SSA 1975, s. 9
Rate	6.3%										SSA 1975, s. 9
Limiting amount	£852.06										S.I. 1979 No. 591, reg. 67

Annual maximum

	£881.30										S.I. 1979 No. 591, reg. 17

[1] Rate applies to all earnings by reference to which the rate band has been selected.

[2] Rate applies only to that part of earnings which exceeds the LEL; the relevant standard rate applies to that part of earnings equal to the LEL.

[3] Rate applies only to that part of earnings which exceeds the UEL; the relevant standard rate (presently, the same rate) applies to a part of earnings which equals the LEL, and the 6.35% rate applies to earnings which exceed the LEL but do not exceed the UEL.

1987–88

Class 1

Earnings			Primary				Secondary				Reference
Weekly	Monthly	Yearly	EB	SR%[1]	RR%[1]	COR%[2]	EB	SR%[1]	RR%[1]	COR%[2]	
£0 – £38.99	£0 – £168.99	£0 – £2,027.99	–	0.00	0.00	0.00	–	0.00	0.00	0.00	SSA 1975, s. 4
£39.00 (LEL) – £64.99	£169.00 (LEL) – £281.99	£2,028.00 (LEL) – £3,379.99	1	5.00	3.85	2.85	1	5.00	5.00	0.90	
£65.00 – £99.99	£282.00 – £433.99	£3,380.00 – £5,199.99	2	7.00	3.85	4.85	2	7.00	7.00	2.90	
£100.00 – £149.99	£434.00 – £649.99	£5,200.00 – £7,799.99	3	9.00	3.85	6.85	3	9.00	9.00	4.90	
£150.00 – £295.00 (UEL)	£650.00 – £1,279.00 (UEL)	£7,800.00 – £15,340.00 (UEL)	3	9.00	3.85	6.85	4	10.45	10.45	6.35	
£295.01 or more	£1,279.01 or more	£15,340.01 or more	–	Ignore earnings above UEL			4	10.45	10.45	10.45[3]	

Class 2

		Reference
Normal weekly rate	£3.85	SSA 1975, s. 7 / S.I. 1979 No. 591, reg. 98
Share fisherman's special rate	£6.55	S.I. 1979 No. 591, reg. 98
Small earnings exception limit	£2,125	—
De-categorisation limit	£800	

Class 3

		Reference
	£3.75	SSA 1975, s. 8

Class 4

		Reference
Lower annual limit	£4,590	SSA 1975, s. 9
Upper annual limit	£15,340	SSA 1975, s. 9
Rate	6.3%	SSA 1975, s. 9
Limiting amount	£881.30	S.I. 1979 No. 591, reg. 67

Annual maximum

		Reference
	£1,407.15	S.I. 1979 No. 591, reg. 17

[1] Rate applies to all earnings by reference to which the rate band has been selected.
[2] Rate applies only to that part of earnings which exceeds the LEL; the relevant standard rate applies to that part of earnings equal to the LEL.
[3] Rate applies only to that part of earnings which exceeds the UEL; the relevant standard rate (presently, the same rate) applies to a part of earnings which equals the LEL, and the 6.35% rate applies to earnings which exceed the LEL but do not exceed the UEL.

1988–89

Class 1

Earnings			Primary				Secondary				Reference
Weekly	Monthly	Yearly	EB	SR%¹	RR%¹	COR%²	EB	SR%¹	RR%¹	COR%²	
£0 – £40.99	£0 – £177.99	£0 – £2,131.99	—	0.00	0.00	0.00	—	0.00	0.00	0.00	
£41.00 (LEL) – £69.99	£178.00 (LEL) – £303.99	£2,132.00 (LEL) – £3,639.99	1	5.00	3.85	3.00	1	5.00	5.00	1.20	
£70.00 – £104.99	£304.00 – £454.99	£3,640.00 – £5,459.99	2	7.00	3.85	5.00	2	7.00	7.00	3.20	SSA 1975, s. 4
£105.00 – £154.99	£455.00 – £671.99	£5,460.00 – £8,059.99	3	9.00	3.85	7.00	3	9.00	9.00	5.20	
£155.00 – £305.00 (UEL)	£672.00 – £1,322.00 (UEL)	£8,060.00 – £15,860.00 (UEL)	3	9.00	3.85	Ignore earnings above UEL	4	10.45	10.45	6.65	
£305.01 or more	£1,332.01 or more	£15,860.01 or more	—					10.45	10.45	10.45³	

Class 2											
Normal weekly rate		£4.05									SSA 1975, s. 7 / S.I. 1979 No. 591, reg. 98
Share fisherman's special rate		£6.55									
Small earnings exception limit		£2,250									S.I. 1979 No. 591, reg. 98
De-categorisation limit		£800									—

Class 3		£3.95									SSA 1975, s. 8

Class 4											
Lower annual limit		£4,750									SSA 1975, s. 9
Upper annual limit		£15,860									SSA 1975, s. 9
Rate		6.3%									SSA 1975, s. 9
Limiting amount		£914.58									S.I. 1979 No. 591, reg. 67

Annual maximum		£1,454.85									S.I. 1979 No. 591, reg. 17

¹ Rate applies to all earnings by reference to which the rate band has been selected.

² Rate applies only to that part of earnings which exceeds the LEL; the relevant standard rate applies to that part of earnings equal to the LEL.

³ Rate applies only to that part of earnings which exceeds the UEL; the relevant standard rate (presently, the same rate) applies to a part of earnings which equals the LEL, and the 6.65% rate applies to earnings which exceed the LEL but do not exceed the UEL.

1989–90

Class 1

Earnings			Primary[4]				Secondary				Reference
Weekly	Monthly	Yearly	EB	SR%[1]	RR%[2]	COR%[2]	EB	SR%[1]	RR%[1]	COR%[2]	
£0 – £42.99	£0 – £186.99	£0 – £2,235.99	–	0.00	0.00	0.00	1	0.00	0.00	0.00	SSA 1975, s. 4
£43.00 (LEL) – £74.99	£187.00 (LEL) – £324.99	£2,236.00 (LEL) – £3,899.99	1	5.00	3.85	3.00	1	5.00	5.00	1.20	
£75.00 – £114.99	£325.00 – £498.99	£3,900.00 – £5,979.99	2	7.00	3.85	5.00	2	7.00	7.00	3.20	
£115.00 – £164.99	£499.00 – £714.99 (UEL)	£5,980.00 – £8,579.99	3	9.00	3.85	7.00	3	9.00	9.00	5.20	
£165.00 – £325.00 (UEL)	£715.00 – £1,409.00 (UEL)	£8,580.00 – £16,900.00 (UEL)	3	9.00	3.85	7.00	4	10.45	10.45	6.65	
£325.01 or more	£1,409.01 or more	£16,900.01 or more	–	Ignore earnings above UEL			4	10.45	10.45	10.45[3]	

Class 2				Reference
Normal weekly rate	£4.25			SSA 1975, s. 7; S.I. 1979 No. 591, reg. 98
Share fisherman's special rate	£5.80			S.I. 1979 No. 591, reg. 98
Small earnings exception limit	£2,250			—
De-categorisation limit	£800			

Class 3				
	£4.15			SSA 1975, s. 8

Class 4				
Lower annual limit	£5,050			SSA 1975, s. 9
Upper annual limit	£16,900			SSA 1975, s. 9
Rate	6.3%			SSA 1975, s. 9
Limiting amount	£971.80			S.I. 1979 No. 591, reg. 67

Annual maximum				
	£1,468.98			S.I. 1979 No. 591, reg. 17

[1] Rate applies to all earnings by reference to which the rate band has been selected.

[2] Rate applies only to that part of earnings which exceeds the LEL; the relevant standard rate applies to that part of earnings equal to the LEL.

[3] Rate applies only to that part of earnings which exceeds the UEL; the relevant standard rate (presently, the same rate) applies to a part of earnings which equals the LEL, and the 6.65% rate applies to earnings which exceed the LEL but do not exceed the UEL.

1990–91

Class 1

	Earnings		Primary			Secondary				Reference
Weekly	Monthly	Yearly	SR	RR%	COR	EB	SR%[1]	RR%[1]	COR%[2]	
£0 – £45.99	£0 – £199.99	£0 – £2,391.99	0.00	0.00	0.00	–	0.00	0.00	0.00	SSA 1975, s. 4
£46.00 (LEL) – £79.99	£200.00 (LEL) – £346.99	£2,392.00 (LEL) – £4,159.99	92p plus 9% of bal'ce	3.85	92p plus 7% of bal'ce	1	5.00	5.00	1.20	
£80.00 – £124.99	£347.00 – £541.99	£4,160.00 – £6,499.99		3.85		2	7.00	7.00	3.20	
£125.00 – £174.99	£542.00 – £758.99	£6,500.00 – £9,099.99		3.85		3	9.00	9.00	5.20	
£175.00 – £350.00 (UEL)	£759.00 – £1,517.00 (UEL)	£9,100.00 – £18,200.00 (UEL)		3.85		4	10.45	10.45	6.65	
£350.01 or more	£1,517.01 or more	£18,200.01 or more	Ignore earnings above UEL			4	10.45	10.45	10.45[3]	

Class 2		Yearly	Reference
Normal weekly rate		£4.55	SSA 1975, s. 7 / S.I. 1979 No. 591, reg. 98
Share fisherman's special rate		£6.15	
Small earnings exception limit		£2,600	S.I. 1979 No. 591, reg. 98
De-categorisation limit		£800	—
Class 3		£4.45	SSA 1975, s. 8
Class 4			
Lower annual limit		£5,450	SSA 1975, s. 9
Upper annual limit		£18,200	SSA 1975, s. 9
Rate		6.3%	SSA 1975, s. 9
Limiting amount		£1044.40	S.I. 1979 No. 591, reg. 67
Annual maximum		£1,498.84	S.I. 1979 No. 591, reg. 17

[1]Rate applies to all earnings by reference to which the rate band has been selected.

[2]Rate applies only to that part of earnings which exceeds the LEL; the relevant standard rate applies to that part of earnings equal to the LEL.

[3]Rate applies only to that part of earnings which exceeds the UEL; the relevant standard rate (presently, the same rate) applies to a part of earnings which equals the LEL, and the 6.65% rate applies to earnings which exceed the LEL but do not exceed the UEL.

APPENDIX 2. PRESS RELEASES

22 August 1977. No. 77/251
National Insurance Advisory Committee to consider draft regulations about ministers of religion

The National Insurance Advisory Committee is to consider draft regulations [see the Social Security (Categorisation of Earners) Regulations 1978 (S.I. 1978 No. 1689)] about the national insurance contributions to be paid by ministers of religion from 6 April next year, at the request of Mr. David Ennals, Secretary of State for Social Services.

The proposed regulations would treat those ministers of religion who are paid wholly or mainly by salary or stipend as if they were employed by the body paying the salary or stipend and establish rules for deciding, where there is more than one source of such payments, which body is to discharge the duties of an "employer". This will be the first time, after 66 years of national insurance, that the majority of salaried clergy will be treated otherwise than as "self-employed". The change, which is being made at the specific request of a committee representing all the main religious bodies, will enable ministers of religion to qualify for the additional pension under the new state scheme for which the contribution arrangements begin on 6 April next year.

8 December 1978. No. 78/407
National insurance contributions regulations

Regulations [S.I. 1978, No. 1703; revoked and consolidated in S.I. 1979 No. 591] made today by Mr. David Ennals, Secretary of State for Social Services, with the concurrence of the Revenue, make provision for the exclusion from gross earnings for the purposes of earnings-related contributions a payment from a profit-sharing scheme to which the FA 1978 applies. They also exclude from gross earnings a payment of expenses made to a disabled person under the Disabled Persons (Employment) Act 1944.

In additon they except from liability for Class 4 national insurance contributions the earnings from employment as a diver or diving supervisor in the North Sea or other designated area on which Class 1 contributions are charged.

The regulations come into operation on 4 January 1979 except for payments from profit-sharing schemes the provisions for which operate from 6 April 1979.

Note
FA 1978, ss. 53–61 make special provision for PAYE income tax on realisation, normally after at least five years, of shares allocated out of profits by a company to trustees to hold for the benefit of an employee. In view of their nature, neither shares appropriated under such a scheme nor the proceeds arising from each appropriation will in future attract liability for national insurance contributions.

Home-to-office expenses paid by an employer normally form part of an employee's gross earnings for national insurance purposes. Travelling expenses paid to a disabled person in sheltered workshops however will not in future attract a liability for contributions; this will bring them into line with people in open employment, for whom state-provided help with travelling expenses does not count as earnings for earnings-related contributions purposes.

FA 1978, s. 29 treats for tax purposes employment as a diver or diving supervisor in the North Sea or other designated area as if it were a trade within Schedule D Case I. This would normally lead to liability for Class 4 national insurance contributions. The earnings from such employment however incur liability for Class 1 earnings-related contributions and are therefore to be exempted from liability for Class 4 contributions.

7 August 1980. No. 80/204
National insurance contributions on service charges in the catering and hotel industries

Under Regulation 19 (1) (c) of the Social Security (Contributions) Regulations 1979, gratuities which are either not paid or not allocated (directly or indirectly) by an employer to his employees are not liable for national insurance contributions. The Department had hitherto assumed that this regulation covered payments derived from service charges. The recent decision that service charges are always liable for national insurance contributions was based on legal advice, that service charges are not a gratuity, and are not therefore covered by the regulation.

14 March 1986. No. 86/86
New national insurance contribution for overseas volunteer development workers

New regulations were today introduced to enable voluntary workers working in developing countries to pay a special voluntary national insurance contribution for their period of service if they:

(*a*) are normally resident in Great Britain;

(*b*) are recruited by a recognised organisation; and

(*c*) are sent to work in a recognised developing country.

A further set of Regulations were also introduced today to enable the special Volunteer Development Workers' contribution to be included when unemployment benefit entitlement is calculated. The special contributions will come into effect from 6 April 1986. It will cost £6.55 per week.

Mr. Tony Newton, Minister of State for Social Security said, "I am pleased that by introducing this special rate of national insurance contribution we are able to put right a long standing anomaly and to do something positive to make life easier for these people who play such a valuable part in the British Overseas Aid Programme".

4 February 1987. No. 87/49
Statutory maternity pay and statutory sick pay—compensation for employers' national insurance contributions

Arrangements for compensating employers for their share of the national insurance contributions payable on statutory maternity pay have been announced today by Mr. John Major, Minister for Social Security. He also announced the rate of compensation for national insurance contributions paid by employers on statutory sick pay from 6 April 1987. Mr. Major was answering a Parliamentary Question from Roger Sims MP (Chislehurst).

Mr. Major said:

"The arrangements for reimbursing employers for their payments of statutory maternity pay and compensating them for the associated secondary (employers) national insurance contributions will be the same as those now operating for statutory sick pay. For the year beginning 6 April 1987 the compensation for secondary national insurance contributions will be a rate of 7 per cent. of the statutory maternity pay paid to employees. This rate will also apply to payments of statutory sick pay. It has been calculated from estimates of aggregate payments of statutory sick pay and statutory maternity pay in 1987–88 and the total secondary National Insurance contributions payable on them.

"I have today made the necessary regulations".

The Regulations are The Statutory Maternity Pay (Compensation of Employers) Regulations 1987 (S.I. 1987 No. 91); The Statutory Sick Pay (Additional Compensation of Employers) Amendment Regulations 1987 (S.I. 1987 No. 92).

Notes

1. Statutory maternity pay is introduced by the Social Security Act 1986. It will combine the present maternity pay (paid by employers) and maternity allowance (paid by DSS). Employers will pay statutory maternity pay in the same way as they already pay statutory sick pay.

2. Statutory sick pay has been paid by employers since April 1983. Employers became entitled to compensation for their share of the national insurance contributions payable on statutory sick pay from April 1985. From April 1986 statutory sick pay has been payable for up to 28 weeks of sickness in any one period of incapacity for work.

July 1990. Department of Social Security
National insurance contributions on employee's petrol expenses

Background

When an employer pays an employee's petrol expenses, NICs must be paid on their value, unless the payment can be shown to be a business expense. The regulation which allows an employer to disregard some or all of employees petrol expenses which he pays is the Social Security (Contributions) Regulations 1979, S.I. 1979 No. 591, reg. 19 (4) (*b*). The regulation excludes "any specific and distinct payment of, or contribution towards, expenses actually incurred by an employed earner in carrying out his employment."

The really important words are "expenses actually incurred". They mean that employers must keep documentary evidence to show that any petrol payments on which NICs have not been charged are actual business expenses. Where petrol expenses, incurred because of both business and private use, are reimbursed only the business expenses which can be supported by documentary evidence can be excluded from NIC liability.

Sometimes an employer supplies petrol directly to an employee from his own stock, *i.e.*, from his company petrol pump. If he does this there is no need to assess NICs on its value. The same will apply if he gives fuel vouchers to an employee which cannot be surrendered for cash, or if an employee is allowed to charge petrol to a garage account in his employer's name. (Where an employee charges petrol to the employer's garage account, the debt is incurred by the employer and only the employer has any liability to pay for the petrol.)

The regulations which allows these methods of supplying petrol to be excluded from NIC liability is the Social Security (Contributions) Regulations 1979, S.I. 1979 No. 591, reg. 19 (1) (*d*). The regulation deals with payments in kind, services and other facilities.

The Employer's Manual on national insurance contributions (NI 269)
The manual describes various methods of providing for an employee's petrol and the way in which they should be treated when considering NICs. The supplement to the employer's manual from October 1989 gives additional information on this. The methods of supply are divided into two basic groups:

(1) ALLOWANCES WHICH ATTRACT NIC LIABILITY

    (*a*) cash allowances;
    (*b*) vouchers which can be exchanged for petrol and/or cash;
    (*c*) petrol bought using an employee's credit card and subsequently paid for by the employer;
    (*d*) payments by an employer to an employee's garage account.

Any part of the above allowances for which documentary evidence is kept to confirm that the petrol was used on the employers business can be disregarded when paying NICs.

(2) METHODS OF SUPPLY WHICH DO NOT ATTRACT NIC LIABILITY

    (*a*) petrol supplied from company stocks;
    (*b*) vouchers which cannot be exchanged for cash;
    (*c*) petrol charged to an employer's garage account;

Payment using an agency card or employer's credit card
Under this heading employers are told that any incidental private use can be disregarded where an employer intends to supply petrol only for business use. An employer needs to ask himself here whether he intends to allow any private motoring by his employee, using the petrol he pays for. If the answer is no, then no NIC liability will arise if, exceptionally, the employee uses the petrol for a private journey. Generally there will be no element of private motoring which can be disregarded simply because there will usually be some element of private use accepted by the employer, *e.g.*, home to office travel.

Employer's credit cards/petrol agency cards
Many employers use this method of supplying petrol to minimise administrative costs. Having obtained legal advice, the Department is satisfied that any petrol supplied using this method is liable for NICs unless documentary evidence can be produced to show that some or all of the petrol was used on business.

NIC liability on payments using this method was first explained in NI 269. Employers who have maintained records since 6 April 1989 will not be liable for any identified business petrol from that date. Where no documentary evidence is available to confirm business use or where the employer cannot demonstrate that his supply is for business purposes only he will be liable for both primary and secondary NICs on all petrol supplied using his credit/agency card.

What records need to be kept to show business expenditure
Employers will have to keep evidence to confirm the amount and cost of petrol, for which they have paid, for individual employees and maintain a log of all miles travelled so that the non-business element can be identified. NICs must be paid on any "non-business" costs met by the employer.

Home to place of work journeys cannot be treated as a business expense for NIC purposes. An employee who drives to and from work in addition to his usual business mileage will have to complete a log showing the business and private mileage separately, *e.g.* petrol purchased 20 gallons, miles driven 600, home to office 200 miles, business mileage 400 miles. Therefore ²/₃ of cost of fuel would be NIC free.

Logs will not be needed where an employee pays for petrol but receives a mileage allowance based on the business miles declared in his claim.

How should the value of any private use petrol be assessed
The value of any private petrol can be assessed either as a proportion of the overall miles travelled (*i.e.* of the petrol bought and the actual consumption) or by using the cars agreed consumption figures (quoted for 56 m.p.h.). Any other reasonable method of assessment can be used providing prior authority is obtained from DSS.

Value and the point at which liability should be discharged
Employers have expressed difficulty over the question of the value of petrol to be used when assessing NIC liability. Petrol used for business includes a charge for VAT which is paid on purchase but which is refundable. When assessing the value of petrol used for private motoring, the

cost to the employer is the value to be used. The net cost of petrol can be used, when an employer is entitled to a VAT refund, on any petrol for private use.

Liability for NICs arises when a payment is made. In most cases this will be self-evident, but when credit cards are used there are difficulties. Where an employee uses his/her own credit card and is reimbursed by the employer, liability will arise in the pay period during which reimbursement is made by the employer.

Where company credit cards/agency cards are used payment of NICs should be made in the pay period when the employer receives the account from the agency/credit card company, whether or not the employer settles the account.

Petrol bought for business use: some incidental private use
The supplement to the Employers Manual gives specific advice on this. If the employer's intention is to pay only for business expenses, then any occasional incidental private use, where this is unavoidable, *e.g.* because of urgent domestic problems, can be ignored and there will be no need to keep a mileage log. An employer must be able to show that petrol paid for is intended for business in order to operate this easement.

Although the Employer's Manual suggests that this approach applies only to purchases using credit/agency cards, it can be used to cover other ways of paying for petrol which attract NIC liability.

Business journeys
Where an employee visits an employer's client or a temporary place of work direct from his home, NIC liability will arise on payments made which exceed the payment to which an employee would have been entitled if the journey was made from his normal place of work. This will apply equally to the value of petrol supplied by a credit/agency card.

Where employees (*e.g.* travelling salesmen) have no base to which they are regularly required to report, NIC liability will not arise on payments made for business journeys where travelling forms an integral part of their duties. This applies equally to the value of petrol supplied by credit/agency cards.

Further information/advice
If further advice is required, please contact your local DSS office.

Index
NI Contributions Appendices

References in this index are to page numbers

Part III Stamp Duty and Stamp Duty Reserve Tax

Contents

All references, in this style **S & S 123** and **S & S A12** , in this Part are to Sergeant and Sims on Stamp Duties and Capital Duty and Stamp Duty Reserve Tax (Ninth edition) and the supplement thereto.

[*N.B.* In relation to the prospective abolition of all stamp duties on transactions in shares (including bearer instruments) and units under unit trust schemes, and of stamp duty reserve tax, see the Revenue Press Release, 20 March 1990 and the commentary on FA 1990.]

Pensions and Yeomanry Pay Act 1884

47 & 48 Vict. c. 55

5. Exemption from stamp duty. (S&S 421)
This provision was extended to the Air Force (S.R. & O. 1918 No. 548) and was amended by FA 1949, s. 52 and Sch. 11, Pt. V, and by FA 1970, s. 36 (8) and Sch. 8, Pt. IV.

Barracks Act 1890

53 & 54 Vict. c. 25

11. Exemption from stamp duty. (S&S 198, 424)
This provision was extended to the Air Force (S.R. & O. 1918 No. 538) and the Navy (FA 1944, s. 46) and was amended by the Defence (Transfer of Functions) (No. 1) Order 1964, S.I. 1964 No. 488, Art. 2 (2) and Sch. 1, Pt. 11.

Stamp Duties Management Act 1891

54 & 55 Vict. c. 38

1. Act to apply to all stamp duties. (S&S 41–42, 455)

Responsibility is conferred on the Commissioners of Inland Revenue (the Commissioners) for administering the collection of all fees and duties which as a matter of law are chargeable as stamp duties, *i.e.* which are collected or received by means of adhesive or impressed stamps, which may include, for example, the payment of Class 2 or Class 3 national insurance contributions (which may be by means of adhesive stamps if the Secretary of State so provides pursuant to the Social Security Act of 1975, Sch. 1, para. 6 (2) and (3)).

Certain provisions of the Acts also apply to national savings stamps (by virtue of the National Savings Stamps Regulations 1969, S.I. 1969 No. 1343), savings certificates (see the Savings Certificates Regulations, S.I. 1972, No. 641) and to national savings stocks (see the National Savings Stock Register Regulations 1976, S.I. 1976 No. 2012).

The Inland Revenue Regulation Act 1890 sets out the general powers of the Commissioners of Inland Revenue with regard to the relevant duties.

Since 1974, the administration of stamp duty payable in Northern Ireland has also been the responsibility of the Commissioners of Inland Revenue in the United Kingdom (see the Northern Ireland Constitution Act 1973, and the Northern Ireland (Modification of Enactments—No. 1) Order 1973, S.I. 1973 No. 2163, made thereunder). The Stamp Office in Belfast continues in full operation under the functional control of the Controller of Stamps in London.

MODE OF RECOVERING MONEY RECEIVED FOR DUTY

2. Moneys received for duty and not appropriated to be recoverable in High Court. (S&S 42)

The Commissioners are empowered by this section to institute legal proceedings in the High Court to compel any person who has received any sum of money in respect of stamp duty payable to the Commissioners to account to them for that sum if it is improperly withheld or retained by that person, together with the costs of the proceedings, unless cause can be shown to the Court why such payments should not be made (in which case the Court is empowered to make such Order as it thinks just).

Under the Crown Proceedings Act 1947, s. 14 (1), the Commissioners can now take summary proceedings to recover money withheld.

In the case of *Lord Advocate* v. *Gordon* (1901) 8 SLT 439, it was held that a solicitor was accountable to the Crown under s. 2 (1) when he deducted, from moneys payable to a client, an amount for stamp duty and subsequently withheld payment to the Revenue for more than three years.

Proceedings are taken in the High Court by originating motion or originating summons to which the person required to account or pay is made respondent or defendant, and the provision of s. 2 (2) that the Crown may sue a writ of summons for this relief is now obsolete.

Compliance with any order of the Court may be enforced by attachment (see *Re Coulson* (1894), cited in *Highmore's Stamp Laws* (4th edn.), p. 17 and *Halsbury's Laws of England* (4th edn.), Vol. 44, para. 605, note 3).

SALE OF STAMPS

3. Power to grant licences to deal in stamps. (S&S 42–43)

Before 1961, the Commissioners could only grant licences for dealing in stamps from particular premises, but s. 3 (1) and (2) were amended by the Post Office Act 1961, s. 25 (1), to remove this requirement.

The Post Office Act 1961, s. 25 also, by the repeal of s. 3 (3) and the words in s. 3 (4), abolished the former requirement that a licence holder must give security to the Commissioners in the sum of £100, in such manner and form as the Commissioners prescribe, for example by a bond.

The section ceased to apply to postage stamps with effect from 3 November 1966.

4. Penalty for unauthorised dealing in stamps, etc. (S&S 43)

This section no longer applies to postage stamps (FA 1966, s. 48 (1) (*a*)).

5. Provisions as to determination of a licence. (S&S 43–44)

A person whose licence to deal in stamps expires (or, if he dies or becomes bankrupt while still a licence holder, his personal representatives or trustee in bankruptcy) has the right to return any stamps in his possession at the time of the expiry of the licence, or at the time of his death or bankruptcy, in which case he is (or they are) entitled to demand a refund from the Commissioners of the amount of duty represented by the stamps.

6. Penalty for hawking stamps. (S&S 44)
Again, this section no longer applies to postage stamps (FA 1966, s. 48 (1) (*a*)).

8. Discount. (S&S 44)

ALLOWANCE FOR SPOILED STAMPS

9. Procedure for obtaining allowance. (S&S 44–48)
Subject to certain conditions, stamp duty can be recovered where it is paid on an instrument which is ineffective or useless, so that the duty would be wasted. Examples include cases where an instrument is prepared on stamped paper and never used, or where errors are made in preparing an instrument so that it cannot be used, or where an instrument turns out to be completely void. Application must be made within two years of the fixing of the stamp and it can only be made in a fairly restricted class of cases, for example where the instrument is void *ab initio* or is never executed by a required party, or is inadvertently spoiled. The duty cannot be recovered in cases where an instrument fails through non-fulfilment of a condition precedent, or where a voidable instrument is avoided or rescinded by some party entitled to do so. It is also not possible to recover the duty where legal proceedings have been commenced in which the instrument would or could have been given in evidence. By contrast, SA 1891, s. 59 contains a much less restrictive provision in relation to the stamp duty charged by that section on certain contracts which are chargeable as conveyances on sale; under sub-s. (6), if the contract is anulled or rescinded or not substantially performed, then any *ad valorem* duty paid to the Commissioners must be returned by them. Also, under this subsection, there is no time limit and no requirement that the instrument shall not have been admitted or admissible in evidence.

By virtue of the provisions of FA 1966, s. 46 (4), any reference in s. 9, and in s. 10, to any stamp is deemed to include (unless the context otherwise requires) a reference to any indication of the payment and the amount of stamp duty referred to in FA 1966, s. 46 (1) (*b*).

Allowances for spoiled stamps are made by the issue of fresh stamps in lieu, by a cash payment or by the issue of a payable order as arranged at the time the claim is made. A cash refund will only be made where the amount of the claim does not exceed £20. It is a condition precedent to allowances being made that the spoiled instrument be surrendered for destruction, and only in very exceptional circumstances will this condition be waived. Furthermore, spoiled instruments must be presented in a complete state without mutilation—no allowances will be made where stamps have been removed from documents. Claims have to be made in writing by the owner of the stamps (*i.e* the person for whose use and business they were purchased) or by his agent or employee authorised by him in writing. Claims are made on Form 52 (Stamps), of which a specimen can be found at S&S 47.

For other provisions in relation to the repayment of stamp duty, see FA 1965, s. 90 (2) and (5).

Allowance of the stamp duty on lost documents will be made either by repayment, where replicas have been stamped, or by free stamping of the replicas; Extra-statutory concession G1. Where the stamp duty is allowed on a document because it has been spoiled or lost and replaced by a replica but the duty has been increased so that the amount to be impressed on the replica is more that the amount allowable on the original, then the additional duty is impressed free of charge: Extra-statutory concession G2.

For submission of claims, see Law Society Press Release of 27 September 1989.

10. Allowance for misused stamps. (S&S 48)
The Commissioners are empowered to treat as spoiled any stamp used which was of greater value than required or was inadvertently used on an instrument not liable to any duty, provided that application is made within two years after the date of the instrument (or, if it is not dated, within two years after execution) and the instrument, if liable for duty, is stamped with the proper duty.

11. Allowance how to be made. (S&S 48)
The Commissioners may make allowances for spoiled or misused stamps by giving other stamps in lieu or, at their discretion, stamps of any other denomination to the same amount in value, or cash.

12. Stamps not wanted may be repurchased by the Commissioners. (S&S 48)
The Commissioners also have discretion to repurchase stamps which are not spoiled or rendered unfit or useless, but merely surplus to requirements, provided that application is made within two years of the stamps being purchased from an authorised or licensed person and with a bona fide intention to use the stamps.

OFFENCES RELATING TO STAMPS

13. Certain offences in relation to dies and stamps provided by Commissioners to be felonies. (S&S 48–49)
As the Forgery Act 1913 did not extend to Scotland, the repeals made by that Act of the words in s. 13 (1) ("forges a die or stamp"), s. 13 (2) ("prints or makes an impression upon any material with

a forged die"), s. 13 (8) ("any forged stamp, or") and s. 13 (9) ("any forged die or stamp or") do not apply as regards Scotland and the words are still in force there.

Sentences of penal servitude and hard labour were abolished by the Criminal Justice Act 1948, s. 1, and references to these powers are now to be construed as powers to sentence to terms of imprisonment only.

By virtue of the Post Office Act 1969, s. 118, this section also applies to offences in relation to postage stamps.

Offences under this section are now triable either summarily or on indictment, instead of only on indictment. Furthermore, all distinctions between a felony and a misdemeanour have been abolished and in matters in which a distinction had previously been drawn the law becomes the law as it relates to misdemeanours.

For the purposes of this section, the expression "forged stamp" is deemed to include a stamp bearing a cancellation mark as well as an unused stamp (see *R.* v. *Lowden* [1914] 1 KB 144). Lack of knowledge that a stamp was forged has been held not to be a lawful excuse for possession unless the stamp was acquired lawfully, *e.g.* at a post office (see *Winkle* v. *Wiltshire* [1951] 1 KB 684, a decision on the interpretation of the Post Office Act 1953, s. 63 (1) (*b*)). It has also been held that a die for making a false stamp which was in the defendant's possession for a purely innocent purpose was still possession without lawful excuse within the meaning of the Post Office (Protection) Act 1884, s. 7 (*c*), the provision repealed and replaced by the Post Office Act 1953, s. 63 (1) (*b*) (see *Dickins* v. *Gill* [1896] 2 QB 310).

16. Proceedings for detection of forged dies, etc. (S&S 51)
A Justice of the Peace is empowered to issue a search warrant on the receipt of information upon oath that there is cause to suspect that an offence under the above sections has been committed, and to allow the seizure of anything found upon execution of the warrant.

See also Revenue Act 1898, s. 12, which applied this section in the same way to the manufacture of paper used for excise licences.

17. Proceedings for detection of stamps stolen or obtained fraudulently. (S&S 51)
Any Justice of the Peace may issue warrants for the seizure of stolen or fraudulently obtained stamps, and for the arrest of the person in whose possession or custody the stamps are found. If any person arrested pursuant to this section is not able to give a satisfactory reason for his possession of the stamps, or prove that they were purchased by him from an authorised or licensed person, then the stamps are to be forfeited and delivered to the Commissioners unless any other person comes forward within the next six months to claim the stamps, proving that the stamps were stolen or fraudulently obtained from him after they had been duly purchased by him.

18. Licensed person in possession of forged stamps to be presumed guilty until contrary is shown. (S&S 51–52)
This is one of the rare instances where, under English law, a person is presumed to be guilty until he proves himself innocent. Any person appointed or licensed to sell or deal in stamps found to be in possession of forged stamps is to be regarded as having them in his possession knowing them to be forged and with intent to sell them, and therefore liable to the appropriate penalty, unless he can prove the contrary to be the case. Furthermore, where the Commissioners suspect that any such person has forged stamps in his possession, they are themselves empowered to issue a search warrant and to authorise the person executing the warrant to make a forcible entry on the relevant premises if they are not admitted voluntarily. It is an offence to refuse to permit any search or seizure pursuant to such a warrant or to assault, oppose, molest or obstruct any person authorised to execute the warrant.

See also FA 1966, s. 48 (1) (*c*), which provides that, in relation to postage stamps, s. 18 (1) is to have effect as if the words "or being or having been licensed to deal in stamps" were omitted.

19. Mode of proceeding when stamps are seized. (S&S 52)
Where stamps are seized pursuant to a warrant, the person in whose possession they are found is entitled to demand a receipt for the stamps seized, and to mark them before they are removed.

20. As to defacement of adhesive stamps. (S&S 52)
Any person who defaces a stamp without authority is liable to a fine.

21. Penalty for frauds in relation to duties. (S&S 52)
Any person who commits an act with intent to defraud the Government is liable to a fine.

MISCELLANEOUS

22. As to discontinuance of dies (S&S 52–53)
The Commissioners can discontinue the use of any die used for the impression of stamps and replace it with a new die, and the change takes effect on the day specified in public notices to be

given in the London, Edinburgh, Dublin and (by virtue of the Government of Ireland (Adaptation of the Taxing Acts) Order 1922, Pt. IV, para. 17 (*d*) (S.R. & O. 1922 No. 80)) Belfast Gazettes. Any instrument first executed by any person after that date, or dated after that date, and stamped with a discontinued die will be deemed not to be properly stamped, except as provided in sub-paragraphs (*a*) and (*b*). Sub-paragraph (*a*) relates to instruments executed outside the U.K. and provides that any such instrument which is stamped with a discontinued die can be produced to the Commissioners within 14 days of its arrival in the U.K. for the discontinued stamped to be cancelled and the instrument to be stamped with the new die. Sub-paragraph (*b*) allows any person in the possession of an instrument rendered useless by virtue of the fact that it has been stamped with a discontinued die to produce it to the Commissioners within six months of the adoption of the new die to enable the old stamp to be cancelled and the instrument to be stamped with the new die.

23. Application of Act to excise labels. (S&S 53)
The provisions in relation to offences in connection with stamps apply to labels used for the purposes of excise duties.

24. Declarations, how to be made. (S&S 53)
Any statutory declaration required for the purposes of the Act is to be made before the Commissioners themselves, or any person authorised by them, or before any Commissioner for Oaths, Justice of the Peace or Notary Public in the United Kingdom, or in any place outside the United Kingdom before any person duly authorised to administer oaths there.

This section also applies to affidavits and oaths (Revenue Act 1898, s. 7 (6)). See also the Solicitors Act 1974, s. 81, whereby solicitors are generally empowered to administer oaths. Similarly, see also the Solicitors (Northern Ireland) Order 1976, Article 78.

25. Mode of granting licences. (S&S 53)

26. Recovery of fines. (S&S 54)
Proceedings in relation to any fines payable under this Act may be instituted, and the fines recovered, in the same manner as a fine or penalty under any Act relating to the excise, or by action in the High Court. The Commissioners have wide discretionary powers of mitigating any fine or penalty under any Act relating *inter alia* to stamp duties and of staying or compounding any proceedings for its recovery, and they or the Treasury may mitigate or remit any such fine or penalty either before or after judgment.

Although fines under the Act may strictly speaking be regarded as punishments for offences, the actual liability is not criminal—a fine is a debt due to the Crown recoverable by proceedings in the High Court (which must be brought within two years of the commission of the offence). Accordingly, the common law rules as to criminal liability do not apply. One consequence of this is that, where an employee does an act in the course of his employment and within the scope of his authority, then his employer may be vicariously liable for the fine (*AG* v. *Carlton Bank* [1899] 2 QB 158). However, this does not mean that two fines can be extracted from two persons both vicariously liable for the single act or omission of another (*Lord Advocate* v. *Thomson* (1897) 24 R. (Ct. of Sess.) 543) and the presumption of an employer's liability can apparently be rebutted by proof of non-complicity (*R.* v. *Dean* (1843) 12 M&W 39).

27. Definitions. (S&S 54)

REPEAL, SHORT TITLE

30. Short title. (S&S 55)

Stamp Act 1891
54 & 55 Vict. c. 39

PART I REGULATIONS APPLICABLE TO INSTRUMENTS GENERALLY

CHARGE OF DUTY UPON INSTRUMENTS

1. Charge of duties in schedule. (S&S 55–56)

This is the charging section. Unless one of the many exemptions applies (see for example the general exemptions from stamp duty set out at the end of SA 1891, Sch. 1, or the special exemptions conferred by the various other Revenue and Finance Acts described below) stamp duties are payable on certain instruments which have legal effect, as specified in Sch. 1 and in the various other Revenue and Finance Acts described below.

Stamp duties are payable on documents and it therefore follows that, if a transaction can be effected orally or by conduct only, there will be no liability to stamp duty because there will be no document to which the stamp can be affixed. This has been reaffirmed many times in a large number of cases since stamp duty was first introduced. See for example Lord Esher MR in *I.R. Comrs.* v. *G. Angus & Co* (1889) 23 QBD 579 at 589, CA, and Lord Reid in *William Cory & Son Ltd.* v. *I.R. Comrs.* [1965] AC 1088.

Many legal transactions can only be effected by a written instrument, for example contracts for the sale and purchase of land (Law of Property (Miscellaneous Provisions) Act 1989, s. 2), and some legal transactions can only be effected by deed, for example powers of attorney (Powers of Attorney Act 1971, as amended by Law of Property (Miscellaneous Provisions) Act 1989, s. 1 (8) and Sch. 1). However, where an oral contract is possible, *e.g.* where chattels are sold and transferred by delivery, no stamp duty will be payable.

The general principle that the charge to stamp duty is a charge on documents rather than on transactions can in certain circumstances cause difficulties, *e.g.* where a transaction is effected partly orally and partly in writing. Consider the case of a contract where the offer is in writing and the acceptance is oral, or vice versa: in the former case there is no stamp duty as the offer by itself does not constitute an agreement, but in the latter case, where an offer is made orally and is accepted in writing, the acceptance concludes the contract and is prima facie stampable (*Hegarty* v. *Milne* (1854) 14 CB 627).

Another problem arises when parties enter into a transaction wholly orally and thereafter record or give effect to it in writing. There is no general provision that such a document should bear the same stamp duty as would have been payable had the parties originally entered into the transaction by means of a written instrument. Notwithstanding the lack of statutory provision, however, the courts have in certain circumstances held that duty is in fact payable where the creation of the memorandum or record and the previous oral transaction can in fact be construed as "all one transaction". In *Garnett* v. *I.R. Comrs.* (1899) 81 LT 633, a case concerning a receipt signed for the payment of the purchase price of a share of partnership assets on a dissolution, Channell J. said (at p. 638) "... the question is whether it is one transaction. If there is a clearly independent transaction and it is not all part of one transaction then it would stand on a different footing." This was cited with approval by Finlay J. in *Cohen & Moore* v. *I.R. Comrs.* [1933] 2 KB 126 (at pp. 137–138), a case involving a deed which purported to be an appointment of new trustees in respect of trusts declared orally some time beforehand, where the deed was held to be chargeable under the heading "Settlement" (repealed by FA 1962, s. 34 (7)).

It is a general principle of the law relating to stamp duty, and indeed of tax law as a whole, that in determining any liability, regard is to be had to the substance of the transaction rather than to its form. This question has been exhaustively considered and ruled upon by the House of Lords in a number of leading cases: *I.R. Comrs.* v. *Burmah Oil Co. Ltd.* [1982] STC 30; *W. T. Ramsay Ltd.* v. *I.R. Comrs.* heard together with *Eilbeck (Inspector of Taxes)* v. *Rawling* [1981] STC 174; *Furniss* v. *Dawson* [1984] STC 153, 55 TC 324; and *Craven (Inspector of Taxes)* v. *White* heard together with *I.R. Comrs.* v. *Bowater Property Developments Ltd.* and *Baylis (Inspector of Taxes)* v. *Gregory* [1988] 3 All E.R. 495. Of those cases, the most important, *Furniss* v. *Dawson*, was primarily concerned with CGT, but the scheme considered by the House of Lords also involved arrangements designed to save stamp duty.

The facts were as follows: The three appellants, who with the wife of one of them controlled two companies, F. & B. and K.G., had agreed in principle that the family would sell their shares in F. & B. and K.G. to W.B.H. (a company having no connection with the family). Pursuant to a scheme which was designed inter alia to defer liability to CGT, a company, G. was specially incorporated in the Isle of Man. The family then sold their shares in F. & B. and K.G. to G. in exchange for shares in G. and on the same day G. sold its shares in F. & B. and K.G. to W.B.H. for cash. The appellants appealed to the Special Commissioners against CGT assessments raised on the basis that the transactions had resulted in disposals by the family giving rise to chargeable gains. The Commissioners decided (contrary to the Revenue's contentions) that, when it bought the shares in F. & B. and K.G., G. acquired beneficial ownership of those shares, with the result that the shares issued to the family by G. fell to be treated as the same shares as the shares in F. & B. and

K.G. which the family had disposed of; and that this prevented a disposal for CGT purposes occurring at that stage. They therefore allowed the appeals and overturned the assessments. The Crown appealed to the Chancery Division where they argued that, in the light of the decisions of the House of Lords in *I.R. Comrs.* v. *Burmah Oil Co. Ltd.* and *W. T. Ramsay Ltd.* v. *I.R. Comrs., Eilbeck (Inspector of Taxes)* v *Rawling*, the two transactions could not be considered in isolation but had to be treated for tax purposes as part of a single composite scheme whereby the taxpayers disposed of their shares in F. & B. and K.G. to W.B.H. The Chancery Division, dismissing the Crown's appeals, held that even if the two steps in the scheme (the sale to G. and the onward sale by G. to W.B.H.) were taken as part of a single composite transaction, the first step in the composite transactions was nonetheless a real step which had enduring legal consequences in that, *inter alia*, G. became the beneficial owner of the shares in F. & B. and K.G. These consequences could not be ignored, nor the exchange agreement disregarded. G. accordingly, acquired control of F. & B. and K.G. when it acquired the shares in those companies, so that there was never a disposal of those shares by the family to W.B.H. Vinelott J. held that the new approach to tax avoidance schemes laid down by the House of Lords in the *Ramsay*, *Rawling* and *Burmah Oil* cases applied only where the steps forming part of the scheme were circular or self-cancelling or where a change in the parties' legal position was a mere change of form without enduring legal consequences. The Crown then appealed to the Court of Appeal, which agreed with Vinelott J. and unanimously dismissed the Crown's appeals. The Crown then appealed to the House of Lords and this time succeeded in their arguments. The House of Lords unanimously agreed that the result of correctly applying the principles laid down in the *Ramsay* case was that there was a disposal by the family in favour of W.B.H. in consideration of a sum of money paid with their consent to G. The House of Lords' reasons ran as follows:

(*a*) In a pre-planned tax saving scheme, no distinction is to be drawn for fiscal purposes, because none exists in reality, between

   (i) a series of steps which are followed through by virtue of an arrangement which falls short of a binding contract, and

   (ii) a like series of steps which are followed through because the participants are contractually bound to take each step *seriatim*.

Where there is a pre-ordained series of transactions or one single composite transaction, whether or not it includes the achievement of a legitimate commercial (*i.e.* business) end, and steps are inserted which have no commercial purposes apart from the avoidance of a liability to tax, the inserted steps are to be disregarded and the end results considered in the light of the relevant taxing statute.

(*b*) Fears that the Crown's arguments would lead to oppressive double taxation were misconceived. There would be no additional CGT on the steps by which the disposal from the family to W.B.H. was achieved, because the fiscal consequences of the introduction of G. are to be disregarded. On any subsequent disposal by the family of their shares in G., the base cost of the G. shares would be the price which they paid for them, namely the value of the shares in F. & B. and K.G. at the date of the scheme transactions.

In the subsequent three cases, heard together, of *Craven (Inspector of Taxes)* v. *White, I.R. Comrs.* v. *Bowater Property Developments Ltd.* and *Baylis (Inspector of Taxes)* v. *Gregory*, [1988] 3 All ER 495 a differently constituted House of Lords took great pains to restrict the scope of the fairly controversial principles laid down in *Ramsay* and *Furniss* v. *Dawson*. In each of these three cases there was a series of linear transactions in which the execution of the final transaction was not certain at the time a transaction with tax saving consequences was effected and the question arose whether the transactions were to be treated for tax purposes as preordained and therefore a single composite transaction so that the tax saving consequences were to be disregarded when tax was assessed.

In *Craven* v. *White* the taxpayers owned a family company, Q Ltd., which in 1973 they decided to sell. Their initial attempts to dispose of the company were not successful but in 1976 they entered into negotiations, first with a public company, O Ltd., for the sale of the company and then, when those negotiations were inconclusive, with CNC for a merger. In anticipation of the merger the taxpayers incorporated M Ltd. in the Isle of Man and agreed that M Ltd. should acquire the share capital of Q Ltd. from the taxpayers in exchange for shares in M Ltd. However, before the merger with CNC was completed, negotiations with O Ltd. were resumed with the result that it was agreed between the taxpayers and O Ltd. that M Ltd. would sell its Q Ltd. shares to a subsidiary of O Ltd. for £2·2m. When the transaction was completed M Ltd., whose only assets were the proceeds of the sale, distributed the proceeds to the taxpayers by means of interest-free loans.

The taxpayers were assessed to capital gains tax for 1976–77 and 1977–78 on the basis that the sale of the shares by M Ltd. had given rise to chargeable gains on disposals by the taxpayers. On appeal by the taxpayers, the Special Commissioners made a finding that the transfer of the Q Ltd. shares to M Ltd., M Ltd.'s sale of those shares a month later to O Ltd.'s subsidiary and the lending of the proceeds of sale to the taxpayers was a single composite transaction but since the agreements between the taxpayers and M Ltd. and between the taxpayers and O Ltd. were both genuine the taxpayers could not be said to have disposed of their shares directly to O Ltd.'s subsidiary.

In *I.R. Comrs.* v. *Bowater Property Developments Ltd.* the taxpayer company entered into negotiations with MP Ltd. for the sale of certain land and in anticipation of the sale the taxpayer company sold the land in equal shares to five associated companies with the aim of taking advantage of the £50,000 exemption from development land tax afforded by the Development Land Tax Act 1976, s. 12. MP Ltd. withdrew from the negotiations but subsequently reopened them and by a contract of sale in which the five associated companies were named as vendors the land was then sold to MP Ltd. at a higher price and on different terms.

The taxpayer company was assessed to development land tax on the basis that it had disposed of the land direct to MP Ltd. On appeal by the taxpayer company, the Special Commissioners discharged the assessment on the grounds that the true disponers of the land were the five associated companies.

In *Baylis* v. *Gregory* the taxpayers were shareholders of a family company. They entered into negotiations for the sale of the company to CSI Ltd. and in anticipation of the sale, made arrangements to incorporate an Isle of Man company with which the company's shares would be exchanged so that when the sale was effected payment of CGT would be postponed indefinitely. Before the Isle of Man company was incorporated CSI Ltd. broke off the negotiations but the taxpayers decided to continue with the incorporation of the Isle of Man company and the exchange of shares. At the time there was no other purchaser in prospect but 18 months later the taxpayers arranged a sale to a new purchaser and eventually the Isle of Man company sold the shares in the family company to that purchaser and then distributed the proceeds of sale to the taxpayers by way of interest-free loans.

The taxpayers were assessed to CGT on the basis that the share exchange was a chargeable disposal by the taxpayers and the sale of the shares by the Isle of Man company was a disposal by the taxpayers for capital gains tax purposes. On appeal, the Special Commissioners found that the share exchange and subsequent sale were not linked and accordingly allowed the appeal.

In all three cases appeals by the Crown to the High Court and then to the Court of Appeal were dismissed. The Crown appealed to the House of Lords. In all three cases the Revenue contended (1) that the crucial requirement for the application of the *Ramsay* and *Furniss* v. *Dawson* principles to a scheme for the avoidance of tax was that the inserted step in the series of transactions, which was for fiscal purposes to be ignored, should be embarked upon for no commercial purpose; and (2) that a series of transactions might properly be regarded as a "single, composite, transaction" if the transactions were intended to take place in a planned sequence and as machinery by which tax could be avoided, albeit in achieving a commercial end. The House of Lords held as follows:

(1) (Lords Templeman and Goff dissenting) The test of whether a series of transactions which contained a tax saving step was nevertheless liable to tax was whether the transactions were preordained, in the sense that, looking at the transactions as a whole, realistically they constituted a single and indivisible whole and were to be treated as such, and was not whether the tax saving step was effected for the purpose of avoiding tax on a contemplated subsequent transaction.

　　A linear series of transactions which contained an intermediate tax saving step would be held to be susceptible to tax if, but only if, (*a*) the series of transactions was, at the time when the intermediate transaction was entered into, preordained in order to produce a given result, (*b*) that transaction had no other purpose than tax mitigation, (*c*) there was at that time no practical likelihood that the preplanned events would not take place in the order ordained, so that the intermediate transaction was not even contemplated practically as having an independent life, and (*d*) the preordained events did in fact take place.

　　Accordingly, the disposal of property by a taxpayer by means of a series of transactions which had the effect of avoiding CGT would not be treated as a composite transaction or a preordained series of transactions by which the taxpayer was deemed for CGT purposes to have made a direct disposal if at the time when the transactions were entered into it was not certain that they would be carried through.

(2) Applying that principle, the appeals would be dismissed for the following reasons:

(*a*) (Lords Templeman and Goff dissenting) In the first appeal, at the time it was agreed that M Ltd. would acquire the share capital of Q Ltd. from the taxpayers in exchange for shares in M Ltd. it was not certain that the sale to O Ltd.'s subsidiary would take place since at that date the taxpayers were not in a position to secure that the sale went through.

　　Accordingly, it could not be said that at that stage there was a preordained series of transactions and therefore the share exchange between the taxpayers and M Ltd. was an independent transaction and there was no disposal for capital gains tax purposes by the taxpayers to O Ltd.'s subsidiary.

(*b*) In the second and third appeals, there was no connection between the disposal by the taxpayers and the eventual sale to a third party and therefore it could not be said that the disposals and sales were part of a preordained series of transactions.

　　Lords Keith and Oliver stressed that, in the application of the *Ramsay* and *Furniss* v. *Dawson* principles, there is no *moral* dimension by which tax avoidance is to be judged so that any step undertaken with a view to the avoidance or mitigation of tax on an anticipated transaction or disposition is for that reason to be ignored or struck down.

See also the decisions, following the above cases, in *Shepherd (Inspector of Taxes)* v. *Lyntress Ltd.; News International plc.* v. *Shepherd (Inspector of Taxes)* [1989] STC 617; *Countess Fitzwilliam and Others* v. *I.R. Comrs.* [1990] STC 65, and *Ensign Tankers (Leasing) Ltd.* v. *Stokes (Inspector of Taxes)* [1989] STC 705.

For an interesting decision in which a scheme that had been sanctioned by the House of Lords before the *Ramsay* case notwithstanding its circular, self-cancelling nature, but has now been struck down on *Ramsay* principles, see *Moodie* v. *I.R. Comrs. and Sinnett (Insp. of Taxes); Sotnick* v. *I.R. Comrs. and Edwards (Inspector of Taxes)* [1990] STC 475.

Because stamp duty is essentially a tax on documents, rather than a tax on transactions, there has been some considerable debate as to whether or not the principles enunciated in the *Ramsay* and *Furniss* v. *Dawson* cases apply to stamp duty. The Commissioners clearly took the view that the principles were applicable to stamp duty and their view received approval from the Chancery Division (Vinelott J.) in the case of *Ingram* v. *I.R. Comrs.* [1985] STC 835.

The facts of that case were as follows: The taxpayer negotiated a price of £145,500 for the purchase of an unencumbered freehold property with vacant possession. With a view to reducing the stamp duty payable on the transfer of the property, the following transactions were entered into:

(1) the vendor and the taxpayer made an agreement for the lease of the property for a term of 999 years at a premium of £145,000 and an annual rent of £25;

(2) the taxpayer agreed to indemnify the vendor against any liability he might incur which he would not have incurred on a straightforward sale of the property;

(3) H. Ltd., owned and controlled by the partners in the taxpayer's firm of solicitors, contracted to buy the freehold of the property for £500;

(4) H. Ltd. agreed a sub-sale of the property to the taxpayer at a price of £600;

(5) the vendor transferred and H. Ltd. confirmed to the taxpayer the property subject to and with the benefit of the terms and provisions of the lease.

Thereafter, the taxpayer presented the transfer for adjudication and the Revenue assessed the duty at 1 per cent. of £145,600. The taxpayer appealed to the High Court, contending that, stamp duty being chargeable on instruments solely, and SA 1891, s. 59 exempting contracts or agreements from the charge to conveyance on sale duty, the transfer, being the conveyance or transfer on sale, was dutiable only in respect of the consideration moving from the sub-purchaser (*i.e.*, the £600). The Crown contended that (1) the stamp duty, despite being payable on instruments and not on transactions, was arrived at by reference to the transaction that the instrument was intended to effect, complete or record; (2) that the substance of the matter must be looked at; (3) that the arrangements entered into constituted a single composite transaction, and (4) that, in substance and in reality, the transfer was the completion document of that single composite transaction and was thus chargeable to *ad valorem* duty on the whole of the consideration. It was held that, although stamp duty was a tax on instruments and not on transactions, the court had a duty to ascertain the substance of the transaction in the case before it, for it was the transaction which gave rise to the charge. Where a taxpayer had entered into a single composite transaction or a pre-ordained series of transactions with the intention of avoiding stamp duty, the Court would disregard the steps which had been inserted for no business purpose since the *Ramsay* principle constituted a judge-made anti-tax avoidance rule which applied to stamp duty. The substance of the transaction was that the taxpayer had entered into a highly artificial single composite transaction with the intention of achieving a pre-ordained end, namely the transfer of the unencumbered freehold of the property. The lease agreement would therefore be disregarded and the two sale agreements accordingly constituted the transaction for the sale of the property to the taxpayer. The stamp duty payable on these instruments would be assessed at £1,456 and the taxpayer's appeal would therefore be dismissed.

It is worthy of note that in a case concerning the former capital duty provisions (*R.* v. *I.R. Comrs., ex parte J. Rothschild Holdings plc* [1986] STC 410) the court was prepared to grant an order for disclosure of internal documents of the Revenue setting out the general practice to be followed in applying statutory provisions. In that case, the applicants in judicial review proceedings sought discovery of documents relating to the practice of the Revenue in applying the now repealed FA 1973, Sch. 19, para. 10 with regard to share exchange transactions. The applicants claimed that there was such a practice and that an officer of the Revenue had confirmed to their solicitor by telephone that the practice was as the applicants asserted. The applicants contended that the Revenue were under a duty to act fairly in exercising their powers under para. 10 and it would be a breach of that duty to depart from a known and understood practice which was consistent with a proper interpretation of the law. The Revenue resisted the application on the grounds that in judicial review proceedings discovery was not automatic as in writ actions, that the application was a "fishing expedition", and that since the applicants could only succeed to the extent that they asserted and relied on a practice which was actually known to them, discovery was not necessary. It was held that the Revenue's practice in operating the relevant statutory provisions was quite likely to illuminate the issues of fact. Discovery was therefore ordered, but limited to internal documents of the Revenue of a general character, excluding any documents which would indicate how individual cases had been dealt with.

When the application for judicial review itself was heard, Vinelott, J., held that the evidence as regards the Revenue's practice in fact showed that there was no established practice, although there were incidents at times in the past when the Revenue had acted as alleged by the applicants. All the Revenue officials who might have taken the call from the applicant's solicitor denied on oath giving the confirmation asserted, and none of them remembered taking the telephone enquiry at all. Although, therefore, the court accepted that the solicitor had made the relevant telephone enquiry, the evidence showed that he had not been given the assurance on Revenue practice that he had thought and believed he had received; it was probable that there had been a misunderstanding which could not be relied on in the circumstances. It was also held that it had been imprudent of the solicitor to rely on an assurance given in the course of a telephone conversation by an unidentified person, and more particularly sincethe question under consideration raised a "nice" point of law and practice and large sums of money were involved. It was accordingly held that there could be no estoppel of the Revenue in such circumstances and the relief asked for by the applicants was refused: *J. Rothschild Holdings plc* v. *I.R. Comrs.* [1988] STC 645. The decision of Vinelott, J., was subsequently upheld by the Court of Appeal—see [1989] STI 140.

Whilst this case related only to Revenue practices in applying statutory provisions, it is to be hoped that the courts will be prepared to extend the principles enunciated in the case to allow discovery in appropriate cases, and hear evidence regarding Revenue practices in applying case law and particularly the principles laid down in *Furniss* v. *Dawson*. However, the decisions of the Queen's Bench Division and the Court of Appeal in *R.* v. *I.R. Comrs., ex parte Taylor* [1988] STC 832 seem to suggest that the principle enunciated in *Rothschild* is of limited application and do not give grounds for optimism. In that case, an order for discovery of internal Revenue documents was refused on the grounds, inter alia, that (in accordance with the decision of Vinelott, J., in the *Rothschild* case) discovery would only be ordered in "a case where discovery is required in order that the justice of the case may be advanced and likewise a case where it is … necessary for disposing fairly of the matter". It seems likely that this formula will be narrowly applied in future.

2. All duties to be paid according to regulations of Act. (S&S 56–57)
As regards the words "except where express provision is made to the contrary", provision was in fact made to the contrary in several cases, but the instruments concerned have now all been removed from the charge to duty.

3. How instruments are to be written and stamped. (S&S 57)
The application of this section was reviewed in *Prudential Assurance Co. Ltd.* v. *I.R. Comrs.* [1935] 1 KB 101, which held that it applied to enable a memorandum endorsed on a life insurance policy, increasing the sum assured, to be regarded as a separate policy stampable *ad valorem* on the amount of the increase. See now FA 1989, in relation to the abolition of life insurance policy duty.

This section does not apply in relation to any bearer instrument issued on or after 9 December 1987 which represents shares in the U.K. company or the foreign company transferable only as part of paired-share units, or rights to allotment of or subscription for such shares; see FA 1988, s. 143 (1).

[*N.B.* In relation to the prospective abolition of all stamp duties on transactions in shares (including bearer instruments) and units under unit trust schemes, and of stamp duty reserve tax, see the Revenue Press Release, 20 March 1990 and the commentary on FA 1990.]

4. Instruments to be separately charged with duty in certain cases. (S&S 57–59)
Subsection (a)
Following the case of *Limmer Asphalte Paving Co.* v. *I.R. Comrs.* (1872) LR 7 Exch. 211, it has been a well settled principle in relation to stamp duty that an instrument is only stampable for its leading and principal object, and that the relevant stamp covers everything accessory to that object. The corollary to this is that an instrument which is exempt from duty by reason of its leading and principal object will not be rendered liable to duty by any provision which is merely accessory to that object. Thus, only one stamp is payable on the conveyance of land on sale, and no further duty will be payable because the conveyance contains covenants on the part of the vendor. Similarly, the *ad valorem* duty chargeable on a lease would normally cover a provision contained in the lease guaranteeing the rent. The difficulty lies in determining what is the leading and principal object and what is merely ancillary. In *General Accident Assurance Corpn.* v. *I.R. Comrs.* (1906) 8 F (Ct of Sess.) 477, a leading Scottish case, Lord President Dunedin stated (at p. 482) "I cannot think of any better test than to take the second so-called contract and see if it would stand alone; and that is to say, to use the current expression, whether it would stand on its own feet".

The general principle applies where there is only one leading and principal object of an instrument, and one or more ancillary matters. It does not apply where an instrument relates to several distinct matters each of which is separately chargeable to stamp duty, as if contained in a separate instrument pursuant to s. 4 (a). The difficulty in construing s. 4 (a) lies in the definition of the word "matters". Arguably, the "matters" referred to are the various heads of charge listed in Sch. 1 (see *Reversionary Interest Society Ltd.* v. *I.R. Comrs.* (1906) 22 TLR 740). The distinction between one matter and several is not, however, easy to draw. See the examples of separate stamps being required, and of separate stamps not being required, cited in **S&S 58–59**.

Where several parties join in one instrument to effect the same transaction, it has been held that only a single stamp is payable where there is a community of interest between the parties, or the transactions are effected with a common purpose. See for example *Allen* v. *Morrison* (1828) 8 B&C

565 (a case involving a power of attorney executed by all the members of a mutual insurance club authorising named persons to sign the club policies). However, if the conditions relating to community of interest or common purpose are not satisfied, two duties must be paid. For example, where executors used one instrument to convey assets, part of residue, to four residuary legatees, it was held that four stamps could be levied (*Freeman* v. *I.R. Comrs.* (1871) LR 6 Ex. 101).

Where an instrument effects two transactions between different parties separate stamps will clearly be payable.

Subsection (b)
This subsection often applies in practice. For example, where a lease provides both for an ascertainable fixed rent and an unascertainable royalty, it will be chargeable with the fixed duty of £2 in respect of the unascertainable royalty and with *ad valorem* duty in relation to the fixed rent.

5. Facts and circumstances affecting duty to be set forth in instruments. (S&S 59–60)
Any person who submits an instrument for stamping may be required by the Commissioners to provide such evidence as they may consider necessary to show that the facts and circumstances affecting the amount of duty are "fully and truly set forth" in the instrument (see *e.g. R.* v. *I.R. Comrs., ex parte Evill* [1951] 2 TLR 857). However, no fine will be payable as long as the full facts are disclosed at the time of stamping, whether in the document itself or by another means, *e.g.* a covering letter. See also s. 12 (2).

Note that, because of the difficulties arising from the potential interaction between stamp duty and the VAT payable in respect of commercial buildings (discussed in relation to ss. 55, 56 and 77 (5), and the "Lease or Tack" head of charge in Sch. 1), it would be unwise in the light of s. 5 to omit from the face of a document submitted for stamping a reference to any VAT that is payable on the consideration expressed in the document.

6. Mode of calculating ad valorem duty in certain cases (S&S 60–61)
This section provides a method of calculating *ad valorem* duty in cases where the consideration consists of stock or securities, or foreign or colonial currency. The duty is calculated on the value, on the date of the instrument, of the money in British currency according to the rate of exchange prevailing on that date, or of the stock or security according to the average price thereof (when there is one).

The Board adopts the CGT basis for valuing shares and securities listed on The Stock Exchange for the purposes of stamp duty, in accordance with the provisions of CGTA 1979, s. 150 (*i.e.* the lower of one quarter of the difference between the lower and higher closing prices added to the lower price (one quarter up) or mid-way between the highest and lowest prices at which the bargains were marked). When no average price can be quoted, by reason of there having been no dealings at the relevant date of the stock or marketable security, reasonable evidence of value must be furnished. As to securities dealt in on The Stock Exchange Unlisted Securities Market, see SP18/80, under which theRevenue consider, as "initial evidence of their value", not only details of bargains done at or near the relevant date, but also "whether a value offered on the basis of those bargains can be accepted as an adequate reflection of the open market value". For valuation of shares generally, and in particular valuation of shares in private companies, see Nigel A. Eastaway and Harry Booth *Practical Share Valuation* (1983, Butterworths).

In *Crane Fruehauf Ltd.* v. *I.R. Comrs.* [1975] 1 All ER 429, CA, it was held that "the date of the instrument", being an instrument of transfer signed under hand conditionally on the issue of the consideration shares, was the date on which the condition was satisfied so that the consideration shares fell to be valued at that date.

USE OF ADHESIVE STAMPS

9. Penalty for frauds in relation to adhesive stamps. (S&S 61–62)
Any person who fraudulently removes or causes to be removed an adhesive stamp from any instrument, or uses that stamp again for any purpose, or sells it or offers it for sale, or alters any other instrument with that stamp affixed (knowing it to have been removed from the original instrument), is liable to a £50 fine.

The expression "instrument" in this section has been extended to include postal packets within the meaning of the Post Office Protection Act 1884 (see the Revenue Act 1898, s. 7) and the expression "stamp" has been extended to insurance stamps (see the Social Security Act 1975, s. 1 (4), Sch. 1, para. 6 (3)).

APPROPRIATED STAMPS AND DENOTING STAMPS

11. Denoting stamps. (S&S 62–63)
Denoting stamps are most commonly used:
  (*a*) on duplicates or counterparts of stamped instruments (in relation to which the Revenue issued a notice concerning the use of denoting stamps in the *Law Society's Gazette*, 7 July 1976, p. 564);

(*b*) on conveyances on sale following contracts of sale bearing *ad valorem* duty under s. 59;

(*c*) on conveyances, transfers, leases or tacks where there is a conveyance or transfer of land subject to an agreement for a lease for a term exceeding 35 years or a grant of a lease or tack subject to such a term, the *ad valorem* duty having been paid on the agreement or lease under FA 1984, s. 111 (1); and

(*d*) on substituted bearer instruments.

A denoting stamp is not a guarantee that the stamp denoted on the original instrument is sufficient. Such guarantee can be obtained only by the process of adjudication under the provisions of s. 12.

Where a document is required to be denoted under s. 11, the Board normally requires the original of the principal document, on which the *ad valorem* duty was paid, to be produced to them for that purpose, except where the original is filed with the Land Registry (in which case a Land Registry Office copy will be accepted for denoting purposes—provided the amount of duty paid is clear from the copy).

[*N.B.* In relation to the prospective abolition of all stamp duties on transactions in shares (including bearer instruments) and units under unit trust schemes, and of stamp duty reserve tax, see the Revenue Press Release of 20 March 1990 and the commentary on FA 1990.]

ADJUDICATION STAMPS

12. Assessment of duty by Commissioners. (S&S 63–76)
The Commissioners may be required, by any person, to express their opinion as to whether an executed instrument is chargeable with any duty, and if so the amount of duty. When required to make an adjudication, the Commissioners are entitled to require such information to be provided to them as they consider necessary to enable them to make an assessment—*R v I.R. Comrs. ex parte Evill* [1951] 2 TLR 857). The procedure on application for adjudication of stamp duty varies somewhat between England and Wales, Scotland and Northern Ireland. For a detailed description of the procedure, together with a description of the information required with certain classes of application, and copies of relevant forms, see **S&S 65–74**.

Adjudication is obligatory:

(*a*) in the case of conveyances or transfers claimed to be exempt from duty under the provisions of FA 1930, s. 42, relating to certain transfers from one associated body corporate to another;

(*b*) in the case of orders made by the court under the Variation of Trusts Act 1958 (as to the practice in such cases see Practice Note [1966] 1 All ER 672);

(*c*) in the case of conveyances or transfers where property is conveyed or transferred to any person in contemplation of a sale of that property under FA 1965, s. 90 (3);

(*d*) in claims for exemption for maintenance and funds for historic buildings under FA 1980, s. 98;

(*e*) for relief on conveyances in consideration of a debt under FA 1980, s. 102;

(*f*) in claims for exemption for conveyances, transfers and leases to charities (FA 1982, s. 129); and

(*g*) in claims for exemption for instruments executed for the purposes of or in connection with acquisitions of the whole or any part of a company's undertaking or share capital, pursuant to FA 1986, ss. 75, 76 or 77.

[*N.B.* In relation to the prospective abolition of all stamp duties on transactions in shares (including bearer instruments) and units under unit trust schemes, and of stamp duty reserve tax, see the Revenue Press Release of 20 March 1990 and the commentary on FA 1990.]

Adjudication was formerly required:

(*i*) under FA 1985, s. 82 (5), in respect of any conveyance or transfer operating as a voluntary disposition *inter vivos*, within the meaning of F(1909–10)A 1910, s. 74, provided that it did not attract stamp duty under the "conveyance or transfer on sale" head of charge in SA 1891, Sch. 1; and

(*ii*) under FA 1985, s. 84, in respect of certain variations made in dispositions out of the estate of a deceased person by the persons who benefit or would benefit under the dispositions, and in respect of certain appropriations made by the personal representatives of a deceased person to satisfy dispositions out of his or her estate.

By virtue of the Stamp Duty (Exempt Instruments) Regulations 1987, made pursuant to FA 1985, s. 87 (2), adjudication is no longer a requirement in respect of such instruments: they will be deemed to be duly stamped if certified in the manner specified in the Regulations. However, whilst adjudication is no longer a requirement, it may still be sought under SA 1891, s. 12 and in view of the complexity of the law, particularly in relation to voluntary dispositions *inter vivos*, parties who are unwilling to give the certificate envisaged by the Regulations may nevertheless still prefer to seek adjudication. See further the commentaries on FA 1985, ss. 82, 84 and 87.

Adjudication was also formerly required in the case of certain conveyances or transfers on sale claimed to be exempt from stamp duty under FA 1927, s. 55 in connection with schemes for the reconstruction or amalgamation of companies which fulfilled certain conditions and in the case of certain transactions of limited companies (principally issues of shares) claimed to be exempt from capital duty under FA 1973, s. 47 (6) and Sch. 19. However, s. 55 was repealed by FA 1986, s. 74 and Sch. 23, Pt. IX in relation to any instrument executed in pursuance of a contract made on or after the day on which the rule of The Stock Exchange that prohibited a person from carrying on business as both a broker and a jobber was abolished (*i.e.* 27 October 1986) and the whole of the capital duty legislation was repealed by FA 1988, s. 132 and Sch. 10, Pt. XI in relation to transactions (or events which would otherwise have caused the loss of a previously granted relief) occurring on or after 22 March 1988 (or on or after 16 March 1988 where the relevant document is not stamped, or the relevant duty is not paid, before 22 March 1988).

The case law in relation to the interpretation of s. 55, as amended, is voluminous (see Eighth Edition of Sergeant & Sims on Stamp Duties (pp. 224–242)) and, although s. 55 has been abolished so that no question of adjudication can now arise, there are two main reasons why it is still relevant. First, SA 1891, s. 14 (4) provides that (for the purpose of determining admissibility in evidence) an instrument must have been duly stamped "in accordance with the law in force at the time when it was first executed". Secondly, many of the cases relating to the interpretation of s. 55 will be relevant to the relief for company reconstructions provided by FA 1986, s. 75. The case law relating to the repealed capital duty provisions (which is also voluminous, see in particular the 1987–88 edition of this Guide and **S&S 475–616**) will also still need to be referred to in relation to historical events under SA 1891, s. 14 (4), and may also be relevant to an interpretation of FA 1986, s. 75. [See, however, the note following sub-paragraph (*g*) above.]

Except as mentioned below, adjudication stamps are conclusive and preclude any question raised as to the sufficiency of the stamp. Adjudication will not, however, prejudice rights that have already been asserted and relied on before adjudication (*Marx* v. *Estates and General Investments Ltd.* [1975] 3 All ER 1064).

Adjudication will not conclusively render a document duly stamped:

(*a*) in the case of a transfer on sale of the fee simple of land, or the grant of a lease of land for a term of seven years or more, or a transfer on sale of any such lease, where the relevant document does not also bear a "produced stamp" under FA 1931, s. 28 and Sch. 2;

(*b*) where a single document is chargeable in respect of several distinct matters, and therefore requires more than one stamp under s. 4, but it has only been adjudicated in respect of one or some of those matters;

(*c*) where a bearer instrument to which FA 1963, s. 60 applies does not also bear a "denoting stamp" under FA 1963, s. 60 (3) [but see again the note following sub-paragraph (*g*) above]; or

(*d*) where the adjudication was obtained by misrepresentation or without a full disclosure of all material facts.

Court orders, etc

As regards orders made under the Companies Act 1985, s. 427, the solicitors having the conduct of the proceedings will be required, on the settling of the order, to give a written undertaking to the court to submit the order (or a duplicate thereof) for the assessment of stamp duty under SA 1891, ss. 12 and 13, and to pay the duty so assessed. In relation to orders under the Variation of Trusts Act 1958, see the Practice Note the text of which is set out in Appendix 10. Similarly, office copies of orders involving schemes of arrangement cannot be lodged at the Companies Registry as required by the Companies Act 1985, s. 425 (3) without their having first been seen by the Revenue, which has to determine the stamp duty position before the matter can be dealt with at the Companies Registry. In *Sun Alliance Insurance Ltd.* v. *I.R. Comrs.* [1971] 1 All ER 135, it was held, in connection with a scheme of arrangement under what was then the Companies Act 1948, s. 206, involving a transfer of the whole of the issued share capital of a company, that the court order sanctioning the scheme was a conveyance or transfer on sale and was liable to *ad valorem* stamp duty. [See, however, the note following sub-paragraph (*g*) above.]

See also SA 1891, s. 62, pursuant to which every decree or order of any court or of any commissioners, whereby any property on any occasion except a sale or mortgage is transferred to or vested in any person, is to be charged to duty as a conveyance or transfer of property.

The Senior Registrar of the Family Division has also issued a practice note stating that the principal or a district probate registry will examine any original deed or other instrument presented to it for the purposes of applying for a grant of representation to ensure that such deed or instrument has been duly stamped, before proceeding with the application, and that, where there is any doubt about the stamping of the instrument, the applicant will be asked to present the instrument to the Controller of Stamps for adjudication before the issue of the grant.

13. Persons dissatisfied may appeal. (S&S 77–80)

Any person dissatisfied with an adjudication may appeal to the High Court, provided that he has paid the duty before doing so. Appeals are by way of case stated, and the Commissioners are responsible for stating the case (although they usually submit it in draft form to the appellants and agree it with them). At the hearing, the court may hear oral evidence to supplement the facts in the stated case (as was done in *Speyer Brothers Ltd.* v. *I.R. Comrs.* [1906] 1 KB 318). Subject to the rules of the court, there may then be a further appeal by either party to the Court of Appeal and thereafter (if the appropriate leave is obtained) to the House of Lords.

The court is to assess the duty and if the appellant succeeds, *i.e.* if the court holds that the duty payable is less than that assessed by the Commissioners and paid by the appellants, an order will be made that the excess stamp duty paid be returned to the appellants, and interest may be awarded on the amount ordered to be repaid. However, there is no corresponding provision that if the court fixes an amount of duty higher than that assessed by the Commissioners and paid by the appellants, the appellants can be ordered to pay the excess, and it seems to be the general view that no appellant can be so ordered. If an appellant succeeds in the High Court and repayment is made to him, and the decision in his favour is reversed in the Court of Appeal, the Court of Appeal can order him to repay the amount recovered by him. See also, in relation to judicial review proceedings in stamp duty cases *J. Rothschild Holdings plc* v. *I.R. Comrs.* [1988] STC 645, discussed under SA 1891, s. 1 (see above).

The Revenue are obliged to pay interest on overpaid duty only if a court orders it to be repaid as a result of an appeal by way of case stated under s. 13. There is no statutory provision under which the Revenue must pay interest or other compensation in respect of a refund made outside the s. 13 procedure. This is to be contrasted with the position for example in relation to income tax, corporation tax and capital gains tax under TA 1988, ss. 824 and 825 (repayment supplements) and also s. 826 (interest on tax overpaid).

This anomaly has recently been recognised: Sir Anthony Battishill (Chairman of the Board of Inland Revenue), giving evidence before the House of Commons Public Accounts Committee, was asked about an ex gratia payment of £548,000 for financial loss due to late repayment of stamp duty. He replied "I really cannot identify the particular case for reasons of confidentiality. Broadly speaking, that concerned a case where stamp duty was assessed by our stamp office, according to the law as they understood it. The company objected, taking a different view of the law. After reconsideration within the Revenue, we conceded that stamp duty was not properly collectible in that case and so it was repaid. Stamp duty does not have, as other taxes have, the facility for paying repayment supplement where the taxpayer has been denied his money. So it was decided, as the error was ours and as it was a serious error, that we should in effect pay the taxpayer the equivalent of repayment supplement for the fact that he had been without his money for the period in which this stamp duty had been in dispute."

There had been an avoidable delay in repaying the duty after the change of Revenue view, and the ex-gratia payment recognised the taxpayer's loss arising from this delay. The amount of stamp duty finally repaid was £3,039,920 and the ex-gratia payment was based on the repayment supplement rates for the appropriate period. (HC Committee of Public Accounts, Minutes of Evidence 30 January 1989, 168i; Question 1297 and Appendix.)

PRODUCTION OF INSTRUMENTS IN EVIDENCE

14. Terms upon which instruments not duly stamped may be received in evidence. (S&S 80–87)
The general rule, set out in s. 14 (4), is that an instrument executed in the U.K. or relating (wherever executed) to any property situated or to any matter or thing done or to be done in any part of the U.K. shall not (except in criminal proceedings) be given in evidence or be available for any purpose whatever unless it is duly stamped in accordance with the law in force at the time when it was first executed.

Judges, arbitrators and referees may not admit in evidence in proceedings before them any stampable document which is unstamped or insufficiently stamped. This duty exists whether or not any objection is raised as to the admissibility of a document.

However, in *Don Francesco* v. *De Meo*, 1908 SC 7, it was stated that a court is only bound to intervene to protect the Revenue where there is good reason to believe that an instrument produced in evidence has not been duly stamped, and need not raise test cases or spend time trying dubious questions of stamp duty law which are not germane to the main issue before it.

It is not permissible even to give secondary evidence of an instrument which has not been duly stamped, and a court, arbitrator or referee cannot, even with the consent of the parties, make any ruling on an insufficiently stamped document.

In relation to documents which are insufficiently stamped, but which can still be stamped at the time they are tendered in evidence, the procedure laid down by s. 14 (1), involving the payment of the relevant amount of duty, the full penalty, and a further penalty of £1, is rarely followed. It is the normal practice of the court to allow an unstamped document to be used upon the personal undertaking of the solicitor acting for the party tendering the document to have the document stamped and pay every appropriate penalty—see *Re Coolgardie Goldfields Ltd.* [1900] 1 Ch. 475 at p. 477, and *Parkfield Trust* v. *Dent* [1931] 2 KB 579. The Bar Council has ruled that, except in Revenue cases, it is unprofessional conduct for counsel to object that a document is not properly stamped unless the judge specifically raises the issue, or unless the insufficiency of stamping affects the validity of the document (Annual Statement of the General Council of the Bar, 1901–2).

The decision of a judge that a document is properly stamped, or does not require a stamp, is final and cannot be challenged (RSC Ord. 59, Rule 11(5)). On the other hand, it is possible to appeal against the decision to reject a document produced in evidence on the grounds that it is not properly stamped (provided that in this case counsel formally tenders the duty). However, it was held in *Routledge* v. *McKay* [1954] 1 All ER 855 that if a lower court overlooks a stamp duty point, it may be taken by the Court on appeal.

"The United Kingdom" means England, Scotland, Wales and Northern Ireland, but it does not include the Channel Islands or the Isle of Man. Under the first limb of s. 14 (4), an instrument executed in the U.K. is stampable whatever it relates to, e.g. a conveyance on sale of land in Australia between two Australians for Australian dollars (*Wright* v. *I.R. Comrs.* (1855) 11 Exch. 458), and an instrument will be regarded as executed in the U.K. if any party to it executes it in the U.K. The second limb of s. 14 (4) is concerned with instruments "relating to any property situate, or to any matter or thing done or to be done in any part of the United Kingdom" and is thus extremely wide.

The leading case concerning the construction of these words is *I.R. Comrs.* v. *Maple & Co. (Paris) Ltd.* [1908] AC 22, involving the transfer by one English company to another English company of property situated in France by means of an instrument expressed to be governed by French law and in the normal French legal form, the consideration for which was, however, the issue of shares in the transferee company. The instrument was held to be dutiable because it related to property situated in the U.K. (the shares in the transferee company to be issued as consideration) and to a thing to be done in the U.K. (the issue and registration of those shares). In a more recent case (*Faber* v. *I.R. Comrs.* (1936) 155 LT 228) an engineer who worked in the U.K. executed a deed of covenant in Canada to pay a specified proportion of the income he received from his job in the U.K. to a Canadian company, in consideration of the issue to him of shares and debentures of that company, and it was held that the deed was dutiable because it related to something "done or to be done in any part of the United Kingdom", namely the carrying on of the engineer's job.

The words "duly stamped in accordance with the law in force at the time when it was first executed" in s. 14 (4) have been taken in practice to mean the time when the relevant instrument first becomes an effective instrument, and not necessarily when the first person to sign does so. In *Clarke* v. *Roche* (1877) 3 QBD 170) it was held that, where an instrument appeared to be sufficiently stamped according to the law in force on the day that it was dated, but it subsequently transpired that the instrument was executed some years before the date, when the stamp duty was different, the instrument was inadmissible. In *Crane Fruehauf Ltd.* v. *I.R. Comrs.* [1974] 1 All ER 811, instruments of transfer signed conditionally upon the issue by the acquiring company of the consideration shares were held to take effect upon satisfaction of the condition and to be stampable by reference to the then value of the consideration shares. Similarly, an instrument delivered in escrow does not attract stamp duty until the condition subject to which it was delivered has been performed (*Terrapin International Ltd* v. *I.R. Comrs.* [1976] 2 All ER 461).

Insufficiently stamped documents are not to "be given in evidence or be available for any purpose whatever", but unstamped instruments have been admitted to refresh a witness's memory (*Birchall* v. *Bullough* [1896] 1 QB 325), to prove fraud (*Re Shaw* (1920) 90 LJKB 204) or an act of bankruptcy (*Re Gunsbourg* (1919) 88 LJKB 562). In an action to set aside an agreement and to restrain the defendant from carrying it into effect the plaintiff was not compelled to stamp it when, if his claim succeeded, the agreement would be void (*Mason* v. *Motor Traction Company* [1905] 1 Ch. 419).

In the case of an instrument that has been lost or destroyed, it is presumed that the instrument was properly stamped and it is for the party taking the objection to prove that it was unstamped. If the party taking the objection can show that some time after execution the instrument was unstamped, then this presumption will be rebutted unless it is revived by the other party proving facts which imply that the document was properly stamped. See, e.g. *Marine Investment Company* v. *Haviside* (1872) LR 5 HL 624 and *Henty and Constable (Brewers) Ltd.* v. *I.R. Comrs.* [1961] 3 All ER 1146, CA.

The transfer of shares in an English or Scottish company registered in an "overseas branch register" (see the Companies Act 1985, s. 362) is deemed to be a transfer of property situated outside the U.K. and will not be liable to duty unless executed in the U.K. (see the Companies Act 1985, Sch. 14, Part II, para. 8). This does not apply in the case of overseas branch registers kept in Northern Ireland. [*N.B.* In relation to the prospective abolition of all stamp duties on transactions in shares (including bearer instruments) and units under unit trust schemes, and of stamp duty reserve tax, see the Revenue Press Release of 20 March 1990 and the commentary on FA 1990.]

For an interesting case in which an unstamped agreement was admitted in evidence in criminal proceedings, despite an objection from counsel for the defendant, see the unreported decision in *Abdel-Rahim* v. *D.P.P.* (1989) QBD CO/1796/87.

STAMPING OF INSTRUMENTS AFTER EXECUTION

15. Penalty upon stamping instruments after execution. (S&S 87–90)
The general principle under the stamp duty legislation is that instruments first executed in the U.K. must be stamped before execution (which is the implication given by the provisions relating to stamping after execution, although there is no express provision to that effect), but this general principle is subject to a number of general qualifications and special exemptions in respect of particular instruments. Certain instruments (instruments chargeable with *ad valorem* stamp duty and described in Sch. 1 as "bond, covenant or instrument of any kind whatsoever", "conveyance or transfer on sale", "lease or tack", or "agreement for lease or tack chargeable under section 75") may, without any penalty, be stamped within 30 days after their first execution, if in the U.K., or 14 days after notice of assessment by the Commissioners where their opinion has been required as to the amount of stamp duty chargeable under the adjudication provisions of s. 12. Instruments first executed outside the U.K. may be stamped without a penalty within 30 days after their first receipt in the U.K. If such an instrument has not been sufficiently stamped within the proper period, the person responsible is liable to pay, in addition to the amount of the unpaid duty pursuant to s. 15 (1), the penalty of £10 imposed by s. 15 (1), plus the fine of £10 imposed by s. 15 (2) (*c*), a further penalty equivalent to the amount of the unpaid duty imposed by s. 15 (2) (*c*), and interest on the amount of the unpaid duty (where that amount exceeds £10) at the rate of 5 per cent. per annum pursuant to s. 15 (1). The fine of £10 and further penalty equivalent to the amount of the unpaid duty imposed by s. 15 (2) (*c*) are only payable if there is no "reasonable excuse for the delay in stamping, or the omission to stamp, or the insufficiency of stamp, . . . afforded to the satisfaction of the Commissioners, or of the court, judge, arbitrator, or referee before whom it is produced", and the Commissioners have in any case a discretion to "mitigate or remit any penalty payable on stamping" pursuant to s. 15 (3) (*b*).
Section 15 (2) (*c*) does not appear to apply to a contract chargeable as a conveyance on sale under SA 1891, s. 59 because such an instrument is not included in the list of instruments in s. 15 (2) (*d*).
Note also the implication to be drawn from the second column of the table in s. 15 (2) (*d*) that the persons listed there as liable to pay the penalties for late stamping will actually be regarded as the persons liable to stamp the documents in question.
FA 1986, s. 69 (5) (depositary receipts) provides that the table in s. 15 (2) (*d*) is to have effect as if it included instruments transferring "relevant securities" where FA 1986, s. 67 (3) applies.
Similarly, FA 1986, s. 72 (3) (clearance services) provides that the table in s. 15 (2) (*d*) is to have effect as if it included instruments transferring "relevant securities" where FA 1986, s. 70 (3) applies.
In each of the last two mentioned cases, the person named in the relevant instrument as transferee is to be the person listed in the second column of the table in s. 15 (2) (*d*).
[*N.B.* In relation to the prospective abolition of all stamp duties on transactions in shares (including bearer instruments) and units under unit trust schemes, and of stamp duty reserve tax, see the Revenue Press Release of 20 March 1990 and the commentary on FA 1990.]

ENTRIES UPON ROLLS, BOOKS, ETC.

16. Rolls, books, etc., to be open to inspection. (S&S 90)
A "public officer" has been defined as a person "who is appointed to discharge a public duty and receives a compensation in whatever shape, whether from the Crown or otherwise" (Best CJ in *Henly* v. *Lyme Corpn.* (1829) 5 Bing. 91 at 107) and includes the trustees and managers of a unit trust scheme, and their agents, officers or servants (see FA 1946, s. 56).

17. Penalty for enrolling, etc., instrument not duly stamped (S&S 91–94)
This section renders liable to a fine (of £10) any person whose office it is to enrol, register, or enter in or upon any rolls, books, or records any stampable document who does so in relation to a document which is not duly stamped. The most important practical effect of this is that the secretary of a company presented with a share transfer for registration should not register it unless he is satisfied that the correct amount of stamp duty has been paid. The section also prevents the Registrar of Companies from accepting for filing such documents as contracts or particulars of contracts relating to the issue of shares for a non-cash consideration unless he is satisfied that they have been duly stamped.
In determining whether an instrument is duly stamped, the person concerned is entitled to go behind what appears on the face of the document (see *Maynard* v. *Consolidated Kent Collieries Ltd.* [1903] 2 KB 121, CA, followed in *Conybear* v. *British Briquettes Ltd.* [1937] 4 All ER 191). Any person who objects to the refusal of the relevant officer to enrol, register or enter any instrument must present the instrument to the Revenue for adjudication, and if necessary appeal, and not apply for a court order compelling enrolment or registration, etc.
The correct view today seems to be that a title resting on registration would apparently not be adversely affected merely because registration was procured by the use of an unstamped instrument (see *Lap Shun Textiles Industrial Company Ltd.* v. *Collector of Stamp Revenue* [1976] AC 530, [1976] 1 All ER 833, PC).

Thus, registration of a transfer of shares while inadequately stamped nevertheless will operate as a legal transfer of the shares into the name of the transferee.

In the case of the purchase by a company of its own shares pursuant to the Companies Act 1985, s. 162, or the Companies (Northern Ireland) Order 1982, Art. 47, the return required to be delivered to the Registrar of Companies is to be charged with stamp duty, and treated for all purposes of SA 1891 as if it were an instrument transferrring the shares on sale to the company in pursuance of the contract (or contracts) of purchase concerned: FA 1986, s. 66 (2). The Registrar of Companies will not therefore register the return unless he has been satisfied that the return has been duly stamped.

The Land Registration Act 1925, s. 14 (3), provides that the Land Registrar must be satisfied, before registering any person who has not previously acquired the estate intended to be registered, that all *ad valorem* stamp duty (if any) which, if the estate had been acquired by him, would have been payable in respect of the instrument vesting that estate in him, has been discharged. See also the Land Registration Rules 1925, rr. 94 and 95 with regard to the procedures to be adopted in relation to registered instruments (**S&S 93–94**).

[*N.B.* In relation to the prospective abolition of all stamp duties on transactions in shares (including bearer instruments) and units under unit trust schemes, and of stamp duty reserve tax, see the Revenue Press Release of 20 March 1990 and the commentary on FA 1990.]

PART II REGULATIONS APPLICABLE TO PARTICULAR INSTRUMENTS

INSTRUMENTS OF APPRENTICESHIP

25. Meaning of instrument of apprenticeship.
The stamp duty payable on instruments of apprenticeship was abolished by FA 1949, s. 35 and Sch. 8, Pt. I.

BILLS OF SALE

41. Bills of sale.
This section expressly prohibits the registration of insufficiently stamped bills of sale.

CHARTER-PARTIES

49. Provisions as to duty on charter-party. (S&S 106)
Charter-parties are now exempt from all stamp duty by virtue of FA 1949, s. 35 and Sch. 8, Pt. I.

CONVEYANCES ON SALE

54. Meaning of "conveyance on sale". (S&S 113–133, 197)
It should be emphasised that s. 54 is not an exclusive definition ("the expression "conveyance on sale" *includes* . . . ") and the Commissioners maintain that a conveyance or transfer may in fact be chargeable under the head of charge "conveyance or transfer on sale" even if it does not come within s. 54 (see *Oughtred* v. *I.R. Comrs.* [1960] AC 206, 222 and 223).

(a) "*every instrument, and every decree or order of any court or of any commissioners*"
The word "instrument" is extremely wide. By virtue of s. 122 (1) it includes "every written document", and it will not matter whether the document is under seal or under hand. It includes court orders (for example an order sanctioning a scheme of arrangement under the Companies Act 1985, s. 425—see *Sun Alliance Insurance Ltd.* v. *I.R. Comrs.* [1972] Ch. 133 at 148 in relation to a scheme under what was then the Companies Act 1948, s. 206). It also includes Acts of Parliament. FA 1895, s. 12 provides that where by statute any property is vested by way of sale in any person, or any person is authorised to purchase property, such person must within three months after the passing of the Act or the day of vesting (if later) or after completion of the purchase produce to the Commissioners for stamping an office copy of the Act or the instrument of conveyance of the property. It also includes "the return which relates to the shares purchased and is delivered to the Registrar of Companies" under the Companies Act 1985, s. 169 where a company purchases its own shares under the powers conferred by the Companies Act 1985, s. 162 (see FA 1986, s. 66 (2)).

[*N.B.* In relation to the prospective abolition of all stamp duties on transactions in shares (including bearer instruments) and units under unit trust schemes, and of stamp duty reserve tax, see the Revenue Press Release of 20 March 1990 and the commentary on FA 1990.]

(b) "*any property, or any estate or interest in any property*"
Property is "that which belonged to a person exclusive of others, and which could be the subject of bargain and sale to another" (*Potter* v. *I.R. Comrs.* (1854) 10 Ex. 147 at 156). The most obvious

examples are a legal estate in land (which can only be conveyed or transferred by deed), goods (which are transferable by delivery but dutiable if included in an instrument of transfer in addition to a sale and purchase agreement) and stocks and marketable securities, including most shares, debentures and units under a unit trust scheme. [But see above note in relation to prospective abolitions.] However, the word "property" has also been held to include the goodwill of a trade or business (*Benjamin Brooke & Co. Ltd.* v *I.R. Comrs.* [1896] 2 QB 356, DC; *I.R. Comrs.* v. *Muller & Co.'s Margarine* [1901] AC 217 at 223, 234, 235, HL), copyrights and trade marks (*Leather Cloth Co.* v *American Leather Cloth Co.* (1865) 11 HL Cas. 523), secret processes (*Re Keene* [1922] 2 Ch. 475), the grant of an exclusive licence to use a U.K. patent (unless containing a power of revocation), book debts (*Measures Brothers Ltd.* v. *I.R. Comrs.* (1900) 82 LT 689, DC), life insurance policies (*Caldwell* v. *Dawson* (1859) 5 Exch. 1) and the benefit of contractual rights (*Western Abyssinian Mining Syndicate Ltd.* v. *I.R. Comrs.* (1935) 14 ATC 286).

Almost anything can be the subject of a conveyance on sale, and therefore attract stamp duty, but the property or the right being transferred must actually exist. In *Limmer Asphalte Paving Co.* v. *I.R. Comrs.* (1872) LR 7 Exch. 211 it was held that a deed purporting to grant an exclusive licence to make asphalte paving "within the counties of Lancaster and Chester" was not chargeable as a conveyance on sale on the grounds that the purported licensor did not in fact have any exclusive right to use the asphalte within those counties, so that "if the company had no such property and could not create it, they could not convey or transfer it".

A conveyance of property situated abroad is required by s. 14 (4) to be stamped if it is executed in the U.K., or if it relates to any property situated, or thing done or to be done in the U.K. For example, a transfer executed in France of property situated in France was nevertheless held to be stampable since the consideration was the issue of shares in an English company (*I.R. Comrs.* v. *Maple & Co. (Paris) Ltd.* [1908] AC 22).

(c) *"upon the sale thereof"*
The conveyance or transfer will be a conveyance or transfer "upon" sale where at the date of the conveyance or transfer there exists a binding agreement for sale (even if that agreement is conditional—*Ridge Nominees Ltd.* v. *I.R. Comrs.* [1962] Ch. 376), or where the conveyance or transfer itself gives rise to the sale, without a pre-existing agreement (*e.g. Escoigne Properties Ltd.* v. *I.R. Comrs.* [1958] AC 549). A conveyance made in contemplation of a sale but before the formation of a binding contract (whether conditional or unconditional) is not a conveyance on sale (*William Cory & Son Ltd.* v. *I.R. Comrs.* [1965] 1 All ER 917) but is nevertheless chargeable with duty at the same rate by reference to the value of the property conveyed (FA 1965, s. 90 (1)). In that case, a claim for repayment may be made to the Commissioners not later than two years after the making or execution of the instrument charged under s. 90 (1) and if the Commissioners are satisfied either:

(a) that the sale has not taken place and the property has been re-conveyed or re-transferred to the original transferor or his personal representative or trustee in bankruptcy, or

(b) that the sale has taken place for a consideration less than the value on which duty was paid,
then the duty or the excess duty (as the case may be) may be repaid.

Instruments falling within the provisions of s. 90 (1) must be adjudicated. It has been suggested that the reference in s. 90 (2) to "the sale in contemplation of which the instrument was made" implies that no duty would be payable in respect of a conveyance in contemplation of sale generally, with no particular purchaser in mind, for example where a person going abroad transfers his portfolio of shares to a stockbroker to enable him to effect any expedient sales during the owner's absence. It is submitted that this is not a correct interpretation of s. 90. If a blank share transfer is delivered to a stockbroker in contemplation of a sale and the sale subsequently does in fact take place, then that sale must have been in the "contemplation" of the transferor at the time the transfer was signed, notwithstanding that the identity of the purchaser was not known. Section 90 refers to *the sale* being contemplated, not *the purchaser*. Where a particular purchaser has been found, a blank share transfer will in fact be treated as a conveyance or transfer on sale and stampable as such (*Fitch Lovell Ltd.* v. *I.R. Comrs.* [1962] 3 All ER 685). [But see again the above note in relation to prospective abolitions.]

It is of course of the essence of every sale that there should be a purchase price. For the purpose of SA 1891, the consideration for a sale may be not only money, but also foreign or colonial currency, stock, including shares and units under a unit trust scheme, marketable and other securities, and debts and transfers either certainly or contingently of any money or stock (see ss. 6, 55 and 57, and FA 1946, s. 54 (1)). However, there is no general rule that a transfer of property for valuable consideration, such as other property or services, is a sale. For example, in *Littlewoods Mail Order Stores Ltd.* v. *I.R. Comrs.* [1962] 2 All ER 279, it was held that an exchange of a freehold reversion in property for the leasehold interests in the same property was not a sale of the freehold property for the rent reserved by the lease.

In *Oughtred* v. *I.R. Comrs.* [1960] AC 206, where a settlement entitled a mother to a life interest in 200,000 shares and her son, subject only to his mother's life interest, to the shares in remainder, it was orally agreed between the mother and the son that the son would exchange his reversionary interest in return for certain other shares owned absolutely by the mother in the same company.

Completion of that agreement involved the execution of a deed transferring the shares absolutely owned by the mother to the son's nominees, a deed of release releasing and discharging the trustees under the settlement, and a deed transferring the 200,000 shares from the trustess to the mother. It was held that the true nature and intended purpose of the third deed was to complete the oral agreement, so that the third deed was accordingly a transfer "on sale" and assessable to *ad valorem* duty on the consideration expressed in the deed, which was the agreed value of the shares absolutely owned by the mother which were transferred by her to her son's nominees. [But see again the above note in relation to prospective abolitions.]

Any conveyance or transfer which gives effect to an agreement for sale is a conveyance on sale, and it is not necessary that the property conveyed or transferred should be precisely the property sold. On the other hand, it is not sufficient that the property conveyed has simply come to represent the property sold, where for example (as in *Henty and Constable (Brewers) Ltd.* v. *I.R. Comrs.* [1961] 3 All ER 1146) shares in a company are sold and, the company being wound up, assets are distributed in specie to the purchaser without his having a transfer of the shares to him. [But see again the above note in relation to prospective abolitions.]

Not only is it the case that the property conveyed or transferred need not be precisely the property sold, but it also seems to have been held on a number of occasions that the transferor need not be the vendor (*A.G.* v. *Brown* (1849) 3 Exch. 662); that the consideration need not be paid or payable to the vendor (*GHR Co.* v. *I.R. Comrs.* [1943] KB 303, where there was a sale by a tenant for life and payment was made to the Settled Land Act trustees); and that the consideration need not be provided by the purchaser or transferee (*Central & District Properties Ltd.* v. *I.R. Comrs.* [1966] 2 All ER 433). In addition, the transfer need not necessarily be to the purchaser, but may also be to some person on his behalf or by his direction (see s. 54).

As can be seen, what constitutes a conveyance or transfer "upon sale" will very much depend upon the nature of the transaction and the documents which are executed. The courts have tried on a number of occasions to state the general principles involved (see *e.g.* Lord Denning in *Oughtred* v. *I.R. Comrs.* [1960] AC 206 at 233; Wills J. in *Chesterfield Brewery Co.* v. *I.R. Comrs.* [1899] 2 QB 7 at 12; Romer LJ. and Maugham LJ. in *Fleetwood-Hesketh* v. *I.R. Comrs.* [1936] 1 KB 351, at 361 and 364–365 respectively; and Wilberforce J. in *Fitch Lovell Ltd.* v. *I.R. Comrs.* [1962] 3 All ER 685 at 696). The most succinct statement was made by Lindley LJ. in *John Foster & Sons* v. *I.R. Comrs.* [1984] 1 QB 518 at 528, where he said: "I do not know what is necessary to constitiute a sale, except a transfer of property from one person to another for money or, for the purposes of the Stamp Act, for stock or marketable securities". In that case, eight partners of a firm executed a deed in favour of a limited company incorporated by them to convey and assign to that company all the property of their partnership; it was held that the deed was a "conveyance on sale" because it was a transfer of property from individuals to a corporation in consideration of "stocks or securities", notwithstanding the fact that the eight partners who conveyed the property were also the individuals who constituted the company.

In distinguishing between sales which are chargeable and partitions or exchanges which are not chargeable, problems have arisen particularly in two areas: those involving family arrangements and partnerships.

(*i*) *Family arrangements* Apart from the case of *Oughtred* v. *I.R. Comrs.* mentioned above, there have frequently been cases involving consideration by the courts of whether particular types of family arrangement can be construed as transactions involving chargeable conveyances or transfers on sale. Usually there is no problem because the arrangement will not involve a consideration in cash or stock or securities—for example in *Cormack's Trustees* v. *I.R. Comrs.* 1924 SC 819 a widow accepted a life annuity in exchange for renunciation of certain legal and equitable rights. There have been cases, however, where family arrangements have been held to be conveyances on sale *e.g.* in the *Marquess of Bristol* v. *I.R. Comrs.* [1901] 2 KB 336, where a settlor conveyed all his unsettled property to the beneficiary of his settled property, the deeds reciting that the beneficiary had undertaken the payment of the mortgages of the transferor's estates and that the transferor was indebted to the beneficiary for certain sums.

Many of the stamp duty problems relating to family arrangements have now been resolved by FA 1985 s. 84 (as to which see below), but this does not apply where, in the case of variations in dispositions of a deceased person's estate (whether by will, under the law relating to intestacy or otherwise), the variation "is made for any consideration in money or money's worth other than consideration consisting of the making of a variation in respect of another of the dispositions".

(*ii*) *Partnerships* Where one or more partners take a new partner into the business in return for a cash payment, and the incoming partner gets a share of the business, then the deed or instrument of partnership will, as a rule, be construed as a conveyance or transfer on sale. If, however, the incoming partner merely brings in a capital sum, this will not necessarily be consideration for a sale, unless one or more of the existing partners withdraws capital in consequence of the incoming partner's contribution. A division of assets between partners on the dissolution of the partnership is not a conveyance on sale. But where only one partner leaves the partnership in consideration of a sum of money paid to him by the continuing partner or partners, the deed of dissolution constitutes a clear conveyance on sale of his share in the partnership to the continuing partners, and is stamped as such.

An assent or conveyance by a personal representative to give effect to a contract of sale entered into by the deceased vendor was held to operate as a conveyance on sale notwithstanding the Administration of Estates Act 1925, s. 36 (4) in *GHR Co. Ltd.* v. *I.R. Comrs.* [1943] KB 303. It has also been held that conveyance on sale duty attaches to an assent by personal representatives to give effect to an appropriation made with the beneficiary's consent in satisfaction of the whole or part of a pecuniary legacy (*Dawson* v. *I.R. Comrs.* [1905] 2 IR 69). A similar decision was reached in the case of an appropriation made in satisfaction of a fixed sum payable on an intestacy (*Jopling* v. *I.R. Comrs.* [1940] 3 All ER 279). However, where personal representatives do not need a legatee's consent to appropriate property, either by virtue of a clause in the will or by virtue of the Administration of Estates Act 1925, s. 41, then conveyance on sale duty will not be chargeable because there is deemed to be no contractual element to the appropriation. The same applies where a legatee is entitled to demand an appropriation in satisfaction whether in whole or in part of a pecuniary legacy. The same applies also to an appropriation in satisfaction of a share of residue notwithstanding dicta supporting the opposite course in *Re Beverly, Watson* v. *Watson* [1901] 1 Ch. 681. Where, however, a widow whose interest on intestacy falls short of the value of the matrimonial home pays the difference in value in order that it may be appropriated to her, then the difference will attract conveyance on sale duty.

(*d*) "*is transferred to or vested in a purchaser, or any other person on his behalf or by his direction.*" Property needs to be vested in the purchaser or someone on his behalf, but it is not necessary for it to be the exact property actually sold nor need it be the vendor that does the vesting. For example, a declaration of trust vesting only the equitable interest may be a conveyance on sale, so that where a contract for sale provides expressly that on payment of the purchase price the vendor will hold the property in trust for the purchaser, then the agreement is a conveyance on sale: *Chesterfield Brewery Co.* v. *I.R. Comrs.* [1899] 2 QB 7; *West London Syndicate Ltd.* v. *I.R. Comrs.* [1898] 1 QB 226 at 240, (reversed on another point [1898] 2 QB 507, CA). An instrument of transfer of shares in which the name of the transferee and the amount of the consideration are left blank is a conveyance or transfer on sale (*Fitch Lovell Ltd.* v. *I.R. Comrs.* [1962] 3 All ER 685. [But see again the above note in relation to prospective abolitions.]

A lease has been held to be a conveyance on sale (in *Littlewoods Mail Order Stores Ltd.* v. *I.R. Comrs.* [1962] 2 All ER 279), but an instrument which purported to be a conveyance of land, but which could not operate as such since it was not executed under seal, and contained a stipulation not to disturb the party intended to take the premises, was held not to be stampable as a conveyance on sale (*R* v. *Ridgwell Inhabitants* (1827) 6 B. & C. 665).

A deed effecting a dissolution of partnership reciting that an outgoing partner had no claim to the partnership assets in consideration of a payment of a fixed sum to be made to him was held to be a conveyance on sale of the relevant part of the partnership property (*Garnett* v. *I.R. Comrs.* (1899) 81 LT 633) and a document worded as a receipt for purchase money may in certain circumstances operate as a conveyance or transfer on sale (*Fleetwood-Hesketh* v. *I.R. Comrs.* [1936] 1 KB 351 at 364 CA). An order by a creditor to a debtor for payment to another may constitute an equitable assignment of a debt (see *e.g. Brice* v. *Bannister* (1878) 3 QBD 569, CA). A letter addressed to a company by a shareholder directing the company to allot certain shares to which he was entitled to certain donees was to a valid equitable assignment (*Letts* v. *I.R. Comrs.* [1956] 3 All ER 588) [But see again the above note in relation to prospective abolitions].

The grant of an option in consideration of a cash sum has also been held to be a conveyance on sale (*George Wimpey & Co. Ltd.* v. *I.R. Comrs.* [1975] 2 All ER 45) notwithstanding the argument that a document bringing property into existence, *i.e.* an option, could not also be treated as having effected a sale of that property.

Conditional transfers of shares in the context of public takeover bids have also in the past given rise to problems. In the case of *Ridge Nominees Ltd.* v. *I.R. Comrs.* [1961] 2 All ER 354, it was held that, where a company makes an offer to shareholders of another company to purchase their shares in that company, the offer being conditional on a specified number of acceptances being received by a certain date, transfers executed by accepting shareholders before the date when the offer becomes unconditional are liable to *ad valorem* stamp duty as conveyances on sale. An attempt was made by B.T.R. plc, in the context of its takeover bid for Thomas Tilling, to mitigate the effects of this decision by using a scheme involving a reorganisation of the share capital of the target immediately after the bid became unconditional. The attempt, however, failed. The facts of *B.T.R. plc* v. *I.R. Comrs.* [1986] STC 433, were as follows:

On 21 May 1983, a final offer of shares or cash was made by the taxpayer company for the ordinary share capital of T., subject to conditions as to acceptance. In addition the offer provided that if T. reorganised its share capital the offer would be adjusted so as to constitute separate offers for the existing ordinary shares and the new ordinary shares allotted pursuant to the reorganisation. The offer was to be conditional on no announcement being made convening a general meeting of T., on or before 21 days after the offer became unconditional, to effect a capital reorganisation. In the event of such an announcement the offer would apply apply in adjusted terms to both the existing and new shares at no greater cost to the taxpayer company. The offer was declared unconditional on 8 June. On 10 June dealing commenced in the shares issued by the taxpayer company in consideration for the T. shares. On the same day T. announced that an extraordinary general meeting was to be held on 29 June for the purpose of passing a resolution for a capital reorganisation. At that meeting it was resolved to capitalise reserves and then to issue three new shares for each T. share held. On the basis of the cash offer the value of one T. share before the reorganisation was 225p; after the reorganisation the value of one T.share was 56·25p. The new shares were issued on documents of title renounceable in favour of the taxpayer company. Five block transfers in respect of irrevocable forms of acceptance and transfer received on various dates before 29 June were presented for stamping. Duty was assessed by reference to the value of the shares before the reorganisation on 29 June on the grounds that the offer became unconditional on 8 June and the forms of acceptance and transfer constituted conveyances on sale of the existing shares as from that date. The taxpayer company appealed against the adjudication contending that the shares transferred by forms of acceptance and transfer were dutiable by reference to the value of the new shares because the offer remained conditional until the reorganisation on 29 June.

It was held that irrevocable forms of acceptance and transfer delivered in response to the offer before it became unconditional, *i.e.* on 8 June 1983, became effective transfers on that date, and acceptances delivered after that date but before 29 June took effect on delivery. Accordingly there were effective transfers which were conveyances on sale of the shares referred to in the adjudication before 29 June and stamp duty was payable as assessed. The appeal would therefore be dismissed.

Reliefs from stamp duty are now available in takeover bid situations under FA 1986, ss. 75, 76 and 77. [But see again the above note in relation to prospective abolitions.]

(e) Computation of consideration

Conveyance on sale duty is payable on the "amount or value of the consideration for the sale", and not on the value of the property conveyed or transferred, so that any change in the value of the property sold between the agreement and completion will not affect the amount of duty payable. The question how the "amount or value of the consideration for the sale" is arrived at may depend upon the statutory provisions governing the matter, which are contained in ss. 55, 56, 57 and 58 (these being sections dealing with particular types of consideration and in particular cases) and FA 1900, s. 10.

There is no general definition of "consideration" in the stamp duty legislation. One area of uncertainty that the lack of a statutory definition gives rise to relates to the potential interaction between stamp duty and the VAT payable in respect of commercial buildings. The Stamp Office take the view, and it seems difficult to contest, that any VAT payable on the purchase price of land and buildings will form part of the "consideration" and be subject to stamp duty accordingly. This view is taken whether the purchase price in the relevant instrument is expressed as an amount *inclusive* of VAT or an amount *plus* VAT. Arguments by practitioners that the Revenue are effectively seeking to impose a "tax upon a tax" have not had a sympathetic hearing from either the Revenue or the Treasury. For a more detailed analysis, see for example the articles by R. S. Nock in *Taxation* dated 5 and 12 April 1990.

Where on a conveyance or transfer on sale the consideration is unascertained at the date of the instrument (*e.g.* where the consideration for the sale of shares is to be a fixed percentage of net profits over a period of years after completion of the sale), or where an agreed purchase price of property is to be the subject of adjustment upwards or downwards according to a valuation which cannot be determined until after completion, the Controller of Stamps seems to take the view that the instrument must be stamped provisionally by reference to an estimated consideration. This is subject to an undertaking given by the solicitors presenting the instrument to re-present it for adjustment of the stamping and payment of any additional duty when the final consideration is known.

It is submitted that this practice is not in accordance with the basic principle of stamp duty law that the Revenue are not entitled to "wait and see" but must assess the duty payable on the facts known at the date of the agreement. There is a distinction between consideration which is incapable of being ascertained at the date of the agreement because, for example, it is based on the *future* profits of a company being acquired, and consideration which is theoretically capable of being ascertained at the date of the agreement, because, for example, it is based on the *past* profits of a company being acquired, but cannot be so ascertained in fact because the relevant accounts or valuation reports have not been prepared at the date of the agreement. It is arguable that the Revenue's practice should, at the most, apply only in the latter case, *i.e.*, where the consideration can be ascertained, as a fixed amount, but has not yet been ascertained because the parties are awaiting, for example, a valuation report or the company's accounts.

If, in the former case, the consideration is genuinely unascertainable at the date of the agreement, the Revenue should at most be able to rely on the "contingency principle" (as, for example, it does in the calculation of the duty payable on leases with contingent rents, discussed below in the commentary on the "Lease or Tack" head of charge in Sch. 1). If consideration will become payable on the happening of some future event, that event is treated for stamp duty purposes as though it had occurred at the date of the relevant instrument. The Stamp Office will first determine whether or not there is a maximum (though variable) amount payable on the contingency and assess duty on that amount, even though it is highly unlikely that the maximum will ever be received. If there is a minimum but no maximum amount payable on the contingency, the document will be dutiable on the basis of that minimum. If there is neither a maximum nor minimum but a fixed amount subject to upward or downward adjustment, the duty will be charged on the basis of the fixed amount. However, if the consideration is genuinely unascertainable at the date of the agreement and no definite figure can be determined by applying the above principles, then there is authority for the view that no duty is payable other than (in appropriate cases) the fixed duty of 50p (Scrutton J. in *Underground Electric Railways and Glyn Mills & Co* v. *I.R. Comrs.* [1914] 3 KB 210 at 220; *Independent Television Authority* v *I.R. Comrs.* [1961] AC 427). [But, in relation to sales of shares, see the above note concerning prospective abolitions.]

The operation of the contingency principle also gives rise to potentially difficult problems in relation to the interaction between stamp duty and VAT. Assuming the Stamp Office is correct in its view that any VAT payable on the purchase price of land and buildings will form part of the "consideration" and be dutiable as such, the question then arises as to whether a potential charge to VAT upon a deferred or contingent purchase price will fall within the scope of the contingency principle. It seems to be the better view that it will not, on the basis that the potential VAT in those circumstances is not a *prima facie* sum that will or may become payable (which would be dutiable under the contingency principle) but a formula that may become applicable in the future subject to variations in accordance with future changes in the rate of tax. See, again, the articles by R. S. Nock referred to above.

In relation to sales of shares, see the above note concerning prospective abolitions.

In calculating the amount or value of the consideration for the sale, the consideration mentioned in the conveyance is not conclusive. For example, where in *Oughtred* v. *I.R. Comrs.* the life tenant of settled shares agreed orally with the reversioner to exchange other shares owned by her for his reversionary interest in the settled shares, and the transaction so far as it related to the settled shares was completed by a transfer for a nominal consideration, the transfer was held liable to *ad valorem* duty on the value of the shares received by the reversioner from the life tenant by way of exchange (*Oughtred* v. *I.R. Comrs.* [1960] AC 206).

55. How ad valorem duty to be calculated in respect of stock and securities. (S&S 133–134)
The value of stock or marketable securities is to be ascertained in the manner set out in s. 6 in every case where there is an "average price" on The Stock Exchange. Where there is no such average price, the Commissioners must reach their own conclusions as to the value of the shares or stock. There seems to be some justification in the relevant body of case law for arriving at the value of the consideration by reference to the value of the property conveyed or transferred (see *e.g. John Foster & Sons* v. *I.R. Comrs.* [1894] 1 QB 516, CA and *Faber* v. *I.R. Comrs.* (1936) 155 LT 228).

[*N.B.* In relation to the prospective abolition of all stamp duties on transactions in shares (including bearer instruments) and units under unit trust schemes, and of stamp duty reserve tax, see the Revenue Press Release of 20 March 1990 and the commentary on FA 1990.]

56. How consideration consisting of periodical payments to be charged. (S&S 134–137)
This section applies where purchase consideration is payable by instalments or where additional periodical payments (whether contingent or not) are to be payable after completion. It does not apply in respect of periodical payments which are inherently incident to the property sold (*e.g.* the rent in the case of leasehold property).

In a case where a company agreed to sell its business to a new company in consideration of money and shares, and it was agreed in addition that the original company would be paid a proportion of the profits of the new company, it was held that the further consideration, though payable contingently, was "money payable periodically in perpetuity or for an indefinite period not terminable with life" within the meaning of s. 56 (2) (*Underground Electric Railways Company of London Limited* v. *I.R. Comrs.* [1906] AC 21).

A provision in a sale and purchase agreement, allowing for the purchase price to be payable in fixed annual instalments for a period of 125 years, to the effect that the whole of the instalments would become immediately payable in the event of a default in payment of any one instalment will not entitle the Commissioners to avoid s. 56 (2) and claim *ad valorem* duty on the whole of the purchase price (*Western United Investment Company Limited* v. *I.R. Comrs.* [1958] 1 All ER 257).

The Court of Appeal re-examined s. 56 (2) in two cases, heard together, involving the assessment of stamp duty payable on the grant of leases (*Blendett* v. *I.R. Comrs.* and *Quietlece* v. *I.R. Comrs.* [1984] STC 95, CA). In the first case, B. Ltd. was granted a long underlease of certain property at a peppercorn rent in consideration of a premium of £240,500 payable as to £50,000 on the execution of the lease and as to the balance on the 23rd anniversary of the lease. In the second case, Q. Ltd. was granted a long lease on similar terms save that the premium of £370,900 was payable as to £50,000 on the execution of the lease and as to the balance in three yearly instalments of £106,966 commencing on the 23rd anniversary of the lease. The companies paid *ad valorem* stamp duty on the instruments amounting to 2 per cent of the initial payment of £50,000 on the basis that the premiums consisted of "money payable periodically for a period exceeding 20 years" within s. 56 (2), and accordingly that stamp duty was payable only on so much of the consideration as would be paid within 20 years from the dates of the leases.

It was held by both Vinelott J. and the Court of Appeal that s. 56 (2) applied to neither of the two leases. In relation to the *Blendett* case, Vinelott J. held that money could not be said to be payable "periodically" unless a payment fell to be made between the payment which marked the beginning and the payment which marked the end of the period; the Court of Appeal held that there could not be said to be "periodical payments" when there were only two payments which were to be made over 20 years apart. In the *Quietlece* case, Vinelott J. held that the phrase "payable periodically for a definite period" envisaged the payment of instalments more than one of which would occur during the 20 years following the date of the instrument, but the Court of Appeal held, to the contrary, that the three instalments did constitute money payable periodically but since the duration of that period did not exceed 20 years s. 56 (2) did not apply.

As will be seen from the commentary on the "Lease or Tack" head of charge in Sch. 1, the better view seems to be that VAT on rent payable in respect of commercial buildings will not itself constitute "rent" and be dutiable as such under that head of charge. If that is right, it has been suggested (by R. S. Nock in *Taxation* dated 12 April 1990) that the Revenue might seek to argue that the VAT constitutes some other form of consideration or premium for the grant of the lease, payable periodically and therefore dutiable under this section.

57. How conveyance in consideration of a debt, etc., to be charged. (S&S 137–139)

Where property is conveyed either in satisfaction of a debt or subject either certainly or contingently to the payment or transfer of any money or stock, duty is payable on the amount of the debt or money or the value of the stock. Thus, if mortgaged property is sold, duty is paid on the purchase price together with the amount outstanding on the mortgage, whether the purchaser assumes personal liability for the debt or not (*I.R. Comrs.* v. *City of Glasgow Bank Liquidators*, 1881 8 R (Ct. of Sess.) 389). Where a creditor takes over the property of his debtor in consideration of the release of his debt, the transaction is also a sale and dutiable under this section (*I.R. Comrs.* v. *North British Railway Company*, 1901 4 F(Ct. of Sess.) 27). Similarly, where a business is purchased, the purchaser undertaking to discharge the business debts of the vendor, the amount of these debts will be added to the consideration (*E. Gomme Ltd.* v. *I.R. Comrs.* [1964] 3 All ER 497).

In the case of *Huntington* v. *I.R. Comrs.* [1896] 1 QB 422 it was held that a conveyance to an equitable mortgagee in pursuance of an order for foreclosure was liable to *ad valorem* duty under this section, but it was also suggested that the "amount or value of the consideration" on which the duty was to be assessed should not exceed the value of the property notwithstanding that the amount of the debt exceeded the value of the property. This suggestion received statutory effect in FA 1980, s. 102.

Where, on the sale of a business, "net assets" are purchased at their valuation, it is important to note that stamp duty will be payable on a gross basis—*i.e.* on the gross value of the fixed and current assets (including book debts) acquired *plus* the amount of the liabilities asumed. Where, therefore, the purchaser of a business undertakes to discharge the business debts of the vendor, it is common to avoid the additional stamp duty which would then be payable by a clause in the sale and purchase agreement to the effect that the purchaser will collect the book debts of the business as agent for the vendor and apply them in discharging the debts of the vendor, the purchaser keeping the balance (if any). This is effective, but it should be noted that if the purchaser also undertakes to make good any deficiency then this may amount to a contingent liability to discharge all the debts and therefore give rise to a claim for duty accordingly.

This section involves a trap for the unwary donor and donee in respect of a gift of property subject to a mortgage. Notwithstanding the abolition of *ad valorem* stamp duty on voluntary dispositions *inter vivos,* where gifted property is subject to a mortgage which the donee undertakes to discharge the conveyance or transfer of the property will be stampable *ad valorem,* as a conveyance or transfer on sale, on the amount of the liability assumed. There will, of course, be no stamp duty if the donor retains liability for the mortgage after making the gift. (See SP 6/90.)

As with s. 56, liabilities which are an integral part of the property conveyed (*e.g.* the rent payable in respect of leasehold property) are disregarded.

Notwithstanding this section, it is the practice of the Commissioners not to claim, in respect of transfers on sale of partly paid shares, that the contingent liability for further calls is part of the consideration for the sale.

[*N.B.* In relation to the prospective abolition of all stamp duties on transactions in shares (including bearer instruments) and units under unit trust schemes, and of stamp duty reserve tax, see the Revenue Press Release of 20 March 1990 and the commentary on FA 1990.]

58. Direction as to duty in certain cases. (S&S 139–142)

Subsections (1), (2) and (3) provide for the separate stamping of the several instruments involved where property contracted to be sold to a single purchaser for a single consideration is conveyed to that purchaser in separate parts or parcels by different instruments, or where property is contracted to be sold to two or more purchasers for a single consideration, and is conveyed in parts or parcels by separate instruments to the individual purchasers, or where there are several instruments of conveyance necessary to complete the purchaser's title to property sold. Subsections (4) and (5) are, subject to the exceptions, relieving provisions to prevent two lots of stamp duty being payable where an immediate sub-sale (or on-sale) is effected by a purchaser of property.

The exceptions in subsection (4) were inserted by FA 1984, s. 112 to counter a tax avoidance device involving a sub-sale of land by the real purchaser to a third party for a nominal sum and an agreement by the third party to grant the purchaser a long lease, followed by a direct conveyance from the original vendor to the third party and a subsequent reconveyance to the original purchaser.

FA 1984, s. 112 also inserted subsection (7) for the purposes of construing the exceptions inserted in subs ss. (4) and (5). It was amended by FA 1985, s. 82 in consequence of the abolition of voluntary disposition duty.

Where the provisions of subs ss. (4) and (5) apply, the conveyance or transfer giving effect to the sub-sale is stampable on the basis of the consideration paid by the sub-purchaser, whether that consideration is greater or less than the consideration paid by the original purchaser. The potential problems arising out of the drafting of the two subsections were given detailed consideration in *Fitch Lovell Ltd* v. *I.R. Comrs.* [1962] 1 WLR 1325 at 1341–1344. The general principle that can be extracted from that case is that the sub-sale relief will not be available in any of the following circumstances:

(a) where the original purchaser takes a conveyance or transfer before entering into the sub-sale agreement;

(b) where the original purchaser enters into the sub-sale agreement before the main purchase agreement;

(c) where the original purchaser so alters the nature of the property conveyed or transferred that it is not "the same"; or

(d) where the consideration provided by the sub-purchaser does not consist solely of cash, stock, etc. equal to the market value of the property conveyed or transferred.

Where sub-sale relief is not available, it seems that two lots of stamp duty will be payable on the instrument of tansfer (one on the consideration moving from the original purchaser and one on the consideration moving from the sub-purchaser).

This section does not seem to provide for what is to happen where, in the case of property contracted to be sold to a single purchaser for a single consideration, it is conveyed in separate parts or parcels at the direction of the purchaser, some to the purchaser himself and some to sub-purchasers. It has been suggested that the transfer of the property direct to the purchaser should be assessed on the basis of the appropriate proportion of the original purchase consideration, *i.e.* not including any pro rata share of the profit the purchaser may have made in respect of any sub-sales. This would seem to be the most logical application of this section and is supported by the decision in *Maples* v. *I.R. Comrs.* [1914] 3 KB 303.

59. Certain contracts to be chargeable as conveyances on sale. (S&S 142–149)
It was held in the case of *I.R. Comrs.* v. *G. Angus & Co*; *I.R. Comrs.* v. *J. Lewis & Sons* (1889) 23 QBD 579 that an agreement for the sale of the goodwill of a busines was not a conveyance on sale for stamp duty purposes. This case resulted in the Customs and Inland Revenue Act 1889, s. 18 and subsequently the Revenue Act 1889, s. 15, now reproduced in this section.

Any agreement for the sale of either:

(a) any equitable estate or interest in any property whatever; or

(b) any estate or interest in any property except (i) land, (ii) property locally situated outside the U.K., (iii) goods, (iv) stock and marketable securities (until the repeals made by FA 1990 are brought into force), or (v) ships,

is liable to duty as if it were an actual conveyance on sale.

A conveyance in favour of the purchaser pursuant to the contract, or in favour of a sub-purchaser pursuant to a subsequent sub-sale agreement, is not chargeable, or in the case of a sub-sale is chargeable only to the extent of the excess consideration paid by the sub-purchaser, and the conveyance has the duty paid on the contract denoted on it or transferred to it.

Where any such contract is not stamped it will nevertheless be treated as sufficiently stamped for all purposes if, within six months or such longer period as the commissioners may think reasonable, a conveyance in conformity with the contract is presented for stamping and duly stamped.

The duty can be reclaimed from the Commissioners if any such contract is rescinded or annulled or for any other reason, *e.g.* by failure of a condition, is not substantially performed.

There is a large body of case law in relation to the interpretation of this section, which in parts has proved to be particularly problematic. The most important of those cases are:

(a) *Farmer & Co.* v. *I.R. Comrs.* [1898] 2 QB 141, in which it was held that the words of exception (*i.e.*, in (i)–(v) of para. (b) above) do not qualify the words "equitable estate or interest" (in para. (a) above) so that, *e.g.*, an agreement for the sale of an *equitable* interest (as opposed to a legal interest) in property situated outside the U.K. will be liable to duty if it falls within s. 14 (4);

(b) *West London Syndicate* v. *I.R. Comrs.* [1898] 2 QB 507, in which it was held that for an agreement to constitute an agreement for the sale of an equitable interest the vendor must be bound to grant, and the purchaser must be bound to accept, an equitable interest in the property, so that an agreement for the sale of a legal interest in land coupled with an option enabling the purchaser to take a declaration of trust in lieu is not an agreement for the sale of an equitable interest within the meaning of the first part of subsection (1);

(c) *Chesterfield Brewery Company* v. *I.R. Comrs.* [1899] 2 QB 7, in which it was held that an agreement to hold property on trust for someone in consideration of the payment of a sum of money, or the transfer of stock or marketable securities, is an agreement for the sale of an equitable interest within this section;

(d) *Fleetwood-Hesketh* v. *I.R. Comrs.* [1936] 1 KB 351, CA, in which it was held that a memorandum of an agreement within the section requires to be stamped in accordance with it, so that an acknowledgement of receipt of the purchase money for a reversion under a will signed by the reversioner was an agreement for the sale of an equitable interest chargeable under this section;

(e) *William Cory Ltd.* v. *I.R. Comrs.* [1965] 1 All ER 917, in which it was held that the grant of an option to purchase property is not a contract to which this section applies;

(f) *George Wimpey & Co. Ltd.* v. *I.R. Comrs.* [1975] 2 All ER 45, in which it was held that a contract for the sale of an option to purchase a legal interest in land can be a contract for the sale of an equitable interest in land;

(g) *Muller & Co's Margarine Ltd.* v. *I.R. Comrs.* [1900] 1 QB 310, CA (affirmed by the House of Lords [1901] AC 217), in which it was held that the goodwill of a business abroad is property locally situated outside the U.K. within the exemption mentioned in this section and therefore not chargeable; and

(h) *English, Scottish and Australian Bank Ltd.* v. *I.R. Comrs.* [1932] AC 238, in which it was held that simple contract debts owed by debtors resident outside the U.K. constituted "property locally situate out of the United Kingdom", so that a contract for their sale was not stampable under s. 59. This case overruled the decision in *Danubian Sugar Factories* v. *I.R. Comrs.* [1901] 1 KB 245, where an agreement for the sale of the benefit of a contract enforceable against a resident of Romania for the transfer of land in Romania was held liable to duty under s. 59 as being "an estate or interest in property" not falling within any of the exceptions. An agreement for the sale of the benefit of a contract is now chargeable under s. 59 provided it is not enforceable only abroad. The House of Lords in the *English, Scottish and Australian Bank* case decided that, as a matter of "well-settled law", choses in action could have a local situation and therefore in certain circumstances be "property locally situate out of the United Kingdom".

Goodwill is a form of property and an agreement for the sale of goodwill is chargeable under this section. It has been held (for example in *Eastern National Omnibus Co.* v. *I.R. Comrs.* [1939] 1 KB 161) that a non-competition undertaking given in return for a monetary consideration was an agreement for the sale of goodwill chargeable under this section.

"Goods, wares or merchandise" form a class of property falling within the exceptions under this section, and an agreement for their sale will not be chargeable. However, problems have arisen in the past as to what exactly is meant by the word "goods". It has been held that an agreement for the sale of tenant's fixtures is neither an agreement for the sale of land nor of goods requiring an agreement in writing under the Statute of Frauds (*Lee* v. *Gaskill* (1876) 1 QBD 700). As a result, the Commissioners claim duty on the apportioned price for tenant's fixtures in the case of an agreement for sale of leasehold property and fixtures, but in the case of freehold property, fixtures form part of the freehold and an agreement for the sale of freehold land and fixtures will therefore fall within the exemption. It has also been held that the owner's interest under hire-purchase agreements of goods (at least in cases where the customer has a purchase option) is not an interest, an agreement for the sale of which is chargeable under s. 59 (*Drages Ltd.* v. *I.R. Comrs.* (1927) 6 ACT 727). Electricity is treated as "goods" for the purposes of this section, so that contracts for the sale of electricity will not be stampable (see Electricity Act 1989, s. 103, a measure introduced in connection with the privatisation of the electricity industry).

An agreement for the sale of book debts is chargeable under this section. In *Measures Brothers* v. *I.R. Comrs.* (1900) 82 LT 689, under an agreement for the sale of the entire business of the company including its book debts, the book debts were to be taken as they were at the end of the vendor company's preceding financial year, the vendor company guaranteed their payment in full before the date fixed for completion, and at the date of the agreement only a small part of the debts due at the end of the preceding year were still owing; it was held that *ad valorem* duty was payable on the consideration apportioned for the book debts as at the end of the financial year, notwithstanding the subsequent repayment.

Cash at a bank represents as a matter of law a debt due from the bank to its customer and, theoretically, when any such cash forms part of the assets of a business agreed to be sold, *ad valorem* duty should be payable on the consideration for it. In practice, however, the Commissioners do not exact duty in the case of cash on current account, but treat it as falling within the exemption. They do charge cash on deposit account.

Ad valorem duty is also not claimed, in practice, on agreements for the sale of mortgage debts.

Because of the differing treatment of assets and property of different kinds, where there is an agreement for the sale of a business, or a number of different assets, an apportionment of the consideration amongst the various assets involved will be required for the purposes of s. 59, and that apportionment must be a *bona fide* apportionment based on the commercial values of the respective assets. The Stamp Office supplies a form (No. 22) (reproduced at **S&S 150**) for use in connection with apportionments, and will frequently require particulars showing detailed break-downs of the various items listed (particularly those listed under the general heading of "loose plant and machinery, stock-in-trade, and other chattels").

Where an existing business is sold to a company in consideration of shares, *i.e.* for a consideration otherwise than in cash, then by virtue of the Companies Act 1985, s. 88, any written agreement must be stamped with the *ad valorem* duty payable before being delivered to the Registrar of Companies; alternatively "particulars" of the agreement must be so stamped and delivered. The Registrar of Companies may require that the duty be adjudicated. It is possible to get round this by arranging for the business to be sold to the company by oral agreement for a cash consideration, the vendors then using the cash to subscribe for the shares (see, *e.g.*, *Re Harmony and Montague Tin and Copper Mining Co., Spargo's Case* (1873) 8 Ch. App. 407).

60. As to sale of an annuity or right not before in existence. (S&S 149, 152)

The scope of this section was considered in *Great Northern Railway Company* v. *I.R. Comrs.* [1901] 1 KB 416, in which it was held that it does not apply to every contract whereby a right is acquired in consideration of a money payment, but that the transaction must be one of sale. Collins L.J. stated (at p. 426) that "to bring an instrument within this section, there must be (*a*) a sale of an annuity or other right, (*b*) that right must not be an already existing right, but must take its origin from the transaction of sale itself, (*c*) the right must be one, the sale of which is capable of being completed by grant or conveyance".

Contrast *Blandy* v. *Herbert* (1829) 9 B&C 396 (where an instrument securing an annuity agreed to be paid in consideration of a transfer of property was held not be an instrument given on the "sale" of an annuity) and *Faber* v. *I.R. Comrs.* (1936) 155 LT 228 (where a covenant by an engineer to pay an annuity to a company in return for the issue and allotment to him of shares and debentures of the company was held to be chargeable as a conveyance on sale under this section).

For an interesting scheme involving the sale of an annuity to a charitable company for tax avoidance purposes, which has now been held to be a fiscal nullity on the basis of the principles enunciated in the House of Lords decision in *W. T. Ramsay Ltd.* v. *I.R. Comrs.* [1981] STC 174 and the cases that followed that decision (further described in the commentary on SA 1891, s. 1), see the decision in *Moodie* v. *I.R. Comrs. and Sinnett (Inspector of Taxes); Sotnick* v. *I.R. Comrs. and Edwards (Inspector of Taxes)* [1990] STC 475.

61. Principal instrument, how to be ascertained. (S&S 152)

In all cases (except one) the parties to a transaction may determine for themselves which of several instruments is to be deemed the principal instrument chargeable to *ad valorem* stamp duty. The exception is where in Scotland there is a disposition or assignation executed by a vendor, and another instrument is executed for completing the title, in which case the disposition or assignation is to be regarded as the principal instrument.

CONVEYANCES ON ANY OCCASION EXCEPT SALE OR MORTGAGE

62. What is to be deemed a conveyance on any occasion, not being a sale or mortgage. (S&S 152)

This section relates to the head of charge "conveyance or transfer of any kind not hereinbefore described" under Sch. 1. If not a sale or mortgage, every instrument, decree or order (of a court or any commissioners) is chargeable under that head where the instrument, decree or order has the effect of transferring or vesting any property on any occasion in any person.

The proviso was extended by FA 1902, s. 9, to the retirement of a trustee as well as the appointment of a trustee, but has been held not to apply to an appointment which expressly vests property in the appointee (*Hadgett* v. *I.R. Comrs.* (1877) 3 Ex. D 46, DC).

DUPLICATES AND COUNTERPARTS

72. Provision as to duplicates and counterparts. (S&S 155–156)

A counterpart (not executed by or on behalf of any lessor or grantor) of a lease may be used in evidence without a denoting stamp, provided it is stamped with 50p or the proper *ad valorem* duty if such duty is less than 50p. The counterpart of any other instrument, and the duplicate of all instruments liable to a duty of more than 50p, are not duly stamped with 50p unless they bear a denoting stamp. In the case of a duplicate or counterpart of a conveyance where the consideration does not exceed £30,000 (and the appropriate certificate is given so that the duty is nil), the duty on the duplicate or counterpart will also be nil.

EXCHANGE AND PARTITION OR DIVISION

73. As to exchange etc. (S&S 156–157)

An instrument effecting an exchange, partition or division is normally charged 50p. Where, however, upon the exchange of real or heritable property (*i.e.* freehold but not leasehold property and not property held upon trust for sale (*I.R. Comrs.* v. *Littlewoods Mail Order Stores Ltd.* [1963]

AC 135) for other real or heritable property, or upon the partition or division of real or heritable property, any consideration exceeding £100 in amount or value is paid or given, or agreed to be paid or given, for equality, then the instrument effecting the exchange, partition or division is charged with the same *ad valorem* stamp duty as on a conveyance on sale for that consideration and with that duty only. Where more than one instrument is used for completing the title of either party in such a transaction, only the principal instrument is charged with *ad valorem* duty; the others are charged in the same manner as in the case of several instruments of conveyance.

It can sometimes be difficult to distinguish between an exchange or partition on the one hand and a sale on the other. In *Portman Trustees* v *I.R. Comrs.* (1956) 35 ATC 349, where mutual sales of property were completed by an instrument described as an exchange which vested the properties in the respective parties, the instrument was held to constitute two conveyances on sale and to be chargeable on the aggregate of the considerations for the conveyances, and not merely on the equality money which was paid.

Where duty is charged on equality consideration, no account need be taken of the provisions relating to conveyances in consideration of debt or subject to liabilities (see notes on s. 57), since an instrument effecting an exchange will *ex hypothesi* not be a conveyance on sale.

LEASES

75. Agreements [for not more than thirty-five years] to be charged as leases. (S&S 167–169)
Originally an agreement for a lease for any term not exceeding 35 years, or for an indefinite term, was to be charged with the same duty as if it were an actual lease, *i.e.* agreements for leases for fixed terms of more than 35 years were exempt. However, FA 1984, s. 111 removed the exception for agreements for leases for fixed terms of more than 35 years, and such agreements are now liable to lease duty.

Where duty is paid on a lease agreement and subsequently a lease is granted which is either in conformity with the agreement or relates to substantially the same property and term as the agreement, then the duty payable on the lease is reduced accordingly. Furthermore, where there is a conveyance or transfer of a freehold or leasehold interest subject to an agreement for a lease for more than 35 years, the conveyance or transfer instrument is not to be taken as duly stamped unless the duty on the agreement is denoted on the conveyance, except where the agreement is directly enforceable against another interest in the land.

FA 1984, s. 111 nullified a device for avoiding stamp duty on sales of houses and other property; this device involved (in its simplest form) the purchaser of property, instead of buying the freehold in the normal way, entering into (for substantially the full sale price) an agreement for a lease of more than 35 years and buying (for a nominal consideration) the freehold subject to that agreement.

77. Directions as to duty in certain cases. (S&S 169–170)
An additional rent which becomes payable if and when a lessee commits a breach of the convenants in the lease is a "penal rent", and no additional duty will be payable in respect of that rent. However, if the lessee has the option either of performing or abstaining from some action or of paying an increased rent, the increased rent will not be a penal rent, and additional duty will be payable accordingly.

No additional duty is to be charged where part of the consideration for the grant of a lease consists either of a covenant by the lessee to make any substantial improvement or addition to the property, or of his having previously done so, or any other covenant relating to the subject matter of the lease. Under the Revenue Act 1909, s. 8, the exemption does not apply in respect of any further consideration in the lease consisting of a covenant which if it were contained in a separate deed would be chargeable with *ad valorem* stamp duty, and accordingly the lease should in any such case be charged with duty in respect of any such further consideration under s. 4.

A deed of variation increasing the rent reserved by a lease, but leaving the original lease in existence, *prima facie* attracts "bond, covenant" duty, but this duty is relieved by s. 77 (5) and is chargeable on the additional rent as if it were a lease or tack (see *Gable Construction Co. Ltd.* v. *I.R. Comrs.* [1968] 2 All ER 968). An appropriately drafted memorandum recording a change of rent under a rent review clause will not attract stamp duty.

It seems to be the current view of the Stamp Office that where a landlord exercises his option under the relevant legislation to standard-rate a lease for VAT purposes, the notification he is required to give to Customs and Excise is an instrument increasing the rent which is dutiable under s. 77 (5). This cannot be correct. First, as will be seen from the commentary on the "Lease or Tack" head of charge in Sch. 1, the better view seems to be that VAT cannot itself constitute "rent". Secondly, even if that were not correct, the option to standard-rate the rent is obviously created by the lease itself and s. 77 (5) does not apply to increases of rent arising by reason of the terms of the lease (which is why an appropriately drafted memorandum recording a change of rent under a rent review clause is not dutiable). For a fuller analysis, see the article by R. S. Nock in *Taxation* dated 12 April 1990.

83. Penalty on issuing, etc., foreign, etc., security not duly stamped. (S&S 170–171)
Any person who, in the U.K., assigns, transfers or negotiates a foreign security or a Commonwealth government security that is not duly stamped is liable to a fine of £20.

[*N.B.* In relation to the prospective abolition of all stamp duties on transactions in shares (including bearer instruments) and units under unit trust schemes, and of stamp duty reserve tax, see the Revenue Press Release of 20 March 1990 and the commentary on FA 1990.]

STOCK CERTIFICATES TO BEARER

109. Penalty for issuing stock certificate unstamped. (S&S 176)
This section has been extended to cover instruments to bearer issued by or on behalf of companies or bodies of persons formed or established in the U.K. In addition, the provision for cancellation of stock certificates to bearer in certain cases is extended to certificates to bearer in respect of a unit under a unit trust scheme when the owner of that unit is registered on any register kept under the scheme.

[*N.B.* In relation to the prospective abolition of all stamp duties on transactions in shares (including bearer instruments) and units under unit trust schemes, and of stamp duty reserve tax, see the Revenue Press Release of 20 March 1990 and the commentary on FA 1990.]

WARRANTS FOR GOODS

111. Provisions as to warrants for goods. (S&S 182–183)
"Warrant for goods" is defined.

PART III SUPPLEMENTAL

MISCELLANEOUS

117. Conditions and agreements as to stamp duty void. (S&S 183)
A purchaser is entitled to have every deed forming a link in the vendor's title duly stamped (*Whiting to Loomes* (1881) 17 Ch. D10, CA).

119. Instruments relating to Crown property. (S&S 183–184)
Crown property is chargeable.

121. Recovery of penalties. (S&S 184)
Fines are sued for in the names specified. See also FA 1986, ss. 68 (6), 71 (6).

122. Definitions. (S&S 184–186)
The definition of "marketable security" has been considered by the courts on a number of occasions. It appears that a security can be "marketable" whether or not it is actually dealt in on any stock exchange, so long as it is capable of being so dealt—see *Texas Land and Cattle Co.* v. *I.R. Comrs.* 1888 16 R (Ct. of Sess.) 69, per Lord Shand. Thus, promissory notes of a type dealt in on The Stock Exchange have been held to be marketable securities (*Brown Shipley & Co.* v. *I.R. Comrs.* [1895] 2 QB 598, 601, and *Speyer Brothers* v. *I.R. Comrs.* [1907] 1 KB 246, 259, [1908] AC 92). In addition, although the Revenue do not in practice treat them as such, in theory the debentures of a private company containing no provision objectionable to The Stock Exchange, such as a restriction on transfer or possibly a prohibition against Stock Exchange dealings, are marketable securities (see *Deddington Steamship Co.* v. *I.R. Comrs.* [1911] 1 KB 1078).
   By virtue of FA 1946, s. 54 (1), the expression "stock" also includes units under a unit trust scheme.

[*N.B.* In relation to the prospective abolition of all stamp duties on transactions in shares (including bearer instruments) and units under unit trust schemes, and of stamp duty reserve tax, see the Revenue Press Release of 20 March 1990 and the commentary on FA 1990.]

REPEAL; COMMENCEMENT; SHORT TITLE

124. Commencement. (S&S 187)

125. Short title. (S&S 187)

SCHEDULES

FIRST SCHEDULE: STAMP DUTIES ON INSTRUMENTS. (Section 1) (S&S 94–188)

It is a fundamental rule of stamp duty law that the thing which is dutiable is the document and not the transaction, so that if there is no document no duty will be chargeable. This Schedule sets out a list, in alphabetical order, of the heads of charge under which documents are chargeable. A number of the heads of charge are followed by a cross-reference (for example "AGREEMENT for a lease or tack, or for any letting . . . see LEASE OR TACK, and section 35"). The commentary on such heads of charge, as set out below, should therefore be read in conjunction with the commentary on the relevant sections. The commentary below contains a full analysis only of those heads of charge not already dealt with.

In cases where an instrument liable to stamp duty falls within two categories or heads of charge (which, with the repeal of a large number of the duties originally imposed, has become rather less frequent), the Crown is entitled to only one of the duties, but it is entitled to choose the higher (*Speyer Brothers* v. *I.R. Comrs.* [1908] AC 92, where it was held that certain documents ranking as both promissory notes and marketable securities were liable to the higher duty which was at the time chargeable on marketable securities). Nevertheless, an instrument chargeable under a specific head of charge will not usually be charged with the larger duty under a more general head of charge (*North of Scotland Bank* v. *I.R. Comrs.* 1931 SC 149, per Lord Blackburn at 154).

Where duties in respect of any of the heads of charge mentioned below have been abolished, the case law relating to that head which evolved before abolition will still be relevant for the purpose of investigating title deeds to properties, or determining admissibility in evidence, and reference to S&S should be made to the relevant case law to the extent that it is not dealt with in the following commentary.

[*N.B.* In relation to the prospective abolition of all stamp duties on transactions in shares (including bearer instruments) and units under unit trust schemes, and of stamp duty reserve tax, see the Revenue Press Release of 20 March 1990 and the commentary on FA 1990.]

AGREEMENT for a lease or tack, or for any letting. **(S&S 94)**

See LEASE or TACK, and s. 75.

AGREEMENT for sale of property. **(S&S 94)**

See CONVEYANCE AND SALE, and s. 59.

ANNUITY, conveyance in consideration of. **(S&S 94)**

See CONVEYANCE ON SALE, and s. 56.

Purchase of:
    See CONVEYANCE ON SALE, and s. 60.

Instruments relating to, upon any other occasion:
    See BOND, COVENANT etc.

ASSIGNMENT or ASSIGNATION. **(S&S 94)**

Upon a sale, or otherwise:
    See CONVEYANCE.

ASSURANCE. **(S&S 94)**

See POLICY.

BEARER INSTRUMENT. **(S&S 95–101)**

[*N.B.* In relation to the prospective abolition of all stamp duties on transactions in shares (including bearer instruments) and units under unit trust schemes, and of stamp duty reserve tax, see the Revenue Press Release of 20 March 1990 and the commentary on FA 1990.]

FA 1963, s. 59 (1), inserted the heading "Bearer Instrument". The duty under the heading was altered and increased by the FA 1970, s. 32 and Sch. 7, para. 6 and FA 1974, s. 49 and Sch. 11, para. 2. It has now been reduced to 1½ per cent. with effect from 27 October 1986 by FA 1986, s. 65.

FA 1963, as amended by FA 1973, defines the various expressions used in connection with the head, and provides for the payment of the duty and the ascertainment of the market value.

Exemption 2 (for a bearer letter of allotment, bearer letter of rights, scrip, scrip certificate to bearer or other similar instrument to bearer where the letter, scrip, certificate or instrument is required to be surrendered not later than six months after issue) was repealed, with one exception, by FA 1986, s. 80 and Sch. 23, Pt. IX (3) in relation to instruments falling within FA 1963, s. 60 (1) and (2) issued or transferred after 24 March 1986. FA 1963, s. 60 (1) made the duty chargeable on the issue of bearer instruments either issued in Great Britain or issued by or on behalf of a company or body of persons corporate or unincorporate formed or established in Great Britain. FA 1963, s. 60 (2) made the duty chargeable on the transfer in Great Britain of stock constituted by or transferable by means of bearer instruments which were not chargeable upon issue pursuant to s. 60 (1). The one exception to the repeal is in relation to bearer instruments falling within FA 1963, s. 60 (1) which are issued by a company in pursuance of a general offer for its shares which became unconditional as to acceptances on or before 18 March 1986.

FA 1963, s. 65 (1) provided that any instrument exempt from duty by virtue of exemption 3 was also exempt from duty under or by reference to the head "conveyance or transfer on sale". The exemption from "conveyance or transfer on sale" duty was repealed by FA 1985, s. 81 (2) in respect of arrangements whereby rights under an instrument to shares in a company are renounced in favour of a person who, together with persons connected with him, has, or will have, control of that company in consequence of the arrangements, *i.e.,* in company takeover situations, where the rights were renounced on or after 1 August 1985 (unless the arrangements concerned included an offer for the rights which became unconditional as to acceptances on or before 27 June 1985). The removal of the exemption in these specific circumstances was designed to end the use of a revised version of the so-called "pref-trick" which had been devised by solicitors to avoid a challenge by the Revenue on the basis of the decision in *Furniss* v. *Dawson* [1984] STC 153. Before that decision, the "pref-trick" in common use involved the existing shares of a company being converted into deferred shares with little or no rights, which were therefore virtually worthless, and the issue of new shares pro rata to the existing shareholders on renounceable letters of allotment which could then be renounced in favour of a purchaser of the company. The letters of allotment would be exempt from stamp duty under exemption 3 where they had a life of not more than six months, and the valueless deferred shares could be transferred for a minimal consideration, and consequently a minimal stamp duty. As a result of *Furniss* v. *Dawson* [1984] STC 153 the Revenue claimed that this device was a tax avoidance scheme which could be attacked on the basis of its substance rather than its form, and the Revenue therefore claimed duty on the transfers of the worthless deferred shares in respect of the total consideration paid by the purchaser for both the new shares renounced in its favour and the deferred shares transferred to it. Consequently, revised versions of the "pref-trick" were introduced which simply left the worthless deferredshares registered in the names of the original owners, and did not transfer them to the purchaser, so that there was no stampable document which needed to be produced to the Revenue which could be assessed on the basis of the whole consideration under *Furniss* v. *Dawson* principles. Section 81 sought to put an end to that revised version by making the renounceable documents themselves stampable in takeover situations, but it did not affect the use of renounceable letters of allotment in other circumstances.

In his Budget speech on 18 March 1986, the Chancellor announced that the exemption from "conveyance or transfer on sale" duty given by FA 1963, s 65 (1) would be repealed, with effect from 27 October 1986, in respect of renounceable letters of allotment used in any circumstances at all, and not just those used in the circumstances set out in FA 1985, s. 81. However, during proceedings on the Finance Bill on 5 June 1986 the Economic Secretary announced that, following consultation, the Government had agreed to withdraw the original clause to that effect from the Bill, and to replace it with a new clause designed to achieve the same result by a different mechanism. As a result of the original clause, where a letter of allotment was renounced stamp duty would have been payable in respect of the renunciation, but the Government realised that the most frequent use of renounceable letters of allotment, after the enactment of FA 1985, s. 81 which nullified their utility in takeover situations, was in connection with rights or bonus issues or new listings. In such cases a very large number of renunciations would take place which it would be difficult for the Stamp Duty Office to deal with quickly enough to enable the ultimate holder to be registered as a member of the relevant company within the normal timescales. To avoid such inconvenient delays the Government withdrew the original clause and introduced a new clause to make renunciations subject to stamp duty reserve tax rather than stamp duty. Consequently, where rights under a renounceable letter of allotment are renounced, the purchasers will not have to get the letters of allotment stamped before they can get their shares, but the provisions of FA 1986, ss. 87 and 88 (as amended) will apply so that a charge to stamp duty reserve tax will arise on the date of renunciation and be payable at the end of the following month. This does not apply, however, to agreements to transfer securities constituted by or transferable by means of *overseas* bearer instruments (FA 1986, s. 90 (3) (*a*)), upon which no stamp duty reserve tax will be payable. For stamp duty reserve tax, see FA 1986, ss. 86 to 99.

Other relevant provisions of FA 1986 are s. 78 (3), (11), (12) and (13), and s. 79 (2), (9), (10), (11) and (12) (stamp duty under the heading "Bearer Instrument" is not chargeable on instruments relating to loan capital issued or transferred after 24 March 1986, except in the case of certain instruments executed in pursuance of a contract made before 19 March 1986) and also s. 95 (2) and s. 97 (3) (depositary receipts and clearance services—exemption from stamp duty reserve tax in respect of the transfer, issue or appropriation of an inland bearer instrument not falling within exemption 3 in the heading "Bearer Instrument").

See also FA 1988, s. 143 in relation to bearer instruments issued in connection with "paired shares" forming part of a joint public offering by a U.K. company and a foreign company (as, for example, was the case in the Eurotunnel "Equity 3" offerings in 1987).

BILL OF SALE. (S&S 103)

Absolute.
  See CONVEYANCE ON SALE.
  And see s. 41.

BOND in relation to any annuity upon the original creation and sale thereof. (S&S 103)

See CONVEYANCE ON SALE, and s. 60.

BOND, COVENANT or INSTRUMENT of any kind whatsoever. **(S&S 103–105)**

The duties under paras. (1) and (2) of this heading (securities for annuities other than superannuation annuities and for certain other periodic sums) have been abolished as from 1 August 1971 except as respects any instrument increasing the rent reserved by another instrument which continues to be chargeable to duty under this head, subject to s. 77 (5).

Accordingly, a deed of covenant in common form for periodical payments does not now attract any stamp duty, unless it is a covenant (other than a charitable covenant) for an unstated or variable amount (in which case the fixed duty of 50p is payable).

See FA 1980, s. 99, in relation to charitable covenants for variable or unstated amounts.

The leading case on the interpretation of paras. (1) and (2) of this heading is *Independent Television Authority* v. *I.R. Comrs.* [1960] 2 All ER 481, HL. In that case it was held that an agreement between the ITA and Associated Rediffusion, pursuant to which Associated Rediffusion was constituted a programme contractor for one of the ITA's television stations for a period of years during which it was obliged to pay certain fees, constituted a "security" under this heading, notwithstanding that the agreement was an executory agreement and that the fees were payable in consideration of services to be rendered by the ITA. It was also held that the contingency that the fees might be subject to increase or decrease in certain circumstances did not affect the calculation of the proper *ad valorem* duty.

Paragraph (3) of this heading was abolished by FA 1989 with effect from 31 December 1989.

BOND given pursuant to the directions of any Act, or of the Commissioners or the Commissioners of Customs, or any of their officers, for or in respect of any of the duties of excise or customs, or for preventing frauds or evasions thereof, or for any other matter or thing relating thereto.

BOND on obtaining letters of administration in ... Ireland, or a confirmation of testament in Scotland ...

[*N.B.* In relation to the prospective abolition of all stamp duties on transactions in shares (including bearer instruments) and units under unit trust schemes, and of stamp duty reserve tax, see the Revenue Press Release of 20 March 1990 and the commentary on FA 1990.]

CONVEYANCE or TRANSFER on sale. **(S&S 106–110)**

Of any property.
 And see ss. 54, 55, 56, 57, 58, 59, 60 and 61 (referred to above).

FA 1963, s. 55 as subsequently amended, provides that, subject to the matters mentioned in that section, "the stamp duty chargeable under the heading "conveyance or transfer on sale" in Sch. 1 shall be charged by reference to the amount or value of the consideration for the sale" at the rates specified in FA 1963, s. 55.

Other legislation provides for special rates of duty in respect of certain types of instrument, as follows:
 (*a*) FA 1963, s. 62 (2)—a transfer of Commonwealth Government stock;
 (*b*) FA 1986, s. 67 (2)—a transfer of relevant securities of a company incorporated in the U.K. to a person who at the time of the transfer falls within s. 67 (6), (7) or (8) (depositary receipts);
 (*c*) FA 1986, s. 70 (2)—a transfer of relevant securities of a company incorporated in the U.K. to a person who at the time of the transfer falls within s. 70 (6), (7) or (8) (clearance services);
 (*d*) FA 1986, s. 76 (2)—a transfer of property, other than shares, by a target company to a company acquiring the whole or any part of the undertaking of the target company for a consideration consisting of or including an issue of shares in the acquiring company to the target company, or to all or any of the target company's shareholders, with no other consideration except cash (not exceeding 10 per cent. of the nominal value of the shares to be issued) or the assumption or discharge by the acquiring company of liabilities of the target company, or both;
 (*e*) FA 1986, ss. 78 (6) and 79 (8)—a transfer of loan capital issued after 24 March 1986 except in the case of certain instruments executed in pursuance of a contact made before 19 March 1986.

In addition, there are a number of statutory provisions which provide for reliefs and exemptions from *ad valorem* "conveyance or transfer on sale" duty, which are discussed in detail in the commentary following the relevant provisions.

See in particular:

FA 1930, s. 42 (stamp duty under this head not chargeable in the case of certain conveyances or transfers on sale between asociated bodies corporate),

FA 1958, s. 35 (5) (no duty chargeable on any agreement made under the New Towns Act 1946, s. 14, by a development corporation under that Act for the transfer of water or sewerage undertakings),

FA 1982, s. 129 (stamp duty exemption to charities and Trustees of the the National Heritage Memorial Fund),

FA 1985, s. 83 (transfer of property in connection with divorce, nullity of marriage or judicial separation—stamp duty exemption under this heading),

FA 1985, s. 84 (variations of dispositions by beneficiaries and appropriations of property by personal representatives within two years of death—stamp duty exemption under this heading),

FA 1986, s. 75 (2), (6) (if certain conditions are satisfied, instruments in respect of business reconstruction schemes are exempt from stamp duty under this heading if executed after 24 March 1986 unless executed in pursuance of an unconditional contract made before 19 March 1986), and

FA 1986, s. 77 (1) (exemption from stamp duty under this heading for instruments transferring shares in one company to another if specified conditions are satisfied).

[*N.B.* In relation to the prospective abolition of all stamp duties on transactions in shares (including bearer instruments) and units under unit trust schemes, and of stamp duty reserve tax, see the Revenue Press Release of 20 March 1990 and the commentary on FA 1990.]
And see s. 62.

CONVEYANCE or TRANSFER of any kind not herein before described. **(S&S 111–113)**

All conveyances or transfers, not being conveyances or transfers on sale, are liable to a fixed duty of 50p under this heading unless exempted from all stamp duty under some other specific provision.

There are four exceptions to the general rule that the duty payable on instruments under this heading is 50p. These appear in the following sections of FA 1986:

- (*a*) 67 (3)—a transfer of relevant securities of a company incorporated in the U.K. to a person who at the time of the transfer falls with s. 67 (6), (7) or (8) (depositary receipts);
- (*b*) 70 (3)—a transfer of relevant securities of a company incorporated in the U.K. to a person who at the time of the transfer falls within s. 70 (6), (7) or (8) (clearance services);
- (*c*) 93 (5) (*a*)—a transfer of chargeable securities to a nominee of the issuer of a depositary receipt;
- (*d*) 96 (3) (*a*)—a transfer of chargeable securities to a provider of clearance services, or his nominee, pursuant to an arrangement for the provisions of such services.

[*N.B.* In relation to the prospective abolition of all stamp duties on transactions in shares (including bearer instruments) and units under unit trust schemes, and of stamp duty reserve tax, see the Revenue Press Release of 20 March 1990 and the commentary on FA 1990.]

COUNTERPART. **(S&S 153)**

See DUPLICATE.

COVENANT in relation to any annuity upon the original creation and sale thereof. **(S&S 153)**

See CONVEYANCE ON SALE, and s. 60.

COVENANT in relation to any annuity (except upon the original creation and sale thereof) or to any other periodical payments. **(S&S 153)**

See BOND, COVENANT, etc.

DECLARATION of any use or trust of or concerning any property by any writing, not being a will, or an instrument chargeable with *ad valorem* duty as a unit trust instrument. **(S&S 153–154)**

[*N.B.* In relation to the prospective abolition of all stamp duties on transactions in shares (including bearer instruments) and units under unit trust schemes, and of stamp duty reserve tax, see the Revenue Press Release of 20 March 1990 and the commentary on FA 1990.]

DISPOSITION of heritable property in Scotland to singular successors or purchasers. **(S&S 155)**

See CONVEYANCE ON SALE.

DISPOSITION of heritable property in Scotland to a purchaser, containing a clause declaring all or any part of the purchase money a real burden upon, or affecting, the heritable property thereby disponed, or any part thereof. **(S&S 155)**

See CONVEYANCE ON SALE.

DISPOSITION in Scotland, containing constitution of feu or ground annual right. **(S&S 155)**

See CONVEYANCE AND SALE, and s. 56.

DISPOSITION in Scotland of any property or of any right or interest therein not described in this schedule. **(S&S 155)**

DUPLICATE or COUNTERPART of any instrument chargeable with any duty. **(S&S 155–156)**

And see s. 72.

EXCHANGE or EXCAMBION—Instruments effecting. **(S&S 156–157)**

See s. 73 for they duty payable in the cases therein specified. The duty payable in any other case is 50p.

FEU CONTRACT in Scotland. (S&S 157)

See CONVEYANCE ON SALE, and s. 56.

INSURANCE. (S&S 157)

See POLICY.

This head of charge was abolished by FA 1989 Sch. 17 with effect from 31 December 1989.

LEASE or TACK. (S&S 158–170)

To fall within this head of charge, the subject matter of the relevant lease or tack must be land, tenements or heritable subjects. The head of charge does not apply to leases or hiring agreements relating to personalty, nor does it apply to a mere licence (as distinguished from a lease), which does not now attract any stamp duty.

For the purposes of this head a lease granted for a fixed term and thereafter until determined is to be treated as a lease for a definite term equal to the fixed term together with such further period as must elapse before the earliest date at which the lease can be determined: FA 1963, s. 56 (3).

The words in the head of charge "moving either to the lessor or to any other person" include the common case of a lease to a builder's nominee under a building agreement, where the lease is granted by the ground landlord at the direction of the builder to his nominee and a premium is paid to the builder.

The words "average rate", referring to the rent, are intended to meet the case of a varying rent over a fixed term.

It would only be possible to calculate the "average rent" if the annual rental for each period of the whole term of the lease were specified in the lease itself. This will quite often not be the case; although rent review procedures will generally be set out in a lease it will almost always be impossible to calculate in advance the annual rental figure which will be produced, unless minimum rent increases are specified. If there is a specified rental for the whole term of the lease which may be varied, upwards or downwards, in accordance with a normal rent review clause it will be assumed that the specified figure will apply over the whole term unless a percentage or amount as a minimum or maximum increase is also specified, in which case that figure or percentage will be taken into account. It will always be the average of the highest ascertainable rents over the whole period of the lease which will be used as the basis of calculation. This principle ("the contingency principle") was applied in the case of *Coventry City Council* v. *I.R. Comrs.* [1979] Ch. 142, [1978] 1 All ER 1107, applying dicta of Collins MR in *Underground Electric Railways Company of London Ltd.* v. *I.R. Comrs.* [1905] 1 KB 174 at 182 and of Lord Radcliffe in *Independent Television Authority* v. *I.R. Comrs.* [1960] 2 All ER 481 at 485 and 486 (as to which see above).

In that case, Coventry City Council entered into an arrangement with the Norwich Union Life Insurance Society whereby one of the Council's development projects was financed by the Society by means of a scheme involving a lease and lease back of the relevant site. The Council granted to the Society a lease of the site for 125 years at an annual rental of £17,500, and on the same day the Society granted back to the Council an underlease of the site for 125 years less one day and covenanted to incur certain expenses and reimburse the Council's development costs up to a maximum of £1,300,000, the rent payable under the underlease being a basic rent of £17,500 p.a. (to match the rent under the headlease) and an annual rent of 8.142 per cent. on the total sums incurred or reimbursed by the Society under its covenant not exceeding £1,300,000. It was held that the annual rent reserved was £17,500 plus 8.142 per cent. of £1,300,000.

As far as the length of the lease is concerned, it has been held that a lease for a term of 99 years if A. B. and C. should so long live is a lease for a term exceeding 35 years and not exceeding 100 years and is not a lease for an indefinite term within the meaning of the heading (*Earl Mount-Edgcumbe* v. *I.R. Comrs.* [1911] 2 KB 24). It has also been held that a lease for a stated term of years is a lease for the length of that stated term notwithstanding that it contains a clause providing for the determination of the lease at an earlier date (*Kushner* v. *Law Society* [1952] 1 KB 264).

The term "rent" is not defined and the description of a payment by the parties to an instrument as "rent" is not conclusive (see for example *Donellan* v. *Read* (1832) 3 B&Ad 899). Payments which are not reserved out of the land are not rent (*Hill* v. *Booth* [1930] 1 KB 381). The meaning of the word "rent" and its distinction from other payments such as royalties was considered in detail in *T. and E. Homes Ltd.* v. *Robinson* [1976] STC 462. If periodical payments for services, heating, lighting, cleaning, maintenance, etc. are payable under the lease they will not be taken into account in calculating the *ad valorem* stamp duty payable whether or not they are reserved as rent.

It is debatable whether VAT payable in respect of the rent of commercial premises can itself be regarded as "rent" and dutiable as such under this head of charge. On the basis of the cases mentioned in the previous paragraph the better view seems to be that it cannot (though this in itself might give rise to a different problem under s. 56, as to which see above). If the "rent" can only include sums reserved out of the land on its demise, and not other sums payable under collateral arrangements, it should exclude any VAT payable. In other words, the VAT should be treated in exactly the same way as a service charge, especially where the lease reserves an amount by way of rent which is *exclusive* of VAT and makes separate provision for the VAT.

If this argument is not right, and VAT on rent is itself dutiable as rent, there will be further difficulties arising out of the operation of the contingency principle, dicussed above. Where for example rent is exempt from VAT at the time the lease is executed, the question will arise as to whether the possibility of the landlord in future exercising his option to standard-rate the rent will cause an additional amount of stamp duty to be payable on the VAT which is contingently payable (and, if so, at what rate of VAT). Similarly, there will be difficulties where the lease reserves a rent which is itself contingent. For a detailed analysis, see the articles by R. S. Nock in *Taxation* dated 5 and 12 April 1990.

Where a lease is at a fixed rent for part of the term and for the remainder of the term at a rent to be agreed upon or fixed in accordance with a specified rent review procedure, the consideration for the lease will be regarded as divided into two parts and the first part, the rent specified for the first portion of the term, will attract *ad valorem* stamp duty on the specified rent (using the "average rate" method where appropriate or necessary), whereas the remainder will attract the fixed duty of £2.

Because of FA 1963, s. 56 (3), a weekly or monthly tenancy agreement will, for stamp duty purposes, be regarded as a lease for an indefinite term, whereas an agreement for one week or one month certain, and thereafter subject to one week's or one month's notice, will be treated as a lease for a definite term of two weeks or two months, as the case may be.

A lease for a fixed term with an option to renew is regarded as a lease for the fixed term only, and if the option is exercised the instrument exercising it will be liable to stamp duty as for a new lease.

When notice to terminate a tenancy is given, and the notice is afterwards withdrawn by agreement, the withdrawal of the notice will also constitute a new tenancy (see *Freeman* v. *Evans* [1922] 1 Ch. 36, CA) and further *ad valorem* stamp duty will be payable. Since it appears to be well established that a lease cannot be retrospective, so that the commencement of a term cannot be earlier than the date the lease is executed (*Bradshaw* v. *Pawley* [1979] 3 All ER 273), the Revenue disregard any period before the date of the lease in calculating the amount of *ad valorem* stamp duty payable.

The distinction between a lease and a licence was considered in detail by the House of Lords in the case of *Street* v. *Mountford* [1985] 2 All ER 289. The facts of that case were that the landlord had granted to the appellant the right to occupy a furnished room under a written agreement which stated (*i*) that the appellant had the right to occupy the room "at a licence fee of £37 per week", (*ii*) that "this personal licence is not assignable", (*iii*) that the "licence may be terminated by 14 days written notice", and (*iv*) that the appellant understood and accepted that "a licence in the above form does not and is not intended to give me a tenancy protected under the Rent Act." The appellant had exclusive possession. The House of Lords held that the test as to whether an occupancy of residential accommodation was a tenancy or a licence was whether, on the true construction of the agreement, the occupier had been granted exclusive possession of the accommodation for a fixed or periodic term at a stated rent, and that unless special circumstances existed which negatived the presumption of a tenancy (e.g. where from the outset there was no intention to create legal relations or where the possession was granted pursuant to a contract of employment) a tenancy arose whenever there was a grant of exclusive possession for a fixed or periodic term at a stated rent—whatever the intention of the parties, as manifested in the agreement. Accordingly, it was held in this case that since the effect of the agreement between the appellant and the landlord was to grant the appellant exclusive possession for a fixed term at a stated rent, and no circumstances existed to negative the presumption of a tenancy, it was clear that the appellant was a tenant.

See the letter from the Controller of Stamps to the Law Society, 2 January 1963.

MORTGAGE, BOND, DEBENTURE, COVENANT (except a marketable security otherwise specially charged with duty), and WARRANT OF ATTORNEY to confess and enter of judgment. (S&S 170–171)

The duties chargeable under this heading have been abolished with regard to instruments executed on or after 1 August 1971 (FA 1971, s. 64, Sch. 14, Part VI). This abolition is subject to two important qualifications.

First, it is subject to s. 4, pursuant to which an instrument containing or relating to several distinct matters is chargeable in respect of each matter so that it will only be relieved from duty by FA 1971, s. 64 (1) to the extent that any matter falls within an abolished head of charge.

Secondly, FA 1971, s. 64(2) expressly provides that "any instrument which, but for subsection (1) above, would be chargeable with duty under a heading mentioned in that subsection shall not be chargeable with any duty under any other heading in the said Schedule." This means that instruments which were chargeable under this heading are not to be chargeable under any of the heads which remain in existence purely because of the abolition of this specific heading. For example, a release of a mortgage which would have been chargeable under para. (5) of this heading will not become chargeable under "release . . . in any other case".

It should be noted, however, that a conveyance or transfer of any assets to a lender as security, and a subsequent re-transfer, will each attract duty under the residual head "conveyance or transfer".

MUTUAL DISPOSITION for conveyance in Scotland. **(S&S 171)**

See EXCHANGE or EXCAMBION.

PARTITION or **DIVISION**—Instruments effecting. **(S&S 171)**

See s. 73 for the duty payable in respect of instruments covered by that section. Any other instruments are chargeable with the fixed duty of 50p.

Note that a partition is not a sale, and the provisions relating to conveyances on sale will not be applicable to instruments of partition (see *Henniker* v. *Henniker* (1852) 1 E&B 54).

POLICY OF LIFE INSURANCE. (S&S 171–175)

This head of charge was abolished by FA 1989, Sch. 17 with effect from 31 December 1989.

RELEASE or **RENUNCIATION** of any property or of any right or interest in any property. **(S&S 175–176)**

With the exception of releases or renunciations upon sale, instruments under this head are charged with a fixed duty of 50p. As a result of the introduction by the F(1909–1910)A 1910, s. 74, of *ad valorem* duty on voluntary dispositions, a release or renunciation of any property or interest in property operating as a voluntary disposition *inter vivos* (for example the voluntary release of a life interest to the remainderman, as in *Platt's Trustees* v. *I.R. Comrs.* (1953) 32 ATC 292) was also liable to *ad valorem* duty. However, voluntary disposition duty was abolished by FA 1985, s. 82 and such releases are chargeable only with 50p, and only releases or renunciations in respect of which a consideration is given are chargeable *ad valorem* as conveyances on sale. However, there must be a release in the nature of an assignment, *e.g.* of an interest in property which would, if the property were land, constitute an estate in the land. It has been held that the following were not such releases: the release by a Scottish widow of her claim to *jus relictae* (*Cormack's Trustees* v. *I.R. Comrs.* 1924 SC 819) and an undertaking not to work coal in a particular area (*Great Northern Railway* v. *I.R. Comrs.* [1901] 1 KB 416).

Releases and renunciations are to be distinguished from disclaimers. Releases or renunciations involve dispositions of property whereas disclaimers are simply the rejection of gifts and operate by way of avoidance (*Re Paradise Motor Co.* [1968] 2 All ER 625, CA). Accordingly, disclaimers, if in writing, do not attract *ad valorem* stamp duty under the head "conveyance or transfer".

Note that this head of charge is not relevant in relation to renounceable letters of allotment of shares, and renunciations thereof, which are dutiable (if at all) under the bearer instrument head of charge, and in respect of which stamp duty reserve tax is payable.

[*N.B.* In relation to the prospective abolition of all stamp duties on transactions in shares (including bearer instruments) and units under unit trust schemes, and of stamp duty reserve tax, see the Revenue Press Release of 20 March 1990 and the commentary on FA 1990.]

RENUNCIATION.

See RELEASE.

SUPERANNUATION ANNUITY. (S&S 176)

See BOND, COVENANT, etc.

SURRENDER. (S&S 177)

Formerly, surrenders were also treated as conveyances or transfers of property operating as voluntary dispositions *inter vivos* within the meaning of F(1909–10)A 1910, s. 74 and chargeable with *ad valorem* duty accordingly. Since voluntary disposition duty has now been abolished, surrenders will only be chargeable under this head with a fixed duty of 50p unless a consideration is received for the surrender, in which case they will be stampable as conveyances on sale.

TACK of lands, etc., in Scotland. **(S&S 177)**

See LEASE OR TACK.

TRANSFER. (S&S 177)

See CONVEYANCE OR TRANSFER.

GENERAL EXEMPTIONS FROM ALL STAMP DUTIES. (S&S 187–188)

Other general exemptions from stamp duty have been added by subsequent legislation; *e.g.*, transfers of stock where payment of principal and interest is guaranteed by the Treasury (FA 1947, s. 57); instruments of apprenticeship, articles of clerkship, bonds on obtaining letters of administration and charter parties (FA 1949, s. 35 and Sch. 8, Part I.)

There are in addition special exemptions in particular circumstances from the duty under the various heads of charge; *e.g.*, exemption from "conveyance or tansfer on sale" duty in respect of share for share acquisitions under FA 1986, s. 77 (1).

In relation to the general exemption contained in Sch. 1, para. (2), there is no general exemption from stamp duty for transfers of aircraft, and a disposition of freight does not appear to be within the exemption in respect of ships or vessels. However, "freight is for many purposes part of the ship inseparably appurtenant thereto"—per Erle C.J. in *Willis* v. *Palmer* (1859) 7 CBNS 340 at 358.

[*N.B.* In relation to the prospective abolition of all stamp duties on transactions in shares (including bearer instruments) and units under unit trust schemes, and of stamp duty reserve tax, see the Revenue Press Release of 20 March 1990 and the commentary on FA 1990.]

Finance Act 1895
58 & 59 Vict. c. 16

PART II STAMPS

12. Collection of stamp duty in cases of property vested by Act or purchased under statutory power. (S&S 188–190)

Where, by virtue of any Act of Parliament, either (*a*) property is vested by way of sale in any person, or (*b*) any person is authorised to purchase property, then that person must, within three months after the passing of the relevant Act of Parliament, or the date of vesting (whichever is the later), or after the completion of the purchase, as the case may be, produce to the Commissioners a Queen's Printer's copy of the statute or some instrument relating to the vesting in the first case, and an instrument of conveyance in the second case, duly stamped with the *ad valorem* stamp duty payable on a conveyance on sale of the property.

Any conveyance required to be produced need not include any goods, wares or merchandise forming part of the property, and if the property consists wholly of goods, wares or merchandise no conveyance need be produced (FA 1949, s. 36 (4)).

In default of production, the duty and interest at the rate of 5 per cent. from the date of vesting or the completion of the purchase of the property, as the case may be, become a debt due to the Crown from the person in default.

The leading cases in relation to this section are:

  (*a*) *A-G* v. *Eastbourne Corporation* [1902] 1 KB 403 at 408, 409, C.A.; affirmed sub. nom. *Eastbourne Corporation* v. *A-G* [1904] AC 155 at 158 (but overruled in relation to the definition of "property" by FA 1949 s. 36 (4));

  (*b*) *A-G* v. *Felixstowe Gas Light Co.* [1907] 2 KB 904 (in which it was held that it is not necessary, for this section to apply, that there shoul be a contract of sale between the parties—the terms of the sale may be imposed by Act of Parliament without a contract);

  (*c*) *Lord Advocate* v. *Caledonian Railway Co.* 1908 SC 566 (in which it was held that a purchase of property by a railway company in pursuance of compulsory powers contained in the relevant special Act fell within this section, and that the date of "completion of the purchase" for the purposes of the section is the date of the final payment of the price to the seller).

There are numerous statutory exclusions from these provisions, mostly in relation to the nationalisation of industries and the setting up of statutory bodies. See for example the Aircraft and Shipbuilding Industries Act 1977, Schs. 3 and 4.

A Minister or local or public authority authorised to acquire land by means of a compulsory purchase order may make a general vesting declaration vesting that land in himself or itself (the Compulsory Purchase (Vesting Declarations) Act 1981, s. 1). Such a declaration may involve a number of properties acquired from several owners, as well as the compulsory purchase of a single property. Liability to stamp duty will depend on whether or not the compensation payable has at the date of execution of the instrument been determined:

  (*a*) in whole, in which case *ad valorem* conveyance on sale duty is charged in respect of the total compensation payable to each owner, the declaration being regarded as a separate transaction between each owner and the Minister or authority so that certificates of value will be admissible, or

  (*b*) in part, in which case *ad valorem* conveyance on sale duty is charged in respect of the ascertainable compensation paid or payable to each owner, and in addition 50p fixed conveyance duty for each owner in respect of the remaining unascertainable consideration, no certificate of value then being admissible, or

  (*c*) not at all, in which case 50p fixed conveyance duty is chargeable in respect of each acquisition, *i.e.*, a separate duty is charged in respect of each owner, no adjudication being necessary.

All such declarations have to be produced to the Revenue under FA 1931, s. 28.

See further, in relation to nationalisation schemes, FA 1946, s. 52.

PART IV MISCELLANEOUS

20. Short title

Finance Act 1898

61 & 62 Vict. c. 10

PART II STAMPS

6. Removal of doubt as to 54 & 55 Vict. c. 39, ss. 54, 57, so far as regards foreclosure decrees. (S&S 190)

The definition of "conveyance on sale" in SA 1891, s. 54 includes a foreclosure decree or order. The maximum amount of *ad valorem* stamp duty payable on any such decree or order is on a sum equal to the value of the property to which the decree or order relates. Any conveyance following upon such decree or order is exempt from *ad valorem* stamp duty.

Revenue Act 1898

61 & 62 Vict. c. 46

PART II STAMPS

7. Amendments of 54 & 55 Vict. c. 39. (S&S 190–191)
Postal packets are within the definition of the word "instrument" in SA 1891, s. 9. Fines incurred under SA 1891, s. 9 may be recovered summarily. SDMA 1891, s. 24 applies to affidavits and oaths as well as to statutory declarations.

10. Amendment of 54 & 55 Vict. c. 38, s. 22. (S&S 191)
After the discontinuance of the use of particular stamp duty office dies, documents stamped with discontinued dies are not duly stamped.

12. Extension of certain sections of 54 & 55 Vict. c. 36, to paper used for excise licences. (S&S 191)
Paper used for excise licences is within SDMA 1891, ss. 14, 15 and 16 in relation to frauds in connection with the manufacture of paper provided by the Inland Revenue for receiving the impression of a stamp duty office die.

Finance Act 1899

62 & 63 Vict. c. 9

PART II STAMPS

5. Extension of stamp duty on share warrants and stock certificates to bearer. (S&S 191)
SA 1891, s. 109 is extended to provide for a penalty for the issue of unstamped stock certificates to bearer by "companies or bodies of persons".

[*N.B.* In relation to the prospective abolition of all stamp duties on transactions in shares (including bearer instruments) and units under unit trust schemes, and of stamp duty reserve tax, see the Inland Revenue Press Release of 20 March 1990 and the commentary on FA 1990.]

Finance Act 1900
63 & 64 Vict. c. 7

PART II STAMPS

10. Conveyances on sale. (S&S 192)
Where further consideration is expressed, in a dutiable conveyance on sale, as consisting of a covenant by the purchaser to make, or of his having made, any substantial improvement of or addition to the property, or as consisting of any covenant relating to the subject matter of the conveyance, such further consideration does not attract additional *ad valorem* stamp duty.

This section has been considered by the courts in detail in relation to the problems which arise in connection with conveyances on sale of building plots where at the date of the contract for sale no building has been erected, or a building has been partly erected, on the site which constitutes or is included in the subject matter of the sale, and where at the date of the conveyance a building has been wholly or partly erected on the site. The leading cases are *M'Innes* v. *I.R. Comrs.* 1934 SC 424, *Kimbers & Co.* v. *I.R. Comrs.* [1936] 1 KB 132, and the three cases, heard together, of *Paul* v. *I.R. Comrs.*, *Span* v. *I.R. Comrs.*, and *Blair* v. *I.R. Comrs.* 1936 SC 443. From these cases, the generally accepted principle appears to be that where the vendor and the contractor responsible for erecting the building are one and the same person, and the building contract is expressed to be conditional on the completion of the purchase of the site, then by virtue of this section the consideration paid for the building (as distinct from the consideration paid for the site) does not attract duty, even where the builder may have begun to build before completion. Where, however, there is in substance a contract to purchase a plot of land with a completed building on it, even where the contract is constituted by separate documents, then the consideration for the building will attract *ad valorem* stamp duty and s. 10 will not apply. If the builder is not also the vendor, then the consideration paid for the building will not attract *ad valorem* conveyance on sale duty even where the landowner and the builder habitually act together.

A statement of the advice received by the Commissioners as to the present state of the law regarding conveyances after the commencement of building operations, broadly speaking indicating that the Revenue will abide by the principles established by the above cases, was published in the *Law Society's Gazette* (1957), p. 450, and has recently been reaffirmed by a Statement of Practice (SP 10/87) issued in December 1987. See further FA 1958, s. 34.

Finance Act 1902
2 Edw. 7 c. 7

PART II STAMPS

9. Amendment of 54 & 55 Vict. c. 39, s. 62. (S&S 192)
SA 1899, s. 62 includes retirements of trustees as well as appointments of trustees.

Finance Act 1930

20 & 21 Geo. 5, c. 28

PART IV STAMPS

**42. Relief from transfer stamp duty in case of transfer of property as between associated companies.
(S&S 361, 365–378)**

Subject to the anti-avoidance provisions contained in FA 1967, s. 27 (3), discussed below, stamp
duty under the heading "conveyance or transfer on sale" is not to be charged on any instrument if it
is shown to the satisfaction of the Commissioners that the effect of the instrument is to transfer a
beneficial interest in property from one "associated body corporate" to another. For this purpose
two bodies corporate (wherever incorporated—*Canada Safeway Ltd* v. *I.R. Comrs.* [1973] Ch.
374) are associated if either one body corporate is the beneficial owner of not less than 90 per cent.
(in nominal amount) of the issued share capital of the other, or a third body corporate is the
beneficial owner of not less than 90 per cent. (in nominal amount) of the issued share capital of both
bodies corporate. Such ownership may be either direct or through another body corporate or other
bodies corporate, or partly direct and partly through another body corporate or other bodies
corporate, in each case in accordance with the rules for determining chains of ownership as set out
in FA 1938, Sch. 4, Pt. I.

The Commissioners must be satisfied that "*the effect*" of the relevant instrument is to convey or
transfer a "*beneficial interest*" in property from one body corporate to another. There is no
problem in the simplest case, where the transferor company is the beneficial owner of the property
at the time the instrument is executed and the instrument in question causes the beneficial
ownership to pass to or vest in the transferee company. Usually, however, the formal instrument of
transfer follows a prior sale and purchase agreement between the two companies by virtue of which
the beneficial interest will already have passed to the transferee before the formal instrument is
executed. In these circumstances, it was held in *Escoigne Properties Ltd* v. *I.R. Comrs.* [1958] AC
549 that the formal instrument qualifies for relief because it would otherwise be stampable in
respect of the value of the beneficial interest which passed by virtue of the prior agreement.

It is fatal to the relief if the beneficial interest was not previously vested in the transferor
company but in an unassociated person or body corporate. This most frequently arises where the
transferor company is in liquidation. A company ceases to be the beneficial owner of its property
when it goes into liquidation: *Ayerst (Inspector of Taxes) v. C and K (Construction) Ltd.* [1976] AC
167 (though not when an administration order is made in respect of the company under the
Insolvency Act 1986–see ICAEW TR 799 "Tax aspects of the Insolvency Act 1986", June 1990,
para. 9 (c) *Simon's Tax Intelligence* 1990, p. 631). Accordingly the transfer of assets by a company
in liquidation to an associated body corporate would vest beneficial ownership in the transferee,
but that beneficial ownership would not pass from the transferor company itself, and relief is
therefore denied in these circumstances—*Holmleigh (Holdings) Ltd* v. *I.R. Comrs.* (1958) 46 TC
435 at 453. The effect, however, of the House of Lords decision in *Escoigne Properties Ltd* v. *I.R.
Comrs.* as mentioned above, is that, where one associated body corporate goes into liquidation
between (*a*) the date of a contract for sale entered into with another associated body corporate and
(*b*) the date of the formal conveyance or transfer, relief cannot be refused. The company which
goes into liquidation must not be the one which is required to be the beneficial owner of 90 per cent.
of the issued share capital of the other body or bodies corporate.

In relation to both the beneficial interest of the transferor in the property to be transferred, and
also the 90 per cent. beneficial ownership relationship between the transferor and the transferee, it
is important to note that a company ceases to be the beneficial owner of shares in a subsidiary or
other assets not only when it has entered into a contract to sell them (*Parway Estates Ltd.* v. *I.R.
Comrs.* (1958) 37 ATC 164), whether conditionally or otherwise (*Brooklands Selangor Holdings
Ltd.* v. *I.R. Comrs.* [1970] 2 All ER 76; *Wood Preservation Ltd.* v. *Prior* [1969] 1 All ER 849; *I.R.
Comrs.* v. *Ufitec Group* [1977] 3 All ER 929), but also if it has entered into arrangements the end
result of which is to sell them.

It can be a difficult question of law to determine at what stage a vendor company ceases to be the
beneficial owner of assets, or a parent company ceases to be the beneficial owner of its shares in a
subsidiary, in order to determine whether intra-group transfers qualify for relief. Even where no
binding agreements are entered into, there may be informal arrangements regarding a series of
transactions which, once begun, are bound to be continued to their conclusion. In such circumstances it has been held that the beneficial interest in shares in a subsidiary which is to be sold, as
well as the beneficial interest in any other property, passes as soon as the arrangements are entered
into. The leading cases are *Leigh Spinners Ltd.* v. *I.R. Comrs.* (1956) 46 TC 425, *Homleigh
Holdings Ltd.* v. *I.R. Comrs.* (1958) 46 TC 435, *Baytrust Holdings Ltd.* v. *I.R. Comrs.*; *Thomas
Firth and John Brown (Investments) Ltd.* v. *I.R. Comrs.* [1971] 3 All ER 76, *Brooklands Selangor
Holdings Ltd.* v. *I.R. Comrs.* [1970] 2 All ER 76, *Wood Preservation Ltd.* v. *Prior* [1969] 1 All ER

849 and *Times Newspapers Ltd.* v. *I.R. Comrs.* [1973] Ch. 155. The decision of the House of Lords in *Furniss* v. *Dawson* is also relevant.

On the other hand, the mere existence of a call option granted to a third party by a parent company over shares in its subsidiary does not deprive the parent company of the beneficial ownership of those shares. In a case which inter alia turned on the meaning of "beneficial ownership" in this context (*J. Sainsbury plc* v. *O'Connor (Inspector of Taxes)* [1990] STC 518), the Revenue contended that, in the case of shares, it involved (i) the unfettered right to dispose of the shares; (ii) the right to the beneficial enjoyment of any dividends declared in respect of the shares; and (iii) the ability to reap the benefit of any increase (and the risk of suffering loss from any diminution) in the intrinsic value of the shares. Millett, J., did not accept that an unfettered freedom of disposition was an essential feature of beneficial ownership: a litigant subject to a Mareva injunction, a party to a joint venture or shareholders' agreement and the grantor not only of an option but even of a mere right of pre-emption or first refusal were all subject to limitations on their freedom of disposition, but—so long as they retained their rights to the beneficial enjoyment of the shares and of any income derived therefrom while they remained undisposed of—it could not be accepted that they were not beneficial owners. Secondly, the court held that, although the right to the beneficial enjoyment of any dividends which might have been declared in respect of shares was an important feature of beneficial ownership, it was not the only, or even the most important, way in which the trading profits of a subsidiary could be enjoyed by its parent, and that the right to the beneficial receipt of any dividends which were declared had to be distinguished from the right to cause them to be declared ("beneficial ownership" had nothing to do with control). Finally, the court rejected the Revenue's submission that beneficial ownership necessarily involved the hope of gain or the risk of loss: even if the beneficial ownership of shares necessarily involved the right to reap the benefit of any increase (and the risk of suffering loss from any diminution) in the value of the shares, there was no requirement that their value had to be capable of fluctuation or must reflect the changing profitability or value of the company; such a requirement would substitute an economic test for a legal one and confuse the existence of legal rights with their value—"beneficial ownership" had nothing to do with value or the economic attributes of ownership. The Revenue's case on "beneficial ownership" stood or fell by the presence of an option agreement. An option was not a conditional contract but an irrevocable offer which was open to acceptance by the exercise of the option. In the meantime, the grantor was under a contractual obligation not to put it out of his power to do what he had offered to do. However, subject thereto, he retained not only equitable ownership but also all the rights of beneficial enjoyment normally attaching to equitable owner-ship.

A parent company may enter into composite multi-layered arrangements with a third party, the end result of which is to be the sale by the parent company to the third party either of the issued share capital of a wholly-owned subsidiary of the parent company or of certain other assets of the parent. This may be after an intra-group transfer either (*a*) by the subsidiary which is to be sold to another group company of assets of the subsidiary which the parent company wishes to retain in the group, or (*b*) by the parent to a subsidiary of the assets to be sold (because for example the parent wishes any capital loss arising on the sale to be vested in that subsidiary). In such circumstances it is possible that the parent company's beneficial interest in the subsidiary or assets to be sold would pass to the third party as soon as the arrangements are entered into, so that the relief on the intra-group transfer of the subsidiary's or the parent's assets would be lost. For these purposes, the arrangements must have a certain degree of commercial inevitability, so that they will of necessity proceed to their conclusion, although there is no contractual commitment to that effect (*Times Newspapers Ltd.* v. *I.R. Comrs.*).

In the first of the above circumstances, where before the sale of a subsidiary there is an intra-group transfer by the subsidiary to the parent of assets which the parent wishes to retain, the arrangements would not fall foul of the anti-avoidance provisions of FA 1967, s. 27 (3) (*c*) (because those provisions only apply where the *transferee* of the assets, *not* the transferor, is to move out of the group and cease to be associated) and relief would only be denied if the negotiations with the purchaser had reached the point where the Stamp Office could successfully argue that at the time of the transfer the parent's beneficial ownership of the subsidiary had already been lost. The Stamp Office take the view that it is not sufficient for the transferor and transferee to be associated at the time of the contract, they must also be associated at the time of the conveyance for which relief is sought under s. 42. In any case, in these circumstances it would presumably not be necessary for an application for relief to be made. Following the abolition of *ad valorem* stamp duty on voluntary dispositions *inter vivos*, and the introduction of the Stamp Duty (Exempt Instruments) Regulations 1987 (S.I. 1987 No. 516), the assets could simply be transferred by the subsidiary to the parent by way of gift.

In the second of the above circumstances, where before the sale of certain assets those assets are transferred to a subsidiary, the arguments would be similar whether or not the transfer is made to the subsidiary with a view to the subsidiary itself being sold or simply with a view to that subsidiary benefiting from a capital loss on the sale. The availability of the relief would still depend upon the absence of sufficiently advanced negotiations with a potential purchaser. If such advanced negotiations existed, the relief would be denied where the subsidiary is not to leave the group but merely benefit from a capital loss, because the subsidiary will never obtain the beneficial interest in the assets. The position would be even worse if such advanced negotiations existed and it was intended that the subsidiary itself be sold, because in that case not only would the parent be deemed to have lost its beneficial ownership of the subsidiary but also the arrangements would fall foul of FA 1967, s. 27 (3) (*c*). But again, the assets could be transferred by way of gift and the need to apply for s. 42 relief would be obviated. Where the subsidiary is not itself to be sold it would be necessary for there to be two conveyances or transfers of the relevant assets (parent to subsidiary and subsidiary to third party) rather than a direct transfer from parent to third party.

In either of the above cases, where transfers for no consideration by a limited company are involved, regard will have to be had to provisions of insolvency law and the law relating to *ultra vires* before any such transaction is carried out.

Alternatively, where assets are being both removed from and injected into a subsidiary which is to be sold, it may be possible to minimise stamp duty, or possibly avoid it altogether, by arranging for mutual exchanges of assets. For example, one piece of land could be removed from the subsidiary and exchanged with another piece of land and the exchange would, prima facie, attract stamp duty only at the rate of 50p unless equality money was paid, in which case that would attract *ad valorem* stamp duty. Note, however, the problem raised by *Portman Trustees* v. *I.R. Comrs.* (1956) 35 ATC 349, discussed in relation to SA 1891, s. 73.

In any claim for exemption under this section, the onus of proof is on the person claiming the relief and the Commissioners require that a statutory declaration be made by a solicitor or an officer of the parent company who has knowledge of the relevant facts. The statutory declaration should set out in full the grounds on which the claim is based showing *inter alia*:

- (*a*) that a claim under FA 1930, s. 42, is made in respect of a specified document/s which should be summarised briefly, and that the effect of the document/s is that laid down by sub-section (2) as amended;
- (*b*) particulars of the bodies corporate concerned (date of incorporation, registered number, capital both nominal and issued);
- (*c*) the reason for the transaction;
- (*d*) how the relationship between the bodies corporate complies with s. 42 (2) or (3) as amended—if the shares are held by a nominee, any instrument evidencing the beneficial ownership of those shares should be produced;
- (*e*) whether it is intended that:
  - (i) the relationship between the bodies corporate satisfying the provisions of s. 42 (2) shall be maintained; and
  - (ii) the transferee shall continue to be the beneficial owner of the assets now acquired by it.
  If this is not so in either case, full particulars of any proposed changes should be given;
- (*f*) the amount of the consideration for the transfer and how it has been or is to be found and satisfied; if by way of inter-company loan, the security and terms of repayment should be stated;
- (*g*) an assurance should also be given that the document/s was/were not executed in pursuance of or in connection with such an arrangement as is described in FA 1967, s. 27 (3).

See the notes issued by the Stamp Office reproduced at **S&S 376–377**.

[*N.B.* In relation to the prospective abolition of all stamp duties on transactions in shares (including bearer instruments) and units under unit trust schemes, and of stamp duty reserve tax, see the Revenue Press Release of 20 March 1990 and the commentary on FA 1990.]

PART VI MISCELLANEOUS AND GENERAL

53. Construction, short title, application and repeal.

Finance Act 1931
21 & 22 Geo. 5 c. 28

PART III LAND VALUE TAX

28. Production to Commissioners of instruments transferring land. (S&S 195–198)

Upon the transfer on sale of the fee simple of land, the grant of a lease of land for a term of seven or more years, or the transfer on sale of any such lease, the transferee, lessee or proposed lessee must produce to the Commissioners the instrument of transfer, or lease, together with the required "Particulars Delivered Form" giving the information set out in Sch. 2. The document is then stamped with a "produced stamp", in addition to any *ad valorem* duty stamp, and without the produced stamp the document is not duly stamped.

This procedure has been substantially amended by virtue of FA 1985, s. 89 and the Stamp Duty (Exempt Instrument) Regulations 1985, S.I. 1985 No. 1688.

SCHEDULE 2 REQUIREMENTS IN CONNECTION WITH PRODUCTION OF INSTRUMENTS OF TRANSFER (Section 28) (S&S 196–198)

This sets out the information to be provided on the "Particulars Delivered Form" to be furnished to the Commissioners.

Finance Act 1938

1 & 2 Geo. 6 c. 46

PART V NATIONAL DEFENCE CONTRIBUTION

42. Further provisions as to subsidiary companies. (S&S 362)

Section 42 (2) and Sch. 4 Pt. I are relevant for FA 1930, s. 42 and FA 1967, s. 27.

SCHEDULE 4 PROVISIONS RELATING TO SUBSIDIARY COMPANIES FOR PURPOSE OF NATIONAL DEFENCE CONTRIBUTION (Section 42). (S&S 362–364)

PART I PROVISIONS FOR DETERMINING AMOUNT OF CAPITAL HELD THROUGH OTHER BODIES CORPORATE

These provisions are best illustrated by examples, as set out below.

(1) Where A. owns 100 per cent. of B. and B. owns 100 per cent. of C., then A. is also deemed to own 100 per cent. of C.

(2) Where A. owns 100 per cent. of B., B. owns 100 per cent. of C. and C. owns 100 per cent. of D., then A. is also deemed to own 100 per cent. of both C. and D. and B. is also deemed to own 100 per cent. of D.

(3) Where A. owns 75 per cent. of B., B. owns 80 per cent. of C. and C. owns 100 per cent. of D., then A, is also deemed to own 60 per cent. (*i.e.* 75 per cent. of 80 per cent.) of C. and D. and B. is also deemed to own 80 per cent. of D.

(4) Where A. owns 75 per cent. of B., B. owns 80 per cent. of C. and C. owns 55 per cent. of D., then A, is also deemed to own 60 per cent. of C. and 33 per cent. of D. and B. is also deemed to own 45 per cent. of D.

(5) Where A. owns 75 per cent. of B. and also 10 per cent. of C. directly, B. owns 80 per cent. of C. and C. owns 60 per cent. of D., then A. is also deemed to own 70 per cent. of C. and 42 per cent. of D. and B. is also deemed to own 48 per cent. of D.

(6) Where A. owns 75 per cent. of B. and also 10 per cent. of C. directly, B. owns 80 per cent. of C. and also 5 per cent. of D. directly and C. owns 60 per cent. of D., then A is also deemed to own 70 per cent. of C. and 45.75 per cent. of D. and B. is also deemed to own 53 per cent. of D.

Finance Act 1946
9 & 10 Geo. 6 c. 64

PART VII STAMP DUTY

52. Exemption from stamp duty of documents connected with nationalisation schemes. (S&S 206)
Transfers of property by Act of Parliament to bodies running nationalised undertakings are exempt from the duty which would otherwise be payable.

54. Units under unit trust schemes to be treated as stock. (S&S 207–208)
Units in a unit trust scheme are "stock" for the purposes of stamp duty. The most important consequences of this are that the £30,000 threshold does not apply to sales or gifts of units, an agreement for the sale of units is not liable to *ad valorem* stamp duty under SA 1891, s. 59 and a conveyance or transfer of property to the trustees in exchange for an allotment of units is a conveyance or transfer on sale of that property.

The nominal amount or nominal value of a unit under a unit trust scheme is treated for stamp duty purposes as being equivalent to the price at which a unit of the same kind could first have been purchased under the scheme.

A unit can be transferred by a unit holder direct to another person, in which case the transfer will bear the same stamp duty as if it were a transfer of a share in a company. The more usual practice, however, is for a unit to be surrendered by the holder to the managers of the scheme, who will either purchase the unit for cash themselves, realise underlying property of the trust and pay the proceeds to the holder, or reissue the unit (or issue a substituted unit) to a new holder for cash. In any such case, both the surrender of the unit to the managers and its reissue (or the issue of a substituted unit) to a new holder are, unless to give effect to a transfer by operation of law, regarded as transfers on sale for stamp duty purposes.

To avoid double duty, the duty payable on the reissue of a unit, or its replacement by a substituted unit, where that unit has been surrendered to the managers within the preceding two months, is limited to 50p. Furthermore where a unit is transferred to the managers by a duly stamped instrument of transfer and, within a period of two months the managers and trustees jointly certify that the unit has been surrendered to the managers and subsequently extinguished upon the realisation of underlying assets so as to redeem it, then the duty paid on the instrument of transfer is refunded to the managers.

[*N.B.* In relation to the prospective abolition of all stamp duties on transactions in shares (including bearer instruments) and units under unit trust schemes, and of stamp duty reserve tax, see the Revenue Press Release of 20 March 1990 and the commentary on FA 1990.]

56. Supplemental provisions. (S&S 208–211)
The expression "public officer" in SA 1891, s. 16 is treated as including the trustees and managers of a unit trust scheme, or any agent of theirs, or any officer or servant of either them or their agent. The reference in SA 1891, s. 19 to the register of a local authority is to be treated as including any register kept under a unit trust scheme.

The Commissioners may make regulations requiring the managers or trustees of unit trusts to keep records in relation to their trusts. The Unit Trust Records Regulations 1946 make it compulsory for the trustees to keep a register of unit holders and generally make administrative provisions so as to ensure that the appropriate stamp duties are paid (in many ways similar to the administrative provisions relating to the share registers of limited companies): see Appendix 1.

The Secretary of State for Trade and Industry also has the power, under the Financial Services Act 1986, s. 81 to make regulations as to the constitution and management of authorised unit trust schemes, the powers and duties of the manager and trustee of any such scheme and the rights and obligations of the participants in any such scheme, which regulations may include (without limitation) provisions:

(*a*) as to the issue and redemption of the units under the scheme;

(*b*) as to the expenses of the scheme and the means of meeting them;

(*c*) for the appointment, removal, powers and duties of an auditor for the scheme;

(*d*) for restricting or regulating the investment and borrowing powers exercisable in relation to the scheme;

(*e*) requiring the keeping of records with respect to the transactions and financial position of the scheme and for the inspection of those records;

(*f*) requiring the preparation of periodical reports with respect to the scheme and the furnishing of those reports to the participants and to the Secretary of State; and

(*g*) with respect to the amendment of the scheme.

Regulations under this section may also make provision as to the contents of the trust deed, including provision requiring any of the matters mentioned above to be dealt with in the deed; but regulations under this section are to be binding on the manager, trustee and participants independently of the contents of the deed and, in the case of the participants, are to have effect as if contained in it. Regulations under this section may also contain such incidental and transitional provisions as the Secretary of State thinks necessary or expedient.

The Authorised Unit Trust Scheme (Pricing of Units and Dealings by Trustee and Manager) Regulations 1988 (SI 1988 No. 280) make provision as to the creation and cancellation by the trustee of units in an authorised unit trust scheme, as to the issue and redemption of units by the manager of such a scheme when acting as principal, and as to the sale and purchase of units by the manager as agent for the trustee. They include provision as to the way in which the property of a scheme is to be valued for the purpose of determining the prices at which units may be created, cancelled, issued or redeemed. They also include provision as to the circumstances in which the manager of a scheme may issue and redeem units at a price which is fixed by reference to a valuation which precedes the transaction and as to the circumstances in which he must issue and redeem units at a price which is fixed by reference to the valuation which next follows the transaction. The regulations make provision as to the circumstances in which the manager may, and as to the circumstances in which he must, give instructions to the trustee with respect to the creation and cancellation of units. They also make provision as to the period within which the trustee must settle with the manager and the manager must settle with the trustee and with participants for units which have been created, cancelled, issued or redeemed and as to the content of contract notes and the publication of unit prices. Provision is made for the suspension of dealings in units, for the conversion of units and for the cancellation of units by the trustee in exchange for property of the scheme.

The registration of the transfer of any unit otherwise than by operation of law without the production of an instrument of transfer is prohibited. An authority with direction to the trustees to treat some other person as the owner of a unit is deemed to be a transfer by virtue of s. 57 (2). Such an instrument of transfer, or authority or direction, cannot be registered unless the instrument is properly stamped by virtue of SA 1891, s. 17.

[*N.B.* In relation to the prospective abolition of all stamp duties on transactions in shares (including bearer instruments) and units under unit trust schemes, and of stamp duty reserve tax, see the Revenue Press Release of 20 March 1990 and the commentary on FA 1990.]

57. Interpretation of Part VII. (S&S 211–213)

"Unit trust scheme", "trust instrument", "trust property", "trust property represented by units", "unit", and "certificate to bearer" are defined.

The most important of these definitions is that of "unit trust scheme", which incorporates the definition contained in the Financial Services Act 1986 (as amended by the Financial Services Act 1986 (Restriction of Scope of Act and Meaning of Collective Investment Scheme) Order 1990, S.I. 1990 No. 349).

The Financial Services Act 1986, s. 75 (8) defines "a unit trust scheme" as "a collective investment scheme under which the property in question is held on trust for the participants", and s. 75 (1) defines "a collective investment scheme", subject to the other provisions of that section, as "any arrangements with respect to property of any description, including money, the purpose or effect of which is to enable persons taking part in the arrangements (whether by becoming owners of the property or any part of it or otherwise) to participate in or receive profits or income arising from the acquisition, holding, management or disposal of the property or sums paid out of such profits or income".

The arrangements must be such that the participants do not have any day to day control over the management of the property in question, whether or not they have the right to be consulted or to give directions; and either the contributions of the participants and the profits or income out of which payments are to be made to them must be pooled, or the property in question must be managed as a whole by or on behalf of the operator of the scheme, or both (s. 75 (2) and (3)).

Where any arrangements provide for pooling (as mentioned above) in relation to separate parts of the property in question, the arrangements are not regarded as constituting a single collective investment scheme unless the participants are entitled to exchange rights in one part for rights in another (s. 75 (4)).

Arrangements are not a collective investment scheme if:

(*a*) the property to which the arrangements relate (other than cash awaiting investment) consists of certain types of investment listed in the Financial Services Act 1986, Sch. 1 (which broadly speaking are: (i) shares or stock of a company; (ii) debentures and similar instruments creating or acknowledging indebtedness, including those issued by a government, local authority or public authority but excluding certain National Savings products; (iii) warrants; (iv) certificates representing securities; (v) units in another unit trust scheme, and (vi) long term insurance contracts); *and*

(*b*) each participant is the owner of a part of that property and entitled to withdraw it at any time; *and* (*c*) there is no pooling and there is common management only because the parts of the property belonging to different participants are not bought and sold separately except where a person becomes or ceases to be a participant (s. 75 (5)).

The following are (by virtue of s. 75 (6)) also not collective investment schemes:

(*a*) arrangements operated by a person otherwise than by way of business;

(*b*) arrangements where each of the participants carries on a business other than investment business and enters into the arrangements for commercial purposes related to that business (thus excluding many partnerships and joint ventures and certain activities by corporate treasurers);

(*c*) arrangements where each of the participants is a body corporate in the same group as the operator;

(*d*) arrangements where:

    (*i*) each of the participants is a *bona fide* employee or former employee (or the wife, husband, widow, widower, child or step-child under the age of 18 of such an employee or former employee) of a body corporate in the same group as the operator; *and*

    (*ii*) the property to which the arrangements relate consists of shares or debentures in or of a member of that group;

(*e*) franchise arrangements, that is to say, arrangements under which a person earns profits or income by exploiting a right conferred by the arrangements to use a trade name or design or other intellectual property or the goodwill attached to it;

(*f*) arrangements the predominant purpose of which is to enable persons participating in them to share in the use or enjoyment of a particular property or to make its use or enjoyment available gratuitously to other persons (*e.g.*, time-share arrangements);

(*g*) arrangements in the nature of depositary receipt schemes, under which the rights or interests of the participants are certificates or other instruments which confer: (*i*) property rights in respect of shares, stock, debentures, warrants etc.; or (*ii*) any right to acquire, dispose of, underwrite or convert an investment, being a right to which the holder would be entitled if he held any such investment to which the certificate or instrument relates; or (*iii*) a contractual right (other than an option) to acquire any such investment otherwise than by subscription; but not including any instrument which confers rights in respect of two or more investments issued by different persons or in respect of two or more different types of investment issued by the same government, local authority or public authority;

(*h*) arrangements the purpose of which is the provision of clearing services and which are operated by an authorised person, a recognised clearing house or a recognised investment exchange;

(*i*) contracts of insurance;

(*j*) occupational pension schemes;

(*k*) arrangements which by virtue of the Financial Services Act 1986, Sch. 1, para. 34 or 35 are not collective investment schemes for the purposes of that Schedule (which broadly speaking are: (*i*) certain business expansion scheme funds; (*ii*) arrangements where all contributions of participants are deposits for the purposes of the Banking Act 1987; (*iii*) arrangements where the interests of the participants are represented by debt instruments or warrants of a single issuer, including arrangements where a participant has interests which are or include interests as a counterparty pursuant to a swap arrangement; (*iv*) arrangements relating to the holding of client money; and (*v*) arrangements under which the interests of participants are interests in a trust fund within the meaning of the Landlord and Tenant Act 1987, s. 42 (1).

The Treasury are enabled to exclude by regulation particular types of scheme from the stamp duty rules applying to unit trusts. The Stamp Duty and Stamp Duty Reserve Tax (Definitions of Unit Trust Scheme) Regulations 1988, S.I. 1988 No. 268, exclude from the definition of "unit trust scheme" for the purposes of stamp duty and stamp duty reserve tax limited partnership schemes (where property is held on trust for the general partners and the limited partners in a limited partnership registered under the Limited Partnerships Act 1907) and approved profit sharing schemes established by companies under FA 1978, Sch. 9, Pt. I.

Where a person authorises or requires the trustees or managers under a unit trust scheme to treat him as no longer interested in a unit under the scheme and authorises or requires them to treat another person as entitled to that unit, he is deemed to transfer that unit and any instrument whereby he gives the authority or makes the requirement is deemed to be a conveyance or transfer on sale, or a conveyance or transfer of "any kind not hereinbefore described" according to the nature of the transaction as between him and the person whom he authorises the trustees or managers to treat as entitled to the unit.

Where a person authorises or requires the trustees or managers under a unit trust scheme to treat him as no longer interested in a unit under the scheme and does not authorise or require them to treat another person as entitled to that unit, he is deemed to transfer that unit to the managers and any instrument whereby he gives the authority or makes the requirement is deemed to be a conveyance or transfer of the unit on sale.

The relationship between s. 57 (2) and s. 57 (3) was considered in *Arbuthnot Financial Services Ltd.* v. *I.R. Comrs.* [1985] STC 211. In this case the taxpayer company were the managers of a unit trust scheme set up under a trust deed dated 24 February 1984 made between the taxpayer company and a corporate trustee. The trust deed provided for the establishment of a number of separate funds (portfolios), including a U.K. portfolio and a Japanese portfolio, and granted the holder of units in a portfolio the right to convert those units to units in any other portfolio. In June 1984 a company holding units in the Japanese portfolio surrendered those units to the taxpayer company for conversion into units in the U.K. portfolio. The Revenue assessed the taxpayer company to stamp duty on the form of conversion under s. 57 (3), on the grounds that the portfolios each constituted a separate unit trust scheme as defined by s. 57 (1) and that the conversion form constituted a deemed transfer of the units in the Japanese portfolio to the managers. The taxpayer company appealed contending that s. 57 (3) should be read together with s. 57 (2); that s. 57 (3), like s. 57 (2), was concerned with cases in which the former unit holder was out of the particular unit trust in question; and that s. 57 (3) applied only when the units were transferred or surrendered to the managers. The taxpayer company further contended that the portfolios were all part of the same unit trust scheme and that in converting its units in the Japanese portfolio to those in the U.K. portfolio it could not be treated as no longer interested in a unit under the unit trust scheme within the requirements of s. 57 (3).

It was held that s. 57 (3) was not dependent on s. 57 (2) and that the requirements of s. 57 (3) were satisfied when the company holding units in the Japanese portfolio, before converting them into units in the U.K. portfolio, had required the taxpayer company as managers to treat it as no longer interested in those units and did not authorise or require the managers to treat another person as entitled to them. Accordingly, the unit holder was to be regarded as having transferred its units to the managers under s. 57 (3) and conveyance on sale duty was therefore chargeable on the conversion form. The taxpayer company's appeal would therefore be dismissed. It was not necessary, in the event, for the court to decide whether or not the different portfolios were all part of a single unit trust scheme, as the taxpayer had contended, but nevertheless it was stated, *obiter*, that the only property which was held for the benefit of investors in a particular portfolio was the property comprised in that portfolio, and no person who did not hold units in a particular portfolio held an interest in that portfolio. The court therefore held that the trust deed embraced as many unit trust schemes as there were portfolios as the Revenue had argued. This must now be seen in the light of the Financial Services Act 1986, s. 75 (4) which (by implication) would seem to give statutory effect to the taxpayer's argument, although it would not have changed the decision in the case. Section 75 (4) provides that, where a collective investment scheme involves different "pools" in relation to different parts of the property included in the scheme, then unless its participants are entitled to exchange rights in one part for rights in another, the scheme will not be regarded as a single scheme (but presumably as a number of separate schemes). Section 75 (4) does not include a corollary provision to the effect that where participants *do* have rights of exchange the scheme will automatically be regarded as a single scheme, but this would seem to be a reasonable inference to draw.

Where the managers under a unit trust scheme authorise or require the trustees under the scheme to treat a person as entitled to a unit thereunder and their power to do so arises from a previous transfer to them of that unit or some other unit, they are deemed to transfer the unit to that person and any instrument whereby they give the authority or make the requirement is deemed to be a conveyance or transfer of the unit, but this provision does not apply to anything done by the managers for the purpose of recognising or giving effect to a transmission of a unit by operation of law.

Unit certificates issued to bearer are treated as bearer instruments and are accordingly stampable under the bearer instruments head of charge.

[*N.B.* In relation to the prospective abolition of all stamp duties on transactions in shares (including bearer instruments) and units under unit trust schemes, and of stamp duty reserve tax, see the Revenue Press Release, 20 March 1990 and the commentary on FA 1990.]

67. Short title, construction, extent and repeals. (S&S 213)

Finance Act 1949
12, 13 & 14 Geo 6. c. 47

PART IV STAMP DUTIES

35. Abolition of and exemptions from other duties. (S&S 215)

36. Amendments as to conveyances on sale. (S&S 215)

Under FA 1895, s. 12, where an Act of Parliament vests property by way of sale in any person, or authorises any person to purchase property, either the Act (in the first case) or the instrument of conveyance (in the second case) must be produced to the Commissioners duly stamped. It was held in *Eastbourne Corpn.* v. *A.-G.* [1904] AC 155 that the expression "property" included goods and other property not normally transferred by conveyance. That decision is nullified by this section and there is no need for a conveyance on sale of "goods, wares or merchandise" to be produced under FA 1895, s. 12.

Finance Act 1958

6 & 7 Eliz. 2 c. 56

PART VI STAMP DUTIES

34. Conveyances on sale, etc. (S&S 107, 219)

Under FA 1963, s. 55 (1) documents otherwise chargeable under the heading "conveyance or transfer on sale" in SA 1891, Sch. 1, are exempt from stamp duty "where the amount or value of the consideration is £30,000 or under and the instrument is certified, as described in section 34 (4) of the Finance Act 1958, at £30,000". This does not apply to documents chargeable in relation to the conveyance or transfer of stock or marketable securities. [But in relation to the prospective abolition of all stamp duties on transactions in shares, see the Revenue Press Release, 20 March 1990 and the commentary on FA 1990.]

A document is to be regarded as being "certified at a particular amount" if it "contains a statement certifying that the transaction effected by the instrument does not form part of a larger transaction or series of transactions in respect of which the amount or value, or aggregate amount or value, of the consideration exceeds that amount." Such a statement is known as a "certificate of value".

If a certificate of value is omitted from an instrument where it could appropriately have been given, the practice of the Commissioners is to allow the certificate to be added subsequently, provided that it is signed by all the persons who are parties to the instrument.

The only sanction for giving an incorrect certificate of value (apart from a liability to pay the correct amount of duty together with any fines or penalties for late stamping) is imposed by SA 1891, s. 5. This provides that every person who, with intent to defraud, executes or prepares any instrument in which all the facts and circumstances affecting the liability of that instrument to duty, or the amount of the duty with which that instrument is chargeable, are not fully and truly set out is liable to a fine of £25.

Normally, the value of all the property included in one transaction between the same parties should be taken into account before the certificate of value is given in relation to the conveyance or transfer of any one item. There is, however, an exception which allows the value of "goods, wares or merchandise" to be disregarded for the purpose of a certificate of value except insofar as there is an actual conveyance or transfer of them.

The question whether or not a transaction does in fact form part of either a larger transaction or a series of transactions can sometimes be quite difficult to determine. The law on this is far from settled, but the question has been judicially considered on a number of occasions in the past. The principal cases are described below.

The purchase at the same auction of a number of different lots does not necessarily constitute a "larger transaction" or a "series of transactions" within the meaning of s. 34 (4), so that a certificate of value could be given in respect of each lot without reference to the value of the other lots purchased (*A-G* v. *Cohen* [1937] 1 KB 478). This case related solely to public auctions, and the Revenue have indicated that in the case of privately negotiated sales, where a number of them take place at the same time, there will be a very strong presumption that the several sales form part of a larger transaction or a series of transactions which the parties will have to produce cogent evidence to rebut.

In *Kimbers & Co.* v. *I.R. Comrs.* [1936] 1 KB 132; *Paul* v. *I.R. Comrs.* 1936 SC 443, it was held that where a sale of property (in these cases a sale of land) is linked to a simultaneous related transaction (in these cases an agreement for the vendor of the land to build a house upon it following the sale to the purchaser), then the value of the related transaction is to be disregarded for the purpose of giving a certificate of value in relation to the sale of the property.

In cases involving the sale and purchase of a new house where contracts are entered into (before, during or after the house has been completed) between the builder or developer on the one hand and a purchaser on the other, the exact nature of the contractual arrangements determines the overall stamp duty liability. Different arrangements could lead to very different liabilities. For example, if the contracts provide for the sale of a plot of land for £15,000 and, separately, for the erection of a house for £35,000 it is possible that no stamp duty liability would arise. On the other hand a purchaser who pays £50,000 for a completed house and the land on which it stands would be liable for £500 of stamp duty.

The law was the subject of a detailed review by the Board of Inland Revenue which culminated, in 1957, in the statement from the Board published in the *Law Society's Gazette* (1957) p. 450 setting out the Board's views of the law and indicating the practice which the Revenue would accordingly follow.

A further review of this practice completed by the Revenue in 1987 resulted in a reaffirmation of the view of the law announced by the Board of Inland Revenue in their 1957 statement. A new Statement of Practice (SP 10/87) was issued to clarify areas of doubt that had arisen during the 30 years since the statement was first published. See also Inland Revenue Press Release, 22 December 1987.

It seems that where in respect of a number of relevant transactions the vendors or the purchasers are not identical or associated, certificates of value may be given in respect of each transaction even if the transactions themselves may be associated. Where, for example, a purchaser sub-sells part of the property purchased by him, a certificate of value in relation to the sub-sale may be given. Also, where there is a single purchaser but a number of different vendors, a certificate of value may be given in respect of each item whether or not each contract is conditional upon completion of the others.

The difficulties arising from the potential interaction between stamp duty and the VAT payable in respect of commercial buildings (discussed in relation to SA 1891, ss. 55, 56 and 77 (5), and the "Lease or Tack" head of charge in Sch. 1) may also cause difficulties in deciding whether or not an appropriate certificate of value can be given.

35. Miscellaneous amendments. (S&S 220)
Section 35 (4) amends FA 1952, s. 74, which relieves from stamp duty certain transfers of water undertakings and other property to joint committees or joint committees of local authorities, and certain conveyances and agreements for such transfers.

Conveyance on sale duty is not chargeable on any agreement made under the New Towns Act 1946, s. 14 by a development corporation for the transfer of the whole or part of the water undertaking or the sewerage undertaking of that corporation.

Finance Act 1960
8 & 9 Eliz. 2 c. 44

PART V MISCELLANEOUS

74. Visiting forces and allied headquarters (stamp duty exemptions). (S&S 221–223)
Exemption from stamp duty is conferred on visiting forces and allied headquarters; this corresponds to the exemption granted to H.M. Forces. For a list of the countries and allied headquarters designated for this purpose, see **S&S 222**.

Stock Transfer Act 1963
1963 c. 18

1. Simplified transfer of securities. (S&S 400–401)
This Act introduced a new system simplifying the means by which registered securities can be transferred. An instrument of transfer can be under hand in the form set out in Sch. 1, executed by the transferor only and not also the transferee, and specifying particulars of the consideration, the description and number or amount of securities, the person by whom the transfer is made, and the full name and address of the transferee, and the execution of the form does not need to be witnessed.

A "brokers' transfer form" could be used in connection with the stock transfer form where a holding of shares sold on the Stock Exchange was to be transferred to more than one purchaser. The brokers' transfer form was superseded under the new system for Stock Exchange transactions introduced by the Stock Exchange (Completion of Bargains) Act 1976.

See also the commentary on FA 1989 and the Companies Act 1989; Inland Revenue Press Release, 14 March 1989 (Appendix 4); and DTI Consultative Paper: Dematerialisation of share certificates and share transfers (Appendix 9).

See also now, in relation to the prospective abolition of all stamp duties on transactions in shares (including bearer instruments) and units under unit trust schemes, and of stamp duty reserve tax, the Revenue Press Release, 20 March 1990 and the commentary on FA 1990.

2. Supplementary provisions as to simplified transfer. (S&S 401–402)
The simplified system of transferring securities is not to affect any right of the directors of a company to refuse to register a transfer on grounds other than in relation to the form of transfer, or any law regulating the execution of documents by companies or other bodies corporate, or any Articles of Association or other instrument regulating the execution of documents by a particular company or body corporate. The result of this is that, although s. 1 provides for the execution of instruments of transfer under hand, execution by a body corporate having a common seal must still be under seal.

See also the commentary on FA 1989 and the Companies Act 1989; Inland Revenue Press Release, 14 March 1989 (Appendix 4); and DTI Consultative Paper: Dematerialisation of share certificates and share transfers (Appendix 9).

See also now, in relation to the prospective abolition of all stamp duties on transactions in shares (including bearer instruments) and units under unit trust schemes, and of stamp duty reserve tax, the Revenue Press Release, 20 March 1990 and the commentary on FA 1990.

3. Additional provisions as to transfer forms. (S&S 402–403)
The Treasury is given power to amend the forms set out in Schs. 1 and 2, or to substitute new forms in their place, by means of statutory instrument. The brokers' transfer form set out in Sch. 2 was superseded under the new system introduced by the Stock Exchange (Completion of Bargains) Act 1976.

See also the commentary on FA 1989 and the Companies Act 1989; Inland Revenue Press Release, 14 March 1989 (Appendix 4); and DTI Consultative Paper: Dematerialisation of share certificates and share transfers (Appendix 9).

See also now, in relation to the prospective abolition of all stamp duties on transactions in shares (including bearer instruments) and units under unit trust schemes, and of stamp duty reserve tax, the Revenue Press Release, 20 March 1990 and the commentary on FA 1990.

4. Interpretation. (S&S 403)

5. Application to Northern Ireland. (S&S 403)

Finance Act 1963
1963 Chapter 25

PART IV STAMP DUTIES
REDUCTION OF DUTIES

55. Reduced duty on conveyance or transfer on sale. (S&S 225–226)

The rates at which stamp duty is to be charged under the heading "conveyance or transfer on sale" in SA 1891, Sch. 1 are specified as follows:

(a) In relation to a conveyance or transfer of stock or marketable securities, the rate is 50p. for every £100 or part of £100 of the consideration for the conveyance or transfer.

(b) In relation to any instrument chargeable by virtue of the heading "Lease or Tack" in SA 1891, Sch. 1, where the consideration consists of rent exceeding £300 a year, the rate is either 50p. for every £50 or part of £50 of the consideration (if the consideration does not exceed £500) or £1 for every £100 or part of £100 of the consideration (if the consideration exceeds £500).

In every other case:

(a) no duty is chargeable if the amount or value of the consideration is £30,000 or under and the instrument contains a "certificate of value" under FA 1958, s. 34 (4);

(b) duty is charged at the rate of 50p. for every £50 or part of £50 of the consideration where the instrument does not contain a certificate of value but the consideration does not exceed £500; and

(c) duty is chargeable at the rate of £1 for every £100 or part of £100 where the instrument does not contain a certificate of value and the consideration exceeds £500.

This section is to have no effect on any statute imposing an upper limit on the amount of *ad valorem* duty chargeable.

[N.B. In relation to the prospective abolition of all stamp duties on transactions in shares (including bearer instruments) and units under unit trust schemes, and of stamp duty reserve tax, see the Revenue Press Release, 20 March 1990 and the commentary on FA 1990.]

56. Reduced duty on leases. (S&S 226)

For stamp duty purposes, a lease granted for a fixed term "and thereafter until determined" is to be treated as a lease for a definite term equal to the fixed term plus a period of time equal to the period which must elapse before the earliest date on which the lease can be terminated.

57. Miscellaneous reductions. (S&S 226)

The stamp duty chargeable under the headings "Bond, Covenant or Instrument of any kind whatsoever" and "Mortgage, Bond, Debenture, Covenant and Warrant of Attorney" is reduced to the duty chargeable before FA 1947, s. 52 doubled the rates.

BEARER INSTRUMENTS

59. Stamp duty on bearer instruments. (S&S 95–101, 227–229)

This section contains various definitions for the purposes of the "bearer instrument" head of charge inserted into FA 1891, Sch. 1. "Stock" is defined as including "securities" and "any interest in, or in any fraction of, stock or in any dividends or other rights arising out of stock and any right to an allotment of or to subscribe for stock". The expressions "inland bearer instrument", "overseas bearer instrument", "deposit certificate" and "bearer instrument by usage" are also defined.

Essentially, the expression "bearer instrument" is explained by the sweeping-up provision in s. 59 (2) (a) (iv) and would seem to mean "any instrument to bearer by means of which any stock can be transferred". Since the expression "stock" includes "any right to an allotment of or to subscribe for stock", this would include for example bearer allotment letters. The position of renounceable letters of allotment is far from clear: whilst they are quite clearly negotiable instruments transferable by delivery when suitably endorsed, they are not issued "to bearer" and probably fall outside the definition. The question is mostly academic, since there are express exemptions for most forms of renounceable allotment letter, but a useful analysis is contained in Monroe and Nock, *The Law on Stamp Duties* (6th edn.).

A bearer instrument is "inland" if it is "issued by or on behalf of any company or body of persons corporate or unincorporate formed or established in the United Kingdom". A bearer instrument will be "overseas" if it is issued by any other person, or is a "bearer instrument by usage", *i.e.*, an instrument the mere delivery of which "is treated by usage as sufficient for the purpose of a sale on the market, whether that delivery constitutes a legal transfer or not".

A "deposit certificate" is "an instrument acknowledging the deposit of stock and entitling the bearer to rights (whether expressed as units or otherwise) in or in relation to the stock deposited or equivalent stock". The expression "deposit certificate for overseas stock" is also defined as a deposit certificate "in respect of stock of any one company or body of persons" not formed or established in the U.K. Accordingly, where a deposit certificate for overseas stock is issued by a U.K. depositary, the certificate will be treated as an inland bearer instrument, since it is the place where the depositary is formed or established that determines the status of the instrument, not the place or incorporation of the company whose stock is deposited.

[*N.B.* In relation to the prospective abolition of all stamp duties on transactions in shares (including bearer instruments) and units under unit trust schemes, and of stamp duty reserve tax, see the Revenue Press Release, 20 March 1990 and the commentary on FA 1990.]

60. Payment of duty. (S&S 95–101, 229–230)
Duty under the "bearer instrument" head of charge is to be chargeable on issue in the case of a chargeable instrument issued in Great Britain or by or on behalf of a company or a body of persons corporate or unincorporate formed or established in Great Britain, provided that the instrument is not a "foreign loan security" (which is chargeable on transfer rather than issue). A "foreign loan security" is an instrument issued outside the U.K. in respect of a non-sterling loan that is neither offered for subscription in the U.K. nor offered for subscription with a view to an offer for sale in the U.K. of securities in respect of the loan.

Any instrument which is chargeable under the "bearer instrument" head of charge but is not chargeable on issue is to be chargeable on the transfer in Great Britain of the stock constituted by or transferable by means of the instrument (provided that "conveyance or transfer on sale duty" would have been payable if effected by an instrument of transfer rather than a bearer instrument).

Instruments chargeable upon issue are to be produced (before being issued) for endorsement with a "denoting stamp", and within six weeks of the date of issue of the instrument a statement has to be delivered to the Commissioners giving details of the date of issue and such other information as the Commissioners require, whereupon the duty has to be paid on the instrument. Any person who does not deliver an instrument for "denoting" is liable to a default fine of up to the aggregate of £50 and the amount of the duty chargeable, and must pay to the Government both the duty chargeable and interest at the rate at 5 per cent. per annum from the date of default.

The Commissioners may request any person delivering an instrument chargeable on transfer to provide them with "such particulars in writing as they may require for determining the amount of duty chargeable". Similar penalties are levied on any person who transfers, or is concerned as broker or agent in the transfer of, any stock in default of these provisions.

A penalty of up to £50 plus twice the amount of the duty is payable by any person who furnishes false particulars under this section, wilfully or negligently.

As to bearer instruments issued in connection with "paired shares" forming part of a joint public offering by a U.K. company and a foreign company (as, for example, was the case in the Eurotunnel "Equity 3" offerings in 1987) see FA 1988, s. 143.

[*N.B.* In relation to the prospective abolition of all stamp duties on transactions in shares (including bearer instruments) and units under unit trust schemes, and of stamp duty reserve tax, see the Revenue Press Release, 20 March 1990 and the commentary on FA 1990.]

61. Ascertainment of market value. (S&S 230–231)
The *ad valorem* duty chargeable on instruments under the "bearer instrument" head of charge is calculated on the basis of the market value of the underlying stocks or marketable securities in the manner specified in this section.

Where the instrument is chargeable on issue, then in cases where the underlying stock was offered for public subscription (whether in registered or in bearer form) within 12 months before the issue of the instrument the amount subscribed is taken as the market value. In any other case, the value is taken on the first day within one month after the issue of the instrument on which the underlying stock is dealt in on a Stock Exchange in the U.K. or (if it is not so dealt in) the value of the underlying stock immediately after the issue of the instrument.

Where the instrument is chargeable only on transfer, then in cases where the transfer is pursuant to a contract of sale the value is taken on the date when the contract is entered into, and in any other case the value is taken on the day preceding that on which the instrument is presented to the Commissioners for stamping or (if it is not so presented) on the date of the transfer.

[*N.B.* In relation to the prospective abolition of all stamp duties on transactions in shares (including bearer instruments) and units under unit trust schemes, and of stamp duty reserve tax, see the Revenue Press Release, 20 March 1990 and the commentary on FA 1990.]

MISCELLANEOUS

62. Commonwealth stock. (S&S 231)
Transfers of "Commonwealth Government stock" are now exempt from duty.

[*N.B.* In relation to the prospective abolition of all stamp duties on transactions in shares (including bearer instruments) and units under unit trust schemes, and of stamp duty reserve tax, see the Revenue Press Release, 20 March 1990 and the commentary on FA 1990.]

63. Securities for annual and other payments. (S&S 231–232)

A collateral instrument is chargeable *ad valorem* as "the only principal or primary security" under the "Bond Covenant or Instrument of any kind whatsoever" or "Mortgage, Bond, Debenture, Covenant and Warrant of Attorney" heads of charge in circumstances where the other instrument or instruments relating to the same subject matter, although normally constituting the "only principal or primary security", is or are not stamped with the *ad valorem* duty.

This nullifies the decision in *I.R. Comrs.* v. *Henry Ansbacher & Co.* [1963] A.C. 191, where a transaction escaped *ad valorem* stamp duty because the principal document was exempt under the specific legislation then in force and the collateral security was held to be chargeable to the fixed duty only. In that case, by a written contract of sale executed under hand, HA agreed to purchase all the ordinary stock units of OT. The contract was exempt from stamp duty as an agreement for the sale of stock under FA 1949, s. 35 (1) (*a*). Moreover, because it was not executed under seal it could not be charged with duty as a "Mortgage, Bond, Debenture, Covenant". The contract provided for part of the consideration for the sale to be deferred until a future date, but that the payment of the deferred consideration was to be secured up to £750,000 by a bank guarantee. The guarantee was duly executed and was expressed to be supplemental to the contract of sale. The Commissioners claimed *ad valorem* duty on the guarantee under the head "Mortgage, Bond, Debenture, Covenant" on the ground that it was "the only or principal or primary security" for payment of £750,000. The House of Lords held that the contract was the primary security, even though not stampable as a "Mortgage, Bond, Debenture, Covenant" because not under seal, and that the guarantee was only the secondary security and therefore not subject to *ad valorem* duty (but, as a Deed, to the fixed duty only).

65. Miscellaneous exemptions. (S&S 232)

Instruments specifically exempt under the exemptions relating to the "bearer instrument" head of charge are also exempt under the "conveyance or transfer on sale" head of charge.

For the purpose of FA 1946, Pt. VII and FA 1962, s. 30 the expression "unit trust scheme" does not include a "common investment scheme" under the Charities Act 1960, s. 22 or a unit trust scheme the units of which are held by charitable bodies.

Applications for legal aid, and legal aid certificates, are not chargeable.

[*N.B.* In relation to the prospective abolition of all stamp duties on transactions in shares (including bearer instruments) and units under unit trust schemes, and of stamp duty reserve tax, see the Revenue Press Release, 20 March 1990 and the commentary on FA 1990.]

67. Prohibition on circulation of blank transfers. (S&S 232)

A fine may be imposed on any person who completes a "transfer in blank" (*i.e.*, a transfer in which the name of the transferee has not been inserted) delivered to him pursuant to a sale of the stock to which its relates and who then parts with possession of it or removes it or causes or permits it to be removed from Great Britain. The maximum fine is £50 plus an amount equal to the stamp duty chargeable in respect of the transfer.

A transfer will be regarded as duly completed only when the name of the transferee has been inserted, that being either the purchaser or a mortgagee of the stock, a nominee of any such person, or an agent of the purchaser.

This does not apply to instruments chargeable under the "bearer instrument" head of charge, or which are exempt by virtue of Exemption 3 to that head of charge.

References to the purchaser of the stock are deemed to include references to any person to whom the rights of the purchaser are transmitted by operation of law. In the case of sub-sales to which SA 1891, s. 58 (4) or (5) apply, references to the purchaser and the sale are to be construed as references to the sub-purchaser and the sub-sale.

[*N.B.* In relation to the prospective abolition of all stamp duties on transactions in shares (including bearer instruments) and units under unit trust schemes, and of stamp duty reserve tax, see the Revenue Press Release, 20 March 1990 and the commentary on FA 1990.]

PART V MISCELLANEOUS

73. Short title, commencement, construction, extent, amendments and repeals. (S&S 233–235)

Finance Act 1965
1965 Chapter 25

PART V MISCELLANEOUS AND GENERAL

90. Stamp duty: conveyances and transfers. (S&S 236–239)

The section nullifies *William Cory & Sons Ltd.* v. *I.R. Comrs.* [1965] 1 All ER 917, where the owners of the issued share capital of the company entered into an agreement pursuant to which they granted an option to purchase their shares. They agreed that "with a view to protecting [the purchasing company's] rights arising out of the grant of the option" they would execute transfers of the shares in favour of the intending purchasers. The intending purchasers agreed that such transfers would not pass any beneficial interest in the shares, that they would hold the shares in trust for the vendors, and that if the option lapsed as a result of its non-exercise the shares would be re-transferred to the vendors. Transfers were accordingly executed and registered and almost immediately afterwards the intending purchasers orally exercised their option (as they were entitled to do). It was held that *ad valorem* stamp duty was not chargeable on the transfers as "conveyances on sale" because the liability of the transfers to stamp duty had to be determined at the time when they were executed, and at the time there was no sale but only an option, with the consequence that the transfers were not transfers "on sale".

Now any instrument whereby property is conveyed or transferred to any person "in contemplation of a sale of that property" is to be treated for stamp duty purposes as a conveyance or transfer on sale for a consideration equal to the value of the property.

The whole or part of the duty charged will be returned if, not later than two years after the making or execution of the instrument, it is shown to the satisfaction of the Commissioners either that the sale has not taken place and the property has been re-conveyed or that the sale has been completed but for a consideration lower than the value on which duty was originally paid.

Any instrument chargeable to duty under subsection (1) is to be adjudicated under SA 1891, s. 12.

This section applies whether or not the relevant instrument conveys or transfers other property in addition to the property in contemplation of the sale of which it is made or executed, but this section is not to affect any stamp duty chargeable in respect of the other property.

To nullify the stamp duty avoidance schemes invented as a result of the House of Lords decision in *Stanyforth* v. *I.R. Comrs.* [1930] A.C. 339, in assessing the value of property for the purposes of a charge no account is to be taken of any power (whether or not contained in the instrument) of the person by whom the property was conveyed or transferred to have that property re-conveyed or re-transferred back to him, or any annuity reserved out of the property, or any life or other interest so reserved, being an interest which is subject to forfeiture. However, if any such power of revocation is exercised and the property is re-conveyed, then a claim may be made to the Commissioners not later than two years after the making or execution of the instrument for the duty or excess duty to be repaid.

[*N.B.* In relation to the prospective abolition of all stamp duties on transactions in shares (including bearer instruments) and units under unit trust schemes, and of stamp duty reserve tax, see the Revenue Press Release, 20 March 1990 and the commentary on FA 1990.]

91. Interest where stamp duty repaid under judgment. (S&S 239–240)

The Court may require that the Commissioners pay interest on any excess duty which is to be repaid by them as a result of an appeal under SA 1891, s. 13 (4).

97. Short title, construction, extent and repeal

Finance Act 1967
1967 Chapter 54

PART V STAMP DUTIES

27. Conveyances and transfers on sale: reduction of duty, and amendment of provisions for exemption. (S&S 364–378)
This section substantially amends FA 1930, s. 42 which exempts from duty conveyances and transfers between associated bodies corporate, where one owns 90 per cent. of the issued share capital of the other or a third owns 90 per cent. of the issued share capital of each.

Subsection (3) and its predecessor, FA 1938, s. 50, were introduced to counteract stamp duty avoidance schemes which had been developed in reliance on the reliefs available pursuant to FA 1930, s. 42. The following cases illustrate the two principal types of scheme developed:

(1) *Shop and Store Developments Ltd.* v. *I.R. Comrs.* [1967] 1 A.C. 472, the facts of which were summarised by Lord Reid as follows: " . . . a family who owned the shares of two companies, referred to as the clothing company and the property company, wished to turn the property company into a public company, to issue a number of shares for sale to the public, to obtain a Stock Exchange quotation and to get out of the proceeds a sum of over £250,000. An elaborate scheme was put into operation to achieve this. The only parts of it which I need to set out were first a sale of certain property by the clothing company (the transferor) to the property company (the transferee) for which the transferee gave to the transferor allotment letters for 2,920,000 new shares of the transferee, and secondly a sale by the transferor of allotment letters for 1,200,000 of those shares to underwriters . . . for £385,000. So as a result of carrying out the arrangement the transferor company had parted with the property and had acquired 1,720,000 shares of the transferee and £385,000." Relief was granted under FA 1930, s. 42 on the transfer of the property by the transferor to the transferee, notwithstanding that the transferor had effectively received £385,000 in cash from a third party as part of the arrangements. As a result of this, it became possible wherever a vendor wished to sell property to a purchaser for the vendor to form a company as a wholly owned subsidiary and sell property to the company in return for shares which it could then renounce in favour of the purchaser for a cash payment.

(2) *Escoigne Properties Ltd.* v. *I.R. Comrs.* [1958] A.C. 549, the facts of which were summarised by Lord Denning as follows: "They took advantage of s. 42 by forming a small company which was a puppet in their hands. It was done in this way: if Company A. wished to sell property to Company B. for £100,000 and avoid stamp duty, Company A. would form a small "bridge" company of 100 £1 shares in which it held all the shares. Company A. would convey the property to the "bridge" company for £100,000 but the price would be left owing. By reason of s. 42 that conveyance would be exempt from stamp duty. Then Company A. would sell the 100 shares in the "bridge" company to Company B. for £100 and stamp duty of a trivial amount would be paid on the transfer. The "bridge" company would then convey the property to Company B. for £100,000 on the terms that the £100,000 should be paid direct to Company A. By reason of s. 42 no stamp duty would be payable on that conveyance. So the sale from Company A. to Company B. was completed without paying any stamp duty on the £100,000." See also, with similar facts, *Curzon Offices Ltd.* v. *I.R. Comrs.* [1944] 1 All ER 606, and *Times Newspapers Ltd.* v. *I.R. Comrs.* [1973] Ch. 155.

The second of the above devices was stopped by FA 1938, s. 50; both were stopped by FA 1967, s. 27 (3).

For the relief to be obtained it must be shown to the satisfaction of the Commissioners not only that the effect of the instrument is to transfer the beneficial interest in property from one associated body corporate to another (as laid down in FA 1930, s. 42) but also that the transfer was not effected in pursuance of any arrangement under which:

(*a*) the consideration or any part of the consideration for the conveyance or transfer was to be provided or received, directly or indirectly, by a person other than a body corporate associated with either the transferor or the transferee; or

(*b*) the beneficial interest in the property conveyed or transferred was previously conveyed or transferred by a person other than a body corporate associated with either the transferor or the transferee; or

(*c*) the transferor and the transferee were to cease to be associated by reason of a change in the percentage of the issued share capital of the transferee in the beneficial ownership of the transferor or a third body corporate.

An arrangement is to be treated as within paragraph (*a*) above if it is one pursuant to which the transferor or the transferee (or a body corporate associated with either of them) was to be enabled to provide any of the consideration, or was to dispose of any of the consideration, in consequence of a payment or other disposition by an outsider.

Arrangements have been held to fall foul of sub-paragraph (*a*) above where the consideration for the intra-group transfer is left outstanding and a third party guarantees it or otherwise arranges to provide for it to be paid (*Curzon Offices Ltd.* v. *I.R. Comrs.* [1944] 1 All ER 163), or where the consideration for the intra-group transfer is raised by the sale of the relevant assets to a third party (*Metropolitan Boot Co. Ltd.* v. *I.R. Comrs.* (1958) 46 TC 435 at 456–457). Arrangements are not caught where the consideration for the intra-group transfer is borrowed from a bank (*Curzon Offices Ltd.* v. *I.R. Comrs.*, supra; *Times Newspapers Ltd.* v. *I.R. Comrs.* [1973] Ch. 155).

For the above purposes the expression "arrangement" does not imply that the parties are contractually bound to carry out all the steps forming part of the "arrangement", nor is it necessary that every step should have been determined by the parties prior to implementing the scheme. Thus in *Shop and Store Development Ltd.* v. *I.R. Comrs.* the property was sold to the property company by the clothing company in return for the allotment of shares before the underwriters became contractually bound to purchase the renounceable allotment letters, and the underwriters could have withdrawn at any time prior to completion of the arrangements. The arrangements must, however, be such that the occurrence of the fatal event is contemplated at the outset, and it is not enough that it would probably be done or occur. Thus a transfer of assets by the receiver of a company to a newly incorporated subsidiary with a view to selling that subsidiary would qualify for relief provided that the receiver at the time of transfer had no prospective purchaser in mind.

[*N.B.* In relation to the prospective abolition of all stamp duties on transactions in shares (including bearer instruments) and units under unit trust schemes, and of stamp duty reserve tax, see the Revenue Press Release, 20 March 1990 and the commentary on FA 1990.]

30. Exemption for bearer instruments relating to stock in foreign currencies. (S&S 245–247)
No stamp duty is chargeable under the heading "bearer instrument" in SA 1891, Sch. 1 on the issue of any instrument relating to stock expressed in any currency other than sterling, or in any units of account defined by reference to more than one currency (whether or not including sterling), or the transfer of the stock constituted or transferable thereby.

Where the stock consists of a loan for the repayment of which there is an option between sterling and one or more other currencies, the exemption is only to apply if the option is exercisable only by the holder of the stock.

Where the capital stock of any company or body of persons is not expressed in terms of any currency, it is treated as if expressed in the currency of the territory under the laws of which the company or body was formed or established. Units in a unit trust scheme or shares in a "foreign mutual fund" are treated as capital stock of a company or body incorporated or formed in the territory by whose law the scheme or fund is governed. A foreign mutual fund is a fund administered under arrangements governed by the law of a territory outside the U.K. whereby subscribers are entitled to participate in profit or income from investments of the fund.

In the case of paired shares (see FA 1988, s. 143) this exemption does not apply to any bearer instrument issued after 8 December 1987 which (*a*) represents shares in the paired foreign company, and (*b*) is *not* issued for the purpose of the simultaneous offers of the paired units to the public in the U.K. and the relevant foreign country. The foreign company is treated as though it were a U.K. company for these purposes.

[*N.B.* In relation to the prospective abolition of all stamp duties on transactions in shares (including bearer instruments) and units under unit trust schemes, and of stamp duty reserve tax, see the Revenue Press Release, 20 March 1990 and the commentary on FA 1990.]

PART VI MISCELLANEOUS

45. Citation, interpretation, construction, extent and repeals. (S&S 247)

Provisional Collection of Taxes Act 1968

1968 Chapter 2

1. Temporary statutory effect of House of Commons resolutions affecting . . . , stamp duty reserve tax . . .

Changes in relation to stamp duty reserve tax can take effect provisionally from the date of the Budget.

Where any resolution is passed by the House of Commons providing for the renewal for a further period of any tax in force or imposed during the previous financial year, or for the variation or abolition of any existing tax, and that resolution contains a declaration that it is expedient in the public interest that the resolution should have statutory effect under the provisions of this Act, then the resolution is to have statutory effect as if contained in an Act of Parliament.

The maximum period during which such a resolution can have effect is a period expiring (in the case of a resolution passed in March or April in any year) on 5 August in the same calendar year, and (in the case of any other resolution) at the end of four months after the date on which it is expressed to take effect or, if no such date is expressed, after the date on which it is passed. Any such resolution is to cease to have statutory effect, even if the period specified above has not expired, if within 25 days of House of Commons sittings after the passing of the resolution a new Bill giving effect to the resolution is not introduced, or an exisiting Bill is not amended so as to do so.

A resolution also ceases to have statutory effect if the provisions giving effect to it are rejected during the passage of the relevant Bill, or any Act comes into force replacing the resolution, or Parliament is dissolved or prorogued.

If a resolution ceases to have statutory effect or the period specified above expires before an Act comes into force replacing the resolution, then any money paid in pursuance of the resolution is to be repaid and any deduction made pursuant to the resolution is to be deemed to have been an unauthorised deduction. Similar provisions apply for the repayment of excess moneys paid, or excess deductions made, if the Act which eventually comes into force is not identical to the resolution.

A resolution with statutory effect under this section cannot be reintroduced during the same session of Parliament.

This section applies only to stamp duty reserve tax. Similar provisions in relation to stamp duty, but with important differences, are made in FA 1973, s. 50. Stamp duty and stamp duty reserve tax are completely separate taxes and the provisions in FA 1986 introducing the latter are not construed as one with SA 1891.

[*N.B.* In relation to the prospective abolition of all stamp duties on transactions in shares (including bearer instruments) and units under unit trust schemes, and of stamp duty reserve tax, see the Revenue Press Release, 20 March 1990 and the commentary on FA 1990.]

Taxes Management Act 1970
1970 Chapter 9

Note: Except where otherwise stated, this commentary relates to TMA 1970 in the form that existed before the changes made by FA 1989, ss. 142–169. Since no new regulations have been made to incorporate the changes into the Stamp Duty Reserve Tax Regulations (S.I. 1986 No. 1711, as amended by S.I. 1988 No. 835 and by S.I. 1989 No. 1301), it is difficult to see how the relevant provisions of TMA 1970, in either their old or their new form, can be made to apply for stamp duty reserve tax purposes. In view of the prospective abolition of stamp duty reserve tax (as to which, see the Revenue Press Release, 20 March 1990 and the commentary on FA 1990) it is unlikely that such new regulations will ever be made.

PART III OTHER RETURNS AND INFORMATION

23. Power to obtain copies of registers of securities. (S&S 661)
The Revenue may request a copy of the whole or part of a register of chargeable securities and must pay for it at the rate of 25p per hundred entries.

25. Issuing houses, stockbrokers, etc. (S&S 661–662)
An issuing house or person acting as such may be required to give particulars of the names and addresses of allottees and the number of shares issued to them.

A stockbroker may be required to give particulars of the parties to a stock exchange deal including the number and value of the securities dealt in. Similar information may be required of a person acting as an agent or broker. There is no obligation to return particulars of transactions effected more than three years before service of the notice.

26. Nominee shareholders. (S&S 662)
A nominee shareholder may be required to supply the name and address of the beneficial shareholder.

PART V APPEALS AND OTHER PROCEEDINGS

PROCEEDINGS BEFORE SPECIAL COMMISSIONERS

50. Procedure. (S&S 662–663)
The Revenue may be represented by an officer of the Board.

Either party may be represented by a solicitor, counsel or a qualified accountant but in practice the Commissioners are likely to hear any agent.

The Commissioners may postpone a hearing if any party has reasonable grounds for the postponement. (*Timings Tools Ltd.* v. *Mellersh* [1981] STI 327). They may also hear grounds of appeal not specified in the notice of appeal if satisfied the omission was not wilful or unreasonable.

51. Power of Commissioners to obtain information from appellant. (S&S 663)
The Commissioners may issue a precept on the taxpayer or other party (other than the Revenue, but see *R.* v. *I.R. Comrs., ex parte J. Rothschild Holdings plc* [1986] STC 410) requiring them to deliver or make available to them or the Revenue such particulars, books or documents as they consider may have a bearing on the appeal. The Revenue may inspect and take copies of such documents. Penalties for non-compliance may be awarded under TMA 1970, s. 53. The Commissioners may determine appeals on the information available if a precept is not complied with (*Schulze* v. *Bensted* (No. 2) (1922) 8 TC 259, *Haythornthwaite (T) & Sons, Ltd.* v. *Kelly* (1927) 11 TC 657 and *Eke* v. *Knight* [1977] STC 198, *Parikh* v. *Birmingham North Comrs.* [1976] STC 365, *Tudor & Onions* v. *Ducker* (1924) 8 TC 591, *H & C Stephenson* v. *Waller* (1927) 13 TC 318, *Stoneleigh Products Ltd.* v. *Dodd* (1948) 30 TC 1, *Rosette Franks (Kings St.) Ltd.* v. *Dick* (1955) 36 TC 100, *Gaileri* v. *Wirral General Comrs. and Others* [1979] STC 216, *Beach* v. *Willesden General Comrs. & Others* [1982] STC 157).

See *Sen* v. *St Anne, Westminster General Comrs.* [1983] STC 415 and *Boulton* v. *Poole General Comrs. and I.R. Comrs.* [1988] STC 709, on penalties for non-compliance.

52. Evidence. (S&S 663)
The Commissioners may *subpoena* anyone other than the appellant to give evidence before them, (*Soul* v. *I.R. Comrs.* (1962) 40 TC 506). An agent or confidential employee of the appellant however cannot be forced to give evidence if he objects. Other witnesses are liable to a penalty of up to £50 for failure to give evidence (*Bales* v. *Rochford Commissioners & I.R. Comrs.* (1964) 42 TC 17).

Any lawful evidence may be introduced at an appeal hearing, but new facts may not be introduced thereafter if the appeal goes to Court, (*Williams* v. *Special Commissioners & I.R. Comrs.* (1974) 49 TC 670, *R.* v. *Great Yarmouth General Comrs.* (*ex parte Amis*) (1960) 39 TC 143, *Bird (RA) & Co Ltd.* v. *I.R. Comrs* (1924) 12 TC 785, *Smart* v. *I.R. Comrs.* (1949) 29 TC 338, *Fen Farming Co Ltd.* v. *Dunsford* (1974) 49 TC 246, *Archer-Shee* v. *Baker* (1928) 15 TC 1) but new points of law may be raised, *Muir* v. *I.R. Comrs.* (1966) 43 TC 367. The appellant may be put on oath and giving false evidence is perjury (*R.* v. *Hood Barrs* (1943) 1 All ER 665). Particulars of other taxpayers may be produced providing there is no breach of confidentiality. *Gamini Bus Co Ltd.* v. *Colombo Income Tax Commissioners* (1952) 31 ATC 467. Hearsay evidence is not allowed (*Forth Investments Ltd.* v. *I.R. Comrs.* [1976] STC 399). A case may be remitted to the Commissioners for further findings, *Brimelow* v. *Price* (1965) 49 TC 41, *Lack* v. *Daggett* (1970) 46 TC 497.

Evidence may be rejected by the Commissioners, *Cain* v. *Schofield* (1953) 34 TC 362, *Moll* v. *I.R. Comrs.* (1955) 36 TC 384, *Jacobs* v. *Eavis* (1956) 36 TC 576, *Hood Barrs* v. *I.R. Comrs.* (No. 4) (1967) 46 ATC 448. If no evidence is submitted determinations may be amended or confirmed, *Noble* v. *Wilkinson; Ridley* v. *Wilkinson* (1958) 38 TC 135, *Pierson* v. *Belcher* (1959) 38 TC 387, *Bookey* v. *Edwards* [1982] STC 135, *Cutmore* v. *Leach* [1982] STC 61.

53. Summary award of penalties. (S&S 664)
The Commissioners may award penalties summarily for failing to comply with a precept or failing to respond to a Commissioners summons. The appropriate penalties are set out in TMA 1970, ss. 52, 98. (*Dawes* v. *Wallington Commissioners & I.R. Comrs.* (1964) 42 TC 200, *Shah* v. *Hampstead Commissioners & I.R. Comrs.* [1974] STC 438, *Chapman* v. *Sheaf Comrs. and I.R. Comrs.* (1975) 49 TC, *Campbell* v. *Rochdale Comrs. and I.R. Comrs.* [1975] STC 311, *Beach* v. *Willesden General Comrs. & Others* [1982] STC 157.)

PART VI COLLECTION AND RECOVERY

DISTRAINT AND POINDING

61. Distraint by collectors. (S&S 664)
A collector may distrain on taxpayer's goods and chattels for the payment of tax. The goods would be kept for five days and, if not redeemed plus costs, would be auctioned.

63. Recovery in Scotland. (S&S 664–665)
The rules as to distraint are adapted to Scottish Law.

COURT PROCEEDINGS

65. Magistrates' courts. (S&S 666)
Tax due of less than £500 may be recovered by summary proceedings in a magistrates' court by a collector. The limit was raised from £250 to £500 by virtue of the Recovery of Tax in Summary Proceedings (Financial Limits) Order 1989 (reproduced in Appendix 1).

66. County courts. (S&S 666)
The collector may proceed in the county courts for outstanding tax of up to the county court limit, the amount for the purposes of the County Courts Act 1984, s. 16.

67. Inferior courts in Scotland. (S&S 666)
The provisions relating to recovery in a magistrates court or county courts do not apply to Scotland, but a debt within the sheriff's court limits (£250) may be sued for by the collector.

68. High Court, etc. (S&S 666)
The collector can sue for greater sums in the High Court or in Scotland in the Court of Session.

SUPPLEMENTAL

69. Interest on tax. (S&S 667)
Interest on tax may be collected as if it were outstanding tax.

PART VII PERSONS CHARGEABLE IN A REPRESENTATIVE CAPACITY ETC.

INCOME TAX

71. Bodies of persons. (S&S 667)
The treasurer is responsible for making the tax returns and any officer is entitled to retain sufficient to pay any tax due out of monies coming into his hands.

72. Trustees, guardians, etc. of incapacitated persons. (S&S 667)
A trustee or guardian of an incapacitated person is accountable or liable to the tax which that person would be accountable or liable for were he not incapacitated. The trustee may retain sufficient funds to meet the tax liability.

73. Further provisions as to infants. (S&S 667)
An infant's parent or guardian is liable to pay the tax in default of payment by the infant and may be proceeded against as if the infant's tax liability were his own.

74. Personal representatives. (S&S 668)
Personal representatives are responsible for settling the deceased's tax liabilities subject to the sufficiency of the deceased's estate.

PART VIII CHARGES ON NON-RESIDENTS

78. Method of charging non-residents. (S&S 668)
A non-resident who has a trustee, guardian etc. or branch or agency in the U.K. is liable to tax as if he were resident in the U.K.

83. Responsibilities and indemnification of persons in whose name a non-resident person is chargeable. (S&S 668)
An agent etc. of a non-resident is responsible for payment of the tax and may retain sufficient to pay this when accounting to his principal.

PART IX INTEREST ON OVERDUE TAX

86. Interest on overdue tax. (S&S 668)
Interest at the rate applicable under FA 1989, s. 178, and the Taxes (Interest Rate) Regulations 1989, S.I. 1989 No. 1297, runs from the accountable date (even if not a business day) until the date of payment. See also the Revenue Press Release, 26 October 1989, reproduced in Appendix 4.

90. Disallowance of relief for interest on tax. (S&S 669)
No income tax relief is available in respect of interest on unpaid tax.

PART X PENALTIES, ETC.

93. Failure to give notice for stamp duty reserve tax. (S&S 669)
The basic penalty for failing to deliver a notice is £50. The penalty proceedings are commenced before the court or Commissioners and there is a further penalty of up to £10 per day until the notice is submitted—*Napier* v. *Farnham General Comrs. and Others* [1978] STI 589, *Garnham* v. *Haywards Heath General Comrs. and Others* [1977] STI 430, *Moschi* v. *Kensington General Comrs. and Others* [1980] STC 1. As to the possible defence of reasonable excuse see TMA 1970, s 118 (2).
    Penalties should not be levied until any appeals have been heard, *A-G for Irish Free State* v. *White* (1931) 38 TC 666. The Commissioners should be presented with the full facts in assessing penalties (*Stableford* v. *Liverpool General Comrs. and Others* [1983] STC 162).
    Other cases on penalties include *Wells* v. *Croydon Comrs.* (1968) 47 ATC 356, *Taylor* v. *Bethnal Green Comrs. and I.R. Comrs.* (1976), [1977] STC 44, *Willey* v. *I.R. Comrs. & East Dereham Comrs.* [1985] STC 56.

95. Incorrect notice etc. for stamp duty reserve tax. (S&S 669)
Where tax has been lost through the taxpayer's fraud or negligence the penalty is £50 plus in the case of negligence the tax lost, and in the case of fraud twice the tax lost. The penalty is in addition to making good the tax lost. These are the maximum penalties unless the Revenue institute criminal proceedings for fraud or perjury. In most cases settlements are arrived at to include a mitigated penalty. See TMA 1970, s. 102.

97. Incorrect notice; supplemental. (S&S 669)
If an innocent mistake in any notice is not put right without unreasonable delay the mistake is deemed to have been caused by negligence and the penalty provisions of TMA 1970, s. 95 apply.

98. Special returns, etc. (S&S 670)
If the taxpayer is required to complete one of the special returns listed in columns 1 and 2 of the table he is liable on non-compliance to a penalty of up to £50, plus up to £10 per day if declared by

the court or the Commissioners. A false return gives rise to a further penalty of up to £250 for negligence or £500 for fraud. No penalty is incurred if the taxpayer takes remedial action before penalty proceedings are commenced in the case of notices specified in column 1 of the table (*B & S Displays Ltd. and Others* v. *Special Comrs.* [1978] STC 331). The £50 initial penalty may still arise despite remedial action in the case of information etc. specified in column 2 of the table.

99. Assisting in giving incorrect notice, etc. (S&S 670)
There is a penalty of up to £500 for assisting in the production of an incorrect notice.

100. Procedure for recovery of penalties. (S&S 670–671)
Proceedings for the recovery of penalties have to be approved by the Board of Inland Revenue. Proceedings may be taken in the High Court or before the Special Commissioners.

101. Evidence for purposes of preceding provisions of Part X. (S&S 671)
A final notice may be treated as evidence of the matters specified.

102. Mitigation of penalties. (S&S 671)
The Board have power to mitigate penalties.

103. Time limit for recovery of penalties. (S&S 671)
Penalty proceedings may be commenced within six years from the date on which the penalty was incurred *e.g.* within six years of the failure to give a notice.

Proceedings for penalties in fraud or wilful default cases must be commenced within three years of the final determination of the tax.

104. Saving for criminal proceedings. (S&S 672)
The power of the Revenue to institute criminal proceedings, usually for fraud or perjury, is reserved and remains unaffected by any settlement of the tax liabilities and penalties (*R.* v. *Hudson* (1956) 36 TC 561; *R* v. *Patel* (1973) 48 TC 647).

105. Evidence in cases of fraud or wilful default. (S&S 672)
It is common Revenue practice to inform the taxpayer at the beginning of an investigation that provided he gives full co-operation to the Revenue the Board will usually accept a negotiated settlement.

Such an inducement towards co-operation does not serve to make any evidence provided by the taxpayer inadmissible for the purpose of criminal or penalty proceedings.

On 5 October 1944 the Chancellor of the Exchequer stated that the practice of the Commissioners of Inland Revenue in regard to instituting criminal proceedings for alleged frauds on the Revenue was governed by [TMA 1970, s. 105] "which makes provision for the admissibility in evidence of any disclosure made in the circumstances there set out. As the section indicates, the Commissioners have a general power under which they can accept pecuniary settlements instead of instituting criminal proceedings in respect of fraud or wilful default alleged to have been committed by a taxpayer. They can, however, give no undertaking to a taxpayer in any such case that they will accept such a settlement and refrain from instituting criminal proceedings even if the case is one in which the taxpayer has made full confession and has given full facilities for investigation of the facts. They reserve to themselves complete discretion in all cases as to the course which they will pursue, but it is their practice to be influenced by the fact that the taxpayer has made a full confession and has given full facilities for investigation into his affairs and for examination of such books, papers, documents or information as the Commissioners may consider necessary."

PART XI MISCELLANEOUS AND SUPPLEMENTAL

COMPANIES

108. Responsibility of company officers. (S&S 672)
The proper officer of a company on whom documents etc. should be served is the secretary unless the company is in liquidation in which case it is the liquidator. For a club the proper officer is the treasurer.

VALUATION

111. Valuation of assets: power to inspect. (S&S 673)
The Board have power to inspect assets for valuation purposes.

DOCUMENTS

114. Want of form or errors not to invalidate notice of determination, etc. (S&S 673)
Minor defects in notices of determination do not invalidate them provided the recipient is not misled (*Martin* v. *I.R. Comrs.* (1938) 22 TC 330 and *Baylis* v. *Gregory* [1986] STC 22).

118. Interpretation. (S&S 673)

Various terms are defined. It should be noted that failure to comply with a time limit is not enforced where the Commissioners grant further time within which the required action is completed, nor while there is reasonable excuse for not doing it (*Thorne* v. *General Comrs. for Sevenoaks* [1989] STC 560).

Finance Act 1970
1970 Chapter 24

PART III STAMP DUTIES

MISCELLANEOUS

32. Abolition of certain stamp duties, and amendments as to rates and other matters. (S&S 251)

33. Composition by stock exchanges in respect of transfer duty. (S&S 251–253)
The Commissioners may enter into an agreement with, or with persons acting on behalf of, any recognised investment exchange or recognised clearing house for the composition of the stamp duty chargeable under or by reference to the heading "Conveyance or Transfer on sale" or "Conveyance or Transfer of any kind not hereinbefore described" in SA 1891, Sch. 1, on such instruments as may be specified in the agreement. For that purpose the expressions "recognised investment exchange" and "recognised clearing house" have the same meaning as in the Financial Services Act 1986.

Such an agreement must provide for every instrument to bear on its face an indication of the stamp duty chargeable thereon, and for the issue in respect of every such instrument by or on behalf of the relevant investment exchange or clearing house of a certificate to the effect that stamp duty to the amount so indicated has been or will be accounted for to the Commissioners. It must also provide for the delivery to the Commissioners by or on behalf of the relevant investment exchange or clearing house of periodical accounts in respect of instruments to which the agreement relates, and for the payment to the Commissioners by or on behalf of the relevant investment exchange or clearing house (on the delivery of any such account) of the aggregate amount of the stamp duty chargeable on the instruments to which the agreement relates during the period to which the account relates.

A fine is payable by any investment exchange or clearing house which is a party to such an agreement and which is in default in delivering any accounts required by the agreement, or in paying any amounts due, and amounts due bear interest from the due date for delivery of the relevant account to the date of actual payment.

[N.B. In relation to the prospective abolition of all stamp duties on transactions in shares (including bearer instruments) and units under unit trust schemes, and of stamp duty reserve tax, see the Revenue Press Release, 20 March 1990 and the commentary on FA 1990.]

36. Citation, interpretation, construction, extent and repeals. (S&S 253)

SCHEDULE 7 STAMP DUTIES (Section 32)

PART II GENERAL AMENDMENTS (S&S 254–257)

Bearer instruments

6 (4).—If an overseas bearer instrument in respect of a loan expressed in sterling has been stamped *ad valorem* or with the denoting stamp referred to in FA 1963, s. 60(3), or with duty under paragraph (4) of the heading "bearer instrument", then duty is not chargeable under that head of charge by reason only that the instrument is varied.

[N.B. In relation to the prospective abolition of all stamp duties on transactions in shares (including bearer instruments) and units under unit trust schemes, and of stamp duty reserve tax, see the Revenue Press Release, 20 March 1990 and the commentary on FA 1990.]

Conveyance or transfer on sale

13.—SA 1891, s. 140 is repealed in relation to compositions for stamp duty on transfers of colonial stock.

Mortgages, etc.

16 (4).—The duty payable on the transfer of, or of the money or stock secured by, any collateral security was not to exceed 10 shillings (50p), provided that a transfer of the principal or primary security had been duly stamped with the duty chargeable under paragraph (4) of the Mortgages head of charge. Duty is no longer payable under the heading "Mortgage" and instruments falling under that head are now exempt from all stamp duty.

Finance Act 1971
1971 Chapter 68

PART V MISCELLANEOUS

64. Stamp duty—abolition of duty on bonds, mortgages etc. (S&S 260–261)

The duties chargeable (*a*) under paragraphs (1) and (2) of the heading "Bond, Covenant, or instrument of any kind whatsoever" (except as regards instruments increasing the rent reserved by another instrument), (*b*) under the heading "Bond of any kind whatsoever not specifically charged with any duty", and (*c*) under the heading "Mortgage, Bond, Debenture, Covenant" are abolished.

These abolitions will only relieve an instrument from duty to the extent that any matter covered by that instrument falls within an abolished head of charge. Thus, if the instrument relates to other distinct matters which are chargeable, then the instrument will still be chargeable to duty by virtue of SA 1891, s. 4.

69. Citation, interpretation, construction, extent and repeals. (S&S 261)

Gas Act 1972
1972 Chapter 60

32. Position of Corporation as respects taxation etc. generally.

33. Special provisions with respect to stamp duty.
Where the Treasury guarantees the redemption of, and the payment of interest on, any British Gas Stock issued by the Corporation, transfers of the stock are exempt from all stamp duty.

[*N.B.* In relation to the prospective abolition of all stamp duties on transactions in shares (including bearer instruments) and units under unit trust schemes, and of stamp duty reserve tax, see the Revenue Press Release, 20 March 1990 and the commentary on FA 1990.]

Finance Act 1973
1973 Chapter 51

PART V STAMP DUTY

50. Temporary statutory effect of House of Commons resolution affecting stamp duties. (S&S 266–267)

This section applies to stamp duty similar provisions as are applied to income tax by virtue of PCTA 1968, s. 1. There are, however, important differences. Income tax is directly enforceable by assessment, so that if a resolution lapses any tax paid while it was in force can easily be repaid to the taxpayer. Stamp duty, on the other hand, is a tax on instruments and the lapse of a resolution cannot affect anything done while it was in force.

If the House of Commons passes a resolution providing for the variation or abolition of an existing stamp duty, and the resolution is expressed to have effect for a certain period and contains a declaration that it is expedient in the public interest that the resolution should have statutory effect, then (subject as mentioned below) the resolution has statutory effect for the period so stated as if it were contained in an Act of Parliament.

The maximum period which can be stated in such a resolution is the period beginning on a date stated in the resolution and ending on (or up to 31 days after) the earliest of:

(*a*) the 25th day of House of Commons sittings without a Bill containing provisions to the same effect as the resolution being read for a second time, or without a Bill being amended so as to include similar provisions;

(*b*) the rejection of the provisions during the passage through the House of Commons of a Bill containing them;

(*c*) the dissolution or prorogation of Parliament; and

(*d*) the expiration of five months from the date on which the resolution takes effect.

A resolution also ceases to have statutory effect if an Act of Parliament varying or abolishing the relevant duty comes into force.

The ending of the period for which a resolution has statutory effect under these provisions does not affect the validity of anything done while it is in force.

PART VI MISCELLANEOUS AND GENERAL

54. Amendments consequential on establishment of The Stock Exchange. (S&S 267)

Various amendments were made as a consequence of the establishment of The Stock Exchange.

59. Citation, interpretation, construction, extent and repeals. (S&S 267–268)

Finance Act 1976
1976 Chapter 40

PART V MISCELLANEOUS AND SUPPLEMENTARY

127. Stamp duty: stock exchange transfers. (S&S 281)
This section prepared the way for the introduction by The Stock Exchange of the TALISMAN system, its computerised settlement and stock transfer system, TALISMAN being a contraction of the words "Transfer Accounting, Lodgement for Investors and Stock Management for jobbers". In relation to any transfer giving effect to a transaction carried out on or after 27 October 1986 (*i.e.*, the date on which the Stock Exchange rule prohibiting a person from carrying on business as both a broker and jobber was abolished or, more commonly, "Big Bang") stamp duty is not to be chargeable on any transfer to a "Stock Exchange nominee", meaning "any person designated for the purposes of this section as a nominee of The Stock Exchange by an order made by the Secretary of State". Under The Stock Exchange (Designation of Nominees) Order 1985 (S.I. 1975 No. 806), which replaced The Stock Exchange (Designation of Nominees) Order 1979 (S.I. 1979 No. 238) following the consolidation of the Companies Acts 1948 to 1983 in the Companies Act 1985, SEPON Ltd. has been designated for the purposes of this section.

[*N.B.* In relation to the prospective abolition of all stamp duties on transactions in shares (including bearer instruments) and units under unit trust schemes, and of stamp duty reserve tax, see the Revenue Press Release, 20 March 1990 and the commentary on FA 1990.]

131. Inter-American Development Bank. (S&S 281–282)
This confers exemption from stamp duty under the "bearer instrument" head of charge in SA 1891, Sch. 1 in relation to any instrument issued by the Inter-American Development Bank.

[*N.B.* In relation to the prospective abolition of all stamp duties on transactions in shares (including bearer instruments) and units under unit trust schemes, and of stamp duty reserve tax, see the Revenue Press Release, 20 March 1990 and the commentary on FA 1990.]

132. Citation, interpretation, construction and repeals. (S&S 282)

The Stock Exchange (Completion of Bargains) Act 1976
1976 Chapter 47

1. Exemption from obligation to prepare share certificates, etc.
This section exempts companies from the requirements to issue share certificates, certificates for debentures or certificates for debenture stock in respect of shares, debentures or debenture stock allotted or transferred to a Stock Exchange nominee.

See also the commentary on FA 1989 and the Companies Act 1989; Inland Revenue Press Release, 14 March 1989 (Appendix 4); and DTI Consultative Paper: Dematerialisation of Share Certificates and Share Transfers (Appendix 9).

See also now, in relation to the prospective abolition of all stamp duties on transactions in shares (including bearer instruments) and units under unit trust schemes, and of stamp duty reserve tax, the Revenue Press Release, 20 March 1990 and the commentary on FA 1990.

7. Short title, interpretation, commencement and extent.

Finance Act 1980

1980 Chapter 48

PART V STAMP DUTY

97. Shared ownership transactions. (S&S 288–289)

Local authorities, housing associations and housing action trusts have introduced shared ownership or equity sharing schemes to enable those people who could not afford to buy their council houses in the normal way to do so in stages, whereby they would purchase part of the house and then pay rental on the balance, with an option to acquire the entire reversion. To avoid such persons paying more stamp duty than they would otherwise have had to if they had bought the whole house, they can elect to pay "conveyance or transfer on sale" duty on the market value of the house, instead of both lease duty on the grant of the lease and conveyance duty on the purchase of the reversion. A private landlord who has taken over a public housing estate can similarly elect as regards leases granted on or after 1 August 1987.

The provisions only apply where a lease is granted for the exclusive use of the lessee or joint lessees, partly in consideration of the rent and partly in consideration of a premium calculated by reference to the market value or a sum calculated by reference to that value (*i.e.*, whether at market value, or at either a premium or discount to market value). The lease must provide for the lessee to acquire the reversion and contain a statement of the market value and a statement to the effect that the parties intend duty to be charged in accordance with these provisions. In addition, the lease must be granted by one of the specified bodies. No duty will be payable upon the sale of the reversion provided that the conveyance of the reversion includes a statement that it has been executed pursuant to a lease stamped in accordance with these provisions.

98. Maintenance funds for historic buildings. (S&S 289–290)

No stamp duty is chargeable on any instrument whereby property ceases to be comprised in a settlement, if as a result of the property or part of it becoming comprised in another settlement (other than by the instrument itself) there is by virtue of IHTA 1984, Sch. 4, para. 9 (1) or 17 (1) no IHT charge in respect of it, or by virtue of para. 9 (4) or 17 (4) only a reduced charge. The provisions are those relating to exemptions for transfers of property into settlements for the maintenance of historic buildings. Where only part of the property becomes comprised in the other settlement referred to, liability to stamp duty in relation to the rest is not affected, provided that the relevant instrument is adjudicated under SA 1891, s. 12.

101. Unit trusts. (S&S 290–291)

No stamp duty is chargeable on any transfer of any unit in an authorised unit trust scheme (as defined in the Financial Services Act 1986) where the funds of that unit trust can be invested neither in any investment the transfer of which would be liable to *ad valorem* stamp duty, nor in such a way that the trustees could earn income chargeable to income tax in their hands, other than profits chargeable under Schedule C arising from U.K. public revenue dividends (*i.e.* interest, annuities and dividends payable on U.K. gilt-edged securities) and interest, discounts and income from securities payable out of the public revenue chargeable under Schedule D Case III rather than under Schedule C.

Under the relevant provisions of the Financial Services Act 1986 an "authorised unit trust scheme" is a unit trust scheme "declared by an order of the Secretary of State for the time being in force to be an authorised unit trust scheme for the purposes of this Act" following an application for authorisation under the procedures laid down in ss. 77 *et seq.* of that Act. For the definition of "unit trust scheme", see the commentary on FA 1946, s. 57.

[*N.B.* In relation to the prospective abolition of all stamp duties on transactions in shares (including bearer instruments) and units under unit trust schemes, and of stamp duty reserve tax, see the Revenue Press Release, 20 March 1990 and the commentary on FA 1990.]

102. Conveyance in consideration of debt. (S&S 291–292)

Under SA 1891, s. 57, where property is conveyed in consideration wholly or in part of any debt due, the debt is to be deemed to form the whole or part, as the case may be, of the consideration in respect of which the conveyance is chargeable with *ad valorem* duty. As a result of a number of cases concerning s. 57 (*e.g., I.R. Comrs.* v. *North British Railway Company* 1901 4 F (Ct. of Sess.) 389; *Huntington* v. *I.R. Comrs.* [1896] 1 QB 422; and *I.R. Comrs.* v. *City of Glasgow Bank Liquidators* 1981 8 R (Ct. of Sess.) 389) it became increasingly uncertain as to the correct treatment of cases where the value of the property transferred was less than the amount of the indebtedness agreed to be discharged.

The Revenue attempted to clarify the position by the issue on 8 November 1978 of Statement of Practice SP 5/78 to the effect that duty would in such circumstances be charged on the amount of the indebtedness agreed to be discharged.

It was generally thought that this practice was unfair and, in an attempt to mitigate its results, it is provided that where the property is conveyed wholly or in part in consideration of a debt due to *the transferee*, then the duty chargeable is limited by reference to the value of the property conveyed if this is less than the amount of the debt, provided that the conveyance is adjudicated under SA 1891, s. 12.

The new relief only applies where a conveyance is made to a creditor in discharge of a debt due to him. In all other cases, SP 5/78 still applies.

Finance Act 1981
1981 Chapter 35

PART VI STAMP DUTY

107. Sale of houses at discount by local authorities etc. (S&S 294–295)
Where there has been a sale of a dwelling house (including the grant of a lease) by any of the bodies specified, and such sale has been at a discount, the conveyance or transfer on sale to give effect to it is liable to stamp duty *ad valorem* (if any) on the post-discount price actually paid. No account is to be taken of any discount that might have to be repaid in certain circumstances, *e.g.*, if the property is resold.

See also the Local Government Reorganisation (Preservation of Right to Buy) Order, S.I. 1986 No. 2092, para. 12.

108. Shared ownership transactions. (S&S 295–296)
FA 1980, s. 97 is amended in relation to stamp duty in "shared ownership transactions", so as to ensure that that section applies to sales at a discount price. The earlier provisions are extended to some leasehold cases that were not previously covered. A private landlord who has taken over a public housing estate is covered as regards leases granted on or after 1 August 1987.

110. Pooled pension funds. (S&S 297)
In the legislation governing the position of unit trusts for stamp duty purposes, references to unit trust schemes include references to common investment arrangements made by the trustees of exempt approved schemes (within the meaning of TA 1988, s. 592 (1)) solely for the purposes of the schemes.

[*N.B.* In relation to the prospective abolition of all stamp duties on transactions in shares (including bearer instruments) and units under unit trust schemes, and of stamp duty reserve tax, see the Revenue Press Release, 20 March 1990 and the commentary on FA 1990.]

PART X MISCELLANEOUS AND SUPPLEMENTARY

139. Short title, interpretation, construction and repeals

British Telecommunications Act 1981
1981 Chapter 38

81. Stamp duty. (S&S 445)
Stamp duty is not chargeable on any instrument certified to the Commissioners by the Corporation, the Post Office, or by any wholly-owned subsidiary of either of them, as having being made or executed in pursuance of s. 10 or Sch. 2, provided that such instrument is adjudicated under SA 1891, s. 12.

Finance Act 1982
1982 Chapter 39

PART V STAMP DUTY

129. Exemption from duty on grants, transfers to charities, etc. (S&S 298)
Where any conveyance, transfer or lease is made or agreed to be made to a body of persons established for charitable purposes only or to the trustees of a trust so established or to the Trustees of the National Heritage Memorial Fund, no stamp duty is chargeable by virtue of the "conveyance or transfer on sale", "conveyance or transfer of any kind not hereinbefore described" or "lease or tack" heads of charge in SA 1891, Sch. 1, provided that the relevant instrument is adjudicated under SA 1891, s. 12.

Finance Act 1983
1983 Chapter 28

PART IV MISCELLANEOUS AND SUPPLEMENTARY

Miscellaneous

46. Historic Buildings and Monuments Commission for England. (S&S 300)

For the purposes of FA 1982, s. 129, the Historic Buildings and Monuments Commission for England is to be treated as a body of persons established for charitable purposes only.

Finance (No. 2) Act 1983
1983 Chapter 49

PART III MISCELLANEOUS AND SUPPLEMENTARY

15. Relief from stamp duty for local constituency associations of political parties on reorganisation of constituencies. (S&S 300–303)

An existing constituency association may dispose of land either (*a*) to a new constituency association which is a successor to the existing constituency association (which it will be if any part of the existing association's areas is comprised in the new association's area), or (*b*) to a body (whether corporate or unincorporate) which is an organ of the political party concerned and, as soon as practicable thereafter, that body disposes of the land to a new constituency association which is a successor to the existing constituency association. In such cases SA 1891, s. 57 (conveyances in consideration of a debt to be charged with *ad valorem* duty as if the debt forms the whole or part of the consideration for the conveyance) do not apply in relation to conveyances or transfers giving effect to any such disposal.

County Courts Act 1984
1984 Chapter 28

79. Agreement not to appeal. (S&S 429)

The parties to a county court action can enter into a written agreement (signed by themselves or their solicitors or agents) that any judgment, direction, decision or order of the judge is to be final and, provided the agreement is entered into before the judgment, direction, decision or order is given or made, then no appeal lies therefrom. Such an agreement requires no stamp.

Finance Act 1984

1984 Chapter 43

PART IV STAMP DUTY

109. Reduction of stamp duty on conveyances and transfers. (S&S 303–304)

Reductions apply:

(*a*) to instruments executed on or after 20 March 1984; and

(*b*) to instruments executed on or after 13 March 1984 which are stamped on or after 20 March 1984; and

(*c*) in the case of an instrument giving effect to a Stock Exchange transaction, if the transaction takes place on or after 12 March 1984 and is one in respect of which settlement is due on or after 13 March 1984.

The rate of duty applicable to a conveyance or transfer of stock or marketable securities has been further amended by FA 1986, s. 64.

[*N.B.* In relation to the prospective abolition of all stamp duties on transactions in shares (including bearer instruments) and units under unit trust schemes, and of stamp duty reserve tax, see the Revenue Press Release, 20 March 1990 and the commentary on FA 1990.]

110. Extension of stamp duty relief on sales at discount. (S&S 304–305)

In relation to the sale of dwelling houses by certain public sector bodies at a discounted price subject to a condition that the discount should be paid in the event of the purchaser re-selling the property within a specified period, stamp duty is payable by reference to the price after deduction of the discount notwithstanding the possibility that the discount may subsequently become payable by the purchaser.

The U.K. Atomic Energy Authority is also added to the list of bodies to which the provisions apply, and the Treasury is empowered by statutory instrument to prescribe other bodies at a later date.

The relevant provisions are also extended to apply where the transfer in question is in relation to a sub-sale at a discount price by a housing association.

See also the Local Government Reorganisation (Preservation of Right to Buy) Order 1986, S.I. 1986 No. 2092, para. 12 and FA 1988, s. 142.

111. Agreements for leases. (S&S 305–306)

Where an interest in land is conveyed or transferred, or a lease is granted, subject to an agreement for a lease exceeding 35 years, the conveyance transfer or lease must bear a denoting stamp to the effect that duty has been paid upon the agreement for lease. However, this applies only where the agreement for lease is directly enforceable against the interest in the land which is conveyed or transferred, or out of which a new lease is granted, and not where the agreement for lease is enforceable against some other interest to which the interest conveyed or transferred, or the lease granted, is superior.

PART VI MISCELLANEOUS AND SUPPLEMENTARY

Miscellaneous

126. Tax exemptions in relation to designated international organisations. (S&S 307–308)

There is complete exemption from stamp duty in relation to the issue of any instrument by, or the transfer of the stock constituted by or transferable by means of any instrument issued by, certain international organisations of which the U.K. or any EC country is a member, provided that the relevant membership agreement provides for the relevant organisation to be granted this type of exemption, and provided the Treasury designates the organisation by statutory instrument.

Similarly, there is an exemption from the stamp duty reserve tax that would otherwise be chargeable under FA 1986, ss. 93 or 94, on securities issued on a U.K. register by any such organisation to a nominee for either a depositary bank or a clearance service (as to which, see Revenue Press Release, 14 June 1990, and the commentary on FA 1990).

[*N.B.* In relation to the prospective abolition of all stamp duties on transactions in shares (including bearer instruments) and units under unit trust schemes, and of stamp duty reserve tax, see the Revenue Press Release, 20 March 1990 and the commentary on FA 1990.]

128. Short title, interpretation, construction and repeals. (S&S 309)

Companies Act 1985

1985 Chapter 6

SCHEDULE 14 (Section 362)

PART II GENERAL PROVISIONS WITH RESPECT TO OVERSEAS BRANCH REGISTERS. **(S&S 428)**

8.—Shares recorded in an overseas branch register (other than a register kept in Northern Ireland) are deemed to be property situated outside the U.K. for the purposes of stamp duty, so that if such shares are transferred by an instrument of transfer executed outside the U.K. no stamp duty will be payable.

Note, however, that by virtue of FA 1986, s. 99 (10) (b), the effect of this paragraph is to be ignored for interpreting the expression "chargeable securities" in relation to FA 1986, ss. 93, 94, and 96, imposing stamp duty reserve tax where a depositary receipt is issued by a person to whom chargeable securities are transferred and where chargeable securities are transferred or issued pursuant to an agreement for the provision of clearance services.

[*N.B.* In relation to the prospective abolition of all stamp duties on transactions in shares (including bearer instruments) and units under unit trust schemes, and of stamp duty reserve tax, see the Revenue Press Release, 20 March 1990 and the commentary on FA 1990.]

Finance Act 1985
1985 Chapter 54

PART III STAMP DUTY

81. Renounceable letters of allotment etc. (S&S 310–312)

The background to this section is described in the commentary on the "bearer instrument" head of charge in SA 1891, Sch. 1.

Where there is an arrangement pursuant to which rights to shares in a company are renounced in favour of a person who (together with persons connected with him) has control of that company, or will have such control in consequence of the arrangement, the instrument is not to be exempt from stamp duty under or by reference to the heading "conveyance or transfer on sale" in SA 1891, Sch. 1 by virtue of the provisions of FA 1963, s. 65 (1).

The provisions also apply where the rights renounced are rights to convertible loan capital and excessive return capital, to which FA 1976, s. 116 (1) does not apply by virtue of FA 1976, s. 126 (2) or (3). The word "shares" includes stock.

A person has control of a company if he has power to control that company's affairs by virtue of holding shares in, or possessing voting power in relation to, that company, or any other body corporate.

"Connected person" has the meaning in CGTA 1979.

The provisions apply to instruments where the rights are renounced under them on or after 1 August 1985, except where the renunciation results from an offer which had become unconditional as to acceptances on or before 27 June 1985.

[*N.B.* In relation to the prospective abolition of all stamp duties on transactions in shares (including bearer instruments) and units under unit trust schemes, and of stamp duty reserve tax, see the Revenue Press Release, 20 March 1990 and the commentary on FA 1990.]

82. Gifts inter vivos. (S&S 312–313)

By virtue of F(1909–10)A 1910, s. 74, any conveyance or transfer operating as a "voluntary disposition *inter vivos*" was formerly chargeable as a conveyance or transfer on sale for a consideration equal to the value of the property conveyed or transferred. A "voluntary disposition *inter vivos*" was defined as "any conveyance or transfer (not being a disposition made in favour of a purchaser or incumbrancer or other person in good faith and for valuable consideration)". For that purpose, the consideration was deemed not to be "valuable" where the Commissioners were of the opinion "that by reason of the inadequacy of the sum paid as consideration or other circumstances the conveyance or transfer confers a substantial benefit on the person to whom the property is conveyed or transferred", except where the consideration was marriage. F(1909–10)A 1910, s. 74 did not apply in certain circumstances, for example where the conveyance or transfer was for a nominal consideration to secure a loan or where the conveyance or transfer did not pass the beneficial interest in the property. However, all such conveyances or transfers were required to be adjudicated under SA 1891, s. 12 and the body of case law regarding the interpretation of s. 74, and the valuation of property for the purpose of s. 74, is voluminous.

For a detailed discussion of this topic see *Sergeant & Sims on Stamp Duties* (8th edn.), pp. 202–214.

F(1909–10)A 1910, s. 74, and the *ad valorem* stamp duty charged thereunder on conveyances or transfers operating as voluntary dispositions *inter vivos*, was abolished by this section.

Notwithstanding the abolition, certain instruments which would have been chargeable under the abolished provisions had still to be adjudicated under SA 1891, s. 12. The effect was to require the adjudication of any conveyance or transfer operating as a voluntary disposition *inter vivos*, within the meaning of the abolished provisions, provided that it did not attract stamp duty under the "conveyance or transfer on sale" head of charge in SA 1891, Sch. 1. This meant that where a transaction was one of sale the conveyance or transfer did not need to be adjudicated, whether or not the sale was at an undervalue, but where the transaction was not one of sale the conveyance or transfer of the property did need to be adjudicated if it fell within the definition of a "voluntary disposition *inter vivos*" under the abolished provisions. The most obvious example of this was in the case of a transfer of property by way of gift, but there are a large number of other transactions which as a matter of law are deemed to involve "conveyances or transfers" and because the consideration is other than cash, stock (including shares and units under a unit trust scheme), marketable or other securities, or debts, they are not "on sale" for the purposes of SA 1891 (see the cases cited in *Sergeant & Sims on Stamp Duties* (8th edn.), pp. 202–214, and in Monroe and Nock, *The Law of Stamp Duties* (6th edn.), pp. 93–96 inclusive). It was therefore sensible in order to avoid adjudication problems in cases of doubt, wherever a "conveyance or transfer" of property (whether by way of gift or otherwise) was contemplated, for the transaction to be effected for a cash or debt consideration. As long as such a consideration was given, the transaction would for stamp duty purposes have been regarded as a "sale" (even if at an undervalue) and the need for adjudication would have been avoided. If consideration was given in the form of stocks or marketable or other securities, although the transaction would then have been one of sale, adjudication would still have been required in order to value the consideration.

Section 82 (5) must now be read in the light of the Stamp Duty (Exempt Instruments) Regulations 1987, (S.I. 1987 No. 516) made pursuant to FA 1985, s. 87.

83. Transfers in connection with divorce etc. (S&S 127, 313)

An instrument executed on or after 26 March 1985 transferring property was to attract the fixed duty of only 50p and not *ad valorem* duty under the heading "conveyance or transfer on sale" in SA 1891, Sch. 1, if it involved the conveyance or transfer of property from one party to a marriage (which it is presumed also included a former marriage) to the other and the instrument:

(*a*) was executed in pursuance of an order of a court made on granting in respect of the parties a decree of divorce, nullity of marriage or judicial separation; or

(*b*) was executed in pursuance of an order of a court made in connection with the dissolution or annulment of the marriage or the parties' judicial separation and was made at any time after the granting of such a decree; or

(*c*) was executed at any time in pursuance of an agreement of the parties made in contemplation of or otherwise in connection with the dissolution or annulment of the marriage or their judicial separation.

All such instruments are now exempt from any duty by virtue of S.I. 1987 No. 516, made under FA 1985, s. 87, provided that the conditions as to certification set out in those Regulations are satisfied.

Most transfers of property on the break-up of a marriage will be by the way of a gift and therefore exempt from stamp duty under s. 82 (gifts *inter vivos*) and the provisions of S.I. 1987 No. 516 relevant to s. 82. However, not all transfers of property from one spouse to another will inevitably escape duty under these provisions. Transfers involving actual consideration, equivalent to cash for stamp duty purposes, will be dutiable as conveyances on sale. For example, a transfer of property subject to a mortgage which the transferee agrees to discharge will be stampable under SA 1891, s. 57. (See SP 6/90.) Even property adjustments involving, for example, an exchange of property between the spouses or former spouses may constitute a transaction for valuable consideration stampable as a conveyance on sale (see *e.g.*, *Re Abbott* [1983] Ch. 45) and therefore not exempt from *ad valorem* duty under s. 82.

The further exemptions given by this section and the relevant provisions of S.I. 1987 No. 516 were designed to remove the above uncertainties. They do, however, have limitations. In particular, the further exemptions apply only to transfers between the parties to the marriage, and not also, for example, to transfers made by one spouse to trustees for the benefit of the children of the marriage.

84. Death: varying dispositions, and appropriations. (S&S 313–314)

Where, within two years after a person's death, any of the dispositions (whether effected by will, under the laws relating to intestacy or otherwise) of the property of which he was competent to dispose are varied by an instrument executed by the person or any of the persons who benefit or would benefit under the relevant disposition, stamp duty under the heading "conveyance or transfer on sale" in SA 1891, Sch. 1 is not chargeable on the instrument.

The exemption applies whether or not the administration of the estate is complete or the property has been distributed in accordance with the original disposition, but it does not apply where the variation is made for any consideration in money or money's worth other than consideration consisting of the making of a variation in respect of another of the original dispositions.

Where property is appropriated by a personal representative in or towards satisfaction of a general legacy of money, stamp duty under the "conveyance or transfer on sale" head of charge is not chargeable on the instrument giving effect to the appropriation.

Where on an intestacy property is appropriated by a personal representative in or towards satisfaction of any interest of a surviving husband or wife in the intestate's estate (including the capital value of life interests redeemed under the Intestates' Estates Act 1952), then stamp duty is not chargeable on an instrument giving effect to the appropriation.

In any such case, the relevant instrument was required to be adjudicated under SA 1891, s. 12, and any instrument qualifying for the exemption was liable only to the fixed duty of 50p. Now, by virtue of S.I. 1987 No. 516 made under FA 1985, s. 87, all such instruments are exempt from any duty (provided that the conditions as to certification set out in those Regulations are satisfied) and need not be submitted for adjudication under SA 1891, s. 12.

Again, a deed of family arrangement will normally be exempt from stamp duty by virtue of the repeal of F(1909–10)A 1910, s. 74 (gifts *inter vivos*) and the provisions of S.I. 1987 No. 516 relevant to documents formerly chargeable under the abolished provisions. However, it is possible for a family arrangement to amount to a sale, and this section and the relevant provisions of S.I. 1987 No. 516 provide specific exemptions to cover any such circumstances.

85. Repeal of certain fixed duties. (S&S 315)
This section, coupled with Sch. 24, abolished a large number of fixed duties chargeable under various heads of charge in SA 1891, Sch. 1, most of which were obsolete and had ceased to be of any practical effect.

87. Certificates. (S&S 315–316, 349–352)
This section provides for the introduction, by way of regulations to be issued by the Commissioners from time to time, of a system of certification rendering adjudication unnecessary. The regulations may provide that as regards instruments of a specified kind, which will normally attract the fixed duty, the inclusion of an appropropriate certificate signed by appropriate parties shall be sufficient to render that instrument as being duly stamped.

The Treasury, in exercise of the powers conferred on them by this section, have made the Stamp Duty (Exempt Instruments) Regulations 1987 (S.I. 1987 No. 516) which came into force on 1 May 1987.

These Regulations (reproduced in Appendix 1) provide that an instrument which:
(*a*) is executed on or after 1 May 1987, and
(*b*) is of a kind specified in the Schedule to the Regulations, and
(*c*) is certified by a certificate which fulfills the conditions set out in the Regulations to be an instrument of that kind,
shall be exempt from duty under the "Conveyance or transfer of any kind not hereinbefore described" and "Disposition in Scotland of any property or of any right or interest therein not described in this Schedule" heads of charge in SA 1891, Sch. 1 and FA 1985, ss. 83 (2) and 84 (8).

The required certificate:
(*a*) must be in writing and—
   (i) be included as part of the instrument, or
   (ii) be endorsed upon or, where separate, be physically attached to the instrument concerned;
(*b*) must contain a sufficient description of:
   (i) the instrument concerned where the certificate is separate but physically attached to the instrument, and
   (ii) the category in the Schedule to the Regulations into which the instrument falls; and
(*c*) (i) must be signed by the transferor or grantor or by his solicitor or duly authorised agent, and
   (ii) where it is not signed by the transferor or grantor or by his solicitor, must contain a statement by the signatory of the capacity in which he signs, that he is authorised so to sign and that he gives the certificate from his own knowledge of the facts stated in it.

Any instrument which is certified in accordance with these Regulations is not required under FA 1985, s. 82 (5) or s. 84 (9) to be adjudicated in accordance with SA 1891, s. 12.

The Schedule to the Regulations provides that an instrument which effects any one or more of the following transactions only is an instrument specified for the purposes of the Regulations:

A. The vesting of property subject to a trust in the trustees of the trust on the appointment of a new trustee, or in continuing trustees on the retirement of a trustee.

B. The conveyance or transfer of property the subject of a specific devise or legacy to the beneficiary named in the will (or his nominee).

C. The conveyance or transfer of property which forms part of an intestate's estate to the person entitled on intestacy (or his nominee).

D. The appropriation of property within FA 1985, s. 84 (4) (death: appropriation in satisfaction of a general legacy of money) or s. 84 (5) or (7) (death: appropriation in satisfaction of any interest of surviving spouse and in Scotland also of any interest of issue).

E. The conveyance or transfer of property which forms part of the residuary estate of a testator to a beneficiary (or his nominee) entitled solely by virtue of his entitlement under the will.

F. The conveyance or transfer of property out of a settlement in or towards satisfaction of a beneficiary's interest, not being an interest acquired for money or money's worth, being a conveyance or transfer constituting a distribution of property in accordance with the provisions of the settlement.

G. The conveyance or transfer of property on and in consideration only of marriage to a party to the marriage (or his nominee) or to trustees to be held on the terms of a settlement made in consideration only of the marriage.

H. The conveyance or transfer of property within FA 1985, s. 83 (1) (transfers in connection with divorce etc.).

I. The conveyance or transfer by the liquidator of property which formed part of the assets of the company in liquidation to a shareholder of that company (or his nominee) in or towards satisfaction of the shareholder's rights on a winding up.

J. The grant in fee simple of an easement in or over land for no consideration in money or money's worth.

K. The grant of a servitude for no consideration in money or money's worth.

L. The conveyance or transfer of property operating as a voluntary disposition *inter vivos* for no consideration in money or money's worth nor any consideration referred to in SA 1891, s. 57 (conveyance in consideration of a debt etc.).

M. The conveyance or transfer of property by an instrument within FA 1985, s. 84 (1) (death: varying disposition).

In their general notes for guidance issued with the new Regulations (see Appendix 8), the Revenue suggested that an appropriate form of words for the certificate would be as follows:

"I/We hereby certify that this instrument falls within category . . . in the Schedule to the Stamp Duty (Exempt Instruments) Regulations 1987" (the gap to be completed with the letter opposite the category of instrument as listed in the Schedule to the Regulations).

All instruments specified in the Regulations, if duly certified, will be deemed to be duly stamped and need not be produced to, or adjudicated by, the Stamp Duty Office. Once certified, the relevant documents can be sent straight to the registrar or other person who needs to act upon them, if any.

Notwithstanding these Regulations, where there is any doubt as to whether or not a particular instrument can be properly endorsed with the appropriate certificate, it remains possible for that instrument to be submitted to the Stamp Duty Office for adjudication pursuant to SA 1891, s. 12. The Stamp Duty Office cannot refuse to adjudicate a document submitted to it simply because on the face of it it appears to come within the list of documents specified in the Schedule to the Regulations. Whilst the new system will undoubtedly reduce the workload of the Stamp Duty Office and generally speed up the completion of transactions of the kind specified in the Regulations, it does transfer the burden of deciding whether or not a document is duly stamped away from the Stamp Duty Office and on to the professional advisers of the parties to a particular transaction. It may be anticipated, therefore, that professional advisers will, in cases of doubt, submit documents for adjudication rather than run the risk of being held to have misinterpreted the Regulations.

The law in relation to a number of the transactions specified in the Schedule to the Regulations is extremely complex, and this is particularly so in relation to category L: "the conveyance or transfer of property operating as a voluntary disposition *inter vivos* for no consideration in money or money's worth nor any consideration referred to in SA 1891, s. 57 (conveyance in consideration of a debt etc.)." The requirement that the conveyance or transfer be "for no consideration in money or money's worth", nor any debt consideration, arguably leaves a residual category of transactions falling within the abolished provisions relating to "voluntary dispositions *inter vivos*" which do still require to be adjudicated.

It will be seen from the commentary in relation to FA 1985, s. 82 (5) that any conveyance or transfer operating as a voluntary disposition *inter vivos*, within the meaning of the abolished provisions, was required to be adjudicated if it was not stampable as a "conveyance or transfer on sale". It was only, therefore, transactions involving a consideration in cash, stock, marketable or other securities, or debts, *i.e.*, transactions "on sale" for the purposes of SA 1891, where the need for adjudication was avoided. If there was no such consideration, the instrument had to be adjudicated. Where, therefore, a transaction involves some consideration "in money's worth" which is not cash, stock, marketable or other securities, or debts, then it will not be "on sale", and will not therefore avoid the need for adjudication under s. 82 (5), nor will it be within category L of the new Regulations. Whatever the correct interpretation of the Regulations, their very obscurity in such matters may result in the parties to a transaction minimising their own risks by withholding the appropriate certificate and submitting the relevant document for adjudication.

Somewhat surprisingly, the Regulations do not themselves impose any penalties or sanctions in relation to the giving of an improper certificate. Therefore, as is the case with "certificates of value" given under FA 1963, s. 55 (1) and FA 1938, s. 34 (4), the only sanction will be imposed by SA 1891, s. 5. This imposes a fine of £25 on every person who, with intent to defraud Her Majesty, executes or prepares any instrument in which all the facts and circumstances affecting the liability of that instrument to stamp duty, or the amount of the duty with which it is chargeable, are not fully and truly set forth. However, in the absence of bad faith, *i.e.*, where there is no intent to defraud Her Majesty and an incorrect certificate is given in good faith that it is correct, the sanction will not be available. In the light of that, and the paltry amount of the penalty, s. 5 is unlikely to prove an effective deterrent.

Only the penalties for late stamping which may be imposed in relation to a document (on which a certificate is given) that subseqeuntly proves to have been stampable may prove an effective deterrent, assuming, that is, that the document proves to have been liable to *ad valorem* duty and not merely the fixed duty of 50p! Otherwise the only effective check on the misuse of certificates will be the good faith and professional conduct of the parties and their advisers.

88. Exchange rates. (S&S 316)

Where the amount on which stamp duty is payable is expressed in a foreign currency, SA 1891, s. 6 provided that the amount was to be converted into sterling at the rate applying on the date of the document. This section removes the exception made by FA 1899, s. 12 which provided for certain specified currencies to be converted at rates published by the Board of Inland Revenue; all foreign currency amounts are converted at the rate applying on the date of the document.

89. Exemption from section 28 of Finance Act 1931. (S&S 316–317, 324–327)
FA 1931, s. 28, requires any transfer on the sale of the fee simple of land, any lease on land granted for a term of seven years or more, and any transfer on sale of any lease for a term of seven years or more, to be produced to the Stamp Office, whether or not duty is payable, together with a form (known as the "Particulars Delivered Form") summarising the details of the transaction. In addition to any *ad valorem* duty stamp, the document is then stamped with a "produced stamp", without which it is not deemed to have been duly stamped.

The Commissioners may make regulations prescribing classes of document in relation to which the above requirements need not be met.

Pursuant to the above power, the Stamp Duty (Exempt Instruments) Regulations 1985, SI 1985 No. 1688 provide that with effect from 1 January 1986 FA 1931, s 28 no longer applies to:

"Instruments by means of which any transfer on sale within the meaning of paragraphs (*a*) or (*c*) of Section 28(1) of the Finance Act 1931 is effected and in respect of which the following conditions are fulfilled:

(*a*) the instrument is executed on or after 1 January 1896;

(*b*) the consideration for the sale is of an amount or value such that no stamp duty is chargeable and the instrument is certified in accordance with s. 34(4) of the Finance Act 1958; and

(*c*) (i) the land in question is registered land; or

(ii) in the case of land which is not registered land it is an instrument:

(*a*) to which Section 123 of the Land Registration Act 1925 applies, or

(*b*) which effects a transfer in the case of which under rule 72 of the Land Registration Rules 1925 the transferee is deemed to be the applicant for first registration."

The new arrangements accordingly apply to all sales of freehold or leasehold property which are required to be registered with the Land Registry and which are below the threshold for stamp duty (currently £30,000).

The new arrangements do not apply to sales of property which attract stamp duty, sales which do not fall to be registered with the Land Registry, the grant of a new lease, or sales of property in Scotland and Northern Ireland, to which different procedures apply.

The regulations do not affect the need to complete a "Particulars Delivered Form," but this, together with the conveyancing documents, is sent direct to the Land Registry and the Land Registry pass the "Particulars Delivered Form" to the Revenue.

The Stamp Office and the Land Registry have jointly issued further detailed instructions, see Appendix 1 under S.I. 1985 No. 1688.

PART V MISCELLANEOUS AND SUPPLEMENTARY

96. European Communities and Investment Bank: exemptions. (S&S 317–318)

98. Short title, interpretation, construction and repeals. (S&S 318)

Finance Act 1986
1986 Chapter 41

[*N.B.* In relation to the prospective abolition of all stamp duties on transactions in shares (including bearer instruments) and units under unit trust schemes, and of stamp duty reserve tax, see the Revenue Press Release, 20 March 1990 and the commentary on FA 1990.]

PART III STAMP DUTY

SECURITIES

64. Stock or marketable securities: reduction of rate. (S&S 328)
The duty payable on transfers of stock or marketable securities is reduced to 50p for every £100 or part of £100 of the consideration where the relevant instrument is executed in pursuance of a contract made on or after 27 October 1986 (the day on which the rule of The Stock Exchange prohibiting a person from carrying on business both as a broker and as a jobber was abolished).

[*Note:* See note at commencement of commentary on this Act.]

65. Bearers: consequential provisions etc. (S&S 328–329)
The rate of duty payable on the issue of bearer instruments is reduced to 1.5 per cent. in respect of (i) inland bearer instruments issued on or after 27 October 1986 and (ii) overseas bearer instruments on the first transfer made in the U.K. on or after that date. The duty (10p per £50 or part of £50) on depositary certificates for overseas stock and overseas bearer instruments by usage remains unchanged, as does the 10p fixed duty on substitute bearer instruments.

[*Note:* See note at commencement of commentary on this Act.]

66. Company's purchase of own shares. (S&S 329)
Shares in a company which are purchased by that company pursuant to the Companies Act 1985, s. 162, can be surrendered and delivered to the company by the relevant shareholder without any instrument of transfer, but pursuant to the Companies Act 1985, s. 169, within a period of 28 days from the date on which the shares are purchased the company must deliver to the Registrar of Companies a return (on Form 169, reproduced at **S&S 330**) giving certain prescribed particulars, together with (where a contract is entered into between the company and the relevant shareholder) a copy of the contract if it is in writing or, if it is oral, a memorandum of its terms.

With effect from 27 October 1986 the 0.5 per cent. rate of duty applies to a purchase by a company of its own shares, and the statutory return required under s. 169 is to be treated as an instrument transferring the shares on sale and liable for stamp duty accordingly. On the other hand, the Stamp Office seems to accept that an agreement by a company for the purchase of its own shares is not an agreement falling within s. 87 (1), so that no charge to stamp duty reserve tax will arise in relation to any such agreement.

[*Note:* See note at commencement of commentary on this Act.]

DEPOSITARY RECEIPTS

67. Depositary receipts. (S&S 332)
Before the enactment of this section, *ad valorem* stamp duty at the normal rate was payable on transfers of shares to a person (usually a bank) who issued depositary receipts in respect of them, or to a person (usually known as the custodian) who was to hold them as nominee for such issuer. Duty was payable either because the transfers themselves amounted to "conveyances on sale" or (where the depositary receipts were initially issued to the transferor, so that there was initially no change in beneficial ownership) because they were treated as transfers "in contemplation of a sale" under SA 1891, s. 90. However, transfers of the depositary receipts subsequently issued (unlike transfers of the underlying shares) seldom attract *ad valorem* stamp duty because the receipts are usually in registered form, with the register of holders being situated overseas, and transfers are normally executed overseas and not brought into the U.K. (as, for example, is the case with the most common variety—American Depositary Receipts, or "ADRs"). The section was enacted to compensate for the fact that (as stated in the Revenue's press release of 18 March 1986) "a substantial slice of the market in certain U.K. shares has been diverted to the market in American Depositary Receipts in New York"; it effectively renders transfers to depositary receipt issuers or their nominees liable to triple the normal amount of *ad valorem* duty.

Section 67 applies to "transfers" (*i.e.*, not direct allotments, deliveries of bearer securities, or renunciations of renounceable letters of allotment, although in certain circumstances an equivalent charge to stamp duty reserve tax will apply) of "relevant securities" (defined in s. 69 (3)) of a company incorporated in the United Kingdom, to a person who at the time of the transfer is:

(*a*) a person whose business is exclusively that of holding relevant securities as nominee or agent for a person whose business is or includes issuing "depositary receipts" (defined in s. 69 (1)) for relevant securities, where the transfer is for the purpose of the issue of depositary receipts; or

(*b*) a person whose business is or includes issuing depositary receipts for relevant securities who is specified for the purposes of these provisions by the Treasury by statutory instrument; or

(*c*) a person who is specified for the purposes of these provisions by the Treasury by statutory instrument whose business is not exclusively that of a nominee (as described in (*a*) above) but whose business includes holding relevant securities as nominee or agent for a person whose business is or includes issuing depositary receipts for relevant securities, and he holds the relevant securities as nominee or agent for such person for the purpose of the issue of depositary receipts.

If the relevant instrument of transfer is chargeable under the heading "conveyance or transfer on sale" in SA 1891, Sch. 1, it is dutiable at the rate of £1.50 for every £100 or part of £100 of the amount or value of the consideration for the sale to which the instrument gives effect.

However, where the transaction is not one of sale, and the relevant instrument of transfer is chargeable under the heading "conveyance or transfer of any kind not hereinbefore described" (*i.e.*, it is chargeable to the fixed duty of 50p.) then, although the rate of duty is the same as that mentioned above (*i.e.*, £1.50 for every £100 or part of £100), it is in this case charged on the *market value* of the securities on the date of execution of the instrument and not on the amount or value of the consideration for the sale.

In any case where:

(i) at the time of the transfer the transferor is a qualified dealer in securities of the kind concerned (defined in s. 69 (6)) or a nominee of such a qualified dealer; and

(ii) the transfer is made for the purposes of the dealer's business; and

(iii) at the time of the transfer the dealer is not a market maker in securities of the kind concerned (defined in s. 69 (7)) and

(iv) the instrument contains a statement that these conditions are fulfilled;

then the duty on instruments stampable under the heading "conveyance or transfer of any kind not hereinbefore described" is reduced to £1 for every £100 or part of £100 of the value of the securities at the date the instrument is executed.

Where securities are issued or transferred for a consideration to be paid in instalments, and the securities are initially held by a person who holds them until the last instalment has been paid and then transfers them to another person by means of an instrument of transfer which would normally be liable only to 50p duty as a "conveyance or transfer of any kind not hereinbefore described", and before the latter instrument is executed an interim instrument evidencing the rights in the shares is delivered to a person of the kind described in paragraphs (*a*)–(*c*) above, then (provided that the instrument of transfer contains a statement that these conditions have been fulfilled) the instrument of transfer is chargeable at the rate of £1 per £100 or part of £100 of the total of the instalments payable on the shares, less those paid before the instrument of transfer is executed. These provisions are designed to prevent the new charge relating to depositary schemes from applying to companies being privatised by the Government, where shares subscribed are frequently payable in instalments (as, for example, in the case of British Gas plc).

When an instrument transfers relevant securities of a company incorporated in the U.K. from one U.K. resident company to another U.K. resident company, both of whose businesses are exclusively those of holding relevant securities as nominee or agent for a depositary (as described in sub-paragraph (*a*) above), then a maximum duty of 50p is payable on that instrument.

All the above provisions apply to any instrument executed on or after 27 October 1986, the day on which the rule of The Stock Exchange prohibiting a person from carrying on business both as a broker and as a jobber was abolished.

For names of nominee companies, see Inland Revenue Press Release, 24 October 1986 and 14 June 1989.

[*Note:* See note at commencement of commentary on this Act.]

68. Depositary receipts: notification. (S&S 333–334)

Any person whose business is or includes issuing depositary receipts for relevant securities of a company incorporated in the U.K. is required to notify the Commissioners of that fact within one month of the date on which he first issues such depositary receipts. Any person whose business includes (but does not exclusively consist of) holding relevant securities of a company incorporated in the U.K. as nominee or agent for a person whose business is or includes issuing depositary receipts, and for the purposes of issuing depositary receipts, is also required to notify the Commissioners of that fact within one month of the date on which he first holds such securities as such nominee or agent and for such purpose. Failure to notify in either case renders the relevant person liable to a fine of up to £1,000.

A company incorporated in the U.K. which becomes aware that any of its shares are held by a person who is required to notify the Commissioners within the above provisions is itself required to notify the Commissioners of that fact within one month of becoming aware of the holding, and failure to do so renders it liable to a fine of up to £100.

The fines imposed by this section are recoverable as civil debts under the provisions of SA 1891, s. 121.

[*Note:* See note at commencement of commentary on this Act.]

69. Depositary receipts: supplementary. (S&S 334–335)

"Depositary receipt for relevant securities" means an instrument acknowledging that a person holds the relevant securities, or evidence of the right to receive them, and that another person is entitled to rights, whether expressed as units or otherwise, in or in relation to relevant securities of the same kind, including the right to receive such securities (or the evidence of the right to receive them) from the person who holds the securities or evidence of the right to receive them. Basically, this effectively means that a depositary receipt is a document entitling the holder or bearer to rights in shares which are held by the receipt issuer or his nominee.

There is an express exclusion for instruments acknowledging rights in or in relation to securites issued or sold on terms providing for payment in instalments and for the issue of the instrument as evidence that an instalment has been paid; as in s. 67, this is designed to avoid the Government's privatisation schemes falling within the charge for depositary schemes.

The Treasury can change the definition of "depositary receipt" for the purposes of ss. 67 and 68.

"Relevant securities" means shares or stock or marketable securities of any company which (unless otherwise stated) need not be incorporated in the U.K.

For the purposes of s. 67 (3) the value of securities at the date the instrument is executed is to be taken as the price they might reasonably be expected to fetch on a sale at that time in the open market.

The penalties contained in SA 1891, s. 15 (2) are rendered applicable to instruments chargeable under these provisions under the heading "conveyance or transfer of any kind not hereinbefore described". The penalties already apply to instruments chargeable as "conveyances or transfers on sale".

A person is treated as a qualified dealer in securities of a particular kind if he is a member of a recognised stock exchange (within the meaning of TA 1988, s. 841) or is designated as a qualified dealer by the Treasury, and deals in securities of the relevant kind.

A person is treated as a market maker in securities of a particular kind if he holds himself out at all normal times in compliance with the rules of The Stock Exchange as willing to buy or sell securities of that kind at a price specified by him, and he is recognised as so doing by the Council of The Stock Exchange. This definition is the same as that contained in FA 1986, ss. 82 (borrowing of stock by market makers) and 94 (stamp duty reserve tax provisions relating to depositary receipts) and is to be contrasted with the definitions in ss. 81 (3) and 89 (3) (stamp duty and stamp duty reserve tax exemptions in relation to sales to market makers) which, as amended, extend to transactions in unlisted securities by authorised persons under the Financial Services Act 1986.

The Treasury can alter the definition of a market maker in securities of a particular kind.

Unfortunately, for the purposes of the above definitions (and the similar definitions used in other contexts in the later provisions of the Act, and in particular s. 81) the expression "securities of the kind concerned" is not further defined. The expression is obviously intended to be used, in its narrowest sense, as meaning a specific class of shares in a specific company and that is the way the expression is construed by the Revenue as a matter of practice. The Revenue also accepts that there can (within the meaning of these definitions) be a "market maker" in relation to an offer for sale or new issue, where the company is making its début on the market, despite the fact that a narrow interpretation would logically preclude this. It has been suggested that the legislation admits a broader interpretation, but such a view, if correct, would obviously make a nonsense of the provisions and is unlikely to be supportable.

All powers of the Treasury to make regulations or orders pursuant to this section are to be exercisable by statutory instrument.

Before FA 1987 it was arguable that where a depositary scheme involved the depositary holding a "pool" of underlying securities in which the receipt holders had a proportionate interest, rather than an interest attaching to specific shares in the pool, the scheme fell within the definition of "unit trust scheme" contained in FA 1946, s. 57 (1). This would have meant that any deed setting up the scheme and relating to its overall operation would have been regarded as a unit trust instrument liable to unit trust instrument duty (since abolished by FA 1988, s. 140) at the rate of 25p for every £100 or part of £100 of the amount or value of the shares comprised in the scheme or added thereto from time to time, unless the scheme could be shown to be in the nature of a contract rather than a trust. Any such charge might have been avoided if there was no instrument setting up the scheme or relating to its overall operation and the terms and conditions were contained in the receipts themselves. However, FA 1987, s. 48 amended FA 1946, s. 57 (1) by importing the definition of "unit trust scheme" in the Financial Services Act 1986, s. 75 and s. 75 (6) (*h*) seems to exclude arrangements of the kind involved in depositary schemes.

The provisions of ss. 67, 68 and 69 apply only to the transfer of the underlying securities into a depositary scheme. The depositary receipts themselves will be stampable either (*a*) on transfer under the "conveyance or transfer on sale" head of charge (if they are in registered form) or (*b*) under the "bearer instrument" head of charge (if, as they normally will be, they are in bearer form) on issue (if they are inland bearer instruments) or on their first transfer in the U.K. (if they are overseas bearer instruments), for which purpose the determining factor will be the place of incorporation of the depositary itself.

[*Note:* See note at commencement of commentary on this Act.]

CLEARANCE SERVICES

70. Clearance services. (S&S 335–337)

The provisions of this section in relation to clearance services were introduced in the light of the existence of computerised settlement systems (such as Euroclear) which enable U.K. shares to be traded without payment of stamp duty, and are almost identical to the provisions of s. 67 in relation to depositary receipts. The section applies where an instrument "transfers" (*i.e.*, excluding direct allotments, deliveries of bearer securities and renunciations of renounceable letters of allotment) "relevant securities" of a company incorporated in the U.K. to a person who at the time of the transfer is:

(*a*) a person whose business is exclusively that of holding shares, stock or other marketable securities (whether relevant securities or not) as nominee or agent for a person whose business is or includes the provision of clearance services for the purchase and sale of such securities, and the transfer is for the purpose of the provision of such services; or

(*b*) a person who is specified for the purposes of these provisions by the Treasury and whose business is or includes the provision of clearance services for the purchase and sale of relevant securities; or

(*c*) a person who is specified for the purposes of these provisions by the Treasury whose business is not exclusively that of holding relevant securities as nominee (as described in sub-paragraph (*a*) above) but whose business includes holding relevant securities as nominee or agent for a person whose business is or includes the provision of clearance services for the purchase and sale of relevant securities at the time of transfer, and holds relevant securities as nominee or agent for such person for the purposes of the provision of such services.

If stamp duty is chargeable on the relevant instrument under the heading "conveyance or transfer on sale" in SA 1891, Sch. 1, the rate at which the duty is charged is to be £1.50 for every £100 or part of £100 of the amount or value of the consideration for the sale.

If stamp duty is chargeable on the instrument under the heading "conveyance or transfer of any kind not hereinbefore described" in SA 1891, Sch. 1, the rate at which the duty is charged is to be £1.50 for every £100 or part of £100 of the value of the securities at the date the instrument is executed rather than the value of the consideration for the instrument.

The rate payable under the heading "conveyance or transfer of any kind not hereinbefore described" is reduced to £1 for every £100 or part of £100 of the value of the securities in any case where:

(i) at the time of the transfer the transferor is a qualified dealer in securities of the kind concerned or a nominee of such qualified dealer; and

(ii) the transfer is made for the purposes of the dealer's business; and

(iii) at the time of the transfer the dealer is not a market maker in securities of the kind concerned; and

(iv) the instrument contains a statement that the above conditions are fulfilled.

Subsection (5) is identical to s. 67 (5), and deals with any case where securities are issued or transferred on sale, upon terms that (in either case) they are to be paid for in instalments, to a person who holds them until the last instalment is paid and then transfers them to another person, and the transfer to the other person is effected by an instrument chargeable under the heading "conveyance or transfer of any kind not hereinbefore described". If, before the latter instrument's execution, an interim instrument evidencing the rights in the securities is received by a person within the description in paragraphs (*a*)–(*c*) above, then (provided that the instrument is certified to the effect that the above conditions are fulfilled) the duty chargeable is £1.50 for every £100 or part of £100 of the total of the instalments payable, less than those paid before the instrument of transfer is executed.

Where an instrument transfers relevant securities of a company incorporated in the U.K. from one nominee of a provider of clearance services to another such nominee, both of which are resident in the U.K., then there is the same limitation on the stamp duty (a maximum of 50p) as that contained in s. 67 (9) in relation to transfers between nominees for persons who issue depositary receipts.

These provisions also apply to instruments executed on or after 27 October 1986, *i.e.*, the day on which the rule of The Stock Exchange prohibiting a person from carrying on business both as a broker and as a jobber was abolished.

For names of nominee companies, see Inland Revenue Press Release, 24 October 1986.

[*Note:* See note at commencement of commentary on this Act.]

71. Clearance services: notification. (S&S 337–338)
A person whose business is or includes the provision of clearance services for the purchase and sale of relevant securities of a company incorporated in the U.K. is required to notify the Commissioners of this fact within one month of commencing to provide such services. A person whose business includes (but does not exclusively consist of) holding relevant securities of a company incorporated in the U.K. as nominee or agent for a person whose business is or includes the provision of clearance services, and for the purpose of such business, must notify the Commissioners of that fact within one month of the date on which he first holds such relevant securities as such nominee or agent and for such purpose. Any person who fails to make the appropriate notification in accordance with these provisions is liable to a fine of up to £1,000.

A company incorporated in the U.K. which becomes aware that any of its shares are held by persons who are required to notify the Commissioners in accordance with the above provisions must itself notify the Commissioners of that fact within one month of the date on which it becomes aware of it, and failure to do so renders the company liable to a fine of up to £100.

All fines imposed by this section are recoverable under SA 1891, s. 121.

[*Note:* See note at commencement of commentary on this Act.]

72. Clearance services: supplementary. (S&S 338)
"Relevant securities" means shares in or stock or marketable securities of any company which (unless otherwise stated) need not be incorporated in the U.K.

For the purpose of s. 70 (3) the value of securities at the date of execution of an instrument is to be deemed to be the price they might reasonably be expected to fetch on a sale in the open market on that date.

The penalties of s. 15 (2) apply to instruments chargeable under these provisions under the heading "conveyance or transfer of any kind not hereinbefore described". The penalties already apply to instruments chargeable under these provisions under the heading "conveyance or transfer on sale".

For the purposes of s. 70 (4) the definition contained in s. 67 (4) of "qualified dealer" and "market maker" apply.

As with depositary schemes, under the definition of "unit trust scheme" which for stamp duty purposes applied before FA 1987, it was possible that any document setting up and governing the overall operation of a clearance system might have been chargeable to the now abolished unit trust instrument duty as a unit trust instrument if the provider of the services held a "pool" of securities in which the members had proportionate rather than specific interests. However, clearance systems seem to be specifically excluded from the definition of "unit trust schemes" by virtue of the Financial Services Act 1986, s. 75 (6) (i).

The expression "clearance services" is not defined. Concern has been expressed that the provision of any nominee services to facilitate dealings in securities could be within its meaning. The Revenue have indicated that this is not the intention, and that their policy is to construe the expression so as to include only arrangements which are expressly marketed as "clearance services". In cases of doubt, the Revenue's guidance should be sought.

[*Note:* See note at commencement of commentary on this Act.]

RECONSTRUCTIONS AND ACQUISITIONS

75. Acquisitions: reliefs. (S&S 381–382, 384–385)
This section applies where a company (the "acquiring company") acquires the whole or part of the undertaking of another company (the "target company") in pursuance of a scheme for the reconstruction of the target company. It replaces the reliefs formally available under FA 1927, s. 55 and FA 1985, ss. 78, 79, and 80.

The reliefs formerly available under FA 1927, s. 55 were available for both reconstructions and amalgamations, which were technically very different. The fact that the new provisions do not refer to "amalgamations" means that the relief will only be available for "reconstructions", so that many forms of corporate reorganisation in respect of which relief was formerly available will not now qualify for exemption from stamp duty. An analysis of the technical construction of both the term "reconstruction" and the term "amalgamation" is required to determine what does qualify and what does not.

For the purposes of FA 1927, s. 55, a scheme for the reconstruction of a company comprised a transfer of the undertaking, or part of the undertaking, of an existing company to a new company, the new company having substantially the same members as had the existing company and carrying on substantially the same business as the business transferred to it (see generally the cases of *Hooper* v. *Western Counties and South Wales Telephone Co. Ltd.* [1892] 68 LT 78; *Re South African Supply and Cold Storage Co.* [1904] 2 Ch. 268; *Brooklands Selangor Holdings Ltd.* v. *I.R. Comrs.* [1970] 2 All ER 76; *Baytrust Holdings Ltd* v *I.R. Comrs.* [1971] 3 All ER 76).

The meaning of the words "scheme for the amalgamation of any companies" for the purpose of FA 1927, s. 55 was considered by the Court of Appeal in *Crane Fruehauf Limited* v *I.R. Comrs.*

[1975] 1 All ER 429. In that case it was held that an amalgamation consists of the combining of the businesses of more than one company in such a way that the businesses remain in substance owned by the same persons, which result could be achieved in one of two ways:

(a) by a transaction involving the business of an existing company (the transferor company) being acquired by another company (the transferee company) in return for an issue of shares in the transferee company to the transferor company or to the shareholders of the transferor company; or

(b) by a transaction involving the acquisition by the transferee company of shares of the transferor company in exchange for shares in the transferee company being issued to the shareholders of the transferor company.

It was also held in *Crane Fruehauf Ltd.* v. *I.R. Comrs.* that a scheme for reconstruction or amalgamation does not lose its character as such if it forms part of a larger scheme involving other transactions, so that in that case a scheme involving an acquisition of shares in return for shares plus cash was held to be a scheme for amalgamation and to retain its character as such notwithstanding that the vendor shareholders were obliged under the overall scheme to sell one third of the consideration shares issued to them.

It was not essential for the purposes of FA 1927, s. 55 that the company whose undertaking was being acquired, or which was being absorbed on amalgamation, should be put into liquidation (see the cases of *Re Walker' Settlement* [1935] Ch. 567, per Romer LJ at 583 and 585, and per Maugham J. at 589; *Lever Brothers Ltd.* v. *I.R. Comrs.* [1938] 2 KB 518 at 524 per Greene MR; and *Nestle Company Ltd* v. *I.R. Comrs.* [1935] Ch. 395 at 403, per Evershed MR).

It was, however, essential that, for there to be a scheme of reconstruction, there should after completion of the transaction be no change in the real ownership of the undertaking transferred (*Brooklands Selangor Holdings Ltd.* v. *I.R. Comrs.* [1970] 2 All ER 76 applying dicta of Lord Hanworth MR in the case of *Oswald Tillotson Ltd* v. *I.R. Comrs.* [1933] 1 KB 134 at 155). As a result, a partition, *i.e.*, the division of a company into two separate parts, the different parts going to different shareholders, is not a reconstruction. It was also essential that a reconstruction should involve the transfer of a *business*, or part of a business, which could be carried on as a genuinely independent trading activity, as a going concern, by the transferee company in the same way as it was carried on by the transferor (*Baytrust Holdings Ltd.* v. *I.R. Comrs.* [1971] 3 All ER 76) so that a mere distribution of assets not required by a company for the purposes of its business will not be within the definition.

The respective meanings of "reconstruction" and "amalgamation" in the context of FA 1927, s. 55 were more recently analysed by Ferris, J., in the case of *Swithland Investments Ltd.* v. *I.R. Comrs.* [1990] STC 469 in relation to a cleverly designed scheme to effect the sale by an existing company of part of its business and to accommodate the different future requirements of its shareholders by a series of transactions some of which were intended to fall within the section. It was held by the judge (applying the principles laid down in the *Baytrust* and *South African Supply and Cold Storage* cases) that the overall scheme actually involved a partition rather than a reconstruction or amalgamation (or a series of reconstructions or amalgamations) and relief was therefore denied.

Under the new s. 75, stamp duty under the heading "conveyance or transfer on sale" in SA 1891, Sch. 1 will not be chargeable on any instrument executed for the purposes of or in connection with the transfer of an undertaking (or part thereof) as part of a scheme of reconstruction, provided that two conditions are satisfied.

The first condition specified is that the registered office of the acquiring company is in the U.K. and the consideration for the acquisition:

(a) consists of or includes the issue of shares in the acquiring company to all the shareholders of the target company; and

(b) includes nothing else (if anything) but the assumption or discharge by the acquiring company of liabilities of the target company.

The second condition is that:

(a) the acquisition is affected for *bona fide* commercial reasons and does not form part of a scheme or arrangement of which the main purposes, or one of the main purposes, is avoidance of liability to stamp duty, income tax, corporation tax or capital gains tax; and

(b) after the acquisition has been made, each shareholder of each of the companies will be a shareholder of the other; and

(c) after the acquisition has been made, the proportion of shares of one of the companies held by any shareholder is the same as the proportion of shares of the other company held by that shareholder.

If these conditions are satisfied the exemption from stamp duty will be available, provided the relevant instruments are adjudicated under SA 1891, s. 12.

The requirement that the consideration must consist of or include the issue of shares in the acquiring company to *all* the shareholders of the target company is a departure from the traditional ideas of a "scheme of reconstruction" for which relief was formerly available under FA 1927, s. 55. Previously, it was only necessary to show that the new company had *substantially* the same members as the existing company (see for example *Brooklands Selangor Holdings Ltd* v. *I.R.*

Comrs. [1970] 2 All ER 76). The exemption will not be available under the new provisions if the holder of even a single share in the existing company does not receive a share or shares in the new company. This will have particular relevance in relation to a scheme of reconstruction where there may be dissentient shareholders under the Companies Act 1985, s. 582, but it will also make it essential to ensure that any nominee shareholders in the existing company also receives shares in the new company, and that no new nominees receive shares in the new company.

In addition, the consideration must consist *only* of shares or the assumption or discharge by the new company of liabilities of the existing company or both. Under FA 1927, s. 55 it was only necessary for 90 per cent. of the consideration to consist of shares or the discharge of liabilities or both, which made it possible for cash to be paid or loan stock to be issued for up to 10 per cent. of the existing company.

The second condition to the exemption involves *inter alia* a requirement that each shareholder of the new company ends up with exactly the same proportion of the issued share capital of the new company as he held in the issued share capital of the existing company, so that the consideration shares in the new company must be issued *exactly pro rata* to the shareholders of the existing company.

The meaning of the words "the consideration for the acquisition" has been judicially reviewed on a number of occasions in connection with the relief formerly available under FA 1927, s. 55. In the case of *Central and District Properties Ltd.* v. *I.R. Comrs.* [1966] 2 All ER 433 the majority view of the Court of Appeal and the House of Lords seemed to have been that consideration provided by an independent third party could be ignored, provided that the transferee company was not under any contractual obligation to procure that third party to make the consideration available. In that case the appellant company was a subsidiary of U. Ltd., 98 per cent. of whose ordinary share capital was held by two directors. The appellant company had a stock exchange quotation, but the parent company, U. Ltd., whose shares were very valuable, had not. In order to render U. Ltd.'s shares more marketable the two directors took steps to enable the whole of the shares of U. Ltd. to be acquired by the appellant company, of which they were also directors but of which they did not have shareholding control, with a view to a "merger" of the companies. Ordinary shares of the appellant company were accordingly sold by U. Ltd. to L. Ltd., an issuing house unconnected by shareholding either with U. Ltd. or the appellant company, so that the appellant company would cease to be a subsidiary of U. Ltd. (a subsidiary company being debarred by the Companies Act 1948, s. 27, from acquiring shares in its parent company). In order to induce 90 per cent. of the preference shareholders of U. Ltd to exchange their preference shares for preference shares of the appellant company, U. Ltd.'s preference shareholders were offered, in the event of the exchange offer becoming unconditional, transferable low priced options over certain ordinary shares of the appellant company. These ordinary shares were provided in part by U. Ltd. selling to L. Ltd. more shares in the appellant company, and as to the rest were to be provided by the two directors transferring shares to L. Ltd. Under FA 1927, s. 55 (1) (c) there would be exemption from *ad valorem* stamp duty on the transfers of shares involved in the "merger" if the "consideration for the acquisition" consisted as to not less than 90 per cent. thereof in the issue of shares by way of exchange. If the value of the option rights was part of the consideration, then less than 90 per cent. of the consideration would consist in the issue of shares by way of exchange, and the *ad valorem* stamp duty exemption would not apply. The inducement put forward to preference shareholders of U. Ltd. was in a circular accompanying an elaborate document entitled "merger proposals" (both documents being dated 25 June 1958) and addressed by the board of U. Ltd. and the appellant company to the shareholders of both companies. The circular stated that if the offers became unconditional L. Ltd. would in due course offer stock units of the appellant company to the preference shareholders of U. Ltd. by way of negotiable letters of entitlement, and that the rights under these could be sold. Accompanying the merger proposals were also the formal offers and other documents. In due course the offers became unconditional. The Commissioners assessed *ad valorem* stamp duty of £109,098 on the transaction on the basis that the condition of exemption provided by FA 1927, s. 55 (1) was not satisfied.

It was held that, taking the transaction as a whole, the appellant company had made itself legally responsible to ensure (or had warranted) that L. Ltd. would carry out the options offers. Accordingly the value of the options was part of the consideration for the acquisition of the preference shares in U. Ltd., the condition of FA 1927, s. 55 (1) (c) was not satisfied, and exemption from *ad valorem* stamp duty under s. 55 (1) was not established. The majority of the House of Lords, *obiter*, expressed the view that for the purposes of s. 55 (1) the natural meaning of the words "consideration for the acquisition" is the *quid pro quo* provided by, or moving from, the acquiring company. Consequently, a truly independent additional inducement from an independent source, at any rate if not devised as part of the scheme of reconstruction or amalgamation, will not be part of the "consideration for the acquisition".

If the transferee company by its contract with the shareholders of the existing company imposes a condition that in certain circumstances those shareholders on-sell a proportion of their consideration shares to a third party, then the consideration for the acquisition comprises the consideration shares which the vendor shareholders retain plus the cash, in the event, they receive for the sale to the third party: *Crane Fruehauf Ltd.* v. *I.R. Comrs.* [1975] 1 All ER 429.

For an issue of shares to form part of "the consideration for the acquisition", the shares must be issued to the recipients as beneficial owners, and where the recipients of the shares were not free to deal with them because they were bound by an agreement to transfer them to a third party, the shares were not issued to the recipients as beneficial owners and therefore did not form part of the consideration (see *Baytrust Holdings Ltd* v. *I.R. Comrs.* [1971] 3 All ER 76; *Thomas Firth and John Brown (Investments) Ltd* v. *I.R. Comrs.*). The word "issue" in the context of consideration shares for an acquisition means that the relevant shareholders must be registered in the register of members of the new company, so that the giving of renounceable letters of allotment will not suffice, and the consideration shares cannot be issued in the names of nominees for the persons entitled to them (see *Crane Fruehauf Ltd.* v. *I.R. Comrs.* and *Oswald Tillotson Ltd.* v. *I.R. Comrs.* cited above, and also *Brotex Cellulose Fibres* v. *I.R. Comrs.* [1933] 1KB 158 and *Murex* v. *I.R. Comrs.* [1933] 1 KB 173).

The above principles were reaffirmed, and the decisions in *Central and District Properties Ltd.* v. *I.R. Comrs.*, *Crane Fruehauf Ltd.* v. *I.R. Comrs.*, and *Baytrust Holdings Ltd.* v. *I.R. Comrs.* applied, in *I.R. Comrs.* v. *Kent Process Control Ltd.* [1989] STC 245.

In *I.R. Comrs.* v. *Kent Process Control Ltd.* the taxpayer company, Introl Ltd. (Introl) and BBK Investments Ltd. (BBK) were each wholly-owned subsidiaries of Brown Boveri Kent plc (the holding company). In 1979, under a scheme for the internal reorganisation of the companies, Introl and BBK agreed to transfer their undertakings, property and assets to the taxpayer company in return for the issue to them of new shares in the taxpayer company as equalled the net asset value of their undertakings and the discharge of their debts and liabilities. In July 1980 the taxpayer company resolved to increase its share capital by the creation of some 5,002,325 shares of £1 each and to allocate such new shares as to 2,765,952 to Introl and 2,236,373 to BBK. On 15 December 1980 Introl and BBK transferred their newly acquired shares to the holding company for a monetary consideration.

In respect of the taxpayer company's application for relief under FA 1927, s. 55 from stamp duty on the transfers to it of the undertakings of Introl and BBK, the Revenue claimed that (*a*) there had been no issue of shares by the taxpayer company to Introl and BBK within s. 55 (1) (*c*), and (*b*) even if there was such an issue "the consideration for the acquisition" by the taxpayer company of the undertakings of Introl and BBK did not "consist as to 90 per cent. thereof in the issue of shares" since it also included a monetary consideration to be provided by the holding company.

As to the first contention the Revenue submitted that Introl's and BBK's transfer of the shares in the taxpayer company to the holding company was one which the holding company could compel in spite of the absence of any formal agreement to that effect and that Introl and BBK were therefore never able to deal with those shares as they wished and accordingly never took them as beneficial owners. It was held as follows:

(1) To prevent Introl and BBK from holding the shares, allocated to them by the taxpayer company, as beneficial owners, the limitation on dealing with the shares must have been imposed by the taxpayer company as part of the consideration for the acquisition of the undertakings of Introl and BBK. Although the holding company could compel Introl and BBK, as its wholly owned subsidiaries, to transfer to it the new shares acquired by them from the taxpayer company, any such obligation to pass on those shares was not part of the consideration moving from the taxpayer company. Accordingly the shares had been issued to Introl and BBK within the meaning of FA 1927, s. 55 (1) (*c*) (i).

(2) The monetary consideration provided by the holding company for the transfer to it of the new shares did not emanate from the taxpayer company and accordingly was not part of the consideration for the acquisition by the taxpayer company of the undertakings of Introl and BBK. As the consideration for the acquisition consisted of 90 per cent. in the issue of the shares the conditions specified in s. 55 (1) had been fulfilled.

(3) The taxpayer company was therefore entitled to relief from stamp duty and the Revenue's claim failed.

The Stamp Duty Office have indicated that they will regard the requirement that the reconstruction be effected for *bona fide* commercial reasons (and not as part of a scheme or arrangement which has as its main purpose or one of its main purposes the avoidance of liability for stamp duty, income tax, corporation tax or capital gains tax) as being satisfied where clearance has been granted under CGTA 1979, s. 88 or TA 1970, s. 267 (3A).

The procedure for claims under ss. 75 to 77 is as follows:

(*a*) A statutory declaration is not required. A claim should be made in a letter signed by a responsible officer of the acquiring company (*e.g.*, the secretary or a director) or the company's professional advisers.

(*b*) The letter should include the following information and be accompanied by:

(i) the name, registered number and authorised and issued capital of the acquiring company at the relevant date;

(ii) the name, registered number and authorised and issued capital of the acquired company at the relevant date;

(iii) details of and the reason for the reconstruction;

(iv) details of the consideration paid and how it was satisfied;

(v) whether an application for clearance under CGTA 1979, s. 88, or TA 1970, s. 267 (3A) has been made to Board of Inland Revenue, and a copy of any application for clearance together with copies of any correspondence with Board of Inland Revenue;

(vi) confirmation that the shares in the acquiring company have been issued to the registered shareholders of the acquired company and that their names have been entered on the register of members of the acquiring company;

(vii) a copy of the certificate of incorporation of all relevant companies and all changes of names;

(viii) particulars of the register of members of the acquired company immediately prior to the transaction;

(ix) particulars of the register of members of the acquiring company immediately after the transaction for which relief is claimed;

(x) a copy of the agreement or offer document; and

(xi) a copy of the instruments of transfer.

(c) A completed Adjudication Application Form Adj 467, stating any related adjudication references known should be sent with the claim to: The Controller of Stamps, Adjudication Section, West Block, Barrington Road, Worthing, West Sussex, BN12 4SF.

The Stamp Office has issued explanatory notes and a set of precedent letters for use in England and Wales, all of which are reproduced in **S&S 386–396**.

[*Note:* See note at commencement of commentary on this Act.]

76. Acquisitions: further provisions about reliefs. (S&S 382–383, 385)

For transactions involving the acquisition of the whole or part of a company's undertaking, the rate of duty under the heading "conveyance or transfer on sale" which would otherwise be payable in respect of the relevant instruments of transfer is reduced from one per cent. to 0·5 per cent.

This section does not require that there must be a scheme of reconstruction or amalgamation, and there is therefore no requirement that the beneficial ownership of the business must remain substantially the same.

Where a company (the "acquiring company") acquires the whole or part of the undertaking of another company (the "target company"), any instrument executed for the purposes of or in connection with the transfer of the undertaking, or part thereof, or the assignment to the acquiring company by a creditor of the target company of any "relevant debts" (secured or unsecured) owed by the target company, is chargeable to stamp duty under the heading "conveyance or transfer on sale" at the rate of 50p for every £100 or part of £100 of the amount or value of the consideration for the sale to which the instrument gives effect, provided that the conditions specified are satisfied.

The conditions are that the registered office of the acquiring company is in the U.K., and that the consideration for the acquisition consists of or includes the issue of shares in the acquiring company to the target company, or to all or any of its shareholders, and nothing else (if anything) except cash amounting to 10 per cent. of the nominal value of the consideration shares, or the assumption or discharge by the acquiring company of liabilities of the target company, or both.

The expression "relevant debt" is defined as any debt in the case of which the assignor is a bank or trade creditor, and any other debt incurred not less than two years before the date on which the instrument is executed.

Any instrument claimed to be eligible for the reduced rate of duty under these provisions must be adjudicated under SA 1891, s. 12. The provisions apply to all instruments executed on or after 27 October 1986.

As to problems which have arisen in interpreting the word "undertaking" and the expression "the consideration for the acquisition", see the notes to s. 75.

The ability to ignore liabilities assumed or discharged by the acquiring company, for the purpose of determining whether or not the reduced rate is available, does not affect the application of SA 1891, s. 57 by virtue of which the amount on which the duty is chargeable is the value of the consideration shares together with the amount of cash paid and the amount of the liabilities taken over or discharged.

Under this section (unlike s. 75) the consideration shares can be issued to the target company or to all or any of its shareholders. The requirement is still, however, that the consideration shares be "issued" to such persons, *i.e.*, that such persons be registered in the register of members.

As to the procedure for claims, see the notes to s. 75.

[*Note:* See note at commencement of commentary on this Act.]

77. Acquisition of target company's share capital. (S&S 383–385)

There is a complete exemption from stamp duty under the heading "conveyance or transfer on sale" in SA 1891, Sch. 1 in relation to any instrument transferring shares in one company (the "target company") to another company (the "acquiring company") if certain conditions are satisfied and the instrument is adjudicated under SA 1891, s. 12.

The conditions are that:

(a) the registered office of the acquiring company is in the U.K.; and (*b*) the transfer forms part of an arrangement (*i.e.*, one single transaction) by which the acquiring company acquires the whole of the issued share capital of the target company (*i.e.*, the exemption will not be available where the acquiring company already holds shares in the target company before the "arrangement"); and

(*c*) the acquisition is effected for bona fide commercial reasons and does not form part of a scheme or arrangement of which the main purpose, or one of the main purposes, is avoidance of liability to stamp duty, stamp duty reserve tax, income tax, corporation tax or capital gains tax; and

(*d*) the consideration for the acquisition consists only of the issue of shares in the acquiring company to the shareholders of the target company; and

(*e*) after the acquisition has been made, each person who immediately before it was made was a shareholder of the target company is a shareholder of the acquiring company; and

(*f*) after the acquisition has been made, the shares in the acquiring company are of the same classes as were the shares in the target company immediately before the acquisition is made; and

(*g*) after the acquisition has been made, the number of shares of any particular class in the acquiring company bear to all the shares in that company the same proportion as the number of shares of that class in the target company bore to all the shares in that company immediately before the acquisition was made; and

(*h*) after the acquisition has been made, the proportion of shares of any particular class in the acquiring company held by any particular shareholder is the same as the proportion of shares of that class in the target company held by him immediately before the acquisition was made.

Note that, unlike in ss. 75 and 76, it is not possible to ignore liabilities assumed or discharged by the acquiring company. The consideration for the acquisition must consist *solely* of the issue of shares and the word "issue", as before, means that the target company or its shareholders must be entered on the register of members of the acquiring company, so that the giving of renounceable letters of allotment or the registration of nominees will cause the exemption to be lost.

The Commissioners have indicated that a clearance obtained under CGTA 1979, s. 88 or TA 1970, s. 267 (3A) will satisfy them in relation to the requirement that the acquisition is effected for bona fide commercial reasons.

It is generally thought that the severity of the restrictions will limit the availability of this relief to situations where a new company is formed specifically to acquire the whole of the issued share capital of an existing company, where the new company and the existing company have identical share capitals. It seems unlikely that the relief will ever be available where two existing companies merge, either by the formation of a new holding company over both of them or where one takes over the other.

As to the procedure for claims, see the notes to s. 75.

[*Note:* See note at commencement of commentary on this Act.]

LOAN CAPITAL, LETTERS OF ALLOTMENT, ETC

78. Loan capital. (S&S 338–339)

The existence of this section is due to a change of mind by the Chancellor of the Exchequer between his Budget speech on 18 March 1986 and the enactment of FA 1986 on 25 July 1986.

The Budget speech announced that the exemption from stamp duty on transfers of most forms of loan stock was to be withdrawn, and a charge at 0·5 per cent. imposed. This announcement was given effect to by a Budget Resolution (No. 33) passed on 24 March 1986 pursuant to FA 1973, s. 50 which enables temporary statutory effect to be given to Budget proposals by way of "Budget Resolution".

Because of a subsequent change of mind by the Government, Resolution 33 was withdrawn with effect from 7 July 1986 and the previous exemption was reinstated. Section 78 contains the text of Resolution 33 and is included only to impose the charge for the interim period.

However, sub-ss. (7), (9), (10) and (14) have a continuing relevance because they were imported into s. 79, which contains the new exemptions.

"Loan capital" means:

(*a*) any debenture stock, corporation stock, or funded debt by whatever name known issued by a body corporate or other body of persons (which here includes a local authority and any body whether formed or established in the U.K. or elsewhere);

(*b*) any capital raised by such a body if the capital is borrowed or has the character of borrowed money, and whether it is in the form of stock or any other form; or

(*c*) stock or marketable securities issued by the government of any country or territory outside the U.K.

This definition is very similar to the definition applicable to the former duty on loan capital under FA 1899, s. 8 (5). The decisions in relation to the repealed provisions are therefore still relevant in interpreting the new definition. The principal cases are:

(1) *A-G* v. *South Wales Electrical Power Distribution Co.* [1920] 1 KB 552, C.A., which held that it is essential that there is some sort of issue or raising of "capital", so that "deferred warrants"

issued by a company in respect of interest it was unable to pay on its debenture stock were not within the definition.

(2) *A-G* v. *Regent's Canal and Dock Co.* [1904] 1 KB 263, which held that an issue by a company of a new series of debenture stock to the holders of its existing debenture stock, which was then extinguished, was within the definition even though no further funds were borrowed.

(3) *Reed International Ltd* v. *I.R. Comrs.* [1975] 3 All ER 218, H.L., which held that a debt was a "funded debt" if it had some degree of permanence or long-term character and other features which would be expected by a creditor whose debt will not be repaid for some time, including the payment of a stipulated rate of interest and various other provisions, and that it was not necessary for the debt to be supported by some fund or to be transferable in separate amounts, or that it should have been created by the conversion of an existing short-term debt.

It has been suggested that short-term borrowing may also be within the definition, if it is of a capital nature (see, *e.g.* Monroe and Nock, *The Law of Stamp Duties,* (6th edn.)) and it is thought that this must be right in view of the inclusion in (*b*) of "any capital raised . . . if the capital is borrowed or has the character of borrowed money, and whether it is in the form of stock or any other form" (*i.e.*, with no indication of a minimum required period for the loan).

"Designated international organisation" means an international organisation which has been designated by an Order made under FA 1984, s. 126.

The effect of s. 78 (and s. 79) is to be ignored in construing FA 1985, s. 81 (3).

References in s. 78 (and s. 79) to FA 1963, s. 60 include FA (Northern Ireland) 1963, s. 9 (1).

[*Note:* See note at commencement of commentary on this Act.]

79. Loan capital: new provisions. (S&S 340–343)

There is a complete exemption from stamp duty under the heading "bearer instrument" in SA 1891, Sch. 1 in respect of the issue of an instrument which relates to loan capital (as defined in s. 78 (7)) or on the transfer of loan capital constitued by, or transferable by means of, such instrument.

There is also an exemption from duty under the heading "conveyance or transfer on sale" in SA 1891, Sch. 1 on an instrument which transfers loan capital issued or raised by the O.E.C.D., the Inter-American Development bank, or any organisation designated under FA 1984, s. 126, or any other loan capital except as mentioned below.

The above exemption does not apply to an instrument transferring any loan capital which, at the time the instrument was executed, carries a right (exercisable then or later) of conversion into shares or other securities, or to the acquisition of shares or other securities, including loan capital of the same description.

The exemption also does not apply to any instrument transferring loan capital which, at the time the instrument is executed or at any earlier time, carries or has carried:

(*a*) a right to interest the amount of which exceeds a reasonable commercial return on the nominal amount of the capital; or

(*b*) a right to interest the amount of which falls or has fallen to be determined to any extent by reference to results of, or of any part of, a business or to the value of any property; or

(*c*) a right on repayment to an amount which exceeds the nominal amount of the capital and is not reasonably comparable with what is generally repayable (in respect of a similar nominal amount of capital) under the terms of issue of loan capital listed in the Official List of The Stock Exchange.

The fact that any interest or premium on loan capital is index-linked does not, however, of itself, prevent the exemption from applying.

Where loan capital falls under any of the headings in respect of which the exemption is not available, then stamp duty under the heading "conveyance or transfer on sale" in SA 1891, Sch. 1 is chargeable at a reduced rate of 50p for every £100 or part of £100 of the amount or value of the consideration for the sale to which the relevant instrument of transfer gives effect. The new provisions apply to inland bearer instruments issued, and overseas bearer instruments transferred, after 31 July 1986, and to transfer instruments executed after 31 July 1986.

It is interesting to note that the various changes of mind by the Chancellor of the Exchequer, and the timing difference between the withdrawal of Resolution 33 and the introduction of the new provisions, meant that non-exempt transfers of loan capital paid duty of 0·5 per cent. between 25 March and 6 July 1986, 1·0 per cent. between 7 July and 31 July 1986, and 0·5 per cent. again from 1 August 1986.

[*Note:* See note at commencement of commentary on this Act.]

80. Bearer letters of allotment etc. (S&S 343)

The "bearer instrument" head of charge in SA 1891, Sch. 1 applies to any instrument which falls within FA 1963, s. 60 (1) and is issued after 24 March 1986, unless it is issued by a company in pursuance of a general offer for its shares and the offer became unconditional as to acceptance on or before 18 March 1986, and to any instrument which falls within FA 1963, s. 60 (2) if the stock constituted by or transferable by means of it is transferred after 24 March 1986.

[*Note:* See note at commencement of commentary on this Act.]

CHANGES IN FINANCIAL INSTITUTIONS

81. Sales to market makers. (S&S 344)

Provided that the relevant instrument is denoted as not chargeable with any duty, stamp duty is not chargeable on any instrument transferring stock on sale to a person or his nominee if it is shown to the satisfaction of the Commissioners that the transaction to which the instrument gives effect was carried out by that person in the ordinary course of his business as a market maker in stock of the kind transferred.

For these purposes, a person will be construed as a "market maker in stock of a particular kind" if either:

(a) he holds himself out at all normal times in compliance with the rules of The Stock Exchange as willing to buy and sell stock of that kind at a price specified by him, and he is recognised as so doing by the Council of The Stock Exchange, or

(b) he is an "authorised person" under the Financial Services Act 1986, Part I, Ch. III; he carried out the transaction in the course of his business of buying, selling, subscribing for or underwriting investments, or offering or agreeing to do so, as a principal; he did not carry out the transaction as part of investment management activities or activities relating to the establishment, operation or winding-up of a collective investment scheme (including acting as a trustee of an authorised unit trust scheme); and the relevant stock was not, at the time the transaction was carried out, dealt in on a recognised investment exchange within the meaning of the Financial Services Act 1986.

This definition is the same as that contained in FA 1986, s. 89 (3) (stamp duty reserve tax exemption in relation to sales to market makers) and is to be contrasted with the definition contained in ss. 69 and 94 (in relation to depositary receipts) and in s. 82 (borrowing of stock by market makers) which apply only to market makers in listed securities.

[*Note:* See note at commencement of commentary on this Act.]

82. Borrowing of stock by market makers. (S&S 344–345)

The relief given by FA 1961, s. 34 for the transfer of "borrowed" stock to a jobber has also been revised to take account of the stock market changes following "Big Bang".

The new relief applies where a person (A.) has contracted to sell stock in the ordinary course of his business as a market maker in stock of that kind and, to enable him to fulfil the contract, he enters into an arrangement under which another person (B.), who is not a market maker in stock of the kind concerned or a nominee or such a market maker, is to transfer stock to A. or his nominee, and in return stock of the same kind and amount is to be transferred (whether or not by A. or his nominee) to B. or his nominee.

The relief also applies where, to enable B. to make the transfer to A. or his nominee, B. enters into an arrangement under which another person (C.), who is not a market maker in stock of the kind concerned or a nominee or such a market maker, is to transfer stock to B. or his nominee, and in return stock of the same kind and amount is to be transferred (whether or not by B. or his nominee) to C. or his nominee.

In these circumstances, the maximum stamp duty chargeable on any instrument effecting a transfer to B. or his nominee or C. or his nominee in pursuance of the relevant arrangement is 50p.

For the purposes of these provisions, a person is a market maker in stock of a particular kind if he holds himself out at all normal times in compliance with the rules of The Stock Exchange as willing to buy and sell stock of that kind at a price specified by him, and he is recognised as so doing by the Council of The Stock Exchange. This definition is the same as that contained in ss. 69 and 94 (in relation to depositary receipts) and is to be contrasted with the definition contained in ss. 81 (3) and 89 (3), (stamp duty and stamp duty reserve tax exemptions in relation to sales to market makers) which, as amended, extend to transactions in unlisted securities by authorised persons under the Financial Services Act 1986. The Treasury has power by statutory instrument to amend the definition.

[*Note:* See note at commencement of commentary on this Act.]

83. Composition agreements. (S&S 345)

Under FA 1970, s. 33, the Revenue has the power to enter into composition arrangements with The Stock Exchange for the payment of stamp duty. Similar arrangements can be made with any "recognised investment exchange" or "recognised clearing house" under the Financial Services Act 1986.

[*Note:* See note at commencement of commentary on this Act.]

84. Miscellaneous exemptions. (S&S 345–346)

Transfers of stock to a recognised clearing house or its nominee, or to a recognised investment exchange or its nominee, which has entered into a composition agreement for the payment of stamp duty, are not chargeable with stamp duty.

[*Note:* See note at commencement of commentary on this Act.]

PART IV STAMP DUTY RESERVE TAX

INTRODUCTION

86. The tax: introduction. (S&S 629–630)

This section introduces "stamp duty reserve tax". This is a misleading name because it is a completely separate tax and the provisions in Pt. IV (ss. 86 to 99) are not to be construed as one with SA 1891. The new tax is directly enforceable by assessment and, unlike conveyance or transfer on sale stamp duty, not by means of stamping documents. Appeals against assessment lie to the Special Commissioners under the TMA 1970, and not by way of adjudication and case stated under SA 1891, ss. 12 and 13.

The new tax was introduced to apply in circumstances where shares are sold but stamp duty is not payable because there is no instrument of transfer chargeable to duty. Contracts for the sale of a legal interest in stock and marketable securities are not chargeable to stamp duty by virtue of SA 1891, s. 59 and it is therefore possible to avoid stamp duty in respect of a sale where no instrument of transfer is taken and the registered holder of the shares remains the same. Accordingly, stamp duty is not payable on sales of listed securities during a Stock Exchange account period (which are all contractual, transfers being made only to the purchaser entitled at the end of the account period), purchases of shares where the shares are registered in the name of a nominee who acts both for the seller and the purchaser, or transfers of letters of allotment. Stamp duty reserve tax was therefore introduced to render such transactions chargeable.

Because stamp duty reserve tax is an entirely separate tax from stamp duty, transactions which are exempt from stamp duty by virtue of specific statutory provisions are not automatically exempt from the new tax. For example, in the case of internal group re-organisations which are exempt by virtue of FA 1930, s. 42, there is no automatic exemption from stamp duty reserve tax. However, where instruments of transfer are executed for such purposes, and are adjudged as not chargeable to any duty by virtue of the exemption, this enables stamp duty reserve tax to be avoided or reclaimed.

The tax is under the care and management of the Board of Inland Revenue. PCTA 1968, s. 1 applies to the tax.

[*Note:* See note at commencement of commentary on this Act.]

THE PRINCIPAL CHARGE

87. The principal charge. (S&S 630–631)

Stamp duty reserve tax is charged in any case where one person (A.) agrees with another (B.) to transfer chargeable securities (whether or not to B.) for consideration in money or money's worth. It does not apply if, within a period of two months beginning on the date of the agreement (or, where it is conditional, the date on which the conditions are satisfied), an instrument is (or instruments are) executed pursuant to the agreement transferring to B. or his nominee all the chargeable securities towhich the agreement relates, and which is (or are) duly stamped in accordance with the enactments relating to stamp duty (if such instrument or instruments, under those enactments, is or are chargeable with stamp duty or otherwise required to be stamped). A charge to the new tax is assessed at the rate of 50p for every £100 or part of £100 of the amount or value of the consideration agreed to be given for the chargeable securities. "Chargeable securities" is defined in s. 99.

An instrument which is stampable but does not attract any duty (provided that, where required, it is adjudicated) is sufficient to relieve a stamp duty reserve tax liability. It also seems to be sufficient if an instrument is executed which is not required to be stamped or adjudicated in any way. There need not be a stamped instrument but only an instrument which, if it needs to be stamped, is stamped.

The agreement may be written or oral, express or implied, conditional or unconditional, and it does not make any difference whether or not the governing law of the contract is English, or whether either or both of the parties to the agreement is or are resident, incorporated or established in the U.K. The agreement must, however, be an agreement *"to transfer"* securities. An agreement for the issue of shares, where no transfer is involved, will clearly not be caught.

In addition, the Stamp Office has indicated that it does not consider either an agreement by a company to purchase its own shares or the grant of an option to purchase shares as falling within s. 87 (1). In the case of a grant of an option to purchase shares, the Revenue's view does not appear to accord with stamp duty case law (which admittedly does not automatically apply for the purposes of stamp duty reserve tax) concerning options. It was held in *George Wimpey Ltd.* v. *I.R. Comrs.* [1975] STC 248 that the grant of an option to purchase property effectively amounted to a conveyance on sale of property (the option itself) liable to *ad valorem* stamp duty. It is therefore arguable that (if the stamp duty cases are held to apply) whilst the grant of an option to purchase shares is clearly not of itself an agreement to transfer those shares, it may be an agreement to transfer the option itself, and (since an option to acquire shares falls within the definition of "chargeable securities" in s. 99, discussed below) give rise to a charge to stamp duty reserve tax on the consideration for the grant. The same argument will not apply to the grant of an option to sell shares (*i.e.*, a "put option") because only an option to *acquire* shares falls within the defintion of "chargeable securities".

The value of any consideration which does not consist of money is to be taken to be the price it might reasonably be expected to fetch on a sale in the open market at the time the agreement is made. "The enactments relating to stamp duty" mean SA 1891 and any enactment which amends or is required to be construed together with that Act.

The duly stamped instrument or instruments of transfer which avoid the tax being paid must be in favour of the purchaser under the agreement, *i.e.*, B., or his nominee or a person who takes the transfer by way of security for a loan to B. Accordingly, where there is a sub-sale to another person a charge will arise, notwithstanding that stamp duty is paid on a transfer of the securities from the original seller to the sub-purchaser. In that case, the charge will be on the consideration paid by B. The agreement by the sub-purchaser to purchase the securities from B. will not be liable for stamp duty reserve tax, unless the instrument of transfer in his favour is not executed or duly stamped, on the basis of the consideration paid by the sub-purchaser (provided the conditions of SA 1891, s. 58 (4) and (5) are satisfied), within the two month period.

Before the insertion of s. 87 (7A), one problem was that in order to give relief from a charge to stamp duty reserve tax, the relevant instrument or instruments of transfer had to be in respect of *all* the chargeable securities to which the agreement related. The effect of this was that if even a single share covered by the agreement was either not the subject of a duly stamped instrument of transfer within the two month period, or was transferred directly to a sub-purchaser, then the original purchaser, *i.e.*, B., was liable to stamp duty reserve tax on *all* the chargeable securities covered by the relevant agreement, in addition to the stamp duty he would have paid on the securities actually transferred to him by duly stamped instruments of transfer. Under s. 87 (7A), however, stamp duty reserve tax is only chargeable on the agreement between the vendor and the original purchaser in respect of the chargeable securities which are transferred direct to the sub-purchaser rather than to the original purchaser.

Under s. 87 (7A) the section takes effect as if there were separate agreements in relation to each parcel of shares—*i.e.*, one or more agreements covering the shares transferred to B. or his nominee within the two-month period, and one or more separate agreements covering the shares either not transferred at all or sub-sold to one or more third parties. This effectively means that the stamp duty reserve tax will only be paid in respect of the shares which are not actually transferred to B. or his nominee. The Inland Revenue press release of 8 April 1987 gives the following example to show how this provision would operate:

A. sells to B. 1,000 shares in X Plc. for £1,500.
B. resells 750 of the shares to C.
A. transfers 750 shares to C. and 250 shares to B.

The agreement between A. and B. is deemed to be two separate agreements, one in respect of 750 shares and one in respect of 250 shares, with the result that B. incurs a stamp duty reserve tax liability on the agreement to purchase 750 shares, *i.e.*, on £1,125 (75 per cent. of £1,500). The *ad valorem* stamp duty on the transfer to B. of the 250 shares relieves, or "franks", the stamp duty reserve tax liability on that agreement.

The position would be the same even if no sub-sale was involved. If, in the above example, B. did not resell any of the shares he agreed to purchase from A., but simply took a transfer of 250 shares (which was duly stamped within the two month period) and left the remaining shares registered in A.'s name, A. then acting as his nominee, the same result would follow—*i.e.*, there would be deemed to be two agreements and the stamp duty reserve tax would only be payable in respect of the 750 shares not transferred to B.

A liability to stamp duty reserve tax is relieved by s. 87 (7B) if the vendor transfers the shares, not to the purchaser or his nominee, but to a person who has agreed to take the shares as security for a loan to the purchaser. The Inland Revenue press release of 8 April 1987 indicated that the purpose of s. 87 (7B) was retrospectively to clarify the position where there is a transfer of shares to a person, *e.g.*, a bank, who is providing a loan *for the purchase* and who is to hold the shares as security for the loan, but s. 87 (7B) is not actually so restricted. It is not necessary that the loan made by the transferee of the shares is for the purpose of enabling the purchaser to buy them; the loan could be for a completely unconnected purpose.

The effect of s. 87 (7B) is to remove the charge to stamp duty reserve tax on the agreement for the purchase of the shares on the basis that *ad valorem* stamp duty will be payable on the transfer of the shares to the lender, assessed on the basis of the purchase price received by the vendor rather than the consideration provided by the lender to the purchaser, *i.e.*, the amount of the loan. Without the enactment of s. 87 (7B), there would have been a potential double tax charge—stamp duty reserve tax on the agreement for the purchase of the shares and *ad valorem* stamp duty on the transfer of the shares to the lender.

The Revenue regard only the principals to an agreement to transfer chargeable securities as falling within the definition of A. and B. for the purposes of s. 87, and not also their respective agents, (even if any such agent is himself liable as a principal on the contract *e.g.*, where acting for an undisclosed principal). The Revenue take the view that only the agreement between the principals themselves will be chargeable with stamp duty reserve tax, and not also the agreement (if any) between the agent and his named principal. This seems to flow from the fact that s. 87 refers to an agreement *to transfer* rather than an agreement *relating to* a transfer. This analysis may not be correct, despite the Revenue's assurances, if the principal is obliged by the terms of his agreement with his agent to effect the eventual transfer; in that case there is an agreement by which the principal (A.) agrees with his agent (B.) to transfer chargeable securities, even if not to the agent, which would appear to be caught by the precise wording of s. 87 (1). Since this alternative analysis would involve a double charge, one on the agency agreement and one on the agreement with the actual purchaser, the Revenue accept that agency agreements will not give rise to a stamp duty reserve tax liability.

[*Note:* See note at commencement of commentary on this Act.]

88. Section 87 : special cases. (S&S 631)
An instrument which is not chargeable to stamp duty by virtue of FA 1976, s. 127 (1) (transfer to The Stock Exchange nominee) or FA 1986, s. 84 (2) and (3) (transfers to recognised investment exchanges and clearing houses, and their respective nominees) is disregarded in construing s. 87 (4) and (5). This means that the execution of such an instrument does not exclude liability for stamp duty reserve tax. Any transfer by such a person to a purchaser or sub-purchaser, if duly stamped, relieves the purchaser or sub-purchaser, but not the original vendor, from liability to stamp duty reserve tax.

An agreement to transfer a renounceable letter of allotment (or similar instrument) with a life of up to six months (which is exempt from stamp duty under Exemption 3 to the "bearer instrument" head of charge in SA 1891, Sch. 1) is subject to stamp duty reserve tax on the date of the agreement (or, with a conditional agreement, on the date it becomes unconditional).

The date on which stamp duty reserve tax is payable on sales of renounceable documents of title was brought forward by FA 1987, Sch. 7, para. 3. Previously, the charge on sales of renounceable documents of title arose on the same date on which the charge arose in respect of any other transfer of chargeable securities, *i.e.*, on the expiry of a period of two months beginning on the date of the agreement (or, in the case of a conditional agreement, on the date of its becoming unconditional). The two months grace period between the sale and the date on which the charge arose was provided to allow stamp duty to be paid and thereby relieve the charge to stamp duty reserve tax. However, no grace period is needed in the case of a sale of renounceable documents of title because in that case there is of course no possibility of the execution, within any period of time, of an instrument of transfer which would relieve the transaction from stamp duty reserve tax. The date on which the charge arises in these cases was therefore brought forward to the date on which the sale is agreed. The new rule applies to all agreements made on or after 1 August 1987. In this case, the change was made without retrospective effect.

The most important consequence of the application of a charge to stamp duty reserve tax on agreements to transfer renounceable letters of allotment and similar instruments (including the renounceable letters of acceptance commonly used, for example, in offers for sale) with a life of less than six months, is its impact (subject to the exemptions provided by s. 89A) on the structuring of the various forms of domestic corporate finance transactions, for example offers for sale or subscription, bonus or rights issues and vendor placings.

The following brief analysis may help in understanding the issues involved.

(1) In an *offer for sale of new shares*, the company allots the new shares to its merchant bank on a nil paid renounceable letter of allotment; this is deemed to be fully paid when the admission of the company's shares to the Official List of The Stock Exchange becomes effective. The merchant bank issues renounceable letters of acceptance to successful applicants, evidencing the allocation made to them and enabling dealings to commence immediately so that an orderly market may be preserved. Following the last day for renunciation of the letters of acceptance the merchant bank renounces its renounceable letter of allotment in favour of the final renouncees of the renounceable letters of acceptance. The agreement to allot the shares to the bank (on the nil paid letter) does not attract a charge because it is an agreement to allot rather than transfer shares; and the initial issue by the bank of a renounceable letter of acceptance to a successful applicant, although constituting an agreement between the bank and that applicant to transfer the right to be allotted the shares, will clearly be within the exemptions provided by s. 89A and so not attract a charge. Each subsequent renunciation of the letter of acceptance will attract a charge. The final renunciation by the bank of its letter of allotment in favour of the ultimate renouncees does not attract a charge, because it does not itself involve an agreement to transfer, or a transfer of, chargeable securities.

(2) In an *offer for subscription of new shares*, the company allots fully paid renounceable letters of allotment to successful applicants and subsequently issues definitive share certificates in favour of the ultimate renouncees. The issue of the letters of allotment does not attract a charge, as agreements to allot rather than transfer, and nor does the issue of the definitive certificates, but each intermediate renunciation attracts a charge.

(3) In a *bonus issue* or a *rights issue*, the company allots the new shares to existing holders on fully paid renounceable letters of allotment or nil paid provisional renounceable letters of allotment and (following, in the latter case, a period for splitting nil-paid and fully-paid rights) issues definitive shares certificates to the ultimate renouncees. In either case the issues of the letters of allotment and the definitive share certificates do not attract a charge, but each intermediate renunciation does (on the consideration paid by the renouncees, *i.e.*, only on the premium in the case of a renunciation of nil-paid rights).

(4) An *offer for sale by existing shareholders* will usually involve a bonus issue to the existing shareholders on renounceable letters of allotment. The shareholders will agree with their merchant bank to sell the new shares to it, for which purpose they will renounce the letters of allotment in blank and execute powers of attorney in favour of a third party authorising him to complete the registration application forms in favour of such persons as the bank may nominate (upon receipt of the net proceeds of sale). The merchant bank, having purchased the letters of allotment, will then offer the new shares for sale, as *principal*, and issue renounceable letters of acceptance to successful applicants. The bank will subsequently direct the completion of registration appliction forms in respect of the letters of allotment (received from the existing shareholders) in favour of the ultimate renouncees of the letters of acceptance. The issue of the letters of allotment to the existing shareholders by the company and the final registration of the ultimate renouncees of the letters of acceptance will not attract a charge, because they do not constitute agreements to *transfer* chargeable securities. The sale by the existing shareholders to the merchant bank (involving the renunciation by the existing shareholders in blank and the execution of powers of attorney) will not attract a charge, because it is clearly within the exemptions provided by s. 89A. However, whether or not the issue of the letters of acceptance by the bank attracts a charge will depend upon whether the bonus shares fall within the definition of "newly subscribed securities" for the purposes of s. 89A (2), as to which, see below. Each intermediate renunciation of the letters of acceptance will attract a charge. Before the enactment of s. 89A both the sale of the new shares by the existing shareholders to their merchant bank and the issue by the bank of renounceable letters of acceptance would certainly have attracted a charge and banks had therefore developed the practice of offering the new shares for sale as *agent* for the existing shareholders, in which case the first charge was avoided because the existing shareholders would renounce their letters of allotment directly in favour of the ultimate renouncees of the letters of acceptance (which the bank issued on their behalf) without there first being a sale to the bank.

Commonly, an offer for sale by existing shareholders will also involve a sale of existing shares already registered in the names of the shareholders, instead of or in addition to new shares created by means of a bonus issue. In that case, the shareholders will again agree to sell the shares to the merchant bank and execute powers of attorney to transfer the shares to such persons as the bank chooses, against payment of the offer for sale price. The bank will then again offer the shares for sale, as *principal*, issue renounceable letters of acceptance to successful applicants, and subsequently deliver share transfers (executed under the aforesaid powers of attorney) in favour of the ultimate renouncees of the letters of acceptance. The agreement between the existing shareholders and the bank and the issue by the bank of the letters of acceptance will clearly be within the exemptions provided by s. 89A (1) and (3) respectively and therefore not attract a charge to stamp duty reserve tax, but each intermediate renunciation of the letters of acceptance will attract a charge. Again, before the enactment of s. 89A the charge which would then have arisen on the initial agreement to sell the shares to the bank was avoided by the bank acting as *agent* rather than as principal in the offer for sale.

Whether or not a merchant bank is involved, either as principal or agent, there seems in the case of an offer for sale of existing shares already registered in the names of vendor shareholders to be an unfortunate double tax charge where renounceable letters of acceptance are used. Stamp duty reserve tax will be payable on all renunciations of the letters of acceptance, although not (by virtue of s. 89A (3)) on their initial issue, and stamp duty will be payable on the eventual transfers of the underlying securities to the persons seeking to be registered. In the case of applicants who have not renounced the letters of acceptance issued to them payment of this duty will be their only liability, since they will not have to pay stamp duty reserve tax in respect of the issue of the letters of acceptance to them. However, in the case of an ultimate renouncee of a letter of acceptance which is not retained by the original applicant, he will be liable both to stamp duty reserve tax on the agreement to transfer to him the renounceable letter and to stamp duty on the transfer of the underlying securities in his favour, because s. 88 (2) and (3) prevents the latter from "franking" the former. Ultimate renouncees of letters of acceptance evidencing rights to existing registered shares are liable for stamp duty reserve tax on the renunciation in their favour notwithstanding the delivery to them of a duly stamped instrument of transfer.

It is understood that the Revenue view the problem of a double charge sympathetically but the problem of how best to provide relief is rendered difficult by the fact that offers for sale usually involve sales of both existing registered shares and new bonus issue shares represented by renounceable letters of allotment. It would be difficult to tell which ultimate renouncees had acquired rights to registered shares (where the double charge would arise) and which had acquired shares represented by letters of allotment (where there would be no double charge, because there would be no stamp duty on the eventual *issue* of the shares concerned).

(5) A *vendor consideration placing* involves the acquisition by a company of assets (other than shares in a listed company pursuant to a public takeover bid, as to which see below) in consideration of an issue of fully paid shares in the company which the vendors wish to sell, to realise cash. The company issues either definitive share certificates (where stamp duty relief on the transfers of the assets is to be sought under FA 1986, s. 76) or renounceable letters of allotment (where s. 76 relief is not available) to the vendors, who then agree to sell the shares to the merchant bank, who in turn on-sell them (as principal) to the placees. If definitive share certificates are used, transfers are executed by the vendors in favour of the placees. Stamp duty on the transfers to the placees will prevent a charge to stamp duty reserve tax arising on the agreement between the bank and the placees, provided they are stamped within two months. If renounceable letters of allotment are used, stamp duty is avoided but stamp duty reserve tax is payable on any renunciations by the placees before definitive share certificates are issued. In either case, the stamp duty reserve tax position in relation to the other elements of the transaction will depend on whether the exemptions provided by s. 89A apply. If definitive share certificates are used stamp duty reserve tax will be payable on the agreement between the vendors and the bank, and if renounceable letters of allotment are used stamp duty reserve tax will be payable on the renunciation by the vendors to the bank and on the renunciation by the bank to the placees, unless in either case the bank's offer to the chosen placees can be said to be an offer to "the public", which (by analogy with the repealed provisions of the Companies Act 1985) seems unlikely.

Alternatively, to avoid any possible stamp duty reserve tax charge the bank could agree with the vendors to place the shares as their agent.

(6) Where shares to be issued in consideration for an acquisition exceed certain proportions of the acquiring company's existing issued share capital, it is a requirement of the Stock Exchange that the consideration shares allotted to the vendors be offered back to the shareholders of the acquiring company. This is achieved either by means of a *vendor rights offer* (which may take the form of an *open offer*) or by means of a *vendor rights issue*. The former method involves a vendor consideration placing with a so-called "claw-back", whereby the acquiring company's merchant bank invites the acquiring company's existing shareholders to apply for a pro-rata proportion of the consideration shares and, to the extent insufficient applications are received, either (in the case of an *open offer*) gives existing shareholders an opportunity to apply for a proportion of the balance or (in the more common case) places the balance with pre-arranged placees. In the case of a *vendor rights issue*, the merchant bank, as principal, will first purchase or agree to purchase the consideration shares from the vendors and then offer them on a *pro rata* basis to the acquiring company's existing shareholders. The offer is made by means of a nil-paid renounceable letter of rights which can be dealt in the market, and at the acceptance and payment day for the offer the shares are either purchased by the offeree shareholders (or their renouncees) or, if a premium over the net issue price and expenses of sale can be obtained, sold in the market for the benefit of the shareholders originally entitled thereto, or, if this is not possible, sold by the merchant bank to sub-underwriters. The persons accepting the offer have their nil-paid renounceable letters of rights endorsed as fully paid upon payment. The stamp duty reserve tax implications for the agreement between the vendors and the bank and the offers by the bank will again depend upon whether the offer by the bank can be said to be an offer "to the public". If the analogy with the repealed provisions of the Companies Act 1985 is valid (see s. 89A) a carefully drafted letter of rights will evidence an invitation "calculated to result, directly or indirectly, in the shares . . . becoming available for . . . purchase by persons other than those receiving the offer . . ." and therefore constitute an offer to the public. In that case, the stamp duty reserve tax implications for these transactions will be similar to those relating to an *offer for sale by existing shareholders*, as described in paragraph 3 above. The purchase of the consideration shares by the bank from the vendors and the issue by the bank of renounceable documents will be within the s. 89A exemptions and therefore not attract a charge, but each intermediate renunciation will attract a charge. The bank could still avoid any uncertainty caused by the lack of a definition of "offer to the public" for the purposes of s. 89A by offering the shares for sale as agent for the vendors.

(7) In a *public takeover bid* involving an exchange of shares, the acquiring company often wishes to offer a *cash alternative*, without having to raise the money to fund the payment, and this is usually structured by means of an offer by the bidder's merchant bank to purchase for cash any of the shares in the bidder which the shareholders of the target company do not wish to keep (the bank usually mitigating its contingent liability to buy the shares by inviting institutions to "sub-underwrite" its purchase). In such cases, either the consideration shares will be registered in the names of the vendors and definitive certificates of title will be issued at the outset, or renounceable documents of title will initially be issued. Until the enactment of FA 1988, s. 142 the former would normally be the preferred course of action in order that capital duty relief could

be obtained on the issue of the consideration shares. If the bank acts as principal in purchasing the relevant shares from acceptors of the cash alternative and selling them to the sub-under-writers, then if definitive certificates are used at the outset there will be a charge to stamp duty reserve tax on acceptances of the bank's offer which is not recoverable by stamped transfers to sub-underwriters, those transfers only relieving the stamp duty reserve tax liability on the agreements between the bank and the sub-underwriters. If renounceable documents of title are used there will be no double charge, since stamp duty reserve tax will be payable on the renunciations to the bank and sub-underwriters but no stamp duty will be payable.

(8) In all the above examples, extra care will need to be taken in relation to any *underwriting* and *sub-underwriting arrangements*, to ensure that they do not give rise to an "agreement to transfer" the underwritten securities, or rights to them, resulting in an additional charge to stamp duty reserve tax. However, provided that the main underwiting agreement is structured so that it imposes on the lead underwriter an obligation to subscribe or purchase, *or procure* subscribers or purchasers for, shares *which are not otherwise taken up* by existing shareholders (*e.g.*, in a rights issue) or members of the public (*e.g.*, in an offer for sale) it is probable that no "agreement to transfer" securities, or rights to them, and hence no charge to stamp duty reserve tax, arises at the time the agreement is entered into. Until it is known exactly how many shares, if any, are not taken up by shareholders or members of the public, underwriting and sub-underwriting agree-ments cannot "crystallise" as agreements to transfer chargeable securities. Moreover, the company or vendors will not, by virtue of an underwriting agreement, have an unconditional obligation to the lead underwriters to issue or sell to them all of the shares which are the subject of the agreement. The company or vendors have not *agreed* to issue or sell, but have merely imposed on the lead underwriters (who in turn have imposed on sub-underwriters) a commit-ment to subscribe or purchase, *if* called on. In theory, the company or vendors could choose *not* to call on the underwriters but to dispose of the unwanted shares elsewhere. If and when the underwriters are in fact called on, then an agreement (binding on the company or vendors) to issue or transfer the unwanted shares arises directly with the lead underwriters at which point there will also be sub-underwriting agreements in place which will enable the lead underwriters to discharge their liability (in whole or in part) to the company or vendors by procuring the sub-underwriters to comply with their obligations under the sub-underwriting agreements, the sub-underwriters at that stage becoming contractually bound direct to the company or vendors. Accordingly, an underwriting and sub-underwriting structure involves, on creation, merely a series of conditional agreements relating to an unknown number of shares, and does not involve any agreement to transfer an interest in securities between any members of the underwriting group (lead underwriters and sub-underwriters). On crystallisation, there comes into effect a number of parallel agreements between the company or vendors on the one hand and each member of the underwriting and sub-underwriting groups on the other, not a series of sub-sales within the group. Only at that point is there a liability to stamp duty reserve tax in the case of existing shares which are transferred (which is relieved to the extent that the underwriters or sub-underwriters take duly stamped transfers).

(9) A further problem may arise as a result of the inter-action between FA 1985, s. 81 and FA 1986, s. 88. Where an offer for sale involves more new shares than the company has existing shares, this is done by an issue of bonus shares on renounceable letters of allotment which are then renounced for sale by the merchant bank as principal. Since FA 1985, s. 81 that renunciation theoretically, giving as it does control of the company to the merchant bank, gives rise to stamp duty. As the agreement between the vendors and the bank also falls within s. 88, this results in a double charge, as the s. 88 charge cannot be relieved by the stamp duty.

The whole mechanics of corporate finance have now become a good deal more complicated, and great care at each stage will need to be taken by a company and its professional advisers.

[*Note:* See note at commencement of commentary on this Act.]

89. Section 87: exceptions for market makers etc. (S&S 631–633)

There is no charge to stamp duty reserve tax if the purchaser under the agreement, *i.e.*, B., enters into the agreement in the ordinary course of his business as a market maker in securities of the kind concerned. There is also no charge to stamp duty reserve tax if the purchaser under the agreement, *i.e.*, B., enters into the agreement in the ordinary course of his business as a market maker in "related quoted options", *i.e.*, options quoted on The Stock Exchange to buy or sell securities of the kind covered by the agreement. The options can be either traded options or traditional options.

For these purposes, a person is a market maker in securities of a particular kind if either:

(*a*) he holds himself out at all normal times in compliance with the rules of The Stock Exchange as willing to buy and sell securities of that kind at a price specified by him, and he is recognised as so doing by the Council of The Stock Exchange or,

(*b*) he is an "authorised person" under the Financial Services Act 1986, Part I, Ch. III who enters into the agreement in the course of his business of buying, selling, subscribing for or underwriting investments, or offering or agreeing to do so, as a principal. He must not enter into the agreement as part of investment management activities or activities relating to the establish-ment, operation or winding-up of a collective investment scheme (including acting as a trustee of an authorised unit trust scheme). The relevant stock must not, at the time the agreement is entered into, be dealt in on a recognised investment exchange within the meaning of the Financial Services Act 1986.

This definition is the same as that contained in FA 1986, s. 81 (3) (stamp duty exemption in relation to sales to market makers) and is to be contrasted with the definition contained in ss. 69 and 94 (in relation to depositary receipts) and in s. 82 (borrowing of stock by market makers) which apply only to market makers in listed securities.

The Treasury may by statutory instrument change the definition of a market maker for these purposes. This exemption only requires *the party to the agreement*, *i.e.*, B., to be a market maker, and not also the transferee of the shares.

There is no charge to stamp duty reserve tax if the purchaser under the agreement, *i.e.*, B., enters into the agreement as a principal in the ordinary course of his business as a broker and dealer in relation to securities of the kind concerned, and before the end of the period of seven days beginning with the date of the agreement (or, if the agreement is conditional, the date on which the conditions are satisfied) B. enters into an unconditional agreement to sell the securities to another person. Clearly, in this case the agreement must be made by the broker and dealer, as B., *and* the securities must also be transferred to him (or to his nominee).

A person is a broker and dealer in relation to securities of a particular kind if he is a member of The Stock Exchange who carries on his business in the U.K. and is not a market maker in securities of that kind. The Treasury may by statutory instrument change this definition.

Rules enable securities bought and sold by a broker-dealer to be "matched" where specific identification is not possible, *e.g.*, because shares are not numbered or the broker's internal systems are unable to identify specific blocks of shares bought and sold. The way in which this works is a combination of "last in, first out" (LIFO) and "first in, first out" (FIFO) principles.

Securities purchased in the seven days preceding the date of the relevant sale are to be treated as sold before securities purchased "outside" (*i.e.*, before *or* after) that seven-day period—*i.e.*, effectively, securities purchased more than seven days before the sale or securities actually purchased after the sale has been made (LIFO). This seems to be designed to prevent both (*a*) the Revenue from contending that (where securities cannot otherwise be identified) a sale matches a purchase made more than seven days earlier, so that the relief is lost, when in fact there are unused purchases in the preceding seven-day period, and also (*b*) any broker and dealer from matching shares which are "sold short" (*i.e.*, sold first and bought subsequently) in a bear market *unless* there are no unused purchases in the seven days prior to the sale. Short sales *per se* do not seem incapable of matching with a subsequent purchase: the sale against which a purchase can be matched must take place "before the end of the period of seven days beginning with" the date of the purchase, and clearly if the sale takes place before the purchase it is not only before the *end* of the relevant period but also before the *beginning* of that period.

Shares sold are wherever possible to be matched with the earliest acquisition of shares of the same kind during the preceding seven days, for which relief has not already been given against an earlier sale (FIFO).

A useful illustration of the way in which these principles work in practice is provided in the Revenue's *Notes for Guidance*, para. 2.17 (see Appendix 7).

[*Note:* See note at commencement of commentary on this Act.]

89A. Section 87: exceptions for public issues. (S&S 633–634)
Until F(No. 2)A 1987 inserted this section, merchant banks were compelled to act as agents (for the company or the vendor shareholders) rather than as principals in order to avoid the incidence of a stamp duty reserve tax liability on as many as possible of the individual stages in domestic corporate finance transactions, described in more detail in the notes to s. 88. This was on the basis that (as noted under s. 87) the Revenue regarded only the principals in a given transaction, and not their respective agents, as falling within the definition of A. or B. for the purposes of a stamp duty reserve tax charge. For a number of reasons, it was generally recognised that this was an unfortunate side-effect of the new tax.

In an offer for sale involving both existing and new shares the public must be confident that none of the shares being offered are in any way more of a risk than the others as a result of potential problems with bad title or default in delivery because of subsequent bankruptcy, death or other reasons. Any uncertainty in respect of particular shares would undermine the marketability of all the shares being offered because applicants for them would not know the source of any individual share which they might receive should their application be successful. If the merchant banks in such cases act as principal, they take on any risk there might be of bad title or failure to deliver and they offer the public a single root of title which the public can confidently accept. They also give successful applicants for the shares a single vendor to sue, should the need ever arise. The potential problems of bad title and default are resurrected by any structure which involves the merchant bank acting as agent.

To meet these arguments the section provides that s. 87 does not apply:

(1) as regards an agreement to transfer securities other than units under a unit trust scheme to B. or B.'s nominee if:

(a) the agreement is part of an arrangement, entered into by B. in the ordinary course of B.'s business as an issuing house, under which B., as principal, is to offer the securities for sale to the public, and

(b) the agreement is conditional upon the admission of the securities to the Official List of The Stock Exchange, and

(c) the consideration under the agreement for each security is the same as the price at which B. is to offer the security for sale, and

(d) B. sells the securities in accordance with the agreement referred to in (a) above;

(2) as regards an agreement if the securities to which the agreement relates are newly subscribed securities other than units under a unit trust scheme and:

(a) the agreement is made in pursuance of an offer to the public made by A. as principal under an arrangement entered into in the ordinary course of A.'s business as an issuing house, and

(b) a right of allotment in respect of, or to subscribe for, the securities has been acquired by A. under an agreement which is part of the arrangement, and

(c) both those agreements are conditional upon the admission of the securities to the Official List of The Stock Exchange, and

(d) the consideration for each security is the same under both agreements,

for which purposes "newly subscribed securities" are securities which, in pursuance of the arrangement referred to in (a) above, are issued wholly for new consideration; and

(3) as regards an agreement if the securities to which the agreement relates are registered securities other than units under a unit trust scheme and:

(a) the agreement is made in pursuance of an offer to the public made by A., and

(b) the agreement is conditional upon the admission of the securities to the Official List of The Stock Exchange, and

(c) under the agreement A. issues to B. or his nominee a renounceable letter of acceptance, or similar instrument, in respect of the securities.

The above changes apply to all agreements to transfer securities made on or after 8 May 1987, and the Treasury are empowered by statutory instrument to amend para. (1) (b), para (2) (c), and para. (3) (b).

Thus, where there is an offer to the public and the relevant shares are to be listed, then provided that the consideration for the relevant transactions matches the public offer price, there will be no stamp duty reserve tax liability in respect of (1) the purchase by an issuing house of any securities other than units under a unit trust scheme (whether held by vendors in registered form, or in respect of which vendors hold renounceable letters of allotment, *e.g.*, as with bonus shares in an offer for sale by existing shareholders) provided that the issuing house actually goes on to sell the shares as arranged, or (2) the sale by an issuing house of newly-issued shares to which it has acquired the rights, or (3) the sale by any person (whether or not an issuing house) of existing registered shares, where the sale is effected by the issue of renounceable letters of acceptance. This, the Revenue hope, will achieve the object desired by corporate finance practitioners, that the interposition of an issuing house as principal should not lead to a stamp duty reserve tax liability which would not arise if the issuing house acted as agent.

Unfortunately, s. 89A as drafted has a number of problems.

First, in each case the relevant agreement must be made in connection with an "offer to the public". That expression is not defined. Indeed, the only statutory guidance as to its meaning is contained in the Companies Act 1985, ss. 59 and 60—the prospectus provisions which have been repealed (to the extent that they relate to securities which are listed or are the subject of an application for listing) by the Financial Services Act 1986, s. 212 (3). The provisions still apply in relation to offers of unlisted securities, but will finally be repealed when s. 212 (3) comes fully into force. A prospectus is defined by the Companies Act 1985, s. 744, effectively as an invitation made to the public to subscribe for or purchase shares or debentures. Such invitations are obviously constituted by offers of securities to the public at large, so that anyone can apply for them, but the Companies Act 1985, s. 59 (1), to the extent that it remains unrepealed, provides that the definition also includes invitations making offers "to any section of the public, whether selected as members or debenture holders of the company concerned, or as clients of the person issuing the prospectus, or in any other manner". However, the Companies Act 1985, s. 60 (1), again to the extent that it remains unrepealed, provides that an invitation is not to be regarded as being made to the public if it can properly be regarded, in all the circumstances, "as not being calculated to result, directly or indirectly, in the shares or debentures becoming available for subscription or purchase by persons other than those receiving the offer or invitation, or otherwise as being a domestic concern of the persons making and receiving it". In the case of a private company, by virtue of the Companies Act 1985, s. 60 (3)–(7) an invitation is treated as being "a domestic concern" if it is confined to existing members and employees of the company, members of their families, or existing debenture holders, or if it is made under an employees' share scheme to beneficiaries or potential beneficiaries of the scheme, even if in either case the invitation is made on terms permitting the offeree to renounce his rights (provided the renunciation is only in favour of a similarly restricted class of person).

Where the specific provisions of the Companies Act 1985, s. 60(3)–(7) do not apply, the interpretation of the exemptions given in s. 60(1) have caused a great deal of difficulty and given rise to a large body of case law.

Rights issues of public companies are *prima facie* "offers to the public" because of the express wording of s. 59(1), but are in certain circumstances treated as not being "offers to the public", and therefore exempt, because not calculated to result in the securities to be issued being subscribed by anyone other than the offerees. This depends upon the terms of the letter of rights. If the letter of rights is non-renounceable, then the rights issue clearly falls within the exemption. In the case of *Government Stock & Other Securities Investment Company Ltd.* v. *Christopher* [1956] 1 WLR 237, at 242, Wynn-Parry J., held that an offer of shares to the shareholders of two companies did not amount to an offer of shares to the public because "the test is not who receives the circular, but who can accept the offer put forward. In this case it can only be persons legally interested as shareholders. . . . In the case of those who accept, non-renounceable letters of allotment will be issued." However, if the letter of rights is renounceable it has been suggested (see, for example, *Pennington's Company Law*, 5th edn., at p. 274) that whether or not the offer constitutes an "offer to the public" depends in part on whether what the recipient transfers by renouncing it is a right to apply for, or accept an offer of, securities, or a title to securities which he has already agreed to take. In the first case, the invitation must be regarded as being calculated to result in someone other than the recipient subscribing for the securities, and therefore an "offer to the public". This would be the case where, for example, a letter of rights states that the recipient is entitled to subscribe for a certain number of securities but that his right to subscribe can be renounced in favour of any other person, and that the securities will be allotted or issued to the person who completes and returns the registration application form. On the other hand, it is arguable that a letter of rights in the form of a provisional letter of allotment cannot be treated as an offer to the public because it purports to allot securities to the recipient, so that if the recipient renounces his right in favour of another person he thereby accepts the securities allotted to him and merely assigns the benefit of the allotment to the renouncee. In that case the person in whose favour the renunciation is made does not subscribe for the securities but acquires title to them by purchase.

The exemption for domestic concerns, although that expression is also somewhat vague, has in practice been held quite clearly to include private placings to a limited number of institutional or other investors. In addition by virtue of the Companies Act 1985, s. 60(8), in the case of public companies where application has been made for the admission of the securities to the Official List of The Stock Exchange, an offer of those securities "to a person whose ordinary business it is to buy or sell shares or debentures (whether as principal or agent)" is not deemed to be an offer to the public.

It is by no means certain that the courts will construe s. 89A by analogy with the above-mentioned partially repealed (and soon to be completely repealed) provisions of the Companies Act 1985, but in the absence of any other guidance it is difficult to see how else s. 89A can be construed. If the courts do adopt such an interpretation, the new provisions will not avoid completely a double charge to stamp duty reserve tax in every situation where a merchant bank acts as principal rather than as agent in corporate finance transactions. The exemptions will apply in offers for sale (either of new shares or by existing shareholders) on an initial flotation, and possibly in vendor rights offers and vendor rights issues (*i.e.*, vendor consideration placings with "claw-back"), but they will not apply to private placings, including the traditional forms of vendor consideration placing (*i.e.*, without "claw-back"), or any other capital raising exercises involving a limited number of investors and the interposition of a merchant bank.

The same difficulty of construction arises in relation to TMA 1970, s. 25(2), which applies (with modifications) to stamp duty reserve tax by virtue of the Stamp Duty Reserve Tax Regulations 1986, reg. 20. The Board of Inland Revenue can under s. 25(2) require issuing houses and others to make a return of all public issues or placings of shares or securities in any company effected by them during a specified period, giving certain particulars. Questions of construction will for this purpose be rather less of a problem because any issue of shares involving a merchant bank will almost always be a placing if it is not a public issue, although rights issues which do not constitute public offers (if the arguments set out above are correct) may not be placings either, and therefore could conceivably be excluded altogether.

One other definitional problem is the use of the expression "issuing house" in s. 89A(1) and (2). Although the expression is generally recognised by corporate finance practitioners, it is not an expression which has a very precise meaning. TMA 1970, s. 25(2), as mentioned above, contains provisions empowering the Board of Inland Revenue to require particular returns to be made by certain persons and includes (by association) "issuing houses" as within the category of persons "carrying on a business of effecting public issues of shares or securities in any company, or placings of shares or securities in any company, either on behalf of the company, or on behalf of holders of blocks of shares or securities which have not previously been the subject of a public issue or placing". Presumably that is the way in which the term "issuing house" will be construed for the purposes of s. 89A, although it again gives rise to the same questions regarding the definition of a "public" issue.

Agreements relating to units under unit trust schemes, and any agreement which is not conditional upon the admission of the relevant securities to the Official List of The Stock Exchange, are specifically excluded. Also, in the case of agreements within s. 89A (1) and (2) (transfers of securities to issuing houses, and the sale by issuing houses of newly-subscribed securities), the price at which the securities are sold to the public by the issuing house must be the same as the price which the issuing house paid for them. In the case of agreements to which s. 89A (1) relates (purchases by an issuing house) it is of course a condition that the issuing house actually on-sells the securities in accordance with the relevant arrangements.

The requirement of s. 89A (2) that "newly-subscribed securities" must be securities issued "wholly for new consideration" is somewhat confusing. On one analysis, this could be construed as meaning that the consideration for the issue of the shares must be a fresh injection of cash or assets into the company, so that the exemption would apply to offers of shares issued for cash or in consideration for acquisitions of assets (in vendor consideration placings) but not offers of shares issued by way of capitalisation of reserves (in a bonus issue) to existing shareholders immediately prior to an offer for sale. The only statutory usage of the term "new consideration" is in TA 1988, s. 254. For the purpose of determining the tax treatment of company distributions, the word "distribution" includes not only a cash dividend but also any other distribution out of the assets of a company *except* (amongst other things) a distribution equal in amount or value to any "new consideration" received by the company for the distribution. In this connection only, "new consideration" is deemed to mean consideration not provided directly or indirectly out of the assets of the company, and in particular is deemed not to include amounts retained by the company by way of capitalising a distribution, unless by way of capitalisation of share premium account where the capitalised premium was itself created by the company receiving new consideration. Bonus issues, other than by way of capitalisation of share premium account, are therefore (for these purposes only) not treated as distributions for "new consideration". However, for the purposes of company law the consideration for an issue of shares by way of bonus is no less valuable than the consideration for an issue of shares in return for cash or assets. Bonus shares are not a gift from the company, *i.e.,* issued for no consideration at all, but are paid up in full or part by the capitalisation of profits or reserves which could otherwise have been distributed to the shareholders as a cash dividend, or (in the case of unrealised profits) retained as a reserve. For company law purposes an issue of bonus shares is treated as an issue for a consideration otherwise than in cash, and an appropriate return and written contract for the allotment have to be delivered to the Registrar of Companies under the Companies Act 1985, s. 88. TA 1988, s. 254 applies for a limited purpose only, but if it is used by analogy for the purposes of s. 89A sales of bonus shares acquired by issuing houses for public offer will not necessarily come within the exemption. If the exemptions do not apply to bonus shares, s. 89A will not solve the principal problem that it was introduced to deal with—the potential double tax charge where issuing houses act as principal in offers for sale involving both existing registered shares and newly allotted shares. It remains to be seen how in practice s. 89A (2) will be applied.

Irrespective of whether or not an offer for sale of existing registered shares involves the interposition of a merchant bank, either as principal or agent, s 89A (3) is drafted in such a way as to relieve one of the two potential double charges to stamp duty and stamp duty reserve tax which would otherwise arise as a result of the use of renounceable letters of acceptance. Although the matter was not entirely free from doubt, it was generally believed that, where renounceable letters of acceptance were issued in respect of existing registered shares, which at the end of the renunciation period were transferred to the new holders, stamp duty reserve tax was payable both on the issue of the renounceable letters of acceptance to successful applicants and on each subsequent purchase of a renounceable document in the market, and that stamp duty was payable on the transfer of the underlying securities to the ultimate renouncee. Before the enactment of s. 89A (3), it seems that, in the case of applicants who did not renounce letters of acceptance issued to them, payment of the stamp duty on the transfers of the underlying securities to them would have relieved them from the stamp duty reserve tax payable in respect of the original issue of the letters of acceptance. However, in the case of letters of acceptance which were renounced, the stamp duty on the ultimate transfers of the underlying securities would not have relieved the stamp duty reserve tax payable either by the original successful applicants (because the shares were not ultimately transferred to them in accordance with s. 89 (4)) or by the ultimate renouncees (because the shares were represented by renounceable documents of title so that s. 88 (2) and (3) prevented the stamp duty reserve tax from being relieved by the stamp duty). Under s. 89A (3) a stamp duty reserve tax liability cannot arise on the issue of renounceable letters of acceptance to successful applicants for existing registered shares (whether those letters of acceptance are subsequently renounced or not) but it neither relieves the stamp duty reserve tax payable by ultimate renouncees nor allows the stamp duty paid on the share transfers in their favour to "frank" that liability. Ultimate renouncees of letters of acceptance evidencing rights to existing registered shares remain liable for stamp duty reserve tax on the renunciation in their favour notwithstanding the delivery to them of a duly stamped instrument of transfer.

Section 89A (3) (*a*) does not require A. to be an issuing house entering into the agreement in the ordinary course of its business, and it therefore applies wherever renounceable letters of acceptance are issued in respect of existing registered shares offered to the public, whether or not a merchant bank is involved.

[Note: See note at commencement of commentary on this Act.]

90. Section 87: other exceptions. (S&S 634–635)
No liability arises to stamp duty reserve tax in relation to an agreement to transfer a unit under a unit trust scheme if the transfer is in favour of the managers of the scheme, or if (at the time the agreement is made) the trustees under the scheme are resident outside the U.K. and the unit being transferred is not registered in a register kept in the U.K. by or on behalf of the trustees.

No liability to stamp duty reserve tax arises in respect of an agreement to transfer securities constituted by, or transferable by means of, either (*a*) an overseas bearer instrument, or (*b*) an inland bearer instrument which does not fall within Exemption 3 to the "bearer instrument" head of charge in SA 1891, Sch. 1 (*i.e.*, renounceable letters of allotment, and similar instruments, where the rights are renounceable not later than six months after issue).

There are specific exclusions in relation to agreements forming part of arrangements for depositary schemes and schemes for the provision of clearance services, which are subject to the special provisions set out in ss. 93 to 97.

The exemption provided in s. 90 (5) and (6) as substituted is wider than the exemption originally granted. The exemption from the principal charge on securities which are held by a nominee for a clearance service was widened, with retrospective effect, by the removal of references to "chargeable securities" (defined in FA 1986, s. 99 (3) as including units in a unit trust scheme) and the substitution of references to "shares, stock or marketable securities", whether or not "chargeable securities". Consequently, the stamp duty definition of "marketable securities" contained in SA 1891, s. 122 (1) was imported. Previously, the exemption would only have been available if all the securities held by the nominee (whose business consisted solely of holding securities as nominee for the clearance service) were chargeable securities.

No liability to stamp duty reserve tax arises in respect of an agreement to transfer securities to a charitable body or trust, to the Trustees of the National Heritage Memorial Fund, or to the Historic Buildings and Monuments Commission for England.

[Note: See note at commencement of commentary on this Act.]

91. Liability to tax. (S&S 635)
Pursuant to this section, as amended by F(No.2)A 1987, the person liable to pay the stamp duty reserve tax is the person who agrees to purchase the shares, *i.e.*, B.

[Note: See note at commencement of commentary on this Act.]

92. Repayment or cancellation of tax. (S&S 635)
If, after the expiry of the two-month period referred to in s. 87 but within a period of six years from the date beginning on the date of the agreement (or, if the agreement is conditional, the date it became unconditional), the conditions for relief are satisfied (*i.e.*, an instrument or instruments transferring all the chargeable securities to B. or his nominee has or have been executed and duly stamped) then the stamp duty reserve tax, if paid, is refundable or, if not paid, ceases to be payable. Refunds of £25 or more carry interest at the rate applicable under FA 1989, s. 178, and the Taxes (Interest Rate) Regulations 1989, S.I. 1989 No. 1297 (and see the Revenue Press Release, 26 October 1989, reproduced in Appendix 4).

All interest paid on repayments of stamp duty reserve tax is exempt from income tax. This brings the stamp duty reserve tax repayment provisions into line with similar provisions for other taxes.

[Note: See note at commencement of commentary on this Act.]

OTHER CHARGES

93. Depositary receipts. (S&S 635–639)
Depositary receipts for stocks and shares are not included in the definition of "chargeable securities" for the purposes of a charge to stamp duty reserve tax, and special provisions make them subject to the tax in appropriate circumstances.

There is a charge to stamp duty reserve tax where, in pursuance of an arrangement, a person (whose business is or includes that of issuing depositary receipts for chargeable securities) has issued or is to issue a depositary receipt for chargeable securities, and chargeable securities of the same kind and amount are transferred or issued to his nominee or agent, or appropriated by his nominee or agent towards the eventual satisfaction of the entitlement of the receipt-holder to receive chargeable securities. It seems to be essential that there should be both an issuer of depositary receipts and a person who acts as his nominee, so that there is no charge to stamp duty reserve tax where the issuer of the depositary receipt does not use a nominee or agent but has the securities transferred direct to him.

The expression "depositary receipt for chargeable securities" is defined in s. 94 and "chargeable securities" in s. 99.

The basic rate of stamp duty reserve tax in these circumstances is £1·50 for every £100 or part of £100 of the following:

(*a*) in a case where the securities are issued, their price when issued;

(*b*) in a case where the securities are transferred for a consideration in money or money's worth, the amount or value or the consideration; and

(*c*) in any other case, the value of the securities.

As to the meaning of the word "value", either of the consideration or (as the case may be) the securities, see s. 94.

Where the securities are transferred by means of an instrument on which stamp duty under the heading "conveyance or transfer of any kind not hereinbefore described" in SA 1891, Sch. 1 is chargeable, the rate is reduced to £1 for every £100 or part of £100 provided that:

(*a*) at the time of the transfer the transferor is a qualified dealer in securities of the kind concerned or a nominee of such a qualified dealer; and

(*b*) the transfer is made for the purposes of the dealer's business; and

(*c*) at the time of transfer the dealer is not a market maker in securities of the kind concerned; and

(*d*) the relevant instrument contains a statement that these conditions have been fulfilled.

As to determining when a person is a qualified dealer or market maker in securities of a particular kind, see s. 94.

Stamp duty reserve tax is calculated by reference to the total of the instalments payable less those already paid where:

(*a*) securities are issued or transferred upon terms that (in either case) they are to be paid for in instalments; and

(*b*) the person to whom they are issued or transferred holds them and transfers them to another person when the last instalment is paid; and

(*c*) stamp duty reserve tax on the latter transfer is calculated on the basis of the value of the securities; and

(*d*) before the execution of the final transfer an instrument is received by a person whose business is or includes holding chargeable securities as nominee or agent for a depositary; and

(*e*) that instrument evidences the rights vested in the shares; and

(*f*) the final transfer contains a statement that the above conditions have been fulfilled.

Unlike in the normal case, where the payment of stamp duty on an appropriate instrument relieves from any liability for stamp duty reserve tax, in the case of a transfer into a depositary scheme where the *ad valorem* stamp duty is less than the stamp duty reserve tax, the stamp duty reserve tax is only relieved to the extent of the stamp duty and the excess is chargeable. If the *ad valorem* stamp duty equals or exceeds the stamp duty reserve tax, then no stamp duty reserve tax is payable, but neither is any excess stamp duty repayable. Effectively, therefore, in the case of transfers into a depositary scheme, the charge is the higher of the *ad valorem* stamp duty and the stamp duty reserve tax.

The person liable for stamp duty reserve tax is the person who has issued or is to issue the depositary receipt, but where such person is not resident in the U.K. and does not have a branch or agency in the U.K., the person liable for the tax is the person to whom the transfer was made.

Where chargeable securities are issued or transferred on sale on terms providing for payment by instalments and for an issue of other chargeable securities, and stamp duty reserve tax would normally be payable in respect of the issue, then no stamp duty reserve tax is payable unless any of the instalments becomes payable by a person whose business is or includes issuing depositary receipts for chargeable securities, or by his nominee or agent, in which case tax becomes payable when an instalment is payable, at the rate of £1·50 for every £100 or part of £100 of the instalment payable. The person liable to pay the instalment is in these circumstances the person liable for the stamp duty reserve tax.

There is a complete exemption from any charge that would otherwise arise under this section on securities issued by certain international organisations of which the U.K. or any EC country is a member (see FA 1984, s. 126).

[*Note:* See note at commencement of commentary on this Act.]

94. Depositary receipts: supplementary. (S&S 639–641)

A depositary receipt for chargeable securities is an instrument acknowledging that a person holds chargeable securities, or evidence of the right to receive them, and that another person is entitled to rights, whether expressed as units or otherwise, in or in relation to chargeable securities of the same kind, including the right to receive such securities (or evidence of the right to receive them) from the person holding such securities or evidence. It does not include an instrument acknowledging rights in or in relation to securities if they are issued or sold on terms providing for payment in instalments and for the issue of the instrument as evidence that an instalment has been paid. The Treasury are given power by statutory instrument to amend this definition.

The value of any consideration not consisting of money is taken to be the price it might reasonably expect to fetch on a sale in the open market at the time the securities are transferred. The value of any securities is taken to be the price they might reasonably be expected to fetch on a sale in the open market at the time they are transferred or appropriated (as the case may be).

A person is a qualified dealer in securities of a particular kind if he deals in securities of that kind and is a member of a recognised stock exchange (within the meaning given by TA 1988, s. 841), or is designated a qualified dealer by the Treasury by statutory instrument.

A person is a market maker in securities of a particular kind if he holds himself out at all normal times in compliance with the rules of The Stock Exchange as willing to buy and sell securities of that kind at a price specified by him, and is recognised as so doing by the Council of The Stock Exchange. This definition is the same as that contained in FA 1986, ss. 69 (stamp duty provisions relating to depositary receipts) and 82 (borrowing of stock by market makers) and is to be contrasted with the definitions in ss. 81 (3) and 89 (3) (stamp duty and stamp duty reserve tax exemptions in relation to sales to market makers) which, as amended, extend to transactions in unlisted securities by authorised persons under the Financial Services Act 1986. The Treasury has power by statutory instrument to amend the definition.

There is a complete exemption from any charge that would otherwise arise under this section on securities issued by certain international organisations of which the U.K. or any EC country is a member (see FA 1984, s. 126).

[*Note:* See note at commencement of commentary on this Act.]

95. Depositary receipts: exceptions. (S&S 641)
The following transactions are excluded from the charge imposed by s. 93:

(*a*) transfers of securities by a person whose business is exclusively that of holding relevant securities as nominee or agent for a person whose business is or includes issuing depositary receipts for relevant securities, and for the purpose of the issue of depositary receipts, to another such person, provided that both transferor and transferee are resident in the U.K.;

(*b*) transfers, issues or appropriations of inland bearer instruments within the meaning of the "bearer instrument" head of charge in SA 1891, Sch. 1 which do not fall within Exemption 3 to that head of charge (*i.e.*, renounceable letters of allotment and similar documents with a life of six months or less); and

(*c*) issues by one company (X.) of securities in exchange for shares of another company (Y.), where either X. already has control of Y. or X. will have control of Y. in consequence of the exchange, or in consequence of an offer as a result of which the exchange is made, for which purpose X. is deemed to have control of Y. if it has power to control Y.'s affairs by virtue of holding shares in, or possessing voting power in relation to, Y. or any other body corporate.

[*Note:* See note at commencement of commentary on this Act.]

96. Clearance services. (S&S 642–644)
This section imposes a charge to stamp duty reserve tax where one person (A.), whose business is or includes the provision of clearance services for the purchase and sale of chargeable securities, has entered into an arrangement to provide such clearance services for another person, and in pursuance of the arrangement, chargeable securities are transferred or issued to A. or to a person whose business is or includes holding chargeable securities as nominee for A.

The expression "clearance services" is not defined and concern has been expressed that the provision of any nominee services to facilitate dealings in securities could be within its meaning. The Revenue have indicated that this is not the intention, and that their policy will be to construe the expression so as to include only arrangements which are expressly marketed as "clearance services". In cases of doubt, the Revenue's guidance should be sought.

The rate payable is £1·50 for every £100 or part of £100 of the following:

(*a*) in a case where the securities are issued, their price when issued;

(*b*) in a case where the securities are transferred for consideration in money or money's worth, the amount or value of the consideration; and

(*c*) in any other case, the value of the securities.

The value of any consideration which does not consist of money is taken to be the price it might reasonably be expected to fetch on a sale on the open market at the time the securities are transferred, and the value of securities is taken to be the price they might reasonably be expected to fetch on a sale in the open market at the time they are transferred.

The duty is reduced to £1 for every £100 or part of £100 where:

(*a*) the securities are transferred by an instrument on which stamp duty under the heading "conveyance or transfer of any kind not hereinbefore described" in SA 1891, Sch. 1 is chargeable; and

(*b*) at the time of transfer the transferor is a qualified dealer in securities of the kind concerned or a nominee of such qualified dealer; and

(*c*) the transfer is made for the purposes of the dealer's business; and

(*d*) at the time of the transfer the dealer is not a market maker in securities of the kind concerned; and

(*e*) the instrument contains a statement that conditions (*b*) to (*d*) are fulfilled.

"Qualified dealer" and "market maker" mean the same as they do for the purposes of s. 93 in connection with depositary schemes.

As with depositary schemes, the stamp duty reserve tax is chargeable by reference to the total of the instalments payable, less those paid before the transfer to the other person is effected in any case where:

(*a*) securities are issued or transferred on sale upon terms (in either case) that they are to be paid for in instalments; and

(*b*) the person to whom they are issued or transferred holds onto them and transfers them to another person when the last instalment is paid; and

(*c*) the latter transfer would attract stamp duty reserve tax on the value of the securities transferred; and

(*d*) before the making of the latter transfer an instrument is received by A. or a person whose business is or includes holding chargeable securities as nominee for A.; and

(*e*) that instrument evidences all the rights vested in the securities; and

(*f*) the transfer to the other person contains a statement to the effect that the above conditions are fulfilled.

Where chargeable securities are issued or transferred on sale upon terms providing for payment in instalments and for an issue of other chargeable securities, no stamp duty reserve tax is chargeable notwithstanding any other provisions of this section unless any instalment becomes payable by A. or his nominee, in which event tax is payable at the rate of £1·50 for every £100 or part of £100 of the instalment payable.

As is the case with depositary schemes, unlike the usual rule that a payment of stamp duty relieves from any liability for stamp duty reserve tax, in the case of clearance services where *ad valorem* stamp duty paid on a transfer of securities is less than the stamp duty reserve tax, the stamp duty reserve tax is only relieved to the extent of the *ad valorem* stamp duty and tax will be payable on the excess. In any case where the *ad valorem* stamp duty equals or exceeds the stamp duty reserve tax, there is no stamp duty reserve tax, but neither is there a corresponding provision that the excess stamp duty be repaid, so that effectively the charge is the higher of the *ad valorem* stamp duty and the stamp duty reserve tax.

In the case of clearance services, stamp duty reserve tax is payable by the person who provides the services, *i.e.*, A., unless at the time of the transfer such person is not resident in the U.K. and has no branch or agency in the U.K., in which case the transferee is liable for the tax. The only exception to this is where stamp duty reserve tax becomes payable on payment of an instalment, in which case the person liable to pay the instalment is liable for the tax.

The expression "chargeable securities" is defined in s. 99.

[*Note:* See note at commencement of commentary on this Act.]

97. Clearance services: exceptions. (S&S 644)
No charge to stamp duty reserve tax under s. 96 in relation to clearance services arises in any of the following cases:

(*a*) Where securities are transferred by one company whose business is exclusively that of holding securities as nominee for a person providing clearance services to another such company, provided that both the transferor and the transferee are resident in the United Kingdom.

(*b*) Where a transfer is effected by an instrument on which stamp duty is not chargeable by virtue of FA 1976, s. 127 (1) (transfer to The Stock Exchange nominee) or FA 1986, s. 84 (2) or (3) (transfer to a recognised investment exchange or a recognised clearing house, or their respective nominees).

(*c*) In a case of a transfer or issue of an inland bearer instrument within the meaning of the heading "bearer instrument" in SA 1891, Sch. 1 which does not fall within Exemption 3 in that heading (renounceable letters of allotment and similar instruments with a life of six months or less).

(*d*) In respect of an issue by one company (X.) of securities in exchange for shares in another company (Y.) where X. already has control of Y., or will have control in consequence of the exchange or in consequence of an offer as a result of which the exchange is made, for which purpose X. is deemed to have control of Y. if X. has power to control Y.'s affairs by virtue of holding shares in, or possessing voting power in relation to, Y. or any other body corporate.

[*Note:* See note at commencement of commentary on this Act.]

GENERAL

98. Administration etc. (S&S 644–645)
The Treasury may make regulations by statutory instrument providing for specific provisions of TMA 1970 to apply in relation to stamp duty reserve tax, with such modifications as the Treasury thinks fit, and making such further provisions with regard to stamp duty reserve tax as the Treasury thinks fit in relation to administration, assessment, collection and recovery.

The regulations made are the Stamp Duty Reserve Tax Regulations 1986 (S.I. 1986 No. 1711 as amended by S.I. 1988 No. 835 and by S.I. 1989 No. 1301): see commentary under Statutory Instruments.

The *Stamp Duty Reserve Tax—Notes for Guidance* issued by the Stamp Office (see Appendix 7) give, particularly in Chapter 7, a good descriptive guide to the administrative and payment procedures.

[*Note:* See note at commencement of commentary on this Act.]

99. Interpretation. (S&S 645–646; A27)

"Chargeable securities" are defined (except for the purposes of ss. 93, 94 and 96 in relation to depositary schemes and clearance services) as "stocks, shares, loan capital and units under a unit trust scheme", the words "unit" and "unit trust scheme" being given the same meaning as in FA 1946, Pt. VII. References to stocks, shares, or loan capital are deemed to include references to any interest in, or in dividends or other rights arising out of, stocks, shares or loan capital (but, interestingly, not units in a unit trust scheme), and any right to an allotment of or to subscribe for, or an option to acquire, stocks, shares or loan capital (again, not units in a unit trust scheme).

Stocks, shares and loan capital which are issued or raised by a body corporate not incorporated in the U.K. (including interests in, rights to an allotment of or to subscribe for, and options to acquire such stocks, shares and loan capital) are excluded unless:

(*a*) in the case of stocks, shares and loan capital, they are registered in a register kept in the U.K. by or on behalf of the relevant body corporate; or

(*b*) in the case of shares, they are paired with shares issued by a body corporate incorporated in the U.K.; or

(*c*) in the case of interests, rights or options, the stocks, shares or loan capital to which such interests, rights or options relate are either stocks, shares or loan capital registered in a register kept in the U.K. or shares paired with shares issued by a body corporate incorporated in the U.K.

For the purpose of deciding if an "option to acquire" stocks, shares or loan capital falls within the exclusion in relation to overseas registered securities, the relevant criterion is the place of registration of the securities to which the option related.

Shares issued by a body incorporated outside the U.K. are deemed to be paired with shares issued by a body incorporated in the U.K. where the Articles of Association of the U.K. company and the equivalent instruments governing the foreign company each provide that no share in the company to which they relate may be transferred otherwise than as part of a unit comprising one share in that company and one share in the other and:–

(i) such units were offered for sale to the public in the U.K. and, at the same time and in equal numbers at a broadly equivalent price, in the country in which the foreign company is incorporated (and as to the difficulties of construing what does, and what does not, constitute an "offer to the public", see notes on FA 1986, s. 89A); or

(ii) provided there has been an earlier public offering complying with (i) above, such units comprise shares in the U.K. company and shares in the foreign company which are allotted and issued (as part of such units) as fully or partly paid bonus shares.

In addition, provided that there has been an earlier public offering complying with (i) above, even where paired share units are subsequently issued in *unequal* numbers in the two countries (for example as a pro rata rights issue where, because of trading between the two countries, the units are no longer held equally in the two countries), the new shares in the foreign company are still deemed to be paired with the new shares in the U.K. company and therefore fall within the definition of "chargeable securities" in sub-s. (4).

Depositary receipts for stocks or shares (but not depositary receipts for loan capital) are excluded from the definition of "chargeable securities". A depositary receipt is taken to be an instrument acknowledging (*a*) that a person holds stocks or shares, or evidence of the right to receive them, and (*b*) that another person is entitled to rights, whether expressed as units or otherwise, in or in relation to stocks or shares of the same kind, including the right to receive such stocks or shares (or evidence of the right to receive them) from the person holding the stocks or shares, or evidence. A depositary receipt does not include an instrument acknowledging rights in or in relation to stocks or shares if they are issued or sold on terms providing for payment in instalments and for the issue of the instrument as evidence that an instalment has been paid (*i.e.*, such instruments *are* chargeable securities). The Treasury has the power by statutory instrument to amend the definition of depositary receipts.

The failure to exclude, from the definition of chargeable securities, depositary receipts for loan capital could give rise to a double tax charge. For example, registered depositary receipts for convertible loan stock would be chargeable on issue under s. 93 and there would be a further charge under s. 87 on each agreement to transfer them.

The most important exclusion from the definition of "chargeable securities" for the purpose of stamp duty reserve tax is "stocks, shares or loan capital the transfer of which is exempt from all stamp duties", (and interests in, rights to and options to acquire stocks, shares or loan capital the transfer of which is exempt from all stamp duties) *e.g.*, gilt-edged securities and most forms of non-convertible loan capital (which are exempt by virtue of FA 1986, s. 79). The Revenue has also indicated in the *Notes for Guidance*, (see Appendix 7) that neither options traded on The Stock Exchange nor financial futures traded on the London International Financial Futures Exchange are "chargeable securities".

For the purposes of FA 1986, ss. 93, 94 and 96 in connection with depositary schemes and clearance services, the definition of "chargeable securities" includes shares of a foreign company (or interests therein or rights thereto) which are paired with U.K. shares, even though it does not include for those purposes shares issued by a foreign company which are registered in a register kept in the U.K. However, where shares of a foreign company (or an interest therein or a right thereto) are transferred into a depositary scheme or clearance service, no stamp duty reserve tax liability arises simply because the shares (or interest or right) are paired with shares in a U.K. company (or an interest therein or a right thereto) provided that they are "newly subscribed shares", meaning shares issued wholly for new consideration in pursuance of an offer for sale to the public. Again, note the difficulties which might arise in construing this definition discussed in relation to FA 1986, s. 89A.

Also, in relation to depositary schemes and clearance services, the effect of s. 99 (10) (*b*) is that shares are not deemed to be "exempt from all stamp duties", and therefore not subject to stamp duty reserve tax on transfer, simply because they are registered in an overseas branch register under the Companies Act 1985, s. 362. Such shares will therefore be chargeable securities, an agreement for the transfer of which would give rise to a charge to stamp duty reserve tax.

[*Note:* See note at commencement of commentary on this Act.]

PART VII MISCELLANEOUS AND SUPPLEMENTARY

114. Short title, interpretation, construction and repeals. (S&S 347)
The stamp duty provisions contained in Pt. III (ss. 64 to 85) are to be construed as one with SA 1891, but the stamp duty reserve tax provisions contained in Part IV (ss. 86 to 99) are not to be so construed.

[*Note:* See note at commencement of commentary on this Act.]

Insolvency Act 1986
1986 Chapter 45

190. Documents exempt from stamp duty. (S&S 423)

In the case of a company registered in England and Wales which is being wound up by a court, or in a creditors' voluntary winding-up, the following documents are exempt from stamp duty: (a) every assurance relating solely to freehold or leasehold property, or to any estate right or interest in any real or personal property, which forms part of the company's assets and which, after execution of the assurance, either at law or in equity, is or remains part of those assets, and (b) every writ, order, certificate, or other instrument relating solely to the property of any such company, or to any proceeding under the winding up.

Similar provisions are made for companies registered in Scotland.

378. Exemption from stamp duty. (S&S 423)

This section exempts documents relating to the bankruptcy of an individual which are similar to those contained in s. 190 in relation to companies in the course of being wound up by the court, or in a creditors' voluntary winding up.

Finance Act 1987
1987 Chapter 16

PART III STAMP DUTY AND STAMP DUTY RESERVE TAX

STAMP DUTY

48. Unit trusts. (S&S 352)

The definition of "unit trust scheme" in FA 1946, s. 57, is replaced by that in the Financial Services Act 1986, s. 75 (8), with a consequential amendment to the definition in s. 57 of "trust instrument".

In addition, Treasury regulations by statutory instrument may exclude specified schemes from the revised definition of "unit trust scheme" and make supplemental and transitional provisions.

[*N.B.* In relation to the prospective abolition of all stamp duties on transactions in shares (including bearer instruments) and units under unit trust schemes, and of stamp duty reserve tax, see the Revenue Press Release, 20 March 1990 and the commentary on FA 1990.]

49. Contract notes. (S&S 352–353)

The remaining provisions of F(1909–10)A 1910, s. 77–79 are repealed. Although FA 1985, s. 86 provided that no duty was payable on contract notes made and executed after 25 March 1985, it did not remove the obligation on brokers and market makers to prepare contract notes.

Notwithstanding the change however, the conduct of business rules that govern transactions by financial intermediaries under rules laid down by the Securities and Investments Board, consequent upon the Financial Services Act 1986, impose similar obligations to prepare contract notes.

[*N.B.* In relation to the prospective abolition of all stamp duties on transactions in shares (including bearer instruments) and units under unit trust schemes, and of stamp duty reserve tax, see the Revenue Press Release, 20 March 1990 and the commentary on FA 1990.]

50. Warrants to purchase Government stock, etc. (S&S 353–354)

Any instrument which vests or transfers an interest in, or a right to be allotted or to subscribe for, or an option to acquire or dispose of, "exempt securities", is exempt from stamp duty under the heading "Conveyance or Transfer on Sale" and the heading "Conveyance or Transfer of any kind not hereinbefore described". There is also an exemption from stamp duty under the "Bearer Instrument" head of charge on the issue or transfer of any such interest, right or option.

"Exempt securities" means "securities" (*i.e.*, stock or marketable securities or loan capital within the meaning of FA 1986, s. 78 (7)) the transfer of which is exempt from all stamp duties, or where there is an exemption from the "Bearer Instrument" head of charge by virtue of FA 1967, s. 30 (relating to securities not denominated in sterling) or its Northern Ireland equivalent, or by virtue of FA 1986, s. 79 (2) (relating to loan capital constituted by or transferable by means of a bearer instrument).

The definition therefore covers the following types of securities:

(*a*) gilt-edged securities;

(*b*) loan capital in bearer form exempt from stamp duty under FA 1986, s. 79 (2);

(*c*) loan capital in registered form exempt from stamp duty under FA 1986, s. 79 (4) (loan capital issued by companies and foreign government);

(*d*) loan capital which falls within the terms of the exemption in FA 1986, s. 79 (3) (loan capital issued by certain international bodies); and

(*e*) bearer securities denominated in a foreign currency exempt from duty under FA 1967 s. 30 (or its Northern Ireland equivalent).

[*N.B.* In relation to the prospective abolition of all stamp duties on transactions in shares (including bearer instruments) and units under unit trust schemes, and of stamp duty reserve tax, see the Revenue Press Release, 20 March 1990 and the commentary on FA 1990.]

51. Bearer instruments relating to stock in foreign currencies. (S&S 354–355)

References to currencies other than sterling or to any units of account referable to more than one currency (such as European Currency Units or ECUs) replace references to currencies of territories outside the scheduled territories following the repeal of the Exchange Control Act 1947.

[*N.B.* In relation to the prospective abolition of all stamp duties on transactions in shares (including bearer instruments) and units under unit trust schemes, and of stamp duty reserve tax, see the Revenue Press Release, 20 March 1990 and the commentary on FA 1990.]

52. Clearance services. (S&S 355)

In FA 1986, s. 70 (6) references to shares, stock or other marketable securities replace references to relevant securities (defined in FA 1986, s. 72 (1) as shares in or stock or marketable securities of any company).

[*N.B.* In relation to the prospective abolition of all stamp duties on transactions in shares (including bearer instruments) and units under unit trust schemes, and of stamp duty reserve tax, see the Revenue Press Release, 20 March 1990 and the commentary on FA 1990.]

53. Borrowing of stock by market makers. (S&S 355)
An error in FA 1986, s. 82 (6) is corrected.

[*N.B.* In relation to the prospective abolition of all stamp duties on transactions in shares (including bearer instruments) and units under unit trust schemes, and of stamp duty reserve tax, see the Revenue Press Release, 20 March 1990 and the commentary on FA 1990.]

54. Shared ownership transactions. (S&S 355–356)
FA 1980, s. 97 and FA 1981, s. 108, which limit the duty payable on a shared ownership lease, are amended.

The list of lessees to which FA 1980, s. 97 applies includes unregistered as well as registered housing associations because the Housing and Planning Act 1986 brought within the shared ownership scheme leases granted by unregistered housing associations.

The reliefs provided by FA 1980, s. 97 and FA 1981, s. 108 are extended to leases granted by a private landlord who has taken over a public housing estate. The Housing Act 1985, s. 171A, inserted by the Housing and Planning Act 1986, preserves a tenant's right to be granted a shared ownership lease when an estate is privatised.

55. Crown exemption. (S&S 356)
Exemptions from stamp duties previously granted to the Secretary of State for the Environment and the Secretary of State for Transport (but not other Secretaries of State) are replaced with a general exemption for all Ministers of the Crown and the Treasury Solicitor. No stamp duty is to be charged under the "Conveyance or Transfer on Sale", "Conveyance or Transfer of any kind not hereinbefore described", or "Lease or Tack" heads of charge on any instrument effecting a conveyance, transfer or lease to a Minister of the Crown or to the Treasury Solicitor. "Minister of the Crown" is as defined in the Ministers of the Crown Act 1975.

STAMP DUTY RESERVE TAX

56. Stamp duty reserve tax. (S&S 357, 677)
Schedule 7, which amends various parts of the stamp duty reserve tax legislation, is introduced.

SCHEDULES

SCHEDULE 7 STAMP DUTY RESERVE TAX (Section 56). (S&S 677–680)

[*N.B.* In relation to the prospective abolition of all stamp duties on transactions in shares (including bearer instruments) and units under unit trust schemes, and of stamp duty reserve tax, see the Revenue Press Release, 20 March 1990 and the commentary on FA 1990.]

1.—The stamp duty reserve tax provisions of FA 1986 are modified.

Principal charge
2.—FA 1986, s. 87 which provides for the main half per cent. reserve tax charge on sales of securities not attracting the normal half per cent. stamp duty is amended.

Where shares are subsold and the number of shares bought exceeds the number of shares subsold, s. 87 is to have effect as if there were separate agreements in respect of each parcel of shares. The effect of this is that reserve tax is only paid in respect of the shares subsold. The following example shows how this provision will operate.
A. sells to B. 1,000 shares in X. plc for £1,500;
B. resells 750 of these shares to C;
A. transfers 750 shares to C. and 250 shares to B.

The agreement between A. and B. is deemed to be two separate agreements, one in respect of 750 shares and one in respect of 250 shares with the result that B. incurs a reserve tax liability on the agreement to purchase 750 shares *i.e.*, on £1,125 (75 per cent of £1,500). The stamp duty payable on the transfer to B. of the 250 shares franks the reserve tax liability on that agreement.

On a strict construction of s. 87 there was a reserve tax charge on the whole of the consideration paid by B. to A. The Revenue indicated that reserve tax would only be sought in respect of that part of the consideration which related to the shares subsold; this is made statutory.

The application of the tax is clarified where there is a transfer of shares to a person (*e.g.*, a bank) who is providing a loan and who is to hold the shares as security for the loan. On a strict construction of s. 87 the transaction gave rise to a double-charge—reserve tax on the purchase agreement and ad valorem stamp duty on the transfer of shares to the person who is to hold them. The transaction was not covered by the provisions in s. 87 which deal with transactions that attract both charges. The transaction is brought within the terms of those provisions with the result that the reserve tax charge is removed. These changes are deemed always to have had effect.

Renounceable letters of allotment, etc.
3.—The date on which reserve tax is payable on sales of renounceable documents of title is brought forward.

FA 1986, s. 88 (which brings these instruments within the scope of the reserve tax) is amended with the result that the charge arises on the date on which the sale is agreed. Formerly, the charge arose two months after the sale and the tax was payable at the end of the month following that in which the charge arises. The effect is therefore to bring forward the date on which reserve tax is payable on the purchase of a renounceable document. The two-month period between the sale and the date on which the charge arises was provided to allow stamp duty to be paid (reserve tax only arises where stamp duty is not paid). This two-month period of grace is not needed in this case because the instruments concerned do not attract stamp duty. The new rule applies to agreements made on or after 1 August 1987.

Market-makers in options
4.—A reserve tax exemption is provided for market makers in options.

A new FA 1986, s. 89 (1A) provides that the principal charge does not apply to the purchase of chargeable securities by a Stock Exchange market maker in quoted options in the ordinary course of the firm's business as a market maker in these options. The definition of "quoted options" covers both traded options and traditional options.

The change is deemed always to have had effect.

Clearance services
5.—The exemption from the principal charge is widened for shares which attract the one and a half per cent. stamp duty or reserve tax charge when they enter a clearance system. The change ensures that the exemption will apply to nominees whose business is to hold securities as nominee for a clearance system whether or not the securities held are within the scope of the reserve tax charge. As the law stood previously the exemption would only apply if the nominee held securities liable to the reserve tax

These provisions are deemed always to have had effect.

Charities etc.
6.—The reserve tax is not to apply to purchases of shares etc. by charities and certain analogous bodies.

FA 1986, s. 70 (exemptions from the principal reserve tax charge) is amended to disapply the reserve tax charge where securities are bought by a charity, a charitable trust or certain analogous bodies. These transactions are exempt from stamp duty and have been treated as exempt from the reserve tax. This paragraph puts the reserve tax practice on to a statutory basis.

This provision is deemed always to have had effect.

Interest on tax repayments
7.—Interest paid on repayments of reserve tax is exempt from income tax. This brings the reserve tax repayment provision into line with similar provisions for other taxes. The exemption is deemed always to have applied.

Finance (No. 2) Act 1987
1987 Chapter 51

PART III MISCELLANEOUS AND SUPPLEMENTARY

99. Stamp duty: options etc. (S&S 357)

The exemption given by FA 1987, s. 50 (from stamp duty under the headings "conveyance or transfer on sale" and "conveyance or transfer of any kind not hereinbefore described") is extended to any instrument which vests or transfers an option to *dispose of* "exempt securities"; it previously applied only to options to *acquire* "exempt securities".

The definition of "exempt securities" for the purposes of s. 50 is extended to include bearer instruments relating to loan capital.

[*N.B.* In relation to the prospective abolition of all stamp duties on transactions in shares (including bearer instruments) and units under unit trust schemes, and of stamp duty reserve tax, see the Revenue Press Release, 20 March 1990 and the commentary on FA 1990.]

100. Stamp duty reserve tax. (S&S 680)

A new s. 89A in FA 1986 gives specific exemptions for agreements entered into in connection with public issues of securities. FA 1986, s. 91 is amended so that the person who is liable to pay stamp duty reserve tax will be the person who agrees to purchase the shares, *i.e.*, B., even where that person is acting as a nominee for another person. Formerly, where B. was a nominee his principal was liable for the tax.

[*N.B.* In relation to the prospective abolition of all stamp duties on transactions in shares (including bearer instruments) and units under unit trust schemes, and of stamp duty reserve tax, see the Revenue Press Release, 20 March 1990 and the commentary on FA 1990.]

Finance Act 1988
1988 Chapter 39

PART IV MISCELLANEOUS AND GENERAL

STAMP DUTY AND STAMP DUTY RESERVE TAX

140. Abolition of stamp duty under the heading "Unit Trust Instrument". (S&S A51)
Trust instruments (whether by deed or not) establishing unit trust schemes were liable to stamp duty at 25p per £100 on the assets initially comprised in the fund. Duty at the same rate was payable on further property added to the trust.

This duty is abolished, in relation to any trust instrument executed on or after 22 March 1988, any trust instrument executed on or after 16 March 1988 which is not stamped before 22 March 1988, any property becoming trust property on or after 22 March 1988, and any property becoming trust property on or after 16 March 1988 in respect of which the trust instrument is not stamped before 22 March 1988.

SA 1891, s. 14 (4) provides effectively that the admissibility of any document as evidence in legal proceedings will depend upon whether or not such document was stamped "in accordance with the law in force at the time of execution". Accordingly, in the case of trust instruments executed, or property becoming trust property, before the dates specified above, the statutory provisions which existed and the case law which evolved in relation to unit trust instrument duty before its abolition will still be relevant.It will also be relevant for the purpose of investigating title to property. Reference to the 1987–88 edition of this Guide (and where appropriate to S&S) should therefore be made whenever it is necessary to review the relevant statutory provisions and case law.

A trust deed or other instrument creating or recording a unit trust will still be subject to the fixed stamp duty of 50p as a declaration of trust.

The abolition of unit trust instrument duty does not affect any liability to pay the stamp duty and stamp duty reserve tax due in the ordinary course of events on transfer documents in relation to property being transferred into a unit trust, or on transfers of and agreements to transfer units.

[*N.B.* In relation to the prospective abolition of all stamp duties on transactions in shares (including bearer instruments) and units under unit trust schemes, and of stamp duty reserve tax, see the Revenue Press Release, 20 March 1990 and the commentary on FA 1990.]

141. Abolition of stamp duty on documents relating to transactions of capital companies. (S&S A52)
The 1 per cent. stamp duty on documents relating to transactions of capital companies (popularly known as "capital duty") imposed by FA 1973 s. 47, and regulated by s. 48 and Sch. 19, was introduced to give effect to the provisions of EC Council Directive 69/335, which the U.K. was obliged to implement on joining the EC. The Directive was amended in 1985 by Directive 85/303 which allowed the duty to be reduced or abolished.

Capital duty is abolished, and FA 1973, ss. 47 and 48 and Sch. 19 are repealed, in respect of any transaction occurring on or after 22 March 1988, any transaction occurring on or after 16 March 1988 in respect of which the relevant document is not stamped before 22 March 1988, any exempt transaction occurring before 22 March 1988 in respect of which an event occurs on or after 22 March 1988 which would cause the relief to be lost, and any exempt transaction occurring before 16 March 1988 in respect of which an event occurs on or after 16 March 1988 which would otherwise cause the relief to be lost and the relevant duty is not paid before 22 March 1988. The U.K. is the first member state of the EC to abolish capital duty.

Again, SA 1891, s. 14 (4) provides for the admissibility of any document as evidence in legal proceedings to be judged in accordance with the stamp duty law in force at the time of the execution of that document, and accordingly the former statutory provisions, and the voluminous case law in relation to those provisions which evolved before abolition, will be relevant in respect of chargeable transactions which took place before the above dates, and in respect of events which occurred before the above dates causing the loss of previously granted reliefs. For a detailed analysis of the former statutory provisions, and the relevant case law, see the 1987-88 edition of this Guide and S&S.

The abolition of capital duty does not affect the statutory requirements to make returns to the Registrar of Companies in respect of issues of share capital and other relevant transactions of U.K. limited companies under the Companies Act 1985. A new form 88 (2) (Revised 1988) has been introduced for notifying the Registrar of Companies of allotments of shares under s. 88 (2) of the Companies Act 1985 in place of the following forms, which were previously required to be stamped under the capital duty provisions:

PUC2 (Revised)   Return of allotments of shares issued for cash.
PUC3 (Revised)   Return of allotments of shares issued wholly or in part for a consideration other than cash.

and in place of the old form 88 (2) (Return of allotment of shares issued by way of capitalisation of reserves (bonus issues)) which did not require to be stamped. Additionally, the old forms PUC1, PUC4, PUC5 and PUC6 are no longer required. See the DTI press release of 8 August 1988 and the Companies (Forms) (Amendment) Regulations 1988 (S.I. 1988 No. 1359) reproduced in Appendix 1.

142. Stamp duty: housing action trusts. (S&S A53)

Housing action trusts established under the Housing Act 1988, Part III, are added to the lists of bodies from whom leases can be taken in shared ownership transactions, or from whom houses can be bought at a discount, in order for the stamp duty relief provisions in those sections to apply.

143. Stamp duty: paired shares. (S&S A54)

Legislative effect is given retrospectively to arrangements announced at the time of the so-called "Equity 3" capital-raising exercise by the Eurotunnel consortium, although ss. 143 and 144 are drafted in general terms so as to apply to any similar situation.

Eurotunnel was put together as an Anglo-French partnership comprising two principal holding companies, one (Eurotunnel Plc) ("EPLC") incorporated in England and the other (Eurotunnel S.A.) ("ESA") incorporated in France. The "Equity 3" capital-raising exercise consisted of simultaneous offers for sale to the public in the U.K. and France of "units", each of which comprised one share with a par value of 40p. in EPLC and one share with a nominal value of FFr. 10 in ESA, and each of which was issued together with a "New Warrant" which itself comprised the right to subscribe for one-tenth of a share in EPLC and one-tenth of a share in ESA, the warrants being exercisable only in integral multiples of 10.

The shares in EPLC and ESA were therefore effectively "twinned". Under the Articles of Association of EPLC, issues or transfers of shares in that company are not permitted unless they are issued or transferred together with the same number of shares in ESA. The *Statuts* of ESA contain a reciprocal restriction. In addition, the Articles of EPLC and the *Statuts* of ESA provide that shares in EPLC and ESA respectively can only be listed or authorised to be dealt in on any stock exchange in the form of units. Listing was subsequently granted by the London Stock Exchange and the Bourse in Paris for all of the issued shares in EPLC and ESA provided that they are in the form of units.

Without special provision, these arrangements would have given rise to complex liabilities to stamp duty and stamp duty reserve tax; the units could not have been treated in the same way as though each unit were a single share. Although the situation was not free from doubt, it seems that broadly speaking more stamp duty would have become payable than was intended, but less stamp duty reserve tax, and to enable each of these liabilities to be separately assessed the units would have had to have been split into their component shares.

As far as stamp duty is concerned, in addition to the duty which would be (and is) payable in the normal way on transfers of units in the U.K., on the whole of the price paid for the units, bearer instrument duty at the rate of 1.5 per cent. would also have been payable because shares in EPLC had to be delivered in France (and some other countries) in bearer form to meet the requirements of the local market. It was therefore proposed to relieve the units from bearer instrument duty. For stamp duty reserve tax purposes, shares in EPLC would have been (and are) "chargeable securities" so that agreements to transfer them would give rise to a stamp duty reserve tax liability, but shares in ESA would not necessarily have fallen within the definition because the company is not a U.K. company, so that there was a possibility that agreements to transfer them would not give rise to a stamp duty reserve tax liability. It was therefore also proposed to change the stamp duty reserve tax legislation so that agreements to transfer units would give rise to a stamp duty reserve tax liability in relation to the whole of the unit and not just its EPLC component part.

This section contains the relieving provision in relation to bearer instrument stamp duty. It applies where the Articles of Association of a U.K. company and the equivalent instruments relating to a foreign company each provide that no share in the company to which they relate may be transferred except as part of a unit comprising one share in that company and one share in the other, and the units are to be or have been offered for sale to the public in the U.K. and at the same time in the country in which the foreign company is incorporated. The provision is a little restrictive: units can comprise only one share in each company whereas it is possible to imagine situations where it might be more convenient for a unit to comprise a greater number of shares. The number of units offered in the foreign country is to be exactly equal to the number of units offered in the U.K. The units must also be offered in the U.K. and the foreign country "at a broadly equivalent price".

In any such circumstances, no bearer instrument stamp duty is to be chargeable on the issue of any bearer instrument representing shares in the U.K. company, or a right to an allotment of or to subscribe for such shares, if the purpose of the issue is to make such shares available for sale as part of "twinned" units pursuant to the public offers in the U.K. or the relevant foreign country, or any other public offer made at the same time and at a broadly equivalent price in a country other than the U.K. or the relevant foreign country.

On the other hand, bearer instrument stamp duty will be payable on the issue by the foreign company of an instrument which represents shares in that company, or a right to an allotment of or to subscribe for such shares, other than for the purpose of making such shares available for sale as part of units pursuant to the offers for sale in the U.K., the relevant foreign country, or any other country as mentioned above. The foreign company is treated as though it were a U.K. company for these purposes.

The foreign company is also to be treated as though it were a U.K. company for the purposes of transfers of units into depositary schemes and clearance services.

No stamp duty will generally be payable on the first issue of the units pursuant to the offers for sale notwithstanding that the U.K. company may as part of the arrangements be issuing bearer instruments to facilitate trading. The issue by the foreign company of bearer instruments will not in any case be chargeable for stamp duty under the existing law. The U.K. company is accordingly treated as though it were a foreign company for the purpose of bearer instrument duty on the issue of bearer instruments as part of the offers for sale.

Where a transferee (or any other holder) of units in registered form exchanges them for units in bearer form, bearer instrument stamp duty will be payable on the value of the units concerned. In the case of the shares in the U.K. company comprised in the unit, bearer instrument stamp duty would in any case be payble under the existing law, and the foreign company is treated as though it were a U.K. company for these purposes.

Similarly the foreign company is treated as though it were a U.K. company so that transfers of units into a depositary scheme or clearance service will bear the higher rate of duty under the relevant sections of FA 1986.

Bearer instruments representing shares in the U.K. company or the foreign company, or a right to an allotment of or to subscribe for such shares, are relieved from the requirement of SA 1891, s. 3 that every instrument written on the same piece of material as another instrument be separately stamped.

The "equal numbers" test in s. 143 (1) (*b*) cannot be satisfied where, following a public offering of paired share units, there is a rights issue of such units. When the rights issue is made the original units will be held unequally in the two countries because of trading between the two countries and a pro rata rights issue is bound to be unequal. This section has therefore been amended to enable the new units issued in these circumstances to have the benefit of the exemption from bearer instruments duty without satisfying the equal numbers test. See the Revenue Press Release, 14 June 1990, and the commentary on FA 1990.

[*N.B.* In relation to the prospective abolition of all stamp duties on transactions in shares (including bearer instruments) and units under unit trust schemes, and of stamp duty reserve tax, see the Revenue Press Release, 20 March 1990 and the commentary on FA 1990.]

Finance Act 1989
1989 Chapter 26

PART III MISCELLANEOUS AND GENERAL

STAMP DUTY ETC.

173. Insurance: abolition of certain duties. (S&S A61)

Stamp duties under the headings "Policy of Life Insurance" and "Bond, Covenant, or Instrument of any kind whatsoever" (superannuation annuities) in SA 1891, Sch. 1 are abolished in respect of instruments made after 31 December 1989. Repeals are consequently made of SA 1891, s. 100 (with effect from 30 November 1989 in relation to subsection (1) and 31 December 1989 in relation to subsection (2)) and s. 118 (with effect from 31 December 1989) and the relevant parts of Sch. 1; FA 1956, s. 38 and its Northern Ireland equivalent; FA 1959, s. 30 (4) and its Northern Ireland equivalent; FA 1966, s. 47 and its Northern Ireland equivalent (in relation to variations of a policy after 31 December 1989, whenever the policy was made); FA 1970, Sch. 7, paras. 7 (4) and 17 and their Northern Ireland equivalents; FA 1982, s. 130; and the relevant parts of TA 1988, Sch. 14, para. 3 (4).

The effect of sub-section (2) is that instruments which were formerly chargeable under paragraph (3) of the "Bond, Covenant or Instrument of any kind whatsoever" head of charge are not to be chargeable under any of the heads of charge which remain in existence purely because of the abolition of this specific head of charge.

174. Unit trusts. (S&S A62)

Amendments are made to FA 1989, s. 101 consequent upon the changes made elsewhere in this Act bringing unit trusts that can only invest in U.K. gilts into the corporation tax regime applicable to other authorised unit trusts, and the resulting disapplication of TA 1988, s. 468 (5). The section as amended restates in express terms the existing exemption from stamp duty applicable to transfers of units in such unit trusts where the funds of such trusts cannot be invested in investments, transfers of which are themselves liable to *ad valorem* stamp duty.

[*N.B.* In relation to the prospective abolition of all stamp duties on transactions in shares (including bearer instruments) and units under unit trust schemes, and of stamp duty reserve tax, see the Revenue Press Release, 20 March 1990 and the commentary on FA 1990.]

175. Stamp duty: stock exchange nominees. (S&S A63)

This and the following section confer on the Treasury regulation-making powers to adapt stamp duty and stamp duty reserve tax to the new methods of transferring shares which are being developed, particularly by the Stock Exchange as it moves towards its proposed "dematerialised" (*i.e.* paperless) system of share transactions, known as "TAURUS". A general discussion of paperless systems for transactions in securities is contained in the DTI Consultative Paper, the text of which is set out in Appendix 9. According to the Budget Press Release of 14 March 1989 (the full text of which is set out in Appendix 4), regulation-making powers were needed by the Treasury as an interim measure to ensure that transfers made by these new methods are liable to stamp duty and stamp duty reserve tax on the same basis as ordinary transactions effected by present methods.

In relation to a paperless transaction the charge would be to stamp duty reserve tax, rather than to stamp duty. However, the Revenue believed that there might be circumstances when for example the present rules could:

(*a*) produce double—or even multiple—charges to stamp duty reserve tax, or a stamp duty liability in addition to a stamp duty reserve tax liability; or

(*b*) mean a transaction fails to qualify for the stamp duty reserve tax reliefs available to a paper-based transaction; or

(*c*) impose collection obligations and procedures which do not fit the new arrangements.

The Revenue therefore believed that the present stamp duty reserve tax rules needed to be adapted in one or more ways.

Regulations under this section may be made by the Treasury (by statutory instrument) to treat the stamp duty charge as not arising if there would otherwise be a charge both to stamp duty reserve tax and *ad valorem* conveyance on sale duty in circumstances to be prescribed by the regulations where a stock exchange nominee is involved.

See also the powers conferred on the Secretary of State by the Companies Act 1989, s. 207.

All of these provisions must now be read in the light of the prospective abolition of all stamp duties on transactions in shares, and of stamp duty reserve tax (as to which see the Revenue Press Release, 20 March 1990 and the commentary on FA 1990).

176. Stamp duty reserve tax: stock exchange nominees. (S&S A63)
For the background to this section, see the commentary on the preceding section, above. Regulations under this section may be made by the Treasury by statutory instrument, where prescribed circumstances exist involving a stock exchange nominee, either:

(*a*) to treat one of the charges as not arising if there would otherwise be two stamp duty reserve tax charges; or

(*b*) to treat the stamp duty reserve tax charge as not arising if there would otherwise be a charge both to stamp duty reserve tax and to stamp duty; or

(*c*) to provide that a statutory provision by virtue of which there is no charge to stamp duty reserve tax shall apply; or

(*d*) to provide that a statutory provision by virtue of which a lower rate of stamp duty reserve tax is chargeable than would otherwise be the case shall apply.

But note the final paragraph in the commentary on s. 175, above.

177. Stamp duty reserve tax: information. (S&S A64)
This section extends the regulation-making powers conferred on the Treasury by FA 1986, s. 98 (1) to enable the Treasury to make regulations entitling the Commissioners to specify the manner or the form in which notices or information are to be given or supplied to them in connection with the routine administration of stamp duty reserve tax.

But, note the final paragraph in the commentary on s. 175, above.

INTEREST, ETC.

178. Setting of rates of interest. (S&S A64)
Rates of interest on unpaid and overpaid stamp duty reserve tax are set automatically in accordance with formulae prescribed in regulations made by statutory instrument subject to annulment by a resolution of the House of Commons.

Regulations may, inter alia, provide for a specific rate of interest to be applicable or for the applicable rate to be determined by reference to a given rate or average of rates, for a specific increase or decrease in the applicable rates, or an increase or decrease calculated by reference to given formulae, for a rate calculated by reference to an average to be rounded up or down, and for specified circumstances in which alterations in rates are or are not to take place.

The Board of Inland Revenue is also empowered by order to specify a rate of interest without the need for a statutory instrument where the rate provided for by regulations made under this section is changed and the new rate is not specified in the regulations.

The Regulations made under this section are the Taxes (Interest Rate) Regulations 1989, S.I. 1989 No. 1297, reproduced in Appendix 1; see also Revenue Press Release of 26 October 1989 reproduced in Appendix 4. But note the final paragraph in the commentary on s. 175 above.

179. Provisions consequential on section 178. (S&S A65)
Consequential amendments are made inter alia to FA 1986, s. 92 (2).

180. Repayment interest: period of accrual.
An amendment is made to FA 1986, s. 92 (2) to bring it into line with enactments relating to other taxes and to confirm that interest on overpaid stamp duty reserve tax is calculated up to the day on which the payable order for repayment is issued. (FA 1986, s. 92 (4), (5) is repealed as set out in Sch. 17, Part XI).

But, again, see above note.

GENERAL

186. Interpretation, etc.

187. Repeals

188. Short Title.

SCHEDULE 17 REPEALS (Section 187)

PART IX STAMP DUTY: INSURANCE

Repeals are made in accordance with s. 173.

PART X RATES OF INTEREST

Repeals are made in accordance with s. 178.

Electricity Act 1989
1989 Chapter 29

103. Stamp duty exemption for certain contracts.
Electricity is treated as goods for the purposes of SA 1891, s. 59, so that a contract for the sale of electricity is not stampable.

Companies Act 1989
1989 Chapter 40

207. Transfer of securities.

The purpose of this section was explained by Mr. Francis Maude as follows:

"I announced on 1 December at col. 369 that I was considering proposing changes to the law that would, if both the company and the shareholder wished, enable shares to be held on computer, without certificates, and to be transferred without the need for paper transfer forms. This process, sometimes referred to as dematerialisation, is important for London's leading position as an international trading market. Paperless schemes will also offer important benefits for wider share ownership by providing a more efficient service to investors.

I issued a consultative document on the proposed changes and I am grateful to all those individuals and organisations who responded. It is essential that any schemes finally developed meet the legitimate needs of all potential users and I welcome the progress made by the international stock exchange as a result of its recent and continuing consultations.

The moves towards paperless trading are intended to reduce transaction risks and costs. In considering possible changes to legislation it is essential to strike the right balance between the interests of shareholders, of companies and of the financial institutions. I have also borne in mind that schemes will develop over time and that competitors may emerge with different approaches from the nominee-based scheme currently being considered by the stock exchange. Against this background it is clearly important that the framework should be flexible.

I hope to bring forward proposals in the form of amendments to the Companies Bill. These will be intended to ensure that the move towards paperless trading does not alter significantly the effect in practice of current company, investor protection and insolvency law. In order to achieve this the Secretary of State would be empowered to make regulations, subject to affirmative resolution, which would then provide a framework within which authorised systems would operate. The purpose of the regulations would be:

(a) to facilitate the introduction and operation of computer based systems for recording the holding of securities (or interests in them) and for their transfer;

(b) to ensure that, as far as reasonably practicable, investors, issuers (i.e. companies) and others are in a correponding position under such a computer-based system as they are under the present paper-based system.

The regulations will make provisions inter alia for ensuring that authorised systems and their participants are properly regulated. They will also ensure that the speed and ease with which information about the identities of owners of shares is made available is comparable to present arrangements; and that investors continue to enjoy broadly the same rights as they do now."

(HC Written Ans., 14 June 1989, Vol. 154, cols. 443–444.)

See also the commentary on FA 1989, ss. 175 and 176, and the DTI Consultative Paper, the text of which is set out in Appendix 9. All of these must now be read in the light of the prospective abolition of all stamp duties on transactions in shares, and of stamp duty reserve tax (as to which, see the Revenue Press Release of 20 March 1990 and the commentary on FA 1990).

Finance Act 1990
1990 Chapter 29

PART III STAMP DUTY AND STAMP DUTY RESERVE TAX

REPEALS

107. Bearers: abolition of stamp duty.

Stamp duty under the heading "Bearer Instrument" in SA 1891, Sch. 1 is prospectively abolished. The abolition will have effect in respect of (i) bearer instruments issued on or after the "abolition day" either in Great Britain or by or on behalf of corporate or unincorporated bodies formed or established in Great Britain, and (ii) transfers of stock in Great Britain on or after the "abolition day" by means of bearer instruments not issued in Great Britain or by or on behalf of corporate or unincorporated bodies formed or established in Great Britain. Equivalent provisions are made in relation to Northern Ireland. For these purposes, "abolition day" has the meaning given in FA 1990, s. 111.

108. Transfer of securities: abolition of stamp duty.

Stamp duty on instruments transferring or vesting (i) stocks, shares or loan capital, (ii) interests in, or in dividends or other rights arising out of, or rights to allotments of or to subscribe for, or options to acquire or to dispose of, stocks, shares or loan capital, or (iii) units under a unit trust scheme, is prospectively abolished.

The abolition will have effect in respect of instruments executed in pursuance of a contract made on or after the "abolition day" or, in the case of instruments which are not executed in pursuance of a contract or which relate to transfers into depositary receipt schemes or clearance services, executed on or after the "abolition day".

For these purposes: (i) "loan capital" is given a very similar meaning to that contained in FA 1986, s. 78 (7), save that all government debt (whether of the U.K., Northern Ireland or a foreign country) is included; (ii) "unit" and "unit trust scheme" are given the meanings applicable under FA 1946, Pt. VII (s. 57) immediately before "abolition day"; and (iii) "abolition day" has the meaning given in FA 1990, s. 111.

109. Stamp duty: other repeals.

A number of miscellaneous and consequential provisions are also made.

The fine of £20 payable by any person who in the U.K. assigns, transfers or negotiates a foreign security or a Commonwealth government security that is not duly stamped will not apply where the assignment, transfer or negotiation is executed or takes place on or after the "abolition day".

The provisions relating to the cancellation of bearer share or stock or unit trust certificates where the holder has been entered on the register are abolished in the case of entries made on or after the "abolition day".

The fine payable by a person who completes a blank share transfer delivered to him pursuant to a sale of the shares to which it relates, and then parts with possession of it or removes it offshore, will not apply where the sale takes place on or after the "abolition day".

No notifications to the Commissioners will be required by issuers of depositary receipts or providers of clearance services, or by their respective nominees or agents, where they issue their first receipts, or provide their first services, or first act as such nominee or agent, on or after the "abolition day", or by companies who first become aware that their shares are held by any such persons on or after that date.

Various ancillary provisions are to cease to have effect as provided by statutory instrument.

For all these purposes, "abolition day" has the meaning given in FA 1990, s. 111.

110. Stamp duty reserve tax: abolition.

Stamp duty reserve tax is prospectively abolished. The abolition will have effect, so far as the principal charge is concerned, where an unconditional agreement to transfer is made on or after the "abolition day" or where a conditional agreement to transfer becomes unconditional on or after the "abolition day". In so far as arrangements involving depositary receipt schemes and clearance services are concerned, the abolition will have effect where the relevant securities are transferred, issued or appropriated on or after the "abolition day", whenever the arrangements were made.

Similar provisions also apply where there are schemes involving payment for securities by instalments in circumstances where stamp duty reserve tax would be payable; the abolition will have effect where the relevant securities are issued or transferred on sale, pursuant to such schemes, on or after the "abolition day".

Again, for all these purposes "abolition day" has the meaning given in FA 1990, s. 111.

111. General.

The "abolition day" will be appointed by statutory instrument. The provisions in relation to the abolitions of stamp duty contained in ss. 107 to 109 are to be construed as one with SA 1891.

PAIRED SHARES

112. Stamp duty.

This section amends FA 1988, s. 143 in relation to "paired share" units offered for sale in the U.K., on or after the day on which FA 1990 received the Royal Assent, in circumstances where there has been an earlier offer of "paired share" units in the two companies concerned. As long as in a previous offer equal numbers of units were offered in the relevant countries, units subsequently offered can be offered in unequal numbers in those countries without losing the exemption given by s. 143 for bearer instrument duty at the rate of 1.5 per cent.

The rationale behind this section is explained in the Inland Revenue's Press Release of 15 June 1990 [see Appendix 4]. The amendment was made to ensure that rights issues of paired share units receive the same stamp duty treatment as the units of paired shares originally issued, which is consistent with the Government's intention of making it possible for units of paired shares to be traded in the same way as shares in a single company. If the shares comprised in a paired unit are issued in both bearer and registered form, under s. 143 as enacted there is an exemption from the bearer instrument duty otherwise chargeable on the issue of the bearer shares in the British company, provided inter alia that the units are issued in equal numbers in both countries. The equal numbers test, however, is one that a rights issue cannot satisfy. When the rights issue is made, the original units will be held unequally in the two countries because of trading between them and a pro rata rights issue is bound to be unequal. This section ensures that rights issues do not have to pass the equal numbers test.

113. Stamp duty reserve tax.

Two amendments are made to the definitions of "chargeable securities" for stamp duty reserve tax purposes in FA 1986, s. 99.

Again, the rationale for the amendments is explained in the Inland Revenue's Press Release of 15 June 1990 [Appendix 4]. The amendments were made to ensure that right issues and bonus issues of paired share units receive the same stamp duty reserve tax treatment as the units of paired shares originally issued, which is consistent with the Government's intention of making it possible for units of paired shares to be traded in the same way as shares in a single company.

Under FA 1986, s. 99 (as amended by FA 1988, s. 144) there is a stamp duty reserve tax charge on the trading of the foreign company's shares as part of the registered units marketed in the U.K., provided inter alia that the units are issued in equal numbers in both countries. The equal numbers test, however, is one that a rights issue cannot satisfy. When the rights issue is made, the original units will be held unequally in the two countries because of trading between them and a pro rata rights issue is bound to be unequal. Accordingly, FA 1986, s. 99 is amended. Where paired share units of a U.K. and a foreign company are offered for sale in the U.K. in circumstances where there has been an earlier offer of such units then, as long as in the earlier offer equal numbers of units were offered in the relevant countries, the units subsequently offered can be offered in unequal numbers in those countries without the shares in the foreign company comprised in the units being excluded from the definition of "chargeable securities" and thereby escaping a stamp duty reserve tax charge on trading.

The inserted FA 1986, s. 99 (6B) ensures that bonus issues of paired share units are chargeable securities for stamp duty reserve tax purposes, provided that there has been an earlier offer of such units to which s. 99 (6A) applied without the amendment made by subsection (2) of this section (i.e. the units were offered in equal numbers in the two countries concerned).

INTERNATIONAL ORGANISATIONS

114. International organisations.

FA 1984, s. 126, enables the Treasury to designate international organisations of which the U.K. is a member for the purpose of specific exemptions from various taxes. This section amends s. 126 to enable such organisations to be given limited exemption from stamp duty reserve tax on the issue of their securities and was enacted as a result of the decision to establish the European Bank for Reconstruction and Development (EBRD) in the U.K. The Articles of Agreement of the EBRD require exemption from all taxes on the bank's securities which arise solely because they are issued by the bank or because of local factors (*i.e.* the place or currency of issue of the securities, or the location of the bank itself). The SDRT charges relieved by this section, which fall within this category, are the higher rate (1.5 per cent.) charges which arise on the issue of chargeable securities on a U.K. register to the nominee for either a depositary bank or a clearance service. The EBRD may decide to make such issues.

PART IV MISCELLANEOUS AND GENERAL

GENERAL
131. Interpretation etc.

132. Repeals.

133. Short title.

SCHEDULE 19 REPEALS (Section 132)

PART VI STAMP DUTY

Repeals are made in accordance with ss. 107, 108 and 109.

PART VII STAMP DUTY RESERVE TAX

Repeals are made in accordance with s. 110.

STATUTORY INSTRUMENTS

S.I. 1986 No. 1711

The Stamp Duty Reserve Tax Regulations 1986. (S&S 649–674)

[N.B. In relation to the prospective abolition of all stamp duties on transactions in shares (including bearer instruments) and units under unit trust schemes, and of stamp duty reserve tax, see the Inland Revenue Press Release of 20 March 1990 and the commentary on FA 1990.]

Citation and commencement
1. The title and commencement date are given.

Interpretation
2. Various terms are defined.
  The "accountable date", which is the due date for payment of the tax, means the last day of the month following that in which the charge arises, except in the case of a charge incurred under the special provisions relating to depositary and clearance schemes, where the time for payment is extended to the last day of the second month following that in which the charge was incurred. Thus, *e.g.*, if an agreement to transfer existing issued shares is entered into on 3 January, the charge will arise on 2 March and will be due and payable either on 30 April or (in the case of transactions involving depositary schemes or clearance systems) 31 May. In the case of an agreement to transfer a renounceable letter of allotment entered into on the same date, *i.e.*, 3 January, the charge will arise on that date and will be due and payable either on 28 February or (as the case may be) on 31 March.
  The "accountable person" is the person who must give notice of a charge and pay the tax (as opposed to the person who is *liable* for the tax, being the purchaser, or "B", under FA 1986, s. 91) and is defined as either the market maker or broker-dealer who purchased the shares or acted as agent for the purchaser, or (if none) the market maker or broker-dealer who sold the shares or acted as agent for the seller, or (if none) the qualified dealer who purchased the shares or acted as agent for the purchaser, or (if none) the qualified dealer who sold the shares or acted as agent for the seller, or (if none) the purchaser himself. Thus, a purchaser who is a private investor (*i.e.*, who is not a market maker, broker-dealer or qualified dealer) will only have to *account for* the tax himself (although he is always ultimately *liable* for it) if he buys shares privately without the involvement (in any capacity) of a market maker, broker-dealer or qualified dealer. The expressions "broker and dealer" and "market maker" have the same meanings as they have (for the time being) for the purposes of FA 1986, s. 89. "Qualified dealer" is a person who, not being a market maker or broker and dealer, is an "authorised person" under the Financial Services Act 1986, Pt. I, Ch. III. Broadly speaking this means a person authorised by virtue of membership of a recognised self-regulating organisation, a person authorised by certification by a recognised professional body, an authorised insurer, an operator or trustee of a recognised collective investment scheme, or a person specifically authorised by the Secretary of State.
  Practical problems with the accountability of a market maker are caused by the difficulty in identifying, in any given transaction, whether the purchaser is for example a charity which is exempt from stamp duty reserve tax or whether a nominee transferee is the purchaser's nominee (in which case there is no charge arising) or a sub-purchaser's nominee (in which case a charge arises on the sale to the original purchaser).
Due date for payment
3. Any tax charged under FA 1986, ss. 86–89 is due and payable on the accountable date, as defined.

Notice of charge and payment
4. An accountable person, as defined, unless alternative arrangements are authorised by the Revenue, must on or before the accountable date give notice of each charge to tax to the Revenue, and pay the tax due. The Board is empowered to prescribe the form of the notice.
  Under the definition of "accountable person" before its amendment by FA 1988, the "accountable person" was normally B (the purchaser) unless B was not a member of the Stock Exchange but A (the vendor) was such a member, in which case the tax had to be accounted for (and paid) by A. In the case of flotations or privatisations, therefore, where A was a vendor shareholder, an issuing house, or a Minister of the Crown, and therefore not a member of the Stock Exchange, each applicant for shares was a B and therefore accountable for the tax. Frequent use was therefore made of Reg. 4, which provides that "where different arrangements are authorised in writing" by the Revenue someone else could become the accountable person. Such arrangements were made, for example, in the case of the privatisations of British Gas Plc., British Airways Plc. and Rolls Royce Plc., whereby, in order to avoid the private individual investor (who in many cases was a first time share buyer) bearing the administrative burden of accounting for stamp duty reserve tax, it

was agreed that the accountable person would be, respectively, the Secretary of State for Energy, the Secretary of State for Transport and the Secretary of State for Trade and Industry.

However, following the changes in the definition of "accountable person" made by FA 1988, such agreements are in most cases not strictly necessary to protect the private individual investor. All issuing houses as members of self-regulating organisations for the purposes of the Financial Services Act 1986 are within the definition of "qualified dealer" and their involvement in an offer for sale either as principal or as agent for the vendor or offerer renders them liable to account for the stamp duty reserve tax where an applicant is a private individual investor. Agreements under Reg. 4 may, however, still be resorted to in practice, as a matter of administrative convenience to avoid issuing houses being accountable for the tax in respect of some applications but not others (*i.e.* where an applicant is a market maker, broker-dealer or qualified dealer).

Power to require information
5. The Board can require any person to provide them with any specified information (including documents or records) within a period of 30 days or more, except that a barrister or solicitor cannot be obliged to disclose privileged information without his client's consent.

Notice of determination
6. The Board can issue a "notice of determination" to any person who appears to them to be the accountable person, or the person liable for the tax, or any person who has submitted a claim to them.

Relief from accountability
7. An accountable person, other than the purchaser, or the principal of a purchaser acting as a nominee, can be relieved from liability to account for and pay the tax provided that he satisfies the Board that he has taken all reasonable steps to recover the tax from the purchaser.

Appeals against determination
8. An appeal may be made, within 30 days of any notice of determination, to the Special Commissioners, or direct to the High Court if this course of action is agreed between the appellant and the Board, or the High Court itself grants leave. The determination of any question relating to the value of land in the U.K. on any appeal under this Regulation is reserved for the Lands Tribunal.

Appeals out of time
9. Leave to appeal after time may be given by the Board or the Special Commissioners if either the Board or the Special Commissioners (as the case may be) are satisfied that there was a reasonable excuse for the appeal not being brought within the time limit and the application has been made promptly thereafter.

Statement of case for opinion of High Court
10. Any appeal from the Special Commissioners is to be made to the High Court by way of case stated. The High Court is given power to hear any question of law arising on the case and reverse, affirm or amended the determination of the Special Commissioners, or make such other order as it thinks fit. The High Court is also given power to send the case stated back to the Special Commissioners for amendment. The Rules of the Supreme Court have been amended by the Rules of the Supreme Court (Amendment No. 3) 1986, S.I. 1986 No. 2289 to accommodate these provisions.

Interest on overpaid tax
11. Interest on overpaid tax is to be paid at the rate applicable under FA 1989, s. 178, and the Taxes (Interest Rate) Regulations 1989 (S.I. 1989 No. 1297) made under that section. See also Revenue Press Release of 26 October 1989 reproduced in Appendix 4. Any such interest is not to constitute income for income tax or corporation tax purposes.

Recovery of tax
12. The Board is not to take proceedings to recover unpaid tax until the amount is agreed or a notice of determination has been issued under Reg. 6 and any appeal to the Special Commissioners or the High Court under Reg. 8 (but not any further appeal) has been determined.

Underpayments
13. Underpayments of tax are also to be payable with interest, but that no additional tax can become payable more than six years after the date of payment or the relevant accountable date, except in the case of fraud, wilful default or neglect.

Overpayments
14. The Board is relieved from any responsibility to repay over-payments of tax more than six years after the date of the payment or the relevant accountable date.

Inspection of records
15. The Board may inspect all books, documents and records in the possession or control of anaccountable person which contain information relating to any relevant transaction in which he was involved.

Evidence
16. Provisions are made in relation to evidence.

Determination of questions on previous view of the law
17. Liability for the tax is to remain unaltered notwithstanding subsequent legal decisions or changes in the view of the law generally received at the time or adopted in practice.

Recovery of over-repayment of tax, etc.
18. Over-repayments of tax and overpayments of interest may be recovered.

Service of documents
19. The service of documents is provided for.

Taxes Management Act 1970: provisions to apply
20. Certain provisions of TMA 1970 are applied, with certain modifications, in relation to stamp duty reserve tax. These include ss. 50 to 53 (procedure before the Special Commissioners), ss. 61 to 63 (giving powers to levy distress for unpaid tax), s. 65 (power to take action in a magistrates' court), ss. 66 to 68 (powers to take action in the county court and high court), ss. 71 to 74 (providing for the collection of tax from persons chargeable in a representative capacity), ss. 78 and 83, (providing for the assessment of non-residents through a trustee, guardian, branch or agent) and ss. 93 and 95 (imposing penalties for failure to give notice, or for fraudulently or negligently giving an incorrect notice).

Inland Revenue Regulation Act 1890: provisions not to apply
21. The Inland Revenue Regulation Act 1890, ss. 21, 22 and 35 (containing provisions in relation to proceedings for the recovery of fines, etc.) are disapplied.

SCHEDULE

This Schedule specifies, in Pt. I, the provisions of TMA 1970 which are to apply and the modifications to such provisions which are to have effect, and sets out, in Pt. II, those provisions as so modified. For the commentary thereon, see under TMA 1970.

Index
Stamp Duty

Abbreviations

Acts are referred to by the following abbreviations

BTA	British Telecommunications Act
CA	Companies Act
CCA	County Courts Act
EA	Electricity Act
ELA	Electric Lighting Act
FA	Finance Act
GA	Gas Act
IA	Insolvency Act
LCA	Land Commission Act
PCTA	Provisional Collection of Taxes Act
RA	Revenue Act
SA	Stamp Act
SDMA	Stamp Duties Management Act
STA	Stock Transfer Act
TeA	Telecommunications Act

Index
Stamp Duty

Statutes which are not annotated do not appear in this index

Appendices

803

APPENDIX 1. STATUTORY INSTRUMENTS

Contents
S.I.

*These regulations are printed in *Butterworths Orange Tax Handbook* 1989–90 and are not printed in this work. For commentary thereon see under "Statutory Instruments" after FA 1990.

1946 No. 1586

The Unit Trust Records Regulations 1946

Unit Trust Schemes

Note
These Regulations were made by the Commissioners of Inland Revenue under FA 1946, s. 56 (3) on 27 September 1946.

Citation
1. These Regulations may be cited as the Unit Trust Records Regulations 1946.

Interpretation
2. (1) In these Regulations references to the date on which a person became the holder of any units are references to the date of the transfer of those units to him whether by virtue of the delivery to him of a certificate to bearer or by virtue of the execution of an instrument of transfer.
(2) The Interpretation Act 1889 shall apply for the interpretation of these Regulations as it applies for the interpretation of an Act of Parliament.

Preservation by Trustees of certificates and instruments of transfer
3. (1) Every registered certificate and every certificate to bearer in respect of units under a Unit Trust Scheme shall before issue be given a serial number by the trustees of the scheme and when surrendered by the holder shall be preserved by the trustees in such a manner as to enable reference to be made readily thereto.
(2) Every instrument of transfer in respect of units under a Unit Trust Scheme shall, when delivered to the trustees of the scheme, be preserved by the trustees in such a manner as to enable reference to be made readily thereto.

Record of units under Scheme
4. The trustees of a Unit Trust Scheme shall keep a record showing the number of units under the scheme representing the trust property, and from time to time as soon as any change occurs in the amount of such property they shall enter in the record the alteration in the number consequential on such change.

Register of holders of registered units
5. The trustees of a Unit Trust Scheme shall keep a register of the holders of registered units under the scheme and shall enter therein the following particulars:
   (1) The name and address of each person who holds any units under the Scheme, the serial number of the certificate or certificates representing the units held by each such person and the number of units to which each such certificaate relates.
   (2) The date or dates on which each such person became the holder of any units and the number of units of which he became the holder on each such date, and
      (*a*) where he became the holder by virtue of an instrument of transfer, or in consequence of the surrender of a certificate to bearer, a sufficient reference to enable the instrument or certificate to be readily produced;
      (*b*) where he became entitled to the units by operation of law, particulars of the name of the person from whom the right to such units was transmitted to him, and of the circumstances in which it was so transmitted or a sufficient reference to some other record kept by the trustees containing those particulars.
   (3) Where any person has ceased to hold any units the date or dates at which he ceased to hold them, and
      (*a*) where he so ceased by virtue of an instrument of transfer, or in consequence of the issue of a certificate to bearer, a sufficient reference to the instrument of transfer to enable it to be readily produced, or as the case may be, a note of the serial number of the certificate to bearer;
      (*b*) where his right to any units has been transmitted to another person by operation of law, particulars of the name of that person, and of the circumstances in which it was so transmitted, or a sufficient reference to some other record kept by the trustees containing those particulars.

Register of certificates to bearer
6. (1) Where any units under a Unit Trust Scheme are represented by a certificate to bearer, the trustees of the scheme shall enter in a separate part of the register referred to in Regulation 5 or in a separate register, the following particulars:
   (i) the fact of the issue of the certificate, and the serial number of the certificate;
   (ii) the number of units included in the certificate; and
   (iii) the date of the issue of the certificate.

(2) Upon the surrender and cancellation of any certificate to bearer a note of the date of surrender shall be added to the entry.

Loose leaf records: Index
7. (1) Registers or records required under these Regulations may be in loose leaf form instead of in bound books provided that adequate precautions are taken to guard against falsification and ensure its discovery.
(2) Unless the register kept under regulation 5 is in such a form as to constitute in itself an index, the trustess of the scheme shall keep in a convenient form an index of the names of the holders.

Opening statement of units
8. (1) The managers of a Unit Trust Scheme shall keep a statement of the units held by them at the opening of business on 1 August, 1946, showing separately the number represented by certificates to bearer and the number not so represented.
(2) Where it is claimed by the managers that any such units
  (*a*) were not at any time before 1 August, 1946, held by any other person, and did not replace any units so held, or
  (*b*) were units of which they had before that date become the holders by virtue of an instrument or instruments of transfer executed within the immediately preceding two months, or
  (*c*) were units of which they had before that date become the holders by virtue of the transfer to them of a certificate or certificates to bearer within the immediately preceding two months,
they shall enter separately in the statement referred to in para. (1) of this Regulation the number of units held by them by virtue of instruments of transfer executed or certificates to bearer transferred to them before 1 June, 1946, the number of units falling under any of the foregoing headings (*a*), (*b*), (*c*) respectively, and, as respects those falling under the headings (*b*) and (*c*), the number of units to which they became entitled on each day within the said two months on which any transfer took place.

Daily record of transactions in units
9. (1) The managers of a Unit Trust Scheme shall keep a record in which they shall enter separately under the following headings their transactions in units day by day on or after 1 August, 1946:
  (i) the number of units comprised in each transfer to the managers by an instrument of transfer or certificate to bearer. Each entry under this heading shall include a sufficient identification of the instrument of transfer or certificate to bearer;
  (ii) the number of units to which the managers become entitled in consequence of any addition to the trust property;
  (iii) the number of units comprised in each transfer by the managers of units to which no other person was entitled at any previous time and which do not replace units to which any other person was entitled;
  (iv) the number of units comprised in each transfer by managers of units to which some other person was entitled at any previous time or which replace such units.
(2) Where an entry under the heading (iv) in paragraph (1) of this regulation represents a transfer of any units previously entered under paragraph (2) of Regulation 8, or heading (i) of paragraph (1) of this Regulation, or a transfer of units replacing such units, the units comprised in the transfer shall be identified with the units included in the previous entry by a cross-reference to the previous entry and an addition to that entry showing the date of the transfer and the number of units included in that entry that are comprised in the transfer, or in such other manner as may be agreed by the Commissioners of Inland Revenue with the managers.
(3) On any units previously entered under paragraph (2) of Regulation 8 or headings (i) and (ii) of paragraph (1) of this Regulation being extinguished, the extinction shall be recorded by an addition to the appropriate previous entry showing the date of extinction, and, where part only of the units included in any such previous entry is extinguished, the number extinguished, or in such other manner as may be agreed by the Commissioners of Inland Revenue with the managers.

Period of preservation of records
10. The registers, statements and other records and documents referred to in these Regulations shall be preserved during the life of the trust scheme and for a period of not less than one year thereafter:
  Provided that nothing in these Regulations shall require instruments of transfer or registered certificates or certificates to bearer to be preserved for a period exceeding three years from the date on which they were finally delivered to the trustees of the scheme.

1985 No. 1172

The European Communities (Tax Exempt Securities) Order 1985

Note
This Order was made by the Treasury under FA 1984, s. 126 (4) and FA 1985, s. 96 (2) on 25 July 1985.

1. This Order may be cited as the European Communities (Tax Exempt Securities) Order 1985.
2. The following bodies are designated for the purposes of section 126 of the Finance Act 1984—

The European Economic Community
The European Coal and Steel Community
The European Atomic Energy Community
The European Investment Bank

3. The European Communities (Loan Stock) (Stamp Duties) Order 1972 is hereby revoked.

Notes
This Order provides for the limited exemptions from income tax, capital transfer tax, capital gains tax and stamp duty contained in FA 1984 s. 126, as amended by FA 1985, s. 96, to be given in respect of securities issued by the European Communities and the European Investment Bank. These exemptions are conferred in order to give effect to a resolution of the Council of Ministers of the member states of the European Economic Community of 24–25 October 1960 in relation to the European Coal and Steel Community, the European Atomic Energy Community and the European Investment Bank and to grant equal treatment to the European Economic Community. In relation to stamp duty the Order supersedes the European Communities (Loan Stock) (Stamp Duties) Order 1972.

1985 No. 1688

The Stamp Duty (Exempt Instruments) Regulations 1985

Note
These Regulations were made by the Commissioners of Inland Revenue under FA 1985, s. 89 on 4 November 1985 and came into operation on 1 January 1986.

1. These Regulations may be cited as the Stamp Duty (Exempt Instruments) Regulations 1985 and shall come into operation on 1st January 1986.
2. In these Regulations unless the context otherwise requires—
"Her Majesty's Land Registry" and "Chief Land Registrar" have the same meaning as in section 126 (1) of the Land Registration Act 1925 and "Registered land" has the same meaning as in section 3 of that Act.
3. For the purposes of section 89 of the Finance Act 1985, the following class of instrument is prescribed—
Instruments by means of which any transfer on sale within the meaning of paragraphs (*a*) or (*c*) of section 28 (1) of the Finance Act 1931 is effected and in respect of which the following conditions are fulfilled—
   (*a*) the instrument is executed on or after 1 January 1986;
   (*b*) the consideration for the sale in question is of an amount or value such that no stamp duty is chargeable and the instrument is certified in accordance with section 34 (4) of the Finance Act 1958; and
   (*c*) (i) the land in question is registered land; or
      (ii) in the case of land which is not registered land it is an instrument—
         (*a*) to which section 123 of the Land Registration Act 1925 applies, or
         (*b*) which effects a transfer in the case of which under rule 72 of the Land Registration Rules 1925 the transferee is deemed to be the applicant for first registration.
4. Where the instrument is of the class of instrument to which Regulation 3 above applies it shall be the duty of the applicant to deliver to the proper office of Her Majesty's Land Registry with his application for registration the instrument of transfer and a document signed by the transferee or by some person on his behalf and showing his address giving all the particulars set out in Schedule 2 to the Finance Act 1931.
5. The Chief Land Registrar shall furnish to the Commissioners of Inland Revenue the said particulars given to him under Regulation 4 above.

Notes
By FA 1931, s. 28 (1) (*a*), (*c*) it is provided that on certain transfers on sale of land the transferee must produce to the Commissioners of Inland Revenue ("the Board") the instrument of transfer as

well as particulars relating to the transfer as set out in Schedule 2 to that Act ("the Schedule 2 particulars"). Under powers conferred on them by FA 1985, s. 89 the Board may by Regulations prescribe for the purposes of that section classes of instrument to which the provisions of FA 1931, s. 28 shall not apply and provide for the Schedule 2 particulars to be furnished to them in accordance with the Regulations.

These Regulations prescribe for the purposes of FA 1985, s. 89 above a class of instrument of transfer which is to be furnished (with the Schedule 2 particulars) to the Chief Land Registrar; they provide also that he shall transmit to the Board the Schedule 2 particulars.

Regulation 1 provides the title and commencement date and reg. 2 defines terms used.

Regulation 3 prescribes the class of instrument and lays down conditions: that no stamp duty is payable (and it is so certified); that the instrument is one executed on or after 1 January 1986; that the land is registered land, or is unregistered land which will fall to be registered on the occasion of the transfer including unregistered land transferred by the instrument to a third party by a purchaser before he registers his transfer.

Regulation 4 provides that the instrument shall be delivered to the Land Registry with a document, duly signed by the applicant for registration, giving the Schedule 2 particulars.

Regulation 5 provides that the Chief Land Registrar shall furnish to the Board the Schedule 2 particulars (given to him under reg. 4).

The Board of Inland Revenue made these Regulations to enable conveyancing documents to be sent direct to the Land Registry where it is clear that no stamp duty is payable.

As the law stood formerly, home buyers in England and Wales, or more normally their solicitors, were required to send to a Stamp Office the conveyance or transfer together with the "Particulars Delivered Form", summarising details of the transaction. In addition to any *ad valorem* duty payable the conveyance or transfer had to be stamped with a special stamp to show that it had been produced to the Stamp Office. Without this special produced stamp the purchaser was unable to get his title to the property accepted. Where, therefore, the sale had to be registered with the Land Registry the conveyances or transfers had to be sent first to the Stamp Office.

The former arrangements were needlessly out of date. They increased the cost of house purchase, involving the Stamp Office in unnecessary work and could result in a purchaser being unable to lodge his application with the Land Registry within the thirty working days protection period provided by the Land Registry (Official Searches) Rules 1981, Rule 2. FA 1985, s. 89 provides for Regulations which now enable documents to be sent direct to the Land Registry where no stamp duty is payable.

The arrangements apply to:

    (i) sales of commercial premises as well as land and houses; and

    (ii) an assignment or surrender of an existing lease.

They do not, however, apply to:

    (i) sales of property which attract stamp duty;

    (ii) sales which do not fall to be registered with the Land Registry;

    (iii) the grant of a new lease (there is nearly always some stamp duty to pay on the grant of a new lease); or

    (iv) sales of property in Scotland and Northern Ireland to which different procedures apply.

The stamp duty threshold for sales of property is £30,000.

The Regulations do not affect the requirement that purchasers mut supply details of the transaction for the Revenue. The "Particulars Delivered Forms" will still have to be completed. These forms must be sent to the Land Registry along with other documents; the Land Registry will pass the "Particulars Delivered Form" on to the Revenue.

The statutory rule which prevents the Land Registry accepting for registration an unstamped document which attracts stamp duty also continues to apply. Where there is any doubt about the liability of an instrument to stamp duty purchasers will still be able to submit the instrument to a Stamp Office and it will still be open to purchasers to ask for the instrument to be "adjudicated".

The Stamp Office and the Land Registry have issued further detailed instructions. Their joint statement is reproduced below.

Production of documents (L(A) 451): new arrangements

Certain conveyancing documents executed on or after 1 January 1986 do not have to be produced to the Stamp Office. You should send these documents, with form L(A) 451, to the Land Registry instead.

Which documents should I send to the Land Registry?
You should send them transfers, conveyances, and assignments on sale, of registered land and land being registered for the first time which are properly certified at £30,000. You should still send other documents requiring production to the Stamp Office.

What is the procedure?

You should

    (*a*) complete form L(A) 451 in the usual way;

    (*b*) attach any plan referred to on form L(A) 451;

    (*c*) send your completed application for registration, together with supporting documents and form L(A) 451, to the appropriate District Land Registry.

You must send form L(A) 451 and your application for registration together

Will the documents still be examined in the same way?

Yes: the Land Registry will check that no stamp duty is payable and that form L(A) 451 has been completed properly just as the Stamp Office did.

Why the change?

The new procedure will help speed up the conveyancing process.

You will find more detailed information on the back of this sheet (*reproduced below*).

STAMP OFFICE   **LAND REGISTRY**

Further details

Commencement

The new arrangements operate from 1 January 1986 and apply to documents dated on or after that date. Please *do not* attempt to use the new system in advance of this starting date, or for documents dated before it.

Documents involved

To come within the scheme, the document must be one which requires registration, needs a PD stamp only, and bears no duty at all. This means registered land transfers of freehold or leasehold property which contain a certificate of value of £30,000. It therefore *excludes*:

    (*a*) leases themselves;

    (*b*) any transfers which need adjudication (even if it is claimed that no duty will be due);

    (*c*) and all transfers without a certificate.

All such documents must still be sent to the Stamp Office. Conveyances inducing compulsory first registration (but in the case of transfers made following such a conveyance but before first registration has been applied for, only that transfer) are treated in the same way as registered transfers. Conveyances inducing compulsory first registration may of course occur outside compulsory registration areas, for example in a right-to-buy case.

Procedure

The PD form should be completed just as before (including, where necessary, by attaching a plan to identify the property), but should be sent to the appropriate District Land Registry along with the transfer, and the Land Registry will deal with it instead of the Stamp Office. The PD form and the plan must be able to stand on their own, in other words there must be no cross-reference to other documents (even the transfer) which are being lodged with the Registry.

The PD form, once checked, is sent to the District Valuer who needs the information for general Inland Revenue purposes.

Any case in which there is a PD query will be sent back to the applicants by the Land Registry. Provided the query is dealt with, this will not prejudice the Land Registry priority of the application.

The PD form should be lodged with the Land Registry within the Land Registry time limit or priority period applicable to the case.

PD forms

The existing forms will continue to be used. (They are in the process of being redesigned; when the redesigned forms come out, all the procedures described above will remain the same).

1986 No. 1711

The Stamp Duty Reserve Tax Regulations 1986

For commentary on these regulations see under "Statutory Instruments" after FA 1990.

1987 No. 516

The Stamp Duty (Exempt Instruments) Regulations 1987

Note
This order was made by the Treasury under FA 1985, s. 87 (2) on 24 March 1987 and came into operation on 1 May 1987.

1. These Regulations may be cited as the Stamp Duty (Exempt Instruments) Regulations 1987 and shall come into force on 1 May 1987.
2. (1) An instrument which—
    (*a*) is executed on or after 1 May 1987,
    (*b*) is of a kind specified in the Schedule hereto for the purposes of this regulation, and
    (*c*) is certified by a certificate which fulfils the conditions of regulation 3 to be an instrument of that kind,
shall be exempt from duty under the provisions specified in paragraph (2) of this regulation.
(2) The provisions specified are—
    (*a*) the headings in Schedule 1 to the Stamp Act 1891—
        "Conveyance or transfer of any kind not hereinbefore described"; or
        "Disposition in Scotland of any property or of any right or interest therein not described in this Schedule";
    (*b*) sections 83 (2) and 84 (8) of the Finance Act 1985.
3. The certificate—
    (*a*) shall be in writing and—
        (i) be included as part of the instrument, or
        (ii) be endorsed upon or, where separate, be physically attached to the instrument concerned;
    (*b*) shall contain a sufficient description of—
        (i) the instrument concerned where the certificate is separate but physically attached to the instrument, and
        (ii) the category in the Schedule hereto into which the instrument falls;
    (*c*) (i) shall be signed by the transferor or grantor or by his solicitor or duly authorised agent, and
        (ii) where it is not signed by the transferor or grantor or by his solicitor, it shall contain a statement by the signatory of the capacity in which he signs, that he is authorised so to sign and that he gives the certificate from his own knowledge of the facts stated in it.
4. The Schedule to these Regulations shall have effect for the specification of instruments for the purposes of regulation 2.
5. An instrument which is certified in accordance with these Regulations shall not be required under section 82 (5) or section 84 (9) of the Finance Act 1985 to be stamped in accordance with section 12 of the Stamp Act 1891 with a particular stamp denoting that it is duly stamped or that it is not chargeable with any duty.

SCHEDULE (Regulation 4)

An instrument which effects any one or more of the following transactions only is an instrument specified for the purposes of regulation 2—
A.   The vesting of property subject to a trust in the trustees of the trust on the appointment of a new trustee, or in the continuing trustees on the retirement of a trustee.
B.   The conveyance or transfer of property the subject of a specific devise or legacy to the beneficiary named in the will (or his nominee).
C.   The conveyance or transfer of property which forms part of an intestate's estate to the person entitled on intestacy (or his nominee).
D.   The appropriation of property within section 84 (4) of the Finance Act 1985 (death: appropriation in satisfaction of a general legacy of money) or section 84 (5) or (7) of that Act (death: appropriation in satisfaction of any interest of surviving spouse and in Scotland also of any interest of issue).
E.   The conveyance or transfer of property which forms part of the residuary estate of a testator to a beneficiary (or his nominee) entitled solely by virtue of his entitlement under the will.
F.   The conveyance or transfer of property out of a settlement in or towards satisfaction of a beneficiary's interest, not being an interest acquired for money or money's worth, being a conveyance or transfer constituting a distribution of property in accordance with the provisions of the settlement.
G.   The conveyance or transfer of property on and in consideration only of marriage to a party to the marriage (or his nominee) or to trustees to be held on the terms of a settlement made in consideration only of the marriage.

H.   The conveyance or transfer of property within section 83 (1) of the Finance Act 1985 (transfers in connection with divorce etc.).
I.   The conveyance or transfer by the liquidator of property which formed part of the assets of the company in liquidation to a shareholder of that company (or his nominee) in or towards satisfaction of the shareholder's rights on a winding-up.
J.   The grant in fee simple of an easement in or over land for no consideration in money or money's worth.
K.   The grant of a servitude for no consideration in money or money's worth.
L.   The conveyance or transfer of property operating as a voluntary disposition inter vivos for no consideration in money or money's worth nor any consideration referred to in section 57 of the Stamp Act 1891 (conveyance in consideration of a debt etc.).
M.   The conveyance or transfer of property by an instrument within section 84 (1) of the Finance Act 1985 (death: varying disposition).

Notes
FA 1985, s. 87 (2) provides that instruments which would otherwise be chargeable with stamp duty of a fixed amount under any provision specified in regulations shall not be so charged if they are of a kind specified in regulations and certified to be instruments of that kind.
   These Regulations specify the provisions under which, subject to conditions, that duty shall not be charged; specify the instruments (executed on or after 1 May 1987) in relation to which the exemption is available; and provide for the certification requirements.
   Regulation 1 provides the title and commencement date.
   Regulation 2 provides the conditions for the exemption.
   Regulation 3 provides for the requirements for the certificate and the conditions which have to be fulfilled.
   Regulation 4 introduces the Schedule which specifies the instruments which may qualify for the exemption provided by regulation 2.
   Regulation 5 dispenses with the requirement of adjudication in accordance with SA 1891, s. 12 as required by of the FA 1985, s. 82 (5) and 84 (9).

1988 No. 268

The Stamp Duty and Stamp Duty Reserve Tax (Definitions of Unit Trust Scheme) Regulations 1988

Note
These Regulations were made by the Treasury under FA 1946, s. 57 and F(No. 2)A (NI) 1946, s. 28 on 18 February 1988.

Citation and commencement
1. These Regulations may be cited as the Stamp Duty and Stamp Duty Reserve Tax (Definitions of Unit Trust Scheme) Regulations 1988 and shall come into force on 11 March 1988.

Interpretation
2. In these Regulations unless the context otherwise requires—
   "limited partnership" means a limited partnership registered under the Limited Partnerships Act 1907 and "general partner" and "limited partner" have the same meanings as in that Act;
   "limited partnership scheme" means a unit trust scheme of the description specified in regulation 4;
   "Part III" means Part III of the Finance (No. 2) Act (Northern Ireland) 1946;
   "Part VII" means Part VII of the Finance Act 1946;
   "participant" in relation to a unit trust scheme, has the meaning given by s. 75 (2) of the Financial Services Act 1986;
   "scheme property" means, in relation to a unit trust scheme, property of any description, including money, which is held on trust for the participants in the scheme;
   "unit trust scheme" means a scheme which, apart from these Regulations, is a unit trust scheme for the purposes of Part VII or Part III as the case may be.

Exception of certain unit trust schemes from Part VII and Part III
3. A unit trust scheme which is—
   (*a*) a limited partnership scheme, or
   (*b*) a profit sharing scheme which has been approved in accordance with Part I of Schedule 9 to the Finance Act 1978,
shall be treated as not being a unit trust scheme for the purposes of Part VII or Part III as the case may be.

Description of a limited partnership scheme
4. A unit trust scheme is a limited partnership scheme when the scheme property is held on trust for the general partners and the limited partners in a limited partnership.

Notes
These Regulations provide for certain unit trust schemes to be excepted from the definitions of unit trust scheme given by FA 1946, s. 57 (1) and F(No. 2)A (NI) 1946, s. 28 (1). As substituted by FA 1987, s. 48, those sections provide that "unit trust scheme" is to have the same meaning as in the Financial Services Act 1986. Two types of unit trust scheme are excepted from the definitions in FA 1946, s. 57 (1) and F(No. 2)A (NI) 1946, s. 28 (1) by these Regulations: limited partnership schemes and approved profit sharing schemes. In these cases the trust instrument relating to the scheme will not be liable to unit trust instrument duty and units under the scheme will not be treated as stock for transfer duty purposes or (by virtue of FA 1986, s. 99 (9)) as chargeable securities for the purposes of stamp duty reserve tax.

1988 No. 654

The Finance Act 1986 (Stamp Duty and Stamp Duty Reserve Tax) (Amendment) Regulations 1988

Note
These Regulations were made by the Treasury under FA 1986, ss. 81 (5) and 89 (5) on 30 March 1988.

1.—(1) These Regulations may be cited as the Finance Act 1986 (Stamp Duty and Stamp Duty Reserve Tax) (Amendment) Regulations 1988 and shall come into force on 29 April 1988.
(2) The day specified in these Regulations for the purpose of Regulations under subsection (5) of section 81 of the Finance Act 1986 in accordance with subsection (6) of that section is 29 April 1988.
2. For section 81 (3) of the Finance Act 1986 there shall be substituted the following subsection—
  "(3) For the purposes of this section a person is a market maker in stock of a particular kind—
    (*a*) if he—
      (i) holds himself out at all normal times in compliance with the rules of The Stock Exchange as willing to buy and sell stock of that kind at a price specified by him, and
      (ii) is recognised as doing so by the Council of The Stock Exchange; or
    (*b*) if—
      (i) he is an authorised person under Chapter III of Part I of the Financial Services Act 1986,
      (ii) he carried out the transaction in the course of his business as a dealer in investments, within the meaning of paragraph 12 of Schedule 1 to the Financial Services Act 1986, as a principal and in circumstances where that paragraph was applicable for the purposes of that Act,
      (iii) he did not carry out the transaction in the course of any of the activities which fall within paragraph 14 or 16 of Schedule 1 to the Financial Services Act 1986, and
      (iv) the stock was not at the time the transaction was carried out dealt in on a recognised investment exchange.".
3. For section 89 (3) of the Finance Act 1986 there shall be substituted the following subsection—
  "(3) For the purposes of this section a person is a market maker in securities of a particular kind—
    (*a*) if he—
      (i) holds himself out at all normal times in compliance with the rules of The Stock Exchange as willing to buy and sell securities of that kind at a price specified by him, and
      (ii) is recognised as doing so by the Council of The Stock Exchange; or
    (*b*) if—
      (i) he is an authorised person under Chapter III of Part I of the Financial Services Act 1986,
      (ii) he makes the agreement in the course of his business as a dealer in investments, within the meaning of paragraph 12 of Schedule 1 to the Financial Services Act 1986, as a principal and in circumstances where that paragraph is applicable for the purposes of that Act,
      (iii) he does not make the agreement in the course of any activities which fall within paragraph 14 or 16 of Schedule 1 to the Financial Services Act 1986, and
      (iv) the securities are not at the time the agreement is made dealt in on a recognised investment exchange within the meaning of the Financial Services Act 1986."

Notes
FA 1986, ss. 81 (3) and 89 (3) contain definitions of "market maker" for the purposes of exemption from stamp duty and stamp duty reserve tax respectively. Sections 81 (5) and 89 (5) provide that the Treasury may by regulations provide that for ss. 81 (3) and 89 (3) there shall be substituted subsections containing different definitions of "market maker" for the purposes of those sections. These Regulations substitute such subsections for ss. 81 (3) and 89 (3).

The purpose of the substituted subsections is to extend the exemptions from stamp duty and stamp duty reserve tax to an "authorised person" under the Financial Services Act 1986, Pt. I, Ch. III in certain circumstances.

The exemption from stamp duty applies to an "authorised person" if he carried out the transaction in the course of his business as a dealer in investments, within the meaning of FSA 1986, Sch. 1, para. 1, as a principal and in circumstances where that paragraph was applicable for the purposes of that Act; he did not carry out the transaction in the course of any of the activities which fall within para. 14 or 16 of FSA 1986, Sch. 1; and the stock was not, at the time the transaction was carried out, dealt in on a "recognised investment exchange".

The exemption from stamp duty reserve tax applies to an "authorised person" if he makes the agreement in the course of his business as a dealer in investments, within the meaning of FSA 1986, Sch. 1, para. 12, as a principal and in circumstances where that paragraph is applicable for the purposes of that Act; he does not make the agreement in the course of any of the activities which fall within para. 14 or 16 of FSA 1986, Sch. 1; and the securities are not, at the time the agreement is made, dealt in on a "recognised investment exchange".

In relation to both stamp duty (by virtue of FA 1986, s. 85 (5)) and stamp duty reserve tax (by virtue of s. 89 (3) (*b*) (iv) as substituted by these Regulations) a "recognised investment exchange" means such an exchange within the meaning of the Financial Services Act 1986.

1988 No. 780 (C. 25)

Finance Act 1987 (Commencement No. 2) Order 1988

Note

This Order was made by the Treasury under FA 1987, s. 49 (2) on 26 April 1988.
1. This Order may be cited as the Finance Act 1987 (Commencement No. 2) Order 1988.
2. Section 49 (1) of the Finance Act 1987 shall come into force on 29 April 1988.

Notes

This Order brings into force on 29 April 1988 the only provision of FA 1987 (s. 49 (1)) which is not already in force or which has not been repealed.

FA 1987, s. 49 (1) provides that F(1909–10)A 1910 ss. 77 to 79 (which contain provisions relating to contract notes), so far as unrepealed, shall cease to have effect.

1988 No. 1359

The Companies (Forms) (Amendment) Regulations 1988

Note

These Regulations were made by the Secretary of State under the Companies Act 1985, ss. 88 (2) (*a*), 744 on 29 July 1988.

1. (1) These Regulations may be cited as the Companies (Forms) (Amendment) Regulations 1988 and shall come into force on 1 August 1988.
(2) In these Regulations, "the 1985 Regulations" means the Companies (Forms) Regulations 1985.
2. (1) The form 88 (2) set out in the Schedule to these Regulations, with such variations as circumstances require, is the form prescribed for the purposes of section 88 (2) (*a*) of the Companies Act 1985.
(2) The form 88 (2) set out in Schedule 3 to the 1985 Regulations is revoked, except to the extent specified in regulation 3 below.
(3) Regulation 5 of the 1985 Regulations is revoked, except to the extent specified in regulation 3 below.
3. (1) Notwithstanding the repeal of section 47 (1) of the Finance Act 1973 and the provisions of regulation 2 (2) and (3) above, the form 88 (2) revoked by regulation 2 (2) above, and the forms prescribed by regulation 5 of the 1985 Regulations (which is revoked by regulation 2 (3) above)—
   (*a*) shall, in any case where the allotment of shares was made before 16 March 1988, be used for the purposes of section 88 (2) of the Companies Act 1985 instead of the form prescribed by these Regulations; and
   (*b*) may, in any other case, be used for those purposes instead of the form prescribed by these Regulations.
(2) Paragraph (1) (*b*) applies only in relation to documents received by the registrar of companies before 1 August 1989.

Note

These Regulations further amend the Companies (Forms) Regulations 1985 as amended by the

Companies (Forms) (Amendment) Regulations 1986 and the Companies (Forms) (Amendment) Regulations 1987.

They prescribe a new Form 88 (2), to take account of the repeal of FA 1973, s. 47 (1) (which provided for the payment of stamp duty on documents relating to chargeable transactions of capital companies). The forms previously prescribed under the provisions of the Companies Act 1985, s. 88 (2) (*a*) are revoked, except in relation:

(*a*) to any allotment of shares made before 16 March 1988, where the previously prescribed forms must be used;

(*b*) to documents received by the registrar of companies before 1 August 1989 which relate to any allotment of shares made on or after 16 March 1988, where the previously prescribed forms may be used.

1989 No. 291

The Finance Act 1986 (Stamp Duty Repeals) Order 1989

Note
This Order was made by the Treasury under FA 1986, Sch. 23, Pt. IX on 1 March 1989.

1. This Order may be cited as the Finance Act 1986 (Stamp Duty Repeals) Order 1989.
2. The repeals under Part IX (4) of Schedule 23 to the Finance Act 1986 shall have effect on 20 March 1989.

Note
By FA 1986, s. 114 (6) and Sch. 23, Pt. IX the enactments and Order specified in the Table below were repealed to the extent specified in the third column of the Table (repeals of stamp duty provisions consequent upon changes in financial institutions), such repeals to have effect as provided by the Treasury by order made by statutory instrument.

TABLE

Chapter or Number	Short title	Extent of repeal
1920 c. 18.	The Finance Act 1920.	Section 42.
1961 c. 36.	The Finance Act 1961.	Section 34.
1961 c. 10 (N.I.).	The Finance Act (Northern Ireland) 1961.	Section 4.
1973 c. 51.	The Finance Act 1973.	In Schedule 21, paragraphs 1 and 3.
S.I. 1973/1323 (N.I. 18).	The Finance (Miscellaneous Provisions) (Northern Ireland) Order 1973.	In Schedule 3, paragraphs 1 and 3.
1976 c. 40.	The Finance Act 1976.	In section 127, in sub-section (1) the words "which is executed for the purposes of a stock exchange transaction", subsections (2) and (3), in subsection (5) the definitions of "jobber" and "stock exchange transaction", and in subsection (7) the words "and this section".
1980 c. 48.	The Finance Act 1980.	Section 100.

This Order provides that the repeals shall have effect on 20 March 1989.

1989 No. 1297

The Taxes (Interest Rate) Regulations 1989

Note
These Regulations were made by the Treasury under FA 1989, s. 178 on 27 July 1989.

Citation and commencement
1. These Regulations may be cited as the Taxes (Interest Rate) Regulations 1989 and shall come into force on 18 August 1989.

Interpretation
2. (1) In these Regulations unless the context otherwise requires:

"established rate" means—

(*a*) on the coming into force of these Regulations, 14 per cent. per annum; and

(*b*) in relation to any date after the first reference date after the coming into force of these Regulations, the reference rate found on the immediately preceding reference date;

"operative date" means the sixth day of each month;

"reference date" means the day of each month which is the twelfth working day before the sixth day of the following month;

"section 178" means section 178 of the Finance Act 1989;

"working day" means any day other than a non-business day within the meaning of section 92 of the Bills of Exchange Act 1882.

(2) In these Regulations the reference rate found on a reference date is the percentage per annum found by averaging the base lending rates at close of business on that date of:

(*a*) Bank of Scotland,

(*b*) Barclays Bank plc,

(*c*) Lloyds Bank plc,

(*d*) Midland Bank plc,

(*e*) National Westminster Bank plc, and

(*f*) The Royal Bank of Scotland plc.

and, if the result is not a whole number, rounding the result to the nearest such number, with any result midway between two whole numbers rounded down.

Applicable rate of interest on unpaid tax, tax repaid and repayment supplement

3. (1) For the purposes of :

(*a*) sections 86 . . . of the Taxes Management Act 1970, . . .

(*f*) section 92 of the Finance Act 1986,

. . .

the rate applicable under section 178 shall, subject to paragraph (2), be 12·25 per cent. per annum.

(2) Where, on a reference date after the coming into force of these Regulations, the reference rate found on that date differs from the established rate, the rate applicable under section 178 for the purposes of the enactments referred to in paragraph (1) shall, on and after the next operative date, be the percentage per annum found by applying the formula specified in paragraph (3) and, if the result is not a multiple of one-quarter, rounding the result down to the nearest amount which is such a multiple.

(3) The formula specified in this paragraph is—

$$(RR - 2 \cdot 5) \ \frac{(100 - BR)}{100} \ ,$$

where RR is the reference rate referred to in paragraph (2) and BR is the percentage at which income tax at the basic rate is charged for the year of assessment in which the reference date referred to in that paragraph falls.

4. . . .

5. . . .

Effect of change in applicable rate

6. Where the rate applicable under section 178 for the purpose of any of the enactments referred to in regulation 3 (1), 4 (1) or 5 (1) changes on an operative date by virtue of these Regulations, that change shall have effect for periods beginning on or after the operative date in relation to interest running from before that date as well as from or from after that date.

Notes

These Regulations, made under powers contained in FA 1989 s 178 ("section 178"), specify the interest rates applicable under that section for periods beginning on or after 18 August 1989.

The Regulations make provision for the interest rates applicable under section 178 to change on the sixth day of any month, in accordance with formulae specified in the Regulations, when the rounded average of the base lending rates of six clearing banks at the close of business 12 working days prior to that date changes from the rounded average of those rates at the close of business on the corresponding day in the previous month. (The base lending rates of the banks in question are published each day in *The Financial Times*.) Section 178 provides that any such change is to be specified by order of the Board of Inland Revenue. Details of the rates so specified will be available from the Public Enquiry Room, Somerset House, Strand, London WC2R 1LB.

Regulation 1 provides for the title to and commencement of the Regulations.

Regulation 2 contains definitions.

Regulation 3 specifies the interest rate applicable under section 178 in relation to unpaid . . . stamp duty reserve tax . . . It makes provision for changes in the applicable interest rate and for the formula to be used in calculating the new rate.

Regulation 6 provides that changes in interest rates by virtue of the Regulations have effect in relation to interest running from before the date the change takes effect as well as in relation to interest running from, or from a date after, that date.

1989 No. 1298

The Finance Act 1989, section 178 (1), (Appointed Day No. 1) Order 1989

Note
This Order was made by the Treasury under FA 1989, s. 178 (7) on 27 July 1989.
1. This Order may be cited as the Finance Act 1989, section 178 (1), (Appointed Day No. 1) Order 1989.
2. (1) The appointed day for the enactments specified in paragraph (2) for periods beginning on or after which section 178 (1) of the Finance Act 1989 shall have effect is 18 August 1989.
(2) The enactments specified in this paragraph are:
. . .
   (*f*) sections 86 . . . of the Taxes Management Act 1970,
   (*l*) section 92 of the Finance Act 1986, . . .

Notes
This Order appoints 18 August 1989 as the day for periods beginning on or after which FA 1989, s. 178 (1) ("section 178 (1)") and repeals contained in Schedule 17 Part X to that Act, are to have effect for the enactments specified in the Order. Section 178 (1) provides that the rate of interest for the purposes of the enactments to which that section applies is to be the rate provided for by regulations made by the Treasury under that section. At the same time as making this Order the Treasury have made the Taxes (Interest Rate) Regulations (SI 1989 No. 1297) [see above] under that section, which also comes into force on 18 August 1989.
   By virtue of FA 1989, s. 179 (4), the amendments made to various enactments by subsections (1), (2) and (3) of that section have effect in relation to any period for which s. 178 (1) has effect for the purposes of those enactments. Accordingly the amendments of the enactments specified in the Order have effect in relation to periods beginning on or after 18 August 1989.

1989 No. 1300

The Recovery of Tax in Summary Proceedings (Financial Limits) Order 1989

Note
This Order was made by the Treasury under TMA 1970, s. 65 (5) on 27 July 1989.

Citation and commencement
1. This Order may be cited as the Recovery of Tax in Summary Proceedings (Financial Limits) Order 1989 and shall come into force on 11 September 1989.

Increase of sums specified in section 65 (1) of the Taxes Management Act 1970
2. In section 65 (1) of the Taxes Management Act 1970 for "£250" in each place where it occurs there shall be substituted "£500".

Notes
This Order increases the limits of the amount of income tax, capital gains tax, corporation tax (and development land tax), and of the amount of any instalment payable under any assessment to any such tax, which is recoverable in summary proceedings in magistrates' courts in England and Wales and Northern Ireland from £250 to £500 with effect from 11 September 1989.
   The increases apply automatically by virtue of the relevant legislative provisions to:
   (*a*) PAYE deductions from emoluments paid to employees made by employers under the Income Tax (Employments) Regulations 1973 (SI 1973 No. 334);
   (*b*) deductions from payments to sub-contractors in the construction industry made by contractors under the Income Tax (Sub-Contractors in the Construction Industry) Regulations 1975 (SI 1975 No. 1960); and
   (*c*) Class 1 and Class 4 contributions under the Social Security Act 1975 and the Social Security (Northern Ireland) Act 1975.

1989 No. 1301

The Stamp Duty Reserve Tax (Amendment) Regulations 1989

Note
These Regulations were made by the Treasury under FA 1986, s. 98 on 27 July 1989.

Citation and commencement
1. These Regulations may be cited as the Stamp Duty Reserve Tax (Amendment) Regulations 1989 and shall come into force on 18 August 1989.

Interpretation

2. In these regulations "the Principal Regulations" means the Stamp Duty Reserve Tax Regulations 1986.

Amendments to the Principal Regulations

3. In regulation 11 (1) of the Principal Regulations for the words "appropriate rate" there shall be substituted—

"rate applicable under section 178 of the Finance Act 1989".

4. In Part I of the Schedule to the Principal Regulations:

(*a*) in the second column of the Table in the modifications alongside "86 (1)" in the first column after the words " "charged by an assessment" " there shall be added "; for the words "prescribed rate" substitute "rate applicable under section 178 of the Finance Act 1989 for the purposes of section 92 (2) of the Finance Act 1986" ";

(*b*) in the first column of the Table "89 (1) (3)", and in the second column the modifications alongside "89 (1) (3)", shall be omitted.

5. In Part II of the Schedule to the Principal Regulations:

(*a*) for subsection (1) of section 86 of the Taxes Management Act 1970 (as modified) there shall be substituted—

"(1) Any tax to which this section applies shall carry interest at the rate applicable under section 178 of the Finance Act 1989 for the purposes of section 92 (2) of the Finance Act 1986 from the accountable date until payment.";

Notes

These Regulations, which come into force on 18 August 1989, amend the Stamp Duty Reserve Tax Regulations 1986 ("the Principal Regulations"). The amendments are consequential upon the coming into force on that date of FA 1989, s. 178 and the Taxes (Interest Rate) Regulations 1989 SI 1989 No. 1297 [see above], of the amendment to FA 1986, s. 92 (2)) made by FA 1989, s. 179 (1) and of the repeal of TMA 1970, s. 89.

Regulation 1 provides for citation and commencement and reg. 2 contains a definition.

Regulation 3 amends reg. 11 (1) of the Principal Regulations by substituting a reference to the "rate applicable under section 178 of the Finance Act 1989".

Regulation 4 (*a*) amends Part I of the Schedule to the Principal Regulations by making an addition to the modifications in the second column alongside "86 (1)" in the first column so as to secure that in TMA 1970, s. 86 (1) (as modified) the "rate applicable under section 178 of the Finance Act 1989 for the purposes of section 92 (2) of the Finance Act 1986" is substituted for the "prescribed rate", and reg. 4 (*b*) provides that the references in the first column to "89 (1) (3)" and the modifications in the second column alongside them shall be omitted from Part I of that Schedule.

Regulation 5 (*a*) amends Part II of the Schedule to the Principal Regulations by restating TMA 1970, s. 86 (1) as further modified and reg. 5 (*b*) provides that s. 89 of that Act shall be omitted from that Part.

851

APPENDIX 2. INLAND REVENUE STATEMENTS OF PRACTICE

Contents
SP

SP5/78 *(8 November 1978)*
Stamp duty

Conveyance in consideration of a debt
Stamp duty on an instrument transferring property in consideration of the discharge of a debt
owing to the transferee is governed by the provisions of SA 1891, s. 57. The Board of Inland
Revenue are advised that where the value of the property transferred is less than the amount of the
indebtedness agreed to be discharged, the latter is the proper measure of the consideration for
stamp duty purposes. The practice of the Office of the Controller of Stamps will be regulated
accordingly and the value of the property transferred will not be treated as limiting the consideration in respect of which stamp duty is charged.

Note
This Statement of Practice has been deleted (Inland Revenue Press Release 10 November 1980)
but see the commentary on FA 1980, s. 102 for the extent to which it is still applicable.

SP3/84 *(13 March 1984)*
Stamp duty: convertible loan stock

The Board of Inland Revenue has issued the following Statement of Practice:
"Transfers of certain loan capital are exempted from stamp duty by FA 1976, s. 126. Sub-section
(2) provides that the exemption is not available where the loan capital carries an unexpired right
of conversion into shares or other securities or to the acquisition of shares or other securities,
including loan capital of the same description. The Board of Inland Revenue are advised that
sub-section (2) does not exclude from the exemption loan capital which carries an unexpired
right of conversion into or acquisition of loan capital which itself comes within terms of the
exemption."

SP9/84 *(7 December 1984)*
Stamp duty: treatment of securities dealt in on the Stock Exchange Unlisted Securities Market

The Revenue are advised that securities dealt in on the Unlisted Securities Market are not "listed
securities" for the purpose of FA 1980, s. 100 (4) (*b*) (stamp duty relief for dealers in unlisted
securities).

Notes
FA 1920, s. 42 as amended by FA 1980, s. 100 provides for a reduction of stamp duty where shares
are transferred on sale to a jobber or a qualified dealer. In the case of a transfer to a qualified dealer
the reduction does not apply to stock which is listed in the Official List of The Stock Exchange. The
Revenue have been advised by Counsel that securities dealt in on the Unlisted Securities Market
are not listed securities for the purpose of this relief. Where therefore these securities are
transferred on sale to a qualified dealer and the other conditions of the relief are met (in particular
the requirement that the dealer disposes of the securities to a buyer within 2 months) the maximum
stamp duty payable will be 50p.
The statement applies to the law as it stands. It is issued without prejudice to further consideration
of the general tax position of USM securities and of the statutory framework which will be
appropriate to the future functioning of the securities market.

SP10/87 *(22 December 1987)*
Stamp duty: conveyances and leases of building plots

Introduction
1. In 1957 the Inland Revenue published the attached statement summarising the law dealing with
the stamp duty payable on conveyances and leases of building plots where, at the date of the
contract, no house was built or a house was only partly built.
2. The Inland Revenue are advised that the 1957 statement still accurately reflects the law on this
subject. That statement has however sometimes been misconstrued or misapplied. This Statement
therefore restates the view the Inland Revenue takes and, subject to the proviso that ultimately
each case depends on its own facts, clarifies the position in a number of respects.

General
3. The principle on which the statement is based is that the conveyance or lease is liable to
ad valorem duty by reference to the amount of consideration fixed by and payable under the
contract of sale to which that instrument gives effect. If there is a single bargain for the sale of a

completed house, the aggregate consideration payable by the purchaser or lessee will provide the measure of the charge to stamp duty. If there is one contract for the sale of the land in its undeveloped state or with a partly erected house, and another (independent) contract for building work, the conveyance or lease is liable to duty by reference to the consideration payable under the former contract alone. In every case the question is whether there is one *contract* or two.

4. No single factor will be conclusive in answering this question, but whether one *document* or two is used is irrelevant. The Revenue's view is that, in general, arrangements for the sale of the land and for building work which are so interlocked that the purchaser or lessee cannot obtain vacant possession of the land until he has paid both the land price and the full building price, provide a strong indication that there is a single bargain for the sale of a completed house as a package deal.

Specific comments
5. The 1957 statement should be read as a whole, but the following points should be borne in mind in considering particular paragraphs.

Paragraph (i)
6. This paragraph covers the situation in which the parties intend to reach separate agreements for the sale of the land and the construction of the house. It applies only where:
  (*a*) no building work has been started at the date of the contract for sale;
  (*b*) independent contracts are made for the sale of the land and the building of the house; and
  (*c*) the purchaser or lessee is entitled to a conveyance or lease in consideration *only* of the land price or the rent.

7. If the purchaser or lessee can only obtain a conveyance or lease for the land price or rent plus some other consideration, such as an undertaking or guarantee that he will pay the building price, condition (*c*) is not satisfied because the additional consideration is also part of the consideration for the sale.

Paragraph (ii)
8. This paragraph deals with the situation in which the parties intend to create a package deal. Since there is no entitlement to a conveyance or lease until after the building has been completed by the vendor or lessor, duty is chargeable on the total price for the land and the completed building.

Paragraph (iii)
9. This paragraph covers the rare situation in which a package deal has been varied, perhaps because one party or the other is unable to perform the original contract. Although there is no entitlement under the contract to a conveyance or lease until the building has been completed by the vendor or lessor (as in paragraph (*ii*)), the contract has been varied both as to the subject matter of the sale and the consideration payable. As a result of the variation the house is sold in its incomplete state at the date of the conveyance or lease for a proportion of the original aggregate purchase price. Duty is payable on that proportion, *i.e.* the revised consideration.

Paragraph (iv)
10. This paragraph was included to cover cases that would fall within (*i*) were it not that a house had been partly erected at the date of the contract for the sale of the land. It follows that the other conditions of paragraph (*i*) must be met: there must be independent contracts and an entitlement to a conveyance or lease giving the purchaser or lessee vacant possession in consideration *only* of the purchase price or rent of the site.

11. *Subparagraph (a)* applies in such a case if the partly erected building has been built by the vendor or lessor. The conveyance or lease is chargeable with *ad valorem* duty on the land price or rent plus the consideration for the building work at the date of the contract. If the purchaser or lessee is obliged to provide additional consideration for the completion of the building before he can obtain possession, that additional consideration forms part of the consideration for the conveyance or lease.

12. *Subparagraph (b)* applies where the partly erected building has been built by the purchaser or lessee. In this case the value of the work done at the date of the contract for sale does not normally form part of the consideration for the conveyance or lease, and in consequence is not normally chargeable to duty.

Paragraph (v)
13. This paragraph emphasises the need to consider all the contractual arrangements between the parties. Any amendment of a printed form of contract and any other agreement, oral or written, between the parties relevant to the arrangements between them forms part of those arrangements and therefore part of the contract.

Procedures for submitting instruments
14. Where a person accepts that a conveyance or lease of a building plot is chargeable on the total price paid for the land and the completed building, it should be submitted for stamping in the usual

way together with a covering letter giving the aggregate price and a remittance for the duty appropriate to that price.

15. Where the total price does not exceed the amount up to which the instrument is liable to nil duty (currently £30,000) and a certificate of value is included, a conveyance may be sent direct to the Land Registry in England and Wales under the Stamp Duty (Exempt Instruments) Regulations 1985 (see Appendix 1), where appropriate, or, in Scotland, to the Keeper of the Registers of Scotland. A lease will need to be stamped in respect of the rent.

16. Where the total price for the land and the completed building exceeds the threshold for duty and the applicant takes the view that duty is payable on some lesser amount than the total price, the instrument should be submitted to the Stamp Office even if such lesser amount does not exceed the threshold and a certificate of value is included. The instrument should be accompanied by a copy of the agreement(s) for sale etc. and a letter stating the amount which the applicant regards as chargeable consideration, identifying separately any amount attributable to building work. Details of any contractual arrangements not covered by the agreement(s) should be given in the covering letter.

ANNEX

A statement from the Board of Inland Revenue was published in the *Law Society's Gazette* (1957), pp. 450–1 in these terms:

"The Board have taken legal advice concerning the stamp duty chargeable on conveyances or leases of building plots in cases where at the date of the contract for sale or lease no house has been erected or a house has been partly erected on the site which constitutes or is included in the subject-matter of the sale or lease, and at the date of the conveyance or lease a house has been wholly or partly erected on the site.

The Board are advised that the law is as follows:

(i) Subject to what is said under paragraph (iv), if under the contract for the sale or lease the purchaser or lessee is entitled to a conveyance or lease of the land in consideration only of the purchase price or rent of the site, the *ad valorem* duty on the conveyance or lease will be determined only by the amount of the purchase price or rent, although it may have been agreed that a house is to be built on the site at the expense of the purchaser or lessee.

In such a case, the concurrent existence of a contract with the vendor or lessor or any other person for the building of a house on the site will not increase the stamp duty chargeable on the conveyance or lease.

(ii) If under the contract the purchaser or lessee is not entitled to a conveyance or lease until a house has been built on the site at his expense and if the house is to be built by the vendor or lessor or by his agent or nominee, the payment of the building price by the purchaser or lessee will be part of the consideration for the conveyance or lease and the building price will be liable to *ad valorem* duty accordingly.

(If the house is to be built by a person who is not the vendor or lessor or his agent or nominee, the payment of the building price will not form part of the consideration for the sale or lease except in so far as paragraph (iv) applies.)

(iii) When the position is as in paragraph (ii), and a purchaser or lessee not entitled to a conveyance or lease until a house has been erected at his expense in fact obtains a conveyance or lease when the house has been only partly erected, *ad valorem* duty is payable on the conveyance or lease on the proportionate amount of the building price attributable to the partial erection of the house computed as at the date of the conveyance or lease.

(iv) (*a*) If, at the date of the contract, a house has been wholly or partly erected by the vendor or lessor or by his agent or nominee or by a builder not employed by the purchaser or lessee, it normally forms part of the subject-matter of the sale or lease and the consideration or apportioned consideration for that building (as existing at the date of the contract) is accordingly liable to *ad valorem* duty.

(*b*) If, at the date of the contract, a house has been wholly or partly erected by the purchaser or lessee or by any person on his behalf the consideration or apportioned consideration for the house wholly or partly erected will not normally form part of the consideration for the sale or lease and accordingly will not be liable to *ad valorem* duty.

(v) The contract referred to above may be contained in more than one instrument or it may be partly written and partly verbal. It includes any contractual arrangement between the parties.

These observations explain, so far as is possible in general terms, the view of the law at present adopted by the Board, but they have not, of course, the force of law, and are promulgated merely with the object of assisting the taxpayer. The Board are not bound by them, and in the circumstances of any particular case may call for special consideration."

SP1/90 *(9 January 1990)*
Company residence

1. Residence has always been a material factor, for companies as well as individuals, in determining tax liability. But statute law has never laid down comprehensive rules for determining where a company is resident and until 1988 the question was left solely to the courts to decide. FA 1988, s. 66 introduced the rule that a company incorporated in the U.K. is resident here for the purposes of the Taxes Act. Case law still applies in determining the residence of companies excepted from the incorporation rule or which are not incorporated in the U.K.

A THE INCORPORATION RULE

2. The incorporation rule applies to companies incorporated in the U.K. subject to the exceptions in FA 1988, Sch. 7 for some companies incorporated before 15 March 1988. Paragraphs 3 to 8 below explain how the Revenue interpret various terms used in the legislation.

Carrying on business
3. The exceptions from the incorporation test in Sch. 7 depend in part on the company carrying on business at a specified time or during a relevant period. The question whether a company carries on business is one of fact to be decided according to the particular circumstances of the company. Detailed guidance is not practicable but the Revenue take the view that "business" has a wider meaning than "trade"; it can include transactions, such as the purchase of stock, carried out for the purposes of a trade about to be commenced and the holding of investments including shares in a subsidiary company. Such a holding could consist of a single investment from which no income was derived.
4. A company such as a shelf company whose transactions have been limited to those formalities necessary to keep the company on the register of companies will not be regarded as carrying on business.
5. For the purposes of the case law test (see B below) the residence of a company is determined by the place where its real business is carried on. A company which can demonstrate that in these terms it is or was resident outside the U.K. will have carried on business for the purposes of Sch 7.

"Taxable in a territory outside the U.K."
6. A further condition for some companies for exception from the incorporation test is provided by Sch. 7, paras. 1 (1) (c), and 5 (1). The company has to be taxable in a territory outside the U.K. "Taxable" means that the company is liable to tax on income by reason of domicile, residence or place of management. This is similar to the approach adopted in the residence provisions of many double taxation agreements. Territories which impose tax on companies by reference to incorporation or registration or similar criteria are covered by the term "domicile". Territories which impose tax by reference to criteria such as "effective management", "central administration", "head office" or "principal place of business" are covered by the term "place of management".
7. A company has to be liable to tax on income so that a company which is, for example, liable only to a flat rate fee or lump sum duty does not fulfil the test. On the other hand a company is regarded as liable to tax in a particular territory if it is within the charge there even though it may pay no tax because, for example, it makes losses or claims double taxation relief.

"Treasury consent"
8. Before 15 March 1988 it was unlawful for a company to cease to be resident in the U.K. without the consent of the Treasury. Companies which have ceased to be resident in pursuance of a Treasury consent, as defined in Sch. 7, para. 5 (1), are excepted from the incorporation rule subject to certain conditions. A few companies ceased to be resident without Treasury consent but were informed subsequently by letter that the Treasury would take no action against them under the relevant legislation. Such a letter is not a retrospective grant of consent and the companies concerned cannot benefit from the exceptions which depend on Treasury consent.

B THE CASE LAW TEST

9. This test of company residence is that enunciated by Lord Loreburn in *De Beers Consolidated Mines* v. *Howe* (5 TC 198) at the beginning of this century:
"A company resides, for the purposes of Income Tax, where its real business is carried on . . . I regard that as the true rule; and the real business is carried on where the central management and control actually abides."
10. The "central management and control" test, as set out in *De Beers*, has been endorsed by a series of subsequent decisions. In particular, it was described by Lord Radcliffe in the 1959 case of *Bullock* v. *Unit Construction Company* 38 TC 712 at p. 738 as being:
"as precise and unequivocal as a positive statutory injunction . . . I do not know of any other test which has either been substituted for that of central management and control, or has been

defined with sufficient precision to be regarded as an acceptable alternative to it. To me ... it seems impossible to read Lord Loreburn's words without seeing that he regarded the formula he was propounding as constituting *the* test of residence".

Nothing which has happened since has in any way altered this basic principle for a company the residence of which is not governed by the incorporation rule; under current U.K. case law such a company is regarded as resident for tax purposes where central management and control is to be found.

Place of "central management and control"

11. In determining whether or not an individual company outside the scope of the incorporation test is resident in the U.K., it thus becomes necessary to locate its place of "central management and control". The case law concept of central management and control is, in broad terms, directed at the highest level of control of the business of a company. It is to be distinguished from the place where the main operations of a business are to be found, though those two places may often coincide. Moreover, the exercise of control does not necessarily demand any minimum standard of active involvement: it may, in appropriate circumstances, be exercised tacitly through passive oversight.

12. Successive decided cases have emphasised that the place of central management and control is wholly a question of fact. For example, Lord Radcliffe in *Unit Construction* said that "the question where control and management abide must be treated as one of fact or 'actuality'" (p. 741). It follows that factors which together are decisive in one instance may individually carry little weight in another. Nevertheless the decided cases do give some pointers. In particular a series of decisions has attached importance to the place where the company's board of directors meet. There are very many cases in which the board meets in the same country as that in which the business operations take place, and central management and control is clearly located in that one place. In other cases central management and control may be exercised by directors in one country though the actual business operations may, perhaps under the immediate management of local directors, take place elsewhere.

13. But the location of board meetings, although important in the normal case, is not necessarily conclusive. Lord Radcliffe in *Unit Construction* pointed out (p. 738) that the site of the meetings of the directors' board had *not* been chosen as "*the* test" of company residence. In some cases, for example, central management and control is exercised by a single individual. This may happen when a chairman or managing director exercises powers formally conferred by the company's Articles and the other board members are little more than cyphers, or by reason of a dominant shareholding or for some other reason. In those cases the residence of the company is where the controlling individual exercises his powers.

14. In general the place of directors' meetings is significant only insofar as those meetings constitute the medium through which central management and control is exercised. If, for example, the directors of a company were engaged together actively in the U.K. in the complete running of a business which was wholly in the U.K., the company would not be regarded as resident outside the U.K. merely because the directors held formal board meetings outside the U.K. While it is possible to identify extreme situations in which central management and control plainly is, or is not, exercised by directors in formal meetings, the conclusion in any case is wholly one of fact depending on the relative weight to be given to various factors. Any attempt to lay down rigid guidelines would only be misleading.

15. Generally, however, where doubts arise about a particular company's residence status, the Revenue adopt the following approach:

(a) They first try to ascertain whether the directors of the company in fact exercise central management and control.

(b) If so, they seek to determine where the directors exercise this central management and control (which is not necessarily where they meet).

(c) In cases where the directors apparently do *not* exercise central management and control of the company, the Revenue then look to establish where and by whom it is exercised.

Parent/subsidiary relationship

16. It is particularly difficult to apply the "central management and control" test in the situation where a subsidiary company and its parent operate in different territories. In this situation, the parent will normally influence, to a greater or lesser extent, the actions of the subsidiary. Where that influence is exerted by the parent exercising the powers which a sole or majority shareholder has in general meetings of the subsidiary, for example to appoint and dismiss members of the board of the subsidiary and to initiate or approve alterations to its financial structure, the Revenue would not seek to argue that central management and control of the subsidiary is located where the parent company is resident. However, in cases where the parent usurps the functions of the board of the subsidiary (such as *Unit Construction* itself) or where that board merely rubber stamps the parent company's decisions without giving them any independent consideration of its own, the Revenue draw the conclusion that the subsidiary has the same residence for tax purposes as its parent.

17. The Revenue recognise that there may be many cases where a company is a member of a group having its ultimate holding company in another country which will not fall readily into either of the categories referred to above. In considering whether the board of such a subsidiary company exercises central management and control of the subsidiary's business, they have regard to the degree of autonomy which those directors have in conducting the company's business. Matters (among others) that may be taken into account are the extent to which the directors of the subsidiary take decisions on their own authority as to investment, production, marketing and procurement without reference to the parent.

Conclusion

18. In outlining factors relevant to the application of the case law test, this statement assumes that they exist for genuine commercial reasons. Where, however, as may happen, it appears that a major objective underlying the existence of certain factors is the obtaining of tax benefits from residence or non-residence, the Revenue examine the facts particularly closely in order to see whether there has been an attempt to create the appearance of central management and control in a particular place without the reality.

19. The case law test examined in this Statement is not always easy to apply. The courts have recognised that there may be difficulties where it it not possible to identify any one country as the seat of central management and control. The principles to apply in those circumstances have not been fully developed in case law. In addition, the last relevant case was decided almost 30 years ago, and there have been many developments in communications since then, which in particular may enable a company to be controlled from a place far distant from where the day-to-day management is carried on. As the statement makes clear, while the general principle has been laid down by the courts, its application must depend on the precise facts.

C DOUBLE TAXATION AGREEMENTS

20. In general our double taxation agreements do not affect the U.K. residence of a company as established for U.K. tax purposes. But where the partner country adopts a different definition of residence, it may happen that a U.K. resident company is treated, under the partner country's domestic law, as also resident there. In these cases, the agreement normally specifies what the tax consequences of this "double" residence shall be.

21. Under the double taxation agreement with the United States, for example, the U.K. residence of a company for U.K. tax purposes is unaffected. But where that company is also a U.S. corporation, it is excluded from some of the reliefs conferred by the agreement. On the other hand, under a double taxation agreement which follows the 1977 OECD Model Taxation Convention, a company classed as resident by both the U.K. and the partner country is, for the purposes of the agreement, treated as resident where its "place of effective management" is situated.

22. The commentary in the OECD Model art. 4 para. 3 records the U.K. view that, in agreements (such as those with some Commonwealth countries) which treat a company as resident in a state in which "its business is managed and controlled", this expression means "the effective management of the enterprise". More detailed consideration of the question in the light of the approach of continental legal systems and of Community law to the question of company residence has led the Revenue to revise this view. It is now considered that effective management may, in some cases, be found at a place different from the place of central management and control. This could happen, for example, where a company is run by executives based abroad, but the final directing power rests with non-executive directors who meet in the U.K. In such circumstances the company's place of effective management might well be abroad but, depending on the precise powers of the non-executive directors, it might be centrally managed and controlled (and therefore resident) in the U.K.

23. The incorporation rule in FA 1988, s. 66 (1) determines a residence which supersedes a different place "given by any rule of law". This incorporation rule determines residence under U.K. domestic law and is subject to the provisions of any applicable double taxation agreement. It does not override the provisions of a double taxation agreement which may make a U.K. incorporated company a resident of an overseas territory *for the purposes of the agreement* (see paras. 20 and 21 above).

SP2/90 *(9 January 1990)*
Guidance notes for migrating companies: notice and arrangements for payment of tax

1. FA 1988, s. 130 requires a company to notify the Board of Inland Revenue of its intention to cease to be resident in the U.K. and to obtain the Board's approval of arrangements for payment of the company's tax liabilities. These notes explain the procedure to be followed, the information required in support of a request for approval and the arrangements which will normally be acceptable to the Board.

2. *Notice*

2.1 A notice under FA 1988, s. 130 (2) (*a*) should be sent to Inland Revenue, International Division (Company Migrations), Room 312, Melbourne House, Aldwych, London WC2B 4LL.

The notice should give the intended date of migration (see para. 5 below). The information required by s. 130 (2) (*b*), (*c*) should normally be sent with the notice (*i.e.* the statement of tax liabilities and proposals for securing payment—see para. 3 (*d*) and (*c*) below).

2.2 As the Board will have to check the statement of tax payable with the company's tax district, it would be useful if a copy of the notice and of the tax computation could be sent to the company's tax district at the same time.

3. *Information to be supplied*

(*a*) The name of the company, its address in the U.K. and its place of incorporation.

(*b*) Its tax district and reference number.

(*c*) A copy of the latest available accounts.

(*d*) A detailed statement of all tax liabilities which are or will be due for periods commencing before the date of migration. The statement should cover corporation tax and advance corporation tax and, if relevant, all taxes mentioned in s. 130 (7) and any accrued interest on tax (s. 130 (8)). It should include any charges which arise as a consequence of the migration itself *e.g.*, under TA 1988, s. 337 (1) and FA 1988, s. 105. (If an unlimited guarantee is to be offered—see para. 4.3—the statement can be restricted to a brief summary of the tax position.)

(*e*) The company's proposals for securing the payment of tax liabilities. These should include the name and address of the proposed attorney and of the proposed guarantor (see paras. 4.1 and 4.2).

(*f*) If a corporate guarantor other than a bank is proposed (see para. 4.2), a copy of its memorandum and articles of association.

4. *Arrangements for securing payment of tax*

4.1 It will normally be necessary to appoint an attorney to act for the company in tax matters, *e.g.* to receive notices of assessment. The attorney must be resident in the U.K. and will usually be an individual who is professionally qualified *e.g.*, as a solicitor or accountant. The Board will need to be satisfied that the migrating company has power to appoint an attorney. Further information and drafts of the power of attorney in a form approved by the Board are available from the above address.

4.2 The precise form of the arrangements will vary from case to case. Normally they will take the form of a guarantee from a company which must be either resident in the U.K. or a U.K. branch of a foreign bank. A guarantor company must of course have power to act as guarantor and the copy of its memorandum and articles is required to satisfy the Board of this.

4.3 The guarantee may be unlimited or limited to a specified sum. An unlimited guarantee is given for the total tax liabilities without specifying the amount. Where the migrating company has an associated U.K. resident company of sufficient substance the Board will normally look for an unlimited guarantee from that company. Where the guarantee is given by a company not associated with the migrating company, usually by a bank, the Board understand that the guarantor will require the guarantee to be limited to a specified sum. Under s. 130 (4) any dispute as to the amount can be referred to the Special Commissioners.

4.4 Where it is not possible for a guarantee in one of the forms indicated above to be provided, other arrangements may be acceptable. Further information is available from the above address.

5. *Date of migration*

5.1 The Board will act as speedily as possible to approve the arrangements but the time required will depend on several factors. If possible the intended date of migration should be not less than two months from the date of the notice. If it is necessary to agree values of assets in order to estimate tax liabilities, the time required may be longer and companies should take this into account. However, where an unlimited guarantee is proposed, it will not usually be necessary to estimate the tax liabilities in detail and it may then be possible to approve the arrangements well within two months of the notice.

5.2 A company may decide to change the intended date of migration either for its own reasons or because, for example, the arrangements will clearly not be approved in time to meet the original date. It should then give notice under FA 1988, s. 130 of the amended date and provide details of any consequential changes in either the amount of tax and interest to be included in the arrangements or the nature of the arrangements themselves.

6. *Non-compliance*

Where a company migrates without the requirements of s. 130 being met, the persons responsible, including individual directors, may be liable for substantial penalties under s. 131. Where tax liabilities of a migrating company remain unpaid, those liabilities may also be recovered from related companies, or from certain directors, under s. 132.

7. *Telephone enquiries*
An initial enquiry may be made to the Public Enquiry Room (071 438 6420/5)—callers should ask for International Division (Company Migrations).

SP6/90 *(27 April 1990)*
Conveyances and transfers of property subject to a debt: SA 1891, s. 57

Introduction
1. Since the abolition of the duty on voluntary dispositions in 1985, many enquiries have been received about the stamp duty chargeable on conveyances etc. subject to a debt where *no* chargeable consideration (*e.g.* money or stock) unrelated to the debt is given by the transferee. This Statement of Practice sets out the Board's view of the correct stamp duty treatment of such conveyances.
2. For the sake of completeness it should be noted that where chargeable consideration unrelated to debt *is* given by the transferee, s. 57 renders the conveyance liable to *ad valorem* duty on the aggregate of that consideration and the debt whether the transferee assumes liability for the debt or not (*IRC* v. *City of Glasgow Bank* (1881) 8 R (Ct of Sess) 389, 18 SLR 242).

SA 1891, s. 57
3. The most commonly misunderstood applications of s. 57 arise where:
　(*a*) a mortgaged property held in the name of one spouse is transferred into the joint names of both spouses;
　(*b*) a mortgaged property held in the name of one spouse or in their joint names is transferred into the sole name of the other;
　(*c*) a mortgaged business property, frequently farmland, is conveyed from a sole proprietor to a family partnership or from a family partnership to a fresh partnership bringing in other members of the family.
4. The critical question is whether the transaction to which the conveyance gives effect is or is not a sale. If it is, s. 57 will apply and the conveyance will be chargeable to *ad valorem* duty on the amount of the debt assumed. If it is not, then s. 57 will not apply and *ad valorem* duty will not be payable.

Express covenants
5. Where property is transferred subject to a debt, the transferee may covenant, either in the instrument or by means of a separate written undertaking, to pay the debt or indemnify the transferor against his personal liability to the lender. Such a covenant or undertaking constitutes valuable consideration and, in view of s. 57, establishes the transaction as a sale for stamp duty purposes.
6. Where the transferor covenants to pay the debt and the transferee does not assume any liability for it, no chargeable consideration has been given and there is no sale. The transfer would then be a voluntary disposition—*i.e.* an unencumbered gift capable of being certified as Category L under the Stamp Duty (Exempt Instruments) Regulations 1987 (S.I. 1987 No. 516)—and so exempt from the 50p charge that would otherwise arise.

Implied covenants
7. Where no express covenant or undertaking is given by the transferee, the Board are advised that, except in Scotland, a covenant by the transferee may be implied. That makes the transaction a sale, as in para. 4.
8. Such an implied covenant may be negated if there is evidence that it was the intention of the parties at the time of the transfer that the transferor should continue to be liable for the whole of the mortgage debt. Where evidence of such a contrary intention exists, the transfer would again be treated for stamp duty purposes as a voluntary disposition.
9. Where property in joint names subject to a debt is transferred to one of the joint holders (though with no cash passing), a covenant by the transferee to indemnify the transferor may be implied even where both parties were jointly liable on the mortgage.

Amount chargeable
10. Where a conveyance of property subject to a debt is chargeable to *ad valorem* duty and the express or implied covenant by the transferee relates only to part of the debt, only the amount of that part is treated as chargeable consideration within s. 57. A certificate of value under FA 1958, s. 34 (4) may, where appropriate, be included in the conveyance where the relevant amount of the debt does not exceed the amount certified.

Other provisions
11. The foregoing does not affect any statutory exemption from duty that may apply, *e.g.* that for

transfers to a charity (FA 1982, s. 129) and that available for certain transfers of property from one party to a marriage to the other in connection with their divorce or separation (FA 1985, s. 83 (1) and Stamp Duty (Exempt Instruments) Regulations 1987, Category H).

Procedure

12. Where the applicant is satisfied that the conveyance or transfer is made on sale, it may be sent or taken for stamping with a remittance for the duty payable. If the transfer contains an appropriate certificate of value—see para. 10—it may be sent direct to the Land Registry in the usual way if appropriate. In either case, if the amount of the debt outstanding is not given in the conveyance or transfer the amount should be stated in a covering letter.

13. Where the conveyance or transfer contains a covenant by the transferor to pay the debt (see para. 6) and is certified as within the Stamp Duty (Exempt Instruments) Regulations 1987, Category L it should also be sent direct to the Land Registry if appropriate.

14. In any other case where the applicant believes that the conveyance or transfer effects a voluntary disposition—see para. 8—it should be presented for adjudication accompanied by a statement of the facts and any supporting evidence.

871

APPENDIX 3. EXTRA-STATUTORY CONCESSIONS

Contents
Concession

G
CONCESSIONS RELATING TO STAMP DUTIES

G1. *Stamp allowance on lost documents*
Allowance of the stamp duty on lost documents is made either by repayment, where replicas have been stamped, or by free stamping of the replicas.

G2. *Stamping of replicas of documents which have been spoilt or lost*
Where the stamp duty is allowed on a document because it has been spoilt or lost and replaced by a replica but the duty has been increased so that the amount to be impressed on the replica is more than the amount allowable on the original, the additional duty is impressed free of charge.

G5. *Transfer of stock from persons to themselves operating as an executors' assent*
Stamp duty is not claimed on transfer of stock in a company registered in England, Wales or Northern Ireland from a person to himself (or from two or more persons to themselves) which operates as an executors' assent. The point does not arise in relation to companies registered in Scotland.

G6. *Transfer of assets between non-profit making bodies with similar objects*
When the reconstruction of a non-profit making body with objects in a field of public interest such as education, community work or scientific research, or the amalgamation of two or more such bodies involves a transfer to the successor body of assets for which there passes no consideration in money or money's worth, the instruments of transfer are treated as exempt from *ad valorem* stamp duty and charged to 50p fixed duty only. There must be sufficient identity between the members of the transferor and transferee bodies and the rules of both must prohibit the distribution of assets to members and provide that on a winding-up the assets can only be transferred to a similar body subject to like restrictions.

APPENDIX 4. PRESS RELEASES

1957. Inland Revenue
Contracts for Conveyance of Land and for the Erection of Buildings

See SP10/87.

2 January 1963. Controller of Stamps
Stamp duty on leases

The basis of assessment
The Revenue have recently given consideration to the basis of assessment of duty on leases which contain one or more of the following provisions:

   (a) a known rent not exceeding £100 p.a. and a further unascertainable rent;
   (b) a term commencing from a date prior to the date of execution;
   (c) a rent or rents fixed for part only of the term, the rent for the remainder of the term to be agreed subsequently.

The question under consideration in regard to leases of type (a) is whether and to what extent the saving provisions of FA 1947, s. 54 (2), are applicable. The Board are advised that *prima facie* such a lease is liable in respect of the rent to the doubled duty imposed by s. 52 of that Act and that the onus lies on the applicant to show that the relief applies. While it is normally apparent as a matter of fact whether "there is no consideration consisting of money, stock or security . . ." and whether "the term does not exceed thirty-five years or is indefinite", it is not normally possible to show, in relation to a lease where the rent is in part at a known rate or average rate not exceeding £100 p.a. and in part unascertainable, that the total rent "is at a rate or average rate not excdedig £100 p.a." Consequently such a lease is chargeable with *ad valorem* duty under "Lease (3)" at the doubled rate and with fixed duty under "Lease (4)" of £2. The advice given to the Board confirms the practice followed since the enactment of the Finance Act, 1947. [N.B. This question was rendered obsolete by FA 1963, which repealed FA 1947, s. 54 (2).]

In regard to leases of type (b) the Board's view is that, in computing the length of the term, any period prior to the date of the lease is to be left out of account on the authority of *Shaw* v. *Kay* (1847) 1 Ex. 412, *Cadogan* v. *Guiness* (1936) Ch. 515, and *Colton* v. *Becollda Property Investments Ltd* [1950] 1 KB 216. These cases do not, however, provide any authority as to the treatment of rent payable in respect of a period prior to the date of the lease: for the sake of consistency and simplicity, the Board have decided that such rent shall be left out of account, so that the treatment approved by the courts in relation to the term will in practice also be applied to the rent. This means, in effect, a continuation of existing practice, although this practice may not have been applied consistently in individual cases in the past.

'Leases of type (c) present great difficulty and the Board are advised that, in the absence of authority, it cannot be said with certainty how the provisions of the lease head of charge should properly be applied. In the absence of such authority and with the object of securing a consistent practice, hitherto lacking, and to bring the assessment of duty as far as possible into line with the facts, the Board have decided that such leases shall be assessed by treating separately the part of the term in respect of whichthe rent is known from in that respect of which it is unknown: *ad valorem* duty under "Lease (3)" will be assessed in respect of the former part as if it were lease at the known rate or average rate of rent for a term of that length, and fixed duty under "Lease (4)" will be assessed in respect of the latter part.

The practice explained above in relation to leases of type (c) will not affect the basis of assessment of leases where there is a rent of one description (*e.g.*, a ground rent) of known amount for the whole of the term and a further rent of another description (*e.g.*, a service rent) ascertainable for part only of the term. In such cases the basis of assessment will continue to be *ad valorem* duty under "Lease (3)" on the average ascertainable annual rent payable throughout the term and fixed duty under "Lease (4)" on the further uncertain rent.

July 1976. Inland Revenue
Denoting of duplicates and counterparts

In the interests of economy and efficiency, the Revenue have decided to introduce a simplified procedure for stamping those duplicate and counterpart documents which require to be denoted under SA 1891, s. 72. At present, the denoting requirements apply to duplicate documents where the original instrument attracts stamp duty of more than 50p and similarly to counterparts except where the original is liable to lease duty.

'Under the present system the original document is stamped with red duty stamps to the value of the duty paid, and the duplicate or counterpart is stamped with a red 50p stamp and a blue stamp containing the words "Duplicate or Counterpart—original stamped with", followed by blue stamps showing the total amount of duty paid on the original document.

'As from 1 August 1976, the Board propose to introduce throughout the U.K. a system of single-die denoting which will dispense with the use of the blue "value" stamps. As from the date, in addition to the red 50p stamp, a single blue die will be impressed on the duplicate or counterpart. This will bear the legend "Duplicate or Counterpart—original fully and properly stamped". The Board are advised that this will satisfy the requirements of SA 1891, s. 72.

The new system is expected to result in a considerable saving in costs to the Department whilst maintaining the service given to the legal profession and the general public.

28 February 1978. Practice Direction of the Principal Registry of the Family Division
Grants of representation

1. Where, for the purposes of applying for a grant of representation, it is necessary for the applicant to produce to the Principal or a District Probate Registry an original deed or other instrument, it is the practice of the Registry to examine the instrument to ensure that it has been properly executed and duly stamped under SA 1891 before proceeding with the application. Where there is any doubt whether the instrument is duly stamped, the applicant will be asked to present the instrument to the Controller of Stamps (Inland Revenue) for adjudication before the issue of the grant.
2. To avoid delay in the issue of the grant in such cases, the Commissioners of Inland Revenue have agreed that the applicant may, if so desired, submit the original instrument to the Adjudication Section of the Office of the Controller of Stamps for preliminary noting, endorsement and return, providing that a written undertaking is at the same time given to the Controller by the solicitor applying for the grant of representation that he will, on or immediately after the issue of the grant, re-submit the original instrument to the Controller for formal adjudication and pay the stamp duty (if any) to which the instrunment is adjudged liable.
3. In every case on the application for a grant, the original instrument (after inspection) will be returned as soon as practicable to the applicant, or his solicitor, by the probate registry. Practitioners are reminded, however, that where the application is for a grant to an assignee or assignees under the Non-Contentious Probate Rules 1954, Rule 22, a copy of the original instrument of assignment must be lodged in the registry (see Rule 22 (3)).

4 October 1978. C.C.A.B. TR. 309
Revenue answer to accountants' complaints on accounts examination procedures (TA 1970, s. 115)

Introduction
1. In March 1977 the accountancy bodies held a meeting with the Revenue to consider the selective examination of business accounts by Inspectors of Taxes introduced in 1977. The opportunity was also taken to clarify a number of other operational matters which had been causing difficulty.
3. These are the agreed notes of the meeting held on 1 June 1978 and, for this purpose, includes notes relating to some matters which were on the agenda but covered separately by correspondence.

Valuation of unquoted shares by Valuation Division
23. The C.C.A.B. pointed out a common difficulty where separate negotiations took place for valuations for stamp duty, CGT and CTT. It was suggested that all valuations required should be agreed at the same time.
24. The value for stamp duty purposes was usually required very quickly after the transaction and if the other values were negotiated at the same time (often on a different basis) then there could be inconvenient delay in the stamp duty valuation. The Revenue promised to refer the points to its Technical Division to see if the processes could be streamlined but it was stressed that nobody wanted a solution which would cause delays in the stamp duty valuations. They have since written as follows:
"The Technical Division can offer no other solution to that given at our meetings, *i.e.* the parties request the Capital Taxes Office or Tax District soon after the transaction to start the valuation procedure. It is insisted that the facts to determine the value for CTT and CGT purposes are not usually available at the stamp duty valuation stage and without them Shares Valuation Division can make no progress.
Technical Division suggest that if the history of specific cases were instanced they could then identify where the material delays arose and perhaps see if there is anything basically wrong with the system."

8 November 1978. Inland Revenue
Conveyance in consideration of a debt

Stamp duty on a transfer of property at arm's length is chargeable by reference to the price paid. Where the price is the discharge of an existing debt owing to the transferee, stamp duty is accordingly chargeable by reference to the amount of indebtedness agreed to be discharged. As the Statement of Practice, SP5/78 (see Appendix 2) makes clear, the Board has had legal advice that it would make no difference if it were to be the fact that that amount was greater than the value of the property transferred.

1 May 1984. Inland Revenue
Stamp duty: purchase by a company of its own shares

In reply to a Parliamentary Question the Financial Secretary to the Treasury gave the following Written Answer yesterday:

"The Companies Act 1981 enables companies to purchase their own shares. A specific exemption from *ad valorem* stamp duty was not provided although it was intended that s. 52 of the Act (Disclosure of Particulars of Purchase and Authorised Contracts) should effectively provide for this. Doubts have arisen as to whether s. 52 achieved this objective.

Ad valorem duty is payable on any conveyance or transfer on sale and SA 1891, s. 54, provides that the expression 'conveyance on sale' includes every instrument whereby any property sold is transferred or vested in the purchaser. The Revenue are advised that although the matter is not free from doubt there are grounds for holding that this section does not apply when a company purchases its own shares. This is the view that the Board proposes to adopt. A Secretary or Registrar of a company may accordingly amend the register without requiring that any delivery statement is stamped with *ad valorem* duty.

The Companies Act 1981 provides an exemption from capital duty for future re-issues of the repurchased shares."

Note
The Financial Secretary has clarified the stamp duty treatment on the purchase by a company of its own shares.

The Companies Act 1981 enabled companies to purchase their own shares. An exemption from capital duty was provided to cover any future issues of the cancelled shares but nothing was said in the Act about transfer duty. The Bill however was amended to remove the need for a document which would attract stamp duty. Doubts have arisen as to whether the amendments achieved their objective. The Financial Secretary has informed the House that the Revenue has been advised that although the position is not freefrom doubt there are grounds for holding that *ad valorem* duty is not payable. This is the view that the Revenue proposes to adopt.

24 October 1986. Inland Revenue
Stamp duty: depositary receipts and clearance services

The Revenue have announced the names of nominee companies to which, on the transfer of shares to them, the one and a half per cent. rate of stamp duty will apply with effect from 27 October 1986.

FA 1986, ss. 67 and 70 provide for stamp duty at the rate of £1.50 per £100 to be charged in the case of transfers (on sale or otherwise) of U.K. shares to certain nominee companies.

The following companies have notified the Revenue that they come within the terms of these provisions:

    (*a*) Section 67 (depositary receipt) cases:
        (i) Beech Street Nominees Ltd.,
        (ii) BNY (Nominees) Ltd.,
        (iii) Chembank Depositary Nominees Ltd.,
        (iv) Guaranty Nominees Ltd.,
        (v) Irving Trust Company (Nominees) Ltd.,
        (vi) Midland Bank (St. Magnus) Nominees Ltd.,
        (vii) National City Nominees Ltd.,
        (viii) Specease Ltd.,
    (*b*) Section 70 (clearance services) cases;
        (i) EC Nominees Ltd.,
        (ii) Stock Exchange (Nominees) Ltd.,
Stamp duty at the one a half per cent. rate will accordingly be payable on transfers to these companies executed on or after 27 October 1986.

Note
FA 1986 provides for a charge of one and a half per cent., both on the conversion of shares in the U.K. companies into depositary receipts, and also on the transfer of these shares into settlement systems whereby they can be bought and sold without payment of stamp duty.

For *transactions* that have taken place since 18 March the charge has been imposed through the stamp duty reserve tax. The liability for that tax falls on banks who have been passing it on to those depositng the shares.

For transfers of shares to nominee companies acting for depositary banks and clearance systems the Finance Act provides from Big Bang (27 October) an alternative way of collecting the charge. When the transfer is to a nominee company that meets certain statutory conditions the charge is to be paid by the depositor in the form of stamp duty (at the special rate) on the transfer document. For the benefit of depositors, their professional advisers and company registrars, this announcement lists the nominee (*i.e.* transferee) companies who have notified the Board that they wish to take advantage of the stamp duty provisions, rather than continuing to rely on the stamp duty reserve tax machinery. The stamp duty reserve tax continues to apply in other cases.

Further announcements will be made as and when other companies notify the Board that they meet the statutory conditions for the stamp duty provisions to apply.

See also Inland Revenue Press Release, 14 June 1989.

16 April 1987. Inland Revenue
Stamp duty—clearance systems

The Revenue have been notified that Stock Exchange (Nominees) Ltd. will cease to act as a nominee for a clearance service operator.

A new company, SE (Global Custody) Ltd, will in future act for the clearance system previously dealt with by Stock Exchange (Nominees) Ltd.

The change takes effect from 5 May 1987.

Note

A clearance service is an arrangement for settling transactions in securities. Securities within the system are held in the name of a nominee company acting for the clearance system.

Once in the system, shares can be traded *without* payment of stamp duty or need for a transfer document.

However, there *is* a stamp duty charge (at one and a half per cent) *on the transfer into the settlement system*.

Transfers executed on or after 5 May to the new company, SE (Global Custody) Ltd., will accordingly attract duty at the one and a half per cent. rate. Transfers to Stock Exchange (Nominees) Ltd. executed on or after that date will attract the normal half per cent. rate of duty.

4 November 1987. Inland Revenue
Application of stamp duty and stamp duty reserve tax to dealers in securities

The Financial Secretary to the Treasury, the Rt. Hon. Norman Lamont M.P., yesterday announced how it is proposed that the stamp duty and reserve tax market maker exemptions will apply when the Financial Services Act regime fully enters into effect next year.

Dealers who become members of the International Stock Exchange of the U.K. and Ireland and who are registered as market makers in particular stocks will be entitled to the present exemptions under existing legislation.

Other dealers would become entitled to these exemptions for transactions in securities which cannot be dealt in on the Stock Exchange under Treasury Regulations to be made later in the year.

Note
1. Yesterday's announcement by the Financial Secretary was made in answer to a Parliamentary Question. The full text of the answer is:
  "It is proposed that the Treasury should make Regulations extending the stamp duty and reserve tax exemptions for market makers provided by FA 1986, ss. 81 and 89 (1) to authorised dealers carrying out transactions in securities which cannot be dealt in on a recognised investment exchange. A draft of the proposed Regulations is being placed in the House of Commons Library."
2. FA 1986, s. 81 provided a stamp duty exemption for purchases of shares by Stock Exchange market makers and FA 1986, s. 89 provided a similar exemption from the reserve tax. The s. 81 exemption replaced a stamp duty relief, first given in 1920 to jobbers.
3. Since 1980 dealers who are not members of the Stock Exchange but who were authorised dealers under the Prevention of Fraud (Investments) Act have been entitled to relief from stamp duty in the same way for dealings in U.S.M. and other unlisted securities. This relief will come to an end when the Prevention of Fraud (Investments) Act on which it is based is repealed on the coming into force of the relevant part of the Financial Services Act. The proposed regulations will provide comparable exemptions from stamp duty and the reserve tax for dealings in off-market securities.
4. Under the Financial Services Act regime dealers will be able to obtain authorisation to carry out investment business from any appropriate self-regulatory organisation or direct from the Securities and Investments Board. Any authorised dealer will be eligible for membership of the International Stock Exchange, which will have recognised investment exchange status when the Financial Services Act regime takes effect.

5. Dealers who become members of the International Stock Exchange and register as market makers in particular stocks will automatically be entitled to the existing stamp duty and reserve tax exemptions for Stock Exchange market makers.

6. Dealers who do *not* become members of the International Stock Exchange will be entitled to the exemptions but *only* in respect of securities which cannot be dealt in on the International Stock Exchange. This means that the exemptions will *not* be available to these dealers for listed securities or securities that are dealt in on the Unlisted Securities Market or the Stock Exchange's Third Market.

7. Dealers who are members of the International Stock Exchange will also be entitled to the exemptions when dealing in off-market securities.

5 November 1987. Inland Revenue
Eurotunnel: stamp duty and stamp duty reserve tax

The Government have announced proposals to simplify the way stamp duty and stamp duty reserve tax apply to the Units which Eurotunnel are offering for sale to the public. The intention is to treat the Units in the U.K. as if they were a single U.K. share.

The Financial Secretary to the Treasury, the Rt. Hon. Norman Lamont M.P., announced the proposals today in the following reply to a Parliamentary Question:

"The companies, the Stock Exchange and other interested parties have discussed the offer with the Inland Revenue. The Eurotunnel group will be offering for sale to the public Units comprising one share in Eurotunnel plc and one share in Eurotunnel SA. They will require that these shares are issued and transferred together, as a single Unit, in order to link U.K. and French participation in the tunnel project. This arrangement would however give rise to complex charges to stamp duties and stamp duty reserve tax. The taxes would sometimes apply to the Unit and sometimes to the Eurotunnel plc share only. These results were not envisaged when the legislation was introduced, and would complicate dealings in the Units. The next Finance Bill will therefore include proposals to make the Unit the chargeable security for stamp duty and reserve tax purposes, and to remove the initial charge to bearer instrument duty on the issue of Units and Warrants to acquire units abroad.

The intention of these changes is to treat the Units for stamp duty and the reserve tax in the same way as a single share."

Note

Stamp duty
1. Stamp duty is generally charged at 0·5 per cent. on documents which transfer shares. Stamp duty will be payable on transfers in the U.K. on the whole price of Eurotunnel Units in the usual way.

Stamp duty reserve tax
2. Stamp duty reserve tax was introduced in 1986. It applies to various transactions in securities where stamp duty would not normally be paid, *e.g.*:
  (*a*) shares bought and then resold before they are actually transferred to the buyer
  (*b*) shares held by a nominee who acts both for buyer and seller
  (*c*) renounceable documents.
3. Shares in Eurotunnel plc will be chargeable securities for stamp duty reserve tax. But shares in Eurotunnel SA would not necessarily be chargeable because it is not a U.K. company. This would lead to the odd result that Units were quoted at a single price on the Stock Exchange, bought and sold as indivisible securities because the companies' articles require them to be transferred together, but had to be split into their component shares for stamp duty and stamp duty reserve tax. The proposed legislation will remove these difficulties. It will allow investors, dealers and the Stock Exchange to treat the Unit as a single security for stamp duty and stamp duty reserve tax purposes.

Bearer instrument duty
4. Shares in Eurotunnel plc will be delivered in France (and some other countries) in bearer form to meet the requirements of those markets for bearer Units. This would attract bearer instrument duty at the rate of 1·5 per cent. As the bearer shares in France correspond to the Eurotunnel SA shares included in the Units in the U.K., the proposal is to relieve them and bearer warrants from U.K. duty.
5. The charge to bearer instrument duty will apply on any subsequent conversion of registered Units to bearer Units, or issue of bearer Units, on the value of the Units.

Scope of the proposals
6. The proposals reflect the novel arrangements chosen for the Equity 3 offer by Eurotunnel.

However if other companies were to adopt the same arrangements in the same circumstances then the same proposals would apply.

22 December 1987. Inland Revenue
Stamp duty: new houses

The Inland Revenue have published today a Statement of Practice (SP10/87 see Appendix 2) setting out their view of the law on the stamp duty payable on the sale of a new house.

The Statement is being issued in response to a number of enquiries and disputes about the correct duty to be paid where the builder and the vendor are the same person.

Notes

Stamp duty on a new house
1. The precise form of the contractual arrangements for the sale and purchase of a new house can make a big difference to the stamp duty bill. For example, someone who pays £15,000 for a plot on which a house costing £35,000 is to be built would in some cases pay no duty (because the land is below the £30,000 stamp duty threshold), whereas a buyer who pays £50,000 for the land and a completed house would pay £500 stamp duty.

Statement of practice
2. A Statement was issued in 1957 summarising the Revenue's view of the law on this matter. In brief this is that if in reality the purchaser is buying a completed house, duty is payable on the total amount paid for the land and the building work, but that if there are two separate transactions (for example the purchaser makes a separate deal to build the house after buying the land) duty is payable on the price of the land only.
3. Conveyances are, however, being submitted for stamping showing a sale price which, the Revenue are advised, is less than the amount on which stamp duty is chargeable. The Statement of Practice confirms that the 1957 Statement is still regarded as a correct summary of the law.

Standard forms of contracts
4. The Revenue has written to builders (or their solicitors) to withdraw assurances which had been given in respect of standard forms of contract which it is now felt do not constitute two separate transactions. Those assurances will however be honoured where purchasers were already committed to buy their houses.

Other conveyances outstanding
5. The Statement of Practice confirms the practice of the Revenue Stamp Office in seeking duty on the full price where the terms of the statement in 1957 lead to this result. Some 400 conveyances of this kind have been held over pending the Board's advice on this point. The Stamp Office will be contacting people whose transfers have not been stamped to invite them to accept an assessment and pay the duty on the full price, or to pay the duty and appeal. The Statement of Practice does not affect in any way a taxpayer's right to appeal against the assessment.
6. However, in view of the misunderstandings which existed at the time of these purchases, the Revenue will
   (*a*) not seek duty on the full amount where there is evidence that the purchaser (or the purchaser's agents) were given wrong advice by the Revenue about the effect of the *specific* contracts; and
   (*b*) consider evidence that the duty would cause hardship.

Settled cases
7. Conveyances which have been stamped in the past are not affected and will not be reopened.

Submission of documents
8. Any document submitted for stamping should be accompanied by all the relevant facts and circumstances. Where the total price of the land and the completed building exceeds the stamp duty threshold and the buyer takes the view that duty is payable on some lesser amount than the total price, the conveyance should be submitted to the Stamp Office together with a copy of the agreement(s) for sale and details of any contractual arrangements not covered in the agreement(s).

5 April 1988. Inland Revenue
Dealers in securities, stamp duty and stamp duty reserve tax regulations under FA 1986

The Treasury have made Regulations extending the exemptions from stamp duty and stamp duty reserve tax for market makers in shares and other securities.

The Regulations do not affect the exemptions for members of the Stock Exchange who register as market makers. Dealers who are not members of the Stock Exchange will become entitled to the same exemptions, but only for transactions in securities which are not dealt in on the Stock Exchange.

The Regulations will come into force on 29 April.

Note

The Regulations were published in draft by the Revenue on 4 November 1987, following an announcement by the Financial Secretary to the Treasury. No comments or suggestions for changing the Regulations were received, and the Regulations have been made as published.

27 April 1988. Inland Revenue
Stamp duty: repeal of the statutory requirement to issue contract notes

A Treasury Order made yesterday brings to an end the requirements under stamp duty law for contract notes to be issued for dealings in securities. The Order has effect from 29 April 1988. Contract notes will still be required under rules laid down by the Securities and Investments Board.

Note

Contract note duty was abolished in 1985. However the statutory obligation under the F(1909–10)A 1910 to issue contract notes was retained until the new requirements following the Financial Services Act were introduced.

6 May 1988. Inland Revenue
Stamp duty reserve tax regulations

The Treasury made yesterday Regulations which amend the administrative rules for stamp duty reserve tax. In particular they change the rules on who should account for tax, and the definition of a qualified dealer for the purposes of those rules. The changes will take effect on 27 May.

Details

The administrative rules for the stamp duty reserve tax were provided in the Stamp Duty Reserve Tax Regulations 1986 (S.I. 1986 No. 1711). The new Regulations amend those rules to take account of changes flowing from the Financial Services Act, and experience of operating the new tax. The main changes are as follows:

(*a*) the Regulations clarify and expand the definition of who is responsible for giving the Inland Revenue an account of any tax due, and for paying it over:

(i) market makers and brokers and dealers will be accountable persons for tax on shares bought for themselves or for a client who is not a market maker or broker and dealer; and failing that

(ii) market makers and brokers and dealers will be accountable persons for tax on shares they sell, whether their own or a client's, to someone who is not a market maker or broker and dealer and failing that

(iii) qualified dealers will be accountable persons for tax on shares they buy for themselves or as agents for a client who is not a qualified dealer; and failing that

(iv) qualified dealers will be accountable persons for tax on shares they sell or act as agents to sell.

(Investors will normally have to account for the tax themselves only when they buy shares privately, without the involvement of a broker or dealer)

(*b*) the Regulations provide a new definition of a "qualified dealer". For the purposes of administering the tax a qualified dealer will be a member of a self-regulating organisation or a person otherwise authorised under the FSA 1986, Pt. I, Ch. III, or a person treated as authorised under the Act's transitional provisions.

8 August 1988. Department of Trade and Industry (88/588)
Allotments of shares: introduction of a new return

The Department of Trade and Industry has replaced the three forms previously required for notifying the Registrar of Companies of allotments of shares under the Companies Act 1985, s. 88 (2) with a single form.

The Companies (Forms) (Amendment) Regulations 1988 (S.I. 1988 No. 1359) came into force on 1 August 1988, introducing a new Form 88 (2) (Revised 1988). This form is to be used instead of forms PUC2, PUC3 and the old form 88 (2). Additionally forms PUC1, PUC4, PUC5 and PUC6 are no longer required.

The new form is necessary because FA 1988 abolished capital duty on transactions occurring after 15 March 1988. It repealed FA 1973 s. 47, which provided for prescription of the PUC forms on which capital duty was paid.

Note

1. The new Form 88 (2) may be used only for transactions occurring after 15 March 1988, but there will be a transitional period of 12 months during which companies may use the old forms PUC2, PUC3 or 88 (2). After 31 July 1989 only Form 88 (2) (Revised) may be used.

2. For transactions occurring before 16 March 1988 the appropriate old Form 88 (2), PUC2 or PUC3 must be used without exception.

3. These changes do not affect the need to submit a contract for sale or Form 88 (3) where shares have been allotted for a consideration other than cash. Stamp duty could be payable, as before, in respect of the value of certain assets. If chargeable, the duty can be paid at any Stamp Office.

16 February 1989. Inland Revenue
Stamp duty: clearance systems

In accordance with stamp duty law, the Revenue have been notified that a new company, MGT(B) Nominees Ltd., is acting as a nominee for a clearance service operator.

Note

A clearance service is an arrangement for settling transactions in securities. Securities within the system are held in the name of a nominee company acting for the clearance system. Once in the system, shares can be traded without payment of the usual half per cent. duty on share transfers. However, there is a stamp duty charge at one and a half per cent. on the initial transfer of securities into the settlement system itself. FA 1986, s. 71 requires a clearance service operator, or his nominee company, to notify the Revenue within a month of the commencement of business.

14 March 1989. Inland Revenue
Stamp duty on shares: adapting to paperless transactions

The Chancellor proposes in his Budget to bring forward Regulation-making powers to adapt stamp duty and stamp duty reserve tax to the new methods of transferring shares likely to appear over the next 12 months, particularly as the Stock Exchange moves towards a system of paperless share transactions.

The Regulations are needed as an interim measure to ensure that these transfers made by new methods are liable to stamp duties on the same basis as ordinary deals which are made by present methods.

Details

1. There are two parallel duties on share transfers; stamp duty and stamp duty reserve tax. The effect in most cases is to impose a single charge of 0·5 per cent. of the price paid.

2. Stamp duty is a tax on documents. At present most share transactions are effected by paper documents and are liable to stamp duty.

3. But several developments in the way deals are carried out are now in the pipeline. For example, new arrangements have been proposed to cover the initial period of dealing following a new share issue. More generally the Stock Exchange is working towards a dematerialised (*i.e.* paperless) system of share transfers, known as "TAURUS".

4. In a paperless world the charge will be to stamp duty reserve tax, rather than stamp duty. But it is likely that the present stamp duty reserve tax rules will need to be adapted in one or more ways. The necessary adaptations cannot be identified until those concerned in the markets have taken firmer decisions on the structure of the new trading system and how it will work. However, it is possible to envisage circumstances when for example the present rules could:

(*a*) produce double—or even multiple—charges to stamp duty reserve tax, or a stamp duty liability in addition to a stamp duty reserve tax one;

(*b*) mean a deal fails to qualify for the stamp duty reserve tax reliefs available to a paper-based transaction;

(*c*) impose collection obligations and procedures which do not fit the new arrangements.

5. The timing, as well as the substance, of the new system for dematerialised share transfers is still in the planning stage and the details are not yet known. Nor are the revised proposals for new issues yet firm. But it is likely that within the next 12 months there will be some transactions taking place on the basis of these planned developments. The Chancellor therefore proposes, as an interim measure, to introduce Regulations as necessary later in the year to adapt stamp duty and stamp duty reserve tax to these initial arrangements once they become known.

6. It is envisaged that any new substantive legislation necessary to cope with TAURUS in its final form, or other new methods of transferring shares, could be introduced in the 1990 Finance Bill. The legislation could then be framed to take account of the final details of the new methods now in the pipeline, and meanwhile not unnecessarily constrain the Stock Exchange's development plans for TAURUS.

7. The powers to make the interim Regulations will be in this year's Finance Bill.

14 June 1989. Inland Revenue
Stamp duty: depositary receipts

In accordance with stamp duty law [FA 1986, s. 67], the Board of Inland Revenue have been notified that the following two companies are acting as nominees for persons issuing depositary receipts:
   BT CTAG Nominees Ltd. (with effect from 15 May 1989);
   SP Nominees Ltd. (with effect from 18 May 1989).

1 August 1989. Inland Revenue
Collection of tax: financial limits for proceedings in the magistrates' courts

A statutory instrument laid yesterday provides that the upper limit for tax debts the Revenue may recover in magistrates' courts in England, Wales and Northern Ireland shall be raised from £250 to £500 with effect from 11 September 1989.

Note
1. This financial limit is laid down in TMA 1970, s. 65 (1), as amended in 1984. It applies to proceedings in England, Wales and Northern Ireland. It does not apply in Scotland which has a different court system.
2. It covers all assessed Revenue taxes and also, by virtue of the relevant regulations, PAYE deductions made by employers, sub-contractor scheme deductions made by contractors in the construction industry, and Class 1 and Class 4 national insurance contributions.
3. The current limit has been in effect since 1984. At present court action to recover tax debts in the £250–£500 range would have to be taken in the county courts.
4. The costs of commencing proceedings, which have to be paid by the debtor, are lower in the magistrates' courts than in county courts. Magistrates' courts are also more widespread and therefore often more easily accessible.
5. The raising of the limit does not affect the amount of anyone's tax liability or their rights of appeal against underlying tax assessments.
6. Court action is only taken after the usual demands have been issued, and the majority of tax debtors faced with the prospect of magistrates' court proceedings pay the sum due without appearing in court.
7. The statutory instrument, which has the title Recovery of Tax in Summary Proceedings (Financial Limits) Order 1989, will be available shortly from HMSO.

1 August 1989. Inland Revenue
Setting Revenue rates of interest

1. The Treasury has, with Ministerial approval, laid regulations giving details of how interest rates used by the Inland Revenue are calculated.
2. The regulations set out the formulae by which Revenue interest rates are calculated. These formulae have been in use for some years though not previously published. The formulae are based on the average of base lending rate of certain clearing banks rounded to the nearest whole number, and are:
   Main Taxes Acts Provisions:
      Base rate plus 2·5 per cent. reduced by basic rate tax
   Official Rate for Schedule E benefits:
      Base rate plus 1·5 per cent.
   IHT and earlier Capital Taxes:
      (Base rate plus 2 per cent. reduced by basic rate tax) minus 1 per cent.
The current rate of interest for each of these taxes using the present average base lending rate of 14 per cent. are 12·25 per cent., 15·5 per cent. and 11 per cent. respectively.
3. The regulations are made under FA 1989, s. 178 which introduces a new procedure for setting Revenue interest rates. Under this procedure, the formulae used for setting the interest rates are to be published by the Treasury in Regulations and the rates then set automatically in accordance with the formulae. The Regulations take effect from 18 August 1989.

Note
1. The Treasury has laid Regulations setting out the formulae to be used for setting the rates of interest used by the Revenue. These formulae have been in use for some years, though not previously published. The rates are based on an average of the base lending rates of the following

High Street Banks—Barclays, Lloyds, Midland, National Westminster, Bank of Scotland, Royal Bank of Scotland, rounded to the nearest whole number with halves rounded downwards. Revenue rates will then change when this average changes, with the new rate coming into effect from the beginning of the next tax month. Changes will be announced in Revenue Press Releases.
2. The formula for the interest rate on unpaid tax and repayments for the main Taxes Acts provisions is base rate plus 2·5 per cent. reduced by basic rate tax. This is based on a broad average of the net of tax cost of borrowing for an average taxpayer. This rate applies to income tax, capital gains tax, development land tax, corporation tax (including advance corporation tax), petroleum revenue tax (including advance petroleum revenue tax), supplementary petroleum duty, stamp duty reserve tax and tax charged by an assessment for the purposes of making good to the Crown a loss of tax wholly or partly attributable to a person's default.
3. The "Official Rate" of interest is used to calculate the benefit of cheap or interest-free loans provided, by reason of their employment, to directors and employees earning £8,500 a year or more, under TA 1988, s. 160. There are exceptions where the loan is such that if any interest were paid on it the interest would be eligible for tax relief and where the total benefit arising from loans assessable on an employee in a tax year does not exceed £200.
4. The formula for the Official Rate of interest is base rate plus 1·5 per cent. This is based on a broad measure of the cost of a wide range of individual borrowing.
5. The interest rate on capital taxes is (base rate plus 2 per cent. reduced by basic rate tax) minus 1 per cent. This rate applies to unpaid tax and repayments of IHT, CTT and estate duty. The formula is based on a broad average of the net of tax cost of borrowing taking into account that these taxing provisions may run on for a great many years.

27 September 1989. The Law Society
Stamp duty repayment claims

The Stamp Allowance Section, which deals with claims for repayment under SDMA 1891, ss. 9–12 in respect of spoiled, misused or unused stamps, has been transferred from London. Except in Scotland, such claims should in future be sent to:
  Stamp Allowance Section
  Office of the Controller of Stamps
  Inland Revenue
  South Block, Barrington Road
  Worthing, West Sussex BN12 4SF
  (Telephone: 0903 508701)
  Claims for free stamping of a replica where an original stamped document has been lost should be made in the first instance to the Stamp Office at which the lost document was stamped.
  In Scotland, claims should continue to be sent to the Edinburgh office [*Law Society's Gazette*, 27 September 1989, p. 43].

26 October 1989. Inland Revenue
1. Interest on unpaid tax and on repayments
2. ...
3. ...

An Order of the Board of Inland Revenue was issued on 20 October 1989 specifying that in accordance with the relevant regulations:
  —the rate of interest charged on tax paid late and paid in respect of tax overpaid has increased from 12·5 per cent. to 13 per cent.
  This is in line with recent changes in market rates. The rate of interest on tax paid late and overpaid tax takes account of the tax treatment of interest and repayment supplement.
  The new rates of interest will take effect from 6 November 1989 whether or not interest has already started to run before that date.

Interest on unpaid tax and on repayments
The rate of interest on unpaid ... stamp duty reserve tax ... is increased from 12·25 per cent. to 13 per cent.

...

Notes
1. FA 1989, s. 178 and the Taxes (Interest Rate) Regulations 1989, SI 1989 No. 1297 lay down the procedure and formulae for calculating Revenue interest rates.
2. The revised interest rates are based on the average base lending rate of 15 per cent., calculated in accordance with the Statutory Instrument.

9 January 1990. Inland Revenue
Statements of Practice: company residence and company migration

The Revenue have today published Statements of Practice dealing with company residence and company migration [see Appendix 2].

The first concerns company residence and incorporates a change introduced by FA 1988. FA 1988, s. 66 sets out that a company incorporated in the U.K. is resident here for the purposes of the Taxes Acts. Case law still applies in determining the residence of companies excepted from this rule or those not incorporated in the U.K. The Statement also deals with companies which are resident under the domestic law of more than one country. The Statement replaces an existing Statement of Practice 6/83 of 27 July 1983.

The second Statement of Practice concerns company migration and reclassifies guidance issued on 4 August 1988.

Notes
1. Hitherto a company has been resident in the U.K. if its "central management and control" is here. This rule derives from case law, particularly the cases of *De Beers Consolidated Mines* v. *Howe* (5 TC 198) and *Bullock* v. *Union Construction Company* (38 TC 712).
2. From 15 March 1988 companies have been resident in the U.K. for tax purposes if they were incorporated in the U.K. This rule was set out in FA 1988, s. 66. However, the above case law still applies to companies which are excepted from the incorporation rule by FA 1988 or companies which were not incorporated in the U.K.
3. FA 1988 also changed the rules for companies migrating from the U.K. With effect from 15 March 1988 FA 1988, s. 105 imposed a charge on a company's unrealised gains when it ceased to be resident in the U.K. and any company intending to migrate is required under FA 1988, s. 130 to notify the Inland Revenue of its intention and get its approval of the arrangements it proposes to make to pay any tax due. A Revenue Press Release "Company migration: guidance for migrating companies" issued on 4 August 1988 gave details of how the new rules would operate.

20 March 1990. Inland Revenue
Stamp duty on shares to be abolished

The Chancellor proposes in his Budget to abolish all stamp duties on transactions in shares from a date late in 1991–92 to coincide as far as possible with the introduction of paperless dealing under the Stock Exchange's new share transfer system ("TAURUS").

Abolition of these duties will also:
(*a*) enhance London's competitiveness as an international centre for equity trading;
(*b*) boost wider share ownership by reducing transaction costs and benefit savers.
This is the sixth major tax to be abolished since 1983. It makes a significant contribution to the overall simplification of the tax system and the reduction of compliance burdens on taxpayers.

DETAILS

Stamp duties on shares: main duties
1. The main duties to be abolished are:
(*a*) stamp duty on individual share transfers, which is levied on U.K. securities at a rate since 1986 of, broadly, 0·5 per cent. of the price paid;
(*b*) stamp duty of 1·5 per cent., which is payable where U.K. shares are converted into depositary receipts ("ADRs") or transferred into clearance services;
(*c*) stamp duty reserve tax, which applies, at the same rates as stamp duty, to some share transactions which are outside the stamp duty net.

Stamp duties on shares: associated charges
2. Also to be abolished are:
(*a*) the stamp duty charges on bearer shares;
(*b*) the 50p fixed duty on share transfers other than sales;
(*c*) stamp duty on all transfers of units under a unit trust scheme.

Timing
3. Legislation to abolish these duties will be in the 1990 Finance Bill. The Chancellor proposes that abolition should be triggered by Treasury Order in due course. He has indicated that this Order will broadly coincide with the start of paperless trading under the Stock Exchange's planned TAURUS system—*i.e.* towards the end of 1991–92 on the current timetable. Until then, duty continues to apply at the existing rates.

Effects of abolition
4. The Government believes abolition of these taxes will:

(*a*) smooth the path for cheaper and more efficient paperless share dealing, by removing the need for the systems involved to take account of stamp duty;

(*b*) increase the liquidity and efficiency of the London equity market, and maintain its competitiveness in the face of planned tax reductions in other financial centres;

(*c*) encourage investment in U.K. equities and so foster wider share ownership;

(*d*) benefit savers, including beneficiaries of pension funds and life policies;

(*e*) further simplify the tax system and ease the compliance burden on individual shareholders, the equity market and company registrars.

Cost

5. The timing means that no cost will arise until late in 1991–92. The cost that year will depend on precisely when the duty is abolished; a 1 January 1992 start would for example produce a 1991–92 cost of £120 million. The full year cost will be around £800 million.

Stamp duty on property

6. The Chancellor is not proposing to make any changes to the stamp duty on the transfer of land and property (including houses).

Notes

Abolition of duties

1. This Government has already abolished

(*a*) Investment income surcharge (1984);

(*b*) National insurance surcharge (1984);

(*c*) Development land tax (1985);

(*d*) the tax on lifetime gifts (1986);

(*e*) capital duty and the associated unit trust instrument duty (1988)

as well as a number of minor duties. Abolition of stamp duty on shares carries this process forward, making a significant contribution to the overall simplification of the tax system.

Stamp duty on shares

2. The *ad valorem* stamp duty on individual transfers of U.K. companies' shares is currently charged at 50p per £100 or part thereof, *i.e.* broadly at 0·5 per cent. There are exemptions for purchases by market-makers and charities. Government stock and most commercial loan capital are outside the scope of the charge.

3. Conversion of U.K. shares into depositary receipts ("ADRs") or their transfer into a clearance service attracts a 1·5 per cent. "season ticket" charge—see para. 8 below.

4. Bearer instruments are normally charged at 1·5 per cent. on a once-and-for-all basis, either on issue (for instruments issued in the U.K.) or on their first transfer in Great Britain.

5. Certain transfers of shares otherwise than on sale can give rise to a fixed 50p charge—for example transfers where there is no change of beneficial ownership.

Stamp duty reserve tax

6. This tax was introduced in 1986 in order to broaden the base of stamp duty on shares, by charging a wider range of transactions. Stamp duty is a tax on *documents*, but stamp duty reserve tax applies to most *agreements* to sell U.K. securities. It therefore brings within the scope of the charge:

(*a*) the purchase and resale of a security within the same Stock Exchange account;

(*b*) the purchase of renounceable letters of allotment or acceptance;

(*c*) the purchase of shares registered in the name of a nominee acting for seller and purchaser;

(*d*) the purchase of shares which are resold before they are taken into the purchaser's name.

7. Stamp duty reserve tax on individual share transfers is charged at the same rate, 0·5 per cent., as stamp duty on shares. For conversion into ADR form etc. there is again a 1·5 per cent. charge to parallel the higher rate of stamp duty—see 8 below.

Depositary receipts and clearance services—the higher rate charges

8. Where shares are transferred into depositary receipt form or into a clearance service, the higher rate of 1·5 per cent. stamp duty or stamp duty reserve tax applies on the initial transfer. This charge is in the nature of a "season ticket"—subsequent transfers of depositary receipts, or of shares within a clearance service, then take place free of stamp duty or stamp duty reserve tax.

Unit trusts

9. Stamp duty arises on the purchase of units by one unit holder from another, and in the more

common situation of a surrender for cash of units to the managers. The rates are broadly the same as the *ad valorem* charge on shares, but special reliefs apply.

14 June 1990. Inland Revenue.
Finance Bill: stamp duty reserve tax: international organisations

The Government today tabled a proposed new clause to the Finance Bill. It provides that international organisations of which the U.K. is a member can be given limited exemption from stamp duty reserve tax on the issue of their securities.

The clause is being introduced now because of the recent decision to establish the European Bank for Reconstruction and Development (EBRD) in the U.K.

The stamp duty reserve tax charges covered by the new clause are the higher rate (1·5 per cent.) charges which arise on the issue of chargeable securities on a U.K. register to the nominee for either a depositary bank or a clearance service. The EBRD may decide to make such issues.

DETAILS

1. Existing legislation, dating from before stamp duty reserve tax was introduced, enables the Treasury to designate international organisations for the purpose of specific exemptions from various taxes on their securities. Agreements of international organisations may require some limited tax privileges. This ensures that a National Exchequer does not benefit merely because an organisation decides to issue securities in one country rather than another.

2. The Articles of Agreement of the EBRD require exemption from all taxes on the bank's securities which arise solely because they are issued by the bank or because of local factors (*i.e.* the place or currency of issue of the securities, or the location of the bank itself). The stamp duty reserve tax charges relieved by the new clause fall within this category.

3. The new provision adds a reference to stamp duty reserve tax arising on the issue of chargeable securities to FA 1984, s. 126. Issues other than to the nominee of a depositary bank or clearance service do not give rise to stamp duty reserve tax. The principal stamp duty reserve tax charge, at 0·5 per cent., which applies to agreements to transfer chargeable securities, does not fall within the exemptions which are required under the EBRD agreement.

Notes

1. By being a party to an international agreement establishing an organisation, the U.K. is, customarily, committed to granting tax privileges as a condition of membership. It is usual for privileges to be granted in respect of any securities issued by the organisation.

2. Three development banks—the African, the Asian and the Caribbean—and the UNCTAD Common Fund for Commodities have previously been designated by the Treasury under FA 1984, s. 126. In none of these cases has the issue of securities called for a stamp duty reserve tax exemption because the securities, although listed in the U.K. have been registered abroad.

3. Clauses 91–95 of the Finance Bill abolish stamp duty reserve tax and stamp duty on shares with effect from a future date. The Chancellor indicated in his Budget statement that abolition would take place late 1991–92, to coincide broadly with the introduction of paperless share dealings.

15 June 1990. Inland Revenue.
Finance Bill: stamp duty and stamp duty reserve tax: paired shares

The Government has tabled two new clauses to the Finance Bill to amend the existing legislation on "paired shares". The new clauses will ensure that rights and bonus issues receive the same stamp duty and stamp duty reserve tax treatment as the units of paired shares originally issued.

This is consistent with the Government's intention of making it possible for units of paired shares to be traded in the same way as shares in a single company.

DETAILS

1. FA 1988, ss. 143, 144 provide that where a British company and a foreign company "pair" their shares on issue certain stamp duty and stamp duty reserve tax consequences follow. Where shares are paired they can be owned and traded only as units of one share in each company.

2. If the shares of each company are issued in both bearer and registered form, there is an exemption from bearer instrument duty otherwise chargeable on the issue of the bearer shares in the British company. The conditions are that the shares should be the subject of an offer to the public and be issued in equal numbers in both countries. A similar exemption exists for bonus issues. The legislation also secures a stamp duty reserve tax charge on the trading of the foreign company's shares as part of the registered units marketed here.

3. The equal numbers test, however, is one that a rights issue cannot satisfy. When the rights issue is made, the original units will be held unequally in the two countries because of trading between them and a pro rata rights issue is bound to be unequal.

4. The new clauses will ensure that rights issues do not have to pass the equal numbers test and that bonus issues of registered units are chargeable securities for stamp duty reserve tax purposes.

APPENDIX 5. FORM OF CERTIFICATE REQUIRED WHERE STOCK TRANSFER FORM IS NOT LIABLE TO *AD VALOREM* STAMP DUTY

Instruments of transfer are liable to a fixed duty of 50p when the transaction falls within one of the following categories:

   (*a*) Transfer vesting the property in new trustees on the appointment of a new trustee of a pre-existing trust, or on the retirement of a trustee.

*(*b*) Transfer by way of security for a loan or re-transfer to the original transferor on repayment of a loan.

   (*c*) Transfer to a beneficiary under a will of specific legacy of stock, etc. (NOTE—Transfers by executors in discharge or partial discharge of a pecuniary legacy are chargeable with *ad valorem* duty on the amount of the legacy so discharged unless the will confers on the executors power so to discharge the pecuniary legacy without the consent of the legatee.)

   (*d*) Transfer of stock, etc., forming part of an intestate's estate to the person entitled to it, not being a transfer in satisfaction or part satisfaction (i) in England and Wales, of the sum to which the surviving spouse has a statutory entitlement under an intestacy where the total value of the residuary estate exceeds that sum, or of the sum due to the surviving spouse in respect of the value of a life interest which he or she has elected to have redeemed; (ii) in Scotland, of any of the monetary rights of the surviving spouse under the provisions of Section 8 (1) (a) (ii), Section 8 (1) (b) or Section 9 (1) of the Succession (Scotland) Act 1964 as amended by the Succession (Scotland) Act 1973.

   (*e*) Transfer to a residuary legatee of stock, etc., forming part of the residue divisible under a will.

   (*f*) Transfer to a beneficiary under a settlement, on distribution of the trust funds, of stock, etc., forming the share or part of the share of those funds to which the beneficiary is entitled in accordance with the terms of the settlement.

   (NOTE—Categories (*e*) and (*f*) do not include a transfer to a beneficiary under a will or settlement who takes not only by reason of being entitled under the will or settlement but also

     (i) following a purchase by him of some other interest in the trust property, *e.g.*, a life interest or the interest of some other beneficiary; in such a case *ad valorem* transfer on sale duty is payable; or

     (ii) where there is an element of gift *inter vivos* in the transaction in consequence of which a beneficiary under a will or settlement takes a share greater in value than his share under the will or settlement, in such a case *ad valorem* voluntary disposition duty is payable.)

   (*g*) Transfer on and in consideration of marriage of stocks, etc., to either party to the marriage or to trustees to be held on the terms of a duly stamped settlement made in consideration of the marriage. (NOTE—A transfer made to the husband or wife after the date of the marriage is not within this category unless it is made pursuant to an ante-nuptial contract.)

   (*h*) Transfer by the liquidator of a company of stocks, etc., forming part of the assets of the company, to the persons who were shareholders, in satisfaction of their rights on a winding-up.

*(*j*) Transfer, not on sale and not arising under any contract of sale and where no beneficial interest in the property passes: (i) to a person who is a mere nominee of, and is nominated only by, the transferor; (ii) from a mere nominee who has at all times held the property on behalf of the transferee; (iii) from one nominee to another nominee of the same beneficial owner where the first nominee has at all times held the property on behalf of that beneficial owner. (NOTE—This category does not include a transfer made in any of the following circumstances; (i) by a holder of stock, etc., following the grant of an option to purchase the stock, to the persons entitled to the option or his nominee; (ii) to a nominee in contemplation of a contract for the sale of the stock, etc., then about to be entered into; (iii) from the nominee of a vendor, who has instructed the nominee orally or by some unstamped writing to hold stock, etc., in trust for a purchaser, to such purchaser.)

(1) "I" or "We".

(2) Insert "(*a*)", "(*b*)" or appropriate category.

(3) Here set out concisely the facts explaining the transaction in cases falling within (*b*) and (*j*) or in any case which does not clearly fall within any of the categories (*a*) to (*j*). Adjudication may be required.

(1)   hereby certify that the transaction in respect of which this transfer is made is one which falls within the category(2)   above.

(3)...
....
....
....

Signature(s)   *Description ("Transferor", "Solicitor", etc.)*

....
....

Date .... 19......

N.B.—A transfer by way of a gift *inter vivos* is chargeable with *ad valorem* stamp duty and must be adjudicated.

  *NOTE— The above certificate should be signed in the case of (*b*) or (*j*) either by (1) the transferor(s) or (2) a member of a stock exchange or a solicitor or an accredited representative of a bank acting for the transferor(s); in cases falling within (*b*) where the bank or its official nominee is a party to the transfer, a certificate, instead of setting out the facts, may be to the effect that "the transfer is excepted from Section 74 of The Finance (1909–10) Act 1910." A certificate in other cases should be signed by a solicitor or other person (*e.g.*, a bank acting as trustee or executor) having a full knowledge of the facts.

APPENDIX 6. STAMP DUTY (I.R.66)

Changes in stamp duty on shares

On 27 October 1986, the day of the so-called Big Bang, major changes take place on The Stock Exchange.

On the same day the rate of stamp duty on share purchases comes down from one per cent. to a half per cent. The new rate applies to contracts entered into on or after that date.

At the same time stamp duty reserve tax comes into operation to bring within the scope of tax certain purchases of shares and other securities which up to now have not attracted duty. Like stamp duty the rate is a half per cent.

This leaflet explains how the Reserve Tax works. It is for guidance only.

Note
This leaflet is Crown copyright, reproduced with the permission of the Controller of Her Majesty's Stationery Office.

Stamp Duty Reserve Tax

When does the tax apply?
It applies if you:
(*a*) buy shares which you resell before they are actually transferred to you, for example if you buy and sell shares within a Stock Exchange account;
(*b*) buy renounceable documents;
(*c*) buy shares which are registered in the name of a nominee who acts both for you and the seller.
Stamp duty would not normally be paid on any of these transactions. Other share purchases do, of course, attract stamp duty.

When does the tax not apply?
It does not apply:
(*a*) if you buy shares on which the ordinary stamp duty is paid;
(*b*) to gilt-edged securites and non-convertible loan stocks;
(*c*) to foreign shares, except if they are held on a U.K. register;
(*d*) if the purchaser is a charity;
(*e*) if you buy units in a unit trust direct from the fund manager;
(*f*) to deals on The Stock Exchange traded options market or the London International Financial Futures Exchange.

What is the rate of tax?
The rate has been set at half a per cent., that is, 50p for every £100 or part of £100 of the price paid. For example, if you pay £1,040 the tax is £5.50. This is the same as the ordinary stamp duty rate that applies from 27 October 1986.

How is the tax paid?
If you are *buying through a broker or dealer*, as would normally be the case, the tax is included on the contract note you receive. You just pay the amount on the contract note, and the person issuing it pays the tax to the Revenue.

If you *buy shares other than through a broker or dealer*, write to the Office of the Controller of Stamps (at the London address below). Give the details of the transaction and enclose the tax. Cheques should be made payable to the Revenue. You do not have to write if on an offer for sale the vendor agrees to pay. The prospectus will make this clear.

If I don't think the tax is payable, what can I do?
If you do not think that the transaction is taxable, write to the Controller of Stamps Office giving your reasons. There is a right of appeal to an independent body of Appeal Commissioners if you cannot agree with the Stamp Office's ruling.

Where can I get more information?
Ask your broker or dealer, if you have one. Or write to:
Office of the Controller of Stamps, SW Wing, Bush House, Strand, London WC2B 4QN *or* Office of the Controller of Stamps (Scotland) 16 Picardy Place, Edinburgh EH4 3NB.

APPENDIX 7. STAMP DUTY RESERVE TAX: NOTES FOR GUIDANCE

February 1990. Office of the Controller of Stamps
[These notes are Crown copyright, reproduced with the permission of the Controller of Her Majesty's Stationery Office. They provide guidance to the Stamp Duty Reserve Tax provisions in FA 1986 and to the Stamp Duty Reserve Tax Regulations 1986, as subsequently amended. They are intended primarily for brokers, dealers and others concerned with accounting for the tax. They have no binding force and do not affect taxpayers' rights of appeal on points concerning their own liability to the tax. The 1986 edition of these notes is withdrawn.]

[*N.B.* In relation to the prospective abolition of all stamp duties on transactions in shares (including bearer instruments) and units under unit trust schemes, and of stamp duty reserve tax, see Revenue Press Release of 20 March 1990 (see Appendix 4) and the commentary on FA 1990.]

CONTENTS

Chapter 1 GENERAL DESCRIPTION

1.1 FA 1986, Pt. IV provides for a tax, known as the stamp duty reserve tax, to be charged on certain agreements to transfer securities. Most of the provisions relating to the collection and recovery of the tax are contained in The Stamp Duty Reserve Tax Regulations 1986 (S.I. 1986 No. 1711). Except where otherwise indicated, all section references in these notes are to FA 1986 and Regulation references are to S.I. 1986 No. 1711.

1.2 The tax applies principally to certain purchases of securities on or after 27 October 1986. It also applies, however, to transactions after 18 March 1986 involving the "conversion" of securities into depositary receipts (see Chapter 5) and the transfer or issue of securities into clearance systems (see Chapter 6).

1.3 Stamp duty reserve tax is administered from the Controller of Stamps Office, Bush House, London and by the stamp duty reserve tax unit at Worthing.

Principal charge

1.4 The tax applies where there is an agreement to transfer "chargeable securities" (see Chapter 3) for money or money's worth, unless there is an instrument of transfer and either:

    (*a*) stamp duty is paid; or

    (*b*) the instrument is exempt from stamp duty.

1.5 The situations in which stamp duty reserve tax liability will most frequently arise will be where a person:

    (*a*) buys a security and resells it within the same Stock Exchange account;

    (*b*) buys renounceable letters of allotment or acceptance;

    (*c*) buys shares which are registered in the name of a nominee who acts both for the seller and the purchaser;

    (*d*) buys shares which are resold before being transferred into his name;

    (*e*) bed and breakfast transactions.

Stamp duty would not normally be paid in any of these circumstances. This list is, however, by no means exhaustive. In any transaction involving chargeable securities where stamp duty is *not* paid you should consider whether stamp duty reserve tax *has* therefore to be paid.

Exemptions

1.6 The principal charge does not apply to:

    (*a*) Government securities *i.e.* gilt-edged stocks (see **3.5**);

    (*b*) non-convertible loan stocks (see **3.5**);

    (*c*) foreign securities or interests in foreign securities, unless they are registered on a register kept in the U.K. (see **3.2–3.4**);

    (*d*) purchases by a charity (see **2.20**);

    (*e*) certain transactions involving units in a unit trust scheme (see **3.6** and **3.7**);

    (*f*) deals on The Stock Exchange's Traded Options Market or the London International Financial Futures Exchange (see **3.10**);

    (*g*) bearer securities (other than certain renounceable letters of allotment etc) (see **3.8**);

    (*h*) the issue of new securities unless to a depository or clearance service nominee.

1.7 There are in addition special exemptions for Stock Exchange market makers (see **2.13–2.15**) and for Stock Exchange broker-dealers where the shares bought are resold within seven calendar days (see **2.16–2.21**) and for certain purchases and sales of shares by issuing houses under public offers for sale.

Rate of tax and chargeable amount

1.8 Tax is chargeable at the rate of 50p for every £100 or part of £100 of the amount or value of the consideration for the sale *i.e.*, at the same rate as applies for stamp duty to purchases of shares.

Payment arrangements

1.9 Where securities are bought on The Stock Exchange the buying broker is responsible for collecting the tax from his client and accounting for it to the Inland Revenue. Where under Stock Exchange rules an investor buys securities direct from a Stock Exchange member firm, that firm is responsible.

1.10 Where a Stock Exchange firm is not involved in a transaction the responsibility for accounting for the tax is that of any qualified dealer who is party to the transaction either as a principal or as an agent for someone other than a qualified dealer. If qualified dealers are involved on both sides of the transaction it is the dealer who is buying or acting for the buyer who is the accountable person. Where a qualified dealer buys from a Stock Exchange member firm, the Stock Exchange member firm must account for the tax.

1.11 In other circumstances, the responsibility for paying the tax rests with the buyer, who will need to write to the Controller of Stamps giving details of the transaction and enclosing the tax. Buyers will not need to do this when on an offer for sale the seller has agreed to pay the tax. The prospectus will make this clear.

When the tax has to be paid

1.12 The charge in respect of registered shares arises two months after the date of the agreement for the sale. The tax is due on the last day of the month following the month in which the charge arises (the accountable date). Thus an agreement in respect of registered shares made on 5 January gives rise to a charge to stamp duty reserve tax on 5 March (assuming that the agreement is not concluded before then by a duly stamped instrument of transfer). The accountable date for this transaction, and for all agreements during the month of January relating to registered shares is 30 April. For Renounceable Letters of Allotment the charge arises immediately and the tax is due on the last day of the following month. Thus an agreement made on 5 March gives rise to a charge to stamp duty reserve tax on 5 March and the accountable date for this transaction, and for all agreements relating to Renounceable Letters of Allotment effected during March, is 30 April. Interest is charged on tax paid late (see Chapter 7).

Other charges

1.13 Stamp duty reserve tax is charged at a special rate where shares are "deposited" with a bank for conversion into depositary receipts (see Chapter 5) and where shares are put into a clearance system (see Chapter 6).

Chapter 2 THE PRINCIPAL CHARGE

2.1 Stamp duty reserve tax applies where one person (A) agrees with another person (B) to transfer chargeable securities for money or money's worth. It applies to agreements made on or after 27 October 1986.

Definition of chargeable securities

2.2 The expression chargeable securities is explained in Chapter 3. Chargeable securities include stocks, shares and rights to stocks and shares in a U.K. company or in those shares of a foreign company which are kept on a register in the U.K. Most categories of loan stock are not chargeable securities.

When a charge arises

2.3 A charge arises when there is an agreement to transfer chargeable securities for money or money's worth unless the securities are transferred to the original purchaser and:

    (*a*) stamp duty is paid on the transfer; or

    (*b*) the transfer is exempt from stamp duty.

2.4 To allow time for an instrument of transfer to be produced s. 87 provides for the charge to arise two months after the date of the agreement, unless in the meantime a duly stamped instrument of transfer has been executed (normally this would be a stock transfer form or, in the case of most Stock Exchange transactions, a TALISMAN bought transfer) transferring the securities either to the person described in **2.1** as B or to B's nominee. Where in the case of a transaction carried out on The Stock Exchange the agreement is concluded between a member firm selling as a principal and a broker-dealer acting as an agent, this condition is regarded as satisfied if within the two month period a duly stamped instrument of transfer is executed transferring the securities to which the agreement relates to the broker-dealer's principal. Where the transaction involves the sale of a renounceable letter of allotment then with effect from 1 August 1987 the charge arises on the date of sale (s. 88 (3)).

Sub-sales
2.5 If the securities to which the agreement relates are not transferred directly to the purchaser (B) or his nominee but to another person (*e.g.*, a sub-purchaser), a charge arises notwithstanding that stamp duty is paid on the transfer of the securities from the original seller to the other person (see the example at **4.5–4.6**).

Conditional agreements
2.6 If the agreement to transfer securities is conditional, the charge does not arise until two months after the condition is satisfied (s. 87 (3)) and, if more than one condition, when the final condition is satisfied.

Rate of tax
2.7 Stamp duty reserve tax is charged at 50p. for every £100 or part of £100 of the price paid for the securities. Where payment is made other than in money—*e.g.*, by way of shares—tax is calculated on the market value of the consideration at the time the agreement was made (s. 87 (7)).

Accountable persons
2.8 The rules governing the payment of the tax are set out in Chaper 7. In most cases the buying broker (or if no broker is acting the dealer who sells the securities) will be responsible for collecting the tax and paying it to the Stamp Office.
2.9 Where a person who is not resident in the U.K. buys chargeable securities from a dealer (*i.e.*, a Stock Exchange market maker or a broker-dealer or a qualified dealer as defined in Regulation 2) the dealer will be accountable for the tax (see **7.3** and **7.5**). When a non-resident with a branch or agent in the U.K. buys securities through the branch or agent, other than from a dealer as above, the non-resident is the accountable person through the branch or agent. (TMA 1970, s. 78, as applied). An agent would only be liable if he acted in relation to the particular transaction.

Purchases from a non-resident
2.10 A charge is not regarded as arising where a non-resident buys chargeable securities from another non-resident and the agreement to transfer is made abroad. Where a person who is resident in the U.K. buys chargeable securities from a non-resident the buyer will be accountable for the tax in the normal way (see **7.6**).

Documents stamped more than two months after the agreement
2.11 Where stamp duty is paid on an instrument transferring securities to which the charge relates more than two months after the date of the agreement, any stamp duty reserve tax paid will be repaid. If the repayment is £25 or more interest will be paid. If stamp duty reserve tax has not been paid the charge is cancelled though any interest or penalties which have arisen may still be chargeable. A claim for a repayment or cancellation must be made within six years of the date of the agreement. If the agreement is conditional, the claim must be made within six years of the condition being satisfied (see also **7.12**).

Exemption for market makers
2.12 Section 89 (1) provides an exemption from stamp duty reserve tax where securities are bought by a market maker. The exemption applies if the purchaser is recognised by The Stock Exchange as a market maker in the kind of securities bought, and the securities are bought in the course of his ordinary business as a market maker in securities of that kind. Where a broker-dealer is recognised by The Stock Exchange as a market maker in some securities but not others, the exemption is limited to purchases of securities in which he is so recognised. An exemption from stamp duty reserve tax where securities are bought by a market maker in traded or traditional options is provided in s. 89 (1A). The market maker must be recognised by the Stock Exchange as a market maker in options to buy or sell securities of the kind transferred and the securities must be bought in the ordinary course of his business as a market maker in those options. There are rules to ensure that purchases excess to hedging requirements are charged to stamp duty reserve tax in the normal way.
2.13 There are enabling powers for the definition of a market maker to be amended. These have been used to provide that the exemption applies also to certain purchases of securities which are not dealt in on The Stock Exchange. The purchaser must be an "authorised person" under the Financial Services Act 1986 and the securities must be bought as a principal in the ordinary course of his business as a dealer in investments. Purchases made in the course of managing assets

belonging to another person or operating a collective investments scheme do not qualify for the exemption. The market maker definition was extended by the FA 1986 (Stamp Duty and Stamp Duty Reserve Tax) (Amendment) Regulations 1988, (S.I. 1988 No. 654) which are available from Her Majesty's Stationery Office.

Exemption for broker-dealers

2.14 Section 89 (2) provides an exemption from stamp duty reserve tax for broker-dealers in respect of securities resold by them within seven days of purchase. To qualify for the exemption:

(*a*) the broker-dealer must be a member of The Stock Exchange who carries on his business in the U.K. and is not a market maker in the kind of securites bought;

(*b*) there must be an agreement to transfer the securities to the broker-dealer or his nominee;

(*c*) the agreement must be made by the broker-dealer acting as principal in the ordinary course of his business as a broker-dealer in the kind of securities bought; and

(*d*) the broker-dealer must, within seven days of making the agreement to buy the securities, have made an unconditional agreement to sell the securities to another person. Where the agreement to buy the securities is conditional, the seven days start to run from the day on which the condition is satisfied.

2.15 There is an identification rule for determining whether securities bought by a broker-dealer have been sold within seven days. Where the securities sold cannot otherwise be identified, they are to be identified with any securities acquired in the seven days ending with the day of sale. Within this period securities acquired earlier are taken before those acquired later (*i.e.* on a FIFO—first in first out—basis) (s. 89 (7)).

How the special rule works

2.16 A sale of securities will be matched with the earliest acquisition of securities of the same kind within the preceding seven days ending with the day of sale for which relief has not already been given against an earlier sale. If there is no such acquisition, relief will not be available.

2.17 For the purposes of this rule, securities are acquired on the day the broker-dealer enters into an agreement for them to be transferred to him or his nominee; or, where the agreement to buy is conditional, the day on which the condition is satisfied. The securities are sold on the day the broker-dealer enters into an unconditional agreement to sell them.

EXAMPLE

Day 1 B-d agrees to buy 300 Xplc
Day 11 B-d agrees to buy 100 Xplc
Day 12 B-d agrees to buy 200 Xplc
Day 13 B-d agrees to buy 200 Xplc

Day 12 B-d agrees to sell 100 Xplc
Day 13 B-d agrees to sell 300 Xplc
Day 19 B-d agrees to sell 50 Xplc

Day 12 sale is set against Day 11 purchase
Day 13 sale is set against Day 12 purchase and against 100 shares of Day 13 purchase. Day 19 sale is set against 50 of the remaining 100 shares of the Day 13 purchase.

Stamp duty reserve tax is paid on the remaining balance of 50 of the Day 13 purchase.

As no securities of the same kind were sold by Day seven stamp duty reserve tax is also charged on the agreement to buy 300 shares on Day one.

2.18 There are enabling powers for the definition of a broker-dealer to be extended to broker-dealers on other recognised exchanges.

2.19 Individual claims will not normally be necessary. The Stock Exchange will be dealing with this on behalf of its members.

Charities, etc.

2.20 Section 90 (7) provides an exemption for purchases by:

(*a*) a body of persons established for charitable purposes only, or

(*b*) the trustees of a trust so established, or

(*c*) the trustees of the National Heritage Memorial Fund, or

(*d*) the Historic Buildings and Monument Commission for England.

Issuing houses

2.21 Section 89 (A) provides various reliefs for purchases and sales by issuing houses sponsoring offers for sale or placings. These are further explained in **4.8** *et seq*.

TAURUS exemptions

2.22 There are enabling powers to adapt stamp duty reserve tax and stamp duty to paperless share transactions and other new methods of share dealing such as The Stock Exchange's proposed TAURUS system (FA 1989, s. 176). Regulations may be introduced to provide that in prescribed circumstances involving a Stock Exchange nominee a stamp duty reserve tax charge may be cancelled where there is also a stamp duty charge or where more than one stamp duty reserve tax charge arises on a single transaction. As yet no Regulations have been made under these powers.

Chapter 3 CHARGEABLE SECURITIES

3.1 As a broad generalisation, securities are chargeable securities for stamp duty reserve tax if transfers of them would normally attract stamp duty. There are some important exceptions; *e.g.*, although a sale of renounceable letters of allotment or acceptance would not normally be stamped, renounceable letters are chargeable securities for stamp duty reserve tax purposes.

Definition of chargeable securities
3.2 Section 99 defines "chargeable securities" to include:
   (*a*) stocks, shares and loan capital issued or raised by bodies incorporated in the U.K.;
   (*b*) stocks, shares and loan capital issued or raised by bodies not incorporated in the U.K. if:
      (i) the stocks etc. are registered in a register in the U.K., or
      (ii) in the case of stocks or shares, they are paired with shares issued by a body corporate
   incorporated in the U.K.
   (*c*) rights to securities within (*a*) and (*b*) above;
   (*d*) units under a unit trust scheme (but see **3.6** and **3.7**).
3.3 Rights included within the definition of chargeable securities are:
   (*a*) an interest in stocks, shares or loan capital or an interest in dividends or other rights arising
   out of stocks, shares etc.,
   (*b*) rights to an allotment of or to subscribe for stocks, shares or loan capital; and
   (*c*) an option to acquire stocks, shares or loan capital.

Exclusions
3.4 The definition of chargeable securities excludes the following:
   (*a*) stocks, shares or loan capital the transfer of which is exempt from all stamp duties;
   (*b*) an interest in, or in dividends or other rights arising from, stocks, shares or loan capital the
   transfer of which is exempt from all stamp duties;
   (*c*) a right to an allotment of, or to subscribe for, or an option to acquire stocks, shares or loan
   capital the transfer of which is exempt from all stamp duties;
   (*d*) an interest in a depositary receipt;
   (*e*) foreign shares not on a U.K. register unless they are paired with the shares of a U.K.
   company.

Loan capital
3.5 Most non-convertible loan capital is exempt from stamp duty on tranfer (ss. 78 and 79) and is not therefore a chargeable security. The expression loan capital is regarded as covering short term loans *e.g.*, loans for five years or less. Thus if an investor buys a security, *e.g.*, a gilt edged security—which is exempt from stamp duty no stamp duty reserve tax arises. Similarly, if an investor buys an allotment letter which gives rights to a security—*e.g.* registered loan capital which is exempt from duty—no stamp duty reserve tax arises on the purchase of the allotment letter.

Other exclusions

Unit trusts
3.6 Although units in a unit trust are chargeable securities, s. 90 (1) excludes from the charge to stamp duty reserve tax transfers of units under a unit trust scheme to the managers of the scheme. Other transfers of units themselves are generally liable to stamp duty and hence stamp duty reserve tax will not normally have to be paid. The issue of new units by a fund manager is not a transfer of securities. Particular care is needed where either mergers or takeovers of unit trusts occur. Depending on the circumstances a variety of stamp duty and stamp duty reserve tax consequences can arise and you should seek specific advice. (Similar difficulties can be met where pension funds merge).
3.7 Transfers of units in a foreign unit trust are excluded from stamp duty reserve tax. A foreign unit trust is one where all the trustees are resident abroad and the units are not registered in a register kept in the U.K. by or on behalf of the trustees (90 (2)).

Bearer instruments
3.8 Bearer instruments liable to bearer instrument duty are excluded from the charge to stamp duty reserve tax (90 (3)). Renounceable letters of allotment and acceptance, which are exempt from bearer instrument duty, are however liable to stamp duty reserve tax (see **3.12**).

Depositary receipts and clearance services
3.9 Agreements to transfer securities which are liable to either the depositary receipt charge (see

Chapter 5) of the clearance service charge (see Chapter 6) are excluded from the principal charge. Purchases of depositary receipts and of securities held within a clearance system by a nominee whose business is exclusively that of holding securities for a person providing a clearance service are also excluded from the principal charge (ss. 90, 99).

Traded options and futures
3.10 Stamp duty reserve tax does not in practice arise on opitions dealt in on The Stock Exchange Traded Options Market where dealing takes the form of writing put or call options. The writing or grant of an option does not constitute a transfer. The exercise of an option may give rise to stamp duty reserve tax if there is no stamped share transfer. The futures dealt in on the London International Financial Futures market are not stocks and shares or interests in them and are not therefore chargeable securities.

Special cases

Charities
3.11 No charge arises on purchases of chargeable securities by a body of persons established for charitable purposes only or by the trustees of a trust so established.

Renounceable letters of allotment etc.
3.12 Agreements to buy renounceable letters of allotment, acceptance etc. (RLAs) are chargeable to stamp duty reserve tax notwithstanding the stamp exemptions in FA 1963, ss. 59, 65.

Transfers to The Stock Exchange's nominee
3.13 Although transfers to The Stock Exchange's nominees SEPON LTD are exempt from stamp duty (FA 1976, s. 127 (1) and s. 84 (1)) this exemption does not by itself preclude a charge to stamp duty reserve tax on a purchase of the securities transferred (s. 88 (1)). Other exemptions *e.g.*, for market makers (see **2.13–2.15**) and broker-dealers (see **2.16–2.19**) may however apply.
3.14 The same position will arise on transfers to other recognised clearing houses, recognised investment exchanges or their nominees to which the exemption from stamp duty in s. 84 is extended under the Financial Services Act regime.

Chapter 4 THE PRINCIPAL CHARGE: SOME PRACTICAL APPLICATIONS

4.1 Stamp duty reserve tax will apply to certain transactions which do not attract stamp duty. The situations in which stamp duty reserve tax will most frequently arise are set out in **1.5**. This Chapter describes how the charge will operate in those cases. It is assumed in each case that the purchaser is not entitled to any special exemptions.

Stock Exchange: intra account transactions
4.2 Where an investor contracts to buy securities and to sell them on within the same Stock Exchange account, the purchaser does not take delivery of the shares and so no stamp duty is paid. The purchase contract gives rise to a charge to stamp duty reserve tax. A charge also arises where an investor contracts to buy securities which he has previously contracted to sell (s. 87).
4.3 Where the number of shares a person contracts to buy exceeds the number of shares he sells, the unsold shares will be delivered to him and stamp duty will be paid on them. In these circumstances the stamp duty reserve tax is chargeable only on the consideration for the shares sold on (s. 87 (7A)).
4.4 The following examples show how stamp duty reserve tax will be charged in intra-account transactions.

EXAMPLE 1
Securities purchased   100 for £1,500
Securities sold   <u>100</u>
Securities transferred
  to original purchaser   nil
£7.50 stamp duty reserve tax is payable on £1,500, the consideration for the purchase.

EXAMPLE 2
Securities purchased   100 for £1,500
Securities sold   <u>75</u>
Securities transferred
  to original purchaser   25 for £375
                              (25 per cent. of £1,500)

£2 stamp duty is payable on £375, the consideration for the securities transferred to the original purchaser.
£6 stamp duty reserve tax is payable on £1,125, the consideration for the purchase of the 75 shares sold on (75 per cent. of £1,500).

EXAMPLE 3

Securities purchased	100 for £1,500
Securities sold	150
Securities to be delivered by purchaser	50

£7.50 stamp duty reserve tax will be payable on £1,500, the consideration for the purchase.

Off-market transactions: sub-sales
4.5 Similar dealing sequences can arise with off-market transactions, in particular where a bank or a dealer is acting as principal. FA 1963, s. 67 prohibits circulation of blank stock transfer forms (*i.e.*, forms which do not show the name of the transferee). Where however a purchaser sells securities before the delivery of the stock transfer form, the securities transferred can be delivered direct from the original vendor to the sub-purchaser. In these circumstances stamp duty is payable only on the consideration paid by the sub-purchaser.
4.6 The purchase by the original buyer will give rise to a charge to stamp duty reserve tax. The sale to the sub-purchaser will only give rise to a stamp duty reserve tax charge if stamp duty is not paid within two months of the agreement.

EXAMPLE
X agrees to sell N securities to Y for £100
Y agrees to sell N securities to Z for £120

N securities are transferred from X to Z by stock transfer form and stamp duty is paid on £120.

As there is no stamped transfer of securities from X to Y, stamp duty reserve tax is charged on £100 (the amount Y agreed to pay X).
See **4.8** *et seq.* (Offers for Sale).

Renounceable documents
4.7 Rights to and interests in securities which are themselves chargeable securities are also chargeable securities for stamp duty reserve tax (see Chapter 3). Renounceable letters of allotment and renounceable letters of acceptance are the commonest examples of these securities.

Offers for sale
4.8 These paragraphs deal with stamp duty reserve tax charges and reliefs in respect of offers for sale to the public. These offers for sale could include any combination of the following:
(*a*) new shares issued by the company for sale to the public;
(*b*) bonus shares issued by the company to its shareholders and renounced by them for sale to the public; and
(*c*) registered shares sold by the company's shareholders to the public.
4.9 These sales are usually sponsored by issuing houses acting either as agents for the issuing company and its shareholders or as principals. If the sponsor acts as agent then the sale of bonus and registered shares are chargeable transactions, being sales of chargeable securities by the vendor shareholders to the public. The issue of new shares is not an agreement to transfer securities and is, accordingly, not chargeable.
4.10 If the sponsor acts as principal then its purchase of bonus and registered shares and its sale of new, bonus and registered shares will all be chargeable transactions. With effect from 8 May 1987 s. 89A provides exemption for such purchases and sales where the shares are to be admitted to the Official List of the Stock Exchange, to enable issuing houses to act as principals without incurring the additional stamp duty reserve tax charges.
4.11 Section 89A (1) exempts purchases of securities (other than unit trust units) by issuing houses and s. 89A (2) exempts the subsequent sale by them of *newly subscribed* securities where:
(*a*) the securities are bought by the issuing house and sold on under the same arrangements to the public;
(*b*) the sale is subject to an Official Listing on the Stock Exchange; and
(*c*) the securities are bought and sold on at the same price.
4.12 It is usual with such offers for sale for the sponsor to pay stamp duty reserve tax on behalf of the company or the vendors under an arrangement with the Revenue (see **7.9**) and accounted for in the normal way.
Subsequent to the offer for sale, the sale of securities in renounceable form is liable and this is explained in **4.15** *et seq*.
4.13 When registered shares are offered for sale on renounceable letters of acceptance, at the end of the renunciation period a transfer of shares is executed by the vendor shareholders in favour of

the persons who then hold renounceable letters of acceptance, renounced or otherwise. The transfer will be impressed with stamp duty, usually paid by the vendors or sponsor. If the original purchaser does not renounce the letter the stamp duty reserve tax charge arising on the purchase will be cancelled by the stamp duty on the transfer. If the letter of acceptance is renounced the stamp duty reserve tax falling on the original purchase remains in place, as do the charges on subsequent purchases of the renounced letter. The stamp duty payable on the eventual transfer will not cancel any stamp duty reserve tax charges arising in respect of such renounced letters of acceptance (s. 88 (3)).

4.14 However, with effect from 8 May 1987, s. 89A (3) provides an exemption for sales of registered shares to the public (or placees) where the sale is effected by the issue of renounceable letters of acceptance (or similar documents) and the sale is conditional upon an Official Listing on the Stock Exchange. The stamp duty reserve tax charges on the subsequent renunciations remain in place as does the stamp duty charge on the eventual transfer document.

Renounceable letters of allotment

4.15 Where a company issues *new* shares (whether in connection with a rights issue or a bonus issue) existing shareholders will normally receive a renounceable letter of allotment. A renounceable letter of allotment is exempt from stamp duties provided its life does not exceed six months. It is, however, a chargeable security for stamp duty reserve tax purposes (**3.12**).

4.16 The *issue* of a renounceable letter does not give rise to the charge to stamp duty reserve tax as there is no agreement to *transfer* securities. The purchase of a renounced letter (including a split letter) however does give rise to a charge to stamp duty reserve tax on the consideration paid. The purchaser is liable for the tax but his broker is normally accountable for it (**7.3–7.8**).

4.17 The issue of a share certificate at the end of the renunciation period to the person surrendering the allotment letter is not chargeable to stamp duty reserve tax.

Renounceable letters of acceptance

4.18 The issue of a renounceable letter of acceptance, under an offer for sale of shares, can give rise to a charge to stamp duty reserve tax unless the conditions in s. 89(A) (3) have been met (see **4.14**). The purchase of a renounced letter (including a split letter) also gives rise to a charge to stamp duty reserve tax. The purchase is liable for the tax but his broker is normally accountable for it.

Instalment arrangements

4.19 Where shares sold are to be paid for over a period of time, special provision may be made to enable the purchasers to sell freely without prejudicing the interest of the seller. An arrangement of this kind typically involves an agreement between the seller and a custodian bank to which the purchaser is also a party. Under the terms of the agreement the shares concerned will be registered in the name of and retained by the custodian bank until the instalments have been paid. A purchaser's rights and obligations in relation to the shares (*i.e.*, his interim rights) are evidenced by letters of acceptance (which are renounceable for a limited period) and interim certificates issued by the custodian bank.

4.20 Where these circumstances apply, the agreement between the vendor and the purchaser gives rise to a stamp duty reserve tax charge. In practice this charge is often borne by the vendor. Sales of the letter of acceptance, during the renunciation period, also give rise to a stamp duty reserve tax charge (see **4.13**). Where after the renunciation period, the letters of acceptance become registered documents and the shares are transferred by a stock transfer form, stamp duty reserve tax will only arise if stamp duty is not paid within two months of the agreement to buy the letter.

4.21 The *issue* of interim certificates (when the acceptance letters are surrenderd) does not give rise to stamp duty reserve tax (but see Chapters 5 and 6 as regards Depositary receipts and Clearance system charges). When interim certificates are transferred by stock transfer form, a charge to stamp duty reserve tax arises only if stamp duty is not paid within two months of the agreement.

4.22 When the final instalment is paid, the shares are transferred from the custodian bank to the shareholder and a charge to stamp duty of 50p arises on each transfer. There is no charge to stamp duty reserve tax.

Underwriting

4.23 Where shares are offered for sale to the public or placees it is customary for the company or vendor shareholders to enter into an agreement with a financial institution whereby the latter agrees to purchase shares not taken up by the public. This underwriting function can in fact be performed by the issuing house sponsoring the offer for sale by agreeing to procure purchasers and to purchase shares for which purchasers cannot be procured. When that condition is satisfied and the number of shares to be taken up by the underwriter is known, the agreement is liable to stamp duty reserve tax in respect of the shares so purchased.

4.24 It is also customary for underwriters to agree with sub-underwriters (sometimes a "chain" of sub-underwriters) to the effect that the latter will take up part of the underwriter's liability to purchase shares not accepted by the public. No chargeable transaction exists at this stage but when unsold shares have to be taken up by the underwriters and sub-underwriters, then any shares taken up by sub-underwriters would result from a chargeable agreement between the issuing company or vendor shareholders and the sub-underwriters and not a sub-sale of shares purchased by underwriters for sale on to sub-underwriters.

4.25 If registered shares are delivered to underwriters or sub-underwriters, the stamp duty paid on the transfer document will cancel the stamp duty reserve tax charge. If bonus shares are issued stamp duty reserve tax will be payable but the issue of new shares will not be an agreement to transfer securities and accordingly will not attract stamp duty reserve tax. If an underwriter or sub-underwriter sells shares taken up then that sale will attract stamp duty reserve tax in addition to the charge on the underwriter's or sub-underwriter's purchase.

Nominee acting for seller and buyer
4.26 Where securities are registered in the name of a nominee and the beneficial interest is sold to a person using the same nominee so that the legal title remains unchanged, a charge to stamp duty reserve tax arises unless the written instructions from the vendor to nominee instructing him to hold the shares as nominee for the purchaser has been duly stamped as a letter of request. This situation arises frequently within the discretionary nominees operated by many qualified brokers and qualified dealers. They will be accountable for the stamp duty reserve tax arising within those nominees, where letters of request are not stamped.

Bed and breakfast transactions
4.27 Where such transactions are carried out, two charges to stamp duty reserve tax arise, one on the sale to the broker or dealer and one on the repurchase. (Since the stock does not move it is unlikely that stamp duty will be paid.) If the transaction is carried out through a Stock Exchange Member Firm, they will be accountable for *both* transactions. Otherwise the qualified dealer who arranges the transactions is accountable. (Again for both transactions.)

Chapter 5   DEPOSITARY RECEIPTS

5.1 United Kingdom shares are traded on a number of foreign stock exchanges in depositary receipt form. The depositary receipt (see **5.27**) is in effect a substitute for the U.K. share certificate. A stamp duty reserve tax charge at a special rate (depositary receipt charge) is imposed when U.K. shares are "deposited for conversion" into depositary receipts (s. 93). The rate is normally one and a half per cent. The charge complements the similar one and a half per cent. stamp duty charge that applies to the transfer of shares to certain nominee holding companies (s. 67). Unlike the stamp duty charge the stamp duty reserve tax charge applied from 19 March 1986. There are provisions to ensure that both the one and a half per cent. stamp duty and the one and a half per cent. stamp duty reserve tax charges will not both arise on the same transaction, and that the principal charge does not arise if there is a depositary receipt charge (s. 90 (4)). There is no stamp duty reserve tax charge when a depositary receipt changes hands. (s. 99 (6)).

MAIN RULES

When the charge arises
5.2 Depositary banks issue receipts against the deposit of securities with a nominee. A depositary receipt charge (see **5.3**) arises where (i) chargeable securities are "deposited" with a nominee of a person whose business is or includes the issuing of depositary receipts and (ii) a receipt is issued. It is assumed for the purpose of these explanatory notes that the person concerned will be a bank. If exceptionally the person concerned is not a bank the notes should be read accordingly.
5.3 The Finance Act does not define a "deposit"; instead it specified (s. 93 (1)) three separate occasions of charge:
   (*a*) the transfer of the chargeable securities to the bank's nominee;
   (*b*) the issue of chargeable securities to such a nominee;
   (*c*) the appropriation by the bank's nominee of chargeable securities it already holds against the issue of a depositary receipt.
5.4 The charge arises if the securities are transferred, issued or appropriated on or after 19 March 1986. The charge does not, however, apply to certain transactions which straddled 18 March *i.e.*, transfers of securities after 18 March where the commitment to deposit them was entered into before that date. It has to be shown that the securities transferred were bought or appropriated for deposit before 19 March but the depositary receipt can have been issued on or after that date (s. 93 (12)).
5.5 The issue of bonus shares to the nominee of the bank issuing the receipt (where there is no consideration) does not give rise to a charge (see **5.6**). The issue of shares for a scrip dividend can however result in a charge, as a right to cash has been exchanged for shares.

Rate of tax and chargeable amount
5.6 Tax is chargeable at the rate of £1.50 per £100 or part of £100, as follows:

(*a*) where the securities are transferred for consideration, on the amount of value of the consideration;

(*b*) where the securities are issued, on their price when issued;

(*c*) in other cases, on the open market value of the securities at the time of the transfer or appropriation.

5.7 A special rate of duty may apply on transfers by a qualified dealer (see **5.19–5.25**) (s. 93 (5)).

Credit for stamp duty

5.8 Section 67 provides for *stamp duty* at £1.50 per £100 to be charged in the case of transfers (on sale or otherwise) of securities in U.K. companies to:

(*a*) a person whose business is exclusively that of holding as nominee or agent securities for a bank's depositary business; or

(*b*) to certain other persons specified by Treasury Order.

This provision applied to transfers executed on or after 27 October 1986.

5.9 Where both a stamp duty reserve tax depositary receipt charge and *ad valorem* stamp duty are payable in respect of a transfer of securities, the stamp duty reserve tax charge is reduced by the amount of the stamp duty paid. Where the stamp duty equals or exceeds the amount of stamp duty reserve tax charge, no tax will be payable. This credit is not available where a fixed duty of 50p. has been paid on the transfer (s. 93 (7)).

5.10 The effect of these rules, therefore, is as follows. A transfer on sale of securities to a depositary bank's nominee company to which the stamp duty charge applies between 19 March and 26 October 1986, will have been stamped (if the consideration was over £500) at the rate of £1 for every £100 or part £100 of the consideration. Because stamp duty has been paid, the stamp duty reserve tax charge in this instance is limited to 50p per £100 or part £100 of the consideration. However, for a transfer on or after 27 October 1986, which is liable to stamp duty at the rate of £1.50 for every £100 of the consideration, or in the case of a transfer other than on sale the value of the securities, the stamp duty charge will in effect cancel out the stamp duty reserve tax charge.

Exemptions

5.11 Since the stamp duty reserve tax charge applies in respect of transactions involving "chargeable securities" as defined for the purpose of the principal charge to stamp duty reserve tax (see Chapter 3), it does not arise where the transaction involves most categories of loan capital (s. 99 (5)) or stocks and shares of companies incorporated outside the U.K. (s. 99 (10)). Exceptionally, the charge does extend to any such shares if they are paired with shares in a U.K. company unless the transaction involves the issue of the paired shares direct to the bank as part of an offer for sale to the public.

5.12 Nor does the charge apply to inland bearer instruments within the meaning of the heading "bearer instrument" in SA 1891, Sch. 1 (s. 95 (2)) other than renounceable letters of acceptance or allotment etc. which are exempt from stamp duties. Where, therefore, applicants allocated shares under the terms of an offer for sale are sent a renounceable letter of acceptance in respect of those shares, a depositary receipt charge will arise if the letter of acceptance is "deposited" (see **5.3**) with a depositary bank in connection with the issue of a depositary receipt. No charge arises when shares are issued to a depositary bank which holds letters of acceptance or allotment. See **5.16–5.18** as regards letters of acceptance issued in connection with certain instalment arrangements.

5.13 An exemption is provided for certain "share for share" exchanges in connection with a takeover, where an acquiring company (company X) issue securities in exchange for shares in another company (company Y). To qualify for the exemption, company X must either have control of company Y, or obtain control as a consequence of the exchange or of an offer as a result of which the exchange is made. Company X is taken to have control of company Y if it has (direct or indirect) voting control of that company (s. 95 (3) and (4)).

5.14 There is also an exemption for transfers of securities between depositaries. There is no charge in respect of transfers between one nominee company whose business consists exclusively of holding securities in connection with a bank's depositary receipt business and another such company, provided both companies are resident in the U.K. (s. 95 (1)). If either company's business does not meet this requirement the exemption does not apply. Segregation of securities held for depositary receipt business by the use of designated accounts is not enough to bring a company within the scope of the exemption. A company can, however, hold foreign shares provided these are held in connection with the issue of a depositary receipt.

5.15 The position is similar for transfers between nominees for companies operating clearance services (see **6.9**). An exemption is not available for transfers between a depositary receipt nominee and a clearance service operator's nominee, even if both nominees only hold securities for the principal's depositary receipt issuing business or the principal's clearance service business, as the case may be.

SPECIAL CASES

Instalment arrangements

5.16 The following paragraphs set out the implications of the depositary receipt charge where shares are sold under an instalment arrangement of the kind described in **4.19**.

5.17 Where letters of acceptance are issued by a custodian bank to a nominee for a depositary, and either the depositary or the nominee is liable to pay the first of the instalments, the usual depositary receipt charge will not apply. Instead, when the depositary or its nominee makes payment of each of the instalments for which it is liable, there is a special charge at the rate of £1.50 for every £100 or part of £100 of the instalment payable (s. 93 (10)). The normal depositary receipt charge will, however, apply where letters of acceptance or interim certificates are transferred to (or appropriated by) the depositary's nominee. The special charge applies to any instalment for which the depositary or its nominee is liable, whether or not letters of acceptance were issued to it.

5.18 There is neither a stamp duty reserve tax depositary receipt charge nor a ss. 67 stamp duty charge when, after payment of all the instalments, the custodian bank transfers the underlying securities to the depositary's nominee (ss. 67 (5), 93 (6)) provided that the transfer instrument is certified to the effect that:

(*a*) the securities transferred are the subject of an instalment arrangement;

(*b*) the transferor is acting as a custodian bank; and

(*c*) the interim certificate held by the depositary bank's nominee evidences all the rights which under the terms of sale subsist at the time of the receipt in the securities sold.

The certificate can be in terms that s. 93 (6) applies.

Qualified dealers

5.19 Relief is available where a qualified dealer transfers to a depositary bank's nominee, securities the dealer previously bought and registered in his own name (or that of his own nominee) (s. 93 (5)). This is designed to ensure that a dealer who buys shares to transfer against the issue of depositary receipts pays no more than one and a half per cent. on the transaction. "Qualified dealer" has a different meaning in this context from the term used in the accountable person rules in Regulation 2 (see **5.22** and **7.8**).

5.20 Where the relief applied in respect of securities transferred to a depositary bank's nominee before 27 October 1986, the stamp duty reserve tax charge will be 50p per £100. For transfers on or after 27 October the charge, either to stamp duty under s. 67 (3) or to stamp duty reserve tax under s. 93 (5), will be £1 per £100. Where a dealer bought shares before 27 October 1986 and paid stamp duty at £1 per £100, there will be a reserve tax charge of £1 per £100 on transferring stock to the depositary bank's nominee company on or after that date.

5.21 For the stamp duty reserve tax relief to apply the following conditions must be met:

(*a*) the transfer to the depositary bank's nominee must be effected by a transfer made otherwise than on sale;

(*b*) the transferor must be a qualified dealer (or his nominee) in securities of the kind concerned;

(*c*) the transfer must be made for the purposes of the transferor's business;

(*d*) at the time of the transfer the dealer must not be a market maker in securities of the kind concerned, and

(*e*) the transfer must be certified to the effect that the above conditions are fulfilled.

5.22 A dealer in securities is a "qualified dealer" if he is either:

(*a*) a member of a recognised stock exchange within the meaning of TA 1970, s. 535 [TA 1988, s. 841] or

(*b*) designated a qualified dealer by order made by the Treasury.

5.23 No orders by the Treasury have yet been made. Appendix 1 lists the stock exchanges recognised under TA 1970, s. 535 [TA 1988 s. 841]. It should be noted that the s. 535 [s. 841] applies to "Any exchange registered with the Securities and Exchange Commission of the United States as a *national* securities exchange". It does not apply to any local exchanges registered with the SEC.

5.24 A market maker in securities of a particular kind is a firm recognised by the Council of the Stock Exchange as a market maker in those securities (s. 94 (6)).

5.25 For the purpose of **5.21**, the transfer may be certified in the following terms:

"I/We hereby certify that I/we am/are [a nominee of] a qualified dealer in securities of the kind hereby transferred (within the meaning of s. 94 (5) Finance Act 1986) and that the conditions in s. 93 (5) (*c*) and (*d*) Finance Act 1986 are fulfilled."

Where the transfer has already taken place and all the conditions are met except the certification condition, the relief will be given if it is confirmed that the transfer otherwise qualifies.

Payment arrangements

5.26 The depositary bank will normally be the person accountable and liable for the tax (s. 93 (8)). The exceptions are where the bank is not resident in the U.K. and has no branch or agent here, when the bank's nominee is liable, and where the charge arises under the special provisions dealing with instalment arrangements, when the person liable to pay the instalment is liable for the tax. Where the responsibility for accounting for the tax falls on the nominee, despositary banks may make arrangements to account for the tax themselves.

Definition of depositary receipt

5.27 A depositary receipt is defined for the purposes of the charge as an instrument acknowledging that a person holds stocks or shares (or evidence of the right to receive them) and that another person is entitled to rights in relation to stocks or shares of the same kind including the right to receive such securities (s. 94 (1)). This definition reflects the legal rights and obligations contained in depositary receipts currently traded. These receipts acknowledge that:

(*a*) the issuing bank holds (*i.e.*, has deposited with it) securities (often described as deposited shares) or rights to receive them;

(*b*) the owner of the receipt is entitled to rights in or over the deposited shares (*e.g.*, to dividends); and

(*c*) the owner of the receipt is entitled on surrender of the receipt to a specific number of deposited shares or rights ro receive them.

5.28 An interim certificate issued in connection with sales of shares where the purchase price is paid by instalments (see **5.16–5.18**) is not a "depositary receipt".

Chapter 6 CLEARANCE SERVICES

6.1 There is a stamp duty reserve tax charge when U.K. securities of the type to which the depositary receipt charge applies (Chapter 5) are transferred or issued to a person providing clearance services or its nominee (clearance service charge). The charge is at the special one and a half per cent. rate and, like the depositary receipt charge, it complements a one and a half per cent. stamp duty charge (570). The rules that govern the clearance service charge are similar to those that apply to the depositaryreceipt charge.

6.2 The charge applies from 19 March 1986. There are provisions to ensure that both the one and a half per cent. stamp duty charge and the one and a half per cent. stamp duty reserve tax charge do not arise on the same transaction and that the principal charge does not arise if there is a clearance service charge (s. 90 (4)). There is an exemption for transfers of securities between clearance systems. The nominee company that holds the securities must, however, meet certain conditions (see **6.9**).

MAIN RULES

When the charge arises

6.3 A clearance service is an arrangement for settling (*i.e.*, clearing) transactions in securities, which may be held indefinitely on the system, despite changes in ownership. Securities within the system are held in the name of the company operating the clearance system or its nominee. The shares concerned can be traded without the need to produce transfer documents though, sometimes, documents akin to depositary receipts are issued to evidence title. The clearance service charge arises where chargeable securities are either transferred or issued to either:

(*a*) the clearance service operator; or

(*b*) its nominee.

6.4 The charge applies to securities transferred or issued on or after 19 March 1986 (s. 96 (13)). The charge does not, however, apply to certain transactions which straddled 18 March (s. 96 (14)). This transitional exemption applies where the following conditions are satisfied:

(*a*) the transferor (or, where the transferor acts as agent, the principal) agreed on or before 18 March 1986 to sell securities of the same kind and amount to a person other than the clearance service operator; and

(*b*) the transfer is effected in pursuance of that agreement.

6.5 The issue of bonus shares to the clearance service operator or its nominee does not give rise to a charge. The issue of shares for a scrip dividend can however result in a charge, as a right to cash has been exchanged for shares.

Rate of tax and chargeable amount

6.6 Tax is charged at the rate of £1.50 for every £100 or part of £100 as follows:

(*a*) where securities are transferred for consideration, on the amount or value of the consideration;

(*b*) where securities are issued, on their price when issued;

(*c*) in any other case, the open market value of the securities at the time of transfer.

A special rate may apply on transfers by a qualified dealer, on terms similar to those that apply to the relief from the depositary receipt charge provided for qualified dealers (see paragraphs 5.19–5.25) (s. 96 (3)).

Credit for stamp duty

6.7 Section 70 provides for *stamp duty* at £1.50 per £100 to be charged in the case of transfers (on sale or otherwise) of securities in U.K. companies to:

(*a*) a person whose business is exclusively that of holding as nominee securities for a clearance service system; or

(b) certain other persons specified by Treasury Order.

This provision applies to transfers executed on or after 27 October 1986.

6.8 Where both a stamp duty reserve tax clearance service charge and *ad valorem* stamp duty are payable in respect of a particular transfer of securities, the stamp duty reserve tax charge is reduced by the amount of stamp duty paid. Where the stamp duty equals or exceeds the amount of the stamp duty reserve tax charge, no tax will be payable. This credit is not available where a fixed duty of 50p has been paid on the transfer (s. 96 (5)).

Exemptions

6.9 There is an exemption for transfers between clearance systems. The securities concerned must, however, be held by and transferred to a U.K. resident company which acts only as a nominee or agent of a clearance service operator and who holds relevant securities only in connection with the provision of the clearance service (s. 97 (1)).

6.10 An exemption is not available for transfers between a depositary receipt nominee and a clearance service opertator's nominee, even if both nominees hold securities only for the principal's depositary receipt issuing business or the principal's clearance service business, as the case may be.

6.11 Section 97 (2) exempts from the charge transactions involving instruments of transfer to The Stock Exchange's nominee company or to any other nominee company of any other investment exchange which enters into an agreement with the Revenue for the composition of stamp duty.

6.12 There are exemptions relating to loan stocks, securities of non-U.K. companies, inland bearer instruments and takeovers similar to the exemption from the depositary receipt charge (see **5.11–5.13**).

SPECIAL CASES

Instalment arrangements

6.13 There are special rules relating to instalment arrangements which mirror those which apply under the depositary receipt charge (see **5.17–5.18**).

Qualified dealers

6.14 As in the case of the depositary receipt charge, relief is available under similar conditions (see **5.19–5.25**) where a qualified dealer transfers to a clearance service operator (or its nominee) securities which the dealer had previously bought and registered in his own name (or that of his own nominee) (s. 96 (3)).

6.15 Transfers qualifying for the relief may be certified in the following terms:

"I/We hereby certify that I/we am/are [the nominee of] a qualified dealer in securities of the kind hereby transferred (within the meaning of Section 94 (5) Finance Act 1986) and that the conditions in Section 96 (3) (c) and (d) Finance Act 1986 are fulfilled."

Payment arrangements

6.16 The clearance service operator will normally be the person accountable and liable for the tax (s. 96 (6)). The exceptions are where the operator is not resident in the U.K. and has no branch or agent here, when the operator's nominee (if it has one) is liable; and where the charge arises under the special provisions dealing with instalment arrangements, when the person liable to pay the instalment is liable for the tax. Where the responsibility for accounting for the tax falls on the nominee, clearance service operators may make arrangements to account for the tax themselves.

Chapter 7 ADMINISTRATION AND PAYMENT

7.1 Stamp duty reserve tax is to be administered centrally from the Controller of Stamps Office, Bush House (South West Wing), Strand, London WC2B 4QN (tel. 071–438 7039/7048). Enquiries should be addressed there. Notification and payments should be made to the stamp duty reserve tax unit, TOBI, South Block, Barrington Road, Worthing BN12 4SF. Other stamp offices will not handle stamp duty reserve tax. Taxpayers in Scotland may address general enquiries about the tax to the Controller (Scotland), 16 Picardy Place, Edinburgh EH3 1NF.

7.2 The responsibility for collecting the tax from the purchaser and paying the tax to the Revenue will normally rest with the purchaser's broker. Ordinary investors will have to account to the Revenue for the tax themselves when buying shares privately *i.e.* not through a market maker, broker-dealer or qualified dealer by notifying the stamp duty reserve tax unit. Special rules apply in the case of the depositary receipt and clearance services. Most of the provisions relating to collection and recovery of the tax are contained in the Stamp Duty Reserve Tax Regulations 1986, S.I. 1986 No. 1711 [see after FA 1990]. These Regulations were amended by the Stamp Duty Reserve Tax (Amendment) Regulations 1988, S.I. 1988 No. 835.

THE PRINCIPAL CHARGE

Responsibility for payment

7.3 Responsibility for payment depends on whether or not securities are brought on The Stock Exchange. Where securities are bought on The Stock Exchange via a broker acting as agent, the buying broker will normally be the person responsible for accounting for it to the Revenue though his client will be liable. The contractual arrangement between the broker and his client does not constitute a *separate* chargeable agreement. Where an investor buys securities direct from a Stock Exchange member firm (*i.e.*, where the firm is selling as a principal) the person ultimately liable in law for the tax will be the investor; but under the Regulations the Stock Exchange firm will be responsible for notifying the Revenue of the charge and accounting for the tax.

7.4 Arrangements are being made with The Stock Exchange for certain stamp duty reserve tax obligations of member firms to be dealt with centrally. Individual member firms will not therefore be required to notify the Revenue of these transactions or account for the tax. They are required to account for the tax to The Stock Exchange, and notify the Revenue about client transactions that are not reported to The Stock Exchange. There are still, however, a range of transactions for which central accounting via the Stock Exchange is not possible. The one most commonly met is in connection with Stock Situations arising in connection with takeovers. (Though deals in Residual Securities can also give rise to problems.)

It often happens that, before settlement of a deal in the target company's shares can take place, the offer becomes unconditional. The deal is then settled in accordance with the acquiring company's offer. Where this involves settlement by shares and cash, cash, renounceables, loan stock or foreign securities the stamp duty arising on the original deal will not be, or not fully, paid. Thus stamp duty reserve tax arises and had to be accounted for direct by the Member Firm.

7.5 Where a Stock Exchange firm is not involved in a transaction the purchaser will be liable for the tax. However, he will be responsible for accounting for it only if a qualified dealer is not involved in the transaction. If a qualified dealer buys securities as a principal or as an agent for someone other than a qualified dealer he will be the accountable person. If the buyer or the buyer's agent is not a qualified dealer but a qualified dealer is selling securities as a principal or as an agent for someone other than a qualified dealer that dealer is required by the Regulations to account for the tax.

7.6 In other circumstances, the purchaser will be both liable for the tax and responsible for accounting to the Revenue. He will need to write to the Controller of Stamps, Stamp Duty Reserve Tax Unit giving details of the transaction and enclosing the tax (see **7.10–7.11**).

7.7 An accountable person can be relieved of his obligations where the Revenue are satisfied that he has, without success, taken all reasonable steps to recover the tax from the liable person (reg. 7). Where the acountable person is relieved of his obligations the person liable for the tax (the purchaser) is required to pay it.

7.8 A "qualified dealer" for the accountable person rules is a dealer who is not a member of The Stock Exchange but who is a member of a self-regulatory organisation or a person otherwise authorised under the Financial Services Act 1986, Part I, Chapter III or a person treated as authorised under that Act's transitional provisions.

Offers for sale

7.9 Generally, a public offer of shares will be made by a seller who is not either a market maker, nor a broker-dealer nor a qualified dealer. In law, the person liable for the tax will then be the purchaser under the Offer and there will be no market maker, broker-dealer or qualified dealer to account for the tax. Where, however, the vendor undertakes to meet any liability and enters into an arrangement with the Revenue to do so, the investor will not need to concern himself with it. Where the Revenue makes such an agreement with the vendor, there will be a statement to that effect in the Prospectus or Offer document. Vendors wishing to do this must obtain the Revenue's agreement beforehand (reg. 4).

What the accountable person has to do

7.10 The principal charge arises in law two months after the "relevant day" (s. 87 (3)). In most cases the relevant day will be the date shown on the contract note. The accountable person has both to notify the Revenue of the charge and to pay the tax before the "accountable date" (reg. 4). The "accountable date" is the last day of the month following that in which the charge arises. Thus, an agreement made on 5 January would give rise to a charge on 5 March (assuming that the agreement is not concluded with a duly stamped instrument of transfer). The accountable date for this transaction (and for all agreements made during January) would be 30 April (but see **1.12** for the payment date where RLAs are involved in the transaction).

7.11 Regulation 4 provides for notices to be in such form as the Board may prescribe or authorise and to contain such information as they may reasonably require for the purposes of the Act.

FA 1989, s. 177 provides that Regulations may also be introduced to prescribe the manner or form in which information is provided, (*e.g.* in a particular computer format where relevant). As yet a form of notice has not been prescribed. Notice can be given either by letter or a computer print-out containing the following information:

    (*a*) date of the agreement;
    (*b*) names of the parties;
    (*c*) the description and number of securities;
    (*d*) consideration paid;
    (*e*) the stamp duty reserve tax payable.

    Cheques should be made payable to the Inland Revenue and should accompany the notification. Both should be sent to the Stamp Duty Reserve Tax Unit, TOBI, South Block, Barrington Road, Worthing BN12 4SF (Tel. 0903 509782).

Repayments where instruments stamped after the two month period
7.12 The principal charge arises where an agreement is not followed within two months by an instrument of transfer which is duly stamped (or exempt from stamp duty) (see **2.4**). If such an instrument is executed and stamped after the end of the two month period but before the tax has been paid, a charge to tax arises, but accountable persons are not required to pay the tax in these circumstances. Details of the transaction should, however, be notified along with other chargeable transactions. Where the instrument is executed and stamped after the accountable date (**2.11**) but within six years of the date of the agreement giving rise to the charge, repayment of the reserve tax can be claimed. Where the tax is not less than £25 it will be repaid with interest (s. 92).

Other repayments
7.13 Where it is proved that too much tax has been paid in respect of a particular transaction, the tax will be repaid with interest at the rate mentioned (regs. 11 and 14). A claim has to be made to the Controller of Stamps within six years of the date of payment or the accountable date, whichever is the later.

Underpayments and overdue tax
7.14 Regulation 13 provides for tax underpaid to be paid with interest. The time limit for recovery of tax underpaid is six years from the date of payment or the accountable date, whichever is the later. In the case of fraud, wilful default or neglect the period of six years runs from the discovery by the Revenue of the fraud etc.

Determination of liability
7.15 Where it is necessary to determine formally various matters relating to a chargeable transaction, *e.g.*, the occurrence of charge, or the liable person, the Revenue may give notice in writing to the person concerned stating that they have determined the matter specified in the notice (reg. 6).

Appeals
7.16 The Regulations give anyone served with a notice of determination the right of appeal. An appeal against a notice of determination should be made within 30 days of the service of the notice (reg. 8). In general, appeals lie to the Special Commissioners. Appeals may be brought out of time, with the consent of the Revenue or the Special Commissioners (reg. 9). Any party to an appeal may question the determination of the appeal by the Special Commissioners on a point of law by requiring the Commissioners to state a case for the opinion of the High Court (in Scotland the Court of Session and in Northern Ireland the Court of Appeal in Northern Ireland). There are provisions to enable appeals to go direct to the High Court, either where this is agreed between the appellant and the Board, or where the High Court, on an application made by the appellant, agrees (reg. 8). Appeals in relation to the value of land lie to the Lands Tribunal.

Recovery of tax
7.17 The Revenue may not recover tax or interest unless the amount has been agreed in writing or determined by a notice of determination (reg. 12). If an appeal has been lodged against a notice, legal proceedings can be taken only for such amounts as have been agreed or formally determined by further notice (which itself is subject to appeal) as not being in dispute. But proceedings may be taken for the tax due in accordance with the decision of the first tribunal or Court to hear the appeal, even though a further appeal has been made against that decision.

Information
7.18 The Revenue may by written notice require any person to furnish them with information needed for the purposes of the tax. Communications between solicitors and barristers and their clients are in general privileged (reg. 5). Accountable persons may be required to make available their records for inspection (reg. 15). The Board is also entitled to obtain information from company registrars, issuing houses, brokers and dealers on the Stock Exchange and nominees (TMA 1970, ss. 23, 25, 26).

7.19 The Taxes Management Act provides for penalties to be charged where there is a failure to give notice of charge, or incorrect notice of statement or claims or furnish information. Penalties can also arise on a failure to notify the Revenue that securities are held for the purpose of issuing depositary receipts or providing clearance services (ss. 68 and 71).

Depositary receipt and clearance service charges

7.20 In the case of a depositary receipt charge or a clearance service charge, the "accountable date" is the last day of the second month following that in which the charge arises. Thus where the charge arises during January, the accountable date is 31 March. In the case of transactions that took place between 19 March and 30 September 1986, the accountable date is 28 November 1986.

7.21 Where the charge arises under ss. 93 (1) to (7) (the main depositary receipt charge) the depositary bank is both accountable and liable for the tax (s. 93 (8) and reg. 2). Where the bank is not resident in the U.K. and has no branch or agency in the U.K., the person liable and accountable is its nominee. Similar rules also apply to charges under s. 96 clearance services charge (ss. 96 (6) and (7) and reg. 2).

7.22 Where shares are sold under an instalment arrangement and the charge arises either under s. 93 (10) (depositary receipt) or s. 96 (8) (clearance services), the person accountable and liable is the person liable to pay the instalment (ss. 93 (10 (c) and 96 (8) (c) and reg. 2).

7.23 Where the person otherwise accountable is the nominee, the Board will, if it is more convenient, be prepared to accept notifications and payments from the depositary bank or the person providing the clearance services, as the case may be.

Appendix 1. TA 1988, s. 841: Recognised stock exchanges

The following list gives the stock exchanges recognised for the purposes of "qualified dealer" relief (see **5.23**).

Australia	[The Australian Stock Exchange and any of its stock exchange subsidiaries;]
Austria	Any stock exchange in Austria which is a stock exchange within the meaning of the Austrian law relating to stock exchanges;
Belgium	Any stock exchange in Belgium which is stock exchange within the meaning of the Belgian law relating to stock exchanges;
Canada	Any stock exchange prescribed for the purposes of the Canadian Income Tax Act;
Denmark	The Copenhagen Stock Exchange;
Finland	The Helsinki Stock Exchange;
France	Any stock exchange set up in France in accordance with the French legislation;
Germany	Any stock exchange approved under the laws relating to stock exchanges in the Federal Republic of Germany;
Hong Kong	Any stock exchange in Hong Kong which is recognised under s. 2A (1) of the Hong Kong Companies Ordinance;
Ireland	Any stock exchange in the Republic of Ireland which is a stock exchange within the meaning of the law of the Republic of Ireland relating to stock exchanges. (On 25 March 1973 these stock exchanges became part of The Stock Exchange [; now the International Stock Exchange of the United Kingdom and the Republic of Ireland.])
Italy	Any stock exchange in Italy which is a stock exchange within the meaning of the Italian law relating to stock exchanges;
Japan	Any stock exchange in Japan which is a stock exchange within the meaning of Japanese law relating to stock exchanges;
Luxembourg	Any stock exchange in Luxembourg which is a stock exchange within the meaning of the Luxembourg law relating to stock exchanges;
Netherlands	Any stock exchange in the Netherlands which is a stock exchange within the meaning of the Netherlands law relating to stock exchanges;
[New Zealand	The New Zealand Stock Exchange;]
Norway	Any stock exchange in Norway which is a stock exchange within the meaning of the Norwegian law relating to stock exchanges;
Portugal	Any stock exchange in Portugal which is a stock exchange within the meaning of the Portuguese law relating to stock exchanges;
Singapore	The Singapore Stock Exchange;
South Africa	The Johannesburg Stock Exchange;
Spain	Any stock exchange in Spain which is a stock exchange within the meaning of the Spanish law relating to stock exchanges;
Sri Lanka	The Colombo Stock Exchange;
[Sweden	The Stockholm Stock Exchange;]
Switzerland	The Basle Stock Exchange;
	The Geneva Stock Exchange;
	The Zurich Stock Exchange;
United States	Any exchange registered with the Securities and Exchange Commission of the United States as a national securities exchange.

APPENDIX 8. THE STAMP DUTY (EXEMPT INSTRUMENTS) REGULATIONS 1987— GUIDANCE AND TECHNICAL NOTES

(April 1987. Controller of Stamps.)

Documents you no longer need to send to the stamp office

The documents

Certain documents dated *on or after* 1 May 1987 will be exempt from stamp duty, subject to a certificate, and will no longer need to be seen in stamp offices. Once certified, the documents can be sent straight to the registrar or other person who needs to act upon them, if any.

For the new regulations to be effective in speeding up business everyone involved in sending documents to stamp offices should know about them. This notice is to tell people about the regulations: please circulate it to all staff in your office.

A technical note for practitioners will be issued in due course and will be available from any stamp office.

The exempt documents will be those listed overleaf.

The Certificate

The certificate should be—
—included as part of the document or
—endorsed upon the document or
—firmly attached to the document (if prepared separately);
include
—the category into which the document falls and
—a sufficient description of the document where the certificate is separate but physically attached.
be signed by the transferor or grantor, or by a solicitor on his behalf. (An authorised agent of the transferor or grantor who is not a solicitor may also sign provided he states the capacity in which he signs, confirms that he is authorised and that he has knowledge of the facts of the transaction.)
A suggested form of words is:
"I/We hereby certify that this instrument falls within category . . . in the Schedule to the Stamp Duty (Exempt Instruments) Regulations 1987"
Insert the letter opposite the category concerned.

The procedure

(a) complete and sign the appropriate certificate (see above and below).
(b) send the certified documents direct to the registrar or other person who needs to act upon them if any.
(c) DO NOT SEND THEM TO STAMP OFFICES.
(d) DO NOT SEND THEM FOR ADJUDICATION.

The exempt categories

A.   The vesting of property subject to a trust in the trustees of the trust on the appointment of a new trustee, or in the continuing trustees on the retirement of a trustee.

B.   The conveyance or transfer of property the subject of a specific devise or legacy to the beneficiary named in the will (or his nominee).

C.   The conveyance or transfer of property which forms part of an intestate's estate to the person entitled on intestacy (or his nominee).

D.   The appropriation of property within section 84 (4) of the Finance Act 1985 (death: appropriation in satisfaction of a general legacy of money) or section 84 (5) or (7) of that Act (death: appropriation in satisfaction of any interest of surviving spouse and in Scotland also of any interest of issue).

E.   The conveyance or transfer of property which forms part of the residuary estate of a testator to a beneficiary (or his nominee) entitled solely by virtue of his entitlement under the will.

F.   The conveyance or transfer of property out of a settlement in or towards satisfaction of a beneficiary's interest, not being an interest acquired for money or money's worth, being a conveyance or transfer constituting a distribution of property in accordance with the provisions of the settlement.

G.   The conveyance or transfer of property on and in consideration only of marriage to a party to the marriage (or his nominee) or to trustees to be held on the terms of a settlement made in consideration only of the marriage.

H.   The conveyance or transfer of property within section 83 (1) of the Finance Act 1985 (transfers in connection with divorce etc.)

I.   The conveyance or transfer by the liquidator of property which formed part of the assets of the company in liquidation to a shareholder of that company (or his nominee) in or towards satisfaction of the shareholder's rights on a winding-up.

J.   The grant in fee simple of an easement in or over land for no consideration in money or money's worth.

K.   The grant of a servitude for no consideration in money or money's worth.
L.   The conveyance or transfer of property operating as a voluntary disposition inter vivos for no consideration in money or money's worth nor any consideration referred to in section 57 of the Stamp Act 1891 (conveyance in consideration of a debt etc.).
M.   The conveyance or transfer of property by an instrument within section 84 (1) of the Finance Act 1985 (death: varying disposition).

June 1987. Controller of Stamps
The Stamp Duty (Exempt Instruments) Regulations 1987—technical note

1. Copies of the above Regulations (S.I.1987, No.516) are obtainable from HMSO. This note is intended as guidance for those concerned in the application of the Regulations and further copies may be obtained from any Stamp Office.

Effect of the Regulations
2. Instruments correctly certified in accordance with the Regulations are exempted from the fixed duty of 50p to which they would otherwise be liable, and should *not* be presented to Stamp Offices either for duty or for adjudication.

Instruments to which the Regulations apply
3. The Regulations apply to instruments executed on or after 1 May 1987 that effect the conveyance or transfer of property of any description that fall within the categories listed in the Schedule (reproduced as an Appendix). The instrument is not excluded from the Regulations if it contains incidental matter where that matter is not itself a transaction.

Requirement for Certification
4. The relevant instruments are exempt from stamp duty provided they are correctly certified as within one or more of the categories listed in the Schedule to the Regulations. An instrument falling within more than one category will be regarded as exempt if correctly certified for either category or both.

Form of Certificate
5. The certificate need not repeat the precise wording of the category in the schedule. It will be sufficient for the certificate to refer to the category concerned by reference to its prefixed letter. A suggested form of words is:
   "I/We hereby certify that this instrument falls within category . . . . in the Schedule to the Stamp Duty (Exempt Instruments) Regulations 1987".

Method of Certification
6. The Regulations provide that the certificate must be included in, endorsed or attached to the instrument. Endorsement after execution is permissible. Where attached to the instrument the certificate must contain in addition to the usual details a sufficient description of the instrument, e.g. title, date, parties and property passing. Where the instrument effects a conveyance or transfer of land the certificate should preferably not be attached to the instrument but be included in or endorsed upon it. Endorsement on the reverse of a stock transfer form is acceptable.

Signatory of the certificate
7. The certificate must be signed by the transferor or grantor or by his solicitor or duly authorised agent. A solicitor may sign in the name of his firm. The term "duly authorised agent" includes a licensed conveyancer as well as a banker, stockbroker or accountant etc. Where the certificate is not signed by the transferor, grantor or his solicitor it must contain a statement by the signatory of the capacity in which he signs, that he is authorised so to sign and that he gives the certificate from his own knowledge of the facts stated in it.

Instruments to which the Regulations do not apply
8. Although the Regulations provide an exemption from the 50p fixed duty payable in a number of the more common situations where property is transferred otherwise than on sale, there will still be cases where duty is not relieved. Examples are:
   (i)   transfer from a beneficial owner to his nominee;
   (ii) transfer from a nominee to the beneficial owner;
   (iii) transfer from one nominee to another nominee of the same beneficial owner;
   (iv) transfer by way of security for a loan or re-transfer to the original transferor on repayment of a loan;
   (v)   transfer from the trustees of a Profit Sharing Scheme to a participant in the scheme.
   Conveyances or transfers within these categories and others not appearing in the Schedule where the duty is 50p under the head of charge "Conveyance of any kind not herein before described" in

the First Schedule to the Stamp Act 1891 should be presented to a Stamp Office in the normal way. Some documents that do not operate to convey any interest in property remain liable to 50p fixed duty under other heads of charge, e.g. Declaration of trust and Surrender. These are not covered by the Regulations and should also be presented to a Stamp Office as before.

Notes to the Scheduled Categories
9. B. Transfers in satisfaction of a general legacy of money should not be included in this category (see category D below).
   C. Transfers in satisfaction of the transferee's entitlement to cash in the estate of an intestate, where the total value of the residuary estate exceeds that sum should not be included in this category (see category D below).
   D. This category comprises:
      (*a*) Appropriations in or towards satisfaction of a general legacy of money (Section 84 (4) Finance Act 1985).
      (*b*) Appropriations in or towards satisfaction of any interest of a surviving spouse in the intestate's estate (Section 84 (5) Finance Act 1985).
      (*c*) Appropriation in Scotland in or towards satisfaction of the right of a husband to jus relicti, of a wife to jus relictae or of children (including adopted children) or remoter issue to legitim (Section 84 (7) Finance Act 1985).
      Transfers within these descriptions are no longer required to be adjudicated if they are certified within category D.
   G. A transfer made to the husband or wife after the date of the marriage is not within this category unless it is made pursuant to an ante-nuptial contract, although it may fall within L.
   L. Gifts of property within this category are no longer required to be adjudicated if they are so certified. Those transfers of property subject to or in satisfaction of a debt which are transfers on sale liable to ad valorem duty are not within this category.
   M. Transfers within this category are no longer required to be adjudicated if they are so certified.

Registrars
10. Certified instruments should be passed direct to Registrars (or any other persons required to act on them), who retain the right to require adjudication if they are in doubt as to the correctness of the certificate.

APPENDIX 9. THE DEMATERIALISATION OF SHARE CERTIFICATES AND SHARE TRANSFERS

November 1988.

Consultative paper

Department of Trade and Industry
1. The purpose of this paper is to seek views on possible changes to the law which would enable shares to be held on computer, without certificates, and to be transferred without the need for paper transfer forms. Comments should be sent to: Room 620, Financial Services Division, Department of Trade and Industry, 10–18 Victoria Street, London SW1H 0NN by Friday 30 December 1988.

Introduction
2. The last major simplifications in the law relating to share certificates and share transfers were the Stock Transfer Act 1963 (which removed the requirement that the transferee execute transfers) and the 1976 Stock Exchange (Completion of Bargains) Act (which paved the way for the Stock Exchange's TALISMAN system and for SEPON). With the increasing trend towards computerisation of many paper based activities the Government has reviewed whether any further changes would be appropriate.
3. The 1985 White Paper "Financial Services in the United Kingdom" (Cmnd. 9432) said:
   "7.21 In financial markets increasingly facilitated by information technology, there may no longer be a need for securities to be held in the physical form of a share certificate. The technology and expertise exist to create a system of fully integrated settlement between providers of financial services and their counter-parties based upon book entry transfers, with the minimum of physical documentation. The Government therefore propose to amend the existing legislation to permit the holding and trading of uncertificated securities. All the safeguards [for investors set out in the Financial Services Act] will still apply. Provision will also be made for investors who wish to continue to hold a form of share certificate or some other proof of ownership."
   The purpose of this consultative paper is to seek views on precisely how these changes, called dematerialisation, should be introduced.

The existing law
4. At present a company is required, by the Companies Act 1985, s. 185 to "complete and have ready for delivery the certificates of all shares, the debentures and the certificate of all debenture stock allotted or transferred" within two months of allotment or of the date on which a duly stamped transfer is lodged with the company, unless the conditions of issue of the securities provide otherwise. A company may only register a transfer of shares if a "proper instrument of transfer" has been delivered to it, or the transfer is an exempt transfer under the Stock Transfer Act 1982 (Companies Act 1985, s. 183). Registration of a transfer that is not duly stamped is an offence under the Stamp Act 1891, s. 17.
5. The *share certificate* is an important document (the Companies Act 1985, s. 186 provides that it shall be *prima facie* evidence of title) and when accompanying a transfer form is a means of authenticating transfer of beneficial title. The *company register* is however a more authoritative record of legal title to shares, and even that register is subject to rectification by the Court (Companies Act 1985, s. 359). Standard forms for *transfer* have been provided under the Stock Transfer Act 1963, most recently in S.I. 1979, No. 277. The liability to stamp duty reserve tax arising from the underlying agreeement for transfer is extinguished upon the execution and stamping of an instrument of transfer which attracts stamp duty.
6. There is a considerable body of case law built up over many decades on the rights and obligations of shareholders, the duties and liabilities of the parties involved in any transfer (including fraudulent transfer) etc.

The Government's approach
7. The Government have had two main considerations in mind when considering the principles of any new scheme. These were:
   (a) there should be no change to the detriment of the shareholder or of the company either in the relationship between them, or in the position of the company's register, as a result of introducing any new system, and the existing structure of rights and liabilities should be the basis for making corresponding provisions governing the obligations and liabilities of an operator;
   (b) the Government should avoid imposing on a new scheme any advantages or disadvantages over the existing paper based system.

The Government's proposals
8. The Government propose to legislate, when Parliamentary time permits, so that when both parties to the transfer wish, and the company has agreed to its shares being transferable in this way:

(*a*) shares held on a recognised computer system may be transferred from one person to another without the need for transfer forms or certificates;

(*b*) companies should be required not to issue certificates to any shareholder who has chosen to make use of the new arrangements;

(*c*) any person shall be free to convert their holding from one system to the other.

It is not proposed to alter in any way the position of the company's register, or to affect the relationship between the shareholder and company to the detriment of either party.

9. The hub of the new system will be the *operator*. It is the operator who will provide the mechanism to enable the new service to be offered, and who will link shareholders with company registrars. The Government does not propose to limit in the legislation the number of operators: instead it will lay down criteria which, if met, would lead to recognition by the Secretary of State as a recognised operator. It would not be a criminal offence to carry on the business of an operator without being recognised, but any such unrecognised system would not benefit from the proposed dispensation from issuing paper certificates and processing paper transfers.

10. The operator would maintain a computerised record of the dematerialised shares held on its system. Changes in ownership would be reported by transferor and transferee to the operator, or the operator's agent if any (see para. 16). The operator would then be required to notify the company in a timely fashion, and to adjust its own records. The process of the company updating its register would be exactly as at present, except that the company would be able to rely on notification from the operator being sufficient assurance of title and authority. It is not proposed to give any special status to the operator's records, which would be effectively a record of equitable title. It should be noted that the company's right to decline to register a new shareholder (*e.g.* because such an act would breach the company's articles) within the existing reasonable period will not be changed. In such circumstances the operator would be bound to adjust its own records accordingly. More generally it would seem appropriate to require the operator or its agents to provide periodic statements of holdings on the system to the owners of the shares.

11. There would need to be arrangements for entry and exit to the dematerialised systems (either as a result of a share transfer, or on surrender/provision of a share certificate). For obvious reasons no single individual share should be held in both certificated and dematerialised form at the same time.

12. The Government believe that investors should be free to decide whether to use any new systems or not. Dematerialised systems will therefore need to operate in parallel to the existing method. It would therefore seem inappropriate to automatically *require* anybody to accept or deliver dematerialised shares in settlement of a transaction. Subject to the results of this consultation exercise the Government therefore propose that delivery or receipt of dematerialised shares should not be sufficient to discharge any contract, unless the contrary was either an explicit term of the contract or could be so implied as representing standard business practice.

13. Furthermore it would seem inappropriate to require that a company's shares must be able to be held in dematerialised form. One possibility would be to make the inclusion of any company's shares on a given dematerialised system subject to approval of the Board of that company. To protect the interests of any holder of dematerialised shares in that company a decision to cease holding them in dematerialised form would most appropriately be the subject of an Ordinary Resolution at a General Meeting of the company. As a further protection it would also be possible to limit the period of notice that a company might be required to give to the operator to, say, not more than one year.

14. Appropriate arrangements will be needed to reduce the risk of fraud in a computerised system to a minimum. An audit trail will clearly be essential. The Government therefore propose that all instructions relating to the transfer of shares must be capable of being evidenced in legible form. Records will need to be kept for an appropriate length of time (10 years).

Requirements for becoming a recognised operator

15. As noted above (para. 9) the operator plays a key role in the system. The Government have therefore felt it appropriate to set out in some detail the type of requirements that any operator would need to meet to become recognised. Subject to the outcome of this consultation exercise the Government would propose that to be recognised by the Secretary of State an operator should:

(*a*) have sufficient financial resources to perform its functions;

(*b*) have rules and practices which ensured that transfers conducted by means of its facilities are conducted in an orderly manner and so as to afford proper protection to investors;

(*c*) either have, or secure provision of, satisfactory arrangements for:

(i) effecting transfers by its agents (see para. 16 below), if any, of such shares as it holds itself out as willing to transfer;

(ii) maintaining a record accurately identifying either legal title or such equitable title as results from transfers subject to entry in the company's register of members;

(iii) facilitating the proper settlement of transactions involving such transfers, either by means of services provided by itself or through clearing arrangements made with a clearing house or investment exchange (although to qualify such a house or exchange must be recognised as such under the Financial Services Act);

(iv) ensuring that proper information on ownership and transfer is provided to the share owners.

(*d*) have adequate arrangements and resources for the effective monitoring and enforcement of compliance with its rules;

(*e*) have effective arrangement for the investigation of complaints;

(*f*) be able and willing to promote and maintain high standards of integrity and to co-operate, by the sharing of information etc., with any person who is responsible for the supervision or regulation of recognised operators or investment business or other financial services;

(*g*) offer a system which ensured that those whose shares were recorded on it were effectively able to exercise the rights and enjoy the benefits of their shareholding.

In reaching a decision on whether an operator should be recorgnised the Government would also wish to consider whether the operator's proposals had the effect of restricting, distorting or preventing competition, and if they did whether that effect was greater than was necessary to give effect to the system.

16. It is possible to envisage not only systems in which the operator has a direct relationship with the shareholder, but also systems where there are one or more intermediaries between the operator and the shareholder. In the case of U.K. based intermediaries, or intermediaries soliciting business from persons in the U.K., some regulation will be required to protect investors. The Government therefore propose that for an operator of a system with intermediaries to be recognised the operator should be required to have rules and practices (including contractual arrangements) that:

(*a*) only permitted intermediaries to act as agents who:

(i) had satisfied the operator that they were fit and proper;

or

(ii) had no permanent place of business in the U.K., and acted as agents either:

    A. solely for parties outside the U.K.;

or

    B. as a result of an unsolicited approach made to the agent by or on behalf of their principal;

(*b*) required any intermediary acting as agent:

(i) to act with due skill, care and diligence in providing any service in connection with the operator's facilities which he provides, or holds himself out as willing to provide;

(ii) to disclose to his principal details of any commissions or inducements he might receive to use the operator's service;

(iii) to keep, and make available for inspection, accounts and records in connection with any transactions he undertakes;

(iv) to make provision for the protection of his principals in the event of cessation of his business as agent in consequence of his death, incapacity or otherwise.

17. In any case the operator will need to make provision for compensation of a transferee who relied on the operator's record of his transferor's title but who fails to secure good title or where the shareholder's shares are transferred without his authority.

18. Being a recognised operator, or an intermediary, need not in itself constitute investment business for the purpose of the Financial Services Act. The Government recognise however that in practice in any system with intermediaries it is likely that some will already be subject to some form of prudential regulation. In the interest of minimising the regulatory burden it would seem appropriate for an operator to be able to take into account any authorisation which an applicant intermediary had under the Financial Services Act, Building Societies Act, Banking Act or Insurance Companies Act. The operator would nevertheless have to make its own judgment as to whether the applicant was fit and proper to act as an intermediary. The operator would also need:

(*a*) to ensure that it, the operator, was immediately forewarned if the parent regulator of an intermediary had cause for concern;

(*b*) to provide a route to authorisation as intermediaries for persons not otherwise regulated; and

(*c*) to provide for continued monitoring of each intermediary's performance and conduct within the system.

Stamp duty

19. As noted in para. 5 above share transfers attract either stamp duty (in cases where there is a stampable document) or an equivalent amount of stamp duty reserve tax. With a dematerialised system where there are no documents of transfer, the charge will be stamp duty reserve tax rather than stamp duty. In order to ensure collection of tax in the most efficient manner possible the Government envisage that any recognised operator would be required to have an agreement with the Board of Inland Revenue to account for stamp duty reserve tax due on transactions within that operator's system. Such an agreement would be similar to the existing arrangement between the International Stock Exchange and the Revenue covering the stamp duty and stamp duty reserve tax arising on transactions through the TALISMAN system.

Investments to be covered

20. This paper has considered the possibility of paperless holding and transfer of shares in companies affected by the British Companies Act. It would also seem appropriate to extend the same possibilities to companies that are incorporated by charter or private act of Parliament.

21. The Stock Transfer Act 1982 led to the establishment of the Central Gilts Office, which is in effect a dematerialised system for gilts. There are obvious difficulties in dematerialising bearer instruments, but the Government would welcome views on whether there are other classes of investment (*e.g.* debenture stock) for which dematerialised systems might be appropriate, and, if this is the case, on the likely timing of introduction of any such systems.

Reserve powers

22. While it is hoped that the situation will never arise the Government have felt it prudent to consider what might happen should they need to withdraw recognition from any operator in the future. The simplest solution would be to require that any dematerialised holdings on that operator's system be rematerialised. However, if there were a number of systems operating it might be helpful if arrangements could be made for transfer to one of those other systems without needing to rematerialise the securities in between. The Government would therefore propose to take appropriate powers, akin to those in the Insurance Companies Act 1982. These would mean that any contract for the transfer of an operator's business to another operator would only be effective if approved by the Secretary of State. The Government would also propose to take a power to make an order for the transfer of one operator's undertaking to another.

APPENDIX 10. CHANCERY DIVISION PRACTICE DIRECTION

Practice Direction (Chancery: stamp duty on orders under the Variation of Trusts Act 1958) (3/89)

Chancery Division, 31 July 1989
1. An undertaking by solicitors with regard to stamping will no longer be required to be included in an order under the Variation of Trusts Act 1958 whether made by a judge or a master. This statement has immediate effect. *Practice Note* [1966] 1 All ER 672, [1966] 1 WLR 345 is withdrawn.
2. Solicitors having the carriage of such orders may wish to be aware that the Commissioners of Inland Revenue consider that the stamp duty position of duplicate orders is as follows.

(I) ORDERS CONFINED TO THE LIFTING OF PROTECTIVE TRUSTS

These orders are not liable to duty at all and should not be presented to a stamp office.

(II) ORDERS AFFECTING VOLUNTARY DISPOSITIONS INTER VIVOS

These orders may be certified under the Stamp Duty (Exempt Instruments) Regulations 1987, S.I. 1987 No. 516, as within category L in the schedule to those regulations, in which case they should not be presented to a stamp office. Without such a certificate they attract 50p. duty under the head "Conveyance or Transfer of any kind not hereinbefore described".

(III) ORDERS OUTSIDE CATEGORIES I AND II ABOVE THAT CONTAIN DECLARATIONS OF TRUST, I.E. THAT EFFECT NO DISPOSITION OF THE TRUST PROPERTY

These orders attract 50p fixed duty under the head "Declaration of trust". They may be presented for stamping at any stamp office in the usual way, or sent for adjudication if preferred.

By direction of the Vice-Chancellor.

Index
Stamp Duty Appendices

References in this index are to page numbers

Part IV Value Added Tax

Contents

All references, in the style **A17.04**, in this Part are to De Voil: Value Added Tax. If a VAT tribunal decision is unreported in the Value Added Tax Tribunal Reports (VATTR), the official tribunal centre reference is stated, *e.g.* LON/86/620. Transcripts may be purchased from the tribunal centres at London, Manchester or Edinburgh. The centres at Belfast, Birmingham, Cardiff and Leeds have been closed.

Post Office Act 1953
1 & 2 Eliz. 2 Chapter 36

16. Application of Customs Acts to postal packets. (A7.18)

Regulations have been made; see the Postal Packets (Customs and Excise) Regulations 1986, S.I. 1986 No. 260.

Provisional Collection of Taxes Act 1968
1968 Chapter 2

1. Temporary statutory effect of House of Commons resolutions affecting . . ., value added tax. (A10.06)
A House of Commons resolution varying VAT provisions expressed to have statutory effect under this Act, passed in March or April in any year, is effective up to 5 August in that year. A resolution passed at any other time is effective for a maximum of four months. If, therefore, a Finance Act were not passed by 5 August any extra VAT collected under this section would become repayable (see VATA 1983, s. 43).

5. House of Commons resolution giving provisional effect to motions affecting taxation. (A10.06)
A Budget resolution can be given immediate effect if the House of Commons so resolves; it lapses unless confirmed by the House within ten days.

Finance Act 1972
1972 Chapter 41

PART VII MISCELLANEOUS

127. Disclosure of information between revenue departments. (A2.21)
Authorised officers of Customs and Excise may disclose information to authorised officers of the
Revenue and vice versa to assist them in performing their duties.

Finance Act 1977
1977 Chapter 36

PART I CUSTOMS AND EXCISE

11. Recovery of duty etc. due in other member States. (A2.22)
An EC member State may request the Commissioners of Customs and Excise to recover a sum due
to that State as if it were a debt due to the Crown; see FA 1980, s. 17.

Action to recover any sum will not be pursued if the defendant can show either that he is about to
institute proceedings to defend the claim in the appropriate member State within a reasonable time
or that he has had a final decision in his favour on the claim before a competent body against which
no appeal lies in the member State. The defendant cannot dispute the liability itself.

Finance Act 1978
1978 Chapter 42

PART V MISCELLANEOUS AND SUPPLEMENTARY

77. Disclosure of information to tax authorities in other member States.
The Commissioners of Inland Revenue or their authorised officers can reveal certain confidential
information to similar authorities in other E.C. States provided that those authorities are bound by
confidentiality rules no less strict than those that apply in the U.K. and the information is requested
for tax purposes or to pursue legal proceedings for tax offences in the other E.C. State. This is
extended to Customs and Excise by FA 1980, s. 17.

Customs and Excise Management Act 1979
1979 Chapter 2

PART I PRELIMINARY

1. Interpretation.
Various terms used in the Act are defined.

5. Time of importation, exportation, etc. (A7.13)
Goods are considered, for customs and excise purposes, to have been imported when the ship enters the limits of a port, the aircraft lands or the goods cross the Irish land boundary. Whales and fresh fish, community transit goods and passengers' baggage brought by sea and are not treated as imported until they enter the port of discharge.

Exportation occurs when goods are put on board a ship or aircraft or when they are cleared by the last Customs and Excise office on their way to the Irish land boundary.

Similar timing rules apply for goods imported and exported by pipe-line.

For modifications as to VAT, see VATA 1983, Sch. 10, para. 4 (2) and Postal Packets (Customs and Excise) Regulations 1986, S.I. 1986 No. 260.

PART II ADMINISTRATION

APPOINTMENT AND DUTIES OF COMMISSIONERS, OFFICERS, ETC.

6. Appointment and general duties of Commissioners, etc. (A2.18)
The Commissioners of Customs and Excise (the "Commissioners") are appointed by the Queen but are subject to the general control of the Treasury. The Commissioners are responsible for the collection and day to day administration of the Customs and Excise revenues and therefore have the authority to appoint and commission officers to carry out their duties.

OFFENCES IN CONNECTION WITH COMMISSIONERS, OFFICERS, ETC.

15. Bribery and collusion. (A18.02)
It is an offence for any Commisioner or officer to take a payment, in money or kind, for agreeing to comply with or failing to take an action which results in the Crown being defrauded. It is also an offence to offer any payment to any Commissioner or officer to induce him to defraud the Crown. The maximum penalty on summary conviction is of level 5 on the standard scale (see s. 171). An officer may arrest a suspect under this section.

16. Obstruction of officers, etc. (A18.02)
Anyone who prevents or tries to prevent an officer from carrying out his duty is guilty of an offence. This includes assaulting an officer or anyone helping him, impeding a search, reclaiming, damaging or destroying anything which is liable to seizure and helping smugglers to escape. On summary conviction a person is liable to a penalty of the prescribed sum (see s. 171) and up to three months' imprisonment; upon conviction on indictment to an unlimited penalty and up to two years' imprisonment. An officer may arrest a suspect under this section.

COMMISSIONERS' RECEIPTS AND EXPENSES

17. Disposal of duties, etc. (A2.16)
The Commissioners must deposit all monies or securities received in Great Britain in an account with the Bank of England. However some of the monies received may be retained to cover disbursements. The Exchequer and Audit Department Act 1866, s. 10 and the Isle of Man Act 1979, s. 2, control how the money is withdrawn from the General Account. There are special arrangements for Northern Ireland.

Disbursements in the Port of London are to be drawn from the General Account as are claims for overpayment of duty made within six years of payment, provided the Commissioners are satisfied the claim is genuine.

Most penalties and proceeds from the sale of seized goods are to be accounted for as if they were duties.

PART III CUSTOMS AND EXCISE CONTROL AREAS

19. Appointment of ports, etc. (A7.06)
The Commisioners appoint customs ports by statutory instrument, and allocate within each customs port places where customs officers are to board or disembark from ships. See S.I. 1956 No. 1796; S.I. 1980 Nos. 482–486, 1367–1369, 1879–1882.

21. Control of movement of aircraft, etc. into and out of the United Kingdom. (A7.06)
The Secretary of State designates customs and excise airports where aircraft may land or depart. See orders made under Air Navigation Order 1980, S.I. 1980 No. 1965 art. 78.

31. Control of movement of goods to and from inland clearance depot, etc.
The Commissioners may by regulation control the movement of goods between their place of importation and the place where they finally leave customs control, and between a place of examination and their place of exportation. See the Control of Movement of Goods Regulations 1984, S.I. 1984 No. 1176.

Any person who fails to comply with the regulations is liable upon conviction by a magistrate to a maximum penalty of level 4 on the standard scale (see s. 171) and the goods can be seized.

PART IV CONTROL OF IMPORTATION

INWARD ENTRY AND CLEARANCE

37. Entry of goods on importation. (A7.07)
The importer of goods (other than fresh fish and whales, free zone goods free of excise duty, passengers' baggage and Community transit goods) must deliver to the local entry process unit details of the importation on the appropriate form accompanied by such commercial information as the Commissioners require.

The options available to an importer of goods are to have them entered for use in the E.C. (or, if excise duty is chargeable, as free zone goods), for warehousing, for transit or transhipment, for processing or in permitted cases, for temporary holding pending re-exportation.

The Commissioners may by a direction refuse to allow certain goods to be warehoused, but all goods chargeable with duty imported by pipe-line must be warehoused.

There are special rules and time limits for presenting import documents to the entry process unit before the goods are actually imported.

37A. Initial and supplementary entries. (A7.07)
An authorised importer (or an authorised agent acting for an importer who is not authorised) may lodge an initial entry to obtain release of the goods provided that the Commissioners have security for any unpaid duty and the duty is paid and the complete entry completed within certain deadlines.

37B. Postponed entry. (A7.07)
An authorised importer (or an authorised agent acting for an importer who is not authorised) who lodges paperwork acceptable to Customs and Excise may have delivery of goods before an entry is made or duty paid provided a record of the goods is maintained, and arrangements are made for security of duty and custody of the goods.

37C. Provisions supplementary to ss. 37A and 37B.
Contravention of the requirements of ss. 37A and 37B could result in an authorised person being prosecuted and fined and his authorised status being suspended or cancelled. He is liable to a penalty of level 4 on the standard scale (see s. 171).

38. Acceptance of incomplete entry. (A7.07)
The proper officer may accept an entry which does not fully comply with s. 37 but the importer must, within time limits set by the Commissioners, deliver to the proper officer the particulars which were omitted from the original entry.

38A. Examination of goods for purpose of making entry. (A7.07)
Importers may apply to the proper officer to be allowed to examine and sample goods, which are in customs and excise charge, for the purpose of making entry provided that the importer accepts any risk and any expense involved.

38B. Correction and cancellation of entry. (A7.07)
An incorrect entry may be corrected or substituted with another at any time while the goods are in customs and excise charge, but not after clearance, notification that the goods are to be examined or discovery by an officer that the entry is incorrect. If the importer can satisfy the Commissioners that the entry was made by mistake or that the goods cannot be cleared for free circulation then the incorrect entry may be cancelled.

41. Failure to comply with provisions as to entry.
Failure to comply with any of the rules in connection with making entry for goods imported shall render a person liable upon summary conviction to a penalty of level 2 on the standard scale (see s. 171) and the goods may be forfeited. These penalties do not however apply if the entry can be corrected or cancelled under s. 38B.

42. Power to regulate unloading, removal, etc. of imported goods.
The Commissioners may make regulations to control vessels, aircraft and persons carrying goods arriving at a port, an airport or on the Northern Ireland land boundary and to regulate how the unloading, landing, movement and removal of goods may be carried out. See Pleasure Craft (Arrival and Report) Regulations 1979, S.I. 1979 No. 564; Aircraft (Customs and Excise) Regulations 1981, S.I. 1981 No. 1259; Ship's Report, Importation and Exportation by Sea Regulations 1981, S.I. 1981 No. 1260; also Customs (Land Boundary) Regulations 1953, S.I. 1953 No. 1532. Failure to comply with such a regulation will render the offender upon summary conviction to a penalty of level 3 on the standard scale (see s. 171) and any related goods concerned in the offence may be forfeited.

PROVISIONS AS TO DUTY ON IMPORTED GOODS

43. Duty on imported goods. (A7.12)
Unless the law provides otherwise, imported goods may not be delivered out of customs and excise control until the duty, if any, is paid on making the entry.

The rate of duty payable is that in force when an entry is accepted or a s. 78 declaration is made. The rate of duty payable on warehoused goods is ascertained in accordance with warehousing regulations (made under CEMA 1979, s. 93). If no entry or declaration is made, the duty payable in relation to Community customs duty is that applicable when the goods entered the Community, and in relation to U.K. duties is that which applied when they were imported into the U.K.

Goods which have customs duty levied because of a failure to comply with a condition or obligation under ss. 47 or 48 have duty charged as if the entry for the goods had been accepted when the failure to comply occurred. Duties of customs on debris from the destruction of goods are chargeable at the rate applicable when the goods were destroyed.

Goods brought into the U.K. as "merchandise in baggage" are subject to the same rate of duty as would apply to those goods if entered as cargo. The Commissioners determine the country of origin if the question arises, unless the question can be resolved by s. 120 or by E.C. rules having the force of law.

Where the entry of goods involves the use of a computer, the time of delivery of the entry is the time when the details on the entry are accepted by the computer.

Where there is a reduction in the rate of customs duty between the time an entry is accepted and the time an entry is made for goods not entered for warehousing, or subject to agricultural levy, then the rate of duty is that applicable in accordance with the warehousing instructions unless clearance of the goods has been delayed by the importer. Where an application is made under s. 38 for a sample of goods to be taken and the entry subsequently made excludes the sample quantity, the rate of duty chargeable on the sample is that which applied when the application to sample was made.

44. Exclusion of section 43(1) for importers etc. keeping standing deposits. (A15.24)
Importers or agents who keep a standing deposit with the Commissioners sufficient to cover any duty payable need not pay duty on making the entry.

45. Deferred payment of customs duty. (A7.04, 17; A15.21–23, 41)
The Commissioners may by regulation approve arrangements whereby payment of customs duty may be deferred. See Customs Duties (Deferred Payment) Regulations 1976, S.I. 1976 No. 1223; Customs and Excise (Deferred Payment) (RAF Airfields and Offshore Installations) (No. 2) Regulations 1988, S.I. 1988 No. 1898.

46. Goods to be warehoused without payment of duty. (A7.32)
Imported goods, which may be entered for warehousing, may be warehoused duty free subject to any conditions imposed by the warehousing regulations (made under CEMA 1979, s. 93).

47. Relief from payment of duty of goods entered for transit or transhipment. (A7.33)
The Commissioners may allow goods entered for transit or transhipment to be removed without payment of duty, subject to any conditions they think appropriate.

48. Relief from payment of duty of goods temporarily imported. (A7.35)
Where the Commissioners are satisfied that goods have been imported temporarily and will be re-exported, the goods may be delivered duty free subject to such conditions as they think appropriate in accordance with regulations. See Temporary Importation (Commercial Vehicles and Aircraft) Regulations 1961, S.I. 1961 No. 1523. For regulations revoked except insofar as they relate to goods imported before 1 January 1986, see Customs Duties (Temporary Importation) (Revocation) Regulations 1987, S.I. 1987 No. 1781. Relief is now governed by Council Regulation (EEC) No. 3599/82.

FORFEITURE, OFFENCES, ETC. IN CONNECTION WITH IMPORTATION

49. Forfeiture of goods improperly imported.
Goods which are imported without payment of customs or excise duty are liable to forfeiture. However, where prohibited or restricted goods are intended for re-exportation, entered for transit or transhipment, or warehoused for exportation or for use as stores, the Commissioners may allow the goods to be dealt with accordingly.

50. Penalty for improper importation of goods.
Attempting to evade payment of duties or import restrictions renders a person liable to arrest. A person is liable upon summary conviction to a fine of up to three times the value of the goods or up to six months' imprisonment or both, or upon conviction on indictment to a fine of any amount or up to two years' imprisonment or to both. Sch. 1 amends these penalties in relation to the importation of drugs as defined in the Misuse of Drugs Act 1971, s. 3. For forgery the maximum term of imprisonment is 10 years.

Attempting to import goods concealed amongst goods of a different description renders the importer liable upon conviction to the greater of a penalty of three times the value of the goods or of level 3 on the standard scale (see s. 171).

Offences and penalties specified in enactments that impose prohibitions or restrictions take priority over this section.

PART VII CUSTOMS AND EXCISE CONTROL: SUPPLEMENTARY PROVISIONS

ADDITIONAL PROVISIONS AS TO INFORMATION

77. Information in relation to goods imported or exported.
An officer may require any person concerned in the importation, exportation or carriage of goods which require an entry, or concerned in the carriage, unloading, landing or loading of goods which are being imported or exported, to produce any information relating to the goods and to allow an officer to inspect and make copies of any documents relating to the goods. Failure to comply renders a person upon summary conviction liable to a penalty of level 3 on the standard scale (see s. 171).

If there is an export restriction, either on any goods to a particular destination or on particular goods to a particular destination, the Commissioners may require the exporter of such goods to make a declaration. If the Commissioners suspect that the declaration is untrue the goods may be detained and, if the declaration is untrue, forfeited. The exporter is liable to a penalty of the greater of three times the value of the goods or of level 3 on the standard scale (see s. 171) unless he can demonstrate that he did not consent to or connive at the goods reaching a destination other than that stated and that he took all reasonable steps to secure that the ulitmate destination was as stated.

77A. Information powers.
Every person involved in the importation or exportation of goods which require lodgement of an entry or specification with the Commissioners is required, upon demand, to give the Commissioners information relating to the goods. An officer may require a person to produce at any place any document relating to the goods or their movement.

An officer may require any person holding documents to produce them without prejudicing a lien on them and he may copy or take extracts from any document produced or if necessary for a reasonable period remove any document. Where a lien on the document is claimed, removal of the document will not break it.

A free copy of any document removed is to be supplied by the officer when it is required for business purposes and expenses may be claimed from the Commissioners for replacing or repairing lost or damaged documents. A person failing to give information or provide a document is liable to a level 3 penalty on the standard scale (see s. 171) upon summary conviction.

78. Customs and excise control of persons entering or leaving the United Kingdom. (A7.65)
Any person entering the U.K. must declare any thing carried with him (in excess of the personal reliefs) which has been obtained outside the U.K. or duty free in the U.K. Any person entering or

leaving the U.K. must answer such questions as an officer may put to him with respect to any thing carried with him and may be required to produce such thing for examination. Failure to declare any thing renders a person upon summary conviciton to a penalty of the greater of three times the value of the thing not declared or produced or of level 3 on the standard scale (see s. 171). Any thing found concealed or not declared or in breach of import or export prohibition or restriction is liable to forfeiture.

79. Power to require evidence in support of information.
Where the duty chargeable depends on any question of where the goods come from or where they were grown, manufactured or produced, then the Commissioners may require the importer of the goods to provide proof to support any statements made or provide evidence of the accuracy of any certificate or document. Failure to provide such evidence may result in the duty being charged without regard to the disputed statement or certificate.

PART VIII WAREHOUSES AND QUEEN'S WAREHOUSES AND RELATED PROVISIONS ABOUT PIPE-LINES

92. Approval of warehouses. (A7.32; A15.41)
The Commissioners may approve a place of security known as an "excise warehouse". The following goods may be deposited, kept and secured therein in accordance with "warehousing regulations" (see below): (1) imported goods chargeable with excise duty; (2) goods for exportation; (3) goods for use as stores; (4) home manufactured or produced goods eligible for warehousing without payment of excise duty; (5) imported goods eligible for warehousing on drawback; and (6) home manufactured or produced goods eligible for warehousing on drawback.

The Commissioners may approve a place of security known as a "customs warehouse". The following goods may be deposited, kept and secured therein in accordance with "warehousing regulations" (see below): (1) imported goods chargeable with customs duty or not otherwise in free circulation; (2) goods for exportation; (3) goods for use as stores; (4) goods for a purpose referred to in an E.C. regulation; and (5) goods on which any excise duty has been paid and which are eligible to be kept, without being warehoused, in a customs warehouse.

A place of security may be approved as both an excise warehouse and a customs warehouse.

The Commissioners may revoke or vary the terms of their approval at any time for reasonable cause.

Any person breaching conditions imposed under this section is liable on summary conviction to a penalty of level 3 on the standard scale (see s. 171).

"Warehousing regulations" are regulations made by the Commissioners under CEMA 1979 s. 93 regarding the deposit, keeping, securing and treatment of goods in a warehouse and the removal of goods therefrom. See Customs Warehousing Regulations 1979, S.I. 1979 No. 207; Excise Duties (Deferred Payment) Regulations 1983, S.I. 1983 No. 947; Beer Regulations 1985, S.I. 1985 No. 1627, Part V; Excise Warehousing (Etc.) Regulations 1988, S.I. 1988 No. 809; Spirits (Rectifying, Compounding and Drawback) Regulations 1988, S.I. 1988 No. 1760. Penalties are prescribed for failure to comply with the regulations or with any condition, restriction or requirement imposed thereunder.

PART VIIIA FREE ZONES

100A. Designation of free zones. (A7.31)
The Treasury may by statutory instrument designate areas of the U.K. as special free zones for customs purposes, and appoint a responsible authority to administer the area. Orders have been made to designate Belfast Airport (S.I. 1984 No. 1206 and S.I. 1986 No. 1643), Birmingham Airport (S.I. 1984 No. 1207), Cardiff (S.I. 1984 No. 1208), Liverpool (S.I. 1984 No. 1209), Prestwick Airport (S.I. 1984 No. 1210) and Southampton (S.I. 1984 No. 1211).

100B. Free zone regulations. (A7.31)
The Commissioners may by regulation control the movement of goods to and from a free zone and the custody and treatment of goods in a free zone. See Free Zone Regulations 1984, S.I. 1984 No. 1177.

100C. Free zone goods: customs duties, etc. (A7.31)
Subject to any contrary Community Law, goods upon which customs duty is payable may be moved into a free zone and remain duty free. This does not apply to goods also chargeable with excise duty unless the excise duty is paid, except as provided by regulations.

The Commissioners may by regulation set the conditions for removal of goods from a free zone without payment of duty, or where goods cease to be free zone goods the appropriate rate of duty and the time when those goods cease to be free zone goods.

Upon the removal of goods from a free zone, the Commissioners may by such regulation control removal without payment of duty, and determine the appropriate rate of duty and when those goods cease to be free zone goods. The regulations may also set out the rate of duty where a person wishes to pay customs duty whilst the goods remain free zone goods. The Commissioners may also control the destruction of free zone goods without payment of customs duty.

The regulations may also give relief from the whole or part of any VAT on the importation of goods into a U.K. free zone and determine when a supply is deemed to take place for the purposes of VAT where goods are or have been free zone goods. The regulations may also determine the VAT treatment of goods produced in a free zone from other goods or which have other free zone goods incorporated in them.

See Free Zone Regulations 1984, S.I. 1984 No. 1177.

100D. Free zone regulations: supplemental. (A7.31)

The Commissioners may make regulations concerning what can and cannot be done and how it should be done, including provisions for the security of the zone. These regulations may also provide for circumstances when goods physically in a free zone are not considered to be free zone goods, and vice versa.

An officer may inspect goods within a free zone and the records which a proprietor of premises in the zone may be required to keep. The regulations may also prescribe forfeiture of the goods as a penalty where there is failure to comply with the conditions under which operations on goods are carried out.

Upon conviction for failure to observe any condition or request under any free zone regulation the penalty is a fine of level 3 on the standard scale (see s. 171) and £20 for each day the failure continues.

See Free Zone Regulations 1984, S.I. 1984 No. 1177.

100E. Control of trading in free zones. (A7.31)

Only persons authorised by the Commissioners may trade within a free zone and the authorisation may be for such time and under such conditions as the Commissioners consider appropriate.

Anyone who contravenes the terms of the authorisation or trades without authorisation is liable, on conviction, to a fine of level 3 on the standard scale (see s. 171).

100F. Powers of search. (A7.31)

An officer may require answers to questions put to any person entering or leaving a free zone about any goods and require that those goods be produced for examination. An officer may search any vehicle entering or leaving a free zone and may also inspect all buildings and goods within a free zone.

PART X DUTIES AND DRAWBACKS—GENERAL PROVISIONS

GENERAL PROVISIONS RELATING TO IMPORTED GOODS

119. Delivery of imported goods on giving of security for duty. (A15.25)

Where the amount of duty payable is not certain at the time of importation of goods entered for home use, the Commissioners may allow delivery of the goods to the importer upon payment of a deposit. Delivery of the goods is allowed even where there is an incomplete entry. When the Commissioners have ascertained the amount of duty payable they will issue the importer with a notice, allow for any deposit and request further payment or repay any excess. Any dispute about the amount payable may be referred by the importer to arbitration only after it has been paid.

127. Determination of disputes as to duties on imported goods. (A17.04)

Where a dispute arises about the correct amount, if any, of duty payable, the importer is required to pay the duty demanded. However, within three months of payment, he may, if the dispute relates to the value of goods require a referee appointed by the Lord Chancellor to arbitrate, or if the dispute relates to any other matter apply to the High Court or equivalent for a declaration of the amount of duty payable. Where a lesser amount is held payable, the Commissioners must repay the amount overpaid together with interest from the time of overpayment at a rate decided by the referee or court. Acceptance of such a repayment settles all claims in respect of that importation other than the costs of the proceedings.

PART XI DETENTION OF PERSONS, FORFEITURE AND LEGAL PROCEEDINGS

GENERAL PROVISIONS AS TO LEGAL PROCEEDINGS

145. Institution of proceedings. (A18.03)

Proceedings under the customs and excise Acts can be ordered only by the Commissioners. Proceedings in England and Wales before a magistrate must be started in the name of an officer but may be continued by any officer. A law officer of the Crown may begin proceedings for an offence in his own name in any case where he thinks it proper. However where a person has been arrested for any offence under the customs and excise Acts, any court before which he is brought may try the case even if the proceedings have not been ordered by the Commissioners or begun in the name of an officer.

146. Service of process. (A18.03)
Any summons to a magistrates' court for proceedings begun under the customs and excise Acts or notice, order or other document may be served by an officer. Delivery shall be to the person or left at his last known address or on any vessel or aircraft on which he may have been or is serving. If the person is a company, service shall be by delivery to the registered address or principal office.

146A. Time limits for proceedings. (A18.03)
Unless customs and excise legislation specifies otherwise, proceedings must be commenced within three years (for a summary offence) or 20 years (for an indictable offence) from the date of the offence. However, summary proceedings must be commenced no later than six months after sufficient evidence to warrant the proceedings came to the knowledge of the prosecuting authority. The date when sufficient knowledge came to the authority's knowledge is proved by way of a certificate from the authority.

147. Proceedings for offences. (A18.03, 07)
In England and Wales a magistrates' court may not summarily try a person charged with an offence without the consent of the Attorney General where the proceedings were instituted by him, or by the Commissioners in any other case. In England and Wales the prosecutor may appeal to the Crown Court against the decision of a magistrates' court whether or not he requires a statement of a case for the opinion of the High Court.

148. Place of trial for offences. (A18.03)
Proceedings may begin in the court having jurisdiction where the person charged lives or is found, or where any thing was detained or seized, or where the offence was committed. If the offence was committed outside U.K. jursidiction the court having jurisdiction will be that for the place where the offender is found or first brought after commission of the offence.

149. Non-payment of penalties, etc.: maximum terms of imprisonment. (A18.07)
A magistrates' court in England and Wales or a court of summary jurisdiction in Scotland or Northern Ireland may impose both a fine and a term of imprisonment. Failure to pay the fine will result in a further period of imprisonment but the aggregate of the periods of imprisonment must not exceed 15 months. For Scotland there is a scale of maximum periods of imprisonment for non-payment of fines.

150. Incidental provisions as to legal proceedings. (A18.03, 06)
Where two or more persons are involved in an offence jointly, each person shall be liable for the full fine and the Commissioners may proceed against those persons jointly or severally. A court in England, Wales or Northern Ireland may reduce any fine. The fact that security by way of a bond or deposit has been given for the payment of duty or for compliance with any condition is no defence in any proceedings for an offence or for a forfeiture.

151. Application of penalties. (A18.03, 04, 07, 44)
The balance of any penalty after deductions made under the Magistrates' Courts Act 1980, s. 139 shall be paid to the Commissioners even though there may be local or special rights applicable to fines imposed by the court.

152. Power of Commissioners to mitigate penalties, etc. (A18.01, 07)
Where the Commissioners are satisfied an offence has been committed, they may compound cases by offering the offender the option of going to court or paying a compromise penalty. Where the compromise penalty is paid and the goods are accepted as seized the matter is closed. The Commissioners may also restore seized goods in such circumstances as they think proper and may reduce any money penalty, or order any person who has been imprisoned to be released before the end of his term.

For the Commissioners' policy with regard to settlements made on or after 1st June 1989, see HC Written Answer, 26 April 1989, Vol. 151 cols. 562, 563.

153. Proof of certain documents. (A18.03, 04, 07, 44)
Any document which appears to be signed by the Commissioners or anyone else with their authority shall be accepted as valid and to have been issued upon production of a copy unless the contrary can be proved. The Documentary Evidence Act 1868 shall apply to any document mentioned in that Act by the Commissioners. A photograph of a document certified by the

Commissioners to be a true copy shall be admissible in criminal or civil proceedings as if the copy was the original document.

154. Proof of certain other matters. (A18.04)

In the course of proceedings under the customs and excise Acts, a declaration that the proceedings were instituted by the Commissioners, or that any person is a Commissioner, officer, constable or member of the armed forces, or that any person was authorised to carry out a duty, or that the Commissioners are or are not satisfied as to any matter, or that any ship is a British ship, or that any goods were destroyed to prevent seizure, shall be sufficient evidence unless the contrary is proved. Where in the course of proceedings any question arises as to the place from which goods have been brought, or whether or not duty has been paid, or whether goods were lawfully unloaded or imported or lawfully loaded or exported, or whether goods are subject to restriction on importation or exportation, then the burden of proof rests with the importer or exporter.

155. Persons who may conduct proceedings. (A18.04)

Any officer authorised by the Commissioners may conduct proceedings before any magistrates' court in England and Wales or court of summary jurisdiction in Scotland or Northern Ireland or before any examining justices being proceedings relating to an assigned matter. Solicitors employed by the Commissioners may act in any proceedings in England, Wales or Northern Ireland relating to an assigned matter.

PART XII GENERAL AND MISCELLANEOUS

GENERAL POWERS, ETC

159. Power to examine and take account of goods. (A7.06)

An officer may examine and list goods which are imported, in a warehouse, in a free zone, in a ship or aircraft, to be used as stores, to be exported or subject to repayment of duty, and may require any container to be opened or unpacked, at such place as the Commissioners decide. The costs of examination and any handling expenses are the responsibilities of the proprietor of the goods (see s. 1). Removing the goods from customs and excise charge before examination renders them liable to seizure and any person intending to defraud or to evade any restriction under any enactment may be arrested. On summary conviction a person is liable to a penalty of the greater of the prescribed sum (see s. 171) or three times the value of the goods or to imprisonment for up to six months, or to both. On conviction on indictment a person is liable to an unlimited penalty, or to imprisonment for up to two years or to both. A person, approved by both the Commissioners and the proprietor, may be appointed to account for goods and that account accepted for any purpose.

164. Power to search persons.

An officer may detain a person ("the suspect") in order to exercise his powers of search if he has reasonable grounds for suspecting that the suspect is carrying prohibited, restricted or duty-evaded goods.

The officer may require a suspect to permit a search of any article which he has with him and to submit to a rub-down, strip or intimate search (as defined). The suspect has a right to have this requirement reviewed by a J.P. (in the case of a strip or intimate search) or by a superior officer (in the case of any personal search), and must be informed of this right before he is searched.

A rub-down or strip search must be carried out by a person of the same sex as the suspect. An intimate search must be carried out by a doctor or nurse.

The search powers may be exercised in relation to a suspect who is: (1) on board a ship or aircraft; (2) leaving a ship or aircraft; (3) entering or leaving the U.K.; (4) within the dock area of a port; (5) at a customs and excise airport; (6) in, entering or leaving an approved wharf, transit shed or free zone; or (7) crossing the land boundary with the Republic of Ireland.

A suspect detained for a search may be detained subsequently under Criminal Justice (Scotland) Act 1987, s. 48 (1) notwithstanding s. 48 (4) of that Act.

GENERAL OFFENCES

167. Untrue declarations, etc. (A18.02)

Anyone who gives false information to an officer, whether orally or in writing, is guilty of an offence and may be arrested and any goods involved may be seized. He is liable to imprisonment and to a penalty on summary conviction of level 4 on the standard scale (see s. 171).

168. Counterfeiting documents, etc. (18.02)

Anyone who is knowingly involved with a false document or seal, used to transact customs and excise business, is guilty of an offence and may be arrested.

171. General provisions as to offences and penalties. (A18.03, 05)

A person convicted by a court is punishable for every offence. The "prescribed sum", referred to in ss. 16 and 159, is defined: it is currently £2,000. Various sections refer to penalties at various levels

on the standard scale. The scale is defined by the Criminal Justice Act 1982, s. 75. In England and
Wales the current figures are, by virtue of ss. 37 and 48 of that Act and an order made under the
Magistrates' Courts Act 1980, s. 143, namely the Criminal Penalties etc. (Increase) Order 1984
(S.I. 1984 No. 447, art. 2 (4), Sch. 4) with effect from 1 May 1984 as follows:

Level 1   £50
Level 2   £100   (see s. 41)
Level 3   £400   (see ss. 42, 50, 77, 77A, 78, 92, 100D, 100E)
Level 4   £1,000 (see ss. 31, 37C, 167)
Level 5   £2,000 (see s. 15)

Where a body corporate has committed an offence through a director, manager or secretary or
anyone acting in such a capacity, that individual also may be taken to court and if guilty punished.

Customs and Excise Duties (General Reliefs) Act 1979
1979 Chapter 3

MISCELLANEOUS RELIEFS FROM CUSTOMS AND EXCISE DUTIES

7. Power to provide for reliefs from duty and value added tax in respect of imported legacies. (A7.61)
The Commissioners may by order give exemption or relief from duty and VAT where a person imports goods as a legatee. Such an order may be in addition to E.C. reliefs.
See Customs and Excise Duties (Relief for Imported Legacies) Order 1984, S.I. 1984 No. 895.

8. Relief from customs or excise duty on trade samples, labels, etc. (A7.62, 63)
Trade samples whether imported as such or taken from a parcel upon importation may enter the country free of customs or excise duties but subject to some conditions. Labels or similar goods may be imported free of customs or excise duty provided they are to be added to other goods which will be exported from the U.K. or the Isle of Man.

9. Relief from customs or excise duty on antiques, prizes, etc. (A7.64)
Awards for meritorious achievement may be imported without payment of customs or excise duty.

PERSONAL RELIEFS

13. Power to provide, in relation to persons entering the United Kingdom, for reliefs from duty and value added tax and for simplified computation of duty and tax. (A7.65, 66)
The Commissioners may by order give exemption or relief from duty and VAT to persons entering the U.K. They may also by order provide for tax and VAT to be calculated at a global rate, but any person can elect that the true rates be used. The order may impose conditions which if not complied with may render the goods liable to forfeiture. See Customs Duty (Personal Reliefs) (No. 1) Order 1968, S.I. 1968 No. 1558; Customs Duty (Personal Reliefs) (No. 1) Order 1975, S.I. 1975 No. 1132; Customs and Excise (Personal Reliefs for Goods Permanently Imported) Order 1983, S.I. 1983 No. 1828; Customs and Excise Duties (Personal Reliefs for Goods Temporarily Imported) Order 1983, S.I. 1983, No. 1829; Customs Duty (Community Reliefs) Order 1984, S.I. 1984 No. 719.

13A. Reliefs from duties and taxes for persons enjoying certain immunities and privileges. (A7.67)
The Commissioners may make orders providing for the remission or repayment of customs duties (including agricultural levies), excise duties chargeable on goods, VAT and car tax on goods and services supplied to, or imported by, the persons specified in s. 13B. The orders may not be construed as authorising the importation of prohibited or restricted goods. No orders have been made to date.

13B. Persons to whom section 13A applies. (A7.67)
Orders under s. 13A may confer relief on: (1) international defence organisations; (2) the staff and dependants of such organisations; (3) military and civilian members of visiting forces, and their dependants; and (4) diplomatic missions.

13C. Offence where relieved goods used, etc., in breach of condition. (A18.02)
A person is guilty of an offence if, with intent to evade payment of tax or duty and in contravention of a condition for relief, he acquires goods for his own or another person's use, allows goods to be used by another person, or disposes of goods to another person. Such a person may be arrested.
The offence may be tried summarily or on indictment. The maximum penalty on summary conviction is: (1) a fine of the greater of £2,000 or three times the value of the goods; (2) six months' imprisonment; or (3) both. The maximum penalty on indictment is: (1) an unlimited fine; (2) seven years' imprisonment; or (3) both.

Isle of Man Act 1979
1979 Chapter 58

1. Common duties. (A2.02)
VAT, except insofar as it relates to gaming machines, is one of the common duties imposed by both the U.K. and the Isle of Man.

2. Isle of Man share of common duties. (A2.16)
The U.K. Commissioners have to pay the Manx Treasury the amount of VAT net of collection expenses collected for goods consumed or used and services supplied in the Isle of Man.

3. Recovery of common duties chargeable in Isle of Man. (A2.22)
VAT not paid in the Isle of Man may be collected in the U.K. and may reduce any repayment the Commissioners should otherwise pay.

4. Enforcement of Isle of Man judgments for common duties. (A2.22)
When a judgment made by the High Court of Justice of the Isle of Man relates to VAT or a penalty relating to VAT then the Foreign Judgments (Reciprocal Enforcement) Act 1933 applies.

5. Offences relating to common duties etc. (A2.02, 63)
These are reciprocal arrangements whereby persons in the Isle of Man may be summoned to court in the U.K. and vice versa.

6. Value added tax. (A2.63)
The U.K. and the Isle of Man are to be treated for the purposes of VAT as one area so that VAT shall only be charged once on any transaction. An Order in Council provides the basis for determining where a person shall be registered, for imposing requirements applicable to both areas, for deciding who will be the representative member of a VAT group and for any supplementary or incidental matter. See VAT (Isle of Man) Orders 1982, S.I. 1982 Nos. 1067, 1068.

10. Exchange of information. (A2.02, 21, 63)
There is no restriction on the disclosure of information between the two customs and excise services.

11. Transfer of functions to Isle of Man authorities.
An Order in Council transfers to an appropriate authority functions of the Commissioners and their officers and functions of the Lieutenant Governor of the Isle of Man or a deputy governor. See Isle of Man (Transfer of Functions) Order 1980, S.I. 1980 No. 399.

12. Proof of Acts of Tynwald etc.
In any proceedings in the U.K. which relate to a common duty any Act of Tynwald may be proved by producing a copy of the Act authenticated by a certificate purporting to be signed by or on behalf of the Attorney General for the Island.

The Bankers' Books Evidence Act 1879 may be used in respect of books and persons in the Isle of Man.

13. Amendments of customs and excise Acts etc.
The references to the U.K., which are extended also to the Isle of Man, are set out in Sch. 1.

14. Short title, interpretation, repeals, commencement and extent.
The meaning of various terms and miscellaneous provisions are set out. Sections 6 and 11 are part of the law of the Isle of Man.

Finance Act 1980

1980 Chapter 48

PART II VALUE ADDED TAX

17. Mutual recovery and disclosure of information between member States. (A2.21, 22, 57)
The provisions of FA 1977, s. 11 (recovery of duties) and FA 1978, s. 77 (exchange and information) are extended to VAT and the Commissioners of Customs and Excise and their officers.

Value Added Tax Act 1983
1983 Chapter 55

1. Value added tax. (A5.01; A6.01; A7.11)

VAT is charged on the supply of goods and services in the U.K. This excludes the illegal supply of drugs: *Vereniging Happy Family Rustenburgerstraat* v. *Inspecteur der Omzetbelasting* (case 289/86), *Mol* v. *Inspecteur der Invoerrechten en Accijnzen* (case 269/86) [1989] 3 CMLR 729, ECJ. For supplies disregarded for VAT purposes, see ss. 29 (supplies between bodies corporate included in a group registration) and 35 (supplies of warehoused goods). For the charge to tax on supplies, see s. 2 (1).

VAT is charged on the deemed supply of goods and services in the U.K. For deemed supplies, see ss. 3 (self-supplies), 7 (reverse charge), 13 (gaming machines), 16 (5) (transactions which are zero-rated), 29A (business transferred as going concern to group member), Sch. 2, para. 7 (assets held at deregistration) and Sch. 6A, paras. 1, 5, 6 (completed buildings and civil engineering works).

VAT is charged on goods imported into the U.K. This excludes the illegal importation of drugs: *Einberger* v. *Hauptzollamt Freiburg (No. 2)* (case 294/82) [1985] 1 CMLR 765, ECJ. For the charge to tax on imports, see s. 2 (4).

2. Scope of tax. (A3.01; A5.21, 22; A7.11; A14.02)

VAT is charged on a supply of goods or services if: (1) it is made in the U.K.; (2) it is a taxable supply (*i.e.* a supply of goods or services made in the U.K. which is not an exempt supply); (3) it is made by a taxable person (*i.e.* a person who is or is required to be registered); and (4) it is made in the course or furtherance of business: see *Trustees of the Mellerstain Trust* v. *C. & E. Comrs.* EDN/89/41 unreported. For supplies made in the U.K., see s. 6. For exempt supplies, see s. 17. For registration, see Sch. 1. For activities amounting to a business, see s. 47.

VAT is a liability of the person making the supply and (subject to the accounting rules) becomes due at the time of supply. For the accounting rules, see Sch. 7, para. 2. For the time of supply, see s. 4.

VAT is charged and paid on imported goods as if it were a duty of customs. For customs legislation applied for this purpose, see s. 24. For reliefs applicable for VAT purposes only, see ss. 16 (3), 18 (3), 19, 25, 26 and Isle of Man Act 1979, s. 6 (2).

3. Meaning of "supply": alteration by Treasury order. (A5.02, 14; A6.16, 41)

Whether a supply is of goods or services is determined in accordance with Sch. 2 paras. 1–4. For the dividing line between a supply of goods and a supply of both goods and services, see *ADP Insulations (Group) Ltd.* v. *C. & E. Comrs.* [1987] VATTR 36; *AZO-Maschinenfabrik Adolf Zimmerman GmbH* v. *C. & E. Comrs.* [1987] VATTR 25.

Generally, "supply" includes all forms of supply but excludes anything done without a consideration. This includes the sale of a stolen car (*C. & E. Comrs.* v. *Oliver* [1980] STC 73) and the supply of prohibited articles other than drugs (*Vereniging Happy Family Rustenburgerstraat* v. *Inspecteur der Omzetbelasting* (case 289/86), *Mol* v. *Inspecteur der Invoerrechten en Accijnzen* (case 269/86) [1989] 3 CMLR 729, ECJ; *C. & E. Comrs.* v. *Oliver* [1980] STC 73. Cf *I.R.C.* v. *Aken* [1988] STC 69). The free gift or use of goods is treated as a supply despite the absence of consideration: see Sch. 2 para. 5. For the nature of consideration, see *Staatssecretaris van Financien* v. *Cooperatiëve Vereniging "Cooperative Aardappelenbewaarplaats GA"* (case 154/80) [1981] 3 CMLR 337, ECJ; *Apple and Pear Development Council* v. *C. & E. Comrs.* (case 102/86) [1988] STC 221, ECJ; *Naturally Yours Cosmetics Ltd.* v. *C. & E. Comrs.* (case 230/87) [1988] STC 879, ECJ; *Trafalgar Tours Ltd* v. *C. & E. Comrs.* [1990] STC 127, CA. Whether or not consideration arises is determined at the time of supply in accordance with the contract made: see *Potters Lodge Restaurant* v. *C. & E. Comrs.* LON/79/286 unreported and *NPD Co. Ltd.* v. *C. & E. Comrs.* [1988] VATTR 40 (restaurant service charge); *Warwick Masonic Rooms Ltd.* v. *C. & E. Comrs.* BIR/79/33 unreported (unsolicited donation). For the quantification of consideration when "money-off" coupons are redeemed, see *Boots Co. plc* v. *C. & E. Comrs.* [1990] STC 387, ECJ and Press Notice No. 27/90, 30 March 1990. See also *Boots Co. plc* v. *C. & E. Comrs.* [1988] STC 138; *Normal Factors Ltd.* v. *C. & E. Comrs.* [1978] VATTR 20; *McDonald's Restaurants Ltd.* v. *C. & E. Comrs.* LON/88/1190 unreported. The fact that the amount receivable is stolen does not prevent a consideration arising: *Benton* v. *C. & E. Comrs.* [1975] VATTR 138. Consideration may be provided by the customer or a third party: *Lord Advocate* v. *Largs Golf Club* [1985] STC 226; *Telemed Ltd.* v. *C. & E. Comrs.* LON/89/377 unreported; *Professional Footballers Association (Enterprises) Ltd.* v. *C. & E. Comrs.* MAN/88/530 unreported; *McDonald's Restaurants Ltd.* v. *C. & E. Comrs.* LON/88/1190 unreported.

Anything done for a consideration which is not a supply of goods is a supply of services. This includes the grant, assignment or surrender of any right. See *Naturally Yours Cosmetics Ltd.* v. *C. & E. Comrs.* (case 230/87) [1988] STC 879, ECJ (procuring a gathering at which goods were sold); *C. & E. Comrs.* v. *Tilling Management Services Ltd.* [1979] STC 365 (procuring a group relief payment); *GUS Merchandise Corpn. Ltd.* v. *C. & E. Comrs.* [1981] STC 569, CA (agreeing to act as agent); *C. & E. Comrs.* v. *Diners Club Ltd.* [1989] STC 407, CA (making payments under a credit card scheme); *C. & E. Comrs.* v. *High Street Vouchers Ltd.* [1990] STI 611 (redemption of vouchers at a discount); *Tarmac Construction Ltd.* v. *C. & E. Comrs.* [1981] VATTR 35 (services under contract of employment); *Gardner Lohmann Ltd.* v. *C. & E. Comrs.* [1981] VATTR 76 (commodity option); *Gleneagles Hotel plc.* v. *C. & E. Comrs.* [1986] VATTR 196 (covenanting to refurbish premises); *Neville Russell (a firm)* v. *C. & E. Comrs.* [1987] VATTR 194 (accepting a lease); *Landmark Cash and Carry Group Ltd.* v. *C. & E. Comrs.* [1980] VATTR 1 (procuring discounts for members); *Portal (Linwood) Ltd* v. *C. & E. Comrs.* MAN/88/188 unreported (right to remove materials after demolishing a building). This does not include carrying out functions which a trader is obliged to carry out on his own behalf: *National Coal Board* v. *C. & E. Comrs.* [1982] STC 863; *British European Breeders Fund* v. *C. & E. Comrs.* [1985] VATTR 12.

The fact that money is received does not lead to the inevitable conclusion that there is a corresponding supply: see *Warwick Masonic Rooms Ltd.* v. *C. & E. Comrs.* BIR/79/33 unreported (unsolicited donation); *Battersea Leisure Ltd.* v. *C. & E. Comrs.* LON/88/1383 unreported (contribution to cost of removing asbestos from building). For payments under out-of-court settlements, see Press Notice No. 82/87, 19 November 1987. For donations to universities, see Press Notice No. 84/88, 10 November 1988. For agricultural grants, see Press Notice No. 58/89, 9 August 1989.

The true nature of money received may give rise to difficulties. See, for example, *Keydon Estates Ltd.* v. *C. & E. Comrs.* LON/88/1225 unreported (whether money received was share of partnership profit or consideration for supply of services fixed by reference to customer's profit on a transaction).

For supplies through intermediaries, see *Philips Exports Ltd.* v. *C. & E. Comrs.* [1990] STC 508 (property in goods vesting for an infinitely short time) and VATA 1983 s. 32 (agents).

The consideration for a supply is determined when the price payable has been agreed by the parties. This is the time when the contract is completed (*e.g.* under a fixed price contract), the time when an invoice is issued (*e.g.* when the customer accepts the price charged under a contract for an unascertained consideration) or the time when agreement is reached (*e.g.* when the customer disputes the amount invoiced under a contract for an unascertained consideration). The consideration shown on an invoice may be reduced by a credit note to reflect the agreed position: *Castle Associates Ltd.* v. *C. & E. Comrs.* MAN/87/448 unreported. A credit note may also reduce the consideration shown on an invoice if it is made to correct a genuine mistake or overcharge, or give a proper credit: *British United Shoe Machinery Co. Ltd.* v. *C. & E. Comrs.* [1977] VATTR 187; *Securicor Granley Systems Ltd.* v. *C. & E. Comrs.* LON/89/695 unreported. A credit note cannot re-write a completed contract. See, for example, *Mannesmann Demag Hamilton Ltd.* v. *C. & E. Comrs.* [1983] VATTR 156 (repossessed machine); *M. E. Braine (Boatbuilders) Ltd.* v. *C. & E. Comrs.* MAN/88/594 unreported (boat taken over after repair); *Rickard* v. *C. & E. Comrs.* LON/88/802 unreported (payment for supply to be treated as loan). Nor can a credit note vary an agreed consideration: *British United Shoe Machinery Co. Ltd.* v. *C. & E. Comrs.* [1977] VATTR 187 (cancellation of charge for management services because it led to irrecoverable input tax in a recipient group company); *Cripwell & Associates* v. *C. & E. Comrs.* CAR/78/131 unreported and many subsequent cases (cancellation of bad debt). For a valid credit note to cancel a charge for unauthorised services, see *Cobojo Ltd.* v. *C. & E. Comrs.* MAN/89/746 unreported. To the extent that an agreed price is understated on an invoice, an additional invoice should be issued: see Notice No. 700 (October 1987) para. 69 (*a*). For the adjustment to a trader's VAT Account when the consideration is adjusted by a credit note or additional invoice, see VAT (Accounting and Records) Regulations 1989, S.I. 1989 No. 2248 reg. 7. A trader could not obtain a refund of VAT overcharged on a tax invoice if, before 1 January 1990, he did not issue a credit note for the VAT concerned to his customer: *Springfield China Ltd.* v. *C. & E. Comrs.* MAN/89/180 unreported, and this seems to apply also from that date under FA 1989 s. 24. This is because the VAT charged is recoverable from the supplier under VATA Sch. 7 para. 6.

Treasury orders may set out what is to be treated as a supply of goods or of services or of neither and may provide the circumstances where business goods put to non-business use are not be treated as a supply of services. For transactions treated as supplies of goods, see VAT (Water) Order 1989, S.I. 1989 No. 1114. For transactions treated as supplies of services, see VAT (Special Provisions) Order 1981, S.I. 1981 No. 1741 art. 13 (reconditioned goods); VAT (Tour Operators) Order 1987, S.I. 1987 No. 1806 (goods and services amounting to a designated travel service). For transactions treated as supplies of neither goods nor services, see VAT (Treatment of Transactions) Order 1973, S.I. 1973 No. 325 (trading stamps); VAT (Cars) Order 1980, S.I. 1980 No. 442 art. 7 (motor cars); VAT (Special Provisions) Order 1981, S.I. 1981 No. 1741 arts. 10–12 (repossessed goods etc., business sold as going concern, assignment of finance agreements); VAT (Treatment of Transactions) Order 1986, S.I. 1986 No. 896 (pawned goods); VAT (Temporarily Imported Goods) (Relief) Order 1986, S.I. 1986 No. 1989 art. 13 (tax suspended goods).

Treasury orders may, in relation to particular transactions which if done by the business for a consideration would be a supply of services, together with other conditions specified, treat such transactions as being supplied in the course or furtherance of the business. No orders have been made.

Treasury orders may specify circumstances where goods acquired or produced by a business are neither supplied by the business nor incorporated in other goods produced by the business but are used in the business as carried on; then they shall be treated as being both supplied to and supplied by the business. See VAT (Cars) Order 1980, S.I. 1980 No. 442 art. 5 (motor cars); VAT (Special Provisions) Order 1981, S.I. 1981 No. 1741 art. 14 (stationery).

Treasury orders may in relation to anything done by the business which if done for a consideration would be a supply of services treat such services as having been supplied to and by the business. See VAT (Self-supply of Construction Services) Order, S.I. 1989 No. 472.

4. Time of supply. (A5.31, 41, 46)
The time a VAT supply occurs is important when deciding which transactions have to be accounted for in the current accounting period and which should be accounted for in a later period. Goods are supplied when they are removed or made available to the customer: see *West End Motors (Bodmin) Ltd.* v. *C. & E. Comrs.* LON/81/218 unreported; *Volvo Trucks (Great Britain) Ltd.* v. *C. & E. Comrs.* [1988] VATTR 11; *Margrie Holdings Ltd.* v. *C. & E. Comrs.* [1986] VATTR 213. However, goods sent out on approval or sale or return are supplied when they are accepted or, if sooner, 12 months after they were removed. A supply of services occurs at the time when the services are performed: see *Trustees for the Greater World Association Trust* v. *C. & E. Comrs.* LON/88/680 unreported; *Mercantile Contracts Ltd.* v. *C. & E. Comrs.* LON/88/786 unreported.

The times indicated above are termed "basic tax points" by Customs and Excise and they are overridden by the tax points provided for in s. 5.

5. Further provisions relating to time of supply. (A5.31, 42–47)
The time of supply is the date of issue of a tax invoice, or receipt of payment or part payment, if this is before the goods are removed or made available to the person supplied or before the service is performed. If within 14 days after the goods being removed or made available to the person supplied, or the service being performed, the supplier issues a tax invoice, the date of the invoice is the time of supply (unless the supplier elects otherwise in writing) provided that no tax invoice has been issued or payment received. If a taxable person who invoices at less frequent intervals so requests, the Commissioners may extend the 14-day period.

Where a taxable person provides a tax invoice to himself for a supply of goods or services made to him by another taxable person, in accordance with regulations made under Sch. 7, para. 2, so that the "self-billed" tax invoice is treated as the invoice required to be provided by the supplier, the date of that self-billing is treated as the date of the supplier's invoice and the self-biller can make the election or request instead of the supplier.

An invoice is issued when it is sent or given to a customer: *C. & E. Comrs.* v. *Woolfold Motor Co. Ltd.* [1983] STC 715. It must contain all the information required to be shown on a tax invoice: *J. D. Fox Ltd.* v. *C. & E. Comrs.* [1988] 2 CMLR 875.

A transfer of money need not involve a simultaneous transfer of future control of the money in order to amount to a payment: *C. & E. Comrs.* v. *Faith Construction Ltd.* [1989] STC 539, CA. See also *Barratt Urban Construction (Northern) Ltd.* v. *C. & E. Comrs.* MAN/87/116 unreported; *Barratt Construction Ltd.* v. *C. & E. Comrs.* EDN/87/32 unreported. A payment gives rise to a tax point if it is made in respect of a supply contemplated by the contract made by the parties, it is treated as a total or partial payment for the supply and it is made to the person who is to supply the goods or services: see *Purshotam M. Pattni & Sons* v. *C. & E. Comrs.* [1987] STC 1; *J. D. Fox Ltd.* v. *C. & E. Comrs.* [1988] 2 CMLR 875; *Bethway & Moss Ltd.* v. *C. & E. Comrs.* [1988] 3 CMLR 44; *Regalstar Enterprises* v. *C. & E. Comrs.* [1989] 1 CMLR 117. A payment by cheque is received when it is presented and met by the drawer's bank: *Rampling* v. *C. & E. Comrs.* [1986] VATTR 62. A payment by way of offset in an inter-company current account seems to be received when the accounting entry is made: see *Legal & Contractual Services Ltd.* v. *C. & E. Comrs.* [1984] VATTR 85; *Schlumberger Inland Services Inc.* v. *C. & E. Comrs.* [1985] VATTR 35, on appeal [1987] STC 228.

At the request of the taxable person the Commissioners may direct that the tax point is to be determined by the occurrence of some event which would be earlier than the physical time of supply mentioned above. The time of supply in such cases is either the beginning or end of a relevant working period as defined for that person.

Where a person is partially exempt and supplies himself with stationery which he himself produced (see S.I. 1981 No. 1741), or a person is a motor car manufacturer or converter and uses his own cars in his business (see S.I. 1980 No. 442), then such uses of stationery or cars are treated as supplies by the business and are treated as taking place when they are first appropriated to business use.

The time of supply for goods taken for private use or other non-business use by the proprietor of a business (see Sch. 2, para. 5) is the time when the goods are taken or set aside for that purpose. Goods temporarily taken out of business use for private use by the proprietor or for other non-business use, but still held as stock (see Sch. 2, para. 5), create a tax point on the last day of each period that the goods remain used or made available for that purpose.

The Commissioners may regulate the time of supply of a continuous supply of services or where goods or services are invoiced only once but payments are made periodically. See VAT (General) Regulations 1985, S.I. 1985 No. 886 regs. 17–28.

"Designated travel services" supplied by a tour operator are subject to the special rules set out in VAT (Tour Operators) Order 1987, S.I. 1987 No. 1086, art. 4.

6. Place of supply. (A5.24)

Only goods or services supplied in the U.K. are chargeable with VAT.

If goods are in the U.K. at the time of supply then they are treated as supplied in the U.K. If they are outside the U.K. at the time of supply then they are outside the scope of VAT. A supply involving the export of goods from the U.K. is a supply in the U.K. Goods imported into the U.K. are supplied outside the U.K.

For services, the place of supply depends on where the supplier of the service belongs (see s. 8). If the supplier belongs in the U.K. then the supply is made in the U.K. If the supplier belongs in another country then the supply is made there. However, the Treasury may by order specify where a supply of services is treated as made. For courses of formal instruction: see VAT (Place of Supply) Order 1984, S.I. 1984 No. 1685. For services supplied by tour operators, see VAT (Tour Operators) Order 1987, S.I. 1987 No. 1806, art. 5.

7. Reverse charge on supplies received from abroad. (A6.31)

Where a person (since 1 April 1987, whether registered or not) receives standard rated type services specified in Sch. 3 from a person who belongs outside the U.K. then the recipient must account for output tax to Customs and Excise as if he had supplied the services himself. From 1 April 1987, this may involve a business that makes exempt supplies in having to register for VAT; such a business no longer finds it advantageous to buy such services abroad instead of in the U.K.

Where the recipient is able to deduct all of his input tax he is allowed to treat the output VAT he charged himself also as an input and thus suffers no VAT loss.

Where, however, he is only able to deduct a proportion of his input tax then he will only be able to deduct the same proportion of this reverse charge VAT as input tax and he has a net VAT loss. The value of reverse charges cannot be added to the value of taxable supplies used in determining the amount of input tax allowable to a partially exempt person.

The consideration paid for the services supplied is the value to which VAT, where applicable, should be added. The time of supply is prescribed by regulations: see VAT (General) Regulations 1985, S.I. 1985 No. 886 reg. 18.

8. Place where supplier or recipient of services belongs. (A5.24; A11.16)

A supplier of services belongs where he has a business or fixed establishment or, if he has no such establishment, where he has his usual place of residence. If he has business establishments in more than one country then the place most directly concerned with the supply is the place where the supplier belongs. An establishment is a business or fixed establishment if it has a sufficient minimum strength in the form of the permanent presence of the human and technical resources necessary for supplying specific services: *Berkholz* v. *Finanzamt Hamburg-Mitte-Alstadt* (case 168/84) [1985] 3 CMLR 667, ECJ.

Where a supply is received by an individual in his private capacity then he is treated as belonging in whatever country he has his usual place of residence.

Where a supply is received by a trader in a country where he has a business or fixed establishment or has his usual place of residence then the supply is made to that country. If the trader has such establishments in more than one country then the supply is received in the country which most directly uses the service. A trader has a business or fixed establishment in a country if he has an establishment there which has a sufficient minimum strength which enables him to receive and use the services concerned. This includes a U.K. registered office. See *Binder Hamlyn* v. *C. & E. Comrs.* [1983] VATTR 171; *Vincent Consultants Ltd.* v. *C. & E. Comrs.* [1988] VATTR 152, [1989] 1 CMLR 374; *Singer & Friedlander Ltd.* v. *C. & E. Comrs.* [1989] VATTR 27, [1989] 1 CMLR 814.

In this section only, the usual place of residence of a corporate body is where it is legally constituted, and a branch or agency is treated as a business establishment.

9. Rate of tax. (A1.18; A10.01, 06)

VAT is charged at the rate of 15 per cent. of the value of the goods or services supplied or the value of goods imported. As to value see ss. 10, 11 and Sch. 4.

The Treasury may by order increase or reduce the rate for up to 12 months by up to 25 per cent. of the existing rate (3.75 per cent.); thus they could by order increase it to a maximum of 18.75 per cent. or reduce it to a minimum of 11·25 per cent.

10. Value of supply of goods or services. (A8.01, 11)

Where a supply is made for a consideration wholly in money, the value is such amount as, with the addition of VAT, equals the consideration, that is the $^{100}/_{115}$ths or $^{20}/_{23}$rds of the consideration. If the consideration is wholly or partly in something other than money the value of the supply is its open market value. Open market value is the value the supply would have in an arm's length money transaction. See *Naturally Yours Cosmetics Ltd.* v. *C. & E. Comrs.* (case 230/87) [1988] STC 879, ECJ; *Churchway Crafts Ltd.* v. *C. & E. Comrs.* LON/80/204 unreported.

A consideration must be apportioned where it relates to two or more supplies. For the right to apportion, see *Automobile Association* v. *C. & E. Comrs.* [1974] STC 192. For examples of apportionment, see *Barton* v. *C. & E. Comrs.* [1974] STC 200 (membership subscription); *Rapid Results College Ltd.* v. *C. & E. Comrs.* [1973] VATTR 197 (correspondence course); *Cheshire Mushroom Farm* v. *C. & E. Comrs.* [1974] VATTR 87 (mushroom growing kit); *Jarmain* v. *C. & E. Comrs.* [1979] VATTR 41 (admission charge). For the manner in which consideration is apportioned, see *River Barge Holidays Ltd.* v. *C. & E. Comrs.* LON/77/345 unreported and *Rogers* v. *C. & E. Comrs.* [1984] VATTR 183 (cost method); *Jarmain* v. *C. & E. Comrs.* [1979] VATTR 41 (open market value method). For examples of cases where apportionment was inappropriate, see *C. & E. Comrs.* v. *Scott* [1978] STC 191 and *C. & E. Comrs.* v. *Bushby* [1979] STC 8 (stabling horses); *British Airways Authority* v. *C. & E. Comrs.* [1977] STC 36, CA (airport concession); *Rowe & Maw* v. *C. & E. Comrs.* [1975] STC 340 (solicitor's travelling costs); *British Airways plc.* v. *C. & E. Comrs.* [1989] STC 182 (in-flight catering). For the apportionment of an admission charge between consideration for a supply and a voluntary donation, see *Glasgow's Miles Better Mid Summer 5th Anniversary Ball* v. *C. & E. Comrs.* EDN/89/95 unreported and Press Notice No. 1026, 24 July 1985. For the aggregation of separate payments forming a single consideration, see *British Railways Board* v. *C. & E. Comrs.* [1977] STC 221, CA (student rail card and rail ticket); *Exeter Golf & Country Club Ltd.* v. *C. & E. Comrs.* [1981] STC 211, CA (club subscription and benefit of interest free loan); *Patrick Eddery Ltd.* v. *C. & E. Comrs.* [1986] VATTR 30 (jockey's retainer and riding fee). For the off-set of separate considerations, see for example, *Naturally Yours Cosmetics Ltd.* v. *C. & E. Comrs.* (case 230/87) [1988] STC 879, ECJ; *Davies* v. *C. & E. Comrs.* [1975] STC 28; *Theatres Consolidated Ltd.* v. *C. & E. Comrs.* [1975] VATTR 13; *Smith & Williamson* v. *C. & E. Comrs.* [1976] VATTR 215. For reduced considerations which did not amount to an off-set, see *National Coal Board* v. *C. & E. Comrs.* [1982] STC 863; *Goodfellow (a firm)* v. *C. & E. Comrs.* [1986] VATTR 119; *J. Hopkins (Contractors) Ltd.* v. *C. & E. Comrs.* MAN/88/50 unreported.

Schedule 4 provides additional rules for determining value.

11. Value of imported goods. (A8.51, 61)

Where goods are imported in an arm's length transaction the value for VAT is the price paid plus all taxes and duties (except VAT), paid outside and inside the U.K. plus all costs for commission, packing, transport and insurance up to the place of importation.

Where goods are imported and there is consideration other than money then the value for VAT is open market value as prescribed by E.C. legislation for valuation of goods for customs purposes plus all taxes, duties, commissions, packing, transport and insurance. For E.C. valuation provisions, see Regulation (EEC) Nos. 1224/80, 1494/80, 1495/80, 1496/80, 3177/80, 3179/80, 1577/81, 3158/83, 1766/85, 3579/85.

Schedule 4 provides additional rules for determining value.

12. Value of certain goods. (A6.55)

The conversion of zero-rated aircraft weighing 8,000 kilogrammes or more or hovercraft into standard-rated vehicles (adapted for recreation or pleasure use) incurs VAT, not only on the process or treatment applied or the goods incorporated into the vehicle but on the whole value of the vehicle as if the converter had supplied it. This does not apply if the person supplied is VAT-registered and gives the converter a certificate to the effect that the conversion is for the purposes of a business carried on by him. The Treasury may by order make provision for reducing the VAT chargeable on supplies of converted aircraft exceeding 8,000 kilogrammes or hovercraft where VAT was previously charged on a supply or importation of the vehicle and such other conditions as are specified in the order are satisfied. No such order is in force.

13. Gaming machines. (A6.54)

Where a machine provides an element of chance the amount paid into it less the amount paid out as winnings by it is the value of the consideration for the supply of services. Where tokens are used to play the machine their value is equal to the amount paid for them.

CREDIT FOR INPUT TAX AGAINST OUTPUT TAX

14. Credit for input tax against output tax. (A13.01, 04, 05, 11–13)

A taxable person is required to account for and pay tax by reference to prescribed accounting periods at the time and in the manner prescribed by regulations. See VAT (General) Regulations 1985, S.I. 1985 No. 886 reg. 60; VAT (Cash Accounting) Regulations 1987, S.I. 1987 No. 1427 regs. 7–9, 12 (1); VAT (Annual Accounting) Regulations 1988, S.I. 1988 No. 886 regs. 3, 6, 7, 8 (2); VAT (Accounting and Records) Regulations 1989, S.I. 1989 No. 2248 regs. 5–8.

At the end of each prescribed accounting period, a taxable person is entitled to deduct from any output tax due from him (*i.e.* tax on supplies which he makes) so much of his input tax as is allowable under s. 15.

Input tax is: (1) tax on goods or services supplied to a taxable person; and (2) tax on imported goods which is paid or payable by a taxable person. In either case, the goods or services must be for use in a business carried on or to be carried on by the taxable person. However, tax is not input tax if the goods or services are for use in providing domestic accommodation for company directors, their relatives, or the spouses of either. Tax erroneously charged on an exempt or zero-rated supply or supply outside the scope of tax is not input tax: *Genius Holding BV* v. *Staatssecretaris van Financiën* (case 342/87) [1990] STI 46, ECJ; *Podium Investments Ltd.* v. *C. & E. Comrs.* [1977] VATTR 121. Tax paid (*e.g.* on a deposit) in respect of a supply which is not made (*e.g.* because the manufacturer ceases trading before making the goods ordered) is not input tax: *Howard* v. *C. & E. Comrs.* LON/80/457 unreported; *Theotrue Holdings Ltd.* v. *C. & E. Comrs.* [1983] VATTR 88. Mere payment of an invoice does not give rise to input tax if the supply was made to someone else. See: *Stirlings (Glasgow) Ltd.* v. *C. & E. Comrs.* [1982] VATTR 116 (employee); *Berbrooke Fashions* v. *C. & E. Comrs.* [1977] VATTR 168 (sub-contractor); *Normal Motor Factors Ltd* v. *C. & E. Comrs.* [1978] VATTR 20 (customer); *Pollingfold Farms* v. *C. & E.* Comrs. LON/76/103 unreported (associated business); *Culverpalm Ltd.* v. *C. & E. Comrs.* [1984] VATTR 199 (agent). However, by concession, exact reimbursements to employees give rise to credit (see Notice No. 700 (October 1987) para. 66 (*e*) (i)), but not round sum allowances: *BBC* v. *C. & E. Comrs.* [1974] VATTR 100. A similar concession applies to new motor cars purchased via an employee or agent by a non-franchised dealer: Customs and Excise Press Notice dated 25 June 1982. For supplies to employees, see *Leesportefeuille "Intiem" CV* v. *Staatssecretaris van Financiën* (case 165/86) [1989] 2 CMLR 856, ECJ. Ordering and paying for goods or services does not give rise to input tax if the goods or services are used for non-business purposes or for the purposes of someone else's business: see *Ashtree Holdings Ltd.* v. *C. & E. Comrs.* [1979] STC 818; *Jackson (a firm)* v. *C. & E. Comrs.* LON/85/70 unreported. The situation may be different where the trader ordering and paying for the goods obtains some direct or indirect benefit: see *Kelly (a firm)* v. *C. & E. Comrs.* LON/87/173 unreported. Whether or not a business is being carried on, or is to be carried on, is a matter of fact. For examples, see *Whitechapel Art Gallery* v. *C. & E. Comrs.* [1986] STC 156 (activity comprising free admission to premises); *H. Lister (Slippers) Ltd.* v. *C. & E. Comrs.* MAN/83/327 (racehorse owner making occasional bloodstock sales); *Chapman (a firm)* v. *C. & E. Comrs.* LON/81/213 unreported (temporary suspension of taxable supplies); *G. B. Turnbull Ltd.* v. *C. & E. Comrs.* [1984] VATTR 247, *Cobb's Craft Service Station Ltd.* v. *C. & E. Comrs.* [1976] VATTR 170 (no taxable supplies made in respect of planned business). Input tax arises only in respect of U.K. and Isle of Man VAT: see *British Iberian International Transport Ltd.* v. *C. & E. Comrs.* LON/85/654 unreported. For repayment of tax incurred in E.C. member states, see Directive 79/1072/EEC and Notice No. 723. For repayment of VAT which is not input tax, see ss. 20 (public authorities), 21 (self-build projects), 23 (overseas traders), 26 (goods imported for private purposes), 27 (government departments) and VAT (General) Regulations 1985, S.I. 1985 No. 886 reg. 37 made under s. 14 (9) (VAT incurred after deregistration).

Input tax is apportioned if goods or services have been acquired partly for business purposes and partly for non-business purposes. Only that part referable to the business purpose is input tax. The test of purpose is subjective, but the credibility of evidence of intention can be tested against the standards and thinking of the ordinary businessman: *Ian Flockton Developments Ltd.* v. *C. & E. Comrs.* [1987] STC 394. Promoting good industrial relations and motivating sub-contractors are business purposes: *RHM Bakeries (Northern) Ltd.* v. *C. & E. Comrs.* [1979] STC 72; *Kelly (a firm)* v. *C. & E. Comrs.* LON/87/173 unreported. For VAT on fuel for private motoring, see FA 1986 s. 9 (5). The manner of apportionment is not prescribed. For contrasting methods, see *MacDonald* v. *C. & E. Comrs.* [1981] VATTR 223 and *Brooks* v. *C. & E. Comrs.* LON/84/29 unreported.

The Commissioners make a payment to a taxable person if his input tax exceeds the amount (if any) of his output tax. Payment may be withheld if returns for earlier periods are outstanding. Payment may be made subject to conditions if the taxable person has not made any taxable supplies in the period concerned or any earlier period.

Input tax credit may be held over until a later period in accordance with regulations. See VAT (General) Regulations 1985, S.I. 1985 No. 886 reg. 62 (1), (2).

A claim for input tax must be made in such time and manner as may be prescribed by regulations. See VAT (General) Regulations 1985, S.I. 1985 No. 886 reg. 62 (1).

Tax on supplies and imports is input tax only if and to the extent that the charge to tax is evidenced and quantified by reference to the documents specified by regulations. See VAT (General) Regulations 1985, S.I. 1985 No. 886 reg. 62 (1A).

Tax on supplies and inports incurred prior to registration or prior to incorporation of a body corporate may be counted as input tax in accordance with regulations. See VAT (General) Regulations 1985, S.I. 1985 No. 886 reg. 37.

Tax may be excluded from credit by Treasury order. See VAT (Cars) Order 1980, S.I. 1980 No. 442 art. 4 (motor cars); VAT (Special Provisions) Order 1981, S.I. 1981 No. 1741 arts. 7 (goods sold under the used goods schemes), 8 (certain goods installed in dwellings) and 9 (goods or services for business entertainment); VAT (Horses and Ponies) Order 1983, S.I. 1983 No. 1099 art. 5 (bloodstock sold under margin scheme); VAT (Tour Operators) Order 1987, S.I. 1987 No. 1806 art. 12 (goods and services re-supplied as designated travel services).

15. Input tax allowable under section 14. (A13.09)

A taxable person is entitled to credit for so much of his input tax for the period as is allowable by regulations as being attributable to: (1) taxable supplies; (2) supplies outside the U.K. which would be taxable supplies if made in the U.K.; and (3) supplies of warehoused goods which would be taxable supplies if not disregarded for VAT purposes. See VAT (General) Regulations 1985, S.I. 1985 No. 886 regs. 29–36.

For attribution under the "first supply rule" adopted by the Commissioners, see *Fishguard Bay Developments* v. *C. & E. Comrs*. LON/87/625 unreported. For the attribution of input tax on self-supplies, see VAT (General) Regulations 1985, S.I. 1985 No. 886 reg. 30B. For the adjustment of input tax on capital items, see ibid., regs. 37A–37E. For deduction of input tax by holding companies, see Press Notice 42/89, 30 May 1989.

RELIEFS

16. Zero-rating. (A7.84; A11.01, A12.06, 08)

No tax is charged on a supply of goods or services which is zero-rated but the supply is in all other respects treated as a taxable supply.

A supply of goods or services is zero-rated if the goods, services or supply are of a description for the time being specified in Sch. 5.

No tax is chargeable on imported goods if they are of a description for the time being specified in Sch. 5, unless provided otherwise in that schedule.

Sch. 5 may be varied by Treasury order.

A transaction which is not otherwise a supply of goods or services is treated as a supply of goods or services made in the U.K. if it is of a description for the time being included in Sch. 5.

A supply of goods is zero-rated if the Commissioners are satisfied that they have been exported or shipped as stores or retail merchandise on a voyage or flight to an overseas destination. However, good shipped as stores on a private voyage or flight are not zero-rated. Conditions may be specified in regulations or imposed by the Commissioners. No regulations have been made.

Goods for export or for letting overseas may be zero-rated in accordance with regulations. See VAT (General) Regulations 1985, S.I. 1985 No. 886 regs. 38 and 49–57.

Exported goods zero-rated under the previous two paragraphs are liable to forfeiture if discovered in the U.K. after the alleged date of export or shipment or if conditions specified in regulations or imposed by the Commissioners have not been observed. VAT which would have been chargeable but for zero-rating is recoverable from the purchaser or person in possession of the goods. All or part of such VAT may be waived. For forfeiture, see Customs and Excise Management Act 1979 s. 139 and Sch. 3.

17. Exemptions. (A9.01, 03)

A supply of goods or services is exempt if it is of a description for the time being specified in Sch. 6. An exempt supply is not chargeable to VAT by virtue of s. 2 (1), (2). Sch. 6 may be varied by Treasury order.

18. Relief on supply of certain second-hand goods. (A14.31)

VAT is charged on the difference between the purchase and selling prices of goods specified in a Treasury order where conditions specified in the order are met. See VAT (Cars) Order 1980, S.I. 1980 No. 442 art. 6 (motor cars); VAT (Special Provisions) Order 1981, S.I. 1981 No. 1741 arts. 4, 5 (works of art, antiques and collectors' pieces; used motor cycles, caravans, boats, outboard motors, electronic organs, aircraft and firearms) and 9 (2) (goods used for business entertainment); VAT (Horses and Ponies) Order 1983, S.I. 1983 No. 1099 (horses and ponies).

19. Relief from tax on importation of goods. (A7.16)

The Treasury may by order provide relief from VAT on imported goods to comply with international arrangements. See VAT (Imported Goods) Relief Orders, S.I. 1977 No. 1790, S.I. 1984

No. 746; VAT (Small Non-Commercial Consignments) Relief Order 1986, S.I. 1986 No. 939; VAT (Temporarily Imported Goods) Relief Order 1986, S.I. 1986 No. 1989; VAT (Goods Imported for Private Purposes) Relief Order 1988, S.I. 1988 No. 1174.

The Commissioners may remit or repay tax chargeable on imported goods in accordance with regulations where the goods are reimported or for re-export. See VAT (General) Regulations 1985, S.I. 1985 No. 886 regs. 38, 42, 44–48.

REFUNDS

20. Refund of tax in certain cases. (A15.62)
VAT may be refunded to the public bodies specified where goods and services are not used for the purposes of a business carried on by them. However, where the VAT relates partly to exempt supplies the VAT has to be apportioned unless it is insignificant. The VAT (Refund of Tax) Orders made are S.I. 1973 No. 2121, 1976 No. 2028, 1985 No. 1101, 1986 No. 336, 1989 No. 1217.

For repayment supplement on refunds, see FA 1985 s. 20.

21. Refund of tax to persons constructing certain buildings. (A15.64)
A person lawfully constructing a building otherwise than in the course or furtherance of his business may claim a refund of tax in respect of certain goods incorporated in the building or its site. In broad terms, the building must be a dwelling, community home or non-business charity building, and the goods must comprise materials, builders hardware, sanitary ware or articles of a kind ordinarily installed by builders as fixtures. See *Waterways Services* v. *C. & E. Comrs.* LON/89/1055 unreported.

The time, form and manner of making a claim is specifed in regulations. See VAT ("Do-It-Yourself" Builders) (Refund of Tax) Regulations 1989, S.I. 1989 No. 2259.

22. Refund of tax in cases of bad debts. (A15.56)
Traders may claim a refund in respect of the VAT-element of debts due from insolvent customers. The following conditions must be met: (1) goods or services must have been supplied for a consideration in money; (2) the trader must have accounted for and paid tax on that supply (see *English Film Co. Ltd.* v. *C. & E. Comrs.* LON/82/134 unreported); (3) the customer must be insolvent within the statutory definition (for claims which did not meet this test see *Castle Wines Ltd.* v. *Finance Board* MAN/83/31 unreported, *Cobb Blyth Associates* v. *C. & E. Comrs.* EDN/81/13 unreported, *Lipton Parker Agency Ltd.* v. *C. & E. Comrs.* LON/82/100 unreported, *Snowdon* v. *C. & E. Comrs.* MAN/79/109 unreported); (4) the value of the supply must not have exceeded open market value; (5) in the case of goods, the property in the goods must have passed to the customer (see CCAB TR 388 dated 1 May 1980); and (6) in the case of a personal insolvency or company liquidation the amount proved in the insolvency must be net of bad debt relief.

A claim is restricted to $^3/_{23}$ of the outstanding debt even if it is the amount of VAT billed which remains unpaid: *A. W. Mawer & Co.* v. *C. & E. Comrs.* [1986] VATTR 87; *Enderby Transport Ltd.* v. *C. & E. Comrs.* MAN/83/304 unreported. A claim is unaffected by a reimbursement by a third party if there is an express or implied term that the debt is not affected thereby: *C. B. S. United Kingdom Ltd.* v. *C. & E. Comrs.* [1987] VATTR 93. A refund does not become repayable if a surplus arises in the insolvency so that the debt proved is paid in full: *C. & E. Comrs.* v. *T. H. Knitwear (Wholesale) Ltd.* [1988] STC 79, CA.

Claims are made in the time, form and manner prescribed by regulations. See VAT (Bad Debt Relief) Regulations 1986, S.I. 1986 No. 335.

No claim may be made in respect of supplies made after FA 1990 received Royal Assent. For the relief available in respect of supplies made on or after 1 April 1989, see FA 1990 s. 10.

REPAYMENT

23. Repayment of tax to those in business overseas. (A15.51)
Persons carrying on a business in another EC member State or, from 1 January 1988, a non-EC ("third") country, may claim from the Commissioners any VAT paid in the U.K. or on any goods imported into the U.K. which would be input tax if they were taxable persons in the U.K. Regulations stipulate the method and mechanics of obtaining a refund. See VAT (Repayment to Community Traders) Regulations 1980, S.I. 1980 No. 1537 and VAT (Repayments to Third Country Traders) Regulations 1987, S.I. 1987 No. 2015.

FURTHER PROVISIONS AS TO IMPORTATION OF GOODS

24. Application of customs enactments. (A2.63)
The provisions of the customs and excise Acts 1979 (defined in CEMA 1979, s. 1), subject to exclusions in this section and VAT (General) Regulations 1985, S.I. 1985 No. 886 regs. 39, 40, apply as if all goods imported were liable to customs or excise duties and as if VAT were one of those duties.

25. Importation of goods by taxable persons. (A15.26)

The Commissioners by regulations may allow taxable persons to account for the VAT due on imported goods at the same time as they account for VAT on their supplies of goods or services. See the VAT (General) Regulations 1985, S.I. 1985 No. 886 reg. 41.

26. Goods imported for private purposes. (A15.52)

Goods imported for private purposes do not entitle a registered person to deduct VAT as input tax, but the Commissioners may allow a claim where a double charge to VAT would otherwise result.

SPECIAL CASES

27. Application to Crown. (A3.11; A4.13; A15.61)

Taxable supplies made by the Crown are treated in the same manner as taxable supplies made by ordinary taxable persons.

Goods or services supplied by a government department are treated as if they were supplied in the course or furtherance of business if the Treasury so directs. For Treasury directions, see *London Gazette,* 28.4.89, pp. 5110–5124.

Government departments may claim a refund of tax in respect of goods and services acquired otherwise than for the purposes of a business or deemed business if the Treasury so directs. The Commissioners may impose conditions concerning the keeping, preservation and production of records. For Treasury directions, see *London Gazette,* 14.12.84, 17.5.85, 2.5.86.

28. Local authorities. (A3.44)

Local authorities are liable to be registered for VAT even if the value of taxable supplies made is below the registration limit.

29. Groups of companies. (A3.06, 18, 56)

Two or more corporate bodies resident in the U.K. are treated as a group if one of them controls all the others or they are all controlled by an individual, company or partnership. For control, see *Mannin Shipping Ltd.* v. *C. & E. Comrs.* [1979] VATTR 83 (individual with casting vote owning 50 per cent. of equity share capital having control); *British Airways Board* v. *C. & E. Comrs.* LON/79/107 unreported (whether company empowered by statute to control another company); *E. Du Vergier & Co. Ltd.* v. *C. & E. Comrs.* [1973] VATTR 11 (whether individuals controlling company carrying on business in partnership). Two or more of them may then apply to be treated for VAT as if they were one person, with one of the companies (the representative member) treated as if it made or received all supplies of goods or sevices made or received by members of the group.

The Commissioners take the view that a company incorporated and resident abroad is eligible for VAT grouping where it has at least one U.K. resident director who has full voting rights and regularly attends board meetings. Dormant companies and companies making only exempt supplies may be included in a VAT group. See Leaflet No. 700/2/83 para. 2. Supplies within the group are disregarded.

An application for group registration or to change or terminate an existing group registration should be made not less than 90 days before it is to take effect. The Commissioners may allow shorter notice: *C. & E. Comrs.* v. *Save & Prosper Group Ltd.* [1979] STC 205. Their refusal to do so is open to appeal: see *Blue Boar Property & Investment Co. Ltd.* v. *C. & E. Comrs.* [1984] VATTR 12; *Legal & Contractual Services Ltd.* v. *C. & E. Comrs.* [1984] VATTR 85. All group registrations, changes and terminations take effect from the beginning of a prescribed accounting period. The Commissioners may refuse an application for group registration, to add a company or to change the representative member, but only to protect the revenue. For the right of appeal, see s. 40 (1) (*h*). Control of a body corporate has the same meaning as in the Companies Act 1985, s. 736.

29A. Supplies to groups. (A6.46)

Where a registered trader transfers as a going concern to a company in a VAT group a business or part of a business together with assets the transfer of which would normally be treated as neither a supply of goods nor a supply of services, the transfer is treated as a supply both to and by the representative member of the group. This does not apply if the representative member of the group is entitled to credit for all of its input tax on supplies during the prescribed accounting period or any longer period in which the assets are transferred, or if the assets were acquired more than three years before the day on which they are transferred. Nor does it apply to the capital items defined in VAT (General) Regulations 1985, S.I. 1985 No. 886 reg. 37B from 1 April 1990.

The transfer value has to be excluded from any calculation to determine the input tax allowable under the partial exemption rules to the representative member of the group.

The value of a supply made to or by the representative member is the price, net of VAT, between a buyer and a seller who have no relationship which could affect the price. An adjustment of tax payable may be allowed where the Commissioners are satisfied that the person transferring the assets did not receive full credit of input tax upon purchase of those assets (for example where the transferor was exempt).

These provisions apply to transfers made on or after 1 April 1987 and apply only to assets subject to the standard rate.

30. Partnerships. (A3.13)

Registration for VAT may be in the name of the firm so that changes in the members of a partnership do not require a new VAT registration. A partner who leaves is treated as remaining a partner until the Commissioners are informed that he no longer is a partner. Such a partner remains liable for returns, etc. for prescribed accounting periods up to and including that during which he is treated as leaving. The other partners can claim from a former partner only a just proportion of the VAT for his last prescribed accounting period.

A notice addressed to a partnership in the firm name is deemed to be served on the partnership. A notice served or deemed to be served on a partnership is deemed to be served on a former partner if it relates to a period during which he was, or was deemed to be, a partner. See *C. & E. Comrs.* v. *Evans* [1982] STC 342; *Ahmed* v. *C. & E. Comrs.* [1988] VATTR 1; *Choudhury* v. *C. & E. Comrs.* LON/87/116 unreported.

31. Business carried on in divisions or by unincorporated bodies, personal representatives, etc. (A3.02, 13, 15, 17)

Registration of any club, association or organisation may be in its name so that reregistration for VAT is not necessary if its members change.

Regulations may: (1) allow registration of bodies corporate in the names of its divisions; (2) identify who is responsible for doing anything required by the Act in relation to partnerships and unincorporated bodies; and (3) secure continuity of registration on the death, incapacity, insolvency etc. of a taxable person. See VAT (General) Regulations 1985, S.I. 1985 No. 886, regs. 9–11.

32. Agents, etc. (A3.48; A6.21)

Where an agent acts for an overseas person the Commissioners may by notice to the agent direct that he is accountable for VAT or required to carry out the duties imposed by this Act. See *Interbet Trading Ltd.* v. *C. & E. Comrs.* [1978] VATTR 235; *Culverhouse* v. *C. & E. Comrs.* LON/86/125 unreported. Goods imported by a VAT registered agent and supplied by him as agent may be treated as imported and supplied by the agent as principal. Where goods or services are supplied through an agent acting in his own name the Commissioners may treat the supply as both to and from the agent. For the identification of a person as an agent, see *C. & E. Comrs.* v. *Johnson* [1980] STC 624; *Potter* v. *C. & E. Comrs.* [1985] STC 45, CA; *Betterware Products Ltd.* v. *C. & E. Comrs.* [1985] STC 648; *C. & E. Comrs.* v. *Paget* [1989] STC 773; *Music & Video Exchange Ltd.* v. *C. & E. Comrs.* LON/88/1154 unreported. For agency disbursements, see *Rowe & Maw (a firm)* v. *C. & E. Comrs.* [1975] STC 340; *Hamilton* v. *C. & E. Comrs.* [1984] VATTR 95.

33. Transfers of going concerns. (A5.16)

Where a business is transferred as a going concern the transferor's turnover is treated as the transferee's turnover in deciding whether the transferee should register. The transferor must hand over and the transferee must keep the records relating to the business for a maximum of six years unless the Commissioners at the request of the transferor otherwise direct.

The Commissioners may by regulation provide for continuity in cases where a business carried on by one taxable person is transferred to another as a going concern and the transferee takes the place of the transferor as the registered person. See VAT (General) Regulations 1985, S.I. 1985 No. 886 reg. 4 (5)–(8).

34. Terminal markets. (A3.19; A11.08)

The Treasury may by order vary VAT provisions as regards dealings and dealers on terminal markers. In particular the order may zero-rate or exempt supplies of goods or services, register a body of persons representing dealers, disregard dealings by dealers so represented, and refund input tax. See VAT (Terminal Markets) Order 1973, S.I. 1973 No. 173.

35. Supplies of dutiable goods in warehouse. (A5.14; A15.41)

A supply of imported goods is not charged to tax if: (1) the goods are warehoused at the time of supply; and (2) the supply takes place prior to payment of the customs duty or excise duty to which the goods are chargeable (or the excise duty if the goods are chargeable to both duties).

Home produced goods subject to excise duty are charged to tax on the only supply, or on the last supply, made before payment of duty while the goods are warehoused. Prior supplies in warehouse are not charged to tax. The value of the supply includes the duty paid and the supply is deemed to be made at the date of payment. Tax is payable by the person responsible for payment of the duty. If the goods are removed from warehouse without payment of duty, the value of the supply excludes duty and tax is payable by the person removing the goods.

The Commissioners may make regulations allowing tax on supplies of home produced goods in warehouse to be accounted for on the relevant person's tax return. No regulations currently have effect under this provision.

"Customs duty" includes agricultural levies payable under European Communities Act 1972 s. 6(5).

"Excise duty" includes additions and reductions made under Excise Duties (Surcharges or Rebates) Act 1979 s. 1.

35A. Buildings and land
This section introduces Sch. 6A. The Treasury may amend Sch. 6A by order. For the making of orders, see s. 45(4). No orders have been made to date.

36. Capital goods. (A15.66)
The Treasury may by order allow VAT to be deducted where plant or machinery is purchased but VAT cannot be credited under s. 14. No order has been made.

37. Trading stamp schemes. (A8.25)
Regulations allow the value of supplies made by trading stamp promoters to be taken as the net of all monies received and paid out. See VAT (Trading Stamps) Regulations 1973, S.I. 1973 No. 293.

37A. Tour operators. (A14.91)
The Treasury may, by order, modify the application of VATA 1983 in relation to goods and services supplied by tour operators. See VAT (Tour Operators) Order 1987, S.I. 1987 No. 1806.

"Tour operator" includes a travel agent operating as a principal and any other person providing services of any kind commonly provided by tour operators or travel agents for the benefit of travellers.

GENERAL

38. Administration, collection and enforcement.
Schedule 7 provides for the administration, collection and enforcement of VAT.

39. Offences and penalties. (A18.11–14, 16, 17)
It is an offence to be knowingly concerned in, or in the taking of steps with a view to, the fraudulent evasion of VAT. Any person who with intent to deceive produces or sends or makes use of any document which is false in a material particular, or furnishes information which he knows to be false, or recklessly makes a statement which is false, commits an offence. Where a person's conduct during a period must have involved the commission by him of any of the offences mentioned above, then, whether or not particulars of those offences are known, he is guilty of an offence. See *R.* v. *McCarthy* [1981] STC 298, CA; *R.* v. *Asif* [1985] STI 317, CA; *R.* v. *Howard* [1990] STI 351, CA. For convictions under the common law offence of cheating the public revenue, see *R.* v. *Mavji* [1986] STC 508, CA; *R.* v. *Redford* [1988] STC 845, CA, *R.* v. *Fisher* [1989] STI 269.

Where an authorised person has reasonable grounds for suspecting that an offence has been committed he may arrest anyone whom he has reasonable grounds to suspect of being guilty.

Anyone who acquires possession or deals in goods or accepts the supply of any services having reason to believe that the VAT will be avoided is guilty of an offence.

40. Appeals. (A17.03–05, 21–23, 87–89)
An independent VAT tribunal may hear appeals against the decisions of the Commissioners on the following matters:

(*a*)   the registration or cancellation of a registration;

(*b*)   the VAT chargeable on a supply of goods or services (see *Emmanuel Church, Northwood, Middlesex* v. *C. & E. Comrs.* [1973] VATTR 76, *Allied Windows (S. Wales) Ltd.* v. *C. & E. Comrs.* (1973) 91 Taxation 101, *Morrisons Central Garage Ltd.* v. *C. & E. Comrs.* EDN/79/ 24 unreported, *Grimsby & District Sunday Football League* v. *C. & E. Comrs.* [1982] VATTR 210);

(*c*)   the input tax which may be due to a person (including repayments claimed by overseas traders: VAT (Repayment to Community Traders) Regulations 1980, S.I. 1980 No. 1537 reg. 11 and VAT (Repayment to Third Country Traders) Regulations, 1987, S.I. 1987 No. 2015 reg. 11; and repayment supplement: *Richard Costain Ltd.* v. *C. & E. Comrs.* [1988] VATTR 106);

(*d*)   the proportion of input tax allowable under VATA 1983 s. 15 (see *S. D. Taylor Ltd.* v. *C. & E. Comrs.* [1985] VATTR 73; *C. H. Beazer (Holdings) plc.* v. *C. & E. Comrs.* [1987] VATTR 164);

(*e*)   a claim by a do-it-yourself builder;

(*f*)   a claim for bad debt relief;

(*g*)   a claim on goods imported for private purposes;

(*h*)   any refusal to allow a group registration or a change in a group registration (including a decision not to allow a retrospective group registration: see *Blue Boar Property & Invest-ment Co. Ltd.* v. *C. & E. Comrs.* [1984] VATTR 12; *Legal & Contractual Services Ltd.* v. *C. & E. Comrs.* [1984] VATTR 85;

(*hh*) any direction for persons to be regarded as one taxable person for VAT purposes (see below);

(*i*) (repealed);

(*j*) any direction by the Commissioners relating to the value of supplies of goods and services;

(*k*) any refusal to allow the value of supplies to be determined by means of a published retail scheme (see *J. Boardmans (1980) Ltd.* v. *C. & E. Comrs.* [1984] VATTR 18; on appeal [1986] STC 10);

(*l*) any requirements relating to computer invoicing;

(*m*) an assessment where a person has made an incomplete or incorrect return or wrongly received a VAT repayment, or failed to account for goods acquired by a business;

(*n*) the requirement to provide security for the protection of the revenue (see *Mr. Wishmore Ltd.* v. *C. & E. Comrs.* [1988] STC 723; *Gayton House Holdings Ltd.* v. *C. & E. Comrs.* [1984] VATTR 111; *Firepower Builders Ltd.* v. *C. & E. Comrs.* LON/88/301 unreported);

(*o*) any liability to a penalty or surcharge for evasion, serious misdeclaration, failure to notify for VAT registration, breaches of walking possession agreements or regulatory provisions, and default surcharges;

(*p*) the amount of any penalty, interest or surcharge notified by assessment;

(*q*) the making of an assessment more than 6 years after a period;

(*r*) the refusal or termination of use of a cash accounting scheme;

(*s*) a claim for repayment of overpaid VAT.

Tribunals have no jurisdiction regarding the length of a prescribed accounting period fixed by the Commissioners (*Punchwell Ltd.* v. *C. & E. Comrs.* [1981] VATTR 93), the detrimental effects of VAT on a trader's business (*Pool* v. *C. & E. Comrs.* LON/76/122 unreported), the granting of concessionary treatment (*Davis Advertising Service Ltd.* v. *C. & E. Comrs.* [1973] VATTR 16), conduct of a control visit or fairness of an assessment (*Coolisle* v. *C. & E. Comrs.* LON/78/242 unreported), extra-statutory concessions (*Cando 70* v. *C. & E. Comrs.* [1978] VATTR 211), Mr. Robert Sheldon's parliamentary statement of 21 July 1978 regarding incorrect advice given to traders (*Farm Facilities (Fork Lift) Ltd.* v. *C. & E. Comrs.* [1987] VATTR 80).

All returns must have been made and amounts shown therein as due paid before an appeal will be heard, unless the appeal relates to the provision of security to protect the revenue. See *R.* v. *VAT Tribunal ex parte Cohen* [1984] STC 361; *Wright & Associates Ltd.* v. *C. & E. Comrs.* [1975] VATTR 168; *Smalley Construction Co. Ltd.* v. *C. & E. Comrs.* MAN/77/170 unreported; *McAllister (a firm)* v. *C. & E. Comrs.* [1981] VATTR 55. For tax in dispute shown on a return, see *R.* v. *VAT Tribunal ex parte Happer* [1982] STC 700, *R.* v. *VAT Tribunal ex parte Minster Associates* [1988] STC 386, *R.* v. *London VAT Tribunal ex parte Theodorou* [1989] STC 292, *Beadle* v. *C. & E. Comrs.* MAN/84/264 unreported. Appeals against assessments which are in respect of output tax or sums deemed to be output tax shall not be heard unless the amount assessed has been paid or deposited with the Commissioners or such payment has been waived on the grounds of hardship. This requirement arises where the real issue between the parties falls within this description: see *Boltgate Ltd.* v. *C. & E. Comrs.* [1982] VATTR 120; *Brian Gubby Ltd.* v. *C. & E. Comrs.* [1985] VATTR 59. For payment, see *Buckley* v. *C. & E. Comrs.* CAR/76/90 unreported; *Mahoney* v. *C. & E. Comrs.* LON/76/50 unreported; *Trust Securities Holdings Ltd.* v. *C. & E. Comrs.* LON/89/1459 unreported. For hardship applications, see *Don Pasquale (a firm)* v. *C. & E. Comrs.* [1990] STI 545, CA (payment to be waived on all or none of the tax assessed); *Dapagem* v. *C. & E. Comrs.* LON/80/442 unreported; *Western General Trading Ltd.* v. *C. & E. Comrs.* LON/83/334 unreported.

In an appeal against a direction for persons to be regarded as one taxable person the tribunal may allow the appeal only if it considers that the Commissioners could not reasonably have been satisfied that the conditions for making a direction had been met. For the supervisory test applied, see *Chamberlain* v. *C. & E. Comrs.* [1989] STC 505; *South West Launderettes Ltd.* v. *C. & E. Comrs.* LON/87/35 unreported.

Where the tribunal increases an assessment raised on the value of supplies estimated by the Commissioners, the tribunal direction shall be deemed to be sufficient notice to the appellant of the correct amount.

Where it is found that an amount paid or deposited with the Commissioners is not due, that amount is repayable together with interest at a rate determined by the tribunal. For the repayment of tax, see *Barratt Construction Ltd.* v. *C. & E. Comrs.* EDN/87/32 unreported. For interest, see *Mahoney* v. *C. & E. Comrs.* LON/76/50 unreported; *Mann* v. *C. & E. Comrs.* LON/82/184 unreported; *Orbit Housing Association* v. *C. & E. Comrs.* LON/84/73 unreported. Where VAT has not been paid or deposited pending an appeal, and is found to be due, the tribunal may direct that it is payable with interest at such rate as it specifies. See *Dormers Builders (London) Ltd.* v. *C. & E. Comrs.* LON/85/283 unreported. For the rate of interest, see *St. Luke's PPC* v. *C. & E. Comrs.* [1983] VATTR 187.

Where a decision of the Commissioners depended on an earlier decision by them not appealable under this section, an appeal against the later decision only can be allowed if the Commissioners would have allowed on appeal against the earlier decision. See *XL (Stevenage) Ltd.* v. *C. & E. Comrs.* [1981] VATTR 192; *Bardsley* v. *C. & E. Comrs.* [1984] VATTR 171.

For judicial review of a decision made by a VAT tribunal, see *R.* v. *C. & E. Comrs. and London VAT Tribunal, ex parte Menzies* [1990] STC 263, CA.

41. Supplies spanning change of rate, etc. (A5.48)

The standard rate may change or a new rate of tax may be introduced in addition to the standard rate. Supplies which were taxable at one tax rate may become taxable at another (*e.g.* zero-rate to standard rate) or may become exempt, or vice versa.

When a change increases or imposes VAT, a taxable person may elect to charge VAT (if any) at the old rate on goods removed or services performed before the date of the change even though the tax would normally be due on the issue of a tax invoice after the change.

When a change reduces or removes VAT a taxable person may elect to charge VAT (if any) at the new rate on goods removed or services performed after the date of the change even though payment was received or a tax invoice issued before that date. If a tax invoice has already been issued it must be corrected. A credit note should be issued within 14 days.

The election as to which rate of VAT to charge is not available to taxable persons who have issued a tax invoice under the self billing arrangements or when goods are sold from the assets of a business in satisfaction of a debt.

42. Adjustment of contracts on changes in tax. (A5.33A)

The consideration for a supply of goods or services specified in a lease or contract must be adjusted, unless the lease or contract specifies otherwise, to reflect a subsequent change in the rate of tax or the fact that tax has become, or ceased to be, chargeable on the supply as a result of a change in the legislation or the making of an election to waive exemption. A lease "specifies otherwise" only if it refers specifically to VAT or this section.

43. Failure of resolution under Provisional Collection of Taxes Act 1968. (A10.06)

If VAT has been paid under a Budget resolution on a supply, and the Budget resolution fails, the value of the supply is not recalculated to determine either the amount of VAT repayable or the amount chargeable.

For example, VAT is increased from 15% to 25% by Budget resolution. The consideration for a supply is £800 plus VAT @ 25% = £200, a total of £1,000. If the Budget resolution fails, the VAT @ 15% is £120 and £80 is repayable: the VAT is not recalculated as £1,000 × 15/115 = £130.43, so that only £69.57 would be repayable.

If a Budget resolution fails, only the net VAT payable can be claimed as input tax.

44. Disclosure of information for statistical purposes. (A2.21; A18.19)

The Commissioners may disclose to the Department of Trade and Industry information for a central register of businesses or any statistical survey. The information which may be provided is the VAT numbers allocated, the names, addresses, status, trade classification and value of supplies. This information may be released provided it is in a form which does not identify any individual business.

Improper disclosure attracts on summary conviction a fine of up to £2,000 or on conviction on indictment up to two years' imprisonment and an unlimited fine.

SUPPLEMENTAL

45. Orders, rules and regulations. (A2.63)

Orders, regulations and rules under this Act are to be made by statutory instrument. All instruments are to be subject to annulment by a resolution of the House of Commons (the negative procedure) except certain orders which have to be laid and require approval of the House of Commons (the positive procedure). The orders that require the positive procedure all increase VAT; they relate to:

(*a*) self supply,

(*b*) unregistered owners of aircraft and hovercraft,

(*c*) increase of VAT rate (see s. 9), disallowance of input tax (other than with regard to tour operators), and withdrawal of zero-rating or exemption, and

(*d*) the variation of VATA 1983, Sch. 6A.

46. Service of notices

Posting a notice, notification requirement or demand to a person's last or usual residence or place of business is sufficient. But see *C. & E. Comrs.* v. *Medway Draughting & Technical Services Ltd.* [1989] STC 346 in relation to surcharge liability notices.

47. Meaning of "business", etc. (A4.01, 11, 12, 14, 51, A5.25)

Business includes any trade, profession or vocation. For the nature of a business, see in particular *C. & E. Comrs.* v. *Morrison's Academy Boarding Houses Association* [1978] STC 1; *National Water Council* v. *C. & E. Comrs.* [1979] STC 157; *Church of Scientology of California* v. *C. & E.*

Comrs. [1979] STC 297; *C. & E. Comrs.* v. *Lord Fisher* [1981] STC 238; *C. & E. Comrs.* v. *Royal Exchange Theatre Trust* [1979] STC 728; *Greater London Red Cross Blood Transfusion Service* v. *C. & E. Comrs.* [1983] VATTR 241; *Singer & Friedlander Ltd.* v. *C. & E. Comrs.* [1989] VATTR 27, [1989] 1 CMLR 814; *The Lord Mayor and Citizens of the City of Westminster* v. *C. & E. Comrs.* [1990] 2 CMLR 81. For public authorities, see *Ufficio Distreltuale delle Imposte Divette di Fiorenzuola d'Arda* v. *Commune di Carpeneto Piacentino* (joined cases 231/81 and 129/88) (1988) Times, 15 November, ECJ; *Comune di Carpaneto Piacentino* v. *Ufficio Provinciale Imposta sul Valore Aggiunto di Piacenza* (case 4/89) (1990) OJ C143, ECJ. For activities which do not give rise to supplies made for a consideration, see *C. & E. Comrs.* v. *Apple and Pear Development Council* [1986] STC 192, HL (statutory levy); *Whitechapel Art Gallery* v. *C. & E. Comrs.* [1986] STC 156 (free admission to premises). For activities kept afloat by charitable donations and subventions, see *Yoga for Health Foundation* v. *C. & E. Comrs.* [1983] VATTR 297, on appeal [1984] STC 630; *Holy Spirit Association for the Unification of World Christianity* v. *C. & E. Comrs.* LON/84/179 unreported. For activities carried on for pleasure and social enjoyment, see *C. & E. Comrs.* v. *Lord Fisher* [1981] STC 238. For hire of assets, see *Three H Aircraft Hire* v. *C. & E. Comrs.* [1982] STC 653; *Coleman* v. *C. & E. Comrs.* [1976] VATTR 24; *Walker* v. *C. & E. Comrs.* [1976] VATTR 10; *Wilcox* v. *C. & E. Comrs.* [1978] VATTR 79. For the distinction between a contract of service and a contract for services, see *New Way School of Motoring Ltd.* v. *C. & E. Comrs.* [1979] VATTR 57; *Chalmers (a firm)* v. *C. & E. Comrs.* LON/82/84 unreported; *Berbrooke Fashions* v. *C. & E. Comrs.* [1977] VATTR 168; *Headley Enterprises* v. *C. & E. Comrs.* LON/82/65 unreported. Employments were held to exist in *Ricarby* v. *C. & E. Comrs.* [1973] VATTR 186, *Cant* v. *C. & E. Comrs.* [1976] VATTR 237, *Holland* v. *C. & E. Comrs.* [1978] VATTR 57 and *Lean & Rose* v. *C. & E. Comrs.* [1974] VATTR 7; *Headline and Just Hair* v. *C. & E. Comrs.* LON/88/1291, 1292 unreported.

Business also includes the facilities supplied to members of clubs, associations, or organisations. For facilities or advantages supplied by clubs etc., see *Royal Highland and Agricultural Society of Scotland* v. *C. & E. Comrs.* [1976] VATTR 38; *Cambuslang Athletic Club* v. *C. & E. Comrs.* EDN/82/39 unreported; *Carlton Lodge Club* v. *C. & E. Comrs.* [1974] STC 507; *British Olympic Association* v. *C. & E. Comrs.* [1979] VATTR 122; *Royal Ulster Constabulary Athletic Association Ltd.* v. *C. & E. Comrs.* [1989] VATTR 17. For activity groups, see *Belvedere & Calder Vale Sports Club* v. *C. & E. Comrs.* MAN/79/129 unreported; *Watchet Indoor Bowling Club* v. *C. & E. Comrs.* LON/80/341 unreported. For subscriptions and other consideration, see *Lord Advocate* v. *Largs Golf Club* [1985] STC 226 (payment by third party); *C. & E. Comrs.* v. *Automobile Association* [1974] STC 192 (apportionment); *C. & E. Comrs.* v. *Little Spain Club Ltd.* [1979] STC 170 (special levy); *Exeter Golf & Country Club Ltd.* v. *C. & E. Comrs.* [1981] STC 211, CA (interest free loan); *Dyrham Park Country Club* v. *C. & E. Comrs.* [1978] VATTR 244 (bond); *South Church Workmen's Club & Institute Ltd.* v. *C. & E. Comrs.* MAN/78/40 unreported (shares).

Admitting persons to premises for a consideration amounts to a business. For a testimonial match, see *Eric Taylor Deceased Testimonial Match Committee* v. *C. & E. Comrs.* [1975] VATTR 8. For admission by programme, contrast *Rochdale Hornets Football Co. Ltd.* v. *C. & E. Comrs.* [1975] VATTR 71 and *Jarmain* v. *C. & E. Comrs.* [1979] VATTR 41.

A body whose aims are of a political, religious, philanthropic, philosophical or patriotic nature may not be considered a business if its subscription covers only the right to participate in its management or receive reports on its activities. See *English Speaking Union of the Commonwealth* v. *C. & E. Comrs.* [1980] VATTR 184.

Where an office is held as part of a trade, profession or vocation (for example, a practising solicitor is a director), remuneration for such services is part of the turnover of the business for VAT purposes. See *Hempsons (a firm)* v. *C. & E. Comrs.* [1977] VATTR 73; *Gardner* v. *C. & E. Comrs.* MAN/88/690 unreported.

Anything done in ending or transferring a business is done in the course or furtherance of a business.

48. Interpretation. (A2.67; A18.06)
Words and phrases used in the Act are defined.
As to fines, see notes to CEMA 1979, s. 171.

49. Refund of tax to Government of Northern Ireland. (A2.16)
VAT paid by the Government of Northern Ireland shall be refunded net of any VAT on deemed business supplies made by them.

50. Consequential, transitional and saving provisions and repeals.
Schedule 9 makes consequential amendments. Schedule 10 contains savings and transitional provisions. Schedule 11 repeals the enactments consolidated in this Act.

SCHEDULES

SCHEDULE 1 REGISTRATION (Section 215)

Liability to be registered

1.—(A3.41, 43; A8.81) A person is liable to registration if: (1) he makes taxable supplies and his taxable turnover for a one year period ending on the last day of any month exceeded £25,400; or (2) a business was transferred to him as a going concern and his taxable turnover for the one year period ending on the date of transfer exceeded £25,400. For taxable turnover where a business is transferred as a going concern, see VATA 1983 s. 33 (1) (*a*). A person is not liable to registration if he satisfies the Commissioners that taxable turnover for next year will not exceed £24,400. For the requirement to satisfy the Commissioners, see *Briggs* v. *C. & E. Comrs.* MAN/85/41 unreported; *Shepherd* v. *C. & E. Comrs.* LON/86/318 unreported. Taxable turnover is disregarded if: (1) it was made under a previous registration while the trader was liable to, or eligible for, registration; and (2) the Commissioners were given all the information they needed to decide whether to cancel the previous registration.

A person is liable to registration if: (1) he makes taxable supplies and there are reasonable grounds for believing, at any time, that taxable turnover for the next 30 days will exceed £25,400: see *XL (Stevenage) Ltd.* v. *C. & E. Comrs.* [1981] VATTR 192; or (2) a business was transferred to him as a going concern and there are reasonable grounds for believing, at the date of transfer, that taxable turnover for the next 30 days will exceed £25,400. For the objective test applied, see *Optimum Personnel Evaluation (Operators) Ltd.* v. *C. & E. Comrs.* LON/86/620 unreported.

Sales of capital assets (other than standard rated interests, rights and licences in land) are disregarded when calculating turnover for registration purposes.

1A.—(A3.14, 24, 49) To avoid registration, or exclude certain supplies from VAT, some traders hived off part of their business to separate ownership. For example, a publican might arrange for his wife to supply the meals in his public house, or different persons might operate a launderette on certain weeks or days. To counter this the Commissioners may direct that the persons named in a notice are to be treated as a single taxable person, carrying on the activities of a business described in the notice. The taxable person is liable to be registered from the date of the notice or such later date as may be specified in the notice.

The Commissioners may only make a direction naming any person if they are satisfied that:

(*a*) the person is making or has made taxable supplies; and

(*b*) those supplies form only part of the activities which should be regarded as those of the business, those activities being carried on concurrently or previously (or both) by other persons (*i.e.* the persons named in the direction should be closely bound to one another by financial, economic and organisational links within the meaning of Directive 77/388/EEC art. 4 (4): *Osman* v. *C. & E. Comrs.* [1989] STC 596); and

(*c*) the total taxable supplies exceed the registration threshold; and

(*d*) one of the main reasons for organising the business in this way is to avoid a liability to be registered for VAT.

See Press Notice No. 1135, 14 August 1986. For examples of directions, see *Chamberlain* v. *C. & E. Comrs.* [1989] STC 505; *Osman* v. *C. & E. Comrs.* [1989] STC 596; *Lyons* v. *C. & E. Comrs.* [1987] VATTR 187; *South West Launderettes Ltd.* v. *C. & E. Comrs.* LON/87/3 unreported. For directions set aside, see *Grisdale* v. *C. & E. Comrs.* MAN/89/141 unreported; *Myres (a firm)* v. *C. & E. Comrs.* MAN/89/157 unreported; *Thompson, Thompson and Giblin* v. *C. & E. Comrs.* MAN/88/819 unreported.

2.—(A3.62) A registered trader ceases to be liable to registration at any time if he satisfies the Commissioners that his taxable turnover for the year then beginning will not exceed £24,400. However, where the Commissioners are satisfied that the reason for the turnover not exceeding £24,400 is that the taxable person is to cease trading for a period of at least 30 days then the person will remain liable to be registered.

Sales of capital assets (other than standard rated interests, rights and licences in land) are disregarded when calculating turnover for deregistration purposes.

Notification of liability and registration

3.—(A3.41) A person liable to registration at the end of any month must notify his liability within 30 days. He is registered from the end of the next following month or from a mutually agreed earlier date.

4.—(A3.43) A person liable to registration at any time must notify his liability within 30 days of that time. He is registered from that time.

4A.—(A3.41, 43) A person liable to registration at the date when a business is transferred to him as a going concern must notify his liability within 30 days of the date of transfer. He is registered from the date of transfer.

4B.—(A3.41) If a person liable to registration at the end of any month is also liable to registration under another provision at the same time, he is registered under the other provision.

Entitlement to be registered
5.—(A3.51, 52) A person who makes or intends to make taxable supplies is entitled to be registered if he so requests. The registration takes effect from the date of his request or a mutually agreed earlier date.
5A.—(A3.53) A person making supplies outside the U.K. that would be taxable if made within the U.K. or makes supplies in warehouse may be registered.

Notification of end of liability or entitlement etc.
7.—(A3.84) Within 30 days of ceasing to make taxable supplies a registered person must notify the Commissioners of that fact so that the registration may be cancelled.
7A.—(A3.53) A person registered under para. 5A who ceases to make disregarded supplies or who begins to make taxable supplies is required to give notice within 30 days.

Cancellation of registration
8A.—(A3.65) When a registered person satisfies the Commissioners that he is no longer liable to be registered he may request that his business should be de-registered.
9.—(A3.65) Any person who has ceased to be liable or entitled to registration may be de-registered at a date agreed with the Commissioners.
10.—(A3.65) The Commissioners can cancel a registration with effect from the day registration commenced if they are satisfied that the trader should not have been registered.

Exemption from registration
11.—(A3.26) Any person who makes zero-rated supplies may be exempted from registration if the Commissioners think fit. The test is whether exemption from registration is in the interests of the revenue: *Fong* v. *C. & E. Comrs.* [1978] VATTR 75. If any change occurs in that business that affects the liability of the supplies then notice has to be given within 30 days.

Power to vary specified sums by order
12.—Treasury orders may change any of the registration and de-registration thresholds.

Supplementary
13.—(A8.83) The value of supplies for registration purposes is the consideration given. The value of supplies for deregistration purposes is the VAT-exclusive amount of consideration given.
14.—(A3.11, 18) The Commissioners may by regulations prescribe the form and contents of any notification. See VAT (General) Regulations 1985, S.I. 1985 No. 886 reg. 4 (1)–(4), (6).
15.—(A3.81; A8.81) Registration means registration in the register kept by the Commissioners. Supplies mean supplies in the course of furtherance of a business and not otherwise.

SCHEDULE 2 MATTERS TO BE TREATED AS SUPPLY OF GOODS OR SERVICES
(Section 3)

1.—(A5.12, 13) Any transfer of the whole property in goods, *i.e.* transfer of ownership and all the rights associated with ownership, is a supply of goods. See *Philips Exports Ltd.* v. *C. & E. Comrs.* [1990] STC 508.
    However, the transfer of any undivided share of the property or the transfer of the possession of goods is a supply of services. Thus, the hire of goods or the supply of the right to goods owned jointly with others is a supply of services. However, a supply of goods is made when all joint owners release their shares under a sale of goods: *Astor* v. *C. & E. Comrs.* [1981] VATTR 174.
    Where the possession of goods is transferred under an agreement for the sale of goods, or under agreements which expressly intend that the property also will pass at some future time no later than when the goods are fully paid, then there is a supply of goods.
2.—(A5.12) A supply of goods occurs where a person applies a process or treatment to another person's goods. See *London Board for Shechita* v. *C. & E. Comrs.* [1974] VATTR 24.
3.—(A5.12) The supply of power, heat, refrigeration or ventilation is a supply of goods.
4.—(A5.12) The grant, assignment or surrender of a major interest in land is a supply of goods.
5.—(A6.11, 12) The transfer of goods belonging to a business, with or without consideration, is a supply of goods. However, a supply is ignored where it is either a gift costing less than £10 made in the course of furtherance of a business (and not part of a series of gifts to the same person), or a gift to an exisitng or possible customer of an industrial sample in a form not ordinarily available for sale to the public. See *RHM Bakeries (Northern) Ltd.* v. *C. & E. Comrs.* [1979] STC 72 (long service award); *Terry's Supermarket* v. *C. & E. Comrs.* CAR/77/410 unreported (stock transferred to associated business).
    Where goods belonging to a business are put to any private use, whether or not for any consideration, there is a supply of services. This does not apply if input tax deduction was prohibited when the goods were acquired: *H. Kühne v Finanzampt München III* (case 50/88) [1989]

STI 676, ECJ. For hotel accommodation, contrast *Ibstock Building Products Ltd.* v. *C. & E. Comrs.* [1987] VATTR 1 (supply made) and *Stormseal (UPVC) Window Co. Ltd.* v. *C. & E. Comrs.* MAN/89/18 (no supply made].

Where there is a supply of goods or services under this paragraph it is treated as made in the course or furtherance of the business. A sole trader or partner must pay VAT on transfers of business goods to his private possession or use of business goods for private purposes.

6.—(A6.26) Where a trader's business goods are sold by another person to satisfy a debt owed by the trader, then the trader is deemed to supply those goods.

7.—(A6.51) When a business ceases, goods which form part of its assets are deemed to be supplied in the course of furtherance of the business before the business ceases, unless:

    (*a*) the business is transferred as a going concern, or

    (*b*) it continues upon the death or incapacity of the proprietor, or

    (*c*) the VAT on the deemed supply is £250 or less.

If input tax is not claimed for these goods, and the goods were not acquired as part of the assets of a business bought as a going concern, and relief under FA 1973, s. 4 (goods held on 1 April 1973) has not been obtained, then there is no supply of these goods.

8.—(A6.11, 12, 26, 51) As regards land, a grant or assignment for a consideration is treated as either a supply of goods (major interest) or a supply of services (other interest). A grant or assignment without consideration is a supply of goods. The use of land for non-business or private purposes is a supply of services. Para. 5 above is to be read accordingly.

For the purposes of paras. 5–7 above, "goods" includes land.

SCHEDULE 3 SERVICES SUPPLIED WHERE RECEIVED (Section 7) (A6.31; A11.41)

The services listed are subject to a "reverse charge" under s. 7 when purchased for business purposes from an overseas trader by a person who belongs in the U.K., and are zero-rated under Sch. 5, Group 9, Items 5 and 6 (*a*) when supplied to certain persons who belong outside the U.K. For "financial services", see *Singer & Friedlander Ltd.* v. *C. & E. Comrs.* [1989] VATTR 27, [1989] 1 CMLR 814. For "means of transport", see *Knut Hamann* v. *Finanzamt Hamburg-Eimsbüttel* (case 51/88) [1990] 2 CMLR 383, ECJ.

SCHEDULE 4 VALUATION—SPECIAL CASES (Sections 10 (6) and 11 (4))

1.—(A8.15) If a person makes a supply at less than open market value to a partially exempt business connected as defined in TA 1970, s. 533 (now TA 1988, s. 839) the Commissioners may direct, by giving notice within three years of the time of supply, that the open market value should be used. See *Oughtred & Harrison Ltd.* v. *C. & E. Comrs.* [1988] VATTR 140.

2.—(A8.62) If a person imports goods at less than market value from a connected person, the Commissioners can issue a direction that open market value is to apply.

3.—(A8.16) If a business sells goods to others who are not VAT registered and the goods will be resold to the public, the Commissioners may direct that the retail open market value of the goods is to be treated as the value of the supplies. For discounts for prompt payment, see *Gold Star Publications Ltd.* v. *C. & E. Comrs.* LON/89/770 unreported. The vires of U.K. legislation was upheld in *Direct Cosmetics Ltd. & Laughtons Photographs Ltd.* v. *C. & E. Comrs.* (joined cases 138 and 139/86) [1988] STC 540, ECJ. For directions upheld, see *Direct Cosmetics Ltd.* v. *C. & E. Comrs.* LON/35/377 unreported; *Moore* v. *C. & E. Comrs.* LON/89/441 unreported.

4, 5.—(A8.06, 51) The value for VAT of goods or services is reduced by the amount of a cash discount offered for prompt payment, whether the discount is taken or not. The value of imported goods is similarly reduced. See *Gold Star Publications Ltd.* v. *C. & E. Comrs.* LON/89/770 unreported.

6.—(A8.24) The face value of a stamp, token or voucher which can be exchanged for goods or services is disregarded for VAT purposes.

For the redemption of stamps, tokens and vouchers, see VATA 1983 s. 3.

7.—(A6.11, 42, 43, 51) The following supplies are valued at cost: (1) goods self-supplied by orders made under s. 3 (5), *i.e.* motor cars and stationery; (2) goods transferred or disposed of without consideration under Sch. 2, para. 5 (1); (3) goods held at deregistration deemed to be supplied under Sch. 2, para. 7. By concession, goods other than stock can be valued at "the price you would expect to have to pay for them in their present condition" for the purposes of (3) (see Leaflet No. 700/11/88 para. 7; *Mendes* v. *C. & E. Comrs.* LON/81/259 unreported).

8.—(A6.12, 16) The following services are valued at the full cost of providing them: (1) services performed without consideration brought within the scope of VAT by order made under s. 3 (4) (no orders have been made); (2) goods used for non-business purposes without consideration under Sch. 2, para. 5 (3). For the basis of valuation, see *Teknequip Ltd.* v. *C. & E. Comrs.* [1987] STC 664.

9.—(A8.21) Where accommodation is supplied in a hotel, boarding house or a similar establishment to an individual for a period exceeding four weeks, the value of the supply may be reduced so that VAT is charged only on the element attributable to facilities. The value of facilities cannot be less than 20 per cent. See *Prior* v. *C. & E. Comrs.* LON/85/417 unreported.

10.—(A8.22, 23) An employer who supplies food, beverages or accommodation to employees has to account for VAT only where there is a money consideration, otherwise the value for VAT is nil. See *Goodfellow (a firm)* v. *C. & E. Comrs.* [1986] VATTR 119.

11.—(A8.07, 51) When a sum is expressed in a currency other than sterling it should be converted using E.C. customs valuation rules, *i.e.* Commission Regulation (EEC) No. 1766/85 of 27 June 1985. The Commissioners publish rates of exchange under this provision on a weekly basis.

12.—(A8.03) Regulations may be made which require payments made by third parties to a transaction to be included in the value of the supply. So far none have been made.

13.—(A8.15, 16, 62) The Commissioners may by written notice vary or withdraw a direction given under para. 1, 2 or 3.

SCHEDULE 5 ZERO-RATING (Section 16)

GROUP 1—FOOD (A11.21, 26, 27)

The provisions in this group are widely drawn to zero-rate food for human consumption, animal feeding stuffs, seeds for such food or feeding stuffs, and live animals used as or yielding food for humans. There are two main exceptions where standard rating for VAT applies: a supply of food in the course of catering (this includes food for consumption on the premises, and hot food takeaways), and non-essential items of diet (broadly comprising specified frozen products, confectionery, alcoholic beverages, non-alcoholic beverages, savoury food products, animal foods and home brew kits).

For "food", see *Soni* v. *C. & E. Comrs.* [1980] VATTR 9; *Marfleet Refining Co. Ltd* v. *C. & E. Comrs.* [1974] VATTR 289; *Ayurueda Ltd.* v. *C. & E. Comrs.* LON/88/1372 unreported.

For "animal feeding stuffs", see *Smith* v. *C. & E. Comrs.* MAN/87/321 unreported; *Chapman & Frearson Ltd.* v. *C. & E. Comrs.* MAN/88/618 unreported.

For "live animals", see *C. & E. Comrs.* v. *Lawson-Tancred* [1988] STC 326; *Chalmers* v. *C. & E. Comrs.* LON/82/99 unreported.

For the nature of a "supply in the course of catering", see *C. & E. Comrs.* v. *Cope* [1981] STC 532; *DCA Industries Ltd.* v. *C. & E. Comrs.* [1983] VATTR 317. For food consumed in the grounds of a café, snack-bar, etc., see *Ivy Café Ltd.* v. *C. & E. Comrs.* MAN/76/73 unreported. For sales from kiosks, etc., see *C. & E. Comrs.* v. *Cope* [1981] STC 532; *R.* v. *C. & E. Comrs. ex parte Sims* [1988] STC 210; *DCA Industries Ltd.* v. *C. & E. Comrs.* [1983] VATTR 317; *Armstrong* v. *C. & E. Comrs.* [1984] VATTR 53; *Crownlion (Seafood) Ltd.* v. *C. & E. Comrs.* [1985] VATTR 188; *Bristol City Football Supporters Club* v. *C. & E. Comrs.* [1975] VATTR 93; *Mylo's of Reading (Catering and Ices) Ltd.* v. *C. & E. Comrs.* LON/86/575 unreported; *Ashby Catering Ltd.* v. *C. & E. Comrs.* MAN/89/144, 426 unreported. For mobile vans, see *James* v. *C. & E. Comrs.* [1977] VATTR 155; *Spragg* v. *C. & E. Comrs.* [1977] VATTR 162; *Cooper* v. *C. & E. Comrs.* MAN/87/269 unreported. For door-to-door salesmen, see *Mowbray* v. *C. & E. Comrs.* [1986] VATTR 266; *Cooper* v. *C. & E. Comrs.* MAN/87/269 unreported; *Zeldaline Ltd.* v. *C. & E. Comrs.* LON/89/87 unreported. For delivery of meals, see *Maheboob Refreshment House* v. *C. & E. Comrs.* LON/83/259 unreported; *Levy* v. *C. & E. Comrs.* LON/85/297 unreported; *C. Chasney Ltd.* v. *C. & E. Comrs.* LON/88/1375 unreported. For vending machines, see *Macklin Services (Vending) West Ltd.* v. *C. & E. Comrs.* [1979] VATTR 31; *Streamline Taxis (Southampton) Ltd.* v. *C. & E. Comrs.* LON/85/499 unreported. For hot take-away food, see *John Pimblett & Sons Ltd.* v. *C. & E. Comrs.* [1988] STC 358, CA; *Redhead* v. *C. & E. Comrs.* MAN/87/321 unreported. For the exemption of catering in schools, hospitals, etc., see Sch. 6 Groups 6 and 7.

For "confectionery", see *Adams Foods Ltd.* v. *C. & E. Comrs.* [1983] VATTR 280; *North Cheshire Foods Ltd.* v. *C. & E. Comrs.* MAN/86/216 unreported; *UB (Biscuits) Ltd.* v. *C. & E. Comrs.* LON/85/560 unreported; *W. Jordans (Cereals) Ltd.* v. *C. & E. Comrs.* LON/88/514 unreported.

For "cakes", see *Marks and Spencer plc.* v. *C. & E. Comrs.* LON/88/1316 unreported.

For the nature of "pet food", see *Popes Lane Pet Food Supplies Ltd.* v. *C. & E. Comrs.* [1986] VATTR 221; *Normans Riding Poultry Farm Ltd.* v. *C. & E. Comrs.* MAN/88/413 unreported.

For apportionment of consideration, see *C. & E. Comrs.* v. *Scott* [1978] STC 191 and *C. & E. Comrs.* v. *Bushby* [1979] STC 8 (stabling horses); *Cheshire Mushroom Farm* v. *C. & E. Comrs.* [1974] VATTR 87 (mushroom-growing kit); *Smiths Foods Ltd.* v. *C. & E. Comrs.* [1983] VATTR 21 (fruit and nut mixture); *British Airways plc.* v. *C. & E. Comrs.* [1989] STC 182 (in-flight catering); *Hermolis & Co. Ltd.* v. *C. & E. Comrs.* LON/88/1429 unreported (meal pack).

GROUP 2—SEWERAGE SERVICES AND WATER (A11.71)

The following are zero-rated: (1) disposal or treatment of foul water or sewerage; (2) emptying domestic cesspools, septic tanks, etc; and (3) domestic water supply. Pure waters (*e.g.* distilled and deionised water) and bottled waters are excluded from zero-rating. For water, see *Scott-Morley* v. *C. & E. Comrs.* LON/80/297 unreported. For supplies made by a launderette, see *Mander Laundries Ltd.* v. *C. & E. Comrs.* [1973] VATTR 136.

GROUP 3—BOOKS, ETC. (A11.73)

The supply of books, newspapers, periodicals, music and maps including the services of lending libraries are all zero-rated. Commercial plans and drawings are, however, standard-rated.

For "books, booklets, brochures, pamphlets and leaflets", see *W. F. Graham (Northampton) Ltd.* v. *C. & E. Comrs.* LON/79/332 unreported (children's cut-out book); *Cronsvale Ltd.* v. *C. & E. Comrs.* [1983] VATTR 313 (leaflet); *Pace Group (Communications) Ltd.* v. *C. & E. Comrs.* MAN/77/210 (pamphlet, brochure); *Evans & Marland Ltd.* v. *C. & E. Comrs.* [1988] VATTR 125 (betting guide); *A. E. Walker Ltd.* v. *C. & E. Comrs.* [1973] VATTR 8, *Butler & Tanner Ltd.* v. *C. & E. Comrs.* [1974] VATTR 72 and *GUS Catalogue Order Ltd.* v. *C. & E. Comrs.* MAN/87/352 (bound and unbound book signatures).

For "newspapers, journals and periodicals", see *Geoffrey E. Snushall (a firm)* v. *C. & E. Comrs.* [1982] STC 537 (monthly property guide); *Stillwell Darby & Co. Ltd.* v. *C. & E. Comrs.* [1973] VATTR 145 (theatre programme); *Rochdale Hornets Football Club Co. Ltd.* v. *C. & E. Comrs.* [1975] VATTR 71 (admission programme); *Evans & Marland Ltd.* v. *C. & E. Comrs.* [1988] VATTR 125 (betting guide).

For "maps, charts and topographical plans", see *Brooks Histograph Ltd.* v. *C. & E. Comrs.* [1984] VATTR 46.

GROUP 4—TALKING BOOKS FOR THE BLIND AND HANDICAPPED AND WIRELESS SETS FOR THE BLIND (A11.62)

The supply to the Royal National Institute for the Blind or other similar charities (whether by sale or lease) of equipment for recording, duplicating or playback of speech for the blind or severely handicapped is zero-rated. So also is the supply to a charity of wireless receiving sets or equipment used to record and playback sound on tape cassettes lent free of charge to blind persons.

GROUP 5—NEWSPAPER ADVERTISEMENTS

Repealed with effect from 1 May 1985.

GROUP 6—NEWS SERVICES (A11.75)

Repealed with effect from 1 April 1989.

GROUP 7—FUEL AND POWER FOR DOMESTIC OR CHARITY USE (A11.77)

The following are zero-rated when supplied for domestic use or for non-business use by a charity: (1) solid substances held out for sale solely as fuel (including coal, coke and fire-lighters, but not matches chargeable with excise duty); (2) coal gas, water gas, producer gases or similar gases (but not road fuel gas chargeable with excise duty); (3) gaseous hydrocarbons (including petroleum gases, but not road fuel gas chargeable with excise duty); (4) heavy hydrocarbon oils in the form of fuel oil, gas oil or kerosene (as defined in Notes 11–14), but not hydrocarbon oil unrelieved from excise duty; and (5) electricity, heat or air-conditioning.

The units of measure listed in Note 2 are always supplied for domestic use. Other units of measure are supplied for domestic use only if supplied for use in: (1) a dwelling; (2) a building used for one of the purposes listed in Note 4; (3) self-catering holiday accommodation, including accommodation advertised or held out as such; (4) a caravan; or (5) a houseboat (as defined in Note 6).

The whole supply is deemed to be supplied for zero-rated use if at least 60 per cent. is supplied for that use. An apportionment is made in other cases.

For coin meters, see *Mander Laundries Ltd.* v. *C. & E. Comrs.* [1973] VATTR 136; *St. Annes on Sea Lawn Tennis Club Ltd.* v. *C. & E. Comrs.* [1977] VATTR 229; *Dyrham Park Country Club Ltd.* v. *C. & E. Comrs.* [1978] VATTR 244; *High Wycombe Squash Club Ltd.* v. *C. & E. Comrs.* [1976] VATTR 156. For rents inclusive of gas, electricity, etc., see, for example, *CMC (Preston) Ltd.* v. *C. & E. Comrs.* MAN/88/78 unreported.

GROUP 8—CONSTRUCTION OF BUILDINGS, ETC. (A11.33, 36, 37, 40)

Item 1
A person who has constructed a building makes a zero-rated supply if he sells the freehold or leases

the building for a term exceeding 21 years. One of the following conditions must be met: (1) the building is designed as one or more dwellings (including garage accommodation) and the purchaser is lawfully entitled to reside there throughout the year; (2) the purchaser certifies that he intends to use the building solely as a community home; or (3) the purchaser, being a charity, certifies that the building will be used solely for non-business purposes or as a community centre. For buildings which do not meet these conditions see VATA 1983, Sch. 5 Group 8A, Sch. 6, Group 1 and Sch. 6A, para. 1; FA 1989, Sch. 3, para. 13 (1)–(3).

"Grant" includes an assignment. For the person making a grant, see *Monsell Youell Developments Ltd.* v. *C. & E. Comrs.* [1978] VATTR 1; *Hulme Trust Educational Foundation* v. *C. & E. Comrs.* [1978] VATTR 179 and Sch. 6A, para. 7.

A person has not constructed a building if he merely carried out works to an existing building. For partly constructed buildings, see *Stapenhill Developments Ltd.* v. *C. & E. Comrs.* [1984] VATTR 1.

Item 2
A supply of services (other than the services of an architect, surveyor, consultant or supervisor, or the hire of goods) is zero-rated if made in the course of carrying out one of the following works: (1) constructing a building designed as one or more dwellings (including garage accommodation); (2) constructing a building for a person who certifies that he intends to use it solely as a community home; (3) constructing a building for a charity which certifies that the building is to be used solely for non-business purposes or as a community centre; or (4) civil engineering works in constructing a permanent park for residential caravans (*i.e.* caravans which can be lawfully used as a residence throughout the year). For works outside these descriptions, see VATA 1983, Sch. 5, Group 8A, 9, 14; FA 1989, Sch. 3, para. 13 (1), (4).

"Construction" does not include: (1) the conversion, reconstruction, alteration or enlargement of an existing building; (2) constructing an extension or annex with internal access to an existing building or (see *C. G. Franklin & Sons Ltd.* v. *C. & E. Comrs.* LON/89/431 unreported); (3) constructing an extension or annex which cannot be separately used, let or disposed of. For "conversion", see *Smith* v. *C. & E. Comrs.* MAN/85/353 unreported; *Bucher* v. *C. & E. Comrs.* LON/85/186 unreported; *St. Andrews Building Co. Ltd* v. *C. & E. Comrs.* EDN/86/12 unreported. For "reconstruction", see *Wimpey Group Services Ltd.* v. *C. & E. Comrs.* [1988] STC 625, CA. For "enlargement", see *C. & E. Comrs.* v. *Great Shelford Free Church (Baptist)* [1987] STC 249 (following which the legislation was amended); *Dale Painting Contractors Newport Ltd.* v. *C. & E. Comrs.* LON/87/288 unreported; *John Rees (Builders) Ltd.* v. *C. & E. Comrs.* LON/86/100 unreported. For the relevance of planning permission, see *C. & E. Comrs.* v. *Perry* [1983] STC 383; *Marath Developments Ltd.* v. *C. & E. Comrs.* MAN/87/35 unreported; *Waterways Services* v. *C. & E. Comrs.* LON/89/1055 unreported.

For "building", see *Walle* v. *C. & E. Comrs.* [1976] VATTR 101.

For "civil engineering work", see *GKN Birwelco Ltd.* v. *C. & E. Comrs.* [1983] VATTR 128; *UDF Ltd.* v. *C. & E. Comrs.* [1981] VATTR 199.

Item 3
The supply of goods to a person is zero-rated if: (1) the supplier makes a zero-rated supply of services to the same person; (2) the services include use or installation of the goods; and (3) the goods comprise materials (but not materials for the construction of fitted furniture other than kitchen furniture), builders hardware, sanitary ware, or other articles of a kind ordinarily installed by builders as fixtures. These descriptions do not include finished or prefabricated furniture (other than furniture designed to be fitted in kitchens), domestic electrical or gas appliances (other than appliances designed to provide space and/or water heating), carpets or carpeting materials.

For "materials", see *C. & E. Comrs.* v. *Smitmit Design Centre Ltd.* [1982] STC 525; *John Turner and Smith Ltd.* v. *C. & E. Comrs.* MAN/74/23 unreported.

For "articles of a kind ordinarily installed by builders as fixtures", see *C. & E. Comrs.* v. *Smitmit Design Centre Ltd.* [1982] STC 525; *British Airports Authority* v. *C. & E. Comrs.* LON/77/144 unreported; *University of Reading* v. *C. & E. Comrs.* LON/89/235 unreported (telephone exchange); Press Notice 1108, 2 May 1986.

For "domestic appliances", see *Garndene Communication Systems Ltd.* v. *C. & E. Comrs.* MAN/86/373 unreported; *Frank Haslam Milan & Co. Ltd.* v. *C. & E. Comrs.* MAN/87/89 unreported.

GROUP 8A—PROTECTED BUILDINGS (A11.34, 38)

Item 1
Where a person who has substantially reconstructed a protected building sells all or any part of the building or its site, or grants a lease for a term exceeding 21 years, the supply is zero-rated. See *Barraclough* v. *C. & E. Comrs.* LON/86/699 unreported.

A "protected building" is a listed building or scheduled monument in respect of which one of the following conditions is met: (1) the building is designed to remain as, or become, one or more dwellings (including garage accommodation) and the purchaser is lawfully entitled to reside there throughout the year; (2) the purchaser certifies that he intends to use the building solely as a community home; or (3) the purchaser, being a charity, certifies that the building will be used solely for non-business purposes or as a community centre. For buildings which do not meet these conditions, see VATA 1983, Sch. 6, Group 1; FA 1989, Sch. 3, para. 13 (1)–(3).

A protected building is regarded as substantially reconstructed if either of the following conditions is met:

(*a*) the works of reconstruction form 60 per cent. of the cost and are such that if supplied by a taxable person they would be zero-rated as approved alterations of a protected building, or

(*b*) the reconstructed building incorporates no more of the original building than the external walls, together with other external features of interest.

Item 2

When a person supplies services (other than those of an architect, surveyor or consultant) during an approved alteration then the supplies are zero-rated.

An approved alteration is any alteration to an ecclesiastical building except any minister's residence or any other alteration which would require authorisation under the Town and Country Planning Act 1971, Pt. IV or its equivalent, or the Ancient Monuments and Archaelogical Areas Act 1979, Pt. I. See *Evans* v. *C. & E. Comrs*. MAN/88/587 unreported. Constructing a separate building within the curtilage of a protected building does not amount to an approved alteration. Where there is an element of repair or maintenance in addition to an approved alteration, the total should be apportioned to determine how much should be zero-rated.

For goods supplied with approved alteration services, see Group 8, Item 3 above.

GROUP 9—INTERNATIONAL SERVICES (A11.41)

The following supplies are zero-rated.

Item 1

Services relating to land situated outside the U.K. This includes services supplied by estate agents, auctioneers, architects and surveyors and the construction, alteration, repair, maintenance or demolition of any building. However, item 1 does not include services specified in Sch. 3, such as those of lawyers, engineers and consultants: see items 5 (E.C.) and 6 (outside E.C.). For "land", see *Brodrick, Wright & Strong Ltd.* v. *C. & E. Comrs*. LON/86/461 unreported.

Item 2

Hiring of any means of transport for use outside of the E.C. which are either exported by the lessor or already outside the Community. For "means of transport", see *Knut Hamann* v. *Finanzamt Hamburg-Eimsbüttel* (case 51/88) [1990] 2 CMLR 383, ECJ.

Item 3

The supply of cultural, artistic, sporting, scientific, educational or entertainment services or exhibition services or services ancillary thereto including organising the performance outside the U.K. of these services, which are performed abroad. See *Patrick Eddery Ltd.* v. *C. & E. Comrs*. [1986] VATTR 30 (jockey's services).

Item 4

Valuing or carrying out work on goods situated abroad where the services are performed abroad.

Item 5

The supply to a business belonging to the E.C. of any of the services mentioned in Sch. 3.

Item 6

The supply to any person outside the E.C. of:

(*a*) the services mentioned in Sch. 3 other than insurance services and dealings with certificates of deposit;

(*b*) insurance by an authorised U.K. insurer of anything but marine-aviation-transport insurance;

(*c*) reinsurance by an authorised U.K. insurer of anything but marine-aviation-transport insurance;

(*d*) services related to insurance or reinsurance zero-rated by this item.

Item 6 does not include most services in Sch. 6 (exemptions) but does include Group 2 (insurance) and Group 5 (finance).

Item 7

The supply of marine-aviation transport insurance by an authorised U.K. insurer in connection with the carriage of passengers or goods to or from a place outside the E.C., and services associated with providing the insurance and handling of claims.

Item 8

The supply by the Export Credits Guarantee Department of insurance against risks in making advances or credits in connection with goods exported outside the E.C., and services associated with providing the insurance and handling of claims.

Item 9

The supply of finance services including dealing with money, security for money, making any advance, granting credit, or hire purchase, conditional sale or credit sale facilities, providing administration and documentation for the transfer of title to goods for a consideration of £10 or less and making arrangements for any of these transactions when such services are in connection with either the export of specific goods or the transhipment of goods with an ultimate destination outside the E.C.

Item 10

The supply of services to a person who belongs outside the U.K. of work on goods which are imported into the U.K. or are acquired within the U.K. for the work to be done and are then actually exported from the U.K. See *Banstead Manor Stud Farm Ltd.* v. *C. & E. Comrs.* [1979] VATTR 154 (stallion covering mare).

Item 11

The supply of services by a person in obtaining for another an export of goods, or any of the supplies in items 1, 2, 3, 4, 5, 6, or 10 or any supply of goods or services made outside the U.K. The services of a travel agent are not zero-rated when they relate to a holiday or journey in the E.C.

GROUP 10—TRANSPORT (A11.51)

The following supplies are zero-rated.

Item 1

The supply (including hire or charter), maintenance or repair of any ship having a gross tonnage exceeding 15 tons which is not designed or adapted for recreation or pleasure use. Charter services are excluded from zero-rating if they wholly comprise one or more of the following services performed in the U.K.: (1) transport of passengers; (2) accommodation; (3) entertainment; or (4) education. For passenger transport, see item 4. For educational services, see Group 9 Item 3.

Item 2

The supply (including hire or charter), maintenance or repair of any aircraft weighing more than 8,000 kg. which is not designed or adapted for recreation or pleasure use. Charter services are excluded from zero-rating if they wholly comprise one or more of the following services performed in the U.K.: (1) transport of passengers; (2) accommodation; (3) entertainment; or (4) education. For passenger transport, see item 4. For educational services, see Group 9 Item 3.

Item 3

The supply (including hire), repair or maintenance of sea rescue vessels and launching and recovery equipment for them; and the construction, alteration, repair or maintenance of slipways for the sole use of such vessels. The supply must be made to a sea-rescue charity. The charity must give a certificate stating that the supply is zero-rated.

Item 4

Transport of passengers: (1) in any vehicle which carries twelve or more passengers; (2) by the Post Office; (3) on any schedule flight; or (4) to or from the U.K. (provided the supply is made in the U.K.). For the application of this item to designated travel services, see VAT (Tour Operators) Order 1987, S.I. 1987 No. 1806 art 10 (1), (1A). "Transport" involves movement from one place to another for some purpose: compare *C. & E. Comrs.* v. *Blackpool Pleasure Beach Co.* [1974] STC 134 (ride on "Big Dipper") and *Quarry Tours Ltd.* v. *C. & E. Comrs.* [1984] VATTR 238. For "vehicle", see *Llandudno Cabinlift Co. Ltd.* v. *C. & E. Comrs.* [1973] VATTR 1; *Quarry Tours Ltd.* v. *C. & E. Comrs.* [1984] VATTR 238. For student travel cards, see *British Railways Board* v. *C. & E. Comrs.* [1977] STC 221, CA. For apportionment of the transport element of a river cruise, see *River Barge Holidays Ltd.* v. *C. & E. Comrs.* LON/77/345 unreported.

Item 5

Transporting freight outside the U.K. or to or from a place outside the U.K. See *Baxter-Martin* v. *C. & E. Comrs.* LON/73/108 unreported; *Bevington* v. *C. & E. Comrs.* LON/76/85 unreported.

Item 6

The handling of ships and aircraft in any port or customs and excise airport, or overseas, and the handling or storage of transported goods in any port or customs and excise airport or on adjacent land. This item excludes the hire of goods. This item also excludes pleasure ships or aircraft and those of less than 15 tons or 8,000 kg. respectively.

Item 7
Pilotage services.

Item 8
Salvage or towage services.

Item 9
The surveying or classification of any ship or aircraft for the purpose of any register, other than of pleasure ships or aircraft of less than 15 tons or 8,000 kg. respectively.

Item 10
The services of agents in obtaining space in any ship or aircraft, other than pleasure ships or aircraft or those of less than 15 tons or 8,000 kg. respectively or any services mentioned in items 1 to 9, 11 and 12.

Item 11
Services performed outside the U.K. in connection with the transport of goods.

Item 12
The supply to a business which belongs outside the U.K. of the following services: handling or storing goods at, or transporting them to or from, the place of import or export, the survey of any ship or aircraft or making arrangement for space on any ship or aircraft. This item includes pleasure ships and aircraft and those of less than 15 tons or 8,000 kg. respectively.

Item 13
Supplying a designated travel service for enjoyment outside the E.C.

GROUP 11—CARAVANS AND HOUSEBOATS (A11.79)

The following supplies are zero-rated.

Item 1
Caravans that cannot be towed on roads by a vehicle of less than 2,030 kg.

Item 2
Houseboats not having a means of self-propulsion designed or adapted for use as places of permanent habitation.

Item 3
The hire or loan of caravans within item 1 or houseboats within item 2, other than as accommodation.

GROUP 12—GOLD (A11.81)

The supply of gold held in the U.K. by a Central Bank to another Central Bank or to a member of the London Gold Market or by such a member to a Central Bank is zero-rated. Gold coins and options are included.

GROUP 13—BANK NOTES (A11.83)

The issue by a bank of a bank note is zero-rated.

GROUP 14—DRUGS, MEDICINES, AIDS FOR THE HANDICAPPED, ETC. (A11.85)

The following supplies are zero-rated.

Item 1
The supply of goods dispensed by a registered pharmacist on a prescription issued by a registered medical practitioner or dentist.

Item 2
The supply of medical, surgical or other appliances including parts designed solely for the relief of

severe abnormality, adjustable beds designed for invalids, sanitary appliances, lifts designed for use with invalid wheelchairs, hoists, lifters and equipment, permanently adapted wheelchair or stretcher-carrying motor vehicles. The supply must be to a handicapped person for domestic or personal use or to a charity to make available to such a person. For "other appliances and equipment", see *Princess Louise Scottish Hospital* v. *C. & E. Comrs.* [1983] VATTR 191; *Hobden* v. *C. & E. Comrs.* LON/85/52 unreported; *Kirton Designs Ltd.* v. *C. & E. Comrs.* LON/86/641 unreported.

Item 3
The supply to a handicapped person of services of adapting goods to suit his purposes.

Item 4
The supply to a charity of services of adapting goods to suit the purposes of a handicapped person.
   Where goods are adapted prior to supply, an apportionment of value is required to find out how much should be zero-rated.

Item 5
The repair or maintenance of any goods specified in items 2, 6, 15 or 16 supplied as described.

Item 6
The supply of goods in connection with a supply described in items 3, 4 or 5.

Item 7
Installation of equipment when supplied to a handicapped person or to a charity.

Item 8
Building ramps or widening doorways within the private residence of a handicapped person.

Item 9
The supply to a charity of any supply mentioned in item 8.

Item 10
The supply to a handicapped person of a service of providing, extending or adapting a bathroom or lavatory in a private residence where such provision is necessary by reason of his condition. See *Strachan* v. *C. & E. Comrs.* MAN/86/155 unreported.

Item 10A
The supply to a charity of a service of providing, extending or adapting a bathroom or lavatory for use by handicapped persons in a residential home. See *Mid Derbyshire Cheshire Home* v. *C. & E. Comrs.* MAN/89/546 unreported.

Item 11
Goods supplied in connection with items 8, 9, 10 or 10A.

Item 12
The hire of a motor vehicle for three years to a person in receipt of a mobility allowance where the lessor's business is predominantly the provision of motor vehicles to such persons.

Item 13
The installation of a lift to facilitate movement between floors within the private residence of a handicapped person. See *Brian Perkins & Co. Ltd.* v. *C. & E. Comrs.* LON/88/952 unreported.

Item 14
The supply of a lift to a charity providing day care facilities for handicapped persons.

Item 15
Goods supplied in connection with items 13 or 14.

Item 16
The supply to a handicapped person or to a charity of an alarm system.

Item 17
The supply of services performed by a control centre responding to calls from an alarm as described in item 16.

GROUP 15—IMPORTS, EXPORTS ETC. **(A11.87)**

The following supplies are zero-rated.

Item 1
Imported goods supplied before a customs entry is made by the purchaser.

Item 2
Goods or services supplied to or by an overseas authority participating in an international collaborative defence project.

Item 3
The supply to an overseas authority, body or trader of jigs, patterns, templates, dies, punches and similar machine tools used in the U.K. solely to make goods for export. This provision relieves the overseas authority, body or trader from the need to register for VAT and reclaim the VAT which would normally be incurred on the transfer of such equipment.

GROUP 16—CHARITIES, ETC. **(A11.66)**

The following supplies are zero-rated.

Item 1
The supply of donated goods by: (1) a charity established to relieve poverty, carry out medical research, care for ill or disabled persons, or protect animals; or (2) a trader who covenants his profits to such a charity. The goods must be donated to the charity or trader for resale.

Item 2
The donation of goods to a charity or trader described in Item 1. The goods must be donated for the purposes of sale or export by the charity or trader.

Item 3
The export of goods by a charity.

Item 4
A supply of relevant goods for donation to a nominated health authority or non-profit-making hospital or research institution, or a charitable institution providing rescue or first aid services. The goods must be purchased with funds provided either by a charity or from voluntary contributions. If the donee is not a charity it must not have contributed to the purchase of the goods. "Relevant goods" are medical, scientific, computer, video, sterilising, laboratory or refrigeration equipment and parts for use in medical research, diagnosis, training or treatment; ambulances and parts; appliances and equipment within Group 14, Item 2; adapted vehicles; and equipment used in rescue or first aid operations.

Item 5
The supply of goods mentioned in item 4 directly to a provider of help mentioned in item 4 where the goods are funded from charitable or voluntary contributions. Also the supply of item 4 goods to a charitable supplier of care or medical or surgical treatment to handicapped persons.

Item 6
The repair or maintenance of the above goods where the goods are owned by the bodies mentioned in items 4 and 5 paid for from charitable sources.

Item 7
The supply of goods in connection with the repair of goods in items 4 and 5 paid for from charitable sources.

Item 8
The supply to a charity of: (1) an advertisement which is for raising money or publicising the object of the charity; or (2) goods or services relating to the preparation of such an advertisement.

Item 9
The supply of any medicinal product used by a charity engaged in medical research or care of humans or animals.

Item 10
The supply to a charity of a substance directly used for synthesis or testing in the course of medical research.

GROUP 17—CLOTHING AND FOOTWEAR (A11.89)

The following supplies are zero-rated.

Item 1
Young children's clothing and footwear not suitable for older persons. There are numerous problems in identifying what is children's wear as opposed to that suitable for a small adult. The Commissioners publish size guides; they also consider that the way in which the goods are held out for sale is relevant. Children's sizes held out for purchase by adults are standard-rated. See *Jeffrey Green & Co. Ltd.* v. *C. & E. Comrs.* [1974] VATTR 94; *Walter Stewart Ltd.* v. *C. & E. Comrs.* [1974] VATTR 131.

Item 2
Protective boots and helmets for industrial use, provided they are not supplied to a trader for use by his employees.

Item 3
Protective helmets worn by motor cycle riders.

SCHEDULE 6 EXEMPTIONS (Sections 7 and 17)

GROUP 1—LAND (A9.11–13)

Granting an interest in land, a right over land or a licence to occupy land is exempt. "Grant" includes an assignment to someone other than the person to whom an interest could be surrendered. See also VATA 1983, Sch. 6A, para. 7. For interests and rights, see *Trewby* v. *C. & E. Comrs.* [1976] STC 122; *Rochdale Hornets Football Club Co. Ltd.* v. *C. & E. Comrs.* [1975] VATTR 71. For licences to occupy land, see in particular *Henley Picture House Ltd.* v. *C. & E. Comrs.* BIR/79/107 unreported; *Tameside Metropolitan Borough Council* v. *C. & E. Comrs.* [1979] VATTR 93; *South Glamorgan County Council* v. *C. & E. Comrs.* LON/84/485 unreported; *Bullimore* v. *C. & E. Comrs.* MAN/86/145 unreported.
   The following grants are excluded from exemption and are chargeable to tax at the standard rate:
   (a) the freehold of a building or civil engineering work prior to completion or within three years after completion unless, in the case of a building, it qualifies for zero-rating;
   (b) rights to take game and fish (the consideration for a freehold, lease, etc. is apportioned if it includes a valuable right to take game or fish);
   (c) sleeping and catering accommodation in a hotel, inn, boarding house etc. or service flat (see *Swindon Masonic Association Ltd.* v. *C. & E. Comrs.* [1978] VATTR 200; *McMurray, Governor of Allen Hall* v. *C. & E. Comrs.* [1973] VATTR 161; *Namecourt Ltd.* v. *C. & E. Comrs.* [1984] VATTR 22; *The Lord Mayor and Citizens of the City of Westminster* v. *C. & E. Comrs.* [1990] 2 CMLR 81; *McGrath* v. *C. & E. Comrs.* MAN/88/87 unreported);
   (d) holiday accommodation in a house, flat, caravan, houseboat or tent, including accommodation held out as such (see *Sheppard* v. *C. & E. Comrs.* [1977] VATTR 272; *American Real Estate (Scotland) Ltd.* v. *C. & E. Comrs.* [1980] VATTR 88; *Cretney (a firm)* v. *C. & E. Comrs.* [1983] VATTR 271);
   (e) seasonal caravan pitches and facilities in connection with them;
   (f) pitches for tents and camping facilities;
   (g) facilities for parking a vehicle (see *Wilson* v. *C. & E. Comrs.* [1977] VATTR 225; *Dowse* v. *C. & E. Comrs.* LON/73/102 unreported);
   (h) rights to fell and remove standing timber;
   (i) housing or storing aircraft and mooring or storing vessels (see *Strand Ship Building Co. Ltd.* v. *C. & E. Comrs.* LON/84/74 unreported);
   (j) rights to occupy accommodation at a place of entertainment;
   (k) facilities for playing sport or taking part in physical recreation, unless the grant is for a continuous period exceeding 24 hours or a series of 10 or more sessions granted to a school, club, association etc. (see *Queen's Park Football Club Ltd.* v. *C. & E. Comrs.* [1988] VATTR 76 and Press Notice No. 72/88, 20 September 1988).
   For the election to waive exemption in respect of grants otherwise exempt under this Group, see VATA 1983, Sch. 6A, para. 2. For the zero-rating of certain freehold and leasehold interests, see VATA 1983, Sch. 5, Groups 8 and 8A. For apportionment of rents in serviced accommodation, see *Business Enterprises (U.K.) Ltd.* v. *C. & E. Comrs.* [1988] VATTR 160 and VATA 1983 Sch. 5 Group 7.

GROUP 2—INSURANCE (A9.16)

The following supplies are exempt. (For the zero-rating of international insurance, see Sch. 5, Group 9, Item 7).

Item 1
The supply of insurance or reinsurance by a person authorised by the Department of Trade to conduct such business. See *John E. Buck & Co. Ltd.* v. *C. & E. Comrs.* LON/83/208 unreported.

Item 2
The supply of insurance or reinsurance by the Export Credits Guarantee Department.

Item 3
Arranging for insurance to be provided by persons in items 1 and 2. The services of insurance brokers and agents fall into this category: see *Company Moves* v. *C. & E. Comrs.* LON/89/977 unreported. For other persons actively concerned in the arrangements, see *Ford* v. *C. & E. Comrs.* [1987] VATTR 130 and ICAEW TR 787, 15 March 1990. Mere publicity services are insufficient: *Dogbreeders Associates* v. *C. & E. Comrs.* LON/89/313 unreported.

Item 4
The handling of claims by brokers and agents and by insurers. This does not include the services of loss and average adjusters, motor assessors and legal srevices incurred in connection with a claim.

GROUP 3—POSTAL SERVICES (A9.21)

The following supplies are exempt.

Item 1
The conveyance of postal packets by the Post Office.

Item 2
The supply of services by the Post Office in connection with the conveyance of postal packets.
   Item 2 does not include the letting on hire of goods so the hiring fee for franking machines is standard-rated.

GROUP 4—BETTING, GAMING AND LOTTERIES (A9.26)

The following supplies are exempt.

Item 1
The provision of facilities for placing bets, or playing games of chance. See *J. Seven Ltd.* v. *C. & E. Comrs.* [1986] VATTR 42; *Grantham (a firm)* v. *C. & E. Comrs.* MAN/79/102 unreported. However admission charges, session and participation charges levied at premises which are licensed, or registered under the Gaming Act 1968, Pt. II, or regulations under the Betting, Gaming, Lotteries and Amusements (Northern Ireland) Order 1985, Art. 76, the provision by a club of gaming facilities for a subscription and the provision of a gaming machine are standard-rated for VAT. See *Rum Runner Casino Ltd.* v. *C. & E. Comrs.* MAN/80/33 unreported (participation charge); *McCann* v. *C. & E. Comrs.* [1987] VATTR 101.

Item 2
The granting of a right to take part in a lottery. A lottery includes any competition for prizes authorised by a licence under the Pool Competitions Act 1971.

GROUP 5—FINANCE (A9.31)

The following supplies are exempt.

Item 1
The issue, transfer or receipt of, or any dealing with money or security for money or any note or order for the payment of money. For services included within this description, see *British Hardware Federation* v. *C. & E. Comrs.* [1975] VATTR 172 (clearing house payment scheme); *Barclays Bank plc.* v. *C. & E. Comrs.* [1988] VATTR 23 (credit checking service); *C. & E. Comrs.* v. *Diners Club Ltd.* [1989] STC 407, CA (payments under charge card scheme).

Item 2
The making of any advance or granting of any credit. The value of the supply is the interest charged.

Item 3
The provision of instalment credit finance in a hire purchase, conditional sale, or credit sale

agreement where a separate charge for finance is made and disclosed to the recipient of the supply of goods.

The value of the supply is the credit charge made.

Item 4
The provision of administrative arrangements in connection with an item 3 supply if the consideration is specified in the agreement and is £10 or less.

Item 5
The making of arrangements for any transaction in item 1, 2, 3 or 4 and underwriting an issue of securities or notes for the payment of money. See *Guy Butler (International) Ltd.* v. *C. & E. Comrs.* [1976] STC 254; *Minister Associates* v. *C. & E. Comrs.* LON/85/326 unreported.

Item 6
The issue, transfer or receipt of, or any dealing with, any security or secondary security being:
   (*a*) shares, stock, bonds, notes (other than promissory notes), debentures, debenture stock or shares in an oil royalty; or
   (*b*) any document relating to money, in any currency, which has been deposited with the issuer or some other person, being a document which recognises an obligation to pay a stated amount to bearer or to order, with or without interest, and being a document by the delivery of which, with or without endorsement, the right to receive that stated amount, with or without interest, is transferable; or
   (*c*) any bill, note or other obligation of the Treasury or of a Government in any part of the world, being a document by the delivery of which, with or without endorsement, title is transferable, and not being an obligation which is or has been legal tender in any part of the world; or
   (*d*) any letter of allotment or rights, any warrant conferring an option to acquire a security included in this item, any renounceable or scrip certificates, rights coupons, coupons representing dividends or interest on such a security, bond mandates or other documents conferring or containing evidence of title to or rights in respect of such a security; or
   (*e*) units or other documents conferring rights under any trust established for the purpose, or having the effect of providing, for persons having funds available for investment, facilities for the participation by them as beneficiaries under the trust, in any profits or income arising from the acquisition, holding, management or disposal of any property whatsoever.
For "dealing", see *Singer & Friedlander Ltd.* v. *C. & E. Comrs.* [1989] VATTR 27, [1989] 1 CMLR 814.

The value of the supply by a principal is the total consideration for the sale of securities together with any gross interest derived from holding the security.

The receipt of a dividend on shares is outside the scope of VAT.

Item 6A
The making of arrangements for, or the underwriting of, any transaction within Item 6 above. This includes the services of persons introducing buyers and sellers of securities within Item 6 above.

Item 7
The operation of any current, deposit or savings account.

The supply of coin or banknotes as collectors items are excluded from this group. See *Milk Marketing Board* v. *C. & E. Comrs.* LON/87/495 unreported.

Any payments made to a credit card operator by a person who accepts a card in payment of goods or services are exempt from VAT. For check trading companies, see Press Notice No. 1045, 21 October 1985.

Item 8
Services by the operator of the scheme in managing an authorised unit trust scheme or a trust based scheme.

GROUP 6—EDUCATION (A9.36)

The following supplies are exempt.

Item 1
The provision of education or research by a school, university or polytechnic. Education includes training in any form of art. It excludes profit-making courses in English as a foreign language and recreational or sporting holiday courses.

Item 2
The provision otherwise than for profit, of:
   (*a*) education or research of a kind provided by a school or university: or

(b) training or re-training for any trade, profession or employment.
As to the phrase "otherwise than for profit", see *C. & E. Comrs.* v. *Bell Concord Educational Trust Ltd.* [1989] STC 264, CA and Press Notice No. 30/89, 30 March 1989. Recreational or sporting activities are excluded from exemption other than as part of a general educational curriculum.

Item 3
Private tuition in subjects normally taught in a school or university to an individual pupil by a teacher acting independently of any organisation. Recreational or sporting subjects are excluded.

Item 4
The supply of goods or services incidental to the supplies in items 1 and 2. For "incidental", see *Archer (No. 2)* v. *C. & E. Comrs.* [1975] VATTR 1; *Woodward Schools (Midland Division) Ltd.* v. *C. & E. Comrs.* [1975] VATTR 123.

Item 5
The supply of instruction supplemental to the provision of education in items 1 and 2.

Item 6
The provision of youth club facilities by either a club or association of youth clubs. See *World Association of Girl Guides and Girl Scouts* v. *C. & E. Comrs.* [1984] VATTR 28.

Item 7
Training courses, conferences, seminars, etc. supplied under schemes arranged by, and paid for by, the Training Commission or Department of Economic Development.

GROUP 7—HEALTH AND WELFARE (A9.41)

The following supplies are exempt. For the exemption of welfare services under directly applicable E.C. legislation, see *Yoga for Health Foundation* v. *C. & E. Comrs.* [1984] STC 630; *International Bible Students Association* v. *C. & E. Comrs.* [1988] STC 412; *The Lord Mayor and Citizens of the City of Westminster* v. *C. & E. Comrs.* [1990] 2 CMLR 81.

Item 1
The supply of services by any of the following registered persons:
   (a) medical practitioners;
   (b) opthalmic opticians or dispensing opticians;
   (c) chiropodists, dietitians, medical laboratory technicians, occupational therapists, physio-
        therapists, radiographers and remedial gymnasts;
   (d) qualified nurses, midwives and health visitors;
   (e) dispensers of hearing aids.
   For the hire of goods in connection with such services, see *Aslan Imaging Ltd.* v. *C. & E. Comrs.* [1989] VATTR 54.

Item 2
The supply of services by or dental prostheses by a registered dentist, a dental auxiliary or a dental technician. For dental technicians, see *Bennett* v. *C. & E. Comrs.* LON/79/231 unreported.

Item 3
The supply of services by a pharmaceutical chemist.

Item 4
The provision of care or medical or surgical treatment and related goods in any hospital or approved institution. For establishments within this description, see *Huntley Hair Transplants Ltd.* v. *C. & E. Comrs.* LON/77/414 unreported. For the meaning of "care", see *Crothall & Co. Ltd.* v. *C. & E. Comrs.* [1973] VATTR 20; *Cameron* v. *C. & E. Comrs.* [1973] VATTR 177; *Nuffield Nursing Homes Trust* v. *C. & E. Comrs.* [1989] VATTR 62 and Press Notice No. 32/89, 5 April 1989. For goods supplied with services, see *Payton* v. *C. & E. Comrs.* [1974] VATTR 140.

Item 5
The provision of a deputy for a medical practitioner.

Item 6
The supply of human blood.

Item 7
The supply of products for therapeutic purposes, derived from human blood.

Item 8
The supply of human organs or tissues for diagnostic or therapeutic purposes or medical research.

Item 9
The supply, otherwise than for profit, by a charity or public body of welfare services, and goods supplied in connection therewith. For supplies made "otherwise than for profit", see Press Notice No. 30/89, 30 March 1989.

Item 10
The supply of goods and services incidental to the provision of spiritual welfare by a religious community to a resident member in return for a consideration paid as a condition of membership. The supply must be made otherwise than for profit: compare VATA 1983, Sch. 6, Group 6.

Item 11
The supply of transport services for sick or injured persons in specially designed vehicles.

GROUP 8—BURIAL AND CREMATION (A9.46)

The following supplies are exempt.

Item 1
The disposal of the remains of the dead. See *UFD Ltd.* v. *C. & E. Comrs.* [1981] VATTR 199.

Item 2
The making of arrangements for or in connection with the disposal of the remains of the dead.

GROUP 9—TRADE UNIONS AND PROFESSIONAL BODIES (A9.51)

The following supplies are exempt.

Item 1
The supply of services and goods related to those services which are within the aims of the organisation in return for a membership subscription by:
  (*a*) a trade union (see *City Cabs (Edinburgh) Ltd.* v. *C. & E. Comrs.* EDN/79/30 unreported; *British Tenpin Bowling Association* v. *C. & E. Comrs.* LON/87/404 unreported);
  (*b*) a professional association (see *Institute of Leisure and Amenity Management* v. *C. & E. Comrs.* [1988] STC 602; *Royal Photographic Society of Great Britain* v. *C. & E. Comrs.* [1978] VATTR 191);
  (*c*) an association for the advancement of a branch of knowledge (see *Bookmakers Protection Association (Southern Area) Ltd.* v. *C. & E. Comrs.* [1979] VATTR 215; *British Organic Farmers* v. *C. & E. Comrs.* [1988] VATTR 64);
  (*d*) an association for fostering professional expertise (see *Institute of Employment Consultants Ltd.* v. *C. & E. Comrs.* LON/86/410 unreported);
  (*e*) an association lobbying the government on legislation and other public matters affecting a profession (see *Bee Farmers Association* v. *C. & E. Comrs.* LON/83/248 unreported).

GROUP 10—SPORTS COMPETITIONS (A9.56)

The following supplies are exempt.

Item 1
The payment of a right to enter a sports competition where the entry fees are allocated wholly to prizes. For an example of match fees outside the scope of this item, see *Wimborne R.F.C.* v. *C. & E. Comrs.* LON/89/755 unreported.

Item 2
The grant by a sporting non-profit-making body of a right to enter a competition provided that nothing charged relates to the use of facilities. For an example of match fees outside the scope of this item, see *Wimborne R.F.C.* v. *C. & E. Comrs.* LON/89/755 unreported.

GROUP 11—WORKS OF ART, ETC. (A9.56)

Disposals of objects either to museums etc. within IHTA 1984, Sch. 3 or accepted in satisfaction of tax are exempt.

GROUP 12—FUND-RAISING EVENTS BY CHARITIES AND OTHER QUALIFYING BODIES

The following supplies are exempt.

Item 1
A supply of goods or services made to a charity is exempt if the supply is made in connection with a fund-raising event organised for charitable purposes by one or more charities.

Item 2
Goods and services supplied by a qualifying body are exempt if the supply is made in connection with a fund-raising event organised exclusively for the body's own benefit. A "qualifying body" is one which does not carry on a business by virtue of VATA 1983, s. 47(3) or a body whose subscription income is exempt from VAT by virtue of VATA 1983, Sch. 6, Group 9. In either case, the body must be non-profit-making.

SCHEDULE 6A—BUILDINGS AND LAND (Section 35A)

Residential and charitable buildings: change of use etc.
1.—(A6.48; A9.13A) The grant of a freehold, lease or licence in a community home or non-business charity building is excluded from zero-rating (under VATA 1983, Sch. 5, Group 8) and exemption (under VATA 1983, Sch. 6, Group 1) if: (1) the grantor acquired or constructed the building under a zero-rated supply; (2) the supply takes place within ten years after the building was completed; and (3) the recipient of the supply does not intend to use the building as a community home or charity building. The supply is chargeable to tax at the standard rate.

A person's interest in a community home or charity building is self-supplied if: (1) he acquired or constructed the building under a zero-rated supply; and (2) he ceases to use the building as a community home or charity building within ten years after the building was completed. The supply is deemed to take place on the date when the change of use occurred. The supply is chargeable to tax at the standard rate. The tax due is an amount equivalent to the tax which would have been charged if the zero-rated supplies received had been chargeable to tax at the standard rate when supplied, and the value of the supply is calculated accordingly. For the attribution of input tax, see VAT (General) Regulations, S.I. 1985, No. 886 reg. 30B.

Election to waive exemption
2.—(A9.14; A13.42) A grant is excluded from exemption under VATA 1983, Sch. 6, Group 1 if: (1) an election to waive exemption has been made in respect of the land concerned; (2) the election has effect when the grant is made; and (3) the grant is made either by the person who made the election or by a relevant associate (see Sch. 6A para. 3 (8)).

A grant made in resepct of a building remains exempt, despite an election, if the building is a dwelling, community home or charity building.

A grant made in respect of land remains exempt, despite an election, if it is made to either: (1) a registered housing association (see Sch. 6A, para. 3 (9)) which intends to construct a dwelling or community home thereon and issues a certificate to that effect; or (2) an individual who intends to construct a dwelling thereon for his own occupation.

Input tax incurred before the date from which an election takes effect is deductible in two circumstances. First, if no exempt supplies were made before that date or, if made, were confined to the period 1 April 1989—31 July 1989 and would have been taxable supplies if made before 1 April 1989. However, input tax incurred before 1 August 1989 is deductible under this provision only if an election takes effect from that date and it is attributable to supplies made on or after 1 April 1989 which would have been taxable supplies if made before that date. Secondly, if the input tax relates to grants (*e.g.* the freehold of a new commercial building) or other supplies (*e.g.* construction services) made to the claimant during the period 1 April 1989–31 July 1989 which would have been zero-rated under VATA 1983, Sch. 5, Group 8, Items 1 or 2, or exempt under Sch. 6, Group 1, Item 1, if made before 1 April 1989 and the election takes effect from 1 August 1989. But see *EC Commission* v. *France* (case 50/87) [1989] 1 CMLR 505, ECJ.
3.—(A9.04) An election to waive exemption takes effect from the day on which it was made or a later day specified therein. However, an election may be backdated to take effect from 1 August 1989 or a later specified day provided the election is made no later than 31 October 1989.

An election may be made in respect of any specified land or any specified description of land.

An election made in respect of all or part of a planned or completed building extends to the whole building and all land within its curtilage. The following are regarded as a single building: (1) buildings linked internally; (2) buildings linked by a covered walkway; and (3) parades, precincts and complexes divided into separate units.

An election made in respect of agricultural land, or a building thereon, does not extend to land which is separated from it by either: (1) land (other than a road, railway, river, etc.) which is not agricultural land; or (2) agricultural land in which neither the person making the election nor a relevant associate has an interest, right or licence.

An election is irrevocable. An election specified in Notice No. 742B (January 1990) para. 45 does not require notification. All other elections must be notified within 30 days and do not take effect unless so notified.

Two bodies corporate ("A" and "B") are "relevant associates" if A makes an election and B is included in the same group election either: (1) at the date when the election takes effect; or (2) at a later time when A retains an interest, right or licence in the land or building concerned. A third body corporate ("C") is a relevant associate of B if B and C are included in the same group registration at a time when B has an interest, right or licence in the land or building concerned (*e.g.* where A has granted a lease to B).

A "registered housing association" is a society, body of trustees or company within Housing Associations Act 1985, s. 1 (1) registered with the Housing Corporation under ibid., s. 3, or an equivalent body in Northern Ireland.

4.—(A5.49; A8.26) Special tax point rules apply to rents received for periods either side of the date when an election to waive exemption takes effect. In practice, rents are time apportioned so that tax is chargeable for the whole period during which the election has effect, but not before.

A special valuation relief applies where an election is made in respect of a building completed before 1 August 1989 and land occupied by a tenant before that date. Tax is chargeable as if rents were reduced by the following proportions for the periods stated—

	Reduction	
Period to which rent relates	Charity tenant	Other tenant
Year ended 31 July 1990	80%	50%
Year ended 31 July 1991	60%	Nil
Year ended 31 July 1992	40%	Nil
Year ended 31 July 1993	20%	Nil

Developers of certain non-residential buildings etc

5.—(A6.47, 50) A developer makes a self-supply under para. 6 below in relation to a building or civil engineering work on the first occasion when he either: (1) grants an exempt freehold, lease or licence in it; or (2) occupies or uses it at a time when he is not a fully taxable person. This event must occur after the day when construction is first planned and before the tenth anniversary of completion.

A self-supply is not made in relation to a building if: (1) it is a dwelling, community home or charity building; (2) construction was commenced before 1 August 1989; or (3) the freehold had previously been transferred under a grant within VATA 1983, Sch. 6, Group 1, Item 1 (*a*) (ii). See also FA 1989, Sch. 3, para. 13 (6) (*a*)–(*c*).

A self-supply is not made in relation to a civil engineering work if: (1) it is a work necessary for the development of a permanent park for residential caravans; (2) construction was commenced before 1 August 1989; or (3) the freehold had previously been transferred under a grant within VATA 1983, Sch. 6, Group 1, Item 1 (*a*) (iv). See also FA 1989, Sch. 3, para. 13 (6) (*b*).

The terms "fully taxable person" and "developer" are defined. "Developer" has an extended meaning in relation to bodies corporate included in a group registration.

6.—(A6.47, 50) A developer is deemed to supply his interest in, right over or licence to occupy a building or civil engineering work in the course or furtherance of business if the conditions in para. 5 above are met. The supply is also deemed to be made to him for the purpose of his business. The supply is deemed to be made on the later of: (1) the last day of the prescribed accounting period in which the grant, occupation or use occurred; and (2) the last day of the prescribed accounting period in which the building became ready for occupation or the civil engineering work became ready for use.

The value of the supply is the aggregate of: (1) the value of grants made or to be made in respect of the land (but excluding rents for future grants which cannot be ascertained at the time of supply); and (2) the value of standard rate construction services made or to be made.

No supply is deemed to be made if the value is less than £100,000.

General

7.—(A9.11; A11.33, 34; A13.11) The grant of freehold, lease or licence may be made by one person (*e.g.* a trustee ("T")) but the benefit of the consideration may accrue to someone else (*e.g.* the members of a partnership or unincorporated association ("X")). Where this is so: (1) the grant made by T is deemed to be made by X; and (2) input tax incurred by T in respect of the grant is deemed to be incurred by X.

8.—Sch. 6A is interpreted in accordance with the notes to VATA 1983, Sch. 5, Group 8 and Sch. 6, Group 1.

SCHEDULE 7 ADMINISTRATION, COLLECTION AND ENFORCEMENT (Section 38)

General
1.—(A2.16, 18) This paragraph determines how the Commissioners account for VAT revenues.

Accounting for and payment of tax
2.—(A14.12, 42–44) The Commissioners may make regulations requiring accounts to be kept, returns to be made and tax invoices to be provided, and specifying the details to be entered on tax invoices and the time within which they must be provided. See VAT (General) Regulations 1985, S.I. 1985 No. 886 regs. 12–16, 58; VAT (Annual Accounting) Regulations 1988, S.I. 1988 No. 886; VAT (Accounting and Records) Regulations 1989, S.I. 1989 No. 2248 regs. 4, 8.

Regulations may permit the Commissioners to set up special schemes for retailers and publish details of them in notices. See VAT (Supplies by Retailers) Regulations 1972, S.I. 1972 No. 1148.

Regulations may redefine the time when tax becomes chargeable and provide for adjustment of accounts and correction of errors. See VAT (General) Regulations 1985, S.I. 1985 No. 886 reg. 58(1); VAT (Accounting and Records) Regulations 1989, S.I. 1989 No. 2248 regs. 5, 7. For refund of overpaid VAT, see FA 1989, s. 24.

Regulations may provide for tax to be accounted and paid by reference to the time of payment for a supply and may modify the time when a reclaim of input tax may be allowed. See VAT (Cash Accounting) Regulations 1987, S.I. 1987 No. 1427.

The Commissioners may by regulation allow non-standard accounting periods. See VAT (General) Regulations 1985, S.I. 1985 No. 886 reg. 58(1).

Regulations may require a creditor selling goods of a debtor in satisfaction of the debt to provide the Commissioners with details of the transaction, to charge tax and to account for it. See VAT (General) Regulations 1985, S.I. 1985 No. 886 reg. 59.

Amounts of less than £1 are to be treated as nil when due either to or from the Commissioners.

Production of tax invoices by computer
3.—(A14.15) Where information is stored on a computer and is transferred to another person electronically, tax invoices are regarded as issued even though no document is ever delivered.

Persons using electronic means to either supply or receive tax invoices must give one month's notice in writing to the Commissioners and comply with any requirements imposed by the Commissioners or specified in regulations. No regulations have been made to date.

Power of Commissioners to assess tax due
4.—(A15.36–40) Where a person fails to make returns, or to keep documents, or to make it possible to verify returns, or makes incomplete or incorrect returns, the Commissioners may to the best of their judgment assess and notify the registered person of the VAT due. For "best judgment", see *Van Boeckel* v. *C. & E. Comrs.* [1981] STC 290; *Spillane* v. *C. & E. Comrs.* [1990] STC 212.

An amount paid or credited by the Commissioners may be assessed if: (1) it ought not to have been paid or credited; or (2) it would not have been paid or credited if the facts had been known or the facts had been as they later turn out to be. The amount is assessed for the prescribed accounting period to which the payment, repayment or refund concerned relates. For the Commissioners' right to assess, see *Farm Facilities (Fork Lift) Ltd.* v. *C. & E. Comrs.* [1987] VATTR 80. For the amount of an assessment, see *International Language Centres Ltd.* v. *C. & E. Comrs.* [1982] VATTR 172; *Potter (a firm)* v. *C. & E. Comrs.* [1983] VATTR 108. For the Commissioners' right to sue without issuing an assessment, see *C. & E. Comrs.* v. *International Language Centres Ltd.* [1986] STC 279.

Underpayments of output tax and over reclaims of input tax in the same accounting period may be assessed together and notified as one assessment.

A person acting in a representative capacity (personal representative trustee in bankruptcy, receiver or liquidator) who fails to make a return or makes an incomplete return may be assessed in respect of the tax due from the person he represents.

The time limits which restrict the issue of an assessment for failure to make a return or make an incomplete return or an incorrectly repaid amount of input tax are the later of two years after the end of the normal quarterly or monthly accounting period, or one year after the facts sufficient to justify making the assessment come to the Commissioners' knowledge. For the time when facts come to the Commissioners' knowledge, see *Spillane* v. *C. & E. Comrs.* [1990] STC 212. For the application of these time limits where a global assessment is made, see *S. J Grange Ltd.* v. *C. & E. Comrs.* [1979] STC 183, CA.

If further facts are discovered in respect of an accounting period which has already been assessed, an additional assessment may be made. However, the Commissioners are allowed only one bite at the same cherry: *Jeudwine* v. *C. & E. Comrs.* [1977] VATTR 115. For the validity of replacement assessments, see *Heyfordian Travel Ltd.* v. *C. & E. Comrs.* [1979] VATTR 139; *Scott* v. *C. & E. Comrs.* MAN/76/181 unreported.

A taxable person may be required to account for goods acquired or imported by the business. Failure to show that the goods are in stock or have been sold or have been exported (even to an overseas branch) or have been lost or destroyed may lead the Commissioners to assess the amount of tax which would have been chargeable on those goods if they had been supplied by the business.

Where a previous assessment has been paid without a proper return being submitted a subsequent assessment may be for a sum greater than the Commissioners would otherwise have considered appropriate.

Where an assessment has been made and notified for failure to make returns or for making incomplete returns, or incorrectly claiming repayments or for failure to account for goods acquired, then, subject to appeal or subsequent withdrawal or reduction, the amount shall be deemed to be tax due from the person assessed and may be recovered accordingly.

As to time limits for assessments, see FA 1985, s. 22.

Power to require security and production of evidence
5.—(A15.08, 83) Before making a repayment of input tax the Commissioners may require the production of documents including tax invoices and may, to protect the revenue, require security for the amount of the repayment. There is no right of appeal: *Strangewood Ltd.* v. *C. & E. Comrs.* [1988] VATTR 35.

The Commissioners may require a taxable person, as a condition of his supplying goods or services, to give security of such amount and in such manner as they determine (cash deposit, bank guarantee, etc.) for the payment of any tax which is or may become due. For the right of appeal, see s. 40(1)(*n*). For examples, see *Mr. Wishmore* v. *C. & E. Comrs.* [1988] STC 723; *Giddian Ltd.* v. *C. & E. Comrs.* [1984] VATTR 161; *Power Rod (U.K.) Ltd.* v. *C. & E. Comrs.* [1983] VATTR 334; *Gayton House Holdings Ltd.* v. *C. & E. Comrs.* [1984] VATTR 111. The Commissioners' statement of case should set out all the reasons for requiring security: *Interseal 2000 Ltd.* v. *C. & E. Comrs.* LON/89/218 unreported.

Where a trader has a past record of business failures leaving VAT debts, the Commissioners are likely to require security. Tribunals have supported the Commissioners in requiring cash equivalent to the estimated tax due from four months trading to be put up as security. For security required on the sole ground that returns were persistently furnished late, see *Longsight Cricket Club* v. *C. & E. Comrs.* MAN/89/90 unreported.

Recovery of tax, etc.
6.—(A14.18; A15.71, 72) VAT due from any person is recoverable as a debt due to the Crown.

Where an invoice shows that tax was chargeable on a supply of goods or services, an amount equal to the tax is recoverable from the person who issued the invoice or, if tax is not separately shown, so much of this total of the invoice as represents tax on the supply. It is irrelevant whether the invoice is a tax invoice, the supply indicated actually takes place, that the amount shown as VAT or any amount calculated to be VAT is chargeable on the supply, or that the person issuing the invoice is a taxable person. If the sum concerned is tax it is recovered as such. If not, it is recoverable as a debt due to the Crown.

The Commissioners may make regulations in England, Wales and Northern Ireland whereby distress may be levied on the goods and chattels of any person failing to pay tax or any amount recoverable as if it were tax. See VAT (General) Regulations 1985, S.I. 1985 No. 886 reg. 65.

In Scotland, the sheriff may grant a summary warrant authorising recovery of unpaid tax (or of an amount treated as tax) by way of: (1) a poinding and sale; (2) an earnings arrestment; or (3) an arrestment and action of furthcoming or sale. An application by the Commissioners must be accompanied by a certificate setting out specified information.

The sheriff officer's fees and outlays in connection with a summary warrant are chargeable against the debtor. However, no fee is chargeable for collecting and accounting for sums paid by the debtor.

The Commissioners make provision for their powers in connection with diligences to be exercised by officers of a specified rank. See VAT (General) Regulations 1985, S.I. 1985 No. 886 reg. 66.

Duty to keep records
7.—(A16.01, 02; A17.58) Taxable persons must keep the records prescribed by regulations. See VAT (Accounting and Records) Regulations 1989, S.I. 1989 No. 2248 reg. 2.

The Commissioners may require records to be kept for up to six years.

The duty to preserve records may be discharged by the preservation of the information contained in another form (*e.g.*, microfilm) provided the Commissioners approve. A copy of a document forming part of the preserved information records shall be admissible in evidence in any civil or criminal proceedings to the same extent as the original document.

The Commissioners may impose conditions on the means of preserving information which appear necessary to ensure that the information will be readily available to them as if the records themselves had been preserved.

Statements on documents produced by computer are not admissible as evidence in England and Wales unless they are in accordance with the Civil Evidence Act 1968, ss. 5 and 6 for civil proceedings, or the Police and Criminal Evidence Act 1984, ss. 68 to 70 for criminal proceedings.

Similar provisions apply for Scotland and Northern Ireland. In criminal proceedings the court may require oral evidence to be given of any matter of which evidence could be given by means of a certificate under the Civil Evidence Act 1968, s. 5 (4) or the Law Reform (Miscellaneous Provisions) (Scotland) Act 1968, s. 13 (4) or the Civil Evidence Act (Northern Ireland) 1971, s. 2 (4).

As to penalties for breaches, see FA 1985, s. 17.

Furnishing of information and production of documents
8.—(A16.34, 35) The Commissioners may make regulations which require taxable persons to notify details of changes in circumstances relating to either the persons or the business with the aim of keeping the VAT register up to date. See VAT (General) Regulations 1985, S.I. 1985 No. 886 reg. 4.

Every person concerned in the supply of goods or services or in the importation of goods by a business shall provide the Commissioners, within such time and in such form as they reasonably require, such information as the Commissioners may reasonably specify. Such person must also produce upon demand to an authorised person at the principal place of business or such other place as the authorised person may reasonably require at any reasonable time any documents relating to the supply of goods or services or importation of goods.

Where an authorised person can require the production of documents from any person concerned in the supply of goods or services or importation of goods he has the power to demand production by any other person who appears to be in possession of them, but where that person claims a lien on the documents, production shall not prejudice the lien. This covers the type of case where an accountant holds the accounting records pending payment of a fee by the client. The authorised person can demand to examine the accountancy records but he cannot pass the records to the client without the accountant's approval. See *C. & E. Comrs.* v. *A. E. Hamlin & Co.* [1983] STC 780; *EMI Records Ltd.* v. *Spillane* [1986] STC 374.

Documents relating to the supply of goods or services or the importation of goods in the course or furtherance of any business includes any profit and loss account and balance sheet.

An authorised person may remove any document produced by the business at a reasonable time and for reasonable period, without compromising any lien, and must provide a receipt on request.

Where a document which is required for the proper conduct of business is removed by an authorised person, a copy of the document must be provided, free of charge, as soon as practicable.

Documents lost or damaged whilst in the Commissioners' care may be the subject of a claim for compensation by the owner for any expenses reasonably incurred in replacing or repairing the documents.

As to penalties for breaches, see FA 1985, s. 17.

Power to take samples
9.—(A16.40) An authorised person may take samples of the goods in the possession of any person who supplies goods with a view to determining how the goods or the materials of which they are made should be treated for the purposes of tax.

Samples are, for example, taken to decide whether or not an item is confectionery, or to decide whether an item of apparel is solely for children to wear.

A sample is disposed of and accounted for in such manner as the Commissioners direct.

Where an item is not returned in good condition within a reasonable time, compensation equal to the cost of the sample or such larger sum as the Commissioners decide may be paid to the person from whom the sample was taken.

Power to require opening of gaming machines
9A.—(A16.38) An authorised person may at any reasonable time require a person operating a gaming machine to open the machine and to carry out any other operation necessary to calculate the value of supplies made in any period.

Entry and search of premises and persons
10.—(A16.31, 33) An officer of customs and excise may enter any business premises at any reasonable time to carry out his duties.

Where an officer of customs and excise has reasonable cause to believe that premises are used in the course of a supply of goods and the goods are on the premises then he may enter those premises at any reasonable time to inspect the premises and any goods therein.

If a justice of the peace (or the equivalent in Scotland) is satisfied from information on oath that a fraud is being, has been or will be committed on any premises or evidence of such an offence is to be found there he may issue a warrant authorising an officer of customs and excise to enter and search those premises, if necessary by force, at any time within one month of the date of issue of the warrant. The officer of customs and excise may be accompanied by any other person he deems necessary. He may also seize and remove documents or other things found on the premises and he may search any person found on the premises whom he has reasonable cause to believe is in possession of documents or things which will be required as evidence in proceedings under s. 39 (1) to (3).

A warrant may specify the number of persons it authorises to act, specify the times of day when it is exercisable or specify that a uniformed police officer must be present.

The officer of customs and excise who is in charge of the search and is authorised by the warrant must at the beginning of the seach make available to the occupier or person in charge of the premises a copy of the warrant or leave a copy in a prominent place if no one is present.

For search warrants generally, see *IRC* v. *Rossminster Ltd.* [1982] STC 42, HL and Police and Criminal Evidence Act 1984, ss. 15, 16.

Order for access to recorded information, etc.
10A.—(A16.36) A justice of the peace (or the equivalent in Scotland) may upon application by an officer of customs and excise make an order that access to recorded information is made available to an officer of customs and excise who may remove such information as he considers necessary on the grounds that the information may be required as evidence in connection with a VAT offence. Access must be given within seven days or such longer period as the order specifies. Where the information is stored in a computer the order may require the information be produced in a form which is visible, legible, and removable. This paragraph does not prejudice the furnishing of information and the entry and search of premises in paragraphs 8 and 10 above. For orders made under this provision, see *R.* v. *Epsom Justices ex parte Bell* [1989] STC 169.

Procedure where documents etc. are removed
10B.—(A16.33, 36) The occupier of premises or the person in charge of premises may request and must be given within a reasonable time a record of what has been removed.

If the officer in charge of an investigation has grounds to believe that the investigation of an offence may be prejudiced he is not required to grant access to or to supply a photograph of any document or thing removed under a warrant.

Otherwise, access under supervision to the thing or document may be granted, and copies made or photographs supplied within a reasonable time.
10C.—(A16.33, 36) A magistrates' court in England and Wales (or the equivalent in Scotland or Northern Ireland) may order the officer of customs and excise to comply, in such manner and within such time as set out in the order, with the production of either a record of what was removed or give access to the thing or document.

Evidence by certificate, etc.
11.—(A17.57; A18.04) A certificate, issued by the Commissioners, that a person was or was not registered for VAT or that any return had or had not been made by any date or that any VAT due had or had not been paid is sufficient evidence of the facts until the contrary is proved.

Any VAT document given to the Commissioners may be photographed. The Commissioners may certify any document to be a photograph and may use the copy in civil or criminal proceedings to the same extent as the original.

Any document which is supposed to be a certificate is accepted as such until the contrary is proved.

SCHEDULE 8 CONSTITUTION AND PROCEDURE OF VALUE ADDED TAX TRIBUNALS
(Section 40)

Establishment of value added tax tribunals
1.—(A2.41) Value added tax tribunals are set up for England and Wales, Scotland and Northern Ireland.

The President
2.—(A2.41) The President of VAT tribunals performs the duties set out in the following provisions in respect of any U.K. VAT tribunal.

The President is appointed by the Lord Chancellor after consultation with the Lord Advocate and is a barrister, advocate of solicitor of more than ten years' standing.

The Lord Chancellor in consultation with the Lord Advocate sets the term and conditions of appointment of the President subject to para. 3. A person who ceases to be President is eligible for re-appointment.
3.—(A2.41) The President may resign at any time but vacates office at the end of the year of service in which he is 72 or, if the Lord Chancellor considers it desirable in the public interest he may continue until his 75th birthday.

The Lord Chancellor may remove the President from office on grounds of incapacity or misbehaviour and the functions of the President may, if he is unable to act or the office is vacant, be undertaken by a person nominated by the Lord Chancellor.

Salary and pensions of Presidents and former Presidents are set by the Lord Chancellor with the approval of the Treasury. Compensation may be paid to Presidents who cease to hold office if the

Lord Chancellor considers it right and there are special circumstances. The amount is set by the Lord Chancellor with the approval of the Treasury.

Sittings of tribunals
4.—(A2.41) The number of VAT tribunals is decided by the Lord Chancellor or in Scotland by the Secretary of State. The tribunals sit at such places as the Lord Chancellor and the Secretary of State from time to time decide.

Composition of tribunals
5.—(A2.41) A chairman sitting alone or with one or two other members constitutes a tribunal.
   A decision may be made by a majority of votes and where the chairman is sitting with one other member the chairman has a casting vote.

Membership of tribunals
6.—(A2.41) The chairman is either the President or at the President's wish a member of a panel of chairmen set up under para. 7 below. Other members are selected from a panel of other members by either the President or member of the panel of chairmen so authorised by the President.
7.—(A2.41) There are panels of chairmen and panels of other members for each of England and Wales, Scotland and Northern Ireland. One member of each panel of chairmen is known as Vice-President of VAT Tribunals.
   The panel of chairmen is appointed by, in England and Wales the Lord Chancellor, in Scotland the Lord President of the Court of Session and in Northern Ireland the Lord Chief Justice of Northern Ireland. Appointments to a panel of other members are made by the Treasury.
   Chairmen are barristers, advocates or solicitors of more than seven years experience, and are appointed for such term and upon such conditions as the persons appointing them decide. A person who ceases to be a chairman is eligible for re-appointment to the office.
   A chairman may resign at any time but vacates office at the end of the year of service in which he is 72 or, if the appointing authority considers it desirable in the public interest, he may continue until his 75th birthday.
   The appointing authority may remove a chairman on grounds of incapacity or misbehaviour.
   Salary of fees and pensions of chairmen and former chairmen and fees of other members are set by the Lord Chancellor with the approval of the Treasury. Compensation may be paid to chairmen who cease to hold office in circumstances the Lord Chancellor considers special. The amount is set by the Lord Chancellor with the approval of the Treasury.

Exemption from jury service
8.—(A2.41) No member of a VAT tribunal is compelled to serve on any jury in Scotland or Northern Ireland.

Rules of procedure
9.—(A2.41; A17.01) The Commissioners may make rules to be followed if an appeal is to be made to a VAT tribunal. See Value Added Tax Tribunal Rules 1986, S.I. 1986 No. 590. For the power to make rules after 1 July 1986, see FA 1985 s. 27 (3).
10.—(A18.81) Failure to comply with a summons to appear before a VAT tribunal made under the rules under para. 9 renders a person liable to a penalty not exceeding £1,000. A penalty may be ordered by the tribunal without proceedings having been commenced. An appeal may be made to the High Court or the Court of Session in Scotland and the Court may confirm or reverse the decision or increase or decrease the penalty awarded. A penalty is recoverable as if it were tax due from the person liable for the penalty.

SCHEDULE 10 SAVINGS AND TRANSITIONAL PROVISIONS (Section 50)

4.—VAT is not chargeable on any supply or importation occurring before 1 April 1973. The date of supply for imported goods for the purpose of this paragraph is the date entry for customs purposes is made or in the case of warehoused goods the date on which they are removed from warehouse.
9.—Special tax point agreements which had been made with the Commissioners before 21 April 1975 are still valid.
16.—Bad debt relief applies to insolvencies occurring after 1 October 1978.

Finance Act 1985
1985 Chapter 54

PART I CUSTOMS AND EXCISE AND VALUE ADDED TAX

CHAPTER I CUSTOMS AND EXCISE

OTHER PROVISIONS

10. Computer records etc. (A18.02)

Where a person is required to give access to or possession of any document to an officer that requirement is within the terms of the Civil Evidence Act 1968, Pt. I.

An officer has at any reasonable time the right of access to any automatic processing machinery, and to be given assistance by any computer personnel to facilitate inspection and checks in connection with any document.

Obstructing an officer, without reasonable excuse, who is exercising his powers renders a person liable to a penalty upon summary conviction of £1,000.

In various Acts creating offences, "document" has the same meaning as in the Civil Evidence Act 1968, Pt. I, or the Scottish or Northern Ireland equivalent. An assigned matter has the same meaning as in CEMA 1979, s. 1 (1).

CHAPTER II VALUE ADDED TAX

OFFENCES ETC.

12. Offences and penalties in criminal proceedings

This section amends VATA 1983, s. 39 (offences and penalties). Where a penalty is increased, the new penalty does not apply to an offence committed before 25 July 1985.

CIVIL PENALTIES

13. Tax evasion: conduct involving dishonesty. (A18.51)

Where a person does or does not do something with the intention of evading VAT that conduct renders that person liable to a penalty equalling the VAT which was sought to be evaded. For the nature of dishonesty and the standard of proof, see *Gandhi Tandoori Restaurant* v. *C. & E. Comrs.* [1989] VATTR 39; *Parker* v. *C. & E. Comrs.* EDN/89/159 unreported.

If a person who is liable to a penalty co-operates in the investigations to identify the true amount of VAT due the penalty may be reduced by the Commissioners or by the VAT tribunal to any amount not being less than 50 per cent. of the VAT due.

Making it known to a person that the Commissioners may take action by way of civil penalty instead of instituting criminal proceedings and that such penalty may be reduced if co-operation by way of a full confession and full facilities for investigation are given, thus inducing the production of documents or statements which might not otherwise have been given, does not make such documents or statements inadmissible in criminal proceedings or in any action to recover the VAT due.

If a person is convicted of a criminal offence for certain conduct, the same conduct does not incur a penalty under this section.

13A. Incorrect certificates. (A18.51A)

The recipient of a supply is liable to a penalty if he incorrectly certifies that all or part of the supply is zero-rated or exempt from VAT. The penalty is an amount equal to the tax undercharged as a consequence of the incorrect certificate. However, no penalty is assessed if either: (1) the recipient satisfies the Commissioners or, on appeal, a VAT tribunal that he has a reasonable excuse for his conduct; or (2) he has been convicted of an offence in respect of it.

14. Serious misdeclaration or neglect resulting in understatements or overclaims. (A18.52, 52B)

Making returns or accepting assessments raised by the Commissioners which understate a person's true liability or overstate the repayment due incurs a 15 per cent. penalty.

Where the potentially lost VAT equals or exceeds 30 per cent. of the true VAT liability or where the potentially lost VAT equals or exceeds whichever is the greater of £10,000 or 5 per cent. of the true VAT liability then the 15 per cent. penalty applies.

The potentially lost VAT in any period is the sum of, if appropriate, the overstated input VAT and the understated output VAT. If, however, there are also errors in favour of the registered person, allowance has to be made for these.

A return is deemed to be correct if an error in it is corrected on a later return in accordance with regulations. See VAT (Accounting and Records) Regulations 1989, S.I. 1989 No. 2248 regs. 5 and 8 (4).

A person is not liable to a penalty if: (1) he has a reasonable excuse for his conduct; (2) he made a full disclosure of any error(s) before discovering that his VAT affairs were being investigated; or (3) he is convicted of a criminal offence or assessed to a penalty for dishonest conduct in respect of the error. For reasonable excuse, see FA 1985 s. 33 (2).

This section came into operation on 31 March 1990. See Finance Act 1985 (Serious Misdeclaration and Interest on Tax) (Appointed Days) Order 1989, S.I. 1989 No. 2270 art. 2.

14A. Persistent misdeclaration resulting in understatements or overclaims. (A18.52A)
If two returns are submitted with an inaccuracy of £100 or 1 per cent. of the true VAT for the period, whichever is the greater, within a period of two years, then Customs and Excise can serve a penalty liability notice specifying a penalty period beginning on the date of the notice and ending two years later. If there is a further inaccuracy of £100 or 1 per cent. within that two year period there is a penalty of 15 per cent. of the tax lost.

15. Failures to notify and unauthorised issue of invoices. (A18.53–55)
Where a person fails to notify a liability to be registered for VAT, either upon exceeding the registration thresholds or by a change in the nature of supplies made by a person exempted from registration, then that person shall be liable to a penalty of £50 or where greater, the following percentages of the VAT due:

(a) Registration no more than nine months late: 10 per cent.
(b) Registration over nine months but no more than 18 months late: 20 per cent.
(c) Registration more than 18 months late: 30 per cent.

An unregistered person who issues an invoice showing an amount as including VAT is liable to a penalty of £50 or where greater 30 per cent. of the net VAT due. A trader is prima facie liable to a penalty if he became liable to registration from a date on or before 25 July 1985 and notified the Commissioners after that date: *C. & E. Comrs.* v. *Shingleton* [1988] STC 190.

A person is not liable to a penalty where the Commissioners, or upon appeal a VAT tribunal, are satisfied that there is a reasonable excuse for his conduct, nor shall he be liable to a penalty where a civil evasion penalty has been imposed under s. 13 above.

For reasonable excuse in relation to failure to notify liability to registration, see in particular: *Zaveri* v. *C. & E. Comrs.* [1986] VATTR 133 (Commissioners failed to send registration forms requested by trader); *Selwyn* v. *C. & E. Comrs.* [1986] VATTR 142 and *Gale* v. *C. & E. Comrs.* [1986] VATTR 185 (registration form posted by trader not received by Commissioners); *Electric Tool Repair Ltd.* v. *C. & E. Comrs.* [1986] VATTR 257, *Jenkinson* v. *C. & E. Comrs.* [1988] VATTR 45 and *Standoak Ltd.* v. *C. & E. Comrs.* LON/86/500 unreported (trader mistakenly believed he had been registered); *Hutchings* v. *C. & E. Comrs.* [1987] VATTR 58 (identity of person liable to registration unclear until time limit expired); *Timeplas Ltd.* v. *C. & E. Comrs.* LON/87/369 and *Burbeary* v. *C. & E. Comrs.* MAN/87/146 unreported (uncertain whether future registration limit applied at relevant time); *Stabler* v. *C. & E. Comrs.* MAN/88/895 unreported (ambiguous letter from Commissioners); *A. M. Autos* v. *C. & E. Comrs.* unreported (records in custody of deceased bookkeeper); also FA 1985 s. 33 (2).

Ignorance of the registration limits and time limits for notification does not amount to a reasonable excuse (*Neal* v. *C. & E. Comrs.* [1988] STC 131) in the absence of exceptional circumstances (*e.g. Mason* v. *C. & E. Comrs.* MAN/88/861 unreported) but this does not apply to ignorance of some legal principle upon which registration depended or regulations of a detailed character (*Geary* v. *C. & E. Comrs.* LON/86/395 unreported; *Dixon* v. *C. & E. Comrs.* MAN/87/218 unreported; *Bailey* v. *C. & E. Comrs.* LON/88/200 unreported).

The Treasury may by order made by statutory instrument increase the penalty due under this section where the value of money has decreased. Such a statutory instrument may be annulled by a resolution of the House of Commons. A new level of penalty cannot be applied to a failure which ended before the new penalty came into effect. No orders have been made to date.

16. Breaches of walking possession agreements. (A18.56)
Where a person has not paid an amount of VAT which is due and has had his goods and chattels distrained upon by a bailiff, the person may enter into a walking possession agreement whereby the sale of the goods and chattels is delayed and they remain in the custody of the person. The person must, however, acknowledge that the property specified in the agreement is under distraint and, except with the consent of the Commissioners who may impose conditions, the person is not allowed to remove the goodsfrom the premises.

Infringement of the walking possession conditions render a person liable to a penalty of 50 per cent. of the tax due but no penalty is due if there is a reasonable excuse for the conduct. This section does not apply in Scotland.

17. Breaches of regulatory provisions. (A18.57–59)
Where a person ceases to make taxable supplies and does not report that fact then that person is liable to penalty of £5 per day for each day the failure occurs. If, however, there have been in the previous two years similar failures to comply with that requirement then the penalty is £10 per day on the second occasion and £15 per day on subsequent failures subject to a maximum penalty of 100 days at the appropriate rate and a minimum of £50. These penalties apply also to failures to comply with any regulations or rules made under VATA 1983, orders made by Treasury under that Act (but excluding rules relating to VAT tribunals) and regulations which relate to VAT made under European Communities Act 1972. Where a person does not set up or keep the records and information as required or instructed he is liable to a penalty of £500.

This section also allows Customs and Excise to calculate manually a penalty for failure to render or pay returns. Where a failure to comply with the regulations consists of not rendering returns or not paying the VAT due on time then the following penalties may apply.

On the first occasion the penalty is the greater of £10 and ¹/₆ of 1 per cent. of the VAT due for each day of failure to comply. On the second occasion, within two years of the first, the penalty is the greater of £20 and ¹/₃ of 1 per cent. of the VAT due per day. On a third or subsequent occasion within two years of the first the penalty is the greater of £30 and ¹/₂ of 1 per cent. of the VAT due per day. The VAT due is taken as that declared on a VAT return for the period in question or the amount assessed by the Commissioners. No penalty may be levied under this section where the Commissioners or a VAT tribunal are satisfied that there is a reasonable excuse for the conduct or where the conduct has led to a conviction for an offence or a penalty under s. 13 or s. 14 above or a default surcharge under s. 19 below.

The Treasury may by order made by statutory instrument increase the penalty due under this section where the value of money has decreased but such a statutory instrument may be annulled by the House of Commons. No orders have been made to date.

18. Interest on tax etc. recovered or recoverable by assessment. (A18.61–63)
Failure to pay the right amount of VAT at the correct time renders a person liable to pay interest on the unpaid VAT for the amount of time that it remains unpaid.

Interest is due on VAT payable in such circumstances as late notification for registration.

Interest is also payable on assessments for underpayments because of errors made by the registered person identified during visits by officers which relate to periods when returns and payments have been made.

An amount which is due for a prescribed accounting period has interest charged on the whole of the amount from the proper statutory date until payment.

Where an unregistered person issues a VAT invoice interest is due from the invoice date until the VAT is paid.

The time when interest begins to be charged where incorrect reclaims of input tax are involved is seven days after the Commissioners authorised the incorrect repayment, and where underpayments are concerned the latest date on which a return for the period in question could have been submitted.

The rate of interest is prescribed by Treasury order. The prescribed rate in force from 1 April 1990 is 13 per cent: see Finance Act 1985 (Interest on Tax) (Prescribed Rate) Order 1990, S.I. 1990 No. 523 art. 2. Interest is paid without deduction of income tax.

This section came into operation on 1 April 1990. See Finance Act 1985 (Serious Misdeclaration and Interest on Tax) (Appointed Days) Order 1989, S.I. 1989 No. 2270 art. 3. It applies to any prescribed accounting period beginning on or after that date.

Whereas s. 14 (misdeclarations resulting in understatements or overclaims) does not apply where the person voluntarily declares the correct amount of VAT due, this section makes no such allowance. Indeed if an attempt was made to evade a charge to interest by including an amount of VAT underpaid on a previous section as due in the current return the person could be liable to a charge of criminal or civil fraud.

19. The default surcharge. (A18.71–73)
Where a VAT return or payment is submitted later than the due date of one month after the end of the return period, and a subsequent return or payment within the next 12 months is also late, a "surcharge liability notice" is issued warning that further late submission within the next 12 months will attract a penalty. If further late returns or payments then occur within 12 months of the issue of the surcharge liability notice, a surcharge is due and the surcharge period is extended for a further 12 months from each late submission. However, a trader is not liable to surcharge if he proves, on the balance of probabilities, that he did not receive the surcharge liability notice served by the Commissioners: *C. & E. Comrs.* v. *Medway Draughting & Technical Services Ltd.* [1989] STC 346.

Whilst a surcharge liability notice is in force the surcharge is set at the greater of £30 or 5 per cent. for the first late submission or payment, increasing by 5 per cent. steps to a maximum of 30 per cent. for subsequent late submissions or payments. Late submission of repayment claims or nil returns extend the surcharge liability notice period and also uplift the potential surcharge rate: see *Linco*

Impex Ltd. v. *C. & E. Comrs.* MAN/88/251 unreported. However, as VAT has not been delayed, the minimum of £30 applies.

In the absence of a VAT return the Commissioners issue a VAT assessment and calculate the surcharge at the appropriate rate on the VAT assessed for the period. The surcharge is adjusted when the return is submitted so as to be calculated on the actual VAT due for that period.

Under-declarations subsequently discovered (*e.g.*, on a VAT inspection) which relate to a surcharge period are subjected to the same rate of surcharge as was applied to the VAT previously reported for that period.

A trader is not liable to surcharge if he satisfies the Commissioners or, on appeal, a VAT tribunal, that his return or remittance was despatched in reasonable time and manner to arrive no later than the due date. For successful appeals, see *Nazeing Glass Works Ltd.* v. *C. & E. Comrs.* LON/88/70 unreported (entry in post book); *Granville Furniture Ltd.* v. *C. & E. Comrs.* MAN/88/226 unreported (firm recollection of witness). For unsuccessful appeals, see *Zilani Clothing* v. *C. & E. Comrs.* MAN/87/494 (cheque dated before due date); *Holmes* v. *C. & E. Comrs.* LON/88/300 unreported (standing instruction to post envelope in due time); *Wines* v. *C. & E. Comrs.* LON/87/796 unreported (recollection of witness). It is insufficient to post a return or remittance *on* the due date: *Kings Portable Buildings Ltd.* v. *C. & E. Comrs.* LON/87/737 unreported.

A trader is not liable to surcharge if he satisfies the Commissioners or, on appeal, a VAT tribunal, that he has a reasonable excuse for despatching his return or remittance late. For successful appeals, see for example: *Silk Interiors Ltd.* v. *C. & E. Comrs.* LON/87/799 unreported (Commissioners sent return to incorrect address); *Computer Presentations Ltd.* v. *C. & E. Comrs.* MAN/88/190 unreported (return mislaid when moving office); *T. & H. Collard Ltd.* v. *C. & E. Comrs.* LON/87/692 unreported (trader believed that time limit had been extended); *Harrison* v. *C. & E. Comrs.* MAN/88/307 unreported (return withheld for inspection at impending control visit); *Midas Publishing Services Ltd.* v. *C. & E. Comrs.* LON/88/739 unreported (envelope mislaid during accident while driving to post office); *Snow & Rock Sports Ltd.* v. *C. & E. Comrs.* LON/88/596 unreported (change of stagger group); *Appleyard Lees & Co.* v. *C. & E. Comrs.* MAN/88/145 unreported (misunderstanding regarding due date); *Corton Bashforth Screenprint Ltd.* v. *C. & E. Comrs.* MAN/88/491 unreported (clerical error in writing cheque). Delays resulting from an unforeseeable event at a material time normally amount to a reasonable excuse: see, for example, *Manchester Scaffolding Ltd.* v. *C. & E. Comrs.* MAN/88/96 unreported (sudden resignation of staff); *Wordsworth Trade Press Ltd.* v. *C. & E. Comrs.* LON/87/639 unreported (illness); *Concours Motor Co. Ltd.* v. *C. & E. Comrs.* LON/88/830 unreported (computer breakdown); *Collyer* v. *C. & E. Comrs.* MAN/87/314 unreported (fire). Delays resulting from foreseeable events do not amount to a reasonable excuse: see for example, *F. & P. Appointments Ltd.* v. *C. & E. Comrs.* LON/88/171 unreported (holiday closedown); *Boston Copying Machines* v. *C. & E. Comrs.* LON/87/697 unreported (key staff on holiday or business trip); *Reid* v. *C. & E. Comrs.* LON/88/277 unreported (complex accounting system); *Photographic Applications Ltd.* v. *C. & E. Comrs.* LON/87/800 unreported (end of financial year); *Warren* v. *C. & E. Comrs.* MAN/88/27 unreported (pressure of work). Thus, an unexpected event may be reasonable in relation to one period but not in relation to the next period: see *Bowen* v. *C. & E. Comrs.* [1987] VATTR 255. Insufficiency of funds is not a reasonable excuse: see FA 1985 s. 33 (2).

A surcharge liability notice is deemed not to have been served if, in relation to a default on which it depended, the trader satisfies the Commissioners that he despatched the return or remittance in reasonable time and manner to arrive no later than the due date or that he had a reasonable excuse for not doing so. In these circumstances, no surcharge arises in respect of the first default occurring within the surcharge period set out in the surcharge liability notice.

Where a penalty is imposed for failing to comply with orders and regulations under s. 17 above no default surcharge is payable.

20. Repayment supplement in respect of certain delayed payments. (A15.08)

When a person is entitled to a repayment of VAT for a prescribed accounting period and the return was rendered on time, but the Commissioners did not issue authority for the repayment to be made within 30 days following the end of the month following the return period, and the return is within £250 or 5 per cent. of the correct amount due to be repaid, then the registered person will receive the greater of £30 or 5 per cent. of the amount due as a supplement. See *Richard Costain Ltd.* v. *C. & E. Comrs.* [1988] VATTR 106, 111.

The Commissioners may make regulations specifying periods to be disregarded in determining the 30-day limit. See VAT (Repayment Supplement) (No. 2) Regulations 1988, S.I. 1988 No. 1343.

If after a repayment supplement has been made, it is discovered that an overclaim of more than £30 has been paid then Customs and Excise will recover the excess supplement.

Assessments, records and information

21. Assessment of amounts due by way of penalty, interest or surcharge. (A15.32, 38; A18.43, 46, 76)

Where any person is liable to a penalty for VAT evasion, misdeclaration or neglect, failure to notify for registration or unauthorised issue of invoices, breach of walking possession agreements or breaches of regulatory provisions, or interest or surcharge the Commissioners may assess the amount due by giving the person notice, even though the conduct giving rise to the penalty may have ceased.

Penalties, interest and surcharges are calculated by reference to a prescribed accounting period (VAT return period) referred to as the relevant period. The relevant period for a s. 13 penalty is the accounting period in which the VAT evaded should have been paid. Where a repayment is dishonestly obtained the relevant period is the accounting period in which the payment was obtained. For a s. 14 penalty the relevant period is the accounting period in which VAT was understated or where a greater repayment is made than is due the accounting period in which the overstatement occurred. For s. 18 interest the relevant period is the accounting period in which the tax or the amount assesed as tax was due. For a s. 19 surcharge the relevant period is the accounting period which creates the surcharge.

Where a penalty, interest or surcharge is calculated by reference to tax which was not paid at the correct time and the tax or the supply which created the tax cannot be attributed to any one period, the penalty interest or surcharge is attributed to accounting periods by the Commissioners to the best of their judgment.

Where a person is assessed to a penalty interest or surcharge and an assessment is made for failure to make returns or making incomplete returns or a repayment was incorrectly claimed or where goods cannot be accounted for, the assessments can be combined and notified as one assessment but the penalty, interest or surcharge must be identified separately.

A penalty for breach of the regulatory provisions or interest on VAT underpaid can be calculated up to the date on the notice. If the penalty or interest continues a further notice of assessment may be raised. Where such a breach of regulations is corrected or tax previously underpaid is paid within the time limit allowed by the Commissioners, the date of correction or payment is that on the notice detailing the failure.

An assessment for a penalty interest or surcharge is recoverable as if it was tax due.

Notice of a penalty, interest or surcharge to a personal representative, trustee in bankruptcy, receiver or liquidator or other person acting as such is treated as notification to the registered person.

22. Assessments: time limits and supplementary assessments. (A15.37, 39)

An assessment under VATA 1983, Sch. 7, para. 4 or s. 21 above may not be more than six years after the end of the accounting period or importation concerned or the event giving rise to a penalty if it is not mentioned in s. 21 (2) above.

An assessment of a penalty which is mentioned in s. 21 (2) above may not be made more than two years after the tax due for the accounting period concerned has been fixed.

Where, as a result of conduct which has been dishonest, VAT has not been paid or a liability to be registered has not been notified or unauthorised invoices have been issued, then an assessment may be made up to 20 years after the end of the accounting period concerned. However, an assessment of a penalty, interest or surcharge may not be made more than three years after a person's death.

Provided the Commissioners act within one year of facts coming to their knowledge which are sufficient to justify an increase in an amount already assessed, a supplementary assessment may be raised if it is within the time limits for the original assessment. See *Bowden* v. *C. & E. Comrs.* [1987] VATTR 255; *Bill Hennessy Associates Ltd.* v. *C. & E. Comrs.* LON/87/640 unreported.

25. Settling appeals by agreement. (A17.61, 66)

A decision of the Commissioners against which notice of appeal has been given may be upheld, varied or discharged by agreement between the appellant and the Commissioners. An oral agreement must be confirmed in writing by either party within 30 days. The same consequences follow as if a tribunal had determined the appeal at the date of the written agreement or written confirmation.

The appellant may repudiate or resile from the agreement by giving written notice within 30 days of the written agreement or written confirmation.

The foregoing provisions apply where an appellant wishes to withdraw his appeal and the Commissioners do not object. The parties are deemed to have come to an agreement that the appeal should be upheld without variation. The agreement is deemed to be made when the appellant notifies the Commissioners that he does not wish to proceed with the appeal. The Commissioners may object by notifying the appellant in writing within 30 days that they are unwilling that the appeal should be treated as withdrawn.

An agent may act on behalf of an appellant in making an agreement with the Commissioners, or in giving or receiving a notice or notification.

26. Certain appeals to lie directly to the Court of Appeal. (A17.76)

The Lord Chancellor may by order provide that some appeals from a VAT tribunal in England, Wales or Northern Ireland, with the consent of the parties, may proceed directly to the Court of Appeal. Such an order may modify the Tribunals and Inquiries Act 1971, s. 13. It is made by statutory instrument subject to annulment by either House of Parliament. See Value Added Tax Tribunals Appeals Order 1986, S.I. 1986 No. 2288.

27. Procedural rules governing appeals. (A17.52)
The Commissioners have to prove that a person's conduct involved dishonesty for the purpose of avoiding VAT in an appeal against a s. 13 assessment.

The power to make rules under VATA 1983, Sch. 8, para. 9 is transferred from the Commissioners to the Lord Chancellor from 1 July 1986: Finance Act 1985 (VAT Tribunal Rules) (Appointed Day) Order 1986, S.I. 1986 No. 934. The rules in force before that day continue to have effect.

Miscellaneous
29. Enforcement of certain decisions of tribunal. (A15.73)
If the decision of a VAT tribunal in England and Wales is registered by the Commissioners under the rules of court, any amount recoverable as tax due or costs awarded to the Commissioners may be enforced by the High Court. For the rules of court, see RSC Ord. 45 r. 14. Equivalent procedures apply in Scotland and Northern Ireland.

30. Appointments to and administration of tribunals.
Sch. 8 has effect from 1 April 1986: see VAT (Tribunals) Commencement Order 1986, S.I. 1986 No. 365. Appointments to sit on tribunals made under the old rules are not affected by the new rules.

33. Interpretation and construction of Chapter II. (A18.45)
Various terms used in the Act are defined.

A reasonable excuse does not include: (1) having no money to pay any VAT (see *C. & E. Comrs.* v. *Palco Industry Co. Ltd.* [1990] STI 544 (cheque dishonoured); but see *C. & E. Comrs* v. *Salevon Ltd.* [1989] STC 907 for the limited exceptions to this general rule); (2) reliance on some other person to perform a task; or (3) dilatoriness or inaccuracy by a person relied on to perform a task. For ill health etc. of a person relied on, see *Bowen* v. *C. & E. Comrs.* [1987] VATTR 255. For advice and opinions from third parties, see *C. & E, Comrs.* v. *Harris* [1989] STC 907; *Taylor and Beech (a firm)* v. *C. & E. Comrs.* MAN/87/2 unreported; *Noble* v. *C. & E. Comrs.* MAN/87/106 unreported; *Butler* v. *C. & E. Comrs.* MAN/87/119, 185 unreported.

Penalties under ss. 13 to 17 are not subject to CEMA 1979, ss. 145 to 155. VATA 1983, s. 45 does not apply to orders made under this Chapter.

SCHEDULE 8 VALUE ADDED TAX TRIBUNALS (Section 30)

Administration
6.—(A2.41) Officers and staff may be appointed under the Courts Act 1971, s. 27 to carry out the administration work of VAT tribunals in England and Wales. The Secretary of State makes arrangements for administrative staff of VAT tribunals in Scotland.

Finance Act 1986
1986 Chapter 41

PART I CUSTOMS AND EXCISE AND VALUE ADDED TAX

CHAPTER II VALUE ADDED TAX

9. Fuel for private use. (A6.56)

In any accounting period beginning after 6 April 1987 where a taxable person who has been supplied with fuel in the course of his business then supplies that fuel to any individual for private use below the cost of the fuel to the business, he is treated as supplying the fuel for the consideration (scale charge) inclusive of VAT set out in Sch. 6, paras. 2 and 3 which is appropriate to the car and the business miles completed. This section does not apply where fuel is supplied at a price equal to or greater than the cost of the fuel to the taxable person.

VAT on fuel for private use is treated as input tax although the fuel is not to be used for the purposes of the business. No apportionment is therefore necessary under VATA 1983, s. 14 (4).

Incidental private use of pool cars which are kept overnight on the employer's premises does not result in a scale charge.

14. Penalty for tax evasion: liability of directors etc. (A18.51)

Where a corporate body is liable to a penalty for conduct involving dishonesty and that conduct is in whole or in part attributable to a person who is or was a director or managing officer of the corporate body the Commissioners may recover from the individual a penalty which may equal the basic penalty on the corporate body. Where the Commissioners penalise an individual the corporate body is liable only for the balance of the basic penalty. The corporate body and the individual officer may appeal to a VAT tribunal against the Commissioners decision as to the reason for and the amount of the basic penalty. Penalties cannot be levied on individuals for dishonest conduct which took place before 25 July 1986.

SCHEDULES

SCHEDULE 6 CONSIDERATION FOR FUEL SUPPLIED FOR PRIVATE USE (Section 9) (A6.56)

The consideration deemed payable by an individual to a VAT registered person for fuel for private use is as set out in the following table.

Up to 1,400 cc				1401–2000 cc				Over 2000 cc			
Quarterly return		Monthly return		Quarterly return		Monthly return		Quarterly return		Monthly return	
Scale Chge	VAT due	Scale Chge	VAT due	Scale Chge	VAT due	Scale Chge	VAT due	Scale Chge	VAT due	Scale Chge	VAT due
£120	£15.65	£40	£5.21	£150	£19.56	£50	£6.52	£225	£29.34	£75	£9.78
Over 4,500 miles		Over 1,500 miles		Over 4,500 miles		Over 1,500 miles		Over 4,500 miles		Over 1,500 miles	
£60	£7.82	£20	£2.60	£75	£9.78	£25	£3.26	£113	£14.73	£38	£4.95

The Treasury may, by order, substitute different rates from the beginning of any prescribed accounting period after the date of the order. No orders have been made to date.

Where an individual changes vehicles within a period and the vehicles are of the same cubic capacity description then the scale charge applicable is that of one vehicle used throughout the period. Where the cubic capacity of the cars used in a period differ only one scale charge is applicable and that charge is the sum of the fractions on a time basis of the appropriate scale charges for each vehicle.

Finance Act 1988
1988 Chapter 39

PART I CUSTOMS AND EXCISE

MANAGEMENT

8. Disclosure of information as to imports.
The Commissioners are empowered to make available for publication the names and addresses of importers for each classification of imported goods on payment of fees. For the publication of information under this provision, see Press Notice 43/89, 1 June 1989.

PART II VALUE ADDED TAX

21. Set-off of credits. (A15.08)
The amount of tax, penalty, interest or surcharge due to Customs and Excise may be set off against any tax credit to be paid by Customs and Excise. See *R. v. C. & E. Comrs. ex parte Richmond* [1989] STC 429.

22. Invoices provided by recipients of goods or services. (A14.22)
The rules concerning recovery of VAT in the case of a self-billing arrangement have been changed. If the invoice understates the VAT liability, Customs and Excise may by notice to both the customer and the supplier elect to recover VAT from the customer instead of the supplier.

Finance Act 1989
1989 Chapter 26

CHAPTER II VALUE ADDED TAX

ZERO-RATING ETC.

18. Buildings and land.
This section introduces Sch. 3.

OTHER PROVISIONS

24. Recovery of overpaid VAT. (A15.58)
The Commissioners must repay VAT paid to them if: (1) it was not due; (2) the person who made the payment makes a claim in the form and manner prescribed by regulations; and (3) he would not be unjustly enriched by the repayment. For regulations, see VAT (Accounting and Records) Regulations 1989, S.I. 1989 No. 2248 reg. 6. For "unjust enrichment" under EC law, see most recently *E.C. Commission* v. *Italy* (case 104/86) [1989] 3 CMLR 25, ECJ; *Les Fils de Jules Bianco SA* v. *Directeur General des Douanes et Droits* (cases 331, 376 and 378/85) [1989] 3 CMLR 36, ECJ; *Deville* v. *Administration des Impots* (case 240/87) [1989] 3 CMLR 611, ECJ.

Claims must be made within six years from discovery (in the case of error) or payment (in other cases). Claims may relate to payments made before or after 1 January 1990.

Claims made before 1 January 1990 are governed by legislation then in force. See *C. & E. Comrs.* v. *Fine Art Developments plc.* [1989] STC 85, HL and *Springfield China Ltd.* v. *C. & E. Comrs.* MAN/89/180 unreported.

This section came into operation on 1 January 1990. See Finance Act 1989 (Recovery of Overpaid Tax and Administration) (Appointed Days) Order 1989, S.I. 1989 No. 2271.

PART III MISCELLANEOUS AND GENERAL

MISCELLANEOUS

182. Disclosure of information. (A18.02)
A person commits an offence if he discloses, without lawful authority, any information concerning the tax affairs of an identifiable person or business.

SCHEDULES

SCHEDULE 3 VALUE ADDED TAX: BUILDINGS AND LAND (Section 18)

Commencement
12.—Part of this Schedule comes into operation on 1 April 1989 and the remainder on 1 August 1989.
13.—**(A6.47, 50; A11.33–40)** Supplies made on or after 1 April 1989 may be zero-rated under VATA 1983, Sch. 5, Groups 8 or 8A (as effective before that date) in two circumstances. First, where the relevant supply is made in accordance with a contract made before 21 June 1988. Secondly, where the developer incurred, before 21 June 1988, a legally binding obligation to carry out a development under planning permission granted before that date and the relevant supply is made before 21 June 1993 under a contract made between those two dates.

An exemption from the charge to tax under VATA 1983, Sch. 6A, para. 5 arises in similar circumstances.

Finance Act 1990
1990 Chapter 29

PART I CUSTOMS AND EXCISE AND VALUE ADDED TAX

CHAPTER I CUSTOMS AND EXCISE

OTHER PROVISIONS

8. Entry of goods on importation.
This section introduces Sch. 3. It applies to goods imported on or after Royal Assent.

CHAPTER II VALUE ADDED TAX

11. Registration. (A3.41, 43; A8.81)
The rules for determining whether a person is liable to registration are simplified from 21 March 1990 and the existing notification requirements modified accordingly.

12. Bad debts. (A15.55)
A person is entitled to a refund if: (1) he supplied goods or services for a money consideration after 31 March 1989; (2) he has accounted for and paid tax on the supply; (3) he has written off all or part of the consideration as a bad debt; (4) two years have elapsed from the time of supply; (5) the value of the supply does not exceed open market value; (6) (in the case of a supply of goods) property in the goods passes to the customer or, through him, to another person; and (7) a claim is made.

A claim is made in respect of the tax element of the outstanding amount, *i.e.* the consideration written off less payment(s) (if any) received to the date of the claim.

Claims are made, evidenced and calculated in accordance with regulations. No regulations have been made to date.

No claim may be made if a refund has been claimed under the existing bad debt relief (see VATA 1983 s. 22). That relief does not apply to any supply made after 25 July 1990. For supplies made between 1 April 1989 and 26 July 1990, claims should be made under VATA 1983, s. 22, if possible, to avoid the two-year wait under this section.

Provisions relating to criminal penalties for fraudulent conduct, civil penalties for dishonest conduct and the rights of appeal are applied to claims under this section.

13. Domestic accommodation. (A13.36)
VAT incurred on the provision of domestic accommodation for company directors and their families ceases to be eligible for input tax credit as regards goods or services supplied or imported on or after Royal Assent.

14. Goods shipped as stores. (A12.21)
Goods supplied after Royal Assent are not zero-rated if they are shipped for use as stores on a private voyage or flight by the person to whom they were supplied.

15. Supplies to groups. (A6.46)
Capital items are not self-supplied from 1 April 1990 when the assets of a business are transferred as a going concern to a partly exempt VAT group.

16. Power to assess. (A15.36)
Payments, refunds and repayments made by the Commissioners under a mistake of fact can be recovered by assessment.

17. Interest on tax etc. recovered or recoverable by assessment. (A18.62)
The rules for charging interest are simplified in relation to tax for prescribed accounting periods exceeding three months. The new rules apply to assessments made after Royal Assent.

SCHEDULES

SCHEDULE 3 ENTRY OF GOODS ON IMPORTATION (Section 8)

1–4. (A7.07) The provisions relating to initial and supplementary entries and postponed entries are extended to benefit all importers. Importers not authorised to furnish such entries must instruct an agent who is authorised, and he makes the entries and gives security on the importer's behalf.

STATUTORY INSTRUMENTS

S.I. 1972 No. 1148

The Value Added Tax (Supplies by Retailers) Regulations 1972

Note

These Regulations make general provisions for special schemes by which a retailer may calculate VAT on his outputs. The detailed schemes A-J are described in leaflets in the 727 series issued by the Commissioners or as determined by agreement with the retailer.

1. These Regulations came into operation on 1 April 1973.

2. The Commissioners may, either by agreement with a retailer or by any method described in a notice determine the method of valuing positive rated supplies made in any prescribed accounting period. The Commissioners may vary the terms by issuing a new notice, amending an existing notice or amending a method by agreement with a retailer. For the legal status of notices, see *GUS Merchandise Corpn. Ltd.* v. *C. & E. Comrs.* [1980] STC 480. For general provisions regarding the retail schemes, see Notice No. 727 (October 1987) and Leaflet Nos. 727/1/87 (retail florists), 727/6/87 (choosing your retail scheme). For the retail schemes, see:

Scheme	Leaflet No.	Cases
A	727/7/87	
B	727/8/87	*Kelly (a firm)* v. *C. & E. Comrs.*
		LON/87/576 unreported
B (Adaptation 1)	727/8A/87	
B (Adaptation 2)	727/8B/87	
C	727/9/87	
D	727/10/87	
E	727/11/87	
E (Adaptation 1)	727/11A/87	
F	727/12/87	
G	727/13/87	
H	727/14/90	
J	727/15/90	

3. The Commissioners may refuse to value supplies by means of a retail scheme where it appears to them that the normal invoicing procedures could be followed or that the use of a scheme would not produce a fair result.

4. Only one scheme may be used by a retailer at any one time unless otherwise allowed by the Commissioners.

5. A retailer must tick the appropriate box on every VAT return, notifying which scheme he is using.

6. Retail schemes must be adopted for a minimum of one year except where the Commissioners otherwise allow and any change in schemes must be made at the end of any complete year beginning at the start of the tax period in which the scheme was adopted. For retrospective changes of scheme, see *Withers & Gibbs (a firm)* v. *C. & E. Comrs.* [1983] VATTR 323; *Patel* v. *C. & E. Comrs.* LON/80/39 unreported; *Vulgar* v. *C. & E. Comrs.* [1976] VATTR 197; *Pollitt (a firm)* v. *C. & E. Comrs.* MAN/89/160 unreported; *Bryan Markwell & Co. Ltd.* v. *C. & E. Comrs.* LON/89/895 unreported. See also Press Notice No. 1049, 12 November 1985.

7. The Commissioners must be notified before cessation of the use of a scheme and a retailer may be required to pay tax on such proportion of credit supplies as the Commissioners consider fair and reasonable at the end of use of a scheme.

8. Retailers who are also pharmacists are to make an adjustment to the calculations made under a retail scheme as described in a notice published by the Commissioners. The Commissioners may vary the manner of adjustment either by issuing a new notice or by agreement with any retailer.

9. Retailers using a scheme are to take such steps as are directed in a notice applicable to them or as the case may be agreed with the Commissioners when there is a change in the tax charged on any supply.

10. Where a retailer supplies both zero rated food and standard rated food in the course of catering, he shall either keep records identifying the proportion of zero rated and all other supplies to the satisfaction of the Commissioners or where such records are impracticable, make an estimate. If at any time the estimate is no longer accurate or to the Commissioners' satisfaction, then tax shall be accounted for on the basis of a new estimate. The Commissioners may direct the use of a further estimate where they are not satisfied that a retailer's new estimate is accurate and direct the starting date.

S.I. 1973 No. 173

The Value Added Tax (Terminal Markets) Order 1973

Note

This order zero rates certain supplies of goods and services in the course of dealings on the terminal markets listed below which involve goods ordinarily dealt with on the markets. Supplies which are zero rated are fixtures transactions (including options) not resulting in a delivery of goods, provided they are supplied by or to a member of one of the markets; and sales of physical goods between members of one market (subject to certain conditions). The order also zero rates the services of any market member acting as a broker in connection with any of these supplies.

1. This order came into operation on 1 April 1973.
2. This order applies to, The London Metal Exchange, The London Rubber Market, The London Cocoa Terminal Market, The London Coffee Terminal Market, The London Sugar Terminal Market, The London Vegetable Oil Terminal Market, The London Wool Terminal Market, The London Gold Market, The London Silver Market, The London Metal Futures Market, The London Grain Futures Market, The London Soya Bean Meal Futures Market, The London Barley Futures Market, The International Petroleum Exchange of London, The LondonPotato Futures Market and the London Platinum and Palladium Market.
3. The following supplies of goods or services in the course of dealings on the above markets are zero rated subject to the conditions below:
   (*a*) a sale by or to a member of the market of any goods ordinarily dealt with on the market;
   (*b*) a grant by or to a member of the market of the right to acquire such goods;
   (*c*) where a sale of goods or the grant of an option is made in dealings between members of the market acting as agents, a supply by those members to their principals of their services in so acting.

The zero rating of such a sale is subject to the condition that the sale is either a sale which as a result of other dealings on the market does not lead to a delivery of the goods by the seller to the buyer, or a sale by or to a member of the market. In the latter case if the market is The London Metal Exchange the transaction must be between members entitled to deal in the "open ring". If the market is The London Cocoa Terminal Market, The London Coffee Terminal Market, The London Meat Futures Market, The International Petroleum Exchange of London, The London Potato Futures Market, The London Soya Bean Meal Futures Market, The London Sugar Terminal Market, The London Vegetable Oil Terminal Market or The London Wool Terminal Market the sale must be registered with the International Commodities Clearing House Limited.

If the market is the London Grain Futures Market, the sale must be registered in the clearing house of The Grain and Future Association Limited. If the market is a Liverpool Barley Futures Market the sale must be registered at the clearing house of the Liverpool Corn Trade Association Limited.

The zero rating of the grant of a right to acquire such goods is subject to the condition that either the right is excercisable at a date later than that on which it is granted or any sale resulting from the exercise of the right would be a sale with respect to which the conditions in the previous paragraph are satisfied.

S.I. 1973 No. 293

The Value Added Tax (Trading Stamps) Regulations 1973

Note

These Regulations make special provision for the valuation for VAT purposes of goods supplied under trading stamps schemes.

1. These Regulations came into operation on 1 April 1983.
2. Words and phrases used in the Regulation are defined.
3. The normal rules for valuing a supply of goods are amended.
4. The value for VAT purposes of the supply of goods by a promoter of a trading stamp scheme is to be calculated as follows:
   (*a*) The amount of money charged in a period to persons to whom supplies of trading stamps (which are to be treated as neither supplies of goods nor services) are made plus all charges in connection with supplies of goods made in exchange for stamps in that period less the amount paid in that period by the promoter to redeem stamps for cash, less amounts paid by the promoter for goods and services other than those which he undertakes to supply in exchange for stamps.
   (*b*) The total number of stamps delivered less the number of stamps redeemed for cash and less the number of stamps that fairly represent the average number not redeemed may also be used as a method.
   (*c*) The average amount charged for each stamp according to its denomination delivered in a

period shall be calculated by reference to the amount of money calculated under the above and the number of stamps shall be ascertained under (*b*) above.

5. Any amount charged by a promoter to a person who receives deliveries of stamps which is fixed by reference to the number of stamps delivered shall be deemed to be a charge for stamps.

6. The regulations shall not apply where the promoter makes a supply of goods or services which is not fixed by reference to the number of stamps delivered.

S.I. 1973 No. 325

The Value Added Tax (Treatment of Transactions) (No. 1) Order 1973

Note

This Order removes from the scope of VAT certain transactions in trading stamps and complements S.I. 1973 No. 293.

1. This Order came into operation on 1 April 1973.

2. Words and phrases used in the Order are defined.

3. The delivery by the promoter of a trading stamp scheme of stamps except where the stamps are delivered to a wholesaler who will package the stamps with standard rated goods is outside the scope of VAT. Also outside the scope of VAT is the delivery of trading stamps by a person other than a promoter in conjunction with a supply by him of goods or services, except deliveries of trading stamps enclosed in packages of goods.

S.I. 1973 No. 2121

The Value Added Tax (Refund of Tax) (No. 2) Order 1973

Note

Regional water authorities were established under the Water Act 1973, s. 2. By this Order these authorities are entitled to a refund of VAT on supplies to or importations by them if not made for the purpose of business. See VATA 1983, s. 20.

1. This Order came into operation on 10 January 1974.

2. The Interpretation Act 1889 applies to this Order.

The following water authorities may reclaim input VAT on supplies made to them or on importations by them which are not for the purpose of business.

   Welsh National Water Development Authority
   North West Water Authority
   Northumbrian Water Authority
   Yorkshire Water Authority
   Anglian Water Authority
   Thames Water Authority
   Southern Water Authority
   Wessex Water Authority
   South West Water Authority
   Severn Trent Water Authority

S.I. 1976 No. 1223

The Customs Duties (Deferred Payment) Regulations 1976

Note

These Regulations provide for deferment of customs duties payable on imported goods and on imported warehoused goods removed from warehouse; they also apply to agricultural levy and to VAT payable on imported goods (see VATA 1983, s. 2(4)) and on such goods removed from warehouse. The Regulations prescribe the period for which deferment is allowed and the action to be taken by those seeking deferment including the giving of security. Provision is also made for cases of over-or under-payment of duty. For the purposes of giving relief by repayment of duty, duty is deemed to have been paid at the time when deferment was permitted.

Citation and commencement
1. These Regulations come into operation on 1 September 1976.

Interpretation
2. Various words and phrases used in the Regulations are defined, the Interpretation Act 1889 applies and approvals granted by a Collector of Customs and Excise under the Customs Duties (Deferred Payments) Regulations 1972 remain valid.

Application
3. These Regulations apply where goods are chargeable with customs duty at the time a customs entry is made.

Approval
4. A person who wishes to be approved for duty deferment must apply to the Commissioners in such form and manner as they shall determine: in practice they require completion of form C1200. He must furnish security for payment of the amount of duty for which deferment is requested, by obtaining from a bank or insurance company a guarantee which is approved by the Commissioners, normally on form C1201.

   If satisfied, the Commissioners will in writing permit the applicant to defer payment of an amount of duty not exceeding that for which security has been given.

   The Regulations provide that the approval may be limited to deferments within named Collections but the Commissioners have extended this to cover entries at any port, airport or warehouse.

   The Commissioners may, if they have reasonable cause, vary or revoke any approval granted under this regulation. Changes in the details given in the application, security given, or the arrangements for payment must be notified to the Commissioners forthwith.

Grant of deferment
5. If an approved person applies in the form and manner determined by the Commissioners, they will defer customs duty until payment day.

Payment
6. Payment of duty upon which deferment has been approved is due on the 15th day of the month following the month of importation, called payment day. The Commissioners will only accept a bank giro direct debit, for which they provide form C1202.
7. If at any time after entry has been made the Commissioners are satisfied that the full amount of duty has not been shown on the entry then, unless they allow otherwise, the balance is payable forthwith, deferment not being allowed. Where customs duty has been overpaid, the Commissioners repay the excess; however, the total amount has to be paid to the Commissioners on payment day.
8. Duty is regarded as having been paid at the time deferment is granted for the purposes of the Acts listed.

S.I. 1976 No. 2028

The Value Added Tax (Refund of Tax) Order 1976

The following bodies are specified for the purposes of FA 1972, s. 15 (now VATA 1983, s. 20) as persons entitled to a refund of VAT on supplies to or importations by them if not made for the purpose of business.
   The Commission for Local Administration in England.
   The Commission for Local Administration in Wales.
   The Commission for Local Administration in Scotland.
   The Commission for Local Authority Accounts in Scotland.

S.I. 1977 No. 1790

The Value Added Tax (Imported Goods) Relief Order 1977

Note
This Order permits the importation by Central Banks of gold without payment of VAT.

To conform with Directive 77/388/EEC, no VAT is payable on the importation of gold including gold coins by Central Banks.

S.I. 1980 No. 442

The Value Added Tax (Cars) Order 1980

Note
This Order consolidates and revokes Orders concerning the treatment for VAT of new and used motor cars. It revokes the article which concerned the non-deductibility of input VAT on certain goods installed in a motor car after VAT has been paid and supplied with it at the standard rate of VAT. Articles 4, 5 and 6 contain provisions concerning the deduction of input VAT on the supply or importation of new or used motor cars, the self-supply of certain motor cars and the charging of VAT, subject to conditions, on the difference between the buying and selling prices on sales of used motor cars. Article 7 removes from the scope of VAT disposals by finance houses and insurers of used motor cars which have been acquired by them in the circumstances specified and disposals without consideration of any motor car on which deduction of input tax was disallowed on its acquisition.

Citation and commencement
1. This Order came into operation on 30 April 1980.

Interpretation
2. A motor car means any motor vehicle of a kind normally used on public roads which has three or more wheels and either is constructed or adapted mainly for the carriage of passengers or has to the rear of the driver's seat roofed accommodation fitted with side windows. For the test applied, see *C. & E. Comrs.* v. *Jeynes* [1984] STC 30; *Withers of Winsford Ltd.* v. *C. & E. Comrs.* [1988] STC 431; For the carriage of passengers, see *Chartcliffe Ltd.* v. *C. & E. Comrs.* [1976] VATTR 165; *Bolinge Hill Farm* v. *C. & E. Comrs.* LON/89/1071 unreported; *A. L. Yeoman Ltd.* v. *C. & E. Comrs.* EDN/89/104 unreported. For roofed accommodation cf. *R.* v. *C. & E. Comrs. ex parte Nissan (U.K.) Ltd.* (1987) Times, 23 November, CA. Excluded are vehicles capable of carrying only one person or suitable for twelve or more persons, vehicles of three tonnes or more unladen weight, caravans, ambulances, prison vans, London taxis and special purpose vehicles with no accommodation for carrying persons except such as is incidental to that purpose. For special purpose vehicles, see *Chartcliffe Ltd.* v. *C. & E. Comrs.* [1976] VATTR 165; *Weatherproof Flat Roofing (Plymouth) Ltd.* v. *C. & E. Comrs.* LON/81/351 unreported; *Knapp* v. *C. & E. Comrs.* LON/79/55 unreported.

Revocation and savings
3. Continuity with earlier orders is provided for.

Disallowance of input tax
4. VAT charged on the supply or importation of a motor car is excluded from input VAT deduction except where (*a*) the supply is a letting on hire; or (*b*) the motor car is supplied or imported for the purpose of its conversion into a vehicle which is not a motor car (for "conversion", see *G. A. Security Systems Ltd.* v. *C. & E. Comrs.* MAN/83/212 unreported; *Direct Link Couriers (Bristol) Ltd.* v. *C. & E. Comrs.* LON/85/481 unreported; *Scargill* v. *C. & E. Comrs.* MAN/82/122 unreported); or (*c*) the motor car is unused and is supplied or imported for the purpose of being sold; or (*d*) the motor car is unused and is supplied or imported for research and development purposes in a car production business which does not involve the conversion of vehicles; or (*e*) the motor car is unused and is supplied to a taxable person whose only taxable supplies are the letting of motor cars on hire to another taxable person whose business consists predominantly of providing motor cars to disabled persons. A sale includes any supply under a hire-purchase agreement.

For disallowance of tax on delivery charges and optional extras, see *Wimpey Construction U.K. Ltd.* v. *C. & E. Comrs.* [1979] VATTR 174 and *Turmeau* v. *C. & E. Comrs.* LON/81/164 (disallowed when supply made by vendor of car); *Broadhead Peel & Co.* v. *C. & E. Comrs.* [1984] VATTR 195 (allowed when supplied by someone else). For cars to be dismantled and parts sold as spares, see *Withers of Winsford* v. *C. & E. Comrs.* [1988] STC 431.

Self-supply
5. Motor cars produced or acquired by a taxable person which are neither supplied by the taxable person nor converted into another vehicle but are used by the taxable person for the purpose of the business (other than solely for research or development in a car production business which does not involve the conversion of vehicles) are treated as both supplied to him and by him. For cars used in research and development, see *Lea-Francis Cars Ltd.* v. *C. & E. Comrs.* MAN/81/113 unreported.

Relief for second-hand motor cars
6. On the supply by any person of a used motor car VAT is chargeable on a value which is the

excess of the consideration for which the motor car is supplied over that upon its acquisition. For imported used cars and self-supplied used cars the cost of acquisition is the value used for charging tax plus that tax. For cars considered to be "used", see *Lincoln Street Motors (Birmingham) Ltd.* v. *C. & E. Comrs.* [1981] VATTR 120; *Finglands Travel Agency Ltd.* v. *C. & E. Comrs.* MAN/82/232 unreported; see also Press Notice, 25 June 1982. For the sale consideration, see *D. E. Siviter (Motors) Ltd.* v. *C. & E. Comrs.* MAN/88/458 unreported (vehicle excise duty); *G. T. Collins & Son* v. *C. & E. Comrs.* LON/88/3134 unreported (hackney carriage licence).

This Article does not apply to (*a*) supplies of letting on hire, (*b*) supplies where the car was produced by the taxable person and the self supply provisions did not apply, (*c*) supplies where an amount attributable to VAT is shown on an invoice or (*d*) supplies by a car dealer unless the records are as specified in a notice published by the Commissioners or are recognised by them as sufficient for these purposes. For the failure to keep records, see *C. & E. Comrs.* v. *J. H. Corbitt (Numismatists) Ltd.* [1980] STC 231, HL (as modified by VATA 1983 s. 40(6)); *Nixon* v. *C. & E. Comrs.* [1980] VATTR 66. A limited relief is available to car dealers who fail to keep all the required records. Tax is charged as if the consideration for the supply was either: (1) the cost price (if the dealer holds the required purchase records); or (2) one-half of the sale price (if the dealer holds the required sale records). The following conditions must be met: (1) the required purchase or sale records must be held; (2) the Commissioners must be satisfied that the mark-up achieved on the sale does not exceed 100 per cent; and (3) the supply must otherwise meet the conditions of the margin scheme.

Treatment of transactions

7. The following are treated as supplies of neither goods nor services and thus are outside the scope of VAT: (*a*) the disposal, by a person who repossesed it under the terms of a finance agreement, of a used motor car in the same state as when repossessed, (*b*) the disposal by an insurer of a used motor car acquired in settlement of a claim in the same state as when acquired, or (*c*) the disposal of a used car for no consideration where input VAT had been disallowed.

S.I. 1980 No. 1537

The Value Added Tax (Repayment of Community Traders) Regulations 1980

Note
These Regulations implement in the U.K. a scheme which operates throughout the Community whereby VAT incurred by registered taxable persons in member States other than those in which they are registered can be refunded. The scheme originated in the Eighth Council Directive of 6 December 1979: 79/1072/EEC.

Citation and commencement
1. These Regulations came into operation on 1 January 1981.

Interpretation
2. Various words and phrases used in the regulations are explained.

Repayment of tax
3. A person within reg. 4 is entitled to a repayment of VAT on goods and services supplied to him and goods imported by him to the same extent as a taxable person is entitled to input tax credit.

Persons to whom these Regulations apply
4. These Regulations apply to a person carrying on business in the E.C. outside the U.K. who is not established in the U.K. and does not make supplies of goods or services in the U.K. other than transport of freight to and from the U.K. or services where the VATA 1983, Sch. 3 reverse charge provisions apply.

Supplies to which these Regulations apply
5. These Regulations apply to any supply of goods or services made after 1 January 1981 or importation made after 1 February 1989 unless the claimant uses them for the purpose of any business in the U.K. or they are to be exported from the U.K. by the claimant.

Tax which will not be repaid
6. VAT is not repaid if it is charged on a supply which is excluded from credit, such as on entertaining, or charged on a supply to a travel agent or tour operator which is for the direct benefit of travellers.

Method of claiming
7. Form VAT 65 must be completed in English and sent to the Commissioners together with a

certificate of status issued by the VAT authority of the member State in which the claimant is established together with the VAT invoice(s), import entries, etc. upon which the claim is based. The certificate of status must be issued within 12 months of the claim for refund of VAT.

Time within which a claim must be made
8. Claims may be made for periods not less than three months and not more than one calendar year. Claims should be lodged within six months of the end of a calendar year. No claim may be made for less than £16. A claim for less than £130 can only be made if it is the only or last claim for a calendar year.

Deduction of bank charges
9. The Commissioners may reduce the amount of VAT repaid by the cost of bank charges they incur in sending the money abroad.

Treatment of claim and repayment claimed
10. A claim under these Regulations is treated like a VAT return for VATA 1983, Sch. 7, para. 4 so the Commissioners can assess tax incorrectly repaid.
11. Repayments under these Regulations are treated as input tax for VATA 1983, s. 40 (1) (c) so that appeals can be made.

False, altered or incorrect claims
12. A claimant who sends a false or altered document with a claim for input tax to the Commissioners may be refused repayment of tax claimed for two years from the date the claim was made.
13. Money paid as the result of an incorrect claim may be adjusted on subsequent claims by reducing the money paid.

S.I. 1981 No. 1741

The Value Added Tax (Special Provisions) Order 1981

Note
This order allows special treatment of certain transactions such as those concerning second-hand goods, goods and services used for the purposes of entertaining U.K. customers, goods incorporated in new buildings other than builder's hardware, transfers of businesses as going concerns, and the self-supply by partly exempt businesses of stationery.

Citation and commencement
1. This order came into operation on 1 January 1982.

Interpretation
2. Various words and phrases used in this order are defined.

Revocations and savings
3. Two orders are revoked and provisions made for continuity.

Relief for certain goods
4. The supply of the following goods are covered by these provisions: works of art, antiques and collectors' pieces; used motor cycles; used caravans; used boats and outboard motors; used electronic organs; used aircraft; and used firearms.

Provisions also apply where: (1) such goods are acquired from a non-VAT registered person, or from a registered person who has accounted for VAT only on his margin, or as part of a transaction which is outside the scope of VAT or (2) works of art etc., are imported without payment of VAT.

This does not apply to a supply of services for the hire of such goods or where a tax invoice is issued showing an amount of VAT in respect of the supply. A taxable person must also keep detailed records and accounts of the purchases and sales in a form specified by the Commissioners in a notice. For the failure to keep records, see *C. & E. Comrs.* v. *J. H. Corbitt (Numismatists) Ltd.* [1980] STC 231, HL (as modified by VATA 1983 s. 40 (6)); *Nixon* v. *C. & E. Comrs.* [1980] VATTR 66.
5. Where the conditions are fully met taxable persons can account for VAT only on the consideration for which the goods were supplied over the consideration for which that person acquired those goods. No VAT is chargeable unless there is such an excess. For calculation of the "margin", see *Wyvern Shipping Co. Ltd.* v. *C. & E. Comrs.* [1979] STC 91; *Grant Melrose & Tennent Ltd.* v. *C. & E. Comrs.* [1985] VATTR 90; *Jocelyn Fielding Fine Arts Ltd.* v. *C. & E. Comrs.* [1978] VATTR 164.

Relief from tax on importation
6. Works of art acquired before 1 April 1973 and antiques of an age exceeding 100 years (except pearls and loose gem stones) and collectors' pieces are not chargeable with VAT on importation.

Disallowance of input tax

7. Where a taxable person makes a supply upon which VAT is charged only on the margin, any input VAT charged on its purchase is disallowed.

8. Articles which are not of a kind ordinarily installed by builders as fixtures except certain items such as kitchen furniture or gas or electric space and water heating systems are disallowed from credit as input tax when supplied by any person involved in building a new dwelling: see VATA 1983, Sch. 5, Group 8.

9. VAT incurred by a taxable person on goods or services used for the purpose of business entertainment is deductible only if the goods or services are used to entertain employees. For "entertainment", see *C. & E. Comrs.* v. *Shaklee International* [1981] STC 776, CA; *Celtic Football & Athletic Co. Ltd.* v. *C. & E. Comrs.* [1983] STC 470; *Football Association Ltd.* v. *C. & E. Comrs.* [1985] VATTR 106; *Ibstock Building Products Ltd.* v. *C. & E. Comrs.* [1987] VATTR 1; *Northern Lawn Tennis Club* v. *C. & E. Comrs.* [1989] VATTR 1; *British Car Auctions Ltd.* v. *C. & E. Comrs.* [1978] VATTR 56; *William Matthew Mechanical Services Ltd.* v. *C. & E. Comrs.* [1982] VATTR 63. For concessions in relation to subsistence and sporting bodies, see Notice No. 748 (October 1989), para. A8.

   Where a taxable person has claimed no input tax on the supply to him of goods used for business entertainment the VAT chargeable on a supply by him of those goods will only be on any excess of sale proceeds over cost.

Treatment of transactions

10. The disposal of goods listed in article 11 is outside the scope of VAT if made by a person who repossesed them under the terms of a finance agreement, or by an insurer who acquired them in the settlement of a claim under an insurance policy if the goods are disposed of in the same condition as they were in when they were repossessed and are acquired from a non-taxable person or a person entitled to use a second-hand goods scheme. This does not apply to reimported goods which were previously exportedfree of tax.

11. This article lists the same goods as those listed in article 4, whether used or not.

12. A transfer by a person of a business as a going concern is treated as neither a supply of goods nor a supply of services and is thus outside the scope of VAT provided the assets are to be used by the transferee in carrying on the same kind of business, and if the transferor is a taxable person the transferee is already or becomes as a result of the transfer a taxable person. Where part of the business is transferred that part must be capable of separate operation. For the meaning of "going concern" generally, see *C. & E. Comrs.* v. *Dearwood Ltd.* [1986] STC 327; *Kenmir Ltd.* v. *Frizzell* [1968] 1 All ER 414; *Reference under Electricity (Balmain Electric Light Co. Purchase) Act 1950* [1957] SR (NSW) 100; *Spijkers* v. *Gebroeders Benedik Abattoir CV* (case 24/85) [1986] 2 CMLR 296, ECJ. Contrast *Hardlife Ladder Co. Ltd.* v. *C. & E. Comrs.* LON/87/218 unreported (trader ceased manufacturing operations and seeking custom); *Thruxton Parachute Club Ltd.* v. *C. & E. Comrs.* LON/84/331 (business insolvent but not yet dead); *Montrose DIY Ltd.* v. *C. & E. Comrs.* EDN/87/98 unreported (purchaser able to carry on vendor's business without interruption).

   The transfer by an owner of goods which are the subject of hire purchase or conditional sale agreement to a bank or other financial institution is treated as neither a supply of goods nor a supply of services and is therefore outside the a scope of VAT.

13. The exchange of a reconditioned article or an unserviceable article of a similar kind by a person in this kind of business is a supply of services.

Self-supply

14. Stationery or similar printed material produced by a business for its own use may have to be treated as both supplied by and supplied to the business. This is to put it in the same position as if it bought the supplies, so that if it is not registered VAT is charged, and if it is partially exempt VAT is charged and only part of it is allowed as input tax.

S.I. 1982 No. 1067

The Value Added Tax (Isle of Man) Order 1982

Note

This Order modifies the law in various Acts relating to VAT in the U.K. to enable the U.K. and the Isle of Man to be treated as a single area for the purposes of VAT.

S.I. 1982 No. 1068

The Value Added Tax (Isle of Man) (No. 2) Order 1982

Note

This Order modifies the law in various statutory instruments relating to VAT in the U.K. to enable the U.K. and the Isle of Man to be treated as a single area for the purposes of VAT.

S.I. 1983 No. 1099

The Value Added Tax (Horses and Ponies) Order 1983

Note

This Order provides for the tax chargeable on supplies of horses and ponies by a taxable person to be charged only on the excess, if any, of the price which that person obtained for a horse or pony over the price he gave for it.

1. This Order came into operation on 1 October 1983.
2. Article 4 applies where a taxable person supplies a horse or pony and upon its acquisition either no VAT was charged or VAT was charged only on the margin of the vendor.
3. This facility is not available to a supply of a hire of a horse or pony nor where a tax invoice is issued showing an amount as being VAT. A taxable person must also keep such records and accounts as the Commissioners may specify in a notice.
4. When the conditions of this Order are met VAT is charged only on the margin that is the excess of the consideration for which the horse or pony is supplied over the consideration for which the horse or pony was acquired.
5. Input tax is excluded from credit on the purchase of any horse or pony where the margin under article 4 applies.

S.I. 1983 No. 1828

The Customs and Excise Duties (Personal Reliefs for Goods Permanently Imported) Order 1983

This Order implements certain E.C. obligations and proivides a system of personal reliefs from duty and value added tax in respect of property imported permanently, where the conditions imposed are complied with.

S.I. 1983 No. 1829

The Customs and Excise Duties (Personal Reliefs for Goods Temporarily Imported) Order 1983

This Order applies to persons normally resident abroad who enter the U.K. intending to remain there temporarily without transferring their normal place of residence and, in pursuance of international and E.C. obligations, it gives relief from customs and excise duties and VAT chargeable on certain goods at importation.

S.I. 1984 No. 746

The Value Added Tax (Imported Goods) Relief Order 1984

Note

This Order provides for relief from VAT chargeable on certain goods permanently imported in conjunction with activities such as commerce, scientific research, philanthropy, international relations, recreation and culture pursuits. Sch. 2 is divided as follows:

     Group 1 Capital Goods and Equipment on Transfer of Activities
     Group 2 Agriculture and Animals
     Group 3 Promotion of Trade
     Group 4 Goods for Testing, Etc.
     Group 5 Health
     Group 6 Charities, Etc.,
     Group 7 Printed Matter, Etc.,
     Group 8 Articles sent for Miscellaneous Purposes
     Group 9 Works of Art and Collectors' Pieces
     Group 10 Transport
     Group 11 War graves, Funerals, Etc.

Items within these groups are interpreted in accordance with notes. Where goods are described by reference to a use or purpose, relief is given only if the goods are put to such use or the purpose is fulfilled.

S.I. 1984 No. 895

The Customs and Excise Duties (Relief for Imported Legacies) Order 1984

Note

This Order provides for relief from VAT chargeable on legacies imported by persons resident in the U.K. or the Isle of Man and non-profit-making bodies where conditions prescribed by the order are complied with.

S.I. 1984 No. 1176

The Control of Movement of Goods Regulations 1984

Note
These regulations lay down the procedure for the movement within the U.K. of (*a*) imported goods to be cleared from Customs control other than the port of importation; (*b*) goods in transit through the U.K.; (*c*) goods for exportation which are made available for customs examination prior to their movement to the port etc.; and (*d*) goods moving between one free zone and another.

Citation and commencement
1. These Regulations came into operation on 6 August 1984.

Revocation
2. The Control of Movement of Goods Regulations 1981 are revoked.

Interpretation
3. Various words and phrases used in the Regulations are defined.
4. These Regulations do not apply where goods are moved under the Community transit procedure.

Restrictions on the movement of goods
5. Subject to reg. 10 imported goods in the charge of customs and excise may not be moved from their place of importation without the authority of the proper officer of customs and excise.
6. Subject to reg. 10 no goods shall be moved between a free zone and a place approved for clearance out of customs control or between free zones unless the movement is authorised by the proper officer.
7. Subject to regs. 9 and 10 goods intended for export which are made available for inspection at an approved place by the proper officer may not be removed from such a place unless the movement is authorised by the proper officer of customs and excise.
8. Applications to move goods (regs. 5, 6 and 7 above) shall be made in writing on documents obtained from and approved by the Commissioners.

Local export control
9. Where notice for movement of goods is given by an exporter to customs and excise and authority is neither given or refused by the date and time for the movement specified, the authority is deemed to have been given on the date immediately before the time so specified in the notice. Where the notice is for more than one movement of goods and the authority of the proper officer required under reg. 7 is neither given nor refused and it is deemed to be given immediately before each movement commences.

Standing permission to remove
10. Where the Commissioners so permit, during a period specified by them, goods which are subject to the conditions as contemplated in regs. 5, 6 and 7 may be moved without an application to the proper officer; and unless the proper officer previously gives or refuses his authority it shall be deemed to be given immediately before each movement commences.

Requirement for removal document
11. Before any removal commences the person in control of the goods is to be in possession of a removal document.

Specification of vehicles etc.
12. The Commissioners may specify the type of vehicles in which any class or description of goods are to be removed and no person shall remove any goods where such a requirement has been imposed unless the vehicle or container complies with the specification or until such requirement has been relaxed.

Specification of routes
13. The Commissioners may specify the routes which goods may travel during a removal.

Security of goods, vehicles and containers
14. Before any goods are removed the vehicle or container carrying them shall be secured by such seals, locks or marks as Commissioners may specify. Seals, locks and marks shall be affixed by the proper officer or by such persons as the Commissioners may authorise.

15. No person may wilfully break, open or remove any seal, lock or mark fixed for any customs and excise purpose on any goods, vehicle or container unless so authorised by a proper officer or in accordance with special permission given by a Commissioner or in an emergency to safeguard the goods or to protect life or property.

Completion of removals, time limits and accidents
16. Save as the Commissioners may otherwise allow, the person in charge of goods being removed shall complete the removal by producing the goods and removal document to the proper officer at the approved place.
17. The person in charge of goods shall complete the removal within such a period as the Commissioners may specify.
18. If as a result of an accident a vehicle or container is delayed or diverted from a specified route the person in charge of the goods shall notify the local office of customs and excise of the circumstances.

S.I. 1984 No. 1177

The Free Zone Regulations 1984

Note
These Regulations prescribe the procedures governing the operation of free zones in the U.K. In relation to such zones the regulations (*a*) allow obligations for security to be placed on responsible authorities; (*b*) provide for the receipt of goods and where appropriate the discharge of existing procedures and establishment of Community status; (*c*) prescribe the scope of permitted operations and the related control requirements; (*d*) provide for the payment of customs duty and agricultural levy and for the delivery of goods from free zones; (*e*) define the control requirements placed upon free zone traders and responsible authorities; and (*f*) provide for the application of value added tax on delivery of any goods manufactured in free zones, whether or not made from imported components. The Regulations do not affect the control of goods in the course of movement to and from free zones.

PART I PRELIMINARY

Citation and commencement
1. These regulations came into operation on 6 August 1984.

Interpretation
2. Words and phrases used in these regulations are defined.

PART II SECURITY OF FREE ZONES

Security and recovery of expenditure by commissioners
3. The Commissioners may by direction impose obligations on the responsible authority for a free zone to ensure the security of that free zone. Where that authority fails to comply with such a direction and the Commissioners incur any expense then that expense can be recovered by the Commissioners from the authority as a civil debt.

Residence in free zones not permitted
4. No person is allowed to take up residence within a free zone.

PART III GOODS CHARGEABLE WITH EXCISE DUTY

Excise goods which may become free zone goods without payment of excise duty
5. Goods chargeable with excise duty may be moved into a free zone witout payment of duty and remain as free zone goods provided the Commissioners agree.

PART IV MOVEMENT OF GOODS INTO FREE ZONE

Goods to become free zone goods
6. Goods moved into a free zone shall not be free zone goods unless their details have been entered in a record kept by the occupier of the premises.

Acknowledgement of Community status of free zone goods
7. The proprietor of free zone goods may within seven days deliver to the proper officer a document and evidence to enable the officer to establish to his satisfaction that the goods are Community goods and if so satisfied the officer will endorse the document to provide a written acknowledgement of such Community status.

Goods from another customs procedure
8. Goods moved into a free zone will not be free zone goods until the proprietor of the goods has presented them to the proper officer and the other customs procedure has been discharged.

PART V OPERATIONS

Operations on free zone goods
9. Operations on free zone goods are subject to this Regulation.
　Operations which combine non-free zone goods with free zone goods are prohibited.
　The Commissioners may allow, subject to such conditions as they may impose, any operation on free zone goods which are Community goods. Other goods are subject to processing under customs control.
　A person intending to carry out any operation shall inform the proper officer of his intention before commencing the process.
　Free zone goods shall not be used or consumed in a free zone unless they are entered for home use.
　Operations carried out on free zone goods which do not comply with Regulations shall cause the goods to be liable to forfeiture.

PART VI ENTRY, REMOVAL AND PAYMENT OF DUTY ETC.

Procedure for entering free zone goods
10. Free zone goods shall be entered by the proprietor of the goods delivering to the proper officer an entry containing such particulars and accompanied by such documents as the Commissioners may direct.

Entry required before removal for home use etc.
11. Subject to Regulation 12 before any free zone goods are removed from a free zone for home use or transfer to another customs procedure, the goods are to be entered for such purpose.

Removal without entry
12. The Commissioners may allow goods to be removed from the free zone for the purposes set out in Regulation 11 without the goods being entered, if such particulars as the Commissioners may direct are entered in a record kept by the proprietor of the goods.

Goods to be removed after entry etc.
13. Goods which have been entered for home use etc. having paid any tax due and with the approval of the proper officer are to be removed, forthwith, from the free zone.

Removal of goods for export etc.
14. Any prohibition or restriction on the export of goods or on their shipment as stores shall apply to goods removed from a free zone for export or shipment as stores.

Restriction on removal of goods
15. No goods shall be removed from a free zone except with the authority of the proper officer.

Payment of duty before removal of goods
16. Save as the Commissioners may otherwise allow, no goods shall be removed from a free zone until any customs duty or agricultural levy has been paid.

Entry of goods which are to remain in a free zone
17. Free zone goods to be used or consumed in a free zone shall be entered for home use. Where the proprietor of free zone goods wishes to pay any customs duty or agricultural levy chargeable on the goods, the goods shall be entered for free circulation.

Payment of duty etc. on goods to remain in a free zone after entry
18. Where goods are entered for consumption in a free zone, any customs duty and agricultural levy chargeable shall be paid at the time the entry is delivered.

Agricultural levy chargeable because of chargeable operation
19. Where agricultural levy is chargeable because of a chargeable operation, a schedule containing particulars of the goods and the operation must be given to the proper officer and any agricultural levy chargeable paid at the same time.

Customs duty etc. deemed to have been paid
20. For the purposes of these Regulations, customs duty and agricultural levy are deemed to have been paid if the customs duties deferred payment system is in operation, or security has been given or the duty is otherwise accounted for.

Destruction of free zone goods
21. Free zone goods may be destroyed and no duty paid, subject to conditions imposed by the Commissioners, but duty will be payable on any resulting scrap or waste which is removed for use in the U.K.

PART VII CONTROLS

Production of goods
22. Goods in a free zone are subject to inspection by the proper officer.

Segregation etc. of goods
23. The proper officer may require goods to be segregated and marked or otherwise identified.

Keeping of records and provision of information
24. The occupier of any premises upon which free zone goods are kept or the responsible authority on his behalf shall keep such records relating to the goods as the Commissioners may direct. The records shall be kept in the free zone for such period as the Commissioners direct, not exceeding three years from the date the goods are removed from the free zone. A proper officer may examine any records relating to the goods and may take copies or make extracts from them or remove them for a reasonable time.

PART VIII CUSTOMS DUTY ETC. CHARGEABLE ON FREE ZONE GOODS

Customs duty chargeable on free zone goods
25. The rate of customs duty or agricultural levy chargeable on free zone goods is that in force at the time of acceptance of the entry. The value for customs purposes of free zone goods is that accepted by the Commissioners at the time of acceptance of the entry of the goods for home use or free circulation. The amount of customs duty or agricultural levy chargeable on free zone goods which have been the subject of inward processing relief and which are entered for home use or free circulation is either the amount calculated in accordance with the Inward Processing Relief Regulations 1977 or that in force when the entry is accepted.

PART IX VALUE ADDED TAX

Tax charge on removal from free zone of manufactured goods
26. Revoked from 10 May 1988 so that, on delivery from a free zone of products manufacturerd in the free zone, import VAT is charged only on the value of any imported goods retained in these products.

Relief from import tax following supply to non-registered person
27. Where free zone goods have been supplied whilst in a free zone to a person who is not registered for VAT and he enters the goods for home use, the amount of tax payable directly to Customs and Excise is to be reduced by the amount of tax paid to the supplier of the goods.

S.I. 1984 No. 1206

The Free Zone (Belfast Airport) Designation Order 1984

Note
This Order designates a free zone at Belfast Airport. It appoints the responsible authority and imposes obligations upon that authority related to the operation of the zone.

S.I. 1984 No. 1207

The Free Zone (Birmingham Airport) Designation 1984

Note
This Order designates a free zone at Birmingham Airport. It appoints the responsible authority and imposes obligations upon that authority related to the operation of the zone.

S.I. 1984 No. 1208

The Free Zone (Cardiff) Designation Order 1984

Note
This Order designates a free zone at Cardiff. It appoints the responsible authority and imposes obligations upon that authority relating to the operation of the zone.

S.I. 1984 No. 1209

The Free Zone (Liverpool) Designation Order 1984

Note
This Order designates a free zone at Liverpool. It appoints the responsible authority and imposes obligations upon that authority relating to the operation of the zone. The zone was extended from 600 to 621 acres by S.I. 1988 No. 533 and to 643 acres by S.I. 1990 No. 139.

S.I. 1984 No. 1210

The Free Zone (Prestwick Airport) Designation Order 1984

Note
This Order designates a free zone at Prestwick Airport. It appoints the responsible authority and imposes obligations upon that authority relating to the operation of the zone.

S.I. 1984 No. 1211

The Free Zone (Southampton) Designation Order 1984

Note
This Order designates a free zone at Southampton. It appoints the responsible authority and imposes obligations upon that authority relating to the operation of the zone.

S.I. 1984 No. 1685

The Value Added Tax (Place of Supply) Order 1984

Note
This Order varies the rules for determining the place of supply of certain educational, recreational and associated services supplied by persons belonging in another country. These services are treated as supplied in the U.K. when they are performed in the U.K.
1. This Order came into operation on 1 January 1985.
2. The rules for determining where a supply of services is made are varied in accordance with the following provisions.

3. A supply of services to which this Order applies is treated as made in the U.K. notwithstanding the supplier belongs abroad.

4. This Order applies to the supply of services of or incidental to the provision of a course of formal instruction, other than the supply of a designated travel service or as part of such a service.

5. A designated travel service is a supply by a tour operator established in a member state of the E.C., of goods or services acquired for his business, to a traveller without material alteration or further processing. See VAT (Tour Operators) Order 1987, S.I. 1987 No. 1806.

S.I. 1985 No. 886

The Value Added Tax (General) Regulations 1985

Note
These Regulations consolidate and revoke previous Orders and add four new regulations (nos. 5 to 8) which set out common conditions applied to businesses who are allowed to register for VAT before making taxable supplies.

PART I PRELIMINARY

Citation and commencement
1. These Regulations came into operation on 1 September 1985.

Interpretation
2. Various words and phrases used in these Regulations are defined. Any reference to a form in the Schedule to these Regulations includes a form approved by the Commissioners.

Revocation and savings
3. The Regulations which are revoked and instructions for continuity with the new Regulations are listed.

PART II REGISTRATION, DISCRETIONARY REGISTRATION AND PROVISIONS FOR SPECIAL CASES

Registration and notification and transfer of a going concern
4. Form VAT 1 is used to notify the Commissioners of a liability to be registered. The form includes a declaration, signed by the person required to notify or request registration, that all the information given is true and complete (see *Electric Tool Repair Ltd.* v. *C. & E. Comrs.* [1986] VATTR 257). All partners in a partnership are required to sign form VAT 2 which details their names and addresses. Within 30 days of a change in the name, constitution or ownership of a business or any other variation which may necessitate the variation or cancellation of a registration, registered persons are required to notify the Commissioners in writing of the change. A registered person who is required to notify the Commissioners that he makes, intends to make, ceases to make or ceases to intend to make, taxable supplies must do so in writing within 30 days.

When a business is transferred as a going concern, the existing registration number can be transferred to the new owner provided that the registration has not already been cancelled, the transferor will after the transfer cease to be registerable, the transferee is either eligible to register or required to register and both the transferor and the transferee apply on form VAT 56. The registration of the transferor is cancelled from the date of the transfer and the transferee is registered with the number previously allocated to the transferor. However, the transferee takes over any liability of the transferor to render returns or account for VAT which existed at the time of transfer. Any right the transferor has to a repayment of input tax becomes the right of the transferee, and a repayment due at the end of an accounting period is satisfied by the Commissioners paying either party. In addition, where the transferee has been registered with the registration number of the transferor during an accounting period subsequent to that in which the transfer actually took place, and any return has been made, tax paid or repayment claimed, it is treated as having been done by the transferee. See *Ponsonby* v. *C. & E. Comrs.* [1988] STC 28.

Notice by partnership
9. There is joint and several liability on the members of a partnership where notice is required to be given under VATA 1983 or these Regulations but that notice when provided by one partner shall discharge the liability. In Scotland the notice must be given and signed in the manner prescribed in the Partnership Act 1890, s. 6.

Representation of club, association or organisation
10. There is joint and several liability on every member holding office of a club, association or organisation, as president, chairman, treasurer, secretary or any similar office, or in default thereof every member holding office as a member of a committee, or in default thereof every member, to give any notice required under VATA 1983 or these Regulations. Notice given by one official, committee member or member is sufficient.

Death, bankruptcy or incapacity of taxable person
11. The Commissioners may treat any person carrying on the business of a taxable person who has died, become bankrupt, is in liquidation or receivership, is under an administration order, or is otherwise incapacitated as the taxable person from the date of the incapacity. The provisions of VATA 1983 and any Regulations apply to that person as if he were a registered person. A person carrying on the business must notify the Commissioners within 21 days of the change. The notification must be in writing, giving the date and nature of the incapacity.

PART III TAX INVOICES

Obligation to provide a tax invoice
12. A registered person making a taxable supply to another taxable person is to provide a tax invoice, except where these Regulations or the Commissioners otherwise provide. Where a taxable person's goods are sold in satisfaction of a debt by another person (*e.g.*, by an auctioneer), the document issued by the other person shall be treated as a tax invoice in the hands of the buyer provided it contains the particulars required of a tax invoice. A registered taxable person may provide himself with a document which relates to a supply of goods or services to him and may with the approval of the Commissioners treat such a document as a tax invoice. This procedure is commonly known as "self billing" and is commonly used where the customer can identify the value of the supply before the supplier. An authenticated receipt issued by a person in the building trade containing all the particulars required on a tax invoice can be treated as a tax invoice provided no other document is issued in respect of that supply which could be construed to be a tax invoice.

Tax invoices, self-billed invoices and authenticated receipts must be provided within 30 days after the time when the supply is treated as made. The Commissioners may allow a longer period made in general or special directions which may coincide with an extension to the tax points or where the information for the invoice is not available.

Contents of tax invoice
13. A registered person required to provide a tax invoice is to include the following particulars:
   (*a*) an identifying number;
   (*b*) the date of the supply;
   (*c*) the name, address and registration number of the supplier;
   (*d*) the name and address of the person to whom the goods or services are supplied;
   (*e*) the type of supply by reference to the following categories:
       (i) a supply by sale,
       (ii) a supply on hire purchase or any similar transaction,
       (iii) a supply by loan,
       (iv) a supply by way of exchange,
       (v) a supply on hire, lease or rental,
       (vi) a supply of goods made from customers' materials,
       (vii) a supply by sale on commission,
       (viii) a supply on sale or return or similar terms, or
       (ix) any other type of supply which the Commissioners may at any time by notice specify;
   (*f*) a description sufficient to identify the goods or services supplied;
   (*g*) for each description, the quantity of the goods or the extent of the services, the rate of tax and the amount payable, excluding tax, expressed in sterling;
   (*h*) the gross total amount payable, excluding tax, expressed in sterling;
   (*i*) the rate of any cash discount offered;
   (*j*) the amount of tax chargeable at each rate, with the rate, to which it relates, expressed in sterling; and
   (*k*) the total amount of the tax chargeable expressed in sterling.
A consignment note, delivery note or similar document, containing all the above details but issued before the time of supply is not to be treated as a tax invoice provided it is so endorsed.

Supplies of exempt or zero-rated goods or services must be distinguished from standard-rated supplies on a tax invoice and separate gross amounts payable shown.

Change of rate, credit notes
14. Where there is a change in the rate of VAT or in the treatment of particular supplies and a tax

invoice for a supply was issued before the change but the supply is the subject of an election under VATA 1983, s. 41 which alters the date VAT is due then a credit note shall be issued within 14 days of the change and contain the following particulars:

(*a*) the identifying number and the date of issue of the credit note;
(*b*) the name, address and registration number of the supplier;
(*c*) the name and address of the person to whom the supply is made;
(*d*) the identifying number and date of issue of the tax invoice;
(*e*) a description sufficient to identify the goods or services supplied; and
(*f*) the amount of tax being credited.

Retailers' invoices
15. Retailers must provide tax invoices for standard-rated supplies when asked by a customer who is a taxable person. Where, however, the value of the supply including VAT made by the retailer is £50 or less, the invoice need only contain the following details: the name, address and registration number of the retailer; the date of the supply; a description sufficient to identify the goods or services supplied; the total amount payable including tax; and the rate of tax in force at the time of the supply

Such less detailed tax invoices must include only supplies which are subject to the same rate of tax and excluding any zero-rated or exempt supplies.

General
16. Regulations 12, 13, 14 and 15 do not apply to (*a*) any zero-rated supply, or (*b*) any supply where the reclaim of input VAT by the customer is blocked by Treasury order (*e.g.*, cars and entertainment) or (*c*) any supply on which VAT is charged although it is not made for consideration (*e.g.*, a gift of goods exceeding £10 in value to another taxable person), or (*d*) any supply involving second hand goods. See *Double Shield Window Co. Ltd* v. *C. & E. Comrs.* MAN/84/227 unreported.

PART IV TIME OF SUPPLY

Goods for private use and free supplies of services
17. Where goods are put to non-business use but remain part of the assets of the business, a supply of services is deemed to be supplied on the last day of the accounting period in which they are supplied or continue to be supplied. The same time of supply would apply to services which are the subject of a Treasury Order under VATA 1983, s. 3 (4).

Services from outside the United Kingdom
18. Services which are regarded as being supplied where they are received are treated as being supplied when they are paid for, or if the consideration is not in money, on the last day of the VAT accounting period in which the services are performed.

Leases treated as supplies of goods
19. Goods are treated as separately and successively supplied if: (1) the grant of a lease or tenancy is treated as a supply of goods; and (2) all or part of the consideration is payable periodically or from time to time. Each supply of goods is deemed to be supplied on the earlier of: (1) the date when part of the consideration is received; and (2) the date when a tax invoice is issued in respect of the grant.

The supplier can issue a tax invoice for a period of one year or less showing the following additional information: (1) the due date for each payment in the period; (2) the VAT-exclusive amount due on each date; (3) the rate of tax in force at the date of issue; and (4) the VAT due at that rate on each amount due. If he does so, each supply of goods is deemed to be supplied on the earlier of: (1) the due date for payment; and (2) the date when payment is received.

The invoice ceases to be treated as a tax invoice in relation to any payment due after a change in the rate of tax which affects the supply invoiced.

Supplies of water, gas or any form of power, heat, refrigeration or ventilation
20. The following supplies are treated as taking place on the earlier of the receipt of a payment or the issue of a tax invoice: (1) water (subject to specified exceptions); (2) coal gas, water gas, producer gases and similar gases; and (3) any form of power, heat, refrigeration or ventilation.

Water within (1) above, gas within (2) above and electricity within (3) above are treated as separately and successively supplied if all or part of the consideration is payable periodically or from time to time. Each supply of goods is deemed to be supplied on the earlier of: (1) the date when part of the consideration is received; and (2) the date when an invoice is issued in respect of the supply.

The supplier can issue a tax invoice for a period of one year or less showing the following additional information: (1) the due date for each payment under the agreement; (2) the VAT-exclusive amount due on each date; (3) the rate of VAT in force at the date of issue; and (4) the

VAT due at that rate on each amount due. If he does so, each supply of goods is deemed to be supplied on the earlier of: (1) the due date for payment; and (2) the date when payment is received.

The invoice ceases to be treated as a tax invoice in relation to any payment due after a change in the rate of tax which affects the supplies invoiced.

Supplier's goods in possession of buyer
21. Goods supplied under an agreement whereby the property in the goods is retained by the vendor until they are paid for and in circumstances where the consideration is not determined until they are paid for, then the time of supply is the earlier of the date of appropriation by the buyer, the date when a tax invoice is issued by the supplier or the date a payment is received by the supplier. This Regulation does not apply to supplies made on sale or return terms. If a tax invoice is issued within 14 days of the above tax points then the date of the tax invoice is the time of supply.

Retention payments
22. Where a contract for a supply of goods or services provides for a retention of the consideration pending performance under the contract, a supply is treated as taking place on the earlier of the receipt of payment or the issue of a tax invoice.

Continuous supplies of services
23. Services are treated as separately and successively supplied if they are supplied for a consideration all or part of which is determined or payable periodically or from time to time. The time of supply is the earlier of the receipt of payment or the issue of a tax invoice.

If payments are due to be made under an agreement which provides for successive payments, the supplier can issue a tax invoice to cover a period not exceeding one year containing the following additional particulars:

(*a*) the date on which each payment is to become due in the period;

(*b*) the amount payable (excluding tax) on each date; and

(*c*) the rate of tax in force at the time of the issue of the tax invoice and the amount of tax chargeable in accordance with that rate on each payment.

Each of the supplies is treated as taking place on the earlier of when a payment becomes due or is received.

Where there is a change in the rate of VAT during the period covered by such a tax invoice it ceases to be treated as a tax invoice for any payment due after the change.

Royalties and similar payments
24. Where the whole consideration for a supply of services was not fixed at the time the services were performed and those services give rise to further payments, a further supply shall be treated as taking place on the earlier of each time a payment is received or a tax invoice is issued.

Supplies of services by barristers and advocates
25. Services supplied by barristers (or advocates) acting as such are treated as taking place on the earliest of the time when the fee is received by the barrister, or when the barrister issues a tax invoice, or the day when the barrister ceases to practice as such.

Supplies in the construction industry
26. The time of supply for services, or services with goods, in the course of construction, alteration, demolition, repair or maintenance of a building or of any civil engineering work under a contract which provides for periodic payments is the earlier of when a payment is received where the consideration is wholly in money, or when the tax invoice is issued.

General
27. Where a supply is treated as made when a tax invoice is issued or a payment is received under Pt. IV of these Regulations (Regs. 17 to 28) VAT is chargeable on only the value of the payment or the invoice.

Supplies spanning change of rate etc.
28. The election available under VATA 1983, s. 41 (2) when the rate of VAT changes is available also to supplies mentioned in Regulations 17 to 26 above.

PART V INPUT TAX AND PARTIAL EXEMPTION

Interpretation and longer periods
29. Various words and phrases used in this Part of the Regulations are defined.

"Exempt input tax" is any input VAT which is attributable wholly or partly to an exempt supply.

The "tax year" is the period of 12 months from 1 April, 1 May or 1 June according to which quarterly accounting period is allocated to a business unless the Commissioners have approved or directed another tax year.

A "registration period" is the period commencing on registration and ending on the day before the begining of a business's first tax year.

Longer accounting periods are used to calculate the amount of input VAT which a trader is permitted to deduct in the course of a year. The first longer period which can apply is the period from the date of registration to 1 April, 1 May or 1 June. Other traders who incur exempt input tax are those who are starting a project which will result in exempt supplies. In such a case the longer period will commence on the date when the first exempt input tax was incurred and will end on 31 March, 30 April or 31 May. Longer periods also end when a person ceases to make taxable supplies.

Attribution of input tax to taxable supplies
30. The amount of input tax to be provisionally attributed to taxable supplies is to be determined by the following method. Input tax on importations and supplies wholly used or to be used in the making of *taxable* supplies may be deducted. Input tax on importations and supplies wholly used or to be used in making *exempt* supplies or in carrying on any activity other than the making of taxable supplies may *not* be deducted. The deductible proportion of any remaining input tax is provisionally calculated by ascertaining the amount of input tax which will be used in making taxable supplies, expressing that as a proportion of the whole amount of input tax, and taking that proportion.

The Commissioners may allow remaining input tax to be apportioned by reference to the ratio of the value of taxable supplies to the value of all supplies. If they do so, the following amounts are excluded from the calculation: (1) sums due on capital goods supplied; (2) sums due on freeholds, leases, licences and financial services supplied (whether exempt or standard rated) which are incidental to the business activities; (3) the non-margin element of second-hand goods sold; and (4) the value of any self-supply made. Alternatively, the Commissioners may direct how the apportionment is to be made in order to secure a fair and reasonable attribution.

For examples of attribution, see *Neuvale Ltd.* v. *C. & E. Comrs.* [1989] STC 395, CA; *C. & E. Comrs.* v. *C. H. Beazer (Holdings) Ltd.* [1989] STC 549 (costs relating to issue and sale of shares); *Sheffield Co-operative Society Ltd.* v. *C. & E. Comrs.* [1987] VATTR 216 (refurbishing premises for letting). For the "first supply rule" used by the Commissioners, see *Fishguard Bay Developments* v. *C. & E. Comrs.* LON/87/625 unreported.

The Commissioners may allow input tax to be provisionally attributed to taxable supplies in accordance with a "special method". For the treatment of self-supplies and the VAT thereon for the purposes of a special method, see VAT (General) (Amendment) (No. 2) Regulations 1989, S.I. 1989 No. 1302, reg. 6.

Attribution of input tax to foreign and warehouse supplies
30A. Input tax incurred by a taxable person on importations by or supplies to him which are to be used by him in whole or part in making supplies outside the U.K. which would be taxable if made in the U.K., or supplies of goods whilst in bonded warehouses but disregarded for VAT, may be attributed to taxable supplies to the extent that the importations or supplies are to be so used.
30B. Input tax on a self-supply is not attributed to that supply. Cf VATA 1983 ss. 7 (3) and 29A (5).

Treatment of input tax attributable to exempt supplies as being attributable to taxable supplies
31. Input tax attributable to certain exempt supplies is treated as attributable to taxable supplies. These exempt supplies are: any deposit of money; the granting of a right over land where in any longer period the input tax attributable to all such supplies is less than £1,000 and no other exempt input tax is incurred by the person granting the right; any services in making arrangements for the provision of insurance; services of arranging any mortgage or any hire purchase type transaction, and the factoring of any debts. However the above exceptions are not available to banks; accepting houses; insurance companies, agents or brokers; investment trusts or unit trusts; investment companies; Stock Exchange brokers/dealers or share dealing companies; trustees of a pension fund; unit trust management companies; building societies; discount houses; finance houses; friendly soceities; money lenders or money brokers; mortgage brokers; pawnbrokers; debt factors; and credit or chargecard companies.
32. All input tax is treated as attributable to taxable supplies if, in any prescribed accounting period or longer period, a taxable person's exempt input tax is less than £100 per month on average; or both £250 per month on average and 50 per cent. of all input tax; or both £500 per month on average and 25 per cent. of all input tax.

Adjustments to input tax on capital items are disregarded when applying the de minimis limits in a longer period.

Adjustment of attribution
33. Where a taxable person is partially exempt and a longer period applies to him he is required to recalculate the amount of input tax reclaimed from the Commissioners on the quarterly returns using figures for the whole year to even out any seasonal fluctuations; he must include any amount of over-deduction or under-deduction in the first return after the end of the tax year.

34. A taxable person may have been credited with an amount of input tax in respect of any importation or supply which has been attributed to an intended taxable supply, and during a period of six years beginning on the first day of the prescribed accounting period in which the attribution was determined there is a change of use so that such a supply or importation is used in carrying on an activity other than the making of taxable supplies. In such cases the taxable person must, on the next return following the date on which the change of use occurred, account for such proportion of the input tax credited as is attributable to the exempt supply or other non-business activity and repay a proportion of input tax to the Commissioners.

35. Conversely, a taxable person may have incurred input tax in respect of any importation or supply which has been attributed to an intended exempt supply, and during a period of six years beginning on the first day of the prescribed accounting period on which the attribution was determined he uses or appropriates for use any such importation or supply in making a taxable supply before the intended exempt supply is made. In such cases he can apply to the Commissioners who will pay him a sum equal to the amount of input tax which is attributable to the taxable supply in accordance with the method which he was required to use when the input tax was first attributed.

Termination and duration of use of a method
36. Save as the Commissioners may otherwise allow or direct a taxable person using any method shall use it for at least two tax years.

Exceptional claims for tax relief
37. The Commissioners may authorise a taxable person to treat as input tax VAT incurred, on goods or services supplied to him or imported by him for the purpose of the business, before the date from which he was registered.

Where the taxable person is a body corporate and goods or services are acquired before the date of incorporation by a person who becames a member, officer or employee of the company, then provided that the individual acquiring the goods or services was not a taxable person and the goods or services are for the purpose of the company's business and have not been used for any other purpose in the interim period then the Commissioners may allow input tax to be reclaimed.

Where goods or services are supplied by the taxable person before VAT registration the Commissioners will not allow input tax to be reclaimed on the purchase of those goods or services. Where goods are consumed by the taxable person before VAT registration the Commisioners may allow input tax to be reclaimed if the goods into which they were incorported are still held by the taxable person. No input tax may be reclaimed on services performed on goods supplied by the business before VAT registration. No input tax may be reclaimed on services supplied to a taxable person (or in the case of a corporate body its representative) more than six months before the date of the taxable person's registration. See *C. Jeffrey Black (Opticians) Ltd.* v. *C. & E. Comrs.* EDN/89/73 unreported.

A claim for input tax may be made on the first return the taxable person completes. The same standard of evidence in support of the claim is required as for input tax generally.

For goods, a stock account showing quantities purchased, quantities used in making other goods, date of purchase and date of sale is required. For services a list is required showing their description, date of purchase and date of any disposal.

A person who has been (or was liable to be) VAT registered and has incurred VAT on services which were for the purpose of the business and were supplied to him after the date of deregistration may make a claim to the Commissioners on form VAT 427 supported by VAT invoices.

PART VA   ADJUSTMENTS TO THE DEDUCTION OF INPUT TAX ON CAPITAL ITEMS

Interpretation
37A. The definitions in reg. 29 apply with the modification that "tax year" includes a "first tax year". An item is a "capital item" if it is held for a business purpose which does not include resale, *i.e.* it is not trading stock.

Capital items to which this part applies
37B. An item is a "capital item" if it falls within one of the following descriptions and its value, as defined in relation to each description, exceeds the amount stated:

		Minimum value
(a)	computer or item of computer equipment	£ 50,000
(b)	interest in land or all or part of a building aquired under a standard rated supply	£250,000
(c)	interest, right or licence self-supplied when all or part of a building ceases to be used for a relevant residential or charitable purpose	£250,000
(d)	interest, right or licence self-supplied when an exempt grant is made of all or part of a building or the occupier ceases to be fully taxable	£250,000

  (*e*) building constructed by the owner and first used after 31
    March 1990   £250,000
  (*f*) building altered or extended so as to increase the floor area
    by 10 per cent. or more   £250,000

Period of adjustment
37C. The proportion (if any) of input tax deducted on a capital item is adjusted over a period of adjustment comprising five successive intervals (in relation to computers, computer equipment and interests in land and buildings granted for less than ten years under a standard rated supply) or ten successive intervals (in other cases).

The first interval applied to a capital item commences on the day of supply, importation, first use or self-supply, or on 1 April 1990, according to the item concerned, and ends on the last day of the current tax year. The date of commencement is varied if the owner first uses the item before the date from which he is registered or the date from which he is included in a group registration.

Each subsequent interval corresponds with the owner's longer period (if he has one) or his tax year (if he does not).

An interval ends if the owner joins a group registration or if he transfers from one group registration to another. Each subsequent interval ends on the last day of the group's longer period (if it has one) or its tax year (if it does not). An interval also ends if the owner leaves a group registration and becomes registered in his own name. The next interval corresponds with his registration period and subsequent intervals end on the last day of his longer period (if he has one) or his tax year (if he does not).

An interval does not end if a business is transferred as a going concern and the vendor's registration is transferred to the new owner. The current interval ends on the last day of the new owner's longer period (if he has one) or his tax year (if he does not). An interval does come to an end, however, if the registration is not transferred. In either case, subsequent intervals end on the last day of the new owner's longer period (if he has one) or his tax year (if he does not).

Method of adjustment
37D. The owner is entitled to a deduction if the extent to which he used a capital asset to make taxable supplies in the first interval increases in a subsequent interval. He is liable to make a payment to the Commissioners in the reverse circumstances. The deduction or payment is calculated as follows:

$$\frac{\text{total input tax on the capital item}}{\text{number of intervals applied to the item } (\textit{i.e. } 5 \text{ or } 10)} \times \text{the adjustment percentage}$$

The owner must calculate the deduction or payment due in respect of any remaining complete interval if he sells the whole of his interest in the item in any but the last interval, or if he deregisters (so that he is deemed to supply the item) in such an interval. The item is deemed to be used wholly for making either taxable supplies or exempt supplies in each of the remaining complete intervals if the supply made or deemed to be made is respectively a taxable supply or an exempt supply.

No further adjustment is made in respect of any remaining complete intervals following the loss, theft or destruction of a capital item or the expiration of an interest in all or part of a building.

The term "total input on the capital item" is defined in relation to each description of capital item. The "adjustment percentage" is the increase or decrease (expressed as a percentage) between taxable use (if any) in the first interval and taxable use (if any) in the current interval.

A deduction or payment made in respect of the current interval is included on the VAT return furnished for the second prescribed accounting period of the next interval unless the Commissioners allow otherwise. The person making the entry is the group which the owner has left (if the interval ended when the owner left the group) or the vendor (if the interval ended when the owner transferred his business as a going concern without transferring his registration to the new owner).

A deduction or payment for intervals following the interval in which a capital item is supplied or deemed to be supplied is included on the same return as the deduction or payment for the interval in which the relevant event occurred.

Ascertainment of taxable use of a capital item
37E. The extent to which a capital item is used to make taxable supplies in a subsequent interval is determined by the reference to the partial exemption method used in the first interval. The Commissioners may allow or direct otherwise.

If the owner makes a zero-rated supply by reference to the premium or first rent payable under a lease of tenancy any subsequent grant or assignment of that lease or tenancy is disregarded in determining the extent to which the building is used to making taxable supply in a subsequent interval.

PART VI IMPORTATION, EXPORTATION AND REMOVAL FROM WAREHOUSE

Interpretation
38. Various terms and expressions used in this Part of the Regulations are defined.

Enactments excepted
39. The Alcoholic Liquor Duties Act 1979, ss. 7 to 10, 22 (4), 42 and 43, the Hydrocarbon Oil Duties Act 1979, ss. 9 and 15 to 20, the Matches and Mechanical Lighters Duties Act 1979, s. 6 (3) and the Tobacco Products Duty Act 1979, s. 2 (2) do not apply for the purposes of the charge to VAT on imported goods.

Regulations excepted
40. Temporary Importation (Equipment on Hire or Loan) Regulations 1970, S.I. 1970 No. 423, Temporary Importation (Magnetic Tapes) Regulations 1971, S.I. 1971 No. 1356, Customs Warehousing Regulations 1979, S.I. 1979 No. 207, reg. 13 (7), Excise Warehousing (Etc.) Regulations 1982, S.I. 1982 No. 612, reg. 13 (6), (7) and Inward Processing Relief Regulations 1977, S.I. 1977 No. 910, reg. 4 (1) do not apply for the purposes of the charge to VAT on imported goods.

Postal importations
41. Goods imported by post (other than by datapost packet) which do not exceed £1,300 in value, imported by a registered taxable person in the course of his business, may be delivered without payment of tax provided that security for the tax has been given to the Commissioners and the VAT registration number is shown on the customs declaration accompanying the package. VAT is to be accounted for on the importation and on any supply of the goods by him on the VAT return for the prescribed accounting period in which the goods were imported.

Temporary importations
42. The Commissioners may permit any goods imported by a non-taxable person before 1 January 1986, which are not on hire or loan, to be delivered without payment of tax if they are satisfied that the goods, or goods incorporating them, are to be exported and such conditions as may be imposed are complied with.

At the time of importation, the goods are to be produced for examination, if required, and cash or a bond deposited as security to ensure compliance with the regulations and conditions imposed.

The goods are not to be used by or supplied to any person in the U.K. except as the Commissioners allow. The proper officer may require production of the goods at any time for examination. The importer must keep such records as the proper officer requires and produce those records on demand to the proper officer.

The goods are to be exported within six months or such longer period as the Commissioners may allow.

Goods imported on hire or loan
43. Revoked.

Importation of certain goods for re-exportation
44. VAT is not chargeable on goods imported for the purpose of repair, renovation, modification, or treatment if they are subsequently re-exported. The ownership of such goods must not be transferred to a U.K. person and they must be identifiable when they are exported as the goods which were imported. The goods must be exported within six months of importation or within such longer period as the Commissioners allow. See Press Notice 1107, 30 April 1986.

Reimportation of certain goods by non-taxable persons
45. VAT chargeable on importation is not payable on goods previously exported provided that the Commissioners are satisfied that (*a*) the importer is not a taxable person or is importing goods otherwise than in the course of business, (*b*) the goods were last exported by him, (*c*) the goods were supplied in or imported into the U.K. and VAT was paid and not refunded and (*d*) the zero-rating provisions upon export did not apply.

The goods must not have been processed abroad apart from any running repairs which did not enhance their value. They must (*a*) at the time of exportation have been intended to be reimported, or (*b*) have been returned for repair or replacement or after rejection by an overseas customer or due to non-delivery to an overseas customer, or (*c*) have been in private use and possession in the U.K. before export.

Reimportation of certain goods by taxable persons
46. VAT chargeable at importation is not payable on goods previously exported if the Com-

missioners are satisfied that the importer is a taxable person, importing goods which were exported by him, which have not been subject to processing abroad other than running repairs, that the goods have been owned by him throughout the time they were abroad or are goods returned from the continental shelf and any tax chargeable on a previous supply or importation has been paid without a claim for refund being made.

Reimportation of motor cars and works of art
47. The VAT chargeable on importation of motor cars and works of art previously exported is not payable if the Commissioners are satisfied that (*a*) in the case of a motor car it was supplied in the U.K. and any tax paid was not refunded upon export and (*b*) in the case of a work of art it was exported before 1 April 1973 or if exportation was after 31 March 1973 it was exported by a person who would not have had to account for tax on the full value of the supply.

Where such cars or works of art have undergone a process or repair abroad which increase their value, tax is to be charged as if the increase in value were the whole value.

Reimportation of goods exported for treatment or process
48. The tax chargeable on reimportation of temporarily exported goods which were sent abroad for repair, process, adaptation, or have been made up or reworked is payable as if that work had been done in the U.K. provided that the Commissioners are satisfied that at the time of imporation the goods were intended to be reimported and ownership remained with a U.K. person throughout the period the goods were abroad.

Supplies to export houses
49. Goods supplied to, but not delivered to the U.K. address of an export house, and which are delivered by the supplier direct to a port, airport, or inland clearance depot for immediate export or to an export packer for delivery direct to a port, airport or inland clearance depot for immediate export may, subject to conditions imposed by the Commissioners, be zero-rated. For "export house", see *Musani Garments Ltd.* v. *C. & E. Comrs.* MAN/86/62 unreported.

Export of freight containers
50. Supplying a freight container which is to be exported may, subject to conditions imposed by the Commissioners, be zero-rated. The conditions are that the container must be exported, and that it must not be used before exportation except in an international transport of freight transaction or a single domestic journey, which is on the route to the place where it is to be loaded with international freight or it is to leave the U.K. The supplier must also obtain from the customer a written undertaking that the container is to be exported and that it will not be used in the U.K. except for the transactions mentioned above. The undertaking made by the customer should also include agreement to keep records demonstrating international transport use, export or other disposal. The Commissioners' conditions are specified in VAT Leaflet No. 703/1/83.

Supplies to overseas persons
51. Where the Commissioners are satisfied that goods intended for export have been supplied to a person not resident or VAT registered in the U.K. and have been exported then, subject to such conditions as the Commissioners may impose, the supply may be zero-rated. The conditions are set out in Notice 703 Part III. See *Henry Moss of London Ltd.* v. *C. & E. Comrs.* [1981] STC 139, CA; *Rayburn Trading Co. Ltd.* v. *C. & E. Comrs.* MAN/87/447 unreported.

Crews of ships and aircraft are excluded from using this provision.

Supplies to persons departing from the United Kingdom
52. Where the Commissioners are satisfied that goods have been supplied and delivered direct to a ship or aircraft for exportation on behalf of a non-E.C. overseas visitor who is a member of the crew, or who is a U.K. resident who intends to leave the E.C. for at least 12 months, and the goods were produced to customs and excise on exportation then, subject to such conditions as the Commissioners may impose, the goods may be zero-rated. For conditions, see Notice No. 704 (March 1985) Part II.

53. Where the Commissioners are satisfied that goods have been supplied and delivered direct to a ship or aircraft for exportation on behalf of a E.C. traveller who is a member of the crew, or who is a U.K. resident who intends to leave the U.K. for an E.C. destination for at least 12 months, the goods may be zero-rated subject to any conditions the Commissioners may impose where the value of the goods including VAT exceeds £58 when destined for the Republic of Ireland, £210 when destined for Greece, £230 when destined for Denmark or £230 for any other member State. For conditions, see Notice No. 704 (March 1985) Part II.

54. When the Commissioners are satisfied that goods have been supplied to a person who is a non-E.C. overseas visitor, or is a non-U.K. Community traveller who intends to remain outside the Community for 12 months, and at the time of supply intends to leave the U.K. within three months with the goods then, subject to conditions the Commissioners may impose and production of the goods to an officer on exportation, the supply may be zero-rated. Crews of ships and aircraft are excluded from using this provision. For conditions, see Notice No. 704 (March 1985) Part I.

55. Where the Commissioners are satisfied that goods have been supplied to a person who is a non-U.K. Community traveller who intends to depart from the U.K. within three months with the goods to an E.C. destination, the supply, subject to such conditions as the Commissioners may impose, shall be zero-rated where the value of the goods including VAT exceeds £58 when destined for the Republic of Ireland, £210 when destined for Greece, £230 when destined for Denmark or £265 for any other member State. Crews of ships and aircraft are excluded from using this provision. For conditions, see Notice No. 704 (March 1985) Part I.

56. The Commissioners may allow an overseas visitor, who intends to leave the U.K. within 15 months and stay away for at least six months, to acquire a new motor vehicle for exportation from a manufacturer within 12 months of his departure free of VAT subject to such conditions as the Commissioners may impose. The conditions are set out in Notice 705 (January 1986).

57. The Commissioners may allow any person, who intends to leave the U.K. within nine months and stay away for at least six months, to acquire a new motor vehicle for exportation from a manufacturer within six months of his departure free of VAT subject to such conditions as the Commissioners may impose. The conditions are set out in Notice 705 (January 1986).

PART VII ACCOUNTING AND PAYMENT

Furnishing of returns

58. Save as the Commissioners may otherwise allow every registered person is requied to provide the Controller with a return on form VAT 100 containing all the information required on the form together with a signed declaration that the return is true and complete. The return must be with the Controller no later than the last day of the month following the end of the prescribed accounting period concerned: see *Aikman* v. White [1986] STC 1; *Hayman* v. *Griffiths* [1987] STC 649; *Richard Costain Ltd.* v. *C. & E. Comrs.* [1988] VATTR 111. The first return starts on the effective date of registration. The Commissioners may vary the length of any return period or the date by which any return must be rendered: see *Spillane* v. *C. & E. Comrs.* LON/85/86 unreported. The Commissioners may also direct a person to send returns to a specified address.

Supplies under Schedule 2, paragraph 6

59. Where goods are supplied by a business under any power exercisable by another person towards satisfaction of a debt owed by the business, an auctioneer or the person selling the goods is required within 21 days of the sale to send a statement to the Controller containing various details. These details are his name and address and, if registered, his registration number; the name, address and registration number of the person whose goods were sold; the date of the sale; the description and quantity of goods sold at each rate of tax; and the amount for which they were sold and the amount of tax charged. That person is also required to pay the amount of tax charged and send to the person whose goods were sold a copy of the statement sent to the Controller. Goods sold under such arrangements are excluded from other VAT returns rendered by the persons involved.

Tax to be accounted for on returns and payment of tax

60. Save as the Commissioners may otherwise allow or direct, any person sending a VAT return must declare all output VAT which is accountable in the period to which the return relates, and pay the net amount shown on the return by the last day of the following month.

Estimation of output tax

61. The Commissioners may allow a person to estimate the output tax due in any period where they are satisfied that he cannot account for the exact amount of output tax chargeable in that period, provided that any such estimated amount shall be adjusted and exactly accounted for in the next period or in such later period as the Commissioners may allow.

Claims for input tax

62. Save as the Commissioners may otherwise allow or direct, a person claiming input tax deduction will do so on the VAT return for the prescribed accounting period in which the tax became chargeable. To do so he must hold a tax invoice where the supply is from another registered person, or an invoice from a supplier overseas where input tax under reverse charge mechanism is claimed, or a copy of the certified customs entry for the goods where the input tax is on the importation of goods, or an authenticated warehouse document where goods have been removed from warehouse. For situations where a tax invoice is not required, see Notice No. 700 (October 1987) para. 66 (2). For cases where false invoices have been accepted, see *Morsham Contractors Ltd.* v. *C. & E. Comrs.* MAN/84/202 unreported; *Presman (Bullion) Ltd.* v. *C. & E. Comrs.* [1986] VATTR 136. For import entries and warehouse removal documents, see Notice No. 702 (January 1988) paras. 14, 25, 29–31. The Commissioners may allow estimated claims for input tax where they are satisfied that the exact amount cannot be determined in that period, but an adjustment to the exact amount of input tax is required in the next period or in such later period as the Commissioners may allow.

Persons acting in a representative capacity
63. Where any registered person dies or becomes incapacitated and control of the business assets passes to another person acting in a representative capacity that other person is to make returns and pay tax to the extent of the assets over which he has control as if he were the incapacitated person.

Correction of errors
64. Errors in accounting for tax or on any return are to be corrected in such manner and within such time as the Commissioners may require. The Commissioners' requirements made under VATA 1983, Sch. 7, para. 7 are set out in Notice No. 700 (October 1987) para. 69. For overdeclarations of output tax for prior periods, see *C. & E. Comrs.* v. *Fine Art Developments plc.* [1989] STC 85, HL; *Betterware Products Ltd.* v. *C. & E. Comrs. (No. 2)* [1988] STC 6; *Woodcock* v. *C. & E. Comrs.* [1989] STC 237. See also FA 1989 s. 24.

PART VIII DISTRESS AND DILIGENCE

Distress
65. If after a demand has been made by an executive officer a person fails to pay VAT which has either been declared or assessed centrally by the Commissioners, a senior executive officer may sign a warrant directing any authorised person, normally an executive officer, to distrain on the goods and chattels of that registered person. Such distress action may not be taken within 30 days of an assessment, other than an assessment which has been raised because no return has been sent in. A person has five days after the distress action to pay the tax. After those five days a bailiff is to independently appraise the goods to be sold at public auction. Any excess after the tax and costs of the distress action have been paid is restored to the registered person. See *Re Memco Engineering Ltd.* [1985] 3 All ER 267.

Diligence
66. In Scotland, a Sheriff may grant a warrant authorising a Sheriff Officer to recover unpaid VAT. An application for a warrant may be made by a collector or officer of Senior Executive Officer rank or above. Lawful acts during a poinding or sale may be done by officers of like seniority. For the granting of warrants, see VATA 1983, Sch. 7, para. 6.

PART IX MISCELLANEOUS

Requirement, direction, demand or permission
67. The Commissioners may give notice as required by these Regulations in writing or otherwise.

S.I. 1985 No. 1101

The Value Added Tax (Refund of Tax) Order 1985

Note
This Order lists the bodies which may be registered for VAT and allowed to reclaim VAT which was not incurred for the purpose of a business. The bodies are: the Inner London Education Authority, the Inner London Interim Education Authority, the Northumbria Interim Police Authority, the London Fire and Civil Defence Authority, the London Residuary Body, a metropolitan county Police Authority, a metropolitan county Fire and Civil Defence Authority, a metropolitan county Passenger Transport Authority, a metroplitan county Residuary Body.

S.I. 1986 No. 260

The Postal Packets (Customs and Excise) Regulations 1986

Note
These regulations set out the customs requirements relating to incoming and outgoing postal packets and to goods contained in them. Incoming and outgoing postal packets transmitted by letter-post are not required to have a separate, full customs declaration if they have a value below £270, and the category of person to whom a seizure notice may be issued is defined.
1. These regulations came into force on 1 March 1986.

2. The meanings of various words and phrases used in these Regulations are explained.

3. Postal Packets (Customs and Excise) Regulations 1975 are revoked.

4. These regulations apply to all postal packets other than postcards which are posted in the U.K. for transmission abroad or which are brought by post into the U.K.

5. Various drafting modifications and exceptions to CEMA 1979 are listed.

6. Dutiable goods may be brought into the U.K. by post only if in (*a*) a parcel, letter, packet, small packet or datapost packet or (*b*) a printed packet where the goods are of a description transmissible in such a packet under the Post Office Overseas Letter Post Scheme 1982, para. 22.

7. Every parcel brought into the U.K. by post must have affixed to it a customs declaration fully and correctly stating the nature, quantity and value of the goods which it contains and other such particulars as the Commissioners and the Post Office may require. The Commissioners may at the request of the Post Office relax these requirements, by allowing a consignment of parcels to be accompanied by a single declaration. However, every packet which exceeds £270 in value must have attached the full and correct declaration and in addition is to bear the top portion of a green label. Packets which do not exceed £270 in value must either have a green label in the prescribed form on which the description, net weight and value of the contents are fully completed, or have a full and correct customs declaration of the kind prescribed. A registered packet containing any article of value may have the customs declaration enclosed in the package.

8. A parcel posted in the U.K. for transmission to any place outside must have affixed to it a customs declaration fully and correctly completed stating the nature, quantity and value of the goods it contains. There is a relaxation for exportation of a number of parcels accompanied by a single customs declaration posted simultaneously addressed to a single addressee. Packets exceeding £270 in value need a green label in the prescribed form and if the postal administration of the country of destination so requires a full customs declaration. Customs declarations may be included in any registered packet. Packets not exceeding £270 in value are required to have attached a green label declaration of the description, net weight and value of the contents or the top portion of a green label together with a full customs declaration.

9. Every mailbag containing printed packets containing goods which are dutiable in the country of destination brought into the U.K. by post for exportation from the U.K. are to have affixed to the bag a green label in the prescribed form.

10. Every postal packet containing goods to be exported by post without payment of any duty is upon its removal to the Post Office to be accompanied by a shipping bill, declaration or other document containing such particulars as the Commissioners may require and have affixed to its outer cover a label saying "exported by post under customs and excise control".

11. Post Office staff are authorised to carry out the duties required in the Customs and Excise Acts to be performed by the importer or exporter of goods as the Commissioners may require.

12. Post Office staff must produce to the proper officer of customs and excise postal packets arriving in the U.K. or about to be despatched from the U.K. and shall open them for customs examination if so required.

13. Post Office staff must, on accepting any packet to be exported, endorse a certificate of the posting of the packet on the appropriate document and give it to the sender.

14. If an officer of customs and excise requires a customs entry to be made in respect of any packet imported, such entry must be made within 28 days otherwise the Post Office shall return the goods to the sender or deliver the goods to the proper officer of customs and excise or with the permission of the Commissioners and under the supervision of the proper officer, destroy them. Where goods have been delivered to the proper officer of customs and excise the goods may be deposited in a Queen's Warehouse.

15. Post Office staff may demand payment of any duty or other sum due to the Commissioners upon delivery of any postal packet. If payment is not made when demanded, then the Post Office may with the agreement of the Commissioners dispose of the goods contained in the packet as it sees fit. Where an amount demanded includes an amount other than duty which is not paid, the Post Office shall deliver the packet to the proper officer of customs and excise.

16. Imported postal packets which do not contain a customs declaration or whose contents do not agree with the customs declaration are liable to forfeiture.

17. Where any postal packet contains goods which are liable to forfeiture Post Office staff shall deliver the packet to the proper officer of customs and excise.

18. These regulations do not authorise any importation or exportation of any article by post contrary to any provisions of the Post Office Overseas Parcel Post Scheme 1982, the Post Office Overseas Letter Post Scheme 1982 or the Post Office Inland Post Scheme 1979.

S.I. 1986 No. 304

The Administrative Receivers (Value Added Tax Certificates) (Scotland) Rules 1986

Note

These rules provide, in relation to Scotland, for the administrative receiver of a company to issue certificates under VATA 1983, s. 22. This enables an unpaid creditor of a company who has accounted for VAT charged on a debt claimed from the company to claim a refund of the tax paid. The creditor must obtain a certificate from the administrative receiver that the assets of the company in his opinion would be insufficient to pay any dividend in respect of debts which are neither secured nor preferred.

Citation, commencement and interpretation
1. These rules came into operation on 1 April 1986.

Application of these Rules
2. These rules apply to a company where a person is appointed to act as its administrative receiver under the Companies Act 1985, s. 467.

Issue of certificate of insolvency
3. It is the duty of the administrative receiver to issue a certificate as soon as he has formed the opinion that if the company went into liquidation the assets would be insufficient to cover the payment of any dividend in respect of debts that are neither secured nor preferential.

Form of certificate
4. The certificate must contain the name of the company and its registered number, the full name of the administrative receiver, the date of his appointment and the date on which the certificate is issued. The certificate must be headed "CERTIFICATE OF INSOLVENCY FOR THE PURPOSES OF SECTION 22 (3) (*b*) OF THE VALUE ADDED TAX ACT 1983".

Notification to creditors
5. The administrative receiver must notify issue of the certificate of insolvency to all the company's unsecured creditors whose address he knows and who have supplied the company with goods or services charged with VAT. He must do this within three months of his appointment or within two months of issuing the certificate, whichever is later. He must also notify any such creditor who comes to light afterwards. He need not provide a copy of the certificate itself.

Preservation of certificate with company's records
6. The certificate must be kept with the company's accounting records for the length of time specified in the Companies Act 1985, s. 222.

S.I. 1986 No. 335

The Value Added Tax (Bad Debt Relief) 1986

Note
These regulations replace with certain amendments the 1978 Regulations. They regulate the administration of relief for the VAT element of bad debts incurred on supplies where the debtor becomes formally insolvent on or after 1 April 1986. They complement the extended class of qualifying insolvencies provided from that date by FA 1985, s. 32 (1). Reg. 6 (1) is new and prescribes the evidence to be held in cases where an administrator or administrative receiver of a company has been appointed and the assets are insufficient to permit any payment to the ordinary unsecured creditors. Reg. 7 prescribes the minumum period of six years for the retention of this evidence. Regs. 8 and 9 prescribe the method to be used for the calculation of the outstanding consideration in cases of mutual debts and part payment respectively. Reg. 10 provides for the repayment of relief by a claimant where certain conditions are breached.

Citation and commencement
1. These regulations came into operation on 1 April 1986.

Interpretation
2. Various words and phrases used in the Regulations are defined.

Revocation and savings
3. This provides for continuity between the old and new Regulations.

The making of a claim to the Commissioners
4. Save as the Commissioners may otherwise allow or direct, a claim for bad debt relief is included in Box 2 of the VAT return for the period in which the required evidence is obtained.

Evidence required of the claimant in support of his claim
5. Save as the Commissioners may otherwise allow, the person making a bad debt relief claim must

hold the document issued by the debtor's representative specifying the total amount of debt proved, copy tax invoices or, where no invoice is necessary, a document which shows the time, nature and the consideration for each taxable supply, and records which show that tax has been accounted for on each supply which related to the relief claim.

6. Where an administrator or administrative receiver is appointed instead of holding a document specifying the total amount of debt proved, the claimant must hold a notice that a certificate has been issued by that person stating that there would be insufficient funds to pay out unsecured creditors.

Preservation of documents and records and duty to produce
7. Save as the Commissioners may otherwise allow, all paperwork relating to a bad debt relief claim must be kept for a period of six years from the date when the return is sent to customs and excise. An authorised person should produce the paperwork for inspection and permit the removal of the documents at a reasonable time and for a reasonable period.

Set-off of amounts between the claimant and the debtor
8. Save as Commissioners may otherwise allow, where the person making the bad debt relief claim owed an amount to the debtor which under the law governing insolvency, the debtor can set-off, or if it cannot be set-off is a payment which can be lawfully demanded by the debtor, then any refund shall be calculated from the reduced outstanding amount. For example, if the debtor owes £575 (£500+£75 VAT) while the creditor owes the debtor £115 (£100+£15 VAT) then the VAT which may be reclaimed from customs and excise is £575−£115=£460×$^3/_{23}$ (VAT @ 15%)=£60.

Determination of outstanding amount of consideration in money
9. Where a claimant has made more than one supply at differing rates of tax to a debtor who has become insolvent and only part of the consideration, which has not been allocated to any particular supply, has been paid then the outstanding debt shall be calculated on a first in first out basis.
  For examples, see Example 3 of Annex A to leaflet No. 700/18/86.

Repayment of a refund
10. Where documents are destroyed within the six year period or not produced to an officer on demand then the bad debt relief claimed must be repaid to the Commissioners. Where a creditor proves in the insolvency for a sum greater than the outstanding amount of the consideration for taxable supplies, the creditor must repay to the Commissioners the difference between the VAT on the taxable supplies and the amount attributed to VAT from the insolvency. The amount concerned is included in Box 1 of the next VAT return.

Proving in the insolvency in Scotland
11. Special rules apply in Scotland to determine whether a claimant has proved in the insolvency.

S.I. 1986 No. 336

The Value Added Tax (Refund of Tax) Order 1986

Note
This Order specifies bodies who are entitled to claim refunds of VAT on supplies to or importations by them made other than for the purpose of business.
1. This Order came into operation on 1 April 1986.
2. The following bodies are entitled to claim refunds of VAT on supplies to or importations by them made other than for the purposes of business:
  a probation committee constituted by the Powers of Criminal Courts Act 1973,
  a magistrates' courts committee established under the Justices of the Peace Act 1979, and
  the charter trustees constituted by the Local Government Act 1972.

S.I. 1986 No. 385

The Administrative Receivers (Value Added Tax Certificates) Rules 1986

Note
These Rules provide in England and Wales for the administrative receiver of a company to issue certificates proving insolvency. An unpaid creditor of a company who has accounted for VAT charged on the debt claimed from the company may claim a refund of tax paid following the issue of a certificate by the administrative receiver that the debts of the company in his opinion would be insufficient to cover the payment of any dividend in respect of debts which are neither secured nor preferential.

Citation and commencement
1. These Rules came into force on 1 April 1986.

Application of these Rules
2. These rules apply to a company where a person is appointed to act as its administrative receiver. Where such a person is appointed under the law of Scotland, see S.I. 1986 No. 304.

Issue of certificate of insolvency
3. It is the duty of the administrative receiver to issue a certificate as soon as he has formed the opinion that if the company went into liquidation the assets would be insufficient to cover the payment of any dividend in respect of debts that are neither secured nor preferential.

Form of certificate
4. The certificate must contain the name of the company and its registered number, the full name of the administrative receiver, the date of his appointment as such and the date on which the certificate is issued. The certificate must be entitled "CERTIFICATE OF INSOLVENCY FOR THE PURPOSES OF SECTION 22 (3) (*b*) OF THE VALUE ADDED TAX 1983".

Notification to creditors
5. The administrative receiver must notify issue of the certificate of insolvency to all the company's unsecured creditors whose address he knows and who have supplied the company with goods or services charged with VAT. He must do this within three months of his appointment or within two months of issuing the certificate, whichever is later. He must also notify any such creditor who comes to light afterwards. He need not provide a copy of the certificate itself.

Preservation of certificate with company's records
6. The certificate must be kept with the company's accounting records for the period specified in Companies Act 1985, s. 222.

S.I. 1986 No. 532

The Value Added Tax (Refund of Tax) (No. 2) Order 1986

Note
This Order specifies the bodies entitled to claim refunds of VAT on supplies to or importations by them not made for the purposes of business, in the same way as could the bodies whose functions are being transferred to them.
1. This Order came into operation on 1 April 1986.
2. Authorities established under the Local Government Act 1985, s. 10 are entitled to claim refunds of VAT on supplies to or importations by them made other than for the purposes of business.

S.I. 1986 No. 590

The Value Added Tax Tribunals Rules 1986

Note
These Rules prescribe the procedure to be followed when an appeal is made to a VAT tribunal against a decision of the Commissioners. Special provision is made for the conduct of "reasonable excuse appeals" and "mitigation appeals" and for appeals against assessments to a penalty for failure to notify for registration. Provision is made for the serving of a notice of appeal at the appropriate tribunal centre and for limiting the time within which appeals are to be brought, although such time may be extended by the tribunal, as may any other time limit.

Provision is also made for an exchange of lists of documents (Rule 20), the use of witness statements (Rule 21), the summoning of witnesses (Rule 22), the procedure at a hearing (Rule 27), the methods of proof at a hearing (Rule 28), the award of costs (Rule 29) and the giving and making of decisions and directions by the tribunal (Rule 30). There is also a provision conferring on the Registrar of the tribunals, or any member of the administrative staff of the tribunals appointed by the Lord Chancellorto perform all or any of the duties of a registrar and certain powers of making interlocutory directions are exercisable by a tribunal or a chairman (Rule 33).

Citation, commencement, revocation and savings
1. These Rules came into operation on 1 May 1986. Any appeal begun under the former Rules may be continued under the corresponding provision of these new Rules. Unless there is contrary intention, documents or proceedings referred to in the old Rules correspond to provisions in these Rules.

Interpretation
2. Various words and phrases are defined.

Method of appealing
3. The first step is to lodge at the local tribunal centre a notice of appeal signed by the registered person or his representative. This must contain the name and addresss of the appellant, the address of the VAT office from which the disputed decision was sent, the date of the document containing the disputed decision and the address to which it was sent, what the disputed decision was, and the grounds for the appeal against that decision. The grounds for appeal should contain sufficient detail to enable the Commissioners to see the basis of the case against them: see *ACP Jig & Tool Co. Ltd.* v. *C. & E. Comrs.* MAN/82/142 unreported. Any letters from the Commissioners which extend the appellant's time to appeal against a disputed decision should be attached to the notice of appeal. The parties to any appeal are the registered person and the Commissioners.

Time for appealing
4. A notice of appeal must be lodged at the appropriate tribunal centre within 30 days of the decision which is disputed unless the Commissioners have previously extended the time limit for appeal, in which case there will be a further 21 days after the final decision made by the Commissioners. For the appropriate tribunal centres, see Explanatory Leaflet, Appendix A. The tribunal may also extend the time within which a notice of appeal may be lodged: see r. 19.

Acknowledgement and notification of an appeal
5. The tribunal centre is to acknowledge receipt of the notice of appeal and send a copy of the notice to the Commissioners.

Notice that an appeal does not lie or cannot be entertained
6. The Commissioners may contend that the matter of dispute is not within the areas which may be heard by a tribunal, and serve notice to the tribunal that the appeal be struck out or dismissed (see Rule 18). Such a claim by the Commissioners is to be copied to the appellant. Where a hearing is on the grounds of reasonable excuse or mitigation, the hearing of the request for the appeal to be dismissed may immediately precede the hearing of the real dispute.

Statement of case, defence and reply in a section 13 penalty appeal
7. Unless a tribunal directs otherwise the Commissioners are required in a section 13 penalty appeal to lodge a statement of case within 42 days of the lodging of the notice of appeal. The statement of case has to set out grounds on which the penalty assessment was made. The appellant has a further 42 days to lodge at the appropriate tribunal centre a statement of case which sets out his defence. The Commissioners may reply within 21 days setting out any matter which makes the defence invalid.

In a section 13 penalty appeal the Commissioners are not required to prove any fact which is admitted by the appellant in his defence.

Statement of case in an appeal other than a section 13 penalty appeal and reasonable excuse and mitigation appeals
8. Unless a tribunal otherwise directs, the Commissioners are required to lodge at the appropriate tribunal centre a statement of case setting out the matter and facts on which they rely to support the disputed decision. For the content, see *Deeds Ltd.* v. *C. & E. Comrs.* LON/82/20 unreported; *AZO-Maschinenfabrik Adolf Zimmerman* v. *C. & E. Comrs.* LON/86/579 unreported. The statement of case must be lodged at the appropriate tribunal centre within 30 days of the date of service of the notice of appeal or the withdrawal or dismissal of any application that an appeal cannot be entertained. This time limit does not apply to reasonable excuse and mitigation appeals and section 13 penalty appeals. For service of a statement of case out of time, see *C. & E. Comrs.* v. *Dormers Builders (London) Ltd.* LON/85/283 unreported; *Optimum Personnel Evaluation (Operations) Ltd.* v. *C. & E. Comrs.* LON/86/620 unreported.

Further and better particulars
9. A tribunal may, giving no less than 14 days notice, direct a party to an appeal to give further details of his case. Where in an appeal the Commissioners wish to contend that an amount specified on an assessment is less than it ought to have been, the statement of case in that appeal must indicate the amount of the alleged deficiency and the manner in which it has been calculated.

Acknowledgement and notification of service of formal documents served in an appeal
10. A copy of the disputed decision must accompany any statement of case served by the Commissioners unless it has been served previously at the tribunal centre by either party to the appeal.

In a reasonable excuse or a mitigation appeal the Commissioners are to serve a copy of the disputed decision at the appropriate tribunal centre as soon as practical after receipt of the notice of appeal unless a copy of the disputed decision has been served previously by the appellant.

An officer at the tribunal centre shall send an acknowledgement of the service of any statement of case, defence, reply or particulars of any appeal to the person making those details known and copy those details to the other party to the appeal.

Method of applying for a direction
11. An application to a tribunal for a direction without the tribunal sitting must be made by giving notice served at the appropriate tribunal centre. This includes directions that an appeal may be entertained without depositing tax with the Commissioners or for the issue or setting aside of a witness summons.

A notice under this rule has to state the name and address of the applicant, state the direction sought or the details of the witness summons to be issued or set aside, and set out the grounds for the application. In addition, any notice of application by an intending appellant is to state the address of the customs and excise office from which the disputed decision was sent, state the date of the disputed decision and the address to which it was sent, set out briefly the disputed decision. It must also have attached a copy of any letter from the Commissioners notifying the date from which the time of appeal against the decision shall run.

An application for an appeal to be heard without payment of the disputed tax shall be served at the appropriate tribunal centre within the period set for service of a notice of appeal.

Applications for tribunal directions may be made only by parties to the appeal or by witnesses summoned to a hearing.

An officer of the tribunal is required to acknowledge receipt of a notice of application to the applicant and copy such notice of application to the other party, if any, stating the date on which the notice of application was made. Within 14 days of such an application the other party is required to indicate whether or not he consents and if not, the reason for dissent.

Partners
12. Partners in a firm which is not a legal person distinct from the partners of whom it is composed may appeal in the name of the firm and, unless a tribunal otherwise directs, the proceedings shall be carried on in the name of the firm with the same consequences as if the appeal or application had been brought in the names of the partners.

Death or bankruptcy of an appellant or applicant
13. Where at any stage of an appeal or application the appellant or applicant dies or becomes bankrupt or for some other reason his interest is assigned to some other person, the appeal or application shall not end there but a tribunal may direct that the representative if he consents in writing may be substituted for the appellant or applicant.

Amendments
14. A tribunal may at any time either of its own motion or on the application of any party to the appeal or any other interested person direct that a notice of appeal, notice of application, statement of case, defence, reply, particulars or other document in proceedings be amended to correct any errors. This does not apply to tribunal decisions or directions.

Transfers between tribunal centres
15. A party to an appeal may apply to a tribunal centre for a direction that the appeal be heard in another tribunal centre.

Withdrawal of an appeal or application
16. An appellant or applicant may withdraw his appeal or application at any time by serving at the appropriate tribunal centre a notice of withdrawal signed by him or on his behalf. An officer of the tribunals is to send a copy of the withdrawal notice to the Commissioners.

The withdrawal of an appeal or application does not prevent a party to the appeal or application from applying for an award of costs or for the payment or repayment of a sum of money with interest or prevent a tribunal from making such an award or direction if it thinks fit.

Appeal or application allowed by consent
17. Where the parties to an appeal or application have agreed on the terms of any decision or direction, a tribunal may give a decision or make a direction in accordance with those terms without a hearing.

Power of a tribunal to strike out or dismiss an appeal
18. A tribunal may strike out an appeal where no appeal against a disputed decision can be heard by a tribunal, and dismiss an appeal where the appeal cannot be entertained by a tribunal.

A tribunal may dismiss an appeal where the appellant has been found guilty of inordinate and inexcusable delay. No appeal shall be struck out or dismissed without a hearing, except by consent under rule 17.

Power of a tribunal to extend time and to give directions
19. A tribunal may of its own motion or on the the application by any party to an appeal or application, extend the time within which the appeal or application or any other person is required to do anything in relation to an appeal or application. A tribunal may extend the time limits without prior notice to any other party and without a hearing. For the basis on which the tribunal reaches a decision, see *Price* v. *C. & E. Comrs.* [1978] VATTR 115; *Ullah* v. *C. & E. Comrs.* BIR/78/53 unreported; also *C. & E. Comrs.* v. *Holvey* [1978] STC 187. A tribunal may on the application of a party to an appeal or application give or make any direction as to the conduct of or as to any matter or thing in connection with the appeal or application which it may think necessary or expedient to ensure the speedy and just determination of the appeal. If any party to an appeal or application or other person fails to comply with any direction of a tribunal it may allow or dismiss the appeal or may summarily award a penalty not exceeding £1,000, or both. A tribunal may of its own motion or on the application of any party to an appeal or application, waive any breach of any provision of these rules or of any decision or direction of a tribunal upon such terms as it may think just.

For applications to stand over an appeal, see *Kinglace Ltd.* v. *C. & E. Comrs.* LON/86/148 unreported. For applications by the Commissioners to extend time for serving their statement of case and list of documents, see *C. & E. Comrs.* v. *Dormers Builders (London) Ltd.* [1986] VATTR 69. For an application for substitution, joinder or intervention, see *Schwarcz* v. *C. & E. Comrs.* [1988] STC 230.

Disclosure, inspection and production of documents
20. A party to an appeal is required to serve at the appropriate tribunal centre a list of the documents in his possession which he proposes to produce at the hearing of the appeal or application.

In a section 13 penalty appeal the list of documents is required within 15 days after the last day of the service by the Commissioners of a reply to a defence. In any other appeal, except a reasonable excuse or mitigation appeal, the list should be produced within 30 days after the service of the notice of appeal or application.

A tribunal may on the application of a party to an appeal direct that the other party shall serve, at the appropriate tribunal centre for the appeal, a list of the documents which are or have been in his possession relating to any question in issue in the appeal and may order him to make and serve an affidavit verifying such a list. If a party wishes to claim that any document included in such a list of documents is privileged from production in the appeal, that claim must be made in the list of documents with a reason why the documents should not be produced.

A tribunal officer shall copy the list of documents and affidavit to the other party to the appeal or application who is entitled to inspect and take copies of the documents set out on the list which are not privileged from production in the appeal.

At the hearing of an appeal or application, either party can be called upon to produce any document which appears on the list of documents which are not privileged from production, when called upon by another party to do so.

Witness statements
21. A statement in writing may be served at the appropriate tribunal centre containing evidence which is proposed to be given by any person at the hearing of the appeal. Such a witness statement must contain the name, address and description of the person proposing to give the evidence and must be signed.

A tribunal officer is to copy such a witness statement to the other party to the appeal stating the date of service, together with a note to the effect that, unless a notice of objection is served no later than 14 days after the date of service, the witness statement may be read at the hearing of the appeal as evidence of the facts stated in the statement without the person who made the witness statement giving evidence. If the other party to the appeal objects he is required to lodge a notice of objection at the appropriate tribunal centre, whereupon a tribunal officer shall copy the notice of objection to the other party and the witness statement shall not be read or admitted as evidence. However, the person who signed the witness statement may still give evidence orally at the hearing. Unless a tribunal otherwise directs a witness statement properly served is admissible as evidence of fact as if the evidence had been given orally at the hearing.

In a section 13 penalty appeal a witness statement should be served within 21 days after the last day in which the Commissioners may reply to a defence. In the case of a mitigation appeal or a reasonable excuse appeal the statement should be served within 21 days of the service of the notice of appeal and in any other appeal within 21 days after the date of the service of statement of case by the Commissioners.

Witness summonses and summonses to third parties
22. A witness may be summoned by a tribunal chairman upon application by a party to an appeal for a witness to give oral evidence or to produce any document in his possession.

Where a party to an appeal wished to inspect any document relating to a hearing which is in the possession of any other person in the U.K. or the Isle of Man, a tribunal chairman or the registrar will at the request of the party to the appeal issue a summons requiring either the third party to attend with the document for inspection, perusal and copying or to post the document to a U.K. or Isle of Man address by first class mail for the party to the appeal to inspect.

A summons may be issued by a tribunal chairman or registrar without reference to any other person other than the applicant and without a hearing.

A summons shall be signed by a chairman or registrar and must be served personally upon the witness or third party by leaving a copy with him and showing the original not less than four days before the day on which attendance is required or the document is to be posted. The summons should be accompanied by a note to the effect that the witness may apply by giving notice to the tribunal centre for a direction that the summons be set aside. A witness summons properly served is valid until the end of the hearing at which attendance is required.

No person has to attend any hearing or to post any document for the purpose of a hearing in accordance with a summons unless a reasonable sum of money sufficient to defray the expenses of attending and returning from the hearing is offered at the time when the summons was served.

Notice of hearings
23. A tribunal officer is to send a notice giving the date, time and place where an appeal will be heard giving at least 14 days notice.

An application made at a hearing will be heard by the tribunal then and no further notice will be given to the parties to the application unless a tribunal otherwise directs. The tribunal officer is to send a notice stating the date, time and place where an application will be heard unless the parties otherwise agree, giving 14 days notice after the date of the notice. The notice must be given, in the case of an application for the issue of a witness summons, to the applicant; in the case of an application to set aside the issue of a witness summons, to the applicant and the party who obtained the issue of the witness summons; and in the case of any other application, to the parties to the application.

Hearings in public or in private
24. Tribunal hearings shall be in public unless on the application of one of the parties a tribunal directs that the hearing of any part of the hearing is to take place in private. For an example, see *Guy Butler (International) Ltd.* v. *C. & E. Comrs.* [1974] VATTR 199. The hearing of any application made otherwise than at or subsequent to the hearing of an appeal is to take place in private unless the tribunal otherwise directs.

Any member of the Council on Tribunals or the Scottish Committee of the Council on Tribunals may attend in that capacity the hearing of any appeal or application, even if heard privately.

Representation at a hearing
25. Anyone other than the Commissioners may conduct their own case or they may be represented by any person appointed for the purpose. The Commissioners may be represented by any person whom they appoint for the purpose.

Failure to appear at a hearing
26. If the appellant or his representative does not turn up for a hearing the tribunal may strike out the appeal or application but may reinstate the appeal on such terms as it may think just if an application is made within 14 days of the decision to strike out being released.

A tribunal may also consider the appeal or the application in the absence of one party but any decision or direction given may be set aside by a tribunal on such terms as they may think just upon application by the missing party received within 14 days of the date when the decision or direction of the tribunal was released. For examples, see *Hallam* v. *C. & E. Comrs.* [1977] VATTR 105; *Cumbershourne Ltd.* v. *C. & E. Comrs.* [1977] VATTR 110.

Procedure at a hearing
27. At the hearing of an appeal or application other than a section 13 penalty appeal the appellant or applicant shall open with his case. The appellant or applicant shall give evidence in support of the appeal and produce documentary evidence. The appellant or applicant may call other witnesses to give evidence in support of the appeal or to produce documentary evidence and to re-examine any such witness following his cross-examination. The other party to the appeal, normally solicitors employed by theCommissioners, may cross-examine any witness called to give evidence in support of the appeal, including the appellant if he gives evidence. The other party to the appeal will then open his case. The other party to the appeal shall give evidence in opposition to the appeal and produce documentary evidence. The other party to the appeal may call witnesses to give evidence in opposition to the appeal or to produce documentary evidence and to re-examine any such witness following his cross-examination. The appellant may cross-examine any witness called to give evidence in opposition to the appeal including the other party to the appeal or application if he gives evidence. The other party to the appeal may make a second address closing his case and the appellant may make the final address closing his case.

At the tribunal hearing of a section 13 penalty appeal, the same order is to take place but the Commissioners change places with the appellant.

During the hearing the chairman and any other member of the tribunal may put any question to any witness called to give evidence, including a party to the appeal if he gives evidence. Hearings may be postponed or adjourned.

Evidence at a hearing
28. A tribunal may allow evidence of any fact to be given in any manner it thinks fit and shall not refuse evidence tendered to it on the grounds that such evidence would be inadmissible in a court of law. Witness statements may be read unless objected to under Rule 21 (4).

Oral evidence may be required on oath or affirmation and tribunal chairman and administrative staff of tribunals have power to administer oaths or take affirmations. For the duty to warn a witness against self-incrimination, see *Stewart Ward (Coins) Ltd.* v. *C. & E. Comrs.* [1986] VATTR 129.

At the hearing of an appeal the tribunal shall allow a party to produce any documents set out in his list of documents and, unless the tribunal otherwise directs, a document which appears to be an original shall be deemed to be the original and any document contained in such a list of documents which appears to be a copy shall be deemed to be a true copy.

Award and direction as to costs
29. A tribunal may direct that a party or applicant is to pay to the other party to the appeal or application either (*a*) within such period as it may specify such sum as it may determine on account of the costs of the other party which are incidental to and are as a result of the appeal or application or (*b*) the costs of such party taxed by a taxing master of the courts. Costs awarded under this rule are recoverable as a civil debt.

Costs follow the event unless misconduct by the winning party makes an award inappropriate: *Rawlins Davey & Wells* v. *C. & E. Comrs.* LON/77/251 unreported. Costs are not normally awarded to an unsuccessful party: see *Smith-Harris (a firm)* v. *C. & E. Comrs.* MAN/74/6 unreported; *Lawton* v. *C. & E. Comrs.* MAN/77/237 unreported. A proportionate award may be made where an appeal is only partially successful: see *Ahmad* v. *C. & E. Comrs.* [1976] VATTR 128. An award may be made if an appeal is settled prior to the hearing: *Rupert Page Developments Ltd* v. *C. & E. Comrs.* LON/76/64 unreported. However, a compromise must deal with the question of costs before an award can be made: *Cadogan Club Ltd.* v. *C. & E. Comrs.* LON/76/202 unreported. A further award can be made only if the tribunal reserved power to do so in the original award: *Chartcliffe* v. *C. & E. Comrs.* [1976] VATTR 165.

For the manner in which a tribunal arrives at the quantum of an award, see *British Institute of Management* v. *C. & E. Comrs.* [1980] VATTR 42; *Harrison* v. *C. & E. Comrs.* [1982] VATTR 7. For the costs of a litigant in person, see *C. & E. Comrs.* v. *Ross* [1990] STC 353; *Wendy Fair Market Club* v. *C. & E. Comrs.* LON/77/400 unreported. The costs of an advocate are allowed but the award excludes VAT if the appellant is a taxable person: see *Taylor (No. 3)* v. *C. & E. Comrs.* MAN/75/5 unreported; *Ahmad* v. *C. & E. Comrs.* [1976] VATTR 128. For the costs of a represented appellant, see *Johnson* v. *C. & E. Comrs.* MAN/77/255 unreported. For the costs of an appellant represented by an officer or employee, see *Jocelyn Fielding Fine Arts Ltd.* v. *C. & E. Comrs.* [1978] VATTR 164, which has been followed in later cases, but see *Investment Chartwork Ltd.* v. *C. & E. Comrs.* [1981] VATTR 114 for a contrary view. The court will overrule a decision of a tribunal in relation to costs only if it is perverse or unreasonable: *Zoungrou* v. *C. & E. Comrs.* [1989] STC 313.

For the exercise of the discretion to direct a taxation of costs, see *Taylor (No. 3)* v. *C. & E. Comrs.* MAN/75/5 unreported; *Bophuthatswana National Commercial Corpn. Ltd.* v. *C. & E. Comrs.* LON/89/362, 426 unreported.

For the Commissioners' policy on costs of unsuccessful appellants see Press Notice No. 1132, 5 August 1986.

Decisions and directions
30. At the conclusion of the hearing the chairman may announce the decision of the tribunal. However, the decision shall be recorded in a written document signed by the chairman containing the findings of fact by the tribunal and its reasons for the decision. Any party to the appeal may request by notice, within one year at the date of the decision, the outcome of the appeal to be recorded in a written direction which is to be signed by a chairman or the registrar.

At the conclusion of the hearing of an application the tribunal chairman may announce the decison of the tribunal but in any event the outcome of the application and any award or direction given is to be recorded in a written direction signed by a chairman or the Registrar. A party to the application may request by notice in writing served at the appropriate tribunal centre within 14 days of the date of such direction a written document signed by a chairman containing the findings of fact and the reason for the tribunal's decision.

The tribunal officer is to send a copy of the decision and of any direction in an appeal to each party to the appeal. Every decision in an appeal must show the date when the copies are released to the parties to the appeal and all copies of any direction recording the outcome must state that date. Every direction is to bear the date when the copies are released to be sent to the parties and all copies must state that date.

A chairman of the registrar may correct any clerical mistake or other error in expressing his intention in a decision or direction signed by him, but if such corrections are made after a copy has been sent to a party, a tribunal officer must send a copy of the corrected document or the page which has been corrected to those parties. See *Betterware Products Ltd* v. *C. & E. Comrs. (No. 2)* [1988] STC 6.

Where a copy of a decison or direction dismissing an appeal is made in the absence of a party who may apply to the appeal or application reinstated, the copy shall contain a comment to that effect.

Appeals from tribunal
30A. A party wishing to appeal against a tribunal decision directly to the Court of Appeal should apply to the tribunal for a certificate within 21 days of the date when the decision of the tribunal was released. The certificate is to confirm that the dispute involves a point of law relating to the construction of legislation which has been fully argued before and considered by the tribunal. For other conditions, see the VAT Tribunals Appeals Order 1986, S.I. 1986 No. 2288.

Service at a tribunal centre
31. Notices of appeal, application or other documents may be served by handing or posting to the appropriate tribunal centre.

A document received at a wrong tribunal centre may be sent by post to the proper tribunal centre or handed or posted back to the person from whom it was received.

Sending of documents to the parties
32. Documents which have to be sent to the Commissioners may be sent by post to the address of the office from which the disputed decision appears to have been sent or handed or sent by post to such address as the Commissioners may from time to time request by general notice served at the appropriate tribunal centre. Any document which has to be sent to any other party may be sent by post to him at his address stated in his notice of appeal or application or sent by post to any person named in his notice of appeal or application as having been instructed to act for him. Where partners appeal or apply to a tribunal in the name of their firm, any document sent by post in a letter addressed to the firm at the address stated in the notice of appeal or to any person named as having been instructed to act for the firm is regarded as having been sent to all such partners.

Any document authorised or required to be sent to any party to an appeal or application or other person may be sent by post in a letter addressed to him at his usual or last known address or addressed to him at such address as he may from time to time by notice specify, served at the appropriate tribunal centre.

Delegation of powers to the Registrar
33. The Registrar of VAT tribunals has the power to give or make any direction by consent of the parties to the appeal or application, power to give or make any direction on the application of one party which is not opposed by the other party to the application, power to issue witness summons, power to postpone any hearing, and power to extend the time for the service of any notice of appeal, notice of application or other document at the appropriate tribunal centre for a period not exceeding one month.

The Registrar also has the power to sign a direction recording the outcome of an appeal and any award or direction given by a tribunal at the conclusion of a hearing of an appeal and to sign any document recording any directions made.

S.I. 1986 No. 896

The Value Added Tax (Treatment of Transactions) Order 1986

Note
This Order removes from the scope of VAT diposals by pawnbrokers of goods to the person who pawned them within three months of the property and the goods passing to the pawnbroker under the Consumer Credit Act 1974, s. 120(1)(a). Any such disposals would otherwise be a supply of goods and would be chargeable with VAT. See Press Notice No. 1112, 3 June 1986.

Citation and commencement
1. This Order came into operation 1 July 1986.

Interpretation
2. Phrases used in the Order are defined.

Treatment of transaction
3. The supply by a taxable person of goods, the property in which has passed to him by virtue of the Consumer Credit Act 1974, s. 120(1)(a) where the supply is to a person who pawned the goods in

the first place, and where the supply is made not later than three months from the date when the taxable person acquired the property in the goods, is to be treated as neither a supply of goods nor supply of services and is therefore outside the scope of VAT.

S.I. 1986 No. 939

The Value Added Tax (Small Non-Commercial Consignments) Relief Order 1986

Note
This Order replaces the VAT (Imported Goods) Relief Order 1980.
The Order increases the maximum quantity of spirits eligible for relief from one quarter bottle (not exceeding .25 litre) to 1 litre.

Citation and commencement
1. This Order came into operation on 1 July 1986.

Revocation
2. The Value Added Tax (Imported Goods) Relief Order 1980 and the 1985 Amendment Order are revoked.

Relief from value added tax
3. No VAT is payable on the importation of goods forming part of a small consignment of a non-commercial character. "Small consignment" means goods with a value not exceeding £75 from the E.C. or £32 in any other case. A consignment must be from one private individual to another without any consideration in money and intended solely for the personal use of the consignee.

Conditions of relief
4. Goods consigned from the E.C. must have borne normal tax. Goods from elsewhere must not be imported regularly.

Quantitative restriction on relief for certain goods
5. The quantities of tobacco products, alcoholic beverages and perfumes which may be imported in small non-commercial consignments are restricted.

Relief not applicable to travellers' baggage
6. Goods carried in the baggage of a person entering the U.K. are subject to different allowances.

SCHEDULE (Article 5)
   (1) Tobacco products, 50 cigarettes or equivalent;
   (2) Alcoholic beverages, 1 litre spirits or 2 litres still wine;
   (3) Perfumes 50 grammes; toilet waters .25 litre or 8 oz.

S.I. 1986 No. 1925

The Insolvency Rules 1986

Note
Rules 2.56 to 2.58 provide in England and Wales for the administrator of a company to issue certificates proving insolvency. An unpaid creditor of a company who has accounted for VAT charged on the debt claimed from the company may claim a refund of tax paid following the issue of a certificate by the administrator that the debts of the company in his opinion would be insufficient to cover the payment of any dividend in respect of debts which are neither secured nor preferential.

Issue of certificate of insolvency
2.56. It is the duty of the administrator to issue a certificate as soon as he has formed the opinion that if the company went into liquidation the assets would be insufficient to cover the payment of any dividend in respect of debts that are neither secured nor preferential.
   The certificate must contain the name of the company and its registered number, the name of the administrator, the date of his appointment as such and the date on which the certificate is issued. The certificate must be entitled "CERTIFICATE OF INSOLVENCY FOR THE PURPOSES OF SECTION 22 (3) (*b*) OF THE VALUE ADDED TAX 1983".

Notice to creditors
2.57. The administrator must notify issue of the certificate of insolvency to all the company's

unsecured creditors whose address he knows and who have supplied the company with goods or services charged with VAT. He must do this within three months of his appointment or within two months of issuing the certificate, whichever is later. He must also notify any such creditor who comes to light afterwards. He need not provide a copy of the certificate itself.

Preservation of certificate with company's records
2.58. The certificate must be kept with the company's accounting records for the length of time specified in the Companies Act 1985, s. 222 and when he vacates office the administrator must tell the directors (or his successor) about the need to preserve the certificate.

S.I. 1986 No. 1989

The Value Added Tax (Temporarily Imported Goods) Relief Order 1986

Note
This Order provides relief from payment of VAT on the temporary importation of the goods listed in Sch. 1, Groups I to XIV and provides relief from VAT for certain goods which are imported for possible sale listed in Sch. 2, Group I.

Citation and Commencement
1. This Order came into operation on 1 January 1987.

Interpretation
2. Words and phrases used in this Order are defined.

Revocation and savings
3. The Value Added Tax (Temporarily Imported Goods) Relief Order 1985 is revoked. Unless contrary intention appears in this Order documents used under the old Order should continue to be used under the corresponding provision in this Order.

Application
4. This Order does not affect temporary importation reliefs given by other Acts nor does this Order allow any person to import any prohibited or restricted goods. Excluded from the relief are means of transport, pallets, containers, and the personal effects of travellers for their use during their stay in the U.K.

Relief for goods imported from another member State
5. Subject to such conditions as the Commissioners may impose, where goods are imported from another member State into the U.K. with a view to their being re-exported, VAT due on importation is not payable where the Commissioners are satisfied that: the goods are to be re-exported without alteration, the goods are in free circulation within the Community and have not been relieved from VAT in the exporting country, the goods belong to an overseas person and they are not consumable goods.
6. Goods imported from another Community State with a view to their re-exportation but which do not qualify for relief may be imported without payment of VAT if, had they been imported into the U.K. from a country outside the Community, relief would have been granted under the provisions of Article 7 below. This does not apply where the conditions laid down in Articles 9 and 10 of the EEC Treaty are met, the goods were acquired without payment of VAT in the exporting country and the importer is not entitled to full credit for input tax.

Relief for goods imported from outside the Community
7. Goods described in Sch. 1 which are intended for re-exportation are not chargeable with VAT, subject to the provisions of this Order.

Goods for possible sale
8. Goods specified in Sch. 2 which are intended for sale in the U.K. are not chargeable with VAT, subject to the provisions of this Order.

Transfer of goods
9. A U.K. person receiving goods which are subject to these temporary importation reliefs may apply to the Commissioners for a direction that on the date of transfer to him the goods were deemed to be exported by the original importer and imported by the transferee subject to such conditions and time limits as the Commissioners may impose.

Security
10. As a condition of granting relief the Commissioners may require a deposit of cash or such other security as appears necessary to them.

Production of goods and records
11. An importer or a transferee of any temporarily imported goods is required to produce the goods for inspection and is required to keep such records relating to the goods as the Commissioners may require.

Time limits
12. Save as the Commissioners may otherwise allow, goods are to be re-exported within 24 months of their importation into U.K.

Treatment of certain transactions
13. Goods which are eligible for relief and are supplied to a person established outside the U.K. should be treated for VAT purposes as neither a supply of goods nor a supply of services.

Termination of relief
14. Relief from payment of tax may no longer apply but tax shall not be payable where goods are re-exported, or placed in a warehouse in a free zone with a view to subsequent re-exportation from the U.K., or are destroyed or approved to be destroyed to the Commissioners' satisfaction.
15. Relief shall no longer apply where there is a breach of any of the provisions of this Order or goods are entered for home use or the goods are destroyed and result in the production of scrap and waste which is declared for home use.
16. Where relief has ceased to apply the amount of tax payable is the amount due at the date of entry or when the relief ceased to be available.

Supplementary provisions
17. Schedules 1 and 2 are interpreted in accordance with the notes therein. Titles of Groups in the Schedules are for ease of reference only.
SCHEDULE 1 (Article 7)

The titles of the groups are set out below.
GROUP I—PROFESSIONAL EQUIPMENT
GROUP II—GOODS FOR DISPLAY OR USE AT AN EXHIBITION, FAIR, SYMPOSIUM
    OR SIMILAR EVENT
GROUP III—TEACHING AIDS AND SCIENTIFIC EQUIPMENT
GROUP IV—MEDICAL, SURGICAL AND LABORATORY EQUIPMENT
GROUP V—MATERIALS FOR USE IN COUNTERING THE EFFECTS OF DISASTERS
GROUP VI—PACKINGS
GROUP VII—COMMERCIAL SAMPLES, ADVERTISING MATERIAL AND GOODS
    FOR DEMONSTRATION PURPOSES
GROUP VIII—WELFARE MATERIAL FOR SEAFARERS
GROUP IX—GOODS FOR USE BY PUBLIC AUTHORITIES ON THE IRISH LAND
    BOUNDARY
GROUP X—ANIMALS
GROUP XI—FILMS, TAPES AND OTHER CARRIER MATERIAL FOR RECORDED
    SOUND
GROUP XII—GOODS FOR USE IN PRODUCTION FOR EXPORT
GROUP XIII—REPLACEMENT MEANS OF PRODUCTION
GROUP XIV—OTHER CASES

SCHEDULE 2 (Article 8)

GROUP I—GOODS FOR POSSIBLE SALE

S.I. 1986 No. 2288

The Value Added Tax Tribunals Appeals Order 1986

Note
This Order enables appeals from value added tax Tribunals to be made direct to the Court of Appeal instead of to the High Court, in prescribed circumstances similar to those applying to appeals from the High Court direct to the House of Lords.
1. This Order came into operation on 12 January 1987.
2. Any party dissatisfied with a decision of a VAT tribunal may appeal direct to the Court of Appeal provided the parties consent, the tribunal certifies that the decision involves a point of law relating to the construction of legislation which has been fully agreed and it has fully considered, and the leave of a single judge of the Court of Appeal has been obtained.

S.I. 1987 No. 1427

The Value Added Tax (Cash Accounting) Regulations 1987

Note
These Regulations provide, subject to certain conditions, for a taxable person to account for and pay VAT on the basis of cash (or other consideration) received and paid and, when a person ceases to be authorised to use such a scheme, the requirements that follow. The Regulations are by way of derogation from Article 17.1 Council Directive 77/388/EEC (O.J. No. L145, 17.5.77, p. 1).

Citation and commencement
1. These Regulations came into operation on 1 October 1987.

Interpretation
2. Various words and phrases used in these Regulations are defined.

Cash accounting scheme
3. The Commissioners can authorise, subject to these regulations and conditions as described in Notice 731/1987, a taxable person to account for VAT in accordance with a scheme by which the operative date for output tax, is the day on which payment is received and input tax, the date on which payment is made or the date of any cheque, if later.

Admission to the scheme
4. A trader is eligible to apply for authorisation if:
   (a) he believes that the value of his taxable supplies will not exceed £250,000 in the coming year from the date of application; and
   (b) he has made all returns which he is required to make; and
   (c) he has either (i) paid all VAT, penalties, interest and surcharge due from him, or (ii) (if he owes £1,000 or less) agreed to pay the outstanding amount by instalments under an arrangement with the Commissioners; and
   (d) he has not, in the previous three years, been convicted of a VAT offence, accepted a compounded settlement for a VAT offence, been assessed for a penalty under FA 1985, s. 13 or had a previous authorisation terminated.
   The Commissioners may refuse authorisation to protect the revenue. Hire purchase, conditional sale and credit sale agreements are excluded from the cash accounting system.
5. The terms of the scheme may be varied by publication of a fresh Notice.
6. An authorised person may start to use the scheme at the beginning of his next prescribed accounting period indicated in the notification of authorisation. He must notify the Commissioners within 30 days if: (1) taxable turnover for the past year, measured at the end of any quarter or prescribed accounting period, exceeded £312,500 and is expected to exceed £250,000 in the year then beginning; or (2) he has reason to believe, at any time, that taxable turnover for the year then beginning will exceed £312,500. He must cease to use the scheme on the next anniversary of joining if (1) applies. The Commissioners may terminate his authorisation if (2) applies.
   An authorised person may leave the scheme if: (1) he derives no benefit from it; or (2) he is unable to modify his accounting system to comply with its terms. He must notify the Commissioners of this in writing. The Commissioners must terminate his authorisation from the end of the prescribed accounting period in which they receive his notification.
7. Any person who ceases to operate the scheme of his own volition, or because of the value of supplies, will then resume accounting for tax in the manner provided for under the VATA 1983.
8. Where an authorised person becomes insolvent and ceases to trade, he shall, within two months, account for tax on supplies made and received in the previous 12 months which have not otherwise been accounted for, subject to any credit for input tax and indicate the amount of tax which is non-preferential.
9. An authorised person or his representative is required to make a return and pay tax on cessation of business, death, bankruptcy or incapacitation and on transfer of the business not covered by VAT (General) Regulations 1985, S.I. 1985 No. 886, reg. 4 (5).

Expulsion from the scheme
10. A person's authorisation may be terminated for a variety of reasons including making a false statement, having been convicted of an offence or accepting a compounded penalty and receiving an assessment or surcharge under FA 1985, ss. 13, 14, 17 and 19. Failure to leave the scheme when required and incorrectly crediting input tax are also grounds for termination of the right to use the scheme.

A person whose authority has been terminated is required to make a return and pay any tax due in respect of his current tax period and on all tax unaccounted for during the terms of his authority to use the scheme, even if he has already withdrawn of his own volition.

Appeals
11. An appeal may be made against any refusal of authorisation or termination in connection with the scheme made under VATA 1983, Sch. 7, para. 2 (3A).

Accounting
12. Tax shall be accounted for, with the exception of circumstances set out in regs. 7 to 9 above, by the prescribed accounting period in which payment is received and input tax credited at the date payment is given. Receipted and dated invoices to substantiate output and input tax must be kept for a period of six years unless the Commissioners authorise a lesser period.

S.I. 1987 No. 1806

The Value Added Tax (Tour Operators) Order 1987

Note
This Order introduces a special scheme for supplies by tour operators, as required by Council Directive 77/388/EEC Article 26 (O.J. No. L145, 13.6.77, p. 1). In this Order the supplies affected by the scheme are defined and changes made to the normal rules on time of supply and tax value to fit in with the general requirements of the scheme.

Articles 10 and 11 provide reliefs. Article 11 introduces into VATA 1983, Sch. 5, Group 10 an additional item which allows supplies of services made under the scheme which are enjoyed outside the E.C. to be zero-rated. Provisions are made to prohibit the deduction of input tax, the avoidance of tax in respect of group registrations and an option not to use the scheme for certain de minimis supplies. Further provisions are made in Articles 5 and 6 to specify the place of supply of supplies or services made under the scheme and introduces the concept of "in-house" supplies or services not covered by the scheme.

Citation and commencement
1. This Order came into force on 1 April 1988.

Supplies to which this Order applies
2. This Order applies to the supply of goods or services by a tour operator where the supply is for the benefit of travellers.

Meaning of "designated travel service"
3. The meaning of the term "designated travel service" used in the Order is explained.

Time of supply
4. The time of supply rules in VATA 1983, ss. 4, 5 do not apply to any supply comprising in whole or in part a designated travel service.

In the Order the tour operator may elect whether the time of supply is based on use or on payment, but once that choice has been made he may only use the method chosen.

Place of supply
5. The place of supply of a designated travel service is the place where the tour operator has established his business. The place of supply of a service other than a designated travel service is the place where the service is performed or provided.
6. This amends VAT (Place of Supply) Order 1984, S.I. 1984 No. 1685.

Value of a designated travel service
7. The value of a designated travel service may be determined by reference to the difference between sums paid to and sums paid by the tour operator.
8. The value of a supply between connected parties can be deemed to be the open market value and the Commissioners are to give notice to that effect to the tour operator.
9. Rules are set out for dealing with input tax on goods and services acquired before this Order took effect.

Tax chargeable on zero-rated and exempt designated travel services
10. VAT is charged at a nil rate on the value of a designated travel service apportioned to a transport of passengers within VATA 1983, Sch. 5, Group 10 item 4 (*a*) or (*c*) (whether the transport takes place inside or outside the U.K.) or within item 4 (*d*) of that Group.

No tax is charged on the value of designated travel service apportioned to a supply of education services, or goods supplied therewith, exempted under VATA 1983, Sch. 6, Group 6.

11. This inserts VATA 1983, Sch. 5, Group 10 item 13 and note 7.

Disallowance of input tax
12. Input tax on goods or services acquired by a tour operator for resupply as a designated travel service are excluded from credit under VATA 1983, ss. 14 and 15.

Disqualification from membership of group of companies
13. A tour operator cannot be part of a group registration if any member of the group has an overseas establishment; or makes supplies outside the U.K. which would be taxable supplies of goods it made within the U.K.; or supplies goods or services which will become a designated travel service.
14. Supplies of designated travel services may be disregarded if the value of such supplies does not exceed 1 per cent. of all supplies made in one year and no supplies of accommodation or transport are made.

S.I. 1987 No. 2015

The Value Added Tax (Repayments to Third Country Traders) Regulations 1987

Note
These Regulations are made under VATA 1983, s. 23 as amended. They provide for the refund of VAT incurred in Member States by a business person from a third country. This complements the relief from VAT currently available to Community traders (S.I. 1980 No. 1537).
    See Council Directive 86/560/EEC (O.J. No. L236, 21.11.86, p. 40) and 79/1072/EEC (O.J. No. L331, 27.12.79, p. 11).

Citation and commencement
1. These Regulations came into force on 31 December 1987.

Interpretation
2. Various words and phrases used in these Regulations are defined.
    A person is treated as being established in any country if he has a business establishment, permanent address or usual place of residence there.
    A person is treated as being established in a country if he carries out business through a branch or agency in that country and for a body corporate where it is legally constituted.

Repayment of tax
3. A trader is entitled to credit of the VAT charged in U.K. as if he were a taxable person in the U.K.

Tax representatives
4. The Commissioners may require a trader to appoint a tax representative to act on his behalf.

Persons to whom these Regulations apply
5. There is a requirement that a reciprocal arrangement for refunds is available to U.K. companies in the country to which the applicant belongs and that the applicant is not established in any Member State, nor makes supplies in the U.K.

Supplies and importations to which these Regulations apply
6. The refund of VAT only applies to supplies made or imported into the U.K. after 1 January 1988 and that such are not intended for the use of the applicant in the U.K. or for export from the U.K.

Tax which will not be repaid
7. There is no credit for VAT if such supplies were disallowed within the U.K. and any VAT charged by a travel agent which is for the benefit of the traveller is equally disallowed.

Method of claiming
8. A claim form is to be sent to the Commissioners supported by documentary evidence of input and a certificate of status issued by the official authority in the country in which the trader is established.

Time within which a claim must be made
9. A claim must be made within the prescribed financial limits of not less than £16 per claim and not less than £130 if for a period less than one year. A claim must not be submitted later than six months after the end of the year in which the VAT was charged and for a period of not less than three months, nor more than 12 months.

Treatment of claim and repayment claimed
10. These Regulations provide for the assessment of VAT and the right to appeal.

S.I. 1988 No. 886

The Value Added Tax (Annual Accounting) Regulations 1988

Note
These Regulations allow a taxable person to be authorised, subject to certain conditions, to account for and pay tax on an annual basis and, set out the requirements for withdrawal from the scheme.

Citation and commencement
1. These Regulations come into force on 1 July 1988.

Interpretation
2. Various words and phrases are defined.

Annual accounting scheme
3. The Commissioners may authorise a taxable person to account for VAT on an annual basis provided that he pays 90 per cent. of his estimated VAT liability for the current accounting year. The amount must be paid by direct debit in nine equal instalments beginning on the last day of the fourth month of that current accounting year. The actual VAT due for the year is adjusted by means of a tenth return submitted by the last day of the second month following the end of that accounting year.

Admission to the scheme
4. A trader is eligible to apply for authorisation if:
   (1) he has been registered for at least one year; and
   (2) he believes the value of his taxable supplies will not exceed £250,000 exclusive of VAT in the coming year; and
   (3) he has made all returns and paid all tax due on both returns and any assessments made; and
   (4) in the year before his application his total input tax did not exceed his output tax; and
   (5) if a company, it is not registered as a group or a division of a group; and
   (6) he has not had an authorisation terminated within the last three years.
The Commissioners may, to protect the revenue, refuse authorisation.
5. The Commissioners in their authorisation will state the date of commencement. The trader must operate the scheme for at least two years unless the value of taxable supplies exceeds or is likely to exceed £312,500 or the Commissioners terminate the authority.
6. When a taxable person leaves the scheme all outstanding VAT must be accounted for.
7. Where a person becomes insolvent and ceases to trade, or ceases business or to be registered, or dies or becomes bankrupt or incapacitated, his authority is terminated. A final return must be submitted and any outstanding tax paid within two months.

Expulsion from the scheme
8. The Commissioners may terminate an authorisation for a variety of reasons including making a false statement, failing to furnish the annual return, failing to pay VAT by the prescribed date, failing to leave the scheme when turnover exceeds the limit or for the protection of the revenue. When an authorisation is terminated all outstanding VAT has to be accounted for and paid.

S.I. 1988 No. 1174

The Value Added Tax (Goods Imported for Private Purposes) Relief Order 1988

Note
This Order provides relief from payment of the full VAT which would be due on importations of goods for private purposes where the value includes VAT paid in a member state. It implements Article 2.2 of Council Directive 77/388/EEC (O.J. No. L145, 13 June 1977) as interpreted by the European Court of Justice in Case 15/81 (*Gaston Schul Douane-expediteur BV* v. *Inspecteur der Invoerrechten en Accijnzen* [1982] ECR 1409) and Case 47/84 (*Staatssecretaris van Financien* v. *Gaston Schuul Douane-expediteur BV* [1985] ECR 1501).

Citation and commencement
1. This Order came into force on 1 August 1988.

Interpretation
2. Various words and phrases used in this Order are defined.

Relief for goods imported from another member state
3. VAT chargeable on the importation of goods into the U.K. from another member state is reduced to take account of VAT paid in that member state. The conditions are that; (*a*) the importer is not a taxable person (or if he is, the goods are for private use), (*b*) the goods were supplied in or imported into a member state, and that supply was the last taxable transaction and (*c*) VAT paid on the goods has not been subject to a refund.

Conditions of relief
4. A claim for relief must be made as directed by the Commissioners and be accompanied by supporting documents showing the value, the rate of VAT and the amount of VAT paid. The goods must be produced to the proper officer for inspection by the importer.

Method of calculating the relief
5. The VAT chargeable on importation is calculated by reducing the value of the goods by the residue of the VAT paid and deducting the residue of the VAT paid from the VAT that would have been chargeable on importation.

The residue is either the whole amount of the VAT paid in a member state or a percentage to allow for any decrease in value between the supply in that state and the exportation.

The value is to be in sterling converted at the rate of exchange in force at the time of importation. Where the VAT paid in the member state is greater than that chargeable on importation into the U.K., there is no refund.

S.I. 1988 No. 1343

The Value Added Tax (Repayment Supplement) Regulations 1988

Note
FA 1985, s. 20 provides that a person is entitled to a repayment supplement if the Commissioners fail to authorise a payment or refund due to him within 30 days of receiving the relevant tax return or claim. These regulations prescribe the circumstances in which the 30 day period is to be extended.
1. The regulations came into operation on 29 July 1988.
2. The "principal Act" means VATA 1983.
3. The VAT (Repayment Supplement) (No. 2) Regulations 1986, S.I. 1986 No. 1279 are revoked.
4, 5. The following periods are disregarded in relation to the matters stated in calculating the 30 day period in which the Commissioners are required to authorise a payment or refund:

Matter	*Period begins*	*Period ends*
(*a*) Commissioners make reasonable inquiries regarding the tax return or claim concerned	Date when the Commissioners first raised the inquiry	Date when a complete answer to the inquiry is received
(*b*) Commissioners correct errors or omissions in the tax return or claim	Date when the error or omission first came to the Commissioners' notice	Date when the error or omission is corrected
(*c*) Trader has failed to furnish tax return(s) for prior period(s) (see *Richard Costain Ltd.* v. *C. & E. Comrs.* [1988] VATTR 111	Period of failure set out in a certificate issued by the Commissioners	
(*d*) Trader has failed to produce documents or give security	Date when written notice of the requirement was served by the Commissioners	Date when the documents are produced or security given

S.I. 1988 No. 1898

The Customs and Excise (Derferred Payment) (RAF Airfields and Offshore Installations) (No. 2) Regulations 1988

Note
These regulations permit deferment of customs and excise duties on dutiable goods imported in passengers' baggage, and prescribe the time limit for payment of deferred duties.
1. These regulations came into operation on 21 November 1988.
2. "The Act" means CEMA 1979.

3. Customs and excise duties payable on goods in passengers' baggage, or carried with him, are deferred if: (1) the passenger enters the U.K. from an offshore gas or oil installation or arrives at an R.A.F. airfield; (2) he declares the goods in the prescribed form and manner; (3) he pays the deferred duties by the 15th day of the month following his arrival or such earlier date as the Commissioners may demand; and (4) the owner of the gas or oil installation provides adequate security.

4. The deferred duty is deemed to be paid when the goods are landed.

5. These regulations do not apply to persons approved for other duty deferment provisions.

6. Earlier regulations are revoked.

S.I. 1989 No. 472

The Value Added Tax (Self-supply of Construction Services) Order 1989

Note

This Order provides for a charge to tax by way of a self-supply where a person carries out specified construction, alteration or demolition works.

1. This Order came into operation on 1 April 1989.

2. "The Act" means VATA 1983.

3. A person is deemed to make a supply of services in the course or furtherance of his business if three conditions are met. First, he performs one of the specified services without consideration in the course or furtherance of his business and for the purpose of that business. Secondly, the value of the services is £100,000 or more. Thirdly, the services would be chargeable to tax at the standard rate if supplied by a third party.

The specified services are:

(*a*) constructing a building;

(*b*) increasing the floor area of a building by 10 per cent. or more;

(*c*) constructing a civil engineering work; and

(*d*) carrying out demolition work in connection with (*a*)–(*c*).

The supply is deemed to be made to the person for the purpose of his business.

To the extent that services are performed by a body corporate included in a group registration, the foregoing provisions apply as if all bodies included in the registration were one person and the supply is deemed to be made and received by the representative member.

4. The services are deemed to be supplied at their open market value. However, the value of services performed on or before 31 March 1989 is effectively treated as nil.

S.I. 1989 No. 1114

The Value Added Tax (Water) Order 1989

Note

This Order provides that all supplies of water (*e.g.* by a water company) are treated as supplies of goods in the same manner as gas, electricity and other forms of heat, power, refrigeration and ventilation.

1. This Order came into operation on 1 August 1989.

2. The supply of water is treated as a supply of goods (insofar as it is not otherwise such a supply) and not as a supply of services.

S.I. 1989 No. 1217

The Value Added Tax (Refund of Tax) Order 1989

Note

This Order extends the list of bodies entitled to VAT refunds on goods and services purchased or imported for non-business purposes.

1. This Order came into operation on 1 September 1989.

2. The National Rivers Authority is entitled to claim VAT refunds on goods and services purchased or imported for non-business purposes.

S.I. 1989 No. 1302

The Value Added Tax (General) (Amendment) (No. 2) Regulations 1989

Note

This regulation specifies how the value of a self-supply, and the tax chargeable thereon, is treated for partial exemption purposes.

1. These regulations came into operation on 1 August 1989.
2. "The principal regulations" means VAT (General) Regulations 1985, S.I. 1985 No. 886.
3–5. The value of self-supply is excluded from the alternative calculation of remaining input tax under the prescribed partial exemption method. Input tax on a self-supply is not attributed to that supply for partial exemption purposes.
6. A taxable person must exclude the following in calculating the provisional attribution of input tax to taxable supplies under a special partial exemption method which he has been authorised to use: (1) the value of a self-supply; and (2) the input tax arising on a self-supply.

S.I. 1989 No. 2248

The Value Added Tax (Accounting and Records) Regulations 1989

Note
These regulations make provision for the keeping of records and accounts by taxable persons.

Citation, commencement and interpretation
1. These regulations came into operation on 1 January 1990. Various words and phrases are defined.

Records
2. A taxable person must keep and preserve the following records: (1) his business and accounting records; (2) his VAT account; (3) copies of tax invoices which he issues; (4) tax invoices which he receives; (5) import and export documents; (6) credit notes etc. which he issues or receives; and (7) documents specified in a notice published by the Commissioners.
3. A taxable person must keep and preserve his records for six years unless the Commissioners allow a shorter period.

The value added tax account
4. A taxable person must keep and maintain a "VAT Account" in relation to each prescribed accounting period divided into a "tax payable portion" and a "tax allowable portion".
    The following entries are made in the tax payable portion: (1) output tax due for the period; (2) corrections for output tax understated or overstated in prior periods; (3) adjustment to output tax on supplies made in prior periods where the consideration for the supply is varied; and (4) adjustments to tax payable made in accordance with the VAT legislation. For adjustments under head (4), see VAT (General) Regulations 1985, S.I. 1985 No. 886, reg. 61 (adjustment to output tax estimated for a prior period); VAT (Bad Debt Relief) Regulations 1986, S.I. 1986 No. 335, reg. 10 (1), (2) (repayment of bad debt relief); Leaflet Nos. 727/8A/87, 727/10/87, 727/15/90 (annual adjustment under Retail Schemes B1, D and J). Cf VAT (General) Regulations, S.I. 1985 No. 886, regs. 41, 60 (*a*) (VAT on postal imports delivered under the postponed accounting system).
    The following entries are made in the tax allowable portion: (1) input tax allowable for the period; (2) corrections for input tax understated or overstated in prior periods; (3) adjustment to input tax on supplies received in prior periods where the consideration for the supply is varied; and (4) adjustments to input tax allowable made in accordance with the VAT legislation. For adjustments under head (4), see VAT (General) Regulations 1985, S.I. 1985 No. 886 regs. 33 (annual partial exemption adjustment), 34 (amended attribution of input tax), 37D (change in taxable use of a capital item) and 62 (2) (adjustment to input tax estimated for a prior period); and VATA 1983 s. 20 (1), Notice No. 749 (September 1986) paras. 8 (*a*), 15 (refund of VAT incurred for non-business purposes by certain bodies). Cf. VAT (Bad Debt Relief) Regulations 1986, S.I. 1986 No. 335, reg. 4 (1) (claim for bad debt relief).

Correction of returns
5. A taxable person may correct his VAT Account if he has misstated input tax credits or output tax liabilities on a tax return and the difference between underdeclarations of liability (*i.e.* understated output tax and/or overstated input tax) and overdeclarations of liability (*i.e.* overstated output tax and/or understated input tax) discovered during a prescribed accounting period does not exceed £1,000.
    Output tax for the current prescribed accounting period shown in the trader's VAT Account is increased by the net amount of output tax understated in prior periods or decreased by the net amount of output tax overstated. Each entry is cross-referenced to the returns in which the errors were made and the documents to which they relate.
    Input tax for the current prescribed accounting period shown in the trader's VAT Account is increased by the net amount of input tax understated in prior periods or decreased by the net amount of input tax overstated. Each entry is cross-referenced to the returns in which the errors were made and the documents to which they relate.

The VAT Account must not be corrected if the net overdeclaration or net underdeclaration exceeds £1,000. For claims in respect of the former, see FA 1989 s. 24. For voluntary disclosure of the latter, see Notice No. 700 (October 1987) para. 69A.

Claims for recovery of overpaid tax
6. A claim for refund of overpaid tax must be made in writing. The amount claimed and the method used to calculate it must be stated. Form VAT 652 can be used.

Adjustments in the course of business
7. The person making a supply must adjust the tax payable portion of his VAT Account if the consideration is varied after the end of the prescribed accounting period in which the supply was made. Output tax for the period in which the variation takes place is increased (if the consideration is increased) or decreased (if the consideration is decreased).

The person receiving a supply must adjust the tax allowable portion of his VAT Account if the consideration is varied after the end of the prescribed accounting period in which the supply was made. Input tax for the period in which the variation takes place is increased (if the consideration is increased) or decreased (if the consideration is decreased).

The period in which the supply was made or received is substituted for the period in which the variation took place if the person making the entry is insolvent.

Calculation of returns
8. A VAT return is completed by entering: (1) the aggregate of entries in the tax payable portion of the VAT Account for the current period in Box 1; and (2) the aggregate of entries in the tax allowable portion of the VAT Account for the current period in Box 2. A VAT return is deemed to correct an earlier account return if a correction is made in accordance with reg. 5 above. For VAT returns, see VAT (General) Regulations 1985, S.I. 1985 No. 886, reg. 58 (1) and (4).

S.I. 1989 No. 2255

The Value Added Tax (Bad Debt Relief) (Amendment) Regulations 1989

Note
These regulations amend the manner in which amounts due to or by the Commissioners in respect of bad debt relief are shown on VAT returns.

S.I. 1989 No. 2256

The Value Added Tax (General) (Amendment) (No. 3) Regulations 1989

Note
These regulations revise the values of goods which can be purchased by community travellers under the retail export schemes and introduce new VAT return forms (forms VAT 100 and VAT 193).

S.I. 1989 No. 2259

The Value Added Tax ("Do-It-Yourself" Builders) (Refund of Tax) Regulations 1989

Note
These regulations prescribe the time limit for claiming refund of VAT on goods incorporated in a building which he has constructed otherwise than in the course or furtherance of business. They also prescribe the form and manner in which claims are made, the information contained in claims and the documentary evidence to accompany claims.

Citation and commencement
1. These regulations came into operation on 1 January 1990.

Interpretation
2. Various words and phrases are defined.

Method and time for making claim
3. A claim is made by furnishing the prescribed form (VAT 431) no later than three months after the relevant building is completed. The following documents must be furnished at the same time unless the Commissioners allow otherwise: (1) a certificate of completion from the local authority or alternative evidence of completion acceptable to the Commissioners; (2) invoices for each

supply of goods incorporated in the building or its site on which tax was paid; (3) import documents for imported goods (if any) incorporated in the building or its site; (4) documents showing that planning permission was granted; and (5) a signed certificate from an architect or quantity surveyor that the goods were, or were likely to have been, incorporated in the building or its site.

Revocation
4. VAT ("Do-It-Yourself" Builders) (Relief) Regulations 1975, S.I. 1975 No. 649 are revoked.

S.I. 1989 No. 2270

The Finance Act 1985 (Serious Misdeclaration and Interest on Tax) (Appointed Days) Order 1989

Note
This Order brings FA 1985 ss. 14 and 18 into operation on 31 March 1990 and 1 April 1990 respectively.

S.I. 1989 No. 2271

The Finance Act 1989 (Recovery of Overpaid Tax and Administration) (Appointed Days) Order 1989

Note
This Order brings FA 1989 ss. 24 and 25 into operation on 1 January 1990 and 4 December 1989 respectively.

S.I. 1989 No. 2272

The Value Added Tax (Finance, Health and Welfare) Order 1989

Note
This Order exempts underwriting services in connection with securities, the management of unit trusts and the provision of private ambulance services.

S.I. 1989 No. 2273

The Value Added Tax (Small Non-Commercial Consignments) Relief (Amendment) Order 1989

Note
This Order increases the maximum value of small consignments of a non-commercial character which can be imported from another E.C. member state without payment of VAT.

S.I. 1989 No. 2355

The Value Added Tax (General) (Amendment) (No. 4) Regulalations 1989

Note
These regulations provide for adjustments to the initial deduction (if any) of input tax allowed on specified capital items when the extent to which they are used in making taxable supplies changes during an "adjustment period" of either five ot ten "intervals" depending upon the description of the item. These adjustments are disregarded in applying the de minimis limits for partial exemption purposes.

S.I. 1990 No. 139

The Free Zone (Liverpool) Designation (Variation) Order 1990

Note
This Order extends the Liverpool Free Zone to include the North Langton and Brocklebank Docks.

S.I. 1990 No. 237

The European Communities (Privileges of the European School) Order 1990

Note
This Order confers privileges on the European School at Culham, and on its staff members. It gives effect to the agreement between the government and the school governors.

PART I GENERAL

1. This Order came into operation on 15 February 1990.
2. Various words and phrases used in the Order are defined.

PART II THE SCHOOL

3, 4. Not relevant to VAT.
5. The European School may claim refund of VAT paid on goods and services of substantial value necessary for its official activities if it complies with conditions imposed under arrangements made by the Secretary of State. No refund is made unless the aggregate value of goods and services exceeds £100.
6. The European School is exempt from VAT chargeable on goods imported for its official activities. It must comply with conditions imposed by the Commissioners for protection of the revenue.

PART III STAFF MEMBERS

7. The exemption from VAT chargeable on imported furniture and effects (including one motor car) given to diplomatic agents under Diplomatic Privileges Act 1964 is extended to staff members of the European School who are not citizens and who are not permanently resident in the U.K.

S.I. 1990 No. 315

The Value Added Tax (Cars) (Amendment) Order 1990

Note
This Order allows a degree of relief to car dealers who are ineligible to use the "margin scheme" for used cars because they hold only some of the necessary records.

S.I. 1990 No. 420

The Value Added Tax (Cash Accounting) (Amendment) Regulations 1990

Note
These regulations relax the conditions for admission to, and voluntary withdrawal from, the cash accounting scheme.

S.I. 1990 No. 523

The Finance Act 1985 (Interest on Tax) (Prescribed Rate) Order 1990

Note
This Order sets the prescribed rate of interest on tax etc. recoverable by assessment at 13 per cent. from 1 April 1990.

S.I. 1990 No. 682

The Value Added Tax (Increase of Registration Limits) Order 1990

Note
This Order increases the limit for cancellation of VAT registration from £22,600 to £24,400 with effect from 1 June 1990.

S.I. 1989 No. 750

The Value Added Tax (Charities) Order 1990

Note
This Order extends zero-rating to: (1) goods donated to, or supplied by, traders covenanting their profits to charity; (2) preparatory work for certain charitable advertising; and (3) a wider range of goods purchased by certain non-profit-making bodies from charitable funds or voluntary contributions.

S.I. 1989 No. 751
The Value Added Tax (Tour Operators) (Amendment) Order 1990

Note
This Order amends the place of supply of passenger transport and pleasure cruises for the purposes of the tour operators margin scheme and re-defines that part of the value of a designated travel service attributable to exempt or zero-rated supplies.

S.I. 1990 No. 752

The Value Added Tax (Transport) Order 1990

Note
This Order extends zero-rating in connection with lifeboats, slipways for lifeboats, and handling services in connection with ships, aircraft and transported goods. The application of zero-rating is modified in relation to passenger transport and the chartering of ships and aircraft.

S.I. 1990 No. 1188

The Value Added Tax (Refund of Tax) (Revocation) Order 1990

Note
The Scottish Special Housing Association ceases to be eligible for refunds on goods and services purchased or imported for non-business purposes.

Index
Value Added Tax

EXCISE DUTY
  free zones. *See* FREE ZONES
  relief from,
    —antiques, on, CED(GR)A 1979, s. 9
    —breach of condition, use of goods in, CED(GR)A 1979, s. 13C
    —goods permanently imported, for, S.I. 1983, No. 1828
    —goods temporarily imported, for, S.I. 1983, No. 1829
    —immunities and privileges, persons enjoying, CED(GR)A 1979, ss. 13A, 13B, FA 1989, s. 28
    —imported legacies, on, CED(GR)A 1979, s. 70; S.I. 1984, No. 895
    —labels, on, CED(GR)A 1979, s. 8
    —personal, CED(GR)A 1979, s. 13
    —prizes on, CED(GR)A 1979, s. 9
    —trade samples, on, CED(GR)A 1979, s. 8
EXCISE WAREHOUSE
  approval of, CEMA 1979, s. 92
EXEMPTIONS
  betting, gaming and lotteries, VATA 1983, Sch. 6, Gp. 4
  building and land, withdrawal from, FA 1989, Sch. 3
  burial and cremation, VATA 1983, Sch. 6, Gp. 8
  educational supplies, VATA 1983, Sch. 6, Gp. 6; S.I. 1989, No. 267
  financial supplies, VATA 1983, Sch. 6, Gp. 5
  fund-raising events, VATA 1983, Sch. 6, Gp. 12; S.I. 1989, No. 470
  groups for purposes of, VATA 1983, Sch. 6
  health and welfare supplies, VATA 1983, Sch. 6, Gp. 7
  incorrect certificates, FA 1985, s. 13A, FA 1989, s. 23
  insurance, VATA 1983, Sch. 6, Gp. 2
  land, VATA 1983, Sch. 6. Gp. 1
  postal services, VATA 1983, Sch. 6, Gp. 3
  professional bodies, VATA 1983, Sch. 6, Gp. 9
  residential and charitable buildings, VATA 1983, Sch. 6A, FA 1989, Sch. 3, para. 6
  sports competitions, VATA 1983, Sch. 6, Gp. 10
  trade unions, VATA 1983, Sch. 6, Gp. 9
  training supplies, S.I. 1988, No. 1282
  works of arts, VATA 1983, Sch. 6, Gp. 11

F

FALSE INFORMATION
  giving of, VATA 1983, s. 39

FINANCE
  supplies exempt from VAT, VATA 1983, Sch. 6, Gp. 5
FOOD
  zero-rating, VATA 1983, Sch. 5, Gp. 1
FOREIGN CURRENCY
  value expressed in, VATA 1983, Sch. 4, para. 11
FREE ZONES
  Belfast Airport, at, S.I. 1984, No. 1206
  Birmingham Airport, at, S.I. 1984, No. 1207
  Cardiff, at, S.I. 1984, No. 1208
  control of trading in, CEMA 1979, s. 100E
  designation of, CEMA 1979, s. 100A
  excise duty,
    —goods chargeable with, in, S.I. 1984, No. 1177, r. 5
    —payment of, CEMA 1979, s. 100C
  goods,
    —agricultural levy, payment of, S.I. 1984, No. 1177, rr. 16, 18–20, 25
    —Community status, acknowledgment of, S.I. 1984, No. 1177, r. 7
    —customs procedure, discharge from, S.I. 1984, No. 1177, r. 8
    —destruction of, S.I. 1984, No. 1177, r. 21
    —duty free, remaining, CEMA 1979, s. 100C
    —entering procedure for, S.I. 1984, No. 1177, r. 11
    —excise goods becoming, S.I. 1984, No. 1177, r. 5
    —inspection of, CEMA 1979, s. 100D; S.I. 1984, No. 1177, r. 22
    —movement of, CEMA 1979, s. 100B; S.I. 1984, No. 1176, r. 6
    —operations on, S.I. 1984, No. 1177, r. 9
    —payment of duty on, S.I. 1984, No. 1177, rr. 16, 18–20, 25
    —recording details of, S.I. 1984, No. 1177, r. 6
    —records on, S.I. 1984, No. 1177, r. 24
    —remaining in zone, where, S.I. 1984, No. 1177, r. 17
    —removal of, CEMA 1979; s. 100C; S.I. 1984, No. 1177, rr. 12–16
    —segregation of, S.I. 1984, No. 1177, r. 23
    —VAT treatment, CEMA 1979, s. 100C; S.I. 1984, No. 1177, rr. 26, 27
  Liverpool, at, S.I. 1984, No. 1209; S.I. 1990, No. 139
  powers of search, CEMA 1979, s. 100F
  Prestwick Airport, at, S.I. 1984, No. 1200

POSTAL PACKETS
customs declarations on, S.I. 1986,
No. 260, rr. 7, 8
customs entry, made for, S.I. 1986,
No. 260, r. 14
documents accompanying, S.I. 1986,
No. 260, r. 10
dutiable goods imported in, S.I. 1986,
No. 260, r. 6
forfeiture of, S.I. 1986, No. 260, rr. 16, 17
mailbags, green label on, S.I. 1986,
No. 260, r. 9
payment of duty on, S.I. 1986, No. 260,
r. 15
Post Office staff, duties of, S.I. 1986,
No. 260, rr. 11–13
POSTAL SERVICES
exemption from VAT, VATA 1983,
Sch. 6, Gp. 3
POWER
supply of, S.I. 1985, No. 886, r. 20
zero-rating, VATA 1983, Sch. 5, Gp. 7
PRESTWICK AIRPORT
free zone at, S.I. 1984, No. 1210
PROCEEDINGS
body corporate, offence committed by,
CEMA 1979, s. 171
evidence in, CEMA 1979, s. 154
fine, joint and several liability for,
CEMA 1979, s. 150
imprisonment, maximum term of,
CEMA 1979, s. 149
institution of, CEMA 1979, s. 145
offences, for, CEMA 1979, s. 147
penalties,
—application of, CEMA 1979, s. 151
—compromise, CEMA 1979, s. 152
—mitigation of, CEMA 1979, s. 152
—non-payment of, CEMA 1979,
s. 149
—scales of, CEMA 1979, s. 171. *See
also* VAT
persons conducting, CEMA 1979, s. 155
place of trial, CEMA 1979, s. 148
proof of documents, CEMA 1979, s. 153
security, provision of, CEMA 1979,
s. 150
service of process, CEMA 1979, s. 146
time limits for, CEMA 1979, s. 146A
PROFESSIONAL BODIES
supplies exempt from VAT, VATA
1983, Sch. 6, Gp. 9

R

RATE OF TAX
determination of, VATA 1983, s. 9
RECORDS
duty to keep, VATA 1983, Sch. 7,
para. 7
required, S.I. 1989, No. 2248, rr. 2, 3

RECOVERY OF TAX
VATA 1983, Sch. 7, para. 6
REFUND OF TAX
assessment, recovered as, FA 1990, s. 15
bad debt, in cases of, VATA 1983, s. 22;
S.I. 1986, No. 304; FA 1990, s. 11.
See also BAD DEBT RELIEF
bodies entitled to, S.I. 1985, No. 1101;
S.I. 1986, No. 336; S.I. 1986,
No. 532
Commission for Local Administration,
to, S.I. 1976, No. 2028
"do-it-yourself" builder, to, VATA
1983, s. 21; S.I. 1989, No. 2259
EC member State, person carrying on
business in, VATA 1983, s. 23
Government of Northern Ireland, to,
VATA 1983, s. 49
National Rivers Authority, to, S.I. 1989,
No. 1217
overpaid tax, claim for, S.I. 1989,
No. 2248, r. 6
public bodies, to, VATA 1983, s. 20
regional water authorities, to, S.I. 1973,
No. 2121
Scottish Special Housing Association, to,
S.I. 1973, No. 522; S.I. 1990, No.
1188
REGISTRATION
business carried on outside UK, VATA
1983, Sch. 1, para. 11A
cancellation of, VATA 1983, Sch. 1,
paras. 8A–10
club or association, notification by, S.I.
1985, No. 886, r. 10
conditional, VATA 1983, Sch. 1, para. 5;
S.I. 1985, No. 886, rr. 5–8
de-registration, VATA 1983, Sch. 1,
para. 2
discretionary, VATA 1983, Sch. 1,
para. 1; S.I. 1985, No. 886, r. 8
exemption from, VATA 1983, Sch. 1,
para. 11
housing associations, of, S.I. 1985,
No. 886, r. 7
invoices, unauthorised issue of, FA 1985,
s. 15
liability to,
—end of, notification of, VATA 1980,
Sch. 1, para. 7, 7A
—failure to notify, FA 1985, s. 15
—notification of, VATA 1983, Sch. 1,
paras. 3, 4, 14
—simplification of rules, FA 1990, s. 10
—single taxable person, direction as
to, VATA 1983, Sch. 1, para. 1A
—turnover, VATA 1983, Sch. 1,
paras. 1, 13, FA 1987, s. 14, S.I.
1987, No. 438
meaning, VATA 1983, Sch. 1, para. 15
notification of, S.I. 1985, No. 886, r. 4
partnership, notification by, S.I. 1985,
No. 886, r. 9

Appendices

APPENDIX 1. PRESS NOTICES ETC.—CUSTOMS AND EXCISE AND OTHERS

June 1980. Press Release
VAT mailing list: changes in methods of distributing information on VAT

For reasons of economy single copies of new or revised VAT notices are no longer sent automatically to every registered trader. As the need arises a new publication, *VAT Notes*, is issued and a copy sent to every registered trader with his return form. *VAT Notes* gives information on new VAT notices, leaflets, etc.; all of which are available from local VAT offices.

The maintenance of a VAT mailing list had a direct connection with the policy of sending only single copies to registered traders. With the change explained above this need has disappeared. As many copies of VAT notices etc. as are required can be obtained from any local VAT office. It has therefore been decided that the VAT Mailing List will not continue in its present form.

If you are a registered person there is no need to take any action. You will automatically receive each edition of *VAT Notes* with your return form. If, however, you are *not* registered and continue to require information on VAT you should write explaining your requirements to Customs and Excise, Room 305, Knolly House, Byward Street, London EC3R 5AY. If you require information from Customs and Excise on topics other than VAT this should be mentioned.

14 June 1982. Press Notice No. 745
VAT: treatment of supplies of gold coin

Customs and Excise announce that supplies of gold coin, which do not involve physical delivery of the goods and which arise from contracts made on or after 15 June 1982, by members of the London Gold Market or of other terminal markets to non-members of the markets will not be regarded as eligible for VAT relief under the provisions of the Terminal Markets Order 1973, as amended. Dealings between market members will continue to be zero-rated.

The liability of the following supplies of gold coin by members of the London Gold Market or by other traders will therefore be as follows:

(a) supplies to private persons belonging in E.C. countries (including U.K.) and the Isle of Man (IoM)—taxable at the standard rate, zero-rated as an exportation of goods if the gold coins are physically exported by the supplier to private persons belonging outside the U.K. and IoM;

(b) supplies to the U.K. and IoM businesses—taxable at the standard rate, but input tax will be recoverable by the recipient of the supply under the normal mechanism of the tax where supplies are received for the purpose of the business and subject to the partial exemption regulations;

(c) supplies to persons in their business capacity belonging in E.C. countries (other than U.K.)—zero-rated as a financial service (Item 5 of Group 9, Zero Rate Schedule), providing the gold coins are unallocated (this includes non-deivery in the U.K. and IoM), zero-rated as an exportation of goods if the gold coins are physically exported by the supplier;

(d) supplies to any person (business or private) belonging outside the E.C. and the IoM—zero-rated as a financial service (Item 6a of Group 9, Zero Rate Schedule), providing the gold coins are unallocated (this includes non-delivery in the U.K. and IoM), zero-rated as an exportation of goods if the gold coins are physically exported by the supplier;

(e) supplies to any person (business or private) abroad (including E.C. and non-E.C. countries) of allocated gold coins held in the U.K. and not physically exported—taxable at the standard rate;

(f) supplies to any person (business or private) of allocated gold coins held outside the U.K. and IoM are outside the scope of U.K. VAT;

(g) supplies of unallocated gold coins held outside the U.K. and IoM will be treated as financial services and the VAT liability will follow that described in (a), (b), (c), and (d), above;

(h) supplies from overseas persons to taxable persons belonging in the U.K. and IoM of unallocated gold coins held outside the U.K. and IoM will be liable to tax as importations the tax being accounted for by the U.K. and IoM customer (FA 1972, s. 8B) [now VATA 1983, s. 7].

25 June 1982. Press Release
VAT: "premium", "nearly new" and "personal import" cars

Customs and Excise have considered the VAT liability of the sale by VAT registered dealers of premium, nearly new and personal import motor cars.

"Premium and Nearly New" cars are vehicles whose market value is higher than the manufacturer's list price because of their scarcity value. Franchised dealers are not permitted by the terms of their franchise to sell a new car to another dealer. Accordingly non-franchised dealers must

secure regular supplies by other means, *e.g.* by employing an agent to purchase a car from a franchised dealer. When cars so obtained are re-sold they are still for VAT purposes unused and therefore cannot benefit from the second-hand car scheme relief because the law requires the car to be used. As the franchised dealer's sales invoices for the car will be made out in the name of the agent the non-franchised dealer cannot reclaim the tax charged as input tax to offset against the output tax due on his sale. The overall effect is that the car is subject to double taxation:

"Personal Import" cars are sometimes acquired by VAT registered dealers from the private importer immediately following their importation. Such cars when sold by dealers are still unused for VAT purposes and therefore do not qualify for the second-hand car scheme relief. As VAT will have been paid on the car when imported into the U.K. the vehicle is subject to double taxation.

Customs and Excise in consultation with the Motor Agents' Association have reviewed the application of VAT to such transactions and have concluded that:

(*a*) if an employee, director or agent or the non-franchised dealer acquires the car on his behalf, output tax will be due on the full selling-price of the car when re-sold. However, the VAT charged by the franchised dealer on the original sale to the employee, director or agent can be counted as input tax by the non-franchised dealer provided he holds the franchised dealer's tax invoice. In the case of 'personal imports' the franchised dealer may count the VAT paid at importation as input tax provided he holds evidence of the tax paid at importation;

(*b*) in all other cases where the car is acquired by the non-franchised dealer from a person with whom he has no direct association, it will be accepted that the car is used and thus eligible for the second-hand car scheme relief when re-sold.

These guidelines are expected to apply in the majority of cases and [came] into operation on 1 July [1982].

With regard to past transactions, Customs and Excise (unless there are exceptional circumstances) will not normally issue assessments for underdeclarations of output tax where the second-hand car scheme relief has been incorrectly applied.

23 August 1982. Press Notice No. 758
VAT: vehicle hire

Customs and Excise announce that with effect from 1 October 1982 vehicle hirers will be required to charge VAT at the standard rate in respect of the total charge payable by the customer for the hire of the vehicle.

This will include any portion of the hire charge which may be attributable to charges for insurers.

The British Vehicle Rental and Leasing Association and the Motor Agents' Association have been consulted about the new arrangements.

Note
Hitherto vehicle hirers who made a charge to their customers for insurance were allowed, under certain conditions, to exempt this charge from VAT. A recent VAT tribunal (LON/80/250) has however ruled that in such circumstances it is the hire of an *insured vehicle* that has been supplied, the consideration for which is the total charge payable by the customer.

20 September 1982. Press Notice No. 761
VAT: goods obtained by fraud

VAT registered traders who have been defrauded of goods may, in certain circumstances be able to recover VAT which they have accounted for as output tax and submitted to Customs and Excise in respect of the transaction.

If the trader reports the fraud to the police and, as a result, a conviction is obtained, he should apply in writing to his local VAT office for authority to adjust his VAT account. The application should be supported by evidence of his complaint to the police and of the conviction for the offence. A verifiable description of the goods in question will also be required.

12 October 1982. Press Notice No. 768
VAT: supplies through subsidiary companies without assets

Customs and Excise now require companies acting as principals, who are not at present accounting for VAT on supplies through the agency of subsidiary companies without assets ("shell" companies), to correct their VAT accounting in accordance with one of three methods:

(*a*) the provisions of FA 1972, s. 24 (3) [now VATA 1983, s. 32 (4)] may be adopted. The supplies by the principal company may be treated as supplies to the shell company and as supplies by the shell company. This is explained in para. 5 (*a*) of Notice 710 [now Notice 700 (October 1987) Part IX]. The principal company must, of course, issue invoices to the shell company, possibly in the form of a monthly invoicing procedure;

(*b*) applying, where eligible, for a group registration to include both the principal and the shell companies;

(*c*) by the principal company invoicing its supplies directly to the customer.

The same principles apply if the principal company is receiving supplies through a shell company. Note that if procedure (*c*) is adopted the shell company may cease to make any taxable supplies and may no longer be liable to be registered.

Companies affected must correct their accounting as soon as practicable. The date may be agreed with the local VAT office.

10 December 1982. Press Notice No. 790
VAT: sales of goodwill

From 1 January 1983 Customs and Excise will treat all sales of the goodwill of a business as taxable supplies except where they are specifically relieved by law.

Unidentifiable goodwill, valued as the residual difference between the business as a whole and the sum of its identifiable assets, is currently treated as outside the scope of VAT.

Normally goodwill is sold as part of the assets of a business transferred as a going concern. Such sales will be relieved from tax if the transfer meets the provisions of the VAT (Special Provisions) Order 1981 (S.I. 1981 No. 1741), art. 12 (1).

Note
Sales of goodwill which can be specifically identified as an asset of the business have always been treated as taxable supplies of services (*e.g.*, use of a trade mark or trading name, lists of customers etc.).

21 February 1983. Press Notice No. 805
VAT: fruit and nut mixtures

Customs and Excise have revised their view of the VAT liability of fruit and nut mixtures following a recent VAT Tribunal decision (see *Smiths Food Ltd.* v. *C. & E. Comrs.* LON/82/298).

A mixture containing ingredients which would be standard rated if sold on their own (for example drained, glacé or crystallised fruits and roasted or salted nuts) may be zero rated as a single supply if the standard rated content does not exceed 25 per cent. by weight. If this proportion is exceeded the standard rated and zero rated constituents are to be treated as separate supplies and taxed accordingly.

10 March 1983. Press Notice No. 807
VAT: sales of taxi licences

From 1 April 1983 Customs and Excise will treat sales of taxi licences as taxable supplies for VAT purposes. As licences transferred in the open market are sold with a vehicle, the sale is taxable as a single supply of goods, *i.e.* the licensed taxi.

However, the sale will be relieved from VAT if the licensed taxi is part of the assets of a business sold as a going concern provided that the usual conditions are met.

Traders who are not registered for VAT are not affected.

Note
Until now sales of taxi licences have been treated as outside the scope of VAT. The change follows consultations with the National Federation of Taxicab Associations.

The VAT (Special Provisions) Order 1981 (S.I. 1981 No. 1741) art. 12 (1) lays down conditions for VAT relief when a business is sold as a going concern.

17 June 1983. Press Notice No. 841
VAT: electric storage radiators

Customs and Excise confirm that fixed electric storage radiators may now be zero-rated, as articles of a kind ordinarily installed by builders as fixtures, in the course of the construction [or alteration]* of a building. This follows a VAT Tribunal decision at the end of last year.

In order to be considered as "fixed", an electric storage radiator must be permanently wired to a fixed spur mains outlet and securely attached to the building, *e.g.* screwed to a wall. Free standing radiators do not qualify for zero-rating.

Note
The Tribunal case mentioned is *Robert Dale (Builders) Ltd.* v. *C. & E. Comrs.* MAN/82/103.
* Words deleted by FA 1984, s. 10 after 31 May 1984 unless the alteration is an approved alteration to a Protected Building.

23 June 1983. Press Notice No. 843
VAT: property transactions within VAT groups

Customs and Excise have issued a statement following a review of the VAT treatment of supplies of properties subsequent to transfers of such properties between members of formally constituted VAT groups.

It is common practice for property companies trading as a group to transfer title to buildings within the group for rationalisation and similar purposes. Where such a group is also registered as a group for VAT purposes under FA 1972, s. 21 [now VATA 1983, s. 29] such supplies between members of the group are disregarded for VAT purposes.

The principal effect of the statement is that where title to buildings passes from one member of the VAT group to another, the VAT liability of supplies made by the group of interests in such properties will no longer be changed as a result of the subsequent departure from the group of the original owner company. This is significant where the building concerned was constructed by the original owner and the group has been making zero-rated supplies of major interest leases, *i.e.*, leases for more than 21 years. Hitherto such supplies would have become exempt as a result of the departure from the group of the original owner, even though the supply was still being made by the same group.

Supplies made following transfers between members of groups which are not formally constituted VAT groups are not affected. No VAT group can have operated as such before 1 April 1973.

Note
The statement referred to was made in a letter from Customs and Excise to the British Property Federation. It read:
"Rental income received by a 'person constructing a building' in respect of a major interest lease in or in any part of that building is the consideration for a zero-rated supply under FA 1972, Sch. 4, Group 8, Item 1. Under 21 (1) of that Act any business carried on by a member of a VAT group is treated as carried on by the representative member. Customs and Excise have long taken the view that where a 'person constructing a building' in receipt of rental income which is consideration for a zero-rated supply in the hands of the representative member of his VAT group, transferred his interest to the representative or any other member of the VAT group, that income remained consideration for a zero-rated supply, but only so long as the original 'person constructing' remained a member of the VAT group. If the original 'person constructing' left the group and/or ceased to exist subsequent to the transfer, rental income received thereafter was regarded as consideration for an exempt supply under FA 1972, Sch. 5, Group 1, Item 1.
As a result of a review Customs and Excise are now able to accept that:
 (*a*) where a 'person constructing a building' transfers his whole interest in that building to a fellow member of a formally constituted VAT group (of which both parties are members at the date of transfer), rental income can still be accounted for by the representative member as consideration for zero-rated supplies even though the original 'person constructing' subsequently leaves the group and/or ceased to exist;
 (*b*) where a 'person constructing a building' grants a major interest lease and then transfers his own interest to another member of the same formally constituted VAT group, further major interest leases subsequently granted by that member in respect of that building may also be regarded as zero-rated. This would be so whether the new lease was granted on the natural expiry of the old one or the old lease was surrendered and a new one granted, and whether or not the new lease was granted to the former tenants.
These views will be applied to future transfers."

12 July 1983. Press Notice No. 846
VAT: liability of external wall cladding

Customs and Excise have reviewed the VAT liability of external wall cladding, *i.e.* the fixing of blocks of reconstituted stone, timber, plastic or other similar materials, on to walls of a building, following a recent VAT tribunal decision.

The first-time application of such cladding to the external surface of an outside wall of a building, may now be zero-rated as an alteration to the building. The application of cladding which repairs, replaces or covers existing cladding, even if that cladding is in a different material, remains standard rated as does the repair of a wall, *e.g.*, repointing prior to the application of cladding.

Note
1. The current law on VAT and building work is contained in FA 1972, Sch. 4, Group 8[, now VATA 1983, Sch. 5, Group 8].

2. The VAT tribunal case referred to is *Herts Insulation Services Ltd.* v. *C & E Comrs.* LON 82/128.

FA 1972 Sch. 4, Group 8, now VATA 1983, Sch. 5, Group 8, amended with effect from 1 June 1984. Zero-rated alterations now confined to protected buildings under VATA 1983, Sch. 5, Group 8A.

1 November 1983. Press Notice No. 865
VAT: sales of services and related supplies

Customs and Excise have approved the general application of special arrangements for determining the place of belonging of a buyer or seller of a security.

The VAT liability of this sale of a security depends on the place of belonging of the purchaser and may be of importance in determining the input tax the seller can reclaim. Supplies of securities are exempt for supplies to persons belonging outside the E.C. and the IoM which are zero-rated.

A special rule applies only if it is not possible to determine the place of belonging of the purchaser. Sales transacted in the E.C. or the IoM are treated as made to persons belonging in the E.C. and are exempt. Sales which are transacted in any other contry are treated as made to persons outside the E.C. and the IoM and are zero-rated. If, in turn, the place of transaction is not known, this can be deemed to be where the security is listed or as a last resort, where the last known broker in the sale belongs. The place of belonging of a purchaser or seller of a security may be determined similarly in order to determine the liability of a broker's services.

The arrangements can be applied to supplies made on or after 1 April 1983.

Note
These arrangements were previously restricted to sales of securities by members of the Investment and Unit Trust Associations. The amendment on 1 April 1983 to the VAT (General) Regulations 1980 (S.I. 1980 No. 1536) reg. 25 (*d*) (whereby taxable persons who are not wholly or mainly in the business of selling securities are required to exclude from their exemption calculations the value of zero-rated as well as exempt supplies of securities) clears the way for this extension.

14 December 1983. Press Notice No. 871
General valuation statements—revised procedures

Customs and Excise announce that from 1 January 1984 general valuation statements made on a form C 109A which has been registered at a particular port or airport can be used at any other port or airport in the U.K. to which a ship or aircraft may be unexpectedly diverted, *e.g.* because of industrial action, adverse weather conditions, etc. These provisions will also apply to misdirected goods or goods diverted for trade reasons.

Importers wishing to use the facility will have to produce a photocopy of the registered form C 109A with full registration details to the Collector of Customs and Excise of the port or airport concerned. Importers who regularly use a port or airport will continue to be required to submit general valuation statements at each place of entry.

Note
Where goods are imported into the customs territory of the European Community the importer is required to produce in addition to a customs entry, a declaration of value (form C 105A; where the value of the consignment is over [£2,000]). To facilitate importers who import goods on a regular basis from the same supplier under the same terms of trading and remove the need to submit value declarations every time goods are imported, Customs and Excise have a 'season ticket' arrangement whereby a form C 109A general valuation statement is registered by the importer at the port or ports used for this regular traffic. Until now each statement has been valid only for the port at which it was registered. Now the system is being modified to allow photocopy general valuation statements to be produced at a place other than that at which the form C 109A is registered. The additional facility will be allowed only in exceptional circumstances, *e.g.* where a consignment is diverted from the usual place of entry because of something like industrial action or inclement weather conditions.

1 March 1984. Press Notice No. 889
VAT: business gifts

Customs and Excise have now agreed, following trade discussions, that a trader who makes a taxable gift of goods, although barred from issuing a tax invoice, may provide the recipient with a "tax certificate" instead. If he uses the donated goods in his business, the recipient will use the certificate as evidence to support the deduction of input tax. The tax certificate is a statement by the

donor that the goods are being supplied free of charge and that he has accounted for the VAT Certificates on traders' normal invoicing paperwork are acceptable, overwritten as follows:
"TAX CERTIFICATE
No payment is necessary for these goods.
Output tax has been accounted for on the supply."

Note
Gifts costing less than £10 are not considered a supply for VAT purposes. Even though gifts costing more than £10 and those forming part of a series or succession are "supplies" for VAT purposes, there is no "consideration" and consequently no tax invoice may be issued.

9 March 1984. Press Notice No. 890
VAT: rights to supply goods or services on passenger vessels

Customs and Excise have now agreed that ship operators who are registered traders and who grant licences to supply goods or services on board their passenger ships, can zero-rate the supply of such rights when the concessionaires belong overseas.
   Last year, it was announced that the supply of rights of this kind should be VAT standard-rated, but following representations by the General Council of British Shipping, the implementation of the liability change was deferred until the position of overseas concessionaires could be resolved.

Note
The granting of shipboard concessions is now considered to be the supply of a right falling within the terms of the VATA 1983, Sch. 3 para. 1 provided that the contract is in the form of a licence. The zero-rating is provided under items 5 or 6 (*a*) of the zero rate Group 9 when the right is supplied to business customers belonging overseas.

5 April 1984. Press Notice No. 904
VAT: construction industry—liability of "mixed work" done prior to 1 June 1984

Customs and Excise understand that, following recent litigation, there may be some uncertainty among builders and their clients about the current VAT treatment of "mixed work". Mixed work is work that involves the supply of a range of building services comprising both alterations and repairs or maintenance. For example, the renovation of an old house may include alteration work such as the re-arrangements of internal walls as well as repair or maintenance work such as re-pointing of the brickwork or the replacement of defective gutters.
   Work of this nature should be treated as follows when determining VAT liability:
   (*a*) where the separate pieces of work within the job can be identified, this should be done and
         each separate element then either zero-rated as alteration or standard-rated as repair or
         maintenance depending on what was involved;
   (*b*) where the separate pieces of work cannot be identified or the contractor elects not to do so,
         then the whole job is standard-rated.
This approach to mixed work has long been normal practice in the building industry and is consistent with the High Court decision in the case of *C. & E. Comrs.* v. *Morrison Dunbar and Another* [1979] STC 406 (often referred to as the "Mecca case").
   In the recent High Court case of *Brian Lawrence Sharman* v. *C. & E. Comrs.* [1983] STC 809 some doubt was cast on whether zero-rating in mixed work jobs should properly be restricted to separately identifiable alterations and the case was remitted back to the Manchester VAT Tribunal for re-hearing. Customs and Excise were proposing to appeal this High Court judgment by Mr. Justice Webster to the Court of Appeal in order to re-establish the necessary certainty. The Building Employers Confederation, which was similarly concerned about the implications of the Sharman judgment, considered that this proposed appeal was desirable to re-establish certainty. However, in the light of the change of liability for construction work announced in the Budget on 13 March 1984, Customs and Excise have decided to abandon their appeal to the Court of Appeal on Sharman especially as not all the elements of the Tribunal's original decision could now be supported in the light of the House of Lords judgment in the case of *C. & E. Comrs.* v. *Viva Gas Appliances Ltd.* [1983] STC 819.
   Customs and Excise will maintain their view of the proper approach to mixed work set out in para. 2 above for supplies made before 1 June 1984. The Building Employers Confederation and other interested trade bodies are being informed.

18 May 1984. Press Notice No. 915
VAT: building alterations

Customs and Excise advise that many of the "beat the Budget" schemes being offered by businesses concerned with double glazing and other building services, do not comply with VAT rules and do not establish a "tax point" prior to 1 June 1984.

From 1 June alteration work, home extensions and double glazing are among supplies which will become chargeable with VAT at the standard rate, *i.e.* 15 per cent. Supplies that are paid for before 1 June will not attract the charge even if the work is carried out after 1 June.

Some firms have seen this as an opportunity to canvas for new business and are offering incentives to potential customers in the form of credit facilities (often via finance houses) or some form of protection for the customer who pays in cash before the job is done. Most of the schemes fail to establish a "tax point" before 1 June.

A customer does not necessarily have to make complete payment for the whole of a job before 1 June. It is a matter for each customer to decide how far to go in paying money for work not yet done. So far as outright payment is received by the supplier before 1 June, it will escape VAT, but VAT will be due on any element remaining for payment on 1 June or later.

Contractors and their customers should bear in mind that to establish a tax point before the work is done, payment for the supply must be received by the supplier visibly and irrevocably. The mere issue of an invoice is not sufficient, nor is any scheme which in reality defers the receipt of payment by the supplier until after 1 June. Any traders or customers who may be entering into contracts in the belief that their scheme zero-rates the supply are advised to contact Customs and Excise to clear up any misunderstandings or doubts that may exist. Traders who fail to establish a "tax point" before 1 June will be liable subsequently for the VAT on their supplies whether or not they are able to recover the tax from their customers.

3 August 1984. Press Notice No. 931
VAT: repossessed goods

Customs and Excise announce that from 1 September 1984, a supplier who takes back goods sold under a hire purchase or conditional sale agreement from a customer who is a VAT-registered trader before all the instalments have been paid, will not be allowed to reduce the value of the original sale for VAT purposes.

Note
Under normal VAT rules, a VAT-registered trader purchasing goods for use in his business can reclaim from Customs and Excise the full value of the VAT charged to him by his supplier. This applies whether the goods are supplied under hire purchase, conditional sale agreements or outright sale. The measure announced today is necessary in order to limit the revenue loss which may result when the original sale value is reduced by the supplier on repossession of the goods. It restricts the terms of concession No. 3 which is published in the VAT Leaflet "Extra-statutory Concessions".

See Notice No. 748 (October 1989) concession A3, for the text of the concession now applied by the Commissioners.

14 September 1984. Press Notice No. 938
VAT: supplies of staff to offshore oil/gas rigs

Customs and Excise have reviewed the VAT position of supplies of staff by employment agencies and bureaux to offshore oil/gas rigs outside U.K. territorial waters.

Because such oil/gas rigs may now be regarded, within the E.C. as separate overseas business establishments, supplies of staff made to them can be zero-rated under existing U.K. VAT legislation. Previously such supplies were standard-rated.

Note
Zero-rating is available under the provisions of VATA 1983, Sch. 3, para. 6 and Sch. 5, Group 9, Item 6 (*a*).
See also Press Notice No. 1002 dated 29 April 1985.

31 December 1984. Press Notice No. 960
VAT: legal services in insurance claims

The Commissioners of Customs and Excise have agreed with the British Insurance Association and other insurance bodies that policy-holders who are registered for VAT can count as input tax VAT incurred on legal services supplied to them in connection with an insurance claim relating to their business.

From 1 January 1985 this will apply whether the solicitor is instructed by the policy-holder or by the insurer on his behalf and whether or not in practice the proceedings are controlled by the insurer. It has also been agreed that, normally, such legal services are supplied to the policy-holder not the insurer even where the insurer exercises his right of subrogation to pursue or defend a claim in the name of the policy-holder.

The Commissioners have also agreed with the insurance bodies that Directions issued to insurance companies to ensure that input tax is not recovered on repairs and replacements are no longer necessary. The Directions, which were issued under Regulation 24 (2) of the VAT (General) Regulations (S.I. 1985 No. 886), are to be treated as withdrawn with effect from 1 January 1985.

Guidance on the VAT treatment of solicitors' and other costs in insurance claims is to be incorporated in a revision of VAT leaflet No. 701/36/84 to be issued early in 1985.

Note
Previously, solicitors' services in relation to subrogated claims were treated as supplied to the insurer for the purposes of his business and, being exempt or partly exempt, the insurer could not recover all the tax incurred. Furthermore, solicitors' services in proceedings initiated by the insurer were treated as supplied to the policy-holder but for the purposes of the insurer's business. In the latter case neither the insurer nor the policy-holder could recover any of the VAT charged by the solicitor. From 12 January 1985 registered policy-holders will be able to recover the tax subject to the normal rules and thus the amount to be indemnified by the insurer will be reduced. The VAT treatment of lawyers' services to insurance companies remains unaltered.

The Commissioners' Directions under Reg. 24 (2) are no longer necessary because repairs and replacements are normally supplied to policy-holders not to their insurers and an insurance company cannot obtain input tax recovery on a third party's supply to a policy-holder.

25 February 1985. Press Notice No. 977
VAT: rent collection services

Customs and Excise advise that with effect from 1 July rent collection services supplied to overseas persons in respect of property in the U.K. will be regarded as liable to VAT at the standard rate even when supplied separately from other property management services.

Property management services supplied to overseas persons have been taxable since 1978, but it has been accepted that rent collection services, if supplied separately, may be zero-rated as financial services coming within VATA 1983, Sch. 3 Item 5. Having reviewed the matter in the light of a recent VAT tribunal case, the Commissioners have decided this treatment is incorrect and cannot be maintained. Rent collection services supplied to U.K. residents have always been standard rated.

Note
VATA 1983, Sch. 3 lists a number of services which are eligible for zero rating under Sch. 5 Group 9 Items 5 or 6 (*a*) when supplied to overseas persons. Services relating to land are specifically excluded from relief and for this reason the service of managing property in the U.K. has not been eligible for zero rating. But financial services are included in the relief, and hitherto it has been accepted that services of rent collection, provided they are supplied separately from any property management services, came within the definition of financial services and could be relieved.

In the course of giving his decision in the tribunal case of *Culverpalm Ltd.* v. *C. & E. Comrs.* LON/84/47 on 18 October 1984 the Chairman, Lord Grantchester, expressed the view that "financial services" were "primarily services relating to money, foreign currency and securities therefor". He did not consider that "financial services" extended to rent collecting.

Having reviewed the matter, the Commissioners agree with this view, and from 1 July 1985 rent collection services will be treated in the same way as property management services, and will no longer be eligible for zero rating.

29 April 1985. Press Notice No. 1002
VAT: zero-rating of supplies of staff to offshore oil/gas rigs

Customs and Excise advise that for the purpose of deciding whether supplies of staff to offshore oil/gas rigs outside the U.K. territorial waters may be zero-rated, such supplies must be made to an Operating Member in order to qualify.

If supplies of staff are made to a person contracted to the Operating Member, even if he performs his services on the rig, the contractor will "belong" where he has his normal business establishment onshore. If this is within the U.K. such supplies are standard-rated.

Note
Press Notice No. 938 (14 September 1984) advised that within the E.C. oil and gas rigs outside U.K.

territorial waters could be regarded as "separate overseas business establishments". This being the case, supplies of staff to them are zero-rated under the provisions of VATA 1983, Sch. 3 para. 6 and Sch. 5, Group 9, Item, 6(*a*).

An Operating Member (OM) is the member appointed by a consortium of Participating Members (PM) to carry out actual exploration/exploitation operations.

31 May 1985. Press Notice No. 1015
VAT: press advertising—international services

Customs and Excise have agreed to a special procedure for use in cases where advertising in foreign media is placed by a U.K.-based representative of the foreign media on behalf of U.K. advertisers or advertising agencies.

Provided that the foreign media representative is an agent and not a principal in the transaction, then the U.K. advertiser or advertising agent will have to account for VAT himself, under the "reverse charge" procedure. This is true whether the overseas supplier invoices the advertiser direct, or indirectly through their representative passing on the charge. However, in the latter case, if the agent does not use the supplier's original invoice, he should instead provide his customer with a statement(not an invoice) endorsed as follows:

     "VALUE ADDED TAX"

       "This statement relates to an imported service. You should account for VAT under Section 7 VAT Act 1983."

This special procedure has been agreed by Customs and Excise in discussion with trade associations.

Note
Where the foreign media representative is a principal, (rather than an agent) then it is he who must account for VAT under the "reverse charge" procedure, the onward supply to his U.K. customer being a normal (standard-rated) transaction.

Under the "reverse charge" procedure, importers of a range of services, including those of advertising, must account for VAT on the transaction as if they had both made and received the supplies themselves.

24 July 1985. Press Notice No. 1026
VAT treatment of donations to charities

The Minister of State Treasury, Mr. Barney Hayhoe M.P. announced in a reply to a Parliamentary Question on Wednesday 17 July that it had been possible to allow an exceptional waiver of VAT on four-fifths of the ticket proceeds of the Live Aid concert at Wembley on 13 July, amounting to about £190,000. The promoters had intended to sell the tickets for £5, plus a voluntary donation of £20, but had made a mistake in not making this clear in the advertising for the concert. To be free of VAT, a donation in addition to an admission charge must be genuinely voluntary, and advertised as such. Because a genuine mistake had been made, Customs and Excise, with the authority of the Chancellor of the Exchequer, decided as an extra-statutory concession not to insist on the VAT on the donational element of the admission charge.

To avoid future mistakes and misunderstandings of this kind, it is felt necessary to restate the VAT position of donations to charities, and to stress that the concession in the Live Aid case does not set a precedent for the treatment of similar fund-raising events in future.

Genuine donations to chartities do not involve a taxable supply of goods or services, and are outside the scope of VAT. But any payment which is in return for a supply of goods or services (including the granting, assignment or surrender of any right) is the consideration for a supply and will not be accepted as a genuine donation except:

     (*a*) donations given in exchange for an emblem for which there is no fixed minimum charge, *e.g.*, a "flag" or Remembrance Day poppy;

     (*b*) memberships subscriptions to a charitable organisation which secure no entitlement to any personal facility or advantage other than the right to participate in the charity's management and to receive formal reports of its activities.

Where a basic minimum charge is stipulated for admission to a charitable function such as a fund-raising concert or dinner, and patrons are invited to make additonal payments as purely voluntary donations, only the basic minimum charge will be liable to VAT provided all the conditions set out in para. 16 of VAT leaflet 701/1/85 *Charities* are met. In summary, the rules provide that for a donation to be treated as not subject to VAT, it must be in addition to a realistic admission charge, and be completely at the discretion of the purchaser of the ticket—and this must be made clear in all publicity and advertising for the event.

If the organisers of any charitable fund-raising event have doubts about the VAT position in their particular circumstances, they are strongly advised to seek guidance in advance from their Local

VAT Office (listed under Customs and Excise in the telephone directory) or from VAT Administration Division G, Branch 1, Room 414M King's Beam House, Mark Lane, London EC3R 7HE (telephone 01 626 1515 extension 5390).

10 September 1985. Press Notice No. 1032
VAT: exceptional cases where the liability of a supply depends on the customer's status

Customs and Excise, following discussion with the Law Society have issued the following statement about their policy in those exceptional cases where the liability to VAT of a supply is governed by the status of the customer to whom the supply is made:

"As a general principle, the determination of liability of VAT is the responsibility of the taxpayer. In certain special cases the VAT liability of supplies of goods or services depends on the status of the customer receiving them. This can present problems for the supplier where the customer, innocently or otherwise, wrongly represents his status. Where this happens Customs and Excise will not hold the supplier responsible for failing to charge the correct amount of tax, providedthey are satisfied that the supplier:

(a) acted in good faith; and
(b) made normal and prudent checks and enquiries about the status of the customer and of any documentation of certification provided by him."

Note
The Law Society was concerned about those exceptional cases where a supplier of goods or services must establish from his customer the facts relevant to the categorisation of of the supply for VAT liability purposes. An example would be where the right to zero rating depends on the customer being handicapped. The Commissioners' statement which has been agreed with the Law Society makes clear that if the customer misleads a supplier about his status, innocently or otherwise, and the supplier acts in good faith, the supplier will not be held accountable for the tax in question. This statement does not change but rather clarifies and publicises the policy already followed in such cases by the Department.

21 October 1985. Press Notice No. 1045
VAT: check trading companies—charges to retailers

Customs and Excise announce that from 1 December 1985 the charges made by check trading companies to participating retailers will be treated as exempt for VAT purposes and will therefore no longer be regarded as a promotional service which is taxable. This follows a similar change of liability in respect of charges made to retailers by credit card, charge card and similar payment card companies announced in the last Budget. The National Consumer Credit Federation has been advised of this ruling.

Note
Check trading is a means of buying goods on credit whereby a check trading company sells a trading check for a special amount to a customer who pays for the check on credit terms over a period of time. The customer then uses the check to purchase goods from a participating retailer. The check trading company retains a percentage of the sum due to the retailer when he presents the check to the company for redemption. It is this charge which is the subject of the revised liability ruling. The change brings the treatment of check trading companies into line with that of credit card companies in respect of the broadly similar services they supply to participating retailers. It will have the effect of reducing their recovery of input tax.

12 November 1985. Press Notice No. 1049
VAT: retail schemes—retrospective changes

Customs and Excise have introduced changes to the operation of the VAT Retail Schemes which will be of particular benefit to small traders.

Where a new business wishes to change scheme retrospectively, this will be allowed for any period up to the date of the first inspection visit by a VAT officer, which will normally be within 18 months of the trader being registered for VAT.

Other traders whose annual turnover is below £120,000 will now be allowed to apply to change retail schemes at any time, with retrospective calculation of tax due up to a maximum of three years, subject to certain conditions.

No refunds of tax arising from retrospective scheme changes will be made unless the sum due exceeds an average of £50 a year.

Applications to change the scheme should be made to the trader's local VAT office.

Note
VAT Retail Schemes are designed to help retail traders to calculate their VAT liability, particularly where supplies at different tax rates are being made.

The changes to the Retail Schemes follow the publication of the White Paper "Lifting the Burden" (Cmnd 9571—July 1985).

11 February 1986. Press Notice No. 1078
VAT: supplies by confirming houses

Customs and Excise advise that with effect from 1 March 1986, the following supplies by confirming houses will be regarded as exempt from VAT:

Supplies of services for which a confirming commission is charged.

Credit facilities granted in return for interest.

However, supplies of confirming services and credit made to persons outside the Isle of Man and the E.C. may be zero-rated.

Confirming houses provide services to importers of goods both in the U.K. and overseas. For a "confirming" commission they guarantee on behalf of the importer to pay the supplier for his goods. If required they will also provide an extended credit facility for which they charge interest.

Previously, some supplies by confirming houses were regarded as liable to VAT at the standard rate of 15 per cent., but it is understood that many confirming houses have been treating all their supplies as zero-rated. The effect of the changes is that from 1 March most confirming houses will be partly exempt traders. They will be unable to recover input tax in respect of their exempt supplies. The British Export Houses Association has been notified accordingly.

Note
Exemption for financial services, including the provision of credit facilities, is contained in VATA 1983, Sch. 6, Group 5. Zero-rating for the same services supplied to persons outside the Isle of Man and the E.C. is in VATA 1983, Sch. 5, Group 9, Item 6 (*a*).

2 May 1986. Press Notice No. 1108
VAT: liability of telecommunication equipment

Customs and Excise have reviewed the liability of telecommunication equipment when installed in the course of the construction of a new building and have decided that from 1 August 1986 most such supplies should be liable to VAT at the standard rate, in the same way as installation in an existing building.

At present such equipment is regarded as VAT zero-rated under VATA 1983, Sch. 5, Group 8, Item 3 as being "articles of a kind ordinarily installed by builders as fixtures". After consultation with a number of manufacturers and trade associations and in the light of legal advice, the Commissioners have decided that the rapid technical advances in recent years mean that most telecommunications equipment is not now a "fixture" in a building, nor is it installed by a "builder".

However, there are two exceptions. The Commissioners will continue to accept zero-rating for the supply and installation of fixed Network Termination Points (*i.e.* where the system is joined to the outside network) and of any necessary fixed cabling involved in distributing the system throughout a new building before its first time occupation.

26 June 1986. Press Notice No. 1121
VAT liability of Sterling Commercial Paper

Customs and Excise have received a number of enquiries about the VAT liability of the issue of and trading in, Sterling Debt Securities known as "Sterling Commercial Paper". These securities have maturities between seven days and one year and they are used by companies as a means of borrowing large sums of short term capital.

Sterling Commercial Paper takes the form of promissory notes and the issue and any subsequent trading of such securities is exempt from VAT under VATA 1983, Sch. 6 Group 5 Item 1. However the supply may be zero-rated under VATA 1983, Sch. 5 Group 9 Item 6 if the recipient belongs in a country other than the IoM, which is not a member state of the E.C. In either event the value of the supply is the charge, if any, made above the face value of the security.

Note
On 29 April 1986 the Bank of England issued a Notice describing new arrangements for the issue of Sterling Commercial Paper. The Bank included in the Note a reference to income tax and corporation tax. This Press Notice clarifies the VAT position of the new securities. Any enquiries

about other aspects of Sterling Commerical Paper should be directed to the Bank's Gilt-Edged Division.

25 July 1986. Press Notice No. 1129
Taxpayer's Charter

Customs and Excise has joined with the Board of Inland Revenue to issue today a Taxpayer's Charter, which provides a statement of the principles which the Department tries to meet in its dealings with taxpayers, setting out the standards which the Department believes the taxpayer has a right to expect and what people can do if they wish to appeal or complain.

The Charter is not a guarantee that things will never go wrong, but it does reflect the longstanding aims of the Department as expressed in its successive Management Plans and in instructions and training for its staff. The publication of the Charter represents a public commitment to those principles in this new and more detailed form which is accessible to members of the Department and to taxpayers alike.

Within the field of the Department's work the Charter covers both the collection and control of internal taxes such as VAT, car tax and excise duties and also of customs duties and agricultural levies on behalf of the E.C. A copy of the Charter is annexed.

Note
The Taxpayer's Charter has been included by the Board of Inland Revenue in its Annual Report for 1985 published today. The next annual report for Customs and Excise, covering the financial year 1985–1986, will be issued in the autumn.

Copies of the Charter are available to the public from Collectors' offices or from local VAT offices.

5 August 1986. Press Notice No. 1132
VAT tribunals—costs of unsuccessful appellants

Customs and Excise are to continue their present practice of only seeking costs in limited circumstances when there are unsuccessful appeals by taxpayers to the independent Value Added Tax Tribunals. This restatement covers both appeals against tax and those against penalties imposed under the provisions of FA 1985 (for example, late notification and default surcharge).

Announcing this in answer to a Parliamentary Question in the House of Commons the Minister of State, Treasury, the Hon. Peter Brooke M.P. said:

"The practice of Customs and Excise in seeking costs in unsuccessful appeals heard by the VAT Tribunals was set out by the Right Honourable member for Ashton-under-Lyne, when he was Financial Secretary of the Treasury, on 13 November 1978. There has been no change in policy since then, but with the new enforcement powers and rights of appeal, particularly on the grounds of reasonable excuse, enacted in the FA 1985, it may be helpful to restate it. As a general rule, Customs and Excise do not seek costs against unsuccessful appellants. They do, however, ask for costs in certain narrowly defined cases so as to provide protection for public funds and the general body of taxpayers. They will therefore seek to continue to ask for costs at those exceptional Tribunal hearings of substantial and complex cases where large sums are involved and which are comparable with High Court cases, unless the appeal involves an important general point of law requiring clarification. They will also continue to consider seeking costs where the appellant has misused the Tribunal procedure—for example in frivolous or vexatious cases, or where the appellant has failed to appear or to be represented at a mutually arranged hearing without sufficient explanation, or where the appellant has first produced at a hearing relevant evidence which ought properly to have been disclosed at an earlier stage and which could have saved public funds had it been produced timeously.

The new penalty provisions and rights of appeal to the Value Added Tax Tribunals has made no change to this policy. Customs and Excise, with the agreement of the council on Tribunals, consider that appeals against penalties imposed under FA 1985, s. 13 on the grounds that a person has evaded VAT and his conduct has involved dishonesty, fall to be considered as being comparable with High Court cases. Where such appeals are unsuccessful, Customs and Excise will normally seek an award of costs.

In all cases the question whether or not costs should be awarded will, of course, remain entirely within the discretion of the Tribunal concerned and the amount of any such award will be fixed either by that Tribunal, or by the High Court as provided by Tribunal procedure rules.

Customs and Excise, in consultation with the Council on Tribunals, will continue to keep their policy under careful scrutiny."

Note
The VAT Tribunals were originally set up at the same time as the introduction of VAT in 1973 to

provide an independent body to decide appeals against decisions and assessments of tax made by Customs and Excise.

Taxpayers may appeal against their liability to or the amount of penalties and surcharges imposed under FA 1985. The relevant current provisions cover:

(*a*) section 13—tax evasion and conduct involving dishonesty;

(*b*) section 15—late registration and unauthorised issue of invoices;

(*c*) section 16 ⎤ —other legal and regulatory requirements, such as the preservation and
     and 17 ⎦   productions of records:

(*d*) section 19—default surcharge (from 1 October [1986]).

See S.I. 1986 No. 590, reg. 29.

14 August 1986. Press Notice No. 1135
VAT: separation of business activities

Customs and Excise advise that where a business has been split wholly or mainly for VAT avoidance purposes, the Commissioners now have power under FA 1986, s. 10 [inserting VATA 1983, Sch. 1, para. 1A] to direct that the persons running a business must register and account for tax as a single taxable person. This applies even if the way in which the various activities of the business have been separated appears to satisfy the criteria published by the Commissioners in 1982 (for details see the *Note* below).

Customs and Excise are, however, required to satisfy themselves that the following conditions are met before they make a direction of this kind:

(*a*) each person to be named in the direction is making (or has made) taxable supplies;

(*b*) the taxable supplies made by each person form only part of the activities of the business to be described in the direction, additional supplies being made (or having been made) by the other person or persons named;

(*c*) the taxable turnover of the business as a whole exceeds the level at which if it was carried on by a single person, that person would incur a liability to VAT registration; and

(*d*) the main reason, or one of the main reasons, for the separation is the avoidance of a liability to VAT registration.

Any person who considers they have been named in a direction unreasonably may appeal to an independent VAT tribunal.

Persons carrying on genuinely separate and distinct small businesses will not be affected.

Note
The criteria for determining the independence of a business were published by Customs and Excise in Press Notice No. 762 (20/9/82). They are:

(*a*) appropriate premises and equipment for the business should be owned or rented by the person carrying on the business;

(*b*) day-to-day records which specifically identify the business should be maintained and, where appropriate, annual accounts prepared;

(*c*) purchase and sale invoices should be in the name of the person making supplies in the course of carrying on the business. (Where constituents of a supply normally regarded as a single compound supply, *e.g.* "bed and breakfast", are claimed to be made by different persons directly to the customer, not only must each part be invoiced separately but the arrangements for the supply must also be seen to be directly between the person claiming to make the supply and the customer);

(*d*) the person carrying on the business should be legally responsible for all trading activities, *i.e.* payments for supplies should be the sole responsibility of the person carrying on the business and proceeds of sale should also be at the sole disposal of that person;

(*e*) any bank account for the business should be in the name of the person carrying on the business, who should also be the sole drawer to the account;

(*f*) wages and National Health contributions in respect of staff employed in the business should be paid by the person carrying on the business; and

(*g*) for income tax purposes the business should be assessed as a separate business.

20 August 1986. Press Notice No. 1137
VAT: meals and accommodation provided by employers to their employees

In a decision released on 16 June (*Robert Wright Goodfellow and Margaret Jane Goodfellow* v. *C. & E. Comrs.* MAN/85/20) the London VAT Tribunal held that the appellants were not accountable for VAT when they provided meals or accommodation to their employees.

The appellants generally paid their employees in accordance with the Wages Order for the time being in force for the industry under the Wages Councils Act 1979. This involved establishing the basic minimum wage applicable to the employee under the Order and then making the appropriate reduction set out in the Order, depending on the catering and accommodation provided. Customs and Excise contended that the reduction in the wage amounted to a monetary consideration for the provision of the catering and accommodation, and was therefore liable to VAT. The tribunal held however that these calculations were no more than steps in arriving at the amount of the weekly wage to be paid: and that there was no agreement between the appellants and their employees that meals or accommodation would be provided in consideration for the reduction in their weekly remuneration. Because there was no monetary consideration, it followed that under the provisions of VATA 1983, Sch. 4, para. 10 the appellants were not liable to VAT on the amount by which the wages were reduced.

Customs and Excise have accepted the decision in the particular circumstances to which it relates. They remain of the view however that VAT registered employers must account for VAT when they provide meals or accommodation to employees for monetary consideration, for example by an agreed deduction from their wages or by means of periodical payments.

Tax incurred on purchases for the provision of meals or accommodation to employees can be deducted as input tax subject to the normal rules.

28 October 1986. Press Notice No. 1148
VAT: business and non-business activities. Restriction of input tax deduction

In a High Court judgment of 11 February 1986, Mr. Justice Kennedy found for the Commissiners that Whitechapel Art Gallery carries out business and non-business activities and that therefore not all the VAT charged on purchases made by the Gallery can be reclaimed as input tax. However Mr. Justice Kennedy then criticised the income-based method of apportionment which has been suggested by the Commissioners, on the grounds that the grants and donations received by the Gallery should not be included in the calculation.

The Commissioners regard the judge's comment concerning grants and donations as applying solely to the circumstances of the Gallery; they do not consider themselves bound by the comment in other cases where input tax has to be apportioned. Where it is necessary to apportion input tax between business and non-business activities, one of the methods which can be employed involves using the ratio between business income and total income. This method will generally only give an answer which is fair and reasonable if any grants and donations received are included in the figure of total income and it is the intention of the Commissioners that grants and donations should continue to be included in cases where this method is used.

Note
Under VATA 1983, s. 14 (4), where goods or services are purchased for both business and non-business purposes, the VAT charged on their purchase has to be apportioned so that only the VAT relating to the business purposes is deducted as input tax.

The Act does not prescribe any particular method of apportionment.

The Commissioners explain the income based method at Appendix 5 to Notice No. 700, *The VAT guide*, but point out that this method is not mandatory. A registered person can adopt a different method if he has first agreed it with the local VAT office.

25 March 1987. Press Notice No. 24/87
VAT: motoring expenses

In answer to a Parliamentary question yesterday, the Minister of State, Treasury (the Hon. Peter Brooke M.P.) explained that the scheme of VAT scale charges starting on 6 April 1987 will apply only to cars and not to other motor vehicles. The charges will apply whenever road fuel is supplied or apportioned by business for private journeys.

The definition of a road vehcile in FA 1986 is wide enough to include vans. However, the derogation for which application was made under Article 27 of the E.C. Sixth VAT Directive was confined to cars; the scale charge will not therefore apply when road fuel is supplied or apportioned by business for private journeys in vans and the present VAT treatment of such journeys will remain unchanged.

Note
The current VAT treatment of fuel used for private journeys, whether in cars or vans, requires either apportionment of input tax incurred on purchases of fuel so that only the tax on the portion used for business journeys is deductible, or payment of output tax after full deduction of input tax. This system will be replaced from 6 April 1987, in respect of cars only, by a system which allows the whole of the input tax to be deducted. However, a scale similar to the Revenue Fuel Benefit scale, will be used to determine the sum on which output tax must be paid in order to take account of the use of fuel for private journeys. Under this scheme some businesses will gain and others may lose as compared with the present system: but the scale is part of a package under which Customs and

Excise will not be proceeding with an earlier intention to require apportionment of repair, maintenance and leasing charges.

The legislation introducing the VAT scale charge system was enacted in FA 1986, s. 9.

24 June 1987. Press Notice No. 46/87
VAT: valuation of goods on removal from warehouse

Customs and Excise advise that consultations are taking place with the European Commission about the impact on valuation for VAT purposes, of new customs valuation rules which are to be introduced on 1 January 1988, for goods being removed from warehouse. Pending the outcome of the consultations the new customs valuation rules need not be applied to certain goods being removed from warehouse.

From 1 January 1988 traders may choose one of two methods by which elements of the VAT value may be converted from foreign currencies for goods which are chargeable with excise duty only, or with both excise duty and a specific customs duty when they are removed from warehouse. The methods are:

(i) calculation of the sterling value for VAT purposes using the exchange rates in force (*a*) at the time the goods were warehoused or (*b*) where a sale of the goods in warehouse is to be used as the basis of valuation, at the time of that sale; or

(ii) calculation of the sterling value for VAT purposes using the new customs duty procedure which requires any amounts in foreign currencies to be converted to sterling at the time, and using the exchange rates in force, when the goods are removed to home use.

For other goods the new customs valuation procedure will apply from 1 January 1988 for both duty and VAT purposes.

The option described above is an interim arrangement subject to modification as a result of the Brussels consultations.

Further information must be obtained from VAT International Division, telephone 01-382 5322 or 5320.

Note
From 1 January 1988 the procedure for establishing the customs value of imported goods on removal from warehouse is to be changed. The intention behind the change is to ensure that the U.K. practice observes more closely the principles of E.C. customs law, which requires amounts expressed in foreign currency to be converted into sterling at the rate in force at the time when goods are put into free circulation. The present procedure for establishing a sterling customs value for goods at the time they are imported into warehouse (known as valuation classification A) is incompatible with these principles and therefore, with limited exceptions (broadly goods already in warehouse classified A), is to be withdrawn from 1 January 1988.

Where values of goods (or other related costs such as freight or insurance) are expressed in foreign currencies, the Sixth VAT Directive and VATA 1983 apply to value added tax the currency conversion provisions contained in E.C. customs law.

Representations have been received that a burden would be imposed on traders if the new customs valuation procedures were to be applied to VAT in the warehousing environment, particularly in those cases where no *ad valorem* duty is payable. In many cases currency conversions would have to be effected, using the rate of exchange designated at the time when goods were removed to home use, solely for VAT purposes.

Specific duties are those charged by reference to units of quantity. Ad valorem duties are those charged by reference to value.

3 November 1987. Press Notice No. 76/87
VAT: extension of time limit for horses temporarily imported for training and racing

Since 1 January 1986 E.C. rules have provided for relief from import VAT in respect of horses temporarily imported for training and racing for a period not exceeding 24 months. Following representations to the European Commission, Customs and Excise have been authorised to extend the time limit by six months, on a case by case basis, for temporarily imported yearlings.

Importers who require extensions should apply in writing to the control officer specified on the import entry between the start of the 22nd month and the end of the 23rd month from the date of importation. Applications must show full particulars of the horse(s) (name, age, sex, colour and breeding) and import entry details (port, date of importation and import entry number). Applications received after the normal period of relief has expired will not be accepted and import VAT will become payable.

Note
The conditions of the VAT relief are set out in Notice 200 *Temporary Importations into the*

European Community and Notice 201 *Temporary Imports from the European Community.* The letter is based upon Directive 85/362/EEC which has been implemented in the U.K. by means of Value Added Tax (Temporarily Imported Goods) Relief Order 1986 (S.I. 1986/1989) under powers contained in VATA 1983. Prior to 1 January 1986 U.K. law provided relief from import VAT for a maximum period of 30 months for yearlings temporarily imported for training and racing.

19 November 1987. Press Notice No. 82/87
VAT: settlement of disputes

Customs and Excise have reviewed their policy on the VAT treatment of payments made under out-of-court settlements of disputes, after proceedings have been commenced by service of originating process (or appointment of an arbitrator).

They now take the view that, where such payments are in essence compensatory and do not relate directly to supplies of goods or services, they are outside the scope of VAT. This will be so even if the settlement is expressed in terms that the payment is consideration for the plaintiff's agreement to abandon his rights to bring legal proceedings. But payments will remain taxable if, and to the extent, that they are the consideration for specific taxable supplies by the plaintiff, *e.g.* where the dispute concerns payment for an earlier supply, or where the plaintiff grants future rights to exploit copyright material under the settlement.

These changes of policy may be applied from 19 November 1987.

Note
Customs and Excise had previously taken the view that all payments under out-of-court settlements were generally taxable. The revised VAT liability brings the VAT treatment of out-of-court settlements into line with the VAT treatment of payments under court orders.

8 March 1988. Press Notice No. 12/88
Customs and Excise/Inland Revenue co-operation

Customs and Excise and the Revenue are to extend arrangements nationwide for exchanging information to combat tax fraud and evasion.

The Financial Secretary to H.M. Treasury (the Rt. Hon. Norman Lamont M.P.), said today, in reply to a parliamentary question:

"Both the Revenue and Customs, in their published responses to Volumes 1 and 2 of the Report of the Keith Committee on the Enforcement Powers of the Revenue Departments, proposed that the matching recommendations on local exchange of information should be accepted. With my authority, exchanges, which were formerly restricted to head office level as a result of a 1972 ministerial undertaking, will from 1 April 1988, take place at local level also. The exchanges will concentrate on larger cases of suspected tax evasion.

Statutory authority for the exchange of information by Inland Revenue and Customs and Excise, for the purpose of assisting them in the performance of their duties, is already provided by FA 1972, s. 127. No new legislation is, therefore, required."

Notes
When VAT was introduced in 1973, statutory provision was made, by FA 1972, s. 127, for exchange of information between the revenue departments, principally in order to allow for co-ordinated action against fraud and evasion. But there was widespread concern about how the provision might be used and ministers gave an assurance that information would be exchanged at head office level only.

In 1977, with a view to combating tax evasion, authority was given for experimental exchange of selected information between local Revenue and VAT offices in the Leeds area. The conclusion from this, which was recorded in volume 2 of the Keith report (Cmnd. 8822 of 1983), was that extending the local exchange of information nationwide would lead to additional revenue yield of approx. £4m. p.a. (at 1983 prices). The Keith Committee found that the general weight of opinion in representations to them was in favour of extension and recommended that the local exchange of information should be extended nationwide and ministerial constraints placed on the use of FA 1972 s. 127 should be removed.

The Revenue and Customs and Excise responses to the report (The Inland Revenue and the Taxpayer, HMSO 1986 and The Collection of Value Added Tax HMSO 1984) proposed acceptance of the recommendation. No comments on this proposal have been received in responses to the consultative documents. The new procedures, which will go ahead from 1 April 1988, will concentrate on larger cases of suspected default.

9 May 1988. Parliamentary proceedings
Guidelines on compounding of offence proceedings under CEMA 1979, s. 152

The following synopsis of Customs and Excise policy on settlement of tax offences was provided to the House of Commons Public Accounts Committee on 9 May 1988 and published as Annex A to Appendix 1 of the Committee's Minutes of Evidence of 25 April 1988 (session 1987–88 HC Paper 452–i).

Introduction
1. Compounding is one of a range of sanctions available to the Commissioners of Customs and Excise. It is a process whereby as an alternative to taking legal proceedings for an offence under the Customs and Excise Acts, they may offer the alleged offender the option of being prosecuted or settling out of court. The terms for compounding usually involve the alleged offender paying an amount at least equal to the tax or duty evaded. Together with other non-judicial penalties available to the Commissioners, such as the seizure of goods, vehicles or equipment used in smuggling or revenue offences and the civil fraud procedures introduced for VAT by FA 1985, it allows the great majority of offences to be punished efficiently and effectively without burdening the courts or tying up staff in lengthy court hearings.
2. For these reasons, a presupposition in favour of offering a compounded penalty wherever appropriate was announced by Treasury Ministers in the following Written Answer on 25 April 1984 (Hansard, col. 542):
"The Commissioners *do not* prosecute, nor apply other main sanctions such as compounding, unless there is a clear *prima facie* case. The decision whether to prosecute or to offer to compound proceedings is taken on the merits of each case. The general factors taken into consideration are the gravity of the offence and the best interests of law enforcement and of the revenue. In view of the pressure on the courts and on departmental resources, it is the Commissioners' policy to offer compounding whenever appropriate. If the offer is refused, they then proceed with the prosecution of the alleged offender."

General policy
3. Our guidelines as to when compounding is considered to be appropriate were summarised in the Report of the Committee on Enforcement Power of the Revenue Departments, chaired by Lord Keith of Kinkel (Cmnd. 9440) at chapter 36.5.3:
"Within this broad framework, certain types of cases are identified by the Department as normally appropriate for prosecution rather than compounding. Thus, prosecution will be preferred where a prison sentence or a substantial fine is the likely outcome or where special factors indicate that proceedings will be desirable in the interests of the enforcement of revenue or other laws, or Community obligations, or for publicity to deter potential offenders. Such special factors might include the need to reduce the incidence of practices which could if unchecked undermine the security of the duty or tax concerned, and this would comprehend cases of organised fraud, some instances of illegal bookmaking, illicit distillation (though with an eye there to health grounds also) and some false tank cases in hydrocarbon oils. Some offences such as the illegal importation of drugs (other than first offences of very small quantities of cannabis), firearms, and the grosser forms of obscenity, especially those involving children, are generally prosecuted because of close interaction with offences under the social law, and because of the perceived need to protect society from the commodities in question. Other cases normally considered inappropriate for compounding include:
(*a*) cases involving assaults on or obstruction of officers;
(*b*) cases in which the offender is known to be subject to a suspended prison sentence or to be on parole;
(*c*) cases where other related offences are being considered, whether by Customs and Excise, the police or another Government department;
(*d*) cases where the suspected offender is an undischarged bankrupt or, if a limited company, is in liquidation;
(*e*) cases involving persistent offenders."
(The Committee went on to endorse this policy).
4. Details of offences settled by compounding or other non-judicial procedures are not normally published, but this may be done exceptionally, as a condition of the compounding. However, only the minority of offences dealt with by prosecution routinely come into the public domain and this is therefore a factor in deciding whether any individual case warrants the greater resource costs of bringing proceedings.

5. In addition to the guidelines summarised in the extract from the Keith Committee report quoted above, the following guidelines apply:

VAT

Offences are normally investigated for criminal proceedings when one or more of the following conditions apply: the evasion of at least £75,000; the offence is perpetrated by lawyers or accountants who, professionally, advise others; there is a conspiracy to evade VAT other than by persons within the same legal entity; there is a falsification designed to create or inflate input credits of £15,000 or more; there was a previous VAT or Customs offence ending in the imposition of a penalty, the compounding of proceedings or a criminal conviction; there is novelty or ingenuity in the offence capable of adoption by others; the evader occupies a prominent position in the field of law or government; the evasion is executed in conjunction with other criminal activities; there is, during the course of any civil enquiries, a deliberate intent to deceive; or, a supply of goods and services takes place without security being given under VATA 1983, Sch. 7 para. 5 (2). Otherwise, use is generally made of civil penalties, introduced following the recommendations of the Keith Committee in FA 1985.

Customs

Criminal proceedings are taken for all drugs cases (other than first offences involving less than 10 grams of resin or herbal cannabis) and almost invariably for cases involving endangered species, projectiles, firearms and ammunition or child pornography. Compounding is generally considered for other types of offence, subject to the general factors mentioned above.

Excise

Only in cases of illicit distillation of spirits is compounding not considered as an alternative to prosecution, because of the social and health implications of the products of illicit stills.

Car tax

Compounding or prosecution is considered, as appropriate, for all types of offence.

24 June 1988. Hansard
VAT: deposits

Mr. Madel—To ask the Chancellor of the Exchequer if he will introduce legislation to provide that, where a company incurs liability for value added tax on deposits taken from customers for goods not yet supplied, valued added tax may be collected on a quarterly basis for all the deposits the company has taken, rather than the company being required to raise a second invoice for each customer's job to account for the value added tax; and if he will make a statement.
Mr. Lilley—Existing legislation already provides for this where a company supplies goods to customers who are not registered for VAT, since there is no obligation in such cases to issue a tax invoice for either the deposit or the main supply. However, if a tax invoice were not issued to a registered customer in respect of VAT charged on a deposit, the customer would not, in turn, be able to reclaim the VAT.
  HC Written Answer, Vol. 135 col. 730

20 September 1988. Press Notice No. 72/88
VAT: letting of facilities for sport and physical recreation

The Commissioners have decided not to appeal against a decision of the Edinburgh VAT Tribunal (*Queen's Park Football Club Ltd.* v. *C. & E. Comrs.* EDN/87/91) that the letting, for 24 hours or less, of an entire football stadium complete with spectating and other facilities, for the playing of a football fixture, was a standard-rated supply. The Commissioners had argued that such lettings were exempt when made to someone who used the premises for staging a sporting event to which there was a charge for admission because the essential nature of the supply was to concede control over the whole stadium to the licensee who would exploit the property for the purpose of the taxable business of admitting the public to a sporting spectacle.

Although as a matter of strict law the Edinburgh Tribunal's decision applies only to the facts of the Queen's Park Football Club case, the Commissioners now accept that similar supplies by owners of other sporting stadia (outdoor or indoor venues) will, from a current date, also be taxable at the standard rate rather than exempt where the letting concerned is for 24 hours or less.

The existing reliefs for the letting of sports and physical recreation facilities for continuous periods of use exceeding 24 hours, and for a series of lets are unaffected. These reliefs are explained in VAT Leaflet 742/1/86.

The relevant VAT law is in VATA 1983, Sch. 6, Group 1, Item 1, exception (*h*).
Note: Exception (h) re-enacted as exception (k) with effect from 1 April 1989.

28 September 1988. Press Notice No. 77/88
Disruption of postal services: information for VAT traders

In the view of the recent disruption of postal services Customs and Excise have decided, after consultation with the Treasury, that default surcharge will not apply to VAT returns for the period ending 31 July 1988 (07/88) which were due to be received by the Controller VAT Central Unit, Southend, on 31 August 1988.

The suspension of the default surcharge provisions applies only to VAT returns for the period 07/88 and includes those 07/88 returns for which special tax periods have been approved by Customs.

Some businesses may receive a tax assessment, in spite of already having submitted a VAT return, because their return has been delayed in the post. The Customs computer system will automatically cancel the assessment as soon as the return is received. No action is required by the taxpayer.

The piecemeal resumption of postal services and the wide variation in the rate of clearing the backlog from different locations has made it impossible to operate the default surcharge equitably for the period ending 31 July 1988 (for which returns and payments were due on 31 August 1988). It has therefore been decided not to take account of this period for surcharge purposes. The arrangement applies also to 07/88 returns where special tax periods have been approved by Customs. (There is provision for traders to apply for tax periods which fit in with their internal accounting arrangements—when approved they are known as special tax periods.)

21 October 1988. Press Notice No. 80/88
Customs and Excise Inland Revenue joint inspection visits

Customs and Excise and the Revenue will not be adopting a suggestion of the Keith Committee to introduce joint VAT and PAYE inspection visits to traders. This follows an analysis of a pilot exercise in the Nottingham area.

Announcing the decision in a written reply to a Parliamentary Question, the Financial Secretary to the Treasury, the Rt. Hon. Norman Lamont, M.P., said yesterday:

"The pilot study, which took place in the last quarter of 1986, was designed to test the Keith Committee's suggestion that joint visits, rather than separate visits for PAYE and VAT purposes, could be mutually beneficial to traders and to the Revenue and Customs and Excise.

The findings are that, while joint visits are feasible and acceptable to most of the traders who received them, in only two per cent. of cases would a joint visit replace two separate visits. So, in most instances, a joint visit would add to, rather than reduce, the inspections of a business's records. Furthermore, a system of joint visits would add substantially to the department's costs.

In the light of these results, it is not proposed to implement a programme of joint visits at this stage. But both departments will continue to improve the information and other services they provide, especially to small businesses."

Note
The pilot study was carried out in response to a recommendation by the Keith Committee on the Enforcement Powers of the Revenue Departments.

The Committee suggested that joint visits would save time and reduce disruption, especially for the smaller trader, and could produce some staff savings for the departments. It was also thought that there might be some areas of mutual interest, for example, if VAT irregularities in the records pointed to irregularities for PAYE. The pilot aimed to discover whether joint visits could work and to assess their advantages and disadvantages.

One hundred traders in the Nottingham area received joint visits in the last quarter of 1986. These were selected as far as possible from the smaller employers—those with 50 employees or less—due to receive separate visits during the period of the pilot. Visits were made by pairs of local Revenue and Customs officers who each carried out their normal PAYE or VAT inspection procedures.

The Inland Revenue Departmental Statement issued in June set out various ways in which it is improving services to the taxpayer. For example, there is a continuous review of forms and explanatory booklets and leaflets to ensure clear and simple explanations of the tax code. Well focused training and the use of improved equipment, including modern computer systems, helps staff provide more accurate and efficient service in dealilng with enquiries. In addition computerised assessing, now being extended nationwide for Schedule D taxpayers, cuts down the scope for errors, provides clearer information on assessment notices and, through better communication between tax officers and Accounts Offices, reduces the chance of delays in sorting out the correct bill.

For its part, Customs and Excise also continually reviews its forms and explanatory notices and leaflets with the aim of providing guidance which can be easily understood. The Department has reviewed the VAT arrangements for small businesses with the result that the cash and annual accounting schemes have been introduced to help this vital sector. In addition a countrywide network of over 120 public enquiry offices has been set up to deal with enquiries on all Customs matters, including VAT.

10 November 1988. Press Notice No. 84/88
VAT and donations to universities

Financial support
The impression seems to have arisen that all payments made to universities by bodies in the private sector are liable to VAT, including sponsorship payments, donations and the endowment of chairs. This is not the case.

There has been no change in the policy or practice of the Commissioners. The underlying principles are quite straightforward. There is no VAT on unconditional gifts of money to universities. Nor does the mere acknowledgement of such support attract VAT, for example the naming of a university chair after the donor. VAT applies only where something is supplied for a consideration: the name given to a payment is not important—it is what happens in reality that determines the VAT position.

So, where a payment is conditional upon the university supplying clearly identifiable benefits in return (such as advertising, publicity or the making available of university sports facilities), there is a supply by the university which is liable to VAT in accordance with the normal rules.

The value for VAT in such cases is normally the whole amount received. But where both parties recognise that a donor intends a single payment both to cover services supplied by the university and to provide a gratuitous donation, only the payment for services is taxed, provided that:
(1) the amount attributed to the supply is realistic in relation to the benefits provided; and
(2) it is clear from any agreement that this amount can be distinguished from the donation element.

Donated equipment
Free gifts of equipment, with no strings attached, are liable to VAT based on their cost to the donor. This is an EC obligation. Where goods are given to universities with an obligation that the recipient must do something in return, the transaction is a form of barter. Each party to the agreement, if registered for VAT, has to account for tax on the open market value of the goods or services supplied.

The correct VAT treatment may vary according to the facts of individual cases and Customs and Excise are happy to advise taxpayers in specific instances.

Note
As a result of representations made on behalf of universities the Commissioners have recognised the need to explain more fully their policy in this area. Individual decisions have been seen as an implicit indication that all funding of universities will be subject to VAT. This is not the case. Most university funding is not subject to tax. Pure donations, *i.e.* financial contributions with "no strings attached", are not liable to VAT. But if the "donor" receives something in addition to the mere acknowledgement of his support, then the university is making a supply which is subject to VAT under the normal rules.

30 March 1989. Press Notice No. 30/89
VAT: supplies of education and welfare made otherwise than for profit—Bell Concord judgment

The Court of Appeal ruled last month, in the case of the *Bell Concord Educational Trust Ltd.* v. *C. & E. Comrs.* [1989] STC 264, that an educational trust which was prohibited by its foundation document from distributing any surpluses and was bound to apply them to the furtherance of the aims of the organisation was operating otherwise than for profit, even though its supplies generated surpluses which were used for future developments or expansion. Its educational courses were consequently exempt from VAT under VATA 1983, Sch. 6, Group 6, item 2. The Commissioners of Customs and Excise have examined the implications of this decision, and this news release outlines the changes in interpretation of the law which they propose to make.

The term "otherwise than for profit" is used in two separate places in the VAT exemption Schedule. Under Group 6, research and education provided by a body other than a university or school may be exempt from VAT only if it is provided otherwise than for profit. Group 7, items 9 and 10 exempt welfare services provided by charities, public bodies and religious communities otherwise than for profit. The phrase has been interpreted as meaning that providers should set their prices at a level which at maximum does no more than recover the full overhead-inclusive cost of supplying the service. The Court of Appeal judgment, however, requires that attention should be paid to the status of the body providing the education or welfare.

Customs and Excise will now accept that supplies are made "otherwise than for profit" if they are made by non-profit-making organisations in circumstances where any surpluses are applied solely to the furtherance of the educational or welfare activity which generated the surplus. Where, however, a non-profit-making organisation is set up to pursue more than one activity, *e.g.* the provision of education and the propagation of some other cause, the education would *not* be supplied otherwise than for profit if surpluses from the educational activity were applied to the maintenance or furtherance of the other activity. Similarly with welfare: if the surpluses from a welfare activity are not to be devoted to the same general area of welfare, the supply is not made otherwise than for profit, even if the surpluses are used for another charitable activity.

The existing criteria will continue to apply in other cases where the body supplying the education or welfare is not constituted on a non-profit making basis.

5 April 1989. Press Notice No. 32/89
VAT: provision of care in hospitals

In a recent decision (*Nuffield Nursing Homes Trust* v. *C. & E. Comrs.* LON/87/162) the VAT Tribunal found in favour of the supplier in ruling that the provision of (accommodation and) catering in a hospital to a parent of a child patient was a supply of care to the patient. Such supplies are therefore exempt from VAT under VATA 1983, Sch. 6, Group 7, item 4 (H.M. Customs and Excise had earlier conceded that the provision of accommodation amounted to the granting of a licence to occupy land and was thus exempted under Group 1, item 1). Free accommodation and catering provided by NHS hospitals are not affected and remain outside the scope of VAT.

The Independent Hospitals Association and the Department of Health have been advised of the decision.

Note
Group 7, item 4, exempts the provision of care or medical or surgical treatment, and any goods supplied in connection therewith, in any hospital or similar institution.

26 April 1989. Hansard
Customs and Excise Management Act 1979

(HC Written Answer, 26 April 1989, Vol. 151 cols. 562, 563).
The following Written Answer was included in the House of Commons Official Report.
Mr. Quentin Davies asked the Chancellor of the Exchequer if he will make a statement on the circumstances in which the Commissioners of Customs and Excise will disclose particulars of cases where proceedings for offences are compounded under CEMA 1979, s. 152.
Mr. Lilley: CEMA 1979, s. 152 is the most recent re-enactment of the Commissioners' long-standing power to compound proceedings, that is to offer an alleged offender the option of paying a penalty out of court rather than be prosecuted. This power is used to resolve the majority of customs or excise offences, and enables them to be dealt with efficiently and effectively without burdening the courts or tying up Customs staff in lengthy court hearings. Hitherto, details of compounded settlements have not usually been made public.
The Commissioners, having reviewed their policy on disclosure of compounded settlements, have decided that in respect of settlements made on or after 1 June 1989, details will be disclosed in the following circumstances:
It will be the Commissioners' invariable practice to disclose details
(*a*) to other Government Departments whose statutory responsibilities are directly affected; and
(*b*) to the courts for sentencing purposes after conviction, in cases where there has been an earlier compounded settlement for a similar matter within the time limits specified for offences by the Rehabilitation of Offenders Act.
The Commissioners will also disclose compounded settlements under two other circumstances
(*c*) to employers when it is apparent that
(i) the nature of the employment has facilitated the offence; or
(ii) where drugs offences or indications of serious alcohol abuse are involved, the nature of the employment or duties requires a high degree of unimpaired judgment or faculties,
(*d*) in response to enquiries from Parliament or the media about cases which have excited public attention, if disclosure is considered to be in the public interest.
In all cases, persons considering an offer to compound for an alleged offence will be warned when the offer is made that details of the settlement may be disclosed in the circumstances set out at (*a*) or (*d*) above.
The Commissioners have considered the recommendations of Lord Keith of Kinkel's committee on the "Enforcement Powers of the Revenue Departments" (Cmnd. 9440), that the names of all persons making compounded settlements and particulars of the settlements should be published, subject to discretion to withhold the names of persons making full spontaneous voluntary dis-

closure of their offences. The policy now to be adopted reflects the Commissioners' conclusion that, other than in the particular circumstances already described, it would not be equitable or make the best use of their resources or those of the courts to depart from the present general principle of non-disclosure. The Commissioners' general policy of non-disclosure of details of their dealings in individual cases will therefore continue to apply to cases which do not come within the circumstances described above.

I am satisfied with this outcome of the Commissioners' review.

30 May 1989. Press Notice No. 42/89
VAT: deduction of input tax by holding companies

Customs have reviewed their policy on the recovery of VAT input tax by holding companies in the light of representations that their interpretation of VAT law in this area was more restrictive than that applied by other E.C. countries: Customs had argued that VAT incurred by holding companies could not be recovered as the purchases of goods and services on which the tax had been charged were not used to make taxable supplies.

As part of the review, Customs have consulted the E.C. Commission and other Member States. These consultations have borne out the contention that a majority of E.C. countries allow the recovery of a proportion of the input tax incurred by holding companies, provided those companies also make taxable supplies. Customs have therefore decided to amend their current policy to bring it into line with practice in these Member States: tax on holding company expenses will now be eligible for deduction in the same way as that incurred on other expenses.

No new legislative powers are required to implement this change.

Deduction of input tax may now be calculated on the following basis:

(*a*) input tax on supplies to holding companies must be attributed to taxable, exempt or other non-taxable outputs to the greatest possible extent, and the normal rules applied;

(*b*) any residual input tax which cannot be directly attributed will be accepted as a general overhead of the taxable person;

(*c*) the amount of residual input tax which can be recovered will be determined in accordance with the use of the related goods or services.

This means that any costs of goods and services which cannot be directly attributed will be treated as a general overhead and the input tax apportioned in accordance with the taxable person's partial exemption method. (It is expected that most costs related to acquisitions and defence against take-overs will fall into the "overhead" category.) This will, in principle, mean full deduction of input tax on these costs by a fully taxable person, and some deduction where the taxable person is partly exempt.

These changes will apply with effect from 1 April 1987. Taxable persons who consider that since that date they have suffered a larger restriction of input tax related to their holding company business than would have been the case under Customs' revised policy should contact their local VAT office. Customs will re-examine any assessments which have been issued restricting input tax relating to holding company activities, and will make any necessary amendments.

Notes

It is a basic principle of E.C. and U.K. VAT law that input tax can be recovered only to the extent that it relates to the making of taxable supplies of goods and services. The activities of a holding company, including the acquisition and disposal of companies, are normally exempt or outside the scope of VAT and therefore do not give rise to any entitlement to deduct input tax.

During 1988 Customs became increasingly concerned at the way some businesses had arranged their holding company affairs to recover a greater amount of input tax than appeared consistent with a strict interpretation of the law. Customs therefore raised VAT assessments on businesses which they considered had overclaimed deduction of input tax. However, in general those assessments were not enforced while Customs consulted the Commission and other Member States on their interpretation of the Sixth Directive, as it applies to deduction of input tax.

There was unanimous agreement that if a holding company made no taxable supplies then no input tax could be recovered on its expenses. However, where a holding company made some taxable supplies the majority allowed some form of apportionment of input tax. In the light of these enquiries Customs have decided to revise their interpretation of the law.

The "partial exemption regulations" are contained in the VAT (General) Regulations, S.I. 1985 No. 886 Part V, as amended by the VAT (General) (Amendment) (No. 2) Regulations, S.I. 1987 No. 510.

9 August 1989. Press Notice No. 58/89
VAT: treatment of certain agricultural grant schemes

Customs and Excise have been considering whether the voluntary surrender of right by landowners and farmers in return for the payment of certain grants should be liable to VAT at the standard rate, e.g. the surrender by a farmer of his milk quota in return for the payment of a grant by the Ministry of Agriculture, Fisheries and Food.

Customs have consulted other member states and the E.C. Commission. These discussions have not yet been finally concluded, and Treasury Ministers have therefore decided that VAT should not be applied in the meantime, and in any case not before 1 April 1991.

Customs' discussions have centred on grant payments to "outgoers" under the milk quota arrangements and the set-aside schemes but the same issues arise on other grant schemes.

The decision to suspend the application of VAT applies to these grant schemes and similar schemes, in particular those listed below:

Ministry of Agriculture, Fisheries and Food
Farm Woodland Schemes
Set Aside Scheme
Agriculture Act 1986, Section 18 (Environmentally Sensitive Areas)
Outgoers under the Milk (Cessation of Production) Act 1985

Department of the Environment
Nature Conservancy Council management agreements
Countryside Premium Scheme for Set Aside Land
Countryside Commission Community Forests Scheme

Forestry Commission
Woodland Grant Scheme
Farm Woodland Scheme
The application of VAT to the sale of milk quota between farmers is not affected by these discussions, and continues to be liable to VAT at the standard rate.

10 August 1989. Press Notice No. 59/89
VAT: repairs under warranty—change in treatment of repairs carried out on behalf of overseas manufacturers

Following representations from interested parties, Customs and Excise have reviewed the VAT treatment of warranty work done by U.K. repairers on behalf of overseas manufacturers and suppliers of goods.

Customs consider that a U.K. repairer may now, in all cases, recover as input tax, subject to the normal rules, any VAT he incurs on expenditure related to repairs carried out on behalf of overseas manufacturers (e.g. purchase of spare parts).

Where a repair is done by a U.K. importer or U.K. distributor who has taken title to the goods, any payment from the overseas supplier to cover the repair costs is regarded as compensation and no VAT is due. But if the repair is carried out by a third party on behalf of an overseas manufacturer, any payment which the repairer receives is the consideration for his supply of services to the manufacturer on which he must account for VAT at the standard rate.

An overseas manufacturer who incurs VAT in these circumstances may be eligible for a refund of the tax under the E.C. Eighth or Thirteenth VAT Directive schemes.

Alternatively, if he has a business establishment in the U.K. he may be able to register for VAT and claim the tax back as input tax, subject to the normal rules. Repairers may, if they choose, apply these changes back-dated to 1 April 1987.

Notes
When a manufacturer repairs defective goods under warranty, the repair is not a supply for VAT purposes since the original supply of the goods was costed to allow for it. However, overseas manufacturers rarely carry out warranty work themselves; their involvement is normally confined to meeting the cost of repairs, which are usually done by the U.K. importer or distributor of the goods as part of his after sales service to customers, or possibly by an independent third party who has been appointed as the manufacturer's authorised repairer in the U.K.

In the past Customs have regarded *all* payments by overseas manufacturers to repairers in respect of warranty work as compensation, and not the consideration for any supply of repair services. No VAT was therefore charged to the manufacturer. Prior to 1 April 1987 this treatment did not normally result in any restriction on the ability of repairers to recover the input tax on their purchases connected with repair work. However, since 1 April 1987 only the input tax related to taxable supplies has been recoverable. The ability of a U.K. importer or distributor to recover input tax has not been affected by the 1987 changes because he takes title to and resupplies the goods produced by the overseas manufacturer. But independent repairers could no longer recover the tax they incurred in carrying out the repairs.

However, Customs have been advised that their current treatment of payments received by independent repairers is incorrect. They now accept that such payments are the consideration for a taxable supply of repair services, and that VAT should therefore be charged to overseas manufacturers. Consequently independent repairers will also be entitled to recover the input tax related to their repair activities, subject to the normal rules.

Overseas businesses which make no taxable supplies in the U.K. and which have no business establishment here may be eligible for a refund of the VAT charged to them on warranty work under schemes introduced under the E.C. Eighth and Thirteenth VAT Directives. This is explained in greater detail in Notice 723: Refunds of VAT in the European Community and other countries. If the overseas business has an establishment in the U.K., it cannot use a refund scheme but may at its own request register for VAT and claim as input tax any incurred in respect of its business overseas.

Note: this notice is printed as amended by Press Notice No. 67/89, 7 September 1989.

4 January 1990. Institute of Taxation
VAT: problems with transitional reliefs on land, property and construction

The Institute of Taxation has been in correspondence with Customs and Excise on the various anomalies and difficulties arising as a result of the transitional reliefs for land and property transactions and construction contracts following the change in VAT liabilities on 1 April 1989.

Numerous potential problems have appeared where companies which have benefited from various transitional reliefs either joined or left a VAT group. On this subject, Customs and Excise have made the following helpful comments.

Customs and Excise have confirmed in the course of correspondence with the Institute that, where a company within a VAT group has a legally binding obligation within the terms of FA 1989 Sch. 3 para. 13, that legally binding obligation is regarded as attaching itself to the Group as a whole via the representative member. On the other hand, a company with a pre-21 June 1988 legally binding obligation which leaves a VAT Group while still having that obligation does not forgo its entitlement to the transitional relief; and such a company joining a VAT group in effect passes its entitlement on to the representative member.

In the course of this correspondence it became clear that there is one particular anomaly regarding pre-21 June 1988 construction contracts between companies in a VAT group. Customs and Excise have agreed that supplies between members of the same VAT group must be disregarded—the existence or otherwise of a legally binding obligation between members of the same VAT group is, therefore, irrelevant. The problem is the VAT (Self-Supply of Construction Services) Order 1989 [SI 1989/472] may create a self-supply VAT cost on construction contracts between members of the same VAT group, even though the contract was signed prior to 21 June 1988.

Michael Squires, Chairman of the Institute's Technical Committee, commented that:

"VAT groups which [were] caught by this anomaly may need urgently to consider de-grouping in order to minimise the VAT cost on on-going contracts or, alternatively, opting to tax the properties which are the subject of intra-VAT group contracts in order that any VAT costs arising out of the VAT (Self-Supply of Construction Services) Order 1989 can be recovered."

15 March 1990. ICAEW TR 787
VAT: insurance services of intermediaries other than brokers: application to practising accountants

1. Practising accountants are frequently involved in arrangements resulting in clients taking out insurance. This will often be life assurance or pensions insurance business as part of personal financial planning, including provision for estate taxes. But other types of insurance can also be involved. Often this results in commissions (or shared commissions) being received by the accountant either from an insurer or from an insurance broker. In practice, most will be accounted for to the client, usually as an abatement of the fee.

2. The commissions are paid by insurers and insurance brokers, whose activities are generally exempt from VAT where the policy holder belongs in the United Kingdom. In many cases the commissions will also be exempt as the making of arrangements for the provision of insurance within VATA 1983, Sch. 6 Group 2 item 3.

3. Guidance on the interpretation of these provisions is found in Customs and Excise Leaflet 701/36/86, para. 26:

"Persons other than insurance brokers—such as accountants, solicitors and estate agents—sometimes provide services which result in insurance being provided to a client. If you are such a person and are involved in negotiating the terms of a specific supply of insurance to a client you are making arrangements for the provision of insurance and the liability of your supplies is the same as those of an insurance broker described in paragraphs 18–22.

"But supplies of services by intermediaries which do not involve negotiating the terms of a specific supply of insurance—for example the mere introduction of a client to an insurance broker or the provision of advisory services are standard rated.

"The consideration for your supply is the gross amount of commission which you recieve as described in paragraph 24 above whatever the liability of your services".

4. In practice commissions or shared commissions received by accountants are exempt provided:

(*a*) commission is received by the accountant from a permitted insurer and the accountant has both assisted the client in identifying the particular need and also in selecting the appropriate policy;

(*b*) shared commission is received from an insurance broker and the accountant undertakes one or more of the following:

(i) agreeing with the client the personal/financial/commercial details on which the policy will be based and passing these to the broker;

(ii) approaching the broker to obtain quotations from a number of insurers and reviewing these in conjunction with the client;

(iii) receiving and transmitting to and from the broker correspondence, particularly proposal forms and policy documents, relating to the insurance contract;

(iv) assisting the client in completing the insurance proposal and/or transmitting premiums to the broker;

(v) examining the actual policy selected and advising the client on the suitability of its terms before final acceptance—particularly as to built-on options and "excess" arrangements.

5. A commission will be taxable where the accountant's role is limited to:

(*a*) Merely giving general advice, including the specification in broad terms of the form of insurance needed;

(*b*) Effecting general introduction to an insurance company and/or broker where future dealings are carried out without the involvement of the accountant. If the accountant is further involved, particularly in any of the steps in para. 4 (ii) above, the commissions will be exempt.

6. In short only rarely will commissions received from insurance companies or brokers be subject to VAT at the standard rate. In practice they are treated as exempt unless there is clear evidence to the contrary.

7. If the accountant receives renewal commission in respect of services which he has carried out previously, the renewal commission will be exempt if the original services were exempt.

8. As stated in para. 1 above commissions received are often accounted for to the client. In this respect attention is drawn to para. 6 of VAT Notes No. 1 1988–89:

"**6.** *Method of accounting for VAT on fees*

Many traders when charging fees to their clients reduce the amount by taking into account commission they receive from third parties. For example, a financial adviser provides guidance on insurance to a client; the insurance company pays the adviser a commission and the adviser passes on the benefit to the client by charging a lower fee. In the past, traders have accounted for output tax on the full value of their supply before any deductions for commission. Customs and Excise have reviewed this ruling, and from now on you need only account for output tax on the fee shown on the invoice".

9. The fee note to the client may be set out in either of the following ways:

	Method A £	Method B £
Fee	110	
Rebate equivalent to commission received	10	
Fee	100	
VAT @ 15%	15	
Total	115	
Fee net of £10 commission		100
VAT @ 15%		15
Total		115

Note: If method A is used it is important that the commission be described as a rebate.

28 March 1990. Hansard
Default surcharge

(HC Written Answer, 28 March 1990, Vol. 170, col. 200)

Mr. David Davis asked the Chancellor of the Exchequeur if the review of the operation and impact of the default surcharge has been completed; and if he would make a statement.

Mr. Ryder: The review we announced in July 1988 has been completed. A very thorough examination of the operation and effectiveness of the default surcharge was carried out and very careful consideration was given to the submissions made by many interested parties. We have, however, no plans for changes at the present time, although the matter will be kept under constant review.

30 March 1990. Press Notice No. 27/90
VAT and "money-off" coupons: Boots Co. plc v. C. & E. Comrs.

The judgment of the European Court of Justice in the case of *Boots plc* v. *C. & E. Comrs.* [Case 126/88 [1990] STC 387, ECJ] was delivered on 27 March. The court decided that money-off coupons, obtained by consumers when they buy goods, are not a consideration when they are used to buy other goods. They are simply evidence of entitlement to a discount. Output VAT is therefore due only on the net amount which the consumer actually pays for the goods.

The Court's decision will affect the VAT treatment of a wide range of business promotion schemes involving coupons and vouchers. Customs will be consulting interested bodies and will shortly be issuing an amendment to Notice 727 Retail schemes, which is the notice which tells retailers about the retail schemes which may be used for working out their output tax liability when accounting for VAT. Customs also intend to re-issue the VAT Leaflet 700/7 "Business promotion schemes" in a revised and much more comprehensive form.

Businesses which believe they may have overpaid VAT in respect of promotion schemes are advised to contact their local VAT office.

Notes
Boots Company plc appealed to the High Court [[1989] STC 138] following a decision of the independent VAT Tribunal that money-off coupons, obtained by consumers when they purchase certain goods (the premium goods) should be included in the taxable amount when they are used to purchase other goods (the redemption goods). The Tribunal agreed with the Commissioners that the redemption goods are supplied in return for a consideration consisting not only of the cash the consumer pays but also of the coupon. Therefore, under U.K. law businesses were required to account for VAT on the normal retail selling price of the redemption goods. The High Court referred certain questions to the ECJ to determine whether U.K. law properly reflected E.C. Law (the Sixth VAT directive).

The court's decision, that the voucher is more than evidence of entitlement to a discount and is of no VAT significance, will mean a reduction in the amount of VAT payable by businesses in respect of a wide range of promotion schemes involving vouchers, and a degree of simplification in the procedure for accounting for VAT. The schemes affected include:
  (*a*) self liquidators;
  (*b*) promotions where proofs of purchase can be redeemed for gift goods without further charge;
  (*c*) loyalty vouchers;
  (*d*) vouchers issued to store card holders;
  (*e*) price reduction coupons.
In February 1989 the House of Lords ruled—in the case of *C. & E. Comrs.* v. *Fine Art Development plc* [[1989] STC 85]—that businesses which had overpaid VAT where entitled to recover overpayments made in error. That right was subsequently confirmed in FA 1989, s. 24 although at the same time the Commissioners were empowered to resist claims from businesses which would result in their unjust enrichment, where for example they had passed the tax on to their customers. The test of unjust enrichment does not apply to claims which were made or notified before 1 January 1990. Any claim for repayment must be supported by evidence of the overpayment.

The court's decision does not affect the treatment of gift tokens. When gift tokens are purchased VAT is due only on any amount by which the price paid exceeds the face value of the tokens. When the tokens are used to purchase goods or services the face value of the tokens forms part of the consideration for those goods or services. This remains the position.

2 May 1990. Hansard
VAT: flights

(HC Written Answer, 2 May 1990, Vol. 171 cols. 541, 542)
Mr. Frank Cook asked Mr. Chancellor of the Exchequer (1) which rate of VAT applies to the carriage of passengers on non scheduled flights, including scenic, pleasure and special passenger transport services in aircraft capable of carrying not fewer than 12 passengers, including pilot and crew, and if he will make a statement; (2) which rate of VAT applies to the carriage of passengers by hot air balloons capable of carrying not fewer than 12 passengers, including pilot and crew, on non scheduled scenic, pleasure and special passenger transport flights; and if he will make a statement.
Mr. Ryder: The VATA 1983 provides zero-rating for the transport of passengers in aircraft designed or adapted to carry not less than 12 passengers, but, in applying that relief, a distinction

has been made between conventional aircraft and hot air balloons. Conventional aircraft are capable of performing the function of conveying passengers with certainty between specified places—the essential characteristic of a supply of transport. However hot air balloons, which are not capable of powered flight, are largely at the mercy of the elements and do not satisfy that criterion. They are, therefore, excluded from the benefit of the relief and flights in them are thus liable to VAT at the standard rate.

3 May 1990. Hansard
Affinity cards: tax implications for charities

(HC Written Answer, 3 May 1990, Vol. 171 col. 610)
Mr. Hanley asked the Chancellor of the Exchequer what representations he has received from charitable organisations about the VAT and corporation tax implications of affinity credit card schemes; and if he will make a statement.
Mr. Ryder: My right hon Friend has received various representations, including a submission from the Charities' Tax Reform Group (CTRG) ... Customs and Excise and the Inland Revenue have also had discussions with the CTRG about the tax implications of charities' affinity card schemes. It has now been agreed that, with the appropriate contractual arrangements, VAT will be charged on the promotional and other services supplied by the charities, but will not apply to contributions made by the credit card companies for which the beneficiaries are not obliged to do anything in return. The corporation tax treatment of individual schemes will depend on the contractual arrangements, but schemes can be set up in such a way that the charity's income from them qualifies for exemption from corporation tax.

30 May 1990. Law Society
Surrenders of land: VAT groups

The Law Society's Revenue Law Committee recently queried the official view that where the assignee of a lease is grouped with the lessor for VAT purposes, the assignment counts as a taxable surrender of the lease (by virtue of VATA 1983, s. 29 (1)), see HM Customs & Excise Notice 742B para. 12 (*c*). The response of H.M. Customs & Excise, in a letter sent to the Law Society was as follows:
"We had originally taken the view, having regard to the actual wording of s. 29 (1) of the VAT Act 1983, that the business of a landlord company within a group registration becomes part of the representative member's business; that the representative member is the landlord for any lettings made by the group as a whole; and that the whole group is a single person for VAT purposes. Hence what appears in para. 12 (*c*) of Notice 742B. However, we have subsequently been persuaded that the [Law Society's interpretation suggesting that para. 12 (*c*) was incorrect] is to be preferred to our original one. We thus accept that an assignment of any interest to a VAT grouped company is an exempt supply unless that company (the assignee) is itself the lessor or licensor."
Such an assignment would be standard-rated, however, if the assignor had exercised his option to waive exemption.

7 June 1990. Hansard
Free zones

(HC Written Answer, 7 June 1990, Vol. 173 cols. 708, 709)
Mr. Hanley asked the Chancellor of the Exchequer what is the outcome of the Treasury's evaluation of the free zone experiment.
Mr. Ryder: A copy of the evaluation report on the U.K. free zone experiment (1984–89) by the Treasury's consultants Roger Tym and Partners is being made available today in the House Libraries. Further copies are available from the Treasury.
The experiment has shown that free zones can be worthwhile and viable enterprises in the U.K. The Government have therefore decided to offer a further designation for ten years from August 1991 to the three currently operating free zones at Birmingham, Liverpool and Southampton. In addition, the Government intend to announce later in the year objective criteria against which further similar designations of free zones under existing EC and U.K. legislation will be considered by Customs & Excise. Applications from potential free zone operators will be invited at that time and will be judged primarily against the criteria of their commercial viability without public sector assistance and sufficient volume of demand to justify the Customs resources required at the free zone.
Finally, the Government have decided in the light of the evaluation report to introduce certain improvements to the free zone regime. Subject to EC approval, VAT zero rating will be allowed

for supplies of imported free zone goods where, under an agreement with the supplier, the customer is required to clear the goods from the free zone. Furthermore, the Customs & Excise guidance on the free zone regime will be updated and consolidated to take account of technical amendments made since the scheme was introduced to ensure that the scheme operates as clearly and simply as possible within the necessary EC and Customs procedures.

APPENDIX 2. EXTRA-STATUTORY CONCESSIONS (NOTICE No. 748)

In certain circumstances where remission or repayment of VAT, customs duty or excise duty is not provided for by law, Customs and Excise may allow relief on an extra-statutory basis.

This Appendix lists Customs and Excise extra-statutory concessions in force at 1 October 1989 so far as they concern VAT.

The concessions are set out in two lists:

    A: VAT concessions

    B: Other Customs and Excise concessions.

Where a concession involves more than one charge, such as VAT and customs duty, it is listed under its primary heading and the other reliefs are indicated in the text.

All the concessions listed in this are for general use. Concessions for individual cases are not included.

This Appendix does not give the detailed conditions for the concessions, but it shows where to find them. All the conditions must be met before a concession can be used. Any doubts can be checked with Customs and Excise. Addresses of local VAT Enquiries Offices and Collectors' Offices are in the phone book under "Customs and Excise". Where contact with Customs and Excise headqurters is required for detailed information, the address and phone number are given in the text.

In certain trades particular arrangements for applying VAT and other charges have been agreed with the appropriate trade associations. These are not extra-statutory concessions and are not listed. More information about these agreements can be obtained from trade associations or from Customs and Excise.

Contents

LIST A: VAT CONCESSIONS

LIST B: OTHER CUSTOMS AND EXCISE CONCESSIONS

B10. *Hydrocarbon oil delivered duty-paid to bonded distrubutors and bonded users. [not reproduced]*
B11. *Hydrocarbon oil delivered duty-paid for refinery boilers. [not reproduced]*
B12. Visiting forces
B13. U.K. products purchased by diplomats
B14. Foreign civil servants
B15. *Excise duty on importations for examination or test. [not reproduced]*
B16. *Reduced alcohol beer. [not reproduced]*

LIST A: VAT CONCESSIONS

Concession

Detailed information

A1. Disposal of assets
(*a*) On deregistration, unless the business is being transferred as a going concern, VAT must be accounted for on the cost of goods forming part of the assets of a business. The cost of any used equipment can be taken as its price if bought in its used state.

For detailed information, see the VAT Leaflet: *Should I cancel my registration?*

(*b*) If goods forming part of the assets of a business are disposed of for no consideration, so that they no longer form part of those assets, VAT must be accounted for on their cost. The cost of any used goods can be taken as their price if bought in their used state.

For detailed information, ask your local VAT Enquiries office.

A2. Bad debts
From 1 April 1986 relief from VAT was extended to cases where an administrative receiver in Great Britain, appointed on or after 1 April 1986, gives a certificate that a company's assets will be insufficient, in a liquidation, for any dividend to be paid to the ordinary unsecured creditors. As a transitory measure, Customs and Excise will also allow relief where a receiver appointed before that date and still in office, or appointed in Northern Ireland, gives a similar certificate.

For detailed information see the VAT Leaflet: *Relief from VAT on bad debts.*

A3. Repossessed goods
When goods supplied under an agreement reserving the supplier's title to the goods until they have been paid for (hire-purchase, conditional sale etc.) are subsequently repossessed, the supplier can, subject to certain conditions, reduce the value of the original supply by issuing a credit note to his customer.

This procedure cannot be used for goods dealt with under one of the VAT second-hand schemes.

For detailed information see the VAT Leaflet: *Hire-purchase and conditional sale: repossessions and transfers of agreements.*

A4. Misunderstanding
In certain circumstances Customs and Excise may, exceptionally, take no further action in respect of VAT undercharged by a registered person as a result of a genuine misunderstanding which does not concern anything clearly covered in guidance published by Customs and Excise or in specific instructions given to that registered person.

For detailed information, ask your local VAT Enquiries office.

A5. Misdirection
If a Customs and Excise officer, with the full facts before him, has given a clear and unequivocal ruling on VAT in writing or, knowing the full facts, has misled a registered person to his detriment, any assessment of VAT due will be based on the correct ruling from the date the error was brought to the registered person's attention.

For detailed information, ask your local VAT Enquiries office.

A6. VAT charged by unregistered persons

Where an amount is shown or represented as VAT on an invoice issued by a person who is neither registered nor required to be registered for VAT at the time the invoice is issued, Customs and Excise require that person to pay an equivalent amount to them. In certain circumstances a person making such a payment may be permitted to deduct from it the amount of VAT incurred on supplies to him of goods and services that were directly attributable to the invoiced supplies. If the goods or services were supplied to a registered person Customs and Excise will, in certain circumstances, allow the recipient to treat the amount shown or represented as VAT as input tax.

For detailed information, ask your local VAT Enquiries office.

A7. Charities etc.

Goods exported by a charity may be treated as if they were exported in the course of a business carried on by the charity. This enables a VAT-registered charity to treat the VAT charged on these goods at the time of purchase as input tax.

For detailed information, ask your local VAT Enquiries office.

A8. Business entertainment

The business entertainment provisions prevent input tax deduction on goods or services provided for business entertainment unless provided to employees. But where recognised representative sporting bodies necessarily provide accommodation and meals to amateur sport persons, the input tax incurred may be deductible.

For detailed information, ask your local VAT Enquiries office.

A9. Insurance

Imported insurance services provided by overseas insurers may be treated as exempt from VAT if the services would have been exempt if supplied by a U.K. insurer permitted to carry on insurance business by the Department of Trade.

For detailed information, see the VAT Leaflet: *Insurance*.

A10. Linked goods schemes

These are promotion schemes where a minor article is linked and sold with a main article at a single price—*e.g.*, a packet of soap powder sold with a washing machine. This is treated as a combined supply at a single price and if the articles are liable to VAT at different rates, the sale value must normally be apportioned. But, provided the promotion is for a limited period and the minor article comes within certain limits it can be treated as taxable at the same rate as the main article.

For detailed information, see the VAT Leaflet: *Business promotion schemes*.

A11. Dealer loader schemes

These are promotion schemes in which additional goods are offered to trade customers in return for orders of a specified size as an inducement to purchase in greater quantities. The supplier can account for tax only on the price required from the customer, but both the main goods ordered and the reward goods must be shown on the tax invoice. If the articles are liable to VAT at different rates, the supplier must apportion the inclusive price on the invoice. If they are liable at the same rate, the price for the combined supply need not be apportioned.

For detailed information, ask your local VAT Enquiries office.

A12. Sailaway boats

Where a boat is supplied to a U.K. resident who intends to export it under its own power within seven days of delivery and keep the boat abroad for a continuous period of at least 12 months the supplier may zero-rate the supply of the boat after it has been exported.

For detailed information, see the VAT Leaflet: *Sailaway boats supplied for export.*

A13. Goods supplied at duty-free shops

Where goods which are liable to VAT are supplied to intending passengers at duty-free shops approved by Customs and Excise, the supplier may be regarded as the exporter and zero-rate the supply of those goods which are exported.

A14. Inland purchases by visiting forces

In order to place inland purchases on the same footing as imported goods, VAT and car tax are waived on certain inland purchases by NATO military agencies, the U.S. Government, SHAPE and its agents, and visiting forces and their personnel.

For detailed information, contact: H.M. Customs and Excise (VI–3), 5th Floor East, New King's Beam House, 22 Upper Ground, London SE1 9PJ. (Telephone: 071-865-5062).

A15. Repayment of import VAT to shipping agents and freight forwarders

From 1 July 1988, import VAT may be repaid directly to shipping agents and freight forwarders where importers go into liquidation leaving the agents unable to recover VAT paid on their behalf. The importers must have gone into a formal state of insolvency within one month of the date of lodgement of the Customs entry, and the goods must have remained under the agent's control throughout their stay in the U.K. and have been re-exported unused.

For detailed information, ask Customs at the place of importation.

A16. Motoring expenses: purchase of road fuel

Where road fuel is provided for private motoring free or below cost, output tax must be accounted for using the scale charges, set out in the *VAT Guide*, Appendix C. But where a registered person chooses to claim no input tax on *any* road fuel used by the business, including fuel used for business motoring, it is not necessary to account for output tax.

A17. Incorrect customer declarations

Where a customer provides an incorrect declaration claiming eligibility for zero-rating under Group 7, 8, 8A or 16 of the Zero Rate Schedule and the supplier, despite having taken all reasonable steps to check the validity of the declaration, nonetheless fails to identify the inaccuracy and, in good faith, makes the supply at zero rate, Customs and Excise will not seek to recover the tax due from the supplier.

For detailed information, ask your local VAT Enquiries office.

A18. American war graves
In order to place inland purchases on the same footing as imported goods, VAT is waived on the supply of goods and services to the American Battle Monuments Commission for the maintenance of the American Military Cemetery and Memorial at Maddingley, Cambridge and Brookwood, Surrey.

For detailed information, contact: H.M. Customs and Excise (VI-3), 5th Floor East, New King's Beam House, 22 Upper Ground, London SE1 9PJ. (Telephone 071-865-5062).

A19. Re-exported motor cars
Import VAT may be repaid to importers of motor cars which have been re-exported following Department of Transport refusal to register for road use for National Type Approval reasons. The car must not have been used by the importer after refusal of NTA, and proof that the car has been re-exported must be provided. The importer must not have sold the car in the U.K. and must claim repayment within three months of the date of importation.

For detailed information ask Customs at the place of importation.

LIST B: OTHER CUSTOMS AND EXCISE CONCESSIONS

Concession

Detailed information

B1. Personal importations of private property
Personal importations of private property (including motor vehicles) that meet the conditions described in Notices 3 and 3A but:
  (*a*) are imported more than six months before or 12 months after a person takes up residence in the U.K.; or
  (*b*) were purchased duty and tax free by:
    (i) diplomats,
    (ii) members of officially recognised international organisations; and
    (iii) members and civilian staff of NATO and U.K. forces; or
  (*c*) the required period of use or possession and use of the goods is not met due to circumstances beyond the importer's control, may be relieved of customs duty, VAT, car tax and other excise duties.

For detailed information about (*a*) ask your Collector's office. For detailed information about (*b*) and (*c*) contact: H.M. Customs and Excise (CDE5), Room 201, Dorset House, Stamford Street, London SE1 9PS. (Telephone: 071-865-4768).

B3. Containers and pallets
  (*a*) *Containers*. VAT may be waived on containers and pallets which are temporarily imported for emptying or filling and subsequent re-exportation. This concession also extends to parts and accessories imported separately for the repair of, or for installation in, temporarily imported containers.
  (*b*) *Pallets*. Duty and VAT be waived on foreign owned pallets which are temporarily imported for emptying or filling and subsequent re-exportation.

For detailed information, see Notice 309: *Containers, pallets and packing.*

B5. Demonstration cars
Subject to certain conditions, VAT and car tax are not charged when British-made cars are demonstrated by manufacturers for sale purposes to visiting forces personnel or to bona-fide export customers.

For detailed information, ask your local VAT Enquiries office.

B12. Visiting forces

(a) *Imported goods.* In accordance with the NATO Status of Forces Agreement and the 1952 Exchange of Notes, relief from customs duty, excise duty and VAT is available on certain imported goods and hydrocarbon oil used by or on behalf of visiting forces.

For detailed information about imports direct to U.S. bases—ask your Collector's Office.

For other reliefs, see:

(a) Notice 316: *Contractors equipment temporarily imported for a NATO infrastructure contract or in connection with the provision and maintenance of U.S. defence facilities in the U.K.; Customs duty and VAT.*

(b) Notice 431: *Relief from customs duty and/or VAT on U.S. Government expenditure in the U.K.*

(c) Notice 431B: *USAF contracts for the conveyance of personnel and school children: repayment of customs duty on road fuel.*

(b) *Gifts.* Duty and VAT are waived on gifts (other than tobacco goods or alcoholic liquor) sent from abroad for the personal use of visiting forces.

(c) *Goods given by visiting forces.* Duty and VAT are waived on gifts made to charitable organisations by U.S. forces.

For detailed information about (b) and (c) contact: H.M. Customs and Excise (VI–3), 5th Floor East, New King's Beam House, 22 Upper Ground, London SE1 9PJ. (Telephone: 071-865-5062).

B13. U.K. products purchased by diplomats

So that home produced goods are not placed at a disadvantage, relief from excise duty and VAT is allowed on the same basis as foreign produced goods on purchases by diplomats of U.K. produced alcoholic drink and tobacco goods.

For detailed information, contact: H.M. Customs and Excise (VI–3), 5th Floor East, New King's Beam House, 22 Upper Ground, London SE1 9PJ. (Telephone: 071-865-5062).

B14. Foreign civil servants

Where no statutory relief applies, customs charges are waived on goods imported at the time of first arrival of foreign and Commonwealth civil servants coming to the U.K. on an official tour of duty.

For detailed information, contact: H.M. Customs and Excise (VI–3), 5th Floor East, New King's Beam House, 22 Upper Ground, London SE1 9PJ. (Telephone: 071-865-5062).

APPENDIX 3. VAT Notices and Leaflets (Leaflet No. 700/13/90)

The following list of VAT publications is derived from Leaflet No. 700/13/90. It has been updated to include new and revised publications announced in VAT Notes No. 1 1990 and in subsequent press notices. The publications can be obtained from any local VAT office.

Notice	Leaflet	Title
700		**The VAT guide**
	700/1/90	Should I be registered for VAT?
	700/2/83	Registration for VAT: Group treatment
	700/3/87	Registration for VAT: Corporate bodies organised in divisions
	700/4/87	Overseas traders and U.K. VAT
	700/5/85	Hire-purchase and conditional sale: repossessions and transfers of agreements
	700/7/81	Business promotion schemes
	700/8/84	Returnable containers
	700/9/87	Transfer of a business as a going concern
	700/10/84	Processing and repair of goods and exchange units
	700/11/90	Should I cancel my registration?
	700/12/90	Filling in your VAT return
	700/13/90	VAT publications
	700/14/86	Supplies of video cassettes: rental and part-exchange
	700/15/90	The Ins and Outs of VAT
	700/17/83	Funded pension schemes
	700/18/86	Relief from VAT on bad debts
	700/21/90	Keeping records and accounts
	700/22/89	Admissions
	700/24/88	Delivery charges
	700/25/84	Taxis and hire cars
	700/26/90	Visits by VAT officers
	700/28/85	Services supplied by estate agents
	700/30/89	Default surcharge appeals
	700/31/86	Pawnbrokers: disposals of pledged goods
	700/33/87	MSC training programmes and schemes to assist the unemployed
	700/34/88	Supplies of staff, including directors and other office-holders
	700/35/88	Business gifts
	700/36/88	Dealer loader promotional schemes
	700/40/88	Persistent misdeclaration penalty
	700/41/88	Later registration—penalties and reasonable excuse
	700/42/88	Serious misdeclaration penalty
	700/43/88	Default interest
(701)	1/77/VMG	Barristers and advocates: tax point on ceasing to practise
	701/1/87	Charities
	701/5/90	Clubs and associations
	701/6/86	Donated medical and scientific equipment etc
	701/7/86	Aids for handicapped persons
	701/8/85	Postage stamps and philatelic supplies
	701/9/85	Terminal markets: dealing with commodities
	701/10/85	Printed and similar matter
	701/12/89	Sales of antiques, works of art etc from stately homes
	701/13/90	Amusement and gaming machine takings
	701/14/89	Food
	701/15/87	Animal feeding stuffs
	701/16/85	Sewerage services and water
	701/19/90	Fuel and power
	701/20/89	Caravans and houseboats
	701/21/87	Gold and gold coins
	701/22/84	Tools for the manufacture of goods for export
	701/23/89	Protective boots and helmets
	701/24/84	Parking facilities
	701/25/86	Pet food
	701/26/84	Betting and gaming
	701/27/90	Bingo
	701/28/84	Lotteries
	701/29/85	Finance
	701/30/87	Education
	701/31/88	Health

Notice	Leaflet	Title
	701/32/85	Burial and cremation
	701/33/89	Trade unions, professional associations and learned societies
	701/34/89	Competitions in sport and physical recreation
	701/35/84	Youth clubs
	701/36/86	Insurance
	701/37/84	Live animals
	701/38/89	Seeds and plants
	701/39/89	VAT liability law
	701/40/84	Abattoirs
	701/41/90	Sponsorship
702		**Imports and warehoused goods**
	702/1/88	Importing goods on which VAT has already been paid in the European Community
	702/3/89	Repayment of import VAT to shipping agents and freight forwarders
	702/4/89	Importing computer software
	702/5/89	Mares temporarily exported for covering abroad: reimportation with or without foals at foot
703		**Exports**
	703/1/89	Freight containers supplied for export
	703/2/87	Sailaway boats supplied for export
	703/3/87	VAT-free purchases of sailaway boats
704		**Retail exports**
	704/1/85	VAT refunds for visitors to the U.K.
	704/2/87	VAT refunds for U.K. residents going abroad and crews of ships and aircraft
705		**Personal exports of new motor vehicles**
706		**Partial exemption**
	706/1/89	Self-supply of stationery
	706/2/90	Capital goods scheme: input tax on computers, land and buildings acquired for use in your business
(708)	708/1/85	Protected buildings (listed buildings and scheduled monuments)
	708/2/89	Construction industry
	708/4/90	Construction: VAT certificates for residential or charity buildings
(709)	709/1/87	Industrial, staff and public sector catering
	709/2/87	Catering and take-away food
	709/3/90	Hotels and holiday accommodation
	709/4/88	Package holidays and other holiday services
	709/5/88	Tour operators' margin scheme
(710)	710/1/83	Theatrical agents and Nett Acts
	710/2/83	Agencies providing nurses and nursing auxiliaries
	710/3/83	Private investigators: expenses charged to clients
711		**Secondhand cars**
	711/1/84	VAT and the secondhand car scheme
712		**Secondhand works of art, antiques and collector's pieces**
	712/2/85	VAT and secondhand works of art, antiques and collectors' pieces
713		**Secondhand motorcycles**
714		**Young children's clothing and footwear**
717		**Secondhand caravans and motor caravans**
719		**VAT refunds for DIY builders**
720		**Secondhand boats and outboard motors**
721		**Secondhand aircraft**
722		**Secondhand electronic organs**
723		**Refunds of VAT in the European Community and other countries**
724		**Secondhand firearms**
726		**Secondhand horses**
727		**Retail schemes**
	727/1/87	Retail florists—Accounting for VAT on Interflora and Teleflorist transactions
	727/6/87	Choosing your retail scheme

Notice	Leaflet	Title
	727/7/87	How to work Scheme A
	727/8/87	How to work Scheme B
	727/8A/87	How to work Scheme B adaptation 1
	728/8B/87	How to work Scheme B adaptation 2
	727/9/87	How to work Scheme C
	727/10/87	How to work Scheme D
	729/11/87	How to work Scheme E
	727/12/87	How to work Scheme E adaptation 1
	727/13/87	How to work Scheme G
	727/14/90	How to work Scheme H
	727/15/90	How to work Scheme J
731		**VAT: cash accounting**
732		**VAT: annual accounting**
741		**International services**
742A		**Property development**
742B		**Property ownership**
	742/1/90	Letting of facilities for sport and physical recreation
	742/2/90	Sporting rights
744		**Passenger transport, international freight, ships and aircraft**
748		**Extra statutory concessions**
Explanatory leaflet		Appeals and applications to the tribunals

Index
Value Added Tax Appendices

All references in this index are to page numbers